2006 edition

No 142

KT-583-182

Annual Abstract
of Statistics

Editor: Dave Sharp

Office for National Statistics

palgrave
macmillan

First published 2006 by
PALGRAVE MACMILLAN

Houndmills, Basingstoke, Hampshire RG21 6XS and 175 Fifth Avenue, New York, NY 10010, USA

Companies and representatives throughout the world.

PALGRAVE MACMILLAN is the global academic imprint of the Palgrave Macmillan division of St. Martin's Press, LLC and of Palgrave Macmillan Ltd. Macmillan® is a registered trademark in the United States, United Kingdom and other countries. Palgrave is a registered trademark in the European Union and other countries.

ISBN 1-4039-9382-3

ISSN 0072–5730

This book is printed on paper suitable for recycling and made from fully managed and sustained forest sources.

A catalogue record for this book is available from the British Library.

10   9   8   7   6   5   4   3   2   1
15   14   13   12   11   10   09   08   07   06

Printed and bound in Great Britain by
William Clowes Ltd, Beccles, Suffolk.

A National Statistics publication

National Statistics are produced to high professional standards set out in the National Statistics Code of Practice. They are produced free from political influence.

About the Office for National Statistics

The Office for National Statistics (ONS) is the government agency responsible for compiling, analysing and disseminating economic, social and demographic statistics about the United Kingdom. It also administers the statutory registration of births, marriages and deaths in England and Wales.

The Director of ONS is also the National Statistician and the Registrar General for England and Wales.

Contact points
For enquiries about this publication, contact the Editor.
Tel: 01633 812464
E-mail: dave.sharp@ons.gsi.gov.uk

For general enquiries, contact the National Statistics Customer Contact Centre.
Tel: 0845 601 3034
(minicom: 01633 812399)
E-mail: info@statistics.gsi.gov.uk
Fax: 01633 652747
Post: Room 1015, Government Buildings,
              Cardiff Road, Newport NP10 8XG

You can also find National Statistics on the Internet at:
www.statistics.gov.uk

Contents

Table		Page
Acknowledgements		**xiii**
Units of measurement		**xiv**
Introduction		**xv**

PART ONE

Area

	Explanatory notes	2
1.1	Area of the United Kingdom, 2004	3

PART TWO

Parliamentary elections

2.1	Parliamentary elections	6
2.2	Parliamentary by-elections	6
2.3	Devolved assembly elections (Wales and Scotland)	7
2.4	Devolved assembly elections (Northern Ireland)	7

International development

	Explanatory Notes	10
3.1	Gross public expenditure on aid (GPEX)	12
3.2	Total bilateral gross public expenditure on aid (GPEX): by main recipient countries and regions	12

Defence

	Explanatory notes	14
4.1	UK Defence expenditure	18
4.2	Intake of UK regular forces from civilian life: by service	18
4.3	Formation of the UK armed forces	19
4.4	Outflow of UK regular forces: by service	19
4.5	UK Defence: service manpower strengths	20
4.6	UK Defence: civilian manpower strengths	21
4.7	Family accommodation and defence land holdings	21
4.8	Location of UK service personnel	22
4.9	UK regular forces: deaths	22
4.10	Strength of uniformed UK medical staff	23
4.11	UK Defence services and the civilian community	23

PART THREE

Population and vital statistics

	Explanatory notes	26
5.1	Population summary: by country and sex	29
5.2	Population changes: by country	30
5.3	Age distribution of the resident population: by sex and country	31
5.4	Marital condition (de jure): estimated population: by age and sex	34
5.5	Geographical distribution of the population	35
5.6	Population: by ethnic group and age, Spring 2002 – Winter 2002/03	36
5.7	Total international migration estimates: citizenship	36
5.8	Estimates of migration into and out of the United Kingdom by usual occupation and sex	37
5.9	Estimates of migration into and out of the United Kingdom by citizenship and country of last or next residence	38
5.10	Acceptances for settlement: by nationality	40
5.11	Applications received for asylum in the United Kingdom, excluding dependants: by nationality	41

Contents

Table		Page
	Vital statistics	
5.12	Marriages: by previous marital status, sex, age and country	42
5.13	Divorce: by duration of marriage, age of wife and country	44
5.14	Divorce proceedings: by country	46
5.15	Births: by country and sex	48
5.16	Birth occurrence inside and outside marriage: by age of mother	50
5.17	Live births: by age of mother and country	51
5.18	Legal abortions: by age for residents	53
5.19	Deaths: by sex and age	54
5.20	Infant and maternal mortality	58
5.21	Death rates: by sex and age	60
5.22	Interim life tables, 2002–04	61
5.23	Adoptions by date of entry in Adopted Children Register: by sex, age and country	62

Education 6

	Explanatory notes	66
6.1	Number of schools by type and establishments of further and higher education	69
6.2	Full-time and part-time pupils in school: by age and sex	70
6.3	Pupils and teachers, and pupil: teacher ratios: by school type	71
6.4	Full-time and part-time pupils with special educational needs (SEN), 2004/05	72
6.5	GCE, GCSE and SCE/NQ and vocational qualifications obtained at a typical age, and by students of any age	73
6.6	Students in further education: by country, mode of study, sex and age, during 2003/04	74
6.7	Students in further education: by country, mode of study, sex and area of learning, 2003/04	75
6.8	Students in higher education: by level, mode of study, sex and age, 2003/04	76
6.9	Students in higher education: by level, mode of study, sex and subject group, 2003/04	77
6.10	Students obtaining higher education qualifications: by level, sex and subject group, 2003/04	78
6.11	Qualified teachers: by type of school and sex	79

Labour market 7

	Explanatory notes	82
7.1	Labour force summary: by sex	87
7.2	Employment status: full-time/part-time, second jobs and temporary employees	88
7.3	Employment: by sex and age	89
7.4	Distribution of the workforce: by sex	90
7.5	Employee jobs: by industry	91
7.6	Weekly hours worked: by sex	95
7.7	Civil Service staff: by ministerial responsibility	96
7.8	Unemployment: number by sex and age group	97
7.9	Unemployment: percentage by sex and age group	98
7.10	Duration of unemployment: by sex	99
7.11	Claimant count: by age and duration	100
7.12	Unemployment rates: by region	101
7.13	Claimant count rates: by region	101
7.14	Claimant count: by region	102
7.15	Economic activity: by sex and age	103
7.16	Economically inactive: by sex and age	104
7.17	Economically inactive: by reason and sex	105
7.18	Labour disputes: by industry	106
7.19	Average earnings and hours of full-time employees: by industry division and sex	107
7.20	Average earnings and hours of full time employees: by sex	109
7.21	Average earnings index: all employees by main industrial sectors	110

Contents

	Table		Page
	7.22	Average earnings index: all employee jobs: by industry	111
	7.23	Gross weekly and hourly earnings of full time employees: by sex	115
	7.24	Average earnings: by age group of full time employees: by sex, 2004	115
	7.25	Trade unions	116
8 Personal income, expenditure and wealth		Explanatory notes	118
	8.1	Distribution of total income before and after tax	119
	8.2	Average income of households before and after taxes and benefits, 2003/04	121
	8.3	Sources of gross household income	121
	8.4	Households and their expenditure at current prices	122
	8.5	Households with selected durable goods	122
9 Health		Explanatory notes	124
		National Health Service	
	9.1	Hospital and family health services: England and Wales	126
	9.2	Hospital and primary care services: Scotland	127
	9.3	Hospital and general health services: Northern Ireland	128
	9.4	Health services: workforce summary	129
	9.5	Health and personal social services: workforce summary	130
		Public health	
	9.6	Deaths: by cause	131
	9.7	Notifications of infectious diseases: by country	135
	9.8	Estimated number of cases of work-related disease reported by specialist physicians to THOR	136
	9.9	Deaths due to occupationally related lung disease	137
	9.10	Injuries to workers: by industry and severity of injury	137
10 Social protection		Explanatory notes	140
	10.1	National Insurance Fund	144
	10.2	Persons who paid National Insurance contributions in a tax year: by sex	144
	10.3	Weekly rates of principal social security benefits	145
	10.4	National Insurance contributions	148
	10.5	Social Security Acts: number of persons receiving benefit	149
	10.6	Jobseeker's Allowance claimants: by benefit entitlement	150
	10.7	Sickness benefit, Invalidity Benefit and Incapacity Benefit claimants: by sex, age and duration of spell	151
	10.8	Sickness, Invalidity and Incapacity Benefit: days of certified incapacity	151
	10.9	Child benefits	152
	10.10	Family Credit/Working Families' Tax Credit	152
	10.11	In-work families with Child Tax Credit or Working Tax Credit awards	152
	10.12	Widows' Benefit (excluding bereavement payment): by type of benefit	152
	10.13	Bereavement Benefit (excluding bereavement payment): by sex, type of benefit and age of widow/er	154
	10.14	Contributory and non-contributory retirement pensions: by sex and age of claimants	155
	10.15	War pensions: estimated number of pensioners	156
	10.16	Income support: (excluding MIG) by Statistical group: number of claimants	156
	10.17	MIG/Pension Credit: number of claimants	156
	10.18	Income support: average weekly amounts of benefit	157
	10.19	MIG/Pension Credit: average weekly amounts of benefit	157
	10.20	Summary of government expenditure on social services and housing	157

Contents

Table		Page
10.21	Government expenditure on education	158
10.22	Government expenditure on the National Health Service	159
10.23	Government expenditure on the welfare services	159
10.24	Government expenditure on social security benefits	160
10.25	Government and other public sector expenditure on housing and community amenities	161

11 Crime and justice

	Explanatory notes	164
11.1	Police force strength: by country and sex	167

England and Wales

11.2	Recorded crime statistics: by offence group	167
11.3	Offenders found guilty: by offence group	168
11.4	Offenders cautioned: by offence group	169
11.5	Offenders found guilty of offences: by age and sex	170
11.6	Persons cautioned by the police: by age and sex	170
11.7	Sentence or order passed on offenders sentenced for indictable offences: by sex	171
11.8	Offenders sentenced to immediate custody for standard list offences: by sex and number of previous convictions	172
11.9	Population in Prison Service establishments under sentence: by sex and number of previous convictions	172
11.10	Receptions and average population in custody	173
11.11	Prison population serving sentences: by age and offence	174
11.12	Expenditure on prisons	176

Scotland

11.13	Crimes and offences recorded by the police: by crime group	177
11.14	Persons proceeded against: by crime group	178
11.15	Persons with a charge proved: by court procedure	178
11.16	Persons with charge proved: by main penalty	179
11.17	Persons with charge proved: by age and sex	179
11.18	Penal establishments: average daily population and receptions	180
11.19	Expenditure on penal establishments	180

Northern Ireland

11.20	Recorded crime statistics: by offence group	181
11.21	Persons found guilty at all courts: by offence group	181
11.22	Juveniles found guilty at all courts: by offence group	181
11.23	Disposals given to those convicted by court	182
11.24	Prisons and Young Offenders Centres	183

12 Lifestyles

	Explanatory Notes	186
12.1	Expenditure by the Department for Culture, Media and Sport	187
12.2	Employment in tourism	187
12.3	Employment in creative industries	188
12.4	Cinema statistics	188
12.5	Films	188
12.6	Domestic tourism	189
12.7	International tourism	189
12.8	Holidays abroad: by destination	189
12.9	Attendance at leisure and cultural activities	190
12.10	Gambling	190

Contents

Table		Page
	PART FOUR	

13 Environment

	Explanatory notes	192
13.1	Estimated atmospheric emissions on a National Accounts basis, 2003	199
13.2	Estimated emissions of greenhouse gases on IPCC basis: 1990 to 2004	199
13.3	Estimated emissions of sulphur dioxide (SO^2): by source	200
13.4	Estimated emissions of PM_{10}: by source	200
13.5	Estimated emissions of nitrogen oxides (NO_x): by source	201
13.6	Estimated emissions of carbon monoxide (CO): by source	201
13.7	Estimated emissions of volatile organic compounds (VOCs): by source	202
13.8	Annual rainfall: by region	202
13.9	Biological and chemical quality of rivers and canals: England, Wales and Northern Ireland	203
13.10	Water quality of rivers and canals: Scotland	204
13.11	Water reservoir stocks: by month	204
13.12	Water industry expenditure	205
13.13	Water pollution incidents	205
13.14	Bathing water: by region	206
13.15	Estimated abstractions from all surface and groundwater sources: by purpose	206
13.16	Radioactive waste stocks and arisings	207
13.17	Estimated total annual waste arisings: by sector	208
13.18	Recycling of selected materials	208
13.19	Noise complaints received by Environmental Health Officers	209
13.20	Material flows	210
13.21	Designated areas: by region, 2005	211

14 Housing

	Explanatory notes	214
14.1	Stock of dwellings: by tenure and country	215
14.2	Tenure: by type of accommodation, 2004/05	215
14.3	Permanent dwellings completed: by tenure and country	216
14.4	Stock of dwellings: Estimated annual gains and losses	217
14.5	Housebuilding completions: by number of bedrooms	217
14.6	Mortgages	218
14.7	County Court mortgage possession orders: by region	218
14.8	Sales and transfers of local authority dwellings	219
14.9	Households in Temporary Accommodation	219

15 Transport and communications

	Explanatory notes	222
15.1	Trips per person per year: by main mode and purpose, 2003/04	225
15.2	Retail Prices Index: transport components, 1994–2004	225
15.3	Domestic freight transport: by mode	226
15.4	Passenger transport: by mode	227
	Road transport	
	Great Britain	
15.5	Motor vehicle traffic: by road class	227
15.6	Public road length: by road type	228
15.7	Road traffic: by type of vehicle	228
15.8	Motor vehicles currently licenced	229
15.9	New vehicle registrations: by taxation class	229
15.10	Driving test pass rates: by sex and type of vehicle licence	230
15.11	Full car driving licence holders: by sex and age	230
15.12	Households with regular use of cars	231

Contents

Table		Page
	Northern Ireland	
15.13	Vehicles with current licences	232
15.14	New vehicle registrations	232
	Great Britain	
15.15	Local bus services: passenger journeys: by area	233
15.16	Local bus services: fare indices: by area	233
15.17	Road accident casualties: by road user type and severity	234
15.18	Freight transport by road: goods moved by goods vehicles over 3.5 tonnes	235
15.19	Freight transport by road: goods lifted by goods vehicles over 3.5 tonnes	236
	Rail transport	
	Great Britain	
15.20	Rail systems summary	237
15.21	National railways freight	238
	Northern Ireland	
15.22	Railways: permanent way and rolling stock	238
15.23	Operating statistics of railways	239
	Air transport	
15.24	Main output of United Kingdom airlines	239
15.25	Air traffic between the United Kingdom and abroad	239
15.26	Operations and traffic on scheduled services: revenue traffic	240
15.27	Accidents on scheduled fixed wing passenger-carrying services	241
15.28	Activity at civil aerodromes	241
	Sea transport	
15.29	United Kingdom ports: foreign, coastwise and one-port traffic	242
15.30	Roll-on/roll-off ferry and Channel Tunnel traffic; road goods vehicles outward to mainland Europe: by country of registration	244
	Passenger movement	
15.31	United Kingdom international passenger movements: by air and sea	244
	Communications	
15.32	Postal services and television licences	245

PART FIVE

16 National accounts

	Explanatory notes	248
16.1	United Kingdom national and domestic product: Main aggregates	251
16.2	United Kingdom gross domestic product and national income: Current prices	252
16.3	United Kingdom gross domestic product: Chained volume measures	253
16.4	Gross value added at current basic prices: by industry	254
16.5	Gross value added at basic prices: by industry: Chained volume indices	255
16.6	Non-financial corporations: allocation of primary income account	256
16.7	Non-financial corporations: secondary distribution of income account	256
16.8	General government: allocation of primary income account	257
16.9	General government: secondary distribution of income account	258
16.10	Households and non-profit institutions serving households: allocation of primary income account	259

Contents

Table		Page
16.11	Households and non-profit institutions serving households: secondary distribution of income account	260
16.12	Households and non-profit institutions serving households: use of disposable income account	260
16.13	The sector accounts: key economic indicators	261
16.14	Household final consumption expenditure at current market prices: by purpose	262
16.15	Household final consumption expenditure: by purpose: Chained volume measures	263
16.16	Individual consumption expenditure: by households, NPISHs and general government: current market prices	264
16.17	Individual consumption expenditure: by households, NPISHs and general government: chained volume measures	266
16.18	Change in inventories: chained volume measures	267
16.19	Gross fixed capital formation at current purchasers' prices: by broad sector and type of asset	268
16.20	Gross fixed capital formation at current purchasers' prices: by type of asset	268
16.21	Gross fixed capital formation: by broad sector and type of asset: chained volume measures	269
16.22	Gross fixed capital formation: by type of asset: chained volume measures	269

Prices **17**

	Explanatory notes	272
17.1	Producer price index of materials and fuels purchased: by all manufacturing and selected industries SIC(92)	274
17.2	Producer price index of output: by all manufacturing and selected industries SIC(92)	275
17.3	Internal purchasing power of the pound	276
17.4	Consumer Prices Index: detailed figures by division	277
17.5	Retail Prices Index	278
17.6	Tax and Price Index	279
17.7	Index of purchase prices of the means of agricultural production	280
17.8	Index of producer prices of agricultural products	281
17.9	Commodity price trends	282

Government finance **18**

	Explanatory notes	286
	Central government	
18.1	Sector analysis of key fiscal balances	289
18.2	Public sector transactions and fiscal balances	290
18.3	Public sector net debt	291
18.4	Consolidated Fund and National Loans Fund: revenue and expenditure; receipts and payments	292
18.5	Taxes paid by UK residents to general government and the European Union	293
18.6	Borrowing and repayment of debt	295
18.7	Consolidated Fund and National Loans Fund: assets and liabilities	296
18.8	British government and government guaranteed marketable securities	298
18.9	Income tax: allowances and reliefs	299
18.10	Rates of Income tax	299
18.11	Rateable values	300
	Local authorities	
	United Kingdom	
18.12	Local authorities: gross loan debt outstanding	300
18.13	Revenue expenditure of local authorities	301

Contents

Table		Page
	England and Wales	
18.14	Financing of revenue expenditure	303
18.15	Local authority capital expenditure and receipts	304
18.16	Capital expenditure and income	305
	Scotland	
18.17	Expenditure of local authorities	306
18.18	Income of local authorities: classified according to source	307
18.19	Income of local authorities from government grants	307
	Northern Ireland	
18.20	Expenditure of local authorities	308

19 External trade and investment

	Explanatory notes	310
19.1	Trade in goods	314
19.2	Import penetration and export sales ratios for products of manufacturing industry	315
19.3	United Kingdom exports: by commodity	317
19.4	United Kingdom imports: by commodity	318
19.5	United Kingdom exports: by area	319
19.6	United Kingdom imports: by area	320
19.7	Services supplied (exports) and purchased (imports), 2003	321
19.8	International trade in services: by country, 2003	322
19.9	Summary of balance of payments, 2004	323
19.10	Summary of balance of payments: balances (credits less debits)	324
19.11	Balance of payments: current account	325
19.12	Balance of payments: summary of international investment position, financial account and investment income	326
19.13	Net outward foreign direct investment by United Kingdom companies: by area and main country	327
19.14	United Kingdom outward foreign direct international investment position: book value of net assets: by area and main country	328
19.15	Net earnings from foreign direct investment overseas by United Kingdom companies: by area and main country	329
19.16	Net inward foreign direct investment in the United Kingdom: by area and main country	330
19.17	United Kingdom inward foreign direct international investment position: book value of net liabilities: by area and main country	331
19.18	Net earnings from foreign direct investment in the United Kingdom: by area and main country	332

20 Research and development

	Explanatory notes	334
20.1	Cost of research and development: by sector	335
20.2	Gross central government expenditure on research and development	335
20.3	Net central government expenditure on research and development: by European Union objectives for research and development expenditure	336
20.4	Intramural expenditure on Business Enterprise research and development: by industry	336
20.5	Sources of funds for research and development within Business Enterprises	337

21 Agriculture, fisheries and food

	Explanatory notes	340
21.1	Production and income account at current prices	342
21.2	Output and input volume indices	344

Contents

Table		Page
21.3	Agriculture land-use	346
21.4	Estimated quantity of crops and grass harvested	347
21.5	Cattle, sheep, pigs and poultry on agricultural holdings	348
21.6	Forestry	349
21.7	Sales for food of agricultural produce and livestock	350
21.8	Stocks of food and feedingstuffs	350
21.9	Processed food and animal feedingstuffs: production	351
21.10	Food and animal feedingstuffs: disposals	352
21.11	Average weekly and hourly earnings and hours of full time male agricultural workers	353
21.12	Average weekly and hourly earnings and hours of agricultural workers: by type, 2004	353
21.13	Workers employed in agriculture: by type	353

Fisheries

21.14	Landings of fish by United Kingdom vessels: live weight and value	354
21.15	Fishing fleet	355

Food consumption

21.16	Estimated household food consumption	356

22 Production

	Explanatory notes	358
22.1	Production and construction: summary table	362
22.2	Manufacturers' sales: by industry	366
22.3	Numbers of local units in manufacturing industries, March 2005	371

Energy

22.4	Production of primary fuels	372
22.5	Total inland energy consumption	372
22.6	Coal: supply and demand	373
22.7	Fuel input and gas output: gas sales	373
22.8	Electricity: generation, supply and consumption	374
22.9	Electricity: plant capacity and demand	375
22.10	Electricity: fuel used in generation	375
22.11	Indigenous petroleum production, refinery receipts, imports and exports of oil	376
22.12	Throughput of crude and process oils and output of refined products from refineries	376
22.13	Deliveries of petroleum products for inland consumption	377

Industrial materials

22.14	Iron and steel: summary of steel supplies, deliveries and stocks	378
22.15	Iron and steel: iron ore, manganese ore, pig iron and iron and steel scrap	379
22.16	Iron and steel: furnaces and production of steel	380
22.17	Non-ferrous metals	381
22.18	Fertilisers	383
22.19	Minerals: production	383

Building and construction

22.20	Building materials and components: production	384
22.21	Construction: value of output in Great Britain	385
22.22	Construction: value of new orders obtained by contractors	385

Manufactured goods

22.23	Total engineering: total turnover of UK based manufacturers	386
22.24	Volume index numbers of turnover and orders for the engineering industries	387
22.25	Motor vehicle production	388

Contents

Table		Page
22.26	Alcoholic drink	388
22.27	Tobacco products: released for home consumption	389

23 Banking, insurance etc

	Explanatory notes	392
23.1	Bank of England	393
23.2	Value of inter-bank clearings	393
23.3	Other banks' balance sheet	394
23.4	Industrial analysis of bank lending to UK residents	397
23.5	Industrial analysis of bank deposits from UK residents	400
23.6	Public sector net cash requirement and other counterparts to changes in money stock during the year	402
23.7	Money stock and liquidity	402
23.8	Selected retail banks' base rate	403
23.9	Average three month sterling money market rates	404
23.10	Average foreign exchange rates	405
23.11	Average zero coupon yields	406
23.12	Average rates on representative British Government Stocks	407

Other financial institutions

23.13	Building societies	408
23.14	Consumer credit	408
23.15	End-year assets and liabilities of investment trust companies, unit trusts and property unit trusts	409
23.16	Self-administered pension funds: market value of assets	409
23.17	Insurance companies: balance sheet market values	410

Insolvency

23.18	Individual insolvencies	412
23.19	Company insolvencies	412
23.20	Industry analysis: bankruptcies	413
23.21	Industry analysis: company insolvencies	414

24 Service industry

	Explanatory notes	416
24.1	Retail businesses	417
24.2	Retail trade: index numbers of value and volume of sales	419
24.3	Motor trades	420
24.4	Catering and allied trades	423

Sources		426
Index		442

Acknowledgements

The Editor would like to thank the following people for their help in producing this book:

Production team:	Nicola Amaranayake
	Michael Crawley
	Sunita Dedi
	Anna Donabie
	Melanie Edwards
	Jonathan Elphick
	Daniel Hern
	Usuf Islam
	Ian Macrory
	Marco Oliver
	David Penny
	Dilys Rosen
	Sathees Sivagnanam
	Steve Whyman
	Brian Yin

Contributors

The Editor also wishes to thank all his colleagues in ONS, the rest of the Government Statistical Service and all contributors in other organisations for their generous support and helpful comments, without whose help this publication would not be possible.

Typesetting by the Desktop Publishing Unit, ONS Titchfield.

Units of measurement

Length

1 millimetre (mm)		= 0.03937 inch
1 centimetre (cm)	= 10 millimetres	= 0.3937 inch
1 metre (m)	= 1,000 millimetres	= 1.094 yards
1 kilometre (km)	= 1,000 metres	= 0.6214 mile
1 inch (in.)		= 25.40 millimetres or 2.540 centimetres
1 foot (ft.)	= 12 inches	= 0.3048 metre
1 yard (yd.)	= 3 feet	= 0.9144 metre
1 mile	= 1,760 yards	= 1.609 kilometres

Area

1 square millimetre (mm²)		= 0.001550 square inch
1 square metre (m²)	= one million square millimetres	= 1.196 square yards
1 hectare (ha)	= 10,000 square metres	= 2.471 acres
1 square kilometre (km²)	= one million square metres	= 247.1 acres
1 square inch (sq. in.)		= 645.2 square millimetres or 6.452 square centimetres
1 square foot (sq. ft.)	= 144 square inches	= 0.09290 square metre or 929.0 square centimetres
1 square yard (sq. yd.)	= 9 square feet	= 0.8361 square metre
1 acre	= 4,840 square yards	= 4,046 square metres or 0.4047 hectare
1 square mile (sq. mile)	= 640 acres	= 2.590 square kilometres or 259.0 hectares

Volume

1 cubic centimetre (cm³)		= 0.06102 cubic inch
1 cubic decimetre (dm³)	= 1,000 cubic centimetres	= 0.03531 cubic foot
1 cubic metre (m³)	= one million cubic centimetres	= 1.308 cubic yards
1 cubic inch (cu.in.)		=16.39 cubic centimetres
1 cubic foot (cu. ft.)	= 1,728 cubic inches	= 0.02832 cubic metre or 28.32 cubic decimetres
1 cubic yard (cu. yd.)	= 27 cubic feet	= 0.7646 cubic metre

Capacity

1 litre (l)	= 1 cubic decimetre	= 0.2200 gallon
1 hectolitre (hl)	= 100 litres	= 22.00 gallons
1 pint		= 0.5682 litre
1 quart	= 2 pints	= 1.137 litres
1 gallon	= 8 pints	= 4.546 litres
1 bulk barrel	= 36 gallons (gal.)	= 1.637 hectolitres

Weight

1 gram (g)		= 0.03527 ounce avoirdupois
1 hectogram (hg)	= 100 grams	= 3.527 ounces or 0.2205 pound
1 kilogram (kg)	= 1,000 grams or 10 hectograms	= 2.205 pounds
1 tonne (t)	= 1,000 kilograms	= 1.102 short tons or 0.9842 long ton
1 ounce avoirdupois (oz.)	= 437.5 grains	= 28.35 grams
1 pound avoirdupois (lb.)	= 16 ounces	= 0.4536 kilogram
1 hundredweight (cwt.)	= 112 pounds	= 50.80 kilograms
1 short ton	= 2,000 pounds	= 907.2 kilograms or 0.9072 tonne
1 long ton (referred to as ton)	= 2,240 pounds	= 1,016 kilograms or 1.016 tonnes
1 ounce troy	= 480 grains	= 31.10 grams

Energy

British thermal unit (Btu)	= 0.2520 kilocalorie (kcal) = 1.055 kilojoule (kj)
Therm	= 10^5 British thermal units = 25,200 kcal = 105,506 kj
Megawatt hour (MWh)	= 10^6 watt hours (Wh)
Gigawatt hour (GWh)	= 10^6 kilowatt hours = 34,121 therms

Food and drink

Butter	23,310 litres milk	= 1 tonne butter (average)
Cheese	10,070 litres milk	= 1 tonne cheese
Condensed milk	2,550 litres milk	= 1 tonne full cream condensed milk
	2,953 litres skimmed milk	= 1 tonne skimmed condensed milk
Milk	1 million litres	= 1,030 tonnes
Milk powder	8,054 litres milk	= 1 tonne full cream milk powder
	10,740 litres skimmed milk	= 1 tonne skimmed milk powder
Eggs	17,126 eggs	= 1 tonne (approximate)
Sugar	100 tonnes sugar beet	= 92 tonnes refined sugar
	100 tonnes cane sugar	= 96 tonnes refined sugar

Shipping

Gross tonnage	= The total volume of all the enclosed spaces of a vessel, the unit of measurement being a 'ton' of 100 cubic feet.
Deadweight tonnage	= Deadweight tonnage is the total weight in tons of 2,240 lb. that a ship can legally carry, that is the total weight of cargo, bunkers, stores and crew.

Introduction

Welcome to the 2006 edition of the *Annual Abstract of Statistics*. This compendium draws together statistics from a wide range of official and other authoritative sources. Their help is gratefully acknowledged.

Regional information, supplementary to the national figures in *Annual Abstract*, appear in *Regional Trends*. The 2006 edition of *Regional Trends* is available electronically on the National Statistics Website free of charge. This can be accessed from the Regional Trends entry under the Compendia and Reference theme, or directly at: www.statistics.gov.uk/statbase/product. asp?vlnk=14356. Earlier editions are available via Palgrave Macmillan.

Current data for many of the series appearing in this Annual Abstract are contained in other ONS publications, such as *Economic Trends, Monthly Digest of Statistics, Population Trends, Health Statistics Quarterly and Financial Statistics*. All are published by Palgrave Macmillan.

The name (and telephone number, where this is available) of the organisation providing the statistics are shown under each table. In addition, a list of Sources is given at the back of the book, which sets out the official publications or other sources to which further reference can be made.

Identification codes

The four-letter identification code at the top of each data column, or at the side of each row is the ONS reference for this series of data on our database. Please quote the relevant code if you contact us requiring any futher information about the data. On some tables it is not possible to include these codes, so please quote the table number in these cases.

Definitions and Classification

Time Series

So far as possible annual totals are given throughout, but quarterly or monthly figures are given where these are more suitable to the type of series.

Explanatory notes

Most sections are preceded by explanatory notes which should be read in conjunction with the tables. Definitions and explanatory notes for many of the terms occurring in

the *Annual Abstract* are also given in the *Annual Supplement to the Monthly Digest of Statistics*, published annually in the January editions. Detailed notes on items which appear in both the *Abstract* and *Financial Statistics* are given in an annual supplement to the latter entitled *Financial Statistics: Explanatory Handbook*. The original sources listed in the Sources may also be consulted.

Standard Industrial Classification

A Standard Industrial Classification (SIC) was first introduced into the United Kingdom in 1948 for use in classifying business establishments and other statistical units by the type of economic activity in which they are engaged. The classification provides a framework for the collection, tabulation, presentation and analysis of data about economic activities. Its use promotes uniformity of data collected by various government departments and agencies. Since 1948 the classification has been revised in 1958, 1968, 1980, 1992 and 2003. One of the principal objectives of the 1980 revision was to eliminate differences from the activity classification issued by the Statistical Office of the European Communities (Eurostat) and entitled 'Nomenclature générale des activités économiques dans les Communautés Européennes', usually abbreviated to NACE. In 1990, the European Communities introduced a new statistical classification of economic activities (NACE Rev 1) by regulation. The regulation made it obligatory for the UK to introduce a new Standard Industrial Classification SIC(92), based on NACE Rev 1. UK SIC(92) was based exactly on NACE Rev 1 but, where it was thought necessary or helpful, a fifth digit was added to form subclasses of the NACE 1 four digit system. Classification systems need to be revised periodically because, over time, new products, processes and industries emerge. In January 2003, a minor revision of NACE Rev 1, known as NACE Rev 1.1, was published in the Official Journal of the European Communities. Consequently, the UK was obliged to introduce a new Standard Industrial Classification, SIC(2003) consistent with NACE Rev 1.1. The UK took the opportunity of the 2003 revision also to update the national Subclasses. Full details are available from Office for National Statistics (2002). UK Standard IndustrialClassification of Economic Activities 2003. TSO: London. ISBN 0 11 621641 7 (price £39.50) and Office for National Statistics (2002). Indexes to the UK Standard Industrial Classification of Economic Activities 2003. TSO: London. ISBN 0 11 621642 5 (price £39.50). A further update is planned for 2007. For further information see http://www.statistics.gov.uk/methods_quality/sic/downloads/subclasses.pdf

Introduction

Revisions to contents

Some of the figures, particularly for the latest year, are provisional and may be revised in a subsequent issue of the *Annual Abstract*.

Symbols and conventions used

Change of basis

Where consecutive figures have been compiled on different bases and are not strictly comparable, a footnote is added indicating the nature of the difference.

Geographic coverage

Statistics relate mainly to the United Kingdom. Where figures relate to other areas this is indicated on the table.

Units of measurement

The various units of measurement used are listed following the Contents.

Rounding of figures

In tables where figures have been rounded to the nearest final digit, the constituent items may not add up exactly to the total.

Symbols

The following symbols have been used throughout:

.. = not available or not applicable (also information suppressed to avoid disclosure).

- = nil or less than half the final digit shown.

National Statistics Online: www.statistics.gov.uk

Web-based access to time series, cross sectional data and metadata from across the Government Statistical Service (GSS), is available using the site search and index functions from the homepage. Download many datasets, in whole or in part, or consult directory information for all GSS statistical resources, including censuses, surveys, periodicals and enquiry services. Information is posted as PDF electronic documents or in XLS and CSV formats, compatible with most spreadsheet packages.

Complete copies of this publication are available to download free of charge on the following web page:

www.statistics.gov.uk/statbase/product.asp?vlnk=94.

Contact point

The Editor welcomes any feedback on the content of the *Annual Abstract*, including comments on the format of the data and the selection of topics. Comments and requests for general information should be addressed to:

Dave Sharp
Social and Economic Micro-Analysis and Reporting Division
Room 2.164
Office for National Statistics
Government Buildings
Cardiff Road
NEWPORT
South Wales NP10 8XG

or

Email: info@statistics.gov.uk
July 2006

Area

Chapter 1

Area

The United Kingdom comprises Great Britain and Northern Ireland. Great Britain comprises England, Wales and Scotland.

Physical Features

The United Kingdom (UK) constitutes the greater part of the British Isles. The largest of the islands is Great Britain. The next largest comprises Northern Ireland and the Irish Republic. Western Scotland is fringed by the large island chain known as the Hebrides, and to the north east of the Scottish mainland are the Orkney and Shetland Islands. All these, along with the Isle of Wight, Anglesey and the Isles of Scilly, form part of the United Kingdom, but the Isle of Man in the Irish Sea and the Channel Islands between Great Britain and France are largely self-governing, and are not part of the United Kingdom. The UK is one of the 25 member states of the European Union (EU).

With an area of about 243 000 sq km (about 94 000 sq miles), the United Kingdom is just under 1 000 km (about 600 miles) from the south coast to the extreme north of Scotland and just under 500 km (around 300 miles) across at the widest point.

- Highest mountain: Ben Nevis, in the highlands of Scotland, at 1 343 m (4 406 ft)

- Longest river: the Severn, 354 km (220 miles) long, which rises in central Wales and flows through Shrewsbury, Worcester and Gloucester in England to the Bristol Channel

- Largest lake: Lough Neagh, Northern Ireland, at 396 sq km (153 sq miles)

- Deepest lake: Loch Morar in the Highlands of Scotland, 310 m (1 017 ft) deep

- Highest waterfall: Eas a'Chual Aluinn, from Glas Bheinn, in the highlands of Scotland, with a drop of 200 m (660 ft)

- Deepest cave: Ogof Ffynnon Ddu, Wales, at 308 m (1 010 ft) deep

- Most northerly point on the British mainland: Dunnet Head, north-east Scotland

- Most southerly point on the British mainland: Lizard Point, Cornwall

- Closest point to mainland continental Europe: Dover, Kent. The Channel Tunnel, which links England and France, is a little over 50 km (31 miles) long, of which nearly 38 km (24 miles) are actually under the Channel.

1.1 Area of the United Kingdom[1], 2004

	sq km		sq km
		Shropshire	3 197
		Staffordshire	2 620
United Kingdom	242 495	Warwickshire	1 975
		West Midlands (Met County)	902
Great Britain	228 919	Worcestershire	1 741
England and Wales	151 012	**East**	19 109
		Luton UA	43
		Peterborough UA	343
England	130 279	Southend-on-Sea UA	42
		Thurrock UA	163
North East	8 573		
		Bedfordshire	1 192
Darlington UA	197	Cambridgeshire	3 046
Hartlepool UA	94	Essex	3 465
Middlesbrough UA	54	Hertfordshire	1 643
Redcar and Cleveland UA	245	Norfolk	5 371
Stockton-on-Tees UA	204	Suffolk	3 800
Durham	2 226	**London**	1572
Northumberland	5 013		
Tyne and Wear (Met County)	540	Inner London	319
		Outer London	1 253
North West	14 106	**South East**	19 069
Blackburn with Darwen UA	137	Bracknell Forest UA	109
Blackpool UA	35	Brighton and Hove UA	83
Halton UA	79	Isle of Wight UA	380
Warrington UA	181	Medway UA	192
		Milton Keynes UA	309
Cheshire	2 083	Portsmouth UA	40
Cumbria	6 768	Reading UA	40
Greater Manchester (Met County)	1 276	Slough UA	33
Lancashire	2 903	Southampton UA	50
Merseyside (Met County)	645	West Berkshire UA	704
		Windsor and Maidenhead UA	197
Yorkshire and the Humber	15 408	Wokingham UA	179
East Riding of Yorkshire UA	2 408	Buckinghamshire	1 565
Kingston upon Hull, City of UA	71	East Sussex	1 709
North East Lincolnshire UA	192	Hampshire	3 679
North Lincolnshire UA	846	Kent	3 544
York UA	272	Oxfordshire	2 605
		Surrey	1 663
North Yorkshire	8 038	West Sussex	1 991
South Yorkshire (Met County)	1 552		
West Yorkshire (Met County)	2 029	**South West**	23 837
East Midlands	15 607	Bath and North East Somerset UA	346
		Bournemouth UA	46
Derby UA	78	Bristol, City of UA	110
Leicester UA	73	North Somerset UA	374
Nottingham UA	75	Plymouth UA	80
Rutland UA	382	Poole UA	65
		South Gloucestershire UA	497
Derbyshire	2 547	Swindon UA	230
Leicestershire	2 083	Torbay UA	63
Lincolnshire	5 921		
Northamptonshire	2 364	Cornwall and the Isles of Scilly	3 563
Nottinghamshire	2 085	Devon	6 564
		Dorset	2 542
West Midlands	12 998	Gloucestershire	2 653
		Somerset	3 451
Herefordshire, County of UA	2 180	Wiltshire	3 255
Stoke-on-Trent UA	93		
Telford and Wrekin UA	290		

Area

1.1 Area of the United Kingdom[1], 2004
continued

	sq km		sq km
Wales	20 733	Dumfries and Galloway	6 426
		Dundee City	60
Blaenau Gwent	109	East Ayrshire	1 262
Bridgend	251	East Dunbartonshire	175
Caerphilly	277	East Lothian	679
Cardiff	140		
Carmarthenshire	2 371	East Renfrewshire	174
		Edinburgh, City of	263
Ceredigion	1 785	Eilean Siar (Western Isles)	3 055
Conwy	1 126	Falkirk	297
Denbighshire	837	Fife	1 325
Flintshire	438		
Gwynedd	2 535	Glasgow City	175
		Highland	25 659
Isle of Anglesey	711	Inverclyde	160
Merthyr Tydfil	111	Midlothian	354
Monmouthshire	849	Moray	2 238
Neath Port Talbot	441		
Newport	190	North Ayrshire	885
Pembrokeshire	1 619	North Lanarkshire	470
		Orkney Islands	990
Powys	5 181	Perth and Kinross	5 286
Rhondda, Cynon, Taff	424	Renfrewshire	262
Swansea	378	Scottish Borders	4 732
Torfaen	126		
The Vale of Glamorgan	331	Shetland Islands	1 467
Wrexham	504	South Ayrshire	1 222
		South Lanarkshire	1 772
		Stirling	2 187
Scotland	77 907	West Dunbartonshire	159
		West Lothian	428
Aberdeen City	186		
Aberdeenshire	6 313		
Angus	2 182	**Northern Ireland**	13 576
Argyll and Bute	6 908		
Clackmannanshire	159		

1 Figures relate to land area only.

Source: Office for National Statistics

Parliamentary elections

Chapter 2

Elections

2.1 Parliamentary elections[1]
United Kingdom

Thousands and percentages

		15 Oct 1964	31 Mar 1966	18 June 1970[1]	28 Feb 1974		10 Oct 1974	3 May 1979	9 June 1983	11 June 1987	9 April 1992	1 May 1997	7 June 2001	5 May 2005
United Kingdom														
Electorate	DZ5P	35 894	35 957	39 615	40 256	DZ6V	40 256	41 573	42 704	43 666	43 719	43 846	44 403	44 246
Average-electors per seat	DZ5T	57.0	57.1	62.9	63.4	DZ6R	63.4	65.5	66.7	67.2	67.2	66.5	67.4	68.5
Valid votes counted	DZ5X	27 657	27 265	28 345	31 340	DZ6N	29 189	31 221	30 671	32 530	33 614	31 286	26 367	27 149
As percentage of electorate	DZ63	77.1	75.8	71.5	77.9	DZ6J	72.5	75.1	71.8	74.5	76.7	71.4	59.4	61.4
England and Wales														
Electorate	DZ5Q	31 610	31 695	34 931	35 509	DZ6W	35 509	36 695	37 708	38 568	38 648	38 719	39 228	39 266
Average-electors per seat	DZ5U	57.8	57.9	63.9	64.3	DZ6S	64.3	66.5	67.2	68.8	68.8	68.0	68.9	69.0
Valid votes counted	DZ5Y	24 384	24 116	24 877	27 735	DZ6O	25 729	27 609	27 082	28 832	29 897	27 679	23 243	24 097
As percentage of electorate	DZ64	77.1	76.1	71.2	78.1	DZ6K	72.5	75.2	71.8	74.8	77.5	71.5	59.3	61.4
Scotland														
Electorate	DZ5R	3 393	3 360	3 659	3 705	DZ6X	3 705	3 837	3 934	3 995	3 929	3 949	3 984	3 840
Average-electors per seat	DZ5V	47.8	47.3	51.5	52.2	DZ6T	52.2	54.0	54.6	55.5	54.6	54.8	55.3	65.1
Valid votes counted	DZ5Z	2 635	2 553	2 688	2 887	DZ6P	2 758	2 917	2 825	2 968	2 931	2 817	2 313	2 334
As percentage of electorate	DZ65	77.6	76.0	73.5	77.9	DZ6L	74.5	76.0	71.8	74.3	74.2	71.3	58.1	60.8
Northern Ireland														
Electorate	DZ5S	891	902	1 025	1 027	DZ6Y	1 037	1 028	1 050	1 090	1 141	1 178	1 191	1 140
Average-electors per seat	DZ5W	74.2	75.2	85.4	85.6	DZ6U	86.4	85.6	61.8	64.1	67.1	65.4	66.2	63.3
Valid votes counted	DZ62	638	596	779	718	DZ6Q	702	696	765	730	785	791	810	718
As percentage of electorate	DZ66	71.7	66.1	76.0	69.9	DZ6M	67.7	67.7	72.9	67.0	68.8	67.1	68.0	62.9
Members of Parliament elected: (numbers)	DZV7	630	630	630	635	DZV8	635	635	650	650	651	659	659	646
Conservative	DZ67	303	253	330	296	DZ6D	276	339	396	375	336	165	166	198
Labour	DZ68	317	363	287	301	DZ6E	319	268	209	229	271	418	412	355
Liberal Democrat[2]	DZ69	9	12	6	14	DZ6F	13	11	23	22	20	46	52	62
Scottish National Party	DZ6A	–	–	1	7	DZ6G	11	2	2	3	3	6	5	6
Plaid Cymru	DZ6B	–	–	–	2	DZ6H	3	2	2	3	4	4	4	3
Other[3]	DZ6C	1	2	6	15	DZ6I	13	13	18	18	17	20	20	22

1 The Representation of the People Act 1969 lowered the minimum voting age from 21 to 18 years with effect from 16 February 1970.
2 Liberal before 1992. The figures for 1983 and 1987 include six and five MPs respectively who were elected for the Social Democratic Party.
3 Including the Speaker.

Source: University of Plymouth for the Electoral Commission: 01752 233205

2.2 Parliamentary by-elections
United Kingdom

	May 1997 - June 2001	General[1,2] Election May 1997	June 2001 - November 2004	General[1] Election June 2001	May 2005 - November 2005	General[1] Election May 2005
Numbers of by-elections	17		6		2	
Votes recorded						
By party (percentages)						
Conservative	27.0	25.1	17.7	21.2	26.8	25.8
Labour	29.7	40.1	40.8	58.3	21.0	29.2
Liberal Democrat	22.1	14.4	31.3	13.7	35.7	32.7
Scottish National Party	6.0	4.1	-	-	14.4	10.4
Plaid Cymru	2.5	2.3	2.7	2.1	-	-
Other	12.7	14.1	7.4	4.7	2.2	1.8
Total votes recorded (percentages)	100.0	100.0	100.0	100.0	100.0	100.0
(thousands)	435	723	140	205	67	92

1 Votes recorded in the same seats in the previous General Election.
2 Proportions of 'other' votes inflated by the fact that votes were cast for the retiring Speaker as 'The Speaker seeking re-election' and not as a party candidate.

Source: University of Plymouth for the Electoral Commission: 01752 233205

2.3 Devolved assembly elections
Wales and Scotland

Thousands and percentages

		6 May 1999	1 May 2003
Welsh Assembly			
Electorate	E28K	2 205	2 230
Average-electors per seat[1]	E28N	55.1	55.7
Valid votes counted	E28Q	1 023	850
As percentage of electorate	E28T	46.4	38.1
Members elected:[2] (numbers)	E2XI	60	60
Conservative	E2WG	9	11
Labour	E2WU	28	30
Liberal Democrat	E2WW	6	6
Plaid Cymru	E2X3	17	12
Other	E2WY	–	1
Scottish Parliament			
Electorate	E28L	4 024	3 879
Average-electors per seat[1]	E28O	55.1	53.1
Valid votes counted	E28R	2 342	1 916
As percentage of electorate	E28U	58.2	49.4
Members elected:[3] (numbers)	E2XJ	129	129
Conservative	E2WH	18	18
Labour	E2WV	56	50
Liberal Democrat	E2WX	17	17
Scottish National Party	E2X4	35	27
Other	E2WZ	3	17

1 This is the average in each first-past-the-post constituency. Additional members are then elected on the basis of a regional 'list' vote.
2 Comprising 40 from constituencies and 20 from the regional 'list'.
3 Comprising 73 from constituencies and 56 from the regional 'list'.

Source: University of Plymouth for the Electoral Commission: 01752 233205

2.4 Devolved assembly elections
Northern Ireland

Thousands and percentages

		25 June 1998	26 Nov 2003
Electorate	E28M	1 179	1 098
Average-electors per seat[1]	E28P	65.5	61.0
Valid votes counted	E28S	810	702
As percentage of electorate	E28V	68.7	64.0
Members elected: (numbers)	E2XK	108	108
Alliance Party	E2X5	6	6
SDLP	E2X6	24	18
Sinn Fein	E2X7	18	24
Democratic Unionist Party	E2X8	20	30
UK Unionist Party	E2X9	5	1
Ulster Unionist Party	E2XA	28	27
Other	E2X2	7	2

1 This is the average in each Westminster constituency. Six members are elected by single transferable vote (STV) in each constituency.

Source: University of Plymouth for the Electoral Commission: 01752 233205

International development

Chapter 3

International development

Overseas development assistance

(Tables 3.1 and 3.2)

The Department for International Development (DFID) is the UK Government Department with lead responsibility for overseas development. DFID's aim is to eliminate poverty in poorer countries through achievement of the Millennium Development Goals (MDGs) by 2015, statistics relating to international development are published on a financial year basis and on a calendar year basis. Statistics on a calendar year basis allow comparisons of aid expenditure with other donor countries.

Aid flows can be measured before (gross) or after (net) deductions of repayments of principal on past loans. These tables show only the gross figures.

Aid is provided in two main ways: Bilateral funding is provided directly to partner countries while multilateral funding is provided through international organisations.

Funds can only be classified as multilateral if they are channelled through an organisation on a list in the OECD – Development Assistance Committee (DAC) Statistical Reporting Directives which identifies all multilateral organisations. This list also highlights some bodies that might appear to be multilateral but are actually bilateral (in particular this latter category includes some international non-governmental organisations such as the International Committee of the Red Cross and some Public-Private Partnerships such as the Global Alliance for Vaccines and Immunisation and the Global Fund to Fight Aids, Tuberculosis and Malaria). The DAC list of multilaterals is updated annually based on members nominations; organisations must be engaged in development work to be classified as multilateral aid channels.[1]

While core funding to multilateral organisations is always classified as multilateral expenditure, additional funding channelled through multilaterals is often classified as bilateral expenditure. This would be the case in circumstances where a DFID country office transfers some money to a multilateral organisation (e.g. UN agency) for a particular programme in that country (or region). That is where DFID has control over what the money is being spent on and/or where it is being spent. Likewise, if DFID responds to an emergency appeal from

an agency for a particular country or area, the funds will be allocated as bilateral spend to that country or region. As a result, some organisations, such as UN agencies have some of their DFID funding classified as bilateral and some as multilateral.

DFID is planning to introduce a new activity reporting system from 2007. The new system will be more flexible and will allow more information to be gathered on aid flows, including details of how much of DFID's bilateral aid programme is channelled through multilateral organisations, and vice versa.

Table 3.1 shows the main groups of multilateral agencies, the International Development Association being the largest in the World Bank Group.

Bilateral assistance takes various forms:

Financial Aid – Poverty Reduction Budget Support (PRBS) – Funds provided to developing countries for them to spend in support of their expenditure programmes whose long-term objective is to reduce poverty; funds are spent using the overseas governments' own financial management, procurement and accountability systems to increase ownership and long term sustainability. This includes PRBS earmarked for a specific sector.

Other Financial Aid – Funding of projects and programmes such as Sector Wide Programmes not classified as PRBS. Financial aid in its broader sense covers all bilateral aid other than technical cooperation and administrative costs but in SID we separately categorise 'Grants and Other Aid in Kind', Humanitarian Assistance and DFID Debt Relief. Aid and Trade Provision which was previously identified in SID has now been merged into 'other financial aid' as it is a rapidly declining flow.

Technical Co-operation – Activities designed to enhance the knowledge, intellectual skills, technical expertise or the productive capability of people in recipient countries. It also covers funding of services which contribute to the design or implementation of development projects and programmes.

This assistance is mainly delivered through research and development, the use of consultants, training (generally overseas partners visiting the UK or elsewhere for a training programme) and employment of 'other Personnel' (non-DFID experts on fixed term contracts). This latter category is growing less significant over time as existing contracted staff reach the end of their assignments.

Grants and Other Aid in Kind – This category comprises support to the development work of UK and international Civil Society Organisations, (increasingly through partnership agreements with Civil Society Organisations) and grants to the

---

[1] Money may be classified as bilateral while a case is being made for a new multilateral organisation to be recognised.

British Council. It also covers equipment and supplies that the UK might provide (e.g. medical supplies) and funding under a Small Grant Scheme intended to allow Heads of Mission in a number of partner countries to fund eligible small projects of developmental value.

Humanitarian Assistance – Provides food aid and other humanitarian assistance including shelter, medical care and advice in emergency situations and their aftermath. Work of the conflict pools is also included.

DFID Debt Relief – This includes sums for debt relief on old DFID aid loans and cancellation of debt under the Commonwealth Debt Initiative (CDI). The non-CDI DFID debt relief is reported on the basis of the 'benefit to the recipient country'. This means that figures shown represent the money available to the country in the year in question that would otherwise have been spent on debt servicing. The CDI debt cancellation is reported on a 'lump sum' basis where all outstanding amounts on a loan are shown at the time the agreement to cancel is made. See Section 5 for more details on debt relief.

CDC Investments – CDC Group plc (or CDC) replaced the former Commonwealth Development Corporation in 1999. CDC was founded in 1948 and is now the UK government's instrument for investing in the private sector in developing economies (it does so through fund management companies, of whom the largest is Actis Capital LLP). CDC has activities in more than 50 developing countries. CDC provides equities and concessional loans to companies in some aid-eligible countries, and these disbursements and repayments are included as UK flows. Although CDC no longer provides loans to governments, it did in the past and these existing loans can become eligible for debt relief.

Non-DFID Debt Relief – Comprises CDC Debt and ECGD Debt. CDC has a portfolio of loans to governments which can become eligible for debt relief under the HIPC (Heavily Indebted Poor Countries) or other debt relief deals. In 2004/05 £35 million of debts owed to CDC were reorganised.

ECGD is an agency of the Department of Trade and Industry which assists UK exporters to win business overseas by providing insurance for exporters and guarantees to banks providing export finance. Countries can acquire debt with ECGD when they default on paying for goods and services.

Other – This includes contributions from other Government Departments to CSO's, British Council and Global Conflict Pool, and small amounts of drug related assistance funded by the Home Office and FCO.

Further details on the UK's development assistance can be found in the Department for International Developments publication Statistics on International Development which can be found on the website www.dfid.gov.uk/pubs/files/sid2005/contents.asp. International Comparisons are available in the OECD Development Assistance Committee's annual report.

Gross public expenditure on aid (GPEX)[1]
United Kingdom

£ Thousand

		1996/97	1997/98	1998/99	1999/00	2000/01	2001/02	2002/03	2003/04	2004/05
Bilateral Assistance										
Department for International Development										
Poverty Reduction Budget Support	LUJS	106 361	96 448	127 634	174 159	263 998	268 200	215 407	339 298	422 941
Other Financial Aid	LUJW	96 299	84 784	133 574	141 165	205 975	263 942	307 117	366 900	328 608
Technical Co-operation Projects	LUOS	457 060	487 003	479 621	518 095	453 421	472 721	557 983	482 076	508 275
Grants and Other Aid in Kind	LUOT	191 152	172 665	189 311	170 124	243 602	296 413	395 927	448 537	526 043
Humanitarian Assistance	LUOU	121 886	94 680	113 159	227 157	219 904	192 760	294 688	308 300	344 015
DFID Debt Relief	LUOV	23 529	23 161	25 659	23 140	20 367	17 682	20 364	15 531	14 932
CDC Investments	LUOX	189 082	249 062	166 716	268 518	201 427	159 352	237 324	350 356	233 320
Debt Relief	EQ4B	..	..	..	..	82 150	251 741	408 063	175 544	281 790
Aid and Trade Provision	LUOW	61 978	60 711	56 898	37 790	..	..	..	..	..
Other	LUOY	34 224	170 171	87 147	100 721	66 978	67 795	79 459	111 197	140 542
Total	LUOZ	1 281 571	1 438 684	1 379 719	1 660 868	1 757 822	1 990 606	2 516 332	2 597 739	2 800 466
Multilateral Assistance										
European Community[2]	LUPA	636 418	557 287	754 549	752 473	727 685	756 885	901 059	1 085 594	1 170 489
World Bank Group	LUPB	174 398	189 851	175 254	167 297	242 965	219 616	221 939	382 594	206 455
IMF Poverty Reduction and Growth Facility	LUPC	20 000	20 000	18 000	17 000	..	11 147	11 434	9 417	1 767
Global Environmental Assistance	EQ4C	16 541	18 832	15 320	17 095	21 143	25 337	27 338	61 213	52 446
HIPC Trust Funds	EQ4D	..	..	..	..	27 518	23 400	17 855	19 949	42 123
UN Agencies	LUPD	130 775	141 300	133 983	175 730	245 299	226 069	188 890	210 219	214 668
Regional Development Banks	LUPE	58 833	60 411	66 295	67 178	54 803	75 382	90 647	80 391	82 165
Other	LUPF	14 124	12 014	15 037	15 355	15 539	16 749	16 728	16 108	27 463
Total	LUPG	1 067 630	1 018 527	1 193 758	1 229 223	1 334 952	1 354 585	1 475 890	1 865 485	1 797 576
Administrative costs	LUPH	82 133	91 436	98 645	104 601	138 507	132 268	154 770	249 675	224 752
Total Gross Public Expenditure on Aid	LUPI	2 431 334	2 548 647	2 672 122	2 994 692	3 231 281	3 477 459	4 146 992	4 712 899	4 822 794

1 See chapter text.
2 The institution, not the member states of the European Union.

Source: Department for International Development: 01355 843612

Total bilateral gross public expenditure on aid (GPEX): by main recipient countries and regions[1]
United Kingdom

£ Thousand

		1996/97	1997/98	1998/99	1999/00	2000/01	2001/02	2002/03	2003/04	2004/05
Main recipients										
India	LUPJ	111 789	114 022	110 374	107 283	125 479	199 163	183 446	243 948	269 266
Iraq	C222	6 282	3 351	5 749	6 585	9 545	7 760	18 853	214 313	54 907
Tanzania	LUPK	56 414	51 437	78 085	75 099	111 736	205 496	98 348	162 372	129 977
Bangladesh	LUPM	44 329	39 078	67 361	71 794	74 017	60 303	73 174	155 371	149 144
Sudan	EU5S	4 534	5 677	24 201	3 196	4 912	5 598	19 222	24 663	83 964
South Africa	LUPT	23 214	28 372	35 110	47 838	36 423	43 812	57 196	93 321	53 735
Afghanistan	C224	9 644	6 873	3 873	5 452	7 465	50 027	76 018	99 595	98 959
Ghana	LUPL	28 474	30 428	62 912	52 032	74 700	54 479	90 709	77 951	136 324
Pakistan	LUPY	59 365	32 654	26 904	23 471	15 872	44 838	46 852	66 299	55 279
Uganda	LUPN	49 207	59 325	64 261	90 286	97 427	68 095	54 041	59 558	61 454
Malawi	LUPP	44 876	30 651	52 629	49 337	55 144	49 563	52 211	57 344	56 429
Ethiopia	C225	8 371	11 867	9 793	7 299	16 484	12 088	44 224	43 665	73 044
China	LUPS	30 956	38 616	39 190	26 260	56 702	50 266	44 386	42 406	42 229
Mozambique	LUPV	26 610	48 311	28 902	70 630	43 304	134 133	39 101	36 713	47 940
Rwanda	EU5T	9 704	6 198	13 568	14 294	32 431	26 818	31 937	26 910	45 028
Egypt, Arab Republic	EU5U	6 299	7 246	4 947	3 546	2 661	2 594	8 415	3 193	42 710
Vietnam	EU5V	5 606	4 329	4 699	5 202	5 633	15 810	18 508	23 264	40 425
Zambia	LUPO	40 529	46 742	33 567	46 779	93 343	59 203	45 140	32 304	163 537
Nigeria	C227	7 866	9 346	11 216	14 597	15 940	20 561	29 287	32 630	78 767
Kenya	EU5W	26 438	30 025	42 163	32 927	62 155	34 243	63 024	28 453	37 824
Total	LUQD	600 507	604 548	719 504	753 907	941 373	1 144 850	1 094 092	1 524 273	1 720 942
Total other countries	LUQE	681 064	834 135	660 215	906 961	816 450	845 757	1 422 241	1 073 467	1 079 525
Regional totals										
Africa	LUQF	445 153	450 076	574 289	630 662	774 594	871 208	893 354	1 060 963	1 270 592
America	LUQG	107 291	271 336	170 125	239 831	180 159	170 742	224 193	105 875	123 544
Asia	LUQH	401 402	391 763	349 939	381 890	410 807	535 377	609 935	969 310	905 186
Europe	LUQI	137 934	114 537	83 171	191 899	113 854	97 609	384 240	74 871	62 344
Pacific	LUQJ	12 458	26 890	20 251	7 248	4 734	6 802	5 279	4 195	3 272
World unallocated[2]	LUQK	177 333	184 081	181 943	209 338	273 675	308 869	399 332	382 526	435 529
Total Bilateral GPEX	LUQL	1 281 571	1 438 683	1 379 719	1 660 868	1 757 823	1 990 607	2 516 333	2 597 740	2 800 467

1 See chapter text.
2 Includes grants to VSO, CSOs, Research Institutions and Commonwealth Organisations based in the UK.

Source: Department for International Development: 01355 843612

Defence

Chapter 4

Defence

This section includes figures on Defence expenditure, on the size and role of the Armed Forces and on related support activities.

Much of the material in this section can be found in *UK Defence Statistics 2005 (The Stationery Office)*.

Defence expenditure (Table 4.1)

UK Defence Expenditure – the move from cash to resource accounting

Up until Financial Year 1998/99, Government expenditure was accounted for on a Cash basis. For the years 1999/00 and 2000/01 there was a transitional period from Cash to Resource Accounting & Budgeting (RAB), whereby Government Departments continued to be controlled on a cash basis, but were required to produce consolidated resource accounts. Since

2001/02 Government expenditure has been accounted for on a resource basis only. The main difference arising from the adoption of RAB is that costs are accounted for as they are incurred, rather than when payment is made (the principle of accruals). This gives rise to timing differences in accounting between the Cash and RAB systems and also to the recognition of depreciation. Additionally, under RAB, departments are required to account for a cost of capital charge, equivalent to an interest charge on the capital (in the form of net assets) held on the Balance Sheet.

> The change from cash based accounting to resource (accruals) based accounting, and the two stage introduction of RAB (outlined below) has affected the time series comparability of the data.
>
> Please refer to *UK Defence Statistics 2002* Chapter 1 – Resource Accounting & Budgeting section for a summary of the key events leading to the introduction of RAB. Back copies of this publication are available at www.dasa.mod.uk/national statistics.

Managing Resources

Under Resource Accounting, Government Departments are accountable for their spending against Resource and Capital Departmental Expenditure Limits (DELs). Spending against the Resource DEL covers current items such as in year personnel costs, equipment/stock consumption, maintenance of land and

buildings etc. The Capital budget, whilst part of the overall DEL, reflects investment spending that will appear on the Department's balance sheet and be consumed over a number of years. Departments are also responsible for Annually Managed Expenditure (AME). This spending is demand led (for example, payment of War Pensions) and therefore cannot be controlled by Departments in the same way.

Stage 1 of RAB covered the financial years 2001/02 and 2002/03. Unlike cash, costs were accrued as they were incurred, rather than when payment was made. For 2001/02 and 2002/03 the Resource DEL did not include the non-cash costs associated with Resource Accounting, such as depreciation and the cost of capital charge. During the stage 1 period these non-cash costs fell within Annually Managed Expenditure (AME) and were not controlled to the same degree as DELs. This arrangement was applied in Stage 1 only and allowed departments an interim period to gain experience of managing the new non-cash costs, to reconsider their holdings of stocks and fixed assets, which impact the non-cash costs, prior to the charge impacting on the more tightly controlled DELs.

Stage 2 of RAB began at the start of the financial year 2003/04. This involved the movement of the primary non-cash costs (depreciation and the cost of capital charge) from AME into the Resource DEL.

> The change in definition of the DELs combined with volatile non-cash costs over the Stage 1 period make time series comparisons over the period 2001/02 – 2003/04 complex. Additionally, the mix of cash and non-cash costs may be subject to change in future years.

Factors affecting Cash to RAB data consistency

i) There are timing differences as to when payments are recognised.

ii) The movement of Non-Cash items of expenditure from AME into the Resource DEL from 2003/04 onwards has the 'apparent' effect of inflating the Resource DEL.

iii) In financial year 2003/04 the Cost of Capital Charge is reduced from 6 per cent to 3.5 per cent.

iv) The discount rate for provisions was changed from 3.5 per cent real to 2.2 per cent real with effect from 1 April 2005.

v) The discount rate for pension's liabilities was changed from 3.5 per cent real to 2.8 per cent real with effect from 1 April 2005.

Under Resource Accounting the individual headings consist of the following:

Equipment support: Internal and contracted out costs for equipment repair and maintenance.

Stock consumption: Consumption of armament, medical, dental, veterinary, oil, strategic weapon systems, clothing, and general stores.

Property management: Estate and facilities management services and costs for buildings' maintenance.

Movements: Cost of transportation of freight and personnel.

Accommodation and utilities: Charges include rent, rates, gas, electricity, water and sewerage costs.

Professional fees: Includes legal and consultancy fees.

Fuel: Relates to fuel consumption by military vehicles, ships and aircraft.

Expenditure on fixed asset categories: Includes disposal receipts but include in particular:

Intangible assets: comprise the development costs of major equipment projects and Intellectual Property Rights.

Assets in the course of construction: largely consist of major weapons platforms under construction in the Defence Procurement Agency (there is a smaller element of buildings under construction). Once construction is complete, those platforms will transfer to the relevant top level budget holder as Fighting Equipment.

Capital spares: are items of repairable material used to replace parts of assets undergoing repair, refurbishment, and maintenance, servicing, modification, enhancement or conversion. Examples include aircraft engines and ships.

Redemption of QinetiQ: Redemption of QinetiQ refers to the proceeds received from the partial redemption of the Redeemable Preference Shares during 2004/05.

Other income: Other Income includes Consolidated Funds Extra Receipts (CFERs) which are income generated by disposals. In previous years CFER income has been already allocated across the categories in Capital DEL.

Other: This category contains the sum of movements, cash release and cost of capital credit on nuclear provisions and also QinetiQ loan repayments. For 2001/02 and 2002/03 AME includes depreciation and the cost of capital charge. The 2002/03 figure includes a supplementary estimate for additional funding to cover the asset write offs in this year.

For 2001/02 through to 2003/04, the 'other' category contains the sum of movements, cash release and cost of capital credit on nuclear provisions and also QinetiQ loan repayments. In addition, for 2001/02 and 2002/03 this category includes depreciation and the cost of capital charge. The 2002/03 figure includes a supplementary estimate for additional funding to cover the asset write off in this year.

Departmental Expenditure Limit (DEL). This changed under Stage 2 RAB when non-cash costs moved to the Resource DEL. The 2002/03 Annually Managed Expenditure figure includes a supplementary estimate for asset revaluation. From 2003/04 Annually Managed Expenditure includes only demand led items such as war pensions.

In order to give a single measure of spending on public services under full resource budgeting, the Defence Spending line is presented as the sum of the resource and capital budgets, net of depreciation and impairments. This reflects the resources required plus the net investment in them, but avoids double counting the writing down of the existing capital stock and the cash outlay on new assets. Control is exercised separately on gross Capital and Resource DEL.

Service personnel

(Tables 4.2, 4.4, 4.5, 4.8 and 4.10)

The Regular Forces consist entirely of volunteer members serving on a whole-time basis, figures for which include both Trained and Untrained personnel and exclude Gurkhas, Full Time Reserve Service personnel, the Home Service battalions of the Royal Irish Regiment, mobilised reservists and Naval Activated Reservists.

Locally Entered Personnel are recruited outside the United Kingdom for whole-time service in special formations with special conditions of service and normally restricted locations. The Brigade of Gurkhas is an example.

The Regular Forces are supported by Reserves and Auxiliary Forces. There are both regular and volunteer Reserves. Regular Reserves consist of former Service personnel with a Reserve liability. Volunteer Reserves are open to both former Service personnel and civilians. The call out liabilities of the various reserve forces differ in accordance with their roles.

All three Services run cadet forces for young people and the Combined Cadet Force, which is found in certain schools where education is continued to the age of 17 or above, may operate sections for any or all of the Services.

Full-Time Reserve Service personnel represent reserves serving full-time in regular posts. This was made possible by the

Defence

Reserve Forces Act 1996. None existed before 1998. FTRS figures include Full Commitment (FC), Home Commitment (HC) and Limited Commitment (LC) individuals.

Home Service battalions of the Royal Irish Regiment. Up until 1 July 1992, this was the Ulster Defence Regiment. The figures for the Territorial Army include Officer Training Corps and non-regular permanent staff.

The figures for cadet forces for each service include the Combined Cadet Force. Naval Service figures include officers and civilian instructors. The Army and Royal Air Force figures exclude officers and civilian instructors.

Intake of UK Regular forces from civilian life: by service

(Table 4.2)

This table shows all intakes to UK Regular Forces including re-enlistments and rejoined reservists.

Formation of the armed forces

(Table 4.3)

This table shows the number of units which comprise the 'teeth' elements of the Armed Forces and excludes supporting units.

Outflow of UK regular forces: by service

(Table 4.4)

This table does not include promotions to officer from other ranks and miscellaneous outflow.

Civilian personnel

(Table 4.6)

In previous years, the Ministry of Defence civilian workforce definition has reflected the historical requirement to understand the number of civil servants being directly funded. However with changes in employment legislation and the requirement to plan the future of the civilian workforce there was a need to change the definition to a more inclusive one better reflecting modern human resources methods and policies. In the longer term it will be used for skills planning, ensuring that the Ministry of Defence has a well-equipped workforce able to provide the best support to the UK Armed Forces.

In summary, the change over previous years is the addition of two further categories of individuals:

Casual staff – those employed on a short–term casual contract;

Those not directly funded – those staff who are employed by the Ministry of Defence, but whose salaries are paid for by another Department/Agency etc. This includes staff on loan to other government departments or working for NATO, as well as those on a career break or long–term sickness absence.

These additions allow two levels of definition to be established:

Definition – Level 1 This includes permanent and casual personnel, Royal Fleet Auxiliaries, but excludes Trading Funds. This is generally used for internal reporting and planning.

Definition – Level 0 This contains all those at Level 1 plus Trading Funds and Locally Engaged Civilians. This is used for external reporting, including National Statistics publications CPS1 and UKDS, and Parliamentary business. For more information on the revised civilian workforce definition, visit: www.dasa.mod.uk/natstats/consultation/consultation.html

As from 1 April 2000 a new top level budget was formed in the Centre called Defence Logistics Organisation, replacing the top level budgets CinC Fleet Support, Quarter Master General and RAF Logistics Command.

The QinetiQ portion of the Defence Evaluation and Research Agency was established as a private company in July 2001. The War Pensions Agency transferred from the Department of Work & Pensions in 2001. The Clyde Dockyards were contractorised in 2002.

1995 Royal Fleet Auxiliary (RFA) figures used in calculating the Level 1 measure are estimates. Data on manually paid staff before 1999 is not available, so estimates are used.

Totals and subtotals have been rounded separately and so may not appear to be the sums of their parts.

Family accommodation and defence land holdings

(Table 4.7)

In November 1996 most of the MOD's housing stock in England and Wales was sold to a private company, Annington Homes Limited. The homes required for use by Service families were leased back with the condition that the MOD release a certain number of houses each year for disposal by Annington. The proceeds of the sale are being used to upgrade the housing stock.

The table also presents statistics of land and foreshore in the United Kingdom owned or leased by the Ministry of Defence or over which it has limited rights under grants or licences. Land declared as surplus to Defence requirements is also included.

Location of Service personnel

(Table 4.8)

The figures for Service personnel in England, Wales, Scotland and Northern Ireland are obtained from a different source from that used to compile the United Kingdom total. Consequently the sum of the national figures can differ from the United Kingdom total. The figures for Northern Ireland include all personnel who are serving on emergency tours of duty but exclude the former Ulster Defence Regiment, now the Home Services element of the Royal Irish Regiment. The figures for overseas countries include service personnel who are on loan to countries in the areas shown. Royal Navy personnel on board ship are included in the United Kingdom figure if the ship was in home waters on the situation date or otherwise against the appropriate overseas area.

UK Regular forces – deaths

(Table 4.9)

Information on deaths is for the regular Armed Forces, including all trained and untrained personnel. The data here exclude the Home Service Battalion of the Royal Irish Regiment, mobilised reservists, full time reservists, Territorial Army and Naval Activated Reservists since DASA do not receive regular notifications of all deaths amongst reservists and non-regulars. The Army figure include those who died whilst serving in the Brigade of Gurkhas, although they have been excluded from the rates owing to the lack of reliable data on date of birth. Rates have been standardised to the 2004 UK Armed Forces age and gender structure.

Health

(Table 4.10)

The Services operate a number of hospitals in this country and in areas abroad where there is a significant British military presence. These hospitals take as patients, members of all three Services and their dependants; in addition, the hospitals in the United Kingdom take civilian patients under arrangements agreed with the National Health Service. Medical support is also supplied by Service medical staff at individual units, ships and stations.

Defence services and the civilian community

(Table 4.11)

The Royal Air Force and Royal Navy provide an essential service to the Search and Rescue (SAR) effort around the UK forming part of the national UK SAR coverage throughout the year for air, land and maritime operations. The military SAR teams'

primary purpose is to recover aircrew from crashed military aircraft although, each year, over 90 per cent of callouts are to civilian incidents. The SAR force currently consists of six x RAF and two x RN SAR Sea King helicopter units and four RAF Mountain Rescue Teams operating from bases around the UK plus specially equipped RAF Nimrod aircraft based in RAF Kinloss in Scotland.

The table includes urgent medical incidents in which the military SAR facilities gave assistance (e.g. inter-hospital transfers).

More than one SAR unit may be called to the same incident; consequently the number of callouts is likely to be greater than the number of incidents.

Persons moved involves moving people from a hostile environment to a safe environment or to a medical facility to receive urgent medical attention. People assisted by RAF Mountain Rescue Teams, but subsequently transported from the scene by helicopter, are recorded as having been rescued by the helicopter unit concerned.

The Royal Navy Fishery Protection squadron operates within the British fishery limits under contract to the Department for Environment, Food and Rural Affairs. Boardings carried out by vessels of the Executive Environment and Rural Affairs Department and the Department of Agriculture for Northern Ireland are not included.

Defence

4.1 UK Defence expenditure[1]

£ million[2]

		2001/02	2002/03	2003/04	2004[3]/05	2005[4]/06
Defence Spending	C228	..	..	31 078	32 597	30 945
Departmental Expenditure Limits (DEL)	SNKJ	24 439	26 144	37 390	38 393	39 386
Resource DEL	E2XV	18 521	19 958	31 317	31 799	32 506
Expenditure on personnel	SNKK	9 456	9 969	10 435	10 936	10 904
Armed forces	SNKL	7 014	7 385	7 974	8 274	8 134
Civilians	SNKM	2 442	2 584	2 461	2 662	2 770
Depreciation/impairments	SNKN	..	..	6 313	5 795	8 441
Cost of capital	SNKO	..	..	3 000	3 139	2 901
Equipment support	SNKP	2 419	3 135	3 804	4 029	3 323
Stock consumption	SNKQ	1 294	1 222	1 060	1 396	1 172
Property management	SNKR	1 222	1 453	1 393	1 525	1 589
Movements	SNKS	718	505	491	423	559
Accommodation and utilities	SNKT	572	544	643	661	766
Professional fees	SNKU	559	468	549	532	462
Fuel	SNKV	160	185	161	189	227
Other	SNKW	2 121	2 477	3 468	3 173	2 162
Capital DEL	E2XW	5 918	6 185	6 073	6 594	6 880
Expenditure on fixed asset categories						
Intangible assets	SNKX	1 031	1 756	1 662	1 579	1 943
Land and buildings	SNKY	−163	−185	−211	128	−224
Fighting equipment	SNKZ	34	320	348	389	23
Plant, machinery and vehicles	SNLA	99	132	66	118	119
IT and communications equipment	SNLB	84	94	37	134	158
Assets in the course of construction	SNLC	4 479	3 601	3 594	4 334	4 344
Transport	E2XX	..	..	..	70	..
Capital spares	SNLD	353	467	581	..	..
Capital loan repayment	E2XY	..	..	−4	−25	−7
Redemption of QinetiQ	E2XZ	..	..	..	−49	..
Unallocated	E2Y2	..	..	..	69	..
Other income	E2Y3	..	..	..	−153	..
Annually Managed Expenditure (AME)	SNLF	14 962	19 293	1 011	626	934
War pensions	SNLG	1 238	1 166	1 116	1 110	1 069
Other	SNLH	13 724	18 127	−105	−484	−135

1 See chapter text.
2 Inclusive of non-recoverable VAT at current prices.
3 Provisional outturn.
4 Planned.

Source: Ministry of Defence/DASA (Procurement): 0117 913 4530

4.2 Intake of UK regular forces from civilian life: by service[1]

Numbers

		1994/95	1995/96	1996/97	1997[2]/98	1998/99	1999/00	2000/01	2001/02	2002/03	2003/04	2004/05
All services:												
Male	KCJB	11 160	15 500	19 230	20 190	22 560	22 390	20 410	20 950	23 040	20 760	15 660
Female	KCJC	1 850	2 170	2 940	3 340	3 440	3 160	2 610	2 700	3 240	2 710	1 900
Total	KCJA	13 010	17 670	22 170	23 530	26 000	25 550	23 020	23 650	26 280	23 470	17 560
Naval service:												
Male	KCJE	960	1 990	3 400	3 970	4 110	4 250	3 990	4 270	4 420	3 530	3 240
Female	KCJF	340	350	560	630	660	700	630	740	800	580	460
Total	KCJD	1 300	2 340	3 960	4 600	4 770	4 950	4 620	5 010	5 220	4 120	3 690
Army:												
Male	KCJJ	9 490	11 530	13 580	13 390	15 010	14 750	13 450	13 620	15 060	13 930	10 780
Female	KCJK	1 190	1 380	1 940	2 010	1 980	1 750	1 320	1 240	1 550	1 260	910
Total	KCJI	10 680	12 910	15 520	15 400	16 990	16 500	14 770	14 850	16 610	15 190	11 690
Royal Air Force:												
Male	KCJM	700	1 980	2 250	2 830	3 450	3 380	2 980	3 070	3 550	3 290	1 640
Female	KCJN	320	450	430	700	800	710	660	720	890	870	530
Total	KCJL	1 020	2 420	2 680	3 530	4 250	4 100	3 630	3 780	4 450	4 160	2 180

1 See chapter text.
2 The definitions of intake used have been standardised from 1997/98 to give a more consistent picture across the three services.

Source: Ministry of Defence/DASA (Tri-Service): 020 7218 0390

4.3 Formation of the UK armed forces[1]
As at 1 April

Numbers

			1995	1996	1997	1998	1999	2000	2001	2002	2003	2004	2005
		Front Line Units											
Royal Navy[2]													
Submarines	KCGA	Vessels	16	15	15	15	15	16	16	16	16	15	15
Carriers and assault ships	KCGB	"	5	5	5	5	6	6	6	4	4	5	6
Destroyers and frigates	KCGC	"	35	36	35	35	35	32	32	32	31	31	28
Mine counter-measure	KCGE	"	18	18	19	19	20	21	23	22	22	19	16
Patrol ships and craft	KCGF	"	32	32	34	28	24	23	23	23	22	26	26
Fixed wing aircraft[3]	KCGG	Squadrons	3	3	3	3	3	1	1	1	1	1	1
Helicopters[4]	KCGH	"	15	15	15	12	12	9	9	8	8	5	5
Royal Marines	KCGI	Commandos	3	3	3	3	3	3	3	3	3	3	3
Regular Army													
Royal Armoured Corps[5]	KCGJ	Regiments	11	11	11	11	11	10	10	10	10	10	10
Royal Artillery	KCGK	"	16	16	15	15	15	15	15	15	15	14	14
Royal Engineers[6]	KCGL	"	10	10	10	10	10	11	11	11	11	11	11
Infantry	KCGM	Battalions	41	41	40	40	40	40	40	40	40	40	40
Special Air Service	KCGN	Regiments	1	1	1	1	1	–	–	–	–	–	–
Army Air Corps[4]	KCGO	"	5	5	5	5	5	–	–	–	–	–	–
Royal Air Force													
Strike/attack	KCGP	Squadrons	6	6	6	6	5	5	5	5	5	5	5
Offensive support[3]	KCGQ	"	5	5	5	5	5	2	2	2	2	2	1
Air defence	KCGR	"	6	6	6	6	5	5	5	5	4	4	4
Maritime patrol	KCGS	"	3	3	3	3	3	3	3	3	3	3	3
Reconnaissance	KCGT	"	5	5	5	5	5	5	5	5	5	5	5
Airborne early warning[7]	KCGU	"	1	2	2	2	2	2	2	2	2	2	2
Air transport and tankers and helicopters[3]	KCGV	"	14	14	13	14	14	8	9	9	9	9	9
Search and rescue	KCGX	"	2	2	2	2	2	2	2	2	2	2	2
Ground based air defence	KCGY	"	5	6	6	6	4	4	..	..	..	..	..
Field	KCGZ	"	5	5	5	5	5	5	..	..	..	..	..
Joint Helicopter Command													
Royal Navy Helicopter	JUAT	"	..	..	..	..	..	4	4	4	4	4	4
Army Aviation	JUAU	Regiments	..	..	..	..	..	5	5	5	5	5	5
Royal Air Force Helicopter	JUAV	Squadrons	..	..	..	..	..	6	6	6	6	6	6
Joint Force Harrier													
Royal Navy	JUAW	"	..	..	..	..	..	3	3	3	3	2	1
Royal Air Force	JUAX	"	..	..	..	..	..	3	3	3	3	3	3

1 See chapter text.
2 Only active vessels are shown.
3 From 2000 excludes aircraft transferred to the Joint Force Harrier squadron.
4 From 2000 excludes helicopters transferred to the Joint Helicopter command.
5 From 2000 includes one Armoured Regiment which is committed to the new Joint Nuclear Biological and Chemical Regiment.

6 Figure for 2000 includes an additional Close Support Regiment formed as a result of the Stategic Defence Review.
7 Figure for 2001 includes an embedded Operational Conversion Unit at the Sentry Operation Establishments.

Source: Ministry of Defence/DASA (Tri-Service): 020 7218 0390

4.4 Outflow of UK regular forces: by service[1]

Numbers

		1994 /95	1995 /96	1996 /97	1997[2] /98	1998 /99	1999 /00	2000 /01	2001 /02	2002 /03	2003 /04	2004 /05
All Services:												
Male	KDNA	31 050	25 750	29 320	21 860	24 500	23 870	22 520	22 360	21 770	21 200	21 330
Female	KDNB	2 990	3 120	3 680	2 490	2 970	2 750	2 430	2 350	2 340	2 200	2 100
Total	KDNC	34 040	28 860	33 000	24 350	27 470	26 620	24 950	24 710	24 100	23 400	23 430
Naval Service:												
Male	KDND	5 500	4 310	6 190	4 650	4 920	5 160	4 480	5 110	4 680	4 230	4 150
Female	KDNE	680	630	940	620	610	630	550	690	620	540	490
Total	KDNF	6 180	4 940	7 130	5 270	5 530	5 800	5 040	5 800	5 300	4 770	4 630
Army:												
Male	KDNI	20 230	13 940	13 760	13 190	15 320	14 620	13 900	13 290	13 420	13 500	13 990
Female	KDNJ	1 650	1 510	1 600	1 280	1 730	1 580	1 330	1 090	1 140	1 090	1 080
Total	KDNK	21 880	15 440	15 350	14 470	17 050	16 200	15 230	14 380	14 560	14 600	15 070
Royal Air Force:												
Male	KDNL	5 310	7 500	9 380	4 020	4 250	4 080	4 140	3 960	3 670	3 470	3 200
Female	KDNM	660	980	1 140	590	640	540	540	570	580	570	530
Total	KDNN	5 970	8 480	10 520	4 610	4 890	4 620	4 680	4 530	4 250	4 040	3 730

1 See chapter text. Comprises all those who left the Regular Forces and includes deaths.
2 The definitions of outflow used have been standardised from 1997/98 to give a more consistent picture across the three services.

Source: Ministry of Defence/DASA (Tri-Service): 020 7218 0390

4.5 UK Defence: service manpower strengths[1]
As at 1 April

Thousands

		1995	1996	1997	1998	1999	2000	2001	2002	2003	2004	2005
UK service personnel												
Full-time trained strength[2]	ZBTR	226.3	211.6	197.4	194.0	..	..	189.2	187.1	188.5	190.2	188.0
Trained Naval Service	ZBTS	48.2	45.6	41.7	40.5	39.3	38.9	38.5	37.5	37.6	37.5	36.3
UK regulars	ZBTT	48.2	45.6	41.7	40.4	39.1	38.5	38.0	36.8	36.6	36.4	35.4
Full-time reserve service	ZBTU	..	..	..	0.1	0.3	0.3	0.5	0.7	1.0	1.1	0.9
Trained Army[2]	ZBTV	108.7	103.6	101.5	100.9	..	..	100.6	100.4	102.0	103.6	102.4
UK regulars	ZBTW	104.5	99.5	97.8	97.5	96.3	96.5	96.3	96.0	97.6	99.4	98.5
Full-time reserve service[2]	ZBTX	..	..	..	..	..	..	0.8	0.9	1.0	0.7	0.4
Gurkhas	ZBTY	4.2	4.0	3.8	3.4	3.4	3.4	3.5	3.4	3.4	3.4	3.5
Trained Royal Air Force	ZBTZ	69.4	62.5	54.2	52.7	51.9	51.2	50.1	49.2	48.9	49.1	49.2
UK regulars	ZBUA	69.4	62.5	54.2	52.7	51.8	51.0	49.8	48.9	48.5	48.7	48.8
Full-time reserve service	ZBUB	..	..	..	..	0.1	0.2	0.3	0.3	0.4	0.4	0.4
Untrained UK regulars	ZBUC	11.2	14.3	17.2	19.7	21.5	21.6	21.5	23.0	24.2	22.5	18.3
Naval Service	ZBUD	2.7	2.8	3.5	4.1	4.6	4.3	4.4	4.9	5.0	4.5	4.5
Army	ZBUE	7.2	9.3	11.1	12.4	13.4	13.6	13.2	14.0	14.5	13.3	10.8
Royal Air Force	ZBUF	1.3	2.2	2.7	3.2	3.5	3.7	3.9	4.1	4.7	4.7	3.0
Locally Entered Personnel (excluding Gurkhas)	ZBUG	0.6	0.6	0.4	0.4	0.4	0.4	0.3	0.4	0.4	0.4	0.4
Royal Irish Regiment Home Service batallions	ZBUH	5.3	5.0	4.8	4.6	4.4	4.2	3.8	3.6	3.5	3.4	3.2
Reserve personnel	ZBUI	329.6	327.3	323.5	319.4	307.0	294.8	284.2	273.4	259.7	246.7	235.6
Regular Reserves	ZBUJ	264.1	264.6	259.4	254.9	247.6	241.6	234.9	224.9	212.6	201.4	191.5
Naval Services	ZBUK	23.3	23.9	24.1	24.8	24.7	24.2	23.5	23.5	23.2	22.8	22.2
Army	ZBUL	195.3	195.5	190.1	186.2	180.5	175.5	169.8	161.1	151.5	141.9	134.2
of which mobilised:	SNEO	..	..	..	0.2	0.1	0.3	0.2	0.3	0.4	0.1	0.2
Royal Air Force	ZBUM	45.5	45.2	45.3	43.9	42.4	41.9	41.6	40.3	37.9	36.6	35.2
of which mobilised:	SNEP	..	..	..	..	–	–	–	–	–	–	..
Volunteer Reserves	ZBUN	65.5	62.6	64.1	64.5	59.4	53.2	49.3	48.5	47.1	45.4	44.1
Royal Naval Reserve and Royal Marine Reserve[3]	ZBUO	3.7	3.5	4.3	4.4	4.5	4.8	4.8	5.0	4.9	4.5	4.4
of which mobilised:	SNEQ	..	..	..	..	..	..	..	..	0.4	0.1	..
Territorial Army	ZBUP	59.7	57.3	57.6	57.6	52.3	45.6	41.9	40.9	39.6	38.3	37.3
of which mobilised:	SNER	..	..	..	0.6	0.5	0.8	0.4	0.5	4.1	2.9	1.5
Royal Auxilliary Air Force	ZBUQ	2.1	1.9	2.2	2.5	2.6	2.7	2.6	2.6	2.6	2.6	2.4
of which mobilised:	SNES	..	..	..	..	–	–	–	0.1	0.8	–	..
Cadet Forces	ZBUR	143.5	152.1	151.0	150.2	151.0	154.5	151.0	152.3	155.6	155.6	153.1
Naval Service	ZBUS	26.5	26.9	26.3	25.9	24.5	24.1	23.8	23.8	23.2	22.6	21.9
Army	ZBUT	65.0	74.2	74.1	73.9	74.6	77.4	75.4	75.8	78.7	80.5	80.9
Royal Air Force	ZBUU	52.2	51.0	50.7	50.5	51.9	53.0	51.8	52.7	53.7	52.5	50.3

1 See chapter text.
2 The recorded Army Officer FTRS strength shows a significant downward revison. This is due to the identification of discrepancies within the underlying raw data supplied to DASA. The process is currently under review and FTRS figures from 2001 have been supplied by the Army Personnel Centre and should be considered as provisional. Figures for 1999 and 2000 were not available at the time of publication.
3 Figures before 1997 do not include University Royal Navy Units.

Source: Ministry of Defence/DASA (Tri-Service): 020 7218 1546

4.6 UK Defence: civilian manpower strengths[1]
As at 1 April

Thousands: Full-time Equivalent

		1995	1996	1997	1998	1999	2000	2001	2002	2003	2004	2005
Ministry of Defence civilians												
Centre												
Non-industrial	KDQE	18.6	21.8	22.9	22.2	21.5	19.7	19.1	20.0	21.2	22.7	24.0
Industrial	KDQF	0.7	0.9	1.2	1.1	1.0	0.9	0.9	0.8	0.7	0.6	0.7
Defence Logistics Organisation												
Non-industrial	ZBTJ	..	..	..	..	..	19.7	17.8	17.3	16.4	16.5	16.5
Industrial	ZBTK	..	..	..	..	..	11.5	8.4	6.3	4.4	4.3	4.1
Naval Service												
Non-industrial	KYCW	14.9	13.6	12.5	12.0	11.3	3.0	3.0	2.9	2.7	2.9	2.6
Industrial	KYCX	10.7	8.6	7.6	6.6	5.3	1.0	0.9	0.8	0.8	0.8	0.7
Royal Fleet Auxiliary	EQS9	2.4	2.2	2.2	2.4	2.4	2.4	2.4	2.4	2.5	2.3	2.3
Army												
Non-industrial	KDQK	23.4	22.9	22.4	21.7	21.6	16.3	16.4	16.0	16.0	14.7	14.5
Industrial	KDQL	15.2	14.4	13.8	12.1	10.6	5.8	5.7	5.5	5.4	5.6	5.5
Royal Air Force												
Non-industrial	KDQM	11.7	11.5	11.5	11.7	12.2	7.1	7.0	7.1	7.0	7.3	7.0
Industrial	KDQN	8.3	8.0	7.8	7.3	7.1	4.5	4.4	4.3	4.4	4.4	4.0
Procurement Executive												
Non-industrial	KDQO	15.7	–	–	–	–	–	–	–	–	–	–
Industrial	KDQP	2.5	–	–	–	–	–	–	–	–	–	–
Level 1 Total	C7PE	124.0	103.8	101.9	97.1	94.1	91.9	86.0	83.6	81.5	82.2	82.0
Non-industrial	C7PF	84.2	69.7	69.4	67.6	66.6	65.8	63.4	63.4	63.3	64.1	64.7
Industrial	C7PG	37.4	31.9	30.3	27.1	25.1	23.7	20.2	17.8	15.7	15.7	15.0
Royal Fleet Auxiliary	EQT2	2.4	2.2	2.2	2.4	2.4	2.4	2.4	2.4	2.5	2.3	2.3
Locally engaged overseas	KDQA	17.3	17.1	15.9	15.2	14.9	14.8	13.3	14.1	13.8	15.4	15.7
Non-industrial	KDQT	6.6	7.1	7.0	6.7	6.7	6.7	6.3	6.5	6.5	7.3	..
Industrial	KDQU	10.7	10.0	8.9	8.4	8.1	8.2	7.0	7.6	7.4	8.1	..
Trading funds	GQHI	..	14.5	15.5	14.0	14.0	14.5	18.8	12.4	12.2	11.4	10.8
Level 0 Total	C7PH	141.3	135.4	133.3	126.3	123.0	121.3	118.2	110.1	107.6	109.0	108.5

1 See chapter text. Individuals on temporary and geographic (T&G) promotion are classed as non-industrial. From 2004, staff who cannot be correctly allocated to Top Level Budgets (TLBs) are included with the Centre figures. (numbering approx 60 in 2004).

Source: Ministry of Defence/DASA (Civilian): 020 7218 6019

4.7 Family accommodation and defence land holdings[1]
As at 1 April

Thousands and thousand hectares

		1995	1996	1997	1998	1999	2000	2001	2002	2003	2004	2005
Family accommodation (thousands)												
United Kingdom: Total	KDPA	69.7	72.1	68.6	67.3	65.5	64.8	59.2	55.8	53.8	52.8	51.9
Land holdings												
United Kingdom												
Land[2]	KDPF	221.0	222.6	221.0	220.0	220.2	219.9	224.3	222.4	221.4	221.3	222.1
Foreshore[2]	KDPH	18.4	18.5	18.6	18.6	18.6	18.6	18.6	18.6	18.6	18.6	18.6
Rights held	KDPJ	122.3	124.3	124.5	124.5	124.8	124.8	124.8	124.9	131.1	131.1	124.9
Defence land												
Used for agricultural purposes	KDPL	107.9	107.4	96.2	103.5	114.5	92.2	98.6	91.8	103.0	100.5	106.3
Used for grazing only	KDPM	61.8	60.7	51.9	59.6	65.5	50.3	66.6	60.0	70.2	68.3	71.0
Full agricultural use	KDPN	46.1	46.7	44.3	43.9	49.0	41.9	32.0	31.8	32.8	32.2	35.3

1 See chapter text.
2 Freehold and leasehold.

Sources: Ministry of Defence/Defence Housing Executive: 020 7305 3051;
Ministry of Defence/Defence Estates: 0121 311 3818

4.8 Location of UK service personnel[1]
As at 1 July

Thousands

		1995	1996	1997	1998	1999	2000	2001	2002	2003	2004	2005
UK Service personnel, Regular Forces:												
UK distribution[2]												
In United Kingdom[3,4]	KDOB	182.2	177.4	171.6	173.4	171.7	170.3	172.0	..	..	..	169.7
England	KDOC	149.4	146.6	142.6	144.6	144.3	143.0	144.1	..	..	..	145.0
Wales	KDOD	5.2	4.3	3.3	3.2	3.3	3.2	2.6	..	..	..	2.9
Scotland	KDOE	16.9	15.5	13.9	14.2	14.9	15.1	14.5	..	..	..	13.2
Northern Ireland	KDOF	9.9	10.5	11.5	11.0	9.0	8.4	9.4	..	..	..	7.0
Global location[2]												
United Kingdom[3]	MKCN	180.7	172.0	167.5	165.0	161.0	163.1	162.8	..	..	..	169.7
Overseas	KDOG	50.0	48.5	42.6	43.1	47.1	43.0	40.9	..	..	..	29.2
Mainland European States[5]	KDOI	..	11.7	6.2	6.9	15.2	8.2	8.6	..	..	..	27.0
Germany[6]	KDOH	33.4	20.8	21.2	20.3	18.0	19.5	17.3	..	..	..	22.2
Balkans	MKCO	..	..	..	..	..	..	..	..	..	..	..
Mediterranean[7]	KDOM	0.6	0.5	0.3	1.2	1.3	1.1	2.3	..	..	..	..
Gibraltar	KDOJ	0.6	0.6	0.5	0.5	0.6	0.6	0.5	..	..	..	0.3
Cyprus	KDOL	4.4	4.0	3.9	3.6	3.6	3.5	3.5	..	..	..	3.1
Far East/Asia[8]	MKCT	1.2	1.2	1.5	0.3	0.3	1.0	0.3	..	..	..	0.3
Africa	MKCP	..	..	..	..	..	..	−	..	..	..	0.6
North America	MKCQ	..	..	..	..	..	..	2.5	..	..	..	0.7
Central/South America	MKCR	..	..	..	..	..	..	−	..	..	..	..
Falkland Islands	MKCS	..	..	..	..	..	..	0.8	..	..	..	0.3
Other locations, including unallocated	KDOQ	9.4	9.8	9.0	10.4	8.2	9.1	5.1	..	..	..	0.8
Locally entered service personnel:[9]												
United Kingdom	KDOS	1.8	1.7	2.1	2.1	2.0	2.1	2.3	2.6	2.6	2.6	2.1
Gibraltar	KDOT	0.2	0.2	0.2	0.4	0.4	0.3	0.4	0.4	0.4	0.4	0.4
Hong Kong	KDOV	1.8	1.6	0.7	..	..	..	..	..	..	..	..
Brunei	KDOW	0.9	0.7	1.0	0.9	0.8	0.8	0.8	0.8	0.8	0.7	0.8
India/Nepal	KDOX	0.5	0.7	0.9	0.5	0.5	0.5	0.4	0.3	0.4	0.4	0.4
Total	KDOK	5.1	4.9	4.7	4.0	3.7	3.7	3.9	4.2	4.1	4.1	3.3

1 See chapter text.
2 Data not available from 2002, because of concerns over the quality of source data. A review of data sources is being undertaken.
3 Figures for global location of service personnel are compiled using different methodologies to those for UK distribution. Comparison is therefore not possible between the two sets of UK personnel figures.
4 Includes personnel within the UK whose location is unknown on the 1st July.

5 Includes the Balkans until 2001.
6 Prior to 1996, figures for the Federal Republic of Germany and Mainland European States were combined.
7 Includes Med Near East and Middle East
8 Prior to 1997 figures include personnel serving in Hong Kong.
9 Including Gurkhas.

Source: Ministry of Defence/DASA (Tri-Service): 020 7218 0390

4.9 UK regular forces: deaths[1]

Numbers and rates per thousand

		1995	1996	1997	1998	1999	2000	2001	2002	2003	2004
Deaths											
Total	SNIA	201	142	160	162	139	147	140	146	170	167
Male	SNIB	192	140	151	154	136	143	137	137	163	161
Female	SNIC	9	2	9	8	3	4	3	9	7	6
Rates per thousand[2]											
Tri-service	SNIH	0.94	0.65	0.80	0.78	0.66	0.72	0.69	0.72	0.82	0.81
Navy	SNII	0.57	0.63	0.87	0.63	0.61	0.62	0.79	0.64	0.90	0.92
Army[3]	SNIJ	0.97	0.74	0.93	0.85	0.72	0.80	0.71	0.84	0.79	0.80
RAF	SNIK	0.84	0.45	0.49	0.64	0.48	0.62	0.49	0.52	0.74	0.60

1 See chapter text.
2 Rates age and gender standarised to 2004 Tri-Service strengths structure.
3 Excludes Gurkhas.

Source: Ministry of Defence/DASA (Health Statistics): 01225 468008

4.10 Strength of uniformed UK medical staff[1]
As at 1 April

Numbers

		1995	1996	1997	1998	1999	2000	2001	2002	2003	2004	2005
Qualified doctors:												
Naval Service	KDMA	260	240	210	210	210	210	220	220	230	240	260
Army	KDMB	470	430	430	440	450	460	470	490	550	600	610
Royal Air Force	KDMC	330	270	220	210	200	180	180	180	190	200	220
All Services	KDMD	1 070	940	870	850	860	860	870	890	970	1 040	1 090
Qualified dentists:												
Naval Service	KDME	70	60	60	60	60	60	60	60	60	60	60
Army	KDMF	150	140	140	140	140	140	150	140	150	150	150
Royal Air Force	KDMG	110	100	90	80	80	80	80	70	70	80	70
All Services	KDMH	340	310	290	280	290	280	290	280	270	290	280
Support staff:[2]												
Naval Service	KDMI	1 410	1 290	1 020	950	1 060	1 100	1 060	1 110	1 180	1 200	1 190
Nursing services	ZBTL	..	..	..	..	220	220	230	260	300	310	320
Support	ZBTM	..	..	..	..	840	880	830	850	880	890	880
Army	KDMJ	3 460	3 280	3 020	3 090	3 120	3 210	3 260	3 320	3 410	3 560	..
Nursing services[3]	ZBTN	..	..	..	..	520	570	610	650	710	770	770
Support	ZBTO	..	..	..	..	2 600	2 640	2 650	2 670	2 700	2 800	..
Royal Air Force	KDMK	1 800	1 400	1 210	1 190	1 360	1 460	1 480	1 500	1 600	1 680	1 660
Nursing services	ZBTP	..	..	..	..	330	400	420	450	470	480	510
Support	ZBTQ	..	..	..	..	1 030	1 060	1 070	1 050	1 130	1 200	1 160
All Services	KDML	6 660	5 980	5 260	5 230	5 540	5 760	5 800	5 930	6 180	6 440	..

1 See chapter text. Includes staff employed at units (including ships) and in hospitals.
2 Includes all members of the Nursing Services/Nursing Corps. From 1999, figures for support staff have been split so that nurses are separate from other support staff.
3 Figures do not include untrained Army Officers.

Source: Ministry of Defence/DASA (Tri- Service): 020 7218 0390

4.11 UK Defence services and the civilian community[1]

Numbers

		1994	1995	1996	1997	1998	1999	2000	2001	2002	2003	2004
Search and rescue operations at home												
Call outs of:	GPYC	2 017	2 297	2 164	1 941	1 898	1 912	1 941	1 763	1 684	1 713	1 638
Royal Navy helicopters	GPXO	560	665	512	495	463	499	499	502	436	424	453
Royal Air Force helicopters	GPXP	1 215	1 392	1 392	1 258	1 257	1 235	1 278	1 115	1 122	1 172	1 079
Contractorised and other helicopters	GPXQ	26	24	27	16	20	–	–	–	–	–	..
Royal Air Force Nimrod aircraft	GPXR	74	78	69	79	71	65	71	54	46	37	37
Other fixed wing aircraft[2]	GPXS	3	6	1	2	2	..	1	1	1	..	2
HM ships and auxilliary vessels[2]	KCMG	6	7	1	3	3	–	–	–	–	–	..
Royal Air Force mountain rescue teams	KCMH	133	125	162	88	82	113	92	91	79	80	67
Persons rescued: total	KCMI	1 390	1 382	1 550	1 226	1 243	1 204	1 316	1 182	1 224	1 270	1 414
By rescue service												
Royal Navy helicopters	GPXT	369	412	356	328	283	355	360	386	314	314	415
Royal Air Force helicopters	GPXU	892	918	1 084	877	937	832	934	781	900	920	980
Royal Air Force mountain rescue teams	GPXV	49	39	100	15	12	17	22	15	10	36	18
Other	GPXW	80	13	10	6	11	..	..	..	..	..	1
By type of rescue												
Rescue	GPXX	464	275	307	219	317	307	276	281	343	271	476
Medrescue	GPXY	766	824	921	721	667	640	713	629	654	785	693
Medivac	GPXZ	123	220	275	224	209	216	241	228	201	174	195
Recovery	GPYA	25	43	34	54	43	32	29	36	21	25	32
Other	GPYB	12	20	13	8	7	9	57	8	5	15	18
Search and rescue incidents: Total	KCMM	1 791	2 036	1 919	1 750	1 697	1 714	1 781	1 608	1 544	1 599	1 504

		1995 /96	1996 /97	1997 /98	1998 /99	1999 /00	2000 /01	2001 /02	2002 /03	2003 /04	2004 /05
Fishery protection											
Vessels boarded	KCMO	1 707	1 884	1 715	1 879	1 716	1 603	1 464	1 375	1 710	1 748

1 See chapter text.
2 Not permanently on stand-by.

Source: Ministry of Defence/DASA (Logistics): 01225 468769/467249

Population and vital statistics

Chapter 5

Population and vital statistics

This section begins with a summary of population figures for the United Kingdom and constituent countries for 1851 to 2026 and for Great Britain from 1801 (Table 5.1). Table 5.2 analyses the components of population change. Table 5.3 gives details of the national sex and age structures for years up to the present date, with projected figures up to the year 2026. Legal marital condition of the population is shown in Table 5.4. The distribution of population at regional and local levels is summarised in Table 5.5.

In the main, historical series relate to census information, while mid-year estimates, which make allowance for under-enumeration in the census, are given for the recent past and the present (from 1961 onwards).

Population

(Tables 5.1 to 5.3)

Figures shown in these tables relate to the population enumerated at successive censuses, (up to 1951), mid-year estimates (from 1961 to 2004) and population projections (up to 2026). Further information can be found on the National Statistics website (www.statistics.gov.uk/popest).

Population projections are 2004-based and were published by the Government Actuary's Department on 20 October 2005. Further information can be found at www.gad.gov.uk/Population/index.asp

Definition of resident population

The estimated resident population of an area includes all people who usually live there, whatever their nationality. Members of HM and US Armed Forces in England and Wales are included on a residential basis wherever possible. HM Forces stationed outside England and Wales are not included. Students are taken to be resident at their term time address.

The projections of the resident population of the United Kingdom and constituent countries were prepared by the Government Actuary, in consultation with the Registrars General, as a common framework for use in national planning in a number of different fields. New projections are made every second year on assumptions regarding future fertility, mortality and migration which seem most appropriate on the basis of the statistical evidence available at the time. The population projections in Tables 5.1 – 5.3 are based on the estimates of

the population of the United Kingdom at mid-2004 made by the Registrars General. On 31 January 2006 responsibility for the United Kingdom population projections transferred to ONS. Future national population projections will be produced by the National Statistics Centre for Demography within ONS on behalf of the Registrars General.

Marital condition (de jure): estimated population

(Table 5.4)

This table shows population estimates by marital status.

Geographical distribution of the population

(Table 5.5)

The population enumerated in the censuses for 1911–1951, and the mid-year population estimates for later years, are provided for standard regions of the United Kingdom, for metropolitan areas, for broad groupings of local authority districts by type within England and Wales, and for some of the larger cities. Projections of future sub-national population levels are prepared from time to time by the Registrar General, but are not shown in this publication.

Migration into and out of the United Kingdom

(Tables 5.7 to 5.9)

A migrant is defined as a person who changes his or her country of usual residence for a period of at least a year, so that the country of destination effectively becomes the country of usual residence.

The main source of international migration data is the International Passenger Survey (IPS). This is a continuous voluntary sample survey that provides information on passengers entering and leaving the UK by the principal air, sea and tunnel routes. Being a sample survey, the IPS is subject to some uncertainty; therefore it should be noted that international migration estimates, in particular the difference between inflow and outflow, may be subject to large sampling errors. The IPS excludes routes between the Channel Islands and Isle of Man and the rest of the world.

The IPS data are supplemented with three types of additional information in order to provide a full picture of total international migration:

1. The IPS is based on intentions to migrate and intentions are liable to change. Adjustments are made for visitor switchers (those who intend to stay in the UK or abroad for less than one year but subsequently stay for longer and become

migrants) and for migrant switchers (those who intend to stay in the UK or abroad for one year or more but then return earlier so are no longer migrants). These adjustments are primarily based on IPS data but for years prior to 2001, Home Office data on short-term visitors who were subsequently granted an extension of stay for a year or longer for other reasons have been incorporated.

2. Home Office data on applications for asylum and dependants of asylum seekers entering the UK are used to estimate inflows of asylum seekers and dependants not already captured by the IPS. In addition, Home Office data on removals and refusals are used to estimate outflows of failed asylum seekers not identified by the IPS.

3. Migration flows between the UK and the Irish Republic are added to these data, as the IPS did not cover this route until recently and the quality of these data are still being assessed. Migration flows are obtained mainly from the Quarterly National Household Survey and are agreed between the Irish Central Statistics Office and ONS.

The international migration estimates in Table 5.7 are derived from all these sources and represent total international migration. The estimates in Tables 5.8 and 5.9 are based on the International Passenger Survey only (without the three adjustments outlined above).

Acceptances for settlement in the United Kingdom

(Table 5.10)

This table presents in geographic regions, the statistics of individual nationalities, arranged alphabetically within each region. The figures are on a different basis from those derived from IPS (Tables 5.8 and 5.9) and relate only to people subject to immigration control. Persons accepted for settlement are allowed to stay indefinitely in the United Kingdom. They exclude temporary migrants such as students and generally relate only to non-EEA nationals. Settlement can occur several years after entry to the country.

Applications received for asylum in the United Kingdom, excluding dependants

(Table 5.11)

This table shows statistics of applications for asylum in the United Kingdom. Figures are shown for the main applicant nationalities by geographic region. The basis of assessing asylum applications, and hence of deciding whether to grant asylum in the United Kingdom, is the 1951 United Nations Convention on Refugees.

Marriages

(Table 5.12)

The figures in this table relate to marriages solemnised in the constituent countries of the UK. They take no account of the growing trend towards marrying abroad.

Divorces

(Tables 5.13 and 5.14)

A marriage may be either dissolved following a petition for divorce and the granting of a decree absolute, or annulled, following a petition for nullity and the awarding of a decree of nullity. The first group of decrees are known as dissolutions of marriage and the second as annulments of marriage. In Table 5.13 the term 'divorce' includes *both* types of decrees, although strictly speaking, it should refer only to dissolutions.

Births

(Tables 5.15 to 5.17)

For Scotland and Northern Ireland the number of births relate to those registered during the year. For England and Wales the figures up to and including 1930-32 are for those *registered*, while later figures relate to births *occurring* in each year.

All data for England and Wales and for Scotland include births occurring in those countries to mothers not usually resident in them. Data for Northern Ireland, and hence UK, prior to 1981 include births occurring in Northern Ireland to non-resident mothers; from 1981, such births are excluded.

Deaths

(Tables 5.19 and 5.21)

The figures relate to the number of deaths registered during each calendar year. However, from 1993 onwards, the figures for England and Wales represent occurrences. This change has little effect on annual totals.

Infant and maternal mortality

(Table 5.20)

On 1 October 1992 the legal definition of a stillbirth was altered from a baby born dead after 28 completed weeks gestation or more, to one born after 24 completed weeks of gestation or more. The 258 stillbirths of 24 to 27 weeks gestation that which occurred between 1 October and 31 December 1992 are excluded from this table.

Population and vital statistics

Life tables

(Table 5.22)

The current set of interim life tables are constructed from the estimated populations in 2002–04 and the births, infant deaths and deaths by individual age occurring in those years for England & Wales and registered in those years for Scotland and Northern Ireland.

The estimates used in these interim life tables are the estimates, or revised estimates, following the 2001 Census issued on the following dates:

Mid-year population estimates	England	Wales	Scotland	Northern Ireland
2002	September 2004	September 2004	June 2003	August 2003
2003	September 2004	September 2004	April 2004	August 2004
2004	August 2005	August 2005	April 2005	July 2005

Adoptions

(Tables 5.23)

The figures shown within these tables relate to the date the adoption was entered in the Adopted Children Register. Figures based on the date of court order are available for England and Wales in the volume *Marriage, divorce and adoption statistics 2003* (no. 31 in the FM2 series) available on the National Statistics website www.statistics.gov.uk or from the enquiry point shown at the foot of the tables.

5.1 Population summary: by country and sex

Thousands

	United Kingdom			England and Wales			Wales	Scotland			Northern Ireland		
	Persons	Males	Females	Persons	Males	Females	Persons	Persons	Males	Females	Persons	Males	Females
Enumerated population: Census figures													
1801	..	..	..	8 893	4 255	4 638	587	1 608	739	869	..	..	..
1851	22 259	10 855	11 404	17 928	8 781	9 146	1 163	2 889	1 376	1 513	1 442	698	745
1901	38 237	18 492	19 745	32 528	15 729	16 799	2 013	4 472	2 174	2 298	1 237	590	647
1911	42 082	20 357	21 725	36 070	17 446	18 625	2 421	4 761	2 309	2 452	1 251	603	648
1921[1]	44 027	21 033	22 994	37 887	18 075	19 811	2 656	4 882	2 348	2 535	1 258	610	648
1931[1]	46 038	22 060	23 978	39 952	19 133	20 819	2 593	4 843	2 326	2 517	1 243	601	642
1951	50 225	24 118	26 107	43 758	21 016	22 742	2 599	5 096	2 434	2 662	1 371	668	703
1961	52 709	25 481	27 228	46 105	22 304	23 801	2 644	5 179	2 483	2 697	1 425	694	731
Resident population: mid-year estimates													
	DYAY	BBAB	BBAC	BBAD	BBAE	BBAF	KGJM	BBAG	BBAH	BBAI	BBAJ	BBAK	BBAL
1969	55 461	26 908	28 553	48 738	23 666	25 072	2 722	5 209	2 503	2 706	1 514	739	776
1970	55 632	26 992	28 641	48 891	23 738	25 153	2 729	5 214	2 507	2 707	1 527	747	781
1971	55 928	27 167	28 761	49 152	23 897	25 255	2 740	5 236	2 516	2 720	1 540	755	786
1972	56 097	27 259	28 837	49 327	23 989	25 339	2 755	5 231	2 513	2 717	1 539	758	782
1973	56 223	27 332	28 891	49 459	24 061	25 399	2 773	5 234	2 515	2 719	1 530	756	774
1974	56 236	27 349	28 887	49 468	24 075	25 393	2 785	5 241	2 519	2 722	1 527	755	772
1975	56 226	27 361	28 865	49 470	24 091	25 378	2 795	5 232	2 516	2 716	1 524	753	770
1976	56 216	27 360	28 856	49 459	24 089	25 370	2 799	5 233	2 517	2 716	1 524	754	770
1977	56 190	27 345	28 845	49 440	24 076	25 364	2 801	5 226	2 515	2 711	1 523	754	769
1978	56 178	27 330	28 849	49 443	24 067	25 375	2 804	5 212	2 509	2 704	1 523	754	770
1979	56 240	27 373	28 867	49 508	24 113	25 395	2 810	5 204	2 505	2 699	1 528	755	773
1980	56 330	27 411	28 919	49 603	24 156	25 448	2 816	5 194	2 501	2 693	1 533	755	778
1981	56 357	27 412	28 946	49 634	24 160	25 474	2 813	5 180	2 495	2 685	1 543	757	786
1982	56 291	27 364	28 927	49 582	24 119	25 462	2 804	5 165	2 487	2 677	1 545	757	788
1983	56 316	27 371	28 944	49 617	24 133	25 484	2 803	5 148	2 479	2 669	1 551	759	792
1984	56 409	27 421	28 989	49 713	24 185	25 528	2 801	5 139	2 475	2 664	1 557	761	796
1985	56 554	27 489	29 065	49 861	24 254	25 606	2 803	5 128	2 470	2 658	1 565	765	800
1986	56 684	27 542	29 142	49 999	24 311	25 687	2 811	5 112	2 462	2 649	1 574	768	805
1987	56 804	27 599	29 205	50 123	24 371	25 752	2 823	5 099	2 455	2 644	1 582	773	809
1988	56 916	27 652	29 265	50 254	24 434	25 820	2 841	5 077	2 444	2 633	1 585	774	812
1989	57 076	27 729	29 348	50 408	24 510	25 898	2 855	5 078	2 443	2 635	1 590	776	814
1990	57 237	27 819	29 419	50 561	24 597	25 964	2 862	5 081	2 444	2 637	1 596	778	818
1991	57 439	27 909	29 530	50 748	24 681	26 067	2 873	5 083	2 445	2 639	1 607	783	824
1992	57 585	27 977	29 608	50 876	24 739	26 136	2 878	5 086	2 445	2 640	1 623	792	831
1993	57 714	28 039	29 675	50 986	24 793	26 193	2 884	5 092	2 448	2 644	1 636	798	837
1994	57 862	28 108	29 754	51 116	24 853	26 263	2 887	5 102	2 453	2 649	1 644	802	842
1995	58 025	28 204	29 821	51 272	24 946	26 326	2 889	5 104	2 453	2 650	1 649	804	845
1996	58 164	28 287	29 877	51 410	25 030	26 381	2 891	5 092	2 447	2 645	1 662	810	851
1997	58 314	28 371	29 943	51 560	25 113	26 446	2 895	5 083	2 442	2 641	1 671	816	856
1998	58 475	28 458	30 017	51 720	25 201	26 519	2 900	5 077	2 439	2 638	1 678	819	859
1999	58 684	28 578	30 106	51 933	25 323	26 610	2 901	5 072	2 437	2 635	1 679	818	861
2000	58 886	28 690	30 196	52 140	25 438	26 702	2 907	5 063	2 432	2 631	1 683	820	862
2001	59 113	28 832	30 281	52 360	25 574	26 786	2 910	5 064	2 434	2 630	1 689	824	865
2002	59 322	28 963	30 359	52 570	25 702	26 868	2 923	5 055	2 432	2 623	1 697	829	868
2003	59 554	29 108	30 446	52 794	25 841	26 953	2 938	5 057	2 435	2 623	1 703	833	870
2004	59 834	29 271	30 563	53 046	25 988	27 057	2 952	5 078	2 446	2 632	1 710	836	874
Resident population: projections (mid-year)[2]													
	C59J	C59K	C59L	C59M	C59N	C59O	C59P	C59Q	C59R	C59S	C59T	C59U	C59V
2006	60 533	29 668	30 864	53 691	26 357	27 334	2 977	5 108	2 463	2 646	1 733	848	884
2011	61 892	30 438	31 454	55 005	27 100	27 904	3 037	5 120	2 470	2 649	1 767	868	900
2021	64 727	31 943	32 784	57 770	28 572	29 198	3 165	5 127	2 471	2 656	1 830	900	930
2026	66 002	32 579	33 423	59 042	29 212	29 831	3 219	5 109	2 457	2 652	1 851	911	940

1 Figures for Northern Ireland are estimated. The population at the Census of 1926 was 1 257 thousand (608 thousand males and 649 thousand females).
2 These projections are 2004-based. See chapter text for more detail.

Sources: Office for National Statistics: 01329 813233; General Register Office for Scotland; Northern Ireland Statistics and Research Agency; Office for National Statistics (projections): 020 7533 5222

Population and vital statistics

5.2 Population changes: by country

Thousands

	Population[1] at start of period	Average annual change				
		Overall annual change	Births	Deaths[2]	Natural change	Net migration and other changes
United Kingdom						
1901 - 1911	38 237	385	1 091	624	467	-82
1911 - 1921	42 082	195	975	689	286	-92
1921 - 1931	44 027	201	824	555	268	-67
1931 - 1951	46 038	213	793	603	190	22
1951 - 1961	50 225	258	839	593	246	12
1961 - 1971	52 807	312	962	638	324	-12
1971 - 1981	55 928	42	736	666	69	-27
1981 - 1991	56 357	108	757	655	103	5
1991 - 2001	57 439	161	731	631	100	61
2001 - 2004	59 113	240	684	603	81	159
2011 - 2021	61 892	284	716	578	139	145
England and Wales						
1901 - 1911	32 528	354	929	525	404	-50
1911 - 1921	36 070	182	828	584	244	-62
1921 - 1931	37 887	207	693	469	224	-17
1931 - 1951	39 952	193	673	518	155	38
1951 - 1961	43 758	244	714	516	197	47
1961 - 1971	46 196	296	832	560	272	23
1971 - 1981	49 152	48	638	585	53	-5
1981 - 1991	49 634	111	664	576	89	23
1991 - 2001	50 748	155	647	556	92	63
2001 - 2004	52 360	229	610	531	79	149
2011 - 2021	55 005	277	643	508	135	142
Scotland						
1901 - 1911	4 472	29	131	76	54	-25
1911 - 1921	4 761	12	118	82	36	-24
1921 - 1931	4 882	-4	100	65	35	-39
1931 - 1951	4 843	13	92	67	25	-12
1951 - 1961	5 096	9	95	62	34	-25
1961 - 1971	5 184	5	97	63	34	-30
1971 - 1981	5 236	-6	70	64	6	-11
1981 - 1991	5 180	-7	66	63	3	-10
1991 - 2001	5 083	-2	60	60	-1	-1
2001 - 2004	5 064	5	52	58	-6	10
2011 - 2021	5 120	1	51	55	-3	4
Northern Ireland						
1901 - 1911	1 237	1	31	23	8	-6
1911 - 1921	1 251	1	29	22	7	-6
1921 - 1931	1 258	-2	30	21	9	-11
1931 - 1951	1 243	6	28	18	10	-4
1951 - 1961	1 371	6	30	15	15	-9
1961 - 1971	1 427	11	33	16	17	-6
1971 - 1981	1 540	-	28	17	11	-11
1981 - 1991	1 543	6	27	16	12	-5
1991 - 2001	1 607	8	24	15	9	-
2001 - 2004	1 689	7	22	14	7	-
2011 - 2021	1 767	6	22	15	7	-1

1 Census enumerated population up to 1951; mid-year estimates of resident population from 1961 to 2001 and mid-2004-based projections of resident population thereafter.
2 Including deaths of non-civilians and merchant seamen who died outside the country. These numbered 577 000 in 1911-1921 and 240 000 in 1931-1951 for England and Wales; 74 000 in 1911-1921 and 34 000 in 1931-1951 for Scotland; and 10 000 in 1911-1926 for Northern Ireland.

Sources: Office for National Statistics (projections): 020 7533 5222; Office for National Statistics: 01329 813233; General Register Office for Scotland; Northern Ireland Statistics and Research Agency

5.3 Age distribution of the resident population: by sex and country

Thousands

| | | United Kingdom | | | | | | | | | | | | | | | |
| | | Population enumerated in Census | | | Estimated mid-year resident population | | | | | | | | Projected mid-year resident population[1] | | | | |
		1901	1931	1951	1961	1971	1981	1991[2]	2001[5]	2002	2003	2004	2006	2011	2016	2021	2026
Persons: All ages	KGUA	38 237	46 038	50 225	52 807	55 928	56 357	57 439	59 114	59 322	59 554	59 834	60 533	61 892	63 304	64 727	66 002
Under 1	KGUK	938	712	773	..	899	730	790	663	661	679	705	707	698	714	722	713
1 - 4[3]	KABA	3 443	2 818	3 553	4 274	3 654	2 726	3 077	2 819	2 753	2 703	2 684	2 764	2 794	2 825	2 881	2 876
5 - 9	KGUN	4 106	3 897	3 689	3 819	4 684	3 677	3 657	3 735	3 689	3 650	3 608	3 503	3 488	3 509	3 557	3 620
10 - 14	KGUO	3 934	3 746	3 310	4 267	4 232	4 470	3 485	3 890	3 912	3 891	3 870	3 757	3 518	3 503	3 524	3 572
15 - 19	KGUP	3 826	3 989	3 175	3 748	3 862	4 735	3 719	3 678	3 761	3 855	3 920	3 986	3 823	3 584	3 569	3 591
20 - 29	KABB	6 982	7 865	7 154	6 570	7 968	8 113	9 138	7 499	7 401	7 379	7 458	7 807	8 428	8 530	8 130	7 880
30 - 44	KABC	7 493	9 717	11 125	10 529	9 797	10 956	12 125	13 405	13 499	13 519	13 471	13 299	12 587	12 299	12 821	13 265
45 - 59	KABD	4 639	7 979	9 558	10 605	10 202	9 540	9 500	11 168	11 316	11 424	11 517	11 757	12 310	13 090	12 945	12 268
60 - 64	KGUY	1 067	1 897	2 422	2 788	3 222	2 935	2 888	2 884	2 890	2 943	3 021	3 246	3 756	3 460	3 838	4 296
65 - 74	KBCP	1 278	2 461	3 689	3 977	4 764	5 195	5 067	4 947	4 969	5 005	5 033	5 052	5 550	6 404	6 610	6 742
75 - 84	KBCU	470	844	1 555	1 885	2 159	2 677	3 119	3 296	3 345	3 401	3 435	3 421	3 531	3 801	4 316	5 063
85 and over	KGVD	61	113	224	346	485	603	873	1 130	1 127	1 104	1 112	1 234	1 407	1 584	1 813	2 117
School ages (5-15)	KBWU	..	..	7 649	..	9 704	9 086	7 818	8 381	8 369	8 330	8 257	8 058	7 738	7 684	7 797	7 898
Under 18	KGUD	..	..	13 248	..	15 798	14 472	13 120	13 357	13 310	13 253	13 221	13 102	12 727	12 630	12 847	12 907
Pensionable ages[4]	KFIA	2 387	4 421	6 828	7 747	9 123	10 035	10 557	10 845	10 916	11 014	11 125	11 368	12 182	12 430	12 740	13 922
Males: All ages	KGWA	18 492	22 060	24 118	25 528	27 167	27 412	27 909	28 832	28 963	29 108	29 271	29 668	30 438	31 205	31 943	32 579
Under 1	KGWK	471	361	397	−	461	374	403	338	339	349	361	362	358	366	369	365
1 - 4[3]	KBCV	1 719	1 423	1 818	2 194	1 874	1 400	1 572	1 445	1 409	1 384	1 375	1 414	1 428	1 444	1 472	1 470
5 - 9	KGWN	2 052	1 967	1 885	1 956	2 401	1 889	1 871	1 913	1 890	1 869	1 848	1 792	1 780	1 789	1 813	1 845
10 - 14	KGWO	1 972	1 892	1 681	2 185	2 175	2 295	1 784	1 993	2 005	1 995	1 985	1 928	1 802	1 790	1 799	1 824
15 - 19	KGWP	1 898	1 987	1 564	1 897	1 976	2 424	1 905	1 879	1 930	1 983	2 017	2 052	1 970	1 845	1 833	1 842
20 - 29	KBCW	3 293	3 818	3 509	3 288	4 024	4 103	4 578	3 744	3 700	3 697	3 748	3 938	4 286	4 358	4 153	4 018
30 - 44	KBCX	3 597	4 495	5 461	5 237	4 938	5 513	6 045	6 645	6 690	6 701	6 675	6 598	6 255	6 136	6 436	6 695
45 - 59	KBUU	2 215	3 753	4 493	5 137	4 970	4 711	4 732	5 534	5 604	5 653	5 694	5 808	6 068	6 449	6 380	6 058
60 - 64	KGWY	490	894	1 061	1 250	1 507	1 376	1 390	1 412	1 414	1 439	1 476	1 585	1 830	1 682	1 863	2 083
65 - 74	KBWL	565	1 099	1 560	1 605	1 999	2 264	2 272	2 308	2 327	2 354	2 374	2 397	2 652	3 065	3 158	3 220
75 - 84	KBWM	196	335	617	675	716	922	1 146	1 308	1 339	1 371	1 394	1 417	1 533	1 700	1 956	2 306
85 and over	KGXD	23	36	70	105	126	141	212	312	316	313	323	378	475	581	708	852
School ages (5-15)	KBWV	..	..	3 895	..	4 982	4 666	4 001	4 294	4 289	4 269	4 233	4 130	3 959	3 923	3 979	4 031
Under 18	KGWD	..	..	6 753	..	8 108	7 430	6 711	6 845	6 822	6 794	6 780	6 717	6 516	6 457	6 564	6 595
Pensionable ages[4]	KFIB	785	1 471	2 247	2 385	2 841	3 327	3 630	3 928	3 982	4 038	4 091	4 192	4 660	5 346	5 822	6 378
Females: All ages	KGYA	19 745	23 978	26 107	27 279	28 761	28 946	29 530	30 281	30 359	30 446	30 563	30 864	31 454	32 099	32 784	33 423
Under 1	KGYK	466	351	376	..	437	356	387	324	323	331	343	345	341	349	352	348
1 - 4[3]	KBWN	1 724	1 397	1 735	2 079	1 779	1 327	1 505	1 375	1 344	1 319	1 309	1 349	1 366	1 381	1 409	1 406
5 - 9	KGYN	2 054	1 930	1 804	1 863	2 283	1 788	1 786	1 822	1 800	1 781	1 760	1 712	1 708	1 721	1 743	1 774
10 - 14	KGYO	1 962	1 854	1 629	2 083	2 057	2 175	1 701	1 897	1 907	1 896	1 884	1 829	1 716	1 712	1 725	1 748
15 - 19	KGYP	1 928	2 002	1 611	1 851	1 887	2 311	1 815	1 799	1 830	1 873	1 903	1 935	1 853	1 740	1 736	1 749
20 - 29	KBWO	3 690	4 047	3 644	3 282	3 945	4 009	4 560	3 755	3 701	3 682	3 710	3 869	4 142	4 172	3 977	3 862
30 - 44	KBWP	3 895	5 222	5 663	5 292	4 859	5 442	6 080	6 760	6 808	6 817	6 796	6 700	6 332	6 163	6 386	6 570
45 - 59	KBWR	2 424	4 226	5 065	5 467	5 231	4 829	4 769	5 634	5 713	5 771	5 823	5 949	6 241	6 640	6 564	6 210
60 - 64	KGYY	577	1 003	1 361	1 539	1 715	1 559	1 498	1 473	1 476	1 504	1 545	1 661	1 926	1 779	1 974	2 213
65 - 74	KBWS	713	1 361	2 127	2 372	2 765	2 931	2 795	2 640	2 641	2 651	2 659	2 655	2 898	3 339	3 452	3 522
75 - 84	KBWT	274	509	937	1 210	1 443	1 756	1 972	1 987	2 006	2 030	2 041	2 004	1 998	2 100	2 360	2 757
85 and over	KGZD	38	77	154	241	359	462	661	817	811	791	789	857	933	1 003	1 105	1 265
School ages (5-15)	KBWW	..	..	3 753	..	4 722	4 421	3 817	4 087	4 081	4 060	4 023	3 928	3 779	3 761	3 818	3 867
Under 18	KGYD	..	..	6 495	..	7 690	7 042	6 409	6 512	6 489	6 459	6 442	6 386	6 212	6 173	6 283	6 313
Pensionable ages[4]	KFIC	1 601	2 950	4 580	5 362	6 282	6 708	6 927	6 917	6 934	6 976	7 034	7 176	7 522	7 084	6 917	7 544

5.3 Age distribution of the resident population: by sex and country

continued

Thousands

		England									Wales							
		Estimated mid-year resident population						Projected population[1]			Estimated mid-year resident population						Projected population[1]	
		1981	1991[2]	2001	2002	2003	2004	2011	2026		1981	1991[2]	2001	2002	2003	2004	2011	2026
Persons: All ages	KCCI	46 821	47 875	49 450	49 647	49 856	50 093	51 967	55 823	KERY	2 813	2 873	2 910	2 923	2 938	2 952	3 037	3 219
Under 1	KCCJ	598	660	558	558	575	597	594	612	KFAC	36	38	32	30	31	32	32	32
1 - 4	KCCK	2 235	2 560	2 366	2 312	2 273	2 260	2 370	2 460	KFBX	136	153	136	132	129	127	130	133
5 - 9	KCCL	3 011	3 019	3 121	3 085	3 054	3 019	2 947	3 082	KFCA	185	186	185	183	181	178	164	172
10 - 14	KCCM	3 666	2 865	3 238	3 260	3 245	3 228	2 945	3 031	KFCB	222	177	196	197	197	195	176	174
15 - 19	KCCN	3 897	3 067	3 045	3 118	3 202	3 261	3 193	3 043	KFCC	233	187	186	191	196	199	195	175
20 - 29	KCEG	6 734	7 651	6 307	6 226	6 208	6 276	7 108	6 726	KFCD	381	415	336	334	336	342	394	357
30 - 44	KCEH	9 175	10 147	11 257	11 351	11 379	11 346	10 675	11 317	KFCE	536	583	608	611	611	608	557	609
45 - 59	KCEQ	7 948	7 920	9 327	9 448	9 533	9 600	10 259	10 377	KFCF	485	486	572	579	583	588	610	583
60 - 64	KCEW	2 449	2 399	2 395	2 397	2 438	2 503	3 127	3 586	KFCG	158	154	154	156	161	166	206	220
65 - 74	KCGD	4 347	4 222	4 113	4 130	4 159	4 181	4 613	5 583	KFCH	272	284	264	265	268	270	308	366
75 - 84	KCJG	2 249	2 626	2 764	2 804	2 852	2 879	2 948	4 231	KFCI	139	164	183	185	187	188	188	283
85 and over	KCKJ	511	739	959	956	936	943	1 189	1 775	KFCK	29	45	59	59	58	60	77	114
School ages (5-15)	KCWX	7 451	6 439	6 985	6 982	6 955	6 897	6 504	6 712	KFCL	453	397	420	419	417	413	377	381
Under 18	KCWY	11 871	10 840	11 146	11 118	11 082	11 065	10 718	10 988	KFCM	721	662	662	659	655	652	615	615
Pensionable ages[4]	KEAA	8 403	8 827	9 055	9 111	9 190	9 280	10 161	11 589	KFEB	525	573	584	589	596	602	666	762
Males: All ages	KEAB	22 795	23 291	24 166	24 288	24 415	24 554	25 615	27 630	KFEI	1 365	1 391	1 409	1 414	1 426	1 434	1 485	1 582
Under 1	KEAC	306	336	285	286	295	306	304	313	KFEJ	18	20	16	16	16	16	17	16
1 - 4	KEAD	1 147	1 307	1 212	1 183	1 164	1 158	1 211	1 258	KFEK	70	78	69	68	66	66	66	68
5 - 9	KEAE	1 547	1 545	1 599	1 580	1 564	1 546	1 504	1 572	KFEL	95	95	95	94	93	91	84	88
10 - 14	KEAF	1 883	1 467	1 658	1 671	1 664	1 657	1 508	1 548	KFFA	113	91	101	101	101	100	90	89
15 - 19	KECA	1 996	1 572	1 558	1 603	1 648	1 679	1 647	1 563	KFFN	119	95	94	97	100	102	100	90
20 - 29	KECB	3 404	3 835	3 155	3 117	3 113	3 156	3 614	3 428	KFHA	193	207	166	164	167	171	202	185
30 - 44	KECC	4 623	5 064	5 600	5 648	5 663	5 644	5 328	5 725	KFHB	270	289	297	297	297	295	270	308
45 - 59	KECD	3 938	3 957	4 624	4 682	4 721	4 752	5 074	5 155	KFHW	240	242	283	286	287	289	297	281
60 - 64	KECE	1 154	1 159	1 176	1 176	1 195	1 225	1 525	1 748	KFQO	73	74	75	77	79	82	101	106
65 - 74	KECF	1 902	1 900	1 928	1 944	1 965	1 981	2 209	2 674	KFQV	118	128	124	125	127	128	149	175
75 - 84	KECG	777	970	1 103	1 128	1 156	1 175	1 287	1 930	KFUK	48	60	73	74	75	76	83	130
85 and over	KECH	119	181	267	270	267	276	403	717	KFUL	7	11	16	16	16	17	26	46
School ages (5-15)	KECI	3 827	3 295	3 578	3 578	3 565	3 536	3 327	3 427	KFUV	232	204	215	215	214	212	194	195
Under 18	KECJ	6 096	5 545	5 712	5 698	5 681	5 674	5 488	5 615	KFVE	370	339	340	338	336	335	315	315
Pensionable ages[4]	KECK	2 798	3 050	3 298	3 342	3 388	3 431	3 900	5 322	KFVF	173	198	212	215	219	222	257	351
Females: All ages	KEJV	24 026	24 584	25 284	25 358	25 441	25 539	26 352	28 194	KFVL	1 448	1 482	1 502	1 509	1 512	1 518	1 552	1 637
Under 1	KEJW	292	324	273	272	280	291	290	298	KFYW	18	19	15	15	15	15	16	16
1 - 4	KEJX	1 088	1 253	1 154	1 129	1 109	1 103	1 159	1 203	KFZJ	66	75	66	65	63	62	63	65
5 - 9	KEKP	1 464	1 474	1 522	1 505	1 491	1 473	1 443	1 510	KGCK	90	91	90	89	88	87	80	84
10 - 14	KEKQ	1 783	1 399	1 580	1 589	1 581	1 571	1 436	1 483	KGCM	109	86	95	96	96	95	86	85
15 - 19	KEKR	1 901	1 495	1 487	1 516	1 554	1 582	1 546	1 481	KGCN	114	91	92	94	95	97	95	85
20 - 29	KEKS	3 330	3 816	3 152	3 108	3 095	3 120	3 493	3 298	KGCO	189	208	170	170	169	171	192	173
30 - 44	KENR	4 553	5 083	5 657	5 703	5 716	5 702	5 347	5 592	KGCP	265	294	312	314	314	312	286	302
45 - 59	KEOQ	4 009	3 964	4 702	4 766	4 812	4 849	5 186	5 222	KGGZ	246	244	289	293	296	299	313	302
60 - 64	KEOZ	1 295	1 239	1 219	1 220	1 243	1 278	1 603	1 839	KGIY	85	80	78	80	82	85	106	114
65 - 74	KEQJ	2 445	2 323	2 185	2 186	2 194	2 200	2 404	2 909	KGKR	154	156	141	140	141	142	159	191
75 - 84	KEQK	1 472	1 656	1 661	1 676	1 696	1 704	1 661	2 301	KGTQ	91	104	110	111	112	112	106	152
85 and over	KEQL	392	558	692	687	669	667	786	1 057	KGTZ	22	34	43	43	42	42	51	67
School ages (5-15)	KEQM	3 625	3 143	3 406	3 405	3 391	3 360	3 176	3 285	KGVG	221	194	204	204	203	201	184	186
Under 18	KEQN	5 775	5 295	5 434	5 420	5 401	5 391	5 230	5 372	KGVH	351	323	323	321	319	317	300	300
Pensionable ages[4]	KEQO	5 605	5 777	5 757	5 769	5 802	5 849	6 261	6 267	KGVK	352	375	372	374	377	380	409	411

5.3 Age distribution of the resident population: by sex and country
continued

Thousands

		Scotland									Northern Ireland							
		Estimated mid-year resident population						Projected population[1]			Estimated mid-year resident population						Projected population[1]	
		1981	1991[2]	2001[5]	2002	2003	2004	2011	2026		1981	1991	2001[5]	2002	2003	2004	2011	2026
Persons: All ages	KGVP	5 180	5 083	5 064	5 055	5 057	5 078	5 120	5 109	KIOY	1 543	1 607	1 689	1 697	1 703	1 710	1 767	1 851
Under 1	KHAQ	69	66	52	51	52	54	51	49	KIOZ	27	26	22	22	21	22	21	20
1 - 4	KHCT	249	258	224	217	212	210	208	199	KIPA	106	106	93	91	89	87	86	84
5 - 9	KHDN	348	320	306	299	294	290	267	256	KIPN	133	131	123	122	121	120	110	109
10 - 14	KHDQ	433	313	323	323	320	319	280	258	KIPP	148	129	132	131	129	128	117	109
15 - 19	KHDT	459	337	318	319	324	328	312	265	KIPQ	146	128	130	132	133	133	123	107
20 - 29	KHDU	771	820	630	619	614	617	672	579	KIPR	227	253	225	222	221	224	254	217
30 - 44	KHDV	971	1 080	1 163	1 158	1 150	1 140	1 003	966	KIPS	273	305	376	378	378	378	353	372
45 - 59	KHFK	880	853	979	993	1 008	1 025	1 098	967	KIPT	227	241	290	296	301	305	342	341
60 - 64	KHOZ	260	265	262	262	265	270	329	370	KIPU	68	70	74	75	78	81	93	119
65 - 74	KHTU	460	441	447	449	452	455	482	603	KIPV	116	120	123	125	126	127	147	190
75 - 84	KHUO	232	259	272	276	281	286	306	419	KIPW	57	69	77	79	81	82	89	130
85 and over	KHUQ	49	70	89	88	86	85	110	176	KIPX	14	19	23	24	24	24	32	53
School ages (5-15)	KHVV	871	697	694	687	679	672	606	567	KIPY	311	285	282	281	278	274	251	239
Under 18	KIMT	1 377	1 150	1 098	1 086	1 074	1 067	987	918	KIQL	504	467	451	447	443	437	407	386
Pensionable ages[4]	KIMU	882	912	944	950	958	968	1 047	1 198	KIQM	224	246	262	266	271	275	309	373
Males: All ages	KIMV	2 495	2 445	2 434	2 432	2 435	2 446	2 470	2 457	KIQN	757	783	824	829	833	836	868	911
Under 1	KIMW	35	34	26	26	26	28	26	25	KIQO	14	13	11	11	11	11	11	10
1 - 4	KIMX	128	132	115	111	108	107	106	102	KIQP	54	54	48	47	46	45	44	43
5 - 9	KIMY	178	164	156	153	151	149	136	130	KIQQ	69	67	63	63	62	62	56	55
10 - 14	KIMZ	222	161	166	165	164	163	143	131	KIQR	76	66	68	67	66	65	60	55
15 - 19	KINA	234	171	161	163	166	168	160	135	KIQS	75	66	66	68	68	68	63	55
20 - 29	KINB	390	410	311	308	306	309	340	293	KIQT	117	127	113	111	111	112	131	113
30 - 44	KINC	483	535	563	560	556	550	484	476	KIQU	137	156	185	186	186	185	173	187
45 - 59	KIND	424	415	483	490	496	503	530	458	KIQV	109	118	144	147	149	151	168	164
60 - 64	KINE	118	124	125	125	126	129	159	172	KIQW	32	32	35	36	38	39	45	57
65 - 74	KINR	194	192	200	202	204	207	225	281	KIRJ	50	53	56	56	57	58	69	91
75 - 84	KINS	77	91	103	106	108	111	126	187	KIRK	21	26	30	31	31	32	37	59
85 and over	KINT	11	16	23	23	23	23	35	68	KIRL	4	5	6	6	7	7	10	21
School ages (5-15)	KINU	446	357	356	352	348	344	309	288	KIRM	160	146	145	144	142	141	129	122
Under 18	KINV	706	588	562	556	550	546	504	467	KIRN	259	239	231	229	227	225	209	197
Pensionable ages[4]	KINW	282	299	327	331	336	341	386	535	KIRO	75	83	92	94	95	97	117	170
Females: All ages	KINX	2 685	2 639	2 630	2 623	2 623	2 632	2 649	2 652	KIRP	786	824	865	868	870	874	900	940
Under 1	KINY	33	32	26	25	25	26	25	24	KIRQ	13	13	10	11	10	11	10	10
1 - 4	KINZ	121	126	109	106	104	103	102	97	KIRR	52	52	45	44	43	42	42	41
5 - 9	KIOA	170	157	149	146	143	141	131	126	KIRS	65	64	60	59	59	58	54	53
10 - 14	KIOB	211	153	157	157	156	156	137	127	KIRT	72	63	65	64	63	62	57	53
15 - 19	KIOC	225	166	156	156	158	160	153	130	KIRU	70	62	64	65	65	65	59	52
20 - 29	KIOO	381	411	319	311	307	308	333	287	KISH	110	126	113	111	110	111	124	104
30 - 44	KIOP	488	545	600	598	595	590	518	491	KISI	137	159	191	192	193	192	181	185
45 - 59	KIOQ	456	437	496	504	512	521	568	509	KISJ	118	123	146	149	152	154	174	177
60 - 64	KIOR	142	141	137	137	139	141	170	197	KISK	37	38	38	39	40	42	48	62
65 - 74	KIOS	265	249	246	247	248	248	258	323	KISL	66	67	68	68	68	69	77	99
75 - 84	KIOT	155	168	169	171	173	175	180	232	KISM	37	44	47	48	49	50	52	71
85 and over	KIOU	38	54	66	65	63	62	74	108	KISN	10	14	17	17	17	17	22	32
School ages (5-15)	KIOV	424	340	339	335	331	328	297	279	KISO	151	139	138	137	135	134	122	117
Under 18	KIOW	671	562	536	530	524	520	483	451	KISP	245	228	220	218	215	213	199	189
Pensionable ages[4]	KIOX	600	612	617	619	622	627	660	663	KISQ	150	163	170	173	175	178	192	203

1 2004-based projections are made as described in the chapter text.
2 Data for mid 1991 for UK, England and Wales and Scotland are revised in light of the 2001 Census.
3 1961 estimates are for ages 0 - 4.
4 The pensionable age population is that over state retirement age. The 2011 figures take account of planned changes in retirement age from 65 for men and 60 for women at present to 65 for both sexes. This change will be phased in between April 2010 and March 2020.
5 The mid-2001 estimates for Scotland and Northern Ireland are based on the 2001 census.

Sources: Office for National Statistics: 01329 813233;
General Register Office for Scotland;
General Register Office for Northern Ireland;
Office for National Statistics (projections): 020 7533 5222

5.4 Marital condition (*de jure*): estimated population: by age and sex
England and Wales

Thousands

		Males							Females					
		1981	1991[1]	2001	2002	2003	2004		1981	1991[1]	2001	2002	2003	2004
All ages:														
Single	KRPL	10 614	11 131	12 270	12 422	12 582	12 756	KUBS	9 424	9 824	10 917	11 051	11 188	11 338
Married	KRPM	12 238	11 636	11 090	11 015	10 940	10 863	KVCC	12 284	11 833	11 150	11 073	11 000	10 935
Widowed	KRPN	698	727	733	731	728	726	KVCD	2 939	2 951	2 745	2 709	2 668	2 628
Divorced	KRPO	611	1 187	1 482	1 535	1 590	1 644	KVCE	828	1 459	1 975	2 035	2 096	2 156
Age groups:														
0 - 14: Single	KRPP	5 181	4 939	5 036	4 999	4 963	4 940	KVCF	4 910	4 720	4 796	4 760	4 722	4 697
15 - 19: Single	KRPQ	2 095	1 659	1 645	1 694	1 743	1 777	KVCG	1 923	1 554	1 560	1 595	1 637	1 668
Married	KRPR	20	8	5	4	4	3	KVCH	93	32	16	13	12	11
Widowed	KRPS	–	–	1	1	1	–	KVCI	–	–	1	1	1	–
Divorced	KRPT	–	–	1	1	1	–	KVCJ	–	–	1	1	–	–
20 - 24: Single	KRPU	1 420	1 717	1 501	1 534	1 573	1 621	KVCK	1 007	1 421	1 390	1 428	1 466	1 499
Married	KRPV	466	242	74	69	69	67	KVCL	811	490	178	166	161	156
Widowed	KRPW	1	–	1	1	1	1	KVCM	2	1	1	1	1	2
Divorced	KRPX	10	12	3	3	3	3	KVCN	27	29	8	8	8	8
25 - 34: Single	KRPY	906	1 652	2 227	2 238	2 253	2 279	KVCO	496	1 135	1 770	1 795	1 820	1 857
Married	KRPZ	2 508	2 028	1 391	1 293	1 206	1 129	KVCP	2 791	2 488	1 768	1 662	1 566	1 481
Widowed	KRQA	4	2	3	3	3	3	KVCQ	13	8	10	9	8	8
Divorced	KRQB	151	237	136	131	126	121	KVCR	218	312	231	219	208	196
35 - 44: Single	KRQC	316	477	963	1 031	1 089	1 142	KVEH	170	280	692	751	805	858
Married	KRQD	2 519	2 632	2 494	2 489	2 471	2 445	KVEI	2 540	2 760	2 649	2 650	2 634	2 614
Widowed	KRQE	12	11	12	12	12	11	KVEJ	41	34	36	35	34	32
Divorced	KRQF	178	384	411	424	435	444	KVEK	222	444	558	571	583	593
45 - 54: Single	KRQG	254	251	419	433	451	474	KVEL	169	144	256	271	289	311
Married	KUAR	2 338	2 347	2 511	2 433	2 379	2 348	KVEM	2 292	2 322	2 548	2 475	2 427	2 400
Widowed	KUBA	38	31	37	35	34	33	KVEN	150	118	111	105	99	96
Divorced	KUBB	134	290	448	455	466	481	KVEO	158	332	557	566	578	594
55 - 59: Single	KUBC	128	101	128	141	151	158	KVEP	108	69	74	81	87	92
Married	KUBD	1 192	1 050	1 156	1 240	1 280	1 287	KVEQ	1 130	982	1 125	1 211	1 258	1 272
Widowed	KUBE	46	34	34	36	37	37	KVER	186	136	112	115	114	112
Divorced	KUBF	49	95	174	195	210	222	KVES	63	107	210	235	256	271
60 - 64: Single	KUBG	98	104	97	97	100	103	KVET	109	80	62	61	62	63
Married	KUBH	1 029	997	980	976	989	1 009	KVEU	936	908	906	909	928	956
Widowed	KUBI	64	63	50	49	48	47	KVEV	284	250	178	172	167	163
Divorced	KUBJ	35	70	125	131	138	147	KVEW	51	82	151	158	168	180
65 - 74: Single	KUBK	149	150	155	154	154	153	KMGN	263	176	130	126	123	120
Married	KUBL	1 594	1 574	1 569	1 582	1 600	1 612	KMGO	1 291	1 317	1 322	1 336	1 354	1 371
Widowed	KUBM	234	229	188	184	179	176	KMGP	978	879	697	675	654	633
Divorced	KUBN	43	74	139	149	159	169	KMGQ	68	107	177	190	204	218
75 and over: Single	KUBO	67	81	99	101	104	107	KMGR	270	246	188	182	178	173
Married	KUBP	573	759	909	928	945	963	KMGS	401	536	639	651	661	673
Widowed	KUBQ	300	357	407	411	415	418	KMGT	1 285	1 526	1 598	1 597	1 590	1 583
Divorced	KUBR	11	25	44	48	52	56	KMGU	23	46	81	86	91	96

1 Mid-1991 marital status estimates are revised in light of the 2001 Census.

Source: Office for National Statistics: 01329 813233

5.5 Geographical distribution of the population

Thousands

		Population enumerated in Census			Mid-year population estimates							
		1911	1931	1951	1961	1971	1981	1991	2001	2002	2003	2004
United Kingdom	KIUR	42 082	46 074	50 225	52 807	55 928	56 357	57 439	59 113	59 322	59 554	59 834
Great Britain	KISR	40 831	44 795	48 854	51 380	54 388	54 815	55 831	57 424	57 625	57 851	58 124
England	KKOJ	33 650	37 359	41 159	43 561	46 412	46 821	47 875	49 450	49 647	49 856	50 093
Standard Regions												
North	KKNA	2 729	2 938	3 009	3 246	3 152	3 117	3 073	3 028	3 026	3 029	3 040
Yorkshire and Humberside	KKNB	3 896	4 319	4 567	4 630	4 902	4 918	4 936	4 977	4 993	5 009	5 039
East Midlands	KKNC	2 467	2 732	3 118	3 108	3 652	3 853	4 011	4 190	4 223	4 252	4 280
East Anglia	KKND	1 191	1 231	1 381	1 489	1 688	1 894	2 068	2 181	2 192	2 219	2 238
South East	KKNE	11 613	13 349	14 877	16 346	17 125	17 011	17 511	18 566	18 645	18 712	18 792
South West	KKNF	2 818	2 984	3 479	3 436	4 112	4 381	4 688	4 943	4 968	4 999	5 038
West Midlands	KKNG	3 277	3 743	4 423	4 762	5 146	5 187	5 230	5 281	5 304	5 320	5 334
North West	KKNH	5 659	6 062	6 305	6 545	6 634	6 459	6 357	6 285	6 296	6 315	6 332
Government Office Regions												
North East	JZBU	..	..	..	..	2 679	2 636	2 587	2 540	2 538	2 539	2 545
North West (including Merseyside)	JZBV	..	..	..	..	7 108	6 940	6 843	6 773	6 783	6 805	6 827
Yorkshire and The Humber	JZBX	..	..	..	..	4 902	4 918	4 936	4 977	4 993	5 009	5 039
East Midlands	JZBY	..	..	..	..	3 652	3 853	4 011	4 190	4 223	4 252	4 280
West Midlands	JZBZ	..	..	..	..	5 146	5 187	5 230	5 281	5 304	5 320	5 334
South West	JZCA	..	..	..	..	4 112	4 381	4 688	4 943	4 968	4 999	5 038
East of England	JZCB	..	..	..	..	4 454	4 854	5 121	5 400	5 422	5 463	5 491
London	JZCC	..	..	..	..	7 529	6 806	6 829	7 322	7 371	7 388	7 429
South East	JZCD	..	..	..	..	6 830	7 245	7 629	8 023	8 044	8 080	8 110
Wales	KKNI	2 421	2 593	2 599	2 635	2 740	2 813	2 873	2 910	2 923	2 938	2 952
Scotland	KGJB	4 761	4 843	5 096	5 184	5 236	5 180	5 083	5 064	5 055	5 057	5 078
Northern Ireland[3]	KGJC	1 251	1 280	1 371	1 427	1 540	1 543	1 607	1 689	1 697	1 703	1 710
Greater London	KKNJ	7 161	8 110	8 197	7 977	7 529	6 806	6 829	7 322	7 371	7 388	7 429
Inner London[1]	KISS	4 998	4 893	3 679	3 481	3 060	2 550	2 599	2 859	2 892	2 905	2 931
Outer London[1]	KITF	2 162	3 217	4 518	4 496	4 470	4 255	4 230	4 463	4 479	4 483	4 498
Metropolitan areas of England and Wales	KITG	9 716	10 770	11 365	11 686	11 862	11 353	11 085	10 888	10 908	10 925	10 956
Tyne and Wear	KGJN	1 105	1 201	1 201	1 241	1 218	1 155	1 124	1 087	1 084	1 083	1 086
West Yorkshire	KGJP	1 852	1 939	1 985	2 002	2 090	2 067	2 062	2 083	2 091	2 096	2 108
South Yorkshire	KGJO	963	1 173	1 253	1 298	1 331	1 317	1 289	1 266	1 269	1 273	1 278
West Midlands	KGJQ	1 780	2 143	2 547	2 724	2 811	2 673	2 619	2 568	2 576	2 578	2 579
Greater Manchester	KGJR	2 638	2 727	2 716	2 710	2 750	2 619	2 554	2 516	2 522	2 531	2 539
Merseyside	KGJS	1 378	1 587	1 663	1 711	1 662	1 522	1 438	1 368	1 365	1 364	1 366
Principal Metropolitan Cities[1]	KITH	3 154	3 906	3 915	4 204	3 910	3 550	3 415	3 344	3 355	3 361	3 379
Newcastle	KGJT	267	286	292	336	312	284	275	266	266	267	269
Leeds	KGJX	446	483	505	710	749	718	707	716	716	715	720
Sheffield	KGJV	455	512	513	581	579	548	520	513	513	513	516
Birmingham	KGKF	526	1 003	1 113	1 179	1 107	1 021	1 005	985	990	992	992
Manchester	KGKJ	714	766	703	657	554	463	433	423	429	432	437
Liverpool	KGKM	746	856	789	741	610	517	476	442	442	442	444
Other metropolitan districts[1]	KITI	6 562	6 864	7 450	7 482	7 952	7 803	7 670	7 544	7 552	7 565	7 577
Non-metropolitan districts of England and Wales	KITJ	19 194	21 072	24 196	26 533	29 761	31 475	32 834	31 239	31 368	31 543	31 708
Non-metropolitan cities[1,2]	KITK	..	..	..	4 670	4 715	4 617	..	..	..	..	–
Incl. Kingston-upon-Hull	KKNZ	278	314	299	302	288	274	263	250	248	248	249
Leicester	KKOA	227	239	285	286	285	283	281	283	284	284	285
Nottingham	KKNX	260	269	308	311	302	278	279	269	271	274	275
Bristol	KKNV	357	397	443	436	433	401	392	390	390	392	394
Plymouth	KITL	207	215	225	240	249	253	251	241	241	241	244
Stoke-on-Trent	KKOD	235	277	275	276	265	252	249	240	239	238	238
Cardiff	KKOB	182	224	244	289	291	281	297	310	313	315	317
Industrial districts[1,2]	KITM	..	..	..	6 004	6 486	6 713	..	..	..	..	..
New Towns[1,2]	KITN	..	..	..	1 552	1 895	2 194	..	..	..	..	..
Resort, port and retirement districts[1,2]	KITO	..	..	..	2 828	3 184	3 368	..	..	..	..	..
Urban and mixed urban/rural districts[1,2]	KITP	..	..	..	7 240	8 821	9 446	..	..	..	..	..
Remoter, mainly rural districts[1,2]	KITQ	..	..	..	4 239	4 661	5 137	..	..	..	..	..
City of Edinburgh local government district	KGKU	320	439	467	..	478	446	436	449	448	448	455
City of Glasgow local government district	KGKT	784	1 088	1 090	..	983	774	629	579	577	577	578
Belfast[3]	KGKV	387	438	444	..	..	316	293	277	274	272	269

1 Details of the classification by broad area type are given in recent issues of the ONS annual reference volume *Key Population and Vital Statistics; local and health authority areas* (Series VS). The ten broad area types include all local authorities in England and Wales.

2 The breakdown of non-metropolitan districts by area type has not been provided from mid-2001 onwards. This is because the effect of boundary changes due to the major local government reorganisation on 1 April 1995 and 1 April 1996 (particularly in Wales) make the comparison of 2001 data with data for earlier years invalid.

3 1931 figures shown for Northern Ireland and the City of Belfast relate to the 1937 Census.

Sources: Office for National Statistics: 01329 813318;
General Register Office for Scotland;
Northern Ireland Statistics and Research Agency

5.6 Population: by ethnic group and age, Spring 2002 - Winter 2002/03[1]
United Kingdom
Average over the period

Percentages and thousands

	0 to 4	5 to 9	10 to 14	15 to 19	20 to 24	25 to 29	30 to 34	35 to 44	45 to 59	60 to 74	75 and over	All ages (=100%) (thousands)
White												
British[2]	5	6	7	6	6	6	7	16	20	14	7	51 010
Other[2]	4	4	4	4	8	12	11	18	18	11	6	1 946
Mixed												
White and Black Caribbean	19	21	16	12	8	5	4	9	-	-	-	234
White and Black African	19	19	12	10	-	11	-	11	-	-	-	72
White and Asian	19	15	14	11	7	7	8	10	4	-	-	129
Other Mixed	14	19	14	9	-	7	-	13	-	-	-	74
Asian												
Indian	7	7	7	8	9	9	10	17	18	8	1	1 016
Pakistani	11	11	11	10	11	9	8	12	11	5	1	718
Bangladeshi	14	12	10	10	10	12	9	11	6	5	-	273
Other Asian	8	7	7	6	8	13	12	17	14	6	-	302
Black												
Black Caribbean	8	7	7	8	6	5	8	25	12	11	3	584
Black African	12	11	8	8	8	8	11	20	10	3	-	541
Black Other	14	-	10	10	11	-	-	16	10	-	-	59
Chinese	4	5	5	9	15	12	9	19	15	6	-	199
Other	8	8	6	6	8	11	10	21	14	5	2	458
All[1]	6	6	7	6	6	6	8	16	19	13	7	59 330

1 Includes ethnic group not stated.
2 These data are presented for Great Britain only and exclude Northern Ireland. Detailed level ethnicity questions are not asked of the White group in Northern Ireland.

Source: Office for National Statistics, Labour Force Survey

5.7 Total international migration estimates:[1] citizenship
United Kingdom

Thousands

	All citizenships	British	Non-British	European Union[2]	Commonwealth Old[3]	Commonwealth New[4]	Other foreign[5]
Inflow							
	C58E	C58H	C58K	C58N	C58Q	C58T	C58W
1996	317.8	93.6	224.2	72.5	29.0	49.2	73.5
1997	326.1	88.9	237.2	71.5	31.2	58.7	75.7
1998	390.3	103.1	287.3	81.8	53.9	51.0	100.5
1999	453.8	116.4	337.4	66.6	54.4	66.5	149.9
2000	483.4	104.1	379.3	63.1	57.2	90.9	168.1
2001	479.6	106.3	373.3	60.4	67.4	83.9	161.6
2002	512.8	94.6	418.2	62.8	65.6	92.9	196.8
2003	512.6	105.8	406.8	64.0	62.7	103.1	177.0
2004	582.1	88.0	494.1	117.3	76.2	143.0	157.7
Outflow							
	C58F	C58I	C58L	C58O	C58R	C58U	C58X
1996	263.7	155.7	108.0	44.0	17.3	14.3	32.4
1997	279.2	148.7	130.6	53.2	20.1	19.8	37.5
1998	251.5	125.8	125.7	48.9	19.7	13.2	44.0
1999	290.8	139.2	151.6	58.6	28.8	12.3	51.9
2000	320.7	161.1	159.6	57.0	32.2	14.9	55.5
2001	307.7	159.2	148.5	49.1	32.1	18.6	48.6
2002	359.4	185.7	173.7	51.7	42.3	15.8	63.9
2003	361.5	190.9	170.6	49.9	41.9	16.6	62.2
2004	359.5	207.6	151.9	43.1	35.1	20.0	53.6
Balance							
	C58G	C58J	C58M	C58P	C58S	C58V	C58Y
1996	54.1	−62.1	116.2	28.5	11.7	34.9	41.1
1997	46.8	−59.8	106.6	18.3	11.2	38.9	38.2
1998	138.8	−22.7	161.6	33.0	34.2	37.9	56.6
1999	163.0	−22.8	185.8	8.0	25.6	54.2	98.0
2000	162.8	−57.0	219.7	6.1	25.0	76.0	112.6
2001	171.8	−53.0	224.8	11.2	35.2	65.4	113.0
2002	153.4	−91.1	244.5	11.1	23.4	77.1	132.9
2003	151.0	−85.2	236.2	14.2	20.8	86.5	114.8
2004	222.6	−119.6	342.2	74.1	41.1	123.0	104.0

1 Based mainly on data from the International Passenger Survey. Includes adjustments for (1) those whose intended length of stay changes so that their migrant status changes; (2) asylum seekers and their dependants not identified by the IPS; and (3) flows between the UK and the Republic of Ireland.
2 Up to and including 2003, estimates are shown for the EU15. For 2004, the estimates are for the EU25. These countries are included in the definition for the whole of 2004, whether migration occurred before or after 1 May.
3 Figures for all years include South Africa in the Old Commonwealth.
4 Figures for all years include Pakistan in the New Commonwealth. For 2004, the New Commonwealth excludes Malta and Cyprus.
5 Figures for all years include Hong Kong.

5.8 Estimates of migration into and out of the United Kingdom by usual occupation[1,2] and sex

Thousands

	Total			Professional and managerial			Manual and clerical			Not gainfully employed[3]		
	Persons	Males	Females	Persons	Males	Females	Persons	Males	Females	Persons	Males	Females
Inflow												
	KGOA	KGOB	KGOC	KGOD	KGOE	KGOF	KGOG	KGOH	KGOI	KGOJ	KGOK	KGOL
1996	261	124	137	86	51	35	55	24	31	120	50	71
1997	273	137	136	89	57	33	42	23	19	141	57	84
1998	318	160	158	112	65	47	71	35	35	136	60	76
1999	354	181	173	131	77	54	77	41	36	146	63	83
2000	364	191	173	163	98	65	64	34	30	137	60	77
2001	372	187	185	142	78	63	77	38	39	154	71	82
2002	386	200	186	142	78	64	83	44	39	161	77	83
2003	431	212	220	144	77	67	98	46	52	189	89	100
2004	518	261	257	175	102	72	131	66	66	212	92	120
Outflow												
	KGPA	KGPB	KGPC	KGPD	KGPE	KGPF	KGPG	KGPH	KGPI	KGPJ	KGPK	KGPL
1996	223	109	114	87	54	32	48	23	24	89	31	58
1997	232	125	107	88	59	29	50	23	26	94	43	51
1998	206	103	103	82	48	34	42	22	21	82	33	48
1999	245	132	114	97	60	38	69	32	37	79	41	39
2000	278	154	124	128	80	48	59	36	23	90	37	53
2001	251	136	115	104	67	37	60	30	30	88	39	49
2002	306	162	144	124	79	45	80	41	40	102	42	59
2003	314	165	149	108	60	49	103	59	44	103	46	57
2004	310	152	158	114	65	49	73	40	33	123	47	76
Balance												
	KGRA	KGRB	KGRC	KGRD	KGRE	KGRF	KGRG	KGRH	KGRI	KGRJ	KGRK	KGRL
1996	37	15	22	−1	−3	2	7	–	7	31	18	13
1997	40	12	29	1	−2	3	−7	−1	−7	47	14	33
1998	113	57	55	30	17	13	28	13	15	54	27	27
1999	109	49	60	33	17	16	8	9	−2	67	22	45
2000	87	38	49	35	18	17	5	−2	8	47	22	24
2001	121	51	69	38	11	26	17	8	10	66	33	34
2002	80	38	42	18	−1	19	3	4	−1	59	35	24
2003	118	47	71	36	17	18	−5	−14	9	87	43	44
2004	208	109	99	61	37	23	58	26	32	89	46	43

1 See chapter text.
2 Refers to regular occupation before migration.
3 Includes housewives, students, children and retired persons.

Source: Office for National Statistics: 01329 813255

5.9 Estimates of migration into and out of the United Kingdom by citizenship and country of last or next residence

Thousands

	All migrants	British citizens						European Union citizens[1] (excluding British)			
			Country of last/next residence						Country of last/next residence		
	Total	Total	European[1] Union	Old[2] Common-wealth	New[3] Common-wealth	United States of America	Other countries	Total	European[1] Union	Other Europe	Other countries
Inflow											
	KEZR	KGLA	KGLB	KGLC	KGLD	KGLE	KGLF	KGLG	KGLH	KGLI	KGLJ
1996	261	97	33	18	16	13	17	55	49	1	5
1997	273	90	36	20	10	7	17	62	56	–	6
1998	318	104	29	29	14	16	16	70	62	–	7
1999	354	117	32	38	16	11	20	60	55	–	5
2000	364	104	34	29	14	8	19	59	53	–	6
2001	372	106	26	31	17	10	22	57	54	–	3
2002	386	94	29	22	10	9	24	59	53	3	3
2003	431	106	40	29	12	10	15	61	54	1	6
2004	518	85	23	24	15	9	16	108	100	–	7
Outflow											
	KEZS	KGMA	KGMB	KGMC	KGMD	KGME	KGMF	KGMG	KGMH	KGMI	KGMJ
1996	223	143	53	38	16	16	21	24	19	–	5
1997	232	135	41	38	13	16	27	32	27	1	4
1998	206	114	37	36	8	15	19	26	21	1	4
1999	245	115	37	41	8	14	14	47	41	–	6
2000	278	141	41	48	9	19	24	46	39	1	6
2001	251	134	43	47	7	15	22	40	34	1	5
2002	306	165	69	44	10	18	24	42	38	–	4
2003	314	170	71	55	9	13	22	42	33	3	5
2004	310	184	68	62	12	16	27	34	30	1	3
Balance											
	KEZT	KGNA	KGNB	KGNC	KGND	KGNE	KGNF	KGNG	KGNH	KGNI	KGNJ
1996	37	−46	−20	−20	–	−3	−3	31	31	1	–
1997	40	−45	−5	−18	−2	−9	−10	30	29	−1	2
1998	113	−10	−8	−7	7	1	−3	44	41	−1	4
1999	109	2	−6	−3	7	−3	6	13	14	–	−2
2000	87	−37	−8	−19	6	−12	−4	13	14	−1	–
2001	121	−28	−17	−15	10	−6	–	17	20	−1	−1
2002	80	−70	−40	−21	–	−9	−1	17	15	3	−1
2003	118	−64	−31	−26	3	−3	−7	19	21	−3	1
2004	208	−99	−46	−38	3	−7	−11	74	70	−1	4

5.9 Estimates of migration into and out of the United Kingdom by citizenship and country of last or next residence

continued

Thousands

| | Commonwealth[4] citizens | | | | | | | | | | Other foreign citizens[1] | | | | |
| | Country of last/next residence | | | | | | | | | | Country of last/next residence | | | | |
	Total	Aust-ralia	Canada	New Zealand	South Africa	Bangl-adesh, India, Sri Lanka	Pakistan	Other African Common-wealth	Carib-bean Common-wealth	Other[5] count-ries	Total	Euro-[1] pean Union	Other Europe	United States of America	Other coun-tries
Inflow															
	KGLK	KGLL	KGLM	KGLN	KTDK	KGLO	KGLP	KGLQ	KGLR	KGLT	KGLU	KGLV	KGLW	KGLX	KGLY
1996	59	14	3	7	4	8	7	6	1	10	49	–	7	15	27
1997	75	14	5	7	5	15	5	6	1	18	45	–	7	11	27
1998	88	24	5	13	11	10	4	10	1	11	56	4	7	18	27
1999	98	26	2	12	12	14	6	14	3	9	79	3	19	15	42
2000	114	23	6	11	14	21	9	13	1	16	87	2	11	13	61
2001	123	32	4	10	12	21	9	18	2	14	87	1	12	12	61
2002	124	22	5	9	20	27	6	23	2	9	109	2	11	16	81
2003	141	20	6	8	20	37	8	23	3	16	124	2	23	16	82
2004	205	26	5	8	29	55	21	39	4	17	120	1	11	14	95
Outflow															
	KGMK	KGML	KGMM	KGMN	KTDL	KGMO	KGMP	KGMQ	KGMR	KGMT	KGMU	KGMV	KGMW	KGMX	KGMY
1996	29	8	2	3	2	2	–	2	–	9	27	1	7	5	14
1997	36	7	1	5	5	2	2	2	1	12	29	2	5	9	13
1998	30	9	1	3	4	2	1	2	–	6	35	2	7	9	18
1999	38	11	2	6	4	1	–	1	–	11	45	–	9	14	21
2000	43	12	3	8	5	2	2	2	1	8	48	3	11	9	24
2001	44	15	3	6	5	3	1	2	1	7	33	1	9	7	16
2002	52	18	6	9	5	3	2	2	–	7	47	2	12	16	18
2003	53	19	2	8	9	4	1	2	–	8	48	2	12	8	26
2004	50	17	4	5	7	3	1	3	–	11	42	5	2	8	28
Balance															
	KGNK	KGNL	KGNM	KGNN	KTDM	KGNO	KGNP	KGNQ	KGNR	KGNT	KGNU	KGNV	KGNW	KGNX	KGNY
1996	30	7	1	4	2	5	7	4	1	–	22	–1	–	10	13
1997	39	7	4	2	1	13	3	4	–	7	16	–2	2	3	14
1998	59	15	3	10	7	7	3	8	1	5	21	2	–	9	9
1999	60	15	–	6	8	13	6	12	3	–2	34	3	10	2	20
2000	71	11	3	3	9	19	8	10	–	7	40	–1	–	4	36
2001	79	17	–	4	7	18	9	16	1	7	53	–	3	5	45
2002	72	4	–1	–	15	24	4	21	2	2	61	–	–2	–	63
2003	87	1	3	–	11	33	7	21	3	8	75	–	11	8	56
2004	154	9	1	4	22	52	20	36	4	6	79	–4	9	6	67

1 Up to and including 2003, estimates are shown for the EU15 (UK, Austria, Belgium, Denmark, Finland, France, Germany, Greece, the Irish Republic, Italy, Luxembourg, Netherlands, Portugal, Spain and Sweden). For 2004, the estimates are for the EU25 (EU15 plus the 10 countries of Cyprus, the Czech Republic, Estonia, Hungary, Latvia, Lithuania, Malta, Poland, Slovakia and Slovenia). These countries are included in the definition for the whole of 2004, whether migration occurred before or after 1 May.

2 Figures for all years include South Africa in the Old Commonwealth.

3 Figures for all years include Pakistan in the New Commonwealth. For 2004, the New Commonwealth excludes Malta and Cyprus.

4 Figures for all years include South Africa and Pakinstan in the Commonwealth. For 2004, the Commonwealth excludes Malta and Cyprus.

5 For 2004 Other countries includes Malta and Cyprus.

Source: Office for National Statistics: 01329 813255

5.10 Acceptances for settlement by nationality[1,2]
United Kingdom

Number of persons

Geographical region and nationality		2002[6]	2003[6]	2004[3]
All nationalities	KGFA	115 825	139 280	139 260
Europe[1]				
Accession States				
Cyprus	KGFN	270	565	160
Czech Republic	LQLS	495	515	520
Estonia	LQLU	50	75	165
Hungary	KGFZ	270	325	100
Latvia	LQLV	75	125	210
Lithuania	LQLW	170	325	610
Malta	KGFP	80	95	25
Poland	KGGA	875	1 290	1 235
Slovakia	LQLT	380	425	255
Slovenia	LQMB	25	20	5
Accession States	EL20	2 690	3 755	3 285
Remainder of Europe				
Bulgaria	KGFW	365	750	625
Croatia	LQMA	310	280	985
Romania	KGGB	390	565	560
Russia	LQLX	1 365	2 160	1 620
Serbia & Montenegro	LQMC	1 540	1 165	9 590
Turkey	KGFT	2 920	4 365	6 060
Ukraine	LQLY	460	805	1 050
Other former USSR	LQLZ	415	625	830
Other former Yugoslavia	LQMD	955	510	285
Other Europe	KOSO	190	315	1 700
Remainder of Europe	EL2P	8 910	11 540	23 315
Europe[1]	KOSP	11 600	15 295	26 600
Americas				
Argentina	KGGF	120	155	95
Barbados	KGGG	100	160	145
Brazil	KGGH	510	695	565
Canada	KGGI	1 300	1 710	1 225
Chile	KGGJ	100	120	65
Colombia	KGGK	805	1 000	1 745
Guyana	KGGM	190	275	170
Jamaica	KGGN	2 675	4 500	2 930
Mexico	KGGO	160	245	130
Peru	KGGP	155	180	110
Trinidad and Tobago	KGGQ	410	655	570
USA	KGGR	4 355	5 620	4 120
Venezuela	KGGT	80	120	85
Other Americas	KOSR	720	1 025	2 175
Americas	KGGU	11 680	16 465	14 130
Africa				
Algeria	KGGV	855	945	1 005
Angola	KOSS	660	620	1 090
Congo (Dem. Rep.)[4]	KOST	1 260	1 475	2 410
Egypt	KGGW	500	615	485
Ethiopia	KGGX	345	285	520
Ghana	KGGY	2 585	4 015	2 305
Kenya	KGHA	1 055	1 585	2 255
Libya	KGHB	445	380	465
Mauritius	KGHC	455	695	530
Morocco	KGHD	520	660	305
Nigeria	KGHE	5 325	7 570	4 620
Sierra Leone	KGHF	855	1 375	1 805

Geographical region and nationality		2002[6]	2003[6]	2004[3]
Africa (continued)				
Somalia	KGHG	10 000	6 305	3 825
South Africa	KGHH	6 135	8 805	7 565
Sudan	KGHI	560	665	745
Tanzania	KGHJ	290	510	570
Tunisia	KGHK	160	220	115
Uganda	KGHL	745	830	960
Zambia	KGHM	330	560	505
Zimbabwe	KGHN	3 530	830	3 765
Other Africa	KOSU	2 550	3 080	3 585
Africa	KGHO	39 165	44 860	39 440
Asia				
Indian sub-continent				
Bangladesh	KGHP	4 725	5 590	3 115
India	KGHQ	8 005	10 955	11 100
Pakistan	KGHR	11 935	12 945	10 025
Indian sub-continent	KGHS	24 665	29 490	24 240
Middle East				
Iran	KGHT	1 715	1 585	1 725
Iraq	KGHU	1 955	1 440	1 720
Israel	KGHV	375	500	505
Jordan	KGHW	170	180	250
Kuwait	KGHX	65	75	90
Lebanon	KGHY	365	310	490
Saudi Arabia	KGHZ	40	75	60
Syria	KGIA	170	280	255
Yemen	KOSV	300	405	420
Other Middle East	KOSW	190	170	525
Middle East	KGIB	5 345	5 020	6 040
Remainder of Asia				
China	KGIC	1 705	2 540	2 315
Hong Kong[5]	KOSX	460	725	540
Indonesia	KGID	225	315	195
Japan	KGIE	1 785	1 850	1 360
Malaysia	KGIF	745	1 150	955
Philippines	KGIG	1 505	3 810	8 200
Singapore	KGIH	220	265	305
South Korea	KOTE	485	735	570
Sri Lanka	KGII	2 935	2 565	4 875
Taiwan	KOSY	200	255	205
Thailand	KGIJ	1 335	2 020	985
Other Asia	KOSZ	4 980	4 215	2 330
Remainder of Asia	KGIL	16 575	20 435	22 830
Asia	KGIM	46 585	54 945	53 115
Oceania				
Australia	KGIN	3 500	4 120	3 240
New Zealand	KGIO	2 645	2 920	2 370
Other Oceania	KOTA	100	85	85
Oceania	KGIP	6 250	7 125	5 690
British Overseas citizens	KGIQ	330	265	75
Nationality unknown	KGIS	215	330	205
All nationalities	KGFA	115 825	139 280	139 260

1 Excluding European Economic Area and Swiss nationals throughout the period covered.
2 Data from 2003 also excludes dependants of EEA and Swiss nationals in confirmed relationships granted permanant residence.
3 Includes nationals of the Czech Republic, Cyprus, Estonia, Hungary, Latvia, Lithuania, Malta, Poland, Slovakia and Slovenia before 1 May, but excludes them from this date.

4 Formerly known as Zaire.
5 Hong Kong (Special Administrative Region of China)includes British overseas territories citizens and stateless persons from Hong Kong and British Nationals (overseas).
6 Data has been revised.

Source: Home Office: 020 8760 8289

5.11 Applications[1] received for asylum in the United Kingdom, excluding dependants, by nationality

Number of principal applicants

		1995	1996	1997	1998	1999[2]	2000[2]	2001	2002	2003	2004[3]
Europe											
Albania	LQME	110	105	445	560	1 310	1 490	1 065	1 150	595	295
Czech Republic	LQMF	15	55	240	515	1 790	1 200	825	1 365	70	20
Macedonia	PTDW	..	15	20	50	90	65	755	310	60	15
Moldova	VQHP	10	..[4]	20	25	180	235	425	820	380	170
Poland	DMLX	1 210	900	565	1 585	1 860	1 015	615	990	95	15
Romania	KEAV	770	455	605	1 015	1 985	2 160	1 400	1 210	550	295
Russia	ZAEQ	..	205	180	185	685	1 000	450	295	280	190
SAM[5]	ZAFA	..	400	1 865	7 395	11 465	6 070	3 230	2 265	815	290
Turkey	KEAW	1 820	1 495	1 445	2 015	2 850	3 990	3 695	2 835	2 390	1 230
Ukraine	ZAER	..	235	490	370	775	770	445	365	300	120
Other Former USSR	ZAES	785	960	1 325	2 235	2 460	2 275	895	1 245	625	340
Other Former Yugoslavia	ZAET	1 565	620	375	535	2 625	2 200	85	90	50	20
Europe Other	ZAEU	770	1 035	1 575	1 260	200	415	335	300	80	30
Total	KEAZ	7 050	6 475	9 145	17 745	28 280	22 880	14 215	13 235	6 295	3 025
Americas											
Colombia	KEBZ	525	1 005	1 330	425	1 000	505	365	420	220	120
Ecuador	KYDB	250	435	1 205	280	610	445	255	315	150	35
Jamaica	PTDX	150	125	130	105	180	310	525	1 310	965	455
Americas Other	PTDY	415	205	165	165	240	155	170	240	230	130
Total	KECT	1 340	1 765	2 825	975	2 025	1 420	1 315	2 290	1 560	740
Africa											
Algeria	KOTB	1 865	715	715	1 260	1 385	1 635	1 140	1 060	550	490
Angola	KECU	555	385	195	150	545	800	1 015	1 420	850	400
Burundi	PTDZ	95	60	85	215	780	620	610	700	650	265
Cameroon	VQHU	85	105	175	95	245	355	380	615	505	360
Congo	PTEA	80	75	90	150	450	485	540	600	320	150
Congo (Dem. Rep.)	KEEH	935	680	690	660	1 240	1 030	1 370	2 215	1 540	1 475
Eritrea	PTEC	245	135	125	345	565	505	620	1 180	950	1 105
Ethiopia	KECW	585	205	145	345	455	415	610	700	640	540
Gambia	DMMA	1 170	245	125	45	30	50	65	130	95	100
Ghana	KECX	1 915	780	350	225	195	285	190	275	325	355
Ivory Coast	DMLZ	245	125	70	95	190	445	275	315	390	280
Kenya	KOTC	1 395	1 170	605	885	485	455	305	350	220	145
Liberia	C53K	390	330	205	70	65	55	115	450	740	405
Nigeria	KECY	5 825	2 900	1 480	1 380	945	835	810	1 125	1 010	1 090
Rwanda	ZAEV	135	80	90	280	820	760	530	655	260	75
Sierra Leone	KOTD	855	395	815	565	1 125	1 330	1 940	1 155	380	230
Somalia	KECZ	3 465	1 780	2 730	4 685	7 495	5 020	6 420	6 540	5 090	2 585
Sudan	KEEE	345	280	230	250	280	415	390	655	930	1 305
Tanzania	DMMC	1 535	225	90	80	80	60	80	40	30	20
Uganda	KEEG	365	215	220	210	420	740	480	715	705	405
Zimbabwe	GRFS	105	130	60	80	230	1 010	2 140	7 655	3 295	2 065
Africa Other	PTEB	360	275	220	305	400	615	555	845	895	910
Total	KEEJ	22 545	11 290	9 515	12 380	18 435	17 920	20 590	29 390	20 370	14 745
Middle East											
Iran	KEEK	615	585	585	745	1 320	5 610	3 420	2 630	2 875	3 455
Iraq	KEEL	930	965	1 075	1 295	1 800	7 475	6 680	14 570	4 015	1 695
Middle East Other	ZAEX	755	600	675	745	1 045	1 330	1 165	1 115	1 080	1 375
Total	KEGY	2 295	2 150	2 335	2 785	4 165	14 415	11 265	18 315	7 970	6 525
Asia											
Afghanistan	DMLY	580	675	1 085	2 395	3 975	5 555	8 920	7 205	2 280	1 395
Bangladesh	ZAEY	685	645	545	460	530	795	510	720	735	510
China	KEGZ	790	820	1 945	1 925	2 625	4 000	2 390	3 675	3 450	2 365
India	KEIL	3 255	2 220	1 285	1 030	1 365	2 120	1 850	1 865	2 290	1 405
Pakistan	KEIM	2 915	1 915	1 615	1 975	2 615	3 165	2 860	2 405	1 915	1 710
Sri Lanka	KEIN	2 070	1 340	1 830	3 505	5 130	6 395	5 510	3 130	705	330
Vietnam	VQIB	5	10	10	35	105	180	400	840	1 125	755
Asia Other	PTEE	385	270	255	615	1 120	1 025	1 040	915	655	375
Total	KEJO	10 685	7 885	8 570	11 940	17 465	23 230	23 480	20 755	13 155	8 850
Nationality not known	KEJP	50	80	105	190	785	450	160	145	55	70
Grand Total	KEJQ	43 965	29 640	32 500	46 015	71 160	80 315	71 025	84 130	49 405	33 960

1 Figures rounded to the nearest 5.
2 May exclude some cases lodged at Local Enforcement Offices between January 1999 and March 2000.
3 Provisional figures.
4 Figure = 1 or 2.

5 Serbia and Montenegro (SAM) replaced Federal Republic of Yugoslavia (FRY) from 5 February 2003. SAM comprises the Republic of Serbia, the Republic of Montenegro, and the Province of Kosovo (administered by the UN on an interim basis since 1999).

Source: Home Office: 020 8760 8274

5.12 Marriages: by previous marital status, sex, age and country

Numbers

		1994	1995	1996	1997	1998	1999	2000	2001	2002	2003	2004
United Kingdom[1,2,3]												
Marriages	KKAA	331 232	322 251	317 514	310 218	304 797	301 083	305 912	286 129	293 021	308 623	311 182
Persons marrying per 1,000 resident population	KKAB	11.4	11.1	10.9	10.6	10.4	10.3	10.4	9.7	9.9	10.4	10.4
Previous marital status												
Bachelors	KKAC	236 619	227 717	221 826	216 237	214 005	211 820	213 777	202 690	206 196	217 534	219 581
Divorced men	KKAD	85 261	85 743	87 113	85 625	82 977	81 750	84 771	76 852	80 040	84 011	84 771
Widowers	KKAE	9 352	8 791	8 575	8 356	7 815	7 513	7 364	6 587	6 785	7 078	6 830
Spinsters	KKAF	237 241	228 462	221 697	216 776	215 399	213 246	215 865	205 048	208 385	219 828	222 396
Divorced women	KKAG	85 220	85 396	87 618	85 648	82 016	80 816	83 166	74 807	78 182	82 181	82 164
Widows	KKAH	8 771	8 393	8 199	7 794	7 382	7 021	6 881	6 274	6 454	6 614	6 612
First marriage for both partners	KMGH	200 910	192 078	185 293	181 135	180 404	178 759	180 020	171 912	174 374	184 661	186 810
First marriage for one partner	KMGI	72 040	72 023	72 937	70 743	68 596	67 548	69 602	63 914	65 833	68 040	68 357
Remarriage for both partners	KMGJ	58 282	58 150	59 284	58 340	55 797	54 776	56 290	50 303	52 814	55 922	56 015
Males												
Under 21 years	KKAI	7 091	6 302	5 497	5 126	5 173	5 234	5 019	4 625	4 396	4 340	4 190
21-24	KKAJ	56 877	49 432	42 488	36 875	32 723	29 390	28 467	25 840	26 293	27 155	26 960
25-29	KKAK	111 108	105 218	101 647	97 345	94 696	90 412	85 870	78 687	74 858	75 580	74 182
30-34	KKAL	65 490	68 245	69 867	70 904	71 096	72 129	73 809	70 657	72 592	75 892	75 125
35-44	KKAM	51 310	53 350	56 513	58 292	59 838	62 114	68 019	65 242	69 747	75 695	78 976
45-54	KKAN	24 136	24 786	26 252	26 472	26 118	26 581	28 791	26 122	27 801	30 387	31 701
55 and over	KKAO	15 220	14 918	15 250	15 204	15 153	15 223	15 937	14 956	17 334	19 574	20 058
Females												
Under 21 years	KKAP	22 903	20 643	18 485	17 254	16 793	16 082	15 938	13 874	13 194	13 510	12 721
21-24	KKAQ	84 171	75 071	66 191	59 549	54 645	50 350	48 578	45 687	45 789	47 400	46 409
25-29	KKAR	102 803	100 644	99 651	97 932	97 181	94 703	92 753	85 647	82 892	84 066	83 992
30-34	KKAS	52 359	54 819	57 752	58 589	59 349	60 446	62 478	59 859	62 279	65 979	66 066
35-44	KKAT	41 213	43 115	45 969	47 267	47 721	50 136	54 697	52 209	56 997	61 682	64 627
45-54	KKAU	19 280	19 720	21 025	21 038	20 708	20 822	22 621	20 459	22 187	24 721	25 728
55 and over	KKAV	8 503	8 239	8 441	8 589	8 400	8 544	8 847	8 394	9 683	11 265	11 649
England and Wales[1,2]												
Marriages	KKBA	291 069	283 012	278 975	272 536	267 303	263 515	267 961	249 227	255 596	270 109	270 700
Persons marrying per 1,000 resident population	KKBB	11.4	11.0	10.9	10.6	10.3	10.1	10.3	9.5	9.7	10.2	10.2
Previous marital status												
Bachelors	KKBC	206 077	198 208	193 306	188 268	186 329	184 266	186 113	175 721	179 121	189 470	190 060
Divorced men	KKBD	76 633	76 967	78 003	76 839	74 029	72 617	75 378	67 678	70 506	74 397	74 690
Widowers	KKBE	8 359	7 837	7 666	7 429	6 945	6 632	6 470	5 828	5 969	6 242	5 950
Spinsters	KKBF	206 332	198 603	192 707	188 457	187 391	185 328	187 717	177 506	180 675	191 170	192 400
Divorced women	KKBG	76 857	76 869	78 939	77 098	73 330	71 971	74 092	66 120	69 234	73 071	72 480
Widows	KKBH	7 880	7 540	7 329	6 981	6 582	6 216	6 152	5 601	5 687	5 868	5 810
First marriage for both partners	KMGK	174 200	166 418	160 680	156 907	156 539	155 027	156 140	148 642	151 014	160 283	161 300
First marriage for one partner	KMGL	64 009	63 975	64 653	62 911	60 642	59 540	61 550	55 943	57 768	60 074	59 860
Remarriage for both partners	KMGM	52 860	52 619	53 642	52 718	50 122	48 948	50 271	44 642	46 814	49 752	49 540
Males												
Under 21 years	KKBI	6 175	5 520	4 877	4 574	4 608	4 629	4 536	4 160	3 952	3 885	3 760
21-24	KKBJ	49 073	42 711	36 713	31 907	28 389	25 424	24 764	22 436	22 961	23 802	23 610
25-29	KKBK	96 862	91 607	88 338	84 644	82 135	78 364	74 367	67 934	64 619	65 568	64 010
30-34	KKBL	57 848	60 014	61 582	62 265	62 323	63 212	64 611	61 409	62 998	66 060	64 930
35-44	KKBM	45 514	47 330	50 038	51 654	52 812	54 528	59 834	56 872	61 196	66 364	68 830
45-54	KKBN	21 794	22 349	23 661	23 688	23 385	23 676	25 470	22 949	24 336	26 785	27 680
55 and over	KKBO	13 803	13 481	13 766	13 804	13 651	13 682	14 379	13 467	15 534	17 645	17 890
Females												
Under 21 years	KKBP	20 250	18 343	16 510	15 439	15 065	14 379	14 421	12 467	11 916	12 270	11 510
21-24	KKBQ	72 937	65 126	57 296	51 766	47 446	43 691	42 265	39 746	39 968	41 567	40 480
25-29	KKBR	89 941	87 680	86 838	85 352	84 399	82 250	80 312	73 799	71 540	72 790	72 350
30-34	KKBS	46 119	48 216	50 799	51 405	51 982	52 721	54 649	51 865	53 970	57 348	57 150
35-44	KKBT	36 651	38 367	40 889	41 838	42 245	44 199	48 245	45 672	49 984	54 103	56 280
45-54	KKBU	17 409	17 791	18 992	18 938	18 575	18 572	20 083	18 071	19 535	21 858	22 530
55 and over	KKBV	7 762	7 489	7 651	7 798	7 591	7 703	7 986	7 607	8 683	10 173	10 410

5.12 Marriages: by previous marital status, sex, age and country
continued

Numbers

		1994	1995	1996	1997	1998	1999	2000	2001	2002	2003	2004
Scotland												
Marriages	KKCA	31 480	30 663	30 242	29 611	29 668	29 940	30 367	29 621	29 826	30 757	32 154
Persons marrying per 1,000 resident population	KKCB	12.3	12.0	11.9	11.7	11.7	11.8	12.0	11.7	11.8	12.2	12.7
Previous marital status												
Bachelors	KKCC	23 004	22 126	21 454	20 994	20 987	21 052	21 201	20 737	20 671	21 477	22 526
Divorced men	KKCD	7 654	7 741	8 048	7 845	7 934	8 142	8 427	8 238	8 475	8 574	8 930
Widowers	KKCE	822	796	740	772	747	746	739	646	680	706	698
Spinsters	KKCF	23 248	22 410	21 799	21 303	21 241	21 308	21 608	21 223	21 180	21 974	22 884
Divorced women	KKCG	7 487	7 542	7 718	7 621	7 754	7 949	8 141	7 825	8 008	8 157	8 622
Widows	KKCH	745	711	725	687	673	683	618	573	638	626	648
First marriage for both partners	KEZV	19 644	18 822	18 071	17 751	17 677	17 680	17 864	17 468	17 426	18 232	19 039
First marriage for one partner	KEZW	6 964	6 892	7 111	6 795	6 874	7 000	7 081	7 024	6 999	6 987	7 332
Remarriage for both partners	KEZX	4 872	4 949	5 060	5 065	5 117	5 260	5 422	5 129	5 401	5 538	5 783
Males												
Under 21 years	KKCI	680	577	452	406	421	490	364	371	367	361	336
21-24	KKCJ	5 693	4 915	4 191	3 494	3 147	2 853	2 720	2 489	2 395	2 507	2 501
25-29	KKCK	10 812	10 209	10 056	9 495	9 439	9 031	8 536	7 949	7 468	7 219	7 365
30-34	KKCL	6 176	6 574	6 574	6 911	6 988	7 179	7 419	7 464	7 692	7 752	7 992
35-44	KKCM	4 864	5 021	5 412	5 649	5 945	6 470	7 018	7 215	7 328	8 007	8 553
45-54	KKCN	2 050	2 124	2 288	2 459	2 412	2 575	2 960	2 816	3 033	3 213	3 503
55 and over	KKCO	1 205	1 243	1 269	1 197	1 316	1 342	1 350	1 317	1 543	1 698	1 904
Females												
Under 21 years	KKCP	1 959	1 728	1 423	1 302	1 289	1 322	1 171	1 111	996	1 007	954
21-24	KKCQ	8 291	7 264	6 474	5 568	5 248	4 778	4 581	4 343	4 171	4 199	4 358
25-29	KKCR	9 895	9 904	9 818	9 574	9 764	9 539	9 495	8 994	8 520	8 321	8 528
30-34	KKCS	5 145	5 401	5 675	5 927	6 036	6 433	6 463	6 618	6 832	7 110	7 235
35-44	KKCT	3 917	4 025	4 378	4 722	4 726	5 150	5 633	5 712	6 115	6 583	7 163
45-54	KKCU	1 648	1 689	1 794	1 844	1 900	1 994	2 279	2 147	2 322	2 589	2 821
55 and over	KKCV	625	652	680	674	705	724	745	696	870	948	1 095
Northern Ireland[3]												
Marriages	KKDA	8 683	8 576	8 297	8 071	7 826	7 628	7 584	7 281	7 599	7 757	8 328
Persons marrying per 1,000 resident population	KKDB	10.6	10.4	10.0	9.7	9.3	9.1	9.0	8.6	9.0	9.1	9.7
Previous marital status												
Bachelors	KKDC	7 538	7 383	7 066	6 975	6 689	6 502	6 463	6 232	6 404	6 587	6 995
Divorced men	KKDD	974	1 035	1 062	941	1 014	991	966	936	1 059	1 040	1 151
Widowers	KKDE	171	158	169	155	123	135	155	113	136	130	182
Spinsters	KKDF	7 661	7 449	7 191	7 016	6 767	6 610	6 540	6 319	6 530	6 684	7 112
Divorced women	KKDG	876	985	961	929	932	896	933	862	940	953	1 062
Widows	KKDH	146	142	145	126	127	122	111	100	129	120	154
First marriage for both partners	KEZY	7 066	6 838	6 542	6 477	6 188	6 052	6 016	5 802	5 934	6 146	6 471
First marriage for one partner	KEZZ	1 067	1 156	1 173	1 037	1 080	1 008	971	947	1 066	979	1 165
Remarriage for both partners	KFBI	550	582	582	557	558	568	597	532	599	632	692
Males												
Under 21 years	KKDI	236	205	168	146	144	115	119	94	77	94	94
21-24	KKDJ	2 111	1 806	1 584	1 474	1 187	1 113	983	915	937	846	849
25-29	KKDK	3 434	3 402	3 253	3 206	3 122	3 017	2 967	2 804	2 771	2 793	2 807
30-34	KKDL	1 466	1 657	1 711	1 728	1 785	1 738	1 779	1 784	1 902	2 080	2 203
35-44	KKDM	932	999	1 063	989	1 081	1 116	1 167	1 155	1 223	1 324	1 593
45-54	KKDN	292	313	303	325	321	330	361	357	432	389	518
55 and over	KKDO	212	194	215	203	186	199	208	172	257	231	264
Females												
Under 21 years	KKDP	694	572	552	513	439	381	346	296	282	233	257
21-24	KKDQ	2 943	2 681	2 421	2 215	1 951	1 881	1 732	1 598	1 650	1 634	1 571
25-29	KKDR	2 967	3 060	2 995	3 006	3 018	2 914	2 946	2 854	2 832	2 955	3 114
30-34	KKDS	1 095	1 202	1 278	1 257	1 331	1 292	1 366	1 376	1 477	1 521	1 681
35-44	KKDT	645	723	702	707	750	787	819	825	898	996	1 184
45-54	KKDU	223	240	239	256	233	256	259	241	330	274	377
55 and over	KKDV	116	98	110	117	104	117	116	91	130	144	144

1 Figures for 2003 are provisional until the FM2 no.31 is published on 28th March 2006.

2 Figures for 2004 are provisional. These may not add precisely due to rounding.

3 Bachelors and spinsters include a small number of persons who "previously went through a form of marriage".

Sources: Office for National Statistics: 01329 813772;
General Register Office for Scotland;
Northern Ireland Statistics and Research Agency

5.13 Divorce: by duration of marriage, age of wife and country

Numbers

		1994	1995	1996	1997	1998	1999	2000	2001	2002	2003	2004[6]
United Kingdom												
Decrees absolute granted[1]:												
Number	ZBRL	173 611	170 050	171 729	161 087	160 057	158 746	154 628	156 814	160 726	166 737	167 138
Duration of marriage:												
0-4 years	ZBRM	37 978	36 594	37 016	33 719	33 087	31 047	28 933	28 306	28 591	28 781	28 746
5-9 years	ZBRN	49 215	48 309	48 670	45 040	44 243	43 357	41 621	42 360	42 924	43 558	42 855
10-14 years	ZBRO	31 177	30 257	30 159	29 085	29 706	30 270	30 166	30 849	31 257	32 564	31 775
15-19 years	ZBRP	21 336	21 040	21 379	20 211	20 078	20 147	19 902	20 568	21 881	23 119	23 898
20 years and over	ZBRQ	33 898	33 840	34 487	33 020	32 935	33 916	34 000	34 729	36 073	38 713	39 844
Not stated	ZBRR	7	10	18	12	8	9	6	2	–	2	20
Age of wife at marriage:												
16-19 years	ZBRS	38 464	35 145	33 590	28 987	27 627	25 440	23 505	22 558	22 107	22 367	20 948
20-24 years	ZBRT	80 594	78 341	78 075	72 971	71 416	69 509	66 215	66 282	66 264	67 070	65 671
25-29 years	ZBRU	30 576	31 611	33 634	33 452	34 195	35 585	36 009	37 418	39 116	41 464	42 544
30-34 years	ZBRV	11 716	12 322	13 122	12 968	13 719	14 420	14 892	15 842	17 374	18 658	19 729
35-39 years	ZBRW	5 979	6 172	6 470	6 155	6 571	6 848	6 993	7 417	8 070	8 742	9 456
40-44 years	ZBRX	3 247	3 335	3 507	3 375	3 360	3 557	3 568	3 778	4 104	4 404	4 550
45 years and over	ZBRY	2 952	3 052	3 239	3 094	3 086	3 291	3 352	3 429	3 572	3 917	4 093
Not stated	ZBRZ	83	72	92	85	83	96	94	90	119	115	147
Age of wife at divorce:												
16-24 years	ZBSA	11 845	10 517	9 298	7 371	6 758	5 671	5 115	4 874	4 998	5 092	4 885
25-29 years	ZBSB	35 824	33 354	32 808	28 814	26 968	24 120	21 280	19 635	18 340	17 633	16 972
30-34 years	ZBSC	39 456	38 839	39 497	37 257	36 795	36 052	34 356	34 194	33 555	32 774	30 754
35-39 years	ZBSD	30 000	30 280	31 497	30 641	31 688	32 605	32 588	33 997	35 050	36 465	35 894
40-44 years	ZBSE	22 847	22 791	22 843	22 246	22 810	23 614	23 879	25 579	27 564	30 154	31 372
45 years and over	ZBSF	33 549	34 187	35 684	34 662	34 947	36 578	37 311	38 442	41 102	44 498	47 108
Not stated	ZBSG	90	82	102	96	91	106	99	93	117	121	153
Divorces in which there were[2,3]:												
No children aged under 16	ZBSH	78 913	78 844	..	..	..	..	..	..	..	..	..
One or more children aged under 16	ZBSI	94 698	91 206	..	..	..	..	..	..	..	..	..
England and Wales												
Decrees absolute granted[1]:												
Number	KKEA	158 175	155 499	157 107	146 689	145 214	144 556	141 135	143 818	147 735	153 490	153 399
Rate per 1,000 married couples	KKEB	13.7	13.6	13.8	13.0	12.9	12.9	12.7	12.9	13.4	14.0	14.1
Duration of marriage:												
0-4 years	KKEC	35 695	34 507	34 924	31 767	31 136	29 307	27 474	26 987	27 344	27 511	27 389
5-9 years	KKED	44 769	44 304	44 609	41 260	40 239	39 676	38 206	39 079	39 730	40 599	39 779
10-14 years	KKEE	28 073	27 365	27 332	26 215	26 698	27 384	27 459	28 176	28 592	29 831	29 086
15-19 years	KKEF	19 200	18 943	19 321	18 027	17 934	18 072	17 870	18 603	19 784	20 923	21 591
20 years and over	KKEG	30 431	30 370	30 912	29 408	29 199	30 108	30 120	30 971	32 285	34 624	35 554
Not stated	KKEH	7	10	9	12	8	9	6	2	–	2	–
Age of wife at marriage:												
16-19 years	KKEI	34 069	31 322	29 927	25 579	24 276	22 486	20 930	20 218	19 828	20 063	18 709
20-24 years	KKEJ	73 291	71 360	71 123	66 167	64 453	62 853	59 874	60 211	60 353	61 057	59 548
25-29 years	KKEK	28 360	29 441	31 396	31 022	31 533	32 867	33 282	34 759	36 387	38 722	39 575
30-34 years	KKEL	11 007	11 585	12 335	12 094	12 788	13 507	13 972	14 890	16 339	17 567	18 545
35-39 years	KKEM	5 615	5 800	6 051	5 767	6 153	6 432	6 562	6 956	7 623	8 249	8 912
40-44 years	KKEN	3 064	3 121	3 254	3 156	3 135	3 331	3 378	3 559	3 841	4 154	4 274
45 years and over	KKEO	2 769	2 870	3 021	2 904	2 876	3 080	3 137	3 225	3 364	3 678	3 836
Age of wife at divorce:												
16-24 years	KKEP	10 956	9 783	8 615	6 871	6 298	5 318	4 839	4 643	4 808	4 867	4 658
25-29 years	KKEQ	32 608	30 563	30 075	26 435	24 586	22 173	19 650	18 231	17 227	16 539	15 867
30-34 years	KKER	35 848	35 538	36 274	33 967	33 446	32 837	31 420	31 489	30 982	30 345	28 368
35-39 years	KKES	27 195	27 550	28 727	27 715	28 605	29 663	29 820	31 164	32 282	33 519	33 013
40-44 years	KKET	20 765	20 739	20 774	20 125	20 521	21 325	21 469	23 190	25 017	27 610	28 558
45 years and over	KKEU	30 796	31 316	32 633	31 564	31 750	33 231	33 931	35 099	37 419	40 608	42 935
Not stated	KKEV	7	10	9	12	8	9	6	2	–	2	–
Divorces in which there were[2]:												
No children aged under 16	ZBSJ	69 684	69 632	70 174	66 019	64 738	65 258	64 359	64 541	66 738	69 681	71 382
One or more children aged under 16	ZBSK	88 491	85 867	86 933	80 670	80 476	79 298	76 776	79 277	80 997	83 809	82 017

5.13 Divorce: by duration of marriage, age of wife and country

continued

Numbers

		1994	1995	1996	1997	1998	1999	2000	2001	2002	2003	2004[6]
Scotland												
Decrees absolute granted[1]												
Number	KKFA	13 133	12 249	12 308	12 222	12 384	11 864	11 143	10 631	10 826	10 928	11 227
Rate per 1,000 married couples	KKFB	11.5	10.8	10.9	11.0	11.3	10.9	10.3	9.7	10.0	10.2	10.5
Duration of marriage:												
0-4 years	KKFC	2 095	1 908	1 914	1 793	1 766	1 588	1 304	1 159	1 128	1 141	1 204
5-9 years	KKFD	3 790	3 399	3 432	3 224	3 360	3 095	2 890	2 721	2 689	2 450	2 536
10-14 years	KKFE	2 592	2 407	2 310	2 385	2 456	2 368	2 168	2 163	2 183	2 222	2 173
15-19 years	KKFF	1 786	1 698	1 709	1 804	1 729	1 686	1 622	1 562	1 705	1 773	1 810
20 years and over	KKFG	2 870	2 837	2 934	3 016	3 073	3 127	3 159	3 026	3 121	3 342	3 504
Not stated	ZBSL	–	–	9	–	–	–	–	–	–	–	–
Age of wife at marriage:												
16-19 years	ZBSM	3 641	3 091	2 939	2 749	2 654	2 374	2 043	1 839	1 845	1 816	1 753
20-24 years	ZBSN	6 197	5 845	5 822	5 714	5 744	5 453	5 142	4 873	4 823	4 869	4 892
25-29 years	KKFJ	1 926	1 887	1 933	2 151	2 314	2 333	2 318	2 233	2 316	2 307	2 462
30-34 years	KKFK	628	654	697	791	824	829	805	827	895	958	1 025
35-39 years	KKFL	329	338	393	360	382	379	378	401	407	432	489
40-44 years	KKFM	163	196	234	199	198	208	170	193	235	219	252
45 years and over	KKFN	166	166	198	173	185	192	193	175	186	212	221
Not stated	KKFO	83	72	92	85	83	96	94	90	119	115	133
Age of wife at divorce:												
16-24 years	KKFP	767	622	583	426	377	301	232	182	180	191	192
25-29 years	KKFQ	2 750	2 353	2 269	2 021	1 957	1 597	1 330	1 109	974	884	869
30-34 years	KKFR	3 045	2 747	2 708	2 736	2 767	2 642	2 381	2 215	2 174	1 943	1 918
35-39 years	KKFS	2 390	2 290	2 307	2 469	2 562	2 450	2 298	2 311	2 281	2 388	2 278
40-44 years	KKFT	1 788	1 734	1 761	1 819	1 951	1 929	1 999	1 963	2 110	2 106	2 341
45 years and over	KKFU	2 310	2 431	2 587	2 667	2 687	2 848	2 810	2 760	2 990	3 297	3 496
Not stated	KKFV	83	72	93	84	83	97	93	91	117	119	133
Divorces in which there were[2,3]:												
No children aged under 16	KKFW	7 390	7 515	..	..	..	..	..	..	..	..	..
One or more children under 16	KKFX	5 743	4 734	..	..	..	..	..	..	..	..	..
Northern Ireland												
Decrees absolute granted:[1,4]												
Number	ZBSO	2 303	2 302	2 314	2 176	2 459	2 326	2 350	2 365	2 165	2 319	2 512
Duration of marriage:												
0-4 years	ZBSP	188	179	178	159	185	152	155	160	119	129	153
5-9 years	ZBSQ	656	606	629	556	644	586	525	560	505	509	540
10-14 years	ZBSR	512	485	517	485	552	518	539	510	482	511	516
15-19 years	ZBSS	350	399	349	380	415	389	410	403	392	423	497
20 years and over	ZBST	597	633	641	596	663	681	721	732	667	747	786
Not stated[5]	EK8B	–	–	–	–	–	–	–	–	–	–	20
Age of wife at marriage:												
16-19 years	ZBSU	754	732	724	659	697	580	532	501	434	488	486
20-24 years	ZBSV	1 106	1 136	1 130	1 090	1 219	1 203	1 199	1 198	1 088	1 144	1 231
25-29 years	ZBSW	290	283	305	279	348	385	409	426	413	435	507
30-34 years	ZBSX	81	83	90	83	107	84	115	125	140	133	159
35-39 years	ZBSY	35	34	26	28	36	37	53	60	40	61	55
40-44 years	ZBSZ	20	18	19	20	27	18	20	26	28	31	24
45 years and over	ZBTA	17	16	20	17	25	19	22	29	22	27	36
Not stated[5]	EK8C	–	–	–	–	–	–	–	–	–	–	14
Age of wife at divorce:												
16-24 years	ZBTB	122	112	100	74	83	52	44	49	10	34	35
25-29 years	ZBTC	466	438	464	358	425	350	300	295	139	210	236
30-34 years	ZBTD	563	554	515	554	582	573	555	490	399	486	468
35-39 years	ZBTE	415	440	463	457	521	492	470	522	487	558	603
40-44 years	ZBTF	294	318	308	302	338	360	411	426	437	438	473
45 years and over	ZBTG	443	440	464	431	510	499	570	583	693	593	677
Not stated[5]	EK8D	–	–	–	–	–	–	–	–	–	–	20
Divorces in which there were[2]:												
No children aged under 16	ZBTH	1 839	1 697	1 676	1 573	1 807	1 649	1 051	1 054	972	1 050	1 218
One or more children aged under 16	ZBTI	464	605	638	603	652	677	1 299	1 311	1 193	1 269	1 282
Not stated[5]	EK8E	–	–	–	–	–	–	–	–	–	–	12

1 Includes decrees of nullities.
2 Children of the family as defined by the Matrimonial Causes Act 1973.
3 Data not available in Scotland.
4 Marital estimates are not available for Northern Ireland - no divorce rate for Northern Ireland and the United Kingdom.
5 Due to some incomplete records.
6 Provisional

Sources: Office for National Statistics: 01329 813339;
General Register Office for Scotland;
Northern Ireland Statistics and Research Agency

5.14 Divorce proceedings: by country

Numbers

		1994	1995	1996	1997	1998	1999	2000	2001	2002	2003	2004[4]
United Kingdom												
Dissolution of marriage[1]												
Decree absolute/decree granted	ZBXR	173 178	169 621	171 309	160 733	159 688	158 418	154 273	156 562	160 529	166 536	166 937
On grounds of:												
Adultery	ZBXS	42 743	41 313	41 127	38 652	37 302	35 545	34 082	33 452	33 389	33 844	32 586
Behaviour	ZBXT	75 029	71 733	72 581	68 546	68 685	67 851	65 687	66 818	68 499	70 866	70 879
Desertion	ZBXU	1 185	1 196	1 101	956	828	748	722	718	727	697	675
Separation (2 years and consent)	ZBXV	41 144	41 969	42 265	39 398	39 627	40 368	39 763	40 699	42 579	44 012	44 819
Separation(5 years)	ZBXW	12 317	12 699	13 547	12 552	12 697	13 389	13 653	14 575	15 076	16 831	17 714
Combination of more than one ground and other	ZBXX	760	711	688	629	549	517	366	300	259	286	264
Decree absolute/decree granted to:												
the wife	ZBXY	123 256	118 869	119 570	111 912	111 556	109 828	106 958	107 345	108 106	114 665	113 971
the husband	ZBXZ	49 507	50 268	51 247	48 393	47 764	48 236	47 069	49 015	52 251	51 691	52 793
both	ZBYA	423	490	493	430	369	358	247	202	173	181	174
Nullity of marriage[2]												
Decree absolute/decree granted	ZBYB	433	429	420	354	369	328	355	252	198	201	201
England and Wales												
Dissolution of marriage												
Petitions filed[3]	KKGA	175 701	174 012	178 117	163 787	165 602	162 137	157 809	172 341	177 224	173 263	167 193
Decree nisi granted[3]	KKGM	154 241	155 739	157 588	148 310	144 231	143 106	143 729	146 932	170 996	167 992	166 042
Decree absolute granted	KKGN	157 756	155 076	156 692	146 339	144 851	144 233	140 783	143 568	147 538	153 294	153 199
On grounds of:												
Adultery	KKGB	41 449	40 178	40 012	37 592	36 319	34 584	33 310	32 839	32 829	33 331	32 035
Behaviour	KKGC	70 932	68 168	68 986	65 047	65 257	64 816	63 182	64 768	66 480	68 944	68 859
Desertion	KKGD	1 062	1 108	1 030	912	790	713	680	689	681	665	654
Separation (2 years and consent)	KKGE	33 996	35 030	35 422	32 638	32 394	33 482	32 820	33 703	35 476	36 931	37 543
Separation(5 years)	KKGF	9 589	9 930	10 626	9 592	9 616	10 193	10 498	11 355	11 896	13 239	13 933
Combination of more than one ground and other	ZBYC	728	662	616	558	475	445	293	214	176	184	175
Decree absolute granted to[2]:												
the wife	ZBYD	112 415	108 764	109 489	102 173	101 583	100 469	98 227	98 992	102 676	106 208	105 381
the husband	ZBYE	44 918	45 823	46 712	43 739	42 902	43 413	42 311	44 378	44 694	46 915	47 651
both	ZBYF	423	489	491	427	366	351	245	198	168	171	167
Nullity of marriage												
Petitions filed[3]	KKGO	822	881	702	485	747	549	452	492	443	463	494
Decree nisi granted[3]	KKGR	705	425	332	248	281	495	274	297	158	204	308
Decree absolute granted	KKGS	419	423	415	350	363	323	352	250	197	196	200
Judicial separation												
Petitions filed[3]	KKGT	1 943	1 694	1 639	1 078	916	906	650	1 078	1 001	826	742
Decrees granted[3]	KKGW	1 350	1 543	1 199	589	519	696	540	925	331	467	419

5.14 Divorce proceedings: by country

continued

		1994	1995	1996	1997	1998	1999	2000	2001	2002	2003	2004[4]
Scotland												
Dissolution of marriage[1]												
Decree granted	ZBYG	13 125	12 243	12 307	12 220	12 383	11 860	11 142	10 631	10 826	10 927	11 226
On grounds of:												
Adultery	ZBYH	1 099	956	943	909	832	770	610	473	428	401	413
Behaviour	ZBYI	3 711	3 203	3 184	3 081	3 005	2 611	2 099	1 639	1 656	1 537	1 546
Desertion	ZBYJ	103	72	61	33	28	18	34	24	43	23	15
Separation (2 years and consent)	ZBYK	6 078	5 846	5 835	5 773	6 121	5 908	5 878	5 943	6 101	6 016	6 122
Separation(5 years)	ZBYL	2 134	2 166	2 284	2 424	2 397	2 553	2 521	2 552	2 598	2 950	3 130
Decree granted to[2]												
the wife	ZBYM	9 278	8 545	8 559	8 266	8 329	7 774	7 191	6 775	4 025	6 927	6 939
the husband	ZBYN	3 855	3 704	3 749	3 956	4 055	4 090	3 952	3 856	6 802	4 001	4 288
Nullity of marriage												
Decree granted	ZBYO	8	6	1	2	1	4	1	–	1	1	1
Northern Ireland												
Dissolution of marriage												
Petitions filed	ZBYP	2 875	2 875	2 695	2 808	2 760	2 414	3 005	2 869	2 929	3 192	2 808
Decree nisi granted	ZBYQ	2 535	2 535	2 419	2 532	2 904	2 393	2 456	2 615	2 454	2 616	2 697
Decree absolute granted	ZBYR	2 296	2 302	2 310	2 174	2 454	2 325	2 348	2 363	2 165	2 315	2 512
On grounds of:												
Adultery	ZBYS	195	179	172	151	151	191	162	140	132	112	138
Behaviour	ZBYT	386	362	411	418	423	424	406	411	363	385	474
Desertion	ZBYU	20	16	10	11	10	17	8	5	3	9	6
Separation (2 years and consent)	ZBYV	1 072	1 093	1 010	991	1 112	978	1 065	1 053	1 002	1 065	1 154
Separation(5 years)	ZBYW	594	603	637	536	684	643	634	668	582	642	651
Combination of more than one ground and other	ZBYX	29	49	70	67	74	72	73	86	83	102	89
Decree absolute granted to:												
the wife	ZBYY	1 562	1 560	1 522	1 473	1 644	1 585	1 540	1 578	1 405	1 530	1 651
the husband	ZBYZ	734	741	786	698	807	733	806	781	755	775	854
both	ZBZA	–	1	2	3	3	7	2	4	5	10	7
Nullity of marriage												
Petitions filed	ZBZB	5	5	5	7	5	1	2	1	5	4	8
Decree nisi granted	ZBZC	3	5	5	2	6	2	5	2	2	5	3
Decree absolute granted	ZBZD	7	–	4	2	5	1	2	2	–	4	–
Judicial separation												
Petitions filed	ZBZE	57	84	63	70	64	50	54	40	27	35	18
Decrees granted	ZBZF	15	30	22	34	40	31	23	25	15	22	12

1 The terms petition filed, decree nisi granted, decree absolute and judicial separation are not used in Scotland. Decree absolute granted to 'both' and 'Combination of more than one ground and other' are not procedures used in Scotland.

2 Information on Decree granted for the wife or husband for Scotland includes nullities (these are identified separately under 'Nullity of marriage'); figures excluding nullities are not available.

3 Data supplied by Her Majesty's Court Service (14 February 2006) with the introduction of Management Information System Data (from 2001).

4 2004 data are provisional until FM2 series no. 31 is published on 28 March 2006.

Sources: Office for National Statistics: 01329 813772;
General Register Office for Scotland;
Northern Ireland Statistics and Research Agency;
Her Majesty's Court Service;
Scottish Courts Administration;
Northern Ireland Courts Administration

5.15 Births:[1] by country and sex

Thousands

	Live births				Rates				
	Total	Male	Female	Sex ratio[2]	Crude birth rate[3]	General fertility rate[4]	TFR[5]	Still-births[6]	Still-birth rate[6]
United Kingdom[7]									
1900 - 02	1 095	558	537	1 037	28.6	115.1	..	..	..
1910 - 12	1 037	528	508	1 039	24.6	99.4	..	..	..
1920 - 22	1 018	522	496	1 052	23.1	93.0	..	..	..
1930 - 32	750	383	367	1 046	16.3	66.5	..	..	..
1940 - 42	723	372	351	1 062	15.0	..	1.89	..	..
1950 - 52	803	413	390	1 061	16.0	73.7	2.21	..	..
1960 - 62	946	487	459	1 063	17.9	90.3	2.80	18.6	19.2
1970 - 72	880	453	427	1 064	15.8	82.5	2.36	11.3	12.7
1980 - 82	735	377	358	1 053	13.0	62.5	1.83	5.0	6.8
1990 - 92	790	405	385	1 051	13.8	63.7	1.81	3.6	4.6
2000 - 02	672	345	328	1 052	11.4	54.7	1.64	3.6	5.4
	BBCA	KBCZ	KBCY	KMFW	KBCT	KBCS	KBCR	KBCQ	KMFX
1994	750	385	365	1 054	13.0	61.6	1.74	4.3	5.8
1995	732	375	357	1 052	12.6	60.1	1.71	4.1	5.6
1996	733	376	357	1 055	12.6	60.2	1.73	4.1	5.5
1997	727	372	354	1 051	12.5	59.6	1.72	3.9	5.3
1998	717	367	350	1 052	12.3	58.8	1.71	3.9	5.4
1999	700	359	341	1 056	11.9	57.3	1.69	3.7	5.3
2000	679	348	331	1 051	11.5	55.4	1.64	3.6	5.3
2001	669	343	326	1 050	11.3	54.3	1.63	3.6	5.3
2002	669	343	327	1 054	11.3	54.2	1.64	3.8	5.6
2003	696	357	339	1 052	11.7	56.2	1.72	4.0	5.7
2004[8]	716	368	348	1 055	12.0	57.7	1.77	4.0	5.5
England and Wales									
1900 - 02	932	475	458	1 037	28.6	114.7	..	..	..
1910 - 12	884	450	433	1 040	24.5	98.6	..	..	..
1920 - 22	862	442	420	1 051	22.8	91.1	..	..	..
1930 - 32	632	323	309	1 047	15.8	64.4	..	27.0	..
1940 - 42	607	312	295	1 057	15.6	61.3	1.81	22.0	..
1950 - 52	683	351	332	1 058	15.6	72.1	2.16	16.0	..
1960 - 62	812	418	394	1 061	17.6	88.9	2.77	15.6	18.9
1970 - 72	764	394	371	1 061	15.6	81.4	2.31	9.7	12.5
1980 - 82	639	328	311	1 053	12.9	61.8	1.81	4.3	6.7
1990 - 92	698	358	340	1 051	13.8	63.8	1.82	3.2	4.5
2000 - 02	598	307	292	1 052	11.4	55.2	1.65	3.2	5.4
	BBCB	KMFY	KMFZ	KMGA	KMGB	KMGC	KMGD	KMGE	KMGF
1994	665	341	323	1 055	13.0	62.0	1.75	3.8	5.7
1995	648	332	316	1 051	12.6	60.5	1.72	3.6	5.5
1996	649	333	316	1 055	12.6	60.6	1.74	3.5	5.4
1997	643	330	314	1 051	12.5	60.0	1.73	3.4	5.3
1998	636	326	310	1 051	12.3	59.2	1.72	3.4	5.3
1999	622	319	303	1 055	12.0	57.8	1.70	3.3	5.3
2000	604	310	295	1 050	11.6	55.9	1.65	3.2	5.3
2001	595	305	290	1 050	11.4	54.7	1.63	3.2	5.3
2002	596	306	290	1 055	11.3	54.7	1.65	3.4	5.6
2003	621	318	303	1 051	11.8	56.8	1.73	3.6	5.7
2004[8]	640	328	311	1 054	12.1	58.2	1.78	3.5	5.5

5.15

Births:[1] by country and sex

continued

Thousands

	Live births				Rates				
	Total	Male	Female	Sex ratio[2]	Crude birth rate[3]	General fertility rate[4]	TFR[5]	Still-births[6]	Still-birth rate[6]
Scotland									
1900 - 02	132	67	65	1 046	29.5	120.6	..	..	..
1910 - 12	123	63	60	1 044	25.9	107.4	..	..	..
1920 - 22	125	64	61	1 046	25.6	105.9	..	..	..
1930 - 32	93	47	45	1 040	19.1	78.8	..	..	..
1940 - 42	89	46	43	1 051	18.5	73.7	..	4.0	..
1950 - 52	91	47	44	1 060	17.9	81.4	2.41	2.0	..
1960 - 62	102	53	50	1 060	19.7	97.8	2.98	2.2	20.8
1970 - 72	84	43	41	1 057	16.1	83.3	2.46	1.1	13.5
1980 - 82	68	35	33	1 051	13.1	62.2	1.80	0.4	6.3
1990 - 92	66	34	32	1 052	13.0	59.2	1.68	0.4	5.7
2000 - 02	52	27	26	1 046	10.3	48.6	1.48	0.3	5.6
	BBCD	KMEU	KMEV	KMEW	KMEX	KMEY	KMEZ	KMFM	KMFN
1994	62	31	30	1 038	12.1	56.0	1.58	0.4	6.1
1995	60	31	29	1 043	11.8	54.6	1.55	0.4	6.6
1996	59	31	29	1 061	11.6	54.1	1.56	0.4	6.4
1997	59	31	29	1 055	11.7	54.4	1.58	0.3	5.3
1998	57	29	28	1 060	11.3	52.7	1.55	0.4	6.1
1999	55	28	27	1 050	10.9	50.9	1.51	0.3	5.2
2000	53	27	26	1 051	10.5	49.2	1.48	0.3	5.6
2001	53	27	26	1 041	10.4	48.8	1.49	0.3	5.7
2002	51	26	25	1 047	10.1	48.1	1.48	0.3	5.4
2003	52	27	26	1 054	10.4	49.4	1.54	0.3	5.6
2004[8]	54	28	26	1 060	10.6	51.0	1.60	0.3	5.8
Northern Ireland[7]									
1900 - 02	..	..	..	..	..	..	..	..	..
1910 - 12	..	..	..	..	..	..	..	..	..
1920 - 22	31	16	15	1 048	24.2	105.9	..	..	..
1930 - 32	26	13	12	1 047	20.5	78.8	..	..	..
1940 - 42	27	14	13	1 078	20.8	73.7	..	..	..
1950 - 52	29	15	14	1 066	20.9	81.4	..	..	..
1960 - 62	31	16	15	1 068	22.5	111.5	3.47	0.7	22.0
1970 - 72	31	16	15	1 074	20.4	105.7	3.13	0.5	14.3
1980 - 82	28	14	13	1 048	18.0	87.5	2.59	0.2	8.4
1990 - 92	26	13	13	1 051	16.1	74.8	2.15	0.1	4.6
2000 - 02	22	11	11	1 054	12.8	58.8	1.78	0.1	5.0
	BBCE	KMFO	KMFP	KMFQ	KMFR	KMFS	KMFT	KMFU	KMFV
1994	24	12	12	1 053	14.7	68.0	1.95	0.2	6.3
1995	24	12	11	1 078	14.4	66.6	1.91	0.1	6.1
1996	24	12	12	1 032	14.7	67.8	1.95	0.2	6.2
1997	24	12	12	1 048	14.4	66.4	1.93	0.1	5.4
1998	24	12	12	1 039	14.1	65.0	1.90	0.1	5.1
1999	23	12	11	1 084	13.7	62.9	1.86	0.1	5.7
2000	22	11	10	1 070	12.8	58.7	1.75	0.1	4.3
2001	22	11	11	1 058	13.0	59.7	1.80	0.1	5.1
2002	21	11	11	1 035	12.6	58.1	1.77	0.1	5.7
2003	22	11	10	1 081	12.7	59.0	1.81	0.1	5.0
2004[8]	22	11	11	1 059	13.0	60.6	1.87	0.1	5.0

1 See chapter text.
2 Males per 1,000 females (calculated using whole numbers).
3 Rate per 1,000 population(calculated using whole numbers).
4 Rate per 1,000 women aged 15 - 44.
5 Total period fertility rate is the average number of children which would be born to a woman if she experienced the age-specific fertility rates of the period in question throughout her child-bearing life span. UK figures for the years 1970-72 and earlier are estimates.
6 On 1 October 1992 the legal definition of a stillbirth was changed from a baby born dead after 28 completed weeks gestation or more to one born dead after 24 completed weeks gestation or more. Between 1 October and 31 December 1992 in the UK there were 258 babies born dead between 24 and

27 completed weeks gestation (216 in England and Wales, 35 in Scotland and 7 in Northern Ireland). If these babies were included in the stillbirth figures given, the stillbirth rate would be 4.7 for the UK and England and Wales, while Scotland and Northern Ireland stillbirth rate would remain as stated.
7 From 1981, data for the United Kingdom and Northern Ireland have been revised to exclude births in Northern Ireland to non-residents of Northern Ireland.
8 Birth rates for 2004 have been calculated using the revised mid-2004 population estimates published on 20 December 2005.

Sources: Office for National Statistics: 01329 813772;
General Register Office for Scotland;
Northern Ireland Statistics and Research Agency

5.16 Birth occurrence inside and outside marriage by age of mother

Thousands

	Inside marriage						Outside marriage					
	All ages	Under 20	20 - 24	25 - 29	Over 30	Mean[1] age (Years)	All ages	Under 20	20 - 24	25 - 29	Over 30	Mean[1] age (Years)
United Kingdom[2]												
	KKEY	KKEZ	KKFY	KKFZ	KKGX	KKGY	KKGZ	KKIC	KKID	KKIE	KKIF	KKIG
1961	890	55	273	280	282	27.7	54	13	17	10	13	25.5
1971	828	70	301	271	185	26.4	74	24	25	13	12	23.8
1981	640	36	193	231	180	27.3	91	30	33	16	13	23.4
1986	596	21	159	231	185	27.9	158	45	60	31	22	23.7
1987	598	18	153	235	192	28.1	178	48	68	37	26	23.9
1988	589	16	144	234	195	28.2	198	51	76	42	29	24.1
1989	570	14	130	228	198	28.4	207	49	79	46	32	24.3
1990	576	13	121	233	209	28.6	223	51	83	53	37	24.5
1991	556	10	109	224	213	28.9	236	50	87	58	41	24.8
1992	540	9	98	216	218	29.1	241	46	86	62	46	25.1
1993	520	8	87	204	221	29.3	242	44	84	64	50	25.4
1994	510	7	78	194	231	29.6	240	41	80	65	55	25.7
1995	486	6	69	180	232	29.8	246	42	79	66	60	25.9
1996	473	6	61	170	237	30.1	260	45	80	69	66	26.0
1997	460	6	55	159	240	30.3	267	47	79	71	71	26.1
1998	447	6	51	149	243	30.5	270	49	77	70	74	26.2
1999	428	6	47	136	239	30.7	272	49	77	68	77	26.3
2000	411	5	44	126	237	30.9	268	47	77	66	78	26.4
2001	401	5	44	116	236	30.9	268	45	77	64	82	26.7
2002	397	5	44	109	239	31.1	272	44	80	62	85	26.7
2003	407	5	44	110	249	31.2	288	45	86	65	92	26.8
2004	413	4	44	110	255	31.3	303	47	90	69	97	26.9
Great Britain												
	KKIH	KKII	KKIJ	KKIK	KKIL	KKIM	KKIN	KKIO	KKIP	KKIQ	KKIR	KKIS
1961	859	53	264	270	272	27.7	53	13	17	10	13	25.5
1971	797	68	293	261	176	26.4	73	24	25	13	12	23.8
1981	614	34	186	223	171	27.2	89	29	32	16	13	23.3
1986	572	20	153	222	177	27.9	155	44	59	30	22	22.9
1987	574	17	147	227	184	28.0	174	46	66	36	25	23.4
1988	566	16	138	226	186	28.2	194	49	74	42	29	23.6
1989	549	13	125	220	190	28.4	202	48	77	45	32	24.2
1990	554	12	116	225	201	28.6	218	49	81	52	36	24.6
1991	535	10	105	216	205	28.9	231	48	85	57	41	24.8
1992	520	9	94	208	210	29.1	235	45	84	61	46	25.1
1993	500	7	84	196	213	29.3	236	42	82	62	49	25.4
1994	492	7	75	188	222	29.6	235	41	78	63	53	25.7
1995	468	6	66	173	223	29.8	240	40	77	65	59	25.9
1996	455	6	59	163	227	30.1	254	44	78	68	65	26.0
1997	442	6	53	152	231	30.3	261	46	76	69	69	26.2
1998	430	6	49	143	233	30.5	263	48	74	68	73	26.3
1999	412	6	46	131	230	30.7	265	48	74	67	76	26.4
2000	396	5	43	121	228	30.9	261	46	74	65	77	26.5
2001	386	5	43	112	227	30.9	261	44	75	62	80	26.6
2002	383	5	43	105	230	31.1	265	43	77	61	84	26.7
2003	393	4	43	106	239	31.2	281	44	83	64	90	26.9
2004	399	4	43	106	245	31.3	295	45	88	67	95	26.9

1 The mean ages presented in this table are unstandardised and therefore take no account of the age structure of the population.
2 From 1981, data for the United Kingdom have been revised to exclude births in Northern Ireland to non-residents of Northern Ireland.

Sources: Office for National Statistics: 01329 813772;
General Register Office for Scotland;
Northern Ireland Statistics and Research Agency

5.17 Live births: by age of mother and country

	Under 20	20 - 24	25 - 29	30 - 34	35 - 39	40 - 44	45 and over	All ages
United Kingdom								
All live births[1]								
	KMDV	KMDW	KMDX	KMDY	KMDZ	KMES	KMET	KMBZ
1994	47 874	157 468	259 367	202 880	70 871	11 432	536	750 480
1995	47 646	147 056	246 017	204 601	73 945	12 008	585	731 882
1996	50 793	141 090	238 857	210 490	78 335	12 832	638	733 163
1997	52 851	133 257	229 429	212 162	84 508	13 731	618	726 622
1998	54 822	127 230	218 072	212 876	88 729	14 453	640	716 888
1999	54 921	124 036	204 808	208 986	91 272	15 210	695	699 976
2000	52 059	120 305	191 583	202 893	95 400	16 032	708	679 029
2001	50 157	121 664	179 776	202 017	97 379	17 271	831	669 123
2002	49 165	123 844	171 852	203 261	101 379	18 273	968	668 777
2003	49 874	129 867	175 473	210 071	109 038	20 233	933	695 549
2004	50 752	134 614	179 050	213 620	114 852	22 107	975	715 996
Age-specific fertility rates								
	KMBR	KMBS	KMBT	KMBU	KMBV	KMBW	KMBX	KMBY
1994	28.7	77.9	112.3	89.1	35.4	6.0	0.3	61.6
1995	28.2	75.4	108.4	88.1	36.1	6.4	0.3	60.1
1996	29.6	75.7	106.6	89.6	37.2	6.8	0.3	60.2
1997	30.2	74.9	104.2	89.8	39.1	7.1	0.3	59.6
1998	30.8	73.6	101.4	90.4	40.0	7.4	0.3	58.8
1999	30.7	71.8	98.0	89.4	40.2	7.6	0.4	57.3
2000	29.2	68.7	93.9	87.7	41.0	7.8	0.4	55.4
2001	27.9	68.0	91.5	88.0	41.3	8.2	0.4	54.3
2002	26.9	68.1	91.3	89.7	42.6	8.4	0.5	54.2
2003	26.6	70.1	95.9	94.5	45.9	9.1	0.5	56.2
2004	26.7	71.5	98.0	99.1	48.6	9.7	0.5	57.7
England and Wales								
All live births								
	KGSA	KGSB	KGSC	KGSD	KGSE	KGSF	KGSG	KGSH
1994	42 026	140 240	229 102	179 568	63 061	10 241	488	664 726
1995	41 938	130 744	217 418	181 202	65 517	10 779	540	648 138
1996	44 667	125 732	211 103	186 377	69 503	11 516	587	649 485
1997	46 372	118 589	202 792	187 528	74 900	12 332	582	643 095
1998	48 285	113 537	193 144	188 499	78 881	12 980	575	635 901
1999	48 375	110 722	181 931	185 311	81 281	13 617	635	621 872
2000	45 846	107 741	170 701	180 113	84 974	14 403	663	604 441
2001	44 189	108 844	159 926	178 920	86 495	15 499	761	594 634
2002	43 467	110 959	153 379	180 532	90 449	16 441	895	596 122
2003	44 236	116 622	156 931	187 214	97 386	18 205	875	621 469
2004	45 094	121 072	159 984	190 550	102 228	19 884	909	639 721
Age-specific fertility rates								
	KGSI	KGSJ	KGSK	KGSL	KGSM	KGSN	KGSO	KGSP
1994	28.9	79.0	112.2	89.4	35.8	6.1	0.3	62.0
1995	28.5	76.4	108.4	88.3	36.3	6.5	0.3	60.5
1996	29.7	77.0	106.6	89.8	37.5	6.9	0.3	60.6
1997	30.2	76.0	104.3	89.8	39.4	7.3	0.3	60.0
1998	30.9	74.9	101.5	90.6	40.4	7.5	0.3	59.2
1999	30.9	73.0	98.3	89.6	40.6	7.7	0.4	57.8
2000	29.3	70.0	94.3	87.9	41.4	8.0	0.4	55.9
2001	28.0	69.0	91.7	88.0	41.5	8.4	0.5	54.7
2002	27.0	69.2	91.6	89.8	43.0	8.6	0.5	54.7
2003	26.8	71.2	96.4	94.8	46.4	9.3	0.5	56.8
2004	26.9	72.7	98.4	99.4	48.9	9.9	0.5	58.2

5.17 Live births: by age of mother and country

continued

Numbers

	Under 20	20 - 24	25 - 29	30 - 34	35 - 39	40 - 44	45 and over	All ages
Scotland								
All live births[1]								
	KGTA	KGTB	KGTC	KGTD	KGTE	KGTF	KGTG	KGTH
1994	4 303	12 637	21 851	16 705	5 346	736	26	61 656
1995	4 280	11 913	20 395	16 803	5 799	811	26	60 051
1996	4 544	11 026	19 511	17 038	6 126	891	32	59 296
1997	4 835	10 607	18 782	17 455	6 740	936	19	59 440
1998	4 802	9 804	17 477	17 207	6 893	1 027	43	57 319
1999	4 755	9 440	16 011	16 722	7 034	1 096	41	55 147
2000	4 599	8 962	14 676	16 233	7 395	1 133	29	53 076
2001	4 444	9 121	13 763	16 206	7 701	1 224	40	52 527
2002	4 195	9 267	12 694	16 038	7 727	1 267	47	51 270
2003	4 155	9 626	12 725	16 085	8 310	1 432	39	52 432
2004	4 172	9 950	13 131	16 085	8 912	1 631	50	53 957
Age-specific fertility rates								
	KGTI	KGTJ	KGTK	KGTL	KGTM	KGTN	KGTO	KGTP
1994	28.5	68.2	106.5	81.3	28.8	4.4	0.2	56.0
1995	28.2	66.6	101.3	80.6	30.4	4.8	0.1	54.6
1996	29.7	64.5	98.5	81.9	31.4	5.2	0.2	54.1
1997	31.0	65.5	97.4	83.9	34.0	5.3	0.1	54.4
1998	30.6	62.8	94.3	83.2	34.1	5.7	0.3	52.7
1999	30.3	61.0	90.4	82.0	34.3	5.9	0.2	50.9
2000	29.3	57.6	86.5	81.3	35.6	6.0	0.2	49.2
2001	28.4	57.8	85.1	82.2	36.9	6.3	0.2	48.8
2002	26.8	58.3	83.3	83.6	37.1	6.4	0.3	48.1
2003	26.3	60.1	86.5	86.8	40.0	7.1	0.2	49.4
2004	26.1	61.8	89.4	90.3	43.3	7.9	0.3	51.0
Northern Ireland								
All live births								
	KMDF	KMDG	KMDH	KMDI	KMDJ	KMDK	KMDL	KMDM
1994	1 545	4 591	8 414	6 607	2 464	455	22	24 098
1995	1 428	4 399	8 204	6 596	2 629	418	19	23 693
1996	1 582	4 332	8 243	7 075	2 706	425	19	24 382
1997	1 644	4 061	7 855	7 179	2 868	463	17	24 087
1998	1 735	3 889	7 451	7 170	2 955	446	22	23 668
1999	1 791	3 874	6 866	6 953	2 957	497	19	22 957
2000	1 614	3 602	6 206	6 547	3 031	496	16	21 512
2001	1 524	3 699	6 087	6 891	3 183	548	30	21 962
2002	1 502	3 619	5 779	6 691	3 203	565	26	21 385
2003	1 483	3 619	5 817	6 772	3 342	596	19	21 648
2004	1 486	3 592	5 935	6 985	3 712	592	16	22 318
Age-specific fertility rates								
	KMDN	KMDO	KMDP	KMDQ	KMDR	KMDS	KMDT	KMDU
1994	25.4	75.0	131.2	104.9	44.3	9.2	0.4	68.0
1995	23.4	73.5	129.1	102.7	45.5	8.4	0.4	66.6
1996	25.7	73.8	129.4	108.3	45.4	8.4	0.4	67.8
1997	26.4	71.1	124.2	109.2	46.6	8.8	0.3	66.4
1998	27.8	69.6	119.0	108.4	47.2	8.2	0.4	65.0
1999	28.6	70.6	112.3	105.6	46.1	8.9	0.4	62.9
2000	25.6	66.0	103.9	100.4	46.2	8.5	0.3	58.7
2001	23.9	67.5	105.1	106.0	48.0	9.1	0.6	59.7
2002	23.3	66.0	102.9	104.2	48.2	9.2	0.5	58.1
2003	22.8	65.5	106.8	107.0	50.2	9.8	0.3	59.0
2004	23.0	62.8	109.8	112.6	56.1	9.5	0.3	60.6

1 The 'All ages' figure for Scotland includes births to mothers whose age was not known. There were 52 such births in 1994, 24 in 1995, 128 in 1996, 66 in 1997, 66 in 1998, 48 in 1999, 49 in 2000, 28 in 2001, 35 in 2002, 60 in 2003 and 26 in 2004.

Sources: Office for National Statistics: 01329 813772;
General Register Office for Scotland;
Northern Ireland Statistics and Research Agency

5.18 Legal abortions[1]: by age for residents

Numbers

	All ages	Under 15	15	16 - 19	20 - 24	25 - 29	30 - 34	35 - 39	40 - 44	45 and over	Not stated
England and Wales											
	C53Z	C542	C543	C544	C545	C546	C547	C548	C549	C54A	C54B
1986	147 619	924	2 970	33 819	45 316	28 656	18 005	12 977	4 521	409	22
1987	156 191	907	2 858	35 167	49 256	31 243	18 960	12 639	4 757	390	14
1988	168 298	859	2 709	37 928	54 067	34 584	20 000	12 681	5 047	412	11
1989	170 463	803	2 580	36 182	54 880	36 604	21 284	12 713	5 020	388	9
1990	173 900	873	2 549	35 520	55 281	38 770	22 431	12 956	5 104	404	12
1991	167 376	886	2 272	31 130	52 678	38 611	23 445	13 035	4 901	408	10
1992	160 501	905	2 095	27 589	49 052	38 430	23 870	13 252	4 844	452	12
1993	157 846	964	2 119	25 806	46 846	38 139	24 690	13 885	4 889	494	14
1994	156 539	1 080	2 166	25 223	44 871	38 081	25 507	14 156	5 008	440	7
1995	154 315	946	2 324	24 945	43 394	37 254	25 759	14 352	4 868	457	16
1996	167 916	1 098	2 547	28 790	46 356	39 311	28 228	16 118	5 027	428	13
1997	170 145	1 020	2 414	29 947	44 960	40 159	28 892	16 858	5 413	482	–
1998	177 871	1 103	2 656	33 236	45 766	40 366	30 449	18 174	5 576	511	34
1999	173 701	1 066	2 537	32 807	45 004	38 492	29 139	18 341	5 755	502	58
2000	175 542	1 048	2 700	33 218	47 099	37 852	28 735	18 589	5 794	459	48
2001	176 364	1 066	2 592	33 431	48 267	36 506	28 782	19 146	6 094	456	24
2002	175 932	1 075	2 658	32 985	48 359	35 795	28 503	19 450	6 531	457	119
2003	181 582	1 171	2 796	34 247	51 201[2]	36 018	28 749	19 868	7 032	500	–
2004	185 415	1 034	2 722	35 386	52 701[2]	37 759	28 064	19 820	7 422	507	–
Scotland											
	C54C	C54D	C54E	C54F	C54G	C54H	C54I	C54J	C54K	C54L	EVH4
1986	9 628	74	236	2 529	2 985	1 744	1 081	708	249	22	–
1987	9 460	70	210	2 417	2 996	1 729	1 082	697	242	17	–
1988	10 128	65	218	2 529	3 304	1 970	1 107	663	257	15	–
1989	10 209	53	209	2 561	3 202	1 968	1 229	706	266	15	–
1990	10 219	54	186	2 539	3 242	2 063	1 161	700	253	21	–
1991	11 068	77	203	2 571	3 486	2 253	1 445	743	262	28	–
1992	10 818	73	174	2 377	3 389	2 291	1 444	799	254	17	–
1993	11 076	92	193	2 300	3 368	2 447	1 492	891	264	29	–
1994	11 392	78	215	2 312	3 486	2 431	1 648	877	315	30	–
1995	11 143	79	233	2 169	3 399	2 438	1 609	887	296	33	–
1996	11 978	87	236	2 362	3 571	2 603	1 801	960	331	27	–
1997	12 109	85	204	2 431	3 444	2 651	1 854	1 093	322	25	–
1998	12 485	73	213	2 707	3 426	2 749	1 807	1 149	339	22	–
1999[3]	12 168	69	182	2 635	3 354	2 554	1 810	1 180	361	23	–
2000[3]	11 997	93	181	2 610	3 355	2 403	1 769	1 177	381	28	–
2001[3]	12 128	66	210	2 722	3 462	2 322	1 818	1 127	378	23	–
2002[3]	11 870	79	194	2 653	3 453	2 172	1 736	1 171	382	29	1
2003	12 304	71	243	2 789	3 690	2 233	1 724	1 113	413	28	–
2004[4]	12 448	102	207	2 906	3 700	2 267	1 663	1 184	385	32	2

1 Refers to therapeutic abortions notified in accordance with the Abortion Act 1967.
2 Records with missing ages were assigned to the 20 - 24 age group.
3 Revised.
4 Provisional.

Sources: Department of Health; Scottish Executive

5.19 Deaths: by sex and age[1]

Numbers

	All ages[2]	Under 1 year	1-4	5-9	10-14	15-19	20-24	25-34	35-44	45-54	55-64	65-74	75-84	85 and over
United Kingdom														
Males														
1900 - 02	340 664	87 242	37 834	8 429	4 696	7 047	8 766	19 154	24 739	30 488	37 610	39 765	28 320	6 563
1910 - 12	303 703	63 885	29 452	7 091	4 095	5 873	6 817	16 141	21 813	28 981	37 721	45 140	29 397	7 283
1920 - 22	284 876	48 044	19 008	6 052	3 953	5 906	6 572	13 663	19 702	29 256	40 583	49 398	34 937	7 801
1930 - 32	284 249	28 840	11 276	4 580	2 890	5 076	6 495	12 327	16 326	29 376	47 989	63 804	45 247	10 022
1940 - 42	314 643	24 624	6 949	3 400	2 474	4 653	4 246	11 506	17 296	30 082	57 076	79 652	59 733	12 900
1950 - 52	307 312	14 105	2 585	1 317	919	1 498	2 289	5 862	11 074	27 637	53 691	86 435	79 768	20 131
1960 - 62	318 850	12 234	1 733	971	871	1 718	1 857	3 842	8 753	26 422	63 009	87 542	83 291	26 605
1970 - 72	335 166	9 158	1 485	1 019	802	1 778	2 104	3 590	7 733	24 608	64 898	105 058	82 905	30 027
1980 - 82	330 495	4 829	774	527	652	1 999	1 943	3 736	6 568	19 728	54 159	105 155	98 488	31 936
1990 - 92	312 521	3 315	623	372	396	1 349	2 059	4 334	6 979	15 412	40 424	87 849	106 376	43 032
2000 - 02	288 261	2 065	365	233	326	1 032	1 502	4 270	7 181	15 370	32 328	66 808	98 363	58 419
	KHUA	KHUB	KHUC	KHUD	KHUE	KHUF	KHUG	KHUH	KHUI	KHUJ	KHUK	KHUL	KHUM	KHUN
1993[1]	317 796	2 746	582	325	401	1 072	1 907	4 442	6 672	15 631	38 734	90 160	105 693	49 431
1994	303 333	2 660	497	319	400	1 041	1 829	4 741	6 661	14 983	36 469	86 896	98 982	47 855
1995	310 722	2 595	447	314	388	1 115	1 810	4 748	6 754	15 644	36 068	85 459	103 324	52 056
1996	305 323	2 562	489	267	352	1 104	1 693	4 746	6 789	15 796	35 033	81 333	102 090	53 069
1997	300 414	2 391	456	300	364	1 111	1 712	4 583	6 667	15 689	33 707	77 870	101 365	54 199
1998	300 160	2 327	463	283	343	1 058	1 539	4 684	6 902	15 825	33 778	75 718	101 468	55 772
1999	300 368	2 318	456	257	319	1 085	1 553	4 516	6 946	15 849	33 338	73 736	101 795	58 200
2000	290 186	2 120	380	253	326	1 042	1 491	4 397	7 081	15 470	32 556	69 499	98 075	57 496
2001	286 760	2 042	347	223	330	1 061	1 508	4 262	7 156	15 515	32 005	66 111	97 816	58 384
2002	287 837	2 032	368	223	321	992	1 508	4 150	7 305	15 126	32 423	64 814	99 198	59 377
2003	288 604	2 029	351	214	289	969	1 467	3 823	7 408	14 689	32 825	63 574	100 933	60 033
2004	277 840	2 017	329	202	286	917	1 373	3 642	7 285	14 342	31 583	60 587	98 365	56 912
Females														
1900 - 02	322 058	68 770	36 164	8 757	5 034	6 818	8 264	18 702	21 887	25 679	34 521	42 456	34 907	10 099
1910 - 12	289 608	49 865	27 817	7 113	4 355	5 683	6 531	15 676	19 647	24 481	32 813	46 453	37 353	11 828
1920 - 22	274 772	35 356	17 323	5 808	4 133	5 729	6 753	14 878	18 121	24 347	34 026	48 573	45 521	14 203
1930 - 32	275 336	21 072	9 995	3 990	2 734	4 721	5 931	15 373	14 255	23 629	39 471	59 520	56 250	18 886
1940 - 42	296 646	17 936	5 952	2 743	2 068	4 180	5 028	11 261	14 255	23 629	42 651	70 907	71 377	24 658
1950 - 52	291 597	10 293	2 098	880	625	1 115	1 717	5 018	8 989	18 875	37 075	75 220	92 848	36 844
1960 - 62	304 871	8 887	1 334	627	522	684	811	2 504	6 513	16 720	36 078	73 118	105 956	51 117
1970 - 72	322 968	6 666	1 183	654	459	718	900	2 110	5 345	15 594	36 177	75 599	109 539	68 024
1980 - 82	330 269	3 561	585	355	425	733	772	2 099	4 360	12 206	32 052	72 618	117 760	82 743
1990 - 92	328 218	2 431	485	259	255	520	714	1 989	4 340	9 707	25 105	61 951	115 467	104 994
2000 - 02	317 356	1 586	283	188	208	446	536	1 877	4 426	10 270	20 549	47 324	101 650	128 012
	KIUA	KIUB	KIUC	KIUD	KIUE	KIUF	KIUG	KIUH	KIUI	KIUJ	KIUK	KIUL	KIUM	KIUN
1993[1]	340 685	2 084	436	239	283	465	659	2 121	4 204	9 973	23 900	63 767	114 905	117 649
1994	324 303	1 989	410	205	232	406	626	2 053	4 285	10 081	22 401	62 069	106 816	112 730
1995	334 771	1 931	370	224	250	449	592	2 140	4 203	10 389	22 093	60 988	110 247	120 895
1996	330 701	1 904	355	214	224	493	589	2 140	4 215	10 301	21 406	57 889	109 578	121 393
1997	329 332	1 862	333	215	239	487	574	1 960	4 323	10 412	20 999	55 687	108 276	123 965
1998	329 012	1 752	347	213	215	486	568	1 971	4 289	10 430	20 874	54 200	107 135	126 532
1999	331 694	1 727	338	195	240	473	553	1 924	4 372	10 430	21 045	52 240	106 841	131 316
2000	318 180	1 671	277	177	203	449	535	1 961	4 509	10 459	20 533	48 994	101 711	126 701
2001	315 508	1 622	297	208	207	439	552	1 821	4 385	10 287	20 481	46 964	100 907	127 338
2002	318 379	1 465	276	180	214	449	521	1 849	4 385	10 063	20 633	46 013	102 333	129 998
2003	322 584	1 657	312	176	221	424	539	1 802	4 482	9 830	20 962	45 364	105 158	131 657
2004	305 242	1 590	257	153	191	445	533	1 715	4 425	9 438	20 452	43 005	100 640	122 398

5.19 Deaths: by sex and age[1]

continued

Numbers

	All ages[2]	Under 1 year	1-4	5-9	10-14	15-19	20-24	25-34	35-44	45-54	55-64	65-74	75-84	85 and over
England and Wales														
Males														
1900 - 02	288 886	76 095	32 051	7 066	3 818	5 611	7 028	15 869	21 135	26 065	31 600	33 568	23 835	5 144
1910 - 12	257 253	54 678	24 676	5 907	3 348	4 765	5 596	13 603	18 665	24 820	32 217	38 016	24 928	6 036
1920 - 22	240 605	39 796	15 565	5 151	3 314	4 901	5 447	11 551	17 004	25 073	34 639	42 025	29 685	6 455
1930 - 32	243 147	23 331	9 099	3 844	2 435	4 354	5 580	10 600	14 041	25 657	41 581	54 910	39 091	8 624
1940 - 42	268 876	19 393	5 616	2 834	2 051	3 832	3 156	9 484	14 744	25 983	50 058	68 791	51 779	11 158
1950 - 52	266 879	11 498	2 131	1 087	778	1 248	1 947	4 990	9 489	23 815	46 948	75 774	69 496	17 677
1960 - 62	278 369	10 157	1 444	812	742	1 523	1 624	3 278	7 524	22 813	54 908	77 000	73 180	23 364
1970 - 72	293 934	7 818	1 259	860	677	1 524	1 788	3 079	6 637	21 348	56 667	92 389	73 365	26 522
1980 - 82	290 352	4 168	657	452	555	1 716	1 619	3 169	5 590	16 909	47 144	92 485	87 338	28 551
1990 - 92	275 550	2 926	545	325	338	1 157	1 757	3 717	6 057	13 258	34 977	77 063	94 672	38 757
2000 - 02	253 706	1 836	323	200	282	862	1 244	3 619	6 104	13 184	27 696	58 114	87 481	52 761
	KHVA	KHVB	KHVC	KHVD	KHVE	KHVF	KHVG	KHVH	KHVI	KHVJ	KHVK	KHVL	KHVM	KHVN
1993[1]	279 561	2 407	510	276	340	912	1 596	3 813	5 784	13 416	33 347	78 881	93 754	44 525
1994	267 555	2 367	432	278	331	843	1 550	4 065	5 769	12 923	31 320	76 270	88 230	43 177
1995	274 449	2 305	391	269	340	910	1 533	4 043	5 880	13 487	30 973	74 970	92 291	47 057
1996	268 682	2 272	441	236	291	925	1 409	4 064	5 843	13 565	30 066	71 046	90 708	47 816
1997	264 865	2 137	412	267	325	947	1 442	3 940	5 707	13 484	28 907	68 024	90 207	49 066
1998	264 707	2 070	413	240	291	875	1 292	4 013	5 895	13 595	29 052	66 099	90 450	50 422
1999	264 299	2 075	405	218	275	902	1 270	3 847	5 934	13 620	28 689	64 296	90 431	52 337
2000	255 547	1 886	335	217	284	872	1 224	3 755	6 048	13 367	27 898	60 593	87 126	51 942
2001	252 426	1 808	318	185	281	882	1 266	3 633	6 065	13 271	27 469	57 492	87 013	52 743
2002	253 144	1 813	315	197	280	833	1 243	3 470	6 198	12 915	27 721	56 258	88 304	53 597
2003	253 852	1 809	305	189	244	808	1 229	3 260	6 318	12 694	28 221	55 118	89 629	54 028
2004	244 130	1 793	287	170	256	775	1 146	3 092	6 191	12 249	27 040	52 536	87 266	51 329
Females														
1900 - 02	269 432	60 090	30 674	7 278	4 010	5 265	6 497	15 065	18 253	21 474	28 424	35 307	29 118	7 977
1910 - 12	242 079	42 642	23 335	5 883	3 519	4 522	5 256	12 742	16 363	20 611	27 571	38 489	31 363	9 782
1920 - 22	229 908	29 178	14 174	4 928	3 456	4 719	5 533	12 244	15 142	20 580	28 633	41 010	38 439	11 871
1930 - 32	233 915	16 929	8 013	3 338	2 293	3 969	5 039	10 716	13 022	21 190	33 798	50 844	48 531	16 234
1940 - 42	253 702	14 174	4 726	2 265	1 695	3 426	4 198	9 470	12 093	20 413	36 814	60 987	61 891	21 550
1950 - 52	252 176	8 367	1 727	732	520	893	1 365	4 131	7 586	16 161	31 875	65 087	81 154	32 579
1960 - 62	266 849	7 409	1 103	527	444	591	700	2 147	5 576	14 389	31 083	63 543	93 548	45 789
1970 - 72	284 181	5 677	1 020	562	396	620	806	1 814	4 585	13 417	31 222	65 817	96 952	61 293
1980 - 82	290 026	3 064	511	301	365	635	670	1 821	3 740	10 420	27 606	63 023	103 676	74 194
1990 - 92	288 851	2 161	420	227	217	455	625	1 718	3 765	8 347	21 466	53 783	101 752	93 914
2000 - 02	279 482	1 412	251	168	182	382	455	1 629	3 805	8 893	17 659	40 734	89 387	114 525
	KIVA	KIVB	KIVC	KIVD	KIVE	KIVF	KIVG	KIVH	KIVI	KIVJ	KIVK	KIVL	KIVM	KIVN
1993[1]	299 238	1 835	374	194	246	394	575	1 802	3 625	8 614	20 423	55 245	100 947	104 964
1994	285 639	1 753	364	187	204	357	535	1 771	3 669	8 688	19 039	53 921	94 197	100 954
1995	295 234	1 677	333	196	210	382	502	1 859	3 644	9 001	18 891	52 987	97 162	108 390
1996	291 453	1 687	320	175	196	430	507	1 852	3 658	8 852	18 244	50 195	96 679	108 658
1997	290 416	1 663	297	177	209	426	490	1 718	3 737	9 016	17 949	48 293	95 508	110 933
1998	290 308	1 555	309	177	189	407	480	1 724	3 678	9 066	17 927	46 894	94 713	113 189
1999	291 819	1 546	300	168	215	385	470	1 668	3 786	9 029	18 031	45 100	93 878	117 243
2000	280 117	1 491	246	156	179	384	466	1 688	3 874	9 090	17 635	42 174	89 310	113 424
2001	277 947	1 432	270	188	178	378	467	1 591	3 768	8 917	17 610	40 465	88 808	113 875
2002	280 383	1 314	236	159	189	384	432	1 608	3 772	8 672	17 733	39 564	90 043	116 277
2003	284 402	1 497	281	153	193	353	461	1 569	3 860	8 514	17 989	38 991	92 670	117 871
2004	268 411	1 426	229	133	163	375	455	1 486	3 794	8 114	17 601	36 928	88 269	109 438

5.19 Deaths: by sex and age[1]
continued

Numbers

	All ages[2]	Under 1 year	1-4	5-9	10-14	15-19	20-24	25-34	35-44	45-54	55-64	65-74	75-84	85 and over
Scotland														
Males														
1900 - 02	40 224	9 189	4 798	1 083	672	1 069	1 292	2 506	2 935	3 591	4 597	4 531	3 117	834
1910 - 12	35 981	7 510	3 935	962	595	826	910	1 969	2 469	3 325	4 356	5 113	3 182	813
1920 - 22	34 649	6 757	2 847	710	489	747	791	1 616	2 128	3 314	4 785	5 624	3 928	911
1930 - 32	32 476	4 426	1 771	610	365	568	706	1 352	1 848	2 979	5 095	6 906	4 839	1 010
1940 - 42	36 384	3 973	1 011	449	321	668	888	1 643	2 090	3 348	5 728	8 556	6 317	1 337
1950 - 52	32 236	1 949	349	175	105	200	265	693	1 267	3 151	5 574	8 544	8 094	1 871
1960 - 62	32 401	1 578	222	121	102	146	185	456	1 013	2 986	6 682	8 505	7 980	2 425
1970 - 72	32 446	944	168	119	93	178	233	396	875	2 617	6 641	10 176	7 383	2 624
1980 - 82	31 723	451	80	56	71	206	233	423	776	2 280	5 601	10 152	8 804	2 591
1990 - 92	29 421	287	57	34	40	137	230	485	744	1 730	4 402	8 611	9 311	3 353
2000 - 02	27 526	165	30	23	30	119	196	523	882	1 775	3 781	7 038	8 535	4 430
	KHWA	KHWB	KHWC	KHWD	KHWE	KHWF	KHWG	KHWH	KHWI	KHWJ	KHWK	KHWL	KHWM	KHWN
1993[1]	30 504	240	50	39	37	107	225	490	725	1 817	4 375	9 031	9 470	3 898
1994	28 416	212	42	27	48	133	212	538	715	1 684	4 114	8 575	8 446	3 670
1995	28 791	197	37	30	30	152	195	563	698	1 746	4 144	8 449	8 604	3 946
1996	29 223	206	41	23	46	139	212	556	755	1 845	4 087	8 259	8 926	4 128
1997	28 305	186	32	22	27	114	208	521	788	1 794	3 876	7 909	8 791	4 037
1998	28 132	183	37	34	39	134	200	524	843	1 796	3 828	7 746	8 585	4 183
1999	28 605	161	31	23	33	138	215	545	818	1 820	3 773	7 569	8 908	4 571
2000	27 511	173	33	24	28	115	198	512	842	1 716	3 789	7 224	8 523	4 334
2001	27 324	155	22	27	35	131	179	510	902	1 820	3 751	6 950	8 433	4 409
2002	27 743	167	34	17	27	111	211	546	901	1 789	3 804	6 940	8 648	4 548
2003	27 832	146	35	15	31	122	186	469	893	1 634	3 787	6 797	8 994	4 723
2004	26 775	160	29	21	23	105	181	449	889	1 676	3 629	6 507	8 733	4 373
Females														
1900 - 02	39 891	7 143	4 477	1 162	747	1 058	1 246	2 625	2 732	3 130	4 485	5 273	4 305	1 508
1910 - 12	36 132	5 854	3 674	981	618	836	910	2 149	2 473	2 909	3 960	5 636	4 588	1 552
1920 - 22	34 449	5 029	2 602	687	489	711	889	1 947	2 266	2 828	4 157	5 587	5 443	1 814
1930 - 32	32 377	3 319	1 602	527	339	568	666	1 508	1 812	2 731	4 380	6 630	6 178	2 117
1940 - 42	33 715	2 852	921	373	283	595	656	1 382	1 672	2 528	4 630	7 674	7 613	2 536
1950 - 52	31 525	1 432	284	115	84	185	293	714	1 127	2 188	4 204	8 157	9 310	3 431
1960 - 62	30 559	1 107	170	80	63	72	87	287	762	1 897	4 115	7 752	9 991	4 177
1970 - 72	30 978	694	118	69	46	73	74	231	608	1 769	4 036	7 823	10 112	5 324
1980 - 82	32 326	337	49	37	44	74	73	213	493	1 456	3 565	7 781	11 333	6 871
1990 - 92	31 747	190	45	20	29	49	72	218	458	1 093	2 966	6 630	11 079	8 898
2000 - 02	30 235	123	24	14	21	50	64	199	493	1 110	2 341	5 326	9 785	10 685
	KIWA	KIWB	KIWC	KIWD	KIWE	KIWF	KIWG	KIWH	KIWI	KIWJ	KIWK	KIWL	KIWM	KIWN
1993[1]	33 545	172	45	34	27	55	60	258	460	1 089	2 793	6 918	11 330	10 304
1994	30 912	170	29	11	19	33	74	229	495	1 102	2 723	6 617	10 008	9 402
1995	31 709	178	26	16	26	50	70	231	435	1 100	2 601	6 449	10 452	10 075
1996	31 448	159	24	31	21	49	67	218	453	1 172	2 573	6 206	10 256	10 219
1997	31 189	130	23	28	21	43	71	199	496	1 128	2 480	5 985	10 164	10 421
1998	31 032	137	26	28	19	55	68	198	485	1 106	2 416	5 955	9 913	10 626
1999	31 676	115	26	20	17	65	58	201	467	1 128	2 431	5 837	10 198	11 113
2000	30 288	132	20	10	21	46	56	222	510	1 086	2 324	5 512	9 875	10 474
2001	30 058	135	20	16	21	47	71	189	480	1 111	2 361	5 235	9 695	10 677
2002	30 360	103	32	15	20	58	65	185	489	1 134	2 339	5 232	9 784	10 904
2003	30 640	119	24	18	20	57	64	181	489	1 062	2 446	5 194	9 977	10 989
2004	29 412	106	19	15	22	52	62	179	492	1 065	2 291	4 924	9 924	10 261

5.19 Deaths: by sex and age[1]

continued

Numbers

	All ages[2]	Under 1 year	1-4	5-9	10-14	15-19	20-24	25-34	35-44	45-54	55-64	65-74	75-84	85 and over
Northern Ireland														
Males														
1900 - 02	11 554	1 958	985	280	206	367	446	779	669	832	1 413	1 666	1 368	585
1910 - 12	10 469	1 697	841	222	152	282	311	569	679	836	1 148	2 011	1 287	434
1920 - 22	9 622	1 491	596	191	150	258	334	496	570	869	1 159	1 749	1 324	435
1930 - 32	8 626	1 083	406	126	90	154	209	375	437	740	1 313	1 988	1 317	388
1940 - 42	9 383	1 258	322	117	102	153	202	379	462	751	1 290	2 305	1 637	405
1950 - 52	8 197	658	105	55	36	50	77	179	318	671	1 169	2 117	2 178	583
1960 - 62	8 080	499	67	38	27	49	48	108	216	623	1 419	2 037	2 131	816
1970 - 72	8 786	396	58	40	32	76	83	115	221	643	1 590	2 493	2 157	881
1980 - 82	8 420	211	37	20	26	77	92	144	202	539	1 414	2 518	2 346	795
1990 - 92	7 550	102	21	13	18	55	73	132	178	423	1 044	2 175	2 393	922
2000 - 02	7 029	64	13	11	14	50	62	128	195	411	851	1 656	2 347	1228
	KHXA	KHXB	KHXC	KHXD	KHXE	KHXF	KHXG	KHXH	KHXI	KHXJ	KHXK	KHXL	KHXM	KHXN
1993[1]	7 731	99	22	10	24	53	86	139	163	398	1 012	2 248	2 469	1 008
1994	7 362	81	23	14	21	65	67	138	177	376	1 035	2 051	2 306	1 008
1995	7 482	93	19	15	18	53	82	142	176	411	951	2 040	2 429	1 053
1996	7 418	84	7	8	15	40	72	126	191	386	880	2 028	2 456	1 125
1997	7 244	68	12	11	12	50	62	122	172	411	924	1 937	2 367	1 096
1998	7 321	74	13	9	13	49	47	147	164	434	898	1 873	2 433	1 167
1999	7 464	82	20	16	11	45	68	124	194	409	876	1 871	2 456	1 292
2000	7 128	61	12	12	14	55	69	130	191	387	869	1 682	2 426	1 220
2001	7 010	79	7	11	14	48	63	119	189	424	785	1 669	2 370	1 232
2002	6 950	52	19	9	14	48	54	134	206	422	898	1 616	2 246	1 232
2003	6 920	74	11	10	14	39	52	94	197	361	817	1 659	2 310	1 282
2004	6 935	64	13	11	7	37	46	101	205	417	914	1 544	2 366	1 210
Females														
1900 - 02	12 735	1 537	1 013	317	277	495	521	1 012	902	1 075	1 612	1 876	1 484	614
1910 - 12	11 397	1 369	808	249	218	325	365	785	811	961	1 282	2 328	1 402	494
1920 - 22	10 415	1 149	547	193	188	299	331	687	713	939	1 236	1 976	1 639	518
1930 - 32	9 044	824	380	125	102	184	226	475	539	774	1 293	2 046	1 541	535
1940 - 42	9 229	910	305	105	90	159	174	409	490	688	1 207	2 246	1 873	572
1950 - 52	7 896	494	87	33	21	37	59	173	276	526	996	1 976	2 384	834
1960 - 62	7 463	371	61	20	15	21	24	70	175	434	880	1 823	2 417	1 151
1970 - 72	7 809	295	45	23	17	25	20	65	152	408	919	1 959	2 475	1 407
1980 - 82	7 917	160	26	17	17	23	29	65	127	329	881	1 813	2 752	1 678
1990 - 92	7 620	80	20	12	9	16	17	53	117	267	672	1 538	2 636	2 182
2000 - 02	7 638	50	9	7	5	13	17	49	129	266	548	1 263	2 479	2 802
	KIXA	KIXB	KIXC	KIXD	KIXE	KIXF	KIXG	KIXH	KIXI	KIXJ	KIXK	KIXL	KIXM	KIXN
1993[1]	7 902	77	17	11	10	16	24	61	119	270	684	1 604	2 628	2 381
1994	7 752	66	17	7	9	16	17	53	121	291	639	1 531	2 611	2 374
1995	7 828	76	11	12	14	17	20	50	124	288	601	1 552	2 633	2 430
1996	7 800	58	11	8	7	14	15	70	104	277	589	1 488	2 643	2 516
1997	7 727	69	13	10	9	18	13	43	90	268	570	1 409	2 604	2 611
1998	7 672	60	12	8	7	24	20	49	126	258	531	1 351	2 509	2 717
1999	8 199	66	12	7	8	23	25	55	119	273	583	1 303	2 765	2 960
2000	7 775	48	11	11	3	19	13	51	125	283	574	1 308	2 526	2 803
2001	7 503	55	7	4	8	14	14	41	137	259	510	1 264	2 404	2 786
2002	7 636	48	8	6	5	7	24	56	124	257	561	1 217	2 506	2 817
2003	7 542	41	7	5	8	14	14	52	133	254	527	1 179	2 511	2 797
2004	7 419	58	9	5	6	18	16	50	139	259	560	1 153	2 447	2 699

1 See chapter text.
2 In some years the totals include a small number of persons whose age was not stated.

Sources: Office for National Statistics: 020 7533 5249;
General Register Office for Scotland;
Northern Ireland Statistics and Research Agency

5.20 Infant and maternal mortality[1]
(i) - By country. (ii) - Infant mortality by country, type of death and sex

| | Deaths of Infants under 1 year of age per thousand live births | | | | | | | | | | | | Maternal deaths per thousand live births[3] | | | |
| | United Kingdom | | | England and Wales[2] | | | Scotland | | | Northern Ireland | | | United Kingdom | England and Wales | Scotland | Northern Ireland |
	Total	Males	Females	Total	Males	Females	Total	Males	Females	Total	Males	Females				
1900 - 02	142	156	128	146	160	131	124	136	111	113	123	103	4.71	4.67	4.74	6.03
1910 - 12	110	121	98	110	121	98	109	120	97	101	110	92	3.95	3.67	5.65	5.28
1920 - 22	82	92	71	80	90	69	94	106	82	86	95	77	4.37	4.03	6.36	5.62
1930 - 32	67	75	58	64	72	55	84	94	73	75	83	66	4.54	4.24	6.40	5.24
1940 - 42	59	66	51	55	62	48	77	87	66	80	89	70	3.29	2.74	4.50	3.79
1950 - 52	30	34	26	29	33	25	37	42	32	40	45	36	0.88	0.79	1.09	1.09
1960 - 62	22	25	19	22	24	19	26	30	22	27	30	24	0.36	0.36	0.37	0.43
1970 - 72	18	20	16	18	20	15	19	22	17	22	24	20	0.17	0.17	0.17	0.12
1980 - 82	12	13	10	11	13	10	12	13	10	13	15	12	0.09	0.09	0.14	0.06
1990 - 92	7	8	6	7	8	6	7	8	6	7	8	6	0.07	0.07	0.10	-
2000 - 02	5	6	5	5	6	5	5	6	5	5	6	5	0.07	0.06	0.12	0.05
	KKAW	KKAX	KKAY	KKAZ	KKBW	KKBX	KKBY	KKBZ	KKCW	KKCX	KKCY	KKCZ	KKDW	KKDX	KKDY	KKDZ
1993	6.3	7.0	5.6	6.3	7.0	5.6	6.5	7.4	5.6	7.1	7.8	6.3	0.06	0.05	0.11	–
1994	6.2	6.9	5.4	6.2	6.9	5.4	6.2	6.8	5.6	6.1	6.5	5.6	0.08	0.08	0.15	–
1995	6.2	6.9	5.4	6.1	6.9	5.3	6.4	6.4	6.1	7.1	7.5	6.6	0.07	0.07	0.10	–
1996	6.1	6.8	5.4	6.1	6.9	5.4	6.2	6.7	5.5	5.8	6.7	4.8	0.07	0.07	0.10	0.04
1997	5.8	6.4	5.3	5.9	6.5	5.3	5.3	6.1	4.5	5.6	5.5	5.8	0.06	0.06	0.07	–
1998	5.7	6.3	5.0	5.7	6.4	5.0	5.6	6.2	4.9	5.6	6.1	5.1	0.07	0.07	0.09	0.04
1999	5.8	6.4	5.1	5.8	6.5	5.1	5.0	5.7	4.3	6.4	6.8	5.9	0.05	0.05	0.13	–
2000	5.6	6.1	5.0	5.6	6.1	5.1	5.7	6.4	5.1	5.1	5.5	4.6	0.07	0.06	0.15	–
2001	5.5	6.0	5.0	5.4	5.9	4.9	5.5	5.8	5.2	6.1	7.0	5.2	0.07	0.07	0.11	0.09
2002	5.2	5.9	4.5	5.2	5.9	4.5	5.3	6.4	4.1	4.7	4.8	4.6	0.06	0.06	0.10	0.05
2003	5.3	5.7	4.9	5.3	5.7	4.9	5.1	5.4	4.7	5.2	6.5	3.9	0.10	0.07	0.10	0.14
2004	5.0	5.5	4.6	5.0	5.5	4.6	4.9	5.8	4.0	5.3	5.4	5.2	0.07	0.07	0.11	0.04

5.20
continued

Infant and maternal mortality[1]
(i) - By country. (ii) - Infant mortality by country, type of death and sex

Deaths per thousand live births

		1994	1995	1996	1997	1998	1999	2000	2001	2002	2003	2004
Total												
United Kingdom:												
Stillbirths[4]	KHNQ	5.8	5.6	5.5	5.3	5.4	5.3	5.3	5.3	5.6	5.7	..
Perinatal[4]	KHNR	8.9	8.9	8.7	8.3	8.3	8.2	8.1	8.0	8.3	8.5	..
Neonatal	KHNS	4.1	4.2	4.1	3.9	3.8	3.9	3.9	3.6	3.5	3.6	3.4
Post neonatal	KHNT	2.1	2.0	2.0	2.0	1.9	1.9	1.7	1.8	1.7	1.7	1.6
England and Wales:												
Stillbirths[4]	KHNU	5.7	5.5	5.4	5.3	5.3	5.3	5.3	5.3	5.6	5.7	..
Perinatal[4]	KHNV	8.9	8.7	8.6	8.3	8.2	8.2	8.2	8.0	8.3	8.5	..
Neonatal	KHNW	4.1	4.1	4.1	3.9	3.8	3.9	3.9	3.6	3.6	3.6	3.5
Post neonatal	KHNX	2.1	2.0	2.0	2.0	1.9	1.9	1.7	1.9	1.7	1.7	1.6
Scotland:												
Stillbirths[4]	KHNY	6.1	6.6	6.4	5.3	6.1	5.2	5.6	5.7	5.4	5.6	5.8
Perinatal[4]	KHNZ	9.0	9.6	9.2	7.8	8.7	7.6	8.4	8.5	7.6	8.0	8.1
Neonatal	KHOA	4.0	4.0	3.9	3.2	3.6	3.3	4.0	3.8	3.2	3.4	3.1
Post neonatal	KHOB	2.2	2.2	2.2	2.1	2.0	1.7	1.8	1.7	2.1	1.7	1.9
Northern Ireland:												
Stillbirths[4]	KHOC	6.3	6.1	6.3	5.4	5.1	5.7	4.3	5.1	5.7	4.9	4.9
Perinatal[4]	KHOD	9.7	10.4	9.4	8.2	8.1	10.0	7.3	8.5	8.9	8.0	8.0
Neonatal	KHOE	4.2	5.5	3.7	4.2	3.9	4.8	3.8	4.5	3.5	3.9	3.6
Post neonatal	KHOF	1.9	1.6	2.0	1.4	1.7	1.6	1.3	1.6	1.2	1.3	1.7
Males												
United Kingdom:												
Perinatal[4]	KHOG	9.6	9.4	9.1	8.7	8.8	8.7	8.7	8.6	8.9	8.8	..
Neonatal	KHOH	4.6	4.6	4.6	4.2	4.2	4.3	4.2	4.0	4.0	3.9	3.8
Infant mortality	KHOI	6.9	6.9	6.8	6.4	6.3	6.4	6.1	6.0	5.9	5.7	5.5
England and Wales:												
Perinatal[4]	KHOK	9.6	9.3	9.0	8.7	8.8	8.6	8.7	8.5	8.9	8.9	..
Neonatal	KHOL	4.6	4.6	4.6	4.2	4.3	4.3	4.2	3.9	4.0	3.8	3.8
Infant mortality	KHOM	6.9	6.9	6.9	6.5	6.4	6.5	6.1	5.9	5.9	5.7	5.5
Scotland:												
Perinatal[4]	KHOO	9.6	10.1	10.0	8.1	9.6	8.4	9.5	9.2	7.9	8.4	8.8
Neonatal	KHOP	4.4	4.1	4.3	3.4	4.0	3.8	4.5	4.0	3.7	3.6	3.6
Infant mortality	KHOQ	6.8	6.4	6.7	6.1	6.2	5.7	6.4	5.8	6.4	5.4	5.8
Northern Ireland:												
Perinatal[4]	KHOS	10.4	10.4	10.1	8.5	8.9	10.5	8.0	9.8	10.0	8.2	8.2
Neonatal	KHOT	4.3	5.7	4.3	4.3	4.4	5.5	4.2	5.3	3.8	4.6	3.7
Infant mortality	KHOU	6.5	7.5	6.7	5.5	6.1	6.8	5.5	7.0	4.8	6.5	5.4
Females												
United Kingdom:												
Perinatal[4]	KHOW	8.2	8.3	8.2	7.9	7.7	7.8	7.5	7.4	7.7	8.2	..
Neonatal	KHOX	3.6	3.7	3.6	3.5	3.3	3.4	3.5	3.3	3.1	3.4	3.1
Infant mortality	KHOY	5.4	5.4	5.4	5.3	5.0	5.1	5.0	5.0	4.5	4.9	4.6
England and Wales:												
Perinatal[4]	KHPA	8.1	8.1	8.2	7.9	7.7	7.8	7.6	7.3	7.7	8.2	..
Neonatal	KHPB	3.6	3.6	3.6	3.6	3.3	3.5	3.5	3.2	3.1	3.4	3.1
Infant mortality	KHPC	5.4	5.3	5.4	5.3	5.0	5.1	5.1	4.9	4.5	4.9	4.6
Scotland:												
Perinatal[4]	KHPE	8.4	9.2	8.4	7.5	7.9	6.7	7.2	7.8	7.2	7.7	7.3
Neonatal	KHPF	3.6	3.9	3.5	2.9	3.2	2.8	3.5	3.5	2.6	3.1	2.5
Infant mortality	KHPG	5.6	6.1	5.5	4.5	4.9	4.3	5.1	5.2	4.1	4.7	4.0
Northern Ireland:												
Perinatal[4]	KHPI	8.9	10.5	8.6	8.0	7.3	9.5	6.5	7.0	7.8	7.8	7.8
Neonatal	KHPJ	4.1	5.2	3.1	4.0	3.4	4.1	3.4	3.6	3.1	3.2	3.5
Infant mortality	KHPK	5.6	6.6	4.8	5.8	5.1	5.9	4.6	5.2	4.6	3.9	5.2

1 See chapter text.
2 From 1937 to 1956 death rates are based on the births to which they relate
  in the current and preceding years.
3 Deaths in pregnancy and childbirth.
4 Deaths per 1,000 live and stillbirths. See chapter introduction.

Sources: General Register Office for Scotland;
General Register Office (Northern Ireland)

5.21 Death rates by sex and age
United Kingdom

Rates per 1,000 population

	All ages	0-4	5-9	10-14	15-19	20-24	25-34	35-44	45-54	55-64	65-74	75-84	85 and over
Males													
1900 - 02	18.4	57.0	4.1	2.4	3.7	5.0	6.6	11.0	18.6	35.0	69.9	143.6	289.6
1910 - 12	14.9	40.5	3.3	2.0	3.0	3.9	5.0	8.0	14.9	29.8	62.1	133.8	261.5
1920 - 22	13.5	33.4	2.9	1.8	2.9	3.9	4.5	6.9	11.9	25.3	57.8	131.8	259.1
1930 - 32	12.9	22.3	2.3	1.5	2.6	3.3	3.5	5.7	11.3	23.7	57.9	134.2	277.0
1940 - 42	..	..	..	..	..	..	..	..	..	..	..	..	..
1950 - 52	12.6	7.7	0.7	0.5	0.9	1.4	1.6	3.0	8.5	23.2	55.2	127.6	272.0
1960 - 62	12.5	6.4	0.5	0.4	0.9	1.1	1.1	2.5	7.4	22.2	54.4	123.4	251.0
1970 - 72	12.4	4.6	0.4	0.4	0.9	1.0	1.0	2.4	7.3	20.9	52.9	116.3	246.1
1980 - 82	12.1	3.2	0.3	0.3	0.8	0.9	0.9	1.9	6.3	18.2	46.7	107.1	224.9
1990 - 92	11.2	2.0	0.2	0.2	0.7	0.9	1.0	1.8	4.6	14.2	38.6	93.0	201.4
2000 - 02	10.0	1.4	0.1	0.2	0.5	0.8	1.0	1.6	4.0	10.4	28.9	75.2	187.7
	KHZA	KHZB	KHZC	KHZD	KHZE	KHZF	KHZG	KHZH	KHZJ	KHZK	KHZL	KHZM	KHZN
1993	11.3	1.7	0.2	0.2	0.6	0.9	1.0	1.7	4.4	13.6	38.6	94.8	208.6
1994	10.8	1.6	0.2	0.2	0.6	0.9	1.0	1.7	4.1	12.8	36.8	90.3	194.8
1995	11.0	1.6	0.2	0.2	0.6	0.9	1.0	1.7	4.2	12.6	36.7	90.0	202.1
1996	10.8	1.6	0.1	0.2	0.6	0.9	1.0	1.7	4.2	12.3	35.2	86.0	199.6
1997	10.6	1.5	0.2	0.2	0.6	1.0	1.0	1.7	4.1	11.8	33.9	83.2	196.7
1998	10.5	1.5	0.1	0.2	0.6	0.9	1.1	1.7	4.1	11.6	33.0	81.8	193.6
1999	10.5	1.5	0.1	0.2	0.6	0.9	1.0	1.7	4.1	11.2	32.2	80.9	195.7
2000	10.1	1.4	0.1	0.2	0.6	0.8	1.0	1.6	4.0	10.7	30.3	76.8	187.9
2001	9.9	1.3	0.1	0.2	0.6	0.8	1.0	1.6	4.0	10.4	28.6	74.8	186.9
2002	9.9	1.4	0.1	0.2	0.5	0.8	1.0	1.6	4.0	10.1	27.8	74.1	188.2
2003	9.9	1.4	0.1	0.1	0.5	0.8	1.0	1.6	3.9	9.9	27.0	73.6	191.7
2004	9.5	1.4	0.1	0.1	0.5	0.7	0.9	1.6	3.8	9.3	25.5	70.6	176.3
Females													
1900 - 02	16.3	47.9	4.3	2.6	3.5	4.3	5.8	9.0	14.4	27.9	59.3	127.0	262.6
1910 - 12	13.3	34.0	3.3	2.1	2.9	3.4	4.4	6.7	11.5	23.1	50.7	113.7	234.0
1920 - 22	11.9	26.9	2.8	1.9	2.8	3.4	4.1	5.6	9.3	19.2	45.6	111.5	232.4
1930 - 32	11.5	17.7	2.1	1.5	2.4	2.9	3.3	4.6	8.3	17.6	43.7	110.1	246.3
1940 - 42	..	..	..	..	..	..	..	..	..	..	..	..	..
1950 - 52	11.2	6.0	0.5	0.4	0.7	1.0	1.4	2.3	5.3	12.9	35.5	98.4	228.8
1960 - 62	11.2	4.9	0.3	0.3	0.4	0.5	0.8	1.8	4.5	11.0	30.8	87.3	218.5
1970 - 72	11.3	3.6	0.3	0.2	0.4	0.4	0.6	1.6	4.5	10.5	27.5	76.7	196.1
1980 - 82	11.4	2.3	0.2	0.2	0.3	0.4	0.5	1.3	3.9	9.9	24.8	67.2	179.5
1990 - 92	11.1	1.5	0.1	0.2	0.3	0.3	0.4	1.1	2.9	8.4	22.1	58.7	157.2
2000 - 02	10.5	1.1	0.1	0.1	0.2	0.3	0.4	1.0	2.6	6.4	17.9	51.1	157.3
	KHZO	KHZP	KHZQ	KHZR	KHZS	KHZT	KHZU	KHZV	KHZW	KHZX	KHZY	KHZZ	KHZI
1993	11.5	1.3	0.1	0.2	0.3	0.3	0.5	1.1	2.8	8.1	22.4	60.6	165.2
1994	10.9	1.3	0.1	0.1	0.2	0.3	0.4	1.1	2.8	7.6	21.7	57.5	154.8
1995	11.2	1.2	0.1	0.1	0.3	0.3	0.5	1.1	2.8	7.5	21.7	57.8	161.4
1996	11.1	1.2	0.1	0.1	0.3	0.3	0.5	1.1	2.7	7.3	21.0	56.4	159.4
1997	11.0	1.2	0.1	0.1	0.3	0.3	0.4	1.1	2.7	7.1	20.5	55.2	160.3
1998	11.0	1.2	0.1	0.1	0.3	0.3	0.4	1.0	2.7	7.0	20.2	54.4	159.8
1999	11.0	1.2	0.1	0.1	0.3	0.3	0.4	1.0	2.7	6.9	19.6	54.2	163.7
2000	10.5	1.1	0.1	0.1	0.3	0.3	0.5	1.0	2.7	6.6	18.5	51.6	155.8
2001	10.4	1.1	0.1	0.1	0.2	0.3	0.4	1.0	2.6	6.4	17.8	50.8	155.8
2002	10.5	1.0	0.1	0.1	0.2	0.3	0.4	1.0	2.6	6.2	17.4	51.0	160.3
2003	10.6	1.2	0.1	0.1	0.2	0.3	0.4	1.0	2.6	6.1	17.1	51.8	166.4
2004	10.0	1.1	0.1	0.1	0.2	0.3	0.4	1.0	2.4	5.8	16.2	49.3	155.2

Sources: Office for National Statistics;
General Register Office for Scotland;
Northern Ireland Statistics and Research Agency

5.22 Interim life tables,[1] 2002-04

| | United Kingdom | | | | England and Wales | | | |
| | Males | | Females | | Males | | Females | |
	l_x	$e^0{}_x$	l_x	$e^0{}_x$	l_x	$e^0{}_x$	l_x	$e^0{}_x$
Age(x)								
0 years	100 000	76.3	100 000	80.7	100 000	76.5	100 000	80.9
5 years	99 328	71.8	99 448	76.2	99 331	72.0	99 445	76.4
10 years	99 271	66.8	99 400	71.2	99 276	67.1	99 398	71.4
15 years	99 197	61.9	99 346	66.2	99 203	62.1	99 344	66.4
20 years	98 956	57.0	99 229	61.3	98 973	57.3	99 232	61.5
25 years	98 573	52.2	99 087	56.4	98 612	52.5	99 096	56.6
30 years	98 149	47.4	98 909	51.5	98 214	47.7	98 923	51.7
35 years	97 638	42.7	98 659	46.6	97 727	42.9	98 678	46.8
40 years	96 987	37.9	98 287	41.8	97 105	38.2	98 317	42.0
45 years	96 050	33.3	97 701	37.0	96 201	33.5	97 745	37.2
50 years	94 603	28.8	96 728	32.4	94 797	28.9	96 794	32.5
55 years	92 370	24.4	95 248	27.8	92 625	24.6	95 347	28.0
60 years	88 967	20.2	93 006	23.4	89 320	20.4	93 162	23.6
65 years	83 438	16.4	89 463	19.3	83 967	16.5	89 718	19.4
70 years	75 271	12.9	83 994	15.3	75 957	13.0	84 384	15.4
75 years	63 303	9.8	75 356	11.8	64 134	9.8	75 888	11.9
80 years	47 067	7.3	62 121	8.7	47 874	7.3	62 745	8.8
85 years	29 048	5.2	44 411	6.2	29 680	5.3	45 043	6.2
90 years	12 945	3.8	24 152	4.3	13 305	3.8	24 595	4.3

| | Scotland | | | | Northern Ireland | | | |
| | Males | | Females | | Males | | Females | |
	l_x	$e^0{}_x$	l_x	$e^0{}_x$	l_x	$e^0{}_x$	l_x	$e^0{}_x$
Age(x)								
0 years	100 000	73.8	100 000	79.1	100 000	75.8	100 000	80.6
5 years	99 294	69.3	99 476	74.5	99 308	71.4	99 461	76.0
10 years	99 236	64.4	99 420	69.5	99 228	66.4	99 416	71.0
15 years	99 154	59.4	99 355	64.6	99 141	61.5	99 367	66.1
20 years	98 816	54.6	99 180	59.7	98 840	56.7	99 262	61.1
25 years	98 234	49.9	98 983	54.8	98 405	51.9	99 104	56.2
30 years	97 543	45.2	98 758	49.9	97 910	47.1	98 915	51.3
35 years	96 744	40.6	98 457	45.1	97 469	42.3	98 668	46.4
40 years	95 778	36.0	97 974	40.3	96 820	37.6	98 314	41.6
45 years	94 508	31.4	97 281	35.5	95 879	32.9	97 657	36.9
50 years	92 662	27.0	96 080	30.9	94 403	28.4	96 706	32.2
55 years	89 837	22.8	94 269	26.5	92 176	24.0	95 232	27.7
60 years	85 536	18.8	91 474	22.2	88 441	19.9	92 906	23.3
65 years	78 389	15.2	87 023	18.2	82 769	16.1	89 336	19.1
70 years	68 833	12.0	80 398	14.5	74 461	12.6	83 685	15.2
75 years	55 727	9.2	70 532	11.2	61 893	9.7	74 955	11.7
80 years	39 768	6.9	56 382	8.3	45 616	7.2	61 967	8.6
85 years	23 267	5.0	38 649	5.9	28 086	5.1	43 801	6.0
90 years	9 700	3.7	20 140	4.1	12 239	3.6	23 646	4.1

Note Column l_x shows the number who would survive to exact **age**(x), out of 100,000 born, who were subject throughout their lives to the death rates experienced in the three-year period indicated. Column $e^0{}_x$ is 'the expectation of life', that is, the average future lifetime which would be lived by a person aged exactly x if likewise subject to the death rates experienced in the three-year period indicated.

1 See chapter text.

Source: Office for National Statistics (interim life tables): 020 7533 5222

5.23 Adoptions by date of entry in Adopted Children Register: by sex, age and country

	All ages		Under 1		1-4		5-9		10-14		15-17	
	Numbers	Percentages	Numbers	Percentages	Numbers	Percentages	Numbers	Percentages	Numbers	Percentages	Numbers	Percentages
United Kingdom												
Persons												
	VOXI	VOXJ	VOXK	VOXL	VOXM	VOXN	VOXO	VOXP	VOXQ	VOXR	VOXS	VOXT
1999	4 951	100	234	5	1 795	36	1 714	35	957	19	251	5
2000	5 503	100	283	5	2 203	40	1 745	32	1 025	19	247	4
2001[1,3]	6 588	100	272	4	2 874	44	2 047	31	1 103	17	292	4
2002	6 240	100	314	5	2 737	44	1 937	31	999	16	253	4
2003[6]	5 429	100	211	4	2 484	46	1 717	32	790	15	227	4
2004	6 079	100	277	5	2 820	46	1 845	30	869	14	268	4
Males												
	VOXU	VOXV	VOXW	VOXX	VOXY	VOXZ	VOYA	VOYB	VOYC	VOYD	VOYE	VOYF
1999	2 428	100	115	5	903	37	833	34	459	19	118	5
2000	2 740	100	144	5	1 115	41	867	32	491	18	123	4
2001[2,4]	3 314	100	138	4	1 483	45	1 006	30	547	17	140	4
2002	3 140	100	176	6	1 425	45	935	30	488	16	116	4
2003[7]	2 635	100	103	4	1 225	46	845	32	351	13	111	4
2004	3 037	100	146	5	1 419	47	931	31	415	14	126	4
Females												
	VOYG	VOYH	VOYI	VOYJ	VOYK	VOYL	VOYM	VOYN	VOYO	VOYP	VOYQ	VOYR
1999	2 523	100	119	5	892	35	881	35	498	20	133	5
2000	2 763	100	139	5	1 088	39	878	32	534	19	124	4
2001[2,5]	3 274	100	134	4	1 391	42	1 041	32	556	17	152	5
2002	3 100	100	138	4	1 312	42	1 002	32	511	16	137	4
2003[8]	2 794	100	108	4	1 259	45	872	31	439	16	116	4
2004	3 042	100	131	4	1 401	46	914	30	454	15	142	5
England and Wales												
Persons												
	GQTP	GQTQ	GQTR	GQTS	GQTT	GQTU	GQTV	GQTW	GQTX	GQTY	GQTZ	GQUA
1999	4 317	100	196	5	1 627	38	1 477	34	803	19	214	5
2000	4 940	100	251	5	2 019	41	1 549	31	906	18	215	4
2001[1]	5 981	100	246	4	2 648	44	1 845	31	983	16	257	4
2002	5 681	100	288	5	2 532	45	1 748	31	900	16	213	4
2003	4 821	100	182	4	2 263	47	1 504	31	684	14	188	4
2004	5 525	100	252	5	2 606	47	1 641	30	782	14	244	4
Males												
	GQUB	GQUC	GQUD	GQUE	GQUF	GQUG	GQUH	GQUI	GQUJ	GQUK	GQUL	GQUM
1999	2 115	100	96	5	816	39	712	34	390	18	101	5
2000	2 452	100	127	5	1 022	42	759	31	434	18	110	4
2001[2]	3 011	100	124	4	1 370	45	904	30	494	16	118	4
2002	2 871	100	160	6	1 324	46	846	29	443	15	98	3
2003	2 340	100	90	4	1 116	48	738	32	301	13	95	4
2004	2 763	100	132	5	1 320	48	826	30	371	13	114	4
Females												
	GQUN	GQUO	GQUP	GQUQ	GQUR	GQUS	GQUT	GQUU	GQUV	GQUW	GQUX	GQUY
1999	2 202	100	100	5	811	37	765	35	413	19	113	5
2000	2 488	100	124	5	997	40	790	32	472	19	105	4
2001[2]	2 970	100	122	4	1 278	43	941	32	489	16	140	5
2002	2 810	100	128	5	1 208	43	902	32	457	16	115	4
2003	2 481	100	92	4	1 147	46	766	31	383	15	93	4
2004	2 762	100	120	4	1 286	47	815	30	411	15	130	5

5.23 Adoptions by date of entry in Adopted Children Register: by sex, age and country

	All ages		Under 1		1-4		5-9		10-14		15-17	
	Numbers	Percentages	Numbers	Percentages	Numbers	Percentages	Numbers	Percentages	Numbers	Percentages	Numbers	Percentages
Scotland												
Persons												
	GQUZ	GQVA	GQVB	GQVC	GQVD	GQVE	GQVF	GQVG	GQVH	GQVI	GQVJ	GQVK
1999	489	100	34	7	135	28	176	36	117	24	27	6
2000	391	100	24	6	140	36	123	31	85	22	19	5
2001³	468	100	18	4	176	38	161	34	92	20	21	4
2002	385	100	13	3	143	37	130	34	73	19	26	7
2003⁶	468	100	25	5	153	33	170	36	88	19	32	7
2004	393	100	21	5	144	37	143	36	67	17	18	5
Males												
	GQVL	GQVM	GQVN	GQVO	GQVP	GQVQ	GQVR	GQVS	GQVT	GQVU	GQVV	GQVW
1999	247	100	17	7	71	29	91	37	54	22	14	6
2000	210	100	13	6	75	36	71	34	43	20	8	4
2001⁴	241	100	11	5	93	39	83	34	40	17	14	6
2002	193	100	8	4	75	39	60	31	37	19	13	7
2003⁷	228	100	11	5	78	34	85	37	43	19	11	5
2004	200	100	13	7	67	34	77	39	34	17	9	5
Females												
	GQVX	GQVY	GQVZ	GQWA	GRFK	GRFL	GRFM	GRFN	GRFO	GRFP	GRFQ	GRFR
1999	242	100	17	7	64	26	85	35	63	26	13	5
2000	181	100	11	6	65	36	52	29	42	23	11	6
2001⁵	227	100	7	3	83	37	78	34	52	23	7	3
2002	192	100	5	3	68	35	70	36	36	19	13	7
2003⁸	240	100	14	6	75	31	85	35	45	19	21	9
2004	193	100	8	4	77	40	66	34	33	17	9	5
Northern Ireland												
Persons												
	VOYS	VOYT	VOYU	VOYV	VOYW	VOYX	VOYY	VOYZ	VOZA	VOZB	VOZC	VOZD
1999	145	100	4	3	33	23	61	42	37	26	10	7
2000	172	100	8	5	44	26	73	42	34	20	13	8
2001	139	100	8	6	50	36	41	29	28	20	12	9
2002	174	100	13	7	62	36	59	34	26	15	14	8
2003	140	100	4	3	68	49	43	31	18	13	7	5
2004	161	100	4	2	70	43	61	38	20	12	6	4
Males												
	VOZE	VOZF	VOZG	VOZH	VOZI	VOZJ	VOZK	VOZL	VOZM	VOZN	VOZO	VOZP
1999	66	100	2	3	16	24	30	45	15	23	3	5
2000	78	100	4	5	18	23	37	47	14	18	5	6
2001	62	100	3	5	20	32	19	31	13	21	7	11
2002	76	100	8	11	26	34	29	38	8	11	5	7
2003	67	100	2	3	31	46	22	33	7	10	5	7
2004	74	100	1	1	32	43	28	38	10	14	3	4
Females												
	VOZQ	VOZR	VOZS	VOZT	VOZU	VOZV	VOZW	VOZX	VOZY	VOZZ	VPAA	VPVD
1999	79	100	2	3	17	22	31	39	22	28	7	9
2000	94	100	4	4	26	28	36	38	20	21	8	9
2001	77	100	5	6	30	39	22	29	15	19	5	6
2002	98	100	5	5	36	37	30	31	18	18	9	9
2003	73	100	2	3	37	51	21	29	11	15	2	3
2004	87	100	3	3	38	44	33	38	10	11	3	3

1 Includes two cases where age was greater than 17 - these have been included in the '15-17' age group.

2 Includes one case where age was greater than 17 - these have been included in the '15-17' age group.

3 Includes four adoptions where age was greater than 17 - these have been included in the '15-17' age group.

4 Includes one adoptions where age was greater than 17 - this has been included in the '15-17' age group.

5 Includes three adoptions where age was greater than 17 - these have been included in the '15-17' age group.

6 Includes three adoptions where age was greater than 17 - these have been included in the '15-17' age group.

7 Includes two adoptions where age was greater than 17 - these have been included in the '15-17' age group.

8 Includes one adoption where age was greater than 17 - this has been included in the '15-17' age group.

Sources: Office for National Statistics: 01329 813772;
General Register Office for Scotland;
Northern Ireland Statistics and Research Agency

Education

Chapter 6

Education

Educational establishments in the United Kingdom are administered and financed in several ways. Most schools are controlled by local authorities (LAs), which are part of the structure of local government, but some are 'assisted', receiving grants direct from central government sources and being controlled by governing bodies which have a substantial degree of autonomy. Completely outside the public sector are non-maintained schools run by individuals, companies or charitable institutions.

For the purposes of UK education statistics, schools fall under the following broad categories:

Mainstream state schools (Grant-aided mainstream schools in Northern Ireland)

These schools work in partnership with other schools and local authorities and they receive funding from LAs. Since 1 September 1999, the categories (typically in England) are:

Community - schools formerly known as 'county' plus some former Grant-maintained (GM) schools;

Foundation - most former GM schools;

Voluntary Aided - schools formerly known as 'aided' and some former GM schools;

Voluntary Controlled - schools formerly known as 'controlled'.

Non-maintained mainstream schools consisting of

(a) Independent schools

Schools which charge fees and may also be financed by individuals, companies or charitable institutions. These include Direct Grant schools, where the governing bodies are assisted by Departmental grants and a proportion of the pupils attending them do so free or under an arrangement by which local authorities meet tuition fees. City technology colleges and Academies (applicable in England only) are also included as independent schools.

(b) Non-maintained schools

Run by voluntary bodies who may receive some grant from central government for capital work and for equipment, but their current expenditure is met primarily from the fees charged to the LAs for pupils placed in schools.

Special schools

Provide education for children with special educational needs (SEN) (Record of Needs, in Scotland) who cannot be educated satisfactorily in an ordinary school. Maintained special schools are run by LAs, while non-maintained special schools are financed as shown at (b) above.

Pupil Referral Units

Pupil Referral Units (PRUs) operate in England and Wales and provide education outside of a mainstream or special school setting, to meet the needs of difficult or disruptive children.

Schools in Scotland are categorised as Education Authority, Grant-Aided, Opted-out/Self-governing (these three being grouped together as 'Publicly funded' schools), Independent schools and Partnership schools.

The home Government Departments dealing with education statistics are:

Department for Education and Skills (DfES);

National Assembly for Wales (NAfW);

Scottish Executive (SE);

Northern Ireland Department of Education (DENI);

Northern Ireland Department for Employment and Learning (DELNI).

Each of the home Education Departments in Great Britain, along with the Northern Ireland Department of Education, have overall responsibility for funding the schools sectors in their own country.

Up to March 2001, further education (FE) courses in FE sector colleges in England and in Wales were largely funded through grants from the respective Further Education Funding Councils. In April 2001, however, the Learning and Skills Council (LSC) took over the responsibility for funding the FE sector in England, and the National Council for Education and Training for Wales (part of Education and Learning Wales – ELWa) did so for Wales. The LSC in England is also responsible for funding provision for FE and some non-prescribed higher education in FE sector colleges; it also funds some FE provided by LA maintained and other institutions referred to as 'external institutions'. In Wales, the National Council – ELWa, funds FE provision made by FE institutions via a third party or sponsored arrangements. The Scottish Further Education Funding Council (SFEFC) funds FE colleges in Scotland, while the Department for Employment and Learning funds FE colleges in Northern Ireland.

Higher education courses in higher education establishments are largely publicly funded through block grants from the HE funding councils in England and Scotland, the Higher Education Council – ELWa in Wales, and the Department of Employment and Learning in Northern Ireland. In addition, some designated HE (mainly HND/HNC Diplomas and Certificates of HE) is also funded by these sources. The FE sources mentioned above fund the remainder.

Statistics for the separate systems obtained in England, Wales, Scotland and Northern Ireland are collected and processed separately in accordance with the particular needs of the responsible Departments. Since 1994/95 the Higher Education Statistics Agency (HESA) has undertaken the data collection for all higher education institutions (HEIs) in the UK. This includes the former Universities Funding Council (UFC) funded UK universities previously collected by the Universities Statistical Record. There are some structural differences in the information collected for schools, further and higher education in each of the four home countries and in some tables the GB/UK data presented are amalgamations from sources that are not entirely comparable.

Stages of education

There are five stages of education: foundation, primary, secondary, further and higher education, and education is compulsory for all children between the ages of five (four in Northern Ireland) and sixteen. The non-compulsory fourth stage, further education, covers non-advanced education, which can be taken at both further (including tertiary) education colleges, higher education institutions and increasingly in secondary schools. The fifth stage, higher education, is study beyond A levels and their equivalent which, for most full-time students, takes place in universities and other higher education institutions.

Foundation education

In recent years there has been a major expansion of pre-school education, and in England, the National Curriculum has been extended to include the Foundation stage and covers children's education from the age of three to the end of reception year, when most are just five and some almost six years old. Children under five attend a variety of settings including state nursery schools, nursery classes within primary schools and, in England and Wales, reception classes within primary schools, as well as settings outside the state sector such as voluntary pre-schools or privately run nurseries.

Primary education

The primary stage covers three age ranges: nursery (under 5), infant (5 to 7 or 8) and junior (up to 11 or 12) but in Scotland and Northern Ireland there is generally no distinction between infant and junior schools. Most public sector primary schools take both boys and girls in mixed classes. It is usual to transfer straight to secondary school at age 11 (in England, Wales and Northern Ireland) or 12 (in Scotland), but in England some children make the transition via middle schools catering for various age ranges between 8 and 14. Depending on their individual age ranges middle schools are classified as either primary or secondary.

Secondary education

Public provision of secondary education in an area may consist of a combination of different types of school, the pattern reflecting historical circumstance and the policy adopted by the local education authority. Comprehensive schools largely admit pupils without reference to ability or aptitude and cater for all the children in a neighbourhood, but in some areas they co-exist with grammar, secondary modern or technical schools. In 2004/05, 88 per cent of secondary pupils in England attended comprehensive schools while all secondary schools in Wales are comprehensive schools. The majority of education authority secondary schools in Scotland are comprehensive in character and offer six years of secondary education; however in remote areas there are several two-year and four-year secondary schools. In Northern Ireland, post primary education is provided by secondary intermediate and grammar schools. In England, the Specialist Schools Programme helps schools, in partnership with private sector sponsors and supported by additional Government funding, to establish distinctive identities through their chosen specialisms and achieve their targets to raise standards. Specialist schools have a special focus on their chosen subject area but must meet the National Curriculum requirements and deliver a broad and balanced education to all pupils. Any maintained secondary school in England can apply to be designated as a specialist school in one of ten specialist areas: arts, business & enterprise, engineering, humanities, language, mathematics & computing, music, science, sports and technology. Schools can also combine any two specialisms.

Special schools

Special schools (day or boarding) provide education for children who require specialist support to complete their education, for example because they have physical or other difficulties. Many pupils with special educational needs are educated in main-stream schools. All children attending special schools are offered a curriculum designed to overcome their learning difficulties and to enable them to become self-reliant.

Further education

The term further education may be used in a general sense to cover all non-advanced courses taken after the period of compulsory education, but more commonly it excludes those staying on at secondary school and those in higher education, i.e. courses in universities and colleges leading to qualifications above GCE A Level, SCE H Grade, GNVQ/NVQ level 3, and their equivalents. Since 1 April 1993 sixth form colleges in England and Wales have been included in the further education sector.

Higher education

Higher education is defined as courses that are of a standard that is higher than GCE A level, the Higher Grade of the Scottish Certificate of Education, GNVQ/NVQ level 3 or the Edexcel (formerly BTEC) or SQA National Certificate/Diploma. There are three main levels of HE course:

(i)   postgraduate courses leading to higher degrees, diplomas and certificates (including postgraduate certificates of education and professional qualifications) which usually require a first degree as entry qualification;

(ii) first degrees which includes first degrees, first degrees with qualified teacher status, enhanced first degrees, first degrees obtained concurrently with a diploma, and intercalated first degrees;

(iii) other undergraduate courses which includes all other higher education courses, for example HND's and Diplomas in HE.

As a result of the 1992 Further and Higher Education Act, former polytechnics and some other higher education institutions were designated as universities in 1992/93. Students normally attend HE courses at higher education institutions, but some attend at further education colleges. Some also attend institutions which do not receive public grant (such as the University of Buckingham) and these numbers are excluded from the tables.

6.1 Number of schools[1] by type and establishments of further and higher education
Academic years

Numbers

		1990/91	1998[2]/99	1999[2]/00	2000[2]/01	2001[2]/02	2002[2]/03	2003[2]/04	2004/05
United Kingdom:									
Public sector mainstream									
Nursery[3,4]	KBFK	1 364	2 369	2 864	3 228	3 227	3 394	3 438	3 425
Primary[5]	KBFA	24 135	23 125	23 036	22 902	22 800	22 638	22 509	22 343
Secondary[6]	KBFF	4 790	4 418	4 405	4 337	4 306	4 284	4 255	4 230
of which 6th form colleges	KPGM	116	..	..	..	..	..	..	..
Non-maintained mainstream[1]	KBFU	2 508	2 482	2 457	2 414	2 409	2 380	2 524	2 476
Special - all	KBFP	1 830	1 522	1 523	1 498	1 483	1 471	1 463	1 434
maintained	KPVX	..	1 428	1 426	1 401	1 387	1 367	1 360	1 327
non maintained	KPGO	..	94	97	97	96	104	103	107
Pupil referral units	KXEP	..	325	325	338	340	390	457	478
Universities (including Open University)[7,8]	KAHG	48	95	95	96	97	96	96	101
All other further and higher education institutions	KJPQ	588	581	574	546	541	520	520	512
Higher education institutions	KPVY	..	58	58	55	58	54	55	47
Further education institutions	KSNY	..	523	516	491	483	466	465	465
of which 6th form colleges	KPGP	..	107	105	103	101	103	102	102
England:									
Public sector mainstream									
Nursery	KBAK	566	520	514	506	494	475	468	456
Primary	KBAA	19 047	18 234	18 158	18 069	17 985	17 861	17 762	17 642
Secondary[6]	KBAF	3 897	3 560	3 550	3 481	3 457	3 436	3 409	3 385
of which 6th form colleges	KPGS	114	..	..	..	..	..	..	..
Non-maintained	KBAU	2 289	2 231	2 204	2 205	2 206	2 180	2 330	2 283
Special - all	KBAP	1 380	1 209	1 197	1 175	1 161	1 160	1 148	1 122
maintained	KPGT	..	1 148	1 134	1 113	1 098	1 088	1 078	1 049
non maintained	KPGU	..	61	63	62	63	72	70	73
Pupil referral units	KXEQ	..	298	295	308	312	360	426	447
Universities (including Open University)[7]	KAHM	37	70	70	72	73	72	72	78
All other further and higher education institutions	KJPR	460	482	458	446	441	422	422	414
Higher education institutions	KPXA	..	47	47	43	45	41	42	34
Further education institutions	KPWC	..	435	411	403	396	381	380	380
of which 6th form colleges	KPGV	..	107	105	103	101	103	102	102
Wales:									
Public sector mainstream									
Nursery	KBBK	54	46	42	41	40	37	34	34
Primary	KBBA	1 717	1 660	1 644	1 631	1 624	1 602	1 588	1 572
Secondary[6]	KBBF	230	229	228	229	227	227	227	227
of which 6th form colleges	KPGY	2	..	..	..	..	..	..	..
Non-maintained	KBBU	71	54	55	54	56	59	60	58
Special (Maintained)	KBBP	61	48	47	45	44	43	43	43
Pupil referral units	KZBF	..	27	30	30	28	30	31	31
Universities[7,8]	KAHS	1	9	9	9	9	9	9	8
All other further and higher education institutions	KJQP	38	28	28	28	28	27	27	27
Higher education institutions	KSNZ	..	4	4	4	4	4	4	4
Further education institutions	KPGZ	..	24	24	24	24	23	23	23
Scotland:									
Public sector mainstream									
Nursery[5]	KBDK	659	1 712	2 213	2 586	2 597	2 782	2 836	2 836
Primary	KBDA	2 372	2 291	2 293	2 278	2 271	2 258	2 248	2 217
Secondary	KBDF	424	392	389	389	387	386	386	386
Non-maintained[1]	KBDU	131	175	176	129	122	119	117	118
Special - all	KBDP	343	218	229	230	230	221	225	224
maintained	KYCZ	343	185	195	195	197	189	192	190
non-maintained	KYDA	..	33	34	35	33	32	33	34
Universities[7]	KAHX	8	14	14	13	13	13	13	13
All other further and higher education institutions	KJRA	64	52	52	53	53	53	53	53
Higher education institutions	KPWE	..	5	5	6	7	7	7	7
Further education institutions	KPHB	..	47	47	47	46	46	46	46
Northern Ireland:									
Grant aided mainstream									
Nursery[4]	KBEK	85	91	95	95	96	100	100	99
Primary[6]	KBEA	999	940	941	924	920	917	911	912
Secondary	KBEF	239	237	238	238	235	235	233	232
Non-maintained	KBEU	17	22	22	26	25	22	17	17
Special (Maintained)	KBEP	46	47	50	48	48	47	47	45
Universities	KIAD	2	2	2	2	2	2	2	2
Colleges of education	KIAE	2	2	2	2	2	2	2	2
Further education colleges	KIAG	24	17	17	17	17	16	16	16

1 From 1997/98 to 1999/00, non-maintained schools in Scotland with more than one department have been counted once for each department e.g. a school with nursery, primary and secondary departments has been counted 3 times. Subsequent figures for Scotland show primary and secondary only.

2 Includes revised data.

3 Excludes voluntary and private pre-school education centres in Northern Ireland (365 in total in 2004/05).

4 Nursery schools figures for Scotland prior to 1998/99 only include data for Local Authority pre-schools. Data thereafter include partnership pre-schools.

5 From 1995/96, includes Preparatory Departments in Norther Ireland Grammar Schools (18 in total in 2004/05).

6 From 1993/94, excludes sixth form colleges in England and Wales which were reclassified as further education colleges on 1 April 1993.

7 From 1993/94, includes former polytechnics and colleges which became universities as a result of the Further and Higher Education Act 1992.

8 From 1995/96, universities includes the members of the University of Wales separately. For 1990/91, its member institutions are counted as one institution.

Source: Education Departments: 01325 392754

6.2 Full-time and part-time pupils in school[1] by age[2,3] and sex
United Kingdom
All schools at January[4]

Thousands

		1995	1996	1997	1998	1999	2000	2001	2002	2003	2004[5]	2005[6]
Age at previous 31 August[7]												
Boys and girls												
2 - 4[9]	KBIF	1 135	1 146	1 148	1 149	1 154	1 184	1 187	1 180	1 189	1 145	1 138
5 - 10	KBIG	4 517	4 583	4 628	4 668	4 661	4 629	4 597	4 537	4 489	4 403	4 378
11	KBIH	718	717	744	746	762	783	771	783	791	784	758
12 - 14	KBII	2 179	2 157	2 151	2 182	2 211	2 256	2 297	2 320	2 343	2 355	2 369
15	KBIK	700	722	716	701	706	705	732	737	751	775	764
16	KBIL	259	279	289	288	283	285	287	298	290	314	304
17	KBIM	181	191	206	217	218	213	219	223	217	238	226
18 and over	KBIN	24	22	22	24	25	27	27	23	24	32	27
Boys												
14	KBIO	376	370	365	368	367	381	384	391	401	394	402
15	KBIP	358	368	365	358	361	359	374	377	384	394	390
16	KBIQ	127	137	141	140	137	138	139	145	140	150	146
17	KBIR	88	92	100	104	104	101	105	107	104	112	107
18 and over	KBIS	13	12	12	13	13	14	15	13	13	17	14
Girls												
14	KBIT	358	355	349	350	352	364	365	373	384	378	384
15	KBIU	342	354	351	343	345	346	358	360	368	379	375
16	KBIV	132	143	148	149	146	147	148	153	150	161	159
17	KBIW	93	99	107	113	114	111	114	116	113	124	119
18 and over	KBIX	11	10	10	11	11	13	12	11	11	15	12
United Kingdom	KBIE	9 714	9 816	9 907	9 975	10 020	10 081	10 116	10 102	10 095	10 048	9 963
England[8]	KBIA	8 013	8 110	8 195	8 261	8 310	8 346	8 374	8 369	8 367	8 335	8 274
Wales	KBIB	504	508	510	513	513	512	512	511	509	506	501
Scotland[2]	KBIC	845	846	848	850	844	874	882	876	874	866	851
Northern Ireland[3]	KBID	351	353	354	352	352	349	348	346	345	341	337

1 From 1 April 2003 excludes 6th form colleges in England and Wales which were reclassified as further education colleges.
2 Figures for Scotland, up to 2002/03, are estimates using the stage rolls.
3 In Northern Ireland a split is not collected by age but is available by year group and so this is used as a proxy.
4 In Scotland, as at the previous September.
5 Revised to include 2003/04 data for Wales.
6 Provisional.
7 1 July for Northern Ireland and 31 December for Scotland.
8 From 1992, figures for independent schools in England include pupils aged less than 2.
9 Includes the so-called "rising 5s" (i.e. those pupils who become 5 during the autumn term).

Source: Education Departments: 01325 392754

6.3 Pupils and teachers, and pupil:teacher ratios:[1] by school type
United Kingdom
At January[2]

Numbers

		2000[3]	2001[3]	2002[3]	2003[3,4]	2004[3,4]	2005[3,5]
All schools or departments							
Total							
Pupils (thousands)							
Full-time and full-time							
equivalent of part-time	KBCA	9 828.3	9 856.3	9 858.1	9 852.2	9 812.6	9 759.4
Teachers[6] (thousands)	KBCB	545.6	553.1	558.3	561.6	561.4	564.8
Pupils per teacher[6]:							
United Kingdom[7]	KBCC	18.1	17.9	17.7	17.6	17.6	17.4
England	KBCD	18.3	18.1	18.0	17.9	17.8	17.5
Wales[7]	KBCE	18.7	18.4	18.1	18.0	18.0	18.0
Scotland	KBCF	15.4	15.4	15.4	14.9	15.0	15.0
Northern Ireland	KBCG	16.9	16.6	16.4	16.3	16.5	16.5
Public sector mainstream schools or departments							
Nursery							
Pupils (thousands)							
Full-time and full-time							
equivalent of part-time	KBFM	75.3	77.5	85.6	84.8	83.9	101.9
Teachers[6] (thousands)	KBFN	3.1	3.4	3.6	3.6	3.5	3.8
Pupils per teacher[6]	KBFO	24.2	23.1	23.6	23.6	23.7	26.5
Primary[8]							
Pupils (thousands)							
Full-time and full-time							
equivalent of part-time	KBFB	5 167.9	5 130.5	5 083.4	5 021.9	4 953.9	4 896.6
Teachers[6] (thousands)	KBFD	228.0	229.6	231.5	228.9	224.9	224.2
Pupils per teacher[6]	KBFE	22.7	22.3	22.0	21.9	22.0	21.8
Secondary[9]							
Pupils (thousands)							
Full-time and full-time							
equivalent of part-time	KBFG	3 859.0	3 915.5	3 948.0	3 994.0	4 014.1	4 001.9
Teachers[6] (thousands)	KBFH	232.9	237.0	241.2	243.3	243.8	246.6
Pupils per teacher[6]	KBFI	16.6	16.5	16.4	16.4	16.5	16.2
Special schools							
Pupils (thousands)							
Full-time and full-time							
equivalent of part-time	KPGE	107.4	106.5	105.4	104.5	102.2	100.4
Teachers[6] (thousands)	KPGG	17.0	17.0	17.0	17.0	16.9	16.8
Pupils per teacher[10]	KPGI	6.3	6.3	6.2	6.1	6.1	6.0

1 'All schools' pupil:teacher ratios exclude Pupil Referral Units and non-maintained special schools.
2 In Scotland, as at the previous September.
3 Nursery schools for Scotland refer to pre-school education centres and are not therefore directly comparable with earlier years.
4 Includes revised data.
5 Provisional.
6 Figures of teachers and of pupil:teacher ratios take account of the full-time equivalent of part-time teachers.

7 Excludes Pupil Referral Units as information on teachers is not collected for Wales.
8 Includes preparatory departments attached to grammer schools in Northern Ireland.
9 Includes voluntary grammar schools in Northern Ireland.
10 England and Scotland only.

Source: Education Departments: 01325 392754

6.4 Full-time and part-time pupils with special educational needs (SEN)[1], 2004/05[2]
United Kingdom
By type of school

Thousands and percentages

	United Kingdom	England[3]	Wales	Scotland	Northern Ireland
All schools					
Total pupils	9 976.3	8 274.5	500.9	857.9	343.0
SEN pupils with statements	286.2	242.6	15.9	16.2	11.5
Incidence (%)[4]	*2.9*	*2.9*	*3.2*	*1.9*	*3.4*
Maintained schools[5]					
Nursery[6]					
Total pupils	154.6	37.4	1.9	103.1	12.1
SEN pupils with statements	1.7	0.4	-	1.3	0.1
Incidence (%)[4]	*1.1*	*1.1*	*0.7*	*1.2*	*0.5*
Placement (%)[7]	*0.6*	*0.2*	*0.1*	*7.8*	*0.6*
Primary[9]					
Total pupils	5 044.9	4 204.5	270.3	398.1	172.0
SEN pupils without statements	768.8	692.5	48.5	..	27.8
SEN pupils with statements	81.0	67.4	5.8	3.9	4.0
Pupils with statements -incidence (%)[4]	*1.6*	*1.6*	*2.1*	*1.0*	*2.3*
Pupils with statements - placement (%)[7]	*28.3*	*27.8*	*36.3*	*24.2*	*34.5*
Secondary					
Total pupils	4 002.2	3 316.1	214.6	318.1	153.4
SEN pupils without statements	514.4	473.5	28.6	..	12.3
SEN pupils with statements	90.6	76.6	6.0	4.8	3.2
Pupils with statements - incidence (%)[4]	*2.3*	*2.3*	*2.8*	*1.5*	*2.1*
Pupils with statements - placement (%)[7]	*31.6*	*31.6*	*37.7*	*29.4*	*27.8*
Special[9,10]					
Total pupils	101.4	85.5	3.8	7.4	4.7
SEN pupils with statements	96.8	83.3	3.7	5.5	4.3
Incidence (%)[4]	*95.5*	*97.4*	*97.1*	*74.7*	*91.9*
Placement (%)[7]	*33.8*	*34.3*	*23.4*	*34.0*	*37.2*
Pupil referral units[9,11]					
Total pupils	14.9	14.5	0.4	..	..
SEN pupils with statements	2.3	2.3	0.1	..	..
Incidence (%)[4]	*15.8*	*15.6*	*21.8*	..	..
Placement (%)[7]	*0.8*	*0.9*	*0.6*	..	..
Other schools					
Independent					
Total pupils	652.0	611.7	9.8	29.8	0.8
SEN pupils with statements	8.3	7.9	0.3	-	..
Incidence (%)[4]	*1.3*	*1.3*	*3.1*	*0.1*	..
Placement (%)[7]	*2.9*	*3.2*	*1.9*	*0.2*	..
Non-maintained special[9]					
Total pupils	6.3	4.9	..	1.4	..
SEN pupils with statements	5.5	4.7	..	0.7	..
Incidence (%)[4]	*87.2*	*97.3*	..	*52.0*	..
Placement (%)[7]	*1.9*	*2.0*	..	*4.5*	..

1 For Scotland, pupils with a Record of Needs including some who had an Individualised Educational Programme.

2 Provisional. Includes 2003/04 nursery schools data for Scotland. Pupil numbers are not compiled on the same basis as those used in table 6.2.

3 Includes new codes for recording SEN status following the introduction of a new SEN Code of Practice from January 2002. Data are therefore not directly comparable prior to 2001/02.

4 Incidence of pupils - the number of pupils with statements within each school type expressed as a proportion of the total number of pupils on roll in each school type.

5 Grant-Aided schools in Northern Ireland.

6 Includes pupils in Voluntary and Private Pre-School Centres in Northern Ireland funded under the Pre-School Expansion Programme which began in 1998/99.

7 Placement of pupils - the number of pupils with statements within each school type expressed as a proportion of the number of pupils with statements in all schools.

8 Includes nursery classes (except for Scotland, where they are included with Nursery Schools) and reception classes in primary schools.

9 England and Wales figures exclude dually registered pupils.

10 Including general and hospital special schools.

11 England and Wales only.

Source: Education Departments: 01325 392754

6.5

GCE, GCSE and SCE/NQ[1] and vocational qualifications obtained at a typical age,[2,3] and by students of any age

United Kingdom

Percentages and thousands

	Pupils in their last year of compulsory education[2]					Pupils/students in education[3]			
						% achieving GCE A Levels and equivalent			
	5 or more grades A*-C[4]	1-4 grades A*-C[4]	Grades D-G[5] only	No graded results	Total (=100%) (Thousands)	2 or more passes[6,7]	1 pass[8]	1 or more passes	Population aged 17 (thousands)
Students at a typical age (percentages and thousands)									
1999/00[1]									
All	50.4	24.5	19.7	5.5	703.7	34.5	6.5	41.0	732.2
Males	45.0	25.0	23.6	6.4	357.7	30.5	6.0	36.6	376.0
Females	55.9	23.9	15.7	4.5	346.0	38.6	7.1	45.6	356.3
2000/01[1]									
All	51.0	24.1	19.4	5.5	729.7	36.5	4.8	41.3	735.4
Males	45.7	24.6	23.1	6.5	372.1	32.3	4.5	36.9	378.5
Females	56.5	23.6	15.5	4.4	357.6	41.0	5.0	46.0	356.9
2001/02[1]									
All	52.5	23.7	18.4	5.4	732.5	37.6	4.7	42.3	735.2
Males	47.2	24.4	22.0	6.4	374.0	33.2	4.5	37.8	377.0
Females	58.0	23.1	14.6	4.3	358.5	42.1	5.0	47.1	358.2
2002/03[1]									
All	53.5	23.1	18.2	5.2	750.2	38.5	3.8	42.3	769.0
Males	48.3	23.6	21.8	6.3	382.7	34.1	3.8	37.9	395.1
Females	58.8	22.7	14.4	4.1	367.6	43.2	3.8	47.0	373.9
2003/04[1]									
All	54.2	22.7	18.8	4.4	772.0	39.2	3.2	42.4	769.5
Males	49.2	23.1	22.4	5.3	392.6	34.7	3.2	37.9	395.8
Females	59.3	22.2	15.0	3.4	379.4	44.0	3.2	47.2	373.8

	GCSE and SCE S Grade/Standard Grade (SG)				GCE A Level and SCE/NQ Higher Grade		
	5 or more grades A*-C[4,9]	1-4 grades A*-C[4,9]	Grades D-G[5,10] only	No graded results[11]	2 or more passes[6,7]	1 pass[8]	Total 1 or more passes
Students of all ages (thousands)							
1999/00[1]							
All	357.7	311.6	224.4	30.3	258.8	65.6	324.4
Males	162.8	150.9	125.3	15.2	118.0	28.7	146.6
Females	194.9	160.7	99.1	15.1	140.9	36.9	177.7
2000/01[1]							
All	375.1	335.0	227.3	31.8	280.8	64.2	345.1
Males	171.8	164.1	127.3	16.0	128.4	29.1	157.5
Females	203.3	170.9	100.1	15.8	152.4	35.2	187.6
2001/02[1]							
All	394.9	381.1	234.2	50.6	286.7	67.8	354.5
Males	182.4	188.7	131.1	27.9	130.0	31.6	161.6
Females	212.4	192.3	103.1	22.7	156.7	36.2	192.9
2002/03[1]							
All	409.4	340.9	234.2	51.7	309.1	60.8	369.9
Males	189.6	168.1	131.2	28.3	140.5	28.7	169.3
Females	219.9	172.9	103.0	23.4	168.6	32.0	200.6
2003/04[1]							
All	420.4	211.2	152.8	33.9	323.5	53.1	376.6
Males	194.3	107.0	91.9	20.8	147.5	24.9	172.4
Females	226.0	104.2	60.9	13.1	176.0	28.3	204.2

1 From 1999/00 National Qualifications (NQ) were introduced in Scotland but are not all shown until 2000/01. NQs include Standard Grades, Intermediate 1 & 2 and Higher Grades. The figures for Higher Grades combine the new NQ Higher and the old SCE Higher and include Advanced Highers.

2 Pupils aged 15 at the start of the academic year, pupils in year S4 in Scotland.

3 Pupils in schools and students in further education institutions generally aged 16-18 at the start of the academic year in England, Wales and Northern Ireland as a percentage of the 17 year old population. Data from 2002/03 for Wales and Northern Ireland however, relate to schools only. Pupils in Scotland generally sit Highers one year earlier and the figures relate to results of pupils in Year S5/S6.

4 Standard Grades 1-3/Intermediate 2 A-C/Intermediate 1 A in Scotland.

5 Grades D-G at GCSE and Scottish Standard Grades 4-6/Intermediate 1 B and C/ Access 3 (pass).

6 3 or more SCE/NQ Higher Grades/ 2 or more Advanced Highers/ 1 Advanced Higher with 2 or more Higher passes in Scotland.

7 Includes Vocational Certificates of Education (VCE) and, previously, Advanced level GNVQ/GSVQ which is equivalent to 2 GCE A levels or AS equivalents/3 SCE/NQ Higher grades.

8 2 AS levels or 2 Highers/ 1 Advanced Higher or 1 each in Scotland, count as 1 A Level pass. Includes those with 1.5 A level passes.

9 Includes GNVQ/GSVQ Intermediate Part 1, Full and Language unit which are equivalent to 2, 4 and 0.5 GCSE grades A*-C/SCE Stamdard grades 1-3 respectively. Figures include those with 4.5 GCSEs.

10 Includes GNVQ/GSVQ Foundation Part 1, Full and Language unit which are equivalent to 2, 4 and 0.5 GCSE grades D-G/SCE Standard grades 4-6 respectively.

11 Figures for Scotland include students in Year S4 only, excluding special schools.

Source: Education Departments: 01325 392754

6.6 Students in further[1] education: by country, mode of study,[2] sex and age,[3] during 2003/04[4],[5]

United Kingdom (home and overseas students)

Thousands

	United Kingdom		England[6]		Wales		Scotland[7]		Northern Ireland[5]	
	Full-time	Part-time	Full-time	Part-time	Full-time	Part-time	Full-time	Part-time	Full-time	Part-time
All persons										
Age under 16	5.3	41.0	2.3	5.4	0.9	5.6	2.0	26.1	0.2	4.0
16	285.4	72.1	253.8	49.5	14.1	4.1	9.8	12.8	7.6	5.7
17	236.6	77.8	208.3	53.9	11.7	4.8	9.3	14.1	7.3	5.0
18	113.7	83.0	97.1	64.3	5.5	4.7	6.9	10.4	4.2	3.5
19	45.4	75.7	38.4	60.0	2.2	4.6	3.2	8.6	1.7	2.5
20	27.5	72.7	23.6	59.4	1.2	4.4	2.0	6.8	0.8	2.1
21	21.7	74.2	19.0	62.1	0.9	4.4	1.5	5.8	0.4	1.9
22	18.8	80.0	16.7	67.7	0.6	4.5	1.2	5.7	0.3	2.0
23	17.6	83.7	15.9	71.7	0.5	4.3	1.0	5.9	0.2	1.8
24	15.7	81.3	14.3	70.1	0.4	3.8	0.8	5.6	0.1	1.7
25	13.9	76.6	12.8	65.9	0.4	3.7	0.7	5.3	0.1	1.6
26	12.7	74.8	11.6	64.7	0.4	3.9	0.6	4.7	0.1	1.5
27	12.5	76.8	11.6	66.6	0.3	3.9	0.6	4.8	-	1.4
28	12.2	78.0	11.3	67.5	0.3	4.0	0.5	5.1	-	1.4
29	12.0	78.7	11.1	68.3	0.3	4.1	0.5	4.9	0.1	1.4
30+	223.1	2 621.7	210.2	2 259.1	4.9	146.9	7.3	178.2	0.6	37.4
Unknown	5.7	22.3	5.6	18.8	0.1	2.9	-	-	-	0.6
All ages	1 079.8	3 770.3	963.5	3 175.0	44.8	214.7	47.8	304.8	23.7	75.7
Males										
Age under 16	3.0	21.8	1.1	2.7	0.6	3.2	1.2	13.5	0.1	2.5
16	139.7	35.3	122.5	24.7	7.3	2.1	5.5	5.8	4.4	2.7
17	115.0	38.6	100.4	26.6	5.7	2.7	4.8	7.0	4.2	2.3
18	57.5	40.7	49.0	29.8	2.7	2.7	3.4	6.3	2.3	1.8
19	24.4	35.0	20.6	26.1	1.2	2.5	1.6	5.1	1.0	1.3
20	14.5	32.0	12.4	25.0	0.7	2.2	1.0	3.8	0.5	1.0
21	10.9	30.7	9.5	25.1	0.4	2.0	0.7	2.8	0.2	0.7
22	9.3	31.4	8.3	26.2	0.3	2.0	0.5	2.5	0.1	0.7
23	8.6	33.0	7.9	28.1	0.2	1.8	0.5	2.5	0.1	0.6
24	7.6	31.8	7.0	27.3	0.2	1.6	0.4	2.4	0.1	0.6
25	6.7	30.0	6.2	25.7	0.2	1.6	0.3	2.2	-	0.6
26	6.1	29.6	5.6	25.6	0.2	1.6	0.3	1.9	-	0.5
27	6.1	29.8	5.7	26.0	0.1	1.5	0.2	1.9	-	0.5
28	5.9	30.5	5.6	26.3	0.1	1.7	0.2	2.0	-	0.5
29	5.7	30.3	5.4	26.4	0.1	1.6	0.2	1.8	-	0.5
30+	108.0	945.2	103.5	812.4	1.8	55.6	2.6	65.2	0.1	12.1
Unknown	2.8	8.6	2.8	7.1	-	1.2	-	-	-	0.3
All ages	531.8	1 434.4	473.5	1 191.0	21.8	87.7	23.4	126.7	13.1	29.0
Females										
Age under 16	2.3	19.2	1.1	2.7	0.3	2.4	0.8	12.6	0.1	1.5
16	145.7	36.9	131.3	24.8	6.8	2.0	4.4	7.0	3.2	3.0
17	121.6	39.2	107.9	27.3	6.0	2.1	4.5	7.1	3.2	2.6
18	56.2	42.3	48.0	34.4	2.8	2.0	3.5	4.1	1.9	1.7
19	21.0	40.7	17.8	34.0	1.0	2.1	1.5	3.4	0.7	1.2
20	13.0	40.6	11.2	34.3	0.6	2.2	1.0	3.0	0.3	1.1
21	10.9	43.5	9.4	37.1	0.5	2.4	0.8	3.0	0.2	1.1
22	9.5	48.5	8.4	41.5	0.3	2.5	0.7	3.2	0.1	1.3
23	9.0	50.7	8.1	43.6	0.3	2.5	0.6	3.4	0.1	1.2
24	8.2	49.4	7.4	42.8	0.3	2.2	0.5	3.2	0.1	1.2
25	7.2	46.6	6.6	40.3	0.2	2.1	0.4	3.1	-	1.1
26	6.6	45.3	6.0	39.1	0.2	2.3	0.4	2.8	-	1.0
27	6.5	46.9	5.9	40.6	0.2	2.4	0.3	3.0	-	1.0
28	6.3	47.5	5.7	41.1	0.2	2.4	0.3	3.1	-	0.9
29	6.2	48.4	5.7	41.9	0.2	2.5	0.3	3.0	0.1	0.9
30+	115.0	1 676.5	106.7	1 446.7	3.1	91.3	4.7	113.1	0.5	25.4
Unknown	2.9	13.7	2.8	11.7	-	1.7	-	-	-	0.4
All ages	548.0	2 335.8	490.0	1 984.0	23.0	127.0	24.5	178.2	10.6	46.7

1 Further education (FE) institution figures are whole year counts except for Northern Ireland, which are on a snapshot basis. Higher education (HE) institution figures are based on the HESA July 'standard registration' count and are not directly comparable with previous years prior to 2001/02.

2 Full-time includes sandwich. Part-time comprises both day and evening, including block release and open/distance learning.

3 Ages as at 31 August 2003 (1 July in Northern Ireland and 31 December in Scotland).

4 Provisional. Includes 2002/03 further education institution data for Wales.

5 2003/04 saw the introduction of a new MIS system across the Northern Ireland Further Education Sector, as a result 2003/04 figures are not comparable with earlier years.

6 Further education institution figures for England include LSC funded students only and are not therefore directly comparable with previous years prior to 2002/03.

7 Figures for Scotland further education colleges are enrolments rather than headcounts.

Source: Education Departments: 01325 392754

6.7 Students in further education:[1] by country, mode of study,[2] sex and area of learning,[3] 2003/04[4],[5]

United Kingdom - Home and overseas students   Thousands

	United Kingdom		England[6]		Wales		Scotland[7]		Northern Ireland[5]	
	Full-time	Part-time	Full-time	Part-time	Full-time	Part-time	Full-time	Part-time	Full-time	Part-time
All persons										
Business Administration, Management & Professional	71.1	361.7	64.4	313.3	-	-	3.8	29.2	3.0	19.1
Construction	44.7	97.2	35.6	80.3	-	-	4.9	13.7	4.1	3.2
Engineering, Technology and Manufacturing	53.2	108.3	45.5	88.5	-	0.1	5.3	16.3	2.4	3.3
English, Languages and Communications	46.7	237.5	43.7	210.0	-	-	3.1	27.5	-	-
Foundation programmes	103.8	400.6	103.2	396.5	-	-	0.6	4.1	-	-
Hairdressing and Beauty Therapy	51.0	79.1	45.2	69.8	-	-	4.0	6.3	1.8	3.0
Health, Social Care and Public Services	184.3	579.6	172.6	516.9	-	-	8.7	57.5	3.0	5.2
Hospitality, Sports, Leisure and Travel	74.8	315.7	67.4	276.1	-	-	4.8	35.0	2.6	4.6
Humanities	69.8	101.3	67.7	92.3	-	-	2.1	9.0	-	-
Information & Communication Technology	82.8	685.2	77.3	607.1	-	-	3.3	63.5	2.1	14.6
Land-based provision	21.2	55.2	19.8	47.7	-	-	1.3	7.2	0.1	0.3
Retailing, Customer Service and Transportation	8.1	61.8	7.8	53.5	-	-	0.2	6.5	0.1	1.7
Science and Mathematics	55.0	101.3	51.5	82.3	-	-	1.1	6.3	2.4	12.7
Visual and Performing Arts & Media	112.5	215.2	105.8	184.8	-	-	4.6	22.6	2.1	7.8
Other Subjects[8]	16.2	81.9	15.9	73.8	0.4	7.9	-	0.2	-	0.1
Unknown	84.5	288.8	40.1	82.2	44.4	206.6	-	-	-	-
All subjects	1 079.8	3 770.3	963.5	3 175.0	44.8	214.7	47.8	304.8	23.7	75.7
Males										
Business Administration, Management & Professional	32.2	115.6	29.8	98.7	-	-	1.0	9.8	1.3	7.1
Construction	42.9	90.4	34.2	75.2	-	-	4.7	12.2	4.1	3.0
Engineering, Technology and Manufacturing	49.5	94.6	42.2	77.1	-	0.1	5.0	14.4	2.3	3.0
English, Languages and Communications	18.3	89.3	16.8	78.4	-	-	1.5	10.9	-	-
Foundation programmes	51.9	162.8	51.6	160.9	-	-	0.3	1.9	-	-
Hairdressing and Beauty Therapy	1.8	8.1	1.6	7.7	-	-	0.1	0.3	-	0.1
Health, Social Care and Public Services	74.9	182.7	73.4	163.2	-	-	1.4	18.8	0.2	0.6
Hospitality, Sports, Leisure and Travel	41.6	115.5	37.6	100.6	-	-	2.7	13.0	1.4	1.9
Humanities	25.6	28.4	24.8	25.6	-	-	0.8	2.8	-	-
Information & Communication Technology	55.3	254.2	51.3	225.8	-	-	2.4	23.2	1.6	5.2
Land-based provision	9.3	24.3	8.5	19.7	-	-	0.8	4.5	-	0.1
Retailing, Customer Service and Transportation	4.6	27.2	4.4	22.0	-	-	0.1	4.6	-	0.6
Science and Mathematics	28.0	32.1	26.4	24.7	-	-	0.5	2.7	1.1	4.7
Visual and Performing Arts & Media	49.7	60.3	46.5	50.4	-	-	2.1	7.4	1.1	2.6
Other Subjects[8]	5.6	32.3	5.5	29.5	0.1	2.7	-	0.1	-	0.1
Unknown	40.6	116.5	19.0	31.6	21.7	84.9	-	-	-	-
All subjects	531.8	1 434.4	473.5	1 191.0	21.8	87.7	23.4	126.7	13.1	29.0
Females										
Business Administration, Management & Professional	38.9	246.0	34.5	214.5	-	-	2.7	19.4	1.7	12.1
Construction	1.8	6.8	1.5	5.1	-	-	0.3	1.5	0.1	0.2
Engineering, Technology and Manufacturing	3.7	13.7	3.4	11.5	-	-	0.2	1.9	0.1	0.3
English, Languages and Communications	28.4	148.2	26.8	131.6	-	-	1.6	16.6	-	-
Foundation programmes	51.9	237.8	51.6	235.6	-	-	0.3	2.2	-	-
Hairdressing and Beauty Therapy	49.2	71.0	43.5	62.1	-	-	3.9	6.0	1.8	2.9
Health, Social Care and Public Services	109.4	396.9	99.2	353.7	-	-	7.4	38.6	2.8	4.6
Hospitality, Sports, Leisure and Travel	33.2	200.2	29.9	175.5	-	-	2.1	22.0	1.2	2.8
Humanities	44.2	72.9	42.9	66.7	-	-	1.3	6.1	-	-
Information & Communication Technology	27.5	431.0	26.0	381.4	-	-	0.9	40.3	0.6	9.3
Land-based provision	11.9	30.9	11.3	28.0	-	-	0.6	2.7	0.1	0.2
Retailing, Customer Service and Transportation	3.5	34.6	3.4	31.6	-	-	-	1.9	-	1.1
Science and Mathematics	27.0	69.2	25.1	57.6	-	-	0.6	3.6	1.3	8.1
Visual and Performing Arts & Media	62.8	154.9	59.3	134.5	-	-	2.5	15.3	1.0	5.2
Other Subjects[8]	10.6	49.6	10.4	44.3	0.2	5.2	-	0.1	-	0.1
Unknown	43.9	172.3	21.2	50.6	22.7	121.7	-	-	-	-
All subjects	548.0	2 335.8	490.0	1 984.0	23.0	127.0	24.5	178.2	10.6	46.7

1 Further education (FE) institution figures are whole year counts except for Northern Ireland, which are collected on a snapshot basis. Higher education (HE) institution figures are based on the HESA July 'standard registration' count and are not directly comparable with previous years prior to 2001/02.

2 Full-time includes sandwich. Part-time comprises both day and evening including block release.

3 Data are shown by area of learning and are not directly comparable with subject groups previously shown, prior to 2002/03.

4 Provisional. Includes 2002/03 further education institution data for Wales.

5 2003/04 saw the introduction of a new MIS system across the Northern Ireland Further Education Sector, as a result 2003/04 figures are not comparable with earlier years.

6 Further education institution figures for England include LSC funded students only and are not therefore directly comparable with previous years prior to 2002/03.

7 Figures for Scotland further education colleges are enrolments rather than headcounts.

8 For UK higher education institutions, includes the previous subject groups not allocated to specific areas of learning, ie: medicine & dentistry, subjects allied to medicine, biological, veterinary, physical, mathematical, computing & social (inc law) sciences, creative arts & design and education.

Source: Education Departments: 01325 392754

6.8 Students in higher [1] education: by level, mode of study,[2] sex and age,[3] 2003/04[4,5,6]
United Kingdom (home and overseas students)

Thousands

	PhD and equivalent		Masters and others		Total Postgraduate		First degree		Other undergraduate		Total higher education[7]	
	Full-time	Part-time	Full-time	Part-time	Full-time	Part-time	Full-time	Part-time	Full-time	Part-time	Full-time	Part-time
All												
Age under 16	-	-	-	-	-	-	-	-	0.1	0.3	0.1	0.3
16	-	-	-	-	-	-	0.3	-	0.7	2.3	1.0	2.3
17	-	-	-	-	-	-	9.9	0.1	4.6	2.2	14.6	2.3
18	-	-	-	-	-	-	163.3	1.1	20.4	6.0	183.8	7.2
19	-	-	0.1	0.1	0.1	0.1	221.1	3.5	26.0	10.0	247.3	13.7
20	-	-	1.2	0.2	1.3	0.2	225.6	5.6	21.7	11.9	248.8	17.9
21	0.7	-	15.6	1.6	16.3	1.7	151.2	8.1	14.8	11.9	182.3	21.8
22	3.0	0.1	26.2	5.6	29.2	5.7	73.5	9.1	10.7	13.4	113.5	28.3
23	5.3	0.3	25.3	9.3	30.6	9.6	39.2	8.3	8.5	14.8	78.3	32.8
24	5.9	1.2	20.0	11.0	26.0	12.2	23.2	7.5	6.8	14.8	56.0	34.5
25	4.6	2.6	14.5	10.7	19.1	13.3	15.2	6.4	5.3	13.6	39.6	33.5
26	3.8	2.6	11.0	10.3	14.7	13.0	11.2	6.0	4.4	13.3	30.3	32.4
27	3.0	2.3	8.9	10.3	11.9	12.6	9.0	5.9	4.1	13.1	25.1	31.6
28	2.6	2.2	7.1	10.2	9.8	12.4	7.4	5.8	3.8	13.2	21.0	31.4
29	2.1	2.0	6.0	10.3	8.1	12.3	6.4	5.7	3.5	13.0	18.0	31.1
30+	14.1	30.8	39.7	182.1	53.9	212.9	67.1	129.6	47.3	339.0	168.5	683.5
Unknown	-	0.1	0.2	2.4	0.2	2.5	0.4	0.2	0.1	10.1	0.7	12.8
All ages	45.2	44.3	175.9	264.1	221.1	308.3	1 024.1	203.1	182.8	502.7	1 428.7	1 017.4
Males												
Age under 16	-	-	-	-	-	-	-	-	-	0.1	-	0.1
16	-	-	-	-	-	-	0.1	-	0.2	1.0	0.4	1.0
17	-	-	-	-	-	-	4.4	0.1	1.9	1.0	6.3	1.0
18	-	-	-	-	-	-	72.6	0.5	9.1	3.4	81.7	3.9
19	-	-	0.1	-	0.1	-	100.6	1.8	12.0	5.7	112.8	7.6
20	-	-	0.6	0.1	0.6	0.1	103.4	3.0	9.8	6.4	113.9	9.5
21	0.4	-	6.4	0.6	6.7	0.6	73.9	4.0	6.4	5.7	87.1	10.4
22	1.7	-	11.4	2.1	13.1	2.2	38.4	4.5	4.5	5.6	56.1	12.4
23	3.1	0.2	11.7	3.7	14.8	3.9	20.7	3.7	3.4	5.6	38.9	13.3
24	3.5	0.6	9.5	4.3	13.0	4.9	12.1	3.2	2.6	5.3	27.6	13.4
25	2.6	1.5	7.1	4.2	9.7	5.7	7.8	2.7	1.9	4.8	19.4	13.2
26	2.0	1.5	5.5	4.2	7.5	5.7	5.5	2.4	1.6	4.7	14.6	12.9
27	1.6	1.3	4.5	4.2	6.1	5.5	4.4	2.3	1.4	4.5	11.9	12.2
28	1.4	1.1	3.7	4.3	5.1	5.4	3.4	2.2	1.3	4.9	9.8	12.5
29	1.1	1.1	3.1	4.5	4.2	5.6	2.8	2.2	1.1	4.6	8.2	12.4
30+	8.3	17.0	21.0	80.7	29.2	97.7	23.1	48.6	12.1	112.9	64.5	259.8
Unknown	-	-	0.1	1.1	0.1	1.1	0.2	0.1	0.1	3.7	0.4	4.9
All ages	25.7	24.5	84.5	113.8	110.3	138.2	473.5	81.3	69.5	179.7	653.7	400.5
Females												
Age under 16	-	-	-	-	-	-	-	-	0.1	0.1	0.1	0.1
16	-	-	-	-	-	-	0.2	-	0.4	1.3	0.6	1.3
17	-	-	-	-	-	-	5.5	0.1	2.7	1.2	8.2	1.3
18	-	-	-	-	-	-	90.7	0.6	11.3	2.6	102.0	3.3
19	-	-	-	-	-	-	120.4	1.7	14.0	4.4	134.5	6.1
20	-	-	0.7	0.2	0.7	0.2	122.2	2.7	11.9	5.6	134.9	8.5
21	0.3	-	9.3	1.1	9.6	1.1	77.2	4.0	8.3	6.3	95.2	11.4
22	1.3	0.1	14.9	3.4	16.1	3.5	35.1	4.6	6.2	7.7	57.4	15.9
23	2.2	0.2	13.6	5.6	15.8	5.8	18.5	4.6	5.1	9.1	39.4	19.6
24	2.5	0.6	10.5	6.7	13.0	7.2	11.2	4.3	4.2	9.5	28.3	21.1
25	2.0	1.1	7.4	6.5	9.4	7.6	7.5	3.8	3.3	8.8	20.2	20.2
26	1.7	1.1	5.5	6.2	7.2	7.3	5.7	3.6	2.8	8.6	15.7	19.6
27	1.4	1.1	4.4	6.1	5.8	7.2	4.7	3.6	2.8	8.6	13.2	19.4
28	1.2	1.0	3.4	5.9	4.7	7.0	4.0	3.6	2.6	8.3	11.2	18.9
29	1.0	0.9	2.9	5.8	3.8	6.7	3.5	3.5	2.4	8.4	9.8	18.6
30+	5.9	13.8	18.8	101.5	24.6	115.2	44.0	81.0	35.2	226.1	104.0	423.6
Unknown	-	-	0.1	1.3	0.1	1.3	0.2	0.2	0.1	6.4	0.3	7.9
All ages	19.5	19.8	91.3	150.3	110.8	170.1	550.6	121.9	113.3	323.0	775.1	616.8

1 Includes Open University students. Part-time figures include dormant modes, those writing up at home and on sabbaticals.

2 Full-time includes sandwich. Part-time comprises both day and evening, including block release and open/distance learning.

3 Ages as at 31 August 2003 (1 July in Northern Ireland and 31 December in Scotland).

4 Provisional. Includes 2002/03 further education institution data for Wales.

5 Figures for higher education (HE) institutions are based on the HESA July 'standard registration' count and are not directly comparable with previous years prior to 2001/02. Figures for further education (FE)

institutions (other than in Scotland FE colleges) are snapshots counted at a particular point in the year (November for FE institutions in England and Northern Ireland, and December for FE institutions in Wales). Students starting courses after these dates will not therefore be counted.

6 FE institution figures for England include Learning and Skills Council (LSC) funded students only.

7 Includes data for higher education students in further education institutions in Wales which cannot be split by level.

Source: Education Departments: 01325 392754

6.9 Students in higher[1] education: by level, mode of study,[2] sex and subject group,[3] 2003/04[4,5,6,7]

United Kingdom: Home and overseas students

Thousands

	Postgraduate level						First degree		Other undergraduate		Total higher education[8]	
	PhD and equivalent		Masters and others		Total Postgraduate							
	Full-time	Part-time	Full-time	Part-time	Full-time	Part-time	Full-time	Part-time	Full-time	Part-time	Full-time	Part-time
All persons												
Medicine & Dentistry	2.9	4.1	3.0	6.6	5.9	10.7	36.0	0.1	0.3	0.2	42.1	10.9
Subjects Allied to Medicine	2.2	2.9	5.3	28.3	7.5	31.2	70.8	33.4	68.7	79.7	147.0	144.2
Biological Sciences	7.3	4.8	6.8	8.9	14.0	13.7	93.7	17.4	3.2	5.7	110.9	36.8
Vet. Science, Agriculture & related	0.8	0.7	1.4	1.3	2.2	1.9	11.1	0.6	4.1	3.2	17.4	5.7
Physical Sciences	6.8	3.4	5.5	4.0	12.3	7.4	46.8	3.3	0.8	3.4	59.8	14.1
Mathematical and Computing Sciences	3.6	2.2	13.4	12.1	17.0	14.4	92.2	15.7	12.0	24.3	121.1	54.3
Engineering & Technology	6.9	4.5	14.2	13.2	21.1	17.7	70.2	10.7	10.1	22.1	101.5	50.6
Architecture, Building & Planning	0.7	0.7	4.8	7.3	5.5	8.1	21.0	6.8	2.9	11.0	29.4	25.8
Social Sciences (inc Law)	4.6	5.1	29.9	26.9	34.6	32.0	139.7	28.7	9.6	40.8	183.9	101.4
Business & Administrative Studies	1.8	2.9	35.6	65.4	37.4	68.2	137.8	18.0	26.4	96.0	201.6	182.3
Mass Communication & Documentation	0.3	0.4	4.9	3.9	5.2	4.3	31.3	1.6	5.6	6.3	42.2	12.1
Languages	2.6	2.8	6.4	5.7	9.1	8.4	72.6	7.5	3.7	36.1	85.4	52.0
Historical and Philosophical Studies	2.7	3.6	4.4	8.0	7.1	11.5	50.5	13.6	1.0	22.6	58.6	47.6
Creative Arts & Design	0.9	1.4	7.8	5.1	8.7	6.5	102.2	4.3	14.0	12.6	124.9	23.4
Education[9]	0.9	4.7	32.4	64.9	33.3	69.6	33.9	8.7	3.5	45.4	70.7	123.8
Other subjects[10]	-	0.1	0.1	2.6	0.2	2.7	14.4	33.0	16.9	93.3	31.4	129.1
Unknown[8]	-	-	-	-	-	-	-	-	0.1	-	0.9	3.2
All subjects	45.2	44.3	175.9	264.1	221.1	308.3	1 024.1	203.1	182.8	502.7	1 428.7	1 017.4
Males												
Medicine and Dentistry	1.2	2.2	1.2	3.0	2.5	5.2	15.0	-	-	-	17.5	5.3
Subjects Allied to Medicine	·0.9	1.2	1.6	7.1	2.6	8.2	15.1	4.6	9.1	9.5	26.8	22.3
Biological Sciences	2.9	2.1	2.5	2.8	5.5	4.9	34.1	5.3	1.7	2.0	41.3	12.2
Vet. Science, Agriculture & related	0.4	0.3	0.7	0.6	1.1	0.9	3.5	0.2	1.6	1.4	6.1	2.6
Physical Sciences	4.5	2.2	3.1	2.2	7.6	4.5	27.7	2.0	0.4	1.9	35.7	8.4
Mathematical and Computing Sciences	2.7	1.7	10.1	8.5	12.8	10.2	70.7	11.5	9.9	13.8	93.4	35.4
Engineering & Technology	5.5	3.7	11.4	10.9	16.9	14.6	59.5	9.7	9.0	20.3	85.4	44.7
Architecture, Building & Planning	0.5	0.5	2.9	4.6	3.4	5.1	15.0	5.4	2.3	8.8	20.7	19.3
Social Sciences (inc Law)	2.4	2.6	13.3	10.7	15.7	13.3	56.8	10.4	2.4	10.5	74.8	34.2
Business & Administrative Studies	1.1	1.8	18.8	34.5	19.8	36.3	68.1	7.7	12.0	35.3	99.9	79.2
Mass Communication & Documentation	0.1	0.2	1.7	1.3	1.8	1.5	13.0	0.7	3.9	3.8	18.8	6.0
Languages	1.1	1.1	2.0	1.8	3.2	2.9	20.3	1.9	1.8	13.9	25.3	18.7
Historical and Philosophical Studies	1.6	2.0	2.1	3.9	3.7	5.9	23.0	5.1	0.3	7.5	27.1	18.5
Creative Arts & Design	0.4	0.7	3.1	2.1	3.5	2.8	39.7	1.4	6.0	4.1	49.3	8.3
Education[9]	0.3	2.0	9.9	18.5	10.2	20.4	6.2	1.5	1.0	11.8	17.4	33.8
Other subjects[10]	-	0.1	-	1.3	0.1	1.4	5.7	13.7	7.9	35.1	13.7	50.2
Unknown[8]	-	-	-	-	-	-	-	-	0.1	-	0.5	1.3
All subjects	25.7	24.5	84.5	113.8	110.3	138.2	473.5	81.3	69.5	179.7	653.7	400.5
Females												
Medicine & Dentistry	1.7	1.9	1.7	3.5	3.4	5.4	21.0	-	0.2	0.2	24.6	5.6
Subjects Allied to Medicine	1.3	1.7	3.7	21.2	4.9	22.9	55.7	28.7	59.6	70.2	120.2	121.9
Biological Sciences	4.3	2.8	4.2	6.1	8.5	8.8	59.7	12.0	1.4	3.8	69.6	24.6
Vet. Science, Agriculture & related	0.4	0.3	0.7	0.7	1.1	1.0	7.6	0.3	2.5	1.8	11.2	3.1
Physical Sciences	2.3	1.2	2.4	1.7	4.7	2.9	19.0	1.2	0.3	1.5	24.1	5.6
Mathematical and Computing Sciences	0.9	0.5	3.3	3.7	4.2	4.2	21.5	4.2	2.0	10.5	27.7	18.9
Engineering & Technology	1.4	0.8	2.8	2.3	4.2	3.1	10.7	1.0	1.1	1.8	16.1	5.9
Architecture, Building & Planning	0.3	0.2	1.9	2.7	2.2	2.9	6.0	1.4	0.5	2.2	8.7	6.5
Social Sciences (inc Law)	2.2	2.4	16.7	16.2	18.9	18.6	82.9	18.3	7.2	30.3	109.1	67.2
Business & Administrative Studies	0.8	1.0	16.8	30.9	17.6	31.9	69.7	10.4	14.5	60.8	101.8	103.0
Mass Communication & Documentation	0.2	0.2	3.3	2.6	3.4	2.8	18.3	0.8	1.7	2.5	23.4	6.1
Languages	1.5	1.7	4.4	3.8	5.9	5.5	52.3	5.6	1.9	22.2	60.1	33.3
Historical and Philosophical Studies	1.1	1.5	2.3	4.1	3.4	5.6	27.5	8.5	0.6	15.1	31.5	29.1
Creative Arts & Design	0.5	0.7	4.7	3.0	5.2	3.7	62.4	2.9	8.0	8.5	75.6	15.1
Education[9]	0.6	2.8	22.5	46.4	23.1	49.2	27.7	7.2	2.5	33.6	53.3	90.0
Other subjects[10]	-	0.1	0.1	1.3	0.1	1.4	8.6	19.3	9.0	58.2	17.7	78.9
Unknown[8]	-	-	-	-	-	-	-	-	-	-	0.4	1.9
All subjects	19.5	19.8	91.3	150.3	110.8	170.1	550.6	121.9	113.3	323.0	775.1	616.8

1 Higher Education Statistics Agency (HESA) higher education institutions include Open University students. Part-time figures include dormant modes, those writing up at home and on sabbaticals.

2 Full-time includes sandwich. Part-time comprises both day and evening, including block release and open/distance learning.

3 For HE students in further education institutions in England, includes those areas of learning which cannot be allocated to specific subject groups shown.

4 Provisional. Includes 2002/03 further education institution data for Wales.

5 2003/04 saw the introduction of a new MIS system across the Northern Ireland Further Education Sector, as a result 2003/04 figures are not comparable with earlier years.

6 FE institution figures for England include Learning and Skills Council (LSC) funded students only.

7 Figures for higher education (HE) institutions are based on the HESA July 'standard registration' count and are not directly comparable with previous years prior to 2001/02. Figures for further education (FE) institutions (other than in Scotland FE colleges) are snapshots counted at a particular point in the year [November for FE institutions in England and Northern Ireland, and December for FE institutions in Wales]. Students starting courses after these dates will not therefore be counted. Figures for Scotland, however, are whole year (not snapshot) enrolments (rather than headcounts).

8 Includes data for higher education students in further education institutions in Wales which cannot be split by level.

9 Including ITT and INSET.

10 Includes Combined and general categories.

Source: Education Departments: 01325 392754

6.10 Students[1,2] obtaining higher education qualifications:[3,4] by level, sex and subject group, 2003/04

United Kingdom

Thousands

			Postgraduate			
	Sub-degree[5]	First degree	PhD and equivalent	Other	Total	Total higher education
All persons						
Medicine & Dentistry	0.1	7.0	1.5	2.9	4.5	11.6
Subjects Allied to Medicine	40.8	24.7	0.9	8.3	9.2	74.7
Biological Sciences	3.6	26.0	2.4	5.7	8.1	37.6
Vet. Science, Agriculture & related	1.2	3.1	0.3	1.1	1.4	5.7
Physical Sciences	1.3	12.0	2.3	3.9	6.1	19.5
Mathematical & Computer Sciences	8.4	25.6	0.9	9.9	10.8	44.7
Engineering & Technology	4.8	19.8	2.0	8.9	10.9	35.6
Architecture, Building & Planning	2.4	6.7	0.2	4.0	4.2	13.4
Social Sciences (inc Law)	18.0	39.5	1.5	26.1	27.6	85.1
Business & Financial Studies	14.1	41.6	0.5	37.5	38.0	93.6
Librarianship & Info Science	1.2	7.9	0.1	4.0	4.1	13.2
Languages	4.0	19.8	0.8	5.1	5.9	29.7
Historical and Philosophical Studies	2.8	14.9	0.9	4.1	5.0	22.6
Creative Arts & Design	4.8	28.3	0.2	5.6	5.8	38.9
Education[6]	10.5	9.5	0.6	38.2	38.8	58.9
Combined, general	3.6	5.7	0.1	1.7	1.7	11.0
All subjects	121.5	292.1	15.3	166.8	182.1	595.6
Males						
Medicine and Dentistry	-	3.1	0.8	1.3	2.0	5.1
Subjects Allied to Medicine	4.8	4.5	0.4	2.0	2.4	11.7
Biological Sciences	1.6	8.9	1.0	1.8	2.9	13.3
Vet. Science, Agriculture & related	0.5	1.1	0.2	0.5	0.7	2.3
Physical Sciences	0.8	6.9	1.5	2.1	3.6	11.3
Mathematical & Computer Sciences	6.0	18.8	0.7	7.0	7.7	32.5
Engineering & Technology	4.3	16.7	1.6	7.2	8.9	29.9
Architecture, Building & Planning	1.7	4.9	0.1	2.3	2.5	9.0
Social Sciences (inc Law)	4.7	15.4	0.8	11.3	12.1	32.2
Business & Financial Studies	6.3	19.0	0.3	19.4	19.8	45.1
Librarianship & Info Science	0.6	3.0	-	1.3	1.4	5.0
Languages	1.4	5.1	0.4	1.6	2.0	8.5
Historical and Philosophical Studies	1.0	6.4	0.5	1.9	2.4	9.8
Creative Arts & Design	2.1	10.7	0.1	2.1	2.3	15.1
Education[6]	2.8	1.8	0.2	11.2	11.4	15.9
Combined, general	1.3	2.4	-	1.1	1.1	4.8
All subjects	40.1	128.6	8.7	74.3	83.0	251.7
Females						
Medicine & Dentistry	0.1	3.9	0.8	1.6	2.4	6.4
Subjects Allied to Medicine	35.9	20.3	0.5	6.3	6.8	63.0
Biological Sciences	2.0	17.1	1.4	3.8	5.2	24.3
Vet. Science, Agriculture & related	0.7	2.0	0.2	0.5	0.7	3.4
Physical Sciences	0.5	5.1	0.8	1.8	2.6	8.2
Mathematical & Computer Sciences	2.3	6.8	0.2	2.9	3.1	12.2
Engineering & Technology	0.5	3.1	0.4	1.7	2.1	5.7
Architecture, Building & Planning	0.7	1.9	0.1	1.7	1.7	4.3
Social Sciences (inc Law)	13.3	24.1	0.7	14.8	15.5	52.9
Business & Financial Studies	7.7	22.6	0.2	18.0	18.3	48.6
Librarianship & Info Science	0.6	4.9	-	2.7	2.7	8.2
Languages	2.5	14.7	0.5	3.5	3.9	21.2
Historical and Philosophical Studies	1.8	8.4	0.4	2.2	2.6	12.8
Creative Arts & Design	2.7	17.6	0.1	3.4	3.5	23.8
Education[6]	7.7	7.8	0.4	27.1	27.4	42.9
Combined, general	2.3	3.2	-	0.6	0.6	6.1
All subjects	81.3	163.5	6.6	92.5	99.1	343.9

1 Includes students on Open University courses. Figures are not comparable to previous years as the Open University have recorded the subject of qualification in the separate subject groups this year and not all in the 'combined, general' category.

2 Includes students qualifying on all modes of study. Previous figures excluded those on a dormant mode of study (around 55,000 students in 2003/04).

3 Excludes qualifications from the private sector.

4 Includes higher education in higher education institutions in the UK only. Excludes higher education qualifications in further education institutions (approximately 8% of the total number of students).

5 Excludes students who successfully completed courses for which formal qualifications are not awarded.

6 Including ITT and INSET.

Source: Education Departments: 01325 392754

6.11 Qualified teachers: by type of school and sex

Thousands

	Public sector mainstream schools		Non-maintained mainstream schools	All special schools	Total[2]
	Nursery and primary	Secondary[1]			
All full-time teachers					
Great Britain					
1990/91	200.3	223.2	44.9	18.2	486.6
1995/96	203.3	212.2	48.6	16.6	480.6
United Kingdom					
1999/00[3]	211.1	223.0	51.2	16.6	502.0
2000/01[4,5]	211.2	225.7	52.3	16.5	505.7
2001/02	211.2	227.1	52.8	16.3	507.3
2002/03[6]	209.0	230.5	53.6	17.1	510.2
2003/04[7]	206.2	229.9	55.8	17.0	508.8
of which:					
England and Wales[8]	176.5	196.7	53.2	14.2	440.6
Scotland	21.7	23.1	2.5	2.1	49.4
Northern Ireland	8.0	10.1	0.1	0.7	18.9
Full-time male teachers					
Great Britain					
1990/91	35.8	116.0	20.6	5.8	178.2
1995/96	33.8	103.4	21.1	5.3	163.5
United Kingdom					
1999/00[3]	32.6	102.9	21.1	5.0	161.6
2000/01[4,5]	32.1	102.9	21.3	5.0	161.3
2001/02	31.8	102.6	21.5	4.9	160.8
2002/03[6]	31.4	102.6	21.6	5.1	160.7
2003/04[7]	31.0	101.5	22.7	5.0	160.3
of which:					
England and Wales[8]	28.0	87.0	21.7	4.4	141.1
Scotland	1.6	10.4	1.0	0.5	13.5
Northern Ireland	1.5	4.0	-	0.1	5.6
Full-time female teachers					
Great Britain					
1990/91	164.5	107.1	24.3	12.4	308.4
1995/96	169.5	108.8	27.4	11.3	317.0
United Kingdom					
1999/00[3]	178.5	120.1	30.2	11.6	340.4
2000/01[4,5]	179.1	122.8	30.9	11.6	344.4
2001/02	179.4	124.5	31.2	11.4	346.5
2002/03[6]	177.7	127.9	32.0	12.0	349.6
2003/04[7]	175.2	128.4	33.1	11.9	348.6
of which:					
England and Wales[8]	148.5	109.7	31.5	9.7	299.4
Scotland	20.1	12.6	1.5	1.6	35.9
Northern Ireland	6.6	6.0	0.1	0.6	13.2
All full time equivalents (FTE) of part-time teachers					
Great Britain					
1990/91	..	..	..	..	30.0
1995/96	18.7	17.6	8.9	1.5	46.7
United Kingdom					
1999/00[3]	20.0	17.3	10.3	1.6	49.2
2000/01[4,5]	21.9	16.7	10.2	1.6	50.4
2001/02	23.4	17.4	10.4	1.8	53.0
2002/03[6]	24.0	17.8	11.1	1.7	54.6
2003/04[7]	25.6	18.8	11.4	1.9	57.7

1 From 1993/94 excludes sixth form colleges in England and Wales which were reclassified as further education colleges on 1 April 1993.
2 Excludes Pupil Referral Units (PRUs).
3 Includes 1998/99 data for Northern Ireland.
4 Includes 1999/00 pre-school data for Scotland.
5 Includes 2001/02 data for Northern Ireland.
6 Includes 2001/02 pre-school and 2003/04 school data for Scotland.
7 Provisional.

8 A gender breakdown of public sector teachers in England and Wales is only available from the Database of Teachers Records (DTR) where some in service teachers may be shown as not in service because their service details are not recorded. A more complete coverage of teachers in England and Wales is available from the Form 618G survey and published in "Statistics of Education: School workforce in England (including teachers' pay for England and Wales)".

Source: Education Departments: 01325 392754

Chapter 7

Labour market

Labour market

Labour Force Survey

(Tables 7.1 to 7.3, 7.6, 7.9, 7.10, 7.12 and 7.15 to 7.17)

The impact of Census 2001 on LFS data

(Tables 7.1 to 7.3, 7.6, 7.9 to 7.10, 7.15 to 7.17)

The first results of the 2001 Census, published on 30 September 2002, showed that previous estimates of the total UK population were about 1 million too high. Please see the introduction for more details. Estimates of employment and unemployment levels from the LFS released before 30 October 2002 are therefore too high, with rates also affected. This has led to the Labour Force Survey (LFS) needing to reweight their estimates to the new population figures.

ONS has published interim reweighted LFS estimates for the UK, which have been used in this chapter. The interim reweighted figures only cover top-level seasonally adjusted series published in the Labour Market Statistics First Release. The non-seasonally adjusted series, used in previous editions of the *Annual Abstract*, were not available in time for this publication.

Future editions of the *Annual Abstract* will continue to show seasonally adjusted data for these tables, in line with other headline publications. These figures are not directly comparable to the non-seasonally adjusted figures previously published in the *Annual Abstract*.

(Tables 7.12 and 5.6)

Interim reweighted figures for Table 7.12, and Table 5.6 in the population chapter, are not yet available and have been produced from unrevised not seasonally adjusted data. They are based on the old population estimates and are not in line with the results of the 2001 Census. Future editions of the *Annual Abstract* will show seasonally adjusted data for Table 7.12, in line with the rest of the chapter.

Background

The LFS is the largest regular household survey in the United Kingdom. LFS interviews are conducted continuously throughout the year. In any 3-month period, a nationally representative sample of approximately 102,000 people aged 16 or over in around 57,000 households are interviewed. Each household is interviewed five times, at 3 monthly intervals. The initial interview is done face-to-face by an interviewer visiting the address. The other interviews are done by telephone wherever possible. The survey asks a series of questions about respondents' personal circumstances and their labour market activity. Most questions refer to activity in the week before the interview.

The concepts and definitions used in the LFS are agreed by the International Labour Organisation (ILO) – an agency of the United Nations. The definitions are used by European Union member countries and members of the Organisation for Economic Co-operation and Development (OECD).

The Labour Force Survey was carried out every two years from 1973 to 1983. The ILO definition was first used in 1984. This was also the first year in which the survey was conducted on an annual basis with results available for every spring quarter (representing an average of the period from March to May). The survey moved to a continuous basis in spring 1992 in Great Britain and in winter 1994/95 in Northern Ireland, with average quarterly results published four times a year for seasonal quarters: spring (March to May), summer (June to August), autumn (September to November)and winter (December to February). From April 1998, results are published 12 times a year for the average of three consecutive months.

The LFS collects information on a sample of the population. To convert this information to give estimates for the population the data must be grossed. This is achieved by calculating weighting factors (often referred to simply as weights) which can be applied to each sampled individual in such a way that the weighted-up results match estimates or projections of the total population in terms of age distribution, sex, and region of residence.

Strengths and limitations of the LFS

The LFS produces coherent labour market information on the basis of internationally standard concepts and definitions. It is a rich source of data on a wide variety of labour market and personal characteristics. It is the most suitable source for making comparisons between countries. The LFS is designed so that households interviewed in each three month period constitute are presentative sample of UK households. The survey covers those living in private households and nurses in National Health Service accommodation. Students living in halls of residence have been included since 1992 as information about them is collected at their parents' address.

However the LFS has its limitations. It is a sample survey and is therefore subject to sampling variability. The survey does not include people living in institutions such as hostels or residential homes. 'Proxy' reporting (when members of the household are not present at the interview, another member of the household answers the questions on their behalf) can affect the quality of information on topics such as earnings, hours worked, benefit receipt and qualifications. Around one third of interviews are conducted 'by proxy', usually by a spouse or partner but sometimes by a parent or other near relation.

Sampling Variability

Survey estimates are prone to *sampling variability*. The easiest way to explain this concept is by example. In the September to November 1997 period, ILO unemployment in Great Britain (seasonally adjusted) stood at 1,847,000. If we drew another sample for the same period we could get a different result, perhaps 1,900,000 or 1,820,000.

In theory, we could draw many samples, and each would give a different result. This is because each sample would be made up of different people who would give different answers to the questions. The spread of these results is the sampling variability. Sampling variability is determined by a number of factors including the sample size, the variability of the population from which the sample is drawn and the sample design. Once we know the sampling variability we can calculate a range of values about the sample estimate that represents the expected variation with a given level of assurance. This is called a confidence interval. For a 95 per cent confidence interval we expect that in 95 per cent of the samples (19 times out of 20) the confidence interval will contain the true value that would be obtained by surveying the entire population. For the example given above, we can be 95 per cent confident that the true value was in the range 1,791,000 to 1,903,000.

Unreliable estimates

Very small estimates have relatively wide confidence intervals making them unreliable. For this reason, ONS does not publish LFS estimates below 10,000.

Non-Response

Non-response can introduce bias to a survey, particularly if the people not responding have characteristics that are different from those who do respond. The LFS has a response rate of around 80 per cent to the first interview, and over 90 per cent of those who are interviewed once go on to complete all five interviews. These are relatively high levels for a household survey. Any bias from non-response is minimised by *weighting* the results.

Weighting (or grossing) converts sample data to represent the full population. In the LFS, the data are weighted separately by age, sex and area of residence to population estimates based on the Census. Weighting also adjusts for people not in the survey and thus minimises non-response bias.

Labour Force Survey concepts and definitions

Discouraged workers – a sub–group of the economically inactive population, defined as those neither in employment nor unemployed (on the ILO measure) who said they would like a job and whose main reason for not seeking work was because they believed there were no jobs available.

Economically active – people aged 16 and over who are either in employment or ILO unemployed.

E*conomic activity rate* – the percentage of people aged 16 and over who are economically active.

Economically inactive – people who are neither in employment nor unemployed. This group includes, for example, all those who were looking after a home or retired.

Employment – people aged 16 or over who did at least one hour of paid work in the referenc e week (whether as an employee or self–employed); those who had a job that they were temporarily away from (on holiday, for example); those on Government–supported training and employment programmes (from spring 1983); and those doing unpaid family work (from spring 1992).

Employees – the division between employees and self–employed is based on survey respondents' own assessment of their employment status.

Full Time – the classification of employees, self–employed and unpaid family workers in their main job as full–time or part–time is on the basis of self–assessment. Up until autumn 1995, people who were on government work–related training programmes are classified as full–time or part–time according to whether their usual hours of work per week were over 30 or 30 and under; from winter 1995/96 onwards, the full–time/part–time classification for this group has been changed to self–assessment, in line with the other groups outlined above. People on Government–supported training and employment programmes who are at college in the survey reference week are classified, by convention, as part–time.

Government–supported training and employment programmes – comprise all people aged 16 and over participating in one of the Government's employment and training programmes (Youth Training, Training for Work and Community Action), together with those on similar programmes administered by Training and Enterprise Councils in England and Wales, or Local Enterprise Companies in Scotland.

Hours worked – respondents to the LFS are asked a series of questions enabling the identification of both their usual hours and their actual hours. Total hours include overtime (paid and unpaid) and exclude lunchbreaks.

Unemployment – Unemployment figures from the Labour Force Survey (LFS), which are based upon the International Labour Organisation (ILO) definition, were re–labelled 'unemployment' rather than 'ILO unemployment' in January 2003. This emphasises that the LFS figures provide the official and only internationally comparable measure of unemployment in the UK. For more details see the National Statistics website at www.statistics.gov.uk/cci/nugget. asp?id=251

The International Labour Office (ILO) measure of unemployment used throughout this supplement refers to people without a job who were available to start work in the two weeks following their LFS interview and who had either looked for work in the four weeks prior to interview or were waiting to start a job they had already obtained. This definition of unemployment is in accordance with that adopted by the 13th International Conference of Labour Statisticians, further clarified at the 14th ICLS, and promulgated by the ILO in its publications.

Unemployment (rate) – the percentage of economically active people who are unemployed on the ILO measure.

Unemployment (duration) – defined as the shorter of the following two periods: (a) duration of active search for work; and (b) length of time since employment.

Part–Time – see full–time Second jobs – jobs which LFS respondents hold in addition to a main full–time or part–time job.

Self–employment – See Employees
Temporary employees – in the LFS these are defined as those employees who say that their main job is non permanent in one of the following ways: fixed period contract; agency temping; casual work; seasonal work; other temporary work.

Unpaid Family Workers – the separate identification from spring 1992 of this group in the LFS is in accordance with international recommendations. The group comprises persons doing unpaid work for a business they own or for a business that a relative owns.

Distribution of workforce

(Table 7.4)

Claimant unemployed – those people who were claiming unemployment–related benefits (contributions or income related Jobseeker's Allowance and/or National Insurance credits) at Jobcentre Plus local offices on the day of the monthly count. The seasonally adjusted claimant unemployment series allows for all relevant changes which, unless adjusted for, would distort comparisons over time.

Workforce jobs (formerly workforce in employment) – comprises employee jobs, self–employment jobs (from the Labour Force Survey), HM Forces and government supported trainees.

HM Forces (provided by Ministry of Defence) – represent the total number of UK service personnel, male and female, in HM Regular Forces, wherever serving and including those on leave.

Self–employed jobs – estimates are based on the results of the Labour Force Survey. The Northern Ireland estimates are not seasonally adjusted.

Government–supported trainees – include all participants on government training and employment programmes who are receiving some work experience on their placement but who do not have a contract of employment (those with a contract are included in the employee jobs series). The numbers are not subject to seasonal adjustment.

Jobseekers allowance claimant count

(Tables 7.13 and 7.14)

This is a count of all those people who are claiming Jobseeker's Allowance (JSA) at Jobcentre Plus local offices. People claiming JSA must declare that they are out of work capable of, available for and actively seeking work during the week in which the claim is made. All people claiming Jobseeker's Allowance (JSA) on the day of the monthly count are included in the claimant count, irrespective of whether they are actually receiving benefits.

Labour disputes

(Table 7.18)

These figures exclude details of stoppages involving fewer than ten workers or lasting less than one day except any in which the aggregate number of working days lost is 100 or more. There may be some under-recording of small or short stoppages; this would have much more effect on the total of stoppages than of working days lost. Some stoppages which affected more than one industry group have been counted under each of the industries but only once in the totals. Stoppages have been classified using *Standard Industrial Classification (SIC)* 1992.

The figures for working days lost and workers involved have been rounded and consequently the sum of the constituent items may not agree with the totals. Classifications by size are based on the full duration of stoppages where these continue into the following year. Working days lost per thousand employees are based on the latest available mid-year (June) estimates of employee jobs.

Earnings

(Tables 7.19 to 7.24)

The total gross remuneration employees receive before any statutory deductions (tax, national insurance). Income in kind and pension funds are excluded.

Annual Survey of Hours and Earnings

(Tables 7.19, 7.20, 7.23 and 7.24)

The Annual Survey of Hours and Earnings (ASHE) is a new survey that has been developed to replace the New Earnings Survey (NES). The ASHE includes improvements to the coverage of employees and to the weighting of earnings estimates. The data variables collected remain broadly the same, although an improved questionnaire will be introduced for the 2005 survey. The change in methodology means that statistics on pay and hours published from the ASHE, including the calculation of ONS's low pay statistics, are discontinuous with previous NES surveys.

To improve coverage and make the survey more representative, supplementary information was collected for the 2004 ASHE survey on businesses not registered for VAT and for people who changed or started new jobs between sample selection and the survey reference period. The 2004 ASHE results are therefore discontinuous with the results for 2003, for which no supplementary information was collected. However, for 2004 two sets of results are available; the headline results that include supplementary information and results that exclude this information. These second set of results are given solely for comparison to earlier results.

The ASHE methodology includes imputation and weighting, the main impact of these changes when applied to existing NES data for 1998 to 2003 are:

- To increase the estimates of the level of average weekly pay over estimates published from the NES.

- For males the increase in estimates of earnings is more than the increase for females. In particular this affects hourly pay excluding overtime, which is used in the calculation of the ONS preferred measure of the gender pay gap. The estimate of hourly pay for males is increased more then the estimate for females, which widens the estimate of the gap between male and female hourly pay.

- Estimates of the level of earnings for people working in London are increased more than estimates for other regions. This widens the estimate of the difference in pay between London and other regions of the UK.

Average earnings index

(Tables 7.21 and 7.22)

The Average Earnings Index (AEI) is designed to measure changes in the level of earnings, i.e. wage inflation in Great Britain. Average earnings are calculated as the total wages and salaries paid by firms, divided by the number of employees paid. Like all indices, changes are measured against a base year, whose index value is set to 100. The current base year is 2000 for Tables 7.21 and 7.22.

Users should note that the data contained in Table 7.22 of the *Annual Abstract* since 2003 are not comparable with that published up until 2002. Table 7.22 now shows the set of 20 industry sectors. That better reflect the current state of the economy, and supersedes the previous set of 26 industry sectors. The new series are available in the format of excluding bonus index, including bonus index, and an annual percentage change for including and excluding bonuses. An article covering the reasons for the change can be found on the National Statistics website www.statistics.gov.uk/labour.

The AEI is published monthly in the Labour Market Statistics First Release. The main indicator of growth, the headline rate, is based on the annual change in the seasonally adjusted index values for the latest 3 months compared with the same period a year ago. The use of a 3-month average reduces the level of volatility seen in the data on a month-on-month basis.

Strengths of the AEI

The AEI, based on monthly survey data, is a timely indicator of changes in the level of earnings.

Limitations of the AEI

The index is not adjusted for any changes in the composition of the workforce such as changes in the share of full-time and part-time workers, or in the share of skilled and unskilled workers. Similarly, the index does not account for changes in the number of hours worked, or any temporary factors that affect earnings.

Labour market

The sample of the Monthly Wages and Salaries Survey on which the AEI is based is not designed to provide information on the level of earnings. The sample is not completely representative of the economy as firms with fewer than 20 employees are excluded, as are the earnings of self employed persons.

The AEI only covers earnings in Great Britain as earnings information is not collected for Northern Ireland and regional data are not available.

Trade unions

(Table 7.25)

The statistics relate to all organisations of employees known to Certification Officer with head offices in the United Kingdom that fall within the appropriate definition of a trade union in the 1992 Trade Union and Labour Relations Act. Included in the data are home and overseas membership figures of contributory and non-contributory members. Employment status of members is not provided and the figures may therefore include some people who are self-employed, unemployed or retired.

The membership part of this table was revised in 2001, so that statistics presented here are on a consistent basis with the GB table produced by the Certification Officer in his Annual Report and with tables produced in the annual *Labour Market Trends* Trade Union article. There is a break in the time series for the figures in this table between the years 1988 (contained within previous publications) and 1989. GB data for 1989–95 are DTI analyses of annual returns, with 1996–1999 as published in the Certification Officer's Annual Report. Data for Northern Ireland for 1989–1991 are DTI analyses of annual returns, with 1992–1999 from the Certification Officer's Annual Report.

7.1 Labour force summary:[1] by sex
United Kingdom
Spring each year. Seasonally adjusted

Thousands and percentages

	All aged 16 and over					Percentages			
	Total[2]	Total economically active	Total in employment	Total unemployed	Economically inactive	Economic activity rate 16-59/64[3]	Employment rate all aged 16 and over[4]	Employment rate 16-59/64[5]	Unemployment rate[6]
All									
	MGSL	MGSF	MGRZ	MGSC	MGSI	MGSO	MGSR	MGSU	MGSX
1995	45 189	28 202	25 731	2 470	16 988	78.2	56.9	71.2	8.8
1996	45 342	28 345	26 000	2 344	16 997	78.4	57.3	71.8	8.3
1997	45 497	28 492	26 448	2 045	17 004	78.4	58.1	72.7	7.2
1998	45 661	28 497	26 713	1 783	17 164	78.3	58.5	73.3	6.3
1999	45 862	28 811	27 052	1 759	17 051	78.7	59.0	73.8	6.1
2000	46 107	29 071	27 434	1 638	17 035	78.9	59.5	74.4	5.6
2001	46 413	29 122	27 691	1 431	17 292	78.5	59.7	74.6	4.9
2002	46 704	29 399	27 866	1 533	17 305	78.6	59.7	74.4	5.2
2003	46 995	29 643	28 167	1 476	17 353	78.7	59.9	74.7	5.0
2004	47 324	29 835	28 409	1 426	17 489	78.6	60.0	74.8	4.8
2005	47 727	30 101	28 676	1 425	17 626	78.5	60.1	74.7	4.7
Men									
	MGSM	MGSG	MGSA	MGSD	MGSJ	MGSP	MGSS	MGSV	MGSY
1995	21 710	15 682	14 091	1 591	6 028	85.0	64.9	76.3	10.1
1996	21 794	15 686	14 163	1 524	6 108	84.9	65.0	76.6	9.7
1997	21 876	15 687	14 405	1 283	6 189	84.7	65.8	77.7	8.2
1998	21 961	15 647	14 571	1 076	6 314	84.2	66.3	78.3	6.9
1999	22 071	15 774	14 704	1 070	6 297	84.4	66.6	78.6	6.8
2000	22 202	15 882	14 908	974	6 320	84.6	67.1	79.3	6.1
2001	22 377	15 867	15 020	847	6 510	84.0	67.1	79.5	5.3
2002	22 550	15 971	15 052	919	6 579	83.9	66.7	79.0	5.8
2003	22 723	16 162	15 259	903	6 561	84.1	67.2	79.3	5.6
2004	22 910	16 192	15 363	829	6 718	83.7	67.1	79.3	5.1
2005	23 136	16 301	15 460	841	6 835	83.4	66.8	79.0	5.2
Women									
	MGSN	MGSH	MGSB	MGSE	MGSK	MGSQ	MGST	MGSW	MGSZ
1995	23 479	12 520	11 640	879	10 959	70.9	49.6	65.8	7.0
1996	23 547	12 658	11 838	820	10 889	71.4	50.3	66.7	6.5
1997	23 621	12 805	12 043	762	10 815	71.8	51.0	67.4	6.0
1998	23 700	12 850	12 143	707	10 850	72.0	51.2	67.9	5.5
1999	23 791	13 037	12 348	689	10 754	72.5	51.9	68.6	5.3
2000	23 905	13 189	12 526	663	10 716	72.9	52.4	69.1	5.0
2001	24 036	13 255	12 672	583	10 781	72.7	52.7	69.4	4.4
2002	24 154	13 428	12 815	614	10 726	73.0	53.1	69.6	4.6
2003	24 272	13 481	12 908	573	10 792	73.0	53.2	69.8	4.3
2004	24 414	13 643	13 046	598	10 771	73.2	53.4	69.9	4.4
2005	24 591	13 800	13 216	584	10 791	73.4	53.7	70.1	4.2

1 See chapter text. The data in this table have been adjusted to reflect the latest 2001 Census population data.
2 Population in private households and student halls of residence.
3 Economically active of working age as a percentage of all persons of working age.
4 Total employed as a percentage of all persons 16 and over.
5 Total employed of working age as a percentage of all persons of working age (men 16-64, women 16-59).
6 Total unemployed as a percentage of all economically active.

Source: Labour Force Survey, Office for National Statistics

7.2 Employment status: full-time/part-time, second jobs and temporary employees[1]
United Kingdom
Spring each year. Seasonally adjusted

Thousands

	All in employment[2]					Total employment[2]		Employees[2]		Self-employed[2]			
	Total	Employees	Self employed	Unpaid family workers	Government supported training and employment programmes[3]	Full-time	Part-time	Full-time	Part-time	Full-time	Part-time	Workers with second jobs[4]	Temporary employees
All													
	MGRZ	MGRN	MGRQ	MGRT	MGRW	YCBE	YCBH	YCBK	YCBN	YCBQ	YCBT	YCBW	YCBZ
1995	25 731	21 752	3 562	139	279	19 449	6 282	16 405	5 347	2 869	692	1 279	1 607
1996	26 000	22 155	3 475	127	244	19 485	6 516	16 548	5 607	2 772	703	1 282	1 646
1997	26 448	22 635	3 479	118	216	19 788	6 660	16 888	5 746	2 744	735	1 242	1 760
1998	26 713	23 052	3 386	103	172	20 001	6 712	17 243	5 809	2 632	754	1 169	1 714
1999	27 052	23 485	3 311	101	156	20 249	6 803	17 561	5 923	2 581	730	1 262	1 681
2000	27 434	23 922	3 260	111	141	20 515	6 918	17 884	6 038	2 526	734	1 172	1 696
2001	27 691	24 161	3 281	99	150	20 708	6 983	18 026	6 135	2 578	703	1 166	1 704
2002	27 866	24 325	3 340	96	106	20 802	7 064	18 143	6 182	2 586	753	1 130	1 574
2003	28 167	24 457	3 532	85	93	20 878	7 288	18 136	6 321	2 684	848	1 131	1 510
2004	28 409	24 556	3 625	100	128	21 023	7 385	18 165	6 391	2 780	845	1 072	1 496
2005	28 676	24 817	3 641	102	116	21 357	7 319	18 449	6 368	2 825	815	1 075	1 457
Men													
	MGSA	MGRO	MGRR	MGRU	MGRX	YCBF	YCBI	YCBL	YCBO	YCBR	YCBU	YCBX	YCCA
1995	14 091	11 223	2 647	43	177	12 959	1 132	10 454	770	2 403	245	534	738
1996	14 163	11 409	2 560	43	151	12 956	1 207	10 551	858	2 314	246	539	727
1997	14 405	11 684	2 551	38	132	13 120	1 285	10 740	944	2 285	266	543	798
1998	14 571	11 967	2 464	29	111	13 274	1 296	11 014	953	2 184	279	509	757
1999	14 704	12 128	2 438	36	103	13 361	1 343	11 125	1 003	2 169	269	529	790
2000	14 908	12 432	2 354	37	85	13 537	1 371	11 402	1 029	2 073	281	489	770
2001	15 020	12 478	2 406	37	99	13 636	1 384	11 422	1 056	2 143	263	476	776
2002	15 052	12 505	2 455	30	62	13 608	1 444	11 411	1 094	2 152	303	465	724
2003	15 259	12 595	2 579	30	55	13 668	1 591	11 407	1 188	2 222	357	461	687
2004	15 363	12 582	2 664	41	76	13 732	1 632	11 371	1 212	2 310	354	456	697
2005	15 460	12 671	2 679	40	70	13 817	1 642	11 422	1 248	2 343	337	466	693
Women													
	MGSB	MGRP	MGRS	MGRV	MGRY	YCBG	YCBJ	YCBM	YCBP	YCBS	YCBV	YCBY	YCCB
1995	11 640	10 529	914	96	101	6 490	5 150	5 952	4 577	467	448	745	870
1996	11 838	10 746	915	84	93	6 529	5 309	5 997	4 750	458	457	743	920
1997	12 043	10 951	928	80	84	6 668	5 375	6 148	4 803	459	469	699	962
1998	12 143	11 085	922	74	62	6 727	5 416	6 230	4 856	448	474	660	957
1999	12 348	11 357	873	66	53	6 888	5 461	6 437	4 920	412	461	733	891
2000	12 526	11 491	906	73	56	6 979	5 547	6 482	5 009	453	453	683	926
2001	12 672	11 683	875	62	51	7 073	5 599	6 604	5 079	435	440	690	928
2002	12 815	11 820	885	66	45	7 195	5 620	6 732	5 088	434	451	665	850
2003	12 908	11 862	953	55	38	7 210	5 698	6 729	5 133	462	491	670	823
2004	13 046	11 974	961	59	52	7 292	5 754	6 794	5 180	470	491	616	799
2005	13 216	12 147	961	62	46	7 540	5 677	7 027	5 120	483	479	609	764

1 See chapter text. The data in this table have been adjusted to reflect the latest 2001 Census population data.
2 People whose main job is full or part-time.
3 Those on employment and training programmes are classified as in employment. Some of those on programmes may consider themselves to be employees or self employed so appear in other categories.
4 Second jobs reported in LFS in addition to person's main full or part-time job.

Source: Labour Force Survey, Office for National Statistics

7.3 Employment: by sex and age[1]
United Kingdom
At Spring each year. Seasonally adjusted

Thousands and percentages

	All aged 16 and over	16-59/64	16-17	18-24	16-24	25-34	35-49	50-64 (m) 50-59 (f)	65+ (m) 60+ (f)
Thousands									
All									
	MGRZ	YBSE	YBTO	YBTR	PXLA	YBTU	YBTX	MGUW	MGUZ
1997	26 448	25 645	696	3 232	3 928	6 998	9 561	5 158	803
1998	26 713	25 938	694	3 199	3 893	6 972	9 675	5 398	776
1999	27 052	26 235	675	3 205	3 880	6 942	9 827	5 585	818
2000	27 434	26 602	670	3 265	3 935	6 887	10 044	5 737	832
2001	27 691	26 872	670	3 292	3 962	6 752	10 222	5 935	820
2002	27 866	26 983	653	3 385	4 038	6 553	10 388	6 003	883
2003	28 167	27 239	660	3 389	4 049	6 389	10 572	6 229	928
Men									
	MGSA	YBSF	YBTP	YBTS	PXLB	YBTV	YBTY	MGUX	MGVA
1997	14 405	14 137	339	1 696	2 035	3 852	5 123	3 127	268
1998	14 571	14 298	344	1 677	2 021	3 848	5 187	3 243	273
1999	14 704	14 418	332	1 679	2 011	3 799	5 257	3 350	286
2000	14 908	14 623	333	1 715	2 048	3 774	5 387	3 415	285
2001	15 020	14 755	335	1 727	2 062	3 702	5 457	3 534	264
2002	15 052	14 764	321	1 769	2 090	3 587	5 536	3 550	288
2003	15 259	14 924	323	1 781	2 104	3 496	5 641	3 683	335
Women									
	MGSB	YBSG	YBTQ	YBTT	PXLC	YBTW	YBTZ	MGUY	MGVB
1997	12 043	11 508	357	1 536	1 893	3 146	4 438	2 031	535
1998	12 143	11 640	351	1 522	1 873	3 124	4 488	2 155	503
1999	12 348	11 817	343	1 527	1 870	3 143	4 570	2 234	532
2000	12 526	11 979	337	1 550	1 887	3 113	4 657	2 322	547
2001	12 672	12 116	336	1 565	1 901	3 049	4 765	2 401	556
2002	12 815	12 219	332	1 616	1 948	1 966	4 852	2 453	595
2003	12 908	12 315	338	1 608	1 946	2 892	4 931	2 546	592
Rates[2]									
All									
	MGSR	MGSU	YBUA	YBUD	PXLD	YBUG	YBUJ	YBUM	YBUP
1997	58.1	72.7	47.9	66.5	62.2	77.7	79.9	64.5	7.9
1998	58.5	73.3	47.9	66.6	62.1	78.4	80.6	65.4	7.6
1999	59.0	73.8	47.0	66.6	62.1	79.3	81.1	66.1	7.9
2000	59.5	74.4	46.7	67.6	62.8	80.1	81.7	66.7	8.0
2001	59.7	74.6	45.6	67.4	62.3	80.0	81.9	67.9	7.9
2002	59.7	74.4	43.4	68.1	62.2	79.6	81.9	67.8	8.4
2003	59.9	74.7	43.3	66.5	61.0	79.5	82.2	69.8	8.8
Men									
	MGSS	MGSV	YBUB	YBUE	PXLE	YBUH	YBUK	YBUN	YBUQ
1997	65.8	77.7	45.9	69.8	64.3	86.4	86.4	67.3	7.3
1998	66.3	78.3	46.7	69.9	64.3	87.5	87.3	67.9	7.4
1999	66.6	78.6	45.5	70.0	64.3	87.8	87.6	68.6	7.7
2000	67.1	79.3	45.5	71.3	65.2	88.8	88.6	68.7	7.6
2001	67.1	79.5	44.5	71.0	64.6	88.7	88.4	70.2	6.9
2002	66.7	79.0	41.7	71.1	64.1	88.0	88.3	69.8	7.5
2003	67.2	79.3	41.3	69.6	62.9	87.8	88.7	71.8	8.6
Women									
	MGST	MGSW	YBUC	YBUF	PXLF	YBUI	YBUL	YBUO	YBUR
1997	51.0	67.4	49.9	63.2	60.2	69.2	73.6	60.6	8.2
1998	51.2	67.9	49.1	63.2	60.0	69.5	74.1	62.1	7.7
1999	51.9	68.6	48.6	63.3	59.9	71.0	74.6	62.8	8.1
2000	52.4	69.1	47.9	64.0	60.4	71.6	74.9	63.8	8.3
2001	52.7	69.4	46.8	63.9	60.0	71.6	75.5	64.7	8.4
2002	53.1	69.6	45.2	65.0	60.3	71.4	75.7	65.1	9.0
2003	53.2	69.8	45.4	63.3	59.2	71.3	75.8	67.1	8.9

1 See chapter text. The data in this table have been adjusted to reflect the latest 2001 Census population data.
2 Total in employment as a percentage of all persons in the relevant group.

Source: Labour Force Survey, Office for National Statistics

7.4 Distribution of the workforce:[1,2] by sex
At mid-June each year. Seasonally adjusted

Thousands

		1995	1996	1997	1998	1999	2000	2001	2002	2003	2004	2005
United Kingdom												
Claimant count	BCJD	2 289.7	2 087.5	1 584.5	1 347.8	1 248.1	1 088.4	969.9	946.6	933.0	853.5	861.8
Males	DPAE	1 752.2	1 593.1	1 214.9	1 029.4	955.0	831.6	739.6	717.1	700.3	636.4	639.8
Females	DPAF	537.5	494.4	369.6	318.4	293.1	256.8	230.3	229.6	232.8	217.1	222.0
Workforce jobs	DYDC	27 765	28 091	28 566	28 720	29 079	29 536	29 842	29 985	30 283	30 572	30 810
Males	KAMS	14 686	14 681	15 033	15 245	15 613	15 745	15 947	15 938	16 198	16 295	16 404
Females	KAMT	13 078	13 410	13 533	13 474	13 466	13 791	13 895	14 047	14 085	14 277	14 406
HM Forces	KAMU	241	230	220	219	218	217	214	214	223	218	209
Males	KAMV	224	214	204	203	201	199	196	197	203	199	191
Females	KAMW	17	16	16	17	17	18	18	18	19	19	18
Self-employment jobs	DYZN	3 820	3 765	3 715	3 583	3 606	3 516	3 520	3 573	3 793	3 866	3 855
Males	KAMZ	2 777	2 743	2 654	2 569	2 592	2 517	2 543	2 569	2 730	2 798	2 774
Females	KANA	1 044	1 021	1 061	1 014	1 014	999	977	1 004	1 063	1 068	1 080
Employees jobs	BCAJ	23 464	23 903	24 460	24 786	25 124	25 685	26 009	26 107	26 175	26 381	26 650
Males	KANC	11 530	11 605	12 070	12 398	12 739	12 956	13 147	13 118	13 210	13 234	13 381
Females	KAND	11 933	12 298	12 390	12 388	12 385	12 729	12 862	12 990	12 966	13 147	13 269
of whom												
Total, production and construction industries	KANF	5 244	5 292	5 398	5 525	5 382	5 349	5 195	4 953	4 749	4 601	4 496
Total, all manufacturing industries	KANG	4 073	4 139	4 191	4 208	4 060	3 959	3 805	3 599	3 411	3 255	3 132
Government-supported trainees	KANH	240	194	171	131	131	119	99	90	92	108	96
Males	KANI	156	119	105	76	81	73	62	54	55	64	58
Females	KANJ	84	75	66	55	50	46	38	36	37	43	38
Great Britain												
Claimant count	DPAG	2 201.8	2 003.7	1 521.1	1 290.3	1 197.3	1 046.3	930.5	910.2	898.5	822.7	833.2
Males	ZSDP	1 687.0	1 528.2	1 165.0	984.6	915.7	799.6	709.7	689.3	673.9	613.0	618.1
Females	ZSDQ	1 687.0	475.5	356.1	305.7	281.6	246.8	220.8	220.9	224.6	209.8	215.1
Workforce jobs	KANQ	27 070	27 411	27 863	28 004	28 356	28 791	29 088	29 224	29 506	29 776	30 000
Males	KANR	14 306	14 314	14 654	14 858	15 225	15 342	15 542	15 533	15 787	15 870	15 973
Females	KANS	12 764	13 097	13 209	13 146	13 131	13 449	13 546	13 691	13 719	13 906	14 026
HM Forces	BCAH	241	230	220	219	218	217	214	214	223	218	209
Males	KANU	224	214	204	203	201	199	196	197	203	199	191
Females	KANV	17	16	16	17	17	18	18	18	19	19	18
Self-employment jobs	KANW	3 716	3 679	3 623	3 495	3 520	3 422	3 425	3 484	3 694	3 755	3 744
Males	KANX	2 692	2 672	2 581	2 495	2 523	2 439	2 463	2 495	2 650	2 708	2 684
Females	KANY	1 024	1 007	1 043	1 000	997	984	962	989	1 044	1 047	1 060
Employee jobs	KANZ	22 889	23 323	23 863	24 173	24 498	25 043	25 357	25 442	25 504	25 701	25 957
Males	KAOA	11 245	11 319	11 773	12 093	12 428	12 638	12 826	12 792	12 884	12 904	13 045
Females	KAOB	11 644	12 004	12 089	12 079	12 070	12 405	12 531	12 650	12 621	12 798	12 912
of whom												
Total, production and construction industries	KAOC	5 115	5 159	5 256	5 382	5 240	5 206	5 053	4 814	4 616	4 470	4 366
Total, all manufacturing industries	KAOD	3 968	4 034	4 083	4 101	3 954	3 856	3 704	3 501	3 319	3 166	3 045
Government-supported trainees	KAOE	224	178	157	117	120	110	92	84	85	101	89
Males	KAOF	145	109	96	67	73	67	57	50	50	59	53
Females	KAOG	79	69	61	50	47	43	35	34	35	42	36

Note. Because the figures have been rounded independently totals may differ from the sum of the components. Also the totals may include some employees whose industrial classification could not be ascertained.

1 The data in this table have not been adjusted to reflect the 2001 Census population data. See chapter text.

2 All figures have been revised. For further information see: http://www.statistics.gov.uk/cci/article.asp?id=1340

Source: Earnings and Employment Division, Office for National Statistics: 01633 812318

7.5 Employee jobs: by industry[1,2]
Standard Industrial Classification 1992
At June each year. Not seasonally adjusted

Thousands

			United Kingdom							Great Britain					
		SIC 1992	2000	2001	2002	2003	2004	2005		2000	2001	2002	2003	2004	2005
All sections	KAOH	A - O	25 658	25 987	26 085	26 146	26 343	26 608	LMAB	25 018	25 337	25 422	25 477	25 665	25 916
Index of production and construction industries	KAOI	C - F	5 336	5 185	4 943	4 739	4 589	4 483	LMAH	5 193	5 042	4 805	4 606	4 459	4 354
Index of production industries	KAOJ	C - E	4 153	4 009	3 797	3 595	3 421	3 290	LMAF	4 044	3 902	3 694	3 497	3 327	3 199
of which, manufacturing industries	KAOK	D	3 954	3 802	3 597	3 410	3 253	3 131	KAPQ	3 850	3 700	3 499	3 317	3 165	3 045
Service industries	KAOL	G - O	20 001	20 524	20 886	21 179	21 528	21 884	LMAJ	19 520	20 031	20 376	20 658	20 995	21 336
Agriculture, hunting and forestry and fishing	KAOM	A/B	321	279	256	228	226	240	KAPS	305	264	242	213	211	226
Agriculture hunting and forestry	KPHI	A	310	270	246	221	219	235	KOVW	295	255	231	207	204	220
Agriculture hunting & related activities	KPHJ	01	304	259	235	210	209	224	KOVX	288	245	221	196	195	210
Fishing	KPHK	B	11	9	10	7	7	5	KOVY	11	9	10	7	7	5
Mining and quarrying	KPHL	C	73	72	68	62	58	57	KOVZ	71	70	66	60	56	55
Mining and quarrying of energy producing materials	KPHM	CA	44	43	41	38	34	34	KOWA	43	43	41	37	34	34
Mining	KAPG	10/12	..	..	..	..	..	..	KOWB	13	13	12	10	8	7
Extraction of crude petroleum	KPHN	11	..	..	..	..	..	..	KOWC	31	30	29	27	25	27
Mining and quarrying except of energy producing materials	KPHO	CB(13/14)	29	29	27	24	23	23	KOWD	28	28	25	23	22	21
Energy and water supply industries	KAOO	C/E	200	207	200	185	168	159	LMAM	194	202	195	180	163	154
Manufacturing	KPHP	D	3 954	3 802	3 597	3 410	3 253	3 131	LMAD	3 850	3 700	3 499	3 317	3 165	3 045
Manufacture of food products Beverages and tobacco	KPHQ	DA	493	478	464	456	444	433	LMAN	474	459	445	437	425	414
Of food	KPHR	151 to 158	..	..	..	..	..	..	KOWH	421	406	393	387	376	368
Of beverages and tobacco	KPHS	159/16	..	..	..	..	..	..	KOWI	53	53	52	50	48	46
Manufacture of textiles and textile products	KPHT	DB	258	224	193	164	143	130	KOWJ	242	210	181	154	136	125
Of textiles	KPHU	17	149	135	119	107	95	88	KOWK	141	127	113	101	91	85
Of made-up textile articles except apparel	KPHV	174	..	..	..	..	..	..	KOWL	34	34	33	31	30	28
Of textiles excluding made-up textile	KPHW	Rest of 17	..	..	..	..	..	..	KOWM	106	93	80	70	61	57
Of wearing apparel,dressing and dyeing of fur	KPHX	18	109	89	74	57	47	42	KOWN	101	83	69	54	45	40
Manufacture of leather and leather products including footwear	KPHY	DC	26	21	18	14	12	11	KOWO	25	20	18	14	12	11
Of leather and leather goods	KPHZ	191/192	..	..	..	..	..	..	KOWP	10	9	8	6	6	5
Of footwear	KPIA	193	..	..	..	..	..	..	KOWQ	15	11	10	8	6	6
Manufacture of wood and wood products	KPIB	DD(20)	83	82	84	83	84	82	LMAP	80	78	80	79	80	79
Manufacture of pulp paper and paper products,publishing and printing	KPIC	DE	464	451	440	426	413	403	LMAQ	458	445	434	420	407	397
Of pulp paper and paper products	KPID	21	100	95	89	87	82	79	KOWT	98	93	87	85	80	77
Publishing printing and reproduction of recorded media	KPIE	22	364	356	351	340	331	325	KOWU	360	352	346	335	327	320
Manufacture of coke refined petroleum products and nuclear fuel	KPIF	DF(23)	26	28	26	25	24	24	KOWV	26	27	26	25	24	24
Manufacture of chemicals,chemical products and man-made fibres	KPIG	DG(24)	238	234	233	226	210	201	LMAR	235	230	229	222	207	198
Manufacture of rubber and plastics	KPIH	DH(25)	237	228	221	213	211	202	LMAS	230	221	214	206	204	195
Manufacture of other non-metallic mineral products	KPII	DI(26)	140	134	127	121	118	114	KOWZ	135	129	121	115	112	108
Manufacture of basic metals and fabricated metal products	KPIJ	DJ	521	491	462	442	417	401	KOXA	515	484	455	436	410	394
Of basic metals	KPIK	27	117	108	98	92	82	74	KOXB	116	108	97	91	81	74
except machinery	KPIL	28	404	383	364	350	335	327	KOXC	398	377	358	344	328	320

7.5 Employee jobs: by industry[1,2]
Standard Industrial Classification 1992
continued   At June each year. Not seasonally adjusted

Thousands

		SIC 1992	United Kingdom						Great Britain					
			2000	2001	2002	2003	2004	2005	2000	2001	2002	2003	2004	2005
Manufacture of Machinery and Equipment not elsewhere classified	KPIM	DK(29)	358	348	326	301	288	286 LMAU	351	341	320	294	281	280
Manufacture of electrical and optical equipment	KPIN	DL	494	481	426	380	351	335 LMAV	481	468	415	370	342	326
Of office machinery and computers	KPIO	30	53	50	42	37	33	31 KOXF	51	48	40	34	30	29
Of electrical machinery and apparatus	KPIP	31	178	169	153	138	127	123 KOXG	175	166	150	135	124	119
Of electric motors etc control apparatus and insulated cable	KPIQ	311 to 313	..	..	..	..	..	.. KOXH	101	96	86	74	66	63
Of accumulators, primary cells, batteries, lamps and electrical equipment	KPIR	314 to 316	..	..	..	..	..	.. KOXI	74	70	64	61	58	56
Radio television and communication equipment	KPIS	32	129	126	99	81	74	67 KOXJ	123	120	95	79	72	65
Of electronic components	KPIT	321	..	..	..	..	..	.. KOXK	45	40	33	29	29	27
Of radio TV and telephone apparatus, sound and video recorders	KPIU	322/323	..	..	..	..	..	.. KOXL	78	80	62	49	42	38
Of medical precision and optical equipment, watches	KPIV	33	134	135	131	124	118	114 KOXM	132	134	130	122	116	113
Manufacture of transport equipment	KPIW	DM	400	388	371	356	342	325 LMAW	387	375	358	345	332	315
Of motor vehicles and trailers	KPIX	34	224	212	210	205	196	181 KOXO	220	207	206	200	193	178
Of other transport equipment	KPIY	35	176	176	160	152	146	144 KOXP	168	168	153	145	139	137
Manufacturing not elsewhere classified	KPIZ	DN(36/37)	216	215	207	203	198	184 KOXQ	212	211	203	199	194	180
Electricity gas and water supply	KPJA	E	127	135	132	123	110	102 KOXR	123	132	129	120	107	99
Electricity gas steam and hot water supply	KPJB	40	..	..	..	..	..	.. KOXT	92	97	95	90	82	75
Collection purification and distribution of water	KPJC	41	..	..	..	..	..	.. KOXU	31	35	33	30	25	24
Construction	KPJD	F(45)	1 183	1 176	1 146	1 144	1 168	1 193 LMAY	1 148	1 140	1 110	1 109	1 131	1 156
Services	KPJE	G - O	20 001	20 524	20 886	21 179	21 528	21 884 KOXX	19 520	20 031	20 376	20 658	20 995	21 336
Wholesale and retail trade; Repair of motor vehicles, motorcycles and personal household goods	KPJF	G (50 - 52)	4 378	4 485	4 537	4 537	4 560	4 602 LMAZ	4 272	4 379	4 424	4 422	4 444	4 484
Sale maintenance and repair of motor vehicles,retail of automotive fuel	KPJG	50	567	565	573	564	556	553 KOXZ	553	550	557	548	542	539
Sale of motor vehicles, motorcycles and parts,motorcycle repair and sale of automotive fuel	KPJH	501/503 - 505	..	..	..	..	..	.. KOYA	387	385	391	381	374	370
Maintenance and repair of motor vehicles	KPJI	502	..	..	..	..	..	.. KOYB	166	165	166	167	168	168
Wholesale trade and commission trade except motor vehicles	KPJJ	51	1 175	1 159	1 134	1 126	1 119	1 139 KOYC	1 153	1 136	1 111	1 104	1 095	1 116
Wholesale on a fee of contract basis	KPJK	511	..	..	..	..	..	.. KOYD	62	60	56	59	59	60
Wholesale agricultural raw materials and live animals	KPJL	512	..	..	..	..	..	.. KPLD	23	24	23	23	23	23
Wholesale food beverages & tobacco	KPJM	513	..	..	..	..	..	.. KPLE	199	192	189	190	188	193
Wholesale household goods	KPJN	514	..	..	..	..	..	.. KPLF	266	270	266	264	267	274
Wholesale of non-agricultural intermediate products waste & scrap	KPJO	515	..	..	..	..	..	.. KPLG	243	233	235	232	232	234
Wholesale machinery eqpt. & supplies	KPJP	516	..	..	..	..	..	.. KPLH	252	251	243	238	230	238
Other wholesale	KPJQ	517	..	..	..	..	..	.. KPLI	107	106	100	98	96	94
Retail trade except of motor vehicles and motorcycles;repair of personal and household goods	KPJR	52	2 636	2 762	2 830	2 846	2 885	2 910 KPLJ	2 567	2 692	2 756	2 770	2 808	2 830
Non-specialised stores selling mainly food beverages & tobacco	KPJS	5211/5221-4,5227	..	..	..	..	..	.. KPLK	999	1 083	1 144	1 143	1 120	1 132
Other non-specialised stores second hand shops & sales not in stores	KPJT	5212/525-526	..	..	..	..	..	.. KPLL	381	379	367	365	362	355

7.5 Employee jobs: by industry[1,2]
Standard Industrial Classification 1992
continued   At June each year. Not seasonally adjusted

Thousands

	SIC 1992	United Kingdom 2000	2001	2002	2003	2004	2005		Great Britain 2000	2001	2002	2003	2004	2005
Alcoholic & other beverages, tobacco KPJU	5225 to 5226	..	..	..	..	..	..	KPLM	68	68	64	56	54	50
Pharmaceutical & medical goods cosmetics & toilet articles KPJV	523	..	..	..	..	..	..	KPLN	89	92	96	93	99	105
Clothing footwear & leather goods KPJW	5242/5243	..	..	..	..	..	..	KPLO	352	355	340	369	410	422
Textile furniture lighting equipment electrical household appliances radio and TV paints glass hardware and household goods not elsewhere classified KPJX	5241/5244-46	..	..	..	..	..	..	KPLP	278	291	303	296	304	301
Books newspapers and stationery, other retail in specialised stores KPJY	5247/5248	..	..	..	..	..	..	KPLQ	378	400	416	421	432	438
Repair of personal and household goods KPJZ	527	..	..	..	..	..	..	KPLR	23	24	26	27	26	28
Hotels and restaurants KPKA	H	1 685	1 698	1 748	1 791	1 838	1 843	LMBA	1 647	1 660	1 708	1 751	1 798	1 801
Hotels camp sites short-stay accom. KPKB	551/552	..	..	..	..	..	..	KPLT	375	370	365	369	379	390
Restaurants KPKC	553	..	..	..	..	..	..	KPLU	493	509	547	575	594	606
Bars KPKD	554	..	..	..	..	..	..	KPLV	543	525	531	540	558	542
Canteens and catering KPKE	555	..	..	..	..	..	..	KPLW	237	256	265	267	267	263
Transport, storage and communication KPKF	I	1 523	1 589	1 581	1 586	1 566	1 582	KPLX	1 497	1 562	1 553	1 559	1 537	1 553
Land transport, transport via pipelines KPKG	60	514	522	518	517	518	527	KPLY	503	510	506	505	505	514
Transport via railways KPKH	601	..	..	..	..	..	..	KPLZ	49	50	49	49	50	54
Other land transport and via pipelines KPKI	602/603	..	..	..	..	..	..	KPMA	453	461	457	457	456	460
Water transport KPKJ	61	19	17	18	17	17	19	KPMB	18	17	17	16	17	19
Air transport KPKK	62	94	93	88	90	85	88	KPMC	93	92	87	90	85	88
Supporting and auxiliary transport activities, activities of travel agents KPKL	63	381	403	403	411	440	454	KPMD	376	398	398	406	435	448
Travel agencies and tour operators KPKM	633	..	..	..	..	..	..	KPME	125	132	128	124	134	127
Post and telecommunications KPKN	64	515	555	554	551	505	494	LMBC	506	545	545	542	496	484
National post and courier activities KPKO	641	..	..	..	..	..	..	KPMG	283	300	295	297	274	274
National post activities KPKP	6411	..	..	..	..	..	..	KPMH	216	229	220	216	200	..
Courier activities KPKQ	6412	..	..	..	..	..	..	KPMI	66	70	75	81	72	..
Telecommunications KPKR	6420	..	..	..	..	..	..	KPMJ	223	246	249	245	223	211
Financial intermediation KPKS	J	1 068	1 088	1 112	1 103	1 078	1 078	LMBD	1 053	1 072	1 095	1 087	1 060	1 061
Financial intermediation except insurance and pension funding KPKT	65	605	616	638	639	619	618	KPML	595	605	627	627	607	606
Insurance and pension funding except compulsory social security KPKU	66	227	228	223	215	198	187	KPMM	225	226	221	213	196	185
Activities auxiliary to financial intermediation KPKV	67	236	244	251	249	261	274	KPMN	233	241	248	246	258	270
Except insurance and pension funding KPKW	671	..	..	..	..	..	..	KPMO	95	107	111	113	122	132
Auxiliary to insurance and pension funding KPKX	672	..	..	..	..	..	..	KPMP	138	134	137	133	135	139
Real estate renting & business activities KPKY	K	3 746	3 933	3 956	3 995	4 106	4 210	KPMQ	3 697	3 881	3 901	3 938	4 046	4 146
Real estate activities KPKZ	70	350	364	369	381	405	426	LMBE	347	360	365	378	401	422
Activities with own property, letting of own property KPLA	701/702	..	..	..	..	..	..	KPMS	213	219	218	224	236	244
Activities on a fee or contract basis KPLB	703	..	..	..	..	..	..	KPMT	133	141	147	154	166	178

7.5
continued

Employee jobs: by industry[1,2]
Standard Industrial Classification 1992
At June each year. Not seasonally adjusted

Thousand

		SIC 1992	United Kingdom							Great Britain					
			2000	2001	2002	2003	2004	2005		2000	2001	2002	2003	2004	2005
Renting of machinery and equipment without operator & of personal & household goods	KPLC	71	154	156	157	151	152	156	KPMU	152	154	155	149	150	153
Construction and civil engineering machinery	KOUU	7132	..	..	..	..	..	..	KPMV	42	45	45	42	41	42
All other goods and equipment	KOUV	Rest of 71	..	..	..	..	..	..	KPMW	109	109	110	107	109	111
Computer and related equipment	KOUW	72	460	503	494	500	489	490	KPMX	455	497	489	495	483	484
Research and development	KOUX	73	100	104	108	106	101	104	KPMY	98	102	106	105	99	103
Other business activities	KOUY	74	2 683	2 806	2 829	2 856	2 959	3 034	KPMZ	2 646	2 767	2 786	2 811	2 911	2 984
Legal, accounting,book-keeping & auditing activities	KOUZ	741	..	..	..	..	..	..	KPNA	698	724	741	778	837	848
Legal activities	KOVA	7411	..	..	..	..	..	..	KPNB	240	240	248	250	254	254
Accounting, book-keeping auditing, tax consultancy	KOVB	7412	..	..	..	..	..	..	KPNC	206	207	195	191	194	198
Market research business and consultancy activities	KOVC	7413/7414	..	..	..	..	..	..	KPND	219	246	270	272	289	290
Management activities of holding companies[3]	KOVD	7415	..	..	..	..	..	..	KPNE	..	..	..	..	101	106
Architectural engineering activities and related technical consultancy, technical testing	KOVE	742/743	..	..	..	..	..	..	KPNF	324	331	332	332	340	346
Advertising	KOVF	744	..	..	..	..	..	..	KPNG	86	93	87	83	80	86
Industrial cleaning	KOVG	747	..	..	..	..	..	..	KPNH	427	425	418	418	414	429
Public administration and defence, compulsory social security	KOVH	L(75)	1 384	1 395	1 432	1 484	1 515	1 542	LMBG	1 325	1 335	1 371	1 421	1 451	1 477
Education	KOVI	M(80)	2 081	2 087	2 136	2 218	2 294	2 327	LMBH	2 016	2 021	2 069	2 149	2 226	2 255
Health and social work	KOVJ	N	2 828	2 900	2 993	3 082	3 185	3 292	LOJV	2 734	2 803	2 893	2 980	3 078	3 181
Human health, veterinary activities	KOVK	851/852	..	..	..	..	..	..	KPNL	1 753	1 805	1 890	1 965	2 026	2 101
Social work activities	KOVL	853	..	..	..	..	..	..	KPNM	980	998	1 003	1 015	1 051	1 079
Other community social and personal service activities,private households with employed persons, extra-territorial organisations and bodies	KOVM	O	1 307	1 348	1 391	1 382	1 385	1 409	LMBK	1 278	1 319	1 361	1 351	1 355	1 378
Sewage and refuse disposal; sanitation	KOVN	90	99	109	106	96	99	104	KPNO	97	106	103	93	97	102
Activities of membership organisations	KOVO	91	219	215	226	224	212	211	KPNP	212	207	218	216	204	203
Recreational cultural and sporting activities	KOVP	92	676	705	730	740	760	771	KPNQ	662	690	715	725	745	756
Motion picture video radio TV news agencies and entertainment activities	KOVQ	921 to 924	..	..	..	..	..	..	KPNR	211	215	226	220	224	222
Library archives museums and other cultural activities	KOVR	925	..	..	..	..	..	..	KPNS	80	79	84	92	89	..
Sporting activities and other recreational activities	KOVS	926/927	..	..	..	..	..	..	KPNT	355	377	392	405	411	..
Other service activities,private households with employed persons, extra territorial organisations	KOVT	93/95/99	312	319	330	321	314	321	KPNU	308	315	325	317	309	317
Washing, dry cleaning of textile and fur products	KOVU	9301	..	..	..	..	..	..	KPNV	45	48	46	46	42	40
Hairdressing, other beauty treatment, physical and well-being activities	KOVV	9302/9304	..	..	..	..	..	..	KPNW	100	100	102	104	105	113

Note. Because the figures have been rounded independently totals may differ from the sum of the components. Also the totals may include some employees whose industrial classification could not be ascertained.

1 See chapter text. The data in this table have not been adjusted to reflect the 2001 Census population data.

2 All figures have been revised. For further information see: http://www.statistics.gov.uk/cci/article.asp?id=1340

3 Head office and holding company local units were reclassified to Class 74.15 (within Section K) from December 2003 as a result of the SIC 2003 update.

Sources: Department of Manpower Services (Northern Ireland); Earnings and Employment Division, ONS: 01633 812318

7.6 Weekly hours worked: by sex[1,2]
United Kingdom
At Spring each year. Seasonally adjusted

Hours

	All workers' weekly hours[3]		Average actual weekly hours of work		
	Total (millions)	Average	Full-time employment[3,4]	Part-time employment[4]	Second jobs[5]
All					
	YBUS	YBUV	YBUY	YBVB	YBVE
1995	856.4	33.4	38.7	15.1	9.1
1996	860.9	33.2	38.7	15.1	8.9
1997	878.0	33.3	38.7	15.2	9.4
1998	885.4	33.2	38.7	15.2	9.1
1999	887.3	32.9	38.2	15.3	9.0
2000	893.3	32.6	37.9	15.4	8.9
2001	906.1	32.8	38.0	15.7	9.4
2002	908.5	32.6	37.9	15.6	9.4
2003	905.4	32.2	37.4	15.6	9.4
2004	908.8	32.0	37.3	15.7	9.1
2005	918.3	32.1	37.2	15.7	9.6
Men					
	YBUT	YBUW	YBUZ	YBVC	YBVF
1995	549.5	39.2	40.8	14.7	10.0
1996	549.9	39.0	40.7	14.8	9.7
1997	558.7	38.9	40.7	14.9	10.7
1998	564.0	38.8	40.7	15.0	9.8
1999	560.4	38.2	40.1	15.0	9.7
2000	564.2	37.9	39.8	15.1	9.4
2001	569.6	38.0	39.9	15.6	10.2
2002	567.0	37.7	39.8	15.0	10.3
2003	564.4	37.0	39.2	15.4	10.5
2004	567.0	37.0	39.1	15.7	10.0
2005	569.4	36.9	39.1	15.6	10.7
Women					
	YBUU	YBUX	YBVA	YBVD	YBVG
1995	306.9	26.4	34.4	15.2	8.5
1996	311.1	26.3	34.5	15.1	8.2
1997	319.2	26.6	34.7	15.3	8.4
1998	321.3	26.5	34.6	15.3	8.6
1999	326.9	26.5	34.5	15.3	8.5
2000	329.2	26.3	34.1	15.4	8.6
2001	336.5	26.6	34.4	15.7	8.8
2002	341.5	26.7	34.4	15.7	8.8
2003	341.0	26.5	34.1	15.6	8.6
2004	341.8	26.2	33.9	15.7	8.4
2005	348.9	26.4	33.7	15.7	8.7

1 See chapter text. The data in this table have been adjusted to reflect the latest 2001 Census population data.
2 Average hours actually worked in the reference week which includes hours worked in second jobs.
3 Main and second job.
4 People whose main job is full-time or part-time.
5 Second jobs reported in the LFS in addition to persons' main full time job.

Source: Labour Force Survey, Office for National Statistics

7.7 Civil Service staff: by ministerial responsibility[1,2]
At 1 April each year

Full-time equivalents (thousands)[3]

		1994	1995	1996	1997	1998	1999	2000	2001	2002	2003	2004
Agriculture, Fisheries and Food	BCDA	11.0	10.6	10.8	10.1	10.8	11.7	10.8	11.4	..	..	..
Cabinet Office	BBGD	12.0	11.7	12.3	7.8	7.7	7.6	6.9	6.9	6.9	7.1	7.0
Chancellor of the Exchequer's Departments:												
Customs and Excise	BCDC	25.0	24.1	23.2	23.1	23.4	22.5	21.9	21.7	21.8	22.2	22.6
Inland Revenue	BCDD	64.0	59.1	56.5	54.4	53.4	61.3	66.3	66.9	68.2	75.6	80.1
Department for National Savings	BCDE	6.0	5.4	4.7	4.3	4.1	0.1	0.1	0.1	0.1	0.1	0.1
Treasury and others	BCDF	5.0	4.3	6.0	5.1	5.1	5.0	5.5	5.5	5.6	5.8	6.1
Total	BCDB	99.0	92.9	90.3	86.8	86.0	89.0	93.8	94.2	95.7	103.7	108.9
Culture, Media and Sport	DMTC	..	..	..	..	0.6	0.6	0.6	0.6	0.7	0.7	0.7
Education	BCDG	2.0	2.5	..	..	..	..	..	..	..	..	..
Education and Employment	BBFT	..	..	40.8	34.1	33.6	34.6	36.5	38.3	..	..	..
Education and Skills	LNFW	..	..	..	..	..	..	..	..	7.2	7.5	7.7
Environment	BCDJ	10.0	9.4	10.9	9.6	..	..	..	..	..	..	..
Environment, Food and Rural Affairs	LNFX	..	..	..	..	..	..	..	..	14.6	14.5	15.4
Environment, Transport and the Regions	CKUZ	..	..	..	..	21.2	21.8	23.2	25.4	..	..	..
Foreign and Commonwealth	BCDK	8.0	7.5	7.1	6.6	5.4	5.5	5.5	5.5	5.7	6.0	6.0
Health	BAKR	7.0	6.2	4.8	4.7	4.6	4.8	7.0	7.2	5.1	4.5	4.2
Home	BCDL	51.0	51.4	50.8	50.4	50.7	50.0	53.6	60.1	61.0	65.6	69.9
International Development	DMUA	..	..	..	..	1.1	1.2	1.2	1.3	1.5	1.6	1.8
Legal Departments	BBGE	29.0	28.7	27.8	26.3	25.4	25.5	24.9	25.0	26.9	28.2	28.8
National Heritage	BBGF	1.0	1.0	1.0	1.0	..	..	..	..	..	..	..
Northern Ireland	BBGG	..	0.2	0.2	0.2	0.2	0.2	0.2	0.2	0.2	0.2	0.2
Office of the Deputy Prime Minister	YEGA	..	..	..	..	..	..	..	..	..	4.6	5.2
Scotland	BCDN	13.0	12.1	11.7	11.8	12.0	12.5	13.6	13.7	14.3	14.8	15.3
Social Security	BAKS	90.0	89.2	91.5	93.1	87.2	81.6	83.5	81.9	..	..	..
Trade and Industry	BCDQ	11.3	11.1	11.2	10.3	10.4	10.5	11.0	11.4	12.0	12.2	11.9
Transport	BCDR	14.0	12.9	11.3	11.4	..	..	..	..	..	20.8	15.9
Transport, Local Government and the Regions	LNFZ	..	..	..	..	..	..	..	..	23.9	..	..
Welsh Office	BCDS	2.0	2.2	2.1	2.2	2.1	2.3	2.7	3.2	3.5	3.7	4.4
Work and Pensions	LNGA	..	..	..	..	..	..	..	..	122.0	124.4	129.0
Total civil departments	BCDU	418.0	400.8	384.6	366.3	359.1	359.1	375.1	384.4	401.2	420.0	432.2
Defence	BCDW	122.0	116.1	109.9	109.2	104.2	100.9	100.3	98.3	89.0	91.3	91.4
Total all departments	BCDX	540.0	516.9	494.5	475.6	463.3	460.0	475.4	482.7	490.2	511.3	523.6
of which												
Non-industrial staff	BCDY	494.0	474.1	458.7	439.6	430.5	429.2	446.0	453.8	462.9	490.2	503.6
Industrial staff	BCDZ	46.0	42.0	35.9	36.0	32.8	30.8	29.4	28.9	27.3	21.1	20.0

1 The figures include non-industrial and industrial staff but exclude casual or seasonal staff and employees of the Northern Ireland Civil Service.
2 A comprehensive list of Machinery of Government changes is listed on the Cabinet Office's web site at: *www.civil-service.gov.uk/statistics*
3 Figures included are measured as 'full-time equivalent' staff. Part-time staff are recorded as a proportion of full-time employees according to the proportion of a full week that they work.

Source: Cabinet Office: 020 7276 1532

7.8 Unemployment: number by sex and age group[1]
United Kingdom
At Spring each year. Seasonally adjusted

Thousands

	All aged 16 and over	16-59/64	16-17	18-24	16-24	25-34	35-49	50-64 (m) 50-59 (w)	65+ (m) 60+ (w)
All									
	MGSC	YBSH	YBVH	YBVN	PXLG	YCGM	YCGS	MGVL	MGVO
1997	2 045	2 021	168	489	657	516	532	317	24
1998	1 783	1 763	159	437	596	465	433	268	20
1999	1 759	1 740	169	424	593	423	456	267	19
2000	1 638	1 621	177	403	580	372	411	258	17
2001	1 431	1 416	146	375	521	327	379	189	14
2002	1 533	1 511	163	393	556	351	386	219	21
2003	1 476	1 459	177	403	580	313	356	210	17
Men									
	MGSD	YBSI	YBVI	YBVO	PXLH	YCGN	YCGT	MGVM	MGVP
1997	1 283	1 271	90	304	394	321	330	226	12
1998	1 076	1 067	85	262	347	275	251	194	..2
1999	1 070	1 062	101	250	351	242	275	193	..2
2000	974	968	96	239	335	214	234	184	..2
2001	847	840	85	221	306	187	208	139	..2
2002	919	909	91	246	337	199	227	147	10
2003	903	895	101	247	348	187	212	149	..2
Women									
	MGSE	YBSJ	YBVJ	YBVP	PXLI	YCGO	YCGU	MGVN	MGVQ
1997	762	750	78	184	262	195	202	91	12
1998	707	696	74	175	249	191	182	75	11
1999	689	678	68	173	241	181	181	74	11
2000	663	654	81	164	245	158	177	74	10
2001	583	576	61	154	215	139	171	51	..2
2002	614	602	72	147	219	152	159	72	11
2003	573	563	76	156	232	126	144	62	10

1 See chapter text. The data in this table have been adjusted to reflect the latest 2001 Census population data.
2 Figure not shown as it is based on a small sample size, and is subject to a margin of uncertainty.

Source: Labour Force Survey, Office for National Statistics

Labour Market

7.9 Unemployment: percentage by sex and age group[1,2]
United Kingdom

At Spring each year. Seasonally adjusted

Percentages

	All aged 16 and over	16-59/64	16-17	18-24	16-24	25-34	35-49	50-64 (m) 50-59 (w)	65+ (m) 60+ (w)
All									
	MGSX	YBTI	YBVK	YBVQ	PXLV	YCGP	YCGV	MGXE	MGXH
1997	7.2	7.3	19.4	13.1	14.3	6.9	5.3	5.8	2.9
1998	6.3	6.4	18.7	12.0	13.2	6.3	4.3	4.7	2.6
1999	6.1	6.2	20.0	11.7	13.3	5.7	4.4	4.6	2.3
2000	5.6	5.7	20.9	11.0	12.9	5.1	3.9	4.3	2.0
2001	4.9	5.0	17.9	10.2	11.6	4.6	3.6	3.1	1.7
2002	5.2	5.3	20.0	10.4	12.2	5.1	3.6	3.5	2.4
2003	5.0	5.1	21.1	10.6	12.6	4.7	3.3	3.3	1.8
Men									
	MGSY	YBTJ	YBVL	YBVR	PXLW	YCGQ	YCGW	MGXF	MGXI
1997	8.2	8.2	20.9	15.2	16.2	7.7	6.1	6.7	4.2
1998	6.9	6.9	19.8	13.5	14.6	6.7	4.6	5.6	..[3]
1999	6.8	6.9	23.3	13.0	14.9	6.0	5.0	5.4	..[3]
2000	6.1	6.2	22.3	12.2	14.1	5.4	4.2	5.1	..[3]
2001	5.3	5.4	20.3	11.4	13.0	4.8	3.7	3.8	..[3]
2002	5.8	5.8	22.1	12.2	13.9	5.2	3.9	4.0	3.3
2003	5.6	5.7	23.8	12.2	14.2	5.1	3.6	3.9	..[3]
Women									
	MGSZ	YBTK	YBVM	YBVS	PXLX	YCGR	YCGX	MGXG	MGXJ
1997	6.0	6.1	18.0	10.7	12.1	5.8	4.3	4.3	2.2
1998	5.5	5.6	17.5	10.3	11.7	5.8	3.9	3.4	2.2
1999	5.3	5.4	16.6	10.2	11.5	5.4	3.8	3.2	2.0
2000	5.0	5.2	19.4	9.5	11.4	4.8	3.7	3.1	1.8
2001	4.4	4.5	15.4	8.9	10.1	4.4	3.5	2.1	..[3]
2002	4.6	4.7	17.8	8.3	10.3	4.9	3.2	2.9	1.9
2003	4.3	4.4	18.4	8.8	10.8	4.2	2.8	2.4	1.6

1 See chapter text. The data in this table have been adjusted to reflect the latest 2001 Census population data.

2 Total unemployment as a percentage of all economically active persons in the relevant age group.

3 Figure not shown as it is based on a small sample size, and is subject to a margin of uncertainty.

Source: Labour Force Survey, Office for National Statistics

7.10 Duration of unemployment: by sex[1,2]
United Kingdom

At Spring each year. Seasonally adjusted

Thousands

		1995	1996	1997	1998	1999	2000	2001	2002	2003	2004	2005
All												
All unemployed	MGSC	2 470	2 344	2 045	1 783	1 759	1 638	1 431	1 533	1 476	1 426	1 425
Duration of unemployment												
Less than 6 months	YBWF	1 021	1 041	973	969	997	961	847	972	955	906	914
6 months & less than 1 year	YBWG	394	393	305	248	263	239	216	230	202	232	213
1 year or more	YBWH	1 055	910	767	566	499	437	368	331	319	288	298
1 year or more as % of total	YBWI	*42.7*	*38.8*	*37.5*	*31.7*	*28.4*	*26.7*	*25.7*	*21.6*	*21.6*	*20.2*	*20.9*
Men												
All unemployed	MGSD	1 591	1 524	1 283	1 076	1 070	974	847	919	903	829	841
Duration of unemployment												
Less than 6 months	MGYK	563	587	533	514	550	518	454	532	546	489	494
6 months & less than 1 year	MGYM	248	249	186	162	162	139	130	154	128	142	139
1 year or more	MGYO	780	688	564	401	358	317	263	234	228	198	208
1 year or more as % of total	YBWJ	*49.0*	*45.1*	*44.0*	*37.2*	*33.4*	*32.6*	*31.1*	*25.4*	*25.3*	*23.8*	*24.8*
Women												
All unemployed	MGSE	879	820	762	707	689	663	583	614	573	598	584
Duration of unemployment												
Less than 6 months	MGYL	458	455	439	455	446	443	393	440	408	417	420
6 months & less than 1 year	MGYN	146	144	120	87	101	101	86	76	74	90	74
1 year or more	MGYP	276	222	203	165	142	120	105	98	90	91	90
1 year or more as % of total	YBWK	*31.3*	*27.1*	*26.6*	*23.3*	*20.6*	*18.0*	*18.0*	*15.9*	*15.8*	*15.2*	*15.4*

1 All aged 16 and over. See chapter text.
2 The data in this table have been adjusted to reflect the latest 2001 Census
  population data.

Source: Labour Force Survey, Office for National Statistics

7.11 Claimant count:[1] by age and duration
Computerised claims only
United Kingdom. Seasonally adjusted

Thousands

		1999	2000	2001	2002	2003	2004	2005
Annual averages								
Males								
All ages								
All durations	AGNG	946.1	826.1	733.6	708.3	693.0	630.9	635.1
Up to 6 months	AGXK	522.8	481.4	449.4	457.4	451.2	408.9	423.4
Over 6 and up to 12 months	ELNP	166.3	142.7	125.4	124.2	127.1	113.7	113.3
All over 12 months	ELON	257.1	202.0	158.8	126.7	114.7	108.3	98.3
All over 24 months	IKBS	128.9	102.4	77.5	50.7	37.6	34.6	33.1
Aged 18 to 24								
All durations	JLGC	205.2	182.3	167.9	168.1	171.9	161.8	174.6
Up to 6 months	JLGD	160.9	149.6	141.4	141.0	143.8	134.3	143.6
Over 6 and up to 12 months	JLGE	34.3	28.3	23.4	23.8	24.5	23.3	25.9
All over 12 months	JLGF	10.0	4.4	3.1	3.3	3.6	4.2	5.0
All over 24 months	JLGH	2.3	0.5	0.3	0.3	0.4	0.5	0.6
Aged 25 to 49								
All durations	AGMA	582.9	506.1	445.9	421.8	404.8	362.4	357.6
Up to 6 months	JLHG	291.3	266.8	248.2	254.9	248.0	221.3	226.0
Over 6 and up to 12 months	JLHH	107.4	92.8	83.1	80.9	82.9	72.9	70.4
All over 12 months	JLHI	184.3	146.5	114.7	86.1	73.8	68.2	61.2
All over 24 months	JLHK	88.0	70.5	52.4	29.2	17.0	14.2	14.2
Aged 50 and over								
All durations	JLHL	158.0	137.7	119.8	118.4	116.3	106.7	103.0
Up to 6 months	JLHM	70.6	65.0	59.9	61.6	59.4	53.2	53.8
Over 6 and up to 12 months	JLHN	24.6	21.6	18.9	19.6	19.7	17.5	17.0
All over 12 months	JLHO	62.8	51.1	41.0	37.3	37.2	35.9	32.1
All over 24 months	JLHQ	38.6	31.5	24.8	21.1	20.2	19.9	18.3
Females								
All ages								
All durations	JLGI	289.9	254.8	227.9	226.8	230.1	214.7	220.0
Up to 6 months	JLGK	189.6	172.5	160.4	163.6	166.3	153.1	159.3
Over 6 and up to 12 months	JLGJ	47.7	40.9	35.1	35.5	37.2	34.9	35.6
All over 12 months	JLGL	52.6	41.4	32.5	27.6	26.5	26.7	25.1
All over 24 months	JLGN	22.9	18.2	13.9	9.7	8.1	8.0	7.9
Aged 18 to 24								
All durations	JLGO	88.9	79.3	73.4	75.0	77.3	73.9	79.0
Up to 6 months	JLGP	71.2	65.7	62.1	62.9	64.9	61.4	65.3
Over 6 and up to 12 months	JLGQ	13.9	11.7	9.8	10.4	10.6	10.5	11.4
All over 12 months	JLGR	3.8	1.9	1.4	1.8	1.8	2.1	2.3
All over 24 months	JLGT	0.8	0.2	0.2	0.2	0.3	0.3	0.4
Aged 25 to 49								
All durations	JLHR	147.0	128.0	113.3	111.4	112.1	102.1	101.8
Up to 6 months	JLHS	90.3	80.8	74.4	76.7	77.3	69.0	70.4
Over 6 and up to 12 months	JLHT	24.6	21.3	18.6	18.5	19.9	18.2	17.7
All over 12 months	JLHU	32.1	25.9	20.4	16.2	14.9	14.9	13.7
All over 24 months	JLHW	13.4	10.9	8.2	4.7	3.1	2.9	3.0
Aged 50 and over								
All durations	JLHX	54.0	47.5	41.3	40.4	40.7	38.7	39.1
Up to 6 months	JLHY	28.1	26.0	23.9	24.1	24.1	22.7	23.6
Over 6 and up to 12 months	JLHZ	9.1	7.9	6.7	6.6	6.8	6.3	6.5
All over 12 months	JLIA	16.7	13.6	10.7	9.7	9.8	9.7	9.1
All over 24 months	JLIC	8.7	7.1	5.5	4.8	4.7	4.8	4.5

1 Count of claimants of unemployment-related benefits.

Source: Office for National Statistics: 020 7533 6094

7.12 Unemployment rates: by region[1,2]
At Spring each year. Not seasonally adjusted

Percentages

		1995	1996	1997	1998	1999	2000	2001	2002	2003	2004	2005
North East	MGXK	11.3	10.8	9.7	8.1	10.0	9.0	7.4	6.8	6.5	5.4	6.4
North West	YCZF	8.9	8.3	6.7	6.5	6.1	5.3	5.0	5.3	4.8	4.3	4.2
Yorkshire and Humber	MGXN	8.6	8.1	8.0	6.9	6.5	6.0	4.9	5.3	5.3	4.3	5.0
East Midlands	MGXO	7.4	7.4	6.3	4.8	5.1	5.1	4.9	4.2	4.0	4.1	4.1
West Midlands	MGXP	8.9	9.2	6.8	6.2	6.7	6.2	5.0	5.4	5.5	5.4	4.3
East	MGXQ	7.5	6.1	5.8	5.0	4.2	3.5	3.6	3.4	3.9	3.9	3.6
London	MGXR	11.6	11.3	9.2	8.2	7.5	7.1	5.8	6.6	6.7	6.5	6.8
South East	MGXS	6.4	6.0	5.2	4.3	3.6	3.3	3.0	3.9	3.7	3.7	3.6
South West	MGXT	7.8	6.3	5.2	4.4	4.7	4.1	3.5	3.5	3.6	3.2	3.2
Wales	MGXU	8.8	8.3	8.2	6.7	7.0	6.0	5.6	5.9	4.3	4.6	4.4
Scotland	MGXV	8.3	8.6	8.4	7.3	7.3	7.5	5.7	6.8	5.4	6.0	5.7
Northern Ireland	MGXW	10.9	9.4	7.4	7.2	7.1	6.9	6.2	5.4	5.2	4.7	4.6

1 All aged 16 and over. See chapter text.
2 The data in this table have been adjusted to reflect the latest 2001 Census population data.

Source: Labour Force Survey, Office for National Statistics

7.13 Claimant count rates: by region[1]
Seasonally adjusted annual averages

Percentages

		1995	1996	1997	1998	1999	2000	2001	2002	2003	2004	2005
United Kingdom	BCJE	7.6	6.9	5.3	4.5	4.1	3.6	3.2	3.1	3.0	2.7	2.7
North East	DPDM	10.8	9.7	7.9	7.0	6.9	6.2	5.6	5.0	4.5	4.0	3.9
North West	IBWC	8.1	7.3	5.7	5.0	4.6	4.1	3.7	3.5	3.2	2.8	2.9
Yorkshire and the Humber	DPBI	8.1	7.4	6.0	5.4	5.0	4.3	3.9	3.6	3.3	2.8	2.9
East Midlands	DPBJ	7.1	6.4	4.6	3.9	3.6	3.3	3.1	2.9	2.8	2.5	2.5
West Midlands	DPBN	7.7	6.8	5.2	4.5	4.5	4.0	3.7	3.5	3.5	3.3	3.4
East	DPDP	6.2	5.7	4.0	3.2	2.9	2.4	2.0	2.1	2.1	2.0	2.1
London	DPDQ	8.9	8.3	6.3	5.1	4.5	3.7	3.3	3.6	3.6	3.5	3.4
South East	DPDR	5.6	4.9	3.3	2.6	2.3	1.9	1.6	1.6	1.7	1.6	1.6
South West	DPBM	6.5	5.9	4.2	3.4	3.0	2.5	2.1	1.9	1.9	1.6	1.6
England	VASQ	7.5	6.8	5.1	4.3	3.9	3.4	3.0	2.9	2.9	2.6	2.6
Wales	DPBP	8.1	7.7	6.1	5.4	5.0	4.4	3.9	3.6	3.3	3.0	3.0
Scotland	DPBQ	7.5	7.1	6.0	5.3	5.0	4.5	3.9	3.8	3.7	3.5	3.2
Northern Ireland	DPBR	11.2	10.6	8.0	7.3	6.3	5.3	4.9	4.4	4.1	3.6	3.3
Great Britain	DPAJ	7.5	6.8	5.2	4.4	4.1	3.5	3.1	3.0	3.0	2.7	2.7

1 The number of unemployment-related benefit claimants as a percentage of the estimated total workforce (the sum of claimants, employee jobs, self-employed, participants on work-related government training programmes and HM Forces) at mid-year. Excluded are claimants under 18, consistent with current coverage. See chapter text.

Source: Office for National Statistics: 020 7533 6094

7.14 Claimant count:[1] by region
Seasonally adjusted

Thousands

	North East	North West	Yorkshire and the Humber	East Midlands	West Midlands	East	London	South East	South West	England	Wales	Scotland	Great Britain	Northern Ireland	United Kingdom
	DPDG	IBWA	DPAX	DPAY	DPBC	DPDJ	DPDK	DPDL	DPBB	IBWK	DPBE	DPBF	DPAG	DPBG	BCJD
1990 Jan	112.5	243.7	159.5	93.8	151.1	74.3	199.4	95.5	86.5	1 215.7	84.4	207.9	1 508.6	97.3	1 605.9
Apr	109.3	238.0	154.0	92.7	145.0	75.3	194.7	95.1	86.5	1 189.9	82.8	200.8	1 474.2	96.0	1 570.2
Jul	109.1	237.7	156.1	96.1	147.1	83.8	203.9	107.2	94.1	1 234.7	83.2	194.3	1 512.6	94.4	1 607.0
Oct	112.3	248.0	165.0	104.8	157.3	98.2	226.6	127.5	106.4	1 345.5	88.7	197.3	1 632.1	93.8	1 725.9
1991 Jan	116.7	261.8	176.4	113.1	171.0	112.5	255.8	149.7	122.2	1 478.8	95.0	200.9	1 775.1	96.0	1 871.1
Apr	126.2	285.9	197.5	132.0	203.5	138.5	303.2	190.5	146.9	1 723.9	108.8	212.7	2 045.7	97.9	2 143.6
Jul	130.5	305.4	211.9	145.5	225.4	158.9	342.3	221.3	165.7	1 906.8	115.5	220.1	2 242.5	98.8	2 341.3
Oct	133.2	318.2	219.6	154.5	240.0	172.4	368.9	240.9	178.6	2 025.9	119.3	224.0	2 369.6	100.5	2 470.1
1992 Jan	133.9	325.4	222.7	160.4	250.6	183.3	389.8	258.4	188.4	2 112.6	121.3	228.0	2 462.2	102.2	2 564.4
Apr	135.7	332.8	227.6	168.0	260.0	196.0	409.6	277.7	199.0	2 205.5	123.4	231.8	2 561.6	103.4	2 665.0
Jul	136.7	335.2	232.4	172.1	266.1	205.1	426.2	288.9	206.6	2 268.9	124.1	235.2	2 628.6	104.6	2 733.2
Oct	141.4	343.6	240.2	178.8	277.4	218.6	448.0	308.4	215.3	2 371.1	129.2	242.4	2 743.3	105.1	2 848.4
1993 Jan	146.2	348.3	247.5	185.2	286.2	229.5	464.6	325.2	222.6	2 454.4	131.4	245.3	2 832.0	105.5	2 937.5
Apr	148.0	345.2	246.5	183.6	285.1	228.2	469.5	321.4	220.0	2 446.6	130.3	243.2	2 821.0	104.5	2 925.5
Jul	148.5	338.0	240.9	180.8	278.7	223.5	466.3	314.0	214.4	2 404.4	129.3	241.2	2 775.6	102.5	2 878.1
Oct	147.5	331.1	237.8	177.8	271.5	216.6	460.4	306.6	208.4	2 356.8	127.8	236.6	2 722.1	101.8	2 823.9
1994 Jan	145.6	325.1	233.7	174.7	262.3	210.0	451.4	296.7	203.6	2 302.3	126.7	236.0	2 665.8	100.2	2 766.0
Apr	141.6	314.5	227.4	170.7	252.0	200.4	440.4	280.9	194.5	2 221.7	123.3	231.7	2 577.4	98.9	2 676.3
Jul	139.1	304.2	222.7	166.3	242.3	191.0	428.1	268.1	188.1	2 148.8	119.0	227.4	2 496.3	97.2	2 593.5
Oct	136.0	291.7	215.9	160.1	230.5	180.5	415.4	251.1	178.9	2 059.0	112.9	218.1	2 391.1	93.8	2 484.9
1995 Jan	133.0	280.1	210.6	153.2	218.5	172.3	401.4	237.9	171.4	1 977.5	108.3	209.3	2 296.0	91.3	2 387.3
Apr	130.0	270.8	206.8	148.1	211.0	167.1	395.0	229.7	166.0	1 923.8	106.2	200.3	2 231.0	88.6	2 319.6
Jul	128.2	266.1	204.6	145.3	206.9	165.0	390.2	225.1	162.5	1 892.8	106.7	195.3	2 195.9	87.6	2 283.5
Oct	126.4	260.9	200.7	142.3	201.3	160.7	383.2	219.1	159.4	1 852.7	105.4	193.5	2 152.9	85.8	2 238.7
1996 Jan	123.1	255.8	197.0	140.0	196.5	157.2	376.8	213.3	155.6	1 814.6	104.0	193.2	2 112.5	85.9	2 198.4
Apr	121.7	254.9	195.7	137.7	194.2	153.5	367.9	207.6	152.3	1 785.1	104.6	194.9	2 085.0	86.1	2 171.1
Jul	116.9	248.2	188.8	131.8	187.6	146.8	357.5	198.9	146.8	1 722.5	101.8	191.9	2 017.0	86.4	2 103.4
Oct	110.5	238.4	181.1	124.9	177.8	138.5	341.6	185.5	137.9	1 635.0	98.2	186.3	1 920.7	81.7	2 002.4
1997 Jan	101.0	218.5	166.4	111.8	160.1	123.5	312.6	163.3	126.0	1 483.2	90.3	173.8	1 747.3	71.1	1 818.4
Apr	95.2	201.3	154.7	102.4	147.3	110.6	284.9	144.4	112.1	1 352.9	82.5	162.2	1 597.6	65.0	1 662.6
Jul	92.4	188.9	148.2	95.0	138.0	102.5	264.3	131.0	100.7	1 261.0	78.1	153.6	1 492.7	61.4	1 554.1
Oct	90.4	177.6	142.0	87.6	131.7	94.3	246.4	120.4	93.0	1 183.4	73.6	146.5	1 403.5	60.6	1 464.1
1998 Jan	87.6	170.6	137.2	82.8	126.1	88.5	234.3	112.3	88.7	1 128.1	70.9	141.6	1 340.6	59.9	1 400.5
Apr	84.1	165.4	134.1	79.9	122.3	85.2	229.4	108.0	85.1	1 093.5	69.3	138.7	1 301.5	57.9	1 359.4
Jul	81.8	163.7	133.3	80.0	121.4	83.7	225.2	105.5	84.1	1 078.7	68.6	139.4	1 286.7	57.3	1 344.0
Oct	82.1	160.9	130.9	79.9	121.4	82.0	219.3	102.5	81.8	1 060.8	68.1	136.9	1 265.8	56.1	1 321.9
1999 Jan	82.6	159.5	129.5	79.0	122.6	80.3	214.5	101.2	81.2	1 050.4	67.8	135.6	1 253.8	55.9	1 309.7
Apr	82.5	157.2	127.0	78.2	123.1	79.1	207.8	98.8	78.4	1 032.1	67.1	133.9	1 233.1	55.0	1 288.1
Jul	80.3	153.8	122.4	75.9	120.2	76.6	202.2	94.4	74.9	1 000.7	63.8	130.2	1 194.7	50.0	1 244.7
Oct	76.7	150.0	118.3	73.6	115.9	73.6	196.5	91.1	71.4	967.1	61.0	126.1	1 154.2	46.5	1 200.7
2000 Jan	75.7	145.7	114.6	73.2	112.1	70.3	189.4	87.2	68.0	936.2	59.3	123.2	1 118.7	44.2	1 162.9
Apr	73.6	139.9	108.9	70.0	108.1	66.9	181.6	81.3	63.8	894.1	57.8	119.0	1 070.9	42.4	1 113.3
Jul	72.0	135.4	104.9	68.7	107.2	62.5	172.0	77.5	61.1	861.3	57.1	115.1	1 033.5	41.2	1 074.7
Oct	69.5	131.0	102.5	67.7	106.5	60.7	165.0	74.3	58.1	835.3	56.4	111.7	1 003.4	41.3	1 044.7
2001 Jan	66.2	127.4	99.9	66.6	104.0	57.2	158.2	69.7	54.9	804.1	54.9	108.8	967.8	40.8	1 008.6
Apr	63.2	124.9	97.6	65.1	100.8	54.8	151.8	66.1	53.6	777.9	52.4	105.3	935.6	39.9	975.5
Jul	61.4	121.5	95.1	63.0	97.4	53.7	151.0	65.1	52.1	760.3	49.8	102.4	912.5	39.3	951.8
Oct	61.5	121.4	93.2	61.6	95.7	54.3	156.3	65.9	51.1	761.0	49.2	104.2	914.4	38.6	953.0
2002 Jan	60.9	121.3	91.4	60.6	95.4	55.4	163.1	68.6	51.1	767.8	48.1	104.3	920.2	38.0	958.2
Apr	59.2	119.4	89.4	59.4	93.6	56.4	166.2	71.0	50.9	765.5	47.5	104.4	917.4	37.5	954.9
Jul	58.5	118.1	89.1	58.6	93.4	57.5	167.3	72.3	50.1	764.9	46.8	101.9	913.6	36.4	950.0
Oct	55.9	116.1	87.6	57.9	93.7	57.2	167.6	72.3	49.3	757.6	46.7	100.1	904.4	35.1	939.5
2003 Jan	54.8	115.9	87.0	58.0	94.3	57.4	168.6	72.9	48.9	757.8	46.3	100.2	904.3	35.0	939.3
Apr	53.5	112.7	84.1	58.8	94.7	55.8	171.3	75.6	48.6	757.8	45.2	99.1	902.1	34.0	936.1
Jul	52.6	112.5	84.2	59.9	94.9	58.7	171.7	76.4	49.1	760.0	45.0	100.6	905.6	34.6	940.2
Oct	51.1	108.7	81.6	58.8	94.2	57.3	170.2	76.0	47.4	745.3	43.1	98.9	887.3	34.7	922.0
2004 Jan	49.6	104.2	78.1	56.1	92.9	56.6	167.8	74.8	45.0	725.1	41.9	96.7	863.7	33.5	897.2
Apr	47.4	101.3	75.4	53.9	90.0	56.2	165.0	71.9	42.9	704.0	41.7	94.4	840.1	31.8	871.9
Jul	45.4	96.7	71.7	51.1	86.8	54.4	162.2	68.8	40.5	677.6	39.5	90.2	807.3	29.8	837.1
Oct	45.4	97.0	71.4	51.1	85.9	55.1	159.3	69.6	40.7	675.5	39.2	89.8	804.5	29.7	834.2
2005 Jan	43.4	94.0	69.6	50.6	85.3	55.0	158.6	68.0	40.5	665.0	38.7	86.8	790.5	29.1	819.6
Apr	44.9	97.7	73.0	52.0	88.0	56.4	161.5	69.5	41.5	684.5	39.8	86.1	810.4	28.8	839.2
Jul	46.3	102.0	76.3	54.4	96.6	58.6	162.5	72.0	42.7	711.4	41.6	84.9	837.9	28.2	866.1
Oct	47.6	106.5	80.1	56.7	99.4	60.3	166.4	74.1	43.1	734.2	43.0	85.8	863.0	28.2	891.2

1 The figures are based on the number of claimants receiving unemployment related benefits and are adjusted for seasonality and discontinuities to be consistent with current coverage. See chapter text.

The latest national and regional seasonally adjusted claimant count figures are provisional and subject to revision in the following month.

Source: Office for National Statistics: 020 7533 6094

7.15 Economic activity: by sex and age[1]
United Kingdom
At Spring each year. Seasonally adjusted

Thousands and percentages

	All aged 16 and over	16-59/64	16-17	18-24	16-24	25-34	35-49	50-64 (m) 50-59 (w)	65+ (m) 60+ (w)
Thousands									
All									
	MGSF	YBSK	YBZL	YBZO	PXMK	YBZR	YBZU	YBZX	YCAD
1997	28 492	27 666	864	3 721	4 585	7 513	10 093	5 475	826
1998	28 497	27 700	854	3 636	4 490	7 437	10 107	5 666	796
1999	28 811	27 974	844	3 629	4 473	7 366	10 283	5 852	837
2000	29 071	28 223	846	3 668	4 514	7 259	10 455	5 995	848
2001	29 122	28 288	817	3 667	4 484	7 078	10 602	6 124	834
2002	29 399	28 494	816	3 778	4 594	6 904	10 775	6 222	905
2003	29 643	28 697	837	3 792	4 629	6 701	10 928	6 440	945
Men									
	MGSG	YBSL	YBZM	YBZP	PXML	YBZS	YBZV	YBZY	YCAE
1997	15 687	15 408	429	2 000	2 429	4 172	5 453	3 354	279
1998	15 647	15 365	429	1 939	2 368	4 122	5 438	3 436	282
1999	15 774	15 480	433	1 929	2 362	4 042	5 533	3 544	295
2000	15 882	15 590	428	1 954	2 382	3 988	5 621	3 599	292
2001	15 867	15 596	420	1 949	2 369	3 890	5 665	3 673	271
2002	15 971	15 673	413	2 015	2 428	3 785	5 764	3 697	298
2003	16 162	15 819	423	2 027	2 450	3 684	5 853	3 832	343
Women									
	MGSH	YBSM	YBZN	YBZQ	PXMM	YBZT	YBZW	YBZZ	YCAF
1997	12 805	12 258	436	1 721	2 157	3 341	4 640	2 121	547
1998	12 850	12 336	425	1 697	2 122	3 315	4 670	2 230	514
1999	13 037	12 494	411	1 700	2 111	3 324	4 751	2 309	543
2000	13 189	12 633	418	1 714	2 132	3 271	4 834	2 396	557
2001	13 255	12 692	397	1 718	2 115	3 189	4 936	2 452	563
2002	13 428	12 821	404	1 763	2 167	3 118	5 011	2 525	607
2003	13 481	12 879	414	1 764	2 178	3 018	5 075	2 608	602
Rates[2]									
All									
	MGWG	MGSO	YCAG	YCAJ	PXMN	YCAM	YCAP	MGWP	MGWS
1997	62.6	78.4	59.4	76.5	72.6	83.5	84.4	68.5	8.1
1998	62.4	78.3	58.9	75.6	71.6	83.6	84.2	68.7	7.8
1999	62.8	78.7	58.8	75.4	71.6	84.2	84.8	69.3	8.1
2000	63.1	78.9	59.0	76.0	72.0	84.4	85.0	69.7	8.2
2001	62.7	78.5	55.6	75.1	70.5	83.9	84.9	70.0	8.0
2002	62.9	78.6	54.2	76.0	70.8	83.9	85.0	70.3	8.6
2003	63.1	78.7	54.9	74.4	69.8	83.4	84.9	72.1	9.0
Men									
	MGWH	MGSP	YCAH	YCAK	PXMO	YCAN	YCAQ	MGWQ	MGWT
1997	71.7	84.7	58.0	82.4	76.7	93.6	92.0	72.2	7.6
1998	71.2	84.2	58.3	80.9	75.4	93.7	91.5	71.9	7.6
1999	71.5	84.4	59.3	80.5	75.6	93.4	92.2	72.5	7.9
2000	71.5	84.6	58.6	81.2	76.0	93.8	92.4	72.4	7.7
2001	70.9	84.0	55.9	80.1	74.3	93.2	91.8	72.9	7.1
2002	70.8	83.9	53.5	81.0	74.5	92.9	91.9	72.7	7.7
2003	71.1	84.1	54.1	79.3	73.3	92.5	92.0	74.7	8.8
Women									
	MGWI	MGSQ	YCAI	YCAL	PXMP	YCAO	YCAR	MGWR	MGWU
1997	54.2	71.8	60.8	70.7	68.5	73.5	76.9	63.3	8.4
1998	54.2	72.0	59.6	70.4	67.9	73.7	77.1	64.3	7.8
1999	54.8	72.5	58.3	70.4	67.7	75.1	77.6	64.9	8.3
2000	55.2	72.9	59.5	70.8	68.2	75.2	77.8	65.9	8.5
2001	55.1	72.7	55.3	70.1	66.8	74.8	78.2	66.1	8.5
2002	55.6	73.0	55.0	70.9	67.2	75.0	78.1	67.0	9.2
2003	55.5	73.0	55.7	69.4	66.4	74.4	78.0	68.7	9.1

1 See chapter text. The data in this table have been adjusted to reflect the latest 2001 Census population data.
2 Total economically active as a percentage of all persons in the relevant age group.

Source: Labour Force Survey, Office for National Statistics

7.16 Economically inactive: by sex and age[1]
United Kingdom
At Spring each year. Seasonally adjusted

Thousands and percentages

	All aged 16 and over	16-59/64	16-17	18-24	16-24	25-34	35-49	50-64 (m) 50-59 (w)	65+ (m) 60+ (w)
Thousands									
All									
	MGSI	YBSN	YCAS	YCAV	PXMQ	YCAY	YCBB	MGWA	MGWD
1997	17 004	7 608	591	1 140	1 731	1 488	1 866	2 523	9 396
1998	17 164	7 697	595	1 171	1 766	1 457	1 891	2 583	9 468
1999	17 051	7 589	591	1 181	1 772	1 384	1 840	2 593	9 462
2000	17 035	7 542	587	1 159	1 746	1 340	1 843	2 612	9 493
2001	17 292	7 729	653	1 217	1 870	1 356	1 883	2 619	9 563
2002	17 305	7 749	689	1 195	1 884	1 325	1 908	2 631	9 555
2003	17 353	7 752	687	1 306	1 993	1 336	1 936	2 487	9 601
Men									
	MGSJ	YBSO	YCAT	YCAW	PXMR	YCAZ	YCBC	MGWB	MGWE
1997	6 189	2 790	310	428	738	283	475	1 294	3 399
1998	6 314	2 889	307	458	765	277	504	1 342	3 426
1999	6 297	2 858	297	468	765	283	467	1 342	3 439
2000	6 320	2 847	302	451	753	262	460	1 371	3 473
2001	6 510	2 970	332	486	818	284	507	1 362	3 540
2002	6 579	3 015	359	471	830	288	507	1 389	3 564
2003	6 561	2 990	357	530	887	298	506	1 298	3 571
Women									
	MGSK	YBSP	YCAU	YCAX	PXMS	YCBA	YCBD	MGWC	MGWF
1997	10 815	4 818	281	712	993	1 205	1 391	1 229	5 998
1998	10 850	4 808	288	712	1 000	1 180	1 387	1 240	6 042
1999	10 754	4 731	294	713	1 007	1 100	1 373	1 251	6 023
2000	10 716	4 695	285	708	993	1 078	1 383	1 241	6 020
2001	10 781	4 758	321	731	1 052	1 073	1 376	1 257	6 023
2002	10 726	4 734	330	724	1 054	1 037	1 401	1 242	5 992
2003	10 792	4 762	330	776	1 106	1 038	1 430	1 189	6 029
Rates[2]									
All									
	YBTC	YBTL	LWEX	LWFA	PXNF	LWFD	LWFG	LWFJ	LWFM
1997	37.4	21.6	40.6	23.5	27.4	16.5	15.6	31.5	91.9
1998	37.6	21.7	41.1	24.4	28.4	16.4	15.8	31.3	92.2
1999	37.2	21.3	41.2	24.6	28.4	15.8	15.2	30.7	91.9
2000	36.9	21.1	41.0	24.0	28.0	15.6	15.0	30.3	91.8
2001	37.3	21.5	44.4	24.9	29.5	16.1	15.1	30.0	92.0
2002	37.1	21.4	45.8	24.0	29.2	16.1	15.0	29.7	91.4
2003	36.9	21.3	45.1	25.6	30.2	16.6	15.1	27.9	91.0
Men									
	YBTD	YBTM	LWEY	LWFB	PXNG	LWFE	LWFH	LWFK	LWFN
1997	28.3	15.3	42.0	17.6	23.3	6.4	8.0	27.8	92.4
1998	28.8	15.8	41.7	19.1	24.6	6.3	8.5	28.1	92.4
1999	28.5	15.6	40.7	19.5	24.4	6.6	7.8	27.5	92.1
2000	28.5	15.4	41.4	18.8	24.0	6.2	7.6	27.6	92.3
2001	29.1	16.0	44.1	19.9	25.7	6.8	8.2	27.1	92.9
2002	29.2	16.1	46.5	19.0	25.5	7.1	8.1	27.3	92.3
2003	28.9	15.9	45.8	20.7	26.7	7.5	8.0	25.3	91.2
Women									
	YBTE	YBTN	LWEZ	LWFC	PXNH	LWFF	LWFI	LWFL	LWFO
1997	45.8	28.2	39.2	29.3	31.5	26.5	23.1	36.7	91.6
1998	45.8	28.0	40.4	29.6	32.1	26.3	22.9	35.7	92.2
1999	45.2	27.5	41.7	29.6	32.3	24.9	22.4	35.1	91.7
2000	44.8	27.1	40.5	29.2	31.8	24.8	22.2	34.1	91.5
2001	44.9	27.3	44.7	29.9	33.2	25.2	21.8	33.9	91.5
2002	44.4	27.0	45.0	29.1	32.8	25.0	21.9	33.0	90.8
2003	44.5	27.0	44.3	30.6	33.6	25.6	22.0	31.3	90.9

1 See chapter text. The data in this table have been adjusted to reflect the latest 2001 Census population data.   2 Total economically inactive as a percentage of all persons in the relevant age group.

Source: Labour Force Survey, Office for National Statistics

7.17 Economically inactive:[1] by reason and sex
United Kingdom
At Spring each year. Seasonally adjusted

Thousands and percentages

	Economic inactivity by reason:							by:		All economically inactive
	Student	Looking after family/home	Temporary sick	Long-term sick	Discouraged workers[2]	Retired	Other	Does not want a job	Wants a job	

Thousands

All
	BEDZ	BEEC	BEBK	BEBN	YCFO	BEEI	BEEL	YBVZ	YBWC	YBSN
1998	1 417	2 568	205	2 201	72	506	728	5 323	2 374	7 697
1999	1 452	2 444	178	2 179	68	524	745	5 285	2 305	7 589
2000	1 406	2 376	184	2 157	63	545	812	5 233	2 309	7 542
2001	1 518	2 391	189	2 207	35	589	800	5 529	2 200	7 729
2002	1 546	2 370	177	2 229	34	591	803	5 488	2 261	7 749
2003	1 646	2 390	193	2 118	35	570	801	5 616	2 136	7 752
2004	1 687	2 333	196	2 160	32	598	841	5 827	2 021	7 848
2005	1 777	2 326	185	2 166	36	606	838	5 864	2 070	7 934

Men
	BEEX	BEAQ	BEDI	BEDL	YCFP	BEDR	BEDU	YBWA	YBWD	YBSO
1998	702	177	94	1 259	44	344	269	1 928	961	2 889
1999	706	171	76	1 235	40	353	277	1 936	922	2 858
2000	681	163	87	1 205	34	377	300	1 923	924	2 847
2001	733	176	90	1 237	23	396	315	2 061	909	2 970
2002	744	182	89	1 246	21	397	337	2 067	949	3 015
2003	813	179	89	1 169	20	392	328	2 093	896	2 990
2004	848	192	95	1 178	21	414	347	2 241	855	3 096
2005	881	190	94	1 210	21	417	366	2 330	849	3 179

Women
	BEBL	BEBO	BEEG	BEEJ	YCFQ	BEEP	BEES	YBWB	YBWE	YBSP
1998	715	2 391	111	943	28	162	458	3 395	1 413	.4 808
1999	746	2 273	102	944	28	171	468	3 348	1 383	4 731
2000	725	2 213	97	952	29	168	512	3 310	1 385	4 695
2001	786	2 215	99	970	11	193	484	3 468	1 290	4 758
2002	801	2 188	88	984	14	193	466	3 421	1 313	4 734
2003	833	2 211	104	949	15	177	472	3 523	1 239	4 762
2004	840	2 141	100	982	11	184	494	3 586	1 166	4 752
2005	896	2 136	91	956	15	189	472	3 533	1 222	4 755

Percentages

All
	BEDJ	BEDM	BEDP	BEDS	BEDV	BEDY	BEEB	BEEE	BEBM	BEAR
1998	18.4	33.4	2.7	28.6	0.9	6.6	9.5	69.2	30.8	100.0
1999	19.1	32.2	2.3	28.7	0.9	6.9	9.8	69.6	30.4	100.0
2000	18.6	31.5	2.4	28.6	0.8	7.2	10.8	69.4	30.6	100.0
2001	19.6	30.9	2.5	28.6	0.4	7.6	10.3	71.5	28.5	100.0
2002	19.9	30.6	2.3	28.8	0.4	7.6	10.4	70.8	29.2	100.0
2003	21.2	30.8	2.5	27.3	0.5	7.3	10.3	72.5	27.5	100.0
2004	21.5	29.7	2.5	27.5	0.4	7.6	10.7	74.2	25.8	100.0
2005	22.4	29.3	2.3	27.3	0.5	7.6	10.6	73.9	26.1	100.0

Men
	BEEH	BEEK	BEEN	BEEQ	BEET	BEEW	BEEZ	BEAS	BEGT	BEBP
1998	24.3	6.1	3.3	43.6	1.5	11.9	9.3	66.7	33.3	100.0
1999	24.7	6.0	2.6	43.2	1.4	12.3	9.7	67.7	32.3	100.0
2000	23.9	5.7	3.0	42.3	1.2	13.3	10.5	67.6	32.4	100.0
2001	24.7	5.9	3.0	41.6	0.8	13.3	10.6	69.4	30.6	100.0
2002	24.7	6.0	2.9	41.3	0.7	13.2	11.2	68.5	31.5	100.0
2003	27.2	6.0	3.0	39.1	0.7	13.1	11.0	70.0	30.0	100.0
2004	27.4	6.2	3.1	38.1	0.7	13.4	11.2	72.4	27.6	100.0
2005	27.7	6.0	3.0	38.0	0.7	13.1	11.5	73.3	26.7	100.0

Women
	BEGZ	BEHC	BEHF	BEHI	BEHL	BEHO	BEBQ	BEHR	BEHU	BEGW
1998	14.9	49.7	2.3	19.6	0.6	3.4	9.5	70.6	29.4	100.0
1999	15.8	48.0	2.2	19.9	0.6	3.6	9.9	70.8	29.2	100.0
2000	15.4	47.1	2.1	20.3	0.6	3.6	10.9	70.5	29.5	100.0
2001	16.5	46.5	2.1	20.4	0.2	4.1	10.2	72.9	27.1	100.0
2002	16.9	46.2	1.9	20.8	0.3	4.1	9.8	72.3	27.7	100.0
2003	17.5	46.4	2.2	19.9	0.3	3.7	9.9	74.0	26.0	100.0
2004	17.7	45.1	2.1	20.7	0.2	3.9	10.4	75.5	24.5	100.0
2005	18.9	44.9	1.9	20.1	0.3	4.0	9.9	74.3	25.7	100.0

1 All persons aged 16 - 59/64. See chapter text.
2 People whose reason for not seeking work was that they believed no jobs were available.

Source: Labour Force Survey, Office for National Statistics

7.18 Labour disputes: by industry[1]
United Kingdom
Standard Industrial Classification 1992

Thousands and numbers

		1998	1999	2000	2001	2002	2003	2004
Working days lost through all stoppages in progress (thousands)	KBBZ	282	242	499	525	1 323	499	905
Analysis by industry								
Mining, quarrying, electricity, gas and water	DMME	–	–	3	25	–	–	5
Manufacturing	BBFX	34	57	52	43	21	63	31
Construction	DMMG	13	49	49	10	17	14	–
Transport, storage and communication	BBFY	139	50	97	107	96	126	44
Public administration and defence	BBFZ	28	35	50	216	488	138	437
Education	BBGA	6	25	50	43	376	131	379
Health and social work	BBGB	16	5	122	73	148	15	4
Other community, social and personal services	DMML	30	7	36	4	107	10	4
All other industries and services	DMMM	15	12	40	4	70	2	2
Analysis by number of working days lost in each stoppage								
Under 250 days	KBFC	8	11	12	9	7	6	7
250 and under 500 days	KBFJ	11	13	9	11	8	6	5
500 and under 1,000 days	KBFL	11	16	21	15	15	13	12
1,000 and under 5,000 days	KBFY	48	69	71	59	47	69	51
5,000 and under 25,000 days	KBFZ	118	133	85	140	104	46	59
25,000 and under 50,000 days	KBGS	–	–	–	72	122	112	–
50,000 days and over	KBGT	86	–	301	220	1 021	248	770
Working days lost per 1 000 employees all industries and services	KBHA	11	10	20	20	51	19	34
Workers directly and indirectly involved (thousands)	KBHB	93	141	183	180	943	151	293
Analysis by industry								
Mining, quarrying, electricity, gas and water	DMMN	1	–	1	3	–	–	1
Manufacturing	DMMO	14	31	28	17	10	18	14
Construction	DMMP	2	18	16	3	17	2	–
Transport, storage and communications	DMMQ	39	42	39	69	33	52	12
Public administration and defence	DMMR	4	17	29	46	171	56	207
Education	DMMS	4	28	17	34	388	15	55
Health and social work	DMMT	2	–	28	6	144	3	1
Other community, social and personal services	DMMU	22	2	13	1	103	3	3
All other industries and services	DMMV	4	2	12	1	76	1	1
Analysis by duration of stoppage								
Not more than 5 days	KBHM	57	129	82	98	828	78	222
Over 5 but not more than 10 days	KBHN	32	8	9	43	57	23	47
Over 10 but not more than 20 days	KBJQ	1	3	8	4	3	31	1
Over 20 but not more than 30 days	KBJR	–	–	–	–	1	–	3
Over 30 but not more than 50 days	KBJS	1	–	83	6	1	–	–
Over 50 days	KBJT	1	–	1	30	55	20	20
Numbers of stoppages in progress: total	KBLG	166	205	212	194	146	133	130
Analysis by industry								
Mining, quarrying, electricity, gas and water	DMMW	1	–	3	3	2	1	3
Manufacturing	DMMX	36	37	38	32	33	43	30
Construction	DMMY	13	20	16	9	3	4	1
Transport, storage and communications	DMMZ	57	91	116	94	51	45	46
Public administration and defence	DMNA	10	17	7	22	20	12	19
Education	DMNB	19	21	18	16	16	15	16
Health and social work	DMNC	6	4	10	12	14	7	4
Other community, social and personal services	DMND	17	8	13	10	11	9	12
All other industries and services	DMNE	7	8	5	9	12	4	4
Analysis of number of stoppages by duration								
Not more than 5 days	KBNH	130	179	187	162	118	113	111
Over 5 but not more than 10 days	KBNI	21	8	14	15	16	10	10
Over 10 but not more than 20 days	KBNJ	3	9	5	7	3	5	4
Over 20 but not more than 30 days	KBNK	4	4	1	1	3	1	2
Over 30 but not more than 50 days	KBNL	3	3	3	4	1	1	1
Over 50 days	KBNM	5	2	2	5	5	3	2

1 See chapter text.

Source: Labour Market Statistics, Office for National Statistics: 01633 819205

7.19 Average earnings and hours of full-time employees by industry division:[1] by sex
United Kingdom
At April. Standard Industrial Classification 1992

	Agriculture, Hunting and Forestry	Fishing	Mining and Quarrying	Manufacturing	Electricity, Gas and Water Supply	Construction	Wholesale and Retail Trade; repair of motor vehicles, cycles, personal and household goods
All employees							
Weekly earnings							
	C9EG	C9EI	C9EK	C9EM	C9EO	C9EP	C9EQ
2001	302.6	397.7	581.1	439.9	532.1	445.6	386.8
2002	336.1	350.7	591.7	455.6	543.0	466.4	403.6
2003	340.5	392.7	657.0	476.5	561.5	489.8	414.6
2004[2]	356.1	415.4	617.6	485.2	579.5	505.5	421.7
	362.5	419.0	633.5	493.1	591.9	509.4	433.3
2005	368.0	426.9	626.1	504.3	610.2	527.4	429.1
Total hours worked							
	C5TJ	C5TK	C5TL	C5TV	C5TW	C5TX	C5U3
2001	43.7	45.4	44.0	41.3	39.9	44.1	40.5
2002	44.7	43.4	43.2	41.0	39.9	43.4	40.5
2003	44.9	42.9	45.3	40.9	39.6	43.4	40.4
2004[2]	44.5	43.8	43.2	41.0	40.0	43.2	40.4
		43.5	43.4			43.1	
2005	44.1	43.6	43.8	40.6	39.3	43.0	40.2
Hourly earnings excluding overtime							
	C9HV	C9HX	C9HZ	C9I3	C9I5	C9I7	C9IA
2001	6.82	8.39	13.62	10.62	13.19	10.04	9.55
2002	7.42	7.93	14.01	11.09	13.41	10.73	9.97
2003	7.44	9.09	14.99	11.62	13.99	11.22	10.26
2004[2]	7.87	9.40	14.61	11.81	14.30	11.69	10.44
	8.03	9.57	14.97	12.01	14.61	11.81	10.74
2005	8.28	9.71	14.65	12.40	15.30	12.21	10.69
Males employees							
Weekly earnings							
	C9FZ	C9F4	C9F6	C9F8	C9FA	C9FC	C9FE
2001	312.4	..	601.4	469.5	568.9	456.4	431.7
2002	350.5	353.4	608.8	482.9	584.7	478.5	453.7
2003	356.2	391.4	671.2	503.2	595.7	503.8	464.4
2004[2]	369.1	426.0	637.5	511.6	607.9	518.2	470.2
	375.4	433.2	653.7	519.4	626.1	521.5	483.2
2005	384.3	441.8	644.6	530.5	644.9	540.5	474.0
Total hours worked							
	C5W8	C5WE	C5WH	C5WK	C5WN	C5WQ	C5WT
2001	44.6	..	44.8	41.9	40.4	44.7	41.5
2002	45.8	44.1	44.1	41.6	40.6	44.0	41.5
2003	46.1	43.4	46.5	41.5	40.1	44.0	41.5
2004[2]	45.6	45.5	44.2	41.6	40.5	43.8	41.4
		45.4	44.4			43.7	
2005	44.8	44.1	44.7	41.2	39.8	43.6	41.2
Hourly earnings excluding overtime							
	C9IS	C9IU	C9IW	C9IY	C9J2	C9J4	C9J6
2001	6.90	..	13.91	11.19	13.94	10.15	10.44
2002	7.56	7.84	14.19	11.62	14.22	10.87	10.97
2003	7.57	8.95	14.97	12.12	14.70	11.39	11.21
2004[2]	7.97	9.24	14.81	12.29	14.82	11.84	11.38
	8.11	9.47	15.16	12.49	15.29	11.95	11.71
2005	8.50	9.91	14.83	12.89	15.92	12.35	11.54
Female employees							
Weekly earnings							
	C9G6	C9G8	C9GA	C9GC	C9GE	C9GG	C9GI
2001	253.5	..	437.6	332.2	410.9	343.9	297.2
2002	272.3	..	478.6	350.8	405.1	356.9	310.1
2003	270.8	..	566.5	372.8	426.0	370.8	321.6
2004[2]	291.1	..	497.1	380.4	466.1	392.9	331.2
	297.5	..	511.0	388.1	453.0	403.8	339.3
2005	297.7	..	516.0	399.2	491.4	411.8	345.8
Total hours worked							
	C7NN	C7NP	C7NR	C7NT	C7NV	C7OA	C7OC
2001	39.5	..	38.6	39.0	38.1	38.4	38.6
2002	39.8	40.0	37.8	38.8	37.7	38.2	38.7
2003	39.6	39.8	37.6	38.7	37.9	38.3	38.3
2004[2]	39.2	36.5	37.2	38.7	38.1	38.2	38.5
			37.3			38.3	
2005	40.8	42.1	38.1	38.4	37.3	38.0	38.4
Hourly earnings excluding overtime							
	C9JO	C9JQ	C9JS	C9JU	C9JW	C9JY	C9K2
2001	6.39	..	11.42	8.50	10.73	8.94	7.70
2002	6.80	..	12.76	9.03	10.69	9.33	8.02
2003	6.81	..	15.17	9.62	11.17	9.69	8.38
2004[2]	7.39	..	13.33	9.82	12.20	10.26	8.60
	7.55	..	13.73	10.02	11.83	10.55	8.82
2005	7.27	..	13.54	10.38	13.17	10.83	9.02

7.19 continued

Average earnings and hours of full-time employees by industry division:[1] by sex
United Kingdom
At April. Standard Industrial Classification 1992

	Hotels and restaurants	Transport, Storage and Communication	Financial Inter-mediation	Real Estate, Renting and Business	Public Administration and Defence; compulsory social security	Educa-tion	Health and Social work	Other community, social and personal service activities
All employees								
Weekly earnings								
	C9ER	C9ES	C9ET	C9EU	C9EV	C9EW	C9EX	C9EY
2001	283.1	443.0	628.8	533.1	437.9	438.8	407.7	424.0
2002	295.9	462.3	671.0	564.4	456.7	459.6	427.7	468.4
2003	311.3	476.3	660.6	568.5	469.9	481.6	446.8	486.8
2004[2]	319.4	494.8	669.4	574.6	498.5	495.4	478.7	500.7
	323.8	504.3	696.3	590.6	496.6	493.6	474.9	515.4
2005	324.8	507.0	692.7	592.8	524.3	518.2	505.2	518.2
Total hours worked								
	C5U4	C5U5	C5U6	C5U7	C5U8	C5V5	C5V8	C5VU
2001	40.6	43.0	36.4	39.4	38.3	35.3	38.6	40.0
2002	40.7	42.7	36.3	39.3	38.5	35.5	38.5	39.6
2003	40.7	43.0	36.1	39.3	39.1	35.6	38.5	39.4
2004[2]	41.2	42.6	36.3	39.3	39.2	35.6	38.6	39.8
	41.1							
2005	41.1	42.9	35.9	39.0	39.1	35.6	38.7	40.0
Hourly earnings excluding overtime								
	C9IC	C9IE	C9IG	C9II	C9IK	C9IM	C9IO	C9IQ
2001	6.96	10.42	17.33	13.59	11.33	12.46	10.54	10.64
2002	7.27	10.93	18.56	14.45	11.77	12.98	11.07	11.89
2003	7.63	11.20	18.32	14.54	11.88	13.55	11.57	12.38
2004[2]	7.74	11.74	18.50	14.69	12.63	13.95	12.39	12.63
	7.86	11.99	19.25	15.10	12.57	13.90	12.29	13.02
2005	7.92	11.88	19.31	15.26	13.29	14.62	13.06	13.03
Males employees								
Weekly earnings								
	C9FO	C9FQ	C9FS	C9FU	C9FW	C9FY	C9G2	C9G4
2001	320.8	463.9	794.1	601.0	488.4	480.8	532.8	482.4
2002	332.9	480.4	855.9	635.3	506.0	504.3	549.9	536.3
2003	351.9	493.5	832.1	636.7	522.5	528.8	581.1	562.2
2004[2]	346.0	514.5	831.7	636.0	550.0	540.9	622.5	574.6
	352.5	522.0	869.2	652.5	547.9	539.3	614.8	593.1
2005	357.6	526.3	860.3	659.5	583.6	569.9	674.0	588.7
Total hours worked								
	C5WW	C5WZ	C7MU	C7MW	C7NF	C7NH	C7NJ	C7NL
2001	41.6	44.1	36.5	40.3	38.9	36.4	39.9	41.1
2002	41.7	43.7	36.4	40.2	39.1	36.6	39.8	40.7
2003	41.8	44.0	36.3	40.1	40.0	36.7	39.4	40.4
2004[2]	42.1	43.5	36.4	40.2	40.1	36.6	39.5	40.9
	42.2				40.0			
2005	41.9	43.8	36.2	39.9	40.1	36.6	39.6	41.1
Hourly earnings excluding overtime								
	C9J8	C9JA	C9JC	C9JE	C9JG	C9JI	C9JK	C9JM
2001	7.70	10.69	21.89	15.04	12.47	13.25	13.35	11.80
2002	8.00	11.12	23.66	15.97	12.86	13.87	13.83	13.30
2003	8.40	11.37	23.01	15.99	12.91	14.48	14.73	14.00
2004[2]	8.22	11.99	22.94	15.96	13.63	14.84	15.77	14.19
	8.38	12.20	23.99	16.39	13.56	14.79	15.57	14.68
2005	8.55	12.09	23.86	16.66	14.44	15.68	17.03	14.47
Female employees								
Weekly earnings								
	C9GK	C9GM	C9HJ	C9HL	C9HN	C9HP	C9HR	C9HT
2001	238.5	372.9	440.5	414.6	357.7	407.1	359.9	343.1
2002	249.8	402.9	463.7	436.3	377.6	425.7	380.1	375.7
2003	262.2	410.0	463.7	446.4	390.9	445.9	394.0	379.1
2004[2]	284.1	422.9	473.9	461.3	420.6	462.1	419.6	397.9
	287.2	439.0	492.5	474.5	418.9	460.2	417.9	405.7
2005	284.7	434.3	499.2	476.1	441.2	482.5	441.8	417.7
Total hours worked								
	C7OE	C7OG	C7OI	C7OK	C7OM	C7OO	C7OQ	C7OS
2001	39.4	39.2	36.3	37.8	37.4	34.4	38.1	38.3
2002	39.5	39.2	36.2	37.8	37.6	34.7	38.1	38.2
2003	39.4	39.1	35.9	37.7	37.8	34.8	38.1	38.0
2004[2]	39.9	39.3	36.2	37.7	37.9	34.9	38.2	38.2
	40.0	39.4	36.1					38.3
2005	40.0	39.4	35.7	37.5	37.8	34.9	38.4	38.4
Hourly earnings excluding overtime								
	C9K4	C9K6	C9K8	C9KG	C9KI	C9KK	C9KS	C9KU
2001	6.04	9.51	12.09	10.96	9.50	11.84	9.44	8.95
2002	6.31	10.28	12.80	11.57	9.99	12.28	9.98	9.87
2003	6.64	10.51	12.88	11.83	10.28	12.83	10.30	9.98
2004[2]	7.07	10.79	13.10	12.23	11.07	13.27	10.97	10.38
	7.16	11.22	13.62	12.58	11.01	13.22	10.93	10.60
2005	7.12	11.02	13.98	12.70	11.62	13.87	11.54	10.90

1 See chapter text. Employees on adult rates whose pay for the survey pay-period was not affected by absence.

2 For 2004, two sets of figures are shown. The first does not include supplementary information and therefore is comparable with earlier years. The second includes supplementary information and so is discontinuous with previous years (where the two figures are equal, only one appears).

Sources: Annual Survey of Hours and Earnings;
Office for National Statistics: 01633 819024

7.20 Average earnings and hours of full-time employees:[1] by sex
United Kingdom
At April

£ and numbers

	All Industries				Manufacturing industries			
	Average weekly earnings	Total hours worked (numbers)	Average hourly earnings		Average weekly earnings	Total hours worked (numbers)	Average hourly earnings	
			including overtime	excluding overtime			including overtime	excluding overtime
All employees								
	C7Q5	C7QX	C7Q7	C7Q9	C7PU	C7QL	C7PV	C7PW
2000	425.2	39.7	10.71	10.71	417.2	41.3	10.10	10.00
2001	449.8	39.7	11.33	11.36	439.9	41.3	10.66	10.62
2002	472.2	39.6	11.94	11.98	455.6	41.0	11.12	11.09
2003	487.1	39.5	12.32	12.34	476.5	40.9	11.65	11.62
2004[2]	498.6	39.5	12.61	12.64	485.2	41.0	11.83	11.81
	506.1		12.80	12.85	493.1		12.03	12.01
2005	517.1	39.4	13.13	13.17	504.3	40.6	12.41	12.40
Male employees								
	C7QA	C7QZ	C7QC	C7QE	C7PX	C7QT	C7PY	C7PZ
2000	471.8	41.0	11.50	11.53	445.6	42.0	10.62	10.54
2001	498.6	41.0	12.16	12.24	469.5	41.9	11.21	11.19
2002	523.4	40.8	12.83	12.92	482.9	41.6	11.62	11.62
2003	539.3	40.8	13.21	13.28	503.2	41.5	12.13	12.12
2004[2]	548.5	40.8	13.45	13.52	511.6	41.6	12.31	12.29
	557.4		13.67	13.76	519.4		12.50	12.49
2005	569.0	40.6	14.01	14.08	530.5	41.2	12.88	12.89
Female employees								
	C7QF	C7SA	C7QH	C7QJ	C7Q2	C7QV	C7Q3	C7Q4
2000	344.9	37.4	9.22	9.20	312.1	38.9	8.02	7.97
2001	367.1	37.5	9.79	9.79	332.2	39.0	8.52	8.50
2002	386.8	37.5	10.32	10.32	350.8	38.8	9.04	9.03
2003	400.7	37.4	10.71	10.70	372.8	38.7	9.64	9.62
2004[2]	417.0	37.5	11.12	11.12	380.4	38.7	9.82	9.82
	422.1		11.26	11.27	388.1		10.02	10.02
2005	436.2	37.4	11.66	11.67	399.2	38.4	10.39	10.38

1 See chapter text. Employees on adult rates whose pay for the survey period was not affected by absence.
2 For 2004, two sets of figures are shown. The first does not include supplementary information and therefore is comparable with earlier years. The second includes supplementary information and so is discontinuous with previous years (where the two figures are equal only one appears).

Sources: Annual Survey of Hours and Earnings;
Office for National Statistics: 01633 819024

7.21 Average earnings index:[1] all employees by main industrial sectors
Great Britain
Analyses by industry based on Standard Industrial Classification 1992

Indices (2000=100)

	Annual averages	Jan-uary	Feb-ruary	March	April	May	June	July	August	Sept-ember	Oct-ober	Nov-ember	Dec-ember
						Not seasonally adjusted							
Whole economy (Divisions 01 - 93)													
	LNMM												
2003	111.7	109.9	113.8	116.8	110.0	110.0	111.2	111.8	110.2	110.4	110.9	111.2	114.7
2004	116.7	118.2	118.1	122.2	115.0	114.8	116.1	115.4	114.8	114.9	115.7	116.2	119.5
2005	121.4	123.3	124.9	127.5	119.9	119.2	120.4	120.5	119.0	118.8	119.1	119.9	124.6
Manufacturing industries (Divisions 15 - 37)													
	LNMN												
2003	111.7	109.1	111.0	117.9	110.5	110.5	110.4	111.8	109.8	110.6	111.5	112.3	115.4
2004	115.9	112.8	114.9	122.1	115.6	115.5	114.9	116.1	113.6	114.2	115.4	115.7	119.8
2005	120.1	116.3	119.2	126.6	120.0	117.5	118.2	119.9	118.1	119.2	120.4	120.5	125.1
Production industries (Divisions 10 - 41)													
	LNMO												
2003	111.6	108.9	110.7	118.2	110.7	110.4	110.9	111.6	109.7	110.4	111.2	112.0	114.9
2004	115.8	112.6	115.1	122.1	115.9	115.2	115.3	115.7	113.4	113.9	115.4	115.6	119.5
2005	120.0	116.3	119.6	126.6	120.2	117.4	118.5	119.6	117.9	118.9	120.1	120.1	125.3
Service industries (Divisions 50 - 93)													
	LNMP												
2003	111.7	110.1	114.9	116.3	109.9	110.0	111.3	111.9	110.4	110.1	110.6	110.7	114.3
2004	116.8	119.8	119.0	122.0	114.7	114.4	116.1	115.1	115.0	114.8	115.6	115.7	119.1
2005	121.6	125.0	126.4	127.6	119.8	119.4	120.7	120.5	119.2	118.3	118.5	119.4	123.8
Private sector services (Divisions 50-99)													
	JJGF												
2003	110.6	109.6	115.9	117.5	108.2	108.5	109.8	110.3	108.1	108.1	108.8	108.7	113.0
2004	115.5	121.0	119.7	123.7	113.1	112.6	114.0	113.1	112.3	112.2	113.5	113.6	117.6
2005	120.2	125.9	127.8	129.1	117.9	116.3	118.7	118.8	116.7	115.7	115.9	116.9	122.1
						Seasonally adjusted							
Whole economy (Divisions 01 - 93)													
	LNMQ												
2003	111.9	109.0	109.8	110.9	110.7	111.4	111.7	112.6	112.6	113.2	113.4	113.7	114.3
2004	116.7	115.6	113.8	115.7	115.7	116.1	116.4	116.4	117.2	117.7	118.6	118.9	119.0
2005	121.5	121.0	119.9	120.3	120.6	120.8	121.1	121.6	121.9	122.1	122.3	122.9	124.0
Manufacturing industries (Divisions 15 - 37)													
	LNMR												
2003	111.9	110.2	110.6	111.8	110.3	111.1	111.4	111.8	112.2	112.8	113.0	113.7	113.6
2004	115.9	114.3	114.5	115.5	115.4	116.0	116.0	116.1	116.0	116.2	116.8	117.1	117.8
2005	120.2	117.7	118.3	120.0	118.9	118.2	119.3	120.1	121.0	121.6	122.0	122.2	122.9
Production industries (Divisions 10 - 41)													
	LNMS												
2003	111.7	110.2	110.3	112.0	110.2	110.9	111.3	111.7	112.0	112.6	112.9	113.5	113.4
2004	115.8	114.1	114.4	115.4	115.3	115.7	115.8	115.9	115.8	116.1	116.6	116.9	117.4
2005	120.0	117.6	118.3	119.6	118.7	118.1	119.0	119.8	120.6	121.2	121.7	121.9	123.0
Service industries (Divisions 50 - 93)													
	LNMT												
2003	112.0	108.9	109.5	110.4	110.8	111.6	111.9	113.0	112.8	113.2	113.4	113.7	114.5
2004	116.7	115.7	113.4	115.7	115.6	115.8	116.4	116.2	117.3	117.9	118.8	119.0	119.3
2005	121.7	121.2	120.2	120.7	120.8	121.2	121.4	121.8	121.9	122.0	122.1	122.9	124.0
Private sector services (Divisions 50-93)													
	JJGH												
2003	110.9	107.4	108.3	109.2	109.7	111.0	110.9	111.9	111.8	112.3	112.5	112.8	113.4
2004	115.7	115.4	111.9	114.6	114.6	115.0	115.3	114.8	116.1	116.8	117.8	117.9	118.2
2005	120.5	120.8	119.0	119.5	119.6	119.4	120.1	120.6	120.8	120.7	120.7	121.5	122.7

1 See chapter text.

Source: Office for National Statistics: 01633 819024

7.22 Average earnings index:[1] all employee jobs: by industry
Great Britain
Not seasonally adjusted

Indices (2000=100)

	Agriculture, forestry and fishing	Mining and quarrying	Food products, beverages and tobacco	Textiles, leather and clothing	Chemicals and man-made fibres	Basic metals and metal products	Engineering and allied industries	Other manufacturing	Electricity, gas and water supply	Construction
							(DK, DL,DM)	(DD,DE,DF, DH,DI,DN)		
SIC 1992	(A,B)	(C)	(DA)	(DB,DC)	(DG)	(DJ)			(E)	(F)
Excluding bonuses										
	JVUZ	JVVA	JVVB	JVVC	JVVD	JVVE	JVVF	JVVG	JVVH	JVVI
2003	118.2	112.6	112.4	112.8	112.1	110.5	112.8	112.2	106.4	113.6
2004	122.7	117.5	117.6	117.1	118.3	115.6	117.1	115.8	110.8	119.8
2003 Apr	116.3	110.5	113.8	111.4	111.3	109.3	112.7	110.9	104.9	112.3
May	115.7	112.3	113.5	111.2	111.3	111.2	113.1	111.6	107.0	111.9
Jun	116.7	111.5	112.1	112.7	112.8	110.8	113.2	112.3	105.4	114.0
Jul	117.1	114.3	112.0	116.0	112.5	111.4	113.3	112.5	107.3	113.6
Aug	118.1	114.8	112.5	113.6	113.1	109.7	112.3	112.3	108.5	111.0
Sep	120.4	114.4	112.6	114.8	113.5	111.4	112.8	113.1	106.9	114.9
Oct	118.6	112.9	112.8	114.0	113.1	112.3	113.7	113.4	107.4	115.2
Nov	119.2	113.3	113.2	113.6	114.1	112.1	114.6	113.8	108.2	116.2
Dec	122.7	115.1	115.8	115.8	115.0	110.9	114.5	114.3	108.0	117.1
2004 Jan	119.8	114.1	115.1	115.1	113.5	113.4	114.1	114.1	109.4	116.3
Feb	120.7	116.2	114.5	114.3	116.1	113.1	114.2	114.5	108.9	117.5
Mar	119.6	114.5	115.8	116.4	117.1	115.2	115.7	115.5	109.7	119.8
Apr	123.7	115.1	117.2	114.4	117.7	113.2	116.7	115.2	112.1	119.2
May	120.1	116.0	118.7	116.1	118.1	115.3	117.2	116.4	111.0	118.7
Jun	123.9	116.2	117.6	117.6	119.5	115.5	117.1	116.0	113.3	119.5
Jul	122.5	116.1	117.8	119.6	119.0	117.3	118.3	116.3	111.4	120.4
Aug	120.5	114.6	118.0	117.2	118.9	116.7	117.5	115.2	110.9	119.7
Sep	123.4	115.9	117.4	118.4	118.1	116.7	117.2	115.9	109.5	120.7
Oct	122.5	127.3	118.1	118.5	120.4	117.6	118.6	116.2	111.3	121.4
Nov	127.2	122.5	119.6	118.5	120.2	117.1	119.0	116.8	110.9	121.9
Dec	128.2	121.3	121.9	119.4	121.2	116.3	119.3	117.2	111.1	122.2
2005 Jan	125.1	120.4	119.4	118.1	120.9	118.5	119.0	116.2	111.2	121.8
Feb	121.5	123.6	118.3	116.1	121.0	119.1	119.5	117.3	111.6	120.4
Mar	124.8	120.4	121.8	118.3	122.0	118.4	120.0	117.5	110.9	121.7
Apr	124.3	123.1	120.7	119.0	118.8	120.9	121.2	118.8	113.4	122.3
May	120.9	123.3	121.8	118.1	118.3	120.0	121.3	119.3	113.4	123.1
Jun	125.9	122.4	120.7	121.0	119.4	121.4	121.3	120.4	115.6	124.4
Jul	122.2	122.1	121.2	119.1	118.5	122.2	122.7	120.3	115.3	125.1
Aug	122.5	122.5	122.0	117.0	119.7	122.2	121.7	121.0	115.2	123.3
Sep	131.7	123.5	122.6	118.9	119.2	123.2	122.5	122.1	113.7	125.7
Oct	130.3	125.2	123.1	121.6	119.4	122.9	123.6	122.3	115.2	126.2
Nov	127.0	127.8	125.3	121.5	121.4	122.4	122.8	122.9	116.0	127.8
Percentage change on the year										
	JVVT	JVVU	JVVV	JVVW	JVVX	JVVY	JVVZ	JVWA	JVWB	JVWC
2004 Apr	6.4	4.1	2.9	2.6	5.8	3.6	3.5	3.8	6.9	6.1
May	3.8	3.3	4.6	4.4	6.1	3.7	3.6	4.3	3.7	6.1
Jun	6.2	4.2	4.9	4.4	5.9	4.3	3.5	3.3	7.5	4.8
Jul	4.6	1.6	5.2	3.1	5.8	5.2	4.4	3.4	3.7	6.0
Aug	2.0	-0.1	4.9	3.2	5.1	6.3	4.6	2.5	2.3	7.8
Sep	2.4	1.3	4.3	3.1	4.1	4.8	3.9	2.5	2.4	5.1
Oct	3.2	12.8	4.7	4.0	6.4	4.7	4.3	2.5	3.7	5.4
Nov	6.7	8.1	5.7	4.4	5.4	4.5	3.8	2.6	2.5	4.9
Dec	4.5	5.4	5.3	3.2	5.4	4.9	4.2	2.5	2.9	4.3
2005 Jan	4.4	5.6	3.8	2.6	6.5	4.5	4.3	1.9	1.6	4.8
Feb	0.7	6.4	3.4	1.6	4.2	5.3	4.6	2.5	2.4	2.5
Mar	4.3	5.2	5.2	1.6	4.2	2.8	3.8	1.7	1.1	1.6
Apr	0.5	7.0	3.0	4.1	0.9	6.8	3.9	3.2	1.2	2.7
May	0.6	6.3	2.6	1.7	0.2	4.0	3.6	2.5	2.2	3.7
Jun	1.6	5.4	2.7	2.9	-0.1	5.2	3.6	3.7	2.0	4.1
Jul	-0.2	5.2	2.9	-0.4	-0.4	4.2	3.8	3.5	3.6	3.9
Aug	1.6	6.9	3.4	-0.2	0.7	4.7	3.6	5.0	3.9	3.1
Sep	6.8	6.5	4.5	0.4	0.9	5.5	4.5	5.3	3.9	4.1
Oct	6.4	-1.7	4.3	2.6	-0.8	4.5	4.2	5.3	3.5	3.9
Nov	-0.1	4.4	4.8	2.5	0.9	4.5	3.2	5.2	4.6	4.8

7.22
continued

Average earnings index:[1] all employee jobs: by industry
Great Britain
Not seasonally adjusted

Indices (2000=100)

	Wholesale trade	Retail trade and repairs	Hotels and restaurants	Transport, storage and communication	Financial interm-ediation	Real estate renting and business activities	Public admini-stration	Education	Health and social work	Other services
Excluding bonuses										
SIC 1992	(G:51)	(G:50,52)	(H)	(I)	(J)	(K)	(L)	(M)	(N)	(O)
	JVVJ	JVVK	JVVL	JVVM	JVVN	JVVO	JVVP	JVVQ	JVVR	JVVS
2003	109.0	111.1	116.2	112.6	111.7	113.3	113.6	115.4	119.3	106.1
2004	112.9	114.0	122.3	118.7	115.2	117.9	118.8	119.5	126.7	112.4
2003 Apr	108.5	110.3	116.3	111.6	111.6	112.1	113.0	115.5	117.7	106.2
May	108.8	113.0	116.2	112.0	112.8	113.0	113.1	114.7	118.0	106.2
Jun	109.4	111.7	116.0	112.9	112.5	113.1	112.9	115.7	119.1	106.2
Jul	109.2	112.2	116.8	113.0	112.2	113.4	114.0	116.9	121.8	106.6
Aug	109.3	112.9	117.7	113.2	111.0	113.3	114.0	117.7	122.3	107.2
Sep	109.1	113.0	116.5	114.0	111.1	113.4	114.4	118.2	120.6	105.9
Oct	109.6	111.1	116.5	114.4	111.5	114.2	114.3	116.8	120.9	106.6
Nov	109.2	110.5	116.9	114.7	112.4	114.5	117.8	116.2	121.1	106.3
Dec	110.7	111.9	121.5	115.5	112.2	114.7	116.1	117.0	121.9	106.8
2004 Jan	110.7	112.9	118.6	116.4	113.9	115.7	115.5	115.4	122.4	111.6
Feb	110.8	111.4	118.1	114.9	113.2	116.5	116.4	116.1	121.5	110.7
Mar	112.2	112.7	119.7	115.9	114.8	117.1	116.4	116.1	122.1	110.0
Apr	112.7	114.6	120.6	117.4	114.9	117.4	117.6	118.8	125.6	110.3
May	113.3	114.5	121.1	117.9	115.1	118.7	118.0	119.2	126.1	110.7
Jun	112.9	114.7	121.9	119.7	115.1	117.5	118.1	119.0	130.2	111.9
Jul	112.8	114.8	123.5	119.1	114.9	118.4	118.2	119.5	128.3	114.1
Aug	113.0	115.4	124.2	119.8	115.2	118.2	119.7	123.2	128.1	114.3
Sep	113.7	115.1	122.7	120.3	115.1	118.2	121.7	123.3	128.6	113.2
Oct	113.5	114.4	124.9	121.5	116.5	118.3	120.7	121.6	128.7	112.8
Nov	114.0	113.2	123.9	120.8	116.7	118.9	122.1	120.6	129.2	115.0
Dec	115.6	114.7	128.4	120.6	117.3	120.1	121.7	121.9	129.2	113.9
2005 Jan	115.6	117.3	122.8	121.4	117.7	120.5	120.5	122.0	129.2	114.7
Feb	115.2	115.5	123.7	120.7	118.3	121.0	121.9	120.8	128.8	114.5
Mar	116.9	115.7	126.8	121.0	121.6	120.7	125.9	120.7	128.9	116.7
Apr	117.3	117.9	125.9	122.4	120.9	122.1	124.3	124.0	132.9	115.3
May	117.6	116.3	126.3	123.3	121.3	122.1	123.0	123.5	132.9	116.8
Jun	117.3	116.0	126.8	125.2	119.2	122.3	123.0	124.0	133.9	119.2
Jul	118.0	117.8	127.1	123.9	121.8	123.5	124.3	124.5	133.0	121.3
Aug	118.1	118.3	127.3	123.4	121.1	123.0	124.7	126.1	132.9	118.8
Sep	118.0	115.8	126.2	125.8	119.5	123.2	125.3	126.8	132.9	118.6
Oct	119.1	116.0	126.7	124.9	121.0	123.7	125.4	126.3	133.2	115.4
Nov	118.6	115.1	127.5	124.9	121.4	124.1	125.7	125.1	135.0	116.6
Percentage change on the year										
	JVWD	JVWE	JVWF	JVYJ	JVYK	JVYL	JVYM	JVYN	JVYO	JVYP
2004 Apr	3.8	3.9	3.7	5.2	3.0	4.8	4.1	2.9	6.7	3.9
May	4.0	1.3	4.2	5.2	2.0	5.0	4.4	3.9	6.8	4.2
Jun	3.3	2.7	5.1	6.1	2.3	3.8	4.7	2.8	9.3	5.4
Jul	3.3	2.3	5.7	5.4	2.4	4.4	3.6	2.2	5.4	7.0
Aug	3.4	2.2	5.6	5.8	3.8	4.3	4.9	4.6	4.8	6.6
Sep	4.2	1.8	5.3	5.6	3.6	4.3	6.4	4.3	6.6	6.9
Oct	3.6	2.9	7.1	6.2	4.5	3.6	5.6	4.1	6.5	5.8
Nov	4.4	2.5	6.0	5.3	3.9	3.9	3.6	3.8	6.7	8.2
Dec	4.5	2.5	5.7	4.4	4.5	4.7	4.8	4.1	5.9	6.7
2005 Jan	4.4	3.9	3.5	4.3	3.3	4.1	4.3	5.8	5.6	2.7
Feb	4.0	3.6	4.7	5.0	4.5	3.8	4.7	4.1	6.0	3.4
Mar	4.2	2.7	5.9	4.3	6.0	3.0	8.1	3.9	5.6	6.1
Apr	4.1	2.9	4.5	4.2	5.2	3.9	5.7	4.4	5.8	4.6
May	3.9	1.6	4.3	4.6	5.4	2.9	4.2	3.7	5.4	5.5
Jun	3.9	1.2	4.0	4.5	3.5	4.1	4.1	4.2	2.9	6.5
Jul	4.6	2.6	2.9	4.0	6.0	4.3	5.1	4.2	3.7	6.4
Aug	4.5	2.5	2.5	3.0	5.1	4.1	4.2	2.4	3.8	4.0
Sep	3.8	0.7	2.9	4.6	3.9	4.2	2.9	2.9	3.4	4.8
Oct	4.9	1.4	1.5	2.8	3.9	4.6	3.9	3.9	3.5	2.3
Nov	4.1	1.6	2.9	3.4	4.0	4.3	2.9	3.7	4.5	1.4

7.22
continued

Average earnings index:[1] all employee jobs: by industry
Great Britain
Not seasonally adjusted

Indices (2000=100)

	Agriculture, forestry and fishing	Mining and quarrying	Food products, beverages and tobacco	Textiles, leather and clothing	Chemicals and man-made fibres	Basic metals and metal products	Engineering and allied industries	Other manufacturing	Electricity, gas and water supply	Construction
SIC 1992	(A,B)	(C)	(DA)	(DB,DC)	(DG)	(DJ)	(DK, DL,DM)	(DD,DE,DF, DH,DI,DN)	(E)	(F)
	JVUF	JVUG	JVUH	JVUI	JVUJ	JVUK	JVUL	JVUM	JVUN	JVUO

Including bonuses

	JVUF	JVUG	JVUH	JVUI	JVUJ	JVUK	JVUL	JVUM	JVUN	JVUO
2003	117.0	118.6	110.4	109.2	114.5	110.4	113.5	110.2	105.4	112.4
2004	121.6	121.9	113.9	114.2	120.1	116.5	118.5	112.2	110.6	119.2
2003 Apr	114.8	132.0	110.0	106.6	115.0	110.0	112.4	107.8	101.8	109.8
May	113.8	114.8	108.2	107.1	109.8	109.8	113.5	108.9	104.1	108.5
Jun	115.0	113.9	107.7	107.2	110.6	109.4	112.8	109.5	118.7	111.3
Jul	115.8	115.4	109.8	111.1	110.9	114.1	113.4	110.1	104.8	111.7
Aug	115.5	116.4	108.9	108.7	112.4	108.2	111.2	108.6	103.9	108.0
Sep	118.0	117.1	110.8	109.6	111.3	108.7	111.8	109.7	102.8	112.9
Oct	117.0	114.6	108.1	109.3	110.6	113.7	113.0	110.6	103.9	113.4
Nov	117.5	115.0	109.5	109.2	112.0	110.8	115.2	111.2	104.0	114.8
Dec	124.0	118.3	114.3	117.3	120.2	110.4	117.0	114.1	104.2	119.2
2004 Jan	118.0	117.3	111.1	111.7	113.5	114.7	114.2	110.9	105.5	114.6
Feb	118.9	129.6	112.0	110.8	120.8	114.1	118.1	111.4	109.3	116.5
Mar	119.6	127.3	120.7	114.2	148.9	114.9	124.4	115.7	119.9	124.6
Apr	122.7	132.6	115.0	110.7	125.6	116.0	117.6	110.9	110.6	117.1
May	119.0	115.8	115.2	113.8	116.9	114.2	117.6	113.3	109.3	118.5
Jun	123.9	116.1	112.4	114.4	117.3	115.1	117.5	112.1	123.1	117.7
Jul	122.2	114.8	112.9	116.9	117.6	120.5	118.1	112.4	109.1	119.5
Aug	118.8	114.2	111.2	113.6	115.0	115.4	116.8	109.7	108.8	116.4
Sep	122.7	118.2	113.4	114.4	113.1	115.4	117.0	110.9	106.5	118.2
Oct	121.4	127.5	110.5	115.4	116.5	120.2	118.1	111.7	108.6	119.0
Nov	126.3	123.8	112.0	114.8	114.1	117.4	119.6	112.4	108.1	124.0
Dec	125.8	125.6	120.5	120.1	121.7	120.5	122.7	115.1	108.4	124.7
2005 Jan	123.4	128.8	112.3	117.0	117.9	122.6	118.7	111.8	110.0	121.3
Feb	119.5	137.2	114.2	116.7	121.6	122.3	124.4	113.5	117.3	119.8
Mar	126.0	148.9	129.2	117.2	150.3	125.0	126.2	120.3	112.0	128.8
Apr	122.0	137.9	116.9	117.1	122.5	126.3	123.4	114.2	113.6	120.5
May	118.0	119.2	114.6	116.0	115.7	119.9	119.9	115.4	114.6	122.6
Jun	122.7	120.5	113.3	120.2	116.5	121.5	121.0	115.5	124.9	123.0
Jul	119.4	117.8	117.8	120.0	115.5	126.9	121.7	116.8	115.0	124.4
Aug	120.1	120.1	116.6	117.2	115.6	122.8	119.3	115.8	112.7	120.9
Sep	143.4	125.6	118.0	118.1	115.8	125.2	120.3	116.7	110.2	124.3
Oct	127.5	121.8	115.3	126.6	115.1	128.8	121.8	118.1	112.7	124.9
Nov	125.8	125.1	118.6	120.8	116.3	124.9	121.7	118.9	111.3	127.5

Percentage change on the year

	JVYQ	JVYR	JVYS	JVYT	JVYU	JVYV	JVYW	JVYX	JVYY	JVYZ
2004 Apr	6.9	0.5	4.5	3.8	9.2	5.5	4.6	2.9	8.7	6.6
May	4.5	0.8	6.4	6.2	6.4	4.0	3.6	4.0	5.0	9.2
Jun	7.7	1.9	4.4	6.7	6.0	5.2	4.1	2.3	3.7	5.7
Jul	5.5	−0.5	2.8	5.2	6.1	5.7	4.2	2.1	4.1	6.9
Aug	2.8	−2.0	2.2	4.5	2.3	6.7	5.0	1.0	4.7	7.7
Sep	4.0	0.9	2.4	4.4	1.6	6.2	4.7	1.1	3.6	4.7
Oct	3.7	11.2	2.2	5.6	5.3	5.8	4.4	1.1	4.5	4.9
Nov	7.5	7.6	2.2	5.1	1.9	5.9	3.8	1.1	3.9	8.0
Dec	1.4	6.2	5.4	2.4	1.2	9.2	4.8	0.9	4.1	4.7
2005 Jan	4.6	9.8	1.1	4.7	3.8	6.9	3.9	0.8	4.3	5.9
Feb	0.5	5.9	2.0	5.4	0.7	7.3	5.3	1.9	7.3	2.8
Mar	5.3	17.0	7.0	2.6	1.0	8.8	1.5	3.9	−6.6	3.3
Apr	−0.5	4.0	1.7	5.8	−2.4	8.9	4.9	3.0	2.7	3.0
May	−0.8	3.0	−0.5	2.0	−1.0	5.0	1.9	1.8	4.8	3.5
Jun	−1.0	3.8	0.8	5.1	−0.6	5.6	3.0	3.1	1.5	4.5
Jul	−2.3	2.6	4.4	2.6	−1.8	5.3	3.0	4.0	5.4	4.1
Aug	1.1	5.2	4.8	3.2	0.6	6.5	2.2	5.6	3.6	3.9
Sep	16.9	6.2	4.1	3.3	2.4	8.5	2.8	5.3	3.5	5.2
Oct	5.1	−4.5	4.4	9.7	−1.2	7.1	3.1	5.7	3.8	5.0
Nov	−0.4	1.1	5.9	5.2	2.0	6.4	1.8	5.8	3.0	2.9

7.22 continued

Average earnings index:[1] all employee jobs: by industry
Great Britain
Not seasonally adjusted

Indices (2000=100)

	Wholesale trade	Retail trade and repairs	Hotels and restaurants	Transport, storage and communication	Financial interm-ediation	Real estate renting and business activities	Public admini-stration	Education	Health and social work	Other services
Including bonuses										
SIC 1992	(G:51)	(G:50,52)	(H)	(I)	(J)	(K)	(L)	(M)	(N)	(O)
	JVUP	JVUQ	JVUR	JVUS	JVUT	JVUU	JVUV	JVUW	JVUX	JVUY
2003	111.3	110.9	119.2	111.3	105.2	109.7	113.1	115.2	119.3	108.4
2004	115.4	113.9	125.7	117.7	109.8	114.3	118.4	119.3	126.6	115.6
2003 Apr	108.7	109.8	118.3	108.5	101.5	106.9	112.3	115.3	117.9	107.5
May	109.1	111.6	120.0	110.6	93.7	109.1	112.5	114.4	118.1	107.8
Jun	111.6	112.1	118.1	117.8	92.0	110.5	112.2	115.6	119.1	108.2
Jul	110.1	112.1	119.4	111.8	97.6	110.7	113.3	116.8	121.9	109.8
Aug	107.8	111.7	119.3	110.4	90.4	108.5	114.4	117.4	122.3	108.2
Sep	108.3	112.6	118.5	110.8	90.3	108.1	113.7	117.9	120.6	106.2
Oct	110.4	110.3	118.7	111.3	91.7	109.4	113.8	116.5	120.9	108.9
Nov	112.7	109.2	120.1	112.1	92.3	108.6	117.1	116.1	121.2	107.6
Dec	118.3	113.8	127.8	115.6	101.7	112.3	115.5	116.9	122.0	110.5
2004 Jan	114.1	111.3	120.7	113.5	164.8	112.1	114.7	115.0	122.3	113.8
Feb	113.7	112.8	123.1	115.1	149.5	113.6	115.6	115.8	121.5	113.2
Mar	122.4	115.4	122.8	116.4	151.6	121.1	115.7	115.9	122.1	113.4
Apr	113.6	114.9	122.6	115.8	99.4	113.7	116.8	118.5	125.7	111.1
May	111.1	113.2	125.1	116.5	93.9	115.1	117.4	118.9	126.0	112.4
Jun	114.7	115.1	124.0	126.1	93.3	113.4	117.3	118.7	130.1	120.9
Jul	114.1	114.0	126.2	117.0	92.1	114.8	117.5	119.3	128.3	116.4
Aug	113.2	114.1	126.6	116.8	90.9	112.7	121.2	123.0	128.0	115.3
Sep	113.9	114.6	125.6	117.3	90.5	111.5	121.1	122.9	128.5	115.6
Oct	114.1	113.8	128.5	118.3	96.3	112.5	120.1	121.3	128.7	116.2
Nov	116.5	112.4	127.8	118.8	93.2	113.4	121.4	120.5	129.2	120.0
Dec	123.7	114.8	135.6	121.0	101.7	117.7	122.3	121.6	129.3	119.1
2005 Jan	117.0	117.0	128.6	118.2	163.7	117.7	119.6	121.7	129.1	119.5
Feb	118.9	117.5	132.0	121.6	173.7	117.3	121.1	120.7	129.2	116.0
Mar	126.3	118.7	134.5	121.7	156.0	124.5	125.3	120.4	129.3	123.7
Apr	120.8	119.0	129.4	122.6	101.0	117.3	123.6	123.9	133.0	118.3
May	116.6	115.9	131.5	131.6	96.2	116.9	122.3	123.2	132.9	120.2
Jun	118.1	116.9	129.9	133.3	96.9	118.3	122.2	123.6	134.0	127.8
Jul	118.7	117.2	130.2	125.5	97.0	120.7	124.2	124.3	133.0	122.2
Aug	115.3	116.9	130.9	121.4	96.1	117.1	126.4	125.9	133.0	120.3
Sep	115.5	114.1	128.5	122.8	94.8	115.3	124.6	126.5	132.8	119.7
Oct	119.9	115.6	129.8	122.0	93.1	116.0	125.2	126.0	133.4	116.3
Nov	119.0	114.7	131.8	123.5	97.1	117.3	125.5	124.8	135.0	118.9
Percentage change on the year										
	JVZA	JVZB	JVZC	JVZD	JVZE	JVZF	JVZG	JVZH	JVZI	JVZJ
2004 Apr	4.5	4.7	3.6	6.7	-2.0	6.3	4.0	2.8	6.6	3.3
May	1.8	1.4	4.3	5.3	0.2	5.5	4.4	3.9	6.7	4.3
Jun	2.8	2.7	5.0	7.1	1.4	2.6	4.6	2.7	9.3	11.8
Jul	3.6	1.7	5.7	4.7	-5.6	3.7	3.7	2.2	5.3	6.0
Aug	5.1	2.1	6.1	5.8	0.6	3.8	5.9	4.7	4.6	6.6
Sep	5.2	1.7	6.0	5.9	0.2	3.1	6.5	4.2	6.6	8.8
Oct	3.3	3.2	8.3	6.3	4.9	2.8	5.5	4.1	6.5	6.7
Nov	3.4	2.9	6.4	6.0	1.0	4.4	3.7	3.8	6.6	11.4
Dec	4.6	0.9	6.1	4.7	–	4.8	5.8	4.1	6.0	7.8
2005 Jan	2.5	5.1	6.5	4.1	-0.7	4.9	4.3	5.8	5.6	5.0
Feb	4.6	4.2	7.3	5.7	16.2	3.2	4.8	4.2	6.4	2.5
Mar	3.2	2.9	9.6	4.5	2.9	2.8	8.3	3.9	5.9	9.1
Apr	6.3	3.5	5.5	5.9	1.6	3.2	5.8	4.5	5.7	6.5
May	5.0	2.4	5.1	13.0	2.4	1.6	4.2	3.6	5.5	6.9
Jun	2.9	1.6	4.8	5.7	3.9	4.3	4.1	4.1	2.9	5.7
Jul	4.0	2.8	3.2	7.3	5.3	5.1	5.6	4.2	3.7	5.0
Aug	1.8	2.4	3.4	4.0	5.8	3.9	4.3	2.3	3.9	4.3
Sep	1.5	-0.4	2.3	4.6	4.8	3.4	2.9	3.0	3.3	3.5
Oct	5.1	1.5	1.0	3.1	-3.3	3.1	4.3	3.9	3.7	0.1
Nov	2.2	2.0	3.1	3.9	4.1	3.4	3.4	3.5	4.5	-0.9

1 See chapter text.

Source: Office for National Statistics: 01633 819024

7.23 Gross weekly and hourly earnings of full-time employees:[1] by sex
United Kingdom
At April

£

	Gross weekly earnings					Gross hourly earnings				
	Lowest decile	Lower quartile	Median	Upper quartile	Highest decile	Lowest decile	Lower quartile	Median	Upper quartile	Highest decile
All employees										
	C5U9	C5UC	C5UF	C5UI	C5UL	C5UO	C5UR	C5UU	C5V2	C5UX
2000	195.8	256.6	359.0	501.8	685.4	4.99	6.40	8.91	13.04	18.37
2001	205.0	268.2	375.9	527.8	731.1	5.20	6.67	9.32	13.73	19.60
2002	214.4	279.2	390.9	551.8	767.8	5.44	6.97	9.74	14.36	20.60
2003	222.7	288.0	404.0	572.6	794.2	5.68	7.23	10.07	14.82	21.27
2004[2]	231.9	301.3	422.8	595.0	827.3	5.91	7.54	10.56	15.41	22.18
	230.3	298.1	419.5	590.9	815.3	5.85	7.45	10.45	15.33	21.86
2005	235.2	305.4	431.2	612.3	850.6	6.00	7.68	10.79	15.92	22.87
Male employees										
	C5UA	C5UD	C5UG	C5UJ	C5UM	C5UP	C5US	C5UV	C5V3	C5UY
2000	220.0	287.9	397.7	549.8	760.1	5.30	6.82	9.56	13.94	19.96
2001	229.5	299.6	415.7	575.8	813.3	5.52	7.13	9.99	14.62	21.43
2002	239.0	310.2	430.1	599.9	857.5	5.78	7.41	10.40	15.32	22.56
2003	246.6	320.3	444.6	622.8	881.9	6.00	7.68	10.75	15.83	23.17
2004[2]	254.5	333.3	463.0	647.8	916.8	6.21	7.99	11.23	16.42	24.08
	250.0	329.6	460.2	640.9	901.8	6.13	7.90	11.12	16.26	23.67
2005	255.6	335.5	471.5	666.6	939.8	6.27	8.08	11.44	16.90	24.77
Female employees										
	C5UB	C5UE	C5UH	C5UK	C5UN	C5UQ	C5UT	C5UW	C5V4	C5UZ
2000	174.3	221.7	298.1	422.6	549.4	4.58	5.80	7.89	11.51	15.87
2001	183.1	231.3	314.3	449.4	585.5	4.82	6.07	8.28	12.15	16.77
2002	192.1	241.8	330.7	474.0	623.7	5.04	6.35	8.70	12.80	17.66
2003	201.3	251.6	343.0	490.2	645.7	5.30	6.63	9.07	13.28	18.33
2004[2]	210.8	265.3	360.8	515.5	678.8	5.53	6.96	9.57	13.96	19.19
	209.4	262.4	356.7	510.3	673.9	5.50	6.91	9.42	13.82	18.97
2005	217.0	271.7	371.8	533.4	707.6	5.72	7.17	9.86	14.49	20.04

1 See chapter text. Employees on adult rates whose pay for the survey period was not affected by absence.
2 For 2004, two sets of figures are shown. The first does not include supplementary information and therefore is comparable with earlier years. The second includes supplementary informaion and so is discontinuous with previous years.

Sources: Annual Survey of Hours and Earnings;
Office for National Statistics: 01633 819024

7.24 Average earnings by age group of full-time employees:[1,2] by sex, 2005
United Kingdom
At April

£ and numbers

	Average gross weekly pay excluding overtime	Average gross weekly overtime pay	Average weekly hours (numbers)		Average gross hourly earnings excluding overtime pay
			Total	Overtime	
All employees					
18 to 21	177.8	0.0	40.3	0.0	4.55
22 to 29	255.1	11.0	39.9	11.0	6.62
30 to 39	399.0	14.7	39.1	14.7	10.55
40 to 49	535.8	19.5	39.4	19.5	14.13
50+	559.7	22.1	39.4	22.1	14.83
All ages	498.2	18.8	39.4	18.8	13.16
Male employees					
18 to 21	175.3	0.0	40.7	0.0	4.46
22 to 29	264.1	14.8	41.0	14.8	6.73
30 to 39	416.7	21.3	40.4	21.3	10.81
40 to 49	569.0	26.1	40.6	26.1	14.74
50+	620.0	30.1	40.7	30.1	16.11
All ages	543.3	25.7	40.6	25.7	14.08
Female employees					
18 to 21	182.2	0.0	39.4	0.0	6.48
22 to 29	244.1	6.3	38.5	6.3	10.25
30 to 39	379.0	7.2	37.7	7.2	13.03
40 to 49	478.2	8.0	37.4	8.0	12.61
50+	460.1	9.0	37.3	9.0	11.88
All ages	428.2	7.9	37.4	7.9	11.67

1 See chapter text. Employees on adult rates whose pay for the survey period was not affected by absence.
2 Data collected including supplementary surveys to improve coverage therefore these data are not directly comparable with those from previous years.

Sources: Annual Survey of Hours and Earnings, Office for National Statistics;
01633 819024

115

7.25 Trade unions[1]
United Kingdom
At end of year

Percentages

		1992	1993	1994	1995	1996	1997	1998	1999	2000	2001	2002
Number of trade unions	KCLB	315	302	281	271	261	257	243	241	230	220	218
Analysis by number of members:												
Under 100 members	KCLC	14.3	15.9	16.4	15.5	13.0	16.0	16.9	18.7	22.2	19.1	20.6
100 and under 500	KCLD	22.9	24.8	23.1	23.2	27.2	22.2	21.4	20.3	17.8	18.6	19.3
500 and under 1,000	KCLE	9.8	7.6	8.9	10.0	8.0	12.1	10.7	9.5	9.6	11.4	10.1
1,000 and under 2,500	KCLF	17.1	15.2	15.3	15.1	17.2	14.8	13.2	14.1	12.2	10.0	10.6
2,500 and under 5,000	KCLG	8.9	8.9	9.3	8.9	7.7	7.8	9.5	9.5	9.1	11.4	10.6
5,000 and under 10,000	KCLH	6.0	6.3	6.4	5.9	5.7	5.8	6.2	5.4	5.7	4.5	5.0
10,000 and under 15,000	KCLI	1.6	2.0	2.1	3.0	2.7	2.7	2.1	1.7	1.7	2.7	3.2
15,000 and under 25,000	KCLJ	3.8	3.0	2.8	2.6	2.3	2.3	2.9	4.1	5.2	5.9	4.1
25,000 and under 50,000	KCLK	6.3	7.0	7.1	7.4	7.7	7.4	8.2	7.9	7.0	6.8	7.3
50,000 and under 100,000	KCLL	2.9	3.0	2.5	2.6	1.9	2.3	2.5	2.1	2.6	2.3	1.8
100,000 and under 250,000	KCLM	3.5	3.3	3.6	3.0	3.1	3.1	2.5	2.1	2.2	2.3	2.8
250,000 and over	KCLN	2.9	3.0	2.5	3.0	3.4	3.5	4.1	4.6	4.8	5.0	4.6
All sizes	KCLP	100	100	100	100	100	100	100	100	100	100	100
Membership												
Analysis by size of union:												
Under 100 members	KCLQ	–	–	–	–	–	–	–	–	–	–	–
100 and under 500	KCLR	0.2	0.2	0.2	0.2	0.3	0.2	0.2	0.2	0.2	0.2	0.2
500 and under 1,000	KCLS	0.2	0.2	0.2	0.2	0.2	0.3	0.2	0.2	0.2	0.2	0.2
1,000 and under 2,500	KCLT	1.0	0.9	0.9	0.9	0.9	0.8	0.7	0.7	0.6	0.5	0.5
2,500 and under 5,000	KCLU	1.1	1.1	1.1	1.1	0.9	0.9	1.1	1.1	0.9	1.2	1.1
5,000 and under 10,000	KCLV	1.5	1.5	1.6	1.4	1.3	1.3	1.4	1.2	1.2	0.9	1.0
10,000 and under 15,000	KCLW	0.6	0.8	0.9	1.3	1.2	1.1	0.9	0.7	0.6	0.9	1.1
15,000 and under 25,000	KCLX	2.3	1.8	1.7	1.5	1.3	1.3	1.6	2.3	2.8	3.3	2.2
25,000 and under 50,000	KCLY	8.0	8.6	8.9	9.1	8.8	8.1	8.4	8.2	7.1	6.8	7.2
50,000 and under 100,000	KCLZ	7.0	7.3	5.9	5.9	3.9	4.5	4.5	3.8	4.6	4.0	3.1
100,000 and under 250,000	KCMA	18.6	18.2	19.3	16.3	15.2	15.3	11.9	9.9	9.8	9.5	10.1
250,000 and over	KCMB	59.4	59.2	59.3	62.0	66.0	66.1	69.1	71.7	72.0	72.5	73.5
All sizes	KCMC	100	100	100	100	100	100	100	100	100	100	100
Total membership (thousands)	KCMD	9 171	8 848	8 297	8 111	7 982	7 841	7 894	7 940	7 823	7 796	7 783

1 See chapter text.

Source: Department of Trade and Industry: 020 7215 5780

Personal income, expenditure and wealth

Chapter 8

Personal income, expenditure and wealth

Distribution of total incomes

(Table 8.1)

The information shown in Table 8.1 comes from the Survey of Personal Incomes for the financial years 2000/01, 2001/02, 2002/03 and 2003/04. This is an annual survey that covers approximately 400,000 individuals across the whole of the UK. It is based on administrative data held by Her Majesty's Revenue and Customs (HMRC) Offices on individuals who could be liable to tax.

The table relates only to those individuals who are taxpayers. The distributions cover only incomes as computed for tax purposes and above a level which for each year corresponds approximately to the single person's allowance. Incomes below these levels are not shown because the information about them is incomplete.   .

Investment income from which tax has been deducted at source is not always known to local tax offices. Estimates of missing bank and building society interest and dividends from United Kingdom companies are included in these tables. The missing investment income is distributed, in a manner consistent with information from the Expenditure and Food Survey and the National Accounts, to individuals for whom there is no investment income already reported by the tax office.

Superannuation contributions are estimated and included in total income. They have been distributed among earners in the Survey of Personal Incomes sample by a method consistent with information about the number of employees who are contracted in or out of the State Earnings Related Pension Scheme and the proportion of their earnings contributed.

When comparing results of these surveys across years, it should be noted that the Survey of Personal Incomes is not a longitudinal survey. However, sample sizes have increased in recent years to increase precision.

Average incomes of households

(Table 8.2)

Original income is the total income in cash of all the members of the household before receipt of state benefits or the deduction of taxes. It includes income from employment, self-employment, investment income and occupational pensions. Gross income is original income plus cash benefits received from government (retirement pensions, child benefit, etc). Disposal income is the income available for consumption. It is equal to gross income less direct taxes which include income tax, national insurance contributions, and council tax. By further allowing for taxes paid on goods and services purchased, such as VAT, an estimate of post-tax income is derived. These income figures are derived from estimates made by the Office for National Statistics, based largely on information from the Expenditure and Food Survey (EFS), and published each year in *Economic Trends*, and available on the National Statistics website.

Retired households are those where the household reference person is retired. The household reference person is defined as retired if 65 years of age or more and male or 60 years of age or more and female, and economically inactive.

Children are defined as persons aged under 16 or aged between 16 and 18, unmarried and receiving full-time non-advanced further education.

Expenditure and Food Survey

(Tables 8.3 to 8.5)

The Expenditure and Food Survey (formerly the Family Expenditure Survey), introduced in 1957, covers all types of private households in the United Kingdom. It is a continuous survey with fieldwork carried out in every month of the year. In 2004–05 around 6,800 households in the UK provided information. The main purpose of the survey is to provide a source for the weighting pattern for the Index of Retail Prices, so it is primarily concerned with household expenditure on goods and services. However, it does have several other important uses.

Although the survey is primarily concerned with the expenditure of private households, much additional information is collected about income and the characteristics of co-operating households. Consequently, the survey provides a unique fund of important economic and social data.

Like all surveys based on a sample of the population, its results are subject to sampling error, and to some bias due to non-response.

The results of the survey are published in an annual report, the latest being *Family Spending* 2004–2005. The report includes a list of definitions used in the survey, items on which information is collected and a brief account of the fieldwork procedure.

8.1 Distribution of total income before and after tax
United Kingdom
Years ending 5 April

| | 2000/2001 Annual Survey | | | | | 2001/02 Annual Survey | | | |
| | Number of individuals (Thousands) | £ million | | | | Number of individuals (Thousands) | £ million | | |
		Total income before tax	Total tax	Total income after tax			Total income before tax	Total tax	Total income after tax
Lower limit of range of income					**Lower limit of range of income**				
All incomes[1]	29 300	594 700	105 600	489 100	All incomes[1]	28 600	611 600	107 000	504 700
Income before tax (£)					Income before tax (£)				
4 385	786	3 690	23	3 660	4 535	525	2 500	12	2 490
5 000	1 360	7 470	139	7 330	5 000	1 070	5 890	98	5 790
6 000	3 270	22 800	986	21 800	6 000	2 890	20 200	696	19 500
8 000	2 960	26 700	2 070	24 600	8 000	2 800	25 200	1 670	23 500
10 000	2 740	30 200	3 030	27 100	10 000	2 650	29 100	2 600	26 500
12 000	2 590	33 600	3 950	29 700	12 000	2 580	33 400	3 600	29 800
14 000	2 340	35 100	4 540	30 500	14 000	2 340	35 100	4 220	30 900
16 000	2 040	34 600	4 730	29 900	16 000	2 040	34 600	4 490	30 100
18 000	1 750	33 300	4 850	28 400	18 000	1 700	32 200	4 440	27 700
20 000	5 400	131 000	20 800	110 200	20 000	5 510	134 300	20 500	113 800
30 000	2 780	103 500	19 700	83 800	30 000	3 160	116 900	21 500	95 400
50 000	961	65 500	16 900	46 600	50 000	1 050	69 800	18 500	51 300
100 000	216	28 800	9 150	19 600	100 000	237	31 500	10 000	21 500
200 000 and over	88	40 600	14 700	25 900	200 000 and over	91	41 000	14 600	26 500
Income after tax (£)					Income after tax (£)				
4 385	891	4 220	30	4 190	4 535	577	2 770	14	2 750
5 000	1 490	8 390	175	8 210	5 000	1 190	6 680	121	6 560
6 000	3 980	29 300	1 540	27 800	6 000	3 440	25 100	1 060	24 100
8 000	3 560	35 200	3 160	32 000	8 000	3 400	33 100	2 570	30 600
10 000	3 370	41 700	4 730	37 000	10 000	3 310	40 500	4 130	36 300
12 000	2 940	43 800	5 650	38 100	12 000	2 940	43 400	5 180	38 200
14 000	2 490	43 300	6 020	37 300	14 000	2 500	43 000	5 640	37 400
16 000	2 060	41 100	6 080	35 000	16 000	2 020	39 800	5 570	34 200
18 000	1 630	36 500	5 640	30 800	18 000	1 670	37 100	5 490	31 600
20 000	4 410	127 500	21 300	106 200	20 000	4 730	136 000	21 830	114 200
30 000	1 820	86 400	19 500	66 900	30 000	2 140	100 000	21 880	78 100
50 000	502	46 500	13 800	32 800	50 000	560	52 200	15 390	36 800
100 000	105	21 200	7 100	14 100	100 000	111	22 500	7 560	14 900
200 000 and over	43	29 700	10 900	18 900	200 000 and over	44	29 400	10 520	18 900

8.1
Distribution of total income before and after tax
United Kingdom
Years ending 5 April

	2002/03 Annual Survey					2003/04 Annual Survey			
	Number of individuals (Thousands)	£ million				Number of individuals (Thousands)	£ million		
		Total income before tax	Total tax	Total income after tax			Total income before tax	Total tax	Total income after tax
Lower limit of range of income					**Lower limit of range of income**				
All incomes[1]	28 900	624 000	108 800	515 200	All incomes[1]	28 500	624 900	110 600	514 300
Income before tax (£)					Income before tax (£)				
4 615	439	2 110	8	2 100	4 615	498	2 390	8	2 380
5 000	1 050	5 760	88	5 670	5 000	1 090	6 000	93	5 900
6 000	2 860	20 100	652	19 400	6 000	2 710	19 100	636	18 400
8 000	2 840	25 600	1 630	23 900	8 000	2 660	23 900	1 570	22 300
10 000	2 660	29 200	2 550	26 600	10 000	2 570	28 300	2 500	25 800
12 000	2 520	32 600	3 470	29 200	12 000	2 430	31 600	3 400	28 200
14 000	2 310	34 600	4 130	30 500	14 000	2 270	33 900	4 130	29 800
16 000	2 060	34 900	4 510	30 400	16 000	1 990	33 700	4 450	29 300
18 000	1 740	33 100	4 540	28 600	18 000	1 730	32 900	4 610	28 300
20 000	5 700	138 900	21 200	117 700	20 000	5 710	139 400	21 800	117 500
30 000	3 300	122 400	22 500	100 000	30 000	3 360	124 500	22 800	101 700
50 000	1 090	72 100	19 100	53 000	50 000	1 110	73 600	19 300	54 200
100 000	249	33 100	10 600	22 500	100 000	256	34 000	10 800	23 200
200 000 and over	91	39 500	13 900	25 700	200 000 and over	95	41 600	14 400	27 200
Income after tax (£)					Income after tax (£)				
4 615	488	2 350	10	2 340	4 615	545	2 620	10	2 610
5 000	1 160	6 510	109	6 400	5 000	1 220	6 820	116	6 710
6 000	3 390	24 800	983	23 800	6 000	3 190	23 500	955	22 500
8 000	3 440	33 400	2 490	30 900	8 000	3 270	31 900	2 470	29 400
10 000	3 280	40 000	4 000	36 000	10 000	3 160	38 600	3 920	34 700
12 000	2 930	43 100	5 090	38 000	12 000	2 890	42 600	5 120	37 500
14 000	2 500	43 000	5 600	37 400	14 000	2 460	42 400	5 660	36 800
16 000	2 110	41 600	5 800	35 800	16 000	2 090	41 300	5 910	35 400
18 000	1 720	38 200	5 620	32 500	18 000	1 720	38 400	5 840	32 600
20 000	4 900	140 900	22 600	118 300	20 000	4 900	141 600	23 300	118 300
30 000	2 270	105 700	23 000	82 600	30 000	2 280	106 000	22 800	83 200
50 000	578	53 800	16 000	37 900	50 000	601	55 700	16 300	39 400
100 000	113	22 800	7 690	15 100	100 000	119	23 800	7 930	15 800
200 000 and over	43	27 900	9840	18 100	200 000 and over	45	29 600	10 200	19 300

1 See chapter text. All figures have been independently rounded.

Source: Board of HMRC: 020 7147 2917

8.2 Average income of households before and after taxes and benefits,[1] 2003/04
United Kingdom

	Retired households		Non-retired households								
	1 adult	2 or more adults	1 adult	2 adults	3 or more adults	1 adult with children	2 adults with 1 child	2 adults with 2 children	2 adults with 3 or more children	3 or more adults with children	All house-holds
Number of households in the population (thousands)	3 403	3 063	3 580	5 356	1 959	1 385	1 765	2 252	834	1 073	24 670
Average per household (£ per year)											
Original income	4 552	10 807	18 002	37 200	43 424	9 173	37 462	38 469	40 188	45 023	26 130
Gross income	10 998	19 599	19 875	39 258	46 281	16 261	39 702	41 187	45 105	49 563	30 226
Disposable income	9 823	17 001	15 240	30 116	36 769	14 733	31 118	32 223	35 687	39 826	24 069
Post-tax income	8 194	13 299	12 126	24 729	29 911	11 685	25 416	25 899	28 880	32 097	19 496

1 See chapter text. Figures taken from the article "Effects of taxes and benefits on household income, 2003/04", published on the National Statistics website *www.statistics.gov.uk/taxesbenefits* and in the July 2005 edition of *Economic Trends*.

Source: Office for National Statistics: 020 7533 5770

8.3 Sources of gross household income[1]
United Kingdom

		1994 /95	1995 /96	1996 /97	1997 /98	1998[2] /99	1999 /00	2000 /01	2001 /02	2002 /03	2003 /04	2004 /05
Number of households supplying data	KPDA	6 853	6 797	6 415	6 409	6 630	7 097	6 637	7 473	6 927	7 048	6 798
Average weekly household income by source (£)												
Wages and salaries	KPCB	237.90	245.00	256.30	280.20	309.20	315.40	336.70	376.80	373.90	384.00	409.70
Self-employment	KPCC	35.30	32.90	37.50	32.90	37.20	46.00	44.50	43.80	44.50	49.80	49.00
Investments	KPCD	16.20	18.10	17.80	18.70	18.80	21.80	20.00	19.60	18.80	16.70	16.50
Annuities and pensions (other than social security benefits)	KPCE	23.50	26.00	26.00	28.90	30.30	32.80	35.00	36.10	39.90	40.90	41.70
Social security benefits[3]	KPCF	49.90	52.40	54.10	55.00	55.80	58.00	60.10	63.50	68.50	72.50	76.90
Other sources	KPCH	6.50	6.60	5.30	5.20	5.70	5.90	6.20	6.70	6.70	6.40	6.90
Total	KPCI	369.30	380.90	396.90	420.80	457.00	479.90	502.50	546.50	552.30	570.30	600.70
Sources of household income as a percentage of total household income												
Wages and salaries	KPCJ	64	64	65	67	68	66	67	69	68	67	68
Self-employment	KPCK	10	9	9	8	8	10	9	8	8	9	8
Investments	KPCL	4	5	5	4	4	5	4	4	3	3	3
Annuities and pensions (other than social security benefits)	KPCM	6	7	7	7	7	7	7	7	7	7	7
Social security benefits[3]	KPCN	14	14	14	13	12	12	12	12	12	13	13
Other sources	KPCP	2	2	1	1	1	1	1	1	1	1	1
Total	KPCQ	100	100	100	100	100	100	100	100	100	100	100

1 See chapter text.
2 From 1998-99 income is based on weighted data.
3 Excluding housing benefits and council tax benefit (rates rebate in Northern Ireland) - see definitions in Appendix B of Family Spending 2004-05.

Sources: Expenditure and Food Survey; Office for National Statistics: 020 7533 5755

Personal income, expenditure and wealth

8.4 Households and their expenditure at current prices[1]
United Kingdom

		1994/95	1995/96	1996/97	1997/98	1998[2]/99	1999/00	2000/01	2001/02	2002/03	2003/04	2004/05
Number of households supplying data	KPDA	6 853	6 797	6 415	6 409	6 630	7 097	6 637	7 473	6 927	7 048	6 798

Average weekly household expenditure on commodities and services (£)

		1994/95	1995/96	1996/97	1997/98	1998[2]/99	1999/00	2000/01	2001/02	2002/03	2003/04	2004/05
Housing	KPEV	46.40	48.30	49.10	51.50	57.20	57.00	63.90	66.60	66.70	69.90	76.70
Fuel and power	KPEW	13.00	12.90	13.40	12.70	11.70	11.30	11.90	11.70	11.70	12.00	12.50
Food	KPEX	50.40	52.90	55.20	55.90	58.90	59.60	61.90	62.30	64.30	64.90	67.30
Alcoholic drink	KPEY	12.30	11.40	12.40	13.30	14.00	15.30	15.00	14.60	14.80	14.70	14.80
Tobacco	KPEZ	5.60	5.80	6.10	6.10	5.80	6.00	6.10	5.60	5.40	5.50	5.00
Clothing and footwear	KCWC	17.10	17.20	18.30	20.00	21.70	21.00	22.00	22.50	22.00	22.40	23.50
Household goods	KCWH	22.70	23.50	26.70	26.90	29.60	30.70	32.60	33.10	33.80	35.10	35.60
Household services	KCWI	15.10	15.10	16.40	17.90	18.90	18.90	22.00	23.80	23.30	24.90	26.30
Personal goods and services	KCWJ	10.80	11.60	11.60	12.50	13.30	13.90	14.70	14.90	15.20	16.20	16.00
Motoring expenditure	KCWK	36.20	37.00	41.20	46.60	51.70	52.60	55.10	58.50	61.70	62.40	62.60
Fares and other travel costs	KCWL	6.60	6.20	7.50	8.10	8.30	9.20	9.50	9.50	9.70	9.60	9.40
Leisure goods	KCWM	13.90	13.20	15.20	16.40	17.80	18.50	19.70	19.90	20.50	21.40	21.40
Leisure services	KCWN	31.20	32.10	34.00	38.80	41.90	43.90	50.60	52.30	53.60	55.00	59.60
Miscellaneous	KCWO	2.30	2.40	2.20	2.00	1.20	1.40	0.70	1.90	2.00	1.90	2.00
Total	KCWP	283.60	289.90	309.10	328.80	352.20	359.40	385.70	397.20	404.70	415.70	432.90

Expenditure on commodity or service as a percentage of total expenditure

		1994/95	1995/96	1996/97	1997/98	1998[2]/99	1999/00	2000/01	2001/02	2002/03	2003/04	2004/05
Housing	KPFH	16	17	16	16	16	16	17	17	16	17	18
Fuel and power	KPFI	5	5	4	4	3	3	3	3	3	3	3
Food	KPFJ	18	18	18	17	17	17	16	16	16	16	16
Alcoholic drink	KPFK	4	4	4	4	4	4	4	4	4	4	3
Tobacco	KPFL	2	2	2	2	2	2	2	1	1	1	1
Clothing and footwear	KPFM	6	6	6	6	6	6	6	6	5	5	5
Household goods	KCWQ	8	8	9	8	8	9	8	8	8	8	8
Household services	KCWR	5	5	5	5	5	5	6	6	6	6	6
Personal goods and services	KCWS	4	4	4	4	4	4	4	4	4	4	4
Motoring expenditure	KCWT	13	13	13	14	15	15	14	15	15	15	14
Fares and other travel costs	KCWU	2	2	2	3	2	3	2	2	2	2	2
Leisure goods	KCWV	5	5	5	5	5	5	5	5	5	5	5
Leisure services	KCWW	11	11	11	12	12	12	13	13	13	13	14
Miscellaneous	KPFR	1	1	1	1	–	–	–	–	–	–	–
Total	KPFS	100	100	100	100	100	100	100	100	100	100	100

1 See chapter text.
2 From 1998-99 averages based on grossed number of households. Expenditure based on weighted data and including children's expenditure.

Source: Expenditure and Food Survey, Office for National Statistics: 0207 533 5755

8.5 Households with selected durable goods[1]
United Kingdom

Percentages

		1994/95	1995/96	1996/97	1997/98	1998[2]/99	1999/00	2000/01	2001/02	2002/03	2003/04	2004/05
Number of households supplying data	KPDA	6 853	6 797	6 415	6 409	6 630	7 097	6 637	7 473	6 927	7 048	6 798
Car	KPDB	69	70	69	70	72	71	72	74	74	75	75
One	KPDC	45	47	43	44	44	43	44	44	44	44	42
Two	KPDD	20	19	22	21	23	21	22	24	25	25	27
Three or more	KPDE	4	4	5	5	5	6	6	6	6	6	6
Central heating, full or partial	KPDF	84	85	87	89	89	90	91	92	93	94	95
Washing machine	KPDG	89	91	91	91	92	91	92	93	94	94	95
Refrigerator or fridge/freezer	KPDH	99	99	..	..	..	..	..	..	..	..	..
Fridge/freezer or deep freezer	KPDI	86	87	91	90	92	91	94	95	96	96	96
Refrigerator	KPDJ	..	..	49	51	52	53	..	..	–	–	–
Dishwasher	GPTL	18	20	20	22	23	23	25	27	29	31	33
Television	KPDK	..	..	..	..	..	..	..	..	..	..	..
Telephone	KPDL	91	92	93	94	95	95	93	94	94	92	93
Home computer	KPDM	..	..	27	29	33	38	44	50	55	58	62
Video recorder	KPDN	76	79	82	84	85	86	87	90	90	90	88
Internet access	ZBUZ	..	..	..	..	10	19	32	40	45	49	53

1 See chapter text.
2 From 1998-99, percentages are based on grossed number of households.

Source: Expenditure and Food Survey, Office for National Statistics: 0207 533 5755

Health

Chapter 9

Health

Hospital and family health services

(Table 9.1)

The courses of treatment are for the General Dental Services (GDS). A course of treatment is complete when the treatment that is required – or such of it that the patient is willing to undergo – has been carried out. A dentist in accepting a patient for continuing care (adults) or capitation (children), undertakes to provide the care and treatment necessary to secure and maintain oral health.

Deaths: analysed by cause

(Table 9.6)

All figures in this table for England and Wales represent the number of deaths *occurring* in each calendar year. All data for Scotland and Northern Ireland relate to the number of deaths *registered* during each calendar year. From 2001, all three constituent countries of the United Kingdom are coding their causes of death using the latest, tenth, revision of the International Statistical Classification of Diseases and Related Health Problems (ICD-10). All cause of death information from 2001 (also for 2000 for Scotland) presented in this table is based on the revised classification.

To assist users in assessing any discontinuities arising from the introduction of the revised classification, bridge-coding exercises were carried out on all deaths registered in 1999 in England and Wales and also in Scotland. For further information about ICD-10 and the bridge-coding carried out by the Office for National Statistics, see the ONS Report: Results of the ICD-10 bridge-coding study, England and Wales, 1999. *Health Statistics Quarterly* 14 (2002), pages 75–83 or the National Statistics website at: www.statistics.gov.uk. For information on the Scottish bridge-coding exercise, consult the Annual Report of the General Register Office for Scotland or their website at: www.gro-scotland.gov.uk. No bridge-coding exercise was conducted for Northern Ireland.

Neonatal deaths and homicide and assault

For England and Wales, neonatal deaths (those at age under 28 days) are included in the number of total deaths but excluded from the cause figures. This has particular impact on the totals shown for the chapters covered by the ranges P and Q, 'Conditions originating in the perinatal period' and 'Congenital malformations, deformations and chromosomal abnormalities'. These are considerably lower than the actual number of deaths because it is not possible to assign an underlying cause of death from the neonatal death certificate used in England and Wales. Also, for England and Wales only, the total number shown for Homicide and assault, X85–Y09, will not be a true representation because the registration of these deaths is often delayed by adjourned inquests.

Occupational ill health

(Tables 9.8 and 9.9)

There are a number of sources of data on the extent of occupational or work-related ill health in Great Britain. For some potentially severe lung diseases caused by exposures which are highly unlikely to be found in a non-occupational setting, it is useful to count the number of death certificates issued each year. This is also true for mesothelioma, a cancer affecting the lining of the lungs and stomach, for which the number of cases with non-occupational causes is likely to be larger (although 122 still a minority). Table 9.9 shows the number of deaths for *mesothelioma* and *asbestosis* (linked to exposure to asbestos), *pneumoconiosis* (linked to coal dust or silica), *byssinosis* (linked to cotton dust) and some forms of *allergic alveolitis* (including farmer's lung). For asbestos-related diseases the figures are derived from a special register maintained by HSE.

Most conditions which can be caused or made worse by work can also arise from other factors. The remaining sources of data on work-related ill health rely on *attribution* of individual cases of illness to work causes. In The Health and Occupation Reporting Network (THOR), this is done by specialist doctors – either occupational physicians or those working in particular disease specialisms (covering musculoskeletal, psychological, respiratory, skin, audiological and infectious disease). Table 9.8 presents data from THOR for the last three years. It should be noted that not all cases of occupational disease will be seen by participating specialists; for example, the number of deaths due to mesothelioma (shown in Table 9.9) is known to be greater than the number of cases reported to THOR.

Injuries at work

(Table 9.10)

The appropriate 'responsible person' is required to report injuries arising from workplace activities to HSE or the local authority under the Reporting of Injuries, Diseases and Dangerous Occurrences Regulations 1995 (RIDDOR 95). This includes fatal injuries, nonfatal major injuries, as defined by the Regulations, and other injuries causing incapacity for work for more than three days. As of 1 April 2001, reports are to be made to an Incident Centre (ICC), based at Caerphilly.

HSE gets to know about virtually all workplace fatalities. However, it is known that employers and others do not report all non-fatal reportable injuries. To estimate the level of under-reporting by employers, HSE place questions each year with the Labour Force Survey (LFS), asking respondents if they have suffered a workplace injury in the past year.

The results from the latest LFS show that in Great Britain employers report around 48 per cent of reportable injuries (2003/04). When compared to the previous year, these results also indicate a drop of in the non-fatal injury rate of 7.0 per cent. The self-employed report around 6.7 per cent of reportable non-fatal injuries.

9.1 Hospital and family health services
England and Wales

			England						Wales				
			2000	2001	2002	2003	2004		2000	2001	2002	2003	2004
Hospital services[1]													
Average daily number of available beds	KNMY	Thousands	186	185	184	184	182	KNHY	15	14	14	14	14
Average daily occupation of beds:													
All departments	KNMX	"	156	157	157	158	136	KNHX	12	12	12	12	12
Psychiatric departments	KNMW	"	34	..	..	..	..	KNGZ	3	3	2	2	2
Persons waiting for admission at 31 March[2]	KNMV	"	1 007	1 035	992	906	822	KNGY	66	71	75	75	66
Finished consultant episodes													
Day case admissions	KNLY	"	3 629	3 588	3 703	3 757	3 757	KNBZ	132	131	107	109	109
Ordinary admissions	KIBS	"	8 636	8 750	9 012	9 417	..	KNEO	579	570	564	593	600
Out-patients													
New cases	KNLX	"	12 466	12 613	12 879	13 431	13 370	KNBY	699	697	737	740	742
Total attendances	KNLW	"	43 569	43 675	43 765	45 120	44 768	KNBX	2 737	2 762	2 843	2 868	2 804
Accident and Emergency:													
New cases	KOTH	"	12 953	12 853	12 945	15 313	16 712	KTCO	854	878	889	916	937
Total attendances	KOTI	"	14 293	14 044	14 046	16 517	17 837	KTCP	986	1 010	1 005	1 036	1 059
Ward attendances	KOTJ	"	1 078	1 089	1 179	..	..	KTCQ	..	..	..	..	..
Family health services[3]													
Medical services:													
Doctors on the list[4]	KNKX	Numbers	..	..	..		..	KNBR	1 795	1 807	1 808	1 822	1 816
Number of UPEs[5]	LQZZ	"	27 704	27 843	28 031	28 568	..	ZCMA	–	–	–	–	..
Number of patients per doctor	KNKW	"	1 853	1 841	1 838	1 845	..	KNBQ	1 676	1 665	1 679	1 659	1 674
Paid to doctors[6]	KNKV	£ million	..	..	..	..	..	KNBP	213	222	241	269	..
Pharmaceutical services:[7,8]													
Number of prescription forms	KWUK	Millions	300	315	326	..	..	VQEU	..	..	..	..	–
Number of prescription items	KWUL	"	552	587	617	650	686	KNBO	43	46	49	51	54
Total cost	KWUM	£ million	5 967	6 488	7 162	..	..	KNBN	434	472	..	..	..
Average total cost per prescription	KWUN	£	10.8	11.1	11.6	..	..	KNBK	9.9	10.0	..	..	..
Income from patients	KWUO	£ million	387	408	423	..	..	KNBM	23	23	23	23	..
Dental services:													
Principals on an FHSA/HA list at 30 September[9]	KIAZ	Numbers	16 276	16 451	16 445	..	..	KIBG	928	931	927	919	927
Number of adult courses of treatments[10]	KIBA	Thousands	26 353	26 318	26 284	..	..	KIBH	1 557	1 564	1 886	1 629	1 689
Number of adult patients accepted into continuing care provision at 30 September[11]	KIBB	"	16 813	16 793	16 739	..	..	KIBI	1 074	1 063	1 065	1 079	1 050
Number of children accepted into capitation at 30 September[11]	KIBC	"	6 845	6 784	6 733	..	..	KIBJ	412	403	400	397	384
Gross expenditure[12]	KIBD	£ million	1 555	–	–	..	..	KIBK	91	95	99	104	107
Paid by patients[12]	KIBE	"	453	–	–	..	..	KIBL	25	25	25	27	26
Paid out of public funds[12]	KIBF	"	1 102	–	–	..	..	KIBM	67	71	74	76	82
General ophthalmic services:													
Sight tests[13]	KNJL	Thousands	9 567	9 807	9 662	..	..	KNBD	659	668	647	646	656
Pairs of spectacles for which NHS vouchers redeemed	KNJK	"	3 575	3 607	3 472	..	..	KNBC	273	273	252	252	251
Cost of services (gross)[12]	KNJJ	£ million	306	311	304	..	..	KNBA	21	22	22	22	23
Paid out of public funds:[12]													
For sight testing	KNJH	"	163	167	166	..	..	KMZZ	10	11	11	11	11
For cost of vouchers[11]	WMPC	"	142	143	137	..	..	KMZX	10	10	9	9	10

1 Data shown reflect data for the financial year commencing the year in the heading (for example, the figures under 1999 reflects 1999/2000 data). Out-patient figures do not include accident and emergency figures or ward attenders which are given separately. Information on general practitioner maternity clinics is not collected separately in England but is included for Wales.

2 People awaiting elective admission at NHS Trusts in England and Wales, as an inpatient or a day case.

3 Welsh FHS expenditure and income is based upon cash payments and receipts in each financial year, as accrued gross expenditure is not available in a common format for all years shown in this series. Welsh Dental Services data excludes refunds of dental charges.

4 For Wales, Principals providing unrestricted services as at 1 October.

5 UPE's include Unrestricted Principals, PMS Contracted GP's and PMS salaried GP's.UPE data are at 1 October.

6 For Wales, includes PFMA but excludes GPFH drugs and payments to providers.

7 Welsh data are based on pricing bureau totals of prescriptions dispensed in a calendar year and paid during the financial year. Data shown reflects data for the year commencing the year in the heading (for example, the figures under 1999 reflects 1999/2000 data). Financial year is from 1 April to 31 March.

8 The data cover all prescription items dispensed by community pharmacists and appliance contractors, dispensing doctors and prescriptions submitted by prescribing doctors for items personally administered. Total cost refers to the cost of the drug less discounts and includes on cost allowance, dispensing fees, container allowance, oxygen payments and VAT. Income from patients relates to financial years and from 2001/2002 is taken from HA annual accounts. Previous years taken from the Appropriation Account. Income includes charges retained by pharmacists & dispensing doctors, sales of pre-payment certificates and recoveries from patients.

9 Principals only. Assistants and vocational trainees are not included. Some dentists may have a contract with more than one Family Health Service /Health Authority. These dentists have been counted once only.

10 Data shown reflect data for the financial year commencing the year in the heading (for example, the figures under 2001 represent 2001/2002 data).

11 Figures for 1998 onwards are affected by the shortening of the registration period to 15 months.

12 Figures for England are based on provisional outturn figures, with gross gross expenditure and patient figures having been adjusted from previous publications to include refunds of dental charges. For Wales, figures are for the financial year and based on the Appropriation account.

13 Number of NHS sight tests paid for by FHSAs/HAs in the period.

Sources: Department of Health;
National Assembly for Wales: 029 2082 5080

Hospital and primary care services
Scotland

			1994	1995	1996	1997	1998	1999	2000	2001	2002	2003	2004
Hospital and community services													
In-patients:[1,2]													
Average available staffed beds	KDEA	Thousands	44.2	42.4	40.6	38.4	36.8	35.2	33.5	32.1	30.9	29.8	28.9
Average occupied beds:													
All departments	KDEB	"	35.9	34.3	32.8	30.9	29.5	28.2	26.9	25.8	25.1	24.2	23.2
Psychiatric and learning disability	KDEC	"	13.2	12.6	11.7	10.8	10.0	9.1	8.3	7.6	7.0	6.4	5.9
Discharges or deaths[3]	KDED	"	952	960	973	965	978	977	965	957	952	939	968
Outpatients:[2,4]													
New cases	KDEE	"	2 503	2 577	2 666	2 675	2 715	2 734	2 766	2 748	2 728	2 730	2 748
Total attendances	KDEF	"	6 145	6 241	6 338	6 272	6 331	6 424	6 451	6 381	6 254	6 192	6 144
Medical and dental staff:[5]	JYXO	Numbers	8 317	8 524	8 774	9 098	9 157	9 367	9 325	9 646	10 256	10 381	10 608
Whole-time	KDEG	"	5 937	6 102	6 433	6 707	7 052	7 202	6 896	7 218	7 759	8 325	8 569
Part-time	KDEH	"	1 827	1 854	1 819	1 886	1 613	1 685	1 966	1 989	2 063	1 633	1 622
Honorary	JYXN	"	563	579	534	522	506	495	495	468	468	438	432
Professional and technical staff:[6]													
Whole-time	KDEI	"	10 062	10 452	10 584	10 740	10 884	11 261	11 261	11 705	12 265	12 942	13 258
Part-time	KDEJ	"	3 753	4 075	4 370	4 738	4 928	5 218	5 483	5 852	6 273	6 708	6 968
Nursing and midwifery staff:[7]													
Whole-time	KDEK	"	32 956	32 693	32 560	32 218	32 156	32 356	32 401	33 334	34 294	34 961	35 369
Part-time	KDEL	"	30 532	30 580	29 917	29 736	29 178	29 242	29 131	29 004	29 015	29 356	29 486
Administrative and clerical staff:[8]													
Whole-time	KDEM	"	15 723	15 815	15 155	14 707	14 564	14 541	14 710	15 361	16 200	17 238	17 775
Part-time	KDEN	"	6 624	7 005	6 986	7 174	7 265	7 456	7 677	8 075	8 630	9 305	9 941
Domestic, transport, etc, staff:[9]													
Whole-time	KDEO	"	9 574	9 037	8 596	8 187	8 090	7 972	7 848	7 625	7 768	8 234	8 305
Part-time	KDEP	"	14 464	14 105	13 554	13 082	12 716	12 424	12 272	11 522	11 915	12 588	12 324
Cost of services (gross)[10]	KDEQ	£ million	3 050.5	3 269.5	3 430.6	3 610.3	3 856.0	4 309.7	4 862.6	5 378.6	5 919.5	..	..
Payments by patients[10]	KDER	"	0.40	0.02	0.01	0.01	0.01	0.01	0.01	–	..	..	..
Payments out of public funds[10]	KDES	"	3 050.1	3 269.5	3 430.6	3 610.3	3 855.9	4 309.7	4 862.6	5 378.6	5 919.5	..	..
Primary care services													
Medical services													
Doctors on the list:[11]													
Principals[12]	KDET	Numbers	3 490	3 524	3 573	3 625	3 660	3 698	3 707	3 756	3 765	3 801	3 782
Assistants	KDEU	"	25	28	22	22	27	19	25	39	37	47	..
Average number of patients per principal doctor[13]	KDEV	"	1 524	1 506	1 488	1 468	1 450	1 441	1 425	1 409	1 392	1 381	1 421
Payments to doctor[14]	KDEW	£ million	291.7	311.9	333.2	356.4	365.9	377.5	404.7	429.6	467.5	..	..
Pharmaceutical services[15]													
Prescriptions dispensed	KDEX	Millions	49.27	51.08	54.62	56.64	58.52	60.36	62.34	65.56	69.13	71.83	74.66
Payments to pharmacists (gross)	KDEY	£ million	434.9	474.2	543.4	588.4	627.2	693.7	731.0	788.6	868.9	946.3	988.0
Average gross cost per prescription	KDEZ	£	8.8	9.3	10.0	10.4	10.7	11.5	11.7	12.0	12.6	13.2	13.2
Dental services													
Dentists on list[16]	KDFA	Numbers	1 684	1 691	1 709	1 710	1 739	1 786	1 808	1 808	1 844	1 869	1 882
Number of courses of treatment completed	KDFB	Thousands	2 647	2 723	2 711	2 825	3 406	3 349	3 406	3 395	3 390	3 433	3 370
Payments to dentists (gross)	KDFC	£ million	128.4	136.1	137.3	139.2	154.9	157.5	160.6	162.9	165.1	172.3	170.4
Payments by patients	KDFD	"	40.0	42.2	41.7	41.4	45.9	47.4	48.8	50.6	52.3	54.7	53.3
Payments out of public funds	KDFE	"	88.4	93.9	95.6	97.8	109.0	110.1	111.8	112.3	112.9	117.6	117.1
Average gross cost per course	KDFF	£	37.0	38.0	38.0	40.1	36.5	38.0	38.0	37.0	38.0	40.0	40.0
General ophthalmic services													
Number of sight tests given[17]	KDFG	Thousands	..	614	618	635	656	657	850	861	877	907	920
Number of pairs of glasses supplied[18]	KDFH	"	..	473	461	474	488	485	494	439	463	458	450
Payments out of public funds for sight testing and dispensing	KDFK	£ million	24.4	25.8	27.7	29.1	29.8	32.0	33.1	..	..	34.9	35.5

1 Excludes joint user and contractual hospitals.
2 In year to 31 March.
3 Includes transfers out and emergency inpatients treated in day bed units.
4 Including attendances at accident and emergency consultant clinics.
5 As at 30 September. Figures exclude officers holding honorary locum appointments. Part-time includes maximum part-time appointments. There is an element of double counting of "heads" in this table as doctors can hold more than one contract. For example, they may hold contracts of different type, eg part time and honorary. Doctors holding two or more contracts of the same type, eg part time, are not double counted. Doctors, whose sum of contracts amounts to whole time, are classed as such.
6 As at 30 September. Comprises Scientific and Professional, Allied Health Professionals and Technical staff.
7 As at 30 September. Includes Health Care Assistans.
8 As at 30 September. Comprises Senior Management and Administrative and Clerical staff.
9 As at 30 September. Comprises Ambulance, Works, Ancillary and Trades.

10 These figures are for Health Boards only and do not include the 2 NHS Trusts in 1995 and 47 in 1995/96. Estimated from financial years.
11 At 1 October.
12 Unrestricted principals in post.
13 Unrestricted principals: establishment.
14 Data relate to financial year, eg 1997 data are for year ending 31 March 1998. As 1994/95 data are unavailable for Dumfries & Galloway Health Board, 1993/94 data have been substituted for that board only.
15 For prescriptions dispensed in calendar year by all community pharmacists (including stock orders), dispensing doctors and appliance suppliers.
16 Comprises principals only.
17 This figure represents sight tests paid for by health boards, hospital eye service referrals and GOS(s) ST (v) claimants. From 1995, data refers to financial year (eg 1995 data is for year ending 31 March 1995). 1994 calander year data is missing.
18 Does not include hospital eye service.

Source: NHS National Services Scotland and The Scottish Executive: 0131 551 8899

9.3 Hospital and general health services
Northern Ireland

			1995	1996	1997	1998	1999	2000	2001	2002	2003	2004
Hospital services[1]												
In-patients:												
Beds available[2]	KDGA	Numbers	10 054	9 464	9 006	8 818	8 639	8 571	8 419	8 301	8 347	8 323
Average daily occupation of beds	KDGB	Percentages	*77.7*	*78.9*	*80.8*	*81.9*	*81.5*	*82.0*	*83.3*	*84.3*	*84.1*	*84.2*
Discharges or deaths[3]	KDGC	Thousands	304	300	305	335	332	333	328	327	332	337
Out-patients:[4]												
New cases	KDGD	"	940	933	952	962	984	994	997	992	1 014	1 027
Total attendances	KDGE	"	2 087	2 070	2 084	2 091	2 111	2 114	2 131	2 122	2 161	2 175
General health services												
Medical services[1]												
Doctors (principals) on the list[5,6]	KDGF	Numbers	1 005	1 028	1 039	1 042	1 054	1 066	1 073	1 091	1 096	1 098
Number of patients per doctor	KDGG	"	1 725	1 698	1 690	1 693	1 678	1 661	1 651	1 632	1 783	1 627
GrossPayments to doctors[7]	KDGH	£ thousand	65 130	67 872	69 889	71 385	78 604	82 471	84 664	88 194	96 894	..
Pharmaceutical services[8]												
Prescription forms dispensed	KDGI	Thousands	12 017	12 802	13 246	13 489	13 454	13 666	14 277	14 622	15 158	15 283
Number of prescriptions	KDGJ	"	19 893	21 203	22 047	22 754	23 249	23 985	24 705	25 501	26 656	27 401
Gross Cost[12]	KDGK	£ thousand	197 579	219 978	236 746	248 845	266 535	278 405	303 489	327 045	362 401	382 789
Charges[15]	KDGL	"	6 455	6 224	6 784	7 007	8 183	8 499	9 074	9 597	9 798	10 262
Net Cost[12]	KDGM	"	191 324	213 950	229 962	241 837	258 353	269 906	294 415	317 448	352 602	372 527
Average gross cost per prescription[12]	KDGN	£	9.93	10.38	10.74	10.94	11.46	11.61	12.28	12.82	13.60	13.97
Dental services[8,9]												
Dentists on the list[5]	KDGO	Numbers	588	584	592	612	632	661	673	689	696	720
Number of courses of paid treatment	KDGP	Thousands	832	928	1 053	1 088	1 086	1 113	1 126	1 123	1 107	1 086
Gross cost	KDGQ	£ thousand	48 780	51 512	53 735	56 835	58 712	61 237	64 454	66 201	66 910	67 294
Patients	KDGR	Thousands	11 530	11 870	12 433	13 686	14 358	15 302	16 041	954	950	945
Contributions (Net cost)	KDGS	£ thousand	37 250	39 642	41 303	43 149	44 354	46 152	48 413	49 376	50 282	50 498
Average gross cost per paid treatment	KDGT	£	59	56	50	52	54	55	57	59	60	62
Ophthalmic services[8]												
Number of sight tests given[10]	KDGU	Thousands	196	212	227	236	305	307	326	334	346	347
Number of optical appliances supplied[11]	KDGV	"	146	153	159	158	158	160	165	168	169	167
Cost of service (gross)[14]	KDGW	£ thousand	8 568	9 555	10 271	10 303	11 509	12 035	12 738	13 473	13 981	14 444
Health and social services[13]												
Medical and dental staff:												
Whole-time	KDGZ	Numbers	2 053	2 107	2 156	2 196	2 231	2 224	2 281	2 411	2 607	2 749
Part-time	KDHA	"	1 154	1 094	1 041	1 009	1 014	580	597	626	620	627
Nursing and midwifery staff:												
Whole-time	KDHB	"	10 896	10 578	10 114	10 117	10 135	9 926	9 828	10 248	10 729	11 137
Part-time	KDHC	"	9 169	8 943	9 015	8 287	8 813	7 591	7 814	8 395	8 706	8 887
Administrative and clerical staff:												
Whole-time	KDHD	"	7 078	7 055	6 915	7 019	7 230	7 373	7 536	7 966	8 370	8 846
Part-time	KDHE	"	2 306	2 518	2 708	2 776	2 910	2 972	3 136	3 372	3 609	3 858
Professional and technical staff:												
Whole-time	KDHF	"	2 862	2 939	2 933	3 014	3 177	3 642	3 762	3 975	4 163	4 528
Part-time	KDHG	"	921	985	1 060	1 146	1 226	1 283	1 369	1 499	1 616	1 731
Social services staff(excluding casual home helps):												
Whole-time	KDHH	"	3 470	3 441	3 349	3 262	3 319	3 017	3 127	3 284	3 461	3 716
Part-time	KDHI	"	2 110	2 250	2 394	2 241	2 358	868	911	986	1 105	1 207
Ancillary and other staff:												
Whole-time	KDHJ	"	3 982	3 812	3 569	3 423	3 426	3 506	3 472	3 426	3 418	3 470
Part-time	KDHK	"	3 685	3 558	3 482	3 558	3 913	4 508	4 925	5 125	5 420	5 588
Cost of services (gross)[14]	KDHL	£ thousand	1 111 507	1 120 563	1 153 741	1 292 348	1 422 920	1 576 657	1 639 283	1 868 538	2 113 453	..
Payments by recipients	KDHM	Thousands	32 685	40 725	49 498	59 484	65 533	71 411	78 478	88 860	87 999	..
Payments out of public funds	KDHN	£ thousand	1 078 822	1 079 838	1 104 243	1 232 864	1 357 387	1 505 246	1 560 805	1 779 678	2 025 454	..

1 Financial Year.
2 Average available beds in wards open overnight during the year.
3 Includes transfers to other hospitals.
4 Includes consultant outpatient clinics and Accident and Emergency departments.
5 At beginning of period.
6 Doctors include assistants.
7 These costs refer to the majority of non-cash limited services: further expenditure under GMS is allocated through HSS Boards on a cash limited basis. Change between 2002 and 2003 is due to advance payments being made in relation to the new GMS contract introduced in April 2004.
8 From 1995 onwards figures are taken from financial year.
9 Due to changes in the Dental Contract which came into force in October 1990 dentists are paid under a combination of headings relating to Capitation and Continuing Care patients. Prior to this, payment was simply on an item of service basis, which made statistics such as 'Number of courses of treatment completed' and Average gross cost per course' relevant and meaningful. This is no longer the case.

10 Excluding sight tests given in hospitals and under the school health service and in the home.
11 Relates to the number of vouchers supplied and excludes repair/replace spectacles.
12 Gross cost is defined as net ingredient costs plus on-cost, fees and other payments.
13 Workforce figures until 1999 refer to 31st December and are taken from the Trust and Board payroll system. Figures from 2000 onwards are at 30th September and are taken from the Trust and Board Human Resource Management Systems. Figures for 2000 onwards exclude all home helps and all agency/bank staff but include Ambulance and Works staff in the Ancillary & Other Staff category. As a result, backward comparison of the workforce is not advisable as definitions differ. Some figures for 2000 have been revised.
14 Figures relate to the costs of the hospital, community health and personal social services, and have been estimated from financial year data.
15 Excludes amount paid by patients for pre-payment certificates

Sources: Central Services Agency Northern Ireland: 028 9032 4431;
Dept of Health, Social Services & Public Safety Northern Ireland: 028 9052 2509;
(Figures on Hospital Services: 028 9052 2800)

9.4 Health services: workforce summary[1]
Great Britain
As at 30 September

Whole-time equivalent

		1995	1996	1997	1998	1999	2000	2001	2002	2003	2004
Health service staff and practitioners											
Medical staff: total	KDBC	60 172	62 176	64 316	67 408	69 089	70 939	73 206	78 024	82 294	89 450
Hospital medical staff: total	KDBD	57 299	59 592	61 937	65 088	66 812	68 767	71 107	76 122	80 537	87 641
Consultant	KDBE	20 246	21 066	21 699	23 139	24 250	25 067	26 106	27 951	29 566	31 628
Staff grade	KADJ	2 037	2 440	2 785	3 458	3 868	4 423	4 720	5 409	5 462	5 648
Associate specialist	KDBF	1 128	1 223	1 340	1 439	1 527	1 572	1 609	1 780	1 993	2 263
Registrar group[2]	KWUG	..	11 898	12 435	12 863	13 299	13 372	13 826	14 530	15 580	17 890
Senior registrar	KDBG	4 540	..	..	..	..	..	..	..	..	..
Registrar	KDBH	7 294	..	..	..	..	..	..	..	..	..
Senior house officer	KDBI	15 661	16 616	17 353	17 760	17 518	17 945	18 377	19 850	21 525	23 567
House officer	KADK	4 003	4 025	4 163	4 287	4 364	4 518	4 560	4 944	4 985	5 276
Hospital practitioner	KDBL	197	212	198	220	230	231	223	248	247	256
Clinical assistant	KDBM	2 182	2 094	1 924	1 907	1 744	1 638	1 684	1 407	1 179	1 064
Other staff	KDBK	11	18	38	16	11	1	1	3	−	50
Public health medicine and community health services medical staff	KDBN	2 873	2 584	2 379	2 320	2 278	2 172	2 100	1 902	1 756	1 809
Dental staff: total	KDBO	3 070	3 127	3 078	3 193	3 147	3 107	3 152	3 357	3 429	3 571
Hospital dental staff: total	KDBP	1 687	1 737	1 696	1 807	1 816	1 781	1 816	1 944	1 981	2 021
Consultant	KDBQ	549	556	524	570	581	580	578	610	664	689
Staff grade	KADL	54	67	86	99	113	118	135	154	158	163
Associate specialist	KDBR	69	65	62	68	70	73	74	75	79	93
Registrar group[2]	LQMZ	..	..	..	309	314	295	311	339	329	344
Senior registrar	KDBS	123	138	169	..	..	..	..	..	..	..
Registrar	KDBT	186	183	125	..	..	..	..	..	..	..
Senior house officer	KDBU	446	490	491	531	496	497	513	572	584	580
Dental house officer	KDBV	86	68	58	59	68	60	61	60	38	31
Hospital practitioner	KDBX	17	23	22	21	23	21	18	20	20	22
Clinical assistant	KDBY	158	145	152	144	146	136	126	112	108	98
Other staff	KDBW	−	3	6	5	6	−	−	1	−	1
Community health dental staff	KDBZ	1 383	1 390	1 382	1 386	1 331	1 326	1 336	1 413	1 448	1 550
Non-medical staff: total	KWUH	804 148	856 732	849 426	855 305	870 921	890 282	927 831	974 390	1 022 837	1 061 640
Nursing and midwifery staff:[3,4] (excluding agency): total	KDCA	387 436	410 693	407 760	409 045	415 786	423 737	437 417	455 361	474 263	485 180
of which: qualified	KSBR	282 200	300 371	298 483	299 654	303 644	309 682	320 685	335 313	349 701	360 910
unqualified	KSBS	99 946	106 181	106 313	106 773	109 687	111 931	114 532	117 582	121 896	121 194
learners	KSBT	4 580	2 804	2 356	2 178	1 961	2 054	2 201	2 387	2 591	3 076
All Professional and Technical staff (excluding works)[5]	KSBM	106 544	118 403	120 439	123 902	128 116	131 943	138 348	146 804	155 507	164 419
Health care assistants	KWUI	13 090	18 025	19 268	22 026	22 746	24 919	30 047	33 301	36 027	37 829
Support staff	KWUJ	74 540	75 836	72 608	71 043	69 883	68 449	69 245	69 628	69 553	69 749
Ancillary, Works & Maintainance	KSBN	29 466	27 603	26 037	25 131	24 468	23 962	23 013	23 430	23 820	24 708
Administrative and Clerical staff	KSBO	172 948	183 049	183 112	184 711	190 421	197 327	209 004	224 490	241 634	256 412
Ambulance staff	KSBP	16 744	18 655	18 751	18 382	18 552	19 209	19 888	20 864	21 449	22 753
Others	KSBQ	3 180	4 159	1 079	906	780	746	711	512	584	590

1 Whote-time equivalent. Figures exclude locums and occasional seasonal staff.
2 Includes Specialist Registrar (SpR), Senior Registrar and Registrar. The SpR grade was introduced formally on 1 April 1996.
3 Excludes bank nurses for Wales.
4 Nursing total includes qualified, unqualified and others only.
5 GP Registrars were formerly referred to as Trainees.

Sources: Information Centre for Health and Social Care;
National Assembly for Wales.;
NHS ISD Scotland;
Scottish Health Service Common Services Agency

9.5 Health and personal social services: workforce summary
Great Britain

Numbers

		1995	1996	1997	1998	1999[3]	2000	2001	2002	2003	2004
Family Health services:											
General medical practitioners[1]											
All practitioners: total[2,3]	GPYL	..	..	..	..	36 954	37 583	38 172	38 656	40 021	41 322
All practitioners (excluding GP Retainers)	LQZN	34 596	34 825	35 204	35 618	35 957	36 233	36 761	37 283	38 769	40 273
Contracted GPs	ENO5	32 084	32 290	32 588	32 909	33 148	33 280	33 487	33 671	34 239	34 332
of which											
GMS Contracted GPs	ENO6	32 084	32 290	32 588	32 225	31 931	31 663	29 318	26 813	23 748	23 805
PMS contracted GPs	ENO7	–	–	–	684	1 217	1 617	4 169	6 858	10 491	10 527
GMS Others	ENO8	722	930	939	849	841	867	717	650	917	1 509
PMS Others	LQZX	–	–	–	30	66	58	279	576	987	1 473
GP Registrars[4]	LQZU	1 790	1 605	1 677	1 830	1 902	2 028	2 278	2 386	2 626	2 959
of which GMS[5]	LQZV	1 790	1 605	1 677	1 772	1 799	1 896	1 937	1 858	1 800	2 011
GP Retainers	GPYM	–	–	–	–	997	1 350	1 411	1 373	1 252	1 049
General dental practitioners: total[6]	KDCQ	18 736	19 139	19 598	20 216	20 833	21 316	21 929	22 194	22 507	22 997
General Dental Service	GPYN	18 736	19 139	19 598	20 216	20 750	21 124	21 462	21 538	21 701	20 826
Personal Dental Service	GPYO	..	..	..	..	83	192	467	656	806	2 171
Ophthalmic medical practitioners [7]	KDCT	789	799	833	863	827	819	754	686	644	..
Ophthalmic opticians [7]	KDCU	7 333	7 582	7 790	8 024	8 423	8 742	8 650	8 761	9 123	..
Personal Social Services staff: total	KDDE	233 900	233 700	229 400	223 500	221 700	217 500	212 000	209 700	211 600	213 300
of which:											
Home help service	KSBU	57 000	55 400	53 600	50 500	47 200	42 900	40 200	37 800	34 900	34 400
Field Social Workers	KSBX	31 900	32 100	33 000	33 400	33 900	34 700	35 200	35 900	37 100	37 900
Day care establishments staff	KADV	31 100	31 600	30 800	30 300	30 800	30 800	29 500	29 500	28 800	28 600
Residential care staff	KADW	68 700	68 000	65 400	62 100	59 200	56 600	53 800	51 500	51 300	48 900

Note Scotland GPs figures included in this table will be slightly different to GPs 'headcount' figures published on the ISD Scotland website as GPs holding more than one contract will be counted in this table by the 'number of contracts held' in each year rather than the 'headcount' of GPs.

1 All GP data as at 1 October except England and Wales as at 30 September from 2000.

2 The 'All practioners' totals for some years do not add up to the sum of their parts, having been adjusted in respect of some Scotish GPs who have posts in two separate categories.

3 All Practioners data for 1999 does not include Scotland retainers as these were first collected in April 2000.

4 GP Registrars were formerly referred to as Trainees.

5 GP Registrars in GMS Partnerships.

6 Includes principals, assistants and trainees. Prison contracts and salaried dentists are excluded. A small proportion of dentists work in both the GDS and PDS. These dentists have been counted only within GDS figures to avoid double counting.

7 Figures for Scotland are as at 31 March, and figures for England and Wales are as at 31 December, of that year. Count of OMPs and OOs holding contracts with FHSAs/HA's/LHBs and/ or Scotish Health Boards to carry out NHS Sight Tests. Practitioners with contracts in both England and Scotland are counted twice for these statistics. The OMP figure for 2003 (644) includes an estimate of 22 OMP's for Scotland, the OMP figure for Scotland being unavailable for 2003.

Sources: The Information Centre for health and social care;
Dental Practice Board;
National Assembly for Wales;
NHS ISD Scotland;
Scottish Health Service Common Services Agency

9.6 Deaths: by cause
International Statistical Classification of Diseases, Injuries and Causes of Death[1]
Ninth Revision 1979 and Tenth Revision 2001 (2000 in Scotland)

Numbers

	ICD-9 code	England and Wales			
		1997	1998	1999	2000
Total deaths		555 281	555 015	556 118	535 664
Deaths from natural causes	001-799	536 453	536 396	537 166	516 803
Certain infectious and parasitic diseases	001-139	3 496	3 410	3 613	3 767
Intestinal infectious diseases	001-009	384	418	476	547
Respiratory and other tuberculosis including late effects	010-018,137	437	453	437	427
Meningococcal infection	036	242	210	217	199
Viral hepatitis	070	165	173	179	200
AIDS (HIV - disease)	042-044	259	163	155	182
Neoplasms	140-239	137 618	138 306	136 181	134 793
Malignant neoplasms	140-208	135 647	136 329	134 135	132 686
Malignant neoplasm of oesophagus	150	5 855	5 952	6 040	6 061
Malignant neoplasm of stomach	151	6 613	6 442	6 139	5 779
Malignant neoplasm of colon	153	10 448	10 170	9 911	9 554
Malignant neoplasm of rectum and anus	154.1-154.8	4 177	4 182	4 059	4 024
Malignant neoplasm of pancreas	157	5 782	5 801	5 956	6 105
Malignant neoplasm of trachea, bronchus and lung	162	29 976	30 199	29 493	29 029
Malignant neoplasm of skin	172	1 378	1 468	1 476	1 536
Malignant neoplasm of breast	174-175	12 047	11 835	11 670	11 433
Malignant neoplasm of cervix uteri	180	1 225	1 158	1 107	1 106
Malignant neoplasm of prostate	185	8 523	8 573	8 533	8 293
Leukaemia	204-208	3 587	3 551	3 680	3 570
Diseases of the blood and blood-forming organs and certain disorders involving the immune mechanism	279-289	2 056	1 978	1 907	1 829
Endocrine, nutritional and metabolic diseases	240-278	7 335	7 501	7 508	7 209
Diabetes mellitus	250	5 890	5 938	5 963	5 773
Mental and behavioural disorders	290-319	9 725	10 430	11 173	10 865
Vascular and unspecified dementia	290	6 731	7 124	7 654	7 173
Alcohol abuse (inc. alcoholic psychosis)	291,303	344	350	347	331
Drug dependence and non-dependent abuse of drugs	292,304-305	736	895	935	1 049
Diseases of the nervous system and sense organs	320-389	9 772	10 035	10 192	9 632
Meningitis (including meningococcal)	320-322	224	216	182	206
Alzheimer's disease	331.0	2 185	2 374	2 406	2 182
Diseases of the circulatory system	390-459	228 446	226 677	219 087	207 228
Ischaemic heart diseases	410-414	122 432	121 037	115 119	108 418
Cerebrovascular diseases	430-438	57 747	57 516	56 051	52 516
Diseases of the respiratory system	460-519	92 517	90 192	97 755	92 461
Influenza	487	347	129	585	509
Pneumonia	480-486	56 719	54 631	59 273	56 329
Bronchitis, emphysema and other chronic obstructive pulmonary diseases	490-492,496	25 097	24 878	26 114	23 538
Asthma	493	1 439	1 366	1 364	1 272
Diseases of the digestive system	520-579	20 406	21 025	21 698	22 134
Gastric and duodenal ulcer	531-533	3 959	3 935	4 011	4 007
Chronic liver disease	571	4 107	4 494	4 718	4 770
Diseases of the skin and subcutaneous tissue	680-709	1 025	1 070	1 152	1 266
Diseases of the musculo-skeletal system and connective tissue	710-739	3 559	3 566	3 554	3 407
Rheumatoid arthritis and juvenile arthritis	714	797	778	697	675
Osteoporosis	733.0-733.1	1 282	1 273	1 335	1 268
Diseases of the genito-urinary system	580-629	6 757	6 946	7 299	7 270
Diseases of the kidney and ureter	580-594	3 767	3 803	3 844	3 799
Complications of pregnancy, childbirth and the puerperium	630-676	35	43	30	38
Certain conditions originating in the perinatal period (excluding neonatals)[1]	760-779	131	124	116	83
Congenital malformations, deformations and chromasomal abnormalities (excluding neonatals)[1]	740-759	1 283	1 247	1 194	1 165
Congenital malformations of the nervous system	740-742	121	124	104	116
Congenital malformations of the circulatory system	745-747	689	643	621	617
Symptoms, signs and abnormal clinical and laboratory findings not elsewhere classified	780-799	12 292	13 846	14 707	13 656
Senility without mention of psychosis (old age)	797	11 028	12 615	13 473	12 458
Sudden infant death syndrome	798.0	327	236	222	180
Deaths from external causes	E800-E999	16 311	16 201	16 517	16 526
All accidents	E800-E929	10 661	10 351	10 625	10 771
Land transport accidents	E800-E829	3 291	3 023	3 098	2 985
Accidental falls	E880-E888	3 885	3 865	3 993	4 281
Accidental poisonings	E850-E869	1 058	1 045	1 030	1 064
Suicide and intentional self-harm	E950-E959	3 424	3 614	3 690	3 480
Homicide and assault[1]	E960-E969	290	285	293	380
Event of undetermined intent	E980-E989	1 914	1 931	1 886	1 872

1 See chapter text

9.6
continued

Deaths: by cause
International Statistical Classification of Diseases, Injuries and Causes of Death[1]
Ninth Revision 1979 and Tenth Revision 2001 (2000 in Scotland)

Numbers

		England and Wales			
	ICD-10 code	2001	2002	2003	2004
Total deaths		530 373	533 527	538 254	512541
Deaths from natural causes	A00-R99	511 667	515 262	519 297	493 835
Certain infectious and parasitic diseases	A00-B99	4 253	4 330	4 763	5 009
Intestinal infectious diseases	A00-A09	777	847	1 063	1 382
Respiratory and other tuberculosis including late effects	A15-A19,B90	446	443	451	388
Meningococcal infection	A39	201	115	118	72
Viral hepatitis	B15-B19	196	170	209	197
AIDS (HIV - disease)	B20-B24	180	198	224	209
Neoplasms	C00-D48	139 135	140 174	139 360	138 062
Malignant neoplasms	C00-97	135 839	136 777	135 955	134 856
Malignant neoplasm of oesophagus	C15	6 107	6 330	6 427	6 298
Malignant neoplasm of stomach	C16	5 606	5 588	5 285	5 098
Malignant neoplasm of colon	C18	9 436	9 504	9 152	9 130
Malignant neoplasm of rectum and anus	C20-C21	3 927	3 907	3 982	3 917
Malignant neoplasm of pancreas	C25	6 011	6 142	6 242	6 294
Malignant neoplasm of trachea, bronchus and lung	C33-C34	28 728	28 806	28 765	28328
Malignant neoplasm of skin	C43	1 470	1 480	1 585	1 597
Malignant neoplasm of breast	C50	11 638	11 557	11 276	11 031
Malignant neoplasm of cervix uteri	C53	1 039	1 001	951	957
Malignant neoplasm of prostate	C61	8 912	8 973	9 166	9 169
Leukaemia	C91-C95	3 781	3 911	3 916	3 828
Diseases of the blood and blood-forming organs and certain disorders involving the immune mechanism	D50-D89	1 000	1 086	1 065	1 014
Endocrine, nutritional and metabolic diseases	E00-E90	7 711	7 897	8 016	7 519
Diabetes mellitus	E10-E14	6 119	6 192	6 316	5 837
Mental and behavioural disorders	F00-F99	14 143	14 444	14 846	14 299
Vascular and unspecified dementia	F01,F03	12 572	12 753	13 401	12 756
Alcohol abuse (inc. alcoholic psychosis)	F10	477	435	469	538
Drug dependence and non-dependent abuse of drugs	F11-F16,F18-F19	798	882	655	718
Diseases of the nervous system and sense organs	G00-H95	14 372	14 796	15 793	14 645
Meningitis (including meningococcal)	G00-G03	189	173	229	182
Alzheimer's disease	G30	4 579	4 771	5 055	4 821
Diseases of the circulatory system	I00-I99	211 842	209 433	205 508	190 603
Ischaemic heart diseases	I20-I25	105 895	102 833	99 790	92 528
Cerebrovascular diseases	I60-I69	58 517	59 068	57 808	52 899
Diseases of the respiratory system	J00-J99	67 391	69 900	75 138	69 213
Influenza	J10-J11	38	38	77	25
Pneumonia	J12-J18	31 636	32 631	34 400	30 649
Bronchitis, emphysema and other chronic obstructive pulmonary diseases	J40-J44	23 700	24 159	25 765	23 204
Asthma	J45-J46	1 268	1 264	1284	1243
Diseases of the digestive system	K00-K93	23 386	24 124	24 948	24 912
Gastric and duodenal ulcer	K25-K27	3 802	3 746	3 678	3 495
Chronic liver disease	K70,K73-K74	5 234	5 376	5 844	5 824
Diseases of the skin and subcutaneous tissue	L00-L99	1 291	1 470	1 661	1 670
Diseases of the musculo-skeletal system and connective tissue	M00-M99	4 588	4 647	4 634	4 393
Rheumatoid arthritis and juvenile arthritis	M05-M06,M08	970	966	907	794
Osteoporosis	M80-M81	1 542	1 605	1 583	1 478
Diseases of the genito-urinary system	N00-N99	7 682	8 452	9 120	9 397
Diseases of the kidney and ureter	N00-N29	3 848	4 072	4 135	4 024
Complications of pregnancy, childbirth and the puerperium	O00-O99	42	34	45	46
Certain conditions originating in the perinatal period (excluding neonatals)[1]	P00-P96	200	208	207	213
Congenital malformations, deformations and chromasomal abnormalities (excluding neonatals)[1]	Q00-Q99	1 280	1 233	1 299	1 274
Congenital malformations of the nervous system	Q00-Q07	119	127	142	116
Congenital malformations of the circulatory system	Q20-Q28	592	541	540	527
Symptoms, signs and abnormal clinical and laboratory findings not elsewhere classified	R00-R99	13 351	13 034	12 894	11 566
Senility without mention of psychosis (old age)	R54	11 900	11 645	11 394	9 905
Sudden infant death syndrome	R95	195	137	136	148
Deaths from external causes	V01-Y89	16 569	16 139	16 693	16 497
All accidents	V01-X59,Y85,Y86	10 733	10 382	10 979	10 735
Land transport accidents	V01-V89	2 949	2 929	2 943	2 693
Accidental falls	W00-W19	2 617	2 509	2 732	2 915
Accidental poisonings	X40-X49	1 037	814	835	927
Suicide and intentional self-harm	X60-X84,Y87.0	3 264	3 269	3 270	3 306
Homicide and assault[1]	X85-Y09,Y87.1	386	373	318	363
Event of undetermined intent	Y10-Y34, Y87.2	1 803	1 754	1 776	1 685

1 See chapter text

9.6
continued

Deaths: by cause
International Statistical Classification of Diseases, Injuries and Causes of Death[1]
Ninth Revision 1979 and Tenth Revision 2001 (2000 in Scotland)

Numbers

	ICD-9 code	ICD-10 code	Scotland					
			1999	2000	2001	2002	2003	2004
			ICD-9	ICD-10				
Total deaths			60 281	57 799	57 382	58 103	58 472	56 187
Deaths from natural causes	001-799	A00-R99	57 831	55 415	54 961	55 689	56 161	53 759
Certain infectious and parasitic diseases	001-139	A00-B99	498	476	558	651	660	688
Intestinal infectious diseases	001-009	A00-A09	31	51	65	96	85	104
Respiratory and other tuberculosis including late effects	010-018,137	A15-A19,B90	65	66	54	52	59	52
Meningococcal infection	036	A39	14	18	12	13	5	8
Viral hepatitis	070	B15-B19	17	14	6	13	23	20
AIDS (HIV - disease)	042-044	B20-B24	23	23	33	33	33	16
Neoplasms	140-239	C00-D48	14 966	15 255	15 475	15 391	15 412	15 336
Malignant neoplasms	140-208	C00-C97	14 789	14 958	15 196	15 051	15 116	15 047
Malignant neoplasm of oesophagus	150	C15	776	708	752	763	776	801
Malignant neoplasm of stomach	151	C16	650	649	678	621	579	615
Malignant neoplasm of colon	153	C18	1 018	1 052	1 062	975	966	917
Malignant neoplasm of rectum and anus	154.1-154.8	C20-21	474	400	405	384	368	383
Malignant neoplasm of pancreas	157	C25	574	633	595	562	641	615
Malignant neoplasm of trachea, bronchus and lung	162	C33-34	3 961	3 948	3 915	4 039	3 893	3 923
Malignant neoplasm of skin	172	C43	131	115	145	132	146	151
Malignant neoplasm of breast	174-175	C50	1 136	1 122	1 150	1 110	1 149	1 093
Malignant neoplasm of cervix uteri	180	C53	122	117	113	100	120	102
Malignant neoplasm of prostate	185	C61	769	773	777	775	786	802
Leukaemia	204-208	C91-C95	313	325	350	330	367	352
Diseases of the blood and blood-forming organs and certain disorders involving the immune mechanism	279-289	D50-D89	204	114	124	122	148	111
Endocrine, nutritional and metabolic diseases	240-278	E00-E90	870	828	891	902	958	972
Diabetes mellitus	250	E10-E14	670	616	695	676	709	760
Mental and behavioural disorders	290-319	F00-F99	1 901	2 309	2 425	2 446	2 637	2 670
Vascular and unspecified dementia	290	F01,F03	783	1 684	1 809	1 763	1 997	1 955
Alcohol abuse (inc. alcoholic psychosis)	291,303	F10	358	330	341	339	356	421
Drug dependence and non-dependent abuse of drugs	292,304-305	F11-F16,F18-F19	230	245	238	294	228	238
Diseases of the nervous system and sense organs	320-389	G00-H95	971	1 315	1 243	1 317	1 303	1 254
Meningitis (including meningococcal)	320-322	G00-G03	19	15	16	6	19	25
Alzheimer's disease	331.0	G30	140	329	324	388	354	399
Diseases of the circulatory system	390-459	I00-I99	24 787	23 657	22 666	22 688	22 102	20 837
Ischaemic heart diseases	410-414	I20-I25	13 337	12 412	11 914	11 692	11 441	10 778
Cerebrovascular diseases	430-438	I60-I69	6 785	6 803	6 621	6 722	6 497	6 155
Diseases of the respiratory system	460-519	J00-J99	8 870	6 547	6 435	6 806	7 454	6 743
Influenza	487	J10-J11	62	131	5	6	15	3
Pneumonia	480-486	J12-J18	4 526	2 312	2 370	2 466	2 859	2 399
Bronchitis, emphysema and other chronic obstructive pulmonary diseases	490-492,496	J40-J44	2 941	2 825	2 836	2 840	3 014	2 752
Asthma	493	J45-J46	119	131	101	131	98	94
Diseases of the digestive system	520-579	K00-K93	2 787	2 922	3 063	3 153	3 215	3 065
Gastric and duodenal ulcer	531-533	K25-K27	337	348	308	350	316	305
Chronic liver disease	571	K70,K73-K74	896	956	1 061	1 128	1 170	1 044
Diseases of the skin and subcutaneous tissue	680-709	L00-L99	90	89	90	118	131	131
Diseases of the musculo-skeletal system and connective tissue	710-739	M00-M99	295	405	357	384	369	350
Rheumatoid arthritis and juvenile arthritis	714	M05-M06,M08	87	126	125	133	103	107
Osteoporosis	733.0-733.1	M80-M81	53	58	56	59	70	52
Diseases of the genito-urinary system	580-629	N00-N99	936	844	969	1 013	1 056	965
Diseases of the kidney and ureter	580-594	N00-N29	619	563	638	627	670	574
Complications of pregnancy, childbirth and the puerperium	630-676	O00-O99	7	8	6	5	7	6
Certain conditions originating in the perinatal period	760-779	P00-P96	137	170	167	155	149	151
Congenital malformations, deformations and chromasomal abnormalities	740-759	Q00-Q99	157	154	172	168	172	134
Congenital malformations of the nervous system	740-742	Q00-Q07	13	25	16	31	23	21
Congenital malformations of the circulatory system	745-747	Q20-Q28	59	56	65	60	63	53
Symptoms, signs and abnormal clinical and laboratory findings not elsewhere classified	780-799	R00-R99	355	322	320	370	388	346
Senility without mention of psychosis (old age)	797	R54	185	161	172	191	236	193
Sudden infant death syndrome	798.0	R95	41	33	32	32	43	28
Deaths from external causes	E800-E999	V01-Y89	2 450	2 384	2 421	2 414	2 311	2 428
All accidents	E800-E929	V01-X59,Y85,Y86	1 359	1 341	1 350	1 315	1 326	1 390
Land transport accidents	E800-E829	V01-V89	326	338	367	321	357	325
Accidental falls	E880-E888	W00-W19	713	675	626	668	668	690
Accidental poisonings	E850-E869	X40-X49	30	34	50	37	30	57
Suicide and intentional self-harm	E950-E959	X60-X84,Y87.0	637	648	609	636	560	606
Homicide and assault	E960-E969	X85-Y09,Y87.1	121	93	92	118	101	121
Event of undetermined intent	E980-E989	Y10-Y34, Y87.2	237	230	278	263	234	229

1 See chapter text

9.6
continued

Deaths: by cause
International Statistical Classification of Diseases, Injuries and Causes of Death[1]
Ninth Revision 1979 and Tenth Revision 2001 (2000 in Scotland)

Numbers

			Northern Ireland					
	ICD-9 code	ICD-10 code	1999	2000	2001	2002	2003	2004
				ICD-9	ICD-10			
Total deaths			15 663	14 903	14 513	14 586	14 462	14 354
Deaths from natural causes	001-799	A00-R99	15 054	14 296	13 968	13 949	13 912	13 711
Certain infectious and parasitic diseases	001-139	A00-B99	47	73	117	134	157	149
Intestinal infectious diseases	001-009	A00-A09	1	4	7	11	13	16
Respiratory and other tuberculosis including late effects	010-018,137	A15-A19,B90	7	7	6	10	11	13
Meningococcal infection	036	A39	4	9	4	7	4	5
Viral hepatitis	070	B15-B19	2	6	-	-	-	1
AIDS (HIV - disease)	042-044	B20-B24	2	1	-	3	2	-
Neoplasms	140-239	C00-D48	3 654	3 647	3 802	3 766	3 882	3 835
Malignant neoplasms	140-208	C00-C97	3 552	3 541	3 696	3 652	3 757	3 757
Malignant neoplasm of oesophagus	150	C15	161	150	155	163	154	138
Malignant neoplasm of stomach	151	C16	187	180	174	164	165	180
Malignant neoplasm of colon	153	C18	303	301	271	270	313	286
Malignant neoplasm of rectum and anus	154.1-154.8	C20-C21	95	84	100	90	103	94
Malignant neoplasm of pancreas	157	C25	142	159	176	194	173	152
Malignant neoplasm of trachea, bronchus and lung	162	C33-C34	781	792	782	802	810	837
Malignant neoplasm of skin	172	C43	33	31	37	38	40	36
Malignant neoplasm of breast	174-175	C50	286	289	316	278	291	320
Malignant neoplasm of cervix uteri	180	C53	36	30	24	25	31	37
Malignant neoplasm of prostate	185	C61	195	213	214	193	217	241
Leukaemia	204-208	C91-C95	104	91	87	93	85	95
Diseases of the blood and blood-forming organs and certain disorders involving the immune mechanism	279-289	D50-D89	24	24	32	24	37	34
Endocrine, nutritional and metabolic diseases	240-278	E00-E90	118	122	200	238	246	248
Diabetes mellitus	250	E10-E14	93	89	145	187	190	189
Mental and behavioural disorders	290-319	F00-F99	190	207	381	411	341	370
Vascular and unspecified dementia	290	F01,F03	75	66	298	329	284	298
Alcohol abuse (inc. alcoholic psychosis)	291,303	F10	46	46	75	74	52	68
Drug dependence and non-dependent abuse of drugs	292,304-305	F11-F16,F18-F19	25	38	2	6	3	2
Diseases of the nervous system and sense organs	320-389	G00-H95	285	245	467	531	481	487
Meningitis (including meningococcal)	320-322	G00-G03	3	6	9	5	3	1
Alzheimer's disease	331.0	G30	98	81	211	246	224	251
Diseases of the circulatory system	390-459	I00-I99	6 422	5 776	5 829	5 729	5 448	5 272
Ischaemic heart diseases	410-414	I20-I25	3 568	3 234	3 148	2 948	2 843	2 775
Cerebrovascular diseases	430-438	I60-I69	1 679	1 469	1 531	1 573	1 531	1 435
Diseases of the respiratory system	460-519	J00-J99	3 161	3 019	1 975	1 883	2 082	1 950
Influenza	487	J10-J11	5	39	-	1	4	1
Pneumonia	480-486	J12-J18	2 130	2 027	1 028	951	1 025	909
Bronchitis, emphysema and other chronic obstructive pulmonary diseases	490-492,496	J40-J44	704	610	584	553	660	609
Asthma	493	J45-J46	38	33	38	36	32	44
Diseases of the digestive system	520-579	K00-K93	507	531	556	581	587	691
Gastric and duodenal ulcer	531-533	K25-K27	80	89	76	62	77	70
Chronic liver disease	571	K70,K73-K74	92	101	133	166	156	189
Diseases of the skin and subcutaneous tissue	680-709	L00-L99	27	21	24	21	15	19
Diseases of the musculo-skeletal system and connective tissue	710-739	M00-M99	54	40	94	90	93	66
Rheumatoid arthritis and juvenile arthritis	714	M05-M06,M08	13	26	31	21	26	15
Osteoporosis	733.0-733.1	M80-M81	11	5	12	19	16	10
Diseases of the genito-urinary system	580-629	N00-N99	242	292	278	333	327	364
Diseases of the kidney and ureter	580-594	N00-N29	173	201	192	246	225	252
Complications of pregnancy, childbirth and the puerperium	630-676	O00-O99	-	-	2	1	3	1
Certain conditions originating in the perinatal period	760-779	P00-P96	69	62	63	62	62	64
Congenital malformations, deformations and chromasomal abnormalities	740-759	Q00-Q99	93	57	83	53	69	61
Congenital malformations of the nervous system	740-742	Q00-Q07	9	14	16	7	12	10
Congenital malformations of the circulatory system	745-747	Q20-Q28	32	19	24	17	16	17
Symptoms, signs and abnormal clinical and laboratory findings not elsewhere classified	780-799	R00-R99	161	180	65	92	82	100
Senility without mention of psychosis (old age)	797	R54	122	146	37	63	63	70
Sudden infant death syndrome	798.0	R95	3	-	2	0	-	-
Deaths from external causes	E800-E999	V01-Y89	609	607	545	637	550	643
All accidents	E800-E929	V01-X59,Y85,Y86	430	364	361	424	364	448
Land transport accidents	E800-E829	V01-V89	134	142	148	144	120	161
Accidental falls	E880-E888	W00-W19	161	131	52	60	44	63
Accidental poisonings	E850-E869	X40-X49	38	25	13	30	30	17
Suicide and intentional self-harm	E950-E959	X60-X84,Y87.0	121	163	141	162	132	128
Homicide and assault	E960-E969	X85-Y09,Y87.1	24	56	20	27	30	32
Event of undetermined intent	E980-E989	Y10-Y34, Y87.2	33	22	17	21	12	18

1 See chapter text

Sources: Office for National Statistics;
General Register Office, Scotland;
Northern Ireland Statistics and Research Agency

9.7 Notifications of infectious diseases: by country

Numbers

		1994	1995	1996	1997	1998	1999	2000	2001	2002	2003	2004[1]
United Kingdom												
Measles	KHQD	23 517	9 017	6 866	4 844	4 540	2 951	2 865	2 661	3 675	2 726	2 695
Mumps	KWNN	3 143	2 400	2 182	2 264	1 917	2 000	3 367	3 433	2 333	4 565	20 740
Rubella	KWNO	9 650	7 674	11 720	4 205	4 064	2 575	2 064	1 782	2 002	1 525	1 552
Whooping cough	KHQE	4 837	2 399	2 721	3 669	1 902	1 461	866	1 059	1 051	509	627
Scarlet fever	KHQC	8 031	6 863	6 101	4 639	4 708	2 956	2 544	2 320	2 749	3 252	2 636
Dysentery	KHQG	7 538	5 498	2 643	2 427	1 934	1 630	1 613	1 495	1 167	1 144	1 300
Food poisoning	KHQH	91 128	92 604	94 923	105 579	105 060	96 866	98 076	95 752	81 562	79 073	78 797
Typhoid and Paratyphoid fevers	KHQB	390	386	291	249	252	278	205	254	183	277	283
Hepatitis	KWNP	4 285	3 823	2 876	3 601	3 781	4 365	4 530	4 419	5 035	5 203	5 065
Tuberculosis	KHQI	6 230	6 176	6 238	6 367	6 605	6 701	7 100	7 204	7 239	6 978	7 167
Malaria	KWNQ	1 219	1 363	1 743	1 549	1 163	1 038	1 166	1 118	866	820	634
England and Wales[2]												
Measles	KHRD	16 375	7 447	5 614	3 962	3 728	2 438	2 378	2 250	3 187	2 488	2 356
Mumps	KWNR	2 494	1 936	1 747	1 914	1 587	1 691	2 162	2 741	1 997	4 204	16 367
Rubella	KWNS	6 326	6 196	9 081	3 260	3 208	1 954	1 653	1 483	1 660	1 361	1 287
Whooping cough	KHRE	3 964	1 869	2 387	2 989	1 577	1 139	712	888	883	409	504
Scarlet fever	KHRC	6 193	5 296	4 873	3 569	3 339	2 086	1 933	1 756	2 159	2 553	2 201
Dysentery	KHRG	6 956	4 651	2 312	2 274	1 813	1 538	1 494	1 388	1 087	1 047	1 203
Food poisoning	KHRH	81 833	82 041	83 233	93 901	93 932	86 316	86 528	85 468	72 649	70 895	70 311
Typhoid and Paratyphoid fevers	KHRB	370	370	276	241	243	276	204	250	175	275	280
Viral hepatitis	KWNT	3 722	3 296	2 437	3 186	3 183	3 424	3 541	3 388	3 859	4 004	3 932
Tuberculosis[3]	KHRJ	5 591	5 608	5 654	5 859	6 087	6 144	6 572	6 714	6 753	6 518	6 723
Malaria	KWNU	1 139	1 300	1 659	1 476	1 110	1 005	1 128	1 081	847	791	609
Total meningitis	KHRO	1 800	2 285	2 686	2 345	2 072	2 094	2 432	2 623	1 545	1 472	1 267
Meningococcal meningitis	KHRP	938	1 146	1 164	1 220	1 152	1 145	1 164	1 020	706	646	554
Meningococcal septicaemia	KWNV	430	707	1 129	1 440	1 509	1 822	1 614	1 238	842	732	691
Ophthalmia neonatorum	KHRI	268	245	246	224	198	163	176	115	91	102	85
Scotland												
Measles	KHSE	6 192	1 307	1 055	762	700	434	395	315	399	181	249
Mumps	KWNW	546	371	368	282	251	216	199	155	259	181	3 593
Rubella	KWNX	2 916	1 258	2 449	818	745	548	349	234	292	130	226
Whooping cough	KHSF	639	399	186	545	225	214	93	106	99	60	95
Scarlet fever	KHSD	1 319	1 065	750	645	883	438	301	281	376	395	207
Dysentery	KHSH	446	575	176	124	103	82	95	85	73	83	89
Food poisoning[4]	KHSI	8 291	9 297	10 234	10 144	9 186	8 517	9 263	8 640	7 693	6 910	6 820
Typhoid and Paratyphoid fevers	KHSB	18	16	14	6	6	2	1	3	4	2	3
Viral hepatitis	KWNY	296	405	360	359	490	863	943	1 008	1 165	1 159	1 074
Tuberculosis[5]	KHSL	546	478	509	433	457	496	469	442	418	422	371
Malaria	KWUC	74	58	70	57	30	20	27	24	17	28	20
Meningococcal infection	KWUD	201	190	201	271	313	329	301	256	175	117	155
Erysipelas	KHSC	118	125	84	95	66	64	41	39	41	28	27
Northern Ireland												
Measles	KHTD	950	263	197	120	112	79	92	96	89	57	90
Mumps	KHTR	103	93	67	68	79	93	1 006	537	77	180	780
Rubella	KHTQ	408	220	190	127	111	73	62	65	50	34	39
Whooping cough	KHTE	234	131	148	135	100	108	61	65	69	40	28
Scarlet fever	KHTC	519	502	478	425	486	432	310	283	214	304	228
Dysentery	KHTG	136	272	155	29	18	10	24	22	7	14	8
Food poisoning	KHTH	1 004	1 266	1 456	1 534	1 942	2 033	2 285	1 644	1 220	1 268	1 666
Typhoid and Paratyphoid fevers	KHTB	2	–	1	2	3	–	–	1	4	–	–
Infective hepatitis	KHTO	267	122	79	56	108	78	46	23	11	40	59
Tuberculosis	KHTI	93	90	75	75	61	61	59	48	68	38	73
Malaria	KWUE	6	5	14	16	23	13	11	13	2	1	5
Acute encephalitis/meningitis	KHTM	144	116	105	91	64	99	130	97	98	78	64
Meningococcal septicaemia	KWUF	39	42	67	56	87	145	123	90	98	76	82
Gastro-enteritis (children under 2 years)	KHTP	888	1 072	745	896	1 371	1 121	1 205	1 106	882	867	695

1 2004 data for Scotland and UK is provisional.

2 The figures show the corrected number of notifications, incorporating revisions of diagnosis, either by the notifying medical practitioner or by the medical superintendent of the infectious diseases hospital. Cases notified in Port Health Authorities are included.

3 Formal notifications of new cases only. The figures exclude chemoprophylaxis.

4 Scotland's food poisoning includes 'otherwise ascertained' for the first time in 1995.

5 Figures include cases of tuberculosis not notified before death.

Sources: Information and Statistics Division, NHS in Scotland;
Communicable Disease Surveillance Centre (Northern Ireland);
HPA Centre for Infections CDSC: 020 8200 6868

9.8 Estimated number of cases of work-related disease reported by specialist physicians to THOR[1]

Great Britain

Numbers

	All physicians			Disease specialist			Occupational physicians		
	2002	2003	2004	2002	2003	2004	2002	2003	2004
Musculoskeletal disorders									
					MOSS			OPRA	
Upper limb	5 223	3 359	4 183	1 665	1 477	1 534	3 558	1 882	2 649
Spine/ back	2 145	1 997	2 027	449	501	394	1 696	1 496	1 633
Lower limb	501	352	580	93	40	175	408	312	405
Other	279	176	252	51	68	29	228	108	223
Total number of diagnoses	8 225	5 981	7 154	2 310	2 123	2 181	5 915	3 858	4973
Total number of individuals[2]	7 988	5 804	6 872	2 242	2 066	2 063	5 746	3 738	4 809
Mental ill health									
					SOSMI			OPRA	
Stress/ anxiety/ depression	6 675	6 529	6 448	1 899	1 705	1 815	4 776	4 824	4 633
Other	978	880	856	666	604	651	312	276	205
Total number of diagnoses	7 653	7 409	7 304	2 565	2 309	2 466	5 088	5 100	4 838
Total number of individuals[2]	7 054	6 747	6 797	2 458	2 175	2 281	4 596	4 572	4 516
Respiratory disease									
					SWORD			OPRA	
Asthma	671	667	555	399	351	386	272	316	169
Malignant mesothelioma	882	875	830	870	869	819	12	6	11
Benign pleural disease	935	1094	1132	899	1082	1120	36	12	12
Other	706	820	825	458	549	567	248	271	258
Total number of diagnoses	3194	3456	3342	2626	2851	2892	568	605	450
Total number of individuals[2]	3118	3357	3237	2562	2764	2799	556	593	438
Skin disease									
					EPIDERM			OPRA	
Contact dermatitis	2928	2617	2374	1972	1668	1750	956	949	624
Skin neoplasia	428	361	616	416	361	615	12	-	1
Other	451	419	325	225	220	215	226	199	110
Total number of diagnoses	3807	3397	3315	2613	2249	2580	1194	1148	735
Total number of individuals[2]	3746	3331	3281	2577	2183	2546	1169	1148	735
Audiological disease									
					OSSA			OPRA	
Sensorineural hearing loss	219	488	291	27	212	33	192	276	258
Other	16	170	41	16	146	12	-	24	29
Total number of diagnoses	235	658	332	43	358	45	192	300	287
Total number of individuals[2]	222	529	321	30	229	34	192	300	287
Infections									
					SIDAW				
Diarrhoeal diseases	..	..	..	2051	959	915	..	..	..
Other	..	..	..	182	106	123	..	..	..
Total number of diagnoses	..	..	..	2233	1065	1038	..	..	..
Total number of individuals[2]	..	..	..	2233	1065	1038	..	..	..

1 THOR: The Health and Occupation Reporting Network (formerly know as ODIN) comprises of the following schemes: MOSS: Musculoskeletal Occupation Surveillance Scheme; SOSMI: Surveillance of Occupational Stress and Mental Illness; SWORD: Surveillance or Work-related and Occupational Respiratory Disease; EPIDERM: Occupational Skin Disease Surveillance by Dermatologists; OSSA: Occupational Surveillance Scheme for Audiologists; SIDAW: Surveillance of Infectious Disease at Work.

2 Individuals may have more than one diagnosis.

Source: Health and Safety Executive: 0151 951 3479/4355

9.9 Deaths due to occupationally related lung disease
Great Britain

Numbers

		1993	1994	1995	1996	1997	1998	1999	2000	2001	2002	2003
Asbestosis (without mesothelioma)[1]	KADY	173	174	166	196	191	165	171	186	233	234	234
Mesothelioma	KADZ	1 152	1 246	1 317	1 322	1 367	1 541	1 615	1 633	1 862	1 866	1 874
Pneumoconiosis (other than asbestosis)	KAEA	281	276	287	223	230	268	321	279	240	271	231
Byssinosis	KAEB	11	7	6	3	5	5	6	4	2	–	3
Farmer's lung and other occupational allergic alveolitis	KAEC	12	10	10	1	5	8	9	7	7	6	7
Total	KAED	1 629	1 713	1 786	1 745	1 798	1 987	2 122	2 109	2 344	2 377	2 349

1 By definition every case of asbestosis is due to asbestos; the association with mesothelioma is also very strong, though there is thought to be a low natural background incidence.

Sources: Office for National Statistics; Health and Safety Executive: 0151 951 3479/4355

9.10 Injuries to workers:[1] by industry and severity of injury
Great Britain
As reported to all enforcing authorities

Numbers

		Section	SIC (92)		Fatal				Major				Over 3 Days[2]		
					2001/02	2002/03	2003/04		2001/02	2002/03	2003/04		2001/02	2002/03	2003/04
Agriculture, hunting, forestry and fishing[3]	KSYS	A,B	01,02,05		39	36	44	KSZN	695	642	574	KTAZ	1 597	1 320	1 007
Energy and water supply industries	KSYT	C,E	10-14,40/41		14	3	10	KSZO	459	443	408	KTBH	2 261	1 890	1 827
Mining and quarrying	KSYU	C	10-14		9	1	8	KSZP	282	276	207	KTBI	1 417	1 086	943
Mining and quarrying of energy producing materials	KSON	CA	10-12		7	..	5	KSZQ	174	163	124	KTBJ	979	751	641
Mining and quarrying except energy producing materials	KSOO	CB	13/14		2	1	3	KSZR	108	113	83	KTBK	438	335	302
Electricity, gas and water supply	KSOP	E	40/41		5	2	2	KSZS	177	167	201	KTBL	844	804	884
Manufacturing	KSOQ	D	15-37		48	43	30	KSZT	7 180	6 789	6 449	KTBM	35 034	33 195	30 042
of food products; beverages and tobacco	KSOR	DA	15/16		7	3	2	KSZU	1 418	1 308	1 209	KTBN	8 779	8 685	7 896
of textile and textile products	KSOS	DB	17/18		..	1	1	KSZV	215	177	195	KTBO	973	903	828
of leather and leather products	KSOT	DC	19		1	..	..	KSZW	19	21	20	KTBP	120	112	52
of wood and wood products	KSOU	DD	20		2	2	2	KSZX	411	343	300	KTBQ	1 107	1 139	795
of pulp, paper and paper products; publishing and printing	KSOV	DE	21/22		3	..	2	KSZY	473	459	388	KTBR	2 365	2 105	1 793
of coke, refined petroleum products and nuclear fuel	KSOW	DF	23		2	1	..	KSZZ	19	18	23	KTBS	103	79	79
of chemicals, chemical products and man-made fibres	KSOX	DG	24		2	2	..	KTAE	406	407	361	KTBT	1 708	1 569	1 501
of rubber and plastic products	KSOY	DH	25		4	4	..	KTAF	608	557	450	KTBU	3 100	3 021	2 093
of other non-metallic mineral products	KSOZ	DI	26		2	4	4	KTAG	404	383	338	KTBV	1 929	1 827	1 469
of basic metals and fabricated metal products	KSYV	DJ	27/28		12	13	9	KTAH	1 333	1 285	1 218	KTBW	5 133	4 731	4 247
of machinery and equipment not elsewhere classified	KSYW	DK	29		3	4	2	KTAI	541	544	392	KTBX	2 731	2 468	1 795
of electrical and optical equipment	KSYX	DL	30-33		..	3	1	KTAJ	371	356	262	KTBY	2 053	1 774	1 196
of transport equipment	KSYY	DM	34/35		2	3	1	KTAK	586	538	594	KTBZ	3 351	3 171	3 144
Manufacturing not elsewhere classified	KSYZ	DN	36/37		8	3	6	KTAL	376	393	699	KTCA	1 582	1 611	3 154
Construction	KSZA	F	45		80	70	71	KTAM	4 595	4 721	4 728	KTCB	9 695	9 578	8 995
Total service industries	KSZB	G-Q	50-99		70	75	81	KTAN	16 011	16 597	19 813	KTCC	81 985	83 152	90 260
Wholesale and retail trade, and repairs	KSZC	G	50-52		13	19	16	KTAO	3 445	3 618	4 045	KTCD	14 376	15 379	15 818
Hotel and restaurants	KSZD	H	55		1	1	5	KTAP	936	997	1 197	KTCE	3 215	3 367	3 900
Transport, storage and communication[4]	KSZE	I	60-64		23	28	33	KTAQ	3 068	3 237	3 729	KTCF	22 531	23 340	24 148
Financial intermediation	KSZF	J	65-67		1	2	..	KTAR	228	252	269	KTCG	857	919	960
Real estate, renting and business activities	KSZG	K	70-74		13	9	11	KTAS	1 623	1 645	2 806	KTCH	4 882	5 206	
Public administration and defence	KSZH	L	75		4	5	4	KTAT	2 183	2 362	3 409	KTCI	14 296	13 941	18 308
Education	KSZI	M	80		2	..	1	KTAU	1 447	1 338	1 064	KTCJ	4 373	4 290	2 732
Health and social work	KSZJ	N	85		2	..	4	KTAV	1 800	1 877	2 113	KTCK	13 061	12 576	13 450
Other community, social and personal services activities	KSZK	O-Q	90-99		11	11	7	KTAW	1 281	1 271	1 181	KTCL	4 394	4 134	3 045
All industries	KSZM				251	227	236	KTAY	28 940	29 192	31 972	KTCN	130 572	129 135	132 131

1 See chapter text.
2 Injuries causing incapacity for normal work for more than 3 days.
3 Excludes sea fishing.

4 Injuries arising from shore based services only. Excludes incidents reported under merchant shipping legislation.

Source: Health and Safety Executive (HSE): 0151 951 4355/3479

Social protection

Chapter 10

Social protection

Social security

(Tables 10.2 to 10.11, 10.13 and 10.15 to 10.19)

Tables 10.2 to 10.6, 10.9 to 10.11 and 10.13 to 10.19 give details of contributors and beneficiaries under the National Insurance and Industrial Injury Acts, supplementary benefits and war pensions.

There are four classes of National Insurance Contributions (NICs):

Class 1   Earnings-related contributions paid on earnings from employment. Employees pay primary Class 1 contributions and employers pay secondary Class 1 contributions. Payment of Class 1 contributions builds up entitlement to contributory benefits which include Basic State Pension; Additional State Pension (State Earnings Related Pension Scheme SERPS and from April 2002, State Second Pension, S2P); Contribution Based Jobseeker's Allowance; Bereavement Benefits; Incapacity Benefit.

Primary class 1 contributions stop at State Pension age, but not Class 1 secondary contributions paid by employers.

There are reduced contribution rates where the employee contracts out of S2P (previously SERPS). They still receive a Basic State Pension but an Occupational or Personal Pension instead of the Additional State Second Pension.

Class 2   Flat rate contributions paid by the self-employed whose profits are above the small earnings exception. Payment of Class 2 contributions builds up entitlement to the contributory benefits which include Basic State Pension; Bereavement Benefits; Maternity Allowance and Incapacity Benefit. But not Additional State Second Pension or Contribution Based Jobseeker's Allowance

Class 2 contributions stop at State Pension age.

Class 3   Flat rate voluntary contributions, which can be paid by someone whose contribution record is insufficient. Payment of Class 3 contributions builds up entitlement to contributory benefits which include Basic State Pension; Bereavement Benefits.

Class 4   Profit-related contributions paid by the self-employed in addition to Class 2 contributions. Class 4 contributions stop at State Pension age.

Under some circumstances people who are not in employment do not have to make voluntary contributions to accrue a qualifying year for Basic State Pension.

Home Responsibilities Protection

Home Responsibilities Protection (HRP) helps to protect the basic State Pension of those precluded from regular employment because they are caring for children or a sick or disabled person at home. To be entitled to HRP, a person must have been precluded from regular employment for a full tax year. HRP reduces the amount of qualifying years a person would otherwise need for a Basic State Pension.

National Insurance Credits

In addition to paying, or being treated as having paid contributions, a person can be credited with National Insurance. Contribution credits help to protect people's rights to State Retirement Pension and other Social Security Benefits.

A person is likely to be entitled to contributions credits if they are; a student in full time education or training, in receipt of Jobseekers Allowance, unable to work due to sickness or disability, entitled to Statutory Maternity Pay or Statutory Adoption Pay, or they have received Carers Allowance.

Credits are automatically awarded for men aged 60 to 65 provided they are not liable to pay Class 1 or 2 NICs and to young people for the tax years containing their 16th, 17th and 18th birthdays.

Jobseeker's Allowance

(Table 10.6)

Jobseeker's Allowance (JSA) replaced Unemployment Benefit and Income Support for unemployed claimants on 7 October 1996. It is a unified benefit with two routes of entry: contribution-based which depends mainly upon national insurance contributions and income-based which depends mainly upon a means test. Some claimants can qualify by either route. In practice they receive income-based JSA but have an underlying entitlement to the contribution-based element.

Sickness Benefit, Invalidity Benefit and Incapacity Benefit

(Tables 10.7 and 10.8)

Incapacity Benefit replaced Sickness Benefit and Invalidity Benefit from 13 April 1995. The first condition for entitlement to these contributory benefits is that the claimants are incapable of work because of illness or disablement. Secondly, that they satisfy the contribution conditions which depend on contributions paid as an employed (Class 1) or self-employed person (Class 2). Under Sickness and Invalidity Benefits the contribution conditions were automatically treated as satisfied if a person was incapable of work because of an industrial accident or prescribed disease. Under Incapacity Benefit those who do not satisfy the contribution conditions in this case do not have them treated as satisfied. Class 1A contributions paid by employers are in respect of the benefit of cars provided for the private use of employees, and the free fuel provided for private use. These contributions do not provide any type of benefit cover.

Since 6 April 1983, most people working for an employer and paying National Insurance contributions as employed persons, receive Statutory Sick Pay (SSP) from their employer when they are off work sick. SSP was payable for a maximum of eight weeks until 5 April 1986, and 28 weeks thereafter. People who do not work for an employer, and employees who are excluded from the SSP scheme, or those who have run out of SSP before reaching the maximum of 28 weeks and are still sick can claim benefit. Any period of SSP is excluded from the tables.

Spells of incapacity of three days or less do not count as periods of interruption of employment, and are excluded from the tables. Exceptions are where people are receiving regular weekly treatment by dialysis, or treatment by radiotherapy, chemotherapy or plasmapheresis where two 2 days in any six consecutive days make up a period of interruption of employment, and those whose incapacity for work ends within three days of the end of SSP entitlement.

At the beginning of a period of incapacity, benefit is subject to three waiting days, except where there was an earlier spell of incapacity of more than three days in the previous eight weeks. Employees entitled to SSP for less than 28 weeks and who are still sick can get Sickness Benefit or Incapacity Benefit Short Term (Low) until they reach a total of 28 weeks provided they satisfy the conditions. After 28 weeks SSP and/or Sickness Benefit (SB), Invalidity Benefit (IVB) was payable up to pension age for as long as the incapacity lasts. From pension age Invalidity Benefit was paid at the person's State Pension rate, until entitlement ceases when SP is paid or at deemed pension age (70 for a man, 65 for a woman). For people on Incapacity Benefit under State pension age there are two short-term rates: the lower rate is paid for the first 28 weeks of sickness and the higher rate for weeks 29 to 52. From week 53 the Long Term rate Incapacity Benefit is payable. The Short Term rate Incapacity Benefit is based on State Pension entitlement for

people over State Pension age and is paid for up to a year if incapacity began before pension age.

The long-term rate of Incapacity Benefit applies to people under State Pension age who have been sick for more than a year. People with a terminal illness or who are receiving the higher rate care component of Disability Living Allowance will get the Long Term rate. The Long Term rate is not paid for people over pension age.

Under Incapacity Benefit, for the first 28 weeks of incapacity, people previously in work will be assessed on the 'own occupation' test – the claimant's ability to do their own job. Otherwise, incapacity will be based on a personal capability assessment, which will assess ability to carry out a range of work-related activities. The test will apply after 28 weeks of incapacity or from the start of the claim for people who did not previously have a job. Certain people will be exempted from this test.

The tables exclude all men aged over 65 and women aged over 60 who are in receipt of State Pension, and all people over deemed pension age (70 for a man and 65 for a woman), members of the Armed Forces, mariners while at sea, and married women and certain widows who have chosen not to be insured for sickness benefit. The tables include a number of individuals who were unemployed prior to incapacity.

The Short Term (Higher) and Long Term rates of Incapacity Benefit are treated as taxable income.

There were transitional provisions for people who were on Sickness or Invalidity Benefit on 12 April 1995. They were automatically transferred to Incapacity Benefit, payable on the same basis as before. Former IVB recipients continue to get Additional Pension entitlement, but frozen at 1994 levels. Also their IVB is not subject to tax. If they were over State Pension age on 12 April 1995 they may get Incapacity Benefit for up to 5 years beyond pension age.

Child Benefits

(Table 10.9)

Child Benefit is paid to those responsible for children. Here 'children' includes all those aged under 16. It also includes young people aged under 19 who are in full-time non-advanced education, or are entered for future external examinations, or are in the period between leaving (or exams finishing) and the week containing the first Monday in September (or similar dates after Easter and in early January, if earlier). It also includes young people aged under 18 who have moved directly from full-time education to being registered for

Social protection

work or training with the Careers service or with Connexions. Awards are also subject to residence criteria being satisfied.

Guardian's Allowance is an additional allowance for people bringing up a child because one or both of their parents has died. They must be getting Child Benefit for the child.

The table shows the number of families in the United Kingdom in receipt of Child Benefit. The numbers shown in the table are estimates based on a random 5 per cent sample of awards current at 31 August and are therefore subject to sampling error. The figures take no account of new claims, or revisions to claims that were received or processed after 31 August even if they are backdated to start before 31 August.

Family Credit/ Working Families' Tax Credit

(Table 10.10)

Working Families' Tax Credit (WFTC) replaced Family Credit from 5 October 1999.

Family Credit was, and Working Families' Tax Credit is, available to families with at least one adult in remunerative work for at least 16 hours per week and who is responsible for at least one child under 16 (under 19 if in full time education up to A-level or equivalent standard). The rate of payment of WFTC depends on the number of such children and expenditure incurred on eligible childcare. It is also higher if the worker works for at least 30 hours per week, or if there are disabled children or severely disabled adults in the family. It is tapered away above an income threshold. Further details can be obtained from the Inland Revenue.

Child and Working Tax Credits (New Tax Credits)

(Table 10.11)

Child and Working Tax Credits (NTC's) replaced Working Families' Tax Credit (WFTC) from 6 April 2003.

CTC and WTC are claimed by individuals, or jointly by couples, whether or not they have children.

Child Tax Credit (CTC) provides support to families for the children (up to the 31 August after their 16th birthdays) and the 'qualifying' young people (in full-time non-advanced education until their 19th birthdays) for which they are responsible. It is paid in addition to Child Benefit.

Working Tax Credit (WTC) tops up the earnings of families on low or moderate incomes. People working for at least 16 hours a week can claim it if they (a) are responsible for at least one child or qualifying young person, (b) have a disability which

puts them at a disadvantage in getting a job, or (c) in the first year of work, having returned to work aged at least 50 after a period of at least six months receiving out-of-work benefits. Other adults also qualify if they are aged at least 25 and work for at least 30 hours a week.

Widow's Benefit and Bereavement Benefit

(Table 10.12 and 10.13)

Widow's Benefit is payable to women widowed on or after 11 April 1988 and up to and including 8 April 2001. There are three types of widow's benefits: Widow's Payment, Widowed Mother's Allowance and Widow's Pension. Women widowed before 11 April 1988 continue to receive Widow's Benefit based on the rules that existed before that date. Bereavement Benefit was introduced on 9 April 2001 as a replacement of Widows Benefit, payable to both men and women widowed on or after 9 April 2001. There are three types of Bereavement Benefits available: Bereavement Payment, Widowed Parent's Allowance and Bereavement Allowance.

Government expenditure on social services and housing

(Table 10.20 to 10.25)

The tables of general government expenditure on social services and housing in the United Kingdom comprise a summary table followed by separate tables for each of the social services and housing. The definition of government expenditure used in these tables follows that in Table 11.2 of the *Blue Book* 2006 Edition, and covers both current and capital expenditure of the central government (including the National Insurance Fund) and local authorities. The housing table also includes the capital expenditure of public corporations concerned with housing. As in the *Blue Book*, government expenditure is measured after deducting fees and charges for services. Expenditure on administration includes the cost of common services (accommodation, stationery and printing, superannuation, etc) some of which is not directly borne by the departments administering each service. Transfers from one part of government to another have been eliminated to avoid double counting. The figures relate to years ended 31 March.

It should be noted that the figures no longer include imputed rents for the use of fixed assets owned and used by general government. In the Blue Book, imputed rents have been replaced by capital consumption. Capital consumption, however, cannot be allocated to individual services and is therefore not included in these tables.

The following notes give brief descriptions of each of the main services shown in the tables.

Education

(Table 10.21)

This covers expenditure by the Education Departments, local education authorities and the University Grants Committee on education in schools, training colleges, technical institutions and universities. It includes expenditure on school meals.

National Health Service

(Table 10.22)

This covers expenditure by central government on hospital and community health, family practitioner and other health services. The expenditure by local authorities on the provision of health centres, health visiting, home nursing, ambulance services, vaccination and immunisation, etc, was transferred to central government on 1 April 1974. Only the net costs of providing these services are included in total government expenditure. Estimates for receipts from patients are shown separately.

Welfare services

(Table 10.23)

Personal social services: This covers local authority expenditure on the aged, handicapped and homeless, child care, care of mothers and young children, mental health, domestic help, etc. Also included are central government grants to voluntary approved schools.

Welfare foods: This covers the cost of providing welfare foods at reduced prices to children and expectant mothers. Only the net costs of providing these services are included in the total government expenditure, payments by the recipients of the services being shown separately.

Social security

(Table 10.24)

This comprises both benefits under the Social Security schemes and non-contributory benefits and allow-ances, administered by the Department for Work and Pensions. The analysis by type of Income Support is not exact; the estimates are derived from average numbers in receipt of benefit and average amounts paid. Unified housing benefit (rent rebates and allowances) is also included as social security expenditure and not as housing expenditure. This is now mainly administered by local authorities who receive grants from central government. War

pensions are now administered by the Ministry of Defence and not included in this table. Child and Working Tax Credits (NTC's) replaced Working Families' Tax Credit (WFTC) from 6 April 2003 and are administered by the Inland Revenue.

Housing

(Table 10.25)

The table shows government expenditure on housing. It includes expenditure made by the central and local government sectors, but excludes expenditure by public corporations. The Housing Revenue Account is classified as a quasi-public corporation, so that most of its current and expenditure and income is included in the corporate rather than government sector. All overhead and administration expenses are included in final current expenditure. Non-capitalised support for public corporations and other market bodies relating to housing is recorded as subsidies. Capital transfers are paid mainly by local government to individuals for repair and improvement of privately owned housing. Current transfers paid include insurance premiums. Gross capital formation includes that of the council houses administered by the Housing Revenue Account. This is net of any sales of housing either through Right to Buy or Large Scale Voluntary Transfers. Housing benefit in the form of rent rebates and rent allowances is not included in the table, as they are regarded as forms of social security.

10.1 National Insurance Fund
(Great Britain and Northern Ireland)
Years ended 31 March

£ million

		1996/97	1997/98	1998/99	1999/00	2000/01	2001/02	2002/03	2003/04	2004/05
Receipts										
Opening balance	KJFB	8 045	7 869	9 763	12 625	14 909	19 868	24 177	27 267	27 816
Contributions	JXVM	42 806	46 755	50 023	51 852	55 627	58 050	59 658	59 827	62 863
State Scheme Premiums[1]	C59W	..	..	..	..	..	..	194	147	115
Grant from Consolidated Fund	KOTF	1 952	966	3	2	..	..	..	..	..
Compensation for SSP/SMP	KJQM	542	601	576	625	688	710	775	1 346	1 470
Transfers from Great Britian	KOTG	75	150	315	230	200	110	350	260	270
Income from investments	KJFE	489	474	667	724	884	1 146	1 457	1 292	1 288
Other receipts	KJFF	85	97	92	127	112	67	80	82	72
Redundancy receipts	KIBQ	26	25	21	21	23	22	24	28	32
Total	JYJO	54 020	56 937	61 462	66 206	72 442	79 972	86 716	90 249	93 926
Expenditure										
Total benefits	JYJP	44 518	45 321	46 822	50 026	50 960	54 550	54 201	56 255	58 572
Unemployment[2]	KJFH	605	..	..	..	..	..	..	..	..
Jobseeker's Allowance (Contributory)[2]	LUQW	341	489	489	475	449	478	519	512	455
Incapacity[3]	JYXL	7 993	7 739	7 574	7 206	6 982	7 074	7 104	7 116	6 910
Maternity	KETY	34	37	39	40	46	57	70	128	153
Widows' pensions	KEWU	1 017	1 021	1 008	1 020	1 008	1 132	1 142	1 033	946
Guardian's allowances and Child's special allowance[4]	KJFK	2	2	2	2	2	2	2	2	1
Retirement pensions[5]	JYJV	34 736	36 396	38 072	41 157	42 350	45 677	45 240	47 339	49 979
Pensioners' lump sum payments	KAAW	132	126	128	126	123	131	124	125	128
Other payments	KAAZ	17	19	18	19	21	29	27	34	30
Administration	KABE	1 065	1 073	1 053	847	1 197	873	1 280	1 794	1 521
Transfers to Northern Ireland	KABF	75	150	315	230	200	110	350	260	270
Redundancy payments	KIBR	134	120	140	174	195	232	255	243	222
Personal Pensions	C59X	..	..	..	..	..	..	3 336	3 847	3 508
Total	JYJU	46 151	47 173	48 837	51 297	52 574	55 795	59 449	62 433	64 123
Accumulated funds	KABH	7 869	9 763	12 625	14 909	19 868	24 177	27 267	27 816	29 804

1 State Scheme Premiums are payable in respect of employed persons who cease to be covered, in certain circumstances, by a contracted out pension scheme.
2 Jobseeker's Allowance (Contributory) was introduced in October 1996 and replaced Unemployment Benefit.
3 Incapacity Benefit replaced Sickness Benefit and Invalidity Benefit from April 1995.
4 Includes Child's special allowance for Northern Ireland
5 Includes personal pensions up to 2001/02.

Source: HM Revenue and Customs: 020 7438 7370

10.2 Persons who paid National Insurance contributions in a tax year:[1] by sex
United Kingdom

Millions

		Total				Men				Women		
		2001/02	2002/03	2003/04		2001/02	2002/03	2003/04		2001/02	2002/03	2003/04
Total[2]	KABI	27.90	28.10	28.00	KEYF	15.46	15.49	15.37	KEYP	12.48	12.63	12.63
Class 1	KABJ	24.91	25.02	25.05	KEYG	13.30	13.30	13.26	KEYQ	11.60	11.72	11.78
Not contracted out[3]	KABK	15.81	16.07	16.35	KEYH	8.71	8.88	9.04	KEYR	7.10	7.18	7.31
Contracted out	KABL	7.46	7.46	7.33	KEYI	3.84	3.75	3.63	KEYS	3.62	3.70	3.69
Mixed contracted in/out[4]	KABM	1.67	1.50	1.38	KEYJ	0.75	0.67	0.59	KEYT	0.88	0.83	0.78
Class 1 Reduced rate (including standard rate)	KABO	0.11	0.09	0.07	KEYL	..	..	..	KEYV	0.11	0.09	0.07
Class 2 exclusively	KABP	2.17	2.20	2.17	KEYM	1.68	1.69	1.65	KEYW	0.48	0.51	0.52
Mixed Class 1 and Class 2	KABQ	0.55	0.57	0.60	KEYN	0.38	0.39	0.41	KEYX	0.17	0.18	0.19
Class 3 exclusively[5]	KABR	0.16	0.15	0.10	KEYO	0.08	0.07	0.05	KEYY	0.08	0.08	0.05

1 See chapter text. The tax year commences on 6 April and ends on 5 April of the following year.
2 Components may not sum to totals as a result of rounding.
3 Includes those persons with an Appropriate Personal Pension (such persons pay contributions at the not contracted out rate but then receive a rebate).
4 Not included in the above rows.
5 Persons who paid a mixture of Class 3 contributions and others are not included in this category.

Source: Department for Work and Pensions: 020 7122 2444

10.3 Weekly rates of principal social security benefits[1]
Great Britain
At April

£

		1995	1996	1997	1998	1999	2000	2001	2002	2003	2004	2005
Unemployment Benefit:[2,3]												
Men and women	KJNA	46.45	48.25	..	..	..	..	..	..	..	..	..
Jobseeker's Allowance:[3]												
Personal allowances												
Single												
Aged under 18	KXDH	..	..	29.60	30.30	30.95	31.45	31.95	32.50	32.90	33.50	33.85
Aged 18 - 24	KXDJ	..	..	38.90	39.85	40.70	41.35	42.00	42.70	43.25	44.05	44.50
Aged 25 or over	KXDK	..	..	49.15	50.35	51.40	52.20	53.05	53.95	54.65	55.65	56.20
Lone parent												
Aged under 18 - usual rate	F92E	..	..	..	..	..	31.45	31.95	32.50	32.90	33.50	33.85
Aged under 18 - higher rate payable in specific circumstances	F92F	..	..	..	..	..	41.35	42.00	42.70	43.25	44.05	44.50
Aged 18 or over	F92G	..	..	..	..	..	52.20	53.05	53.95	54.65	55.65	56.20
Couple												
Both aged under 18[4]	KXDL	..	..	58.70	30.30	30.95	31.45	31.95	32.50	32.90	33.50	33.85
Both under 18, one disabled	KXDI	..	..	38.90	39.85	40.70	41.35	42.00	42.70	43.25	44.05	44.50
Both under 18, with a child	F92H	..	..	..	..	..	62.35	63.35	64.45	65.30	66.50	67.15
One under 18, one 18 - 24	KXDI	..	..	38.90	39.85	40.70	41.35	42.00	42.70	43.25	44.05	44.50
One under 18, one 25+	F92I	..	..	..	..	..	52.20	53.05	53.95	54.65	55.65	56.20
Both aged 18 or over	KXDM	..	..	77.15	79.00	80.65	81.95	83.25	84.65	85.75	87.30	88.15
Dependant children and young people												
Aged under 11 - 16	KXDN	..	..	16.90	17.30	20.20	26.60	31.45	33.50	38.50	42.27	43.88
Aged 16 - 18	KXDP	..	..	29.60	30.30	30.95	31.75	32.25	34.30	38.50	42.27	43.88
Invalidity allowance[5]												
High rate	KJND	12.40	12.90	13.15	13.60	14.05	14.20	14.65	14.90	15.15	15.55	16.05
Middle rate	KJNE	7.80	8.10	8.30	8.60	8.90	9.00	9.30	9.50	9.70	10.00	10.30
Low rate	KJNF	3.90	4.05	4.15	4.30	4.45	4.50	4.65	4.75	4.85	5.00	5.15
Increase for dependants[5]												
Adult	KJNG	35.25	36.60	37.35	38.70	39.95	40.40	41.75	42.45	43.15	44.35	45.70
Each child[6]	KJNH	11.05	11.15	11.20	11.30	11.35	11.35	11.35	11.35	11.35	11.35	11.35
Incapacity Benefit:[5]												
Short term (Lower) Under pension age	KOSB	44.40	46.15	47.10	48.80	50.35	50.90	52.60	53.50	54.40	55.90	57.65
Increase for adult dependant	KOSC	27.50	28.55	29.15	30.20	31.15	31.50	32.55	33.10	33.65	34.60	35.65
Short term (Lower) Over pension age	KOSD	56.45	58.65	59.90	62.05	64.05	64.75	66.90	68.05	69.20	71.15	73.35
Increase for adult dependant	KOSE	33.85	35.15	35.90	37.20	38.40	38.80	40.10	42.45	41.50	42.65	43.95
Short term (Higher)	KOSF	52.50	54.55	55.70	57.70	59.55	60.20	62.20	63.25	64.35	66.15	68.20
Increase for dependants:												
Adult	KOSG	27.50	28.55	29.15	30.20	31.15	31.50	32.55	33.10	33.65	34.60	35.65
Child[6]	KOSH	11.05	11.15	11.20	11.30	11.35	11.35	11.35	11.35	11.35	11.35	11.35
Long term	KOSI	58.85	61.15	62.45	64.70	66.75	67.50	69.75	70.95	72.15	74.15	76.45
Increase for dependants:												
Adult	KOSJ	35.25	36.60	37.35	38.70	39.95	40.40	41.75	42.45	43.15	44.35	45.70
Child[6]	KOSK	11.05	11.15	11.20	11.30	11.35	11.35	11.35	11.35	11.35	11.35	11.35
Incapacity age addition:[7]												
Higher rate	KOSL	12.40	12.90	13.15	13.60	14.05	14.20	14.65	14.90	15.15	15.55	16.05
Lower rate	KOSM	6.20	6.45	6.60	6.80	7.05	7.10	7.35	7.45	7.60	7.80	8.05
Attendance Allowance:												
Higher rate	KJNI	46.70	48.50	49.50	51.30	52.95	53.55	55.30	56.25	57.20	58.80	60.60
Lower rate	KJNJ	31.20	32.40	33.10	34.30	35.40	35.80	37.00	37.65	38.30	39.35	40.55
Disability Living Allowance:												
Care component												
Higher rate	KXDC	46.70	48.50	49.50	51.30	52.95	53.55	55.30	56.25	57.20	58.80	60.60
Middle rate	KXDD	31.20	32.40	33.10	34.30	35.40	35.80	37.00	37.65	38.30	39.35	40.55
Lower rate	KXDE	12.40	12.90	13.15	13.60	14.05	14.20	14.65	14.90	15.15	15.55	16.05
Mobility component												
Higher rate	KXDF	32.65	33.90	34.60	35.85	37.00	37.40	38.65	39.30	39.95	41.05	42.30
Lower rate	KXDG	12.40	12.90	13.15	13.60	14.05	14.20	14.65	14.90	15.15	15.55	16.05

10.3
continued

Weekly rates of principal social security benefits[1]
Great Britain
At April

£

		1995	1996	1997	1998	1999	2000	2001	2002	2003	2004	2005
Maternity Benefit:												
Maternity allowances for insured women[8]												
Higher rate	KOSN	52.50	54.55	55.70	57.70	59.55	60.20	..	..	..	..	..
Lower rate[9]	KJNL	45.55	47.35	48.35	50.10	51.70	52.25	..	..	..	..	..
Standard rate[10]	GPTJ	..	..	..	..	..	..	62.20	75.00	100.00	102.80	106.00
Threshold[11]	GPTK	..	..	..	..	..	..	30.00	30.00	30.00	30.00	30.00
Guardian's Allowance	KJNN	11.05	11.15	11.20	11.30	11.35	11.35	11.35	11.35	11.55	11.85	12.20
Widow's Benefit:												
Widow's pension	KJNO	58.85	61.15	62.45	64.70	66.75	67.50	72.50	75.50	77.45	79.60	82.05
Widowed mother's allowance	KJNP	58.85	61.15	62.45	64.70	66.75	67.50	72.50	75.50	77.45	79.60	82.05
Addition for each child	KJNQ	11.05	11.15	11.20	11.30	11.35	11.35	11.35	11.35	11.35	11.35	11.35
Bereavement Benefit:												
Bereavement allowance	WMPF	..	..	..	..	..	..	72.50	75.50	77.45	79.60	82.05
Widowed parent's allowance	WMOZ	..	..	..	..	..	..	72.50	72.50	77.45	79.60	82.05
Addition for each child	WMPA	..	..	..	..	..	..	11.35	11.35	11.35	11.35	11.35
State Pension contributory:[12]												
Single person	KJNR	58.85	61.15	62.45	64.70	66.75	67.50	72.50	75.50	77.45	79.60	82.05
Married couple	KJNS	94.10	97.75	99.80	103.40	106.70	107.90	115.90	120.70	122.80	127.25	131.20
State Pension non contributory:												
Man or woman	KJNT	35.25	36.60	37.35	38.70	39.95	40.40	43.40	45.20	45.45	47.65	49.15
Married woman	KJNU	21.10	21.90	22.35	23.15	23.90	24.15	24.95	27.00	27.70	28.50	29.40
Industrial Injuries Benefit:												
Disablement pension at 100 per cent rate	KJNW	95.30	99.00	101.10	104.70	108.10	109.30	112.90	114.80	116.80	120.10	123.80
Widow's or widower's pension	KJNX	58.85	61.15	62.45	..	..	..	..	..	..	..	..
Increase for dependants:[13]												
Adult	KJNY	28.65	29.75	..	..	..	..	..	..	..	..	..
Child Benefit:												
First child	KJOA	10.40	10.80	11.05	11.45	14.40	15.00	15.50	15.75	16.05	16.50	..
Subsequent children	KETZ	8.45	8.80	9.00	9.30	9.60	10.00	10.35	10.55	10.75	11.05	..
Family Credit[14]												
(maximum awards payable):[15]												
Families with 1 child												
Birth to September following 11th birthday	KJOB	56.50	58.20	59.70	61.15	64.95	..	..	..	..	..	..
From September following 11th birthday to September following 16th birthday	KJOC	64.00	65.90	67.60	69.25	70.70	..	..	..	..	..	..
From September following 16th birthday to day before 19th birthday	KJOD	68.55	70.60	72.45	74.20	75.95	..	..	..	..	..	..
Increase for each additional child												
Birth to September following 11th birthday	KJOF	11.40	11.75	12.05	12.35	15.15	..	..	..	..	..	..
From September following 11th birthday to September following 16th birthday	KJOG	18.90	19.45	19.95	20.45	20.90	..	..	..	..	..	..
From September following 16th birthday to day before 19th birthday	KJOH	23.45	24.15	24.80	25.40	25.95	..	..	..	..	..	..
War pension:												
Ex-private (100 per cent assessment)	KJOJ	101.10	105.00	107.20	111.10	114.70	116.00	119.80	121.80	..	..	..
War widow	KJOK	76.35	79.35	81.00	83.90	86.60	87.55	90.45	92.00	..	..	..

10.3

Weekly rates of principal social security benefits[1]
Great Britain
At April

£

		1995	1996	1997	1998	1999	2000	2001	2002	2003	2004	2005
Income Support:												
Personal allowances[16]												
Single												
aged 16-17 usual rate	KJOW	28.00	28.85	29.60	30.30	30.95	31.45	31.95	32.50	32.90	33.50	33.85
aged 16-17 higher rate in specific circumstances	KABS	36.80	37.90	38.90	39.85	40.70	41.35	42.00	42.70	43.25	44.05	44.50
aged 18-24	KJOX	36.80	37.90	38.90	39.85	40.70	41.35	42.00	42.70	43.25	44.05	44.50
aged 25 or over	KJOY	46.50	47.90	49.15	50.35	51.40	52.20	53.05	53.95	54.65	55.65	56.20
Couple												
both aged under 18[4]	KJOZ	..	..	..	..	..	31.45	31.95	32.50	32.90	33.50	33.85
both aged under 18, one disabled	F92J	..	..	..	..	..	41.35	42.00	42.70	43.25	44.05	44.50
both aged under 18, with a child	F92K	..	..	..	..	..	62.35	63.35	64.45	65.30	66.50	67.15
One aged under 18, one 18-24	F92L	..	..	..	..	..	41.35	42.00	42.70	43.25	44.05	44.50
One aged under 18, one 25+	F92M	..	..	..	..	..	52.20	53.05	53.95	54.65	55.65	56.20
Both aged 18 or over	KJPA	73.00	75.20	77.15	79.00	80.65	81.95	83.25	84.65	85.75	87.30	88.15
Lone parent												
aged 16-17 usual rate	KJPB	28.00	28.85	29.60	30.30	30.95	31.45	31.95	32.50	32.90	33.50	33.85
aged 16-17 higher rate in specific circumstances	KABT	36.80	37.90	38.90	39.85	40.70	41.35	42.00	42.70	43.25	44.05	44.50
aged 18 or over	KJPC	46.50	47.90	49.15	50.35	51.40	52.20	53.05	53.95	54.65	55.65	56.20
Dependant children and young people[16]												
1994 to 1996												
aged under 11	KJPD	15.95	16.45	..	..	..	..	..	..	..	..	..
aged 11-15	KJPE	23.40	24.10	..	..	..	..	..	..	..	..	..
aged 16-17	KJPF	28.00	28.85	..	..	..	..	..	..	..	..	..
aged 18	KABU	36.80	37.90	..	..	..	..	..	..	..	..	..
From 1997 to 1999												
Birth to September following												
11th birthday	KXDQ	..	..	16.90	17.30	20.20						
From September following												
11th birthday to September following 16th	KXDR	..	..	24.75	25.35	25.90						
From September following												
16th birthday to day before 19th	KXDS	..	..	29.60	30.30	30.95						
Dependant children and young people - from 2000												
Birth to September following 16th birthday	WMOD	..	..	..	..	..	26.60	31.45	33.50	38.50	42.27	43.88
From September following 16th birthday to day before 19th	WMOP	..	..	..	..	..	31.75	32.25	34.30	38.50	42.27	43.88
Pension Credit[17]												
Standard minimum guarantee:												
single	C59Y	..	..	..	..	..	..	..	..	102.10	105.45	109.45
couple	C59Z	..	..	..	..	..	..	..	..	155.80	160.95	167.05
Additional amount for severe disability												
single	C5A2	..	..	..	..	..	..	..	..	42.95	44.15	45.50
couple (one qualifies)	C5A3	..	..	..	..	..	..	..	..	42.95	44.15	45.50
couple (both qualifies)	C5A4	..	..	..	..	..	..	..	..	85.90	88.30	91.00
Additional amount for carers	C5A8	..	..	..	..	..	..	..	..	25.10	25.55	25.80
savings credit												
threshold single	C5A9	..	..	..	..	..	..	..	..	77.45	79.60	82.05
threshold couple	C5AA	..	..	..	..	..	..	..	..	123.80	127.25	131.20
maximum single	C5AB	..	..	..	..	..	..	..	..	14.79	15.51	16.44
maximum couple	C5AC	..	..	..	..	..	..	..	..	19.20	20.22	21.51

1 See chapter text
2 Persons under the age of 18 are entitled to the appropriate adult rate.
3 Jobseeker's Allowance, introduced 7 October 1996, replaced Unemployment Benefit and Income Support for the unemployed.
4 From 12 April 1999 the personal allowance for couples where both members are not yet 18 or one of the couples is aged 18 or over depends on the couple's circumstances. They may be entitled to a couple allowance or a single person's allowance dependant on certain criteria.
5 Incapacity benefit introduced from 13 April 1995, has replaced sickness benefit and invalidity benefit.
6 For the first child only the Child Dependency increase is reduced by £1.30 to £9.90 because of child benefit.
7 The rate of age addition depends on age at date of onset of incapacity: higher rate for under age 35 and lower rate for age 35-44.
8 Following a EU Directive, employee's maternity benefit is aligned with the state benefit they would receive if off work sick.
9 Women who were either not employed or self-employed received the lower rate.

10 New Standard rate introduced from April 2000.
11 MA Earnings Threshold introduced April 2000.
12 Retirement pensioners over 80 receive 25p addition.
13 An allowance for one adult dependent was payable, where appropriate, with unemployment benefit, sickness benefit, retirement pension, injury benefit and maternity allowance.
14 Family credit was replaced by In-work Families with Child or Working Child Tax Credit awards. Some children have protected rights. Further information is available from the Department for Work and Pensions.
15 Maximum award does not include the 30 hour credit.
16 In addition to personal allowances, a claimant may also be entitled to premiums. The types of premiums are family, lone parent, pensioner, higher pensioner, disability, severe disability and disabled child.
17 Pension Credit replaced Minimum Income Guarantee (MIG) for Income Support for those aged 60 and over on 6th Ocotober 2003.

Sources: Department for Work and Pensions;
Information and Analysis Directorate : 0191 225 7373;
HM Revenue and Customs: 020 7438 7370;
Ministry of Defence/DASA (Pay & Pensions): 020 7218 4271

10.4 National Insurance contributions
United Kingdom

	Employee's standard contibutions[1]		Employer's standard contributions[1]	
	not contracted-out rate	contracted-out rate[2]	not contracted-out rate	contracted-out rate[3]
Class 1				
Weekly earnings				
1999/00				
Below 66.00 (LEL)	-	-	-	-
66.00-82.99	10.0%	8.4%	-	-
83.00-500.00	10.0%	8.4%	12.2%	9.2%
Above 500.00 (UEL)	£43.40	£36.46	12.2%	12.2%
2000/01				
Below 67.00 (LEL)	-	-	-	-
67.00-75.99 (PT)	-	See note 4	-	See note 5
76.00-83.99 (ST)	10.0%	8.4%	-	
84.00-535.00 (UEL)	10.0%	8.4%	12.2%	9.2%
Above 535.00 (UEL)	£45.90	£38.41	12.2%	12.2%
2001/02				
Below 72.00 (LEL)	-	-	-	-
72.00-86.99 (PT/ST)	-	See note 4	-	See note 5
87.00-575.00 (UEL)	10.0%	8.4%	11.9%	8.9%
Above 575.00 (UEL)	£48.80	£40.75	11.9%	11.9%
2002/03				
Below 75.00 (LEL)	-	-	-	-
75.00-88.99 (PT/ST)	-	See note 4	-	See note 6
89.00-585.00 (UEL)	10.0%	8.4%	11.8%	8.3%
Above 585.00 (UEL)	£49.60	£41.44	11.8%	11.8%
2003/04				
Below 77.00 (LEL)	-	-	-	-
77.00-88.99 (PT/ST)	-	See note 4	-	See note 6
89.00-595.00 (UEL)	11.0%	9.4%	12.8%	9.3%
	£55.66	£47.37		
Above 595.00 (UEL)	1%	1%	12.8%	12.8%
2004/05				
Below 79.00 (LEL)	-	-	-	-
79.00-90.99 (PT/ST)	-	See note 4	-	See note 6
91.00-610.00 (UEL)	11.0%	9.4%	12.8%	9.3%
	£57.09	£48.59		
Above 610.00(UEL)	1.0%	1.0%	12.8%	12.8%
2005/06				
Below 82.00 (LEL)	-	-	-	-
82.00-93.99 (PT/ST)	-	See note 4	-	See note 6
94.00-630.00 (UEL)	11.0%	9.4%	12.8%	9.3%
	£58.96	£50.38		
Above 630.00(UEL)	1.0%	1.0%	12.8%	12.8%

	1999/00	2000/01	2001/02	2002/03	2003/04	2004/05	2005/06
Class 2							
Flat rate weekly	£6.55	£2.00	£2.00	£2.00	£2.00	£2.05	£2.10
Small earnings exception[7] (per annum)	£3,770	£3,825	£3,955	£4,025	£4,095	£4,215	£4,345
Class 3							
Flat-rate voluntary weekly contributions	£6.45	£6.55	£6.75	£6.85	£6.95	£7.15	£7.35
Class 4 (Self-employed; profit-related)							
Rate on profits between LPL and UPL	6.0%	7.0%	7.0%	7.0%	8.0%	8.0%	8.0%
Rate on profits above UPL	..	..	..	..	1.0%	1.0%	1.0%
Lower profits limit (LPL)	£7,530	£4,385	£4,535	£4,615	£4,615	£4,745	£4,895
Upper profits limit (UPL)	£26,000	£27,820	£29,900	£30,420	£30,940	£31,720	£32,760

Note: LEL: Lower Earnings Limit; UEL: Upper Earnings Limit. PT: Primary Threshold; ST: Secondary Threshold.

1 Married women opting to pay contributions at the reduced rate at 3.85% before 2003-04 and 4.85% from 2003-04 earn no entitlement to contributory National Insurance benefits as a result of these contributions. No women have been allowed to exercise this option since 1977, but around 70,000 women who have been continually married or widowed and in the labour market since that time have retained their right to pay the reduced rate.

2 The contracted-out rebate for employees' contributions is applied only between LEL and UEL. Earnings below LEL are charged at the appropriate not contracted-out rate (which depends on total earnings). Earnings above the UEL are not subject to employee NICs before 2003-04.

3 The rates shown only apply to Contracted-Out Salary Related schemes. (COSR). Earnings below the LEL and above the UEL are charged at the appropriate not-contracted out rate. The employers' contracted-out rate applies only between the LEL and the UEL.

4 The contracted-out rebate for primary contributions is 1.6 per cent of earnings between the LEL and the UEL for all forms of contracting-out.

5 The contracted-out rebate for secondary contributions is 3.0 per cent of earnings between the LEL and the UEL.

6 The contracted-out rebate for secondary contributions is 3.5 per cent of earnings between the LEL and the UEL.

7 If earnings from self-employment are below this annual limit and the contributor applies for and is granted a small earnings exception Class 2 contributions need not be paid. Class 2 or 3 contributions may be paid voluntarily.

Source: HM Revenue and Customs: 020 7147 3082

10.5 Social Security Acts: number of persons receiving benefit[1]
Great Britain
At any one time

Thousands

Persons receiving:		1995	1996	1997	1998	1999	2000	2001	2002	2003	2004	2005
Unemployment Benefit[2]	KJHA	414.6	397.8	..	..	..	..	..	..	..	..	..
Jobseeker's Allowance[2,3]	JYXM	..	..	1 406.3	1 181.2	1 105.8	1 071.2	948.9	919.2	927.8	820.1	844.9
Sickness and Invalidity Benefit[4,5]	KJHB	1 894.1	..	..	..	..	..	..	..	..	..	..
Incapacity benefit[6]	KXDT	..	1 812.8	1 749.2	1 671.2	1 557.1	1 568.7	1 583.4	1 592.5	1 579.3	1 556.7	1 519.3
Attendance Allowance[7]	KXDU	1 046.5	1 120.6	1 183.2	1 225.6	1 243.8	1 382.3	1 427.0	1 428.1	1 450.7	1 492.4	1 525.0
Disability Living Allowance[7]	KXDW	1 534.2	1 729.2	1 886.5	1 995.9	2 061.3	2 192.6	2 305.8	2 423.9	2 498.0	2 606.7	2 715.5
Widows' Benefits[8]	KJHF	323.2	308.9	296.4	278.7	267.6	264.9	254.8	223.4	191.5	163.3	138.9
Bereavement Benefits[8]	VQAA	..	..	..	..	..	..	..	41.5	47.7	51.0	54.5
National Insurance												
State pension contributory[5]:												
Males[9]	KJHH	3 590.1	3 688.2	3 786.5	3 880.4	3 956.3	4 039.4	4 083.9	4 148.5	4 211.1	4 275.1	4 327.2
Females[9]	KJHL	6 686.4	6 733.5	6 783.2	6 850.7	6 886.3	6 928.0	6 959.7	6 971.9	7 036.6	7 115.4	7 179.6
Total[9]	KJHG	10 276.5	10 421.7	10 569.7	10 731.1	10 842.6	10 967.4	11 043.6	11 120.3	11 247.8	11 390.4	11 506.8
State pension non contributory[5]:												
Males[8]	KJHI	5.4	5.7	5.6	5.5	5.1	5.2	5.1	5.3	5.4	5.4	5.3
Females[8]	KJHJ	21.8	22.3	20.9	19.8	18.8	18.0	18.2	18.1	17.8	17.3	16.7
Total[8]	KJHK	27.2	28.0	26.5	25.2	23.9	23.2	23.3	23.3	23.1	22.7	22.0
Industrial Injuries Disablement												
Pensions assessments[9,10]	KJHN	235.2	249.2	257.8	269.1	278.2	280.8	280.4	264.8	267.1	266.5	266.6
Reduced Earnings Allowance/												
Retirement Allowance assessments[9,10]	KEYC	152.1	154.9	155.6	152.8	153.5	153.5	152.3	144.3	143.0	139.3	136.3
Family Credit[11]	ZCGF	607.6	693.0	748.0	767.5	791.2	–	..	..	..	..	..
Income Support (Excluding MIG)[2,12]	KABV	5 667.7	5 545.8	3 958.0	3 853.1	3 814.4	2 241.6	2 264.6	2 245.5	2 239.7	2 196.6	2 140.5
Pension Credit[12]	C5AP	..	..	..	..	..	..	..	..	..	2 489.9	2 680.2
Housing Benefit and Council Tax Benefit												
Housing Benefit Total[13]	EW3X	4 734.4	4 775.9	4 639.4	4 474.7	4 313.1	4 033.3	3 874.4	3 812.6	3 796.4	3 879.4	3 957.1
Social Landlord[14]	KABY	2 964.3	2 898.3	2 792.3	2 664.1	2 518.5	3 218.4	3 131.1	3 093.8	3 081.7	3 135.5	3 166.8
Private Landlord	KABZ	1 770.1	1 877.6	1 847.1	1 810.6	1 794.6	815.0	743.3	718.8	714.7	743.9	790.3
Council tax benefit[15]	KJPO	5 623.9	5 611.2	5 498.3	5 325.7	5 166.1	4 830.1	4 673.4	4 601.7	4 627.8	4 800.2	4 959.6
War pensions[5]	KJHR	315.4	327.5	320.7	302.0	306.0	295.7	284.3	272.7	260.7	247.5	235.2

1 See chapter text. Caseload counts at a specific date in the year which varies from benefit to benefit.
2 Figures are given at May each year and based on WPLS data.
3 Jobseeker's Allowance introduced 7 October 1996, replacing Unemployment Benefit and Income Support for the unemployed.
4 A relatively small number of claims do not result in the payment of benefit but are included here because they indicate notified incapacity for work.
5 Includes overseas cases. As at end of March.
6 Incapacity Benefit replaced Sickness Benefit and Invalidity Benefit from 13 April 1995. Figures are taken at the last day in February from 100% data.
7 AA and DLA figures based on WPLS data from 2002. Prior to 2002 a consistent series for caseload, based on WPLS levels, has been created by combining older information, available from the previously published 5% sample data, with the WPLS data.
8 Includes overseas cases up to 2002.
9 A person may be in receipt of either IIDB or REA or both.
10 Figures from 2000 to 2001 are based on 10% data at March, 2002 and 2003 are at March from 100%, from 2004 are as at May.
11 Family Credit was replaced by Working Families' Tax Credit from October
12 Pension Credit replaced MIG on 6th October 2003 and extended Income Support entitlement to customers aged 60+. MIG claimants have been excluded from the IS figures in order to keep the series consistent.
13 Housing Benefit figures excludes any Extended Payment cases.
14 Social landlord figures include registered social landlord tenants.
15 Figure excludes Second Adult Rebate Claims

Sources: Department for Work and Pensions; Information and Analysis Directorate : 0191 225 7373; HM Revenue and Customs: 020 7438 7370; Ministry of Defence/DASA (Pay & Pensions): 020 7218 4271

10.6 Jobseeker's Allowance[1,2,3,4] claimants: by benefit entitlement
Great Britain

As at May   Thousands

		1999	2000	2001	2002	2003	2004	2005
All Persons								
All with benefit - total	KXDX	1 105.8	976.2	854.5	828.0	835.8	738.0	768.5
Contribution-based JSA only	KXDY	158.2	148.8	148.1	162.7	168.0	138.2	147.2
Contribution based JSA & income-based JSA	KXDZ	27.1	19.0	18.4	19.4	19.0	14.2	14.2
Income-based JSA only payment	KXEA	920.4	808.4	688.1	645.9	648.8	585.6	607.1
No benefit in payment	KXEB	118.7	95.0	94.4	91.1	92.0	82.1	76.4
Total	KXEC	1 224.5	1 071.2	948.9	919.2	927.8	820.1	844.9
Males								
All with benefit - total	KXED	862.3	757.8	664.2	635.0	634.4	556.2	575.5
Contribution-based JSA only	KXEE	109.0	104.6	105.2	116.0	119.5	99.0	105.0
Contribution based JSA & income-based JSA	KXEF	24.4	17.3	16.9	17.5	16.7	12.9	13.3
Income-based JSA only payment	KXEG	728.9	635.9	542.1	501.5	498.2	444.3	457.2
No benefit in payment	KXEH	79.2	63.6	62.3	62.3	63.2	55.6	52.5
Total	KXEI	941.5	821.4	726.5	697.4	697.6	611.8	628.0
Females								
All with benefit - total	KXEJ	243.4	218.5	190.3	193.0	201.4	181.9	193.0
Contribution-based JSA only	KXEK	49.2	44.2	42.8	46.7	48.5	39.2	42.3
Contribution based JSA & income-based JSA	KXEL	2.7	1.8	1.5	1.9	2.3	1.3	0.9
Income-based JSA only payment	KXEM	191.5	172.5	146.0	144.5	150.6	141.4	149.9
No benefit in payment	KXEN	39.5	31.3	32.1	28.8	28.9	26.4	23.8
Total	KXEO	283.0	249.8	222.4	221.8	230.3	208.3	216.9

1 See chapter text. Jobseeker's Allowance (JSA) has two routes of entry: contribution-based which depends mainly upon national insurance contributions and income-based which depends mainly on a means test. Some claimants can qualify by either route. In practice they receive income-based JSA but have an underlying entitlement to the contribution-based element.
2 Figures are given at May each year and have been derived by applying 5% proportions to 100% totals taken from the DWP 100% Work and Pensions Longitudinal Study (WPLS).
3 Figures are rounded to the nearest hundred and quoted in thousands.
4 Totals may not sum due to rounding.

Sources: Department for Work and Pensions;
Information and Analysis Directorate: 0191 225 7373

10.7 Sickness Benefit, Invalidity Benefit and Incapacity Benefit[1,2] claimants: by sex, age and duration of spell

Great Britain. At end of May

Thousands

		2000	2001	2002	2003	2004	2005
Males							
All durations: All ages	KJJA	1 488.2	1 518.7	1 531.8	1 530.1	1 522.5	1 496.0
Under 20	KJJB	11.6	11.9	22.2	22.2	22.4	21.8
20-29	KJJC	124.5	131.1	135.6	139.9	143.7	144.0
30-39	KJJD	234.2	247.2	252.3	255.8	254.9	246.8
40-49	KJJE	288.7	299.2	305.6	312.8	318.9	321.6
50-59	KJJF	475.5	482.9	478.7	472.7	464.1	452.9
60-64	KJJG	353.3	346.1	337.3	326.5	318.2	308.8
65 and over	KJJH	0.3	0.2	0.1	0.2	0.2	0.1
Over six months: All ages	KJJI	1 307.0	1 334.4	1 354.8	1 356.4	1 355.0	1 342.2
Under 20	KJJJ	5.0	3.8	13.7	13.5	13.9	13.7
20-29	KJJK	89.5	94.6	100.2	105.4	110.1	113.5
30-39	KJJL	194.8	206.8	212.6	216.4	216.8	212.5
40-49	KJJM	253.0	263.6	270.6	277.7	284.8	289.4
50-59	KJJN	430.5	438.6	437.8	433.1	426.2	418.0
60-64	KJJO	333.9	326.8	319.8	310.2	303.1	295.0
65 and over	KJJP	0.3	0.2	0.1	0.1	0.1	0.1
Females							
All durations: All ages	KJJQ	872.1	910.6	946.6	971.4	992.1	999.3
Under 20	KJJR	14.8	14.3	21.9	21.9	21.8	20.8
20-29	KJJS	91.6	93.4	97.2	101.0	105.1	108.4
30-39	KJJT	165.3	172.5	175.7	178.0	178.2	173.8
40-49	KJJU	232.5	243.8	253.2	262.6	271.1	277.1
50-59	KJJV	367.6	386.6	398.6	407.9	415.8	419.2
60 and over	KJJW	0.3	–	–	–	–	–
Over six months: All ages	KJJX	758.2	793.3	830.5	855.4	877.9	891.6
Under 20	KJJY	6.9	5.0	12.3	12.4	12.5	12.2
20-29	KJJZ	68.9	70.5	74.8	79.0	83.4	88.0
30-39	KJKA	140.6	147.5	150.9	153.4	154.4	151.9
40-49	KJKB	204.8	215.5	224.8	233.9	242.7	249.4
50-59	KJKC	336.8	354.9	367.8	376.7	384.9	390.1
60 and over	KJKD	0.3	–	–	–	–	–
Unknown Gender							
All durations	EW44	1.0	0.9	0.8	0.7	0.6	0.4
Over 6 months	EW45	0.5	0.4	0.5	0.4	0.4	0.2

1 See chapter text. Figures are given at May each year and are based on WPLS data.

2 Figures will Include a small number of overseas cases.

Sources: Department for Work and Pensions;
Information and Analysis Directorate: 0191 225 7373

10.8 Sickness, Invalidity and Incapacity Benefit: days of certified incapacity

Great Britain analysis by age at end of period[1]

Years starting on first Monday in April[2]

Millions

		1992/93	1993/94	1994[3]/95	1995/96	1996/97	1997/98	1998/99	1999/00	2000/01	2001/02	2002/03
Age at 31 March[4]												
Males: All ages	KJKH	445.5	468.8	507.9	596.2	576.3	563.5	538.6	526.7	531.7	536.1	540.3
Under 20	KJKI	1.5	1.6	1.8	3.4	3.1	3.5	3.7	3.3	2.6	3.5	5.4
20 - 29	KJKJ	24.5	27.0	30.4	43.7	42.4	43.2	41.7	38.3	38.9	40.4	44.3
30 - 39	KJKK	41.4	46.6	56.0	72.3	73.9	77.7	78.2	75.8	81.3	84.0	85.1
40 - 49	KJKL	64.6	72.7	78.9	98.5	98.5	97.7	97.6	98.0	103.9	106.0	106.8
50 - 59	KJKM	121.7	129.8	141.4	172.0	170.7	172.2	170.0	161.9	165.9	168.5	168.1
60 - 64	KJKN	102.4	107.3	112.6	127.9	127.8	126.7	124.3	126.0	125.8	120.2	116.3
65 and over	KJKO	80.4	83.9	86.8	78.4	59.9	41.7	23.0	23.4	13.3	13.4	14.4
Females: All ages	KJKP	190.7	211.4	237.5	279.5	285.8	292.8	294.8	315.0	325.1	338.7	344.6
Under 20	KJKQ	2.1	2.4	2.6	4.8	4.1	4.4	4.5	4.0	3.5	3.9	5.4
20 - 29	KJKR	22.1	22.1	23.9	31.9	32.0	32.1	31.3	30.7	30.3	32.3	34.4
30 - 39	KJKS	28.5	32.7	37.6	48.0	49.8	51.4	53.4	54.9	58.9	59.9	61.3
40 - 49	KJKT	46.6	51.5	58.9	72.1	74.0	75.8	77.1	79.1	82.8	88.9	89.8
50 - 59	KJKU	71.3	79.1	88.4	101.0	107.5	115.3	120.0	134.3	142.2	145.9	146.0
60 and over	KJKV	20.1	23.6	26.1	21.7	18.4	13.8	8.4	12.0	7.3	7.9	7.7

1 See chapter text. The end of the statistical year up to 1993/94 was the Saturday before the first Monday in April.

2 Up to and including 1994/95 years start first Monday in April. The 1995/96 year started 13 April and ended 31 March. From 1996/97 years start 1 April.

3 The statistical year for 1994/95 was extended to 12 April 1995, the day before the introduction of the new Incapacity Benefit which replaced Sickness and Invalidity Benefit.

4 Until 1995/96 then at 1 March.

Sources: Department for Work and Pensions;
Taken from 1% extract;
Information and Analysis Directorate: 0191 225 7373

10.9 Child benefits[1]

Thousands

		Great Britain As at 31 December						United Kingdom As at 31 August					
		1995	1996	1997[2]	1998[2]	1999		2000	2001	2002	2003	2004	2005
Families receiving allowances:													
Total	KJMU	6 996	7 024	6 956	6 976	7 102	VOWX	7 340	7 335	7 336	7 342	7 353	7 375
With 1 child	KJMV	2 970	2 983	..	..	3 015	VOWY	3 128	3 143	3 162	3 189	3 219	3 260
2 children	KJMW	2 783	2 794	..	..	2 822	VOWZ	2 898	2 891	2 894	2 890	2 885	2 882
3 children	KJMX	928	929	..	..	943	VOXA	977	970	954	942	931	920
4 children	KJMY	231	236	..	..	241	VOXB	251	247	242	239	235	233
5 or more children	KJMZ	84	82	..	..	82	VOXC	86	84	83	82	82	80
Families receiving Guardian's Allowance	VOXG	2.1	2.2	2.3	2.3	2.3	VOXH	2.5	2.3	2.5	2.6	2.9	2.8

1 See chapter text.
2 Figures provided by Child Benefit Centre Management Information Statistics as a new scan was being developed.

Source: HM Revenue and Customs: 020 7147 3021

10.10 Family Credit/ Working Families' Tax Credit[1,2]

Thousands

		Great Britain As at 31 December							United Kingdom As at 30 November			
		1993	1994	1995	1996	1997	1998		1999	2000	2001	2002
Families in receipt:												
Total	KJTO	518.3	578.0	646.5	716.7	751.4	779.7	ZCMK	965.3	1 167.8	1 293.7	1 377.3
Two-parent families: total	KJTP	291.0	324.6	356.9	390.2	388.0	383.4	ZCML	467.6	565.9	617.2	639.8
With 1 child	KJTQ	73.3	80.1	89.7	98.6	96.6	95.4	ZCMM	116.8	144.8	151.6	159.0
2 children	KJTR	110.1	122.4	135.1	146.1	144.4	141.7	ZCMN	178.4	220.1	243.5	252.7
3 children	KJTS	66.9	76.4	83.4	91.1	91.4	89.1	ZCMO	107.8	129.2	142.9	147.3
4 children or more children	ZIYM	40.7	45.8	48.6	54.4	55.6	57.3	ZCMP	64.6	71.8	79.2	80.8
One-parent families: total	KJTW	227.3	253.4	289.6	326.5	363.4	396.3	ZIYI	497.8	601.8	676.5	737.6
With 1 child	KJTX	117.8	133.8	152.2	170.4	189.3	203.4	ZIYJ	259.6	313.7	349.5	381.2
2 children	KJTY	79.2	86.0	99.1	111.2	121.8	136.1	ZIYK	169.6	207.6	238.7	261.6
3 or more children	KJTZ	30.4	33.5	38.3	45.0	52.3	56.9	ZIYL	68.6	80.5	88.3	94.8

1 See chapter text. Family Credit was replaced by Working Families Tax Credit (WFTC) in October 1999. The WFTC figures for December 1999 include Family Credit awards made before October 1999 and still current (both FC and WFTC awards last for 26 weeks).
2 WFTC was replaced by Child Credit and Working Tax Credit on 6th April 2003. See table 10.11.

Sources: Board of Inland Revenue: 020 7438 7370; Department for Work and Pensions; Information and Analysis Directorate: 0191 225 7373

10.11 In-work families with Child Tax Credit or Working Tax Credit awards[1]
United Kingdom

Thousands

		2003[2]
In-work families with award:	C5PF	4 647
With children	C5PG	4 368.5
Receiving Working Tax Credit[3] and Child Tax Credit	C5PH	1 588.6
Receiving Child Tax Credit only	C5PI	2 726.8
Zero award[4]	C5PJ	53.1
Without children	C5PK	278.5
Receiving Working Tax Credit	C5PL	187.7
Zero award[4]	C5PM	90.7

1 Child and Working Tax Credits replaced Working Families' Tax Credit on 6th April 2003. See chapter text.
2 Figures for 2003 are based on awards current at 5th January 2004.
3 Includes 57.7 thousand families (31.8 thousand couples and 25.9 thousand singles) whose Working Tax Credit (WTC) is less than or equal to the childcare element and is therefore all paid together with Child Tax Credit (CTC).

4 Claimed, and eligible for, CTC or WTC at the reference date, but with zero awards based on their circumstances at that date and their annual income reported by that date. These families may have positive awards at other times in the year, based on their circumstances then, and may finally qualify for positive annual awards based on all their circumstances in the year and their current year incomes.

Source: Board of Inland Revenue: 020 7084 5501

10.12 Widows' Benefit (excluding bereavement payment[1,2]): by type of benefit Great Britain

Number in receipt of windows benefit as at May 2005

Thousands

		2000	2001	2002	2003	2004	2005
All Widows' Benefit (excluding bereavement allowance)							
All ages	KJGA	264.9	255.0	223.4	191.4	163.3	138.9
Unknown Age	EW4O	0.2	0.2	0.2	0.1	–	–
18 - 24	EW4P	0.1	0.1	0.1	–	–	–
25 - 29	EW4Q	0.9	0.8	0.5	0.3	0.2	0.1
30 - 34	EW4R	3.5	3.2	2.3	1.7	1.1	0.8
35 - 39	EW4S	8.2	7.8	6.4	5.0	3.9	2.9
40 - 44	EW4T	13.4	12.7	10.8	9.1	7.5	6.1
45 - 49	EW4U	26.0	24.7	20.1	16.3	13.3	11.0
50 - 54	EW4V	65.2	62.6	50.2	40.6	33.3	26.9
55 - 59	EW4W	117.1	113.6	103.4	90.9	77.6	66.8
60 - 64	EW4X	30.3	29.3	29.4	27.4	26.4	24.3
Widowed parents' allowance - with dependant children							
All ages	KJGG	49.5	47.7	40.8	34.1	28.2	23.2
Unknown Age	EW4Y	0.1	0.1	0.1	–	–	–
18 - 24	EW4Z	0.1	0.1	0.1	–	–	–
25 - 29	EW52	0.9	0.8	0.5	0.3	0.2	0.1
30 - 34	EW53	3.4	3.1	2.3	1.6	1.1	0.8
35 - 39	EW54	7.9	7.5	6.2	4.9	3.8	2.8
40 - 44	EW55	12.3	11.8	10.0	8.4	7.0	5.7
45 - 49	EW56	12.6	12.3	10.8	9.3	7.8	6.7
50 - 54	EW57	8.8	8.7	7.6	6.6	5.7	4.8
55 - 59	EW58	3.2	3.1	3.0	2.7	2.3	2.0
60 - 64	EW59	0.2	0.2	0.2	0.3	0.3	0.2
Widowed parents' allowance - without dependant children							
All ages	KJGM	3.1	2.9	2.4	2.0	1.3	1.1
Unknown Age	EW5A	–	–	–	–	–	–
18 - 24	EW5B	–	–	–	–	–	–
25 - 29	EW5C	–	–	–	–	–	–
30 - 34	EW5D	0.1	0.1	0.1	–	–	–
35 - 39	EW5E	0.3	0.3	0.2	0.2	0.1	0.1
40 - 44	EW5F	0.6	0.6	0.5	0.4	0.3	0.2
45 - 49	EW5G	0.8	0.7	0.6	0.5	0.4	0.3
50 - 54	EW5H	0.8	0.7	0.6	0.5	0.3	0.3
55 - 59	EW5I	0.4	0.4	0.4	0.3	0.2	0.2
60 - 64	EW5J	0.1	0.1	–	0.1	–	–
Age -related bereavement allowance							
All ages	KJGS	154.9	150.8	138.5	124.2	110.1	96.5
Unknown Age	EW5K	–	–	–	–	–	–
18 - 24	EW5L	–	–	–	–	–	–
25 - 29	EW5M	–	–	–	–	–	–
30 - 34	EW5N	–	–	–	–	–	–
35 - 39	EW5O	–	–	–	–	–	–
40 - 44	EW5P	0.5	0.4	0.3	0.2	0.2	0.1
45 - 49	EW5Q	12.6	11.7	8.7	6.6	5.1	4.0
50 - 54	EW5R	54.0	51.7	40.9	32.8	26.7	21.3
55 - 59	EW5S	78.6	77.5	77.7	73.5	66.3	59.0
60 - 64	EW5T	9.2	9.5	10.9	11.1	11.8	12.1
Bereavement allowance (Not age related)[3]							
All ages	KJGW	57.4	53.6	41.6	31.2	23.6	18.1
Unknown Age	EW5U	0.1	–	–	–	–	–
18 - 24	EW5V	0.1	–	–	–	–	–
25 - 29	EW5W	–	–	–	–	–	–
30 - 34	EW5X	–	–	–	–	–	–
35 - 39	EW5Y	–	–	–	–	–	–
40 - 44	EW5Z	–	–	–	–	–	–
45 - 49	EW62	–	–	–	–	–	–
50 - 54	EW63	1.6	1.5	1.1	0.8	0.6	0.5
55 - 59	EW64	34.9	32.6	22.3	14.4	8.8	5.6
60 - 64	EW65	20.7	19.5	18.2	16.0	14.2	12.0

1 Definitions and Conventions: "-" Nil or Negligible; "." Not applicable; Caseload figures are rounded to the nearest hundred and displayed in thousands.

2 Caseload (Thousands) All Claimants of Widows Benefit are female. No new claims for WB have been accepted since April 2001 when it was replaced by Bereavement Benefit.

3 Figures include overseas cases.

Sources: DWP Information Directorate: Work and Pensions Longitudinal Study 100% data; Information and Analysis Directorate: 0191 225 7373

10.13 Bereavement Benefit[1] (excluding bereavement payment): by sex, type of benefit and age of widow/er

Great Britain. Number in payment at March

Thousands

		Males				Females		
		2003	2004	2005		2003	2004	2005
All Bereavement Benefit (excluding bereavement allowance)								
All ages	WLSX	16.9	16.8	17.5	WLTC	30.8	34.2	37.0
18 - 24	EVW9	..	..	..	EVY2	0.1	0.1	0.1
25 - 29	EVX2	0.1	–	0.1	EVY3	0.4	0.4	0.5
30 - 34	EVX3	0.4	0.4	0.4	EVY4	1.1	1.4	1.6
35 - 39	EVX4	1.2	1.3	1.2	EVY5	2.3	3.0	3.5
40 - 44	EVX5	2.2	2.4	2.5	EVY6	3.3	4.6	5.6
45 - 49	EVX6	3.1	3.2	3.3	EVY7	5.3	6.4	7.3
50 - 54	EVX7	3.3	3.2	3.3	EVY8	7.2	7.6	7.8
55 - 59	EVX8	3.5	3.5	3.6	EVY9	11.1	10.7	10.8
60 - 64	EVX9	3.1	2.9	3.1	EVZ2	–	–	–
Widowed parents' allowance - with dependant children								
All ages	WLUD	9.6	10.2	10.6	WLUH	12.9	17.4	21.1
18 - 24	EVZ3	–	–	–	EW24	0.1	0.1	0.1
25 - 29	EVZ4	0.1	–	0.1	EW25	0.3	0.4	0.5
30 - 34	EVZ5	0.4	0.4	0.4	EW26	1.1	1.4	1.6
35 - 39	EVZ6	1.2	1.2	1.2	EW27	2.2	2.9	3.5
40 - 44	EVZ7	2.2	2.3	2.4	EW28	3.3	4.5	5.6
45 - 49	EVZ8	2.5	2.7	2.8	EW29	3.1	4.3	7.3
50 - 54	EVZ9	1.9	2.0	2.1	EW2A	1.9	2.7	7.8
55 - 59	EW22	1.1	1.2	1.2	EW2B	0.8	1.1	10.8
60 - 64	EW23	0.3	0.3	0.4	EW2C	–	–	–
Widowed parents' allowance - without dependant children								
All ages	WLVK	0.1	0.1	0.1	WMMR	0.3	0.4	0.4
18 - 24	EW2D	–	–	–	EW2M	–	–	–
25 - 29	EW2E	–	–	–	EW2N	–	–	–
30 - 34	EW2F	–	–	–	EW2O	–	–	–
35 - 39	EW2G	–	–	–	EW2P	0.1	0.1	0.1
40 - 44	EW2H	–	–	–	EW2Q	0.1	0.1	0.1
45 - 49	EW2I	–	–	–	EW2R	0.1	0.1	0.1
50 - 54	EW2J	–	–	–	EW2S	0.1	0.1	0.1
55 - 59	EW2K	–	–	–	EW2T	–	–	–
60 - 64	EW2L	–	–	–	EW2U	–	–	–
Age-related bereavement allowance								
All ages	WMOB	2.1	1.9	1.9	WMOC	8.1	7.5	6.9
18 - 24	EW2V	–	–	–	EW36	–	–	–
25 - 29	EW2W	–	–	–	EW37	–	–	–
30 - 34	EW2X	–	–	–	EW38	–	–	–
35 - 39	EW2Y	–	–	–	EW39	–	–	–
40 - 44	EW2Z	–	–	–	EW3A	–	–	–
45 - 49	EW32	0.6	0.5	0.5	EW3B	2.1	1.9	1.8
50 - 54	EW33	1.3	1.2	1.2	EW3C	5.2	4.8	4.4
55 - 59	EW34	0.2	0.2	0.2	EW3D	0.8	0.7	0.6
60 - 64	EW35	–	–	–	EW3E	–	–	–
Bereavement allowance (not age related)								
All ages	WMOX	5.0	4.7	4.9	WMOY	9.5	8.9	8.6
18 - 24	EW3F	–	–	–	EW3O	–	–	–
25 - 29	EW3G	–	–	–	EW3P	–	–	–
30 - 34	EW3H	–	–	–	EW3Q	–	–	–
35 - 39	EW3I	–	–	–	EW3R	–	–	–
40 - 44	EW3J	–	–	–	EW3S	–	–	–
45 - 49	EW3K	–	–	–	EW3T	–	–	–
50 - 54	EW3L	–	–	–	EW3U	–	–	–
55 - 59	EW3M	2.2	2.2	2.2	EW3V	9.5	8.9	8.6
60 - 64	EW3N	2.8	2.5	2.7	EW3W	–	–	–

1 Bereavement Benefit replaced Widow's Benefit and is payable to both men and women widowed on or after 9 April 2001. Figures include overseas cases.

Source: Work and Pensions longitudinal study (WPLS) 100%: 0191 225 7874

10.14 Contributory and non-contributory retirement pensions:[1] by sex and age of claimant

Great Britain. Numbers in payment at end of May · Thousands and percentages

		2002	2003	2004	2005
Men:					
Age-groups:					
65-69	KJSB	1 308.3	1 329.3	1 352.7	1 355.3
Percentage	KJSC	*31.5*	*31.5*	*31.6*	*31.3*
70-74	KJSD	1 129.0	1 136.7	1 140.2	1 148.8
Percentage	KJSE	*27.2*	*27.0*	*26.6*	*26.5*
75-79	KJSF	864.0	867.2	875.2	886.5
Percentage	KJSG	*20.8*	*20.6*	*20.4*	*20.5*
80-84	KJSH	532.0	565.3	593.7	592.8
Percentage	KJSI	*12.8*	*13.4*	*13.9*	*13.7*
85-89	KJSJ	233.3	226.0	221.4	245.9
Percentage	KJSK	*5.6*	*5.4*	*5.2*	*5.7*
90 and over	KJSL	85.9	90.6	95.6	100.1
Percentage	KJSM	*2.1*	*2.1*	*2.2*	*2.3*
Unknown age	EW3Y	1.4	1.3	1.5	2.8
Percentage	EW3Z	–	–	–	0.1
Total all ages	KJSA	4 153.9	4 216.4	4 280.3	4 332.2
Women:					
Age-groups:					
60-64	KJSO	1 371.0	1 401.8	1 449.4	1 484.4
Percentage	KJSP	*19.6*	*19.9*	*20.3*	*20.6*
65-69	KJSQ	1 409.8	1 429.4	1 452.0	1 461.2
Percentage	KJSR	*20.2*	*20.3*	*20.4*	*20.3*
70-74	KJSS	1 333.3	1 328.9	1 318.7	1 313.7
Percentage	KJST	*19.1*	*18.8*	*18.5*	*18.3*
75-79	KJSU	1 175.3	1 162.0	1 156.6	1 157.6
Percentage	KJSV	*16.8*	*16.5*	*16.2*	*16.1*
80-84	KJSW	893.3	939.9	974.3	951.7
Percentage	KJSX	*12.8*	*13.3*	*13.7*	*13.2*
85-89	KJSY	514.1	491.4	473.1	510.3
Percentage	KJSZ	*7.4*	*7.0*	*6.6*	*7.1*
90 and over	KJTA	289.3	298.8	307.3	314.4
Percentage	KJTB	*4.1*	*4.2*	*4.3*	*4.4*
Unknown age	EW42	3.6	2.3	1.3	3.1
Percentage	EW43	0.1	–	–	–
Total all ages	KJSN	6 989.7	7 054.5	7 132.7	7 196.4

1 See chapter text. Including pensions payable to persons residing overseas.

Sources: Department for Work and Pensions; Work and Pensions Longitudinal Study (WPLS); Information and Analysis Directorate: 0191 225 7373

Social protection

10.15 War pensions: estimated number of pensioners[1]
Great Britain

At 31 March each year

Thousands

		1995	1996	1997	1998	1999	2000	2001	2002	2003	2004	2005
Disablement	KADH	260.30	265.37	264.59	259.16	248.93	240.76	231.62	222.25	212.59	201.97	192.15
Widows and dependants	KADI	49.54	58.37	60.05	58.49	55.85	54.92	52.71	50.48	48.13	45.56	43.09
Total	KADG	309.84	323.74	324.64	317.65	306.06	295.67	284.33	272.72	260.73	247.52	235.24

1 See chapter text. From 1914 war, 1939 war and later service.

Source: Ministry of Defence/DASA (Pay & Pensions): 020 7218 0031

10.16 Income support[1] (excluding MIG)[2] by statistical group[3]:number of claimants
Great Britain

Thousands[4]

		2000	2001	2002	2003	2004	2005
All income support claimants (excluding MIG)[5]	F8YY	2 241.6	2 264.6	2 245.5	2 239.7	2 196.6	2 140.5
Incapacity Benefits	F8YZ	1 111.5	1 179.6	1 195.9	1 212.1	1 201.8	1 188.7
Lone Parent	F8Z2	913.0	893.2	864.5	851.1	821.2	787.2
Carer	F8Z3	72.1	72.7	75.4	77.3	78.3	78.5
Others on Income Related Benefits	F8Z4	145.0	119.1	109.7	99.2	95.3	86.0

1 Figures are given at May each year and are taken from the DWP 100% Work and Pensions Longitudinal Study (WPLS).
2 Figures exclude MIG claimants. Pension Credit replaced MIG on 6th October 2003 and extended Income Support entitlements to customers aged 60 and over.
3 Statistical groups are defined as follows:
Incapacity Benefits- claimants aged under 60 on Incapacity Benefit or Severe Disablement Allowance;
Lone Parent - single claimants aged under 60 with dependants not in receipt of IB/SDA;
Carer- claimants aged under 60 entitled to Carer's Allowance;
Other Income Related Benefit- claimants not in one of the above categories.
4 Figures are rounded to the nearest hundred and quoted in thousands.
5 Totals may not sum due to rounding.

Sources: Department for Work and Pensions;
Information and Analysis Directorate: 0191 225 7373

10.17 MIG/Pension Credit[1,2]:number of claimants
Great Britain

End of May

Thousands[3]

		2000[4]	2001[4]	2002[4]	2003[4]	2004[5]	2005[5]
All Pension Credit	F8Z5	..	..	..	..	2 489.9	2 680.2
Guarantee Credit Only	F8Z6	..	..	..	..	734.8	766.7
Guarantee Credit Only and Savings Credit	F8Z7	..	..	..	..	1 269.3	1 321.1
Savings Credit	F8Z8	..	..	..	..	482.5	592.3
(Residual)[6] MIG Case	F8Z9	1 607.0	1 777.0	1 738.0	1 778.0	0.3	–

1 Source Data: Work and Pensions Longitudinal Data in each May from 2000 - 2005.
2 Pension Credit was introduced on 6th October 2003 and replaced Monthly Income Guarantee (Income Support for people aged 60 or over). The vast majority of people who were in receipt of MIG transferred to PC in October 2003.
3 Figures are rounded to the nearest hundred and expressed in thousands.
4 Columns 2000 - 2003 represent MIG caseloads.
5 Columns 2004 onwards represent Pension Credit Caseloads.
6 When MIG was replaced by Pension Credit in October 2003 some cases continued to be MIG cases. These were cases where the partner aged under 60 continued as the claimant. These cases are minimal and are reducing each quarter.

Sources: Department for Work and Pensions;
Information and Analysis Directorate: 0191 225 7373

10.18 Income support: average weekly amounts of benefit[1,2]
Great Britain
As at May

£ per week

		2000	2001	2002	2003	2004	2005
All income support claimants (excluding MIG)[3]	F8ZF	77.95	84.31	84.78	91.05	91.11	85.83
Incapacity benefits[4]	F8ZG	70.18	74.21	72.27	76.07	77.66	76.92
Lone Parent[4]	F8ZH	91.72	101.39	105.87	116.54	115.00	102.90
Carer[4]	F8ZI	53.31	69.33	71.41	76.57	76.73	72.29
Others on income related benefits[4]	F8ZJ	63.06	65.40	64.27	66.70	66.69	65.25

1 Figures are given at May each year and are taken from the DWP Work and Pensions Longitudinal Study (WPLS).
2 Average amounts are rounded to the nearest penny.
3 Figures exclude MIG claimants. Pension Credit replaced MIG on 6 October 2003 and extended Income Support entitlement to customers aged 60 and over.
4 Statistical groups are defined as follows:
Incapacity Benefits- claimants under 60 on incapacity benefit or Severe Disablement Allowance;
Lone Parent- single claimants aged under 60 with dependants not in receipt of IB/SDA;
Carer- claimants aged under 60 entitled to Carer's Allowance;
Other Income Related Benefit- claimants not in one of the above categories.

Sources: Department for Work and Pensions; Information and Analysis Directorate: 0191 225 7373

10.19 MIG/Pension Credit: average weekly amounts of benefit[1,2]
Great Britain
As at May

£ per week[3]

		2000[4]	2001[4]	2002[4]	2003[4]	2004[5]	2005[5]
All Pension Credit	F8ZA	..	..	..	..	42.31	43.64
Guarantee Credit Only	F8ZB	..	..	..	..	71.92	75.45
Guarantee Credit and Savings Credit	F8ZC	..	..	..	..	37.51	39.88
Savings Credit only	F8ZD	..	..	..	..	10.04	10.84
(Residual) MIG Case[6]	F8ZE	47.40	50.00	49.45	50.38	46.27	..

1 Figures are given in each May from 2000 - 2005 and are taken from the DWP Work and Pensions Longitudinal Study (WPLS).
2 Pension Credit was introduced on 6th October 2003 and replaced Minimum Income Guarantee (Income Support for people aged 60 or over).
3 Average amounts are shown as pounds per week and rounded to the nearest penny.
4 Columns 2000-2003 represent MIG average amounts.
5 Colums 2004 onwards represent Pension Credit Average amounts.
6 When MIG replaced pension credit in October 2003 some cases continued to be MIG cases. These were cases where the partner aged under 60 continued as the claimant. These cases are minimal and are reducing each quarter.

Sources: Department for Work and Pensions; Information and Analysis Directorate: 0191 225 7373

10.20 Summary of government expenditure on social services and housing[1]
Years ended 31 March

£ million

		1994 /95	1995 /96	1996 /97	1997 /98	1998 /99	1999 /00	2000 /01	2001 /02	2002 /03	2003 /04
Education[2]	KJAA	35 390	36 807	37 950	39 077	38 981	40 895	44 350	49 820	53 320	59 323
National Health Service	KJAB	39 879	40 691	42 383	43 878	47 194	48 362	53 039	59 880	66 314	74 928
Welfare services	CSWL	9 016	10 312	11 521	11 713	11 984	12 168	12 995	14 031	16 337	20 287
Social security benefits	KJAE	87 941	90 534	92 217	92 146	93 929	97 077	98 899	106 504	109 017	102 487
Housing	QYXD	8 306	8 402	6 994	6 717	6 128	5 047	5 313	6 647	6 371	7 443
Total government expenditure	KJAG	180 532	186 746	191 065	193 531	198 216	203 549	214 596	236 882	251 359	264 468
Current expenditure	KJAH	173 030	179 199	184 749	187 667	193 846	199 789	210 128	231 342	246 427	255 938
Capital expenditure	KJAI	7 502	7 547	6 316	5 864	4 370	3 760	4 468	5 540	4 932	8 530
Total government expenditure	KJAG	180 532	186 746	191 065	193 531	198 216	203 549	214 596	236 882	251 359	264 468
Central government	KJAK	130 819	134 954	137 487	142 670	158 494	163 098	171 010	189 104	200 919	203 706
Local authorities	KJAL	49 713	51 792	53 578	50 861	39 722	40 451	43 586	47 778	50 440	60 762
Total government expenditure	KJAG	180 532	186 746	191 065	193 531	198 216	203 549	214 596	236 882	251 359	264 468
Total government expenditure on social services and housing as a percentage of GDP[3]		26.16	25.63	24.66	23.50	22.74	22.15	22.25	23.50	23.67	23.60

1 See chapter text.
2 Includes school meals.
3 GDP adjusted to take account of change from rates to community charge.

Source: Office for National Statistics: 020 7533 5990

10.21 Government expenditure on education[1]
Years ended 31 March

£ million

		1993 /94	1994 /95	1995 /96	1996 /97	1997 /98	1998 /99	1999 /00	2000 /01	2001 /02	2002 /03	2003 /04
Current expenditure												
Nursery and primary schools	KEZN	8 712	9 094	9 352	9 697	10 405	23 069	24 441	27 066	30 280	31 160	35 428
Secondary schools	KJBC	8 615	8 875	8 844	9 194	9 322	..	..	..	..	..	..
Special schools	KJBD	1 420	1 451	1 493	1 578	1 655	..	..	..	..	..	..
Higher Education Funding Council[2,3]	CSWM	4 908	5 192	5 472	5 729	5 693	4 726	5 166	5 843	5 638	6 164	6 595
Further Education Funding Council[4]	CSWO	3 072	3 200	3 392	3 694	3 718	5 064	5 216	5 194	6 822	6 012	6 746
Continuing Education	CSWP	380	294	1 801	1 891	1 960	..	..	..	..	..	..
Other education expenditure	KJBH	905	963	948	1 277	1 355	4 611	4 278	3 881	3 996	6 430	6 436
Related current expenditure:												
School welfare[5]	KJBJ	346	359	328	336	372	..	..	..	..	..	..
School meals[6]	KJBK	149	147	148	147	138	..	..	..	..	..	..
Youth service and physical training	KJBL	392	401	396	389	389	..	..	..	..	..	..
Maintenance grants and allowances to pupils and students[7]	KJBM	1 972	2 204	1 660	1 440	1 289	..	..	..	..	..	..
Transport of pupils	KJBN	444	486	507	526	584	..	..	..	..	..	..
Miscellaneous expenditure	KJBO	10	31	31	49	45	..	..	..	..	..	..
Total current expenditure[8]	KJBQ	31 325	32 697	34 372	35 947	36 925	37 470	39 101	41 984	46 736	49 766	55 205
Capital expenditure												
Nursery and primary schools	KEZP	414	517	497	482	546	1 357	1 472	1 730	2 048	2 260	2 850
Secondary schools	KJBT	485	565	482	515	601	..	..	..	..	..	..
Special schools	KJBU	31	37	51	52	44	..	..	..	..	..	..
Higher Education Funding Council[2,3]	CSWQ	406	412	424	74	61	31	113	208	342	405	494
Further Education Funding Council[4]	CSWR	194	201	187	33	29	44	97	253	459	491	465
Continuing Education	CSWS	6	8	8	5	−	−	−	−	−	..	..
Other education expenditure	KJBY	12	45	25	24	30	57	111	174	234	398	309
Related capital expenditure	KJBZ	23	25	17	20	24	22	..	..	..	..	..
Total capital expenditure[8]	KJCA	1 571	1 810	1 691	1 205	1 335	1 511	1 793	2 365	3 083	3 554	4 118
VAT refunds to local authorities	KJBP	648	860	747	801	818	816	906	..	..	..	..
Total expenditure												
Central government	KJCB	8 186	9 490	10 853	11 388	12 167	11 422	13 177	14 421	16 735	18 114	20 109
Local authorities	KJCC	25 354	25 900	25 954	26 562	26 910	27 559	27 718	29 929	33 085	35 206	39 214
Total government expenditure[9]	KJAA	33 540	35 390	36 807	37 950	39 077	38 981	40 895	44 350	49 820	53 320	59 323
Total government education expenditure as a percentage of GDP[10]		5.15	5.13	5.05	4.90	4.75	4.47	4.45	4.60	4.94	5.02	5.29

1 See chapter text. From 1998/99 figures have been taken from HM Treasury Public Expenditure Statistical Analyses. They are not comparable with earlier years which used different sources. Schools expenditure no longer separately identifiable

2 Includes tuition fees.

3 Includes expenditure on higher education institutions in Northern Ireland.

4 Includes expenditure on further education institutions in Northern Ireland.

5 Expenditure on the school health service is included in the National Health Service.

6 Expenditure on school meals in England has been recharged across other expenditure headings.

7 Excludes the secondment of teachers on further training. Includes student loans expenditure.

8 Due to rounding constituent figures may not sum to totals.

9 Excludes additional adjustment to allow for Capital consumption made for National Accounts purposes. From 1995/96, figures include expenditure on training programmes in England (such as Work Based Training for Young People) reclassified as education. Therefore the figures are not comparable with earlier years.

10 GDP includes adjustments to remove the distortion caused by the abolition of domestic rates.

Sources: Department for Education and Skills;
Office for National Statistics: 020 7533 5990

10.22 Government expenditure on the National Health Service[1]
Years ended 31 March

£ million

		1994/95	1995/96	1996/97	1997/98	1998/99	1999/00	2000/01	2001/02	2002/03	2003/04
Current expenditure[2]											
Hospitals and Community Health Services[3] and Family Health Services[4]	KJQA	37 698	38 514	39 425	40 993	43 600	48 275	52 599	59 081	65 368	73 843
less Payments by patients:											
Hospital services	KJQC	−111	−42	−42	−48	−84	−138	−138	−155	−172	−194
Pharmaceutical services	KJQD	−342	−383	−376	−396	−391	−405	−425	−478	−528	−596
Dental services	KJQE	−464	−494	−447	−475	−470	−483	−506	−568	−628	−709
Total	KJQG	−917	−919	−865	−919	−945	−1 026	−1 068	−1 199	−1 326	−1 498
Departmental administration	KJQH	256	242	265	245	227	231	324	364	402	454
Other central services	KJQI	2 304	2 538	3 124	3 242	4 980	1 601	1 931	2 885	2 858	3 229
Total current expenditure	KJQJ	39 341	40 375	41 949	43 561	46 910	48 055	52 707	59 508	65 975	74 529
Capital expenditure[2]	KJQK	538	316	434	317	284	307	332	372	339	399
Total government NHS Expenditure[2]	KJAB	39 879	40 691	42 383	43 878	47 194	48 362	53 039	59 880	66 314	74 928
Total NHS expenditure as a percentage of GDP[5]		*5.78*	*5.58*	*5.47*	*5.33*	*5.41*	*5.26*	*5.50*	*5.94*	*6.24*	*6.69*

1 See chapter text.
2 By central government.
3 Including the school health service.
4 General Medical Services have been included in the expenditure of the Health Authorities. Therefore, Hospitals and Community Health Services and Family Practitioner Services (now Family Health Services) are not identifiable separately.
5 GDP adjusted to take account of change from rates to community charge.

Source: Office for National Statistics: 020 7533 5990

10.23 Government expenditure on the welfare services[1]
Years ended 31 March

£ million

		1993/94	1994/95	1995/96	1996/97	1997/98	1998/99	1999/00	2000/01	2001/02	2002/03	2003/04
Personal social services												
Central government current expenditure	KJCG	216	197	140	101	73	53	50	49	56	65	81
Local authorities current expenditure:												
Running expenses	CTKQ	7 113	8 400	9 716	10 947	11 131	11 378	11 563	12 405	13 353	15 530	19 285
Capital expenditure	KJCI	190	235	229	210	204	199	145	132	147	196	243
Total	KJAC	7 519	8 832	10 085	11 258	11 408	11 630	11 758	12 586	13 556	15 791	19 609
Welfare foods service												
Central government current expenditure on welfare foods (including administration)	KJCK	182	185	228	264	306	355	411	411	477	547	681
less Receipts from the public	KJCL	−1	−1	−1	−1	−1	−1	−1	−2	−2	−2	−3
Total	KJAD	181	184	227	263	305	354	410	409	475	545	678
Total government expenditure	CSWL	7 700	9 016	10 312	11 521	11 713	11 984	12 168	12 995	14 031	16 337	20 287
Total government expenditure as a percentage of GDP[2]		*1.18*	*1.31*	*1.42*	*1.49*	*1.42*	*1.37*	*1.32*	*1.35*	*1.39*	*1.54*	*1.81*

1 See chapter text.
2 GDP adjusted to take account of change from rates to community charge.

Source: Office for National Statistics: 020 7533 5990

10.24 Government expenditure on social security benefits[1]
Years ended 31 March

£ million

		1993 /94	1994 /95	1995 /96	1996 /97	1997 /98	1998 /99	1999 /00	2000 /01	2001 /02	2002 /03	2003 /04
Government current expenditure												
National Insurance fund:												
Retirement pensions	EKXK	28 481	28 925	30 162	32 146	33 643	35 782	37 918	39 361	43 222	48 863	51 169
Lump sums to pensioners	KJDB	122	123	124	129	118	120	123	128	134	137	–
Widows and Guardians allowances	CSDH	1 041	1 034	1 018	974	992	973	990	982	1 113	1 092	1 005
Unemployment Benefit	CSDI	1 623	1 277	1 099	588	1	–	−1	−1	–	–	–
Jobseeker's Allowance[2]	CJTJ	–	–	–	379	590	474	462	435	441	520	257
Sickness Benefit[3]	CSDJ	294	426	12	–	–	–	–	–	–	–	–
Invalidity Benefit[3]	CSDK	7 146	8 042	271	–	–	–	–	–	–	–	–
Incapacity Benefit[3]	CUNL	–	–	7 615	7 668	7 471	7 295	6 897	6 677	6 836	6 837	6 801
Maternity Benefit	CSDL	32	17	28	32	36	39	40	52	56	69	125
Statutory sick pay	CSDQ	688	24	24	24	28	28	28	36	32	–	–
Statutory maternity pay	GTKZ	440	498	476	500	516	552	585	611	652	708	–
Total	ACHH	39 867	40 366	40 829	42 440	43 395	45 263	47 043	48 281	52 486	58 226	59 357
Redundancy Fund	GTKN	110	208	128	108	88	116	148	196	194	280	240
Social Fund	GTLQ	189	183	216	203	200	360	920	1 957	1 859	1 925	2 159
Non-contributory benefits:												
War pensions [4]	KJDP	913	1 083	1 247	1 352	1 284	1 262	1 254	1 201	1 182	..	..
Family benefits:												
Child Benefit	KJDQ	6 347	6 294	6 332	6 645	7 095	7 327	8 212	8 528	8 685	8 897	..
One parent benefit	KJDR	282	289	310	317	9	–	–	–	–	–	–
Family Credit	KAAA	1 208	1 441	1 739	2 084	2 338	2 430	1 927	−788	–	–	–
Income support/Supplementary benefits:												
Income Support	KAAB	16 997	16 387	16 650	14 438	11 998	11 793	12 227	13 076	14 222	10 003	10 432
Other non-contributory benefits:												
Old persons' pensions	KJDX	36	35	36	30	29	29	28	28	27	29	30
Lump sums to pensioners	KJDY	14	13	15	15	17	17	17	17	17	17	17
Attendance Allowance	KJDZ	1 795	1 963	2 194	2 393	2 640	2 682	2 834	2 957	3 121	3 259	3 456
Invalid Care Allowance	KJEA	442	526	617	736	745	783	814	849	924	999	1 055
Mobility Allowance	KJEB	–	–	–	–	–	–	–	–	–	–	–
Disability Living Allowance	EKXL	2 772	3 125	3 802	4 498	5 018	5 367	5 653	6 021	6 567	7 081	7 609
Disability Working Allowance	EKYE	7	11	19	34	44	49	40	–	–	–	–
Severe Disablement Allowance	KJEC	703	776	820	906	1 007	984	1 016	1 024	1 034	960	934
Industrial Injury benefits	EKXM	687	706	731	744	754	–	–	–	–	–	–
Housing Benefit	KJED	9 163	10 345	10 773	11 276	11 315	11 311	11 247	11 616	11 910	12 980	12 720
Administration	KJEE	4 273	4 190	4 076	3 998	4 170	4 349	3 737	3 936	4 253	4 364	4 478
Total government expenditure	KJAE	85 805	87 941	90 534	92 217	92 146	93 929	97 077	98 899	106 504	109 017	102 487
Total government benefit expenditure as a percentage of GDP[5]		13.17	12.74	12.43	11.90	11.19	10.78	10.57	10.26	10.56	10.26	9.14

1 See chapter text.
2 Jobseeker's allowance was introduced in October 1996 to replace Unemployment benefit and Income Support for the unemployed.
3 Sickness benefit and Invalidity benefit were replaced by a single incapacity benefit in 1995.
4 From 2002/03 War Pensions are administered by the Ministry of Defence.
5 GDP adjusted to take account of change from rates to community charge.

Source: Office for National Statistics: 020 7533 5990

10.25 Government and other public sector expenditure on housing and community amenities[1]

Years ended 31 March

£ million

		1994/95	1995/96	1996/97	1997/98	1998/99	1999/00	2000/01	2001/02	2002/03	2003/04	2004/05
Final consumption expenditure												
Compensation of employees	QYSV	952	852	704	745	870	864	897	976	984	981	1 068
Other current expenditure on goods and services	QYSW	735	782	484	1 047	999	1 092	1 340	1 448	1 508	1 821	3 020
Capital consumption	QYSY	394	544	960	1 035	1 096	1 195	1 242	1 358	1 481	1 440	1 463
Total	QYSZ	2 081	2 178	2 148	2 827	2 965	3 151	3 479	3 782	3 973	4 242	5 551
Subsidies												
Paid to public corporations	C5AN	243	256	237	248	223	214	168	143	161	233	..
Paid to local authorities	CTMN	814	687	717	711	737	466	438	347	241	203	164
Other subsidies	C5DR	207	215	216	214	−19	21	21	5	18	46	..
Other current transfers	QZNY	19	15	43	14	40	184	185	270	238	389	105
Gross Fixed Capital Formation	QYVH	1 822	2 173	909	466	−146	−1 109	−894	102	−694	−815	−135
Capital transfers												
LA improvement grants	ADCE	1 105	846	918	1 157	1 181	1 130	902	985	969	1 110	901
LA capital grants to public corporations	ADCF	1	1	2	29	13	17	36	16	16	52	314
Central Government grants to Housing Associations	GTDI	1 507	1 243	1 140	761	883	1 022	986	1 143	1 220	2 211	1 986
Others	C5AO	507	788	664	290	251	−49	−8	−146	229	−228	−219
Total government expenditure	QYXD	8 306	8 402	6 994	6 717	6 128	5 047	5 313	6 647	6 371	7 443	..
Total public sector housing expenditure as a percentage of GDP		1.20	1.15	0.90	0.82	0.70	0.55	0.55	0.66	0.60	0.66	..

1 See chapter text.

Source: Office for National Statistics: 020 7533 5990

Crime and justice

Chapter 11

Crime and justice

There are differences in the legal and judicial systems of England and Wales, Scotland and Northern Ireland which make it impossible to provide tables covering the United Kingdom as a whole in this section. These differences concern the classification of offences, the meaning of certain terms used in the statistics, the effects of the several Criminal Justice Acts, and recording practices.

Recorded crime statistics

(Table 11.2)

Crimes recorded by the police provide a measure of the amount of crime committed. The statistics are based on counting rules, revised with effect from 1 April 1998, which are standard for all the police forces in England, Wales and Northern Ireland and now include all indictable and triable-either-way offences together with a few summary offences which are closely linked to these offences. The new rules have changed the emphasis of measurement more towards one crime per victim, and have also increased the coverage of offences. These changes have particularly impacted on the offence groups of violence against the person, fraud and forgery, drugs offences and other offences.

For a variety of reasons many offences are either not reported to the police or not recorded by them. The changes in the number of offences recorded do not necessarily provide an accurate reflection of changes in the amount of crime committed.

In order to further improve the consistency of recorded crime statistics, and to take a more victim oriented approach to crime recording, the National Crime Recording Standard (NCRS) was introduced in England, Wales and Northern Ireland from 1 April 2002. Some police forces implemented the principles of NCRS in advance of its implementation across all forces in April 2002. The NCRS had the effect of increasing the number of offences recorded by the police.

Similarly, the Scottish Crime Recording Standard was introduced by the eight Scottish police forces with effect from 1 April 2004. This means that no corroborative evidence is required initially to record a crime related incident as a crime if so perceived by the victim. Again, the introduction of this new recording standard was expected to increase the numbers of minor crimes recorded by the police, such as minor crimes of vandalism and minor thefts and offences of petty assault and breach of the peace. However, it was expected that the SCRS would not have much impact on the figures for the more serious crimes such as serious assault, sexual assault, robbery or housebreaking.

Further information is available from the Home Office: *Crime in England and Wales 2002/2003*, ed: Jon Simmons and Tricia Dodd.

Court proceedings and police cautions

(Tables 11.3 to 11.7, 11.13 to 11.17, 11.20 to 11.22)

The statistical basis of the tables of court proceedings is broadly similar in England and Wales, Scotland and Northern Ireland; the tables show the number of persons found guilty, recording a person under the heading of the principal offence of which he is found guilty, excluding additional findings of guilt at the same proceedings. A person found guilty at a number of separate court proceedings is included more than once.

The statistics on offenders cautioned in England and Wales cover only those who, on admission of guilt, were given a formal caution by, or on the instructions of, a senior police officer as an alternative to prosecution. Written warnings by the police for motor offences and persons paying fixed penalties for certain motoring offences are excluded. Formal cautions are not issued in Scotland. There are no statistics on cautioning available for Northern Ireland.

The Crime and Disorder Act 1998 created provisions in relation to reprimands and final warnings, new offences and orders which have been implemented nationally since 1 June 2000. They replace the system of cautioning for offenders aged under 18. Reprimands can be given to first-time offenders for minor offences. Any further offending results in either a final warning or a charge.

For persons proceeded against in Scotland, the statistics relate to the High Court of Justiciary, the Sheriff Court and the District Court. The High Court deals with serious solemn (i.e. Jury) cases and has unlimited sentencing power. The Sheriff Court is limited to imprisonment of three years for solemn cases, or three months (six months when specified in legislation for second or subsequent offences and 12 months for certain statutory offences) for summary (i.e. non-Jury) cases. The District Court deals only with summary cases and is limited to 60 days imprisonment and level 4 fines. Stipendiary Magistrates sit in Glasgow District Court and have the summary sentencing powers of a Sheriff.

In England and Wales, indictable offences are offences which are:

(a) *Triable only on indictment*. These offences are the most serious breaches of the criminal law and must be tried at the Crown Court. 'Indictable-only' offences include murder, manslaughter, rape and robbery.

(b) *Triable either way*. These offences may be tried at the Crown Court or Magistrates' Court.

The Criminal Justice Act 1991 led to the following main changes in the sentences available to the courts in England and Wales:

(a) introduction of combination orders,

(b) introduction of the 'unit fine scheme' at Magistrates' courts,

(c) abolishing the sentence of detention in a young offender institution for 14 year old boys and changing the minimum and maximum sentence lengths for 15 to 17 year olds to 10 and 12 months respectively, and

(d) abolishing partly suspended sentences of imprisonment and restricting the use of a fully suspended sentence.

The Criminal Justice Act 1993 abolished the 'Unit Fine Scheme' in Magistrates' courts which had been introduced under the Criminal Justice Act 1991.

A *charging standard for assault* was introduced in England and Wales on 31 August 1994 with the aim to promote consistency between the police and prosecution on the appropriate level of charge to be brought.

The Criminal Justice and Public Order Act 1994 created several new offences in England and Wales, mainly in the area of Public Order, but also including male rape (there is no statutory offence of 'male rape' in Scotland, although such a crime may be charged as serious assault). The Act also:

(a) extended the provisions of section 53 of the Children and Young Persons Act 1993 for 10 to 13 year olds,

(b) increased the maximum sentence length for 15 to 17 year olds to 2 years,

(c) increased the upper limit from £2,000 to £5,000 for offences of criminal damage proceeded against as if triable only summarily,

(d) introduced provisions for the reduction of sentences for early guilty pleas, and

(e) increased the maximum sentence length for certain firearm offences.

Provisions within the Crime (Sentences) Act 1997 (as amended by the Powers of Criminal Courts Sentencing Act 2000), in England and Wales, and the Crime and Punishment (Scotland) Act 1997, in Scotland, included:

(a) an automatic life sentence for a second serious violent or sexual offence unless there are exceptional circumstances (this provision has not been enacted in Scotland);

(b) a minimum sentence of seven years for an offender convicted for a third time of a class A drug trafficking offence unless the court considers this to be unjust in all the circumstances, and, in England and Wales,

(c) the new section 38A of the Magistrates' Courts' Act 1980 extending the circumstances in which a magistrates' court may commit a person convicted of an offence triable either way to the Crown Court for sentence – it was implemented in conjunction with section 49 of the Criminal Procedure and Investigations Act 1996, which involves the magistrates' courts in asking defendants to indicate plea before the mode of trial decision is taken and compels the court to sentence or commit for sentence any defendant who indicates a guilty plea.

Under the Criminal Justice and Court Service Act 2000 new terms were introduced for certain orders. Community rehabilitation order is the new name for a probation order. A community service order is now known as a community punishment order. Finally, the new term for a combination order is community punishment and rehabilitation order. In April 2000 the secure training order was replaced by the detention and training order. Section 53 of the Children and Young Persons Act 1993 was repealed on 25 August 2000 and its provisions were transferred to Sections 90–92 of the Powers of Criminal Courts (Sentencing) Act 2000. Reparation and Action plan order were implemented nationally from 1 June 2000. Drug treatment and testing order was implemented nationally from October 2000. And Referral order was implemented nationally from April 2000. These changes are now reflected in Table 11.7.

The system of Magistrates' courts and Crown Courts in Northern Ireland operates in a similar way to that in England and Wales. A particularly significant statutory development, however, has been the Criminal Justice (NI) Order 1996 which introduces a new sentencing regime into Northern Ireland, largely replicating that which was introduced into England and Wales by the Criminal Justice Acts of 1991 and 1993. The order makes many changes to both community and custodial sentences, while introducing new orders such as the combination order, the custody probation order and orders for release on licence of sexual offenders.

Crime and justice

Prior to 30 August 2005, for the purposes of criminal proceedings, a juvenile meant a person aged 10 years or more but under 17. After the 30th August 2005, the youth justice system was extended to 17 year olds. As the information relates to data for 2003 and earlier, figures relate to 10–16 year olds only.

Previous convictions of prisoners

(Tables 11.8 and 11.9)

Standard list offences consist of all the indictable offences plus some of the more serious summary offences. From 1 January 1996 a number of summary motoring offences became standard list offences. Excluding the new standard lists from the analysis presented in the table would slightly alter the percentages with previous convictions.

Information on previous convictions of prisoners published prior to 1995 was based upon Prison Service records. However, details of a prisoner's previous conviction were often not recorded (eg. this information was missing for 44 per cent of the 1990 male receptions under sentence). To overcome this problem the Home Office Offenders Index (a computerised database containing details of convictions for standard list offences) is now being used to provide information on prisoners' previous convictions. Unfortunately, this means that the most up-to-date information on previous convictions is not directly comparable with that previously published. Standard list offences include indictable offences and some of the more serious summary offences so the coverage is not as complete. The published information also does not relate to 'prison receptions' but to those sentenced to immediate custody for standard list offences (which accounted for 98 per cent of those sentenced to custody in 2002).

The problems with non-availability of previous history information are much less acute using the Offenders Index data source. Previous convictions were found for 95 per cent of the 1993 prison population sample. Some of the cases where information is missing would be accounted for by prisoners who are not sentenced for a standard list offence and have no previous record for such offences.

Expenditure on penal establishments in Scotland

(Table 11.19)

The results shown in this table are reported on a cash basis for financial years 1991–92 to 2000–01 in line with funding arrangements. Financial year 2001–02 is reported on a resource accounting basis in line with the introduction of Resource Budgeting. Capital Charges were introduced with Resource Accounting and Budgeting.

11.1 Police force strength: by country and sex
End of year

Numbers

		1995[1]	1996[1]	1997[1]	1998[1]	1999[1]	2000[1]	2001[1]	2002[1]	2003[1]	2004[1]	2005[1]
England and Wales												
Police Officer Strength(FTE)												
Men	KERB	107 716	106 756	106 271	105 145	103 956	101 801	102 321	104 483	106 996	110 150	110 597
Women	KERC	17 464	18 087	18 780	19 611	19 885	20 155	21 155	22 784	24 430	26 956	28 898
Seconded:[2]												
Men	KERD	1 856	1 859	1 882	1 836	2 017	–	1 914	2 031	1 689	1 811	1 514
Women	KERE	186	198	225	222	238	–	292	305	251	284	222
Officers Absent from Service:[3]												
Men	KERF	–	–	–	–	–	–	–	–	375	394	522
Women	KERG	–	–	–	–	–	–	–	–	709	969	1 042
Special constables												
Men	KERH	12 885	12 838	12 886	11 977	10 860	9 623	8 630	8 014	7 718	7 645	8 074
Women	KERI	7 141	6 937	6 988	6 279	5 624	4 724	4 108	3 584	3 319	3 343	3 844
Scotland												
Regular police Strength[4,6]:												
Men	KERK	12 630	12 627	12 752	12 753	12 545	12 374	12 547	12 513	12 590	12 685	12 798
Women	KERL	1 693	1 885	2 037	2 227	2 265	2 325	2 602	2 738	2 897	2 898	3 203
Central service:[4,5,6]												
Men	KERM	96	94	85	85	88	95	87	116	131	166	195
Women	KERN	7	8	4	6	9	13	10	12	17	29	29
Seconded:												
Men	KERO	108	105	101	101	85	130	140	133	166	192	216
Women	KERP	16	16	13	10	12	18	14	18	24	30	31
Additional regular police:												
Men	HFVM	85	81	71	88	85	80	83	80	79	88	79
Women	HFVN	5	5	1	9	6	4	5	12	10	13	21
Special constables[6] Strength:												
Men	KERS	..	1 411	1 336	1 286	1 229	981	924	812	711	773	718
Women	KERT	..	467	450	437	422	355	336	307	280	328	437
Northern Ireland												
Regular police[7,9] Strength:												
Men	KERU	7 528	7 526	7 562	7 523	7 406	6 844	6 227	6 057	6 171	6 108	6 016
Women	KERV	887	897	923	933	987	966	1 009	1 080	1 266	1 418	1 547
Reserve[8] Strength:												
Men	KERW	3 976	3 727	3 587	3 469	3 199	2 962	2 629	2 223	1 983	1 824	1 431
Women	KERX	709	675	719	705	641	607	556	510	453	485	410

1 Figures for England and Wales are as 31 March and are based on full-time equivalent strength excluding those on career breaks or maternity/ parternity leave. Figures for Scotland are as at 31 December until 1994 and from 1995 onwards as at 31 March. From 1999, figures for Northern Ireland reflect the position at the end of the financial year, i.e. 1999 and 2000 figures are as at 31 March 2000 and 31 March 2001 respectively. Prior to this figures were as at 31 December.

2 Figures exclude secondments outside the police service in England and Wales (eg to the private sector or to law enforcement agencies overseas). It is not possible to provide the gender breakdown of secondments in 2000. However the total number of secondments in this year was 2,214.

3 Figures include those officers on career breaks or maternity/paternity leave. Prior to 2003, these figures were not collected centrally.

4 'Strength' includes central service and seconded police.
5 Instructors at Training Establishments, etc, formerly shown as secondments.
6 Scottish Crime Squad, officers on courses, etc.
7 Does not include officers on secondment.
8 Includes part-time reserve and full-time reserve, 826 as at 31 March 2006 (500 males and 326 females).
9 Also includes student officers.

Sources: Home Office: 020 7273 2583;
The Scottish Executive Justice Department: 0131 244 2148;
The Police Service of Northern Ireland: 028 9065 0222 ext 24135

11.2 Recorded crime statistics: by offence group[1]
England and Wales

Thousands

		1994	1995	1996	1997	1998[2,3] /99		1998[3] /99	1999 /00	2000 /01	2001[4] /02	2002[4] /03	2003 /04	2004 /05
Violence against the person	BEAB	218.4	212.6	239.3	250.8	230.8	LQMP	502.8	581.0	600.9	650.3	834.9	955.8	1 035.0
Sexual offences	BEAC	32.0	30.3	31.4	33.2	34.9	LQMQ	36.2	37.8	37.3	41.4	48.6	52.1	60.9
Burglary	BEAD	1 256.7	1 239.5	1 164.6	1 015.1	951.9	LQMR	953.2	906.5	836.0	878.5	888.8	818.6	680.0
Robbery	BEAE	60.0	68.1	74.0	63.1	66.2	LQMS	66.8	84.3	95.2	121.4	108.0	101.2	88.7
Theft and handling stolen goods	BEAF	2 564.6	2 452.1	2 383.9	2 165.0	2 126.7	LQMT	2 191.4	2 223.6	2 145.4	2 267.0	2 365.2	2 268.1	2 027.5
Fraud and forgery	BEAG	145.3	133.0	136.2	134.4	173.7	LQMU	279.5	334.8	319.3	314.9	330.1	317.9	278.9
Criminal damage	BEAH	928.3	914.0	951.3	877.0	834.4	LQMV	879.6	945.7	960.1	1 064.5	1 109.3	1 205.6	1 185.4
Drug offences[5]	LQMO	..	..	..	..	21.3	LQYT	135.9	121.9	113.5	121.4	141.1	141.1	142.3
Other offences[5]	BEAI	47.7	29.4	33.6	36.6	42.0	LQYU	63.6	65.7	63.2	65.7	72.5	74.2	63.9
Total	BEAA	5 253.0	5 100.2	5 036.6	4 598.3	4 481.8	LQYV	5 109.1	5 301.2	5 170.8	5 525.0	5 898.6	5 934.6	5 562.7

1 See chapter text.
2 Estimates.
3 The counting rules were revised on 1 April 1998
4 The National Crime Recording Standard (NCRS) was introduced in England and Wales from 1 April 2002. For more details about the inflationary effects of the NCRS on the 2001/02 and 2002/03 figures see chapter text.

5 Prior to 1 April 1998 the offence of drug trafficking was included in the 'Other offences' group. From 1 April 1999, under the new counting rules, drug trafficking became part of a new 'Drug offences' group which, now includes possession and other drug offences. For 1998/99 under the old counting rules, drug trafficking has been separated out and listed under drugs offences.

Source: Home Office: 020 7273 2583

11.3 Offenders found guilty: by offence group[1]
England and Wales
Magistrates' courts and the Crown Court

Thousands

		1994	1995	1996	1997	1998	1999	2000	2001	2002	2003	2004
All ages[2]												
Indictable offences												
Violence against the person:	KJEJ	37.6	29.1	30.0	34.6	35.7	34.4	34.0	35.3	37.7	38.0	39.1
Murder	KESB	0.2	0.2	0.3	0.3	0.3	0.3	0.3	0.3	0.3	0.3	0.4
Manslaughter	KESC	0.2	0.2	0.3	0.3	0.3	0.3	0.3	0.3	0.3	0.2	0.3
Wounding	KESD	36.1	27.4	28.3	32.7	35.2	33.9	33.5	33.5	35.7	35.9	35.0
Other offences of violence against the person	KESE	1.0	1.2	1.2	1.3	1.3	1.3	1.3	1.2	1.4	1.5	1.9
Sexual offences	KESF	4.5	4.7	4.4	4.5	4.6	4.3	3.9	3.8	4.4	4.4	4.8
Burglary	KESG	38.0	35.3	32.2	31.7	30.8	29.3	26.2	24.8	26.7	25.7	24.3
Robbery	KESH	4.9	5.2	5.9	5.6	5.5	5.6	6.0	6.8	7.7	7.3	7.5
Theft and handling stolen goods	KESI	121.6	116.1	114.5	118.3	125.7	131.2	128.0	127.0	127.3	119.1	110.6
Fraud and forgery	KESJ	18.4	17.2	16.3	17.0	19.8	20.3	19.2	18.3	18.1	18.0	18.1
Criminal damage	KESK	10.0	9.6	9.8	10.5	10.9	10.9	10.2	10.7	11.0	11.2	11.7
Drugs	KBWX	27.8	31.6	34.1	40.7	48.8	48.7	44.6	45.6	49.0	51.2	54.5
Other offences (excluding motoring)	KESL	39.4	42.2	43.5	47.6	49.6	47.9	44.5	44.2	48.0	51.4	54.7
Motoring offences	KESM	12.0	11.2	9.9	9.5	9.0	8.1	7.6	7.7	8.2	8.7	8.0
Total	KESA	314.1	302.2	300.6	320.1	341.7	342.0	325.5	324.2	338.3	335.1	317.8
Summary offences[3]												
Assaults[4]	KESO	21.9	29.3	30.0	32.0	35.3	37.5	37.4	37.7	40.7	45.6	53.4
Betting and gaming	KESP	–	–	–	–	–	–	–	–	–	–	–
Offences with pedal cycles	KBWY	1.0	1.1	1.3	1.5	2.1	1.3	0.8	0.6	0.5	0.6	0.7
Other Highways Acts offences	KBWZ	3.4	2.6	2.8	3.2	3.1	2.9	2.7	2.4	2.2	1.9	1.8
Breach of local or other regulations	KESQ	9.4	6.7	5.9	6.4	5.8	6.5	5.0	4.3	3.9	3.4	3.1
Intoxicating Liquor Laws:												
Drunkenness	KESR	20.2	19.8	24.2	28.8	30.8	28.7	27.2	26.2	26.9	27.7	21.1
Other offences	KESS	0.7	0.7	0.5	0.6	0.6	0.5	0.4	0.3	0.4	0.7	0.8
Education Acts	KEST	2.8	3.1	3.5	3.7	5.0	5.1	5.1	5.6	5.8	5.8	6.5
Game Laws	KESU	0.6	0.4	0.4	0.3	0.4	0.3	0.2	0.2	0.3	0.2	0.2
Labour Laws	KESV	0.1	0.1	–	0.1	0.1	0.1	0.1	–	–	0.1	–
Summary offences of criminal damage and malicious damage	KESW	22.7	22.6	23.4	24.7	26.5	27.9	28.0	26.9	28.3	29.8	31.5
Offences by prostitutes	KESX	7.7	6.8	6.6	6.6	6.0	4.0	4.1	3.7	4.2	3.9	2.9
Railway offences	KESY	5.6	6.2	9.1	11.4	12.6	15.2	17.4	22.6	29.4	34.8	35.0
Revenue Laws[3]	KESZ	126.2	123.8	139.1	143.5	174.7	165.8	175.0	146.9	167.8	172.5	175.5
Vagrancy Acts	KETB	1.9	1.6	2.0	2.0	2.2	2.7	3.3	3.2	3.8	3.8	2.9
Wireless Telegraphy Acts[3]	KETC	162.9	113.8	164.9	77.0	76.6	55.8	105.7	83.8	96.6	79.9	89.3
Other summary offences	KETD	67.8	71.5	74.7	74.7	80.9	79.3	78.1	77.8	76.4	82.9	97.9
Motoring offences (summary)[3]	KETA	638.7	642.4	649.0	649.3	665.2	632.9	607.5	583.3	595.8	662.6	707.9
Total	KESN	1 093.5	1 052.4	1 137.4	1 065.8	1 128.0	1 066.5	1 098.2	1 025.5	1 083.0	1 156.1	1 230.7
Persons aged 10 to under 18[3,5]												
Indictable offences												
Violence against the person:	KETF	5.8	4.7	5.3	5.9	5.9	6.2	6.4	6.9	6.9	6.6	6.9
Murder	KBXA	–	–	–	–	–	–	–	–	–	–	–
Manslaughter	KBXB	–	–	–	–	–	0.2	–	–	–	–	–
Wounding	KBXC	5.7	4.7	5.3	5.8	5.9	5.9	6.3	6.8	6.8	6.5	6.5
Other offences of violence against the person	KCAA	–	–	–	0.1	0.1	–	0.1	0.1	0.1	0.1	0.3
Sexual offences	KETG	0.4	0.4	0.4	0.5	0.5	0.5	0.5	0.5	0.6	0.4	0.6
Burglary	KETH	8.9	9.1	8.6	8.6	8.5	7.8	6.8	6.3	6.4	5.8	5.9
Robbery	KETI	1.7	2.0	2.4	2.3	2.2	2.0	2.2	2.8	2.8	2.6	3.0
Theft and handling stolen goods	KETJ	14.4	18.2	19.0	19.6	21.9	22.7	21.0	20.6	18.4	16.5	16.8
Fraud and forgery	KETK	0.5	0.6	0.7	0.8	1.0	1.1	1.0	1.0	1.2	0.8	0.8
Criminal damage	KETL	2.0	2.1	2.2	2.3	2.3	2.7	2.6	2.9	2.9	2.9	3.2
Drugs	KCAB	1.1	1.3	1.6	1.8	2.7	3.1	3.7	4.3	5.0	5.1	4.5
Other offences (excluding motoring)	KETM	2.8	3.3	3.8	4.2	4.2	4.3	4.4	4.4	4.4	4.3	4.6
Motoring	KETN	0.3	0.4	0.4	0.4	0.4	0.4	0.6	0.7	0.8	0.8	0.7
Total	KETE	37.9	42.2	44.4	46.4	49.7	50.6	49.2	50.3	49.1	46.0	47.0
Summary offences[3]												
Offences with pedal cycles	KETP	0.1	0.2	0.2	0.2	0.3	0.3	0.2	0.2	0.2	0.2	0.2
Breach of local or other regulations	KETR	0.1	0.2	0.3	0.2	0.2	0.2	0.2	0.2	0.1	0.1	0.1
Summary offences of criminal damage and malicious damage	KETS	2.9	3.4	3.9	4.4	5.2	6.1	6.7	6.9	7.0	7.2	8.3
Railway offences	KETT	0.3	0.4	0.4	0.5	0.5	0.5	0.4	0.4	0.4	0.3	0.4
Other summary offences	KETU	9.7	7.2	8.8	10.1	12.1	11.7	11.3	11.6	11.7	10.3	11.0
Motoring offences (summary)[3]	KCAC	8.6	9.3	10.8	10.8	11.3	12.6	14.5	16.7	17.1	17.8	17.0
Total	KETO	21.7	25.6	30.3	22.0	36.8	39.6	42.2	45.2	45.4	46.6	49.2

1 See chapter text.
2 Includes 'Companies', etc.
3 It is estimated that in 1995 there was a shortfall of 75,100 offenders found guilty for certain summary offences.

4 A new charging standard was introduced for assault in 1994.
5 Figures for persons aged 10 to under 18 are included in the totals above.

Source: Home Office: 020 8760 1404

11.4 Offenders cautioned: by offence group[1]
England and Wales

Thousands

		1994	1995	1996	1997	1998	1999	2000	2001	2002	2003	2004
All ages[2]												
Indictable offences												
Violence against the person	KELB	21.8	20.4	21.8	23.6	23.5	21.2	19.9	19.5	23.6	28.8	36.6
Murder	KCAD	–	–	–	–	–	–	–	–	–	–	–
Manslaughter	KCAE	–	–	–	–	–	–	–	–	–	–	–
Wounding	KCAF	21.4	20.1	21.4	23.3	22.9	20.6	19.3	18.9	22.9	27.9	35.0
Other violence against the person	KCAG	0.4	0.3	0.4	0.4	0.6	0.6	0.6	0.6	0.7	0.9	1.2
Sexual offences	KELC	2.0	2.3	2.0	1.9	1.7	1.5	1.3	1.2	1.1	1.4	1.6
Burglary	KELD	10.2	10.5	10.2	9.4	8.4	7.7	6.6	6.4	5.8	5.6	5.6
Robbery	KELE	0.6	0.6	0.6	0.7	0.6	0.6	0.6	0.5	0.4	0.4	0.5
Theft and handling stolen goods	KELF	93.6	104.9	93.6	82.8	83.6	75.4	67.6	63.5	54.2	54.5	61.9
Fraud and forgery	KELG	7.5	7.9	7.5	7.2	7.4	7.2	6.2	5.8	5.3	5.5	6.0
Criminal damage	KELH	3.1	3.8	3.1	2.8	2.7	3.0	3.2	3.4	3.1	3.7	5.5
Drug offences	KCAI	47.5	48.2	47.5	56.0	58.7	49.4	41.1	39.4	44.9	45.7	32.6
Other offences	KELI	4.4	4.0	4.4	5.0	5.0	4.6	4.4	4.2	4.4	5.3	6.0
All offenders cautioned	KELA	190.8	202.6	190.8	189.4	191.7	170.6	150.9	143.9	142.9	150.7	156.3
Summary offences												
Assaults[3]	KELK	4.2	8.1	9.1	9.1	..	17.0	17.2	18.2	17.3	19.8	26.1
Betting and gaming	KELL	–	–	–	–	–	–	–	–	–	–	–
Offences with pedal cycles	KCAK	0.8	0.8	0.9	0.9	0.8	0.6	0.3	0.2	0.1	0.1	0.3
Other Highways Acts offences	KCAL	0.9	0.9	0.8	0.8	0.8	0.7	0.4	0.3	0.2	0.3	0.3
Breach of local or other regulations	KELM	1.1	0.9	0.8	0.9	0.9	0.7	0.5	0.3	0.3	0.2	0.3
Intoxicating Liquor Laws:												
Drunkenness	KELN	37.7	22.9	25.9	25.7	22.8	20.3	18.1	16.6	16.2	18.1	13.5
Other offences	KELO	1.0	1.0	0.9	0.9	0.7	0.4	0.2	0.3	0.3	0.3	0.3
Education Acts	KELP	–	–	–	–	–	–	–	–	–	0.1	0.1
Game Laws	KELQ	0.1	0.1	0.1	0.1	0.1	0.1	–	–	–	–	–
Labour Laws	KELR	–	–	–	–	–	–	–	–	–	–	–
Summary offences of criminal damage and malicious damage	KELS	23.1	25.1	27.7	27.6	28.3	28.7	26.8	26.7	24.7	27.6	33.3
Offences by prostitutes	KELT	3.6	3.3	3.5	3.5	3.5	2.1	1.3	1.0	1.8	1.3	1.6
Railway offences	KELU	0.2	0.3	0.2	0.1	–	–	–	–	–	–	–
Revenue Laws	KELV	0.2	0.2	0.1	0.1	0.1	0.1	–	–	–	–	–
Vagrancy Acts	KELX	1.0	1.0	0.6	0.6	1.2	0.8	0.4	0.3	0.3	0.3	0.2
Wireless Telegraphy Acts	KELY	–	–	–	–	–	–	–	–	–	–	–
Other summary offences	KELZ	24.6	24.2	24.7	22.3	37.0	24.1	22.5	21.9	21.0	22.9	23.5
All offenders cautioned	KELJ	98.7	88.7	95.4	92.7	96.2	95.6	88.1	85.9	82.4	91.1	99.5
Persons aged 10 to under 18[4]												
Indictable offences												
Violence against the person	KEMB	9.4	9.4	9.4	9.6	9.5	8.5	8.3	8.7	9.3	11.0	13.6
Murder	KCAN	–	–	–	–	–	–	–	–	–	–	–
Manslaughter	KCAO	–	–	–	–	–	–	–	–	–	–	–
Wounding	KCAP	9.4	9.4	9.4	9.6	9.4	8.4	8.2	8.6	9.2	10.9	13.5
Other violence against the person	KCCE	–	–	–	–	0.1	0.1	0.1	0.1	0.1	0.1	0.1
Sexual offences	KEMC	0.7	0.8	0.7	0.7	0.6	0.6	0.5	0.5	0.4	0.5	0.5
Burglary	KEMD	8.2	8.5	8.2	7.5	6.7	6.1	5.4	5.3	4.6	4.4	4.2
Robbery	KEME	0.6	0.5	0.6	0.6	0.5	0.5	0.5	0.5	0.4	0.4	0.4
Theft and handling stolen goods	KEMF	48.2	57.4	48.2	40.9	44.0	39.6	36.9	35.2	28.1	28.3	33.1
Fraud and forgery	KEMG	1.5	1.6	1.5	1.4	1.6	1.7	1.5	1.3	1.1	1.0	1.0
Criminal damage	KEMH	2.0	2.4	2.0	1.8	1.7	1.9	2.1	2.3	1.9	2.3	3.1
Drug offences	KCCF	7.9	8.7	7.9	9.7	11.0	9.6	7.9	8.5	9.5	9.6	8.3
Other offences	KEMI	1.3	1.3	1.3	1.5	1.5	1.4	1.3	1.3	1.3	1.4	1.6
All offenders cautioned	KEMA	79.9	90.6	79.9	73.7	77.2	69.8	64.3	63.5	56.6	58.7	65.9
Summary offences												
Offences with pedal cycles	KEMK	0.5	0.4	0.5	0.5	0.4	0.3	0.2	0.1	0.1	0.1	0.2
Breach of local or other regulations	KEMM	0.4	0.3	0.3	0.3	0.3	0.2	0.2	0.1	0.1	0.1	0.1
Summary offences of criminal damage and malicious damage	KEMN	12.5	12.8	13.8	13.5	14.2	14.7	14.4	15.2	12.6	14.3	17.1
Railway offences	KEMO	0.1	0.1	0.1	0.1	–	–	–	–	–	–	–
Other summary offences	KEMP	15.6	10.3	10.8	9.1	13.8	9.9	9.2	9.5	8.5	9.2	10.1
All offenders cautioned	KEMJ	29.2	30.0	33.2	30.8	32.5	34.2	33.2	34.5	29.9	33.3	39.1

1 See chapter text.
2 Includes 'Companies', etc.
3 A new charging standard was introduced for assault in 1994.
4 Figures for persons aged 10 to under 18 are included in the totals above.

Source: Office for Criminal Justice Reform: 020 8760 1404

11.5 Offenders found guilty of offences: by age and sex[1]
England and Wales
Magistrates' courts and the Crown Court

Thousands

		1994	1995	1996	1997	1998	1999	2000	2001	2002	2003	2004
Males												
Indictable offences												
All ages	KEFA	273.2	263.2	261.1	276.5	292.9	291.7	276.5	275.5	287.1	283.4	268.4
10 and under 15 years	KEFB	6.9	7.1	6.6	7.1	8.1	8.9	8.7	9.0	8.8	8.0	8.5
15 and under 18 years	KEFC	28.7	30.2	32.5	33.6	35.2	35.1	33.8	34.4	33.7	31.4	31.8
18 and under 21 years	KEFD	50.3	47.4	46.3	48.4	51.8	52.6	49.9	48.2	46.6	43.8	39.9
21 years and over	KEFE	187.4	178.6	175.6	187.3	197.9	195.0	184.0	183.9	198.0	200.2	188.2
Summary offences[2]												
All ages	KEFF	871.0	862.0	903.6	880.9	929.0	886.6	881.0	826.6	866.4	937.1	990.0
10 and under 15 years	KEFG	2.3	2.9	2.8	3.0	3.9	5.1	5.8	6.2	6.1	6.1	6.7
15 and under 18 years	KEFH	17.7	20.5	24.6	25.9	28.5	30.3	32.2	34.5	34.6	35.3	36.5
18 and under 21 years	KEFI	82.9	84.0	88.4	91.0	96.3	94.8	93.0	92.2	94.7	99.9	98.2
21 years and over	KEFJ	768.2	754.6	787.9	761.0	800.3	756.5	750.0	693.6	731.0	795.8	848.8
Females												
Indictable offences												
All ages	KEFK	39.5	37.5	38.0	42.2	47.3	49.0	47.7	47.4	50.0	50.2	48.4
10 and under 15 years	KEFL	1.0	1.0	1.0	1.0	1.4	1.4	1.5	1.6	1.6	1.6	1.7
15 and under 18 years	KEFM	3.8	4.0	4.2	4.6	5.1	5.2	5.2	5.3	5.1	4.9	5.0
18 and under 21 years	KEFN	6.2	5.7	5.7	6.3	7.1	7.6	7.5	7.0	6.9	6.2	5.7
21 years and over	KEFO	28.6	26.8	27.2	30.4	33.7	34.7	33.5	33.5	36.5	37.5	35.9
Summary offences[2]												
All ages	KEFP	211.5	180.5	222.9	174.9	188.3	171.0	208.3	190.2	208.7	210.5	231.2
10 and under 15 years	KEFQ	0.2	0.4	0.4	0.5	0.6	0.8	0.9	0.9	1.1	1.2	1.5
15 and under 18 years	KEFR	1.5	1.8	2.6	3.4	3.8	3.4	3.3	3.6	3.6	4.0	4.6
18 and under 21 years	KEFS	9.6	10.4	12.1	11.1	12.1	10.8	11.8	11.1	11.6	12.6	13.0
21 years and over	KEFT	200.2	167.9	207.9	160.0	171.7	155.4	192.3	174.7	192.4	192.7	212.2
Companies, etc												
Indictable offences	KEFU	1.4	1.5	1.5	1.3	1.5	1.3	1.3	1.3	1.2	1.4	1.1
Summary offences[2]	KEFV	10.9	9.9	10.9	10.0	10.7	8.9	8.8	8.6	7.9	8.6	1.9

1 See chapter text.
2 It is estimated that in 1995 there was a shortfall of 75,100 offenders found guilty for certain summary offences.

Source: Office for Criminal Justice Reform: 020 8760 1404

11.6 Persons cautioned by the police: by age and sex[1]
England and Wales

Thousands

		1994	1995	1996	1997	1998	1999	2000	2001	2002	2003	2004
Males												
Indictable offences												
All ages	KEGA	153.6	149.3	142.6	143.3	142.9	126.1	109.7	103.8	104.4	109.8	110.0
10 and under 15 years[2]	KEGB	32.3	29.2	25.1	22.9	23.7	22.0	20.3	19.7	16.7	16.9	18.7
15 and under 18 years[2]	KEGC	35.5	35.3	33.0	32.0	32.0	28.7	25.0	24.5	23.3	24.1	25.9
18 and under 21 years	KEGD	25.0	24.8	24.3	25.2	25.7	22.7	20.1	18.5	18.9	19.4	16.7
21 years and over	KEGE	60.7	60.0	60.2	63.2	61.5	52.7	44.3	41.2	45.6	49.4	48.7
Summary offences												
All ages	KEGF	83.6	73.8	79.2	75.7	76.9	76.1	69.6	68.0	63.8	70.9	76.0
10 and under 15 years[2]	KEGG	10.5	10.1	10.3	9.9	10.6	11.7	12.0	12.7	10.3	10.9	12.6
15 and under 18 years[2]	KEGH	14.7	15.4	18.0	16.1	16.1	16.1	14.9	15.2	13.3	15.1	17.2
18 and under 21 years	KEGI	11.3	11.1	13.0	12.9	13.2	13.0	11.9	11.0	11.0	12.4	12.3
21 years and over	KEGJ	47.0	37.1	37.9	36.9	37.0	35.3	30.9	29.0	29.2	32.5	33.9
Females												
Indictable offences												
All ages	KEGK	56.2	53.3	48.2	46.0	48.8	44.5	41.2	40.1	38.5	41.0	46.3
10 and under 15 years[2]	KEGL	15.2	14.0	10.8	9.2	11.1	9.8	10.0	10.1	8.4	8.6	10.6
15 and under 18 years[2]	KEGM	12.4	12.2	10.9	9.5	10.3	9.3	9.0	9.3	8.3	9.1	10.7
18 and under 21 years	KEGN	6.1	6.0	5.6	5.7	5.9	5.7	5.2	4.9	4.8	4.9	5.2
21 years and over	KEGO	22.4	21.1	20.9	21.5	21.4	19.6	17.0	15.9	17.0	18.4	19.9
Summary offences												
All ages	KEGP	15.1	14.8	16.2	17.0	19.2	9.4	18.5	18.0	18.6	20.2	23.5
10 and under 15 years[2]	KEGQ	1.5	1.7	1.8	1.7	2.1	2.5	2.8	2.9	2.7	3.0	3.9
15 and under 18 years[2]	KEGR	2.5	2.7	3.2	3.2	3.7	3.9	3.7	3.8	3.6	4.3	5.4
18 and under 21 years	KEGS	1.9	1.9	2.1	2.3	2.6	2.7	2.5	2.3	2.4	2.7	2.9
21 years and over	KEGT	9.2	8.6	9.1	9.9	10.8	10.3	9.6	9.0	9.8	10.2	11.3

1 See chapter text.
2 From 1 June 2000 the Crime and Disorder Act 1998 came into force nationally and removed the use of cautions for persons under 18 and replaced them with reprimands and final warnings.

Source: Office for Criminal Justice Reform: 020 8760 1404

11.7 Sentence or order passed on offenders sentenced for indictable offences: by sex[1]
England and Wales
Magistrates' courts and the Crown Court

Percentages and thousands

		1994	1995	1996	1997	1998	1999	2000	2001	2002	2003	2004
Males												
Sentence or order												
Absolute discharge	KEJB	0.8	0.8	0.8	0.7	0.7	0.6	0.6	0.6	0.8	0.9	0.8
Conditional discharge	KEJC	17.4	16.2	15.6	15.5	15.3	15.0	14.1	13.4	12.4	13.0	12.2
Fine	KEJF	31.8	30.0	28.6	28.2	28.4	27.7	25.7	24.5	23.9	24.0	20.9
Community rehabilitation order	KEJD	10.2	10.0	9.9	10.0	10.0	10.1	10.1	10.7	10.6	10.1	9.5
Supervision order	KEJE	2.4	2.7	2.9	2.7	2.7	2.7	2.4	2.3	2.1	1.8	2.0
Community punishment order	KEJG	11.1	10.6	9.9	9.5	9.3	9.3	9.5	9.0	8.6	8.3	8.8
Attendance centre order	KEJH	2.0	2.0	1.9	1.8	1.7	1.8	1.5	1.2	0.7	0.6	0.6
Community punishment and rehabilitation order	KIJW	2.7	3.0	3.5	3.7	3.8	3.7	3.6	2.6	2.6	2.6	2.8
Curfew order	LUJP	..	..	0.1	0.1	0.2	0.3	0.5	0.7	1.1	1.6	2.7
Reparation order	SNFI	..	..	..	..	..	..	0.7	1.3	0.8	0.4	0.4
Action plan order	SNFJ	..	..	..	..	..	..	0.9	1.7	1.1	0.7	0.8
Drug treatment and testing order	SNFK	..	..	..	..	..	..	0.1	1.2	1.4	1.9	2.3
Referral order	SNFL	..	..	..	..	..	..	..	..	3.0	4.0	4.4
Fully suspended	KEJL	0.7	0.7	0.8	0.8	0.7	0.6	0.7	0.6	0.5	0.5	0.6
Imprisonment												
Sec 90-92	LUJQ	0.1	0.1	0.2	0.3	0.2	0.2	0.2	0.2	0.2	0.2	0.2
Detention and training order	LUJR	..	..	..	..	..	..	1.4	1.9	1.8	1.5	1.6
Young offender institution	KEJK	4.9	5.6	6.1	6.1	6.0	6.2	5.2	4.5	4.2	3.6	3.8
Unsuspended	KEJM	13.6	16.0	17.2	17.9	18.2	18.7	19.9	20.0	20.9	20.6	21.5
Other sentence or order	KEJN	2.3	2.2	2.4	3.0	2.6	3.1	3.1	3.4	3.3	3.5	4.1
Total number of offenders (thousands) = 100 per cent	KEJA	272.6	262.9	260.8	275.4	292.4	291.3	277.1	274.6	285.6	282.3	267.5
Females												
Sentence or order												
Absolute discharge	KEKB	0.9	0.8	0.9	0.8	0.7	0.7	0.6	0.6	0.9	1.0	0.8
Conditional discharge	KEKC	34.4	32.4	30.6	29.4	28.7	26.9	24.9	23.9	22.0	22.5	21.8
Fine	KEKF	25.6	24.1	22.5	21.8	21.3	20.8	20.1	18.6	17.9	18.5	16.7
Community rehabilitation order	KEKD	17.5	18.0	19.0	19.1	19.1	19.4	19.6	19.1	19.2	17.0	15.4
Supervision order	KEKE	2.4	2.7	2.9	2.9	3.1	2.9	2.8	2.7	2.1	2.1	2.1
Community punishment order	KEKG	6.4	6.6	6.5	6.5	6.5	7.1	7.5	7.3	6.8	6.6	7.6
Attendance centre order	KEKH	0.8	1.0	1.0	1.0	0.9	0.9	0.8	0.6	0.4	0.3	0.3
Community punishment and rehabilitation order	KIJX	2.1	2.4	3.0	3.2	3.4	3.3	3.0	2.1	2.1	1.8	1.9
Curfew order	LUJT	..	..	–	0.1	0.1	0.3	0.4	0.6	0.8	1.4	2.2
Reparation order	SNFX	..	..	..	..	..	..	0.8	1.6	0.8	0.4	0.5
Action plan order	SNFZ	..	..	..	..	..	..	1.0	2.0	1.2	0.8	0.8
Drug treatment and testing order	SNGA	..	..	..	..	..	..	0.1	1.4	1.7	2.4	3.2
Referral order	SNGB	..	..	..	..	..	..	..	..	3.9	5.1	5.6
Fully suspended	KEKL	1.1	1.4	1.5	1.6	1.5	1.3	1.3	1.2	1.1	1.0	1.3
Imprisonment												
Sec 90-92	LUJU	–	0.1	0.1	0.1	..	0.1	0.1	0.1	0.1	0.1	0.1
Detention and training order	LUJV	..	..	..	..	..	..	0.6	0.8	0.8	0.7	0.7
Young offender institution	KEKK	1.1	1.5	1.8	1.9	2.2	2.4	2.2	2.0	1.9	1.7	1.4
Unsuspended	KEKM	5.9	7.4	8.4	9.4	10.0	11.0	11.5	12.1	12.7	12.8	13.2
Other sentence or order	KEKN	1.7	1.8	2.0	2.2	2.5	3.0	2.9	3.5	3.4	3.8	4.3
Total number of offenders (thousands) = 100 per cent	KEKA	39.5	37.5	38.0	42.1	47.2	49.0	47.8	47.3	49.9	50.2	48.3

1 See chapter text.

Source: Office for Criminal Justice Reform: 020 8760 1404

11.8 Offenders sentenced to immediate custody for standard list offences: by sex and number of previous convictions[1]

England and Wales | Percentages[2] and numbers

	Nil	1 - 2	3 - 6	7 - 10	11 and over	Total sentenced for standard list offences	Total sentenced to custody for all offences
Year and sex							
1999							
Males	32	22	19	10	17	95 500	97 800
Females	49	23	15	6	7	7 300	7 500
Total	34	22	19	9	16	102 800	105 300
2000							
Males	30	17	14	11	28	95 700	98 300
Females	40	17	15	10	17	7 700	7 900
Total	31	17	14	11	27	103 400	106 200
2001							
Males	22	15	17	13	33	95 905	98 200
Females	33	15	18	14	20	7 903	8 100
Total	23	15	17	13	32	103 808	106 300
2002							
Males	14	12	19	16	39	100 389	102 800
Females	22	12	23	17	26	8 675	8 800
Total	14	12	19	16	38	109 064	111 600
2003							
Males	15	11	18	16	40	96 629	98 860
Females	23	13	23	14	27	8 670	8 810
Total	16	11	19	16	39	105 299	107 670

1 See chapter text. Counting one conviction per court appearance.
2 The percentages are based on samples of 6 096, 17 771, 6 863, 7 231 and 7 219 males and 426, 1 361, 603 618 and 648 females in the years 1999, 2000, 2001, 2002 and 2003 respectively. Percentages are rounded and therefore may not add to 100.

Source: Home Office: 020 7217 1941

11.9 Population in Prison Service establishments under sentence: by sex and number of previous convictions[1,2]

England and Wales, on 30 June each year: | Percentages[3] and numbers

	Previous convictions not found[4]	Nil	1 - 2	3 - 6	7 - 10	11 and over	Number of prisoners
Year and sex							
1999							
Males	8	12	15	21	15	28	47 989
Females	16	27	18	17	9	13	2 486
Total	9	13	15	21	15	27	50 475
2000							
Males	9	14	15	19	14	29	50 437
Females	10	32	15	17	10	14	2 633
Total	9	15	15	19	14	28	53 070
2001							
Males	9	15	13	19	14	29	51 623
Females	13	33	15	16	10	13	2 909
Total	9	16	14	19	13	28	54 532
2002							
Males	9	15	13	18	14	30	53 936
Females	12	36	13	16	9	13	3 336
Total	9	17	13	18	14	29	57 272
2003							
Males	10	15	13	18	14	30	55 906
Females	13	35	14	15	10	13	3 074
Total	10	16	13	17	14	29	58 980

1 Excludes fine defaulters.
2 In some cases it was not possible to find details on previous convictions. This can happen when a prisoner is not sentenced for a standard list offence and has no previous record for such offences. See chapter text.

3 The percentages are based on samples of 12 341, 12 833, 13 225, 13,814 and 17 115 for males in 1999, 2000, 2001, 2002 and 2003 respectively. All females are sampled. Percentages are rounded and therefore may not add to 100.
4 These numbers are based on a weighted sample and may therefore differ slightly from the exact figures published elsewhere.

Source: Home Office: 020 7217 1941

11.10 Receptions and average population in custody
England and Wales

Numbers

		1994	1995	1996	1997	1998	1999	2000	2001	2002	2003	2004
Receptions												
Type of inmate:												
Untried	KEDA	57 079	55 287	58 888	62 066	64 697	64 572	54 892	53 467	58 708	58 696	54 556
Convicted, unsentenced	KEDB	34 563	32 039	34 987	36 424	43 387	45 893	43 889	46 851	53 301	53 246	50 115
Sentenced	KEDE	83 657	89 173	82 861	87 168	91 282	93 965	93 671	91 978	94 807	93 495	95 161
Immediate custodial sentence	KEDF	61 188	69 016	74 306	80 832	85 908	90 238	91 195	90 523	93 615	92 245	93 326
Young offenders	KEDG	14 956	16 244	17 593	18 743	19 599	21 020	21 333	20 969	20 236	18 179	18 264
Up to 12 months	KEDH	10 520	11 308	11 285	11 867	12 942	14 330	14 639	14 234	12 891	11 850	11 855
12 months up to 4 years	KEDJ	3 921	4 393	5 497	5 949	5 921	5 904	5 877	5 856	6 355	5 412	5 426
4 years up to and including life	KEDL	515	543	811	927	736	786	817	879	990	917	983
Adults	KFBO	46 232	52 772	56 713	62 089	66 309	69 218	69 862	69 554	73 379	74 066	75 062
Up to 12 months	KEDV	28 197	33 053	34 864	38 702	42 513	45 662	46 759	46 146	47 870	48 962	49 814
12 months up to 4 years	KEDW	14 146	15 328	16 560	17 546	18 100	17 751	17 290	17 116	18 313	17 968	17 988
4 years up to and including life	KEDX	3 889	4 391	5 289	5 841	5 696	5 805	5 813	6 292	7 196	7 136	7 260
Committed in default of payment												
of a fine	KEDY	22 469	20 157	8 555	6 336	5 374	3 727	2 476	1 455	1 192	1 250	1 835
Young offenders	KEEA	3 268	2 846	885	555	568	366	216	138	110	116	155
Adults	KAFQ	19 201	17 311	7 670	5 781	4 806	3 361	2 260	1 317	1 082	1 134	1 680
Non-criminal prisoners	KEDM	4 507	3 789	3 128	3 204	3 290	3 271	3 153	4 630	2 674	3 142	3 669
Immigration Act 1971	KEDN	1 641	1 825	1 857	2 122	2 348	2 443	2 455	4 035	2 093	2 457	3 041
Others	KEDO	2 866	1 964	1 271	1 082	942	828	698	595	581	685	628
Average population												
Total in custody	KEDP	48 794	51 047	55 281	61 114	65 298	64 771	64 602	66 301	70 861	73 038	74 657
Total in prison service												
establishments	KFBQ	48 621	50 962	55 281	61 114	65 298	64 771	64 602	66 301	70 778	73 038	74 657
Police cells[1]	KFBN	173	85	–	–	–	–	–	–	83	–	–
Untried	KEDQ	9 047	8 352	8 374	8 453	8 157	7 947	7 098	6 924	7 727	7 862	7 735
Convicted, unsentenced	KEDR	3 181	2 954	3 238	3 678	4 411	4 571	4 177	4 314	5 064	5 060	4 750
Remanded for medical												
examination	KEDS	15	9	6	8	9	8	..	40	..	..	–
Others	KEDT	3 166	2 945	3 232	3 670	4 402	4 563	..	4 274	..	..	–
Sentenced	KEDU	35 753	39 040	43 043	48 413	52 176	51 691	52 685	54 051	57 222	59 007	61 071
Immediate custodial sentence	KFBR	35 308	38 636	42 863	48 272	52 045	51 596	52 620	54 006	57 184	58 959	61 012
Young offenders	KFBS	5 258	5 752	6 700	7 821	8 490	8 335	8 435	8 559	8 777	8 422	8 290
Up to 12 months[2]	KFBU	2 736	1 721	1 788	1 820	1 964	1 997	2 414	2 330	2 051	1 899	1 941
12 months up to 4 years[3]	KFBV	1 902	2 987	3 748	4 466	4 795	4 674	4 517	4 562	4 867	4 525	4 293
4 years up to and including life	KFBW	620	1 042	1 164	1 534	1 730	1 665	1 504	1 667	1 860	1 997	2 053
Adults	KFCO	30 050	32 902	36 162	40 451	43 555	43 261	44 186	45 447	48 408	50 536	52 721
Up to 12 months[2]	KFCP	8 051	4 930	5 136	5 428	5 898	5 635	6 053	5 904	5 755	6 000	6 238
12 months up to 4 years[3]	KFCQ	9 164	11 976	13 383	15 073	16 079	15 048	15 161	15 525	16 845	16 664	17 053
4 years up to and including life	KFCR	12 835	15 998	17 644	19 950	21 580	22 578	22 971	24 021	25 808	27 871	29 427
Committed in default of payment												
of a fine	KFCS	446	403	180	141	131	95	64	45	37	48	59
Young offenders	KFEW	62	54	22	13	15	9	4	6	2	3	4
Adults	KFEX	384	349	158	128	116	86	60	39	35	45	55
Non-criminal prisoners	KEEB	640	615	626	571	554	558	641	1 012	847	1 107	1 100
Immigration Act 1971	KEEC	487	483	516	485	476	485	576	955	777	995	1 032
Others	KEED	153	132	111	87	78	73	63	57	70	112	67

1 Mostly untried prisoners.
2 Figures before 1995 relate to sentence length defined as 'up to 18 months'.
3 Figures before 1995 relate to sentence length defined as '18 months up to 4 years'.

Source: Home Office: 020 7217 5567

11.11 Prison population serving sentences: by age and offence[1]
England and Wales

Numbers

	15 - 17	18 - 20	21 - 24	25 - 29	30 - 39	40 - 49	50 - 59	60 and over	Total
At 30 June 1999									
Offences									
Males									
Total	1 643	5 633	8 245	10 080	14 072	5 552	2 678	1 053	48 956
Violence against the person	250	1 070	1 548	2 033	3 260	1 428	608	238	10 435
Sexual offences	48	99	236	485	1 448	1 133	935	546	4 930
Burglary	447	1 441	2 207	2 230	1 899	322	73	7	8 626
Robbery	410	1 126	1 384	1 272	1 556	353	58	16	6 175
Theft, handling, fraud and forgery	208	585	886	1 065	1 418	529	279	57	5 027
Drugs offences	36	338	866	1 614	2 720	1 132	476	121	7 303
Other offences	185	742	968	1 120	1 422	541	197	49	5 224
Offence not known	59	232	150	261	349	114	52	19	1 236
Females									
Total	67	224	427	491	798	301	108	20	2 436
Violence against the person	17	65	50	77	125	63	25	7	429
Sexual offences	-	2	1	-	5	7	1	1	17
Burglary	7	27	37	38	41	6	2	-	158
Robbery	15	24	36	33	41	6	3	-	158
Theft, handling, fraud and forgery	11	33	113	99	159	58	24	5	502
Drugs offences	2	50	131	184	340	129	35	4	875
Other offences	13	9	45	43	68	26	16	-	220
Offence not known	2	14	14	17	19	6	2	3	77
At 30 June 2000									
Offences									
Males									
Total	1 788	5 911	8 691	10 060	14 454	5 720	2 749	1 140	50 514
Violence against the person	256	1 092	1 658	1 964	3 440	1 480	690	226	10 807
Sexual offences	58	139	261	460	1 424	1 157	937	635	5 070
Burglary	453	1 426	2 165	2 291	2 040	359	77	13	8 824
Robbery	399	1 087	1 343	1 315	1 556	387	57	14	6 158
Theft, handling, fraud and forgery	312	798	1 006	1 118	1 419	483	233	53	5 422
Drugs offences	43	405	949	1 591	2 765	1 188	480	106	7 526
Other offences	225	818	1 180	1 161	1 616	598	236	76	5 909
Offence not known	43	148	131	160	194	67	38	16	797
Females									
Total	65	266	457	563	863	335	102	15	2 666
Violence against the person	22	46	56	71	122	62	26	6	410
Sexual offences	-	1	1	1	7	5	2	2	20
Burglary	10	24	33	45	40	5	1	-	158
Robbery	13	43	39	39	50	10	1	-	195
Theft, handling, fraud and forgery	7	61	117	154	196	74	24	4	638
Drugs offences	6	58	151	200	354	141	34	2	947
Other offences	5	26	47	40	70	31	9	1	229
Offence not known	2	7	13	12	23	7	5	-	69
At 30 June 2001									
Offences									
Males									
Total	1 918	5 864	9 051	9 964	14 538	6 044	2 723	1 211	51 313
Violence against the person	343	1 180	1 810	1 997	3 432	1 631	702	252	11 347
Sexual offences	53	145	265	406	1 368	1 172	953	686	5 048
Burglary	383	1 176	2 039	2 190	2 158	389	61	15	8 410
Robbery	429	1191	1 436	1 309	1 652	360	60	12	6 449
Theft, handling, fraud and forgery	318	742	1 086	1 080	1 362	510	217	55	5 370
Drugs offences	47	423	1 126	1 686	2 828	1 278	479	113	7 980
Other offences	285	840	1 146	1 163	1 541	616	213	66	5 868
Offence not know	61	165	143	133	196	90	40	13	841
Females									
Total	63	305	493	589	906	406	119	18	2 899
Violence against the person	18	63	55	72	123	81	24	6	441
Sexual offences	0	2	1	1	7	10	2	2	25
Burglary	9	29	44	29	36	5	2	0	153
Robbery	10	53	63	54	55	13	1	0	248
Theft, handling, fraud and forgery	12	53	100	155	178	64	29	4	594
Drugs offences	3	72	183	215	411	193	49	4	1130
Other offences	8	27	40	50	82	32	9	2	249
Offence not known	3	7	8	14	14	9	4	0	59

11.11
continued
Prison population serving sentences: by age and offence[1]
England and Wales

Numbers

	15 - 17	18 - 20	21 - 24	25 - 29	30 - 39	40 - 49	50 - 59	60 and over	Total
At 30 June 2002									
Offences									
Males									
Total	1 986	5 821	9 722	10 196	15 415	6 630	2 832	1 365	53 967
Violence against the person	336	1 187	1 942	1 937	3 490	1 769	749	267	11 678
Sexual offences	58	167	262	406	1 347	1 241	996	794	5 270
Burglary	396	1 130	2 159	2 331	2 379	448	58	15	8 917
Robbery	503	1 285	1 647	1 390	1 865	443	66	10	7 208
Theft, handling, fraud and forgery	302	570	1 055	1 105	1 416	480	213	62	5 203
Drugs offences	43	431	1 255	1 763	3 142	1 496	495	129	8 754
Other offences	275	875	1 195	1 103	1 555	640	205	73	5 921
Offence not known	72	174	207	162	222	113	50	15	1 016
Females									
Total	103	356	596	662	1 030	439	134	19	3 339
Violence against the person	27	67	73	85	163	84	33	6	538
Sexual offences	-	1	-	1	11	6	3	1	23
Burglary	9	37	58	54	68	12	1	-	239
Robbery	19	63	89	65	60	14	3	1	314
Theft, handling, fraud and forgery	22	56	103	139	168	68	20	4	581
Drugs offences	8	94	206	256	474	216	60	6	1 319
Other offences	12	32	52	50	73	34	9	1	262
Offence not known	6	7	16	13	13	5	4	-	63
At 30 June 2003									
Offences									
Males									
Total	1 724	5 740	10 112	10 441	16 304	7 252	2 975	1 413	55 962
Violence against the person	310	1 257	2 112	2 068	3 733	1 932	780	290	12 482
Sexual offences	42	183	310	390	1 376	1 353	1 023	838	5 514
Burglary	289	919	2 003	2 204	2 555	527	71	11	8 579
Robbery	436	1 370	1 910	1 546	2 022	514	69	12	7 879
Theft, handling, fraud & forgery	291	543	1 020	1 060	1 437	472	201	45	5 069
Drugs offences	43	452	1 256	1 791	3 215	1 579	528	127	8 993
Other offences	271	884	1 329	1 218	1 760	787	263	69	6 581
Offence not known	42	133	172	164	205	89	40	21	865
Females									
Total	57	305	670	702	1 100	492	123	28	3 477
Violence against the person	10	61	91	66	155	82	32	7	506
Sexual offences	-	-	2	1	11	7	3	2	26
Burglary	1	24	64	60	77	12	2	-	240
Robbery	21	60	105	100	93	24	4	-	407
Theft, handling, fraud & forgery	10	56	117	128	199	70	18	11	609
Drugs offences	6	73	226	271	453	253	54	8	1 343
Other offences	7	27	58	66	108	39	6	-	311
Offence not known	2	3	8	10	5	4	4	-	36
At 30 June 2004									
Offences									
Males									
Total	1 706	5 585	10 095	10 738	17 021	7 858	3 013	1 508	57 523
Violence against the person	326	1 353	2 247	2 272	3 965	2 107	799	304	13 373
Sexual offences	55	193	329	424	1 433	1 416	1 030	865	5 747
Burglary	242	855	1 807	2 141	2 662	608	71	11	8 397
Robbery	449	1 254	1 865	1 691	2 127	583	70	17	8 056
Theft, handling, fraud and forgery	272	502	903	1 045	1 479	573	180	63	5 017
Drugs offences	51	471	1 383	1 789	3 258	1 615	537	150	9 256
Other offences	286	848	1 390	1 249	1 895	868	284	87	6 908
Offences not known	25	108	171	126	202	87	41	10	769
Females									
Total	58	300	632	727	1 056	507	152	20	3 453
Violence against the person	15	70	98	89	192	95	36	9	603
Sexual offences	0	0	3	3	8	7	4	2	27
Burglary	6	19	59	83	56	22	3	0	247
Robbery	8	65	93	90	114	20	2	0	392
Theft, handling, fraud and forgery	11	28	100	140	171	67	25	1	543
Drug offences	6	78	197	245	392	246	65	6	1 235
Other offence	11	37	75	72	108	44	13	2	361
Offences not known	2	3	8	7	15	7	4	0	46

1 Includes persons committed in default of payment of a fine.

Source: Home Office: 020 7217 5567

11.12 Expenditure on prisons
England and Wales
Operating cost and total capital employed, years ending 31 March

£ thousand

		1998 /99	1999 /00	2000 /01	2001 /02	2002 /03	2003 /04	2004 /05
Expenditure								
Staff costs	KWUV	995 200	1 044 700	1 094 500	1 138 400	1 259 500	1 364 200	1 439 900
Accommodation costs	KXCO	163 400	149 300	153 700	193 100	200 000	194 000	185 400
Other operating costs	KXCP	538 800	584 300	654 200	706 100	756 200	653 000	694 600
Depreciation	KXCQ	146 100	115 700	117 200	128 100	132 600	129 600	143 800
Cost of capital	KXCR	262 500	254 900	259 900	284 900	292 700	164 400	170 300
Total expenditure	KXCS	2 106 000	2 148 900	2 279 500	2 450 600	2 641 000	2 505 200	2 634 000
Income								
Contributions from industries	KXCT	−8 300	−10 400	−10 600	−11 600	−10 100	−11 000	−10 600
Other operating income	KXCU	−8 500	−9 600	−10 300	−13 100	−15 500	−21 000	−38 400
Income from other Government Departments[1]	GDPM	..	..	−123 900	−180 600	−210 200	−368 000	−381 500
Total income	KXCV	−16 800	−20 000	−144 800	−205 300	−235 800	−400 000	−430 500
Net operating costs	KXCW	2 089 200	2 128 900	2 134 700	2 245 300	2 405 200	2 105 200	2 203 500
Total capital employed	KXCX	4 345 100	4 382 600	4 726 200	4 859 600	4 821 500	5 228 600	5 116 700

1 Income from the Youth Justice Board (a non-departmental public body of the Home Office) for the provision of juvenile custody within the Prison Service and Department for Education and Skills for the provision of education services.

Source: Home Office: 020 7217 5567

11.13 Crimes and offences recorded by the police: by crime group[1]
Scotland

Thousands

		1995 /96	1996 /97	1997 /98	1998 /99	1999 /00	2000 /01	2001 /02	2002 /03	2003 /04	2004[4] /05
Non-sexual crimes of violence											
against the person	BEBC	15.0	14.2	13.4	14.7	15.8	14.8	15.7	16.1	15.2	14.7
Serious assault, etc	KAFS	7.1	6.6	6.2	6.7	7.3	6.9	7.5	7.6	7.5	7.8
Robbery	KAFU	5.4	5.1	4.6	5.0	4.9	4.3	4.6	4.6	4.2	3.7
Other	KAFV	2.5	2.5	2.6	3.0	3.6	3.6	3.5	3.8	3.5	3.2
Crimes involving indecency	BEBD	5.7	5.9	7.4	7.1	5.9	5.7	6.0	6.6	6.8	7.3
Rape and attempted rape[2]	OXBQ	0.6	0.6	0.8	0.8	0.8	0.7	0.8	0.9	1.0	1.1
Indecent assault[2]	OXBR	1.1	1.1	1.3	1.3	1.1	1.0	1.2	1.4	1.4	1.5
Lewd and indecent behaviour	KAFY	2.6	2.5	3.0	2.9	2.3	2.4	2.4	2.8	2.6	2.8
Other	KAFZ	1.5	1.7	2.4	2.1	1.7	1.6	1.6	1.6	1.7	1.9
Crimes involving dishonesty	BEBE	319.3	285.8	266.9	277.0	275.6	253.3	242.9	224.8	211.0	210.4
Housebreaking	KAGB	72.0	61.6	55.6	55.8	52.9	47.7	45.5	40.6	36.4	35.0
Theft by opening lockfast places	KAGC	8.3	8.4	10.5	12.1	11.6	10.6	8.2	7.8	7.4	7.9
Theft from a motor vehicle (OLP)	EPI4	58.2	48.9	39.8	39.5	38.0	32.0	32.7	30.4	26.8	20.4
Theft of a motor vehicle	KAGD	37.2	32.5	27.9	29.3	28.9	25.6	23.1	20.9	17.6	15.6
Shoplifting	KAGE	28.6	26.2	27.0	30.8	32.1	32.3	31.6	28.3	27.9	28.5
Other theft	KAGF	87.4	81.7	80.0	80.1	81.2	76.6	76.0	73.2	72.5	77.6
Fraud	KAGG	17.1	15.8	16.2	18.4	20.6	20.0	17.4	15.8	15.3	18.3
Other	KAGH	10.7	10.7	9.9	11.1	10.3	8.4	8.4	7.9	7.0	7.1
Fire-raising, vandalism, etc	BEBF	88.8	86.0	81.0	77.6	81.2	85.8	94.9	97.6	103.7	128.6
Fire-raising	KAGJ	3.4	3.2	2.7	2.5	2.3	2.4	2.9	3.8	4.2	4.7
Vandalism, etc	KAGK	85.4	82.8	78.3	75.2	78.9	83.4	92.0	93.8	99.6	123.9
Other crimes	BEBG	49.3	48.7	52.3	57.7	57.0	58.9	66.8	73.2	77.5	77.1
Crimes against public justice	KAGM	16.5	16.3	16.6	17.7	18.4	18.6	20.9	22.7	25.8	25.6
Handling offensive weapons[3]	KAFT	6.9	6.5	6.2	7.1	8.1	8.1	9.0	9.4	9.3	9.5
Drugs	KAGN	25.7	25.8	29.4	32.8	30.4	32.1	36.8	40.9	42.3	41.8
Other	KAGO	0.2	0.1	0.1	0.1	0.1	0.1	0.1	0.2	0.2	0.2
Total crimes	KAGQ	478.1	440.7	421.0	434.1	435.5	418.5	426.2	418.3	414.2	438.1
Miscellaneous offences	BEBH	137.5	149.3	156.6	153.3	151.9	154.9	163.5	169.6	181.0	214.3
Petty assault	KAGS	47.4	48.3	50.2	51.6	54.6	54.1	55.4	55.0	57.4	73.7
Breach of the peace	KAGT	67.7	71.5	73.3	71.7	71.3	70.2	72.7	74.7	77.9	90.0
Drunkenness	KAGU	9.7	9.8	9.6	8.4	7.6	7.8	7.8	7.3	7.5	7.2
Other	KAGV	12.6	19.8	23.4	21.6	18.4	22.8	27.6	32.6	38.2	43.4
Motor vehicle offences	BEBI	311.6	311.1	339.6	367.2	347.5	340.1	362.6	348.0	426.7	418.7
Dangerous and careless driving	KAGX	18.2	17.1	16.2	15.8	13.2	12.0	12.2	12.7	12.0	13.1
Drunk driving	KAGY	11.1	11.8	11.1	10.6	10.9	10.8	11.5	11.8	11.6	11.1
Speeding	KAGZ	82.5	85.6	95.6	119.7	123.4	113.9	126.8	117.2	199.2	210.1
Unlawful use of a motor vehicle	KAHA	84.9	78.3	77.3	76.0	80.7	83.3	88.7	92.9	91.3	71.1
Vehicle defect offences	KAHB	54.7	56.9	62.3	63.8	48.0	46.8	45.5	46.5	37.2	27.0
Other	KAHC	60.2	61.4	77.0	81.3	71.2	73.3	77.9	66.9	75.4	86.3
Total offences	KAHD	449.1	460.4	496.2	520.5	499.4	495.0	526.1	517.5	607.6	633.0
Total crimes and offences	BEBB	927.2	901.1	917.2	954.6	934.9	913.5	952.3	935.8	1 021.8	1 071.1

1 See chapter text.

2 The category of 'sexual assault' was split into 'rape and attempted rape' and 'indecent assault' with effect from 2001, allowing the Police Statutory Performance Indicator of serious violent crime to be readily calculated. The Statutory Performance Indicator of serious violent crime includes all non-sexual crimes of violence and rape & attempted rape.

3 'Handling offensive weapons' used to be included in the group 'non-sexual crimes of violence'.

4 The introduction of the Scottish Crime Recording Standard on 1 April 2004 has increased the number of minor crimes recorded, such as minor crimes of theft, vandalism, petty assault and breach of the peace.

Source: The Scottish Executive Justice Department: 0131 244 2226

11.14 Persons proceeded against: by crime group[1]
Scotland

Numbers

		1993	1994	1995	1996	1997	1998	1999	2000	2001	2002	2003[2]
Non-sexual crimes of violence	KEHC	2 022	1 867	1 786	2 008	2 028	1 940	2 080	1 958	2 035	2 237	2 387
Homicide	KEHD	114	94	111	133	108	88	107	95	101	94	83
Serious assault, etc	KEHE	856	831	809	944	1 037	1 002	1 086	1 050	1 121	1 298	1 410
Robbery	KEHG	785	737	664	720	665	627	682	625	632	625	631
Other violence	KEHH	267	205	202	211	218	223	205	188	181	220	263
Crimes of indecency	KEHI	1 509	1 427	1 306	979	1 200	1 328	910	658	622	565	598
Rape and attempted rape	HFVU	72	54	56	55	52	62	51	43	69	42	62
Sexual assault	KEHJ	79	82	79	69	84	86	82	66	52	56	82
Lewd and libidinous practices	KEHK	309	333	291	300	334	324	316	252	289	291	264
Other indecency	KEHL	1 049	958	880	555	730	856	461	297	212	176	190
Crimes of dishonesty	KEHM	31 034	30 021	28 197	26 965	25 666	24 728	23 293	20 866	21 446	21 804	19 773
Housebreaking	KEHN	5 219	5 064	4 470	3 838	3 275	2 977	3 021	2 686	2 711	2 735	2 532
Theft by opening lockfast places	KEHO	2 817	2 844	2 458	2 327	2 092	1 802	1 658	1 497	1 501	1 472	1 289
Theft of motor vehicle	KEHP	2 399	2 492	2 411	2 357	2 146	1 853	1 642	1 449	1 376	1 426	1 295
Shoplifting	KEHQ	7 437	6 633	6 510	7 080	7 194	7 611	7 649	7 419	8 123	8 931	7 993
Other theft	KEHR	7 129	6 427	6 318	6 052	5 960	5 701	5 260	4 493	4 284	3 876	3 487
Fraud	KEHS	2 188	2 511	2 307	2 011	2 010	1 974	1 635	1 458	1 490	1 451	1 422
Other dishonesty	KEHT	3 845	4 050	3 723	3 300	2 989	2 810	2 428	1 864	1 961	1 913	1 755
Fire-raising, vandalism, etc	KEHU	4 896	4 781	4 878	5 176	4 951	4 645	4 115	3 949	4 017	4 130	4 505
Fire-raising	KEHV	146	172	142	144	119	122	108	103	120	135	166
Vandalism, etc	KEHW	4 750	4 609	4 736	5 032	4 832	4 523	4 007	3 846	3 897	3 995	4 339
Other crime	KEHX	12 841	13 817	14 730	15 389	14 609	13 760	13 166	12 522	13 769	13 401	15 027
Crime against public justice	KFBK	6 592	6 913	7 316	6 935	5 346	4 738	4 622	4 845	5 317	4 998	5 095
Handling offensive weapons[3]	KEHF	1 552	1 491	1 782	2 240	2 194	2 062	2 080	2 238	2 695	2 589	2 799
Drugs offences	KFBL	4 675	5 386	5 599	6 183	7 027	6 927	6 439	5 426	5 736	5 801	7 105
Other	KFBM	22	27	33	31	42	33	25	13	21	13	28
Total crimes	KEHB	52 302	51 913	50 897	50 517	48 454	46 401	43 564	39 953	41 889	42 137	42 290
Miscellaneous offences	KEHZ	48 762	44 011	45 810	46 816	45 502	41 582	34 502	33 442	34 404	36 001	38 391
Common assault	KEIA	11 765	11 404	11 956	12 330	12 455	11 952	10 886	10 242	10 845	11 297	12 032
Breach of the peace	KEIB	17 456	16 775	17 989	19 411	19 416	18 109	14 398	13 226	13 775	14 124	14 733
Drunkenness	KEIC	1 735	1 429	1 313	1 103	928	725	478	434	371	384	411
Breach of social work orders	HFVT	2 197	2 385	2 783	3 176	3 554	4 180	4 564	4 691	4 446	4 974	3 985
Other miscellaneous offences	KEID	15 609	12 018	11 769	10 796	9 149	6 616	4 176	4 849	4 967	5 222	7 230
Motor vehicle offences	KEIE	61 742	63 254	60 000	55 754	56 552	51 894	49 494	44 757	44 032	46 891	49 925
Dangerous and careless driving	KEIF	5 426	4 839	4 962	4 847	4 732	3 908	3 369	2 816	3 217	3 419	4 027
Drunk driving	KEIG	7 632	7 426	7 595	8 065	8 519	7 287	6 899	6 691	6 792	8 854	8 280
Speeding[2]	KEIH	15 558	16 693	15 125	12 672	12 213	12 536	14 262	11 315	9 977	9 636	12 034
Unlawful use of vehicle	KEII	20 804	21 680	20 288	19 726	20 339	18 772	16 638	16 922	17 804	18 892	19 457
Vehicle defect offences	KEIJ	3 007	3 262	3 340	3 209	3 323	2 659	2 004	1 576	1 252	1 398	1 770
Other motor vehicle offences	KEIK	9 315	9 354	8 690	7 235	7 426	6 732	6 322	5 437	4 990	4 692	4 357
Total offences	KEHY	110 504	107 265	105 810	102 570	102 054	93 476	83 996	78 199	78 436	82 892	88 316
Total crimes and offences	KEHA	162 806	159 178	156 707	153 087	150 508	139 877	127 560	118 152	120 325	125 029	130 606

1 See chapter text.
2 Figures for 2003 for some categories dealt with by the High Court - including homicide, rape and major drugs cases - may be underestimated slightly due to late recording of disposals on SCRO.

3 'Handling an offensive weapon' has been moved from 'Non-sexual crimes of violence' to 'other crime'.

Source: Scottish Executive Justice Department: 0131 244 2229

11.15 Persons with a charge proved: by court procedure[1]
Scotland

Numbers

		1993	1994	1995	1996	1997	1998	1999	2000	2001	2002	2003
Court procedure												
High Court[2]	KEIQ	1 235	964	1 096	1 099	1 120	1 049	1 176	1 105	1 114	994	990
Sheriff Court	KEIU	82 936	84 278	84 602	85 438	83 332	78 603	74 530	70 938	75 977	82 290	82 870
District Court[3]	KEIV	68 966	63 784	61 336	57 672	57 260	53 217	45 890	41 844	38 382	41 745	46 742
Stipendiary Magistrate Court[3]	KEIW	9 667	10 146	9 670	8 878	8 794	7 008	5 963	4 265	4 846	..	..
Total called to court[4]	KEIZ	162 806	159 178	156 707	153 087	150 508	139 877	127 560	118 152	120 325	125 029	130 606

1 See chapter text.
2 Including cases remitted to the High Court from the Sheriff Court. Figure for 2003 may be an underestimate due to late recording of disposals on SCRO.

3 District Court figures for 2002 and 2003 include the Stipendiary Magistrates Court.
4 Includes court type not known.

Source: Scottish Executive Justice Department: 0131 244 2229

11.16 Persons with charge proved: by main penalty[1]
Scotland

Numbers

Main penalty		1993	1994	1995	1996	1997	1998	1999	2000	2001	2002	2003
Restriction of liberty order[2]	ZBRE	..	..	..	..	..	71	206	215	201	495	945
Supervised attendance order[3]	ZBRF	..	..	..	8	73	68	107	75	48	74	31
Drug treatment and testing order[4]	OEWA	..	..	..	..	..	..	..	80	277	448	560
Absolute discharge	KEXA	989	839	939	1 000	1 065	957	986	967	987	1 097	889
Admonition or caution	KEXB	16 976	16 243	15 857	15 859	15 041	13 893	12 916	11 805	11 973	12 585	12 808
Probation	KEXC	5 722	6 145	6 145	6 435	6 817	7 146	7 351	7 377	8 181	9 186	8 530
Remit to children's hearing	KEXD	83	124	172	193	219	177	136	106	159	210	185
Community service order	KEXE	5 079	5 320	5 339	5 711	5 709	5 246	4 889	4 690	4 879	5 011	4 584
Fine	KEXF	116 918	112 748	110 337	105 384	103 861	94 917	83 482	76 238	75 672	77 624	83 631
Compensation order	KEXG	1 578	1 535	1 527	1 415	1 304	1 298	1 154	1 111	1 138	1 282	1 736
Insanity, hospital, guardianship order	KYAN	138	133	136	159	164	131	138	109	113	115	95
Prison	KEXI	10 832	11 583	11 561	12 134	11 663	11 489	11 682	11 047	12 432	13 202	13 195
Young offenders' institution	KEXJ	4 461	4 472	4 646	4 744	4 563	4 464	4 496	4 321	4 249	3 677	3 386
Detention of child	KEXM	30	36	48	45	29	20	17	11	16	23	26
Total persons with charge proved[5]	KEXO	162 806	159 178	156 707	153 087	150 508	139 877	127 560	118 152	120 325	125 029	130 606

1 See chapter text.
2 A community sentence introduced by Section 5 of the Crime and Punishment (Scotland) Act 1995 and available on a pilot basis to 3 Scottish sheriff courts since August 1998. This sentence was made available to High Court, Sheriff Courts and Stipendiary Magistrates court from 1 May 2002.
3 The pilot scheme under the Crime and Punishment (S) Act 1995, where fines for 16 & 17 year olds were replaced by supervised attendance orders, was discontinued in December 1999. The majority of supervised attendance orders recorded from the year 2000 onwards were disposals relating to the breach of an existing order.

4 Drug treatment and testing orders are new measures made available on a pilot basis to the High Court and to Sheriff Courts for residents in Glasgow (from October 1999), Fife (from July 2000) and Aberdeen/Aberdeenshire (From December 2001).
5 Total for 2003 includes a small number where penalty is unkown.

Source: Scottish Executive Justice Department: 0131 244 2229

11.17 Persons with charge proved[1]: by age and sex
Scotland

Numbers

		1993	1994	1995	1996	1997	1998	1999	2000	2001	2002	2003
Males	KEWA	136 127	136 533	133 330	130 961	129 519	120 530	110 442	101 343	103 824	106 167	109 969
Under 16	KEWB	138	171	180	149	138	135	75	55	76	125	96
16 to 20	KEWC	32 589	30 708	30 113	31 704	31 319	29 317	26 949	24 362	25 170	24 769	24 706
21 to 30	KEWD	56 052	56 519	54 184	52 218	50 714	46 149	41 716	38 585	39 813	40 892	41 122
Over 30	KEWE	45 701	47 788	47 648	45 799	46 299	44 061	40 831	37 596	38 340	40 338	44 041
Age not known	KEWF	1 647	1 347	1 205	1 091	1 049	868	871	745	425	43	4
Females	KEWG	25 405	21 650	22 412	21 308	20 246	18 670	16 548	16 374	16 148	18 507	20 211
Under 16	KEWH	6	8	17	12	11	5	6	9	5	3	16
16 to 20	KEWI	3 589	2 939	3 098	3 302	3 424	3 361	3 275	3 052	2 918	3 031	3 018
21 to 30	KEWJ	10 557	9 190	9 284	8 461	8 095	7 458	6 496	6 285	6 383	7 186	7 663
Over 30	KEWK	10 611	9 002	9 439	8 894	8 266	7 532	6 499	6 769	6 725	8 277	9 513
Age not known	KEWL	642	511	574	639	450	314	272	259	117	10	1
Males and Females	KEWM	161 532	158 183	155 742	152 269	149 765	139 200	126 990	117 717	119 972	124 674	130 180
Under 16	KEWN	144	179	197	161	149	140	81	64	81	128	112
16 to 20	KEWO	36 178	33 647	33 211	35 006	34 743	32 678	30 224	27 414	28 088	27 800	27 724
21 to 30	KEWP	66 609	65 709	63 468	60 679	58 809	53 607	48 212	44 870	46 196	48 078	48 785
Over 30	KEWQ	56 312	56 790	57 087	54 693	54 565	51 593	47 330	44 365	45 065	48 615	53 554
Age not known	KEWR	2 289	1 858	1 779	1 730	1 499	1 182	1 143	1 004	542	53	5
Companies	KEWS	1 263	991	961	812	737	675	551	399	308	341	406
Total persons with charge proved[2]	KEWT	162 806	159 178	156 707	153 087	150 508	139 877	127 560	118 152	120 325	125 029	130 606

1 See chapter text.
2 Includes gender unknown.

Source: Scottish Executive Justice Department: 0131 244 2229

11.18 Penal establishments: average daily population and receptions
Scotland[1]

Numbers

		1996/97	1997/98	1998/99	1999/00	2000/01	2001/02	2002/03	2003/04	2004/05
Average daily population										
Male	KEPB	5 803	5 874	5 830	5 765	5 676	5 929	6 193	6 307	6 447
Female	KEPC	189	186	199	210	207	257	282	314	332
Total	KEPA	5 993	6 059	6 029	5 975	5 883	6 186	6 475	6 621	6 779
Analysis by type of custody										
Remand	KEPD	1 021	927	971	976	881	1 019	1 247	1 246	1 216
Persons under sentence: total	KEPE	4 970	5 129	5 056	4 997	5 001	5 165	5 226	5 375	5 561
Adult prisoners[2]	KEPF	4 168	4 357	4 347	4 317	4 346	4 537	4 624	4 802	5 001
Young offenders[2]	KEPI	797	773	708	679	655	628	601	573	560
Persons recalled from supervision/licence[3]	KEPN	46	51	78	100	145	202	250	310	356
Others[3]	KEPO	15	18	21	28	36	37	6	6	5
Persons sentenced by court martial[3]	KEPP	1	1	–	2	–	–	–	–	1
Civil prisoners[3]	KEPQ	1	2	1	1	1	1	2	–	1
Receptions to penal establishments										
Remand	KEPR	15 452	14 685	15 713	14 626	14 062	15 725	19 198	18 963	18 892
Male	KEPS	14 443	13 677	14 527	13 450	13 042	14 402	17 455	17 111	17 085
Female	KEPT	1 009	1 008	1 186	1 176	1 020	1 323	1 743	1 852	1 807
Persons under sentence: total	KEPU	23 499	21 910	22 376	20 336	19 136	18 953	20 084	19 357	18 584
Male	KEPV	22 231	20 698	20 952	19 125	17 953	17 755	18 779	18 013	17 272
Female	KEPW	1 268	1 212	1 424	1 211	1 183	1 198	1 305	1 344	1 312
Imprisoned: Adults:										
directly	KEPX	10 256	9 697	9 887	9 217	8 943	9 470	10 571	10 255	10 299
in default of fine[4]	KEPY	8 358	7 650	7 907	7 030	6 450	5 882	6 081	6 063	5 404
Sentenced to young offenders' institution:										
directly	KEQA	3 058	2 811	2 824	2 582	2 436	2 312	2 207	1 949	1 908
in default of fine[4]	KEQB	1 776	1 695	1 606	1 328	1 116	1 109	1 016	825	694
Persons recalled from supervision/licence[5]	JYYD	51	57	152	179	191	180	209	265	279
Persons sentenced by court martial	KEQH	6	6	2	3	2	2	3	1	5
Civil prisoners[4]	KEQI	23	22	10	17	10	8	11	10	7

1 All figures are now reported as financial years, as Scotland is now publishing all figures on a financial year basis.
2 1998 figures have been revised to reflect improved treatment of missing data.
3 Persons recalled from supervision/licence and others are included in persons under sentence. Persons sentenced by court martial and civil prisoners are not included in persons under sentence.

4 Includes compensation orders.
5 Now covers all recalls including recalls from supervision release orders and default of compensation orders.

Source: The Scottish Executive Justice Department: 0131 244 2225

11.19 Expenditure on penal establishments[1]
Scotland

Years ended 31 March

£ thousand

		1994/95	1995/96	1996/97	1997/98	1998/99	1999/00	2000/01	2001/02	2002/03	2003/04	2004/05
Departmental Expenditure												
Manpower and Associated Services	KPHC	140 009	135 941	143 107	137 890	144 660	170 347	160 242	172 490	168 593	169 784	181 931
Prisoner and Associated Costs	KPHD	11 679	12 373	13 377	16 313	18 891	22 930	23 501	24 652	23 363	51 070	42 767
Capital Expenditure	KPHE	15 636	15 377	22 577	22 136	23 697	28 918	24 283	24 955	36 519	34 617	72 812
Gross Expenditure	KPHF	167 324	163 691	179 061	176 339	187 248	222 195	208 026	222 097	228 475	255 471	297 510
Less Receipts	KPHG	3 042	2 800	2 600	2 810	8 160	6 668	8 380	8 194	3 485	3 298	3 312
Net Departmental Expenditure	KPHH	164 282	160 891	176 461	173 529	179 088	215 527	199 646	213 903	224 990	252 173	294 198
Plus Annually Managed Expenditure Capital Charges	DSJI	..	..	..	..	..	..	..	31 341	40 432	41 728	48 497
Total Net Expenditure	DSNX	164 282	160 891	176 461	173 529	179 088	215 527	199 646	245 244	265 422	293 901	342 695

1 See chapter text.

Source: The Scottish Executive Justice Department: 0131 244 2225

11.20 Recorded crime statistics: by offence group[1]
Northern Ireland

Thousands

		Old counting rules						New counting rules						
		1994	1995	1996	1997	1998 /99		1998 /99	1999 /00	2000 /01	2001 /02	2002 /03	2003 /04	2004 /05
Violence against the person	RVCP	4.8	5.2	5.6	5.2	6.6	RVCQ	18.5	21.4	21.4	26.1	28.5	29.0	29.3
Sexual offences	RVCR	1.3	1.7	1.7	1.4	1.5	RVCS	1.6	1.3	1.2	1.4	1.5	1.8	1.7
Burglary	RVCT	16.9	16.5	16.1	14.3	15.5	RVCU	15.5	16.1	15.8	17.1	18.7	16.4	13.4
Robbery	RVCV	1.6	1.5	1.7	1.7	1.4	RVCW	1.4	1.4	1.8	2.2	2.5	2.0	1.5
Theft	RVCX	33.2	33.5	32.8	29.5	34.6	RVCY	35.4	37.0	36.9	41.7	41.9	35.7	31.1
Fraud and forgery	RVCZ	5.1	4.9	4.1	3.8	5.3	RVDA	6.8	7.9	8.0	8.6	8.8	6.3	5.2
Criminal damage	RVDB	3.1	3.8	4.8	4.7	9.8	RVDC	27.7	31.2	32.3	40.0	36.6	32.4	31.4
Offences against the state	RVDD	0.4	0.3	0.4	0.5	0.5	RVDE	0.6	0.7	0.8	1.2	1.8	1.3	1.2
Other notifiable offences	RVDF	1.4	1.5	1.2	1.1	1.5	RVDG	1.7	2.1	1.7	1.4	2.4	3.2	3.3
of which drug offences	RVDH	1.3	1.4	1.1	1.0	1.4	RVDI	1.4	1.7	1.5	1.1	1.9	2.6	2.6
Total	RVDR	67.9	68.8	68.5	62.2	76.6	RVDS	109.1	119.1	119.9	139.8	142.5	128.0	118.1

1 See chapter text.

Source: The Police Service of Northern Ireland

11.21 Persons found guilty at all courts: by offence group[1]
Northern Ireland

Numbers

		1993	1994	1995	1996	1997	1998	1999	2000	2001	2002	2003
Violence against the person	KYCT	1 674	1 498	1 685	1 597	1 594	1 596	1 699	1 858	1 621	1 790	1 965
Sexual offences	KEVG	126	148	182	184	130	128	90	130	112	84	108
Burglary	KYBW	1 114	979	951	801	715	647	703	703	496	595	602
Robbery	KYBX	159	168	195	161	161	134	129	122	121	152	192
Theft	KYBY	3 254	3 044	3 128	2 765	2 596	2 342	1 995	2 111	1 831	1 695	1 803
Fraud and forgery	KYBZ	633	568	533	467	491	426	476	403	398	362	314
Criminal damage	KYCA	1 145	1 134	1 008	1 076	1 163	1 043	931	1 060	917	957	1 034
Offences against the state	KYCB	184	137	166	147	165	198	178	174	158	215	274
Other indictable	KYCC	606	669	863	899	739	936	943	700	495	453	527
Total indictable[2]	KYCD	8 895	8 345	8 711	8 097	7 759	7 450	7 144	7 261	6 149	6 303	6 819
Summary[3]	KYCE	4 307	4 369	4 137	4 402	4 435	4 062	3 598	3 967	3 735	3 453	3 514
Motoring[4]	KYCF	21 882	21 502	20 124	18 177	18 770	15 369	15 782	15 390	14 466	14 344	16 342
All offences	KYCG	35 084	34 216	32 972	30 676	30 964	26 881	26 524	26 618	24 350	24 100	26 675

1 See chapter text.
2 From 2000, includes 'indictable-only' motoring offences.

3 Excludes motoring offences.
4 Prior to 2000, includes all motoring offences. From 2000, includes summary and triable-either-way motoring offences.

Source: Northern Ireland Office: 028 9052 7534

11.22 Juveniles found guilty at all courts:[1] by offence group
Northern Ireland

Numbers

		1993	1994	1995	1996	1997	1998	1999	2000	2001	2002	2003
Violence against the person	KYCH	43	49	51	75	49	97	73	77	66	82	75
Sexual offences	KAHF	7	8	7	4	8	12	12	4	1	6	5
Burglary	KYCI	155	180	170	137	124	108	117	125	73	77	89
Robbery	KYCJ	4	9	22	13	18	4	7	15	8	14	10
Theft	KYCK	280	283	345	338	334	304	227	254	244	212	173
Fraud and forgery	KYCL	14	14	21	14	11	4	10	2	9	3	7
Criminal damage	KYCM	94	117	116	121	136	139	102	143	152	132	162
Offences against the state	KYCN	1	8	9	6	10	11	12	8	10	20	26
Other indictable	KYCO	2	6	14	24	10	20	17	10	12	7	19
Total indictable[2]	KYCP	600	674	755	732	700	699	577	638	575	553	566
Summary[3]	KYCQ	125	131	180	182	198	187	163	180	203	194	174
Motoring[4]	KYCR	44	74	74	58	57	98	97	82	102	89	94
All offences	KYCS	769	879	1 009	972	955	984	837	900	880	836	834

1 See chapter text. Juveniles are aged 10 - 16 years inclusive.
2 From 2000, includes 'indictable-only' motoring offences.
3 Excludes motoring offences.

4 Prior to 2000 includes all motoring offences. From 2000, includes summary motoring offences.

Source: Northern Ireland Office: 028 9052 7534

11.23 Disposals given to those convicted by court
Northern Ireland

Numbers

		1993	1994	1995	1996	1997	1998	1999	2000	2001	2002	2003
Magistrates court - all offences												
Prison[1]	KYAO	1 027	945	1 046	1 003	989	996	1 278	1 356	1 048	1 107	1 133
Custody Probation Order[1]	EOG9	..	..	..	..	..	..	..	..	..	..	7
Young offenders centre	KYAP	575	499	483	443	430	326	243	191	209	288	395
Training school[2]	KYAQ	125	193	169	147	148	136	13	..	..	..	..
Juvenile Justice Centre order[2]	OEUX	..	..	..	..	..	..	22	78	72	58	48
Total immediate custody	KYAR	1 727	1 637	1 698	1 593	1 567	1 458	1 556	1 625	1 329	1 453	1 583
Prison suspended	KYAS	1 529	1 558	1 674	1 722	1 506	1 025	1 080	1 247	1 215	1 278	1 407
YOC suspended	KYAT	447	447	385	444	461	139	104	93	77	100	201
Attendance centre	KYAU	94	89	101	91	66	55	14	20	37	84	91
Probation/supervision[3]	KYAV	881	1 017	1 137	1 134	1 155	1 473	1 246	1 096	1 070	1 005	974
Community service order	KYAW	536	551	547	591	561	622	678	726	587	643	623
Combination order	OEUZ	..	..	..	..	..	38	7	48	24	36	96
Fine[4]	KYAX	25 166	24 390	22 726	20 614	21 313	17 956	18 076	17 716	16 439	15 968	17 546
Recognizance	KYAY	858	961	1 001	1 203	1 267	1 134	1 089	1 357	810	912	1 091
Conditional discharge	KYAZ	2 021	1 830	1 928	1 679	1 597	1 538	1 439	1 286	1 559	1 497	1 526
Absolute discharge	KYBA	690	661	608	509	424	303	223	242	209	163	201
Other	KYBC	13	17	10	15	8	123	221	57	61	104	215
Total	KYBD	33 962	33 158	31 815	29 595	29 925	25 864	25 733	25 513	23 417	23 243	25 554
Crown court - all offences												
Prison[1]	KYBE	555	471	533	469	475	520	386	521	407	410	238
Custody Probation Order[1]	EOH2	..	..	..	..	..	..	..	..	..	..	331
Young offenders centre	KYBF	130	87	76	106	111	63	67	32	42	23	51
Training school[2]	KYBG	2	5	6	–	4	2	–	..	..	..	..
Juvenile Justice Centre order[2]	VQEV	..	..	..	..	..	–	–	–	–	2	–
Total immediate custody	KYBH	687	563	615	575	590	585	453	553	449	435	620
Prison suspended	KYBI	211	277	265	253	220	199	185	313	262	220	240
YOC suspended	KYBJ	37	43	63	71	60	49	41	48	37	35	50
Combination order	ZAEP	..	..	..	..	..	13	6	7	5	18	34
Attendance centre	KYBK	–	1	–	–	–	–	–	–	–	1	–
Probation/supervision[3]	KYBL	73	58	60	49	47	70	43	68	48	49	63
Community service order	KYBM	48	59	60	54	37	33	24	29	45	25	27
Fine[4]	KYBN	33	23	27	39	40	25	20	40	38	32	49
Recognizance	KYBO	5	16	–	7	10	7	–	4	11	12	8
Conditional discharge	KYBR	19	15	64	30	31	23	17	38	36	20	24
Absolute discharge	KYBS	3	2	1	–	1	6	–	3	–	6	1
Other	KYBU	6	1	2	3	3	7	2	2	2	4	5
Total	KYBV	1 122	1 058	1 157	1 081	1 039	1 017	791	1 105	933	857	1 121

1 Custody Probation Orders cannot be separately identified from 'prison' sentences from 1998 to 2002. Thus during this timeframe, figures for prison include custody probation orders.

2 The Juvenile Justice Centre order replaced the training school order from 31st January 1999.

3 Supervision orders were abolished with the introduction of the Criminal Justice (Children) NI Order 1998.

4 From 2000, fine incorporates 'fine plus disqualification' and 'fine plus penalty points'.

Source: Northern Ireland Office: 028 9052 7534

11.24 Prisons and Young Offenders Centres
Northern Ireland

Receptions and average population

Numbers

		1994	1995	1996	1997	1998	1999	2000	2001	2002	2003	2004
Receptions:												
Reception of untried prisoners	KEOA	2 043	2 003	2 292	2 188	2 284	2 497	2 197	1 922	2 337	2 439	2 440
Reception of sentenced prisoners:												
Imprisonment under sentence of immediate custody	KEOB	1 029	1 070	1 070	1 062	949	963	1 001	791	916	1 032	975
Imprisonment in default of payment of a fine	KEOC	1 190	1 248	1 374	1 513	1 530	1 423	1 261	1 090	990	1 140	1 296
Total	KEOD	2 219	2 318	2 444	2 575	2 479	2 386	2 262	1 881	1 906	2 172	2 271
Reception into Young Offender Centres:												
Detention under sentence of immediate custody	KEOE	346	371	362	331	347	346	282	252	315	268	287
Detention in default of payment of a fine	KEOF	276	351	373	366	385	417	389	303	250	313	351
Total	KEOG	622	722	735	697	732	763	671	555	565	581	638
Other receptions[1]	KEOL	13	45	27	42	70	38	56	58	57	117	106
Daily average population:												
Unconvicted[2]	KEON	440	322	337	376	383	377	317	272	347	393	456
Convicted[3]	KEOP	1 459	1 440	1 302	1 256	1 124	867	751	638	679	767	818
Total	KEOM	1 899	1 762	1 639	1 632	1 507	1 244	1 068	910	1 026	1 160	1 274

1 Non-criminal prisioners including those imprisoned for non-payment of maintenance, non-payment of debt, contempt of court or are being held under the terms of an Immigration Act.
2 Prisoners on remand or awaiting trial and prisoners committed by civil process.
3 Includes those sentenced to immediate custody and fine defaulters.

Source: Northern Ireland Office: 028 9052 7534

Lifestyles

Chapter 12

Lifestyles

Expenditure by the Department for Culture, Media and Sport

(Table 12.1)

The figures in this table are taken from the Department's Annual Report and are outturn figures for each of the headings shown (later figures are the estimated outturn). The Department's planned expenditure for future years is also shown.

Cinema statistics

(Table 12.3)

This table now includes data from CAA/Gallup/Nielsen EDI which replaces the previous ONS Inquiry data which are no longer collected.

Tourist attractions

(Table 12.5)

The figures in this table are compiled using data from the Survey of Visits to Visitor Attractions. The tourist attractions included within the headings shown are as follows:

Country parks: Country parks and forest parks.

Farms: Farms, rare breeds, shire horse centres and farm animals.

Gardens: Gardens, arboretums and botanical gardens.

Historic properties: Historic houses, palaces, castles, forts, historic monuments, places of worship, archaeological sites, historic ships and other historic properties.

Leisure and theme parks: Leisure parks and theme parks.

Museums and art galleries: Museums and/or art galleries and science centres.

Steam and heritage railways: Steam railways and heritage railways.

Visitor and heritage centres: Visitor and heritage centres.

Wildlife attractions: Nature reserves, wetlands, wildlife trips, safari parks, zoos, aquariums and aviaries.

Workplaces: Distilleries, vineyards, breweries and industrial or craft premises.

Domestic tourism

(Table 12.6)

The figures in this table are compiled using data from the United Kingdom Tourism Survey (UKTS) and represent trips of one or more nights away from home. The UKTS changed survey methodology in 2000. Data from 1995 to 1999 were reworked to allow comparisons to be made with 2000 and later data.

International tourism and holidays abroad

(Tables 12.7 and 12.8)

The figures in these tables are compiled using data from the International Passenger Survey. A holiday abroad is a visit made for holiday purposes. Business trips and visits to friends and relatives are excluded.

Attendances at leisure and cultural activities

(Table 12.9)

The definitions used in this table differ from those normally used to define regular attendees by the Department for Culture, Media and Sport.

Gambling

(Table 12.10)

The National Lottery figures in this table are the latest figures at the time of going to press which have been released by the National Lottery Commission, and represent ticket sales (money staked) for each of the games which comprise the lottery. The figures have been adjusted to real terms using the Retail Prices Index.

The National Lottery commenced on 19 November 1994, with the first instant ticket being sold in March 1995. Various other games have been started since, the latest shown in the table being the Euromillions game. The sum of the individual games may not agree exactly with the figures for total sales. Total sales also includes the Easy Play games which commenced in 1998, but were dropped in 1999.

The other gambling figures in this table are obtained from the Gaming Board and H.M. Revenue and Customs. The figures have been adjusted to real terms using the Retail Prices Index.

The money staked at bingo clubs refers to licensed clubs only. Prior to 1994–95 the figures for bingo clubs relate to the year ending August.

12.1 Expenditure by the Department for Culture, Media and Sport[1]

£ million

	Museums, galleries and libraries[2]	The arts (England)	Sports (UK)	Historic buildings, monuments, and sites (England)	The Royal Parks (UK)	Tourism (UK)	Broadcasting and media (UK)	Administration and research	Other gambling and gaming bodies	Commemorative services (Queen's Golden Jubilee)	European regional development fund	Culture online
	GQIF	KWFP	KWFQ	KWFR	LQYY	KWFS	KWFT	GQIG	SNKA	SNKB	JYXQ	GQII
1995/96	399	200	54	164	25	45	98	20	–	..	6	..
1996/97	336	195	52	162	23	46	97	21	–	..	16	..
1997/98	321	196	50	156	22	45	43	21	–	..	26	..
1998/99	363	192	46	138	23	44	99	23	–	..	33	..
1999/00	377	230	51	144	27	48	104	28	–	–	28	–
2000/01	411	239	52	144	24	48	104	29	–	–	35	1
2001/02	313	254	67	139	42	68	105	33	–1	–	27	1
2002/03	416	286	126	149	26	75	109	38	2	6	19	–
2003/04	775	328	74	349	25	58	112	42	2	–	25	1
2004/05[3]	579	379	125	162	31	55	128	54	4	–	6	2
2005/06[4]	564	411	123	165	25	56	120	50	3	–	6	–
2006/07[4]	582	418	154	176	26	54	120	49	3	–	7	–
2007/08[4]	601	419	174	181	26	54	120	48	3	–	7	–

1 See chapter text.
2 Includes museums and galleries (England), libraries (UK) and museums library archives (UK).
3 Data are estimated outturn.
4 Data are plans.

Source: Department for Culture, Media and Sport: 020 7211 6121

12.2 Employment in tourism[1]
United Kingdom
Non seasonally adjusted. At June each year

Thousands

	Hotels and other tourist accommodation	Restaurants, bars and canteens	Transport	Travel agents, tour operators	Recreation services	Rest of the economy	All tourism related industries		
								Of which:	
							All	Employee jobs	Self-employment jobs
	EUR7	EUR8	EUR9	EUS2	EUS3	EUS4	EUS5	EUS6	EUS7
2000	230.0	556.1	132.2	135.2	73.2	205.2	1 331.9	1 214.4	117.5
2001	226.8	567.2	134.5	144.5	72.6	207.5	1 353.0	1 231.1	121.9
2002	222.0	586.8	133.4	138.8	78.4	208.2	1 367.4	1 247.1	120.3
2003	226.4	610.4	133.8	137.5	79.6	210.0	1 397.7	1 270.9	126.8
2004	229.6	618.2	131.5	146.8	82.7	211.1	1 419.9	1 293.8	126.1

1 See chapter text

Sources: Department for Culture, Media and Sport: 020 7211 6121; using data from Labour Force Survey, Office for National Statistics

12.3 Employment in creative industries
Great Britain

Thousands

	Advertising	Architecture	Crafts	Design and designer fashion	Film, video and photography	Music and the visual and performing arts	Publishing	Software computer games and electronic publishing	Television and radio	Art/antiques trade	All
	EUS8	EUS9	EUT2	EUT3	EUT4	EUT5	EUT6	EUT7	EUT8	EUT9	EUU2
1995	189.1	97.3	115.3	79.5	53.1	227.9	327.2	285.9	96.5	19.8	1 491.6
1996	173.0	106.1	97.4	85.5	47.5	224.3	314.4	318.6	96.8	19.4	1 483.0
1997	201.0	95.8	95.0	80.7	52.7	237.8	308.5	379.4	97.6	20.2	1 568.7
1998	204.2	101.5	119.8	88.8	52.5	229.5	317.1	426.0	101.5	19.8	1 660.7
1999	200.9	101.5	96.8	93.5	51.5	266.1	317.0	488.6	92.5	20.8	1 729.3
2000	206.0	102.6	111.3	98.5	58.5	233.3	283.9	544.6	109.8	20.9	1 769.4
2001	220.5	103.4	115.1	103.0	64.3	235.8	293.3	567.7	104.1	20.9	1 828.1
2002	215.4	102.9	114.1	115.0	58.9	250.8	286.8	556.7	108.8	21.4	1 830.7
2003	213.8	103.1	108.7	113.2	65.9	254.2	305.2	581.2	110.9	22.5	1 878.8
2004	200.0	102.6	112.9	110.4	53.9	243.9	274.3	593.9	110.6	22.5	1 825.0

Sources: Department for Culture, Media and Sport: 020 7211 6121;
using data from Labour Force Survey, Office for National Statistics

12.4 Cinema statistics[1,2]
United Kingdom

	Sites (numbers)	Screens (numbers)	Total number of admissions[3] (millions)	Gross box office takings (£ million)	Revenue per admission[3] (£)	Revenue per screen (£ thousand)
	JMHX	JMHY	JMHZ	JMIA	JMIB	JMIC
1996	742	2 166	123.5	407.2	3.30	188.0
1997	747	2 383	138.9	486.2	3.50	204.0
1998	761	2 638	135.2	504.9	3.73	191.4
1999	751	2 825	139.1	549.7	3.95	194.6
2000	754	3 017	142.5	572.8	4.02	189.9
2001	766	3 248	155.9	645.0	4.14	198.6
2002	775	3 402	175.9	755.3	4.29	222.0
2003	776	3 433	167.3	742.0	4.44	216.1
2004	773	3 475	171.3	769.6	4.49	221.4

1 See chapter text.
2 Includes Isle of Man and the Channel Islands.
3 Admissions are based on all cinemas taking advertising.

Source: CAA/Gallup/Nielsen EDI

12.5 Films
United Kingdom

Numbers and £ million

	Production of UK films		Expenditure on feature films (Current prices)				
	Films produced in the UK (numbers)	Production costs (1998 prices)	UK box office	Video rental	Video retail	Subscriptions to movie channels	Box office, video, subscription channels
	KWGD	KWGE	KWHU	KWHV	KWHW	KWHX	KWHY
1994	84	436.0	364	339	698	540	1 941
1995	78	421.0	385	351	789	721	2 246
1996	128	726.0	426	382	803	1 319	2 930
1997	116	558.0	506	369	858	..	1 733
1998	88	487.0	515	437	981	..	1 892
1999	100	570.0	606	408	960	..	1 896
2000	98	793.0	628	444	1 200	..	2 176
2001	96	..	692	465	1 539	..	..
2002	119	550.0	755	476	2 050	..	..
2003	173	1 158.0	742	450	2 421	..	..
2004	133	812.0	770	461	2 667	..	..

Source: UK Film Council

12.6 Domestic tourism[1]
United Kingdom

	Number of trips (millions)	Number of nights spent (millions)	Expenditure at current prices (£ million)	Average nights spent (numbers)	Average expenditure per trip (£)
	GQGY	GQGZ	GQHA	GQHB	GQHC
1995	147.8	526.0	20 072	3.6	135.8
1996	154.2	532.8	22 041	3.5	142.9
1997	162.2	555.3	24 137	3.4	148.8
1998	148.8	516.0	22 814	3.5	153.3
1999	173.1	568.6	25 635	3.3	148.1
2000	175.4	576.4	26 133	3.3	149.0
2001	163.1	529.6	26 094	3.2	160.0
2002	167.3	531.9	26 699	3.2	159.6
2003	151.0	490.5	26 482	3.2	175.4
2004[2]	126.6	408.9	24 357	3.2	192.4

1 See chapter text.
2 There are concerns that the data for 2004 are not truly representative of the United Kingdom population. The data for 2004 should be used and interpreted with caution.

Source: United Kingdom Tourism Survey, VisitBritain: 020 8563 3317

12.7 International tourism[1]

Thousands and £ million

	Visits to the UK by overseas residents (thousands)	Spending in the UK by overseas residents		Visits overseas by UK residents (thousands)	Spending overseas by UK residents	
		Current prices	Constant 1995 prices		Current prices	Constant 1995 prices
	GMAA	GMAK	CQPR	GMAF	GMAM	CQPS
1995	23 537	11 763	11 763	41 345	15 386	15 386
1996	25 163	12 290	11 954	42 050	16 223	15 897
1997	25 515	12 244	11 542	45 957	16 931	18 652
1998	25 745	12 671	11 573	50 872	19 489	21 847
1999	25 394	12 498	11 133	53 881	22 020	24 676
2000	25 209	12 805	11 102	56 837	24 251	27 281
2001	22 835	11 306	9 528	58 281	25 332	27 710
2002	24 180	11 737	9 641	59 377	26 962	29 311
2003	24 715	11 855	9 451	61 424	28 550	28 677
2004	27 755	13 047	10 146	64 194	30 285	31 459
2005	29 950	14 260	10 714	66 250	32 155	33 630

1 See chapter text.

Sources: International Passenger Survey, Office for National Statistics;
020 7533 5765

12.8 Holidays abroad:[1] by destination

Percentages

		1971	1981	1991	1997	1998	1999	2000	2001	2002	2003	2004
Spain[2]	JTKC	34.3	29.8	21.3	26.3	27.5	27.2	27.8	27.9	28.5	29.8	28.4
France	JTKD	15.9	18.1	25.8	23.1	20.2	19.7	18.3	18.3	19.0	18.1	17.3
Greece	JTKF	4.5	6.6	7.6	4.7	5.3	6.5	6.8	7.8	7.0	6.6	5.7
United States	JTKE	1.0	5.5	6.8	6.7	7.0	7.5	7.3	6.3	5.4	5.5	6.1
Italy	JTKG	9.2	5.0	3.5	4.2	4.0	4.1	4.2	4.3	4.6	5.0	5.0
Ireland	JTKI	..	3.7	3.0	3.6	3.5	5.5	4.6	4.1	4.1	3.7	3.8
Portugal	JTKH	2.6	4.0	4.8	4.0	3.6	3.7	3.9	3.6	4.0	4.0	3.5
Cyprus	JTKL	1.0	2.7	2.4	2.2	2.6	2.4	3.3	3.5	3.0	2.7	2.6
Netherlands	JTKK	3.6	2.6	3.5	2.8	2.7	2.4	2.2	2.6	2.8	2.6	2.6
Turkey	JTKJ	..	2.3	0.7	3.1	3.0	2.1	1.8	2.0	2.2	2.3	2.3
Belgium	JTKM	..	2.2	2.1	2.2	2.3	1.9	1.8	2.1	2.0	2.2	1.8
Germany	JTKN	3.4	1.2	2.7	1.7	1.8	1.6	1.7	1.4	1.5	1.2	1.6
Austria	JTKP	5.5	1.1	2.4	1.1	1.3	1.0	1.0	1.1	1.4	1.1	1.4
Malta	JTKO	..	1.0	1.7	1.2	1.3	1.0	1.1	1.0	1.0	1.0	1.0
Other countries	JTKQ	19.0	14.2	11.8	13.2	13.9	13.3	14.1	13.8	13.6	14.2	16.8

1 See chapter text.
2 Excludes the Canary Islands prior to 1981.

Sources: International Passenger Survey, Office for National Statistics;
020 7533 5765

12.9 Attendance at leisure and cultural activities[1]
Great Britain
At Spring

Percentages

		1994/95	1995/96	1996/97	1997/98	1998/99	1999/00	2000/01	2001/02	2002/03	2003/04	2004/05
Attendance by men at:												
Cinema	JSPR	53	53	55	55	57	58	57	58	62	59	65
Plays	JSPS	22	21	21	20	20	21	20	21	22	23	22
Art galleries and exhibitions	JSPT	22	22	22	20	20	21	21	22	23	24	24
Classical music	JSPU	12	12	12	11	10	11	12	12	12	13	12
Ballet	JSPV	5	4	4	4	4	4	4	4	5	5	5
Opera	JSPW	6	6	6	6	5	6	6	6	6	6	7
Contemporary dance	JSPX	3	3	3	4	3	3	3	3	4	5	4
Taking part in sporting events - regularly[2]	EU5X	..	..	..	..	..	50	48	49	50	52	54
Watching sporting events	JSPY	89	88	87	87	86	85	85	78	76	73	76
Pop/rock concerts	C3Q8	..	..	..	..	..	..	..	..	25	26	26
Attendance by women at:												
Cinema	JSQA	51	50	52	54	57	54	54	57	60	62	65
Plays	JSQB	26	25	26	25	23	25	25	26	27	27	27
Art galleries and exhibitions	JSQC	21	22	23	22	22	22	22	23	25	24	25
Classical music	JSQD	12	13	12	13	12	12	12	13	13	14	14
Ballet	JSQE	9	9	9	8	8	9	8	8	9	10	10
Opera	JSQF	7	7	7	7	7	7	7	7	8	8	8
Contemporary dance	JSQG	4	5	5	5	5	5	5	6	6	7	7
Taking part in sporting events - regularly[2]	EU5Y	..	..	..	..	..	42	40	40	44	42	42
Watching sporting events	JSQH	72	72	69	67	66	65	65	56	58	55	60
Pop/rock concerts	C3Q9	..	..	..	..	..	..	..	..	21	23	24
Attendance by all persons at:												
Cinema	JSQJ	52	51	54	55	57	56	55	57	61	61	65
Plays	JSQK	24	23	24	22	22	23	23	24	24	25	25
Art galleries and exhibitions	JSQL	21	22	22	21	21	22	21	22	24	24	24
Classical music	JSQM	12	12	12	12	11	12	12	12	13	13	13
Ballet	JSQN	7	7	7	6	6	6	6	6	7	8	8
Opera	JSQO	7	6	7	6	6	6	6	6	7	8	7
Contemporary dance	JSQP	4	4	4	5	4	4	4	5	5	6	6
Taking part in sporting events - regularly[2]	EU5Z	..	..	..	..	..	46	44	45	47	47	48
Watching sporting events	JSQQ	80	80	78	78	76	75	75	67	68	63	68
Pop/rock concerts	C3QA	..	..	..	..	..	..	..	..	23	25	25

1 Percentage of resident population aged 15 and over attending 'these days'. See chapter text.
2 From 2002 the question asked to the respondent was changed.

Source: Target Group Index, BMRB International: 020 8433 4125

12.10 Gambling[1]
United Kingdom

£ million at 2003/04 prices[2]

		1993/94	1994/95	1995/96	1996/97	1997/98	1998/99	1999/00	2000/01	2001/02	2002/03	2003/04
Money staked on gambling												
National Lottery - Total[3]	C229	..	1 417	6 404	5 603	6 325	5 809	5 450	5 315	5 029	4 670	4 614
Lotto including on-line	C3PU	..	1 404	4 526	4 564	5 408	5 064	4 641	4 416	4 038	3 479	3 225
Instants[4]	C3PV	..	13	1 878	1 039	917	744	612	590	606	592	641
Thunderball	C3PW	..	..	..	..	..	..	197	257	254	287	351
Lottery Extra	C3PX	..	..	..	..	..	..	..	51	131	90	78
HotPicks	C3PY	..	..	..	..	..	..	..	..	..	222	244
Christmas draw	C3PZ	..	..	..	..	..	..	..	..	..	..	15
Euromillions	C3Q2	..	..	..	..	..	..	..	..	..	..	15
Daily Play	C3Q3	..	..	..	..	..	..	..	..	..	..	45
Lotteries (excluding the National Lottery)[5]	C3Q4	55	49	96	136	144	179	114	114	114	134	127
Bingo clubs	C3Q5	1 014	1 017	1 101	1 148	1 170	1 159	1 179	1 190	1 221	1 256	1 381
Football pools	C3Q6	1 191	1 121	727	548	400	286	221	185	151	124	112
Off-course betting[6]	C3Q7	8 232	8 233	7 671	7 972	7 869	7 916	7 996	7 689	9 969	17 985	32 265

1 See chapter text.
2 Adjusted to real terms using the Retail Prices Index.
3 Includes Easy Play tickets which are not shown separately.
4 From 2003/04 includes Inter-active games.
5 From 2002/03 includes Hotspot lotteries.
6 From 2001/02 includes Fixed Odds Betting Terminals.

Sources: National Lottery Commission;
Gaming Board for Great Britain: 020 7306 6253;
Department for Culture, Media and Sport: 020 7211 6121

Environment

Chapter 13

Environment

Air emissions

(Table 13.1 to 13.7)

Emissions of air pollutants arise from a wide variety of sources. The National Atmospheric Emissions Inventory (NAEI) is prepared annually for the Government and the devolved administrations by the National Environmental Technology Centre (NETCEN), with the work being co-ordinated by Defra. Information is available for a range of point sources, including the most significant polluters. However, a different approach has to be taken for diffuse sources such as transport and domestic emissions where this type of information is not available and estimates for these are derived from statistical information and from research on emission factors for stationary and mobile sources. Although for any given year considerable uncertainties surround the emission estimates for each pollutant, trends over time are likely to be more reliable.

UK national emission estimates are updated annually and any developments in methodology are applied retrospectively to earlier years. Adjustments in the methodology are made to accommodate new technical information and to improve international comparability.

Three different classification systems are used in the tables presented here: a National Accounts basis (Table 13.1); the format required by the Inter-governmental Panel on Climate Change (IPCC) (Table 13.2); and the EMEP format used by the United Nations Economic Commission for Europe (UNECE) (Tables 13.3 to 13.7).

The EMEP source categories are detailed below, together with details of the main sources of these emissions.

Energy industries: Public electricity and heat production, Petroleum refining, manufacture of solid fuels and other energy industries

Manufacturing industries and construction: iron and steel, autogenerators, foundries, sinter production, other industrial fuel combustion including ammonia, fletton brick and cement production.

Road transport: Passenger cars, light duty vehicles, Buses, HGVs mopeds, motorcycles; gasoline evaporation from vehicles, tyre and brake wear.

Other transport: Civil aviation (Domestic cruise, take off and landing cycles), Railways locomotives, National navigation, fishing vessels, and Other mobile sources including agricultural machinery; gardening, construction and aircraft support equipment and mobile industrial equipment powered by diesel or petrol engines.

Commercial and institutional: Public sector industrial and commercial combustion, and railways stationary combustion.

Residential: Residential plant, household and gardening (mobile).

Agriculture and forestry fuel use: Stationary, off road vehicles and other machinery.

Military aircraft and shipping: military road vehicles are included in road transport.

Fugitive emissions from fuels: Solid fuel transformation, exploration production, transport, venting and flaring.

Industrial processes: Emissions from industrial processes other than fuel combustion

Solvent and other product use: Paint application, degreasing and dry cleaning, chemical products, manufacture and processing , wood impregnation and tyre manufacture.

Agriculture: Culture with and without fertilisers; enteric fermentation and manure management of animals.

Land-use change and forestry: Emissions from managed and unmanaged forests, and forest and grassland conversion.

Waste treatment and disposal: Treatment of domestic, industrial and other waste, including landfill, but excluding incineration with energy recovery; and including accidental fires.

In Tables 13.3 and 13.5, the figures on emissions from individual large combustion plants (LCPs) for 1991 onwards are totals of those reported by the Environment Agency to the Department for Environment Food and Rural Affairs (Defra). For 1970–1990, estimates are made assuming all power station emissions from coal, fuel oil and orimulsion stations are included, plus 79 per cent of refineries' emissions, 12 per cent of iron and steel emissions and 38 per cent of other (Table 13.3), and 88 per cent of refineries' emissions, 11 per cent of iron and steel emissions and 40 per cent of other industrial combustions in fuel extraction and transformation (Table 13.5). It is not possible to calculate LCP figures from the categories presented in these tables as refineries and other industrial combustion are both included in more than one category.

Estimated atmospheric emissions on a National Accounts basis

(Table 13.1)

The National Accounts figures in Table 13.1 differ from those on an IPCC basis in that they include estimated emissions from fuels purchased by UK residents either at home or abroad, including emissions from UK international shipping and aircraft operators and exclude emissions in the UK resulting from the activities of non-residents.

Greenhouse gases include carbon dioxide, methane, nitrous oxide, hydro-fluorocarbons, perfluorocarbons and sulphur hexafluoride which are expressed in thousand tonnes of carbon dioxide equivalent.

Acid rain precursors include sulphur dioxide, nitrogen oxides and ammonia which are expressed as thousand tonnes of sulphur dioxide equivalent.

PM10 are carbon particles in the air arising from incomplete combustion.

Estimated total emissions of greenhouse gases on a IPCC basis

(Table 13.2)

The IPCC classification is used to report greenhouse gas emissions under the Framework Convention on Climate Change and includes land use change and all emissions from domestic aviation and shipping, but excludes international marine and aviation bunker fuels. Estimates of the relative contribution to global warming of the main greenhouse gases, or classes of gases, is presented weighted by their global warming potential. The Kyoto basket total differs slightly from sum of individual pollutants as the basket uses a narrower definition for the Land Use Change and Forestry sector, and includes emissions from UK Overseas Territories. Total emissions of greenhouse gases are now reported as a net value (emissions minus removals) after including land use change.

In tables 13.3 to 13.7 the agriculture and forestry fuel use category previously contained fishing fuel use, fishing is now included within coastal shipping under other transport.

Emissions of PM[10]

(Table 13.4)

Emissions of PM[10] includes particles which pass through a size selective inlet with a 50 per cent efficiency cut-off at 10µm aerodynamics diameter.

Emissions of nitrogen oxides

(Table 13.5)

Most of the figures in this table are based on a single NO_x emission factor for each fuel which is held constant over time. Emissions are expressed as nitrogen dioxide equivalent.

Emissions of carbon monoxide

(Table 13.6)

Most of the figures in this table are based on a single carbon monoxide emission factor for each fuel held constant over time.

Emissions of volatile organic compounds

(Table 13.7)

Most of the figures in this table are based on a single volatile organic compound emission factor for each source held constant over time.

Annual rainfall

(Table 13.8)

The Centre for Ecology and Hydrology, Wallingford and the British Geological Survey jointly maintain the National Hydrological Monitoring Programme which provides assessments of hydrological conditions and water resources variability across the UK. For further details visit: www.ceh.ac.uk/data/nrfa/water_watch.html

The UK climate is inherently variable but rainfall patterns over the last 20 years have been particularly volatile with major departures from the seasonal average characterising much of the country for extended periods. Much of England and Wales suffered protracted drought conditions in the early and mid-1990s with an especially arid episode in the spring and summer of 1995. Thereafter, most rain-bearing frontal systems followed more southerly tracks bringing abundant rainfall to southern Britain in particular. The 1998–2002 period is the wettest five-year sequence for England and Wales in a series from 1766. As a consequence, water resources remained very healthy but significant flood episodes were frequent and their impact widespread across southern Britain. This was particularly true during the winter of 2000/01 when flooding was extensive and protracted, with very sustained groundwater flooding in some impermeable southern catchments. Further notable flooding occurred in early 2003 but it heralded a notably dry and extremely warm summer. Rainfall for England and Wales over the February–October period was the 2nd lowest since 1921 and an intense drought affected all regions by the late autumn.

However, water resources are largely dependant on winter and spring rainfall (most summer rainfall is lost to evaporation) and in 2003, the wetness of the preceding winter provided abundant replenishment to reservoirs and aquifers, greatly moderating the impact of the ensuing rainfall deficiency. By contrast, two successive very dry winter and early spring periods in 2004/05 and 2005/06 resulted in a sustained deterioration in the water resources outlook and severe drought stress across much of the South-East by early 2006.

Biological and chemical quality of rivers and canals

(Table 13.9)

The chemical quality of river and canal waters is monitored in a series of separate national surveys in England and Wales and Northern Ireland. The General Quality Assessment (GQA) Scheme used in the surveys provides a rigorous and objective method for assessing the basic chemical quality of rivers and canals based on three determinants – dissolved oxygen, biochemical oxygen demand (BOD), and ammoniacal nitrogen. The GQA grades river stretches into six categories (A–F) of chemical quality and these in turn have been grouped into four broader groups – good (classes A and B), fair (C and D), poor (E) and bad (F).

To provide a more comprehensive picture of the health of rivers and canals, biological testing has also been carried out. The biological grading is based on the monitoring of tiny animals (invertebrates) which live in or on the bed of the river. Research has shown that there is a relationship between species composition and water quality. Using a procedure known as the River Invertebrate Prediction and Classification System (RIVPACS), species groups recorded at a site were compared with those which would be expected to be present in the absence of pollution, allowing for the different environmental characteristics in different parts of the country. Two different summary statistics (known as ecological quality indices (EQI)) were calculated and then the biological quality was assigned to one of six bands based on a combination of these two statistics.

River length stretches were allocated to Government Office Regions using a 1995 digitised map. This provides consistently smaller total river lengths for local areas than the equivalent Environment Agency figures. This is because of differences between stretch lengths used by the Environment Agency and those calculated using the map, and because it was not possible to link all stretch codes to the map, so some stretches were excluded. It should be noted that the monitoring network only covers stretches the Environment Agency are required to

monitor, that is rivers and streams with a flow greater than 1m3 /second. On this basis 40,000km of river network are monitored in England and Wales out of an estimated total river length of 150,000km. No canals are classified in Northern Ireland. The figures in Table 13.9 are rounded to the nearest 10km and may not sum to totals.

Water quality of rivers and canals

(Table 13.10)

In Scotland, river and canal water quality is based upon the Scottish River Classification Scheme of 20 June 1997 which combines chemical, biological, nutrient and aesthetic quality using the following classes: excellent (A1), good (A2), fair (B), poor (C) and seriously polluted (D). The figures in the table are also rounded to the nearest 10km and may not sum to totals.

During 2000 a new digitised river network (DRN) was developed, based on 1:50,000 ordnance survey data digitised by the Institute of Hydrology – now CEH – Wallingford. The new network ensures consistency between all SEPA areas and includes the Scottish Islands which were not previously covered. Data based on this network are published for the first time in the 2004 edition of Annual Abstract and are not consistent with data which have previously been published. The DRN includes:

> all mainland and islands rivers with a catchment area of 10 km2 or more. This is known as the 'baseline network'.

> mainland and islands stream stretches with a catchment of less than 10 km2 which are classified as fair, poor or seriously polluted and have been monitored. These are added to the baseline network to give a 'classification network'.

It is intended that future emphasis will be placed on the baseline network, which is likely to be reportable for the purposes of the EC Water Framework Directive. Efforts to improve the quality of the downgraded smaller streams will continue, but once this has been sustainably achieved, their monitoring may be reduced. Many of these streams are the subject of current attention because of their influence on the quality of larger classification network rivers.

Using the DRN scheme, data for every routine sampling point are automatically applied to an identified river stretch of predetermined length. The loss in total river length in moving to the DRN (i.e. despite the first time inclusion of islands rivers) arises mainly from the exclusion from classification of thousands of small remote headwater streams which were never monitored, but assumed to be of excellent quality. The smaller reduction in length of downgraded waters arises mainly from using 1:50,000 maps for the DRN; in the former system lengths were hand measured from 1:10,000 maps, so more minor channel bends were included.

Water reservoir stocks

(Table 13.11)

Reservoir levels normally rise and fall with the seasons. Typically, maximum stocks occur in the late winter/early spring and minimum stocks in the late autumn. Consistent with the recent rainfall patterns (Table 13.8), enhanced variability has been a feature of reservoir stocks over the recent past. Exceptionally dry conditions in 1995 resulted in overall reservoir storage for England and Wales falling to below 50 per cent of capacity in the autumn, with particularly depressed stocks in parts of Yorkshire. Generally, reservoir stocks remained considerably below average over the ensuing two years as a result of limited winter rainfall. Stocks recovered briskly in the autumn of 1997 and remained mostly very healthy over the next five years. Drought conditions in 2003 then saw overall stocks decline to below 60 per cent of average by the late autumn when reservoir storages were particularly depleted in the South East. Many reservoirs failed to return to capacity during the dry, mild winter of 2004/05 and limited replenishment over the succeeding winter resulted in a fragile water resources outlook in much of central and southern England. The overall stocks for England and Wales disguise important regional and more local variability in reservoir storage. By the spring of 2006, the most seasonally depleted stocks were generally associated with gravity-fed reservoirs in the drier parts of England where concentrations of population, commercial activity and intensive agriculture generate the highest water demand.

Water industry expenditure

(Table 13.12)

The table is informed by the annual and regulatory accounts of water and sewerage companies and water companies of England and Wales. Figures are given based on current cost rather than historical cost accounting principles. The elements which make up operating expenditure are as follows: manpower costs, other costs of employment, power, agencies, associated companies, Environment Agency charges, bulk supply imports, general and support, customer services, scientific services, other business activities, local authority rates, water charges, local authority sewerage agencies, materials and consumables, hired and contracted services, charge for bad and doubtful debts, depreciation, infrastructure renewals expenditure, infrastructure renewals accrual, exceptional items

and other operating costs. Capital expenditure figures are the addition to tangible fixed assets including management and general expenditure but excluding infrastructure renewals expenditure. Adopted assets at nil cost are also included.

Water pollution incidents

(Table 13.13)

The Environment Agency responds to complaints and reported incidents of pollution in England and Wales. Each incident is then logged and categorised according to its severity. The category describes the impact of each incident on our water, land and air. The impact of an incident on each medium is considered and reported separately. If no impact has occurred for a particular medium, the incident is reported as a Category 4. Before 1999, the reporting system was used only for water pollution incidents, thus the total number of substantiated incidents was lower as it did not include incidents not relating to the water environment.

Bathing waters

(Table 13.14)

Under the EC Bathing Water Directive 76/160/EEC, eleven physical, chemical and microbiological parameters are measured including total and faecal coliforms which are generally considered to be the most important indicators of the extent to which water is contaminated by sewage. The mandatory value for total coliforms is 10,000 per 100 ml, and for faecal coliforms 2,000 per 100 ml. For a bathing water to comply with the coliform standards, the Directive requires that at least 95 per cent of samples taken for each of these parameters over the bathing season are less than or equal to the mandatory values. In the UK a minimum of 20 samples are normally taken at each site. In practice this means that where 20 samples are taken, a maximum of only one sample may exceed the mandatory value for the bathing water to comply, and where less than 20 samples are taken none may exceed the mandatory value for the bathing water to comply.

The bathing water season is from mid-May to end-September in England and Wales, but shorter in Scotland and Northern Ireland. Bathing waters which are closed for the season are excluded for that year.

The table shows Environment Agency (EA) regions for England and Wales. The boundaries of which are based on river catchment areas and not county borders. In particular, the figures shown for Wales are the EA Welsh Region, the boundary of which does not coincide with the boundary of Wales.

Environment

Surface and groundwater abstractions

(Table 13.15)

From 1991 data were collected on a different basis. Figures are therefore not strictly comparable with those in previous years. Some regions report licensed and actual abstracts for financial rather than calendar years. As figures represent an average for the whole year expressed as daily amounts, differences between amounts reported for financial and calendar years are small.

The following changes have occurred in the classification of individual sources:

Public water supply: The 1991 figures include some private water supply.

Spray irrigation: This category includes small amounts of non-agricultural spray irrigation.

Mineral washing: From 1999 was not reported as a separate category, licences for mineral washing are now contained in 'Other industry'.

Private water supply: was shown as separate category from 1992 and includes private abstractions for domestic use and individual households.

Fish farming, cress growing, amenity ponds: Includes amenity ponds, but excludes miscellaneous from 1991.

Other: The figure for 1991 included some private domestic water supply wells and boreholes, public water supply transfer licences and frost protection use.

Radioactive wastes

(Table 13.16)

Solid radioactive wastes are not discharged to the environment but stored and conditioned by processes such as supercompaction, cementation or turning into glass. Such wastes cover a wide range of materials and can be classified, according to the nature and quantity of radioactivity associated with them, as high level wastes (HLW), intermediate level wastes (ILW) or low level wastes (LLW). HLW result from the reprocessing of irradiated nuclear fuel and are intensely radioactive. They contain over 95 per cent of all the radioactivity in wastes from nuclear establishments. HLWs are of relatively small in volume, but have a high heat output as a result of the energy from radioactive decay. ILW include the irradiated metal cladding for nuclear reactor fuel, reactor components, and chemical process residues and filters. They have a lower radioactivity and heat output than HLW but their

radioactivity content exceeds the upper limits for LLW. LLW includes concrete, rubble and soil from building demolition, discarded protective clothing and worn out or damaged plant and equipment. LLW do not normally require shielding against radiation emissions during handling and transport. LLW volumes are reported, in most cases, as the volumes before supercompaction and grouting before disposal.

The table shows recent trends in the volume of radioactive waste stocks for particular groups of nuclear sites. Data are presented in two physical states – as stored and conditioned. 'As stored' is the form in which the waste is currently stored. For the majority of LLW, storage is short term prior to disposal. 'Conditioned' is the form of waste suitable for long-term storage (i.e. vitrified) in the case of HLW or ultimate disposal to deep underground repositories in the case of ILW. There is no simple relationship between as-stored and conditioned volumes of waste, since the effects of conditioning can vary with different wastes. Conditioning of HLW has yet to start at Dounreay. Volume indicates predicted final conditioned volume. Estimates of conditioned wastes are indicative only and should be interpreted with care.

The table excludes waste from defence establishments prior to 1991. Such ILW and LLW will add no more than 20 per cent to the volumes of radioactive waste from civil sources before 1991.

Annual waste arisings

(Table 13.17)

Agriculture: The estimate is derived from a survey of agricultural waste commissioned by Environment Agency/ Defra and relates to Great Britain.

Mining and quarrying: The minerals waste estimate is based on ratios of waste to product.

Sewage sludge: The estimate of sewage sludge arisings has been made on the basis of dry weight (wet weight can be estimated on the basis of 4 per cent solid content on average – giving a total of 26,450,000 tonnes).

Dredged material: The data for dredged material are for all UK waters.

Municipal waste: The UK estimate for municipal waste is based on survey returns made by local Authorities in England and Wales.

Commercial and industrial: UK totals estimated from figures for England and Wales, based on survey by the Environment Agency.

Demolition and construction: UK total estimated from figures for England and Wales, based on survey by the Department for Communities and Local Government.

Noise complaints

(Table 13.19)

The table shows trends in the number of complaints received by local authority Environmental Health Officers (EHOs) in England and Wales. The figures are from those authorities making returns and are calculated per million people based on the population of the authorities making returns.

Most complaints about traffic noise are usually addressed to highways authorities or Department for Transport (DfT) Regional Directors, and will not necessarily be included in the figures. Similarly, complaints about noise from civil aircraft are generally received by aircraft operators, the airport companies, the DfT or Civil Aviation Authority. Complaints about military flying are dealt with either by Station Commanding Officers or by Ministry of Defence headquarters. It is also true that railway noise will be reported elsewhere. Thus the figures in this table will not necessarily include these complaints and are likely to be considerably understated. Therefore the information reported to the EHOs is considered to give, at best, only a very approximate indication of the trend in noise complaints from these sources.

Over time some of the categories shown in this table have changed. These have included:- Up until 1996/97 Section 62 of the Control of Pollution Act 1974 covered noise in the streets – it primarily included the chimes of ice-cream vendors and the use of loudspeakers other than for strictly defined purposes. From 1997/98 all complaints about noise in the street are included with 'vehicles machinery and equipment in streets'. From 1997/98 complaints about road works are included with 'vehicles machinery and equipment in streets'. The use of the category 'Other' was discontinued in England and Wales from 1997/98. It included some complaints not covered by the other specified sources, but also those where the source was not certain or was due to more than one source. From 1997/98 in England and Wales more vigorous procedures have allocated complaints to the most appropriate source.

Material flows

(Table 13.20)

Economy-wide material flow accounts record the total mass of natural resources and products that are used by the UK economy, either directly in the production and distribution of products and services, or indirectly through the movement of materials which are displaced in order for production to take place.

The direct movement of materials into the economy derives primarily from domestic extraction, that is from biomass (agricultural harvest, timber, fish and animal grazing), fossil fuel extraction (such as coal, crude oil and natural gas) and mineral extraction (metal ores, industrial minerals such as pottery clay, and construction material such as crushed rock, sand and gravel). This domestic extraction is supplemented by the imports of products, which may be of raw materials such as unprocessed agricultural products, but can also be semi-manufactured or finished products. In a similar way the UK produces exports of raw materials, semi-manufactured and finished goods which can be viewed as inputs to the production and consumption of overseas economies.

Indirect flows of natural resources consist of the unused material resulting from domestic extraction such as mining and quarrying overburden and the soil removed during construction and dredging activities. They also include the movement of used and unused material overseas which is associated with the production and delivery of imports. Water – except for that included directly in products – is excluded from the accounts.

There are three main indicators used to measure inputs. The *Direct Material Input (DMI)* measures the input of used materials into the economy, that is all materials which are of economic value and are used in production and consumption activities (including the production of exports). *Domestic material consumption (DMC)* measures the total amount of material directly used in the economy, ie it includes imports but excludes exports. The *Total Material Requirement (TMR)* measures the total material basis of the economy, that is the total primary resource requirements of all the production and consumption activities. It includes not only the direct use of resources for producing exports, but also indirect flows from the production of imports and the indirect flows associated with domestic extraction. Although TMR is widely favoured as a resource use indicator, the estimates of indirect flows are less reliable than those for materials directly used by the economy, and the indicator therefore needs to be considered alongside other indicators.

Designated areas

(Table 13.21)

National Parks, Areas of Outstanding Natural Beauty (AONB's) in England, Wales and Northern Ireland and National Scenic Areas in Scotland are the major areas which have been designated to protect their landscape importance. National Scenic Areas in Scotland are the equivalent of AONB's in England, Wales and Northern Ireland.

Environment

Some areas may be in more than one category. All areas shown in the table are at March 2005, except for Green Belt land which relates to 1 January 1997.

The area for Green Belt land is based on a new methodology in which the extent of Green Belt land is captured in digital form. This approach provides much more reliable figures than those previously published in earlier years.

Further details regarding tables 13.2 to 13.7, 13.9, 13.13 to 13.18 and 13.21 can be found in Defra's e-*Digest of Environmental Statistics* (on the Defra website at: www.defra. gov.uk/environment/statistics/index.htm). If you would like to discuss the tables, Adrian Redfern can be contacted at Defra on 020 7082 8608.

13.1 Estimated atmospheric emissions on a National Accounts basis,[1] 2003
United Kingdom

Thousand tonnes

| | Greenhouse gases[2] | Acid rain precursors[3] | Emissions affecting air quality | | | | | | | | |
			PM$_{10}$	Carbon monoxide	Volatile organic compounds[4]	Benzene	Butadiene	Lead	Cadmium (Tonnes)	Mercury (Tonnes)
Agriculture	48 413	490.05	17.77	24.94	76.34	0.09	0.02	0.11	0.010	0.008
Mining and quarrying	30 500	65.21	10.50	47.61	198.6	0.32	0.02	0.21	0.051	0.019
Manufacturing	129 267	436.82	35.92	771.39	355.29	2.95	0.51	97.74	3.992	3.410
Electricity, gas and water supply	192 598	938.24	11.27	92.32	54.66	0.60	0.02	22.83	0.629	1.786
Construction	7 392	21.92	6.15	39.58	56.72	0.07	0.05	4.11	0.040	0.010
Wholesale and retail trade	17 523	44.84	5.22	50.53	74.08	0.17	0.15	0.16	0.030	0.005
Transport and communication	95 745	855.09	18.38	155.34	46.43	3.22	0.78	4.19	3.163	0.180
Other business services	6 964	14.89	2.07	45.62	4.89	0.06	0.04	0.14	0.055	0.005
Public administration	9 514	33.32	1.16	28.36	2.36	1.70	1.51	0.43	0.060	0.035
Education, health and social work	10 992	17.11	0.82	6.28	1.76	0.04	0.00	0.34	0.072	0.027
Other services	15 807	45.05	1.51	33.05	12.89	0.92	0.04	0.36	0.034	1.861
Domestic	157 612	312.08	38.14	1 549.67	291.80	11.03	1.11	6.13	0.366	0.185
Total	722 328	3 275	149	2 845	1 176	21	4	137	9	8
Of which, emissions from road transport	127 804	479	38.6	1 366.26	162.74	2.02	1.91	2.02	0.42	0.004

1 See chapter text.
2 Thousand tonnes of carbon dioxide equivalent.
3 Thousand tonnes of sulphur dioxide equivalent.
4 Excluding methane, but including benzene and 1,3-butadiene.

Sources: National Environmental Technology Centre;
Office for National Statistics: 020 7533 5904

13.2 Estimated emissions[1] of greenhouse gases on an IPCC basis[2]: 1990 to 2004
United Kingdom

Million tonnes (Carbon dioxide equivalent[3])

		1990	1994	1995	1996	1997	1998	1999	2000	2001	2002	2003	2004
Net CO_2 emissions/removals	JZCK	592.1	559.1	549.7	571.4	548.4	550.2	540.8	546.3	561.5	544.9	556.4	559.1
Methane(CH_4)	GXDO	91.9	80.5	79.9	77.9	73.9	70.0	63.2	59.9	54.3	52.2	47.2	45.9
Nitrous oxide(N_2O)	GXDP	68.3	58.6	57.0	58.8	60.5	57.6	44.4	44.2	42.1	40.4	40.1	40.7
Hydrofluorocarbons(HFCs)	JZCN	11.38	14.01	15.49	16.72	19.18	17.27	10.83	9.08	9.67	9.89	10.19	8.86
Perfluorocarbons(PFCs)	JZCO	1.40	0.49	0.47	0.49	0.42	0.42	0.40	0.50	0.43	0.32	0.30	0.35
Sulphur hexafluoride(SF_6)	JZCP	1.03	1.18	1.24	1.27	1.23	1.26	1.43	1.80	1.42	1.51	1.32	1.13
Kyoto greenhouse gas basket[4]	F92X	763.3	713.1	702.6	725.3	702.5	695.9	660.3	661.1	668.8	649.0	655.1	656.2
1990 Baseline[5]	GXJK	768.3	..	..	..	..	..	..	..	..	..	..	..
Percentage change for basket from 1990 baseline	GXDR	−0.6	−7.2	−8.5	−5.6	−8.6	−9.4	−14.0	−13.9	−12.9	−15.5	−14.7	−14.6

1 Net emissions weighted by global warming potential. Emissions inventories based on the methodology developed by the Intergovernmental Panel on Climate Change (IPCC) are used to report UK emissions to the Climate Change Convention.
2 See chapter text.
3 12 tonnes of carbon is equivalent to 44 tonnes of carbon dioxide.
4 Kyoto basket total differs slightly from sum of individual pollutants above as the basket uses a narrower definition for the Land Use Change and Forestry sector, and includes emissions from UK Overseas Territories.

5 The base year used for the Kyoto Protocol consists of 1990 emissions of CO_2 (without LUCF), CH_4 and N_2O and 1995 emissions of HFCs, PFCs and SF_6. In addition there is a small allowance (equal to 0.1 million tonnes carbon for net emissions from deforestation in 1990, as allowed under Article 3.7 of the Kyoto Protocol). It is used as the baseline against which progress is measured, to meet the UK commitment of a 12.5 per cent reduction in greenhouse gas emissions, required by the Kyoto Protocol.

Sources: National Environmental Technology Centre;
for Department for Environment, Food and Rural Affairs 020 7082 8608

13.3 Estimated emissions of sulphur dioxide (SO_2): by source[1]
United Kingdom

Thousand tonnes

		1970	1980	1990	1994	1995	1996	1997	1998	1999	2000	2001	2002	2003	2004
By source category (UNECE/EMEP)		*Percentage of total in 2004*													
Energy industries	EU62	*68*	3 349	3 296	2 888	1 902	1 738	1 469	1 144	1 160	849	888	796	733	730	565
Manufacturing industries and construction	EU63	*19*	1 850	908	422	398	317	255	249	222	180	147	183	154	140	158
Road transport	EU64	*-*	46	43	64	64	52	38	28	23	14	7	4	4	4	4
Other transport	EU65	*4*	45	32	31	33	32	32	30	28	25	23	18	17	28	35
Commercial and institutional	EU66	*-*	412	193	79	69	50	48	40	27	20	14	17	9	8	4
Residential	EU67	*4*	521	226	113	97	71	76	67	57	54	47	49	42	31	33
Agriculture and Forestry fuel use	EU68	*-*	45	27	11	12	10	10	8	7	7	4	4	4	4	4
Military aircraft and shipping	EU69	*1*	9	9	9	8	8	8	8	6	6	6	6	5	4	5
Fugitive emissions from fuels	EU6A	*1*	62	39	28	23	17	19	19	17	10	9	10	7	9	10
Industrial processes	EU6B	*2*	59	59	46	40	43	42	41	41	36	26	23	18	16	14
Waste treatment and disposal	EU6C	*-*	8	8	7	4	4	3	1	1	1	1	2	1	1	1
Total	EU6D	*100*	6 407	4 838	3 699	2 649	2 343	1 999	1 635	1 591	1 202	1 173	1 111	994	973	833
Emissions from large combustion plants																
Large combustion plants	EU6E		3 732	3 457	2 934	1 969	1 756	1 468	1 107	1 208	881	873	762	658	715	539
Index (1980=100)	ZBZL		108	100	85	57	51	42	32	35	25	25	22	19	21	16

1 See chapter text.

Sources: National Environmental Technology Centre; Environment Agency; for Department for Environment, Food and Rural Affairs 020 7082 8608

13.4 Estimated emissions of PM_{10}: by source[1]
United Kingdom

Thousand tonnes

		1970	1980	1990	1994	1995	1996	1997	1998	1999	2000	2001	2002	2003	2004
By source category (UNECE/EMEP)		*Percentage of total in 2004*													
Energy industries	EVH5	*7*	84	83	74	54	43	40	37	29	23	26	19	11	10	11
Manufacturing industries and construction	EVH6	*16*	69	39	37	34	33	32	31	31	28	25	26	24	24	24
Road transport	EVH7	*23*	42	51	60	56	54	51	47	45	43	39	38	37	36	35
Other transport	EVH8	*1*	2	2	2	2	2	2	2	2	2	2	2	2	2	2
Commercial and institutional	EVH9	*-*	17	8	5	3	3	3	3	2	2	1	2	1	1	1
Residential	EVI2	*17*	210	95	50	41	33	35	34	35	35	29	32	30	25	26
Agriculture and Forestry fuel use	EVI3	*5*	11	10	11	11	11	11	11	11	10	10	10	9	9	8
Military aircraft and shipping	EVI4	*-*	–	–	–	–	–	–	–	–	–	–	–	–	–	–
Fugitive emissions from fuels	EVI5	*1*	1	3	2	2	2	2	2	2	2	1	1	1	1	1
Industrial processes	EVI6	*12*	27	23	28	26	25	25	24	22	21	20	20	19	19	19
Solvent and other product use	EVI7	*4*	7	7	8	7	6	6	6	6	6	6	5	5	5	5
Agriculture	EVI8	*9*	11	12	13	12	12	13	15	14	14	14	14	14	14	14
Waste treatment and disposal	EVI9	*4*	8	8	8	7	7	7	6	6	6	6	10	6	6	6
Other	EVJ2	*1*	1	1	1	1	1	1	1	1	1	1	1	1	1	1
Total	EVJ3	*100*	490	342	299	258	232	227	219	205	193	180	180	160	155	154

1 See chapter text.

Sources: National Environmental Technology Centre; Environment Agency; for Department for Environment, Food and Rural Affairs 020 7082 8608

13.5 Estimated emissions of nitrogen oxides (NO$_x$): by source[1]
United Kingdom

Thousand tonnes

By source category (UNECE/EMEP)		Percentage of total in 2004	1970	1980	1990	1994	1995	1996	1997	1998	1999	2000	2001	2002	2003	2004
Energy industries	EVJ6	27	1 334	937	853	590	557	512	432	428	385	413	433	431	457	445
Manufacturing industries and construction	EVJ7	16	585	423	369	358	344	320	319	319	309	291	295	264	267	263
Road transport	EVJ8	37	765	989	1 324	1 141	1 098	1 068	1 014	960	900	818	749	691	634	595
Other transport	EVJ9	6	79	87	96	91	90	97	95	93	89	88	74	71	96	97
Commercial and institutional	EVK2	1	66	43	34	36	35	37	34	33	33	30	31	26	29	19
Residential	EVK3	7	121	109	104	110	104	119	109	112	111	112	116	114	114	116
Agriculture and Forestry fuel use	EVK4	4	72	74	76	77	77	77	78	76	75	72	70	67	63	58
Military aircraft and shipping	EVK5	1	32	32	35	28	28	28	28	22	23	22	21	20	16	20
Fugitive emissions from fuels	EVK6	-	1	7	14	14	14	11	5	4	5	4	4	4	3	3
Industrial processes	EVK7	-	13	14	11	7	5	4	5	4	4	4	3	2	3	3
Agriculture	EVK8	-	10	15	9	–	–	–	–	–	–	–	–	–	–	–
Land-use change and forestry	EVK9	-	..	..	–	–	–	–	–	–	–	–	–	–	–	–
Waste treatment and disposal	EVL2	-	8	8	7	5	5	5	2	2	2	2	3	2	2	2
Total	EVL3	100	3 085	2 737	2 933	2 456	2 355	2 278	2 121	2 052	1 937	1 857	1 799	1 693	1 685	1 621
Emissions from large combustion plants																
Large combustion plants (LCPs)	EVL4		939	955	848	572	524	471	371	369	320	343	359	316	368	355
Index (1980=100)	ZBZN		98	100	89	60	55	49	39	39	34	36	38	33	39	37

1 See chapter text.

Sources: National Environmental Technology Centre; Environment Agency; for Department for Environment, Food and Rural Affairs 020 7082 8608

13.6 Estimated emissions of carbon monoxide (CO):[1] by source
United Kingdom

Thousand tonnes

By source category (UNECE/EMEP)		Percentage of total in 2004	1970	1980	1990	1994	1995	1996	1997	1998	1999	2000	2001	2002	2003	2004
Energy industries	EVL5	3	173	140	131	126	123	121	70	81	73	83	80	77	84	84
Manufacturing industries and construction	EVL6	22	1 271	655	780	753	769	775	764	753	782	675	794	765	620	642
Road transport	EVL7	47	5 353	5 390	5 480	4 455	4 180	3 999	3 664	3 337	3 003	2 500	2 128	1 856	1 597	1 368
Other transport	EVL8	2	91	58	45	45	45	49	54	54	61	68	71	62	61	68
Commercial and institutional	EVL9	-	55	28	15	11	9	10	10	8	8	7	8	7	6	5
Residential	EVM2	17	4 504	2 152	1 197	1 116	859	878	807	763	763	651	717	619	491	509
Agriculture and Forestry fuel use	EVM3	1	38	38	39	39	39	39	39	39	38	38	37	37	37	37
Military aircraft and shipping	EVM4	-	11	11	13	10	10	10	9	8	8	7	7	8	7	7
Fugitive emissions from fuels	EVM5	1	92	87	60	55	55	54	49	48	41	39	28	21	23	19
Industrial processes	EVM6	5	162	158	225	219	223	225	230	208	201	182	183	131	142	149
Agriculture	EVM7	-	288	449	266	–	–	–	–	–	–	–	–	–	–	–
Land-use change and forestry	EVM8	-	..	..	6	5	5	6	6	6	7	8	10	8	8	7
Waste treatment and disposal	EVM9	1	28	28	29	28	28	28	27	28	29	28	50	28	29	29
Other	EVN2	-	6	6	6	6	6	6	6	6	6	6	6	6	6	6
Total	EVN3	100	12 072	9 201	8 292	6 867	6 350	6 200	5 734	5 338	5 021	4 293	4 119	3 625	3 110	2 930

1 See chapter text.

Sources: National Environmental Technology Centre; Environment Agency; for Department for Environment, Food and Rural Affairs 020 7082 8608

13.7 Estimated emissions of volatile organic compounds (VOCs): by source[1]
United Kingdom

Thousand tonnes

		Percentage of total in 2004	1970	1980	1990	1994	1995	1996	1997	1998	1999	2000	2001	2002	2003	2004
By source category (UNECE/EMEP)																
Energy industries	EVN4	1	8	9	8	8	8	9	7	5	5	7	6	7	6	6
Manufacturing industries and construction	EVN5	4	43	38	39	38	39	39	39	40	38	39	38	38	37	36
Road transport	EVN6	14	524	652	867	700	634	560	506	436	376	303	249	210	175	144
Other transport	EVN7	1	6	6	6	6	6	6	7	6	7	7	6	6	6	7
Commercial and institutional	EVN8	-	1	1	1	1	1	1	1	1	1	1	1	1	1	1
Residential	EVN9	5	327	162	100	88	77	77	73	72	72	62	64	59	52	53
Agriculture and Forestry fuel use	EVO2	1	12	12	13	13	13	13	13	13	12	12	12	11	11	11
Military aircraft and shipping	EVO3	-	2	2	2	2	2	2	2	1	1	1	1	1	1	1
Fugitive emissions from fuels	EVO4	20	173	356	381	385	357	341	369	330	303	310	295	280	230	208
Industrial processes	EVO5	14	193	220	256	232	239	233	214	195	165	155	148	143	142	145
Solvent and other product use	EVO6	39	590	577	670	578	538	527	513	496	463	433	415	402	397	397
Agriculture	EVO7	-	31	46	26	–	–	–	–	–	–	–	–	–	–	–
Waste treatment and disposal	EVO8	1	25	27	27	25	25	24	23	22	20	19	17	16	16	15
Total	EVO9	100	1 936	2 111	2 396	2 077	1 939	1 832	1 766	1 617	1 463	1 348	1 252	1 175	1 073	1 024

1 See chapter text.

Sources: National Environmental Technology Centre; Environment Agency; for Department for Environment, Food and Rural Affairs 020 7082 8608

13.8 Annual rainfall: by region
United Kingdom

Millimetres and percentages

		1961 - 1990 rainfall average (= 100%) millimetres	Annual rainfall as a percentage of the 1961-1990 average										
			1995	1996	1997	1998	1999	2000	2001	2002	2003	2004	2005
Region[1]													
United Kingdom	JSJB	1 080	95	85	95	117	115	124	97	119	83	112	100
North West	JSJC	1 201	81	78	90	115	109	129	92	118	84	113	94
Northumbria	JSJD	853	91	81	93	120	103	129	104	122	79	117	108
Severn Trent	JSJE	754	87	80	96	116	121	133	105	120	82	111	93
Yorkshire	JSJF	821	82	83	92	114	109	135	99	124	81	113	95
Anglian	JSJG	596	90	78	95	120	115	130	125	120	87	117	90
Thames	JSLK	688	99	78	89	119	112	140	118	130	82	104	80
Southern	JSLL	778	96	82	99	111	107	149	115	131	86	98	80
Wessex	JSLM	839	107	90	101	119	121	140	103	136	86	101	92
South West	JSLN	1 173	98	94	100	121	116	131	94	124	80	101	92
England	JSLO	823	90	81	94	116	112	133	105	122	82	108	91
Wales[2]	JSLP	1 355	89	86	94	122	117	135	100	120	84	110	96
Scotland	JSLQ	1 436	100	85	95	117	116	113	91	113	84	117	110
Northern Ireland	JSLR	1 059	102	103	98	119	117	115	85	133	88	103	101

1 The regions of England shown in this table correspond to the original nine English regions of the National Rivers Authority (NRA); the NRA became part of the Environment Agency upon its creation in April 1996.

2 The figures in this table relate to the country of Wales, not the Environment Agency Welsh Region.

Sources: The Met Office; Centre for Ecology and Hydrology, Wallingford: 01491 838800

13.9 Biological[1] and chemical[2] quality of rivers and canals[3]
England, Wales and Northern Ireland

Kilometres and percentages

| | | Length surveyed | | | | | | | Percentage of total | |
| | | Good | | Fair | | | | | | |
	Years	A	B	C	D	Poor E	Bad F	Total	Good or fair	Poor or bad
Biological quality										
North East	1990	590	770	300	160	140	30	1 990	91	9
	2004	950	750	210	100	50	10	2 080	97	3
North West	1990	450	1 200	630	340	700	460	3 770	69	31
	2004	960	1 630	980	610	430	70	4 700	89	11
Yorkshire and the Humber	1990	790	500	340	250	210	220	2 330	81	19
	2004	1 450	880	560	390	220	70	3 590	92	8
East Midlands	1990	340	790	1 140	320	160	40	2 800	93	7
	2004	860	1 190	920	270	120	0	3 360	96	4
West Midlands	1990	440	580	560	350	120	80	2 130	91	9
	2004	900	1180	870	410	290	100	3 750	89	11
East	1990	620	1 130	930	240	100	20	3 040	96	4
	2004	1 460	1 190	560	150	60	0	3 430	98	2
London	1990	-	30	80	80	80	20	290	65	35
	2004	10	90	110	100	50	10	360	83	17
South East	1990	1 020	1 180	700	240	130	30	3 290	95	5
	2004	1 770	1 520	670	220	40	0	4 220	99	1
South West	1990	2 380	2 300	720	220	120	60	5 800	97	3
	2004	3 720	1 770	560	130	50	30	6 260	99	1
England[4]	1990	6 980	9 010	5 640	2 300	1 850	990	26 770	89	11
	2004	12 850	11 020	5 780	2 540	1 420	290	33 900	95	5
Wales	1990	1 240	1 380	480	180	50	10	3 330	98	2
	2004	1 360	2 320	810	100	40	0	4 630	99	1
Northern Ireland	1991	710	950	410	100	10	-	2 190	100	-
	2004	720	2 070	1 830	710	120	10	5 460	98	2
Chemical quality										
North East	1990	230	560	170	70	70	30	1 130	92	8
	2004	890	830	230	40	60	10	2 060	97	3
North West	1990	660	590	520	440	610	200	3 030	73	27
	2004	2 020	1 280	1 100	570	370	90	5 430	92	8
Yorkshire and the Humber	1990	590	1 050	400	370	610	160	3 180	76	24
	2004	1 060	1 460	740	400	340	20	4 030	91	9
East Midlands	1990	50	560	1 120	700	550	80	3 060	79	21
	2004	490	1 440	1 030	380	200	10	3 540	94	6
West Midlands	1990	190	1 150	840	610	540	80	3 420	82	18
	2004	790	1 350	980	380	290	50	3 820	91	9
East	1990	50	690	1 350	790	570	70	3 510	82	18
	2004	210	1 300	1 170	520	360	10	3 560	90	10
London	1990	-	50	120	110	110	10	390	71	29
	2004	0	120	100	100	80	10	410	79	21
South East	1990	330	1 380	1 350	550	610	60	4 290	84	16
	2004	740	1 680	1 180	520	290	10	4 410	93	7
South West	1990	1 590	2 320	1 280	720	380	60	6 360	93	7
	2004	2 570	2 500	920	300	200	20	6 500	97	3
England[4]	1990	4 200	9 160	7 670	4 640	4 300	770	30 740	84	16
	2004	9 390	12 700	7 790	3 450	2 340	240	35 910	93	7
Wales	1990	1 830	1 210	270	130	60	30	3 520	98	2
	2004	3 440	1 080	130	60	70	0	4 790	98	2
Northern Ireland	1991	100	640	680	170	60	20	1 680	95	5
	2004	580	2 270	1 350	390	280	50	4 920	93	7

1 Based on the River Invertebrate Prediction and Classification System (RIVPACS).
2 Based on the General Quality Assessment (GQA) chemical classification system.
3 See chapter text.

4 Figures for the English regions will not add to the national figure for England because a small amount of river lengths which are located along the border between England and Wales are counted in both the national figures for England and Wales.

*Sources: Environment Agency;
Environment and Heritage Service*

13.10 Water quality of rivers and canals[1]
Scotland

Kilometres and percentages

	Excellent A1	Good A2	Unclassified assumed good	Fair B	Poor C	Seriously polluted D	Total	Good or fair[2]	Poor or seriously polluted
			Length surveyed					Percentage of total	

Scottish Environment Protection Agency Regions

Highlands, Islands and Grampian

	DYO4	DYO5	DYO6	DYO7	DYO8	DYO9	DYP2	DYP3	DYP4
1999	..	..	..	480	150	30	11 400	..	2
2000	960	1 650	8 260	390	140	10	11 400	99	1
2001	1 420	1 560	7 950	380	90	20	11 420	99	1
2002	2 020	3 480	5 140	660	90	10	11 400	99	1
2003	2 610	4 310	3 950	430	90	10	11 390	99	1
2004	3 330	5 010	2 570	370	110	10	11 390	99	1

South East Scotland

	DYP5	DYP6	DYP7	DYP8	DYP9	DYQ2	DYQ3	DYQ4	DYQ5
1999	1 120	1 890	2 700	900	450	20	7 090	93	7
2000	1 430	2 270	2 120	920	390	20	7 160	94	6
2001	1 520	2 450	1 670	1 000	520	20	7 170	93	7
2002	2 260	2 800	610	980	510	10	7 160	93	7
2003	2 570	2 810	430	990	360	10	7 160	95	5
2004	2 550	2 810	300	1 170	310	20	7 160	95	5

South West Scotland

	DYQ6	DYQ7	DYQ8	DYQ9	DYR2	DYR3	DYR4	DYR5	DYR6
1999	580	2 260	2 340	1 200	470	40	6 890	93	7
2000	780	2 170	2 440	1 150	320	30	6 900	95	5
2001	930	2 320	2 340	960	320	40	6 920	95	5
2002	1 000	2 370	2 230	930	310	40	6 880	95	5
2003	1 630	2 430	1 530	960	300	40	6 880	95	5
2004	1 780	2 790	940	1 050	300	30	6 880	95	5

Scotland

	DZ38	DZ39	DZ3A	DZ3B	DZ3C	DZ3D	DZ3E	DZ3F	DZ3G
1999	..	..	..	2 580	1 080	90	25 380	..	5
2000	3 170	6 090	12 820	2 450	850	70	25 450	96	4
2001	3 870	6 320	11 960	2 340	930	80	25 510	96	4
2002	5 280	8 660	7 990	2 560	900	60	25 440	96	4
2003	6 820	9 540	5 900	2 370	750	50	25 440	97	3
2004	7 660	10 610	3 810	2 590	720	50	25 430	97	3

1 See chapter text.
2 Classes A1, A2, B and unclassified.

Source: Scottish Environmental Protection Agency: 01786 457700

13.11 Water reservoir stocks:[1] by month
England and Wales

Percentages

		1995	1996	1997	1998	1999	2000	2001	2002	2003	2004	2005
January	JTAS	95.1	61.2	79.1	90.5	95.8	95.8	94.8	86.5	95.1	79.9	91.2
February	JTAT	97.9	71.3	75.6	93.1	97.0	95.9	94.4	93.7	95.0	93.8	92.3
March	JTAU	98.3	81.8	91.6	92.3	96.5	97.4	95.0	95.5	92.1	92.1	92.1
April	JTAV	97.3	84.9	92.3	96.9	96.9	95.2	95.5	94.5	92.3	94.4	93.6
May	JTAW	92.7	86.2	87.1	97.0	97.0	97.0	96.7	91.9	88.6	94.7	95.0
June	JTAX	87.6	88.1	87.7	93.9	95.4	95.7	91.9	97.0	93.1	90.5	93.0
July	JTAY	79.5	82.2	87.8	95.1	92.0	93.8	85.1	94.9	87.0	84.8	85.6
August	JTAZ	69.1	73.4	81.3	93.5	82.6	88.5	80.7	91.1	81.1	78.5	77.9
September	JTBA	52.8	63.0	73.8	88.3	76.9	83.2	77.9	85.9	69.9	82.4	71.5
October	JTBB	47.3	54.6	70.6	86.6	79.7	88.0	77.0	77.3	60.4	84.2	67.4
November	JTBC	51.6	63.3	69.1	93.3	81.7	95.2	85.5	82.9	53.0	87.5	77.2
December	JTBD	56.5	77.3	76.4	93.1	84.9	96.7	87.9	91.8	60.9	86.2	83.8

1 Reservoir stocks are the percentage of useable capacity based on a representative selection of reservoirs; the percentages relate to beginning of each month.

Sources: Water PLCs;
Environment Agency;
Centre for Ecology and Hydrology, Wallingford: 01491 838800

13.12 Water industry expenditure[1]
England and Wales

£ million

		1993/94	1994/95	1995/96	1996/97	1997/98	1998/99	1999/00	2000/01	2001/02	2002/03	2003/04
Operating expenditure												
Water supply	KQQX	2 113.5	2 215.0	2 319.6	2 314.9	2 339.3	2 386.1	2 448.1	2 391.0	2 426.9	2 544.2	2 676.5
Sewerage services	KQQY	1 757.0	1 764.0	1 738.4	1 780.7	1 854.6	1 971.3	2 069.8	2 087.1	2 167.6	2 265.2	2 319.4
Capital expenditure												
Water supply	KQSX	1 386.7	1 081.0	1 074.5	1 314.3	1 467.2	1 294.1	1 290.0	935.0	1 132.5	1 347.1	1 346.4
Sewerage	KQSY	410.7	381.0	375.6	479.9	455.2	507.5	488.5	352.0	362.4	507.2	617.6
Sewage treatment and disposal	KQSZ	735.3	763.0	773.0	959.4	1 296.3	1 374.5	1 440.8	1 040.9	996.0	1 066.2	1 235.6

1 See chapter text.

Source: Office of Water Services: 0121 625 1312

13.13 Water pollution incidents[1]
United Kingdom

Numbers

		1992	1993	1994	1995	1996	1997	1998		2001[2]	2002[2]	2003	2004
Categories 1 to 3													
Environment Agency Regions													
North West	JZIA	3 270	3 656	3 532	3 717	2 818	2 160	2 201	MKDB	1 734	1 805	1 534	1 091
North East	JZIB	3 059	3 642	2 576	2 143	2 404	1 993	MKDC	1 952	1 789	1 971	1 692
Midlands	JZKR	4 420	4 876	4 895	4 259	4 305	4 411	4 061	MKDD	2 862	2 843	2 464	1 955
Anglian	JZKS	2 462	2 625	2 819	2 156	2 417	2 411	2 163	MKDE	1 606	1 716	1 616	1 418
Thames	JZKT	1 955	2 071	2 006	1 972	1 959	1 917	1 819	MKDF	1 510	1 630	1 447	1 211
Southern	JZKU	1 089	1 355	1 316	1 235	1 189	1 174	1 138	MKDG	1 585	1 511	1 543	1 218
South West	JZKV	4 278	4 129	4 340	4 558	3 042	2 847	2 603	MKDH	2 292	1 929	1 882	1 689
Welsh	JZKW	2 798	2 945	3 264	2 990	2 285	2 247	1 885	MKDI	1 475	1 287	1 356	1 309
England and Wales	JZKX	23 331	25 299	25 415	23 463	20 158	19 571	17 863	MKDJ	15 016	14 510	13 813	11 583
Scotland[3]	JZKY	3 020	3 081	3 170	2 752	2 878	3 356	2 329	MKDK	1 829	1 409	1 708	1 480
Northern Ireland	JZKZ	..	..	..	..	2 087	1 826	1 644	MKDL	1 546	1 510	1 551	1 227
By category in England and Wales													
Category 1	MKCW	388	331	229	199	156	194	128	MKDM	118	82	94	114
Category 2	MKCX	..	6 768	6 567	2 194	1 510	1 354	1 238	MKDN	860	784	685	594
Category 3	MKCY	..	18 200	18 619	21 070	18 492	18 023	16 497	MKDO	14 038	13 644	13 034	10 875
Category 4[2,4]	MKCZ	..	..	..	..	..	..	..	MKDP	18 706	15 370	15 813	13 613
Total substantiated incidents[4]	MKDA	23 331	25 299	25 415	23 463	20 158	19 571	17 863	MKDQ	33 722	29 880	29 626	25 196

1 See chapter text. Substantiated incidents to water, unless otherwise specified.
2 From 1999, categories 1-3 do not include all substantiated incidents to water. An additional category (Category 4) was introduced which includes all incidents which were substantiated, but which had no impact on the water environment. Therefore, data are not comparable to previous years

3 Data for all years refer to financial years.
4 Category 4 and Total substantiated incidents include incidents to other media (air, land), which did not involve the water environment.

Sources: Environment Agency;
Scottish Environment Protection Agency;
Environment and Heritage Service

13.14 Bathing water:[1] by region
United Kingdom

Numbers and percentages

		Identified bathing waters (numbers)						Numbers complying						Percentage complying
		2001	2002	2003	2004	2005		2001	2002	2003	2004	2005		2005
Coastal bathing waters														
Environment Agency Regions														
United Kingdom	GPKA	546	547	554	556	559	GPKN	520	535	545	543	550	GPLA	98
North East	GPKB	55	56	55	55	55	GPKO	55	55	53	53	53	GPLB	96
North West	GPKC	34	34	34	34	34	GPKP	30	33	33	33	32	GPLC	94
Anglian	GPKE	37	38	38	38	39	GPKR	36	38	38	38	39	GPLE	100
Thames	GPKF	5	5	8	8	8	GPKS	5	5	8	8	8	GPLF	100
Southern	GPKG	79	79	79	79	79	GPKT	78	78	79	78	79	GPLG	100
South West	GPKH	187	186	188	190	190	GPKU	184	183	186	187	189	GPLH	99
England	GPKI	397	398	402	404	405	GPKV	388	392	397	397	400	GPLI	99
Wales	GPKJ	75	75	78	78	80	GPKW	70	75	77	78	80	GPLJ	100
Scotland	GPKL	58	58	58	58	58	GPKY	49	53	55	54	55	GPLL	95
Northern Ireland	GPKM	16	16	16	16	16	GPKZ	13	15	16	14	15	GPLM	94
Inland bathing waters														
United Kingdom	JTIG	11	11	11	11	11	JTIH	11	11	11	11	11	JTII	100

Compliance with EC Bathing Water Directive coliform standards during the bathing season

1 See chapter text.

Sources: Environment Agency;
Scottish Environment Protection Agency;
Environment and Heritage Service, Northern Ireland

13.15 Estimated abstractions from all surface and groundwater sources: by purpose[1]
England and Wales

Megalitres per day

		1993	1994	1995	1996	1997	1998	1999	2000	2001	2002	2003
Public water supply	JZLA	16 651	16 735	17 346	17 453	16 820	16 765	16 255	16 990	16 231	16 937	16 920
Spray irrigation	JZLB	164	283	352	369	292	282	325	291	259	248	315
Agriculture (excl spray irrigation)	JZLC	139	115	103	136	108	111	142	152	108	120	132
Electricity supply industry[2,3]	JZLD	26 581	27 732	29 510	31 294	33 307	34 587	29 490	31 546	32 263	35 447	31 378
Other industry	JZLE	6 017	4 292	3 808	4 960	4 352	4 964	5 428	5 433	4 772	4 883	6 623
Mineral washing	JZLF	198	222	262	250	297	223	..	..	..	..	..
Fish farming, cress growing, amenity ponds	JYXG	3 818	3 985	4 268	4 338	4 211	5 495	4 867	4 709	4 657	3 215	3 077
Private water supply	JZLG	81	82	98	171	162	175	91	102	92	54	61
Other	JZLH	93	194	223	531	408	289	526	559	108	77	86
Total	JZLI	53 742	53 640	55 970	59 503	59 957	62 891	57 123	59 782	58 489	60 981	58 593

1 See chapter text.
2 In South West region in 1992, Hydroelectric licences were classified as "Other", in 1993 they were classified as "Other industry" and from 1994 they were classified correctly as "Electricity supply".

3 A new power station was commissioned in the Thames region in 1994 and began abstracting from tidal waters in 1995. In the Southern region a power station was demolished and rebuilt in 1998-1999.

Source: Environment Agency: 01225 487635

13.16 Radioactive waste stocks and arisings[1,2,3]
Great Britain

Stocks in cubic metres

		1986	1987	1988	1989	1991	1994	1998	2001
High level waste									
As stored	JTCG	1 351	1 430	1 463	1 575	1 686	1 639	1 804	1 961
Sellafield	JTBE	1 200	1 250	1 250	1 320	1 415	1 476	1 577	1 766
Dounreay[4]	JTBF	151	180	213	255	271	163	227	195
Conditioned	JTCH	436	517	594	674	681	653	717	765
Sellafield	JTBG	430	445	509	572	573	640	701	740
Dounreay[4]	JTBH	6	72	85	102	108	13	16	25
Intermediate level waste									
As stored	JTCI	41 887	43 602	47 783	45 313	51 558	61 494	70 948	75 415
Sellafield	JTBI	28 200	29 000	32 900	30 500	33 100	40 000	47 620	51 913
Dounreay	JTBJ	1 620	1 740	1 810	1 900	2 278	3 316	3 636	3 558
Other BNFL sites[5]	JTBK	78	78	73	74	92	61	55	61
Other UKAEA[6]	JTBL	2 340	2 620	2 680	2 630	3 000	3 117	3 370	2 808
Power stations[7]	JTBM	9 520	9 780	9 920	9 820	10 762	11 938	12 580	12 624
Amersham plc	JTBN	129	384	400	389	380	290	293	358
URENCO[8]	JTBO	–	–	–	–	–	27	1	1
Ministry of Defence	JTBP	..	..	..	..	1 946	2 745	3 393	4 092
Conditioned	JTCJ	56 211	59 479	66 020	81 762	78 512	66 102	74 131	74 466
Sellafield	JTBQ	43 600	44 500	51 600	64 100	57 084	37 360	43 942	47 874
Dounreay	JTBR	3 230	3 050	3 100	3 330	3 606	7 092	6 052	5 679
Other BNFL sites[5]	JTBS	99	85	84	81	92	100	121	130
Other UKAEA[6]	JTBT	2 680	2 800	2 800	5 460	5 655	5 808	6 058	3 020
Power stations[7]	JTBU	6 220	8 520	7 870	8 210	9 494	12 606	14 959	14 531
Amersham plc	JTBV	382	524	566	581	605	597	293	345
URENCO[8]	JTBW	–	–	–	–	–	54	1	1
Ministry of Defence	JTBX	..	..	..	..	1 976	2 485	2 705	2 886
Low level waste									
As stored	JTCK	2 429	2 343	1 002	13 752	6 252	7 882	7 983	14 584
Sellafield	JTBY	120	540	523	601	423	1 633	1 913	1 580
Dounreay	JTBZ	–	–	–	12 000	2 686	–	1 086	5 639
Other BNFL sites[5]	JTCA	827	669	151	259	1 042	2 833	2 046	3 474
Other UKAEA[6]	JTCB	810	831	91	229	393	555	226	489
Power stations[7]	JTCC	672	303	237	663	454	780	937	1 682
Amersham plc	JTCD	–	–	–	–	55	5	–	–
URENCO[8]	JTCE	–	–	–	–	–	–	79	70
Ministry of Defence	JTCF	..	..	..	..	1 199	2 076	1 696	1 650

1 See chapter text.
2 Up to 1991 as at 1st January and from 1994 as at 1st April.
3 Excludes waste from defence establishments before 1991.
4 The fall between 1991 and 1994 is due to increased evaporation of liquid waste and its planned vitrification.
5 Includes Calder Hall, Chapelcross, Capenhurst and Springfields.

6 UKAEA (United Kingdom Atomic Energy Authority) includes wastes from minor producers. Some of this is stored at Harwell, while low level waste suitable for disposal goes to Drigg.
7 Includes all BNFL Magnox stations (except Calder Hall and Chapelcross), British Energy power stations and Berkeley Centre.
8 In 1993, BNFL's enrichment business at Capenhurst was transferred to the newly formed Urenco (Capenhurst) Ltd.

Sources: Electrowatt Ekono (UK) Ltd for;
Department for Environment, Food and Rural Affairs 020 7082 8608

13.17 Estimated total annual waste arisings: by sector
United Kingdom

Million tonnes

Sector		Status[2]	Annual arisings						Percentage of total arisings 2002[1]
			1999	2000	2001	2002	2003		
Agriculture[3]	JSNA	C	..	..	..	..	0.4	JSNP	0.1
Minerals (Mining and quarrying)[4]									
colliery	JSNB	NC	10	9	9	8	8	JSNU	2.4
coal	JSNC	NC	8	7	7	7	6	JSNV	2.1
china clay	JSND	NC	21	21	20	19	19	JSNW	5.7
clay	JSNE	NC	14	13	12	12	12	JSNX	3.6
slate	JSNF	NC	7	10	11	15	18	JSNY	4.5
quarrying	JSNG	NC	37	36	37	34	34	JSNZ	10.2
Sewage sludge[5,6]	JSNH	C	..	..	..	1	1	JSOA	0.3
Dredged material[7]	JSNI	C	33	..	..	17	..	JSOB	5.1
Municipal waste[8]	JSNJ	C	33	34	35	36	35	JSOC	..
of which household	JSNK	C	30	30	31	31	31	JSOD	9.3
Commercial[9]	JSNL	C	..	..	..	35	..	JSOE	10.5
Industrial[9]	JSNM	C	..	..	..	45	..	JSOF	13.5
Demolition and construction[10]	JSNN	C	82	..	105	..	109	JSOG	32.7
Total (latest available year)	JSNO		..	..	..	333	..	JSOH	100

1 2003 figures used if 2002 not available.
2 NC = Not classed as a controlled waste under the terms of the Environmental Protection Act (Controlled Waste Regulations) 1992. C = controlled wastes under the terms of the Environmental Protection Act (Controlled Waste Regulations) 1992.
3 Estimate is for Great Britain, derived from a survey of agricultural waste commissioned by Environmental Agency/Defra. Agricultural waste is currently excluded from national waste legislation but new regulations were introduced from September 2005 to introduce similar controls that already exist for other forms of waste under the Waste Framework Directive.

4 Minerals waste is not subject to control by the EU Waste Framework Directive.
5 Dry weight arisings. Wet weight can be estimated on the basis of 4 per cent solid content on average giving a total of 26,450,000 tonnes.
6 Water UK (formerly Water Services Association and Water Companies Association).
7 The data are for all UK waters.
8 UK estimates based on survey returns made by local authorities in England and Wales.
9 Estimates from EA survey based on England and Wales.
10 Estimates from ODPM/EA survey based on England and Wales.

Sources: Department for Environment, Food and Rural Affairs 020 7082 8608;
Environment Agency;
Water UK

13.18 Recycling[1] of selected materials
United Kingdom

Scrap reused as a percentage of consumption

		1993	1994	1995	1996	1997	1998	1999[2]	2000	2001	2002	2003
Aluminium packaging	C4VH	..	..	..	..	..	..	..	..	24	25	26
Copper	JYWS	35	32	34	36	37	38	47	45	46	..	..
Ferrous	JYWQ	42	42	40	44	45	35	35	34	31	29	33
Glass	JYWW	22	22	22	22	21	22	27	33	34	34	35
Lead	JYWT	67	74	71	73	69	66	64	67	64	60	60
Paper and board	JYWV	32	34	37	38	38	38	38	38	37	38	38
Plastics	C22N	2	3	3	3	3	3	5	6	6	8	10
Waste paper used in newsprint	C22O	31	33	35	44	47	52	55	60	64	65	68
Zinc	JYWU	21	20	20	19	19	18	18	17	16	14	..

1 The ratios shown reflect the amount of secondary material used (scrap collected less exported scrap plus imported scrap) in the UK in a year as a proportion of consumption in that year.
2 Ferrous recycling level for 1999 is estimated.

Sources: Department for Environment, Food and Rural Affairs 020 7082 8608;
Alupro;
World Bureau of Metal Statistics;
HM Revenue & Customs;
Corus;
British Glass Manufacturers Confederation;
Environment Agency;
British Paper & Board Industry Federation;
British Plastics Federation;
The Paper Federation of Great Britain

13.19 Noise complaints received by Environmental Health Officers[1]
England and Wales

Number per million people

		1998 /99	1999 /00	2000 /01	2001 /02	2002 /03	2003 /04	2004 /05
Not controlled by the Environmental Protection								
Act 1990:								
Road traffic	JZLJ	39	38	44	37	36	32	..
Aircraft	JZLK	109	121	26	101	104	120	..
Railway	JTHH	14	17	16	12	18	21	..
Total	JUZR	162	176	86	150	158	173	..
Controlled by the Environmental Protection								
Act 1990:								
Industrial/commercial premises	JZLN	1 280	1 368	1 381	1 273	1 315	1 480	1 260
Industrial	EAC3	..	..	..	..	301	284	219
Commercial/leisure[2]	EAC4	..	..	..	..	1 014	1 196	1 041
Construction/Demolition sites	SNLE	248	292	325	347	325	335	343
Domestic premises	JZLP	4 330	5 149	5 001	5 540	5 573	5 973	5 903
Vehicles, machinery and equipment in streets	JZLQ	252	269	365	372	377	346	330
Miscellaneous[3]	EAC2	..	..	..	..	..	..	433
Total	JZLR	6 110	7 078	7 072	7 532	7 590	8 134	8 269

1 See chapter text.
2 Includes railway noise and airports (non aircraft).
3 From 2004/05 includes 'traffic' which consists of commercial vehicles, cars
   motorbikes, fixed-wing aircraft in flight and helicopters in flight.

Source: The Chartered Institute of Environmental Health

13.20 Material flows[1]
United Kingdom

Million tonnes

		1970	1975	1980	1985	1990	1995	2000	2001	2002	2003	2004
Domestic extraction												
Biomass												
Agricultural harvest	JKUN	42	38	47	47	46	47	51	45	51	48	47
Timber	JKUO	3	3	4	5	6	8	7	8	8	8	8
Animal grazing	JKUP	49	49	49	48	47	45	43	43	43	43	43
Fish	JKUQ	1	1	1	1	1	1	1	1	1	1	1
Total	JKUR	96	92	101	100	101	100	102	97	102	100	99
Minerals												
Ores	JKUS	12	5	1	1	–	–	–	–	–	–	–
Clay	JKUT	38	33	25	23	21	18	15	14	14	14	15
Other industrial minerals	JKUU	14	11	11	11	11	10	8	9	8	9	9
Sand and gravel	JKUV	122	131	110	112	128	106	106	105	98	96	95
Crushed stone	JKUW	156	169	150	160	212	200	176	183	173	170	170
Total	JKUX	342	349	298	307	373	334	305	311	293	288	288
Fossil fuels												
Coal	JKUY	149	129	130	94	94	53	31	32	30	28	25
Natural gas	JKUZ	11	37	39	37	43	71	111	109	106	106	96
Crude oil	JKVA	–	2	80	128	92	130	126	117	116	106	95
Total	JKVB	161	168	249	259	229	254	268	257	252	240	217
Total domestic extraction	JKVC	598	608	648	666	702	688	675	665	648	628	604
Imports												
Biomass	JKVD	38	33	30	31	38	40	42	46	47	49	50
Minerals	JKVE	30	32	24	34	41	50	51	54	55	55	60
Fossil fuels	JKVF	123	111	74	76	89	73	83	99	95	102	127
Other products	JKVG	5	7	14	15	19	23	34	34	32	34	36
Total	JKVH	197	184	141	157	187	188	210	232	228	240	273
Exports												
Biomass	JKVI	3	5	8	11	13	15	17	13	15	19	18
Minerals	JKVJ	17	20	26	22	25	39	44	43	42	44	48
Fossil fuels	JKVK	23	19	60	102	67	103	115	118	119	103	98
Other products	JKVL	5	7	8	11	12	17	20	20	20	20	20
Total	JKVM	47	51	101	146	117	173	196	193	196	187	184
Indirect flows												
From domestic extraction,[2] excluding soil erosion	JKVN	576	575	633	627	693	633	574	578	565	547	543
Of which:												
Unused biomass	JKVO	25	23	32	35	37	37	40	35	40	38	37
Fossil fuels	JKVP	169	202	287	274	309	276	231	241	225	209	204
Minerals and ores	JKVQ	185	155	120	120	144	116	97	95	92	90	90
Soil excavation and dredging	JKVR	197	195	195	199	203	203	206	207	208	210	211
From production of imports	JKVS	394	395	368	423	457	527	614	711	648	671	692
Summary aggregates												
Physical Trade Balance (export - imports)	F8YL	−150	−133	−40	−11	−70	−15	−14	−39	−32	−53	−89
Direct material input (Domestic extraction + imports)	JKVT	796	792	789	822	889	876	886	898	876	869	877
Domestic material consumption (Domestic extraction + imports - exports)	JKVU	748	741	688	677	772	703	690	704	680	682	693
Total material requirement (Direct material input + indirect flows)	JKVV	1 765	1 762	1 790	1 872	2 039	2 036	2 074	2 186	2 089	2 088	2 112

1 See chapter text.
2 Indirect flows from domestic extraction relate to unused material which is moved during extraction, such as overburden from mining and quarrying.

Source: Office for National Statistics: 020 7533 5904

13.21 Designated areas:[1] by region, 2005[2]

	National Parks		Areas of Outstanding Natural Beauty[3]		Green Belt Land		Defined Heritage Coasts length (km)
	Area (thousand hectares)	Percentage of total area in region	Area (thousand hectares)	Percentage of total area in region	Area (thousand hectares)	Percentage of total area in region	
United Kingdom	2 026	8	3 406	14	2 032	8	1 568
North East	111	13	146	17	53	6	138
North West	262	18	157	11	252	18	6
Yorkshire and the Humber	315	20	92	6	264	17	80
East Midlands	89	6	52	3	80	5	-
West Midlands	20	2	128	10	267	21	..
East	30	2	112	6	237	12	121
London	-	-	..	..	36	22	..
South East	54	3	636	33	356	19	74
South West	167	7	712	29	106	4	638
England	1 048	8	2 035	15	1 650	13	1 057
Wales	410	20	84	4	..	..	511
Scotland	568	9	1 002	13	155	2	..
Northern Ireland	-	-	285	20	227	16	..

1 See chapter text.
2 At March 2005, except for Green Belt land which relates to 1 January 1997.
3 National Scenic Area in Scotland. The South East includes London.

Source: Department for Environment, Food and Rural Affairs 020 7082 8608

211

Housing

Chapter 14

Housing

Permanent dwellings completed

(Table 14.1)

Local housing authorities include the Commission for the New Towns and New Towns Development Corporations, Communities Scotland and the Northern Ireland Housing Executive. The figures shown for housing associations include dwellings provided by housing associations other than the Communities Scotland and the Northern Ireland Housing Executive and provided or authorised by government departments for the families of police, prison staff, the Armed Forces and certain other services.

Households in Temporary Accommodation

(Table 14.9)

Comprises households in accommodation arranged by local authorities pending enquiries or after being accepted as owed a main homeless duty under the 1996 Act (includes residual cases awaiting re-housing under the 1985 Act). Excludes 'homeless at home' cases.

Private sector accommodation: Comprises dwellings operated by Registered Social Landlords or local authorities on lease or under licence from the private sector, or placed directly with a private sector landlord.

14.1 Stock of dwellings:[1] by tenure and country

Thousands

		1994	1995	1996	1997	1998	1999	2000	2001	2002	2003	2004
England												
Owner occupied	JUTY	13 553	13 700	13 865	14 041	14 237	14 433	14 635	14 818	14 950	15 098	15 279
Rented	JUUC	6 586	6 606	6 603	6 582	6 541	6 495	6 440	6 388	6 381	6 370	6 334
Local Authority	JUTZ	3 666	3 565	3 470	3 401	3 309	3 178	3 012	2 812	2 706	2 457	2 335
Privately	JUUA	2 141	2 184	2 191	2 196	2 192	2 171	2 155	2 152	2 208	2 292	2 334
Registered Social Landlords	JUUB	779	857	942	985	1 040	1 146	1 273	1 424	1 467	1 621	1 665
All dwellings	JUUD	20 140	20 305	20 468	20 623	20 779	20 978	21 075	21 207	21 331	21 467	21 613
Wales												
Owner occupied	JUUE	862	870	878	885	894	902	911	920	930	942	955
Rented	JUUI	352	354	356	357	357	357	356	354	352	347	341
Local Authority	JUUF	213	210	207	204	201	197	193	188	183	177	162
Privately	JUUG	101	102	104	105	106	108	109	111	112	113	115
Registered Social Landlords	JUUH	38	42	45	48	50	52	54	55	57	57	64
All dwellings	JUUJ	1 214	1 224	1 233	1 243	1 251	1 259	1 267	1 274	1 282	1 289	1 296
Scotland												
Owner occupied	JUUK	1 258	1 293	1 327	1 366	1 401	1 436	1 474	1 468	1 507	1 549	1 583
Rented	JUUO	953	938	921	900	883	869	851	855	837	816	806
Local Authority	JUUL	721	692	668	631	608	584	558	535	515	389	378
Privately	JUUM	155	155	154	154	154	155	156	176	176	177	178
Registered Social Landlords	JUUN	77	91	99	115	121	130	137	144	146	250	250
All dwellings	JUUP	2 210	2 230	2 248	2 267	2 285	2 305	2 324	2 323	2 344	2 366	2 389
Northern Ireland[2]												
Owner occupied	JUUQ	411	409	422	434	446	455	489	..	491	507	523
Rented	JUUU	189	188	186	183	180	180	184	..	172	166	156
Local Authority	JUUR	155	152	148	142	137	131	130	..	117	109	97
Privately	JUUS	21	22	23	26	27	32	34	..	34	35	37
Registered Social Landlords	JUUT	13	14	15	15	16	17	20	..	21	22	22
All dwellings	JUUV	600	597	608	618	626	636	674	..	663	673	679
United Kingdom[3]												
Owner occupied	JUVY	16 027	16 239	16 445	16 675	16 932	17 183	17 437	17 701	17 839	18 054	18 306
Rented	JUWC	8 108	8 102	8 085	8 046	7 981	7 915	7 846	7 777	7 760	7 720	7 647
Local Authority	JUVZ	4 795	4 651	4 521	4 421	4 283	4 120	3 920	3 688	3 541	3 258	2 983
Privately	JUWA	2 417	2 462	2 472	2 478	2 478	2 460	2 451	2 453	2 530	2 616	2 663
Registered Social Landlords	JUWB	896	989	1 092	1 147	1 220	1 335	1 475	1 636	1 689	1 846	2 001
All dwellings	JUWD	24 135	24 341	24 529	24 721	24 913	25 098	25 283	25 478	25 599	25 774	25 953

1 At 31 March for England and Wales and at 31 December for Scotland. At 31 March for Northern Ireland, but data prior to 2002 are at 31 December.
2 To include estimates for vacants in the tenure figures the total dwelling stock figures in Northern Ireland have been apportioned according to the % of occupied dwellings.
3 Calculated from data for England, Wales and Northern Ireland for the current year with Scotland data for the previous year, except for 2001 and earlier where Northern Ireland data for the previous year are used.

Sources: Department for Communities and Local Government;
National Assembly for Wales;
Scottish Executive;
Department for Social Development (Northern Ireland)

14.2 Tenure: by type of accommodation, 2004/05
Great Britain

Weighted Percentages

	House or bungalow			Flat or maisonette		
	Detached	Semi-detached	Terraced	Purpose-built	Other[1]	All dwellings[2]
Owner-occupied						
Owned outright	35	37	21	5	1	100
Owned with mortgage	29	36	28	4	1	100
All owner-occupied	31	37	26	5	1	100
Rented from social sector						
Council[3]	1	28	33	36	2	100
Housing association	3	22	41	31	3	100
All rented from social sector	2	26	35	34	3	100
Rented privately[2]						
Furnished	3	20	35	28	14	100
Unfurnished[4]	15	20	35	15	15	100
All rented privately	12	20	35	19	15	100
All tenures	24	33	29	12	3	100

1 Includes other type of accommodation, such as mobile homes.
2 Includes rent free accommodation. Tenants whose accommodation goes with the job of someone in the household have been allocated to 'rented privately'. Squatters are also included.
3 Council includes local authorities and Scottish Homes.
4 Includes partly furnished.

Source: General Household Survey, Office for National Statistics

14.3 Permanent dwellings completed:[1] by tenure and country

Numbers

	United Kingdom				England and Wales			
	All dwellings	Local authorities[2]	Private enterprise	Registered Social Landlords[3]	All dwellings	Local authorities[2]	Private enterprise	Registered Social Landlords[3]
	KAAD	KAAE	KAAF	KAAG	KAAH	KAAI	KAAJ	KAAK
1980	241 999	88 534	131 989	21 476	214 934	78 539	116 179	20 216
1981	206 985	68 554	118 647	19 784	180 147	58 633	104 069	17 445
1982	182 853	40 091	129 022	13 740	159 407	33 544	113 893	11 970
1983	209 018	39 161	153 038	16 819	181 391	31 625	134 901	14 865
1984	220 414	37 573	165 555	17 286	191 112	31 338	145 263	14 511
1985	207 465	30 420	163 395	13 650	178 284	24 359	142 020	11 905
1986	216 544	25 377	178 008	13 159	187 710	20 496	156 056	11 158
1987	226 234	21 833	191 250	13 151	198 732	17 435	169 895	11 402
1988	242 359	21 448	207 423	13 488	214 156	16 921	185 733	11 502
1989	221 463	19 323	187 542	14 598	190 990	15 332	163 344	12 314
1990/91	198 074	16 550	162 182	19 342	171 031	13 425	141 166	16 440
1991/92	191 825	10 027	160 664	21 134	165 553	7 447	139 583	18 523
1992/93	178 915	4 433	144 367	30 115	152 452	2 706	123 045	26 701
1993/94	185 960	3 611	145 914	36 435	157 813	1 726	122 779	33 308
1994/95	197 169	2 970	156 547	37 652	168 301	997	133 002	34 302
1995/96	198 213	3 045	156 697	38 471	164 581	954	130 891	32 736
1996/97	185 626	1 538	153 137	30 951	156 334	474	128 682	27 178
1997/98	190 709	1 519	160 636	28 554	157 987	325	134 327	23 335
1998/99	176 640	881	152 857	22 902	146 367	223	125 955	20 189
1999/00	184 656	347	160 168	24 141	150 061	88	132 027	17 946
2000/01	176 499	382	152 267	23 850	141 444	226	123 798	17 420
2001/02	175 104	225	153 132	21 747	138 040	131	123 027	14 882
2002/03	183 752	301	163 706	19 745	146 029	205	131 800	14 024
2003/04	190 135	207	171 558	18 370	151 894	207	137 604	14 083
2004/05	205 991	131	183 168	22 692	163 362	131	146 119	17 112

	Scotland				Northern Ireland			
	All dwellings	Local authorities[2]	Private enterprise	Registered Social Landlords[3]	All dwellings	Local authorities[2]	Private enterprise	Registered Social Landlords[3]
	BLFI	BAEZ	BLFK	BLFO	BLGI	BAFA	BLGK	BLGO
1979	23 782	4 755	15 175	3 852	7 253	3 436	3 574	243
1980	20 611	7 488	12 242	881	6 456	2 563	3 568	325
1981	20 011	7 062	11 021	1 928	6 827	3 082	3 557	188
1982	16 423	3 733	11 523	1 167	7 033	3 032	3 606	395
1983	17 929	3 492	13 166	1 271	9 698	4 093	4 971	634
1984	18 838	2 647	14 115	2 076	10 464	3 594	6 177	693
1985	18 411	2 828	14 435	1 148	10 770	3 235	6 940	595
1986	18 637	2 301	14 870	1 466	10 197	2 580	7 082	535
1987	17 707	2 634	13 904	1 169	9 795	1 764	7 451	580
1988	18 272	2 815	14 179	1 278	9 931	1 715	7 511	705
1989	20 190	2 283	16 287	1 620	10 283	1 708	7 911	664
1990/91	19 457	1 801	15 305	2 351	7 586	1 324	5 711	551
1991/92	18 956	1 619	15 528	1 809	7 316	961	5 553	802
1992/93	18 902	778	15 563	2 561	7 561	949	5 759	853
1993/94	20 985	997	17 407	2 581	7 162	888	5 728	546
1994/95	22 136	1 095	18 195	2 846	6 732	878	5 350	504
1995/96	24 382	729	18 956	4 697	9 250	1 362	6 850	1 038
1996/97	20 386	241	17 182	2 963	8 906	823	7 273	810
1997/98	22 541	114	17 938	4 489	10 181	1 080	8 371	730
1998/99	20 635	120	18 762	1 753	9 638	538	8 140	960
1999/00	24 196	69	19 024	5 103	10 399	190	9 117	1 092
2000/01	23 387	112	17 957	5 318	11 668	44	10 512	1 112
2001/02	23 577	65	18 033	5 479	13 487	29	12 072	1 386
2002/03	23 308	94	18 519	4 695	14 415	2	13 387	1 026
2003/04	23 730	–	20 003	3 727	14 511	–	13 951	560
2004/05	26 861	–	22 109	4 752	15 768	–	14 940	828

1 See chapter text.
2 Including the Commission for the New Towns Development Corporations, Communities Scotland, the Northern Ireland Housing Executive.
3 Dwellings provided by housing associations other than Communities Scotland and the Northern Ireland Housing Trust and provided or authorised by government departments for families of police, prison staff, the armed forces and certain other services.

Sources: Department for Communities and Local Government;
Scottish Executive;
National Assembly for Wales;
Department for Social Development, Northern Ireland

14.4 Stock of dwellings: Estimated annual gains and losses
England

Thousands of dwellings

		1993 /94	1994 /95	1995 /96	1996 /97	1997 /98	1998 /99	1999 /00	2000[2] /01	2001 /02	2002 /03	2003 /04
Dwelling stock at start of financial year	GRWM	19 987	20 139	20 305	20 468	20 622	20 778	20 927	21 075	21 207	21 331	21 467
Gains to dwelling stock:												
Housebuilding completions	GRWN	147.7	158.0	154.6	146.2	149.6	138.6	141.4	133.1	129.8	137.7	143.4
Conversions (net gain)[1]	GRWO	7.5	9.9	8.9	8.6	2.8	4.2	3.5	2.8	5.1	3.8	5.1
Change of use	GRWP	..	..	..	..	11.6	15.9	13.9	10.1	16.1	19.0	17.6
Non-permanent dwellings additions	GRWQ	..	..	..	..	0.2	0.2	0.3	0.3	0.3	0.7	2.0
Losses from dwelling stock:												
Slum clearance (non LA owned dwelling demolished)	GRWR	3.9	3.0	2.7	2.9	1.3	1.3	1.4	1.7	1.6	1.2	1.3
Other demolitions[1]	GRWS	5.2	5.8	4.8	4.1	12.8	13.2	15.8	18.3	24.7	22.0	18.8
Change of use	GRWT	..	..	..	..	0.7	1.4	0.8	0.7	0.8	1.2	1.2
Non-permanent dwelling losses	GRWU	..	..	..	..	0.1	0.2	0.1	0.3	0.3	0.2	1.3
New gain in year	GRWV	146.2	159.0	156.0	147.8	149.3	143.0	140.9	125.3	123.9	136.6	145.4
Adjustment[3]	VQDN	6.6	6.6	6.6	6.6	6.6	6.6	6.6	6.6	–	–	–
Dwelling stock at end of financial year	GRWW	20 139	20 305	20 468	20 622	20 778	20 927	21 075	21 207	21 331	21 467	21 613

1 Figures prior to 1997/98 include change of use, and zero for net non-permanent dwellings.
2 Figures for 2000/01 conversions, change of use and non permanent dwellings are based on reported figures and do not include estimates for missing returns.
3 Series has been adjusted so that the 2000/01 estimates matches the 2001 Census.

Source: Department for Communities and Local Government

14.5 Housebuilding completions: by number of bedrooms

Percentages

		1994 /95	1995 /96	1996 /97	1997 /98	1998 /99	1999 /00	2000 /01	2001 /02	2002 /03	2003 /04	2004 /05
England												
1 bedroom	JUWJ	12	11	8	7	7	7	7	7	6	8	10
2 bedrooms	JUWK	32	32	29	27	27	26	27	25	29	33	38
3 bedrooms	JUWL	34	35	36	38	36	35	34	31	30	29	29
4 or more bedrooms	JUWM	22	23	26	28	30	32	32	37	34	30	23
All houses and flats	JUWN	100	100	100	100	100	100	100	100	100	100	100
Wales												
1 bedroom	JUWO	7	8	5	4	3	5	5	4	6	6	7
2 bedrooms	JUWP	30	30	27	24	21	19	18	19	18	20	21
3 bedrooms	JUWQ	47	44	47	46	46	43	42	39	35	37	35
4 or more bedrooms	JUWR	15	18	21	26	31	34	34	38	41	37	37
All houses and flats	JUWS	100	100	100	100	100	100	100	100	100	100	100

Sources: Department for Communities and Local Government;
National Assembly for Wales

14.6 Mortgages
United Kingdom

		1993	1994	1995	1996	1997	1998	1999	2000	2001	2002	2003
Mortgages[1] (Thousands)	JUTH	10 137	10 410	10 521	10 637	10 738	10 821	10 982	11 173	11 270	11 364	11 452
Arrears and repossessions[1] (Thousands)												
Loans in arrears at end-period												
By 6-12 months	JUTI	165	134	127	101	74	74	57	48	41	34	29
By over 12 months	JUTJ	152	117	85	67	45	35	30	21	18	16	13
Properties repossessed in period	JUTK	59	49	49	43	33	34	30	23	17	12	8
Type of mortgage for house purchase[2] (Percentages)												
Standard repayment	JUTL	20.9	25.7	33.7	38.3	39.6	42.7	46.1	59.9	71.9	81.4	78.4
Endowment	JUTM	64.3	61.0	50.6	37.5	35.3	33.1	26.6	17.1	10.4	4.8	3.2
Other[3]	JUTN	14.7	13.3	15.7	24.2	25.1	24.3	27.3	23.0	17.7	13.8	18.4

1 Estimates cover only members of the Council of Mortgage Lenders; these account for 98 per cent of all mortgages outstanding.
2 Includes new mortgages advanced by building societies and other major lenders. Includes sitting tenants.
3 Includes interest only, PEP/ISA and pension.

Sources: Department for Communities and Local Government; Council of Mortgage Lenders

14.7 County Court mortgage possession orders:[1] by region

Thousands

		1996	1997	1998	1999	2000	2001	2002	2003	2004
Actions entered										
England and Wales	JURS	79.8	67.0	84.8	81.6	73.0	67.4	64.1	67.0	77.9
North East	JURT	3.5	3.0	4.3	4.2	4.0	3.5	3.3	3.0	3.5
North West	JURU	12.6	10.9	14.2	13.8	12.4	12.4	11.4	10.2	10.7
Yorkshire and the Humber	JURV	7.6	6.9	8.2	8.1	7.8	7.2	6.2	6.0	6.6
East Midlands	JURW	5.9	4.9	6.4	6.8	5.7	5.3	4.7	4.9	5.8
West Midlands	JURX	7.6	6.7	8.1	9.5	9.8	7.8	6.8	7.4	8.6
East	JURY	8.3	6.7	8.5	7.3	6.2	5.7	5.5	6.4	7.9
London	JURZ	11.4	9.2	11.4	10.0	8.1	7.7	8.8	10.7	13.5
South East	JUSA	11.6	9.1	11.2	9.4	8.6	8.6	8.4	9.5	11.5
South West	JUSB	6.3	5.7	7.3	7.0	5.2	4.5	4.3	4.6	5.4
England	JUSC	74.9	63.1	79.6	76.1	67.7	62.7	59.4	62.6	73.7
Wales	JUSD	4.9	3.9	5.4	5.5	5.3	4.7	4.7	4.4	4.2
Northern Ireland[2]	JUSE	1.2	1.2	1.6	1.9	1.7	1.6	1.6	1.7	2.2
Suspended orders										
England and Wales	JUSF	43.4	34.6	40.8	36.6	31.7	29.1	24.4	23.9	26.1
North East	JUSG	2.0	1.6	2.3	2.3	1.9	1.7	1.3	1.2	1.2
North West	JUSH	7.6	5.5	6.4	6.0	5.7	5.5	4.8	3.9	3.7
Yorkshire and the Humber	JUSI	3.9	3.5	4.3	4.1	3.7	3.4	2.5	2.2	2.4
East Midlands	JUSJ	3.0	2.6	3.1	2.8	2.4	2.4	1.8	1.8	2.1
West Midlands	JUSK	3.9	3.4	3.8	4.1	3.7	3.6	2.8	2.8	3.1
East	JUSL	4.0	3.0	3.9	3.5	2.5	2.3	2.0	2.2	2.6
London	JUSM	6.4	4.7	5.3	4.5	3.1	2.7	2.7	3.2	3.9
South East	JUSN	6.6	5.4	5.8	4.4	3.9	3.4	3.0	3.2	3.8
South West	JUSO	3.3	2.7	3.0	2.8	2.3	1.9	1.6	1.6	1.8
England	JUSP	40.7	32.2	37.9	34.4	29.1	27.0	22.6	22.2	24.6
Wales	JUSQ	2.7	2.4	2.8	2.2	2.6	2.1	1.8	1.7	1.5
Northern Ireland[2]	JUSR	..	..	0.2	0.3	0.2	0.2	0.2	0.3	0.5
Orders made										
England and Wales	JUSS	27.8	22.5	25.3	23.5	20.4	18.7	16.9	16.7	20.3
North East	JUST	1.1	1.0	1.2	1.1	1.1	1.2	0.9	0.8	0.9
North West	JUSU	4.0	3.3	3.7	3.7	3.7	3.8	3.3	2.7	2.7
Yorkshire and the Humber	JUSV	2.6	2.3	3.1	3.0	2.4	2.3	1.8	1.6	1.7
East Midlands	JUSW	2.0	1.7	1.7	1.8	1.6	1.6	1.4	1.2	1.6
West Midlands	JUSX	2.1	2.0	2.4	2.3	2.3	2.2	1.8	1.8	2.2
East	JUSY	3.4	2.5	2.6	2.2	1.6	1.4	1.3	1.5	2.0
London	JUSZ	4.8	3.4	3.5	3.4	2.1	1.8	2.2	2.8	3.8
South East	JUTA	4.0	3.1	3.4	2.7	2.6	1.9	1.9	2.2	2.9
South West	JUTB	2.4	1.9	2.1	2.0	1.3	1.1	1.0	1.0	1.4
England	JUTC	26.4	21.2	23.7	22.0	18.7	17.3	15.6	15.6	19.2
Wales	JUTD	1.4	1.3	1.7	1.5	1.6	1.4	1.3	1.1	1.1
Northern Ireland[2]	JUTE	..	..	0.5	0.7	0.6	0.7	0.5	0.6	1.2

Note In 2001 the data extraction method changed. From 2001 the data are collected electronically from Caseman, the main administrative system in the county courts. Previously they were collected from Stats Module, a manual form completed monthly by all county courts.

1 Local authority and private.
2 Mortgage possession actions are heard in Chancery Division of Northern Ireland High Court.

Sources: The Court Service: 020 7210 1752; Northern Ireland Court Service: 028 9032 8594

14.8 Sales and transfers of local authority dwellings
Great Britain

Thousands

		1994	1995	1996	1997	1998	1999	2000	2001	2002	2003	2004
Right to buy sales	JUQV	65.2	49.6	45.0	58.1	56.0	66.8	71.3	66.5	78.6	94.2	74.8
Large scale voluntary transfers	JUQW	41.0	47.7	29.9	21.1	36.9	88.7	111.4	100.8	102.5	98.2	67.6
Other sales and transfers[1]	JUQX	4.6	3.2	3.0	3.4	2.7	3.3	2.4	1.6	1.4	0.6	1.6
Total sales and transfers	JUQY	110.8	100.5	77.9	82.6	95.6	158.8	185.1	168.9	182.5	193.0	144.0

1 Excludes new town and Scottish Homes sales and transfers.

Sources: Department for Communities and Local Government;
National Assembly for Wales;
Scottish Executive

14.9 Households in Temporary Accommodation[1]
England

As at 31 March of each year

Thousands

		1995	1996	1997	1998	1999	2000	2001	2002	2003	2004	2005
Bed and breakfast hotels	JUWF	4 480	4 750	4 100	4 820	6 570	8 680	10 860	12 710	12 440	7 090	6 780
Hostels/women's refuges	JUWG	10 380	10 090	9 680	9 730	9 840	10 300	10 610	9 570	10 060	10 780	10 280
Private sector accommodation[2]	JXVN	14 130	11 410	11 360	12 090	16 210	17 060	21 900	20 660	28 370	42 390	46 530
Other accommodation[3]	JXVO	17 360	16 990	16 110	20 880	23 960	29 130	31 830	37 270	38 180	37 420	37 490
All accommodation	JUWI	46 350	43 240	41 250	47 520	56 580	65 170	75 200	80 200	89 040	97 680	101 070

1 Households in temporary accommodation arranged by the local authority pending enquiries, or after being accepted as owed a main duty under homelessness legislation. Excludes 'homeless at home' cases who have remained in their existing accommodation after acceptance but have the same rights to suitable alternative housing as those in accommodation arranged directly by authorities.
2 Private sector properties leased by social sector landlords, and households placed directly with a private sector landlord. From 2002 some self-contained B&B Annexe-style units, previously recorded under B&B now more appropriately attributed to Private Sector accommodation.
3 Includes local authorities' and Registered Social Landlords' own stock.

Source: Department for Communities and Local Government

Transport and communication

Chapter 15

Transport and communication

Road data

(Tables 15.4, 15.5, 15.6 and 15.7)

The Department for Transport (DFT) has undertaken significant development work over the last two years to improve its traffic estimates and measurement of traffic flow on particular stretches of the road network. This work has previously been outlined in a number of publications (*Road Traffic Statistics: 2001* SB(02)23, *Traffic in Great Britain Q4 2002* Data SB(03)5 and *Traffic in Great Britain Q1 2003* SB(03)6).

The main point to note is that figures for 1993 to 2004 have been calculated on a different basis from years prior to 1993. Therefore, figures prior to 1993 are not directly comparable with estimates for later years. Estimates on the new basis for 1993 and subsequent years were first published by the DFT on 8 May 2003 in *Traffic in Great Britain Q1* 2003 SB(03)6.

A summary of the main methodological changes to take place over the last couple of years appears below:

Traffic estimates are now disaggregated for roads in urban and rural areas rather than between built-up and non built-up roads. Built-up roads were defined as those with a speed limit of 40mph or lower. This created difficulties in producing meaningful disaggregated traffic estimates because an increasing number of clearly rural roads were subject to a 40mph speed limit for safety reasons. The urban/rural split of roads is largely determined by whether roads lie within the boundaries of urban areas with a population of 10,000 or more with adjustments in some cases for major roads at the boundary.

Traffic estimates are based on the results of many 12-hour manual counts in every year which are grossed up to estimates of annual average daily flows using expansion factors based on data from automatic traffic counters on similar roads. These averages are needed so that traffic in off-peak times, at weekends and in the summer and winter months (when only special counts are undertaken) can be taken into account when assessing the traffic at each site. For this purpose roads are now sorted into 22 groupings (previously there were only seven) and this allows a better match of manual count sites with our automatic count sites. These groupings are based on a detailed analyses of the results from all the individual automatic

count sites and take into account regional groupings, road category (i.e. both the urban/rural classification of the road and the road class) and traffic flow levels. The groupings range from lightly-trafficked, rural minor roads in holiday areas such as Cornwall and Devon, to major roads in Central London.

With the increasing interest in sub-regional statistics, we have undertaken a detailed study of traffic counts on minor roads carried out in the last ten years. This has been done in conjunction with a Geographic Information System to enable us to establish general patterns of minor road traffic in each local authority. As a result of this, we have been able to produce more reliable estimate of traffic levels in each authority in our base year of 1999. This in turn has enabled us to produce better estimates of traffic levels back to 1993, as well as more reliable estimates for 1999 onwards.

The DFT created a database for major roads based on a Geographic Information System and Ordnance Survey data. This was checked by local authorities and discussed with Government Regional Offices and the Highways Agency to ensure that good local knowledge supplemented the available technical data.

Road class

(Tables 15.5 and 15.6)

Urban major and minor roads, from 1993 onwards are defined as being within an urban area with a population of more than 10,000 people, these are based on the 2001 urban settlements. The definition for 'urban settlement' is 'Urban and rural area definitions: a user guide which can be found on the Department for Communities and local Government (DCLG) web site at: www.odpm.gov.uk/stellent/groups/odpm_planning/documents/page/odpm_plan_609188.hcsp.

Rural major and minor roads, from 1993 onwards, are defined as being outside an urban settlement.

New vehicle registrations

(Table 15.9)

Special concession group

Various revisions to the vehicle taxation system were introduced on 1 July 1995 and on 29 November 1995. Separate taxation classes for farmers' goods vehicles were abolished on 1 July 1995; after this date new vehicles of this type were registered as HGVs. The total includes 5,900 vehicles registered between 1 January and 30 June in the (now abolished) agricultural and special machines group in classes which were not eligible to register in the special concession group. The old agricultural and special machines taxation group was abolished at end June 1995. The group includes agricultural and mowing machines, snow ploughs and gritting vehicles. Electric vehicles are also included in this group and are no longer exempt from VED. Steam propelled vehicles were added to this group from November 1995.

Other licensed vehicles

Includes three wheelers, pedestrian controlled vehicles, general haulage and showmen's tractors and recovery vehicles. Recovery vehicle tax class introduced January 1988.

Special vehicles group

The special vehicles group was created on 1 July 1995 and consists of various vehicle types over 3.5 tonnes gross weight but not required to pay VED as heavy goods vehicles. The group includes mobile cranes, works trucks, digging machines, road rollers and vehicles previously taxed as showman's goods and haulage. Figure shown for 1995 covers period from 1 July to 31 December only.

National Travel Survey data

(Tables15.1, 15.11)

The 2004 National Travel Survey (NTS) is the latest in a series of household surveys designed to provide a databank of personal travel information for Great Britain. The survey is part of a continuous survey that began in July 1988, following ad hoc surveys since the mid-1960s. The survey is designed to pick up long-term trends and is not suitable for monitoring short-term trends.

The drawn sample size for 2002 onwards was nearly trebled compared with previous years following recommendations in a National Statistics Review of the National Travel Survey. This enables key results to be presented on a single year basis for the first time since the survey became continuous.

Changes to the methodology in 2002 mean that there are some inconsistencies with data for earlier years. The 2003 results presented in the table should be regarded as provisional.

During 2004, individuals in over 8,100 households provided details of their personal travel by filling in travel diaries over a period of seven days, compared with nearly 3,500 households in 2001. Previously, data have been shown for a three year time period because of the smaller sample size.

Travel details provided by respondents include trip purpose, method of travel, time of day and trip length. The households also provided personal information, such as their age, sex,

working status, and driving licence holding, and details of the cars available for their use.

Because estimates made from a sample survey depend upon the particular sample chosen they generally differ from the true values of the population. This is not usually a problem when considering large samples (such as all car trips in Great Britain), but may give misleading information when considering data from small samples.

The most recent editions of all NTS publications are available on the DfT website at www.dft.gov.uk/transtat/personaltravel. Bulletins of key results are published annually. The most recent bulletin is *National Travel Survey: 2004*. More detailed data for 2002/2003 combined was published in *Focus on Personal Travel*: 2005 Edition.

Households with regular use of cars

(Table 15.12)

The mid-year estimates of the percentage of households with regular use of a car or van are based on combined data from the National Travel Survey (NTS), the Expenditure and Food Survey (EFS) (previously the Family Expenditure Survey) and the General Household Survey (GHS), where available. Data by area type are based on data from the NTS only.

Activity at civil aerodromes

(Table 15.28)

Figures exclude Channel Island airports. 'Other' covers local pleasure flights, scheduled service, positioning flights and non-transport charter flights for reward (for example: aerial survey work, crop dusting and delivery of empty aircraft) and 'Non-commercial' covers test and training flights, private, aeroclub, military and official flights, and Business Aviation etc.

International passenger movements by air and sea

(Table 15.31)

Figures shown in the table are for arrivals plus departures.

EC Europe includes Azores, Madeira, Canary and Cape Verde Islands, Austria, Finland and Sweden joined the EC in 1995, but are included in the EC section for all years to show a consistent time series. Other Western Europe includes Iceland and the Faroe Islands.

For Pleasure cruises, passengers are included at both departure and arrival if their journeys begin and end at the United Kingdom seaports.

Transport and communication

Postal services and television licences

(Table 15.32)

Data for letters, postal orders and telegrams sent, is shown up to 31 March of each year and data for television licences is at 31 March each year.

Letters posted category includes printed papers, newspapers, postcards and sample packets, Airmail includes letters without special charge for air transport. Business reply and freepost is now known as Response Services.

15.1 Trips per person per year: by main mode[1] and purpose, 2003/04
Great Britain

Numbers

	Walk	Bicycle	Car/van driver	Car/van passenger	Motor-cycle	Other private
Commuting	16	5	88	15	2	1
Business	3	-	24	2	-	-
Education	30	1	2	20	-	4
Escort education	21	-	22	6	-	-
Shopping	50	2	80	41	-	-
Other escort	10	-	51	28	-	-
Other personal business	28	1	41	23	-	1
Visiting friends at home	25	2	43	40	-	-
Visiting friends elsewhere	12	-	11	13	-	-
Social/entertainment	10	1	26	24	-	1
Holidays/day trips	2	2	13	14	-	1
Other, including just walk	39	-	-	-	-	-
All purposes	**245**	**15**	**400**	**226**	**3**	**8**

	Local bus	Non-local bus	London Under-ground	Surface rail	Taxi/minicab	Other public	All modes
Commuting	11	-	3	6	1	1	148
Business	1	-	1	1	-	-	33
Education	10	-	-	1	1	-	68
Escort education	1	-	-	-	-	-	50
Shopping	17	-	-	1	2	-	193
Other escort	2	-	-	-	-	-	92
Other personal business	6	-	-	1	1	-	102
Visiting friends at home	6	-	-	1	1	-	118
Visiting friends elsewhere	2	-	-	-	3	-	43
Social/entertainment	3	-	-	1	1	-	67
Holidays/day trips	1	1	-	1	-	-	35
Other, including just walk	-	-	-	-	-	-	40
All purposes	**59**	**1**	**6**	**13**	**11**	**2**	**989**

1 Main mode that is used for the longest part of the trip.

Source: Department for Transport 020 7944 3097

15.2 Retail Prices Index: transport components: 1994 - 2004
Great Britain

Constant prices

Indices (1994=100)

	All items	Purchase	Maintenance	Petrol/oil	Tax and insurance	All motoring	Rail fares	Bus fares	Fares & other travel costs
	ENX3	ENX4	ENX5	ZCFV	ENX6	ZCFW	ZCFX	ENX7	ENX8
1994	100.0	100.0	100.0	100.0	100.0	100.0	100.0	100.0	100.0
1995	103.4	101.7	101.9	105.1	97.5	101.8	104.4	103.7	102.5
1996	105.9	105.0	106.5	110.5	94.3	104.9	108.3	107.5	105.6
1997	109.3	107.5	112.3	121.4	98.2	110.5	110.9	111.4	109.1
1998	113.0	106.3	116.9	127.5	106.8	113.9	115.4	115.0	111.5
1999	114.8	101.8	121.5	138.2	115.5	116.7	119.6	119.2	115.0
2000	118.1	96.3	126.5	156.4	127.8	121.1	121.7	124.0	118.8
2001	120.3	94.9	132.7	148.4	134.5	120.5	126.4	129.2	122.6
2002	122.2	93.1	139.6	143.7	136.6	119.5	129.2	133.2	126.0
2003	125.8	90.4	147.9	148.9	142.5	121.1	131.5	138.8	135.0
2004	129.5	87.6	156.8	157.2	143.1	122.2	136.5	145.9	139.7

Source: Consumer Prices and Inflation Division, ONS: 020 7944 4276

15.3 Domestic freight transport: by mode
Great Britain

		1994	1995	1996	1997	1998	1999	2000	2001	2002	2003	2004
Goods moved (billion tonnes kilometres)												
Petroleum products												
Road[1]	ZBZP	5.1	5.7	6.1	5.8	5.2	5.0	6.4	5.8	5.2	5.5	5.7
Rail[2]	ZBZQ	1.8	1.8	..	..	1.6	1.5	1.4	1.2	1.1	1.2	1.2
Water[3]	ZBZR	43.0	42.5	45.9	38.3	45.2	48.6	52.7	43.5	51.7	46.9	..
of which: coastwise	ZBZS	28.9	31.4	38.7	33.8	36.4	33.3	26.0	23.1	24.2	23.3	..
Pipeline	ZBZT	12.0	11.1	11.6	11.2	11.7	11.6	11.4	11.5	10.9	10.5	10.7
All modes	ZBZU	61.9	61.1	63.6	55.3	63.6	66.6	71.9	62.0	68.9	64.1	..
Coal and coke												
Road[1]	ZBZV	2.9	2.7	2.5	2.7	2.0	2.2	1.5	2.1	1.5	1.5	1.2
Rail[2]	ZBZW	3.3	3.6	3.8	4.4	4.5	4.8	4.8	6.2	5.7	5.8	7.0
Water[3]	ZBZX	1.4	2.3	0.6	0.6	0.5	0.5	0.2	0.5	0.3	0.5	..
All modes	ZBZY	7.6	8.6	6.9	7.7	7.0	7.5	6.5	8.8	7.5	7.8	..
Other traffic												
Road[1]	ZBZZ	135.7	141.2	145.3	148.6	152.4	149.6	150.2	149.0	150.6	152.4	153.0
Rail[2]	ZCAA	7.9	7.9	11.3	12.5	11.2	11.9	11.9	12.0	11.9	11.9	12.4
Water[3]	ZCAB	7.8	8.3	8.7	9.2	11.2	9.6	14.6	14.8	15.2	13.5	..
All modes	ZCAC	151.4	157.4	165.3	170.3	174.8	171.1	176.5	175.8	177.7	177.8	..
All traffic												
Road[1]	KCTA	143.7	149.6	153.9	157.1	159.5	156.7	158.0	156.9	157.3	159.3	159.8
Rail[2]	KCTB	13.0	13.3	15.1	16.9	17.3	18.2	18.1	19.4	18.7	18.9	20.7
Water[3]	ZCAD	52.2	53.1	55.3	48.1	56.9	58.7	67.4	58.8	67.2	60.9	..
Pipeline	KCTE	12.0	11.1	11.6	11.2	11.7	11.6	11.4	11.5	10.9	10.5	10.7
All modes	KCTF	220.9	227.1	235.9	233.3	245.4	245.2	254.9	246.6	254.1	249.6	..
Percentage of all traffic												
Road[1]	ZCAE	*65*	*66*	*65*	*67*	*65*	*64*	*62*	*64*	*62*	*64*	..
Rail[2]	ZCAF	*6*	*6*	*6*	*7*	*7*	*7*	*7*	*8*	*7*	*8*	..
Water[3]	ZCAG	*24*	*23*	*23*	*21*	*23*	*24*	*26*	*24*	*26*	*24*	..
Pipeline	ZCAH	*5*	*5*	*5*	*5*	*5*	*5*	*4*	*5*	*4*	*4*	..
All modes	ZCAI	*100*	*100*	*100*	*100*	*100*	*100*	*100*	*100*	*100*	*100*	..
Goods lifted (million tonnes)												
Petroleum products												
Road[1]	ZCAJ	68	71	75	73	61	61	75	74	59	64	67
Rail[2]	ZCAK	8	6	..	..	..	..	..	..	..	..	..
Water[3]	ZCAL	70	72	71	69	76	72	72	60	67	64	..
of which: coastwise	ZCAM	43	47	54	52	55	52	40	34	36	35	..
Pipeline	ZCAN	161	168	157	148	153	155	151	151	146	141	158
All modes[5]	ZCAO	307	317	303	290	290	288	298	285	272	269	..
Coal and coke												
Road[1]	ZCAP	42	34	32	37	26	28	22	21	17	22	14
Rail[2]	ZCAQ	43	45	52	50	45	44	46	46	41	42	52
Water[3]	ZCAR	4	4	3	4	3	3	3	3	2	2	..
All modes	ZCAS	89	83	87	91	70	75	71	70	60	66	..
Other traffic												
Road[1]	ZCAT	1 579	1 596	1 623	1 630	1 646	1 572	1 593	1 565	1 632	1 639	1 750
Rail[2,6]	ZCAU	47	50	50	55	57	48	50	48	46	47	50
Water[3]	ZCAV	66	67	67	69	70	70	62	68	70	67	..
All modes	ZCAW	1 692	1 713	1 740	1 754	1 773	1 690	1 705	1 681	1 748	1 753	..
All traffic												
Road[1]	KCTG	1 689	1 701	1 730	1 740	1 733	1 661	1 689	1 660	1 708	1 725	1 831
Rail[2]	KCTH	97	101	102	105	102	92	95	94	87	89	102
Water[3]	ZCAX	140	143	142	142	149	144	137	131	139	133	..
Pipeline	KCTK	161	168	157	148	153	155	151	151	146	141	158
All modes	KCTL	2 087	2 113	2 131	2 135	2 131	2 052	2 072	2 037	2 080	2 088	..
Percentage of all traffic												
Road[1]	ZCAY	*81*	*80*	*81*	*81*	*81*	*81*	*81*	*81*	*82*	*83*	..
Rail[2]	ZCAZ	*5*	*5*	*5*	*5*	*5*	*4*	*5*	*5*	*4*	*4*	..
Water[3]	ZCBA	*7*	*7*	*7*	*7*	*7*	*7*	*7*	*6*	*7*	*6*	..
Pipeline	ZCBB	*8*	*8*	*7*	*7*	*7*	*8*	*7*	*7*	*7*	*7*	..
All modes	ZCBC	*100*	*100*	*100*	*100*	*100*	*100*	*100*	*100*	*100*	*100*	..

1 All goods vehicles, including those under 3.5 tonnes gross vehicle weight. These estimates were revised following a survey in 1993.
2 Figures for rail are for financial years.
3 Figures for water are for UK traffic.
4 Figures for goods moved by rail is a new series from 1998.
5 Excludes rail data from 1996.
6 Figures for goods lifted by rail have been revised from 1999.

Source: Department for Transport

15.4 Passenger transport:[1] by mode
Great Britain

Billion passenger kilometres		1994	1995	1996	1997	1998	1999	2000	2001	2002	2003	2004
Road												
Buses and coaches[2]	GRXK	44	43	43	44	45	46	47	47	47	47	48
Cars, vans and taxis[2]	GRXG	614	618	625	632	635	641	639	654	678	677	679
Motor cycles	GRXH	4	4	4	4	4	5	5	5	5	6	6
Pedal cycles	GRXI	4	4	4	4	4	4	4	4	4	5	4
All road	GRXJ	666	669	676	684	688	696	695	710	734	735	736
Rail[3]	KCTN	35	37	39	42	44	46	47	47	48	49	51
Air	KCTM	6	6	6	7	7	7	8	8	8	9	10
All modes[4]	GRXM	706	712	721	733	738	750	749	765	791	793	797
Percentages												
Road												
Buses and coaches[2]	GRXN	6	6	6	6	6	6	6	6	6	6	6
Cars, vans and taxis[2]	GRXO	87	87	87	86	86	85	85	85	86	85	85
Motor cycles	GRXP	1	1	1	1	1	1	1	1	1	1	1
Pedal cycles	GRXQ	1	1	1	1	1	1	1	1	1	1	1
All road	GRXR	94	94	94	93	93	93	93	93	93	93	92
Rail[3]	ZCBJ	5	5	5	6	6	6	6	6	6	6	6
Air	ZCBK	1	1	1	1	1	1	1	1	1	1	1
All modes[4]	GRXU	100	100	100	100	100	100	100	100	100	100	100

1 See chapter text.
2 Data for 2004 are provisional.
3 Financial years. Former British Rail companies and Urban Rail systems.

4 Excluding travel by water within the United Kingdom (including the Channel Islands), estimated at 0.7 billion passenger kilometres in 2000.

Source: Department for Transport

15.5 Motor vehicle traffic[1]: by road class
Great Britain

Billion vehicle kilometres

		1994	1995	1996	1997	1998	1999	2000	2001	2002	2003	2004
Motorways	JSZV	70.7	73.9	78.3	82.1	85.7	87.8	88.4	90.8	92.6	93.0	96.6
Rural major roads												
Trunk	JSZW	56.5	57.9	60.4	62.5	63.3	64.7	64.2	65.9	64.6	61.5	59.7
Principal	JSZX	60.0	61.6	63.1	64.1	65.4	66.0	65.8	67.4	71.8	77.7	81.6
All	JSZY	116.5	119.5	123.5	126.6	128.7	130.7	130.0	133.3	136.4	139.3	141.3
Urban major roads												
Trunk	JSZZ	13.8	13.8	13.9	13.8	13.8	14.0	14.0	7.6	7.4	6.7	6.0
Principal	JTAA	64.7	66.2	67.0	67.1	67.5	67.9	67.7	74.2	74.8	75.1	76.8
All	JTAB	78.5	80.1	80.9	80.9	81.3	81.9	81.7	81.8	82.2	81.7	82.8
Minor roads												
Minor rural roads	JTAC	57.6	57.8	58.9	60.0	60.4	61.3	61.5	61.6	64.4	64.4	65.9
Minor urban roads	JTAD	98.1	98.5	99.6	100.7	102.4	105.3	105.5	106.9	110.8	111.9	112.0
All	JTAE	155.7	156.2	158.5	160.7	162.8	166.6	167.0	168.5	175.3	176.4	177.9
All roads	JTAF	421.5	429.7	441.1	450.3	458.5	467.0	467.1	474.4	486.5	490.4	498.6

1 See chapter text.

Source: Department for Transport: 020 7944 3095

227

Transport and communications

15.6 Public road length:[1] by road type
Great Britain

Kilometres

		1994	1995	1996	1997	1998	1999	2000	2001	2002	2003	2004
Trunk motorway	JSZD	3 170	3 197	3 253	3 333	3 376	3 404	3 422	3 431	3 433	3 432	3 478
Principal motorway	JSZE	72	72	45	45	44	45	45	45	45	46	46
Rural major roads:												
Trunk[2]	JSZF	10 500	10 510	10 598	10 690	10 585	10 611	10 627	10 607	9 973	9 027	8 641
Principal[2]	JSZG	24 609	24 759	24 592	24 636	24 783	24 852	24 866	24 915	25 559	26 498	26 889
Total	JSZH	35 109	35 269	35 190	35 326	35 369	35 463	35 493	35 522	35 532	35 525	35 530
Urban major roads:												
Trunk[2]	JSZI	1 146	1 133	1 117	1 108	1 096	1 087	1 074	762	705	587	506
Principal[2]	JSZJ	9 893	9 902	9 885	9 923	9 931	10 019	10 040	10 370	10 436	10 539	10 632
Total	JSZK	11 039	11 035	11 002	11 031	11 027	11 106	11 114	11 132	11 141	11 127	11 138
Rural minor roads:												
B roads	JSZL	24 618	24 610	24 603	24 594	24 586	24 579	24 570	24 562	24 554	24 547	24 640
C roads	JSZM	73 031	73 124	73 218	73 312	73 405	73 500	73 593	73 688	73 783	73 878	73 363
Unclassified	JSZN	110 265	110 481	110 698	110 915	111 132	111 350	111 568	111 787	112 006	112 231	109 561
All	JSZO	207 914	208 215	208 518	208 820	209 123	209 429	209 731	210 037	210 343	210 656	207 565
Urban minor roads:												
B roads	JSZP	5 608	5 611	5 615	5 618	5 622	5 626	5 630	5 633	5 638	5 641	5 538
C roads	JSZQ	10 900	10 922	10 943	10 966	10 986	11 009	11 031	11 054	11 076	11 098	10 859
Unclassified	JSZR	111 747	112 081	112 417	112 754	113 093	113 432	113 772	114 114	114 456	114 816	113 520
All	JSZS	128 254	128 614	128 975	129 338	129 702	130 068	130 432	130 802	131 169	131 556	129 917
All minor roads	JSZT	336 168	336 828	337 494	338 158	338 825	339 496	340 163	340 838	341 512	342 212	337 482
All roads	JSZU	385 557	386 401	386 983	387 893	388 641	389 515	390 237	390 969	391 663	392 342	387 674

1 See chapter text. A number of minor revisions have been made to the lengths of major roads for all years.
2 Figures for trunk and principal roads in England, from 2001 onwards, are affected by the detrunking programme.

Sources: National Road Traffic Survey;
Department for Transport 020 7944 3095

15.7 Road traffic:[1] by type of vehicle
Great Britain

Billion vehicle kilometres

		1994	1995	1996	1997	1998	1999	2000	2001	2002	2003	2004
Cars and taxis	JTAH	345.0	351.1	359.9	365.8	370.6	377.4	376.8	382.8	392.9	393.1	398.1
Motor cycles etc.	JTAI	3.8	3.7	3.8	4.0	4.1	4.5	4.6	4.8	5.1	5.6	5.2
Larger buses and coaches	JTAJ	4.6	4.9	5.0	5.2	5.2	5.3	5.2	5.2	5.2	5.4	5.2
Light vans[2]	JTAK	43.3	44.5	46.2	48.6	50.8	51.6	52.3	53.7	55.0	57.9	60.8
Goods vehicles:												
2 axles rigid	JTAL	10.8	10.7	10.9	11.0	11.1	11.6	11.7	11.5	11.6	11.7	11.7
3 axles rigid	JTAM	1.4	1.6	1.6	1.6	1.9	1.7	1.7	1.8	1.8	1.8	1.9
4 or more axles rigid	JTAN	1.5	1.5	1.5	1.5	1.6	1.5	1.5	1.5	1.5	1.6	1.6
3 and 4 axles artic.	JTAO	3.6	3.3	3.3	3.2	3.0	3.0	2.7	2.5	2.3	2.2	2.2
5 axles artic.	JTAP	5.8	6.4	6.6	7.1	7.3	7.2	6.7	6.4	6.4	6.2	6.5
6 or more axles artic.	JTAQ	1.8	2.0	2.3	2.5	2.9	3.3	4.1	4.5	4.8	5.0	5.4
All	JTAR	24.8	25.4	26.2	26.9	27.7	28.1	28.2	28.1	28.3	28.5	29.4
All motor vehicles	JURA	421.5	429.7	441.1	450.3	458.5	467.0	467.1	474.4	486.5	490.4	498.6
Pedal cycles	JURB	4.0	4.1	4.1	4.1	4.0	4.1	4.2	4.2	4.4	4.5	3.9

1 See chapter text.
2 Not exceeding 3,500 kgs gross vehicle weight.

Sources: National Road Traffic Survey;
Department for Transport 020 7944 3095

15.8 Motor vehicles currently licenced
Great Britain
At end of year

Thousands

	Private and light goods										Body type cars	
	Body type cars	Other vehicles	Motor cycles, scooters and mopeds	Public transport vehicles[1]	Goods vehicles	Special machines/ special conces- sionary	Other vehicles	Crown and exempt vehicles[3]	Special vehicles group	All vehicles[4]	All	Percent- age of company cars
	BMBJ	BMBK	BMBB	BMBE	BMBD	KSBY	BMBF	BMBL	KSBZ	BMBI	ZCGR	ZCGS
1994	20 479	2 192	630	107	434	309	50	1 030	..	25 231	21 199	10.4
1995[2]	20 505	2 217	594	74	421	274	44	1 169	28	25 369	21 394	10.4
1996	21 172	2 267	609	77	413	254	40	1 424	48	26 302	22 238	10.3
1997	21 681	2 317	626	79	414	249	38	1 522	48	26 974	22 832	10.5
1998	22 115	2 362	684	80	412	243	37	1 558	47	27 538	23 293	10.4
1999	22 785	2 427	760	84	415	241	36	1 573	47	28 368	23 975	10.0
2000	23 196	2 469	825	86	418	233	34	1 590	46	28 898	24 406	10.3
2001	23 899	2 544	882	89	422	233	33	1 602	45	29 747	25 126	9.7
2002	24 543	2 622	941	92	425	243	32	1 855	46	30 557	25 782	9.0
2003	24 985	2 730	1 005	96	426	258	32	1 887	47	31 207	26 240	8.4
2004	25 754	2 900	1 060	100	434	–	32	1 929	50	32 259	27 028	8.5

1 Includes taxis for years up to 1994. Taxation group now restricted to only vehicles with 9 or more seats.
2 The vehicle taxation system was subject to substantial revision from 1 July 1995.
3 Vehicles in this taxation class are exempt from duty and form part of the crown and exempt class with effect from January 2002.
4 Contains 44,000 vehicles still taxed in classes abolished from 1 July 1995.

Source: Department for Transport 020 7944 3077

15.9 New vehicle registrations by taxation class
Great Britain

Thousands

		1994	1995	1996	1997	1998	1999	2000	2001	2002	2003	2004
Total	BBKD	2 249.0	2 306.5	2 410.1	2 597.7	2 740.3	2 765.8	2 870.9	3 137.7	3 229.4	3 231.9	3 185.4
Private and light goods												
Private cars	BMAA	1 809.1	1 828.3	1 888.4	2 015.9	2 123.5	2 100.4	2 174.9	2 431.8	2 528.8	2 497.1	2 437.4
Other vehicles	BMAE	182.6	195.7	205.0	228.4	244.5	241.6	254.9	277.9	286.8	323.5	347.3
Total	BMAK	1 991.7	2 024.0	2 093.4	2 244.3	2 368.0	2 342.0	2 429.8	2 709.7	2 815.6	2 820.7	2 784.7
Motor cycles, etc:												
Up to 50 c.c.	KCUH	6.9	6.3	8.9	14.2	22.6	36.2	49.4	45.6	35.6	34.9	27.1
Other	KCUI	57.7	62.6	80.7	107.1	120.7	132.2	133.5	131.5	126.6	122.4	106.6
Total	BMAL	64.6	68.9	89.6	121.3	143.3	168.4	182.9	177.1	162.2	157.3	133.7
Public road passenger vehicles												
Buses, coaches, taxis, etc												
Not over 8 seats[1]	KCUJ	2.5	1.3	..	..	..	..	..	..	..	..	..
Over 8 seats	KCUK	4.2	5.2	6.5	6.6	7.4	8.0	7.5	6.8	7.8	8.4	8.3
Total	BBJZ	6.7	6.5	6.5	6.6	7.4	8.0	7.5	6.8	7.8	8.4	8.3
Heavy general goods and farmers[2]												
Goods vehicles: by weight	BBJY	41.1	48.0	45.5	41.8	49.1	48.3	50.4	48.6	44.9	48.4	48.0
Special concession group[3]	BBKA	35.3	33.3	25.7	21.7	15.2	17.3	16.9	19.8	23.1	24.1	25.0
Other licensed vehicles[4]	KCUM	1.3	1.0	1.0	1.5	1.5	1.5	1.2	1.2	1.3	1.2	0.9
Special vehicles group[5]	DMNR	..	3.3	8.1	8.6	7.6	7.6	6.5	7.0	7.2	8.1	7.6
Exempt from licence duty												
Crown vehicles	KCUN	4.1	3.3	1.2	0.7	1.1	1.1	1.0	1.0	1.4	1.4	1.4
All other exempt vehicles[2,6]	KCUO	104.3	118.1	139.1	150.7	146.6	170.4	173.9	166.5	166.1	162.1	150.8
Total	KCUP	108.4	121.4	140.3	151.4	147.7	171.6	174.9	167.5	167.5	163.5	152.2

1 From 1 July 1995 separate taxation of public transport vehicles with 8 or fewer seats was abolished. After this date new vehicles of this type were registered as PLG.
2 Until June 1995 included Agricultural vans and Lorries and Showman's goods vehicles licensed to draw trailers. From 1st July 1995 separate taxation group for Farmers and Showman were abolished.
3 Various revisions to the vehicle taxation system were introduced on 1 July 1995 and on 29 November 1995. Separate taxation classes for farmers goods vehicles were abolished on 1 July 1995; after this date new vehicles of this type were registered as HGV's. The total includes 5,900 vehicles registered between 1 January and 30 June in the (now abolished) agricultural special machine group in classes which were not eligable to register in the special concession group. The old agricultural and special machines taxation group was abolished at end of June 1995. The group

includes agricultural and mowing machines, snow ploughs and gritting vehicles. Electric vehicles are also included in this group and are no longer exempt from VED. Steam propelled vehicles were added to this group from November 1995.
4 Includes three wheelers, pedestrian controlled vehicles, general haulage and showmen's tractors and recovery vehicles. Recovery vehicle tax class introduced January 1988.
5 The special vehicle group was created on1 July 1995 and consists of various vehicle types over 3.5 tonnes gross weight but not required to pay VED as heavy goods vehicles. The group includes mobile cranes, works trucks, digging machines, road rollers and vehicles previously taxed as showman's goods and haulage. Figure shown for 1995 covers period from 1 July to 31 December only.
6 Between 1980 and 30 June 1995 electric vehicles were exempt from duty. From 1 July 1995 electric vehicles pay VED as part of the special concession group.

Source: Department for Transport: 020 7944 3077

Transport and communications

15.10 Driving test pass rates: by sex and type of vehicle licence
Great Britain

Percentages

		1989 /90	1991 /92	1998 /99	1999 /00	2000 /01	2001 /02	2002 /03	2003 /04	2004 /05
Males										
Motorcycle	JTRB	72	69	69	67	68	67	66	67	66
Car	JTRC	58	57	51	48	48	47	47	46	46
Bus	JTTG	–	–	48	49	47	46	44	46	43
Lorry	JTTH	–	–	52	53	53	50	50	49	47
All males	JTTI	–	–	–	51	51	50	49	48	47
Females										
Motorcycle	JTTJ	68	63	63	55	56	55	54	53	53
Car	JTTK	47	46	42	40	40	40	40	40	39
Bus	JTTL	–	–	47	46	45	40	40	45	46
Lorry	JTTM	–	–	50	49	53	47	46	48	45
All females	JTTN	–	–	–	40	41	41	40	40	40
All										
Motorcycle	JTTO	–	–	68	66	66	66	65	65	64
Car	JTTP	–	–	46	44	44	43	43	43	42
Bus	JTTQ	–	–	48	49	48	45	44	46	44
Lorry	JTTR	–	–	52	53	54	56	49	49	46
All persons	JTTS	–	–	–	46	46	46	45	44	43

Source: Driving Standards Agency 0115 901 2873

15.11 Full car driving licence holders by sex and age[1]
Great Britain

Percentages and millions

	17-20	21-29	30-39	40-49	50-59	60-69	70 or over	Estimated number of licence holders (millions)
All adults								
1975/76	28	59	67	60	50	35	15	19.4
1985/86	33	63	74	71	60	47	27	24.3
1991/93	49	75	81	78	70	57	34	29.1
1992/94	48	75	82	79	72	57	33	29.3
1996/98	43	73	82	82	76	64	38	30.4
1999/01	36	73	83	84	78	71	44	31.7
	C98J	C98K	C98L	C98M	C98N	C98O	C98P	C98Q
2002[2]	32	67	82	84	81	70	45	32.1
2003[2]	28	68	82	84	79	73	45	32.3
2004	26	65	83	83	81	72	47	32.2[3]
Males								
1975/76	36	78	85	83	75	58	32	13.4
1985/86	37	73	86	87	81	72	51	15.1
1991/93	58	84	90	88	87	80	59	17.1
1992/94	54	83	91	88	88	81	59	17.1
1996/98	48	79	89	90	88	82	64	17.2
1999/01	41	81	89	91	88	86	69	17.6
	C98R	C98S	C98T	C98U	C98V	C98W	C98X	C98Y
2002[2]	34	74	88	91	89	85	68	17.7
2003[2]	31	74	88	91	90	87	69	17.9
2004	29	69	89	89	91	87	72	17.9[3]
Females								
1975/76	20	43	48	37	24	15	4	6.0
1985/86	29	54	62	56	41	24	11	9.2
1991/93	40	68	73	68	54	37	17	12.1
1992/94	42	68	73	70	57	37	16	12.1
1996/98	38	68	75	73	63	48	20	13.2
1999/01	31	66	77	77	69	57	25	14.0
	C98Z	C992	C993	C994	C995	C996	C997	C998
2002[2]	31	60	77	79	74	56	28	14.4
2003[2]	24	62	77	78	69	59	27	14.4
2004	24	61	78	77	71	58	27	14.4[3]

1 See chapter text.
2 Data is supplied on a different basis than in previous years.
3 Data are provisional.

Source: Department for Transport: 020 7944 3097

15.12 Households with regular use of cars[1]
Great Britain

Percentages and millions

	No car	One car	Two cars	Three or more cars	Total (millions)
	ZCGA	ZCGB	ZCGC	ZCGD	ZCGE
1993	31	45	20	4	22.9
1994	32	45	20	4	23.1
1995	30	45	21	4	23.3
1996	30	45	21	4	23.5
1997	30	45	21	5	23.7
1998	28	44	23	5	23.9
1999	28	44	22	5	24.1
2000	27	45	23	5	24.4
2001	26	45	23	5	24.1
2002	26	44	24	5	24.3
2003	26	44	25	5	..

	No car	One car	Two or more cars	Total
Government Office Regions, 2003				
Great Britain	26	44	30	100
North East	37	44	19	100
North West	28	45	27	100
Yorkshire and the Humber	30	44	26	100
East Midlands	22	46	32	100
West Midlands	25	42	33	100
East	18	44	38	100
London	36	43	20	100
South East	17	42	41	100
South West	19	47	34	100
England	25	44	31	100
Wales	25	46	29	100
Scotland	31	43	25	100

	No car	One car	Two or more cars	Total
Area type, 2004				
Great Britain	26	45	29	100
London	41	41	18	100
Metropolitan areas	34	44	22	100
Other urban areas with population:				
Over 250,000	24	46	29	100
25,000 - 250,000	26	48	26	100
10,000 - 25,000	25	46	29	100
3,000 - 10,000	23	44	33	100
Rural areas	11	41	48	100

1 Includes cars and light vans normally available to the household.

Sources: Office for National Statistics;
Department for Transport 020 7944 3097

Transport and communications

15.13 Vehicles with current licences[1]
Northern Ireland

Numbers

		1994	1995	1996[2]	1997	1998	1999	2000	2001[5]	2002	2003	2004
Private cars, etc	KNKA	514 760	521 610	540 083	575 923	584 706	608 316	615 180	644 968	666 731	711 913	737 198
Cycles and tricycles	KNKB	8 775	8 775	8 775	8 775	8 775	8 775	8 775	8 775	8 775	8 775	8 775
Public road passenger vehicles:												
Taxis up to 4 seats	KNKD	623	739	..	..	..	..	..	..	..	..	−
Buses, coaches, over 4 seats	KNKE	2 455	1 353	2 090	2 144	2 175	2 204	2 266	2 315	2 322	2 353	2 378
Total	KNKC	3 078	2 092	2 090	2 144	2 175	2 204	2 266	2 315	2 322	2 353	2 378
General (HGV) goods vehicles:	KNKF	14 810	16 338	17 401	18 172	18 312	17 075	17 864	19 415	20 244	22 100	23 062
Farmers' goods vehicles[3]	KNKJ	5 904	..	..	..	..	..	..	..	..	..	..
Agricultural tractors and engines, etc[3]	KNKM	7 317	9 074	5 911	6 378	5 906	5 505	5 048	4 901	5 731	7 503	8 674
Other	KNKN	354	1 257	1 019	1 188	1 193	1 446	1 287	1 366	1 347	1 588	1 708
Vehicles exempt from duty:												
Government owned	KNKP	4 818	3 872	3 753	3 705	3 785	4 032	3 822	6 427	6 383	6 172	6 116
Other:												
Ambulances	KNKQ	104	250	371	389	425	417	452	318	299	325	355
Fire engines	KNKR	194	301	292	291	285	286	290	181	174	170	178
Other exempt[4]	KNKS	35 837	47 626	58 340	64 447	66 981	68 277	70 405	72 209	73 648	76 715	78 973
Total	KNKO	40 953	52 049	62 756	68 832	71 476	73 012	74 969	79 135	80 504	83 382	85 622
Total	KNKT	595 951	611 562	639 286	683 569	695 431	720 645	730 730	767 305	794 477	852 742	883 261

1 Licences current at any time during the quarter ended December.
2 Due to a revision of taxation classes, 1996 data are not directly comparable with previous years.
3 Owned by a farmer and available for hauling produce and requisites for his farm. From 1 July 1995 farmers goods taxation classes have been abolished.

4 Changes in the Mobility Allowance (DWP) have contributed to the increase in Other exempt.
5 Taxation classes have been revised.

Source: Driver and Vehicle Licensing, Northern Ireland: 028 7034 1461

15.14 New vehicle registrations
Northern Ireland

Numbers

		1994	1995	1996	1997	1998	1999	2000	2001	2002	2003	2004
Private cars, etc	KNLA	70 765	73 718	77 817	83 968	91 141	89 078	84 973	88 592	83 402	87 506	85 190
Cycles and tricycles	KNLB	1 943	2 362	2 803	3 376	4 307	5 310	6 010	5 591	5 596	6 804	4 601
Public road passenger vehicles	KNLC	1 143	622	724	714	486	568	565	451	439	609	467
Goods vehicles:												
General haulage vehicles:												
Under 3.5 tonnes	KNLH	6 908	7 357	7 232	8 468	10 107	11 054	12 617	13 274	12 007	10 716	11 090
3.5 tonnes and over	KNLJ	2 668	2 935	3 492	3 521	3 572	3 697	3 502	4 534	3 669	3 776	3 987
Agricultural tractors[1]	KNLM	1 558	1 619	1 292	1 364	971	987	1 313	301	1	9	2
Vehicles exempt from duty	KNLR	6 423	8 333	10 520	10 885	10 718	11 083	10 789	12 126	12 515	11 907	12 881
General haulage and special types	JTAG	..	..	..	..	..	..	..	..	15	12	11
Total	KNLS	91 408	96 946	103 880	112 296	121 302	121 777	119 769	124 869	117 644	121 339	118 229

1 Agricultural tractors driven on public roads. From April 2001 tractors were exempt.

Source: Driver and Vehicle Licensing, Northern Ireland: 028 7034 1461

15.15 Local bus services: passenger journeys: by area

Millions

		1994 /95	1995 /96	1996 /97	1997 /98	1998 /99	1999 /00	2000 /01	2001 /02	2002 /03	2003 /04	2004 /05
Great Britain	ZCET	4 402	4 366	4 333	4 313	4 231	4 278	4 319	4 352	4 444	4 564	4 609
London	KILS	1 155	1 193	1 230	1 281	1 266	1 294	1 347	1 422	1 527	1 692	1 782
English Metropolitan Counties	KILT	1 331	1 292	1 246	1 232	1 195	1 178	1 166	1 154	1 145	1 114	1 083
English Shire Counties	KILU	1 271	1 259	1 260	1 243	1 242	1 250	1 247	1 222	1 210	1 189	1 167
All outside London	ZCES	3 247	3 173	3 103	3 032	2 965	2 984	2 972	2 930	2 917	2 871	2 828
England	ZCER	3 757	3 744	3 736	3 755	3 702	3 722	3 761	3 798	3 882	3 995	4 032
Scotland	KILV	513	494	467	438	413	442	443	449	452	457	465
Wales	KILW	132	127	130	120	116	114	116	104	110	111	113

Source: Department for Transport 020 7944 3076

15.16 Local bus services: fare indices: by area
Current prices

Indices (1995=100)

		1994 /95	1995 /96	1996 /97	1997 /98	1998 /99	1999 /00	2000 /01	2001 /02	2002 /03	2003 /04	2004 /05
Great Britain	KNEU	96.7	101.2	106.3	112.0	117.1	122.0	126.4	130.6	134.5	139.1	145.7
London	KNEP	96.2	101.1	105.4	109.3	113.7	117.2	117.2	115.5	114.8	116.9	126.8
English Metropolitan Counties	KILD	96.4	101.5	106.9	113.3	118.7	124.6	129.9	137.4	142.7	148.0	154.2
English Shire Counties	KILE	97.0	101.1	106.0	111.5	116.7	122.0	128.6	135.1	141.7	148.5	155.7
All outside London	ZCEQ	96.8	101.2	106.6	112.8	118.2	123.4	129.2	135.3	140.8	146.3	152.5
England	ZCEP	96.7	101.2	106.1	111.4	116.5	121.5	125.9	130.3	134.2	139.1	146.2
Scotland	KILF	96.9	100.8	108.0	116.5	121.8	125.3	129.9	131.8	134.5	136.8	140.4
Wales	KILG	97.4	100.7	104.4	110.1	116.3	122.2	127.5	133.5	139.5	145.5	152.4
Retail Prices Index (1995=100)	KNEV	97.5	100.7	103.1	106.5	109.9	111.6	114.9	116.6	119.1	122.4	126.2

Source: Department for Transport 020 7944 3076

15.17 Road accident casualties: by road user type and severity
Great Britain

Numbers

		1994	1995	1996	1997	1998	1999	2000	2001	2002	2003	2004
Child pedestrians:												
Killed	ZCDH	160	132	131	138	103	107	107	107	79	74	77
Killed or seriously injured	KIJS	4 610	4 400	4 132	3 954	3 737	3 457	3 226	3 144	2 828	2 381	2 339
All severities	ZCDI	19 263	18 590	18 510	18 407	17 971	16 876	16 184	15 819	14 231	12 544	12 234
Adult pedestrians:												
Killed	ZCDJ	953	897	858	835	803	760	750	712	688	695	589
Killed or seriously injured	KIJT	8 114	7 716	7 300	6 925	6 592	6 221	6 112	5 745	5 644	5 422	5 005
All severities	ZCDK	28 129	27 178	26 827	26 223	25 827	24 806	24 481	23 463	23 258	22 531	21 404
Child pedal cyclists:												
Killed	ZCDL	42	48	54	33	32	36	27	25	22	18	25
Killed or seriously injured	KIJU	1 234	1 249	1 231	1 016	915	950	758	674	594	595	577
All severities	ZCDM	8 075	8 133	8 217	7 899	6 930	7 290	6 260	5 451	4 809	4 769	4 682
Adult pedal cyclists:												
Killed	ZCDN	129	164	148	150	126	135	98	111	107	95	109
Killed or seriously injured	KIJV	2 710	2 673	2 517	2 542	2 345	2 172	1 954	1 951	1 801	1 776	1 697
All severities	ZCDO	16 097	16 140	15 778	16 181	15 326	14 834	13 630	12 974	11 712	11 643	11 366
Motorcyclists[1] and passengers:												
Killed	ZCDP	444	445	440	509	498	547	605	583	609	693	585
Killed or seriously injured	ZCDQ	6 666	6 615	6 208	6 446	6 442	6 908	7 374	7 305	7 500	7 652	6 648
All severities	BMDH	24 354	23 524	23 133	24 492	24 610	26 192	28 212	28 810	28 353	28 411	25 641
Car drivers and passengers:												
Killed	ZCDS	1 764	1 749	1 806	1 795	1 696	1 687	1 665	1 749	1 747	1 769	1 671
Killed or seriously injured	ZCDT	23 892	23 461	24 048	23 191	21 676	20 368	19 719	19 424	18 728	17 291	16 144
All severities	ZCDU	195 154	194 027	205 336	211 448	210 474	205 735	206 799	202 802	197 425	188 342	183 858
Bus/coach drivers and passengers:												
Killed	ZCDV	21	35	11	14	18	11	15	14	19	11	20
Killed or seriously injured	KCUZ	815	836	695	601	631	611	578	562	551	500	488
All severities	ZCDW	10 090	9 278	9 345	9 439	9 839	10 252	10 088	9 884	9 005	9 068	8 820
LGV drivers and passengers:												
Killed	ZCDX	64	69	61	64	67	65	66	64	70	72	62
Killed or seriously injured	ZCDY	1 101	1 106	989	928	949	867	813	811	780	765	631
All severities	ZCDZ	7 558	7 200	7 215	7 476	7 672	7 124	7 007	7 304	7 007	6 897	6 166
HGV drivers and passengers:												
Killed	ZCEA	41	57	63	45	60	52	55	54	63	44	47
Killed or seriously injured	ZCEB	571	635	555	573	560	540	571	500	524	429	406
All severities	ZCEC	3 370	3 331	3 245	3 302	3 444	3 484	3 597	3 388	3 178	3 061	2 883
All road users:[2]												
Killed	BMDC	3 650	3 621	3 598	3 599	3 421	3 423	3 409	3 450	3 431	3 508	3 221
Killed or seriously injured	ZCEE	50 190	49 154	48 097	46 583	44 255	42 545	41 564	40 560	39 407	37 215	34 351
All severities	BMDA	315 359	310 687	320 578	327 803	325 212	320 310	320 283	313 309	302 605	290 607	280 840

1 Includes mopeds and scooters.
2 Includes other motor or non-motor vehicle users, and unknown road user type and casualty age.

Source: Department for Transport 020 7944 3078

15.18

Freight transport by road: goods moved by goods vehicles over 3.5 tonnes[1]
Great Britain

Billion tonne kilometres

		1994	1995	1996	1997	1998	1999	2000	2001	2002	2003	2004[3]
By mode of working												
Mainly public haulage	KNND	100.8	106.5	109.1	112.2	114.3	110.9	113.0	114.7	110.6	114.3	110.8
Mainly own account	KNNC	37.0	37.2	37.7	37.4	37.6	38.3	37.5	34.7	39.2	37.4	41.4
All modes	KNNB	137.8	143.7	146.8	149.6	151.9	149.2	150.5	149.4	149.8	151.7	152.2
By gross weight of vehicle												
Rigid vehicles:												
3.5-17 tonnes	ZCIL	19.9	18.7	19.5	19.2	17.8	17.9	15.8	13.1	11.9	10.1	9.1
17-25 tonnes	ZCIM	6.1	5.6	5.3	4.7	4.2	4.3	4.8	5.7	6.3	6.8	7.9
25 tonnes and over	ZCIN	12.4	13.3	13.5	14.3	14.7	15.3	15.4	15.6	17.3	18.3	18.9
All rigids	ZCIO	38.4	37.5	38.3	38.1	36.6	37.5	36.0	34.5	35.6	35.2	35.9
Articulated vehicles:												
3.5-33 tonnes	ZCIP	16.9	15.9	15.9	14.3	14.4	14.0	14.0	12.8	9.9	8.8	7.0
33 tonnes and over	ZCIQ	82.5	90.2	92.6	97.1	100.9	97.7	100.4	102.1	104.4	107.7	109.4
All articulated vehicles	ZCIR	99.4	106.1	108.5	111.4	115.3	111.7	114.4	114.9	114.3	116.5	116.4
All vehicles												
3.5-25 tonnes	ZCIS	26.6	24.7	25.3	24.3	22.5	22.7	21.3	19.3	18.7	17.3	17.3
25 tonnes and over	KNNG	111.2	119.0	121.5	125.2	129.4	126.5	129.2	130.1	131.1	134.4	134.9
All weights	ZCIT	137.8	143.7	146.8	149.6	151.9	149.2	150.5	149.4	149.8	151.7	152.2
By commodity												
Food, drink and tobacco	ZCIU	36.5	37.5	39.3	40.8	42.5	41.5	44.3	41.4	43.1	42.2	41.7
Wood, timber and cork	ZCIV	3.3	3.2	3.8	3.5	3.6	3.8	3.7	3.9	3.8	4.1	4.5
Fertiliser	ZCIW	1.3	1.4	1.5	1.3	1.2	1.4	1.2	1.2	1.2	1.2	0.8
Crude minerals	ZCIX	14.1	13.5	13.5	13.6	13.3	12.7	12.4	13.0	13.9	13.8	14.1
Ores	ZCIY	1.4	1.5	1.3	1.7	1.1	1.3	1.2	1.2	1.1	1.2	1.4
Crude materials	ZCIZ	2.0	1.9	2.1	2.1	2.6	2.6	2.6	2.3	2.7	2.3	3.3
Coal and coke	ZCJA	2.9	2.7	2.5	2.7	2.0	2.2	1.5	2.1	1.5	1.5	1.2
Petrol and petroleum products	ZCJB	5.1	5.7	6.1	5.8	5.2	5.0	6.4	5.8	5.2	5.5	5.7
Chemicals	ZCJC	8.1	7.4	7.7	8.2	7.9	7.4	6.8	7.2	6.5	6.8	6.3
Building materials	ZCJD	10.0	10.7	9.6	11.1	10.7	10.6	10.6	11.7	10.9	12.0	12.1
Iron and steel products	ZCJE	6.7	7.8	7.2	7.9	7.7	6.8	6.8	5.7	5.3	5.4	5.4
Other metal products[2]	ZCJF	2.0	1.7	1.7	1.5	1.7	1.7	1.7	1.4	1.5	1.5	1.9
Machinery and transport equipment	ZCJG	6.8	7.4	7.7	8.4	9.1	8.7	9.1	8.9	8.5	8.7	8.9
Miscellaneous manufactures[2]	ZCJH	13.4	13.3	14.2	14.2	15.9	15.7	15.1	15.4	16.2	15.8	16.3
Miscellaneous transactions[4]	ZCJI	24.3	27.8	28.4	26.8	27.5	27.9	27.1	28.2	28.4	29.5	28.8
All commodities	ZCJJ	137.8	143.7	146.8	149.6	151.9	149.2	150.5	149.4	149.8	151.7	152.2

1 Rigid vehicles or articulated vehicles (tractive unit and trailer) with gross
  vehicle weight over 3.5 tonnes.
2 Includes not elsewhere specified.
3 Figures for 2004 are not fully comparable with those for 2003 and earlier
  years. Detailed comparisons should therefore be made with caution.
4 Includes not elsewhere specified and commodity not known.

Source: Department for Transport 020 7944 3093

15.19 Freight transport by road: goods lifted by goods vehicles over 3.5 tonnes[1]
Great Britain

Million tonnes

		1994	1995	1996	1997	1998	1999	2000	2001	2002	2003	2004
By mode of working												
Mainly public haulage	ZCJK	980	987	1 011	1 044	1 041	991	1 038	1 052	1 019	1 053	1 101
Mainly own account	ZCJL	618	622	618	599	589	576	556	529	608	590	643
All modes	ZCJM	1 597	1 609	1 628	1 643	1 630	1 567	1 593	1 581	1 627	1 643	1 744
By gross weight of vehicle												
Rigid vehicles:												
3.5-17 tonnes	ZCJN	317	298	306	294	268	254	229	203	188	159	160
17-25 tonnes	ZCJO	202	162	133	120	106	86	87	86	90	100	113
25 tonnes and over	ZCJP	332	373	371	380	401	408	424	443	491	506	539
All rigids	ZCJQ	852	833	811	793	776	748	741	733	768	765	812
Articulated vehicles:												
3.5-33 tonnes	ZCJR	142	139	138	124	125	113	107	97	81	69	60
33 tonnes and over	ZCJS	604	637	679	726	729	706	746	751	778	809	872
All articulated vehicles	ZCJT	746	776	817	850	854	819	852	848	859	878	932
All vehicles												
3.5-25 tonnes	ZCJU	527	467	447	419	382	346	325	294	283	265	277
25 tonnes and over	ZCJV	1 070	1 142	1 181	1 224	1 248	1 221	1 268	1 287	1 343	1 378	1 467
All weights	ZCJW	1 597	1 609	1 628	1 643	1 630	1 567	1 593	1 581	1 627	1 643	1 744
By commodity												
Food, drink and tobacco	ZCJX	302	308	326	342	346	333	346	321	339	333	351
Wood, timber and cork	ZCJY	24	24	27	26	27	28	26	28	28	32	42
Fertiliser	ZCJZ	10	11	13	10	9	11	10	9	11	12	7
Crude minerals	ZCKA	355	319	320	329	327	297	308	298	333	327	364
Ores	ZCKB	18	18	18	25	18	20	16	16	17	21	22
Crude materials	ZCKC	16	16	18	17	20	20	18	20	21	19	25
Coal and coke	ZCKD	42	34	32	37	26	28	22	21	17	22	14
Petrol and petroleum products	ZCKE	68	71	75	73	61	61	75	74	59	64	67
Chemicals	ZCKF	51	50	51	53	53	47	49	50	41	47	46
Building materials	ZCKG	156	161	142	156	161	159	165	165	167	165	185
Iron and steel products	ZCKH	47	54	52	55	54	48	49	44	39	41	43
Other metal products[2]	ZCKI	17	17	15	16	18	17	16	14	14	16	19
Machinery and transport equipment	ZCKJ	57	61	59	71	73	67	69	70	68	66	70
Miscellaneous manufactures[2]	ZCKK	84	85	88	90	96	91	97	97	105	98	111
Miscellaneous transactions[3]	ZCKL	351	379	393	343	342	340	328	353	367	379	378
All commodities	ZCKM	1 597	1 609	1 628	1 643	1 630	1 567	1 593	1 581	1 627	1 643	1 744

1 Rigid vehicles or articulated vehicles (tractive unit and trailer) with gross vehicle weight over 3.5 tonnes.
2 Includes not elsewhere specified.
3 Includes not elsewhere specified and commodity not known.

Source: Department for Transport 020 7944 3093

15.20 Rail systems summary

		1994/95	1995/96	1996/97	1997/98	1998/99	1999/00	2000/01	2001/02	2002/03	2003/04	2004/05
Passenger journeys (millions)												
National Rail network[1,8]	ZCKN	735	761	801	846	892	931	957	960	976	1 014	1 088
London Underground	KNOE	764	784	772	832	866	927	970	953	942	948	976
Docklands Light Railway	ZCKO	12	14	17	21	28	31	38	41	46	48	50
Glasgow Underground	ZCKP	15	14	14	14	15	15	14	14	13	13	13
Nexus (Tyne and Wear Metro)[2]	ZCKQ	37	36	35	35	34	33	33	33	37	38	37
Blackpool trams[3]	EL9L	5	5	5	5	4	4	4	5	4	4	4
West Midlands Metro[4]	ZCKR	–	–	–	–	–	5	5	5	5	5	5
Croydon Tramlink[5]	GEOE	–	–	–	–	–	–	15	18	19	20	22
Manchester Metrolink[6]	ZCKS	12	13	13	14	13	14	17	18	19	19	20
Stagecoach Supertram (Sheffield)	ZCKT	2	5	8	9	10	11	11	11	12	12	13
Nottingham NET[7]	C3MI	–	–	–	–	–	–	–	–	–	–	8
All rail	ZCKU	1 582	1 632	1 665	1 776	1 862	1 972	2 065	2 058	2 074	2 122	2 236
of which: light rail	GENZ	68	73	78	84	89	99	124	131	142	147	159
Passenger revenue (£ million at current prices)												
National Rail network	KNDL	2 171	2 379	2 573	2 821	3 089	3 368	3 413	3 548	3 663	3 901	4 158
London Underground	KNOA	718	765	797	899	977	1 058	1 129	1 151	1 138	1 161	1 241
Docklands Light Railway	ZCKV	6	9	12	14	20	22	29	32	36	37	40
Glasgow Underground	ZCKW	7	8	8	9	9	10	10	10	10	10	11
Nexus (Tyne and Wear Metro)	ZCKX	19	20	21	22	23	24	24	25	29	31	33
Blackpool trams[3]	EL9M	4	5	4	5	4	4	4	5	5	4	4
West Midlands Metro	ZCKY	–	–	–	–	–	–	3	4	5	5	5
Croydon Tramlink	GEOF	–	–	–	–	–	–	12	13	15	16	18
Manchester Metrolink	ZCKZ	10	11	13	14	..	..	18	20	20	21	22
Stagecoach Supertram (Sheffield)	ZCLA	2	4	5	6	6	7	7	8	10	9	11
Nottingham NET	C3MJ	–	–	–	–	–	–	–	–	–	–	6
All rail	ZCLB	2 937	3 201	3 433	3 790	4 128	4 493	4 649	4 815	4 930	5 195	5 550
of which: light rail	GEOA	41	49	55	61	53	57	97	107	120	122	140
Passenger kilometres (millions)												
National Rail network[1,8]	KNDZ	28 700	30 000	32 100	34 700	36 280	38 472	38 179	39 141	39 678	40 937	42 369
London Underground	KNOI	6 051	6 337	6 153	6 479	6 716	7 171	7 470	7 451	7 367	7 340	7 606
Docklands Light Railway	ZCLC	55	70	86	103	144	172	200	207	232	235	245
Glasgow Underground	ZCLD	43	41	40	45	47	47	46	44	43	43	43
Nexus (Tyne and Wear Metro)	ZCLE	271	261	254	249	238	230	229	238	275	284	283
Blackpool trams[3]	EL9N	..	..	..	..	..	13	13	15	14	11	12
West Midlands Metro	ZCLF	–	–	–	–	–	50	56	50	50	54	52
Croydon Tramlink	GEOG	–	–	–	–	–	–	96	99	100	105	112
Manchester Metrolink	ZCLG	79	81	86	88	117	126	152	161	167	169	204
Stagecoach Supertram (Sheffield)	ZCLH	8	20	29	34	35	37	38	39	40	42	44
Nottingham NET	C3MK	–	–	–	–	–	–	–	–	–	2	37
All rail	ZCLI	35 207	36 811	38 748	41 698	43 577	46 318	46 479	47 445	47 966	49 222	51 008
of which: light rail	GEOB	413	432	455	474	534	628	784	809	878	903	990
Route kilometres open for passenger traffic (numbers)												
National Rail network	ZCLJ	14 359	15 002	15 034	15 024	15 038	15 038	15 042	15 042	15 042	14 883	14 328
London Underground	ZCLK	392	392	392	392	392	408	408	408	408	408	408
Docklands Light Railway	ZCLM	22	22	22	22	22	26	26	26	26	26	26
Glasgow Underground	ZCLN	11	11	11	11	11	11	11	11	11	11	11
Nexus (Tyne and Wear Metro)	ZCLO	59	59	59	59	59	59	59	78	78	78	78
Blackpool trams[3]	EL9O	18	18	18	18	18	18	18	18	18	18	18
West Midlands Metro	ZCLP	–	–	–	–	–	–	20	20	20	20	20
Croydon Tramlink	GEOH	–	–	–	–	–	–	28	28	28	28	28
Manchester Metrolink	ZCLQ	31	31	31	31	31	39	39	39	39	39	39
Stagecoach Supertram (Sheffield)	ZCLR	22	29	29	29	29	29	29	29	29	29	29
Nottingham NET	C3ML	–	–	–	–	–	–	–	–	–	14	14
All rail	ZCLS	14 914	15 564	15 596	15 586	15 600	15 628	15 680	15 699	15 699	15 554	14 999
of which: light rail	GEOC	152	159	159	159	159	171	219	238	238	252	252
Stations served (numbers)												
National Rail network	ZCLT	2 489	2 497	2 498	2 495	2 499	2 503	2 508	2 508	2 508	2 507	2 508
London Underground	KNOO	245	245	245	245	246	253	253	253	253	253	253
Docklands Light Railway	ZCLU	27	28	28	29	29	34	34	34	34	34	34
Glasgow Underground	ZCLV	15	15	15	15	15	15	15	15	15	15	15
Nexus (Tyne and Wear Metro)	ZCLW	46	46	46	46	46	46	46	58	58	58	58
Blackpool trams[3]	EL9P	124	124	124	124	124	124	124	124	124	124	124
West Midlands Metro	ZCLX	–	–	–	–	–	23	23	23	23	23	23
Croydon Tramlink	GEOI	–	–	–	–	–	–	38	38	38	38	38
Manchester Metrolink	ZCLY	26	26	26	26	26	36	36	36	37	37	37
Stagecoach Supertram (Sheffield)	ZCLZ	37	45	45	46	47	47	47	48	48	48	48
Nottingham NET	C3MM	–	–	–	–	–	–	–	–	–	23	23
All rail	ZCLL	3 009	3 026	3 027	3 026	3 032	3 081	3 124	3 137	3 138	3 160	3 161
of which: light rail	GSOC	260	269	269	271	272	310	348	361	362	385	385

1 Franchised train operating companies from February 1996 following rail privatisation.
2 Tyne & Wear Metro extension to Sunderland opened in March 2002.
3 Blackpool Trams shown as a self-contained system.
4 West Midland Metro opened in 1999.
5 Croydon Tramlink opened in 2000.
6 Transfer of 20 stations from the rail network to Manchester Metrolink.
7 Nottingham Express Transit (NET) opened in March 2004.
8 National Rail passenger journeys & passenger kilometres have been revised by the SRA.

Sources: Network Rail, former Railtrack, SRA, TfL; light rail operators and RTEs

15.21 National railways freight[1]
Great Britain

Billion tonne kilometres

		1994/95	1995/96	1996/97	1997/98	1998/99	1999/00	2000/01	2001/02	2002/03	2003/04	2004/05
Freight moved by commodity												
Coal	ZCGG	3.3	3.6	3.9	4.4	4.5	4.8	4.8	6.2	5.7	5.8	7.0
Metals	ZCGH	1.7	1.7	..	..	2.1	2.2	2.1	2.4	2.7	2.4	2.6
Construction	ZCGI	2.5	2.3	..	..	2.1	2.0	2.4	2.8	2.6	2.7	2.8
Oil and petroleum	ZCGJ	1.8	1.8	..	..	1.6	1.5	1.4	1.2	1.1	1.2	1.2
Other traffic	ZCGK	3.8	3.9	11.3	12.5	7.1	7.6	7.4	7.0	6.5	6.8	7.0
All traffic	VOXD	13.0	13.3	15.1	16.9	17.3	18.2	18.1	19.4	18.7	18.9	20.7
Freight lifted by commodity												
Coal	ZCGL	42.5	45.2	52.2	50.3	45.3	44.3	45.7	46.1	40.7	42.0	51.7[2]
Metals	ZCGM	16.9	15.1	..	..	..	..	..	..	..	..	..
Construction	ZCGN	16.8	11.5	..	..	..	..	..	..	..	..	..
Oil and petroleum	ZCGO	8.1	6.3	..	..	..	..	..	..	..	..	..
Other traffic	ZCGP	13.0	22.6	49.6	55.1	56.8	47.6	49.7	48.3	46.4	46.9	50.2[2]
All traffic	VOXE	97.3	100.7	101.8	105.4	102.1	91.9	95.4	94.4	87.0	88.9	101.9[2]

1 Due to changes in the way freight traffic has been estimated following the privatisation of British Rail, figures since 1996/97 are not strictly comparable with those for previous years. The series calculation was revised again from 1998/99 and from 1999/00 owing to revisions made by freight operators.
2 Break in series, increase largely due to change in coverage.

Source: Department for Transport: 020 7944 4977

15.22 Railways: permanent way and rolling stock
Northern Ireland
At end of year

Numbers

		1994	1995	1996	1997	1998	1999	2000	2001	2002	2003	2004
Length of road open for traffic[1] (Km)	KNRA	331	333	335	335	335	335	356	334	334	334	299
Length of track open for traffic (Km)												
Total	KNRB	503	506	506	505	526	526	547	480	480	480	445
Running lines	KNRC	462	464	464	464	484	484	505	464	464	464	427
Sidings (as single track)	KNRD	41	42	42	42	42	42	42	16	16	16	18
Locomotives												
Diesel-electrics	KNRE	11	11	8	6	5	6	6	6	6	5	6
Passenger carrying vehicles												
Total	KNRF	112	112	112	112	120	108	108	106	106	100	108
Rail motor vehicles:												
Diesel-electric, etc	KNRG	30	30	30	30	28	30	30	29	28	28	28
Trailer carriages:												
Total locomotive hauled	KNRH	28	28	28	28	38	21	21	25	22	22	22
Ordinary coaches	KNRI	26	26	26	26	36	19	19	23	20	20	20
Restaurant cars	KNRJ	2	2	2	2	2	2	2	2	2	2	2
Rail car trailers	KNRK	54	54	54	54	54	54	54	52	50	50	52
Rolling stock for maintenance and repair	KNRT	41	41	41	41	26	18	18	18	18	39	46

1 The total length of railroad open for traffic irrespective of the number of tracks comprising the road.

Source: Department for Regional Development, Northern Ireland: 028 9054 0801

15.23 Operating statistics of railways
Northern Ireland

		Unit	1994	1995	1996	1997	1998	1999	2000	2001	2002	2003	2004
Maintenance of way and works													
Material used:													
Ballast	KNSA	Thousand m^2	33.2	22.5	27.0	51.3	38.5	40.0	47.0	80.0	40.0	130.0	70.0
Rails	KNSB	Thousand tonnes	1.80	1.76	2.12	0.37	2.50	3.00	3.50	2.50	1.00	4.50	1.00
Sleepers	KNSC	Thousands	22.40	22.90	27.50	5.10	32.00	30.00	40.00	50.00	5.00	40.00	28.00
Track renewed	KNSD	Km	12.00	16.00	20.00	2.40	22.50	7.00	29.00	15.00	5.00	25.75	2.00
New Track laid	KPGD	Km	3.2	2.5	–	–	–	–	21.0	–	–	–	–
Engine kilometres													
Total[1]	KNSE	Thousand Km	3 640	4 000	4 100	4 100	4 100	4 100	4 100	4 056	4 056	4 170	4 110
Train kilometres:													
Total	KNSF	"	3 210	3 570	3 670	3 670	3 670	3 670	3 670	3 626	3 626	3 704	3 610
Coaching	KNSG	"	3 206	3 566	3 666	3 666	3 666	3 666	3 666	3 622	3 622	3 700	3 610
Freight	KNSH	"	4	4	4	4	4	4	4	4	4	4	–

1 Including shunting, assisting, light, departmental, maintenance and repair.

Source: Department for Regional Development, Northern Ireland: 028 9054 0801

15.24 Main output of United Kingdom airlines

Available tonne kilometres (millions)

		1994	1995	1996	1997	1998	1999	2000	2001	2002	2003	2004
All services	KNTA	27 714	29 904	32 210	35 538	40 021	42 002	43 379	42 370	40 550	42 784	43 883
Percentage growth on previous year	KNTB	*10.2*	*7.4*	*7.7*	*10.3*	*12.5*	*5.0*	*3.6*	*−2.4*	*−4.3*	*5.5*	*2.6*
Scheduled services	KNTC	20 360	22 016	23 793	26 504	29 756	31 815	32 938	31 866	30 433	31 513	32 422
Percentage growth on previous year	KNTD	*9.4*	*8.1*	*8.1*	*11.4*	*12.3*	*6.9*	*3.5*	*−3.3*	*−4.5*	*3.6*	*2.9*
Non-scheduled services	KNTE	7 265	7 695	8 044	9 034	10 265	10 186	10 440	10 505	10 117	11 271	11 461
Percentage growth on previous year	KNTF	*13.0*	*5.9*	*4.5*	*7.3*	*13.3*	*−0.7*	*4.1*	*0.6*	*−3.7*	*11.4*	*1.7*

Source: Civil Aviation Authority: 020 7453 6246

15.25 Air traffic between the United Kingdom and abroad[1]

Thousands

		1994[2]	1995	1996	1997	1998	1999	2000	2001	2002	2003	2004
Flights												
United Kingdom airlines												
Scheduled services	KNUA	325.8	342.1	373.0	410.3	443.7	480.9	520.3	536.7	531.3	517.7	546.5
Non-scheduled services	KNUB	195.0	204.8	198.0	208.2	218.7	212.6	216.2	208.5	218.6	211.0	198.6
Overseas airlines[3]												
Scheduled services	KNUC	351.3	363.3	390.0	399.6	426.4	467.6	467.6	496.8	487.5	487.0	544.2
Non-scheduled services	KNUD	35.1	31.5	31.3	32.5	34.8	31.7	31.7	26.0	36.7	27.1	28.8
Total	KNUE	907.2	941.7	992.3	1 050.6	1 123.6	1 192.8	1 235.8	1 268.0	1 274.1	1 242.8	1 318.1
Passengers carried												
United Kingdom airlines												
Scheduled services	KNUF	32 578.0	34 934.7	37 902.2	41 854.7	46 747.7	50 148.5	54 522.8	53 591.7	54 360.0	56 476.7	63 216.1
Non-scheduled services	KNUG	19 501.0	20 484.5	26 304.4	28 699.5	31 616.6	32 603.8	33 185.9	34 009.1	33 935.7	33 385.6	32 195.7
Overseas airlines[3]												
Scheduled services	KNUH	35 134.5	34 568.5	36 992.1	39 900.7	42 554.5	46 628.0	46 627.9	51 107.8	51 317.6	54 504.0	60 278.0
Non-scheduled services	KNUI	3 509.5	4 244.2	4 416.3	4 413.0	4 569.7	4 156.5	4 156.5	3 966.1	3 956.3	3 947.1	4 068.3
Total	KNUJ	90 723.0	94 231.9	105 615.0	114 867.9	125 488.5	133 536.8	138 493.1	142 674.7	143 569.6	148 313.4	159 758.1

1 Excludes travel to and from the Channel Islands.
2 Due to the introduction of European licencing, off shore helicopter movements are no longer included in this figure.
3 Includes airlines of overseas UK Territories.

Source: Civil Aviation Authority: 020 7453 6246

15.26 Operations and traffic on scheduled services: revenue traffic
United Kingdom airlines[1]

		Unit	1994	1995	1996	1997	1998	1999	2000	2001	2002	2003	2004
All services													
Aircraft stage flights:													
Number	KNFA	Numbers	621 272	658 958	702 492	749 806	797 682	835 031	878 582	921 556	911 518	895 095	926 498
Average length	KNFB	Kilometres	1 023	1 032	1 047	1 079	1 111	1 134	1 156	1 138	1 149	1 215	1 227
Aircraft-kilometres flown	KNFC	Millions	663	680	735	809	886	947	1 016	1 049	1 047	1 088	1 137
Passengers uplifted	KNFD	"	44	48	51	56	62	65	70	70	72	76	83
Seat-kilometres used	KNFE	"	104 295	115 347	124 847	136 388	151 969	160 336	170 469	158 651	156 494	164 806	173 722
Cargo uplifted:[2]	KNFF	Tonnes	618 067	643 181	690 806	782 855	831 436	860 291	897 184	742 705	768 736	800 645	842 912
Tonne-kilometres used:		Millions											
Passenger	KNFH	"	9 789	11 172	12 190	13 287	14 755	15 518	16 507	15 258	15 035	15 419	15 580
Freight	KNFI	"	3 378	3 567	3 832	4 454	4 663	4 925	5 160	4 548	4 941	5 187	5 297
Mail	KNFJ	"	147	151	176	172	178	153	179	102	57	55	75
Total	KNFG	"	13 315	14 890	16 198	17 913	19 596	20 596	21 846	19 908	20 032	20 660	20 952
Domestic services													
Aircraft stage flights:													
Number	KNFK	Numbers	301 652	318 884	331 109	336 218	352 936	354 864	353 525	365 881	359 400	345 954	373 858
Average length	KNFL	Kilometres	315	317	320	330	333	337	344	350	350	357	360
Aircraft-kilometres flown	KNFM	Millions	95	101	106	111	118	120	121	128	126	123	135
Passengers uplifted	KNFN	"	13	14	15	16	17	17	18	18	20	21	22
Seat-kilometres used	KNFO	"	5 334	5 754	6 204	6 646	6 948	7 184	7 542	7 645	8 322	8 904	9 263
Cargo uplifted:[2]	KNFP	Tonnes	32 670	33 659	35 432	30 679	31 879	25 964	24 644	19 498	16 755	17 248	14 862
Tonne-kilometres used:		Millions											
Passenger	KNFR	"	417	485	528	569	593	610	640	649	703	738	757
Freight	KNFS	"	6	7	7	6	6	6	6	4	4	3	3
Mail	KNFT	"	7	7	6	6	6	4	4	4	3	3	3
Total	KNFQ	"	430	499	542	581	605	620	650	656	709	744	762
International services													
Aircraft stage flights:													
Number	KNFU	Numbers	319 620	339 714	371 400	413 588	444 746	480 167	525 057	555 675	552 118	549 141	552 640
Average length	KNFV	Kilometres	1 693	1 703	1 695	1 688	1 729	1 723	1 704	1 656	1 670	1 758	2 148
Aircraft-kilometres flown	KNFW	Millions	541	579	630	698	769	827	895	921	921	965	1 002
Passengers uplifted	KNFX	"	31	34	36	40	45	48	52	52	52	56	61
Seat-kilometres used	KNFY	"	98 961	109 593	118 642	129 743	145 022	153 153	162 927	151 006	148 172	155 903	164 459
Cargo uplifted:[2]	KNFZ	Tonnes	585 397	609 522	655 374	752 176	799 557	834 327	872 540	723 206	751 975	783 397	828 051
Tonne-kilometres used:		Millions											
Passenger	KNJX	"	9 352	10 686	11 662	12 718	14 162	14 908	15 867	14 610	14 332	14 681	14 824
Freight	KNJY	"	3 372	3 560	3 825	4 448	4 657	4 919	5 154	4 544	4 937	5 184	5 294
Mail	KNJZ	"	141	144	170	166	172	149	176	98	54	51	72
Total	KNJW	"	12 865	14 391	15 656	17 333	18 991	19 976	21 197	19 252	19 322	19 916	20 190

1 Includes services of British Airways and other UK private companies.
2 Cargo has re-defined as freight and mail.

Source: Civil Aviation Authority: 020 7453 6246

15.27 Accidents on scheduled fixed wing passenger-carrying services[1,2]
United Kingdom airlines

| | | Passenger casualties | | Crew casualties | | Thousand aircraft stage flights per fatal accident | Million aircraft-kms. flown per fatal accident | Thousand passengers carried per passenger killed | Million passenger kms. flown per passenger killed | Fatal accidents | | Passengers killed per hundred million passenger-kms. |
	Number of fatal accidents	Killed	Seriously injured	Killed	Seriously injured					per 100 000 aircraft stage flights	per hundred million aircraft-kms.	
1950-54	7	194	9	28	4	107.4	61.8	46.1	50.1	0.93	1.62	2.00
1955-59	7	123	28	29	8	158.3	92.1	155.2	158.5	0.63	1.09	0.63
1960-64	5	104	35	21	6	303.7	182.2	373.4	390.6	0.33	0.55	0.26
1965-69	6	273	2	32	2	282.7	194.9	222.2	255.2	0.35	0.51	0.39
1970-74	2	167	5	14	2	889.5	737.1	464.3	657.7	0.11	0.14	0.15
1975-79	1	54	6	9	-	1 773.0	1 523.5	1 688.2	3 239.9	0.06	0.07	0.03
1980-84	-	-	4	-	1	-	-	-	-	-	-	-
1985-89	2	47	79	1	8	1 220.0	1 014.5	3031.0	6 262.9	0.08	0.10	0.02
1990-94	-	-	1	-	9	-	-	-	-	-	-	-
1995-99	1	9	1	3	3	3 699.9	4 026.0	31 265.6	76 539.4	0.03	0.02	0.001
	KCVN	KCVO	KCVP	KCVQ	KCVR							
2000	-	-	1	-	-	-	-	-	-	-	-	-
2001	-	-	-	-	-	-	-	-	-	-	-	-
2002	-	-	-	-	3	-	-	-	-	-	-	-
2003	-	-	1	-	1	-	-	-	-	-	-	-
2004	-	-	2	-	-	-	-	-	-	-	-	-

1 Excluding accidents involving the deaths of third parties only.
2 Following a review of historical data for this table, some revisions have been made to earlier years.

Source: Civil Aviation Authority: 01293 573446

15.28 Activity at civil aerodromes
United Kingdom[1]

Thousands and tonnes

		1996	1997	1998	1999	2000	2001	2002	2003	2004	2005
Movement of civil aircraft (thousands)											
Commercial											
Transport	KNQC	1 686	1 764	1 871	1 959	2 045	2 095	2 094	2 160	2 277	2 406
Other[2]	KNQD	128	143	162	159	159	150	120	117	116	120
Total	KNQB	1 814	1 907	2 033	2 118	2 204	2 245	2 214	2 277	2 393	2 526
Non-commercial[3]	KNQE	1 281	1 330	1 343	1 263	1 186	1 207	1 100	1 186	1 135	1 129
Total	KNQA	3 095	3 237	3 376	3 381	3 390	3 452	3 314	3 463	3 528	3 655
Passengers handled											
Terminal	KNQG	135 810	146 657	158 856	168 363	179 885	181 231	188 761	199 950	215 681	228 214
Transit	KNQH	1 486	1 405	1 226	1 156	1 167	1 087	1 054	990	950	984
Total	KNQF	137 296	148 062	160 082	169 519	181 052	182 318	189 815	200 940	216 631	229 198
Commercial freight handled[4] (tonnes)											
Set down	KNQJ	886 507	981 861	1 072 127	1 135 065	1 174 635	1 093 142	1 124 026	1 172 552	1 267 411	1 282 724
Picked up	KNQK	885 080	960 859	1 008 358	1 053 902	1 139 292	1 052 379	1 071 407	1 035 680	1 103 539	1 080 620
Total	KNQI	1 771 587	1 942 720	2 080 485	2 188 967	2 313 927	2 145 521	2 195 433	2 208 232	2 370 950	2 363 344
Mail handled											
Set down	KNQM	80 937	88 366	88 766	92 974	101 743	98 690	90 738	86 415	108 481	102 344
Picked up	KNQN	105 964	115 066	113 993	114 752	123 352	117 389	99 747	93 096	112 424	110 576
Total	KNQL	186 901	203 432	202 759	207 726	225 095	216 079	190 485	179 511	220 905	212 920

1 Figures exclude Channel Island Airports.
2 Local pleasure flights and non-transport charter flights for reward (for example; aerial survey work, crop dusting and delivery of empty aircraft).
3 Test and training flights, charter service positioning flights, private, aero-club and official flights & business aviation etc,.
4 With effect from 2001, passengers, freight and mail handled exclude traffic carried on air taxi operations.

Source: Civil Aviation Authority: 020 7453 6258

241

15.29 United Kingdom ports: foreign, coastwise and one-port traffic

Thousand tonnes

		1993	1994	1995	1996	1997	1998	1999	2000	2001	2002	2003
Foreign												
liquid bulk traffic												
Imports	EL9Q	68 824	63 512	58 512	59 309	61 060	61 346	56 528	70 788	74 495	62 811	66 447
Exports	EL9R	96 616	113 936	111 651	106 169	104 654	106 041	110 591	118 509	110 321	107 516	100 772
All	EL9S	165 440	177 448	170 164	165 478	165 714	167 387	167 120	189 297	184 816	170 327	167 218
Dry bulk traffic												
Imports	EL9T	58 053	58 297	62 121	63 905	68 208	68 333	65 219	65 652	77 360	67 575	72 644
Exports	EL9U	18 546	19 652	19 632	19 549	19 596	20 840	18 905	19 739	17 206	18 026	20 559
All	EL9V	76 598	77 949	81 753	83 454	87 805	89 173	84 124	85 391	94 565	85 600	93 203
Container and roll-on traffic												
Imports	EL9W	45 519	49 930	51 668	52 008	58 822	61 191	64 272	64 753	65 721	68 371	69 199
Exports	EL9X	36 079	38 942	41 694	43 711	48 805	49 029	49 616	49 323	47 334	47 313	47 291
All	EL9Y	81 598	88 873	93 362	95 719	107 628	110 220	113 889	114 076	113 054	115 685	116 490
Semi-bulk traffic												
Imports	EL9Z	15 145	16 988	16 445	15 987	16 097	16 878	15 967	17 174	17 059	18 523	17 284
Exports	ELA2	5 183	5 349	4 891	5 267	5 142	4 897	4 519	4 411	3 737	3 613	3 848
All	ELA3	20 329	22 337	21 337	21 253	21 239	21 775	20 486	21 584	20 796	22 136	21 131
Conventional traffic												
Imports	ELA4	1 916	1 359	1 555	1 493	1 506	1 531	1 595	2 500	3 730	3 645	3 699
Exports	ELA5	1 066	1 109	932	1 094	1 100	854	735	1 145	1 786	1 705	1 535
All	ELA6	2 982	2 468	2 487	2 587	2 607	2 385	2 330	3 645	5 515	5 349	5 234
All foreign traffic												
Imports	ELA7	189 457	190 087	190 302	192 702	205 694	209 279	203 581	220 866	238 364	220 924	229 273
Exports	ELA8	157 490	178 988	178 801	175 790	179 298	181 661	184 367	193 127	180 383	178 173	174 003
All	ELA9	346 947	369 075	369 103	368 492	384 992	390 940	387 948	413 993	418 747	399 097	403 276
Coastwise traffic												
Liquid bulk traffic												
Inwards	ELB2	41 893	44 178	48 393	52 354	49 981	51 514	48 164	36 677	37 008	38 694	36 973
Outwards	ELB3	44 557	46 135	51 459	57 146	53 753	52 622	51 966	41 696	36 049	37 535	35 371
All	ELB4	86 450	90 313	99 852	109 501	103 734	104 136	100 131	78 373	73 058	76 229	72 344
Dry bulk traffic												
Inwards	ELB5	8 433	9 098	9 352	7 613	6 678	7 599	6 792	8 243	8 032	7 245	7 956
Outwards	ELB6	7 923	8 230	9 968	7 942	6 963	7 882	7 229	8 201	7 112	7 785	8 438
All	ELB7	16 357	17 329	19 319	15 555	13 642	15 480	14 021	16 444	15 144	15 030	16 395
Container and roll-on traffic												
Inwards	ELB8	8 754	9 542	9 820	9 623	10 522	11 236	11 542	12 186	11 797	11 854	11 788
Outwards	ELB9	9 056	9 941	10 205	9 716	10 786	10 660	11 396	11 506	11 064	11 341	11 426
All	ELC2	17 810	19 484	20 025	19 339	21 307	21 895	22 938	23 692	22 861	23 195	23 214
Semi-bulk traffic												
Inwards	ELC3	234	199	172	187	166	176	203	247	364	324	373
Outwards	ELC4	312	269	266	251	188	477	221	311	570	546	544
All	ELC5	547	467	437	438	354	653	424	558	934	870	917
Conventional traffic												
Inwards	ELL6	118	262	161	139	161	212	274	96	74	99	194
Outwards	ELM5	177	224	238	261	314	306	285	139	131	124	368
All	ELN2	295	486	399	400	475	518	559	236	206	223	562
All coastwise traffic												
Inwards	ELN3	59 433	63 279	67 898	69 917	67 508	70 736	66 975	57 448	57 276	58 215	57 285
Outwards	ELN4	62 027	64 799	72 134	75 316	72 004	71 946	71 098	61 853	54 926	57 331	56 147
All	ELN5	121 460	128 078	140 032	145 233	139 512	142 682	138 073	119 302	112 202	115 546	113 432

Source: Department for Transport; 020 7944 3087

15.29 United Kingdom ports: foreign, coastwise and one-port traffic

continued

Thousand tonnes

		1993	1994	1995	1996	1997	1998	1999	2000	2001	2002	2003
One-port traffic												
Liquid bulk traffic												
Inwards	ELN6	10 063	13 725	10 848	10 861	6 871	10 587	20 220	24 937	18 245	25 886	22 328
Outwards	ELN7	9 137	8 850	8 882	8 847	8 560	4 365	126	485	647	693	563
All	ELN8	19 200	22 575	19 731	19 708	15 431	14 951	20 346	25 422	18 892	26 579	22 892
Dry bulk traffic												
Inwards	ELN9	12 616	13 952	14 964	13 260	14 123	14 436	15 051	12 503	14 362	15 197	14 389
Outwards	ELO2	1 126	312	105	98	106	98	41	41	68	67	70
All	ELO3	13 743	14 263	15 069	13 357	14 229	14 534	15 092	12 544	14 430	15 264	14 460
Non-oil traffic with UK off-shore installations												
Inwards	ELO4	1 123	900	914	984	851	1 063	1 136	589	643	606	490
Outwards	ELO5	3 751	3 238	3 382	3 468	3 515	4 332	3 019	1 199	1 452	1 234	1 112
All	ELO6	4 875	4 138	4 296	4 453	4 366	5 394	4 155	1 789	2 095	1 840	1 602
All one-port traffic												
Inwards	ELO7	23 802	28 577	26 726	25 105	21 844	26 085	36 407	38 030	33 250	41 688	37 208
Outwards	ELO8	14 015	12 400	12 369	12 413	12 181	8 794	3 186	1 725	2 167	1 994	1 745
All	ELO9	37 818	40 977	39 095	37 518	34 026	34 880	39 593	39 755	35 417	43 682	38 953
Foreign and domestic traffic												
Liquid bulk traffic												
Inwards	ELP2	120 780	121 415	117 754	122 524	117 912	123 446	124 913	132 402	129 748	127 391	125 748
Outwards	ELP3	150 311	168 921	171 992	172 163	166 967	163 028	162 684	160 690	147 017	145 744	136 706
All	ELP4	271 090	290 336	289 746	294 687	284 879	286 474	287 597	293 092	276 765	273 134	262 454
Dry bulk traffic												
Inwards	ELP5	79 102	81 347	86 437	84 778	89 009	90 367	87 062	86 398	99 754	90 016	94 990
Outwards	ELP6	27 596	28 194	29 705	27 588	26 666	28 820	26 175	27 981	24 386	25 878	29 067
All	ELP7	106 698	109 542	116 141	112 366	115 675	119 187	113 237	114 379	124 140	115 894	124 057
Container and roll-on traffic												
Inwards	ELP8	54 273	59 473	61 487	61 631	69 344	72 427	75 814	76 939	77 518	80 225	80 987
Outwards	ELP9	45 136	48 884	51 899	53 427	59 591	59 689	61 013	60 829	58 398	58 654	58 717
All	ELQ2	99 409	108 357	113 387	115 058	128 935	132 115	136 827	137 768	135 915	138 879	139 704
Semi-bulk traffic												
Inwards	ELQ3	15 380	17 187	16 617	16 174	16 263	17 054	16 170	17 421	17 423	18 847	17 657
Outwards	ELQ4	5 496	5 618	5 157	5 518	5 330	5 374	4 740	4 721	4 307	4 159	4 392
All	ELQ5	20 876	22 805	21 774	21 692	21 593	22 428	20 910	22 142	21 730	23 006	22 049
Conventional traffic												
Inwards	ELQ6	2 034	1 621	1 716	1 632	1 667	1 744	1 869	2 596	3 804	3 744	3 893
Outwards	ELQ7	1 243	1 332	1 170	1 355	1 414	1 159	1 020	1 284	1 917	1 828	1 903
All	ELQ8	3 277	2 953	2 886	2 987	3 082	2 903	2 889	3 880	5 721	5 572	5 796
Non-oil traffic with UK off-shore installations												
Inwards	ELQ9	1 123	900	914	984	851	1 063	1 136	589	643	606	490
Outwards	ELR2	3 751	3 238	3 382	3 468	3 515	4 332	3 019	1 199	1 452	1 234	1 112
All	ELR3	4 875	4 138	4 296	4 453	4 366	5 394	4 155	1 789	2 095	1 840	1 602
All foreign and domestic traffic												
Inwards	ELR4	272 692	281 943	284 926	287 724	295 046	306 100	306 963	316 344	328 890	320 828	323 766
Outwards	ELR5	233 532	256 187	263 304	263 519	263 484	262 402	258 651	256 706	237 477	237 497	231 896
All	ELR6	506 224	538 130	548 230	551 243	558 530	568 502	565 614	573 050	566 366	558 325	555 662

15.30 Roll-on/roll-off ferry and Channel Tunnel traffic; road goods vehicles outward to mainland Europe: by country of registration

Thousands

		1994	1995	1996	1997	1998	1999	2000	2001	2002	2003	2004
Powered vehicles:												
United Kingdom	ZCGT	453.1	486.0	531.1	543.2	544.3	562.7	544.8	517.6	493.3	473.9	493.1
Austria	ZCGU	..	9.7	8.6	5.4	10.2	14.9	17.0	42.0	45.8	42.9	30.0
Belgium/Luxembourg	ZCGV	37.1	45.7	41.0	53.6	74.5	96.7	114.1	119.3	121.4	104.3	112.4
Denmark	ZCGW	5.0	4.5	4.6	5.5	7.3	8.7	9.5	12.0	16.9	13.7	17.1
Finland	ZCGX	..	0.3	0.2	0.1	0.6	0.7	0.9	3.1	2.0	1.1	0.1
Germany	ZCGY	28.1	28.0	30.4	39.3	52.4	73.1	111.5	132.0	148.2	155.7	164.7
France	ZCGZ	163.2	154.9	181.7	234.2	272.4	319.1	338.8	352.4	363.1	363.2	388.0
Greece	ZCHA	1.3	1.8	2.1	2.6	1.9	2.6	2.9	2.6	2.8	3.6	4.0
Irish Republic	ZCHB	32.4	31.0	30.1	32.3	38.8	44.7	48.5	46.6	44.6	30.8	27.6
Italy	ZCHC	22.7	29.3	28.9	30.4	35.3	45.8	67.8	91.1	127.8	132.4	120.1
Netherlands	ZCHD	76.3	84.6	87.2	107.0	125.4	153.3	185.1	187.5	186.3	210.2	252.1
Spain	ZCHE	35.2	38.4	39.4	45.1	56.3	67.7	81.8	93.9	102.2	105.9	109.8
Sweden	ZCHF	..	0.7	0.9	8.9	10.3	1.0	1.4	1.8	1.8	1.4	1.4
Portugal	ZCHG	3.7	3.4	3.1	5.1	6.7	9.2	10.7	10.2	11.0	9.4	8.9
European Union[1] (excluding UK)	ZCHH	405.2	432.2	458.1	569.5	692.1	837.3	990.0	1 094.5	1 173.9	1 174.6	1 236.2
Non-European Union	ZCHI	34.2	29.0	26.3	28.0	33.3	24.9	24.9	43.2	76.7	97.6	107.6
Unknown	ZCHJ	4.0	3.0	2.2	5.7	4.8	6.3	17.7	20.5	18.1	19.1	17.0
All countries	ZCHK	896.5	950.2	1 017.7	1 146.4	1 274.8	1 453.7	1 605.4	1 711.9	1 801.5	1 814.7	1 956.8
Unaccompanied trailers	ZCHL	701.6	677.4	626.4	740.0	737.5	737.8	712.9	686.4	726.0	780.4	782.2
Powered vehicles and unaccompanied trailers	ZCHM	1 598.1	1 627.6	1 644.1	1 886.4	2 012.3	2 191.4	2 318.3	2 398.3	2 527.5	2 595.1	2 739.0

1 New Member State countries that joined the EU on 1st May 2004. There is no individual breakdown available before 1999 for these countries.

Source: Department for Transport; 0117 987 8484

15.31 United Kingdom international passenger movements by air and sea[1]

Thousands

		1993	1994	1995	1996	1997	1998	1999	2000	2001	2002	2003
By air												
European Union[2]	ZCDD	51 506	58 042	59 987	60 949	66 089	73 360	79 003	84 930	87 534	91 419	97 768
Other Western Europe	ZCDE	8 507	8 797	9 364	9 473	10 385	11 089	11 246	11 897	12 062	12 053	12 477
Rest of the world	ZCDF	27 335	28 915	31 542	34 499	37 594	40 263	42 619	45 293	42 591	42 611	43 400
All air passenger movements	KMUP	87 348	95 754	100 893	104 921	114 068	124 712	132 868	142 120	142 187	146 082	153 644
By sea												
Irish Republic, European continent and Mediterranean Sea area	ZCDG	34 685	36 733	34 321	34 543	36 258	33 226	31 381	28 516	27 754	28 726	26 523
Rest of the world	BMMF	37	34	33	24	29	23	26	26	27	32	25
Pleasure cruises[3]	KMRQ	193	236	207	233	..	..	445	461	469	540	698
All sea passenger movements	KMUO	34 915	37 002	34 562	34 792	36 288	33 249	31 852	29 003	28 249	29 298	27 246

1 See chapter text.
2 As constituted before 1 May 2004.
3 Cruise passengers, like other passengers are included at both departure and arrival if their journeys begin and end at United Kingdom seaports.

Sources: Civil Aviation Authority; Department for Transport.

15.32 Postal services and television licences[1]
United Kingdom

Millions and thousands

		1995	1996	1997	1998	1999	2000	2001	2002	2003	2004	2005
Letters, etc posted (millions)	KMRA	17 468	18 322	18 101	18 350	18 878	19 711	20 076	20 648	21 979	22 837	24 341
of which:												
Registered and insured	KMRB	21.5	23.5	25.6	28.7	31.6	30.2	32.3	36.1	38.5	41.4	45.3
Airmail (Commonwealth and foreign)	KMRC	567.1	655.1	684.5	658.4	693.2	672.3	659.2	600.7	541.6	512.0	457.9
Business reply and freepost items	KMRD	477.6	493.1	505.8	524.7	503.6	475.3	487.4	486.2	434.4	397.7	401.1
Postal orders												
Total issued (thousands)[2]	KMRH	37 901	35 542	33 404	31 907	30 289	30 153	30 931	29 150	28 666	28 888	29 344
Television licences (thousands)												
In force on 31 March	KMQL	20 732	21 105	21 305	21 723	22 240	22 625	22 839	23 157	23 486	23 899	24 162
of which:												
Colour	KMQM	19 957	20 505	20 849	21 344	21 944	22 413	22 684	23 040	23 392	23 824	24 103

1 See chapter text.
2 Excluding those issued on HM ships, in many British possessions and in other places abroad. Up to 1998 includes Postal Orders issued Overseas and by Ministry of Defence.

Sources: Royal Mail: 01246 547012;
Capita Business Services Limited: 0117 3021003;
Post Office Counters Limited: 020 7921 9384

245

National accounts

Chapter 16

National accounts

National accounts

(Tables 16.1 to 16.22)

The tables which follow are based on those in the *Blue Book* 2005 Edition. Some of the figures are provisional and may be revised later; this applies particularly to the figures for 2003 and 2004.

The accounts are based on the European System of Accounts 1995 (ESA95). The *Blue Book* contains an introduction to the system of the UK accounts outlining some of the main concepts and principles of measurement used. It explains how key economic indicators are derived from the sequence of accounts and how the figures describing the whole economy are broken down by sector and by industry. A detailed description of the structure for the accounts is provided in a separate ONS publication *United Kingdom National Accounts*: *Concepts, Sources and Methods* (TSO 1998). Further information on the financial accounts is given in the *Financial Statistics Explanatory Handbook*.

In the tables in this chapter on national income, analyses by industry are based, as far as possible, on the Standard Industrial Classification Revised 1992. The principal aggregate measured in these tables is the Gross domestic product (GDP). This is a concept of the value of the total economic activity taking place in UK territory. It can be viewed as incomes earned, as expenditures incurred, or as production. Adding all primary incomes received from the rest of the world and deducting all primary incomes payable to non-residents produces Gross national income (previously known as gross national product). This is a concept of the value of all incomes earned by UK residents.

ESA95, the internationally compatible accounting framework, provides a systematic and detailed description of the UK economy. It includes the sector accounts which provide, by institutional sector, a description of the different stages of the economic process from production through income generation, distribution and use of income to capital accumulation and financing; and the input-output framework, which describes the production process in more detail. It contains all the elements required to compile such aggregate measures as GDP, gross national income (GNI) and saving.

Gross domestic product and national income

(Tables 16.1, 16.2, 16.3)

Table 16.1 shows the main national accounts aggregates, both at current prices and chained volume measures.

Table 16.2 shows the various money flows which generate the gross domestic product and gross national income. The output approach to GDP shows the total output of goods and services, the use of goods and services in the production process (intermediate consumption) and taxes and subsidies on products. The expenditure approach to GDP shows consumption expenditure by households and government, gross capital formation and expenditure on UK exports by overseas purchasers. The sum of these items overstates the amount of income generated in the United Kingdom by the value of imports of goods and services; this item is therefore subtracted to produce gross domestic product at market prices. The income approach to GDP shows gross operating surplus, mixed income and compensation of employees (previously known as income from employment). Taxes are added and subsidies are deducted to produce the total of the income-based components at market prices.

Table 16.2 also shows the primary incomes received from the rest of the world, which are added to GDP and primary incomes payable to non-residents, which are deducted from GDP, to arrive at Gross national income. Primary income comprises compensation of employees, taxes less subsidies on production and property and entrepreneurial income.

Table 16.3 shows the expenditure approach to the chained volume measure of GDP. When looking at the change in the economy over time the main concern is usually whether more goods and services are actually being produced now than at some time in the past. Over time changes in current price GDP show changes in the monetary value of the components of GDP and, as these changes in value can reflect changes in both price and volume, it is difficult to establish how much of an increase in the series is due either to increased activity in the economy or to an increase in the price level. As a result, when looking at the real growth in the economy over time it is useful to look at volume estimates of GDP. In chained volume series, volume measures for each year are produced in prices of the previous year. These volume measures are then 'chain-linked' together to produce a continuous time series.

Industrial analysis

(Tables 16.4, 16.5)

The analysis of gross value added by industry at current prices shown in Table 16.4 reflects the estimates based on the Standard Industrial Classification, revised 1992 (SIC92). The table is based on current price data reconciled through the input-output process for 1992 to 2003. The estimates are valued at basic prices, that is, the only taxes included in the price will be taxes paid as part of the production process, such as business rates, and not any taxes specifically levied on the production of a unit of output, for example VAT.

Table 16.5 shows chained volume measures of gross value added at basic prices by industry. Chained volume measures of gross value added (output approach) provides the lead indicator of economic change in the short term. The output analysis of gross value added is estimated in terms of change and expressed in index number form. It is therefore inappropriate to show as a statistical adjustment any divergence of an output measure of GDP derived from it from other measures of GDP. Such an adjustment does, however, exist implicitly.

Sector analysis – Distribution of income accounts and capital account

(Tables 16.6 to 16.13)

The National Accounts accounting framework includes the sector accounts which provide, by institutional sector, a description of the different stages of the economic process from production through income generation, distribution and use of income to capital accumulation and financing.

Tables 16.6 to 16.12 show the allocation of primary income account and the secondary distribution of income account for the non-financial corporations, financial corporations, government and households sectors. Additionally, Table 16.12 shows the use of income account for the households sector and Table 16.13 provides a summary of the capital account. The full sequence of accounts is shown in the *Blue Book*.

The allocation of primary income account shows the resident units and institutional sectors as recipients rather than producers of primary income. It demonstrates the extent to which operating surpluses are distributed to the owners of the enterprises. The resources side of the allocation of primary income accounts includes the components of the income approach to measurement of GDP. The balance of this account is the gross balance of primary income (B.5g) for each sector, and if the gross balance is aggregated across all sectors of the economy the result is *Gross national income*.

The secondary distribution of income account describes how the balance of income for each sector is allocated by redistribution; through transfers such as taxes on income, social contributions and benefits and other current transfers. The balancing item of this account is gross disposable income (B.6g). For the households sector, the chained volume measure of gross disposable income is shown as real household disposable income.

Table 16.12 shows, for the households sector, the use of disposable income where the balancing item is saving (B.8g). For the non-financial corporations sector the balancing item of the secondary distribution of income account, gross disposable income (B.6g) is equal to saving (B.8g).

The summary capital account (Table 16.13) brings together the saving and investment of the several sectors of the economy. It shows saving, capital transfers, gross capital formation and net acquisition of non-financial assets for each of the four sectors.

Household and non-profit institutions serving households (NPISH) consumption expenditure at current market prices and chained volume measures

(Tables 16.14 to 16.17)

Household and NPISH consumption expenditure is a major component of the expenditure measure of gross domestic product both at current prices (Table 16.2) and chained volume measures (Table 16.3).

Household final consumption expenditure includes the value of income-in-kind and imputed rent of owner-occupied dwellings but excludes business expenditure allowed as deductions in computing income for tax purposes. It includes expenditure on durable goods, for instance motor cars, which from the point of view of the individual might more appropriately be treated as capital expenditure. The only exceptions are the purchase of land and dwellings and costs incurred in connection with the transfer of their ownership and expenditure on major improvements by occupiers, which are treated as personal capital expenditure.

The estimates of household consumption expenditure include purchases of second-hand as well as new goods, *less* the proceeds of sales of used goods.

The most detailed figures are published quarterly in *Consumer Trends* (available as a web-only publication on the National Statistics website www.statistics.gov.uk).

National accounts

Change in inventories (previously known as value of physical increase in stocks and work in progress)

(Table 16.18)

This table gives a broad analysis by industry, and, for manufacturing industry, by asset, of the value of entries less withdrawals and losses of inventories (stocks).

Gross fixed capital formation

(Table16.19 to 16.22)

Gross fixed capital formation comprises expenditure on the replacement of, and additions to, fixed capital assets located in the United Kingdom, including all ships and aircraft of UK ownership.

16.1 United Kingdom national and domestic product[1]
Main aggregates
At current prices and chained volume measures, reference year 2002

Indices (2002=100) and £ million

		1996	1997	1998	1999	2000	2001	2002	2003	2004
INDICES (2002=100)										
VALUES AT CURRENT PRICES										
Gross domestic product at current market prices ("money GDP")	YBEU	72.8	77.3	82.1	86.4	91.0	95.1	100.0	105.5	111.1
Gross value added at current basic prices	YBEX	73.1	77.4	82.0	85.9	90.4	94.9	100.0	105.5	111.0
CHAINED VOLUME MEASURES										
Gross domestic product at market prices	YBEZ	84.0	86.7	89.5	92.2	95.9	98.0	100.0	102.5	105.8
Gross national disposable income at market prices	YBFP	80.7	84.4	88.3	89.8	93.5	96.4	100.0	102.6	106.0
Gross value added at basic prices	CGCE	84.3	86.9	89.9	92.7	96.4	98.3	100.0	102.5	105.6
PRICES										
Implied deflator of GDP at market prices	YBGB	86.7	89.2	91.7	93.7	94.8	97.0	100.0	102.9	105.0
VALUES AT CURRENT PRICES (£ million)										
Gross measures (before deduction of fixed capital consumption) at current market prices										
Gross Domestic Product ("money GDP")	YBHA	763 561	810 601	860 520	905 438	953 576	996 758	1 048 456	1 105 919	1 164 941
Employment, property and entrepreneurial income from the rest of the world (receipts *less* payments)	YBGG	781	3 276	12 304	−1 460	4 583	11 371	23 679	24 192	26 163
Subsidies (receipts) *less* taxes (payments) on products from/to the rest of the world	-QZOZ	−3 116	−2 919	−3 651	−3 288	−3 838	−3 772	−2 424	−2 431	−1 571
Other subsidies on production from/to the rest of the world	-IBJL	253	206	246	309	292	298	519	..	..
Gross National Income (GNI)	ABMX	761 487	811 166	869 414	901 028	954 656	1 004 939	1 070 230	1 129 075	1 190 619
Current transfers from the rest of the world (receipts *less* payments)	-YBGF	−1 902	−3 209	−4 966	−4 435	−6 253	−3 426	−6 711	−8 135	−9 752
Gross National Disposable Income	NQCO	759 585	807 957	864 448	896 593	948 403	1 001 513	1 063 519	1 120 940	1 180 703
Adjustment to current basic prices										
Gross Domestic Product (at current market prices)	YBHA	763 561	810 601	860 520	905 438	953 576	996 758	1 048 456	1 105 919	1 164 941
Adjustment to current basic prices (*less* taxes *plus* subsidies on products)	-NQBU	−83 084	−90 573	−97 077	−106 051	−112 071	−113 346	−117 660	−124 187	−131 115
Gross Value Added (at current basic prices)	ABML	680 477	720 028	763 443	799 387	841 505	883 412	930 796	981 732	1 033 573
Net measures (after deduction of fixed capital consumption) at current market prices	-NQAE	−86 633	−88 395	−91 348	−97 063	−101 929	−105 990	−112 453	−116 227	−122 702
Net domestic product	NHRK	676 991	722 300	769 277	808 503	851 802	890 920	936 500	990 596	1 042 862
Net national income	NSRX	674 917	722 865	778 171	804 093	852 882	899 101	958 274	1 012 949	1 068 046
Net national disposable income	NQCP	673 015	719 656	773 205	799 658	846 629	895 675	951 563	1 004 814	1 058 294
CHAINED VOLUME MEASURES (Reference year 2002, £ million)										
Gross measures (before deduction of fixed capital consumption) at market prices										
Gross Domestic Product	ABMI	880 854	908 655	938 101	966 551	1 005 542	1 027 905	1 048 456	1 074 858	1 109 145
Terms of trade effect ("Trading gain or loss")	YBGJ	−18 221	−9 835	−4 618	−3 225	−5 650	−7 609	−	2 970	2 569
Real gross domestic income	YBGL	862 633	898 820	933 483	963 326	999 892	1 020 296	1 048 456	1 077 828	1 112 143
Real employment, property and entrepreneurial income from the rest of the world (receipts *less* payments)	YBGI	880	3 622	13 317	−1 551	4 796	11 623	23 679	23 592	25 027
Subsidies (receipts) *less* taxes (payments) on production from/to the rest of the world	-QZPB	−5 402	−1 758	−2 496	−2 458	−3 466	−3 199	−2 424	−2 414	−1 563
Other subsidies on production from/to the rest of the world	-IBJN	171	134	158	219	224	433	519	459	513
Gross National Income (GNI)	YBGM	859 945	901 155	944 300	959 454	1 001 046	1 028 934	1 070 230	1 099 465	1 136 120
Real current transfers from the rest of the world (receipts *less* payments)	-YBGP	−2 142	−3 547	−5 375	−4 710	−6 543	−3 502	−6 711	−7 933	−9 328
Gross National Disposable Income	YBGO	857 814	897 616	938 925	954 746	994 501	1 025 437	1 063 519	1 091 532	1 127 119
Adjustment to basic prices										
Gross Domestic Product (at market prices)	ABMI	880 854	908 655	938 101	966 551	1 005 542	1 027 905	1 048 456	1 074 858	1 109 145
Adjustment to basic prices (*less* taxes *plus* subsidies on products)	-NTAQ	−96 749	−99 734	−101 730	−104 308	−108 284	−112 638	−117 660	−120 869	−126 209
Gross Value Added (at basic prices)	ABMM	784 314	809 136	836 619	862 521	897 570	915 383	930 796	953 989	982 760
Net measures (after deduction of fixed capital consumption) at market prices	-CIHA	−92 187	−94 460	−97 553	−101 696	−104 678	−107 376	−112 453	−113 851	−118 436
Net national income at market prices	YBET	767 917	807 050	847 225	858 200	896 966	922 148	958 274	985 826	1 018 058
Net national disposable income at market prices	YBEY	765 801	803 517	841 848	853 492	890 417	918 656	951 563	977 893	1 008 730

1 See chapter text.

Source: Office for National Statistics: 020 7533 6031

16.2 United Kingdom gross domestic product and national income[1]
Current prices

£ million

		1997	1998	1999	2000	2001	2002	2003	2004	2005
Gross domestic product: Output										
Gross value added, at basic prices										
Output of goods and services	NQAF	1 519 332	1 611 353	1 691 073	1 795 250	1 873 132	1 961 221	2 061 932	..	..
less intermediate consumption	-NQAJ	−799 304	−847 910	−891 686	−953 745	−989 720	−1 030 425	−1 080 200	..	..
Total Gross Value Added	ABML	720 028	763 443	799 387	841 505	883 412	930 796	981 732	1 033 573	..
Value added taxes (VAT) on products	QYRC	55 109	56 702	61 719	64 464	67 549	71 374	77 665	81 747	..
Other taxes on products	NSUI	43 003	46 933	50 512	54 086	52 246	52 890	53 584	56 892	..
less subsidies on products	-NZHC	−7 539	−6 558	−6 180	−6 479	−6 449	−6 604	−7 062	−7 524	..
Gross Domestic Product at market prices	YBHA	810 601	860 520	905 438	953 576	996 758	1 048 456	1 105 919	1 164 941	..
Gross domestic product: Expenditure										
Final consumption expenditure										
Actual individual consumption										
Household final consumption expenditure	ABPB	503 606	536 921	570 634	603 457	635 651	667 361	697 764	731 859	..
Final consumption expenditure of NPISH	ABNV	19 422	20 897	21 941	23 238	24 778	25 998	27 248	28 903	..
Individual government final consumption expenditure	NNAQ	88 213	92 706	99 802	106 011	115 352	127 606	139 697	151 155	..
Total actual individual consumption	NQEO	611 241	650 524	692 377	732 706	775 781	820 965	864 709	911 917	..
Collective government final consumption expenditure	NQEP	60 323	61 547	66 703	73 036	75 670	83 361	92 080	95 815	..
Total final consumption expenditure	ABKW	671 564	712 071	759 080	805 742	851 451	904 326	956 789	1 007 732	..
Households and NPISH	NSSG	523 028	557 818	592 575	626 695	660 429	693 359	725 012	760 762	..
Central government	NMBJ	91 889	94 756	100 039	107 607	114 935	128 563	141 176	148 900	..
Local government	NMMT	56 647	59 259	65 945	71 060	75 854	82 110	90 382	97 944	..
Gross capital formation										
Gross fixed capital formation	NPQX	133 587	150 938	155 486	161 810	165 667	172 558	175 946	190 501	..
Changes in inventories	ABMP	4 621	5 026	6 060	5 271	6 189	2 909	4 203	5 939	..
Acquisitions less disposals of valuables	NPJO	−27	429	229	3	396	214	−37	−37	..
Total gross capital formation	NQFM	138 181	156 393	161 775	167 084	172 252	175 681	180 112	196 403	..
Exports of goods and services	KTMW	232 887	231 034	239 494	267 347	273 116	274 945	282 231	293 949	..
less imports of goods and services	-KTMX	−232 031	−238 978	−254 911	−286 597	−300 061	−306 496	−313 213	−332 927	..
External balance of goods and services	KTMY	856	−7 944	−15 417	−19 250	−26 945	−31 551	−30 982	−39 040	−46 897
Statistical discrepancy between expenditure components and GDP	RVFD	−	−	−	−	−	−	−	−216	..
Gross Domestic Product at market prices	YBHA	810 601	860 520	905 438	953 576	996 758	1 048 456	1 105 919	1 164 941	..
Gross domestic product: Income										
Operating surplus, gross										
Non-financial corporations										
Public non-financial corporations	NRJT	7 769	8 183	7 701	7 361	7 150	6 483	7 102	6 469	..
Private non-financial corporations	NRJK	172 071	175 460	179 711	186 330	186 726	190 747	200 743	215 252	..
Financial corporations	NQNV	15 793	19 528	13 834	12 336	12 173	30 066	36 948	40 640	..
Adjustment for financial services	-NSRV	−22 503	−27 866	−26 731	−33 581	−33 517	−41 207	−45 488	−49 873	..
General government	NMXV	8 727	8 597	8 711	9 068	9 412	9 795	10 191	10 703	..
Households and non-profit institutions serving households	QWLS	42 969	47 745	51 306	54 074	59 187	62 620	67 476	70 949	..
Total operating surplus, gross	ABNF	224 826	231 884	234 738	235 708	241 233	258 750	277 165	294 225	..
Mixed income	QWLT	51 723	52 706	54 587	57 745	61 898	66 149	69 771	73 116	..
Compensation of employees	HAEA	429 212	464 024	494 597	531 962	563 358	588 591	617 641	648 826	..
Taxes on production and imports	NZGX	113 298	119 450	128 713	135 597	137 870	143 086	150 430	158 104	..
less subsidies	-AAXJ	−8 458	−7 544	−7 197	−7 436	−7 601	−8 120	−9 088	−9 712	..
Statistical discrepancy between income components and GDP	RVFC	−	−	−	−	−	−	−	−191	..
Gross Domestic Product at market prices	YBHA	810 601	860 520	905 438	953 576	996 758	1 048 456	1 105 919	1 164 941	..

16.2 United Kingdom gross domestic product and national income[1]
Current prices
continued

		1997	1998	1999	2000	2001	2002	2003	2004	2005
Gross Domestic Product at market prices	YBHA	810 601	860 520	905 438	953 576	996 758	1 048 456	1 105 919	1 164 941	..
Compensation of employees										
receipts from the rest of the world	KTMN	1 007	840	960	1 032	1 087	1 121	1 116	1 171	..
less payments to the rest of the world	-KTMO	−924	−850	−759	−882	−1 021	−1 054	−1 057	−1 100	..
Total	KTMP	83	−10	201	150	66	67	59	71	80
less Taxes on products paid to the rest of the world										
plus Subsidies received from the rest of the world	-QZOZ	−2 919	−3 651	−3 288	−3 838	−3 772	−2 424	−2 431	−1 571	..
Other subsidies on production	-IBJL	206	246	309	292	298	519	..	..	..
Property and entrepreneurial income										
receipts from the rest of the world	HMBN	95 129	103 029	99 290	133 787	139 487	123 641	125 154	140 914	..
less payments to the rest of the world	-HMBO	−91 936	−90 715	−100 951	−129 354	−128 182	−100 029	−100 218	−114 264	..
Total	HMBM	3 193	12 314	−1 661	4 433	11 305	23 612	24 936	26 342	27 328
Gross National Income at market prices	ABMX	811 166	869 414	901 028	954 656	1 004 939	1 070 230	1 129 075	1 190 619	..

1 See chapter text.

Source: Office for National Statistics: 020 7533 6031

16.3 United Kingdom gross domestic product[1]
Chained volume measures, reference year 2002

£ million

		1996	1997	1998	1999	2000	2001	2002	2003	2004
Gross domestic product: expenditure approach										
Final consumption expenditure										
Actual individual consumption										
Household final consumption expenditure	ABPF	531 853	551 112	572 348	598 792	625 145	644 895	667 361	684 841	709 702
Final consumption expenditure of non-profit										
institutions serving households	ABNU	21 089	21 699	23 306	23 260	25 270	25 247	25 998	26 229	26 761
Individual government final consumption expenditure	NSZK	104 403	105 948	107 339	109 554	111 763	114 159	117 238	120 288	..
Total actual individual consumption	YBIO	665 475	686 764	710 964	739 989	770 711	793 253	820 965	842 181	871 276
Collective government final consumption expenditure	NSZL	71 121	68 979	69 644	74 198	78 798	79 417	83 361	89 338	92 653
Total final consumption expenditure	ABKX	734 858	754 395	779 623	813 451	848 923	872 197	904 326	931 520	963 929
Gross capital formation										
Gross fixed capital formation	NPQR	128 565	137 125	154 927	158 104	163 709	167 563	172 558	172 573	181 506
Changes in inventories	ABMQ	1 850	4 013	4 910	6 422	5 267	6 196	2 909	4 602	5 933
Acquisitions less disposals of valuables	NPJP	−44	−4	61	31	3	373	214	−6	−11
Total gross capital formation	NPQU	130 549	141 544	160 074	164 438	169 029	174 175	175 681	177 170	186 135
Gross domestic final expenditure	YBIK	863 882	895 152	939 976	978 031	1 017 985	1 046 424	1 080 007	1 108 689	1 151 316
Exports of goods and services	KTMZ	209 857	227 173	234 247	244 205	266 536	274 274	274 945	278 159	290 989
Gross final expenditure	ABME	1 072 404	1 122 457	1 173 915	1 221 942	1 284 619	1 320 810	1 354 952	1 386 848	1 442 305
less imports of goods and services	-KTNB	−198 346	−217 664	−237 859	−256 657	−279 807	−293 213	−306 496	−311 990	−332 953
Statistical discrepancy between										
expenditure components and GDP	GIXS	–	–	–	–	–	–	–	–	−207
Gross Domestic Product at market prices	ABMI	880 854	908 655	938 101	966 551	1 005 542	1 027 905	1 048 456	1 074 858	1 109 145
of which External balance of goods and services	KTNC	11 511	9 509	−3 612	−12 452	−13 271	−18 939	−31 551	−33 831	−41 964

1 See chapter text.

Source: Office for National Statistics: 020 7533 6031

16.4 Gross value added at current basic prices: by industry[1,2]
United Kingdom

£ million

		1996	1997	1998	1999	2000	2001	2002	2003	2004
Agriculture, hunting, forestry and fishing	EWSH	12 031	10 223	9 469	9 270	8 803	8 571	9 213	10 127	..
Production										
Mining and quarrying										
Mining and quarrying of energy producing materials										
Mining of coal	QTOQ	1 045	988	817	644	611	549	534	513	354
Extraction of mineral oil and natural gas	QTOR	17 124	15 436	13 203	14 844	22 432	21 541	20 711	20 216	27 449
Other mining and quarrying	QTOS	1 599	1 695	1 645	1 716	1 794	1 763	1 474	1 554	2 046
Total mining and quarrying	EWSL	19 768	18 118	15 666	17 203	24 839	23 852	22 719	22 282	..
Manufacturing										
Food; beverages and tobacco	QTOU	19 718	20 143	20 047	20 220	20 260	20 920	21 058	21 726	22 570
Textiles and textile products	QTOV	7 219	7 645	6 982	6 451	6 043	5 590	5 098	4 531	5 192
Leather and leather products	QTOW	892	845	823	808	752	648	594	466	405
Wood and wood products	QTOX	2 006	2 217	2 327	2 248	2 336	2 371	2 517	2 703	2 561
Pulp, paper and paper products; publishing and printing	QTOY	18 074	18 314	18 932	19 869	20 558	20 412	20 341	19 863	20 020
Coke, petroleum products and nuclear fuel	QTOZ	2 536	2 381	2 575	2 665	2 514	2 572	2 446	2 656	3 439
Chemicals, chemical products and man-made fibres	QTPA	15 798	15 222	15 073	15 336	15 181	16 190	16 193	16 143	15 645
Rubber and plastic products	QTPB	7 190	7 981	8 175	7 944	7 842	7 891	7 878	7 835	8 003
Other non-metal mineral products	QTPC	5 181	5 181	5 018	4 952	5 015	5 092	5 336	5 478	5 800
Basic metals and fabricated metal products	QTPD	16 398	17 075	17 632	16 674	16 024	15 682	14 947	14 713	15 644
Machinery and equipment not elsewhere classified	QTPE	12 437	13 361	13 591	12 732	12 343	12 273	12 062	12 056	11 962
Electrical and optical equipment	QTPF	18 431	19 854	20 116	20 782	20 804	18 782	16 841	16 035	16 881
Transport equipment	QTPG	14 263	15 510	16 039	15 923	15 876	15 967	16 001	15 543	18 864
Manufacturing not elsewhere classified	QTPH	5 387	6 002	6 282	6 422	6 557	6 706	6 589	6 384	7 654
Total manufacturing	EWSP	145 530	151 733	153 616	153 026	152 102	151 098	147 901	146 127	..
Electricity, gas and water supply	EWST	16 223	16 081	16 087	15 968	16 112	16 044	16 481	17 113	..
Total production	QTPK	181 521	185 932	185 370	186 198	193 053	190 994	187 101	185 522	200 807
Construction	EWSX	34 715	36 994	39 132	41 843	45 324	50 272	54 784	60 891	..
Service industries										
Wholesale and retail trade (including motor trade); repair of motor vehicles, personal and household goods	QTPM	79 207	85 828	92 949	99 297	103 746	110 873	115 044	121 514	128 382
Hotels and restaurants	QTPN	20 515	22 586	24 535	26 458	28 045	29 520	31 191	32 633	33 757
Transport, storage and communication										
Transport and storage	QTPO	35 002	37 304	39 840	40 955	43 062	44 006	45 035	47 436	46 738
Communication	QTPP	18 711	20 091	22 606	24 165	27 201	27 611	29 330	30 895	31 541
Total	EWTF	53 713	57 395	62 445	65 120	70 263	71 617	74 366	78 332	..
Financial intermediation	QTPR	41 598	41 530	46 285	41 366	42 649	43 918	63 261	71 499	70 258
Adjustment for financial services (FISIM)	-NSRV	–22 694	–22 503	–27 866	–26 731	–33 581	–33 517	–41 207	–45 488	–49 873
Real estate, renting and business activities										
Letting of dwellings including imputed rent of owner occupiers	QTPS	47 288	50 477	56 645	59 921	63 326	68 853	72 593	77 585	78 367
Other real estate, renting and business activities	QTPT	82 123	93 018	107 547	118 948	130 934	142 439	151 006	161 795	176 301
Total	QTPU	129 412	143 497	164 191	178 870	194 260	211 292	223 599	239 380	254 669
Public administration and defence (PAD)[3]	EWTN	39 647	39 736	39 530	40 789	42 658	44 408	47 028	50 266	..
Education[3]	QTPW	36 819	39 018	41 397	44 709	47 826	51 591	55 396	59 032	62 610
Health and social work	QTPX	43 982	46 091	48 754	52 106	55 960	58 916	62 643	66 657	69 308
Other social and personal services, private households with employees and extra-territorial organisations	EWTV	30 011	33 701	37 255	40 092	42 497	44 956	48 378	51 801	..
Total service industries	QTPZ	452 210	486 879	529 473	562 077	594 325	633 575	679 698	725 192	755 518
All industries	ABML	680 477	720 028	763 443	799 387	841 505	883 412	930 796	981 732	1 033 573

1 See chapter text. Components may not sum to totals as a result of rounding.
2 Because of differences in the annual and monthly production inquiries, estimates of current price output and value added by industry derived from the current price input-output supply-use balances are not consistent with the equivalent measures of constant price growth given in Table 16.5. These differences do not affect GDP totals. For further information see "Experimental Constant Price Input-Output Supply-Use Balances: An approach to improving the quality of the national accounts" Nadim Ahmad, *Economic Trends*, July 1999 (No. 548).

3 Central government expenditure on education is included in PAD in 1995. For 1996 onwards it is included in Education.

Source: Office for National Statistics: 020 7533 6031

16.5 Gross value added at basic prices: by industry[1,2,3,4]
Chained volume indices
United Kingdom

Indices (2002=100)

	Weight per 1000[1]		1996	1997	1998	1999	2000	2001	2002	2003	2004
	2002										
Agriculture, hunting, forestry and fishing	9.9	GDQA	90.7	92.8	95.4	98.6	98.0	89.1	100.0	98.3	99.3
Production											
Mining and quarrying											
Mining and quarrying of energy producing materials											
Mining of coal	0.6	CKZP	173.5	164.2	139.1	123.3	105.3	106.4	100.0	94.5	80.7
Extraction of mineral oil and natural gas	25.1	CKZO	104.4	103.6	106.4	111.4	107.5	101.3	100.0	94.4	86.2
Other mining and quarrying	2.0	CKZQ	78.9	77.8	83.3	89.6	93.0	87.3	100.0	101.4	102.5
Total mining and quarrying	27.7	CKYX	104.1	103.1	105.2	109.6	106.1	100.3	100.0	94.9	87.2
Manufacturing											
Food; beverages and tobacco	23.8	CKZA	98.3	100.2	99.0	98.9	98.2	99.0	100.0	99.9	101.6
Textiles and textile products	6.3	CKZB	148.8	145.5	135.3	125.6	122.7	107.3	100.0	100.1	90.1
Leather and leather products	0.7	CKZC	146.0	153.2	133.3	125.9	111.1	114.3	100.0	81.6	60.5
Wood and wood products	2.7	CKZD	104.2	101.1	99.8	95.6	98.1	98.4	100.0	100.8	103.2
Pulp, paper and paper products; publishing and printing	23.2	CKZE	97.3	98.1	98.9	99.1	99.5	99.9	100.0	98.5	97.9
Coke, petroleum products and nuclear fuel	2.9	CKZF	113.5	116.9	109.3	98.5	103.7	97.8	100.0	92.4	97.7
Chemicals, chemical products and man-made fibres	18.4	CKZG	83.0	85.5	86.3	89.4	94.2	100.0	100.0	100.9	104.1
Rubber and plastic products	9.0	CKZH	104.9	105.4	108.7	108.2	108.3	104.3	100.0	100.8	99.4
Other non-metallic mineral products	5.8	CKZI	98.9	101.9	99.4	99.1	102.1	102.9	100.0	105.8	108.6
Basic metals and fabricated metal products	17.8	CKZJ	105.3	107.6	106.8	104.3	106.5	104.2	100.0	97.7	100.9
Machinery and equipment not elsewhere classified	13.9	CKZK	111.6	110.8	110.5	103.9	103.8	105.9	100.0	101.7	107.4
Electrical and optical equipment	21.3	CKZL	90.5	93.1	97.9	108.4	124.5	115.2	100.0	96.5	98.3
Transport equipment	18.1	CKZM	97.4	101.8	106.6	109.4	105.9	103.4	100.0	105.6	111.6
Manufacturing not elsewhere classified	7.6	CKZN	96.1	97.9	99.4	101.9	100.5	99.4	100.0	100.2	100.0
Total manufacturing	171.6	CKYY	98.9	100.7	101.3	102.1	104.6	103.2	100.0	100.1	101.9
Electricity, gas and water supply	18.2	CKYZ	90.3	90.7	93.6	96.1	98.2	100.5	100.0	101.2	103.3
Total production	217.6	CKYW	98.7	100.0	101.1	102.3	104.2	102.6	100.0	99.5	100.3
Construction	56.7	GDQB	89.7	92.1	93.1	93.4	94.6	96.3	100.0	105.2	108.7
Service industries											
Wholesale and retail trade (including motor trade); repair of motor vehicles, personal and household goods	125.5	GDQC	81.5	83.8	87.1	89.5	92.3	95.2	100.0	102.9	108.0
Hotels and restaurants	33.3	GDQD	85.7	89.1	93.0	96.7	98.0	97.4	100.0	105.9	111.2
Transport, storage and communication											
Transport and storage	49.8	GDQF	78.7	83.1	89.2	89.8	95.7	97.3	100.0	100.8	104.4
Communication	31.3	GDQG	55.4	62.8	68.4	79.8	91.7	98.5	100.0	105.4	106.7
Total	81.0	GDQH	69.0	74.7	80.6	85.8	94.1	97.8	100.0	102.6	105.3
Financial intermediation	48.5	GDQI	80.5	83.9	88.0	91.0	95.8	100.9	100.0	101.8	105.7
Adjustment for financial services (FISIM)	−38.1	GDQJ	75.8	79.0	84.0	86.1	92.7	97.2	100.0	110.8	125.3
Real estate, renting and business activities											
Letting of dwellings, including imputed rent of owner occupiers	77.8	GDQL	89.2	91.0	93.9	96.6	96.1	98.8	100.0	102.2	104.2
Other real estate, renting and business activities	160.4	GDQK	69.3	75.4	82.3	85.5	92.1	97.2	100.0	105.7	113.8
Total	238.3	GDQM	75.5	80.3	85.9	89.0	93.4	97.7	100.0	104.6	110.7
Public administration and defence (PAD)[4]	55.6	GDQO	89.7	88.1	88.1	92.1	96.3	97.5	100.0	103.5	105.3
Education[4]	58.7	GDQP	92.3	92.2	93.0	96.0	97.8	98.6	100.0	100.5	100.5
Health and social work[4]	62.3	GDQQ	84.5	85.5	87.5	89.8	93.9	96.6	100.0	103.2	107.4
Other social and personal services, private households with employees and extra-territorial organisations	51.0	GDQR	80.4	82.4	88.2	90.5	93.9	97.1	100.0	101.2	104.7
Total service industries	715.8	GDQS	80.0	83.0	87.0	90.3	94.3	97.4	100.0	102.7	106.4
All industries	1 000.0	CGCE	84.3	86.9	89.9	92.7	96.4	98.3	100.0	102.5	105.6

1 See chapter text. The weights are in proportion to total gross value added (GVA) in 2002 and are used to combine the industry output indices to calculate the totals for 2003 and 2004. For 2002 and earlier, totals are calculated using the equivalent weight for the previous year (eg totals for 2002 use 2001 weights).
2 As GVA is expressed in index number form, it is inappropriate to show as a statistical adjustment any divergence from the other measures of GDP. Such an adjustment does, however, exist implicitly.
3 See footnote 2 to Table 16.4.
4 The GVA for PAD, education and Health and social work in this table follows the SIC(92) and differs from that used in Table 2.3 in *United Kingdom National Accounts* (the *Blue Book*) which is based on Input-Output groups. The administration costs of the NHS are included in PAD in this table but are included in Health and social work in Table 2.3. Central government expenditure on teachers is included in this table but, for 1995 only, are included in PAD in Table 16.4.

Source: Office for National Statistics: 020 7533 6031

16.6 Non-financial corporations[1]
Allocation of primary income account[2]
United Kingdom. ESA95 sector S.11

£ million

		1996	1997	1998	1999	2000	2001	2002	2003	2004
Resources										
Operating surplus, gross	NQBE	169 365	179 840	183 643	187 208	193 453	193 736	197 215	207 826	221 721
Property income, received										
Interest	EABC	9 648	9 964	13 741	10 764	14 322	12 694	9 564	9 785	12 269
Distributed income of corporations	EABD	22 919	26 548	25 086	21 501	26 631	36 868	32 210	..	..
Reinvested earnings on direct foreign investment	HDVR	13 417	11 747	10 979	16 214	20 118	22 950	26 893	12 492	24 181
Attributed property income of insurance policy-holders	FAOF	423	386	463	338	489	280	302	..	..
Rent	FAOG	114	118	118	117	117	117	118	..	..
Total	FAKY	46 522	48 764	50 389	48 905	61 366	73 630	67 466	72 782	80 264
Total resources	FBXJ	215 887	228 604	234 032	236 113	254 819	267 366	264 681	280 608	301 985
Uses										
Property income, paid										
Interest	EABG	25 376	27 215	32 045	31 857	38 228	40 021	37 175	36 789	41 829
Distributed income of corporations	NVCS	76 136	80 805	78 299	87 100	83 202	100 810	91 868	..	..
Reinvested earnings on direct foreign investment	HDVB	6 117	5 187	3 117	2 776	7 348	1 699	1 614	3 955	6 729
Rent	FBXO	815	756	584	564	1 319	1 896	1 853	..	..
Total	FBXK	111 519	117 192	116 307	124 496	134 033	150 911	132 266	140 190	150 090
Balance of primary incomes, gross	NQBG	104 368	111 412	117 725	111 617	120 786	116 455	132 415	140 418	151 895
Total uses	FBXJ	215 887	228 604	234 032	236 113	254 819	267 366	264 681	280 608	301 985
After deduction of fixed capital consumption	-DBGF	−53 427	−53 210	−54 453	−56 740	−58 588	−60 287	−62 460	−64 435	−66 897
Balance of primary incomes, net	FBXQ	50 941	58 202	63 272	54 877	62 198	56 168	69 955	75 912	86 866

1 See chapter text.
2 Before deduction of fixed capital formation.

Source: Office for National Statistics: 020 7533 6031

16.7 Non-financial corporations[1]
Secondary distribution of income account
United Kingdom. ESA95 sector S.11

£ million

		1996	1997	1998	1999	2000	2001	2002	2003	2004
Resources										
Balance of primary incomes, gross	NQBG	104 368	111 412	117 725	111 617	120 786	116 455	132 415	140 418	151 895
Social contributions										
Imputed social contributions	NSTJ	3 059	3 034	3 454	3 845	4 175	4 357	4 575	4 229	3 864
Current transfers other than taxes, social contributions and benefits										
Non-life insurance claims	FCBP	5 508	4 190	4 849	4 151	4 456	4 565	7 789	..	..
Miscellaneous transfers	NRJY	537	557	595	611	622	619	616	..	..
Total	NRJB	5 508	4 190	4 849	4 151	5 923	5 000	5 528	6 199	6 464
Total resources	FCBR	112 935	118 636	126 028	119 613	130 884	125 812	142 518	150 846	162 223
Uses										
Current taxes on income, wealth etc.										
Taxes on income	FCBS	23 348	28 932	27 256	22 948	26 406	26 151	24 493	23 555	26 682
Social benefits other than social transfers in kind	NSTJ	3 059	3 034	3 454	3 845	4 175	4 357	4 575	4 229	3 864
Current transfers other than taxes, social contributions and benefits										
Net non-life insurance premiums	FCBY	5 508	4 190	4 849	4 151	4 456	4 565	7 789	..	..
Miscellaneous current transfers	FDBI	1 518	479	444	569	413	411	422	434	446
Total, other current transfers	FCBX	7 026	4 669	5 293	4 720	6 336	5 411	5 874	6 535	6 887
Gross Disposable Income	NRJD	79 502	82 001	90 025	88 100	93 967	89 893	107 576	116 527	124 790
Total uses	FCBR	112 935	118 636	126 028	119 613	130 884	125 812	142 518	150 846	162 223
After deduction of fixed capital consumption	-DBGF	−53 427	−53 210	−54 453	−56 740	−58 588	−60 287	−62 460	−64 435	−66 897
Disposable income, net	FCCF	26 075	28 791	35 572	31 360	35 379	29 606	45 116	52 021	60 276

1 See chapter text.

Source: Office for National Statistics: 020 7533 6031

16.8 General government[1]
Allocation of primary income account
United Kingdom. ESA95 sector S.13 Unconsolidated

£ million

		1996	1997	1998	1999	2000	2001	2002	2003	2004
Resources										
Operating surplus, gross	NMXV	8 435	8 727	8 597	8 711	9 068	9 412	9 795	10 191	10 703
Taxes on production and imports, received										
Taxes on products										
Value added tax (VAT)	NZGF	46 579	51 712	52 474	57 908	60 260	63 974	68 566	74 925	80 093
Taxes and duties on imports excluding VAT										
Import duties	NMXZ	–	–	–	–	–	–	–	–	–
Taxes on imports excluding VAT and import duties	NMBT	–	–	–	–	–	–	–	–	–
Taxes on products excluding VAT and import duties	NMYB	37 380	40 621	44 815	48 442	51 956	50 146	50 946	51 629	54 746
Total taxes on products	NVCC	83 959	92 333	97 289	106 350	112 216	114 120	119 512	126 554	134 820
Other taxes on production	NMYD	15 045	15 186	15 815	16 482	17 047	18 075	18 822	19 181	19 705
Total taxes on production and imports, received	NMYE	99 004	107 519	113 104	122 853	129 309	132 274	138 450	145 894	154 525
less Subsidies, paid										
Subsidies on products	-NMYF	–3 991	–4 679	–3 863	–3 587	–3 983	–4 546	–4 276	–4 798	–5 087
Other subsidies on production	-LIUF	–728	–711	–745	–679	–622	–570	–997	–1 434	–1 516
Total	-NMRL	–4 719	–5 390	–4 608	–4 272	–4 498	–5 058	–5 266	–6 243	–6 603
Property income, received										
Total Interest	NMYL	7 883	7 335	7 912	7 334	7 344	7 336	6 663	7 047	6 307
Distributed income of corporations	NMYM	6 883	6 544	7 455	7 102	7 203	7 286	6 662	6 539	6 068
Property income attributed to insurance policy holders	NMYO	28	33	48	33	54	24	22	19	19
Rent										
from sectors other than general government	NMYR	780	721	547	528	1 283	1 862	1 879	1 561	1 423
Total	NMYU	15 574	14 633	15 962	14 997	15 884	16 508	15 226	15 166	13 817
Total resources	NMYV	118 294	125 489	133 292	142 684	149 968	153 241	158 343	165 072	172 527
Uses										
Property income, paid										
Total interest	NRKB	31 874	33 792	34 824	30 700	30 639	27 965	25 463	27 033	27 115
Total	NMYY	31 874	33 792	34 824	30 700	30 639	27 965	25 463	27 033	27 046
Balance of primary incomes, gross	NMZH	86 420	91 697	98 468	111 984	119 329	125 276	132 880	138 039	145 481
Total uses	NMYV	118 294	125 489	133 292	142 684	149 968	153 241	158 343	165 072	172 527
After deduction of fixed capital consumption	-NMXO	–8 435	–8 727	–8 597	–8 711	–9 068	–9 412	–9 795	–10 191	–10 703
Balance of primary incomes, net	NMZI	77 985	82 970	89 634	102 863	109 903	115 622	122 824	127 636	134 541

1 See chapter text.

Source: Office for National Statistics: 020 7533 6031

16.9 General government[1]
Secondary distribution of income account
United Kingdom. ESA95 sector S.13 Unconsolidated

£ million

		1996	1997	1998	1999	2000	2001	2002	2003	2004
Resources										
Balance of primary incomes, gross	NMZH	86 420	91 697	98 468	111 984	119 329	125 276	132 880	138 039	145 481
Current taxes on income, wealth etc.										
Taxes on income	NMZJ	99 267	107 717	123 670	129 545	140 002	147 280	142 777	144 115	155 029
Other current taxes	NVCM	13 510	14 778	15 953	17 191	18 223	19 626	21 236	23 397	25 008
Total	NMZL	112 777	122 495	140 057	146 676	158 529	167 291	163 692	166 999	180 037
Social contributions										
Actual social contributions										
Employers' actual social contributions	NMZM	27 344	29 038	30 593	33 060	36 292	38 233	38 798	45 420	48 928
Employees' social contributions	NMZN	21 700	24 121	25 234	26 390	27 506	28 785	29 694	34 598	38 115
Social contributions by self- and non-employed persons	NMZO	1 771	1 848	1 729	1 784	1 973	2 112	2 284	2 799	2 820
Total	NMZP	50 815	55 007	57 556	61 234	65 771	69 130	70 776	82 817	89 863
Imputed social contributions	NMZQ	6 293	6 408	6 981	6 927	7 395	7 577	8 348	6 933	6 038
Total	NMZR	57 108	61 415	64 537	68 161	73 166	76 707	79 124	89 750	95 901
Other current transfers										
Non-life insurance claims	NMZS	371	349	499	410	403	353	400	295	310
Current transfers within general government	NMZT	59 403	59 461	60 367	64 760	66 398	71 901	77 259	85 153	91 799
Current international cooperation	NMZU	2 424	1 739	1 384	3 176	2 084	4 568	3 112	3 570	3 604
Miscellaneous current transfers from sectors other than general government	NMZX	411	459	433	308	228	398	320	273	588
Other current transfers	NNAA	62 609	62 008	62 683	68 654	69 113	77 220	81 091	89 291	96 301
Total resources	NNAB	318 914	337 615	365 745	395 475	420 137	446 494	456 787	484 079	517 720
Uses										
Social benefits other than social transfers in kind	NNAD	113 206	117 103	117 654	121 214	125 724	136 257	138 892	147 553	155 340
Other current transfers										
Net non-life insurance premiums	NNAE	371	349	499	410	403	353	400	295	310
Current transfers within general government	NNAF	59 403	59 461	60 367	64 760	66 398	71 901	77 259	85 153	91 799
Current international cooperation	NNAG	1 814	1 700	1 705	1 667	2 418	2 434	2 573	2 715	3 176
Miscellaneous current transfers to sectors other than general government	NNAI	11 679	13 025	14 829	16 303	17 625	18 353	24 218	28 780	31 745
Of which: GNP based fourth own resource	NMFH	2 454	2 458	3 920	4 632	4 379	3 858	5 335	6 772	7 549
Other current transfers	NNAN	73 267	74 535	77 400	83 140	86 844	93 041	104 450	116 943	127 069
Gross Disposable Income	NNAO	131 838	145 176	169 861	190 260	206 709	216 294	212 569	218 741	234 474
Total uses	NNAB	318 914	337 615	365 745	395 475	420 137	446 494	456 787	484 079	517 720
After deduction of fixed capital consumption	-NMXO	−8 435	−8 727	−8 597	−8 711	−9 068	−9 412	−9 795	−10 191	−10 703
Disposable income, net	NNAP	123 403	136 449	161 027	181 139	197 283	206 640	202 513	208 338	224 618

1 See chapter text.

Source: Office for National Statistics: 020 7533 6031

16.10 Households and non-profit institutions serving households[1]
Allocation of primary income account
United Kingdom. ESA95 sectors S.14 and S.15

£ million

		1996	1997	1998	1999	2000	2001	2002	2003	2004
Resources										
Operating surplus, gross	QWLS	40 053	42 969	47 745	51 306	54 074	59 187	62 620	67 476	70 949
Mixed income, gross	QWLT	50 375	51 723	52 706	54 587	57 745	61 898	66 149	69 771	73 116
Compensation of employees										
Wages and salaries	QWLW	351 075	374 378	404 933	431 327	462 704	489 950	509 546	526 949	551 327
Employers' social contributions	QWLX	52 048	54 917	59 081	63 471	69 408	73 474	79 112	90 751	97 570
Total	QWLY	403 123	429 295	464 014	494 798	532 112	563 424	588 658	617 700	648 897
Property income										
Interest	QWLZ	23 630	26 445	29 928	24 153	28 233	26 823	20 878	20 985	26 480
Distributed income of corporations	QWMA	36 905	39 668	39 602	41 558	45 643	51 061	44 458	45 959	49 122
Attributed property income of insurance policy holders	QWMC	48 356	51 068	53 408	53 200	53 107	53 080	52 096	55 023	54 619
Rent	QWMD	103	105	105	105	105	105	106	108	110
Total	QWME	108 994	117 286	123 043	119 016	127 088	131 069	117 538	122 075	130 331
Total resources	QWMF	602 545	641 273	687 508	719 707	771 019	815 578	834 965	877 022	923 293
Uses										
Property income										
Interest	QWMG	38 275	41 862	51 219	47 434	52 875	52 141	51 513	53 579	63 745
Rent	QWMH	210	216	216	215	215	215	216	220	224
Total	QWMI	38 485	42 078	51 435	47 649	53 090	52 356	51 729	53 799	63 969
Balance of primary incomes, gross	QWMJ	564 060	599 195	636 073	672 058	717 929	763 222	783 236	823 223	859 324
Total uses	QWMF	602 545	641 273	687 508	719 707	771 019	815 578	834 965	877 022	923 293
After deduction of										
fixed capital consumption	-QWLL	−21 108	−22 970	−24 428	−27 329	−29 805	−32 203	−35 482	−36 471	−39 444
Balance of primary incomes, net	QWMK	542 941	576 217	611 504	644 539	687 868	730 784	747 919	787 021	819 745

1 See chapter text.

Source: Office for National Statistics: 020 7533 6031

16.11 Households and non-profit institutions serving households[1]
Secondary distribution of income account
United Kingdom. ESA95 sectors S.14 and S.15

£ million

		1996	1997	1998	1999	2000	2001	2002	2003	2004
Resources										
Balance of primary incomes, gross	QWMJ	564 060	599 195	636 073	672 058	717 929	763 222	783 236	823 223	859 324
Imputed social contributions	RVFH	429	410	478	450	476	502	530	505	495
Social benefits other than social transfers in kind	QWML	144 458	150 825	154 424	161 176	168 394	178 480	184 763	195 083	203 198
Other current transfers										
Non-life insurance claims	QWMM	19 360	14 004	15 224	13 762	16 150	15 607	17 177	15 220	15 986
Miscellaneous current transfers	QWMN	20 010	20 517	21 181	22 229	24 232	25 302	29 908	33 192	35 518
Total	QWMO	39 370	34 521	36 405	35 991	40 382	40 909	47 085	48 412	51 504
Total resources	QWMP	748 317	784 951	827 380	869 675	927 181	983 113	1 015 614	1 067 223	1 114 521
Uses										
Current taxes on income, wealth etc										
Taxes on income	QWMQ	74 163	75 242	89 697	96 460	105 604	112 283	111 862	112 579	120 655
Other current taxes	NVCO	12 907	13 977	15 123	16 330	17 363	18 724	20 360	22 555	24 171
Total	QWMS	87 070	89 219	104 820	112 790	122 967	131 007	132 222	135 134	144 826
Social contributions										
Actual social contributions										
Employers' actual social contributions	QWMT	41 843	44 660	47 697	51 801	56 872	60 554	65 135	78 582	86 673
Employees' social contributions	QWMU	50 145	53 460	54 761	57 179	59 030	60 662	62 393	66 263	69 479
Social contributions by self and non-employed	QWMV	1 771	1 848	1 729	1 784	1 973	2 112	2 284	2 799	2 820
Total	QWMW	105 587	115 511	124 239	128 989	138 279	140 844	146 432	..	..
Imputed social contributions	QWMX	10 205	10 257	11 384	11 670	12 536	12 920	13 977	12 169	10 897
Total	QWMY	103 964	110 225	115 571	122 434	130 411	136 248	143 789	159 813	170 162
Social benefits other than social transfers in kind	QWMZ	899	880	950	922	948	977	1 006	987	984
Other current transfers										
Net non-life insurance premiums	QWNA	19 360	14 004	15 224	13 762	16 150	15 607	17 177	15 220	15 986
Miscellaneous current transfers	QWNB	8 434	9 346	9 677	10 033	10 646	11 019	11 276	11 641	12 327
Total	QWNC	27 794	23 350	24 901	23 795	26 796	26 626	28 453	26 861	28 313
Gross Disposable Income[2]	QWND	528 590	561 277	581 138	609 734	646 059	688 255	710 144	744 428	770 529
Total uses	QWMP	748 317	784 951	827 380	869 675	927 181	983 113	1 015 614	1 067 223	1 114 521
After deduction of fixed capital consumption	-QWLL	−21 108	−22 970	−24 428	−27 329	−29 805	−32 203	−35 482	−36 471	−39 444
Disposable income, net	QWNE	507 471	538 299	556 569	582 215	615 998	655 817	674 827	708 226	729 025

1 See chapter text.
2 Gross household disposable income revalued by the implied households and NPISH's final consumption expenditure deflator. For more details see table 6.1.4 on page 217 in *United Kingdom National Accounts* (the *Blue book*).

Source: Office for National Statistics: 020 7533 6031

16.12 Households and non-profit institutions serving households[1]
Use of disposable income account
United Kingdom. ESA95 sectors S.14 and S.15

£ million and percentages

		1996	1997	1998	1999	2000	2001	2002	2003	2004
Resources										
Disposable income, gross	QWND	528 590	561 277	581 138	609 734	646 059	688 255	710 144	744 428	770 529
Adjustment for the change in net equity of households in pension funds	NSSE	15 073	14 488	13 603	13 629	13 853	16 526	17 906	21 586	25 046
Total resources	NSSF	543 663	575 765	594 741	623 363	659 912	704 781	728 050	766 014	795 575
Uses										
Final consumption expenditure										
Individual consumption expenditure	NSSG	492 470	523 028	557 818	592 575	626 695	660 429	693 359	725 012	760 762
Saving, gross	NSSH	51 193	52 737	36 923	30 788	33 217	44 352	34 691	41 002	34 813
Total uses	NSSF	543 663	575 765	594 741	623 363	659 912	704 781	728 050	766 014	795 575
Saving ratio (percentages)	RVGL	9.4	9.2	6.2	4.9	5.0	6.3	4.8	5.4	4.4

1 See chapter text.

Source: Office for National Statistics: 020 7533 6031

16.13 The sector accounts: key economic indicators[1]
United Kingdom

£ million and indices (2002=100)

		1996	1997	1998	1999	2000	2001	2002	2003	2004
Net lending/borrowing by:										
Non-financial corporations	EABO	4 993	−3 930	−6 678	−14 105	−10 565	−15 981	4 864	15 361	17 426
Financial corporations	NHCQ	−1 775	−418	−1 234	−13 264	−22 883	−16 707	8 631	16 222	22 236
General government	NNBK	−32 054	−17 799	105	10 385	14 282	8 459	−15 730	−35 491	−37 822
Households and NPISH's	NSSZ	22 772	21 343	3 875	−5 463	−3 714	3 531	−12 525	−10 387	−23 181
Rest of the world	NHRB	6 064	804	3 498	23 487	22 892	20 979	15 619	14 652	21 311
Private non-financial corporations										
Gross trading profits										
Continental shelf profits	CAGJ	15 702	13 978	11 696	13 864	21 458	20 397	18 742	..	..
Others	CAED	136 579	149 176	153 282	157 101	156 678	154 292	161 586	172 608	186 208
Rental of buildings	FCBW	8 948	9 254	9 724	10 742	11 657	12 304	12 885	13 652	14 225
less Holding gains of inventories	-DLQZ	−958	−361	753	−1 801	−2 941	434	−2 856	−4 148	−4 113
Gross operating surplus	NRJK	160 295	172 071	175 460	179 711	186 330	186 726	190 747	200 743	215 252
Households and NPISH										
Household gross disposable income	QWND	528 590	561 277	581 138	609 734	646 059	688 255	710 144	744 428	770 529
Implied deflator of household and NPISH individual										
consumption expenditure indicies (2002=100)	YBFS	89.1	91.3	93.7	95.3	96.4	98.6	100.0	102.0	103.3
Real household disposable income:										
Chained volume measures (Reference year 2002)	RVGK	593 437	614 644	620 482	640 038	670 474	698 377	710 144	730 113	745 918
Indices (2002=100)	OSXR	83.6	86.5	87.4	90.1	94.4	98.3	100.0	102.8	105.1
Gross saving	NSSH	51 193	52 737	36 923	30 788	33 217	44 352	34 691	41 002	34 813
Households total resources	NSSJ	629 511	663 978	687 447	723 165	765 923	820 133	855 656	905 711	946 730
Saving ratio (percentages)	RVGL	*9.4*	*9.2*	*6.2*	*4.9*	*5.0*	*6.3*	*4.8*	*5.4*	*4.4*

1 See chapter text.

Source: Office for National Statistics: 020 7533 6031

16.14 Household final consumption expenditure: by purpose[1]
Current market prices

United Kingdom

£ million

		1996	1997	1998	1999	2000	2001	2002	2003	2004
Durable goods										
Furnishings, household equipment and routine maintenance of the house	LLIJ	14 321	15 250	15 873	16 566	18 006	19 275	20 470	22 313	23 968
Health	LLIK	1 453	1 549	1 717	1 881	1 997	2 109	2 411	3 096	3 454
Transport	LLIL	26 469	29 404	30 851	31 888	33 221	35 764	36 224	37 450	38 364
Communication	LLIM	276	302	440	512	601	636	644	722	836
Recreation and culture	LLIN	10 592	11 920	12 953	14 262	14 878	15 970	16 471	17 953	19 674
Miscellaneous goods and services	LLIO	3 094	3 295	3 320	3 398	3 403	3 750	4 204	4 196	4 466
Total durable goods	UTIA	56 205	61 720	65 154	68 507	72 106	77 504	80 424	85 730	90 762
Semi-durable goods										
Clothing and footwear	LLJL	28 865	30 270	31 540	32 661	34 759	36 212	38 351	40 624	43 102
Furnishings, household equipment and routine maintenance of the house	LLJM	8 429	9 061	9 751	10 577	11 677	12 400	13 361	13 620	14 506
Transport	LLJN	2 293	2 529	2 925	3 018	2 772	2 783	3 112	3 534	3 804
Recreation and culture	LLJO	12 887	14 664	17 292	19 049	20 405	21 606	23 910	25 543	27 447
Miscellaneous goods and services	LLJP	1 581	1 700	1 816	1 926	2 018	2 427	2 886	3 611	4 132
Total semi-durable goods	UTIQ	54 055	58 224	63 324	67 231	71 631	75 428	81 620	86 932	92 991
Non-durable goods										
Food & drink	ABZV	53 025	53 812	55 192	57 025	58 598	59 974	61 493	62 729	64 420
Alcohol & tobacco	ADFL	20 439	21 553	22 459	24 458	24 617	25 158	25 966	27 316	27 833
Housing, water, electricity, gas and other fuels	LLIX	22 757	22 656	22 094	21 800	22 265	23 076	23 444	24 194	27 006
Furnishings, household equipment and routine maintenance of the house	LLIY	2 433	2 495	2 505	2 657	2 786	2 972	3 169	3 347	3 417
Health	LLIZ	2 746	2 828	2 975	3 111	3 268	3 613	3 855	3 917	3 975
Transport	LLJA	14 589	15 604	16 615	18 210	19 987	19 391	19 129	19 959	20 590
Recreation and culture	LLJB	11 192	11 788	12 136	12 665	12 959	13 107	13 392	13 588	13 745
Miscellaneous goods and services	LLJC	8 014	8 383	8 727	9 121	9 463	9 884	11 272	12 716	14 036
Total non-durable goods	UTII	135 195	139 119	142 703	149 047	153 943	157 175	161 720	167 766	175 022
Total goods	UTIE	245 455	259 063	271 181	284 785	297 680	310 107	323 764	340 428	358 775
Services										
Clothing and footwear	LLJD	620	631	698	714	720	730	741	750	739
Housing, water, electricity, gas and other fuels	LLJE	64 943	69 321	76 020	81 393	85 785	92 829	97 794	103 622	108 229
Furnishings, household equipment and routine maintenance of the house	LLJF	2 545	2 686	2 873	3 046	3 206	3 327	3 448	3 573	3 987
Health	LLJG	3 233	3 380	3 614	3 783	3 943	4 254	4 512	4 641	5 147
Transport	LLJH	26 929	29 667	32 115	34 121	37 002	38 397	41 332	42 653	45 287
Communication	LLJI	9 083	9 682	10 462	11 493	12 755	13 521	14 031	14 873	15 753
Recreation and culture	LLJJ	20 737	21 612	23 005	23 756	24 175	25 321	27 590	29 062	30 801
Education	ADIE	6 405	7 440	7 814	8 943	9 534	9 409	9 381	9 540	9 950
Restaurants and hotels	ADIF	54 848	57 166	61 804	64 413	68 539	71 493	76 298	78 174	81 823
Miscellaneous goods and services	LLJK	39 174	42 053	44 966	48 809	53 177	56 739	57 907	58 290	59 327
Total services	UTIM	228 517	243 638	263 371	280 471	298 836	316 020	333 034	345 178	361 043
Final consumption expenditure in the UK by resident and non-resident households (domestic concept)	ABQI	473 972	502 701	534 552	565 256	596 516	626 127	656 798	685 606	719 818
Final consumption expenditure outside the UK by UK resident households	ABTA	14 377	14 942	16 913	19 690	21 654	22 907	24 435	26 314	27 739
less Final consumption expenditure in the UK by households resident in the rest of the world	CDFD	−14 038	−14 037	−14 544	−14 312	−14 713	−13 383	−13 872	−14 156	−15 698
Final consumption expenditure by UK resident households in the UK and abroad (national concept)	ABPB	474 311	503 606	536 921	570 634	603 457	635 651	667 361	697 764	731 859

1 See chapter text. Additional detail is published in *Consumer Trends* and table A7 of *UK Economic Accounts*, available from the National Statistics website *www.statistics.gov.uk/statbase/Product.asp?vlnk=1904*.

Source: *Office for National Statistics: 020 7533 6031*

16.15 Household final consumption expenditure: by purpose[1]
Chained volume measures, reference year 2002

United Kingdom

£ million

		1996	1997	1998	1999	2000	2001	2002	2003	2004
Durable goods										
Furnishings, household equipment and routine maintenance of the house	LLME	14 749	15 510	16 008	16 656	18 324	19 416	20 470	22 169	23 429
Health	LLMF	3 003	2 871	2 737	2 573	2 444	2 327	2 411	2 878	2 859
Transport	LLMG	25 246	26 881	28 381	29 880	32 069	35 511	36 224	37 975	39 237
Communication	LLMH	165	207	322	428	538	586	644	725	862
Recreation and culture	LLMI	6 073	6 962	8 445	10 670	12 421	14 742	16 471	19 808	24 018
Miscellaneous goods and services	LLMJ	3 361	3 552	3 504	3 526	3 489	3 793	4 204	4 047	4 217
Total durable goods	UTIC	50 154	53 890	58 010	63 127	68 966	76 305	80 424	87 602	94 622
Semi-durable goods										
Clothing and footwear	LLNG	24 404	25 389	26 649	28 388	31 487	34 386	38 351	41 273	45 181
Furnishings, household equipment and routine maintenance of the house	LLNH	8 236	8 788	9 422	10 290	11 611	12 357	13 361	13 773	14 646
Transport	LLNI	2 504	2 675	3 031	3 076	2 801	2 825	3 112	3 465	3 658
Recreation and culture	LLNJ	11 879	13 398	15 725	17 883	19 901	21 107	23 910	26 526	29 456
Miscellaneous goods and services	LLNK	1 556	1 678	1 792	1 908	2 027	2 408	2 886	3 567	4 101
Total semi-durable goods	UTIS	48 662	51 955	56 555	61 460	67 788	73 078	81 620	88 604	97 042
Non-durable goods										
Food & drink	ADIP	55 540	56 518	57 314	59 086	61 090	60 403	61 493	61 883	63 237
Alcohol & tobacco	ADIS	25 875	26 193	25 916	26 681	25 796	25 594	25 966	26 364	26 618
Housing, water, electricity, gas and other fuels	LLMS	22 462	22 607	22 480	22 184	22 770	23 522	23 444	23 753	25 268
Furnishings, household equipment and routine maintenance of the house	LLMT	2 388	2 487	2 456	2 551	2 727	2 941	3 169	3 421	3 624
Health	LLMU	3 166	3 136	3 210	3 282	3 363	3 647	3 855	3 919	3 992
Transport	LLMV	18 983	18 611	18 855	19 000	18 443	18 866	19 129	19 256	18 833
Recreation and culture	LLMW	12 573	12 994	13 129	13 426	13 371	13 253	13 392	13 310	13 282
Miscellaneous goods and services	LLMX	8 607	8 667	8 568	8 784	9 370	9 712	11 272	12 884	14 376
Total non-durable goods	UTIK	149 268	150 982	151 708	154 753	156 812	157 898	161 720	164 790	169 230
Total goods	UTIG	244 675	254 042	264 381	278 130	293 016	307 121	323 764	340 996	360 894
Services										
Clothing and footwear	LLMY	770	755	798	783	771	756	741	720	684
Housing, water, electricity, gas and other fuels	LLMZ	90 989	92 082	93 992	95 052	95 975	96 544	97 794	98 572	99 700
Furnishings, household equipment and routine maintenance of the house	LLNA	3 524	3 564	3 629	3 668	3 617	3 519	3 448	3 382	3 556
Health	LLNB	4 514	4 499	4 455	4 393	4 465	4 535	4 512	4 495	4 768
Transport	LLNC	35 032	36 548	37 961	40 164	41 856	39 742	41 332	41 359	42 270
Communication	LLND	7 760	8 456	9 257	10 434	12 059	13 754	14 031	14 739	15 503
Recreation and culture	LLNE	24 990	25 324	26 179	26 419	26 665	27 821	27 590	28 090	28 891
Education	ADMJ	8 899	9 834	9 784	10 590	10 676	9 938	9 381	8 870	8 831
Restaurants and hotels	ADMK	69 233	69 552	72 067	72 464	74 430	74 480	76 298	76 422	78 258
Miscellaneous goods and services	LLNF	50 018	51 296	51 727	54 139	56 080	57 721	57 907	56 558	55 205
Total services	UTIO	294 133	300 529	308 754	317 323	326 168	328 770	333 034	333 207	337 666
Final consumption expenditure in the UK by resident and non-resident households (domestic concept)	ABQJ	535 991	552 238	571 145	594 023	618 257	635 579	656 798	674 203	698 560
Final consumption expenditure outside the UK by UK resident households	ABTC	12 983	15 131	17 405	20 287	22 409	23 065	24 435	24 378	25 993
less Final consumption expenditure in the UK by households resident in the rest of the world	CCHX	−16 675	−16 163	−16 222	−15 560	−15 566	−13 748	−13 872	−13 740	−14 851
Final consumption expenditure by UK resident households in the UK and abroad (national concept)	ABPF	531 853	551 112	572 348	598 792	625 145	644 895	667 361	684 841	709 702

1 See chapter text. Additional detail is published in *Consumer Trends* and table A7 of *UK Economic Accounts*, available from the National Statistics website *www.statistics.gov.uk/statbase/Product.asp?vlnk=1904*.

Source: *Office for National Statistics: 020 7533 6031*

16.16 Individual consumption expenditure: by households, NPISHs and general government[1] Current market prices

United Kingdom. Classified by function (COICOP/COPNI/COFOG)[2]

£ million

		1996	1997	1998	1999	2000	2001	2002	2003	2004
FINAL CONSUMPTION EXPENDITURE OF HOUSEHOLDS										
Food and non-alcoholic beverages	ABZV	53 025	53 812	55 192	57 025	58 598	59 974	61 493	62 729	64 420
Food	ABZW	47 323	47 976	49 134	50 670	51 875	52 882	54 144	55 120	56 708
Non-alcoholic beverages	ADFK	5 702	5 836	6 058	6 355	6 723	7 092	7 349	7 609	7 712
Alcoholic beverages and tobacco	ADFL	20 439	21 553	22 459	24 458	24 617	25 158	25 966	27 316	27 833
Alcoholic beverages	ADFM	8 174	8 905	9 096	10 166	10 395	10 700	11 344	12 045	12 263
Tobacco	ADFN	12 265	12 648	13 363	14 292	14 222	14 458	14 622	15 271	15 570
Clothing and footwear	ADFP	29 485	30 901	32 238	33 375	35 479	36 942	39 092	41 374	43 841
Clothing	ADFQ	25 158	26 500	27 799	28 932	31 048	32 223	33 927	35 878	37 794
Footwear	ADFR	4 327	4 401	4 439	4 443	4 431	4 719	5 165	5 496	6 047
Housing, water, electricity, gas and other fuels	ADFS	87 700	91 977	98 114	103 193	108 050	115 905	121 238	127 816	135 235
Actual rentals for housing	ADFT	18 784	19 821	21 155	22 584	23 595	25 302	25 828	26 973	27 663
Imputed rentals for housing	ADFU	39 863	42 758	47 689	51 401	54 378	59 581	63 279	67 825	71 213
Maintenance and repair of the dwelling	ADFV	8 398	9 351	9 960	10 234	10 512	11 340	12 306	12 612	13 629
Water supply and miscellaneous dwelling services	ADFW	4 558	4 772	4 961	5 201	5 033	5 059	5 222	5 477	5 711
Electricity, gas and other fuels	ADFX	16 097	15 275	14 349	13 773	14 532	14 623	14 603	14 929	17 019
Furnishings, household equipment and routine maintenance of the house	ADFY	27 728	29 492	31 002	32 846	35 675	37 974	40 448	42 853	45 878
Furniture, furnishings, carpets and other floor coverings	ADFZ	10 471	11 072	11 667	12 437	13 758	14 362	15 591	17 370	19 042
Household textiles	ADGG	3 227	3 404	3 676	3 972	4 465	4 636	5 086	5 129	5 332
Household appliances	ADGL	4 609	4 997	5 080	5 038	5 156	5 758	5 715	5 659	5 885
Glassware, tableware and household utensils	ADGM	2 887	3 129	3 410	3 722	4 231	4 609	4 710	4 683	4 833
Tools and equipment for house and garden	ADGN	1 998	2 179	2 332	2 586	2 722	2 977	3 355	3 676	3 978
Goods and services for routine household maintenance	ADGO	4 536	4 711	4 837	5 091	5 343	5 632	5 991	6 336	6 808
Health	ADGP	7 432	7 757	8 306	8 775	9 208	9 976	10 778	11 654	12 576
Medical products, appliances and equipment	ADGQ	4 199	4 377	4 692	4 992	5 265	5 722	6 266	7 013	7 429
Out-patient services	ADGR	1 827	1 894	2 010	2 107	2 178	2 344	2 422	2 467	2 713
Hospital services	ADGS	1 406	1 486	1 604	1 676	1 765	1 910	2 090	2 174	2 434
Transport	ADGT	70 280	77 204	82 506	87 237	92 982	96 335	99 797	103 596	108 045
Purchase of vehicles	ADGU	26 469	29 404	30 851	31 888	33 221	35 764	36 224	37 450	38 364
Operation of personal transport equipment	ADGV	27 378	29 830	32 045	34 450	37 059	37 028	38 816	40 353	42 189
Transport services	ADGW	16 433	17 970	19 610	20 899	22 702	23 543	24 757	25 793	27 492
Communication	ADGX	9 359	9 984	10 902	12 005	13 356	14 157	14 675	15 595	16 589
Postal services	CDEF	960	951	919	899	873	870	878	894	892
Telephone & telefax equipment	ADWO	276	302	440	512	601	636	644	722	836
Telephone & telefax services	ADWP	8 123	8 731	9 543	10 594	11 882	12 651	13 153	13 979	14 861
Recreation and culture	ADGY	55 408	59 984	65 386	69 732	72 417	76 004	81 363	86 146	91 667
Audio-visual, photographic and information processing equipment	ADGZ	11 974	13 481	15 132	16 312	17 034	17 580	18 051	19 335	21 031
Other major durables for recreation and culture	ADHL	2 548	2 854	3 089	3 582	3 944	4 325	4 672	5 142	5 439
Other recreational items and equipment; flowers, garden and pets	ADHZ	12 758	14 448	16 237	17 655	18 636	20 216	22 475	24 006	25 693
Recreational and cultural services	ADIA	19 246	20 078	21 395	22 127	22 535	23 586	25 796	27 136	28 733
Newspapers, books and stationery	ADIC	8 882	9 123	9 533	10 056	10 268	10 297	10 369	10 527	10 771
Package holidays[3]	ADID	–	–	–	–	–	–	–	–	–
Education										
Education services	ADIE	6 405	7 440	7 814	8 943	9 534	9 409	9 381	9 540	9 950
Restaurants and hotels	ADIF	54 848	57 166	61 804	64 413	68 539	71 493	76 298	78 174	81 823
Catering services	ADIG	46 219	48 232	52 668	55 190	59 001	62 322	66 573	68 096	70 991
Accommodation services	ADIH	8 629	8 934	9 136	9 223	9 538	9 171	9 725	10 078	10 832
Miscellaneous goods and services	ADII	51 863	55 431	58 829	63 254	68 061	72 800	76 269	78 813	81 961
Personal care	ADIJ	11 361	11 887	12 574	13 229	13 883	14 626	16 444	18 244	20 285
Personal effects not elsewhere classified	ADIK	4 083	4 351	4 490	4 673	4 748	5 455	6 140	6 547	7 111
Social protection	ADIL	8 220	8 241	8 332	8 446	8 643	8 963	9 219	9 679	9 829
Insurance	ADIM	15 064	16 387	17 911	20 257	22 238	25 423	25 456	24 417	23 350
Financial services not elsewhere classified	ADIN	6 966	7 935	8 582	9 856	11 819	11 539	11 769	12 237	13 796
Other services not elsewhere classified	ADIO	6 169	6 630	6 940	6 793	6 730	6 794	7 241	7 689	7 590
Final consumption expenditure in the UK by resident and non-resident households (domestic concept)	ABQI	473 972	502 701	534 552	565 256	596 516	626 127	656 798	685 606	719 818
Final consumption expenditure outside the UK by UK resident households	ABTA	14 377	14 942	16 913	19 690	21 654	22 907	24 435	26 314	27 739
less Final consumption expenditure in the UK by households resident in the rest of the world	CDFD	–14 038	–14 037	–14 544	–14 312	–14 713	–13 383	–13 872	–14 156	–15 698
Final consumption expenditure by UK resident households in the UK and abroad (national concept)	ABPB	474 311	503 606	536 921	570 634	603 457	635 651	667 361	697 764	731 859

16.16
continued

Individual consumption expenditure: by households, NPISHs and general government[1] Current market prices
United Kingdom. Classified by function (COICOP/COPNI/COFOG)[2]

£ million

		1996	1997	1998	1999	2000	2001	2002	2003	2004
FINAL CONSUMPTION EXPENDITURE OF UK RESIDENT HOUSEHOLDS										
Final consumption expenditure of UK resident households in the UK and abroad	ABPB	474 311	503 606	536 921	570 634	603 457	635 651	667 361	697 764	731 859
FINAL INDIVIDUAL CONSUMPTION EXPENDITURE OF NPISH										
Final individual consumption expenditure of NPISH	ABNV	18 159	19 422	20 897	21 941	23 238	24 778	25 998	27 248	28 903
FINAL INDIVIDUAL CONSUMPTION EXPENDITURE OF OF GENERAL GOVERNMENT										
Health	QYOT	41 966	42 999	45 843	49 739	52 537	57 962	63 272	69 791	75 722
Recreation and culture	QYSU	3 444	3 465	3 465	3 736	3 898	4 049	4 335	4 513	4 272
Education	QYSE	26 059	26 736	27 878	29 484	31 521	33 900	37 535	39 876	42 727
Social protection	QYSP	14 379	15 013	15 520	16 843	18 055	19 441	22 464	25 517	28 028
Housing	QYXO	–	–	–	–	–	–	–	..	..
Final individual consumption expenditure of general government	NNAQ	85 848	88 213	92 706	99 802	106 011	115 352	127 606	139 697	151 155
Total, individual consumption expenditure/ actual individual consumption	NQEO	578 318	611 241	650 524	692 377	732 706	775 781	820 965	864 709	911 917

1 See chapter text.
2 "Purpose" or "function" classifications are designed to indicate the "socio-economic objectives" that institutional units aim to achieve through various kinds of outlays. COICOP is the Classification of Individual Consumption by Purpose and applies to households. COPNI is the Classification of the Purposes of Non-Profit Institutions Serving Households and COFOG the Classification of the Functions of Government. The introduction of ESA95 coincides with the redefinition of these classifications and data will be available on a consistent basis for all European Union member states.
3 Package holidays data are dispersed between components (transport etc).

Source: Office for National Statistics: 020 7533 6031

16.17 Individual consumption expenditure: by households, NPISH and general government[1] Chained volume measures, reference year 2002

United Kingdom. Classified by function (COICOP/COPNI/COFOG)[2]

£ million

		1996	1997	1998	1999	2000	2001	2002	2003	2004
FINAL CONSUMPTION EXPENDITURE OF HOUSEHOLDS										
Food and non-alcoholic beverages	ADIP	55 540	56 518	57 314	59 086	61 090	60 403	61 493	61 883	63 237
Food	ADIQ	49 625	50 629	51 399	52 850	54 372	53 297	54 144	54 260	55 444
Non-alcoholic beverages	ADIR	5 953	5 927	5 957	6 271	6 739	7 107	7 349	7 623	7 793
Alcoholic beverages and tobacco	ADIS	25 875	26 193	25 916	26 681	25 796	25 594	25 966	26 364	26 618
Alcoholic beverages	ADIT	8 458	9 107	9 153	10 155	10 321	10 671	11 344	11 845	12 242
Tobacco	ADIU	18 034	17 482	17 104	16 677	15 537	14 941	14 622	14 519	14 376
Clothing and footwear	ADIW	25 117	26 099	27 398	29 136	32 240	35 134	39 092	41 993	45 865
Clothing	ADIX	21 228	22 042	23 221	24 877	27 902	30 490	33 927	36 515	39 839
Footwear	ADIY	3 963	4 135	4 249	4 308	4 345	4 645	5 165	5 478	6 026
Housing, water, electricity, gas and other fuels	ADIZ	113 644	114 845	116 481	117 154	118 706	120 071	121 238	122 325	124 968
Actual rentals for housing	ADJA	25 785	25 974	26 063	26 097	26 079	26 146	25 828	25 892	26 007
Imputed rentals for housing	ADJB	56 542	57 469	59 319	60 583	61 257	61 994	63 279	64 302	65 290
Maintenance and repair of the dwelling	ADJC	10 635	11 188	11 416	11 424	11 311	11 760	12 306	12 217	12 844
Water supply and miscellaneous dwelling services	ADJD	5 097	5 105	5 026	5 035	5 186	5 179	5 222	5 273	5 226
Electricity, gas and other fuels	ADJE	15 122	14 833	14 589	14 087	14 860	14 982	14 603	14 641	15 601
Furnishings, household equipment and routine maintenance of the house	ADJF	28 694	30 178	31 366	33 053	36 231	38 217	40 448	42 745	45 255
Furniture, furnishings, carpets and other floor coverings	ADJG	11 477	11 810	12 214	12 869	14 235	14 576	15 591	17 041	18 217
Household textiles	ADJH	3 088	3 243	3 476	3 775	4 397	4 573	5 086	5 173	5 305
Household appliances	ADJI	4 187	4 606	4 736	4 771	5 055	5 697	5 715	5 811	6 133
Glassware, tableware and household utensils	ADJJ	2 902	3 116	3 378	3 695	4 272	4 649	4 710	4 677	4 810
Tools and equipment for house and garden	ADJK	1 928	2 085	2 246	2 524	2 685	2 961	3 355	3 807	4 165
Goods and services for routine household maintenance	ADJL	5 268	5 422	5 382	5 470	5 618	5 764	5 991	6 236	6 625
Health	ADJM	10 484	10 342	10 290	10 183	10 235	10 504	10 778	11 292	11 619
Medical products, appliances and equipment	ADJN	5 974	5 846	5 839	5 794	5 774	5 971	6 266	6 797	6 851
Out-patient services	ADJO	2 640	2 620	2 557	2 490	2 462	2 491	2 422	2 400	2 579
Hospital services	ADJP	1 883	1 887	1 902	1 906	2 003	2 044	2 090	2 095	2 189
Transport	ADJQ	80 940	84 108	87 734	91 631	94 750	96 970	99 797	102 055	103 998
Purchase of vehicles	ADJR	25 246	26 881	28 381	29 880	32 069	35 511	36 224	37 975	39 237
Operation of personal transport equipment	ADJS	35 893	36 488	37 412	37 810	37 340	37 440	38 816	38 516	38 085
Transport services	ADJT	20 666	21 399	22 508	24 454	25 696	24 014	24 757	25 564	26 676
Communication	ADJU	7 880	8 625	9 563	10 856	12 594	14 335	14 675	15 464	16 365
Postal services	CCGZ	1 017	989	951	931	888	874	878	867	840
Telephone & telefax equipment	ADQF	165	207	322	428	538	586	644	725	862
Telephone & telefax services	ADQG	6 822	7 529	8 352	9 532	11 180	12 879	13 153	13 872	14 663
Recreation and culture	ADJV	52 212	55 841	61 370	67 255	71 748	76 653	81 363	87 734	95 647
Audio-visual, photographic and information processing equipment	ADJW	7 063	8 110	9 989	12 381	14 420	16 267	18 051	21 415	26 053
Other major durables for recreation and culture	ADJX	2 798	3 035	3 231	3 683	4 057	4 425	4 672	4 986	5 110
Other recreational items and equipment; flowers, gardens and pets	ADJY	12 056	13 502	15 185	16 818	18 129	19 713	22 475	24 923	27 317
Recreational and cultural services	ADJZ	23 054	23 405	24 251	24 543	24 862	26 001	25 796	26 257	27 015
Newspapers, books and stationery	ADKM	10 441	10 485	10 605	10 840	10 780	10 518	10 369	10 153	10 152
Package holidays[3]	ADMI	–	–	–	–	–	–	–	–	–
Education										
Education services	ADMJ	8 899	9 834	9 784	10 590	10 676	9 938	9 381	8 870	8 831
Restaurants and Hotels	ADMK	69 233	69 552	72 067	72 464	74 430	74 480	76 298	76 422	78 258
Catering services	ADML	58 060	58 399	61 109	61 765	63 949	64 970	66 573	66 461	67 760
Accommodation services	ADMM	11 241	11 219	11 004	10 732	10 495	9 510	9 725	9 961	10 498
Miscellaneous goods and services	ADMN	63 480	65 141	65 526	68 262	70 897	73 582	76 269	77 056	77 899
Personal care	ADMO	13 002	13 077	13 125	13 430	14 178	14 644	16 444	18 160	20 124
Personal effects not elsewhere classified	ADMP	4 293	4 554	4 630	4 756	4 806	5 476	6 140	6 396	6 882
Social protection	ADMQ	11 437	10 919	10 558	10 179	9 782	9 500	9 219	9 140	8 793
Insurance	ADMR	19 939	20 729	21 332	23 132	24 115	26 099	25 456	23 684	21 955
Financial services not elsewhere classified	ADMS	7 185	7 864	7 836	9 008	10 452	10 727	11 769	12 555	13 699
Other services not elsewhere classified	ADMT	8 652	8 878	8 923	8 339	7 783	7 276	7 241	7 121	6 446
Final consumption expenditure in the UK by resident and non-resident households (domestic concept)	ABQJ	535 991	552 238	571 145	594 023	618 257	635 579	656 798	674 203	698 560
Final consumption expenditure outside the UK by UK resident households	ABTC	12 983	15 131	17 405	20 287	22 409	23 065	24 435	24 378	25 993
less Final consumption expenditure in the UK by households resident in the rest of the world	CCHX	–16 675	–16 163	–16 222	–15 560	–15 566	–13 748	–13 872	–13 740	–14 851
Final consumption expenditure by UK resident households in the UK and abroad (national concept)	ABPF	531 853	551 112	572 348	598 792	625 145	644 895	667 361	684 841	709 702

16.17
continued

Individual consumption expenditure: by households, NPISH and general government[1] Chained volume measures, reference year 2002

United Kingdom. Classified by function (COICOP/COPNI/COFOG)[2]

£ million

		1996	1997	1998	1999	2000	2001	2002	2003	2004
FINAL CONSUMPTION EXPENDITURE OF UK RESIDENT HOUSEHOLDS										
Final consumption expenditure of UK resident households in the UK and abroad	ABPF	531 853	551 112	572 348	598 792	625 145	644 895	667 361	684 841	709 702
FINAL INDIVIDUAL CONSUMPTION EXPENDITURE OF NPISH										
Final individual consumption expenditure of NPISH	ABNU	21 089	21 699	23 306	23 260	25 270	25 247	25 998	26 229	26 761
FINAL INDIVIDUAL CONSUMPTION EXPENDITURE OF GENERAL GOVERNMENT										
Health	EMOA	53 280	54 099	55 065	56 805	58 517	61 019	63 272	65 611	68 758
Recreation and culture	QYXK	3 760	3 779	3 716	3 930	4 051	3 968	4 470	4 717	..
Education	EMOB	35 159	35 612	35 939	36 520	36 876	37 100	37 535	37 732	37 944
Social protection	QYXM	20 901	21 005	21 121	21 108	21 194	21 365	22 464	23 151	23 460
Housing	QYXN	–	–	–	–	–	–	–	–	..
Final individual consumption expenditure of general government	NSZK	104 403	105 948	107 339	109 554	111 763	114 159	117 238	120 288	..
Total, individual consumption expenditure/ actual individual consumption	YBIO	665 475	686 764	710 964	739 989	770 711	793 253	820 965	842 181	871 276

1 See chapter text.
2 "Purpose" or "function" classifications are designed to indicate the "socio-economic objectives" that institutional units aim to achieve through various kinds of outlays. COICOP is the Classification of Individual Consumption by Purpose and applies to households. COPNI is the Classification of the Purposes of Non-Profit Institutions Serving Households (NPISH) and COFOG the Classification of the Functions of Government. The introduction of ESA95 coincides with the redefinition of these classifications and data will be available on a consistent basis for all European Union member states.
3 Package holidays data are dispersed between components (transport etc).

Source: Office for National Statistics: 020 7533 6031

16.18

Change in inventories[1,2] Chained volume measures, reference year 2002

United Kingdom

Reference year 2002, £ million

	Mining and quarrying	Manufacturing industries				Electricity, gas and water supply	Distributive trades		Other industries[4]	Change in inventories
		Materials and fuel	Work in progress	Finished goods	Total		Wholesale[3]	Retail[3]		
	FADO	FBID	FBIE	FBIF	DHBH	FADP	FAJM	FBYH	DLWV	ABMQ
1995	−181	458	1 087	888	2 404	−173	529	893	945	4 538
1996	−68	−93	−206	5	−287	12	606	703	1 045	1 850
1997	81	360	−1 268	303	−534	87	1 526	881	2 306	4 013
1998	376	643	−558	325	467	−130	489	1 088	3 229	4 910
1999	−316	609	−114	−422	102	−134	1 566	1 624	4 057	6 422
2000	−254	649	503	426	1 577	235	1 762	1 382	310	5 267
2001	96	−407	514	168	276	49	710	1 015	4 050	6 196
2002	−28	−390	−4	−364	−758	−99	611	1 618	1 565	2 909
2003	−57	−92	−505	−130	−727	20	230	1 143	3 993	4 602
2004	−40	−135	−659	−79	−873	−86	1 263	1 628	4 041	5 933

1 See chapter text. Estimates are given to the nearest £ million but cannot be regarded as accurate to this degree.
2 Components may not sum to totals due to rounding.
3 Wholesaling and retailing estimates exclude the motor trades.
4 Quarterly alignment adjustment included in this series.

Source: Office for National Statistics 020 7533 6031

16.19 Gross fixed capital formation at current purchasers' prices: by broad sector and type of asset[1,2]

United Kingdom. Total economy

£ million

		1996	1997	1998	1999	2000	2001	2002	2003	2004
Private sector										
New dwellings, excluding land	DFDF	20 205	22 017	23 317	23 921	25 604	27 085	31 455	34 804	40 927
Other buildings and structures	EQBU	20 843	25 349	28 515	31 008	31 776	32 675	33 210	35 046	38 383
Transport equipment	EQBV	11 322	12 065	15 442	14 419	12 959	14 097	15 537	13 945	13 599
Other machinery and equipment and cultivated assets	EQBW	47 491	49 108	57 592	58 067	61 136	57 862	53 048	49 149	50 264
Intangible fixed assets	EQBX	3 278	3 395	3 555	3 624	4 004	4 320	4 628	..	..
Costs associated with the transfer of ownership of non-produced assets	EQBY	6 726	7 647	7 453	9 859	11 207	12 696	15 398	16 361	18 058
Total	EQBZ	109 300	120 157	135 781	138 913	143 699	144 826	152 019	..	..
Public non-financial corporations										
New dwellings, excluding land	DEER	163	123	49	8	–	–	–	–	–
Other buildings and structures	DEES	2 171	1 647	1 334	1 681	1 761	1 850	2 303	2 017	1 274
Transport equipment	DEEP	225	190	171	154	168	160	104	68	100
Other machinery and equipment and cultivated assets	DEEQ	406	402	438	586	503	576	734	1 054	1 006
Intangible fixed assets	DLXJ	585	595	605	625	551	397	556	623	737
Costs associated with the transfer of ownership of non-produced assets	DLXQ	101	267	352	−8	5	59	−41	−245	−266
Total	FCCJ	3 651	3 224	2 949	3 046	2 988	3 042	3 656	3 517	2 861
General government										
New dwellings, excluding land	DFHW	2 148	1 788	1 856	1 771	1 790	2 721	3 044	3 658	3 469
Other buildings and structures	EQCH	9 891	8 580	9 304	8 982	10 076	10 804	11 914	14 633	15 980
Transport equipment	EQCI	672	675	693	610	550	599	573	758	953
Other machinery and equipment and cultivated assets	EQCJ	2 205	1 755	1 605	1 845	1 691	2 090	2 639	2 876	3 133
Intangible fixed assets	EQCK	273	259	387	396	367	334	358	367	351
Costs associated with the transfer of ownership of non-produced assets	EQCL	−2 432	−2 275	−1 730	−2 062	−2 382	−2 623	−2 948	−4 079	−3 231
Total	NNBF	12 757	10 782	12 115	11 542	12 092	13 925	15 580	18 213	21 125
Total gross fixed capital formation	NPQX	126 273	133 587	150 938	155 486	161 810	165 667	172 558	175 946	190 501

1 See chapter text.
2 Components may not sum to totals due to rounding.

Source: Office for National Statistics: 020 7533 6031

16.20 Gross fixed capital formation at current purchasers' prices: by type of asset[1,2]

United Kingdom. Total economy

£ million

		1996	1997	1998	1999	2000	2001	2002	2003	2004
Tangible fixed assets										
New dwellings, excluding land	DFDK	22 516	23 928	25 222	25 700	27 394	29 806	34 499	38 462	44 409
Other buildings and structures	DLWS	32 825	35 455	39 041	41 680	43 878	45 381	47 308	52 036	..
Transport equipment	DLWZ	12 219	12 930	16 306	15 183	13 677	14 856	16 214	14 771	14 663
Other machinery and equipment and cultivated assets	DLXI	50 102	51 265	59 635	60 498	63 330	60 528	56 421	53 079	54 798
Total	EQCQ	117 742	123 699	140 316	143 052	148 014	150 519	154 561	158 008	169 088
Intangible fixed assets	DLXP	4 136	4 249	4 547	4 645	4 966	5 016	5 588	5 901	6 395
Costs associated with the transfer of ownership of non-produced assets	DFBH	4 395	5 639	6 075	7 789	8 830	10 132	12 409	12 037	14 583
Total gross fixed capital formation	NPQX	126 273	133 587	150 938	155 486	161 810	165 667	172 558	175 946	190 501

1 See chapter text.
2 Components may not sum to totals due to rounding.

Source: Office for National Statistics: 020 7533 6031

268

16.21 Gross fixed capital formation: by broad sector and type of asset[1,2,3]
Chained volume measures, reference year 2002
United Kingdom. Total economy

£ million

		1996	1997	1998	1999	2000	2001	2002	2003	2004
Private sector										
New dwellings, excluding land	DFDP	27 832	29 471	29 802	28 832	28 931	29 195	31 455	32 474	35 547
Other buildings and structures	EQCU	23 888	29 033	32 233	33 196	33 155	33 351	33 210	35 253	37 392
Transport equipment	EQCV	11 240	12 271	15 453	14 190	12 734	13 979	15 537	13 873	13 426
Other machinery and equipment and cultivated assets	EQCW	35 008	37 634	46 586	49 624	54 941	55 021	53 048	50 071	52 719
Intangible fixed assets	EQCX	3 745	3 897	3 836	3 804	4 149	4 312	4 674	4 815	4 807
Costs associated with the transfer of ownership of non-produced assets	EQCY	15 854	16 134	13 566	14 829	14 468	14 343	15 398	14 342	14 312
Total	EQCZ	112 474	123 255	140 346	143 705	148 676	150 540	153 322	150 828	158 135
Public non-financial corporations										
New dwellings, excluding land	DEEW	190	141	55	9	–	–	–	–	–
Other buildings and structures	DEEX	2 593	1 942	1 505	1 838	1 887	1 913	2 303	1 984	1 184
Transport equipment	DEEU	250	201	177	158	169	160	104	64	95
Other machinery and equipment and cultivated assets	DEEV	271	271	337	480	447	551	734	1 081	1 049
Intangible fixed assets	EQDE	675	665	654	666	570	403	556	606	696
Costs associated with the transfer of ownership of non-produced assets	EQDF	−86	−220	−261	4	8	67	−41	−234	−266
Total	EQDG	3 961	3 440	3 086	3 165	3 070	3 081	3 656	3 501	2 758
General government										
New dwellings, excluding land	DFID	2 679	2 193	2 197	1 982	1 913	2 812	3 044	3 582	3 318
Other buildings and structures	EQDI	11 912	10 366	10 546	9 918	10 823	11 190	11 914	14 115	14 415
Transport equipment	EQDJ	754	791	750	656	597	662	573	732	724
Other machinery and equipment and cultivated assets	EQDK	1 340	1 107	1 167	1 478	1 462	1 975	2 639	2 952	3 321
Intangible fixed assets	EQDL	300	308	415	409	371	331	358	389	693
Costs associated with the transfer of ownership of non-produced assets	EQDM	−6 739	−5 698	−3 722	−3 359	−3 225	−3 006	−2 948	−3 526	−2 366
Total	EQDN	12 001	10 456	11 515	11 295	12 008	13 954	15 580	18 244	20 562
Total gross fixed capital formation	NPQR	128 565	137 125	154 927	158 104	163 709	167 563	172 558	172 573	181 506

1 See chapter text.
2 For the years before 2002, the total differs from the sum of their components.
3 Components may not sum to totals due to rounding.

Source: Office for National Statistics: 020 7533 6031

16.22 Gross fixed capital formation: by type of asset[1,2,3]
Chained volume measures, reference year 2002
United Kingdom. Total economy

£ million

		1996	1997	1998	1999	2000	2001	2002	2003	2004
Tangible fixed assets										
New dwellings, excluding land	DFDV	30 762	31 796	32 029	30 783	30 797	32 006	34 499	36 056	38 879
Other buildings and structures	EQDP	38 239	41 331	44 319	44 990	45 883	46 465	47 427	51 352	52 990
Transport equipment	DLWJ	12 197	13 223	16 363	14 991	13 487	14 786	16 214	14 669	14 257
Other machinery and equipment and cultivated assets	DLWM	36 689	39 016	48 053	51 575	56 825	57 545	56 421	54 104	57 512
Total	EQDS	114 443	121 853	139 282	141 877	147 307	151 037	154 561	156 181	163 191
Intangible fixed assets	EQDT	4 723	4 872	4 904	4 878	5 091	5 047	5 588	5 810	6 196
Costs associated with the transfer of ownership of non-produced assets	DFDW	9 924	11 399	10 636	11 520	11 275	11 408	12 409	10 582	11 611
Total gross fixed capital formation	NPQR	128 565	137 125	154 927	158 104	163 709	167 563	172 558	172 573	181 506

1 See chapter text.
2 For the years before 2002, the total differs from the sum of their components.
3 Components may not sum to totals due to rounding.

Source: Office for National Statistics: 020 7533 6031

Prices

Chapter 17

Prices

Producer price index numbers

(Tables 17.1 and 17.2)

The producer price indices (PPIs) were published for the first time in August 1983, replacing the former wholesale price indices. Full details of the differences between the two indices were given in an article published in *British Business*, 15 April 1983. The producer price indices are calculated using the same general methodology as that used by the wholesale price indices.

The high level index numbers in Tables 17.1 and 17.2 are constructed on a net sector basis. That is to say, they are intended to measure only transactions between the sector concerned and other sectors. Within the sector, transactions are excluded. Index numbers for the whole of manufacturing are thus not weighted averages of sector index numbers.

The index numbers for selected industries in Tables 17.1 and 17.2 are constructed on a gross sector basis, i.e. all transactions are included in deriving the weighting patterns, including sales within the same industry.

All the index numbers are compiled exclusive of value-added tax. Excise duties on cigarettes, manufactured tobacco and alcoholic liquor are included, as is the duty on hydrocarbon oils except where specified otherwise.

The indices relate to the average prices for a year. The movement in these prices are weighted to reflect the relative importance of the composite products in a chosen year (known as the base year), currently 2000.

Since July 1995, PPIs have been published fully reclassified to the 1992 version of the Standard Industrial Classification (SIC).

Further details are available from the National Statistics website: www.statistics.gov.uk/ppi.

Purchasing power of the pound

(Table 17.3)

Changes in the internal purchasing power of a currency may be defined as the 'inverse' of changes in the levels of prices; when prices go up, the amount which can be purchased with a given sum of money goes down. Movements in the internal purchasing power of the pound are based on the consumers' expenditure deflator (CED) prior to 1962 and on the General index of retail prices (RPI) from January 1962 onwards. The CED shows the movement in prices implied by the national accounts estimates of consumers' expenditure valued at current and at constant prices, whilst the RPI is constructed directly by weighting together monthly movements in prices according to a given pattern of household expenditure derived from the Expenditure and Food Survey. If the purchasing power of the pound is taken to be 100p in a particular month (quarter, year), the comparable purchasing power in a subsequent month (quarter, year) is:

$$100 \quad x \quad \frac{\text{earlier period price index}}{\text{later period price index}}$$

where the price index used is the CED for years 1946–1961 and the RPI for periods after 1961.

Consumer prices index

(Table 17.4)

The consumer prices index (CPI) is the main United Kingdom domestic measure of inflation for macro-economic purposes. Like the RPI (see below) it measures the average change from month to month in the prices of consumer goods and services purchased in the UK, but there are differences in coverage and methodology. A detailed description of these differences is given in the paper entitled *The New Inflation Target: the Statistical Perspective*. This paper is available on the National Statistics website: www.statistics.gov.uk/StatBase/Product. asp?vlnk=10913.

Since 10 December 2003, the Government inflation target for the UK has been defined in terms of the CPI measure of inflation. Prior to that the CPI had been published in the UK as the harmonised index of consumer prices (HICP); the two shall remain one and the same index.

The HICPs are calculated in each Member State of the European Union (EU), according to rules specified in a series of European Regulations developed by the EU statistical office in conjunction with the EU Member States. The HICPs are used to compare inflation rates across the EU. Since January 1999 it has also been used by the European Central Bank (ECB) as the measure of price stability across the euro area. Additional information on HICPs is available from the National Statistics website: www.statistics.gov.uk/hicp

CPI inflation rates prior to 1997 and index levels prior to 1996 are estimated. See article on National Statistics website:*www. statistics.gov.uk/cci/article.asp?ID=31*. Also the coverage of CPI categories for health, education and miscellaneous goods and services have been extended between 2000 and 2002. Details are given in articles available on the website: www.statistics. gov.uk/cci/searchres2.asp?ct=6&term=HICP

Further details on the CPI are available from the National Statistics website: www.statistics.gov.uk/cpi

Retail prices index

(Table 17.5)

The retail prices index (RPI) is the most familiar general purpose measure of inflation in the UK, measuring the percentage changes month by month in the average level of prices of the goods and services purchased by the great majority of households in the United Kingdom. The uses of the RPI include indexation of pensions, state benefits and index-linked gilts. The expenditure pattern on which the index is based is revised each year using information from the Expenditure and Food Survey. The expenditure of certain higher income households and households of retired people dependent mainly on social security benefits is excluded.

The index covers a large and representative selection of more than 650 separate goods and services, for which price movements are regularly measured in around 150 locations throughout the country. Around 120,000 separate price quotations are used in compiling the index.

Further details are available from the National Statistics website: www.statistics.gov.uk/rpi

Tax and price index (TPI)

(Table 17.6)

The purpose and methodology of the TPI were described in an article in the August 1979 issue (No 310) of *Economic Trends* (The Stationery Office). The TPI measures the change in gross taxable income needed for taxpayers to maintain their purchasing power, allowing for changes in retail prices. The TPI thus takes account of the changes to direct taxes (and employees' National Insurance contributions) facing representative cross-section of taxpayers as well as changes in the retail prices index (RPI).

When direct taxation or employees' National Insurance contributions change, the TPI will rise by less than or more than the RPI according to the type of changes made. Between Budgets, the monthly increase in the TPI is normally slightly larger than that in the RPI, since all the extra income needed to offset any rise in retail prices is fully taxed.

Index numbers of agricultural prices

(Tables 17.7 and 17.8)

The Indices of producer prices of agricultural products are currently based on the calendar year 2000. They are designed to provide short-term and medium-term indications of movements in these prices. All annual series are base-weighted Laspeyres type, using value weights derived from the Economic Accounts for Agriculture prepared for the Statistical Office of the European Union. Prices are measured exclusive of VAT. For Table 17.7 it has generally been necessary to measure the prices of materials (inputs) ex-supplier. For Table 17.8, it has generally been necessary to measure the prices received by producers (outputs) at the first marketing stage. The construction of the indices enables them to be combined with similar indices for other member countries of the European Union to provide an overall indication of trends within the Union which appears in the Union's Eurostat series of publications.

Index numbers at a more detailed level and for earlier based series are available from the Department for Environment and Rural Affairs, Food Chain Analysis Division, Food Statistics Branch, Room 146 Foss House, Kingspool 1-2 Peasholme Green, York, YO1 7PX Tel 01904 455253.

Prices

17.1 Producer price index of materials and fuels purchased: by all manufacturing and selected industries SIC(92)[1]

United Kingdom: Annual averages

Indices (2000=100)

			1998	1999	2000	2001	2002	2003	2004	2005
Net sector										
Materials and fuel purchased by manufacturing industry[2]	RNNK	6292000050	94.3	93.1	100.0	98.8	94.4	95.7	99.5	111.0
Materials	PLKX	6292000010	93.6	92.3	100.0	98.1	93.7	95.2	98.7	108.1
Fuels[2]	RNNL	6292000060	103.8	103.6	100.0	107.1	103.4	102.1	109.9	150.6
Materials and fuels purchased by manufacturing industry- seasonally adjusted[2]	RNPE	6292008950	94.3	93.1	100.0	98.8	94.4	95.7	99.4	111.0
Materials and fuels purchased by manufacturing industry other than food, beverages, petroleum and tobacco[2]	RNNQ	6292990050	100.0	96.4	100.0	98.7	94.0	93.7	95.4	102.9
Materials	RWCJ	6292990010	99.7	95.8	100.0	98.1	93.2	93.0	94.2	98.9
Fuel[2]	RNNS	6292990060	103.9	103.7	100.0	106.8	103.1	101.8	109.6	150.1
Materials and fuels purchased by manufacturing industries other than food, beverages, petroleum and tobacco- seasonally adjusted[2]	RNPF	6292998950	100.0	96.4	100.0	98.7	94.0	93.7	95.4	102.9
Gross sector[3]										
All manufacturing	RBBO	6192000000	98.3	96.3	100.0	99.3	97.1	98.4	102.1	109.6
Other mining and quarrying products[4]	RABE	6112140000	87.5	90.2	100.0	96.9	92.3	93.1	96.0	107.6
Manufacture of food products	RBBQ	6192151600	104.0	102.3	100.0	103.2	102.3	105.2	108.5	109.3
Food products and beverages	RABF	6112150000	104.0	102.3	100.0	103.3	102.3	105.2	108.6	109.3
Tobacco products	RABG	6112160000	102.3	100.8	100.0	100.0	101.2	106.9	107.0	107.9
Manufacture of textiles	RBBR	6192171800	102.8	98.7	100.0	100.5	98.4	99.2	99.6	103.3
Textiles	RABH	6112170000	102.7	98.7	100.0	100.5	98.6	99.8	100.0	105.3
Wearing apparel	RABI	6112180000	103.1	98.5	100.0	100.4	97.8	98.0	98.7	99.7
Manufacture of leather	RBBS	6192190000	99.8	97.9	100.0	101.9	100.0	101.1	102.0	105.7
Manufacture of wood and wood products	RBBT	6192200000	105.6	100.2	100.0	99.2	96.5	96.8	99.5	103.8
Manufacture of pulp, paper, publishing and printing	RBBU	6192212200	98.5	97.0	100.0	100.9	99.2	99.4	100.4	103.8
Pulp and paper products	RABL	6112210000	98.7	96.0	100.0	100.7	97.5	96.5	96.9	100.6
Printed matter and recording material	RABM	6112220000	98.4	97.4	100.0	101.0	100.0	100.8	102.2	105.3
Manufacture of coke	RBBV	6192230000	51.1	65.4	100.0	92.0	89.2	95.4	109.1	150.9
Manufacture of chemical products	RBBW	6192240000	99.6	96.1	100.0	101.1	99.4	103.0	105.5	114.2
Manufacture of rubber products	RBBX	6192250000	99.3	96.6	100.0	99.1	97.7	99.5	102.6	110.7
Manufacture of other non-metallic mineral products	RBBY	6192260000	97.6	97.4	100.0	100.5	99.6	100.7	103.0	111.6
Manufacture of basic metals	RBBZ	6192272800	100.2	94.8	100.0	98.5	96.6	99.8	111.8	122.9
Basic metals	RABV	6112270000	98.9	93.4	100.0	98.6	96.8	101.3	115.7	126.9
Fabricated metal products	RABW	6112280000	101.3	96.1	100.0	98.4	96.4	98.6	108.4	119.5
Manufacture of machinery and equipment not elsewhere classified	RBCA	6192290000	100.9	97.8	100.0	98.9	97.1	97.8	102.4	109.2
Manufacture of electrical and optical equipment	RBCB	6192303300	104.6	99.8	100.0	97.2	92.5	88.8	87.7	90.1
Office machinery and computers	RABY	6112300000	104.7	99.5	100.0	95.5	87.4	80.7	78.5	79.3
Electrical machinery and apparatus not elsewhere classified	RACB	6112310000	101.6	98.1	100.0	98.5	95.8	94.5	96.1	101.4
Radio, television and communication equipment	RACC	6112320000	103.8	99.0	100.0	98.1	94.5	92.1	92.4	96.6
Medical, precision, optical instruments and clocks	RACD	6112330000	103.2	99.0	100.0	98.2	95.2	92.3	90.6	93.3
Manufacture of transport equipment	RBCC	6192343500	102.1	99.6	100.0	99.1	97.3	98.1	100.1	105.3
Motor vehicles, trailers and semi-trailers	RACE	6112340000	103.1	100.3	100.0	99.3	98.1	99.3	101.5	106.8
Other transport equipment	RACF	6112350000	99.8	97.8	100.0	98.7	95.4	95.5	97.0	102.0
Manufacturing not elsewhere classified	RBCD	6192363700	101.4	97.8	100.0	99.1	97.8	99.9	104.4	109.8
Electricity including Climate Change Levy	RCVR	7167850000	107.5	107.5	100.0	96.2	92.5	89.3	95.2	127.1
Gas including Climate Change Levy	RCVW	7167860000	92.4	91.9	100.0	140.7	136.5	141.3	155.5	226.7
Collected and purified water	PQNB	7167870000	97.7	102.4	100.0	101.6	103.4	107.0	113.9	131.1

1 See chapter text.
2 These indices include the Climate Change Levy which was introduced in April 2001.
3 The Climate Change Levy is excluded from the detailed industry input index.
4 These indices include the Aggregates Levy which was introduced in April 2002.

Source: Office for National Statistics: 01633 812106

17.2 Producer price index of output: by all manufacturing and selected industries SIC(92)[1]

United Kingdom: Annual averages

Indices (2000=100)

			1998	1999	2000	2001	2002	2003	2004	2005
Net sector										
Output of manufactured products	PLLU	7209200000	98.1	98.5	100.0	99.7	99.8	101.3	103.8	106.7
All manufacturing excluding duty	PVNP	7209200010	99.4	99.0	100.0	99.7	99.7	101.2	103.7	106.8
All manufacturing excluding duty - seasonally adjusted	PVNQ	7209200890	99.4	99.0	100.0	99.7	99.8	101.2	103.7	106.8
Products of manufacturing industries other than the food, beverages, petroleum and tobacco manufacturing industries - not seasonally adjusted	PLLV	7209299000	101.3	100.2	100.0	99.4	99.3	100.6	102.5	104.6
All manufacturing excluding food, beverages, tobacco and petroleum - seasonally adjusted	PLLW	7209299890	101.3	100.2	100.0	99.4	99.3	100.6	102.5	104.7
Gross sector										
Manufactured products excluding duty	POKE	7109200000	98.3	97.8	100.0	99.4	99.1	100.8	104.0	108.8
Manufactured products excluding food, drink, tobacco and petroleum	POKF	7109299000	101.5	100.1	100.0	99.4	99.3	100.5	103.0	106.1
Other mining and quarrying products[2]	ROFV	7112148000	94.8	96.2	100.0	104.4	120.3	126.9	129.1	129.8
Food products, beverages and tobacco excluding duty	POKH	7111151600	100.3	100.5	100.0	101.9	103.3	104.6	106.9	108.3
Food products, beverages and tobacco including duty	RBGA	7111151680	97.8	99.1	100.0	102.0	103.3	104.7	107.3	108.9
Food products and beverages including duty	RPUN	7112150080	100.4	100.4	100.0	101.5	102.6	103.6	105.9	107.1
Food products excluding beverages	RBGD	7112159900	101.1	100.9	100.0	101.7	102.7	103.7	106.0	107.1
Alcoholic beverages including duty	RPUX	7113159080	97.3	98.7	100.0	101.6	103.1	103.7	106.8	108.3
Tobacco products including duty	RPUS	7112160080	81.8	91.6	100.0	105.0	107.8	111.2	115.3	119.8
Textiles and textile products	POKI	7111171800	100.3	99.9	100.0	99.2	98.8	98.7	98.5	99.9
Textiles	POKZ	7112170000	101.0	100.2	100.0	99.4	99.2	99.4	99.2	101.2
Wearing apparel: Furs	POLA	7112180000	98.8	99.2	100.0	99.0	97.9	97.2	97.0	97.4
Leather and leather products	POKJ	7111190000	100.4	99.2	100.0	102.5	102.7	102.9	102.9	104.5
Wood and wood products	POKK	7111200000	104.9	101.5	100.0	99.9	100.0	101.8	105.2	110.0
Pulp, paper and paper products, recorded media and printing services	POKL	7111212200	98.4	98.2	100.0	101.5	102.1	104.0	106.0	108.6
Pulp, paper and paper products	POLD	7112210000	98.2	96.8	100.0	101.0	100.3	100.1	99.7	99.0
Printed matter and recorded media	POLE	7112220000	98.5	98.8	100.0	101.7	102.7	105.5	108.4	112.1
Chemicals, chemical, products and manmade fibres	POKN	7111240000	98.5	97.2	100.0	100.2	100.5	103.9	106.7	111.4
Rubber and plastic products	POKO	7111250000	102.2	100.4	100.0	100.3	100.4	100.5	101.5	106.3
Other non-metallic mineral products	POKP	7111260000	97.6	99.3	100.0	101.9	105.0	107.8	109.6	113.9
Base metals and fabricated metal products	POKQ	7111272800	102.5	98.7	100.0	99.9	99.5	101.3	108.8	118.2
Base metals	POLJ	7112270000	103.1	94.7	100.0	98.4	96.0	99.2	113.1	126.6
Fabricated metal products, except machinery and equipment	POLK	7112280000	102.2	100.6	100.0	100.6	101.1	102.3	106.8	114.3
Machinery and equipment not elsewhere classified	POKR	7111290000	98.3	99.1	100.0	100.9	101.8	101.9	103.3	106.4
Electrical and optical equipment	POKS	7111343500	112.2	106.2	100.0	94.7	90.0	87.5	86.6	85.9
Office machinery and computers	POLM	7112300000	146.6	124.1	100.0	75.2	64.6	57.1	52.2	46.7
Electrical machinery and apparatus not elsewhere classified	POLN	7112310000	102.3	101.3	100.0	99.9	100.4	100.6	102.8	106.1
Radio, television and communication equipment and apparatus	POLO	7112320000	109.4	104.2	100.0	97.3	88.0	84.3	82.1	80.1
Medical precision and optical instruments, watches and clocks	POLP	7112330000	98.7	99.2	100.0	101.1	102.4	103.3	103.6	104.0
Transport equipment	POKT	7111343500	99.0	100.9	100.0	98.4	98.8	99.2	100.3	102.4
Motor vehicles, trailers and semi-trailers	POLQ	7112340000	101.9	102.3	100.0	96.6	96.3	96.1	97.2	98.6
Other transport	POLR	7112350000	92.9	98.0	100.0	102.3	103.8	105.8	107.0	110.5
Furniture: other manufactured goods not elsewhere classified	POLS	7112360000	101.7	100.9	100.0	100.3	100.9	103.8	104.4	104.4

1 See chapter text.
2 These indices include the Aggregates Levy which was introduced in April 2002. These indices do not feed into Net Sector output (PLLU).

Source: Office for National Statistics: 01633 812106

17.3 Internal purchasing power of the pound[1,2]
United Kingdom

Pence

	Year in which purchasing power was 100p																			
	1986	1987	1988	1989	1990	1991	1992	1993	1994	1995	1996	1997	1998	1999	2000	2001	2002	2003	2004	2005
	BAMS	BAMT	BAMU	BAMV	BAMW	BASX	CZVM	CBXX	DOFX	DOHR	DOLM	DTUL	CDQG	JKZZ	ZMHO	IKHI	FAUI	SEZH	C687	E9AO
1986	100	104	109	118	129	136	142	144	147	152	156	161	167	169	174	177	180	185	191	196
1987	96	100	105	113	124	131	136	138	141	146	150	155	160	162	167	170	173	178	183	188
1988	92	95	100	108	118	125	130	132	135	139	143	147	152	155	159	162	165	170	175	180
1989	85	88	93	100	109	116	120	122	125	129	133	137	141	144	148	150	153	157	162	167
1990	78	81	85	91	100	106	110	112	114	118	121	125	129	131	135	137	140	144	148	152
1991	73	76	80	86	94	100	104	105	108	112	114	118	122	124	128	130	132	136	140	144
1992	71	74	77	83	91	96	100	102	104	108	110	114	118	119	123	125	127	131	135	139
1993	70	72	76	82	90	95	98	100	102	106	109	112	116	118	121	123	125	129	133	136
1994	68	71	74	80	88	93	96	98	100	103	106	109	113	115	118	120	122	126	130	133
1995	66	68	72	77	85	90	93	94	97	100	102	106	109	111	114	116	118	122	125	129
1996	64	67	70	75	83	87	91	92	94	98	100	103	107	108	112	113	115	119	122	126
1997	62	65	68	73	80	85	88	89	92	95	97	100	103	105	108	110	112	115	119	122
1998	60	63	66	71	77	82	85	86	88	92	94	97	100	102	105	106	108	111	115	118
1999	59	62	65	70	76	81	84	85	87	90	92	95	98	100	103	105	107	110	113	116
2000	57	60	63	68	74	78	81	83	85	88	90	92	96	97	100	102	103	106	110	113
2001	56	59	62	66	73	77	80	81	83	86	88	91	94	95	98	100	102	105	108	111
2002	56	58	61	65	72	76	79	80	82	85	87	89	92	94	97	98	100	103	106	109
2003	54	56	59	64	70	74	76	78	79	82	84	87	90	91	94	96	97	100	103	106
2004	52	55	57	62	68	72	74	75	77	80	82	84	87	89	91	93	94	97	100	103
2005	51	53	56	60	66	70	72	73	75	78	80	82	85	86	89	90	92	94	97	100

1 See chapter text. These figures are calculated by taking the inverse ratio of the respective annual averages of the Retail Prices Index (RPI).

2 To find the purchasing power of the pound in 1995, given that it was 100 pence in 1990, select the column headed 1990 and look at the 1995 row. The result is 85 pence.

Source: Office for National Statistics: 020 7533 5874

17.4 Consumer Prices Index:[1] detailed figures by division
United Kingdom

Indices (1996=100)

	Food and non-alcoholic beverages	Alcoholic beverages and tobacco	Clothing and footwear	Housing, water, electric-ity, gas & other fuels	Furniture, household equipment & routine mainte-nance	Health	Transport	Commun-ication	Recreation and culture	Education	Restaur-ants and hotels	Miscell-aneous goods and services	CPI (overall index)
COICOP Division	01	02	03	04	05	06	07	08	09	10	11	12	
Weights 2004	106	46	62	103	75	22	151	26	150	16	137	106	1000
	CHVK	CHVL	CHVM	CHVN	CHVO	CHVP	CHVQ	CHVR	CHVS	CHVT	CHVU	CHVV	CHVJ
2003 Sep	107.1	132.0	68.7	114.6	98.5	125.4	117.4	85.0	104.4	151.3	128.3	121.0	110.2
Oct	107.3	132.2	68.4	114.9	97.6	125.8	117.2	84.7	104.3	154.5	128.5	122.5	110.4
Nov	107.6	131.1	68.6	115.0	98.4	125.9	116.4	84.2	104.1	154.5	128.9	122.5	110.3
Dec	108.0	130.7	67.8	115.2	99.5	125.0	118.5	84.2	104.0	154.5	129.1	122.7	110.7
2004 Jan	107.6	131.5	65.7	115.4	96.6	125.4	117.9	84.2	103.2	154.5	129.3	123.6	110.1
Feb	107.9	131.5	65.5	115.5	97.7	125.1	118.5	84.7	103.0	154.5	129.4	123.9	110.4
Mar	107.9	131.8	65.6	116.0	98.2	125.4	118.5	84.8	103.1	154.5	130.1	123.9	110.6
Apr	107.6	133.5	65.4	117.6	97.9	126.0	119.4	85.1	103.4	154.5	130.5	123.7	111.0
May	108.0	133.8	65.6	117.9	98.7	126.2	121.1	85.0	103.1	154.5	130.9	123.8	111.4
Jun	107.1	133.8	64.9	118.1	98.5	126.4	121.2	84.7	103.6	154.5	131.2	123.7	111.3
Jul	106.4	134.2	62.3	118.3	96.4	126.6	122.7	83.7	103.4	154.5	131.4	124.1	111.0
Aug	106.1	134.7	63.1	118.6	97.0	126.5	123.2	83.6	103.4	154.5	131.7	124.4	111.3
Sep	106.4	134.9	64.7	118.9	98.0	127.1	121.3	82.8	103.4	158.2	131.8	124.7	111.4
Oct	106.7	134.8	64.8	119.9	97.2	127.6	121.2	82.9	103.3	162.2	132.2	126.3	111.7
Nov	107.1	134.1	65.0	120.7	98.0	127.7	121.2	82.6	103.2	162.2	132.6	126.4	111.9
Dec	107.8	133.4	64.2	121.4	100.2	127.5	123.3	82.3	103.4	162.2	132.9	126.7	112.5
2005 Jan	108.0	134.8	61.8	122.1	96.2	128.4	121.2	82.2	102.8	162.2	133.1	128.0	111.9
Feb	108.8	135.4	61.7	122.3	96.6	128.5	122.3	82.4	102.3	162.2	133.4	128.1	112.2
Mar	109.7	134.7	62.2	122.7	98.2	128.7	123.2	82.3	102.3	162.2	133.8	128.4	112.7
Apr	108.7	136.2	62.0	125.2	96.9	129.4	123.9	82.4	102.8	162.2	134.9	129.0	113.1
May	109.5	136.8	62.0	125.4	97.7	129.7	125.2	82.0	102.5	162.2	135.3	129.2	113.5
Jun	109.5	136.9	61.8	125.6	97.9	129.8	125.3	82.2	102.4	162.2	135.5	129.4	113.5
Jul	108.3	137.2	59.3	126.2	97.0	130.9	128.4	81.5	101.9	162.2	135.9	130.5	113.6
Aug	108.5	137.1	60.3	126.1	97.1	131.2	129.9	81.9	101.4	162.2	136.4	130.7	114.0
Sep	108.5	136.9	61.3	126.6	97.8	131.0	128.6	81.8	101.7	165.6	136.7	131.0	114.2
Oct	108.3	137.4	61.3	127.8	97.0	131.4	128.2	81.6	101.8	169.9	137.1	131.6	114.3
Nov	109.0	137.5	61.7	128.5	98.0	131.4	126.2	81.6	101.6	169.9	137.2	131.9	114.3
Dec	109.7	136.8	61.5	129.2	100.2	130.5	126.7	81.5	101.6	169.9	137.5	132.0	114.7

Percentage change on a year earlier

	CJYS	CJYT	CJYU	CJYV	CJYW	CJYX	CJYY	CJYZ	CJZA	CJZB	CJZC	CJZD	CJYR
2003 Sep	2.2	1.9	−3.4	2.0	−0.3	3.6	3.3	1.1	−1.7	8.7	3.0	2.7	1.4
Oct	2.2	2.2	−3.3	2.1	−0.3	3.6	3.3	0.4	−2.0	4.7	2.9	2.8	1.4
Nov	2.6	1.6	−4.3	2.2	−0.3	3.6	3.7	−0.4	−2.3	4.7	3.0	2.9	1.3
Dec	3.0	1.8	−3.6	2.2	−0.6	3.0	3.0	−0.2	−2.2	4.7	3.0	2.6	1.3
2004 Jan	2.6	1.7	−2.5	2.3	−0.2	2.6	3.1	−0.4	−2.5	4.7	2.9	4.2	1.4
Feb	2.2	1.6	−4.0	2.2	0.3	2.0	3.0	0.2	−2.8	4.7	2.9	4.3	1.3
Mar	1.9	1.9	−4.5	2.7	−0.7	2.2	2.2	0.2	−2.6	4.7	3.1	4.1	1.1
Apr	1.2	2.1	−4.7	3.4	0.4	2.2	1.4	0.7	−2.2	4.7	3.0	3.9	1.2
May	1.0	2.0	−4.5	3.7	−0.1	2.0	3.7	0.5	−2.0	4.7	3.0	3.9	1.5
Jun	0.8	1.9	−4.7	3.8	0.3	2.0	3.9	1.0	−1.1	4.7	2.9	3.6	1.6
Jul	0.1	2.1	−4.9	3.6	−0.7	1.3	3.9	−1.1	−0.8	4.7	2.8	3.3	1.4
Aug	−0.2	2.0	−5.7	3.8	−0.3	1.1	3.8	−1.2	−1.0	4.7	2.9	3.2	1.3
Sep	−0.7	2.2	−5.8	3.8	−0.5	1.4	3.3	−2.6	−1.0	4.6	2.7	3.1	1.1
Oct	−0.6	2.0	−5.3	4.4	−0.4	1.4	3.4	−2.1	−1.0	5.0	2.9	3.1	1.2
Nov	−0.5	2.3	−5.2	5.0	−0.4	1.4	4.1	−1.9	−0.9	5.0	2.9	3.2	1.5
Dec	−0.2	2.1	−5.3	5.4	0.7	2.0	4.1	−2.3	−0.6	5.0	2.9	3.3	1.6
2005 Jan	0.4	2.5	−5.9	5.8	−0.4	2.4	2.8	−2.4	−0.4	5.0	2.9	3.6	1.6
Feb	0.8	3.0	−5.8	5.9	−1.1	2.7	3.2	−2.7	−0.7	5.0	3.1	3.4	1.6
Mar	1.7	2.2	−5.2	5.8	−	2.6	4.0	−2.9	−0.8	5.0	2.8	3.6	1.9
Apr	1.0	2.0	−5.2	6.5	−1.0	2.7	3.8	−3.2	−0.6	5.0	3.4	4.3	1.9
May	1.4	2.2	−5.5	6.4	−1.0	2.8	3.4	−3.5	−0.6	5.0	3.4	4.4	1.9
Jun	2.2	2.3	−4.8	6.4	−0.6	2.7	3.4	−3.0	−1.2	5.0	3.3	4.6	2.0
Jul	1.8	2.2	−4.8	6.7	0.6	3.4	4.6	−2.6	−1.5	5.0	3.4	5.2	2.3
Aug	2.3	1.8	−4.4	6.3	0.1	3.7	5.4	−2.0	−1.9	5.0	3.6	5.1	2.4
Sep	2.0	1.5	−5.3	6.5	−0.2	3.1	6.0	−1.2	−1.6	4.7	3.7	5.1	2.5
Oct	1.5	1.9	−5.4	6.6	−0.2	3.0	5.8	−1.6	−1.5	4.7	3.7	4.2	2.3
Nov	1.8	2.5	−5.1	6.5	−	2.9	4.1	−1.2	−1.6	4.7	3.5	4.4	2.1
Dec	1.8	2.5	−4.2	6.4	−	2.4	2.8	−1.0	−1.7	4.7	3.5	4.2	2.0

1 See chapter text. Prior to 10 December 2003, the consumer prices index (CPI) was published in the UK as the harmonised index of consumer prices (HICP).

Source: Office for National Statistics: 020 7533 5874

277

17.5 Retail Prices Index[1]
United Kingdom

Indices (13 January 1987=100)

	All items (RPI)	All items excluding					Food and catering	Alcohol and tobacco	Housing and household expenditure	Personal expenditure	Travel and leisure	Consumer durables	All items excluding mortgage interest payments & indirect taxes (RPIY)[3]
		mortgage interest payments (RPIX)	mortgage interest payments and depreciation	housing	food	seasonal food[2]							

Weights

	CZGU	CZGY	DOGZ	CZGX	CZGV	CZGW	CBVV	CBVW	CBVX	CBVY	CBVZ	CBWA	
1997	1 000	961	932	814	864	981	185	114	351	96	254	122	
1998	1 000	955	923	803	870	982	178	105	359	95	263	121	
1999	1 000	958	928	807	872	980	179	100	358	95	268	127	
2000	1 000	960	924	805	882	982	170	95	355	101	279	126	
2001	1 000	954	914	795	884	982	169	97	362	96	276	125	
2002	1 000	964	924	801	886	980	166	99	363	94	278	126	
2003	1 000	961	919	797	891	983	160	98	365	92	285	126	
2004	1 000	961	914	791	889	981	160	97	367	93	283	121	
2005	1 000	950	901	776	890	981	159	96	387	89	269	122	

Annual averages

	CHAW	CHMK	CHON	CHAZ	CHAY	CHAX	CHBS	CHBT	CHBU	CHBV	CHBW	CHBY	CBZW
1997	157.5	156.5	156.4	152.9	160.5	158.5	150.4	183.2	158.4	137.7	159.0	117.3	151.5
1998	162.9	160.6	160.3	156.2	166.5	163.8	153.4	192.3	166.2	139.9	162.8	115.9	154.5
1999	165.4	164.3	163.6	158.9	169.4	166.5	155.4	202.6	167.7	139.6	165.6	112.3	157.1
2000	170.3	167.7	166.4	161.3	175.1	171.4	156.7	210.3	176.2	137.2	170.3	108.0	159.9
2001	173.3	171.3	169.5	163.7	178.0	174.3	162.2	216.9	180.0	135.7	172.0	105.0	163.7
2002	176.2	175.1	172.5	166.0	181.1	177.2	164.8	222.3	184.6	133.2	174.2	101.9	167.5
2003	181.3	180.0	176.2	168.9	186.7	182.4	167.9	228.0	194.3	133.2	177.0	99.8	172.0
2004	186.7	184.0	179.1	170.9	192.8	187.9	170.0	233.6	207.4	131.5	178.1	97.7	175.5
2005	192.0	188.2	182.6	173.7	198.7	193.3	172.9	239.8	219.4	131.0	179.2	95.3	179.4

Monthly figures

2002 Dec	178.5	177.2	173.8	167.2	183.9	179.6	165.1	223.7	190.2	133.6	174.8	102.6	169.8
2003 Jan	178.4	177.1	173.5	166.8	183.8	179.5	165.3	224.6	189.7	130.6	176.1	98.4	169.8
Feb	179.3	177.9	174.4	167.8	184.6	180.4	166.1	224.9	190.3	132.9	176.7	99.9	170.6
Mar	179.9	178.7	175.2	168.7	185.3	181.0	166.6	225.6	190.8	133.8	177.5	101.4	171.4
Apr	181.2	180.0	176.5	169.0	186.7	182.3	167.2	227.4	193.1	133.9	178.4	100.3	171.8
May	181.5	180.2	176.6	169.1	186.8	182.4	168.2	228.3	193.9	133.8	177.4	100.8	171.9
Jun	181.3	180.0	176.4	168.8	186.8	182.4	167.8	228.7	194.2	133.0	177.2	99.9	171.7
Jul	181.3	179.9	176.1	168.5	186.7	182.4	168.0	229.0	194.7	130.6	177.1	97.8	171.6
Aug	181.6	180.4	176.5	168.9	187.1	182.7	168.1	229.6	194.8	132.5	177.2	98.7	172.2
Sep	182.5	181.3	177.2	169.7	188.0	183.5	168.9	229.7	196.3	134.6	177.0	100.4	173.2
Oct	182.6	181.3	177.2	169.6	188.0	183.6	169.2	230.0	196.7	134.3	176.7	99.7	173.1
Nov	182.7	181.4	177.2	169.6	188.1	183.7	169.4	229.4	197.4	134.5	176.2	100.0	173.1
Dec	183.5	181.8	177.6	169.9	189.0	184.5	169.9	229.1	199.4	133.4	176.7	100.3	173.5
2004 Jan	183.1	181.4	177.1	169.3	188.6	184.2	169.7	229.8	198.9	130.9	177.1	97.0	173.2
Feb	183.8	182.0	177.7	170.0	189.3	184.9	170.1	230.0	200.0	131.6	177.6	98.0	173.9
Mar	184.6	182.5	178.1	170.4	190.2	185.7	170.2	231.2	201.9	132.1	177.4	98.5	174.3
Apr	185.7	183.6	179.1	170.8	191.6	186.9	170.2	233.4	204.5	132.2	177.8	98.2	174.9
May	186.5	184.3	179.7	171.4	192.4	187.6	170.6	233.8	205.8	132.3	178.5	98.6	175.6
Jun	186.8	184.2	179.5	171.2	193.0	188.1	169.8	234.2	207.4	131.7	178.5	98.5	175.6
Jul	186.8	183.8	178.9	170.5	193.1	188.2	169.2	234.7	208.3	129.0	178.8	95.6	175.1
Aug	187.4	184.3	179.3	170.9	193.8	188.8	169.1	235.2	209.3	130.1	179.1	96.4	175.7
Sep	188.1	184.7	179.4	171.1	194.6	189.5	169.3	235.3	211.3	132.0	178.1	97.7	176.1
Oct	188.6	185.1	179.8	171.3	195.1	189.9	169.9	235.5	212.5	132.2	177.9	97.2	176.6
Nov	189.0	185.4	180.1	171.6	195.5	190.3	170.4	235.0	213.4	132.6	177.9	97.6	176.9
Dec	189.9	186.4	180.9	172.5	196.4	191.2	171.2	234.7	215.6	131.8	178.6	99.1	177.9
2005 Jan	188.9	185.2	179.8	171.2	195.2	190.1	171.6	236.0	214.3	129.4	177.1	94.5	176.7
Feb	189.6	185.9	180.4	171.9	195.9	190.8	172.4	236.9	214.9	130.2	177.6	95.0	177.4
Mar	190.5	186.8	181.4	173.0	196.8	191.6	173.4	236.8	216.3	131.4	178.1	96.7	178.3
Apr	191.6	187.8	182.4	173.3	198.2	192.9	172.7	239.4	218.3	131.4	179.3	95.6	179.0
May	192.0	188.2	182.7	173.7	198.6	193.2	173.7	240.2	219.0	131.4	179.1	95.9	179.4
Jun	192.2	188.3	182.8	173.8	198.8	193.4	173.6	240.5	219.7	131.4	178.9	95.8	179.5
Jul	192.2	188.3	182.7	173.5	199.1	193.7	172.4	241.0	220.2	128.8	180.2	94.0	179.5
Aug	192.6	188.6	183.0	173.8	199.5	194.1	172.7	241.0	220.5	130.3	180.2	94.1	179.8
Sep	193.1	189.3	183.7	174.6	200.0	194.5	172.7	241.1	220.7	131.6	181.0	95.1	180.5
Oct	193.3	189.5	183.8	174.7	200.4	194.8	172.7	241.8	221.4	131.8	180.8	94.7	180.7
Nov	193.6	189.7	184.0	174.9	200.5	195.0	173.4	241.9	222.5	132.2	179.6	95.4	180.9
Dec	194.1	190.2	184.5	175.5	201.0	195.5	174.1	241.6	224.5	131.9	179.0	97.0	181.5

1 See chapter text.
2 Seasonal food is defined as items of food the prices of which show significant seasonal variations. These are fresh fruit and vegetables, fresh fish, eggs and home-killed lamb.

3 There are no weights available for RPIY.

Source: Office for National Statistics: 020 7533 5874

17.6 Tax and Price Index[1]
United Kingdom

Tax and Price Index: (January 1987=100)

DQAB

	1991	1992	1993	1994	1995	1996	1997	1998	1999	2000	2001	2002	2003	2004	2005
January	123.6	128.1	128.7	132.1	137.2	141.6	143.6	147.1	150.5	152.7	156.7	156.5	161.4	166.9	172.1
February	124.3	128.8	129.6	132.9	138.2	142.3	144.2	147.9	150.8	153.7	157.6	157.0	162.3	167.6	172.8
March	124.9	129.3	130.2	133.4	138.8	143.0	144.6	148.4	151.2	154.6	157.8	157.7	163.0	168.4	173.7
April	125.4	129.6	131.3	135.3	140.3	141.7	143.8	149.7	151.2	155.7	156.3	158.6	164.9	168.9	174.1
May	125.8	130.2	131.8	135.8	141.0	142.0	144.4	150.6	151.7	156.3	157.4	159.1	165.2	169.7	174.5
June	126.5	130.2	131.7	135.8	141.2	142.1	145.0	150.5	151.7	156.7	157.6	159.1	165.0	170.0	174.7
July	126.2	129.6	131.4	135.1	140.4	141.5	145.0	150.1	151.1	156.1	156.5	158.8	165.0	170.0	174.7
August	126.5	129.7	132.1	135.8	141.3	142.2	146.0	150.8	151.5	156.1	157.2	159.3	165.4	170.6	175.1
September	127.0	130.3	132.7	136.1	142.0	143.0	146.9	151.5	152.3	157.3	157.8	160.6	166.3	171.3	175.6
October	127.5	130.8	132.6	136.4	142.2	143.0	147.1	151.6	152.6	157.2	157.5	160.9	166.4	171.8	175.8
November	128.1	130.6	132.4	136.5	141.2	143.1	147.2	151.5	152.8	157.7	156.8	161.2	166.5	172.2	176.1
December	128.2	130.1	132.7	137.2	142.1	143.6	147.6	151.5	153.4	157.8	156.6	161.5	167.3	173.1	176.6

Retail Prices Index: (January 1987=100)

CHAW

	1991	1992	1993	1994	1995	1996	1997	1998	1999	2000	2001	2002	2003	2004	2005
January	130.2	135.6	137.9	141.3	146.0	150.2	154.4	159.5	163.4	166.6	171.1	173.3	178.4	183.1	188.9
February	130.9	136.3	138.8	142.1	146.9	150.9	155.0	160.3	163.7	167.5	172.0	173.8	179.3	183.8	189.6
March	131.4	136.7	139.3	142.5	147.5	151.5	155.4	160.8	164.1	168.4	172.2	174.5	179.9	184.6	190.5
April	133.1	138.8	140.6	144.2	149.0	152.6	156.3	162.6	165.2	170.1	173.1	175.7	181.2	185.7	191.6
May	133.5	139.3	141.1	144.7	149.6	152.9	156.9	163.5	165.6	170.7	174.2	176.2	181.5	186.5	192.0
June	134.1	139.3	141.0	144.7	149.8	153.0	157.5	163.4	165.6	171.1	174.4	176.2	181.3	186.8	192.2
July	133.8	138.8	140.7	144.0	149.1	152.4	157.5	163.0	165.1	170.5	173.3	175.9	181.3	186.8	192.2
August	134.1	138.9	141.3	144.7	149.9	153.1	158.5	163.7	165.5	170.5	174.0	176.4	181.6	187.4	192.6
September	134.6	139.4	141.9	145.0	150.6	153.8	159.3	164.4	166.2	171.7	174.6	177.6	182.5	188.1	193.1
October	135.1	139.9	141.8	145.2	149.8	153.8	159.5	164.5	166.5	171.6	174.3	177.9	182.6	188.6	193.3
November	135.6	139.7	141.6	145.3	149.8	153.9	159.6	164.4	166.7	172.1	173.6	178.2	182.7	189.0	193.6
December	135.7	139.2	141.9	146.0	150.7	154.4	160.0	164.4	167.3	172.2	173.4	178.5	183.5	189.9	194.1

Percentage changes on one year earlier[1]

	1992	1993	1994	1995	1996	1997	1998	1999	2000	2001	2002	2003	2004	2005
Tax and Price Index[1]														
January	3.6	0.5	2.6	3.9	3.2	1.4	2.4	2.3	1.5	2.6	−0.1	3.1	3.4	3.1
February	3.6	0.6	2.5	4.0	3.0	1.3	2.6	2.0	1.9	2.5	−0.4	3.4	3.3	3.1
March	3.5	0.7	2.5	4.0	3.0	1.1	2.6	1.9	2.2	2.1	−0.1	3.4	3.3	3.1
April	3.3	1.3	3.0	3.7	1.0	1.5	4.1	1.0	3.0	0.4	1.5	4.0	2.4	3.1
May	3.5	1.2	3.0	3.8	0.7	1.7	4.3	0.7	3.0	0.7	1.1	3.8	2.7	2.8
June	2.9	1.2	3.1	4.0	0.6	2.0	3.8	0.8	3.3	0.6	1.0	3.7	3.0	2.8
July	2.7	1.4	2.8	3.9	0.8	2.5	3.5	0.7	3.3	0.3	1.5	3.9	3.0	2.8
August	2.5	1.9	2.8	4.1	0.6	2.7	3.3	0.5	3.0	0.7	1.3	3.8	3.1	2.6
September	2.6	1.8	2.6	4.3	0.7	2.7	3.1	0.5	3.3	0.3	1.8	3.5	3.0	2.5
October	2.6	1.4	2.9	3.5	1.3	2.9	3.1	0.7	3.0	0.2	2.2	3.4	3.2	2.3
November	2.0	1.4	3.1	3.4	1.3	2.9	2.9	0.9	3.2	−0.6	2.8	3.3	3.4	2.3
December	1.5	2.0	3.4	3.6	1.1	2.8	2.6	1.3	2.9	−0.8	3.1	3.6	3.5	2.0
Retail Prices Index														
January	4.1	1.7	2.5	3.3	2.9	2.8	3.3	2.4	2.0	2.7	1.3	2.9	2.6	3.2
February	4.1	1.8	2.4	3.4	2.7	2.7	3.4	2.1	2.3	2.7	1.0	3.2	2.5	3.2
March	4.0	1.9	2.3	3.5	2.7	2.6	3.5	2.1	2.6	2.3	1.3	3.1	2.6	3.2
April	4.3	1.3	2.6	3.3	2.4	2.4	4.0	1.6	3.0	1.8	1.5	3.1	2.5	3.2
May	4.3	1.3	2.6	3.4	2.2	2.6	4.2	1.3	3.1	2.1	1.1	3.0	2.8	2.9
June	3.9	1.2	2.6	3.5	2.1	2.9	3.7	1.3	3.3	1.9	1.0	2.9	3.0	2.9
July	3.7	1.4	2.3	3.5	2.2	3.3	3.5	1.3	3.3	1.6	1.5	3.1	3.0	2.9
August	3.6	1.7	2.4	3.6	2.1	3.5	3.3	1.1	3.0	2.1	1.4	2.9	3.2	2.8
September	3.6	1.8	2.2	3.9	2.1	3.6	3.2	1.1	3.3	1.7	1.7	2.8	3.1	2.7
October	3.6	1.4	2.4	3.2	2.7	3.7	3.1	1.2	3.1	1.6	2.1	2.6	3.3	2.5
November	3.0	1.4	2.6	3.1	2.7	3.7	3.0	1.4	3.2	0.9	2.6	2.5	3.4	2.4
December	2.6	1.9	2.9	3.2	2.5	3.6	2.8	1.8	2.9	0.7	2.9	2.8	3.5	2.2

1 See chapter text.

Source: Office for National Statistics: 020 7533 5874

17.7 Index of purchase prices of the means of agricultural production[1]
United Kingdom
Annual averages

Indices (2000=100)

		Weights	1994	1995	1996	1997	1998	1999	2000	2001	2002	2003	2004
Goods and services currently consumed[2]	C3FU	100	102.4	105.7	110.7	105.5	99.5	98.1	100.0	104.3	103.7	106.5	114.0
Seeds	C3FV	3.3	116.1	136.7	136.3	119.2	119.2	109.0	100.0	109.2	105.5	116.0	110.3
Energy, lubricants	C3FW	8.1	81.1	79.7	82.2	82.1	75.1	82.4	100.0	96.7	92.4	100.5	108.8
Fuels for heating	C3FX	1.0	65.6	67.9	81.9	77.3	61.6	66.6	100.0	95.5	87.2	104.5	118.3
Motor fuel	C3FY	5.1	71.0	69.6	71.0	73.1	66.7	77.8	100.0	96.7	91.6	100.7	110.3
Electricity	C3FZ	1.8	117.7	114.1	113.4	109.6	104.8	102.9	100.0	96.9	96.2	96.5	98.9
Lubricants	C3G2	0.2	84.8	84.8	84.9	86.2	88.5	98.1	100.0	101.2	106.2	112.7	113.1
Fertilisers and soil improvers	C3G3	9.1	95.5	103.1	109.5	106.6	95.3	93.3	100.0	115.8	110.3	119.0	133.5
Straight nitrogen	C3G4	3.9	97.4	109.8	121.5	104.4	87.0	82.9	100.0	129.1	120.2	133.1	148.5
Compound fertilisers	C3G5	4.6	94.3	98.0	100.3	109.6	101.9	101.3	100.0	106.7	103.0	109.1	124.4
Other fertiliser (mainly lime and chalk)	C3G6	0.4	83.9	85.2	92.0	93.5	95.9	96.7	100.0	100.5	104.0	103.4	103.8
Plant protection products	C3G7	7.2	110.4	108.8	115.8	116.6	108.2	105.8	100.0	96.8	95.8	95.7	100.6
Animal feedstuffs	C3G8	26.4	127.4	130.6	140.6	125.4	106.5	99.1	100.0	107.4	103.5	104.9	111.6
Feed wheat	C3G9	2.2	154.6	166.2	168.5	133.4	113.6	102.2	100.0	110.8	97.3	107.4	119.3
Whole barley	C3GA	2.1	155.0	161.0	159.5	125.3	108.5	111.5	100.0	101.8	89.5	103.2	112.8
Whole oats	C3GB	0.2	153.7	140.8	153.7	123.3	98.0	104.7	100.0	97.8	90.7	85.1	94.3
Maize glutten feed	C3GC	0.4	139.3	144.3	160.7	117.8	95.3	100.2	100.0	110.0	102.9	122.9	123.8
Oilcake	C3GD	2.1	110.7	109.1	139.8	131.5	91.9	83.5	100.0	109.4	100.4	109.5	112.0
White fish meal	C3GE	0.4	90.4	104.0	133.0	125.3	137.9	93.2	100.0	115.1	134.7	129.1	120.3
Other straight feedstuffs	C3GF	3.3	123.3	133.3	142.6	121.7	98.2	91.8	100.0	114.1	109.3	109.9	115.1
All straight feedstuffs	C3GG	10.6	134.0	141.1	151.5	127.3	104.1	97.1	100.0	109.7	101.3	108.1	114.9
Feedstuffs non-concentrates	C3GH	0.1	134.0	141.1	151.5	127.3	104.1	97.1	100.0	109.7	101.3	108.1	114.9
Compound feedstuffs for:	C3GI	15.8	122.9	123.7	133.3	124.1	108.1	100.4	100.0	105.8	104.9	102.7	109.3
Cattle and calves	C3GJ	6.2	121.7	120.8	130.5	122.0	105.0	99.9	100.0	106.4	105.9	102.5	108.1
Pigs	C3GK	3.5	130.5	132.9	142.0	130.5	112.8	101.9	100.0	105.9	103.3	101.0	107.7
Poultry	C3GL	5.0	120.6	121.7	131.5	121.7	108.7	100.6	100.0	105.9	104.5	104.9	112.8
Sheep	C3GM	1.1	116.4	119.1	129.2	126.5	108.3	98.0	100.0	102.2	106.2	99.4	106.0
Maintenance and repair of plant	C3GN	7.9	81.4	83.4	87.6	91.0	93.4	96.6	100.0	104.3	109.4	116.0	122.5
Maintenance and repair of buildings	C3GO	3.6	89.6	94.8	95.7	97.3	98.5	97.7	100.0	101.9	105.1	108.3	113.4
Veterinary services	C3GP	3.2	97.7	98.1	98.9	100.1	101.1	101.2	100.0	98.6	97.8	101.6	104.6
Other goods and services	C3GQ	31.2	92.9	95.7	98.0	95.6	98.5	99.9	100.0	102.5	105.5	105.2	114.0
Goods and services contributing to investment in agriculture	C3GR	100	89.7	91.9	95.3	98.1	99.8	100.2	100.0	99.0	100.0	101.5	104.4
Materials	C3GS	71.5	92.1	93.5	97.9	100.5	101.6	101.7	100.0	97.3	97.0	97.5	99.4
Machinery and other equipment	C3GT	28.4	85.8	88.3	92.2	95.0	97.7	99.2	100.0	97.4	95.7	95.1	96.1
Machinery and plant for cultivation	C3GU	8.0	79.2	81.5	89.7	93.3	97.7	99.1	100.0	99.6	98.6	98.7	103.8
Machinery and plant for harvesting	C3GV	14.3	88.3	91.1	93.9	96.8	98.4	100.0	100.0	92.3	88.8	88.2	87.3
Farm machinery and installations	C3GW	6.0	88.7	90.4	91.6	93.2	96.1	97.5	100.0	106.3	108.2	106.8	107.0
Tractors	C3GX	28.6	93.3	93.2	98.5	101.0	101.6	102.4	100.0	96.8	98.4	101.4	106.1
Other vehicles	C3GY	14.5	101.8	104.2	107.6	110.0	109.1	105.1	100.0	98.3	96.7	94.4	92.4
Buildings	C3GZ	19.5	84.2	88.6	90.1	93.2	95.6	96.6	100.0	103.3	107.8	112.1	118.1
Engineering and soil improvement operations	C3H2	9.0	87.9	91.2	86.1	89.8	94.8	96.9	100.0	101.4	107.2	110.3	113.3

1 See chapter text.
2 The sum of the percentages of categories included does not add up to 100% due to the exclusion of some minor categories.

Source: Department for Environment, Food and Rural Affairs: 01904 455253

17.8 Index of producer prices of agricultural products[1]
United Kingdom
Annual averages

		Weights	1994	1995	1996	1997	1998	1999	2000	2001	2002	2003	2004
All products[2]	C3H6	100	127.7	139.2	135.2	117.1	107.0	103.6	100.0	108.3	103.3	109.9	113.2
All crop products	C3H7	40.2	128.7	147.4	130.5	108.9	111.7	109.0	100.0	112.0	104.0	110.7	115.0
Cereals (including cereal seeds)	C3H8	13.3	156.0	166.5	166.2	132.4	113.8	111.0	100.0	107.8	95.0	105.2	114.2
Wheat for:													
breadmaking	C3H9	1.1	153.6	159.8	164.5	139.5	122.8	112.9	100.0	109.6	101.4	110.6	120.8
other milling	C3HA	1.5	151.6	162.8	165.0	133.7	116.0	110.9	100.0	107.5	92.9	104.1	116.8
feeding	C3HB	6.4	155.2	167.0	167.3	135.4	114.0	110.5	100.0	110.5	96.7	105.6	117.7
Barley for:													
feeding	C3HC	2.5	155.1	161.1	157.7	123.9	109.2	112.9	100.0	102.6	89.1	103.7	110.7
malting	C3HD	1.4	167.8	187.3	180.9	128.2	115.1	108.9	100.0	104.8	96.5	107.1	101.6
Oats for:													
milling	C3HE	0.1	163.6	158.5	161.1	128.8	104.9	109.9	100.0	109.8	89.0	90.7	96.3
feeding	C3HF	0.2	153.9	145.0	156.0	119.0	97.0	106.1	100.0	98.5	91.2	86.7	94.4
Potatoes:	C3HG	4.5	153.3	264.6	118.0	63.5	138.8	143.5	100.0	131.0	90.0	105.6	140.3
early	C3HH	0.4	134.5	93.2	68.2	46.3	100.7	51.9	100.0	114.5	73.0	90.0	124.8
main crop	C3HI	4.1	154.8	280.6	121.2	63.4	141.1	151.5	100.0	132.5	90.6	106.0	141.6
Industrial crops	C3HJ	4.3	139.5	147.9	154.4	127.9	118.4	103.4	100.0	111.9	114.4	120.3	121.6
Oilseed rape (non set-aside)	C3HK	1.2	157.1	151.9	164.4	135.6	140.0	102.0	100.0	119.2	121.2	140.3	136.1
Sugar beet	C3HL	2.2	139.3	150.1	152.5	124.9	111.4	108.7	100.0	107.3	114.8	112.1	115.4
Fresh vegetables	C3HM	7.7	100.0	107.5	105.3	97.4	105.2	99.2	100.0	113.6	112.7	125.5	113.7
Cauliflowers	C3HN	0.4	95.2	92.3	89.3	79.1	87.9	82.4	100.0	103.9	117.7	119.8	102.4
Lettuce	C3HO	0.7	112.4	108.7	96.5	114.0	98.6	102.9	100.0	129.2	128.6	151.5	130.2
Tomatoes	C3HP	0.7	88.2	92.9	106.6	86.9	91.8	100.3	100.0	100.1	107.6	135.6	99.8
Carrots	C3HQ	0.7	109.7	142.4	130.9	88.1	125.4	119.3	100.0	166.5	150.4	157.2	144.7
Cabbage	C3HR	0.4	81.0	100.7	104.4	83.2	94.5	94.2	100.0	123.0	109.8	119.7	109.3
Beans	C3HS	0.2	103.6	87.4	88.9	87.3	107.8	102.8	100.0	124.3	118.0	119.1	128.7
Onions	C3HT	0.5	181.3	149.0	107.3	122.8	165.8	104.7	100.0	128.6	126.7	136.1	138.8
Mushrooms	C3HU	1.3	97.0	107.7	110.6	99.1	98.9	98.1	100.0	91.0	95.9	100.6	94.4
Fresh fruit	C3HV	1.9	97.2	101.9	105.5	109.1	105.4	100.0	100.0	99.0	113.9	124.2	112.4
Dessert apples	C3HW	0.3	104.2	120.6	132.7	124.7	110.5	104.3	100.0	109.8	111.3	124.6	120.9
Dessert pears	C3HX	0.1	109.9	121.5	122.7	118.2	110.4	108.7	100.0	128.7	124.8	115.3	114.6
Cooking apples	C3HY	0.2	101.8	105.2	122.9	135.6	150.9	100.7	100.0	105.6	109.4	152.1	142.5
Strawberries	C3HZ	0.7	113.1	100.3	102.6	106.9	93.7	102.4	100.0	94.5	121.7	124.4	97.1
Raspberries	C3I2	0.2	73.4	102.9	92.8	103.3	114.3	104.9	100.0	102.9	128.9	125.7	114.3
Seeds (excluding cereal seeds)	C3I3	0.5	129.1	148.2	155.0	130.9	98.6	97.7	100.0	104.0	95.7	112.8	107.9
Flowers and plants	C3I4	5.9	98.4	99.0	98.3	102.4	103.1	105.3	100.0	105.3	106.8	107.9	105.3
Other crop products	C3I5	0.7	116.8	135.9	139.8	122.2	98.7	97.0	100.0	106.0	98.9	108.1	106.3
Animals and animal products	C3I6	59.8	127.0	133.7	138.3	122.6	103.9	99.9	100.0	105.8	102.7	109.4	112.0
Animals for slaughter	C3I7	35.3	123.5	126.0	132.3	118.0	97.2	95.2	100.0	101.3	103.2	109.3	111.7
Calves	C3I8	0.1	277.4	240.5	218.6	179.3	149.4	115.1	100.0	94.2	120.2	143.9	140.8
Clean cattle	C3I9	9.7	136.7	137.5	117.3	107.1	95.0	101.7	100.0	100.8	103.8	106.7	113.4
Clean pigs	C3IA	7.0	105.9	126.5	146.0	117.5	85.8	83.4	100.0	103.6	98.7	99.0	109.3
Sows and boars	C3IB	0.2	145.3	184.2	201.0	157.1	81.1	81.0	100.0	107.4	93.8	101.9	121.7
Clean sheep and lambs	C3IC	5.2	117.5	120.5	142.7	131.0	97.1	90.2	100.0	101.3	118.5	132.5	131.5
Ewes and rams	C3ID	0.4	138.7	137.0	189.6	198.5	116.3	81.3	100.0	152.4	149.6	188.2	183.5
All poultry	C3IE	11.5	120.1	113.0	126.7	116.8	103.3	99.0	100.0	98.6	97.2	99.4	101.2
Chickens	C3IF	7.9	131.3	120.2	136.3	126.6	105.9	101.3	100.0	100.1	99.5	100.2	103.4
Turkeys	C3IG	2.9	92.7	94.2	102.6	89.5	91.3	90.0	100.0	94.4	89.5	97.8	95.0
Cows' milk	C3IH	20.1	131.1	147.2	147.7	130.6	114.4	108.3	100.0	113.7	101.0	106.4	109.0
Eggs	C3II	3.2	137.2	127.6	142.3	121.1	109.4	98.0	100.0	104.9	109.5	130.7	135.1
Other animal products:	C3IJ	1.1	136.6	146.8	144.9	129.4	108.0	103.0	100.0	107.7	100.0	107.4	110.4
Wool (clip)	C3IK	0.2	191.8	189.0	173.5	150.1	98.6	93.5	100.0	87.0	96.4	108.4	107.3

1 See chapter text.
2 The sum of the percentages of all the categories does not add up to 100%
due to the exclusion of some minor categories.

Source: Department for Environment, Food and Rural Affairs: 01904 455253

17.9 Commodity price trends[1]
United Kingdom

			1994	1995	1996	1997	1998	1999	2000	2001	2002	2003	2004
Wheat £ per tonne	KVAA	Average ex-farm price[2,3]	106.4	115.6	112.5	91.8	77.8	75.4	68.1	76.9	65.6	77.3	..
Barley £ per tonne	KVAB	Average ex-farm price[2,3]	105.4	107.6	103.7	86.3	79.2	74.2	70.1	72.1	64.8	75.5	..
Oats £ per tonne	KVAC	Average ex-farm price[2,3]	108.4	101.4	107.4	82.3	66.4	71.1	65.0	67.7	56.6	62.1	..
Rye £ per tonne	KVAD	Average ex-farm price[2]	112.80	107.90	113.90	..	..	..	..	78.10	61.40	71.80	86.40
Hops £ per tonne	KVAE	Average farm-gate price	4 005	3 595	3 360	3 550	3 679	4 003	3 861	3 532	2 832	3 104	2 679
Potatoes £ per tonne	KVAF	Average farm-gate price[4]	125.80	187.70	100.50	66.10	121.50	119.10	83.30	111.30	81.00	102.00	..
Sugar beet £ per tonne	KVAG	Producer price[5]	34.70	38.30	37.70	32.90	31.90	26.40	27.80	30.80	29.60	35.00	..
Oilseed rape £ per tonne	KVAH	Average market price[6]	185.40	177.70	186.90	160.20	164.30	112.90	120.40	148.40	148.20	171.60	..
Apples £ per tonne	KPUE	Dessert average farm-gate price[7]	391.4	437.3	493.6	525.0	476.1	405.0	357.8	352.2	385.2	460.3	357.3
" "	KVAI	Dessert average market price	447.4	465.7	523.5	462.0	431.5	405.4	408.7	418.2	453.1	551.3	526.1
" "	KVAJ	Culinary average market price	446.4	405.9	462.8	517.7	575.5	384.1	378.1	422.4	419.4	652.6	..
" "	KPUJ	Culinary average farm-gate price	232.3	248.2	286.8	335.1	297.3	209.9	215.3	175.7	285.7	471.7	592.0
Pears £ per tonne	KPUG	Average farm-gate price	412.6	453.0	445.7	441.9	405.1	426.4	283.3	352.1	402.9	344.0	354.9
" "	KVAK	Average market price	436.8	462.9	461.9	429.5	431.5	405.4	408.7	418.2	453.1	551.3	437.2
Tomatoes £ per tonne	LQMH	Average farm-gate price[7]	234.4	247.8	270.9	236.8	216.3	211.3	751.6	724.9	793.7	1 042.3	750.0
" "	KVAL	Average market price[7]	674.5	624.4	756.7	549.3	578.2	583.6	569.9	651.3	736.3	824.8	647.2
Cauliflowers £ per tonne	KPUI	Average farm-gate price[7]	685.0	585.1	742.4	546.9	594.6	576.3	274.1	285.3	331.0	331.7	301.7
" "	KVAM	Average market price[7]	317.7	328.9	363.0	309.8	284.8	242.5	282.9	304.9	365.6	368.2	330.8
Cattle (rearing) £ per head	KVAN	1st quality Hereford/cross bull calves[8,9,10]	182.10	166.30	131.80	147.00	107.90	88.20	79.50	..	84.90	112.70	113.70
"	KVAO	1st quality beef/ cross yearling steers[9,10]	471.00	475.00	445.00	427.00	369.00	382.00	400.05	..	403.85	451.54	395.90
Cattle (fat) p per kg liveweight	KVAP	Clean cattle[11]	121.71	123.15	105.52	96.89	86.10	92.12	89.68	87.53	91.38	95.15	101.18

			1994	1995	1996	1997	1998	1999	2000	2001	2002	2003	2004
Sheep (store) £ per head	KVAQ	1st quality lambs, hoggets and tegs[8]	40.02	44.46	46.83	53.42	31.28	28.62	34.50	..	..	36.03	37.70
Sheep (fat) p per kg estimated dressed carcase weight	KVAR KVAS	Great Britain[12] Northern Ireland[13]	236.88 221.95	236.40 214.41	283.13 260.46	239.02 228.23	192.46 179.06	180.27 165.71	196.44 182.67	.. ..	233.40 228.80	271.08 239.91	262.55 227.83
Pigs £ per kg deadweight	KVAT	Average price clean pigs	99.60	118.80	137.70	110.80	80.60	78.60	94.40	97.80	93.30	102.60	102.80
Broilers p per kg carcass weight	KVAU	Average producer price	87.1	84.0	90.9	86.2	76.7	72.1	70.7	70.6	68.8	68.6	72.7
Milk p per litre	KVAV	Average net return to producers[14]	23.20	24.90	25.00	22.10	19.40	18.30	16.90	19.30	17.10	18.00	18.50
Eggs p per dozen	KVAW	Average producer price[15]	42.31	38.23	45.70	39.33	36.36	34.42	39.35	40.76	42.11	46.07	48.93
Wool p per kg	KHWQ	Average producer price for clip paid to producers by the British Wool Marketing Board	98.90	95.00	86.90	74.90	48.00	46.60	51.30	47.00	50.00	55.70	54.60

1 This table gives indications of the movement in commodity prices at the first point of sale. The series do not always show total receipts by farmers; for some commodities additional premiums or deficiency payments are made to achieve support price levels.
2 Weighted average ex-farm prices of United Kingdom cereals.
3 Data from 1997 onwards have been revised and are not directly comparable with earlier years.
4 Weighted average price paid to growers for early and main crop potatoes in the United Kingdom (includes all potatoes and a value for sacks).
5 Returns to growers figures since 1986 prices per 'adjusted' tonne at 16% sugar content.
6 Typical contract price adjusted to delivered basis and 40 per cent oil content.
7 Weighted average wholesale prices for England and Wales. Average farm-gate price for England and Wales, crop year (June-May).

8 Average prices at representative markets in England and Wales.
9 Consists of Hereford/cross, Charolais/cross, Limousin/cross, Simmental/cross, Belgian/cross, other continental cross, other beef/dairy cross, other beef/beef cross.
10 From 2002 no differentiation between class 1 and class 2 animals.
11 Based on Meat and Livestock Commission all clean cattle prices.
12 Average of Great Britain weekly market prices as used to determine the level of ewe premium.
13 Average of Northern Ireland weekly market prices used to determine the level of ewe premium.
14 Derived by dividing total value of output by the total quantity of output available for human consumption.
15 Average price of all Class A eggs weighted according to quantity in each grade.

Source: Department for Environment, Food and Rural Affairs: 01904 455332

Government
finance

Chapter 18

Government finance

Public sector

(Tables 18.1 to 18.3 and 18.5)

In Table 18.1 the term public sector describes the consolidation of central government, local government and public corporations. General government is the consolidated total of central government and local government. The table shows details of the key public sector finances' indicators, consistent with the European System of Accounts 1995 (ESA95), by sub sector.

The concepts in Table 18.1 are consistent with the format for public finances in the Economic and Fiscal Strategy Report (EFSR), published by HM Treasury on 11 June 1998, and The Budget. The public sector current budget is equivalent to net saving in national accounts *plus* capital tax receipts. Net investment is gross capital formation, *plus* payments *less* receipts of investment grants, *less* depreciation. Net borrowing is net investment less current budget. Net borrowing differs from the net cash requirement (see below) in that it is measured on an accruals basis whereas the net cash requirement is mainly a cash measure which includes some financial transactions. Table 18.2 shows the Public sector key fiscal balances. The table shows the component detail of the public sector key fiscal balance by economic category. The tables are consistent with The Budget.

Table 18.3 shows public sector net debt. Public sector net debt consists of the public sector's financial liabilities at face value minus its liquid assets – mainly foreign currency exchange reserves and bank deposits. General government gross debt (consolidated) in Table 18.3 is consistent with the definition of general government gross debt reported to the European Commission under the requirements of the Maastricht Treaty.

More information on the concepts in Table 18.1, 18.2 and 18.3 can be found in a guide to monthly public sector finance statistics, GSS Methodology Series No 12, the ONS First Release Public Sector Finances and *Financial Statistics Explanatory Handbook*.

Table 18.5 shows the taxes and national insurance contributions paid to central government, local government, and to the institutions of the European Union. The table is the same as Table 11.1 of the *National Accounts UK: the Blue Book*. More information on the data and concepts in the table can be found in Chapter 11 of the *Blue Book*.

Consolidated Fund and National Loans Fund

(Tables 18.4, 18.6 and 18.7)

The central government embraces all bodies for whose activities a Minister of the Crown, or other responsible person, is accountable to Parliament. It includes, in addition to the ordinary government departments, a number of bodies administering public policy but without the substantial degree of financial independence which characterises the public corporations; it also includes certain extra-budgetary funds and accounts controlled by departments.

The government's financial transactions are handled through a number of statutory funds, or accounts. The most important of these is the Consolidated Fund which is the government's main account with the Bank of England. Up to 31 March 1968 the Consolidated Fund was virtually synonymous with the term 'Exchequer' which was then the government's central cash account. From 1 April 1968 the National Loans Fund, with a separate account at the Bank of England, was set up by the National Loans Act, 1968. The general effect of this Act was to remove from the Consolidated Fund most of the government's domestic lending and the whole of the government's borrowing transactions and to provide for them to be brought to account in the National Loans Fund.

Revenue from taxation and miscellaneous receipts, including interest and dividends on loans made from Votes, continue to be paid into the Consolidated Fund.

After meeting the ordinary expenditure on Supply Services and the Consolidated Fund Standing Services, the surplus or deficit of the Consolidated Fund (Table 18.4), is payable into or met by the National Loans Fund. Table 18.4 also provides a summary of the transactions of the National Loans Fund. The service of the National Debt, previously borne by the Consolidated Fund, is now met from the National Loans Fund which receives (a) interest payable on loans to the nationalised industries, local authorities and other bodies, whether the loans were made before or after 1 April 1968 and (b) the profits of the Issue Department of the Bank of England, mainly derived from interest on government securities, which were formerly paid into the Exchange Equalisation Account. The net cost of servicing the National Debt after applying these interest receipts and similar items is a charge on the Consolidated Fund as part of the standing services. Details of National Loans Fund loans outstanding are shown in Table 18.7. Details of borrowing and repayments of debt, other than loans from the National Loans Fund, are shown in Table 18.6.

Income tax

(Table 18.9, 18.10)

Following the introduction of Independent Taxation from 1990–91 the married couple's allowance was introduced. It is payable in addition to the personal allowance and between 1990–91 and 1992–93 went to the husband unless the transfer condition was met. The condition was that the husband was unable to make full use of the allowance himself and in that case he could transfer only part or all of the married couple's allowance to his wife. In 1993–94 all or half of the allowance could be transferred to the wife if the couple had agreed beforehand. The wife had the right to claim half the allowance. The married couple's allowance, and allowances linked to it, were restricted to 20 per cent in 1994–95 and to 15 per cent from 1995–96. From 2000–01 only people born before 6 April 1935 are entitled to married couple's allowance.

The age allowance replaces the single allowance, provided the taxpayer's income is below the limits shown in the table. From 1989–90, for incomes in excess of the limits, the allowance is reduced by £1 for each additional £2 of income until the ordinary limit is reached (before it was £2 for each £3 of additional income). The relief is due where the taxpayer is aged 65 or over in the year of assessment.

The additional personal allowance could be claimed by a single parent (or by a married man if his wife was totally incapacitated) who maintained a resident child at his or her own expense. Widow's bereavement allowance was due to a widow in the year of her husband's death and in the following year provided the widow had not remarried before the beginning of that year. Both the additional personal allowance and the widow's bereavement allowance were abolished from April 2000.

The blind person's allowance may be claimed by blind persons (in England and Wales, registered as blind by a local authority) and surplus blind person's allowance may be transferred to a husband or wife. Relief on life assurance premiums is given by deduction from the premium payable. From 1984–85, it is confined to policies made before 14 March 1984.

From 1993–94 until 1998–99 a number of taxpayers with taxable income in excess of the lower rate limit only paid tax at the lower rate. This was because it was only their dividend income and (from 1996–97) their savings income which took their taxable income above the lower rate limit but below the basic rate limit, and such income was chargeable to tax at the lower rate and not the basic rate.

In 1999–2000 the 10 per cent starting rate replaced the lower rate and taxpayers with savings or dividend income at the basic rate of tax are taxed at 20 per cent and 10 per cent respectively. Before 1999–2000 these people would have been classified as lower rate taxpayers.

Rateable values

(Table 18.11)

Major changes to local government finance in England and Wales took effect from 1 April 1990. These included the abolition of domestic rating – replaced by the community charge (replaced in 1993 by the council tax), the revaluation of all non-domestic properties, and the introduction of the Uniform Business Rate. Also in 1990, a new classification scheme was introduced which has resulted in differences in coverage. Further differences are caused by legislative changes which have changed the treatment of certain types of property. There was little change in the total rateable value of non-domestic properties when all these properties were revalued in April 1995. Rateable values for offices fell and there was a rise for all other property types shown in the table. There was a further revaluation in 2000 when total rateable values increased by 28 per cent compared to the end of the 1995 list.

With effect from 1 April 2005 all non-domestic properties were revalued. Overall there was an increase in rateable values of over 17 per cent compared to the end of the 2000 list.

Revenue Expenditure

(Table 18.13)

Revenue expenditure is made up of two distinct elements, current expenditure and debt financing. Current expenditure is essentially the cost associated with running local authority services, such as the salaries and wages of employees, or the purchase of goods such as books for schools, or services such as places in residential care homes. Revenue expenditure also includes day-to-day running costs such as heating, lighting and cleaning of local authority buildings or the running and maintenance of local authority vehicles. This expenditure is offset by income from sales, fees, charges and other non-grant income. Revenue expenditure is financed by central government, in the form of general and specific grants, locally raised council tax and contributions from reserves.

Net revenue expenditure is gross revenue expenditure less that expenditure funded by specific grants other than police grants. Budget requirement is net revenue expenditure less than expenditure funded from local authority reserves. Debt financing is the repayment of debt and the associated interest payable on loans raised to finance past capital expenditure. It also includes any direct revenue contributions to capital expenditure.

Gross Revenue Expenditure

(Table 18.14)

Gross revenue expenditure is the net current element of revenue expenditure, *plus* the capital charges element of revenue expenditure. It is effectively all revenue expenditure, excluding that financed by income from sales, fees and charges and other non-grant sources, but including that financed by specific government grants.

There were increases for all property types, with the largest rise in rateable values for the 'other commercial' category, consisting of commercial properties other than shops or cafes and offices. For the 'other commercial' category, shops and cafes, theatres and music halls and the educational and cultural category there were higher rises for the introduction of the 2005 list than for the introduction of the 2000 list. For all other categories the 2005 list rises were lower.

18.1 Sector analysis of key fiscal balances[1]
United Kingdom
Not seasonally adjusted

£ million[2]

		1994/95	1995/96	1996/97	1997/98	1998/99	1999/00	2000/01	2001/02	2002/03	2003/04	2004/05
Surplus on current budget[3]												
Central Government	ANLV	−30 283	−23 067	−20 714	15	11 903	23 645	24 862	13 659	−8 854	−18 343	−16 927
Local government	NMMX	2 016	458	−20	−367	−225	−2 430	−2 099	−2 149	−1 899	−1 660	−1 376
General Government	ANLW	−28 267	−22 609	−20 734	−352	11 517	21 246	22 675	11 518	−10 423	−19 826	−18 452
Public corporations	FDDP	−4 893	−2 166	−998	−888	−1 145	−962	−1 118	−1 182	−2 561	−1 295	−915
Public sector	ANMU	−33 160	−24 775	−21 732	−1 240	10 442	20 229	21 492	10 253	−13 080	−21 285	−19 383
Net investment[4]												
Central government	-ANNS	14 951	14 454	9 715	8 042	8 357	8 325	9 319	11 964	16 142	17 565	20 700
Local government	-ANNT	2 157	−208	−873	−482	−132	−1 487	−2 393	−849	−4 305	−2 819	−123
General Government	-ANNV	17 108	14 246	8 842	7 560	8 203	6 840	6 895	11 098	11 803	14 609	20 581
Public corporations	-ANNU	−7 058	−4 281	−3 141	−2 259	−1 387	−2 071	−1 428	−978	−259	−975	−597
Public sector	-ANNW	10 050	9 965	5 701	5 301	6 556	4 841	5 671	10 291	12 158	14 515	20 643
Net borrowing[5]												
Central government	-NMFJ	45 234	37 521	30 429	8 027	−3 407	−15 349	−15 486	−1 720	24 632	35 595	37 896
Local government	-NMOE	141	−666	−853	−115	93	943	−294	1 300	−2 406	−1 160	1 283
General Government	-NNBK	45 375	36 855	29 576	7 912	−3 314	−14 406	−15 780	−420	22 226	34 435	39 179
Public corporations	-CPCM	−2 165	−2 115	−2 143	−1 371	−242	−1 109	−310	204	2 302	320	318
Public sector	-ANNX	43 210	34 740	27 433	6 541	−3 886	−15 388	−15 821	38	25 238	35 800	40 026
Net cash requirement												
Central government[6]	RUUX	39 660	36 153	25 199	2 751	−6 344	−10 664	−37 251	3 366	24 214	42 717	37 455
Local government	ABEG	−961	−1 139	−843	−820	−404	979	−611	−423	−2 715	−2 712	1 282
General Government	RUUS	38 699	35 014	24 356	1 931	−6 748	−9 685	−37 862	2 943	21 499	40 005	38 737
Public corporations	ABEM	−2 011	−3 529	−1 637	−669	699	1 712	1 539	694	3 722	−273	32
Public sector	RURQ	36 688	31 485	22 719	1 262	−6 049	−7 973	−36 323	3 637	25 221	39 732	38 769
Public sector debt												
Public sector net debt (£ billion)	RUTN	289.3	321.3	347.5	352.1	350.0	343.0	309.8	314.6	346.3	381.5	421.0
Public sector net debt as a percentage of GDP	RUTO	*40.8*	*42.7*	*43.6*	*41.5*	*39.2*	*36.4*	*31.4*	*30.4*	*31.8*	*33.2*	*35.1*

1 National accounts entities as defined under the European System of Accounts 1995 (ESA95) consistent with the latest national accounts. See chapter text.
2 Unless otherwise stated
3 Net saving *plus* capital taxes.
4 Gross capital formation *plus* payments *less* receipts of investment grants *less* depreciation.

5 Net investment *less* surplus on current budget. A version of General government net borrowing is reported to the European Commision under the requirements of the Maastricht Treaty.
6 Central government net cash requirement (own account).

Source: Office for National Statistics: 020 7533 5984

18.2 Public sector transactions and fiscal balances[1]
United Kingdom

£ million

		1994/95	1995/96	1996/97	1997/98	1998/99	1999/00	2000/01	2001/02	2002/03	2003/04	2004/05
Current receipts												
Taxes on income and wealth	ANSO	87 804	96 422	102 261	114 933	123 859	133 715	144 164	145 139	143 121	145 375	161 729
Taxes on production	NMYE	90 173	95 981	99 484	109 385	115 349	125 322	129 605	133 442	139 842	148 704	154 980
Other current taxes[2]	MJBC	11 312	12 130	13 162	14 214	15 468	16 541	17 519	19 247	20 752	23 159	24 472
Taxes on capital	NMGI	1 409	1 518	1 558	1 684	1 805	2 054	2 236	2 383	2 370	2 521	2 944
Social contributions	ANBO	42 832	45 007	47 219	51 692	54 746	56 935	62 068	63 162	63 529	75 148	79 335
Gross operating surplus	ANBP	14 519	17 543	17 059	16 904	16 608	16 439	16 350	16 545	16 458	17 520	17 121
Interest and dividends from private sector and Rest of World	ANBQ	4 133	4 435	4 369	4 497	5 038	4 487	6 449	5 239	4 937	4 853	5 669
Rent and other current transfers[3]	ANBS	1 107	1 125	1 325	1 041	835	908	1 809	2 221	2 417	1 949	2 050
Total current receipts	ANBT	253 289	274 161	286 437	314 350	333 708	356 401	380 200	387 378	393 426	419 229	448 300
Current expenditure												
Current expenditure on goods and services[4]	GZSN	137 267	142 252	146 304	148 794	156 843	168 273	182 454	195 320	216 059	235 551	250 797
Subsidies	NMRL	5 321	5 421	5 598	5 400	4 259	4 236	4 586	4 992	5 269	6 525	6 977
Social benefits	ANLY	97 715	100 445	104 059	105 873	106 568	110 252	114 314	123 871	124 042	132 401	138 183
Net current grants abroad[5]	GZSI	553	458	−751	102	−847	−253	−146	−1 861	−626	−1 002	−580
Other current grants	NNAI	9 275	10 325	12 693	13 519	15 199	15 975	18 330	19 073	26 036	29 750	32 876
Interest and dividends paid to private sector and Rest of World	ANLO	23 489	26 765	28 128	29 732	29 370	25 380	26 462	22 565	21 619	22 867	24 526
Total current expenditure	ANLT	273 620	285 666	296 031	303 420	311 392	323 863	346 000	363 960	392 399	426 092	452 779
Saving, gross plus capital taxes	ANSP	−20 331	−11 505	−9 594	10 930	22 316	32 538	34 200	23 418	1 027	−6 863	−4 479
Depreciation	-ANNZ	−12 829	−13 270	−12 138	−12 170	−11 944	−12 254	−12 643	−13 082	−14 011	−14 258	−14 888
Surplus on current budget	ANMU	−33 160	−24 775	−21 732	−1 240	10 442	20 229	21 492	10 253	−13 080	−21 285	−19 383
Net investment												
Gross fixed capital formation[6]	ANSQ	19 114	19 135	14 255	13 460	13 976	13 154	14 715	16 943	20 185	20 351	25 385
Less depreciation	-ANNZ	−12 829	−13 270	−12 138	−12 170	−11 944	−12 254	−12 643	−13 082	−14 011	−14 258	−14 888
Increase in inventories and valuables	ANSR	−662	21	34	139	231	−472	−126	−10	−74	107	−21
Capital grants to private sector and Rest of World	ANSS	4 854	4 432	4 032	4 388	4 920	4 768	4 277	7 258	6 535	8 934	10 719
Capital grants from private sector and Rest of World	-ANST	−427	−353	−482	−516	−367	−427	−756	−989	−1 091	−1 500	−1 211
Total net investment	-ANNW	10 050	9 965	5 701	5 301	6 556	4 841	5 671	10 291	12 158	14 515	20 643
Net borrowing[7]	-ANNX	43 210	34 740	27 433	6 541	−3 886	−15 388	−15 821	38	25 238	35 800	40 026
Financial transactions determining net cash requirement												
Net lending to private sector and Rest of World	ANSU	−1 167	−1 749	−655	−224	309	2 301	2 942	2 407	2 625	2 576	832
Net acquisition of UK company securities	ANSV	−6 374	−2 344	−3 992	−1 526	565	−498	859	−562	465	433	112
Accounts receivable/payable	ANSW	75	3 139	−285	−656	418	5 522	−22 054	2 373	−2 749	4 537	1 154
Adjustment for interest on gilts	ANSX	−1 036	−1 895	−382	−2 349	−2 446	−1 295	−2 630	−361	−1 447	−1 186	−2 322
Other financial transcations[8]	ANSY	1 980	−406	600	−524	−1 009	1 385	381	−258	1 089	−2 428	−1 033
Public sector net cash requirement	RURQ	36 688	31 485	22 719	1 262	−6 049	−7 973	−36 323	3 637	25 221	39 732	38 769

1 See chapter text.
2 Includes domestic rates, council tax, community charge, motor vehicle duty paid by household and some licence fees.
3 ESA95 transactions D44, D45, D74, D75 and D72-D71: includes rent of land, oil royalties, other property income and fines.
4 Includes non-trading capital consumption.

5 Net of current grants received from abroad.
6 Including net acquisition of land.
7 Net investment *less* surplus on current budget.
8 Includes statistical discrepancy, finance leasing and similar borrowing, insurance technical reserves and some other minor adjustments.

Source: Office for National Statistics: 020 7533 5984

18.3 Public sector net debt[1]
United Kingdom

£ million

		1996/97	1997/98	1998/99	1999/00	2000/01	2001/02	2002/03	2003/04	2004/05
Central government sterling gross debt:										
British government stock										
Conventional gilts	BKPK	231 869	232 292	223 105	218 687	204 285	200 833	206 119	232 877	261 373
Index linked gilts	BKPL	51 535	58 729	62 289	65 740	70 316	70 417	75 966	78 982	86 749
Total	BKPM	283 404	291 021	285 394	284 427	274 601	271 250	282 085	311 859	348 122
Sterling Treasury bills	BKPJ	4 996	2 106	4 721	4 453	3 521	9 700	15 000	19 300	20 350
National savings	ACUA	61 754	63 271	64 346	63 331	62 611	62 275	63 087	66 522	68 495
Tax instruments	ACRV	853	706	574	535	491	478	376	407	351
Other sterling debt[2]	BKSK	26 345	25 108	26 027	26 550	27 773	25 647	29 722	31 627	28 096
Central government sterling gross debt total	BKSL	377 352	382 212	381 062	379 296	368 997	369 350	390 270	429 715	465 414
Central government foreign currency gross debt:										
US$ bonds	BKPG	4 294	4 180	4 338	4 388	4 924	2 107	–	1 632	1 587
DM bonds[3]	EYST	1 828	–	–	–	–	–	–	–	–
ECU bonds	EYSJ	1 777	1 606	1 672	1 500	–	–	–	–	–
ECU/Euro Treasury notes	EYSV	3 199	2 891	3 010	2 701	2 486	1 225	–	–	–
ECU/Euro Treasury bills	EYSN	2 488	2 249	2 341	–	–	–	–	–	–
Other foreign currency debt	BKPH	752	537	456	364	291	243	172	105	57
Central government foreign currency gross debt total	BKPI	14 338	11 463	11 816	8 954	7 701	3 575	172	1 738	1 644
Central government gross debt total	BKPW	391 690	393 675	392 878	388 250	376 698	372 925	390 442	431 453	467 058
Local government gross debt total	EYKP	49 856	50 193	51 039	51 702	52 517	52 561	51 324	50 512	53 115
less										
Central government holdings of local government debt	-EYKZ	–42 348	–43 172	–45 045	–46 563	–47 789	–47 530	–44 836	–41 540	–42 339
Local government holdings of central government debt	-EYLA	–155	–170	–273	–77	–31	–29	–184	–510	–62
General government gross debt (consolidated)	BKPX	399 043	400 526	398 599	393 312	381 395	377 927	396 746	439 915	477 772
Public corporations gross debt	EYYD	16 069	15 262	14 084	7 938	8 804	8 412	17 951	11 754	12 476
less:										
Central government holdings of public corporations debt	-EYXY	–15 314	–14 590	–10 732	–4 307	–4 714	–4 308	–4 171	–5 188	–5 740
Local government holdings of public corporations debt	-EYXZ	–1	–	–4	–123	–124	–122	–121	–120	–121
Public corporations holdings of central government debt	-BKPZ	–7 103	–7 313	–6 436	–6 126	–5 927	–4 615	–4 279	–3 924	–4 097
Public corporations holdings of local government debt	-EYXV	–134	–139	–108	–141	–106	–60	–50	–84	–100
Public sector gross debt (consolidated)	BKQA	392 560	393 746	395 403	390 553	379 328	377 234	406 076	442 353	480 190
Public sector liquid assets:										
Official reserves	AIPD	25 547	21 293	22 147	21 498	30 423	28 055	26 387	25 266	25 813
Central government deposits[4]	BKSM	2 083	2 293	1 762	1 879	2 797	2 802	2 900	3 879	3 868
Other central government	BKSN	–	–	–	4 756	15 670	10 743	8 141	7 077	3 044
Local government deposits[4]	BKSO	11 313	11 828	12 301	10 221	11 522	11 570	12 535	14 530	16 560
Other local government short term assets	BKQG	3 256	3 693	4 335	5 468	5 719	5 990	6 061	5 599	5 118
Public corporations deposits[4]	BKSP	2 145	1 849	2 058	1 463	1 642	1 808	1 432	2 046	2 717
Other public corporations short term assets	BKSQ	686	668	1 300	1 128	1 212	1 180	1 586	1 729	1 392
Public sector liquid assets total	BKQJ	45 030	41 624	45 365	47 569	69 558	62 676	59 743	60 856	59 157
Public sector net debt	BKQK	347 530	352 122	350 038	342 984	309 770	314 558	346 333	381 497	421 033
as percentage of GDP[5]	RUTO	*43.6*	*41.5*	*39.2*	*36.4*	*31.4*	*30.4*	*31.8*	*33.2*	*35.1*

1 See chapter text.
2 Including overdraft with Bank of England.
3 Matured on 28 October 1997.
4 Bank and building society deposits.
5 Gross domestic product at market prices from 12 months centred on the end of the month.

Source: Office for National Statistics: 020 7533 5984

18.4 Consolidated Fund and National Loans Fund:[1] revenue and expenditure; receipts and payments

United Kingdom, years ending 31 March

£ million

		1995/96	1996/97	1997/98	1998/99	1999/00	2000/01	2001/02	2002/03	2003/04	2004/05
Consolidated Fund											
Revenue											
Inland Revenue	KCWZ	97 100.9	103 892.4	117 632.8	128 249.8	139 384.0	149 084.8	149 112.4	145 898.0	145 555.5	158 975.4
Customs and Excise	KCXA	76 668.6	82 351.6	89 839.6	94 018.3	97 291.5	102 168.0	104 854.8	108 719.8	115 656.3	120 924.0
Motor vehicle duties	KCXB	4 043.6	4 217.5	4 543.0	4 666.3	4 893.0	4 642.1	4 402.3	4 399.4	4 712.3	4 750.9
National Non-Domestic Rates	KPOI	13 373.4	14 269.3	14 036.9	15 878.3	13 403.8	15 482.0	16 009.3	17 592.9	16 579.3	16 000.0
Miscellaneous receipts	KCXE	10 289.3	12 634.6	14 176.6	10 737.1	8 799.0	29 329.4	7 796.6	9 425.0	10 548.9	12 672.4
Total revenue	KCXF	201 475.8	217 365.4	240 228.9	253 549.8	263 771.3	300 706.3	282 175.4	286 035.1	293 052.3	313 322.7
Expenditure											
Supply services	KCXG	211 403.3	214 226.0	209 440.8	213 439.2	226 989.6	241 685.1	271 998.6	290 183.0	313 071.9	325 542.7
Debt interest[2]	KCXH	18 423.1	20 702.3	21 605.7	21 320.8	18 535.3	16 629.2	15 325.6	14 680.9	14 502.4	16 965.9
Payments to Northern Ireland	KCXI	3 903.5	3 685.2	4 581.5	4 709.3	3 104.4	..	..	..	..	..
Payments to the European Union, etc	KCXJ	7 650.7	6 875.3	7 039.9	8 060.7	7 001.8	8 417.1	4 785.8	6 504.0	7 496.3	8 460.7
Other expenditure[3]	KCXL	−14.0	876.2	−53.8	−62.1	223.7	170.1	257.9	−72.4	203.8	266.7
Total expenditure	KCXM	241 366.5	246 365.0	242 614.1	247 467.9	255 854.8	266 901.5	292 367.9	311 295.5	335 274.4	351 236.0
Deficit met from the National Loans Fund	KCXN	39 890.7	28 999.6	2 385.2	−6 081.9	−7 916.5	−33 804.8	10 192.5	25 260.4	42 222.1	37 913.3
National Loans Fund											
Receipts											
Profits of the Issue Department of the Bank of England - income[4]	KZAW	1 275.5	1 200.9	1 604.8	1 600.9	1 327.3	1 603.0	1 362.9	1 240.2	1 247.8	1 632.4
Other miscellaneous receipts	KZAX	4.4	3.6	5.0	5.0	4.4	6.0	7.3	10.6	8.2	7.8
Interest on loans	KCXO	4 598.7	4 393.5	5 103.6	4 409.7	4 533.3	6 215.4	5 901.2	5 791.5	5 558.7	5 066.3
Service of the National Debt - balance met from the Consolidated Fund	KCXP	18 423.2	20 702.3	21 605.7	21 320.8	18 535.3	16 629.2	15 325.6	14 680.9	14 502.4	16 965.9
Gilt Edged Official Operations Account net income	KJDO	..	..	..	..	127.5	..	..	..	..	..
Total	KCXQ	24 301.8	26 300.3	28 319.1	27 336.4	24 527.8	24 453.6	22 597.0	21 723.2	21 967.1	23 672.4
Exchange Equalisation Account-sterling capital	KCXR	2 750.0	2 150.0	3 650.0	1 880.0	975.0	−5 205.0	4 849.0	4 620.0	330.0	−140.0
Net borrowing[5]	KCXS	37 688.8	27 547.9	..	..	4 997.3	..	4 884.8	11 004.4	45 590.1	23 327.3
International Monetary Fund-maintenance of sterling holdings	KCXT	..	82.1	707.0	181.2	..	..	..	98.2	25.9	299.1
Profits of the Issue Department of the Bank of England: capital appreciation	KZAY	..	18.8	21.2	19.3	1.7	2.5	6.4	9.0	9.0	16.3
Reduction of National Debt Commissioners' Liability in respect of the National Savings Bank Investment Account	KCXU	..	..	..	..	..	..	..	..	..	..
Change in balances and other items	KCXV	..	..	..	..	..	..	..	..	..	..
NILO Gilt-Edged operations A/C	KJDL	2 500.0	2 000.0	2 500.0	2 500.0	5 000.0	..	..	..	..	..
Debt Management Account	GPJW	..	..	..	..	..	20 000.0	..	7 000.0	..	15 000.0
Total	KCXW	67 240.6	58 099.1	35 197.3	31 916.9	35 501.8	39 251.1	32 337.2	44 454.8	67 922.1	62 175.1
Payments											
Service of the National Debt:											
Interest	KJDM	24 004.0	25 942.5	27 877.8	26 792.1	24 073.7	23 855.8	22 041.2	21 297.2	21 477.2	22 950.4
Management and expenses	KCXY	297.8	357.8	441.3	544.3	454.1	597.8	555.8	426.0	490.0	722.0
Total	KCXZ	24 301.8	26 300.3	28 319.1	27 336.4	24 527.8	24 453.6	22 597.0	21 723.2	21 967.2	23 672.4
Consolidated Fund deficit met from the National Loans Fund	KCYA	39 890.7	28 999.6	2 385.2	−6 081.9	−7 916.5	−33 804.8	10 192.6	25 260.4	42 222.1	37 913.3
Net repayment[5]	KCYB	..	..	2 482.1	3 558.2	..	7 083.4	..	..	..	..
Net lending[6]	KCYC	334.1	280.6	−4.2	1 766.3	1 255.9	1 496.5	−786.2	−2 532.4	−3 287.4	581.0
International Monetary Fund-maintenance of value of sterling holding	KCYD	202.1	..	..	..	126.1	21.2	315.2	..	..	..
International Monetary Fund-additional subscription	KCYE	..	..	..	2 826.5	..	..	..	..	..	..
NILO Gilt-Edged Operations A/C	KJDN	2 500.0	2 500.0	2 000.0	2 500.0	2 500.0	..	..	..	..	..
Discharge of Treasury Liability to the Bank of England Issue Department	KPUK	11.9	18.6	15.1	11.4	8.5	1.2	18.6	3.6	20.2	8.5
Debt Management Account	ZAFB	..	..	..	..	15 000.0	40 000.0	..	..	7 000.0	..
Total	KCYF	67 240.6	58 099.1	35 197.3	31 916.9	35 501.8	39 251.1	32 337.2	44 454.8	67 922.1	62 175.2

1 See chapter text.
2 Payment to National Loans Fund representing its payments for the service of the National Debt *less* its receipts of interest on loans outstanding, etc.
3 Includes net issues to Contingencies Fund.
4 Prior to 1996-97, receipts from the Bank of England for appreciation of the assets of the Issue Department were included in the total amount for the profits of the Issue Department.

5 See Table 18.6.
6 Minus sign indicates a net issue repayment.

Source: HM Treasury: 020 7270 4761

18.5 Taxes paid by UK residents to general government and the European Union[1]
Total economy sector S.1

£ million

		1995 /96	1996 /97	1997 /98	1998 /99	1999 /00	2000 /01	2001 /02	2002 /03	2003 /04	2004 /05
Generation of income											
Uses											
Taxes on production and imports											
Taxes on products and imports											
Value added tax (VAT)											
Paid to central government	NZGF	44 275	46 649	52 113	53 911	58 899	61 054	65 148	69 402	76 961	80 373
Paid to the European Union	FJKM	4 942	4 661	3 531	4 105	3 451	4 172	3 592	2 518	2 574	1 905
Total	QYRC	49 217	51 310	55 644	58 016	62 350	65 226	68 740	71 920	79 506	82 130
Taxes and duties on imports excluding VAT											
Paid to CG: import duties[2]	NMBS	–	–	–	–	–	–	–	–	–	..
Paid to EU: import duties	FJWE	2 468	2 290	2 261	2 042	2 049	2 103	2 024	1 893	1 957	2 206
Total	QYRB	2 468	2 290	2 261	2 042	2 049	2 103	2 024	1 893	1 957	2 205
Taxes on products excluding VAT and import duties											
Paid to central government											
Customs and Excise revenue											
Beer	GTAM	2 637	2 631	2 699	2 733	2 848	2 798	2 907	2 952	3 084	3 098
Wines, cider, perry & spirits	GTAN	2 983	2 999	3 057	3 301	3 652	3 814	4 068	4 430	4 526	4 788
Tobacco	GTAO	7 405	7 701	7 622	7 551	7 796	7 638	7 639	8 046	8 092	8 135
Hydrocarbon oils	GTAP	15 679	17 171	19 451	21 553	22 510	22 630	21 916	22 147	22 786	23 313
Car tax	GTAT	–	–	–	–	–	–	–	–	–	–
Betting, gaming & lottery	CJQY	1 591	1 460	1 539	1 527	1 500	1 517	1 317	977	898	876
Air passenger duty	CWAA	354	359	522	845	882	956	802	804	799	874
Insurance premium tax	CWAD	648	685	1 179	1 248	1 511	1 751	1 921	2 189	2 316	2 362
Landfill tax	BKOF	–	113	364	322	456	475	501	545	636	680
Other	ACDN	–	–	–	–	–	–	–	–	–	–
Fossil fuel levy	CIQY	1 272	880	256	164	84	52	92	9	–	–
Gas levy	GTAZ	171	199	188	–44	–	–	–	–	–	–
Stamp duties	GTBC	2 018	2 414	3 456	4 623	6 898	8 165	6 983	7 549	7 544	8 932
Levies on exports (Third country trade)	CUDF	–	–	–	–	–	–	–	–	–	–
Camelot payments to National Lottery											
Distribution Fund	LIYH	1 527	1 263	1 572	1 665	1 593	1 542	1 520	1 382	1 311	1 354
Purchase Tax	EBDB	–	–	–	–	–	–	–	–	–	–
Hydro-benefit	LITN	28	31	32	32	38	44	44	44	43	40
Aggregates Levy	MDUQ	–	–	–	–	–	–	–	293	341	327
Other taxes and levies	GCSP	–	–	–	–	–	–	–	–	–	–
Total paid to central government	NMBV	36 313	37 906	41 937	45 520	49 768	51 382	49 710	51 367	52 376	54 813
Paid to the European Union											
Sugar levy	GTBA	36	37	72	44	46	43	27	25	19	24
European Coal & Steel Community levy	GTBB	–	–	–	–	–	–	–	–	–	–
Total paid to the European Union	FJWG	36	37	72	44	46	43	27	25	19	24
Total taxes on products excluding VAT & import duties	QYRA	36 349	37 943	42 009	45 564	49 814	51 425	49 737	51 392	52 395	54 803
Total taxes on products and imports	NZGW	88 034	91 543	99 914	105 622	114 213	118 754	120 501	125 205	133 858	139 138
Production taxes other than on products											
Paid to central government											
Consumer Credit Act fees	CUDB	166	113	168	158	140	150	143	160	146	146
National non-domestic rates	CUKY	13 481	13 010	13 283	13 764	14 353	15 168	16 252	16 728	16 941	17 371
Old style non-domestic rates	NSEZ	124	126	136	130	123	132	131	136	140	146
Levies paid to CG levy-funded bodies	LITK	134	147	162	171	241	207	175	144	150	192
Selective employment tax	CSAH	–	–	–	–	–	–	–	–	–	–
National insurance surcharge	GTAY	–	–	–	–	–	–	–	–	–	–
London Regional Transport levy	GTBE	–	–	–	–	–	–	–	–	–	–
IBA levy	GTAL	–	–	–	–	–	–	–	–	–	–
Motor vehicle duties paid by businesses	EKED	1 331	1 365	1 405	1 503	1 559	1 230	751	736	720	813
Regulator fees	GCSQ	57	54	57	61	69	72	62	60	60	60
Climate change levy	LSNT	–	–	–	–	–	–	822	813	816	759
Total	NMBX	15 293	14 815	15 211	15 787	16 485	16 959	18 336	18 777	19 049	19 607
Paid to local government											
Old style non-domestic rates	NMYH	100	114	124	131	144	150	161	176	192	208
Total production taxes other than on products	NMYD	15 393	14 929	15 335	15 918	16 629	17 109	18 497	18 953	19 241	19 815
Total taxes on production and imports, paid											
Paid to central government	NMBY	95 881	99 370	109 261	115 218	125 178	129 455	133 281	139 666	148 511	154 748
Paid to local government	NMYH	100	114	124	131	144	150	161	176	192	208
Paid to the European Union	FJWB	7 446	6 988	5 864	6 191	5 546	6 318	5 643	4 436	4 550	4 135
Total	NZGX	103 427	106 472	115 249	121 540	130 842	135 863	138 998	144 158	153 023	158 789

18.5
Taxes paid by UK residents to general government and the European Union[1]
Total economy sector S.1

£ million

		1995/96	1996/97	1997/98	1998/99	1999/00	2000/01	2001/02	2002/03	2003/04	2004/05
Secondary distribution of income											
Uses											
Current taxes on income, wealth etc											
Taxes on income											
Paid to central government											
Household income taxes	DRWH	74 974	75 191	81 895	89 739	96 967	106 866	108 556	110 432	112 550	122 497
Petroleum revenue tax	DBHA	968	1 729	963	502	853	1 518	1 310	958	1 179	1 284
Windfall tax	EYNK	–	–	2 610	2 614	–	–	–	–	–	–
Other corporate taxes	BMNX	20 748	25 715	29 844	31 263	36 164	35 878	35 338	31 809	31 918	37 830
Total	NMCU	96 690	102 635	115 312	124 091	133 989	144 270	145 196	143 183	145 456	161 803
Other current taxes											
Paid to central government											
Motor vehicle duty paid by households	CDDZ	2 686	2 802	3 045	3 116	3 296	3 039	3 540	3 600	3 797	3 935
Old style domestic rates	NSFA	79	104	115	114	117	108	109	104	100	94
Licences	NSNP	11	10	11	8	8	2	–	–	–	–
National non-domestic rates paid by non-market sectors	BMNY	–	930	929	971	1 002	997	1 065	1 011	994	994
Total	NMCV	2 776	3 846	4 100	4 209	4 423	4 146	4 714	4 715	4 996	5 023
Paid to local government											
Old style domestic rates	NMHK	60	61	64	62	68	76	80	85	92	100
Community charge	NMHL	–	–	–	–	–	–	–	–	–	–
Council tax	NMHM	9 294	10 059	10 850	12 037	12 918	14 155	15 371	16 809	18 911	20 215
Total	NMIS	9 354	10 120	10 914	12 099	12 986	14 231	15 451	16 894	19 003	20 284
Total	NVCM	12 130	13 966	15 014	16 308	17 409	18 377	20 165	21 609	23 894	25 307
Total current taxes on income, wealth etc											
Paid to central government	NMCP	99 466	106 481	119 412	128 327	138 407	148 408	149 918	147 914	150 537	166 830
Paid to local government	NMIS	9 354	10 120	10 914	12 099	12 986	14 231	15 451	16 894	19 003	20 284
Total	NMZL	108 820	116 601	130 326	140 426	151 393	162 639	165 369	164 808	169 540	187 114
Social contributions											
Actual social contributions											
Paid to central government											
(National Insurance Contributions)											
Employers' compulsory contributions	CEAN	24 533	25 950	27 761	29 779	31 717	35 087	35 702	35 465	41 024	44 051
Employees' compulsory contributions	GCSE	18 889	19 611	22 073	23 255	23 623	24 973	25 308	25 732	31 026	31 478
Self- and non-employed persons' compulsory contributions	NMDE	1 585	1 658	1 858	1 712	1 823	2 008	2 151	2 331	2 880	2 868
Total	AIIH	45 007	47 219	51 692	54 746	56 935	62 068	63 162	63 529	75 148	79 335
Capital account											
Changes in liabilities and net worth											
Other capital taxes											
Paid to central government											
Inheritance tax	GILF	1 484	1 517	1 649	1 764	2 016	2 181	2 346	2 323	2 486	2 874
Tax on other capital transfers	GILG	34	41	35	41	38	55	37	47	35	48
Development land tax and other	GCSV	–	–	–	–	–	–	–	–	–	–
Total	NMGI	1 518	1 558	1 684	1 805	2 054	2 236	2 383	2 370	2 521	2 944
Total taxes and compulsory social contributions											
Paid to central government	GCSS	241 872	254 628	282 049	300 096	322 776	342 107	348 656	353 358	376 626	403 760
Paid to local government	GCST	9 454	10 234	11 038	12 230	13 130	14 381	15 612	17 070	19 195	20 523
Paid to the European Union	FJWB	7 446	6 988	5 864	6 191	5 546	6 318	5 643	4 436	4 550	4 135
Total	GCSU	258 772	271 850	298 951	318 517	341 452	362 806	369 911	374 864	400 283	428 508
Total taxes and social contributions as percentage of GDP	GDWM	35.5	35.1	36.3	36.5	37.1	37.6	36.7	35.3	35.7	36.3

1 See chapter text.
2 These taxes existed before the UK's entry into the EEC in 1973

Sources: HM Treasury;
Office for National Statistics: 020 7533 5991

18.6 Borrowing and repayment of debt[1]
United Kingdom
Years ending 31 March

£ million

		1995/96	1996/97	1997/98	1998/99	1999/00	2000/01	2001/02	2002/03	2003/04	2004/05
Borrowing											
Government securities: new issues	KQGA	34 150.3	40 800.8	28 484.4	12 048.0	26 426.5	25 789.8	43 433.4	54 068.9	53 220.9	57 290.5
National savings securities:											
National savings certificates	KQGB	3 425.9	3 695.5	4 435.2	3 028.7	1 962.7	3 086.2	2 580.7	2 434.3	1 940.4	1 696.4
Capital bonds	KQGC	504.8	450.8	619.0	469.6	35.4	29.0	40.9	107.3	65.0	25.2
Income bonds	KQGD	780.7	1 272.7	1 043.4	1 371.7	653.4	760.5	625.6	484.8	415.3	426.6
Deposit bonds	KQGE	..	..	..	..	..	..	..	..	−	..
British savings bonds	KQGF	..	..	..	..	..	..	..	..	..	..
Premium savings bonds	KQGG	2 040.6	2 552.5	3 158.8	3 652.8	3 449.4	3 296.0	3 859.6	4 604.5	7 530.1	5 737.8
Save As You Earn	KQGH	50.8	34.1	20.7	11.4	5.0	0.3	..	..	−	..
Yearly plan	KQGI	94.1	..	..	5.2	..	..	..	..	−	..
National savings stamps and gift tokens	KQGJ	..	..	..	..	..	..	..	..	−	..
National Savings Bank Investments	KQGK	1 312.1	1 478.7	1 282.3	1 085.0	901.6	955.3	864.9	1 012.4	809.9	817.5
Children's Bonus Bonds	KGVO	144.9	352.4	255.3	205.0	58.5	53.4	45.0	54.0	51.7	66.8
First Option Bonds	KIAR	826.4	1 139.8	1 152.9	1 001.8	34.3	..	..	..	..	..
Pensioners Guaranteed Income Bond	KJDW	2 104.2	2 863.8	1 126.9	201.0	590.7	687.2	603.5	662.9	274.2	323.9
Treasurer's account	KWNF	..	21.1	39.9	17.1	13.6	12.5	15.2	19.4	13.9	11.1
Individual Savings Account	ZAFC	..	..	..	..	257.8	265.9	397.8	405.6	335.4	276.4
Fixed Rate Savings Bonds	ZAFD	..	..	..	..	175.9	284.7	192.7	193.0	82.0	86.3
Guaranteed Equity Bonds	ECPU	..	..	..	..	..	..	27.2	274.8	227.9	317.1
Easy Access Savings Account	C3OM	..	..	..	..	..	..	..	..	126.9	903.5
Certificate of tax deposit	KQGL	76.2	109.4	84.1	66.4	121.4	76.5	77.6	59.6	145.2	114.8
Nationalised industries', etc temporary deposits	KQGM	36 870.6	53 198.2	46 375.9	39 962.4	40 343.3	56 106.6	62 150.0	55 395.1	47 958.6	25 022.0
Sterling Treasury bills (net receipt)	KQGO	2 606.1	..	..	3 546.2	..	..	..	..	−	..
ECU Treasury bills (net receipt)	KQGP	..	..	..	..	..	..	..	..	−	..
ECU Treasury notes (net receipt)	KDZZ	..	..	..	..	721.1	..	..	..	..	..
Ways and means (net receipt)	KQGQ	1 162.3	511.1	..	183.6	5 599.0	12 126.0	12 095.3	3 899.9	22 700.2	..
Other debt : payable in sterling :											
Interest free notes	KQGR	247.4	99.2	32.4	2 130.9	373.5	972.7	1 427.2	754.0	1 213.2	662.3
Other debt : payable in external currencies	KHCY	..	2 565.2	..	..	..	..	..	..	1 792.5	..
Total receipts	KHCZ	86 397.4	111 145.3	88 111.2	68 986.8	81 723.1	104 502.6	128 436.6	124 430.5	138 903.3	93 778.2
Repayment of debt											
Government securities: redemptions	KQGS	4 652.7	14 488.4	20 678.9	18 575.5	19 815.8	33 722.2	43 642.3	42 109.9	35 087.4	25 130.1
Statutory sinking funds	KQGT	2.2	2.2	2.1	2.0	2.0	2.0	1.9	1.9	1.8	1.8
Terminable annuities:											
National Debt Commissioners	KQGU	..	..	..	..	..	..	..	..	..	..
National savings securities:											
National savings certificates	KQGV	2 258.4	3 263.7	4 058.5	3 449.0	2 405.2	4 546.8	4 177.7	4 146.7	2 769.1	1 979.6
Capital bonds	KQGW	509.0	698.3	1 160.5	888.3	324.2	375.0	175.9	155.9	116.9	121.1
Income bonds	KQGX	1 256.9	1 394.0	1 148.9	880.8	1 686.3	857.0	933.8	1 144.2	977.1	879.5
Deposit bonds	KQGY	72.5	64.8	72.6	84.2	70.2	71.1	45.4	369.4	4.4	..
Yearly Plan	KQGZ	101.9	96.3	113.2	120.0	141.8	18.4	4.5	3.0	2.0	..
British savings bonds	KQHA	..	..	..	..	..	..	..	..	..	..
Premium savings bonds	KQHB	590.1	869.3	1 203.1	1 398.4	1 923.8	1 872.6	1 942.9	2 343.3	2 967.4	3 492.4
Save As You Earn	KQHC	98.7	70.1	68.2	37.1	34.5	22.9	8.0	3.2	0.5	..
National savings stamps and gift tokens	KQHD	..	..	..	..	..	..	..	..	−	1.2
National Savings Bank Investments (repayments)	KQHE	1 755.8	1 837.0	2 175.7	2 027.0	1 886.3	1 654.1	1 415.8	1 350.1	1 342.7	1 554.0
Children's Bonus Bonds	KGVQ	0.1	257.8	187.9	183.2	69.3	95.0	114.5	92.6	79.8	84.5
First Option Bonds	KIAS	732.7	833.9	1 283.0	1 055.5	298.1	225.2	111.6	77.4	62.2	33.4
Pensioners Guaranteed Income Bond	KPOB	104.5	185.0	318.8	897.8	935.3	2 003.8	1 640.4	703.9	538.5	445.0
Treasurer's account	KWNG	..	1.2	11.8	13.7	16.4	13.9	16.5	16.9	14.2	16.2
Individual Savings Account	ZAFE	..	..	..	..	12.3	39.9	70.3	105.9	157.6	202.2
Fixed Rate Savings Bonds	ZAFF	..	..	..	..	2.8	62.1	110.1	133.6	153.1	92.1
Guaranteed Equity Bonds	JUWE	..	..	..	..	..	..	..	3.9	3.3	..
Easy Access Savings Account	C3ON	..	..	..	..	..	..	..	..	126.9	189.3
Certificates of tax deposit	KQHF	466.0	478.9	229.0	199.9	159.9	120.1	91.4	161.5	113.1	171.9
Tax reserve certificates	KQHG	..	..	..	..	..	..	..	..	−	..
Nationalised industries', etc temporary deposits	KQHH	35 263.1	51 979.3	46 835.7	41 776.9	41 089.4	56 004.0	63 127.9	55 695.6	47 757.7	25 949.5
Debt to the Bank of England	KPOC	..	..	..	..	..	..	..	..	..	..
Sterling Treasury bills (net repayment)	KQHJ	..	4 009.6	1 928.5	..	3 014.8	6 194.2	..	..	−	..
ECU Treasury bills (net repayment)	KJEG	..	..	..	..	2 492.9	..	..	..	..	..
ECU Treasury notes (net repayment)	KSPA	439.1	318.3	3.3	13.2	..	1 391.9	1 359.6	1 453.1	−	..
Ways and means (net repayment)	KQHK	..	..	5 815.4	..	..	..	..	..	−	9 760.2
Other debt: payable in sterling :											
Interest free notes	KQHL	301.3	87.6	1 215.5	850.5	246.4	458.2	1 723.3	1 393.3	990.5	300.4
Other	KQHM	..	..	..	..	..	..	..	..	..	..
Other debt : payable in external currencies	KQHN	103.6	2 661.7	2 082.7	92.0	98.1	1 835.6	2 838.1	1 960.3	47.0	46.5
Total payments	KQHO	48 708.6	83 597.4	90 593.3	72 545.0	76 725.8	111 586.0	123 551.9	113 426.1	93 313.2	70 450.9
Net borrowing	KQHP	37 688.8	27 547.9	..	..	4 997.3	..	4 884.7	11 004.4	45 590.1	23 327.3
Net repayment	KHDD	..	..	2 482.1	3 558.2	..	7 083.4	..	..	−	..

1 See chapter text.

Source: HM Treasury: 020 7270 4761

18.7 Consolidated Fund and National Loans Fund: assets and liabilities[1]
United Kingdom
At 31 March each year

£ million

		1995	1996	1997	1998	1999	2000	2001	2002	2003
CONSOLIDATED FUND										
Total estimated assets	KQIA	33 992.4	33 809.0	36 177.4	36 061.0	36 148.0	33 932.1	35 967.9	37 458.5	39 694.1
Subscriptions and contributions to international financial organisations	KQIB	5 898.1	6 470.8	6 528.9	6 660.8	7 059.7	6 903.6	7 298.4	7 564.4	8 540.3
International Bank for Reconstruction and Development	KQIC	265.2	271.6	265.0	262.5	266.0	267.1	279.2	279.0	268.2
International Finance Corporation	KQID	62.0	73.1	74.9	72.9	75.6	76.5	85.8	85.7	77.2
International Development Association	KQIE	3 005.5	3 205.8	3 372.7	3 562.2	3 733.3	3 900.0	4 134.0	4 347.8	4 567.5
African Development Bank	KQIF	141.2	148.3	162.9	180.0	199.1	215.7	229.8	259.8	293.9
Asian Development Bank	KQIG	201.5	214.6	240.4	272.5	304.6	339.3	365.5	393.3	420.4
Caribbean Development Bank	KQIH	32.6	34.2	34.1	34.6	36.8	40.7	41.9	44.0	49.1
European Investment Bank	KQII	1 876.4	2 166.6	2 036.5	1 840.7	2 083.1	1 706.6	1 767.3	1 742.1	2 419.2
European Bank for Reconstruction and Development	KPOD	146.3	189.4	175.6	164.2	179.2	170.0	187.4	197.6	239.3
Inter-American Development Bank	KQIJ	107.2	119.6	117.5	219.3	127.8	130.6	145.7	147.3	135.6
International Fund for Agricultural Development	KQIK	42.7	44.2	46.1	48.8	51.0	53.7	56.4	59.1	62.1
Multilateral Investment Guarantee Agency	KQIL	3.2	3.4	3.2	3.1	3.2	3.3	5.4	8.7	7.8
Loans from Votes	KQIP	13 599.7	12 967.0	13 684.7	14 050.0	11 546.3	3 970.3	7 015.3	9 006.1	11 097.1
Issues of public dividend capital:	KQIQ	11 467.0	12 161.1	12 424.8	13 157.1	16 238.5	21 338.3	20 083.6	19 546.2	18 982.3
Army Base Repair Organisation (ABRO)	C3QV	..	..	..	..	..	..	..	..	19.4
Royal Mint	KQIV	7.0	7.0	7.0	7.0	7.0	7.0	7.0	5.5	5.5
Welsh Development Agency	KQIY	10.9	9.8	9.8	8.8	8.6	9.1	9.1	11.0	12.7
British Shipbuilders	KQJA	1 598.3	1 598.5	1 598.5	1 598.3	50.0	21.0	21.0	21.0	21.0
Patent Office	KIAT	6.3	6.3	6.3	6.3	6.3	6.3	6.3	6.3	6.3
NHS Trusts	KIAU	9 603.1	10 173.8	10 349.7	11 078.0	14 158.7	19 216.6	19 539.2	19 184.1	18 600.7
Companies House	KIAV	15.9	15.9	15.9	15.9	15.9	15.9	15.9	15.9	15.9
Central Office of Information	KIAW	0.3	0.3	0.3	0.3	0.3	0.3	0.3	0.3	0.3
Chessington Computer Centre	KPOE	3.5	3.5	..	..	..	..	..	..	..
OGC Buying Solutions[2]	KWNH	0.1	0.4	0.4	0.4	0.4	0.4	0.4	0.4	0.4
Defence Aviation Repair Agency	JRVU	..	..	..	..	..	..	..	42.3	42.3
Defence Evaluation and Research Agency	KWNI	128.8	253.0	274.5	274.5	275.4	275.4	275.4	..	..
Defence Scientific Technology Laboratory	JRVV	..	..	..	..	..	..	..	50.4	50.4
Fire Service College	KWNJ	16.7	16.7	16.7	16.7	16.7	16.7	16.7	16.7	16.7
Forensic Science Service	GPVB	..	..	..	..	–	18.0	18.0	18.0	18.0
Hydrographic Office	GPVC	..	..	..	..	..	13.3	13.3	13.3	13.3
Land Registry	KWNK	55.4	55.4	61.5	61.5	61.5	61.5	61.5	61.5	61.5
Medicines Control Agency	KWNL	1.6	1.6	1.6	1.6	1.6	1.6	1.6	1.6	..
Meteorological Office	KZAZ	..	..	58.9	58.9	58.9	58.9	58.9	58.9	58.9
NHS Estates	GPVD	..	..	..	..	..	0.4	0.4	0.4	0.4
Registers of Scotland	KZBA	..	..	4.3	4.3	4.3	..	..	..	..
Vehicle Inspectorate	KWNM	19.1	19.1	20.3	20.3	20.3	20.3	20.3	20.3	20.3
Driving Standards Agency	LQMI	..	..	..	3.5	3.5	3.5	3.5	3.5	3.5
Ordnance Survey	GPVE	..	..	..	..	..	14.0	14.0	14.0	14.0
Queen Elizabeth II Conference Centre	LQMJ	..	..	..	0.8	0.8	0.8	0.8	0.8	0.8
Contingencies Fund - capital	KQJB	447.0	297.0	977.0	577.0	277.0	277.0	277.0	277.0	..
Balance on revenue accounts	KQJC	1 433.6	1 096.1	954.9	1 546.0	1 026.5	1 442.9	1 293.6	1 064.8	1 074.4
Privatisation receipts	KIAX	1 147.0	817.0	1 607.1	70.1	..	..	..	..	..
Total liabilities	KQJD	..	333 927.9	364 803.0	364 950.8	363 625.5	354 807.7	327 180.6	341 162.2	366 453.7
Liability to balance National Loans Fund	KQJE	286 055.9	331 164.9	362 506.5	362 582.5	361 065.3	351 626.3	324 336.7	338 550.1	362 496.5
Payment from Votes:	KQJF	64.3	63.4	62.4	61.3	60.2	59.0	57.7	56.4	54.9
Married quarters for Armed Forces	KQJG	64.3	63.4	62.4	61.3	60.2	59.0	57.7	56.4	54.9
Liability to Post Office Post-war credits outstanding and interest due - estimated	KQJI	46.0	45.9	45.9	45.9	45.9	45.8	45.8	45.8	45.8
Revenue paid over in advance of collection	KQJJ	37.0	..	28.2	13.8	177.9	259.7	301.7	635.6	1 293.7
Inland Revenue	KQJK	–	–	–	–	177.9	259.7	301.7	635.6	1 293.7
Customs and Excise	KQJL	..	..	28.2	..	..	..	..	..	..
Vehicle Excise Duty	KQJN	37.0	..	..	13.8	..	..	..	..	..
Promissory notes issued by Minister of Overseas Development	KQJQ	996.7	1 005.8	1 021.9	822.1	963.1	783.1	939.9	891.9	954.7
International Development Association	KQJR	656.5	663.2	673.6	484.0	612.3	445.6	553.1	509.7	589.4
African Development Fund	KQJS	93.2	86.2	95.3	95.2	105.6	89.1	141.6	145.5	152.3
Asian Development Bank	KQJT	–	–	–	–	–	1.9	2.5	2.4	2.3
Asian Development Fund	KQJU	140.5	127.6	136.0	120.5	105.4	87.8	78.6	73.2	68.3
Caribbean Development Bank	KQJV	1.3	1.4	1.3	1.3	1.3	1.3	1.5	1.5	1.4
Special Development Fund	KQKC	9.5	10.6	13.2	15.8	16.4	16.9	15.9	13.8	17.3
Inter-American Development Bank	KQJY	1.3	2.0	1.8	1.9	1.0	2.0	1.4	0.7	0.2

18.7

Consolidated Fund and National Loans Fund: assets and liabilities[1]
United Kingdom
At 31 March each year

£ million

		1995	1996	1997	1998	1999	2000	2001	2002	2003
Promissory notes issued by										
Minister of Overseas Development (continued)										
Fund for special operations	KQJZ	13.1	11.3	8.8	6.3	2.6	2.1	1.1	..	..
International Fund for Agricultural Development	KQKA	15.8	14.2	12.3	14.2	16.5	18.4	15.6	12.9	9.9
International Bank for Reconstruction and Development	KQKB	39.2	60.7	71.7	81.9	94.3	105.9	112.5	114.6	88.5
European Bank for Reconstruction and Development	KIAY	20.9	21.0	6.1	..	7.7	12.1	16.1	17.6	19.8
United Nations Environment Programme	KJEH	5.4	7.6	1.8	1.0	..	..	..	..	5.3
Other contributions and instalments due in respect of international subscriptions, etc	KQYX	1 499.6	1 647.9	1 138.1	1 425.2	1 313.1	1 669.2	1 174.0	955.1	1 608.1
NATIONAL LOANS FUND										
Total assets	KQKD	349 159.5	390 681.8	419 548.9	418 444.7	421 635.7	426 239.2	425 955.6	434 544.6	448 006.3
Total National Loans Fund loans outstanding	KQKE	47 496.1	46 600.9	46 746.8	46 742.6	48 513.6	49 788.8	51 037.6	50 251.4	47 719.0
Loans to Public Corporations:										
Royal Mail Group plc	KQKF	..	..	..	..	..	..	500.0	500.0	550.0
Scottish Nuclear Ltd	KQKM	194.1	96.1	..	..	..	..	..	..	..
Railtrack	KTCR	1 287.7	..	..	..	..	..	..	..	..
European Passenger Services	KTCS	99.0	761.2	..	..	..	..	..	..	..
Civil Aviation Authority	KQKQ	453.3	476.1	447.5	420.9	365.7	342.5	92.5	9.8	8.8
British Railways Board	KQKS	749.2	718.3	601.2	573.7	546.2	518.7	481.3	..	..
British Waterways Board	KQKU	18.3	18.2	18.2	18.2	18.2	18.2	16.7	16.3	14.7
New Towns - Development Corporations and Commission	KQLD	1 008.8	314.3	122.2	36.2	8.0	8.0	8.0	8.0	7.9
Scottish Homes	KQLF	397.3	395.0	392.5	259.8	190.9	179.0	161.6	149.7	138.1
Housing Corporation (England)	KQLH	869.9	926.3	848.7	4.0	4.0	3.0	3.0	2.0	2.0
Housing for Wales	KQLI	69.2	59.0	..	..	..	..	..	..	..
Land Authority for Wales	KQLL	3.2	3.2	1.3	1.3	..	..	..	..	..
Scottish Enterprise	KQLM	1.3	0.6	0.5	0.1	..	..	..	..	..
Welsh Development Agency	KQLN	0.9	1.1	1.2	1.2	0.9	0.6	0.3	0.2	0.1
Land Registry Trading Fund	KPOF	..	..	..	..	..	..	..	..	..
Development Board for Rural Wales	KQLO	8.8	7.9	4.1	4.0	4.0	4.0	4.0	4.0	4.0
Royal Mint	KQLP	–	–	–	–	–	2.0	5.0	14.8	11.3
Crown Agents	KQLS	2.0	1.9	..	..	..	..	..	..	..
Her Majesty's Stationery Office	KQLT	..	7.0	..	..	..	..	..	..	..
Urban Development Corporations	KQLU	..	..	..	..	..	..	..	..	..
Harbour Authorities	KQLV	0.8	0.7	0.6	0.5	0.4	0.2	0.1	0.1	0.1
UK Atomic Energy Authority	KQLX	147.3	141.0	..	..	..	..	..	..	..
Ordnance Survey	GPVF	..	..	..	..	..	15.5	13.9	12.3	11.0
Central Office of Information	KJEI	0.5	0.3	..	..	..	..	..	..	..
Registers of Scotland	KZBB	..	..	6.4	5.6	5.1	4.5	4.0	3.7	3.6
East of Scotland Water Authority	KZBC	..	..	163.0	229.0	288.0	283.0	268.0	258.0	248.0
North of Scotland Water Authority	KZBD	..	..	155.0	189.2	242.0	236.5	236.5	236.5	231.5
West of Scotland Water Authority	KZBE	..	..	185.0	304.9	425.6	412.4	412.4	412.4	412.4
Loans to local authorities	KQLY	40 440.7	40 969.2	42 134.0	42 951.1	44 742.7	46 099.2	47 239.1	47 093.4	44 640.3
Loans to private sector:										
Housing associations	KGVS	13.2	12.7	0.5	0.5	0.5	0.5	0.5	..	..
Loans within central government:										
Northern Ireland Exchequer	KGVW	1 666.3	1 627.4	1 602.5	1 681.1	1 611.2	1 602.0	1 533.1	1 473.9	1 380.4
Married quarters for Armed Forces	KGVX	64.3	63.4	62.4	61.3	60.2	59.0	57.7	56.4	54.9
Other assets:										
Exchange Equalisation Account - capital	KGVZ	5 550.0	2 800.0	650.0	..	..	475.0	5 680.0	831.0	30.0
Subscriptions and contributions to international financial organisations:										
International Monetary Fund	KGXE	7 172.2	7 102.6	6 241.2	5 895.6	9 048.1	9 067.4	9 496.6	9 494.5	9 293.8
Gilt-Edged Official Operations Account										
-advances outstanding	KPUF	2 500.0	2 500.0	3 000.0	2 500.0	2 500.0	..	..	..	..
-surplus not paid to the National Loans Fund	KPUH	..	..	..	141.6	190.8	..	..	..	..
Borrowing included in national debt but not brought to account by 31 March	KGXF	385.2	513.4	404.7	568.6	317.9	281.6	405.9	417.5	467.1
Debt Management Account -advances outstanding	GPVG	..	..	..	..	..	15 000.0	35 000.0	35 000.0	28 000.0
Consolidated Fund liability	KCYI	286 055.9	331 164.9	362 506.2	362 596.4	361 065.3	351 626.3	324 335.5	338 550.2	362 496.5
Total liabilities										
National Loans Fund - national debt outstanding	KCYJ	349 159.5	390 681.8	419 548.9	418 444.7	421 635.7	426 239.2	425 955.6	434 544.6	448 006.3

1 See Chapter text.
2 Formerly The Buying Agency.

Source: HM Treasury: 020 7270 4761

18.8 British government and government guaranteed marketable securities[1]
Nominal values of official and market holdings by maturity[2,3]
At 31 March each year

£ million

		1995	1996	1997	1998	1999	2000	2001	2002	2003	2004	2005
Total holdings	KQMO	232 486	262 262	290 259	297 366	291 788	290 629	285 915	278 808	292 777	321 051	355 553
Up to 5 years	KQMP	69 011	81 122	90 357	86 094	95 112	95 131	92 090	92 780	106 074	88 678	110 477
Over 5 and up to 15 years	KQMQ	101 960	111 510	125 401	131 758	124 603	116 910	120 101	106 044	101 465	131 665	124 754
Over 15 years (including undated)	KQMR	61 515	69 630	74 501	79 515	72 074	78 587	73 724	79 984	85 238	97 500	120 322
Official holdings:[3]												
Total	HHAW	6 614	7 186	6 858	6 345	6 394	6 204	8 210	7 558	10 650	9 118	6 613
Up to 5 years	HHAY	2 007	2 345	2 850	2 499	2 600	2 849	4 652	3 928	4 797	3 321	2 422
Over 5 and up to 15 years	HHAZ	3 700	3 774	3 041	2 726	2 989	2 567	3 009	2 844	4 115	4 015	2 806
Over 15 years (including undated)	HHBA	907	1 068	967	1 120	805	788	549	786	1 738	1 540	1 385
Market holdings:												
Total	HHBB	225 872	255 075	283 402	291 021	285 394	284 425	277 705	271 250	282 127	311 933	348 940
Up to 5 years	HHBD	67 004	78 777	87 508	83 595	92 512	92 282	87 438	88 852	101 277	85 357	108 055
Over 5 and up to 15 years	HHBE	98 260	107 736	122 360	129 032	121 614	114 343	117 092	103 200	97 350	127 650	121 948
Over 15 years (including undated)	HHBF	60 608	68 562	73 536	78 395	71 269	77 800	73 175	79 198	83 500	95 960	118 936

1 The government guaranteed securities of nationalised industries only. A relatively small amount of other government guaranteed securities is excluded.

2 Securities with optional redemption dates are classified according to the final redemption date. The nominal value of index-linked British Government Stock has been raised by the amount of accrued capital uplift.

3 Official holdings were changed following the introduction of the central bank sector in the UK national accounts. These holdings now principally include those of the Debt Management Office and other government departments. The Issue and Banking Departments of the Bank of England are classified within the central bank sector and are therefore part of market holdings.

Source: Office for National Statistics: 020 7533 5984

18.9 Income tax: allowances and reliefs[1]
United Kingdom

£

		1994/95	1995/96	1996/97	1997/98	1998/99	1999/00	2000/01	2001/02	2002/03	2003/04	2004/05
Personal allowances												
Personal allowance	KDZP	3 445	3 525	3 765	4 045	4 195	4 335	4 385	4 535	4 615	4 615	4 745
Married couple's (both partners under 65)[2]	KDZR	1 720	1 720	1 790	1 830	1 900	1 970	..	..	..	..	..
Age allowance:												
Personal (aged 65-74)	KSOH	4 200	4 630	4 910	5 220	5 410	5 720	5 790	5 990	6 100	6 610	6 830
Personal (aged 75 or over)	KSOI	4 370	4 800	5 090	5 400	5 600	5 980	6 050	6 260	6 370	6 720	6 950
Married couple's (either partner between 65-74 but neither partner 75 or over)[2,3]	KEDI	2 665	2 995	3 115	3 185	3 305	5 125	5 185	5 365	5 465	5 565	5 725
Married couple's (either partner 75 or over)[2]	KEIY	2 705	3 035	3 155	3 225	3 345	5 195	5 255	5 435	5 535	5 635	5 795
Minimum married couple's allowance	C58D	1 720	1 720	1 790	1 830	1 900	1 970	2 000	2 070	2 110	2 150	2 210
Income limit[4]	KEOO	14 200	14 600	15 200	15 600	16 200	16 800	17 000	17 600	17 900	18 300	18 900
Additional personal allowance[2]	KEPG	1 720	1 720	1 790	1 830	1 900	1 970	..	..	..	..	..
Widow's bereavement allowance	KEPH	1 720	1 720	1 790	1 830	1 900	1 970	..	..	..	..	..
Blind person's allowance												
Single or married (one spouse blind)	KSOJ	1 200	1 200	1 250	1 280	1 330	1 380	1 400	1 450	1 480	1 510	1 560
Married (both spouses blind)	KSOK	2 400	2 400	2 500	2 560	2 660	2 760	2 800	2 900	2 960	3 020	3 120
Life Assurance Relief												
Percentage of gross premium	KFDR	12.5 or Nil	12.5 or Nil	12.5 or Nil	12.5 or Nil	12.5 or Nil	12.5 or Nil	12.5 or Nil	12.5 or Nil	12.5 or Nil	12.5 or Nil	12.5 or Nil

1 See chapter text.
2 The allowance was restricted to 20 per cent in 1994-95, 15 per cent from 1995-96 and 10 per cent from 1999-00.
3 At least one of the partners must be aged 65 before April 2000 to be entitled to the married couple's allowance (MCA). From 2000-01 only people born before 6 April 1935 are entitled to MCA.
4 If the total income, less allowable deductions of a taxpayer aged 65 or over exceeds the limit, the age-related allowances are reduced by £1 for each £2 of income over the aged income level until the basic levels of the personal and married couple's allowances are reached.

Source: Board of Inland Revenue: 020 7147 3082

18.10 Rates of Income tax
United Kingdom

	1995/96		1996/97		1997/98		1998/99		1999/00	
	Bands of taxable income (£)[1]	Rate of tax - Percentages	Bands of taxable income (£)[1]	Rate of tax - Percentages	Bands of taxable income (£)[1]	Rate of tax - Percentages	Bands of taxable income (£)[1]	Rate of tax - Percentages	Bands of taxable income (£)[1]	Rate of tax - Percentages
Lower rate or starting rate[2]	1 - 3 200	20	1 - 3 900	20	1 - 4 100	20	1 - 4 300	20	1 - 1 500	10[4]
Basic rate	3 201 - 24 300	25[3]	3 901 - 25 500	24[4]	4 101 - 26 100	23[4]	4 301 - 27 100	23[4]	1 501 - 28 000	23[6]
Higher rate	over 24 300	40	over 25 500	40	over 26 100	40	over 27 100	40	over 28 000	40[7]

	2000/01		2001/02		2002/03		2003/04		2004/05	
	Bands of taxable income (£)[1]	Rate of tax - Percentages	Bands of taxable income (£)[1]	Rate of tax - Percentages	Bands of taxable income (£)[1]	Rate of tax - Percentages	Bands of taxable income (£)[1]	Rate of tax - Percentages	Bands of taxable income (£)[1]	Rate of tax - Percentages
Starting rate	1 - 1 520	10[5]	1 - 1 880	10[5]	1 - 1 920	10[5]	1 - 1 960	10[5]	1 - 2 020	10[5]
Basic rate	1 521 - 28 400	22[6]	1 880 - 29 400	22[6]	1 920 - 29 900	22[6]	1 960 - 30 500	22[6]	2 020 - 31 400	22[6]
Higher rate	over 28 400	40[7]	over 29 400	40[7]	over 29 900	40[7]	over 30 500	40[7]	over 31 400	40[7]

1 Taxable income is defined as gross income for income tax purposes less any allowances and reliefs available at the taxpayer's marginal rate.
2 In 1999/00 the starting rate replaced the lower rate.
3 The basic rate of tax on dividend income is 20%.
4 The basic rate of tax on dividends and savings income is 20%.
5 The starting rate also applies to savings and dividends.
6 The basic rate of tax on dividends is 10% and savings income is 20%
7 The higher rate of tax on dividends is 32.5%.

Source: Board of Inland Revenue: 020 7147 3082

18.11 Rateable values[1]
England and Wales
At 1 April each year

		1995	1996	1997	1998	1999	2000	2001	2002	2003	2004	2005
Number of properties (Thousands)												
Commercial	KMIN	1 223	1 228	1 225	1 223	1 219	1 223	1 230	1 234	1 236	1 239	1 300
Shops and cafes	KMIO	562	497	491	488	484	478	476	473	469	466	462
Offices	KMIP	252	255	255	257	258	261	269	273	279	284	287
Other	KMIQ	409	476	479	478	477	484	485	487	488	490	551
On-licensed premises	KMIR	60	59	59	59	60	61	61	60	60	60	66
Entertainment and recreational:	KMIS	87	87	87	81	80	79	79	80	80	80	78
Cinemas	KMIT	1	1	1	1	1	1	1	1	1	1	1
Theatres and music-halls	KMIU	1	1	1	1	1	1	1	1	1	1	1
Other	KMIV	86	85	86	80	79	76	76	77	77	78	76
Public utility	KMIW	9	8	8	9	9	8	8	8	8	8	8
Educational and cultural	KMIX	41	41	41	41	41	41	42	42	42	43	45
Miscellaneous	KMIY	56	55	55	56	61	67	70	70	72	74	74
Industrial	KMIZ	248	249	249	250	250	250	251	250	250	250	252
Total	KMIH	1 723	1 726	1 725	1 719	1 720	1 729	1 740	1 745	1 749	1 754	1 756
Value of assessments (£ million)												
Commercial	KMHG	19 626	19 822	19 859	19 733	19 652	26 320	27 255	27 622	27 713	27 878	34 679
Shops and cafes	KMHH	7 780	6 094	5 959	5 860	5 840	6 801	6 972	6 953	6 863	6 845	8 257
Offices	KMHI	5 587	5 630	5 641	5 624	5 575	8 625	9 191	9 388	9 555	9 591	10 840
Other	KMHJ	6 260	8 098	8 259	8 249	8 237	10 894	11 092	11 281	11 295	11 441	15 583
On-licensed premises	KMHK	968	969	970	980	997	1 311	1 347	1 345	1 334	1 320	1 667
Entertainment and recreational	KMHL	1 009	1 018	1 033	1 040	1 045	1 310	1 369	1 430	1 416	1 362	1 467
Cinemas	KMHM	32	32	36	39	45	79	92	104	106	96	117
Theatres and music-halls	KMHN	21	21	21	21	20	24	25	26	26	26	34
Other	KMHO	956	965	975	979	980	1 207	1 252	1 300	1 284	1 240	1 316
Public utility	KMHP	3 455	3 469	3 488	3 380	3 361	3 828	3 411	3 460	3 444	3 410	3 680
Educational and cultural	KMHQ	1 873	1 883	1 894	1 773	1 672	1 829	1 872	1 902	1 895	1 904	2 359
Miscellaneous	KMHR	1 429	1 500	1 494	1 464	1 439	2 142	2 172	2 220	2 218	2 022	2 582
Industrial	KMHS	5 550	5 584	5 561	5 540	5 463	6 249	6 202	6 157	6 034	5 935	6 651
Total	KMHA	33 912	34 245	34 299	33 909	33 649	42 985	43 626	44 136	44 053	43 831	51 419

1 See chapter text.

Source: Board of Inland Revenue: 020 7438 6314

18.12 Local authorities: gross loan debt outstanding[1]
At 31 March each year

£ billion

		2001	2002	2003	2004	2005
United Kingdom						
Total debt	KQBR	52.2	52.2	51.2	50.5	52.9
Public Works Loan Board	KQBS	47.1	46.9	44.6	41.3	42.4
Northern Ireland Consolidated Fund	KQBT	0.3	0.3	0.3	0.3	0.3
Other debt	KQBU	4.8	5.0	6.3	8.8	10.5
England						
Total debt	C3OO	38.5	38.3	38.2	37.7	40.1
of which Public Works Loan Board	C3OP	34.8	34.4	33.4	31.1	32.2
Wales						
Total debt	C3OQ	3.5	3.6	3.7	3.6	3.7
of which Public Works Loan Board	C3OR	3.2	3.3	3.3	3.1	3.1
Scotland						
Total debt	KQBX	9.9	10.0	8.8	8.8	8.7
of which Public Works Loan Board	KQBY	*9.1*	*9.3*	*7.9*	*7.1*	*6.8*
Northern Ireland						
Total debt	KQBZ	0.3	0.3	0.3	0.3	0.3
of which Northern Ireland Consolidated Fund	KQBT	0.3	0.3	0.3	0.3	0.3

1 The sums shown exclude inter-authority loans.

Sources: Department for Communities and Local Government: 020 7944 4176;
Public Works Loan Board: 020 7862 6610;
Department of Finance and Personnel for Northern Ireland: 028 9185 8130

18.13 Revenue expenditure of local authorities

£ million

	2002/03 outturn	2003/04 outturn	2004/05 budget	2005/06 budget
England				
Education[1]	28 405	31 201	32 510	34 960
Transport	3 407	4 495	5 363	4 984
of which:				
Highways	1 948	2 341	2 203	2 204
Public transport	1 490	1 397	3 159	3 160
Social Services[2]	12 931	14 817	15 585	16 874
Housing (excluding HRA)[3]	7 504	8 670	12 590	13 763
Cultural, environmental and planning	7 420	7 990	8 137	8 772
of which:				
Cultural	1 921	2 680	2 819	2 820
Environmental	3 786	3 457	3 786	3 787
Planning and development	1 217	1 428	1 532	1 533
Police	8 246	9 192	9 739	10 313
Fire	1 698	1 844	2 029	2 110
Courts	356	431	398	57
Central services	2 311	2 948	2 941	3 457
Other	366	141	582	156
Net current expenditure	72 645	81 729	89 874	95 446
Capital financing	1 922	2 209	2 544	2 721
Capital Expenditure charged to Revenue Account	694	936	524	868
Interest receipts	-851	-765	-717	-834
Other non-current expenditure[4]		2 508	3 038	2 800
Specific grants outside Aggregate External Finance (AEF)	-11 019	-11 897	-15 649	-17 274
Revenue expenditure	65 898	75 250	79 376	83 995
Specific and special grants inside AEF	-8 901	-13 447	-12 240	13 014
Net revenue expenditure	56 996	61 803	67 136	70 980
Other adjustments	-30	-52	-2	12
Use of reserves	177	1 266	-573	-510
Budget requirement	57 144	63 016	66 561	70 481
SSA reduction grant	-	-	-	-
Police grant	-3 808	-4 079	-4 168	-4 353
Revenue support grant	-19 889	-24 215	-26 964	-26 663
Central Support Protection Grant	-	-	-	-
Council Tax Benefit Subsid Limitation Scheme	-	-	-	-
Redistributed business rates	-16 632	-15 611	-15 004	-18 004
General Greater London Authority Grant	-28	-36	-36	-37
Other items	-138	-130	-90	-104
Council tax requirement	16 648	18 946	20 299	21 320
Scotland				
Net revenue expenditure on general fund	8 565	9 283	9 847	..

18.13 Revenue expenditure of local authorities
continued

£ million

	2002/03 outturn	2003/04 outturn	2004/05 outturn	2005/06 budget
Wales[5]				
Education	1 738.7	1 920.7	2 011.3	2 100.9
Personal social services	856.6	987.3	1 069.2	1 114.5
Council fund housing, including housing benefit[6]	329.6	371.2	632.4	679.1
Local environmental services[7]	227.6	262.2	289.6	331.6
Roads and transport	217.3	240.8	256.7	260.2
Libraries, culture, heritage, sport and recreation	207.6	217.5	239.4	169.6
Planning, economic development and community development	69.8	86.1	98.6	112.9
Magistrates', coroners' and other courts[8]	25.7	28.8	30.3	2.8
Council tax benefit and administration and local tax collection[9]	33.9	36.0	30.0	28.0
Debt financing costs: counties	238.0	250.8	258.8	288.2
Central administrative and other revenue expenditure: counties[10,11]	182.2	201.7	191.2	294.0
Total county and county borough council expenditure	4 127.1	4 603.2	5 107.3	5 381.8
Police operational expenditure	451.6	485.5	500.7	554.0
Other police expenditure[10]	8.1	24.9	37.5	14.7
Total police expenditure	459.8	510.4	538.2	568.7
Fire operational expenditure	106.4	107.3	117.6	130.9
Other fire expenditure[10]	2.6	8.2	6.9	5.2
Total fire expenditure	109.0	115.5	124.5	136.1
National park operational expenditure	10.7	11.3	13.6	14.8
Other national park expenditure[10]	2.1	2.5	2.1	2.4
Total national park expenditure	12.8	13.8	15.7	17.2
Gross revenue expenditure	4 708.6	5 242.8	5 785.7	6 103.8
less specific and special government grants (except council tax benefit grant)	-778.8	-1 004.7	-1 380.8	-1 366.3
Net revenue expenditure	3 929.8	4 238.2	4 404.9	4 737.5
Putting to (+)/drawing from (-) reserves	27.8	23.3	5.7	-69.5
Buget requirement	3 957.6	4 261.4	4 410.6	4668.0
Plus discretionary non-domestic rate relief	1.9	2.2	2.2	2.5
less revenue support grant	-2 340.5	-2 533.4	-2 591.0	-2 751.4
less police grant	-196.1	-209.2	-225.8	-235.2
less re-distributed non-domestic rates income	-643.0	-660.0	-672.0	-672.0
less transitional grant	-4.8	..	..	..
Council tax requirement	775.7	861.0	924.1	1 012.0
of which:				
Paid by council tax benefit grant from the Department for Work and Pensions	120.0	133.0	155.0	156.6
Paid directly by council tax payers	655.6	727.9	769.1	855.4

1 Includes mandatory student awards and inter-authority education recoupment.
2 Includes supported employment.
3 Includes mandatory rent allowances and rent rebates.
4 Includes:
(i) Gross expenditure on council tax benefit.
(ii) Expenditure on council tax reduction scheme.
(iii) Discretionary (non-domestic) rate relief.
(iv) Flood defence payments to the Environment Agency
(v) Bad debt provision.
5 Service expenditure is shown excluding that financed by sales, fees and charges, but including specific grants.
6 Includes rent rebates granted to HRA tenants for 2004-5 onwards (previously part of the housing revenue account, 100% funded by the Department for Work and Pensions. Includes housing benefit and private sector housing costs such as provision for the homeless. Excludes council owned housing.

7 Includes cemetery and crematoria, community safety, environmental health, food safety and waste collection / disposal.
8 Responsibility for magistrates courts transferred to the Department for Constitutional Affairs on 1 April 2005.
9 Net of council tax benefit grant.
10 Includes central administrative costs of corporate management, democratic representation and certain costs such as those relating to back-year or additional pension contributions which should not be allocated to individual services. The figure also includes capital expenditure charged to the revenue account and is net of any interest expected to accrue on balances.
11 The figure includes agricultural services, central services to the public such as birth registration, coastal and flood defence, community councils and licensing.
Sources: Department for Communities and Local Government: 020 7944 4158; Scottish Executive, Statistical Support for Local Government: 0131 244 7033; National Assembly for Wales: 029 2082 5355

18.14 Financing of revenue expenditure
England and Wales
Years ending 31 March

£ million

		1995/96	1996/97	1997/98	1998/99	1999/00	2000/01	2001/02	2002/03	2003/04	2004[1]/05	2005[1]/06
England[2]												
Revenue expenditure												
Cash £m	KRTN	44 827	46 532	47 256	50 189	53 651	57 329	61 952	65 906	75 250	79 376	83 995
Government grants												
Cash £m	KRTO	23 335	23 003	23 840	25 291	26 421	27 809	31 469	32 634	41 404	43 408	44 067
Percentage of revenue expenditure	KRTP	52	49	50	50	49	49	50	50	55	55	52
Non- domestic rates												
Cash £m	KRTQ	11 361	12 743	12 034	12 531	13 619	15 407	15 144	16 639	15 611	15 004	18 004
Percentage of revenue expenditure	KRTR	25	27	25	25	25	27	24	25	21	19	21
Community charges and council taxes												
Cash £m	KRTS	9 777	10 461	11 241	12 332	13 278	14 200	15 246	16 648	18 946	20 299	21 320
Percentage of revenue expenditure	KRTT	22	22	24	25	25	25	25	25	25	26	25
Wales[3]												
Gross revenue expenditure	ZBXH	2 932	2 990	3 121	3 246	3 424	3 605	4 350	4 709	5 243	5 786	6 104
General government grants[4]	ZBXI	1 873	2 001	1 957	2 009	2 093	2 234	2 345	2 541	2 743	2 817	2 987
Specific government grants[5]	ZBXG	70	73	75	84	80	94	601	779	1 005	1 381	1 366
Share of redistributed non-domestic rates	ZBXJ	520	459	584	612	656	638	697	643	660	672	672
Community charge/council tax income[6]	ZBXK	394	449	483	542	596	670	716	776	861	924	1 012
Other[7]	ZBXL	75	9	22	..	−1	−31	−10	−30	−25	−8	67

1 Budget estimates.
2 Produced on a non-Financial Reporting Standard 17 (FRS17) basis.
3 Gross revenue expenditure is total local authority expenditure on services, plus capital charges, but net of any income from sales, fees, and charges and other non-grant sources. It includes expenditure funded by specific grants within and outside aggregate external finance (AEF). The figures have been adjusted to account for FRS17 pension costs.
4 Includes all unhypothecated grants, namely revenue support grant, police grant, council tax reduction scheme grant, transitional grant and the adjustment to reverse the transfer.
5 Comprises specific and supplementary grants, excluding police grant.
6 This includes community council precepts, and income covered by charge/council tax benefit grant, but excludes council tax reduction scheme
7 This includes use of, or contributors to, local authority reserves and other minor adjustments.

Sources: Department for Communities and Local Government: 020 7944 4158;
National Assembly for Wales: 029 2082 5355

18.15 Local authority capital expenditure and receipts
England

Final outturn: Years ending 31 March

£ million

		1999 /00	2000 /01	2001 /02	2002 /03	2003 /04	2004[1] /05
Expenditure[2]							
Education	KRUD	1 139	1 533	2 064	2 287	2 780	3 087
Personal Social Services	KRUE	134	156	158	199	260	285
Transport	KRUC	1 086	1 410	1 877	2 461	2 552	2 906
Housing	KRUB	2 406	2 779	3 110	3 828	3 485	3 987
Arts and libraries	GEKZ	195	194	213	208	196	227
Agriculture and fisheries	GELA	48	45	38	65	72	66
Sport and recreation	KRUH	241	291	314	307	263	305
Other[3]	GELB	1 299	1 341	1 513	1 631	2 056	2 725
Fire and civil defence	GELC	50	46	62	72	68	81
Police and probation	GELD	286	291	359	408	513	561
Magistrates courts	GELE	28	22	33	40	37	46
Total	KRUR	6 912	8 109	9 741	11 508	12 282	14 276
Receipts[4]							
Education	KRUT	102	119	146	233	221	210
Personal social services	KRUV	51	63	71	75	74	75
Transport	KRUU	105	98	138	107	92	101
Housing	KRUS	2 249	2 441	2 245	3 474	3 622	3 193
Arts and libraries	GELF	2	19	19	22	5	10
Agriculture and fisheries	GELG	48	44	42	49	53	45
Sport and recreation	KRUX	8	12	12	21	7	11
Other[3]	GELH	960	600	801	975	1 145	931
Fire and civil defence	GELI	5	8	7	10	18	6
Police and probation	GELJ	118	104	86	70	78	71
Magistrates court	GELK	2	4	12	4	6	8
Total	KRVB	3 651	3 512	3 579	5 040	5 322	4 661

1 Provisional outturn. The figures shown here have been adjusted based on historical differences between provisional and final outturn
2 Includes aquisition of share or loan capital.
3 Environmental services, consumer protection and employment services.
4 Includes disposal of share or loan capital and disposal of other investments.

Source: Department for Communities and Local Government: 020 7944 4076

18.16 Capital expenditure and income
England

£ million

	Expenditure			Income				
	Expenditure on land works, etc	Capital assigned to repayment of debt	All expenditure	Loans	Government grants	Miscellaneous	All income	Gross debt at end of year
Financial year								
	KRVC	KRVD	KRVE	KRVF	KRVG	KRVH	KRVI	KRVJ
1972/73	2 418	213	2 631	2 030	122	531	2 682	16 105
1973/74	3 286	225	3 511	2 781	143	619	3 544	18 300
1974/75[1]	3 712	127	3 839	3 209	128	498	3 835	18 884
1975/76	3 917	198	4 115	3 285	177	647	4 109	21 930
1976/77	3 783	312	4 095	3 097	249	803	4 149	24 534
1977/78	3 487	352	3 839	2 677	255	981	3 913	26 282
1978/79	3 621	390	4 011	2 627	351	1 139	4 117	27 103
1979/80	4 249	331	4 580	2 992	385	1 367	4 745	30 187
1980/81	4 476	413	4 889	2 900	492	1 864	5 256	32 076
1981/82	4 061	563	4 623	2 527	470	2 177	5 174	34 069
1982/83	5 090	634	5 724	3 358	416	3 100	6 874	36 231
1983/84	5 890	562	6 452	3 538	379	3 294	7 211	38 698
1984/85	6 352	515	6 867	3 381	327	3 283	6 991	40 554
1985/86	5 748	348	6 096	3 008	360	3 239	6 607	40 138
1986/87	5 899	328	6 227	2 814	388	3 878	7 081	43 033
1987/88	6 091	486	6 577	2 953	297	4 286	7 536	44 904
1988/89	7 166	658	7 824	2 985	270	6 122	9 376	47 295
1989/90	9 590	474	10 064	2 919	440	6 110	9 469	48 695

	Gross capital expenditure	Income					Capital receipts set aside[2]	Credit ceiling[3]	Provision for credit liabilities[3]
		Credit approvals used	Government grants	Capital receipts	Other income	Total income			
Financial year									
At 1 April 1990	-	-	-	-	-	-	4 241	42 167	4 241
	KRVK	KRVL	KRVM	KRVN	KRVO	KRVP	KRVQ	KRVR	KRVS
1990/91	6 869	2 786	907	3 165	542	7 400	2 022	41 125	5 677
1991/92	6 572	3 140	1 041	2 251	674	7 106	1 353	41 234	6 502
1992/93	6 567	3 229	1 210	2 110	619	7 168	908	37 051	6 282
1993/94	7 124	2 948	1 279	3 310	651	8 188	356	37 941	6 041
1994/95	6 950	2 722	1 176	2 458	724	7 080	1 409	37 673	6 921
1995/96	6 910	2 264	1 484	1 966	1 278	6 992	1 160	37 103	7 677
1996/97	6 419	2 120	1 388	2 183	1 132	6 823	1 039	37 261	8 172
1997/98	6 298	2 099	1 262	2 349	1 129	6 839	1 186	36 711	7 540
1998/99	6 630	2 334	1 160	2 662	1 413	7 569	1 130	36 782	7 108
1999/00	6 912	2 301	1 161	3 651	1 487	8 600	1 483	36 364	7 201
2000/01	8 109	3 216	1 298	3 512	2 219	10 245	1 642	36 628	7 231
2001/02	9 741	2 551	2 027	3 579	2 994	11 151	1 403	36 732	7 081
2002/03	11 508	3 216	2 474	5 040	2 858	13 588	1 922	36 608	6 940
2003/04	12 282	3 909	2 642	5 322	3 852	15 725	2 161	37 511	6 774

1 Reorganisation of local government in April 1974 transferred responsibility for various services to regional health and water authorities.
2 Excluding Social Housing Grant and European Regional Development Fund (ERDF) grants.
3 At end of year.

Source: Department for Communities and Local Government: 020 7944 4076

18.17 Expenditure of local authorities
Scotland
Year ending 31 March

£ thousand

		1995/96	1996/97	1997/98	1998/99	1999/00	2000/01	2001/02	2002/03	2003/04	2004/05
Out of revenue:[1] Total	KQTA	9 690 424	9 196 125	9 566 936	10 033 985	10 439 999	10 924 634	11 553 927	12 858 533	13 658 834	14 527 867
General Fund Services:	KQTB	7 324 381	7 151 759	6 679 396	7 021 038	7 429 626	7 884 168	8 428 217	9 290 268	10 139 679	10 964 598
Education	KQTC	2 654 158	2 629 961	2 512 725	2 649 170	2 855 945	3 037 780	3 283 827	3 533 853	3 872 786	4 180 675
Libraries, museums and galleries	KQTD	149 427	138 483	121 387	124 648	131 696	134 174	138 318	152 308	160 540	161 650
Social work	KQTE	1 222 693	1 289 928	1 315 387	1 394 142	1 519 191	1 632 843	1 793 732	2 173 752	2 400 652	2 621 134
Law, order and protective services	KQTF	866 567	816 315	931 795	952 940	1 006 000	1 047 034	1 088 791	1 130 693	1 226 067	1 306 085
Roads and Transport[2]	KQTG	676 116	716 570	440 712	546 945	527 018	564 738	506 326	601 454	611 721	635 329
Environmental services	KQTH	351 689	329 674	343 565	349 413	373 050	393 333	414 975	484 177	525 556	581 220
Planning	KQTI	226 073	210 827	163 380	179 078	198 285	194 771	223 414	265 315	282 572	299 182
Leisure and recreation	KQTJ	451 952	426 422	364 853	368 023	375 579	387 115	401 904	426 495	472 120	494 237
Other services	KQTL	591 766	562 462	456 219	430 790	435 155	465 612	572 136	515 661	585 425	681 288
Other general fund expenditure[3]	KQTM	133 940	31 117	29 373	25 889	7 707	26 768	4 794	6 560	2 240	3 798
Housing	KQTN	1 924 930	2 000 684	1 658 935	1 754 686	1 821 380	1 886 189	1 954 444	2 224 209	2 295 005	2 459 146
Trading services:	KQTO	575 053	74 799	75 976	79 644	87 321	80 355	61 899	74 062	92 782	106 445
Water supply	KQTP	274 773	..	..	..	..	..	..	..	..	..
Sewerage	KQTQ	233 525	..	..	..	..	..	..	..	..	..
Passenger transport	KQTR	794	2 849	1 524	121	336	162	343	427	441	282
Ferries	KQTS	7 744	6 831	7 512	8 930	9 709	10 005	9 650	11 493	11 768	13 759
Harbours, docks and piers	KQTT	15 301	13 482	12 884	15 697	15 923	13 604	10 912	12 222	13 405	12 407
Road bridges	KQTV	11 755	12 759	16 064	16 408	8 231	8 606	6 914	7 267	11 235	13 276
Slaughterhouses	KQTW	1 000	794	850	228	4	..	..	..	..	..
Markets	KQTX	10 336	14 278	13 479	13 161	14 106	23 844	16 657	17 995	14 824	15 353
Other trading services	KQTY	19 825	23 806	23 663	25 099	39 012	24 134	17 423	24 658	41 109	51 368
Loan charges:[4] Total	KQTZ	1 451 179	1 121 448	1 126 637	1 152 728	1 109 379	1 100 690	1 114 161	1 269 994	1 131 368	997 678
Allocated to :											
General Fund services	KMHV	710 801	639 380	651 982	710 371	701 515	708 822	739 351	738 870	772 852	772 648
Housing	KMHW	504 162	475 507	471 274	438 556	402 936	386 512	369 943	525 201	348 180	212 440
Trading services	KMHX	236 216	6 561	3 381	3 801	4 928	5 356	4 867	5 923	10 336	12 590
On capital works:[5] Total	KQUA	1 528 167	889 572	813 900	815 981	816 473	802 672	929 631	972 049	1 052 310	1 264 031
General Fund Services:	KQUB	767 795	540 127	540 096	541 769	557 119	538 843	610 485	662 869	767 122	1 006 150
Education	KQUC	114 128	101 898	112 753	125 341	136 508	127 781	143 268	157 439	172 227	199 387
Libraries, museums and galleries	KQUD	16 757	11 602	9 974	13 231	10 261	5 834	8 683	19 018	12 043	24 796
Social work	KQUE	30 298	20 658	19 660	22 554	22 097	21 539	31 359	30 116	31 966	33 450
Law, order and protective services	KQUF	35 847	41 326	37 701	37 727	37 132	35 761	39 901	53 268	65 477	65 154
Roads and Transport	KQUG	187 988	116 881	108 227	113 954	108 500	117 485	147 975	147 357	200 278	258 071
Environmental services	KQUH	14 580	10 226	21 193	18 397	14 936	17 944	16 396	17 957	20 567	40 773
Planning	KQUI	103 221	51 182	69 648	50 854	52 045	47 684	33 312	40 241	36 496	61 544
Leisure and recreation	KQUJ	57 243	36 232	29 692	40 926	52 365	44 516	39 240	50 558	71 486	74 116
Administrative buildings and equipment	KQUK	14 693	40 014	45 374	35 107	35 824	34 633	53 189	68 438	48 896	64 414
Other services	KQUL	193 040	110 108	85 814	83 678	87 451	85 666	97 162	78 477	107 686	184 445
Housing	KQUM	517 593	345 713	270 005	268 135	255 019	255 189	300 054	284 418	261 715	241 107
Trading Services:	KQUN	242 779	3 732	3 799	6 077	4 335	8 640	19 092	24 762	23 473	16 774
Water supply	KQUO	107 064	..	..	..	..	..	..	..	..	..
Sewerage	KQUP	131 684	..	..	..	..	..	..	..	..	..
Ferries	KQUR	355	521	770	268	1 030	23	467	1	111	608
Harbours, docks and piers	KQUS	1 218	934	1 175	1 626	1 389	6 192	15 898	20 361	19 503	12 024
Airports	KQUT	763	1 149	439	..	..	607	663	1 031	609	572
Road bridges	KQUU	805	277	973	2 791	600	964	882	2 386	2 395	442
Slaughterhouses	KQUV	63	112	69	54	12	..	40	116	82	–
Other trading services	KMHY	827	739	373	1 338	1 304	854	1 142	867	773	3 128

1 Gross expenditure *less* inter-authority and inter-account transfers.
2 Including general fund support for transport (LA and NON-LA).
3 General fund contributions to Housing and Trading services (excluding transport), are also included in the expenditure figures for these services. From 1996/97 water and sewerage are excluded from other general fund expenditure.

4 From 1997/98 loan charges are not included within individual service totals.
5 Expenditure out of loans, government grants and other capital receipts.

Source: Scottish Executive, Statistical Support for Local Government: 0131 244 7033

18.18 Income of local authorities: classified according to source
Scotland
Year ending 31 March   £ thousand

		1994/95	1995/96	1996/97	1997/98	1998/99	1999/00	2000/01	2001/02	2002/03	2003/04	2004/05
Revenue account												
Rates[1]	KQXA	1 198 575	1 310 721	1 313 531	1 326 129	1 437 646	1 440 522	1 662 691	1 553 926	1 718 104	1 804 423	1 895 941
Council tax	KPUC	918 502	976 465	9 681 531	70 405	1 146 366	1 193 693	1 273 316	1 363 399	1 459 212	1 532 071	1 614 808
Government grants												
Revenue Support Grant	KQXC	3 741 567	3 716 567	3 649 694	3 520 461	3 483 815	3 537 043	3 440 842	3 935 328	4 557 867	5 037 140	5 266 054
Rate rebate grant	KQXG	39 860	4 456	496	..	..	..	..	..	..	..	..
Council tax rebate grants	KPUD	186 219	193 937	226 132	260 424	274 940	275 789	279 459	285 131	293 606	307 733	344 899
Other grants and subsidies	KQXI	1 179 327	1 236 160	1 347 706	1 480 890	1 642 045	1 778 216	1 891 839	2 061 297	2 141 543	2 479 311	2 823 820
Sales	KQXJ	59 182	64 284	59 059	46 874	39 595	43 660	49 826	..	..	..	..
Fees and charges[2]	KQXK	1 471 320	1 528 270	1 539 611	1 625 952	1 668 223	1 682 385	1 776 455	1 789 428	1 954 337	1 785 672	1 845 161
Other income[3]	KQXL	209 819	207 005	238 985	290 427	324 932	398 894	453 458	490 574	712 423	515 897	709 226
Capital account												
Sale of fixed assets	KQXM	529 528	500 838	499 143	327 569	335 037	303 582	149 504	165 016	207 388	222 844	355 069
Revenue contributions to capital	KQXP	134 156	197 606	119 641	149 423	204 982	213 564	210 912	147 760	239 778	212 533	219 593
Transfer from special funds	KMHZ	10 679	9 035	2 652	36 929	26 959	125 365	27 317	37 087	39 650	52 619	82 991
Other receipts[4]	KMGV	38 736	29 571	45 067	32 118	45 028	39 014	45 351	90 360	75 846	114 745	130 575

1 Excluding government grants towards rate rebates and domestic element of revenue support grant (RSG). Including domestic water rate receipts.

2 From 2001-02 onwards, fees & charges incorporates sales.
3 From 1996-97 Other Income includes income from Health Boards and Trusts, Other Public Bodies and Interest on Revenue Balances.
4 Figures include public sector contributions from 2001-02 onwards.

Source: Scottish Executive, Statistical Support for Local Government: 0131 244 7033

18.19 Income of local authorities from government grants[1]
Scotland
Year ending 31 March   £ thousand

		1995/96	1996/97	1997/98	1998/99	1999/00	2000/01	2001/02	2002/03	2003/04	2004/05
General fund services	KQYA	468 660	487 734	557 536	690 569	818 537	935 452	1 032 591	952 692	1 029 338	1 207 912
Education	KQYB	17 186	18 324	61 960	92 368	225 668	324 340	380 726	251 333	217 743	287 226
Libraries, museums and galleries	KQYC	123	137	326	627	507	634	1 137	5 359	1 517	763
Social work	KQYD	50 230	57 576	59 892	62 167	71 611	78 611	86 533	114 591	205 229	240 665
Law, order and protective services	KQYE	312 812	330 767	359 811	366 961	382 246	401 485	423 636	445 275	476 681	512 501
Roads and Transport[2]	KQYF	4 788	403	237	97 649	68 429	57 702	49 900	57 664	27 280	35 038
Environmental services	KQYG	42	119	159	89	71	301	2 272	5 407	18 120	39 971
Planning and Economic Development	KQYH	3 030	3 337	4 885	2 695	4 311	4 375	20 351	19 434	21 517	20 767
Leisure and recreation	KQYI	1 830	1 509	1 856	1 509	1 491	2 377	3 322	2 968	3 732	5 830
Other services	KQYK	78 619	75 562	68 410	66 504	64 203	65 627	64 714	50 661	57 519	65 151
Housing	KQYL	762 172	856 435	920 700	948 232	959 276	956 239	1 028 529	1 188 626	1 449 616	1 614 976
Trading services	KQYM	4 557	..	..	..	403	148	177	225	357	932
Water supply	KQYN	4 459	..	..	..	..	..	..	..	..	..
Other trading services	KQYP	98	..	..	..	403	148	177	225	357	932
Grants not allocated to specific services[3]	KMGY	3 721 023	3 650 190	3 520 461	3 483 815	3 537 043	3 440 842	3 935 328	4 557 867	5 037 140	5 266 054
Total	KMGZ	4 956 412	4 994 362	4 998 697	5 122 616	5 315 259	5 332 681	5 996 625	6 699 410	7 516 451	8 089 874

1 Including grants for capital works.
2 The significant increase in 1998/99 is due to the different reporting of a grant in aid of expenditure on rail passenger services in the Strathclyde Passenger Transport area.
3 Revenue support grant, community charge grant and community charge rebate grants.

Source: Scottish Executive, Statistical Support for Local Government: 0131 244 7033

18.20 Expenditure of local authorities
Northern Ireland
Years ending 31 March

£ thousand

		1993/94	1994/95	1995/96	1996/97	1997/98	1998/99	1999/00	2000/01	2001/02	2002[1]/03	2003[2]/04
Libraries, museums and art galleries	KQVB	5 647	7 214	8 481	10 956	13 928	14 571	19 900	23 097	24 181	32 728	29 916
Environmental health services:												
Refuse collection and disposal	KQVC	39 952	42 109	41 284	52 267	56 246	56 360	62 226	65 289	73 336	90 148	94 614
Public baths	KQVD	1 562	1 648	1 703	1 838	2 585	2 634	1 750	1 724	1 423	..	..
Parks, recreation grounds, etc	KQVE	91 258	101 319	100 418	111 884	115 302	118 396	158 304	170 999	184 406	194 224	193 265
Other sanitary services	KQVF	32 074	34 582	35 706	39 545	39 682	42 923	44 214	45 552	48 784	52 075	55 402
Housing (grants and small dwellings acquisition)	KQVG	873	553	472	489	545	358	37	28	27	12	21
Trading services:												
Cemeteries	KQVI	5 352	5 984	5 489	5 120	5 626	5 887	5 973	6 151	6 538	7 208	7 936
Other trading services (including markets, fairs and harbours)	KQVJ	7 123	6 587	4 254	8 672	7 016	10 779	9 366	7 209	7 769	18 281	17 463
Miscellaneous	KQVK	46 825	51 741	54 987	63 792	63 375	161 790	86 649	89 881	98 244	85 688	91 365
Total expenditure	KQVA	230 666	251 737	252 794	294 563	304 305	413 698	388 419	409 930	444 708	480 364	489 983
Total loan charges	KQVL	19 194	20 797	21 122	24 363	34 823	26 413	..	..	..	..	..

1 Includes estimates for Fermanagh district council.
2 Includes estimates for Down district council.

Source: Department of the Environment for Northern Ireland: 028 9054 0711

External trade and investment

Chapter 19

External trade and investment

External trade

(Table 19.1 and 19.3 to 19.6)

The statistics in this section are on a Balance of Payments (BoP) basis; compiled from information provided to HM Revenue and Customs by importers and exporters on an Overseas Trade Statistics (OTS) basis, which values exports 'f.o.b.'(free on board) and imports 'c.i.f.' (including insurance and freight). In addition to deducting these freight costs and insurance premiums from the OTS figures, coverage adjustments are made to convert the OTS data to a BoP basis. Adjustments are also made to the level of all exports and EU imports to take account of estimated under-recording. The adjustments are set out and described in the annual ONS *Pink Book (United Kingdom Balance of Payments)*. These adjustments are made to conform to the definitions in the 5th edition of the *IMF Balance of Payments Manual.*

Aggregate estimates of trade in goods, seasonally adjusted and on a BoP basis are published monthly in the ONS First Release UK Trade. More detailed figures are available from the ONS Databank and are also published in the *Monthly Review of External Trade Statistics* (Business Monitor MM24). Detailed figures for EU and non-EU trade on an OTS basis are published by The Stationery Office in Overseas Trade Statistics of the United Kingdom.

A fuller description of how trade statistics are compiled can be found in *Statistics on Trade in Goods* (Government Statistical Service Methodological Series).

Overseas Trade Statistics

HM Revenue and Customs provide accurate and up to date information via the website www.uktradeinfo.com. They also produce the publication *Overseas Trade Statistics*.

Import penetration and export sales ratios

(Table 19.2)

The ratios were first introduced in the August 1977 edition of *Economic Trends* in an article 'The Home and Export Performance of United Kingdom Industries'. The article described the conceptual and methodological problems involved in measuring such variables as import penetration.

The industries are grouped according to the 1992 Standard Industrial Classification. The four different ratios are defined as follows:

Ratio 1:   percentage ratio of imports to home demand

Ratio 2:   percentage ratio of imports to (home demand *plus* exports)

Ratio 3:   percentage ratio of exports to total manufacturers' sales

Ratio 4:   percentage ratio of exports to (total manufacturers' sales *plus* imports).

Home demand is defined as total manufacturers' sales plus imports minus exports. *This is only an approximate estimate as different sources are used for the total manufacturers' sales and the import and export data. Total manufacturers' sales are determined by the ProdCom inquiry and import and export data are provided by HM Revenue and Customs.*

Ratio 1 is commonly used to describe the import penetration of the home market. Allowance is made for the extent of a domestic industry's involvement in export markets by using Ratio 2; this reduces as exports increase.

Similarly Ratio 3 is the measure normally used to relate exports to total sales by UK producers and Ratio 4 makes an allowance for the extent that imports of the same product are coming into the UK.

International trade in services

(Tables 19.7 and 19.8)

These data relate to overseas trade in services and cover both production and non-production industries (excluding the Public Sector). In terms of types of services traded this equates to trade in royalties, various forms of consultancy, computing and telecommunications services, advertising and market research and other business services. A separate inquiry covers the Film and Television industries. The surveys cover receipts from the provision of services to residents of other countries (exports) and payments to residents of other countries for services rendered (imports).

Sources of data

The International Trade in Services (ITIS) surveys (which consist of a quarterly component addressed to the largest businesses and an annual component for the remainder) are based on a sample of companies derived from the Inter-departmental Business register. The companies are asked to show the amounts for their imports and exports against the geographical area to which they were paid or from which they were received – irrespective of where they were first earned.

The purpose of the ITIS survey is to record international transactions which impact on the UK's Balance of Payments, hence companies are asked to exclude from their earnings trade expenses such as the cost of services purchased abroad. Exports and imports of Services are excluded where they are included within an invoice for the import or export of goods; in this case they will already be counted in the estimate for Trade in Goods. However, earnings from third country trade, i.e. from arranging the sale of goods between two countries other than the UK and where the goods never physically enter the UK (known as merchanting), are included. Earnings from commodity trading are also included. Together these two comprise 'Trade Related Services'.

'Royalties' are the largest part of the total trade in services collected in the ITIS survey: these cover transactions for items such as printed matter, sound recordings, performing rights, patents, licences, trademarks, designs, copyrights, manufacturing rights, the use of technical 'know-how' and technical assistance.

Balance of payments

(Tables 19.9 to 19.12)

Tables 19.9 to 19.12 are derived from *the ONS Pink Book*. The following general notes to the tables provide brief definitions and explanations of the figures and terms used. Further notes are included in the *Pink Book*.

Summary of Balance of Payments

The Balance of Payments consists of the current account, the capital account, the financial account and the International Investment Position. The *current account* consists of trade in goods and services, income and current transfers. *Income* consists of investment income and compensation of employees. The *capital account* mainly consists of capital transfers and the *financial account* covers financial transactions. The *International Investment Position* covers balance sheet levels of UK external assets and liabilities. Every credit entry in the balance of payments accounts should, in theory, be matched by a corresponding debit entry so that total current, capital and financial account credits should be equal to, and therefore offset by, total debits. In practice there is a discrepancy termed *net errors and omissions*.

The Current Account

Trade in goods

The goods account covers exports and imports of goods. Imports of motor cars from Japan, for example, are recorded as debits in the trade in goods account whereas exports of vehicles manufactured in the UK are recorded as credits. Trade in goods forms a component of the expenditure measure of Gross Domestic Product (GDP).

Trade in services

The services account covers exports and imports of services (e.g. civil aviation). Passenger tickets for travel on UK aircraft sold abroad, for example, are recorded as credits in the services account whereas the purchases of airline tickets from foreign airlines by UK passengers are recorded as debits. Trade in services, along with trade in goods, forms a component of the expenditure measure of Gross Domestic Product (GDP).

Income

The income account consists of compensation of employees and investment income and is dominated by the latter. Compensation of employees covers employment income from cross-border and seasonal workers which is less significant in the UK than in other countries. Investment income covers earnings (e.g. profits, dividends and interest payments and receipts) arising from cross-border investment in financial assets and liabilities. For example, earnings on foreign bonds and shares held by financial institutions based in the UK are recorded as credits in the investment income account, whereas earnings on UK company securities held abroad are recorded as investment income debits. Investment income forms a component of Gross National Income (GNI) but not Gross Domestic Product (GDP).

Current transfers

Current transfers are composed of central government transfers (e.g. taxes and payments to, and receipts from, the European Union) and other transfers (e.g. gifts in cash or kind received by private individuals from abroad or receipts from the EU, where the UK government acts as an agent for the ultimate beneficiary of the transfer). Current transfers do not form a component either of Gross Domestic Product (GDP) or of Gross National Income (GNI). For example, payments to the UK farming industry under the EU Agricultural Guarantee Fund are recorded as credits in the current transfers account while payments of EU agricultural levies by the UK farming industry are recorded as debits in the current transfers account.

External trade and investment

Capital Account

Capital account transactions involve transfers of ownership of fixed assets, transfers of funds associated with acquisition or disposal of fixed assets and cancellation of liabilities by creditors without any counterparts being received in return. The main components are migrants transfers, EU transfers relating to fixed capital formation (regional development fund and agricultural guidance fund) and debt forgiveness. Funds brought into the UK by new immigrants would, for example, be recorded as credits in the capital account, while funds sent abroad by UK residents emigrating to other countries would be recorded as debits in the capital account. The size of capital account transactions are quite minor compared with the current and financial accounts.

Financial Account

While investment income covers earnings arising from cross-border investments in financial assets and liabilities, the financial account of the balance of payments covers the flows of such investments. Earnings on foreign bonds and shares held by financial institutions based in the UK are, for example, recorded as credits in the investment income account, but the acquisition of such foreign securities by UK based financial institutions are recorded as net debits in the financial account or portfolio investment abroad. Similarly the acquisitions of UK company securities held by foreign residents are recorded in the financial account as net credits or portfolio investment in the UK.

International Investment Position

While the financial account covers the flows of foreign investments and financial assets and liabilities, the International Investment Position records the levels of external assets and liabilities. While the acquisition of foreign securities by UK based financial institutions are recorded in the financial account, as net debits, the total holdings of foreign securities by UK-based financial institutions are recorded as levels of UK external assets. Similarly the holdings of UK company securities held by foreign residents are recorded as levels of UK liabilities.

Foreign direct investment

(Tables 19.13 to 19.18)

Direct investment refers to investment that adds to, deducts from or acquires a lasting interest in an enterprise operating in an economy other than that of the investor, the investor's purpose being to have an effective voice in the management of the enterprise. (For the purposes of the statistical inquiry, an effective voice is taken as equivalent to a holding of 10 per cent or more in the foreign enterprise.) Other investments in which the investor does not have an effective voice in the management of the enterprise are mainly portfolio investments and these are not covered here. Cross-border investment by public corporations or in property (which is regarded as direct investment in the national accounts) is not covered here, but is shown in the balance of payments. Similarly foreign direct investment earnings data are shown net of tax in Tables 19.15 and 19.18 but are gross of tax in the balance of payments.

Direct investment is a financial concept and is not the same as capital expenditure on fixed assets. It covers only the money invested in a related concern by the parent company and the concern will then decide how to use the money. A related concern may also raise money locally without reference to the parent company.

The investment figures are published on a net basis, that is, they consist of investments net of disinvestments by a company into its foreign subsidiaries, associate companies and branches.

Definitional changes from 1997

The new European System of Accounts (ESA95) definitions were introduced from the 1997 estimates. The changes were as follows:

(i) Previously for the measurement of direct investment, an effective voice in the management of an enterprise was taken as the equivalent of a 20 per cent shareholding. This is now 10 per cent.

(ii) The Channel Islands (Jersey, Guernsey etc.) and the Isle of Man have been excluded from the definition of the economic territory of the UK. Prior to 1987 these islands were considered to be part of the United Kingdom.

(iii) Interest received or paid was replaced by interest accrued in the figures on earnings from direct investment. There is deemed to be little or no impact arising from this definitional change on the estimates.

New register sources available from 1998 have led to revisions for the figures from that year onwards. These sources gave an improved estimate of the population satisfying the criteria for foreign direct investment.

The definitional changes have been introduced from 1997 and the register changes from 1998. The data prior to these years have not been reworked in Tables 19.13 to 19.18. For clarity, the Offshore Islands are identified separately on the tables. The breaks in the series for the other definitional changes are not quantified but are relatively small. More detailed information on the effect of these changes appears in the Business Monitor, MA4 – *Foreign Direct Investment* 2004, which was published in February 2006 and is available on the National Statistics website.

Sources of data

The figures in Tables 19.13 to 19.18 are based on annual inquiries into foreign direct investment for 2004. These were sample surveys which involved sending around 1250 forms to UK businesses investing abroad and 2,250 forms to UK businesses in which foreign parents and associates had invested. The tables also contain some revisions to 2003 as a result of new information coming to light in the course of the latest surveys. Further details from the latest annual surveys, including analyses by industry and by components of direct investment, are available in Business Monitor MA4. Initial figures were published on the National Statistics website in a First Release, Foreign Direct Investment 2004, in December 2005. Data for 2005 will be published in a First Release in December 2006, followed by the full Business Monitor MA4 in February 2007.

Country allocation

The analysis of inward investment is based on the country of ownership of the immediate parent company. Thus, inward investment in a UK company may be attributed to the country of the intervening overseas subsidiary, rather than the country of the ultimate parent. Similarly, the country analysis of outward investment is based on the country of ownership of the immediate subsidiary. As an example, to the extent that overseas investment in the UK is channelled through holding companies in the Netherlands, the underlying flow of investment from this country is overstated and the inflow from originating countries is understated.

Further information

More detailed statistics on foreign direct investment are available on request from Simon Harrington, Office for National Statistics, Financial & Accounting Surveys Division, Room 2.301, Government Buildings, Cardiff Road, Newport, South Wales, United Kingdom, NP10 8XG. Telephone: 01633 813314, Fax: 01633 812855, e-mail simon.harrington@ons.gsi.gov.uk.

External trade and investment

19.1 Trade in goods[1]
United Kingdom
Balance of payments basis

£ million and indices (2002=100)

		1994	1995	1996	1997	1998	1999	2000	2001	2002	2003	2004
Value (£ million)												
Exports of goods	BOKG	135 143	153 577	167 196	171 923	164 056	166 166	187 936	190 055	186 511	188 615	190 933
Imports of goods	BOKH	146 269	165 600	180 918	184 265	185 869	195 217	220 912	230 703	233 598	236 479	251 347
Balance on trade in goods	BOKI	−11 126	−12 023	−13 722	−12 342	−21 813	−29 051	−32 976	−40 648	−47 087	−47 864	−60 414
Price index numbers												
Exports of goods	BQKR	109.4	113.2	113.9	108.0	102.7	100.6	101.7	100.0	100.0	101.8	102.0
Imports of goods	BQKS	108.1	115.0	114.8	107.1	100.7	100.2	103.5	102.6	100.0	99.3	98.7
Terms of trade[2]	BQKT	*101.2*	*98.4*	*99.2*	*100.8*	*102.0*	*100.4*	*98.3*	*97.5*	*100.0*	*102.5*	*103.3*
Volume index numbers												
Exports of goods	BQKU	66.1	72.6	78.2	84.7	85.6	88.3	99.1	101.7	100.0	99.7	101.0
Imports of goods	BQKV	56.3	59.8	65.4	71.8	77.9	83.2	90.9	95.9	100.0	102.0	108.6

1 See chapter text. Statistics of trade in goods on a balance of payments basis are obtained by making certain adjustments in respect of valuation and coverage to the statistics recorded in the *Overseas Trade Statistics*. These adjustments are described in detail in *The Pink Book 2005*.

2 Export price index as a percentage of the import price index.

Source: Office for National Statistics: 020 7533 6064

19.2

Import penetration and export sales ratios for products of manufacturing industry[1,2]

United Kingdom: Standard Industrial Classification 1992

Ratios

			2002	2003	2004
Ratio 1 Imports/Home Demand		SIC Division			
Other mining and quarrying	BBAM	14	163	179	157
Food products and beverages	BBAN	15	24	26	26
Tobacco products	BBAO	16	21	19	17
Textiles	BAZJ	17	70	74	77
Wearing apparel: Dressing and dyeing of fur	BAZK	18	93	97	100
Tanning and dressing of leather: Luggage, handbags, saddlery, harness and footwear	BBAP	19	96	105	106
Wood products of wood and cork (except furniture) articles of straw and plaiting materials	BBAQ	20	36	38	37
Pulp, paper and paper products	BBAR	21	41	41	37
Publishing, printing and reproduction of recorded media	BBAS	22	6	6	6
Chemicals and chemical products	BAZL	24	80	87	87
Rubber and plastic products	BBAT	25	32	33	34
Other non metallic mineral products	BBAU	26	24	25	25
Basic metals	BBAV	27	74	80	85
Fabricated metal products (except machinery and equipment)	BBAW	28	74	27	25
Machinery and equipment not elsewhere classified	BBAX	29	64	68	65
Office machinery and computers	BBAY	30	149	136	142
Electrical machinery not elsewhere classified	BBAZ	31	70	73	73
Radio, television and communication equipment and apparatus	BBBA	32	265	152	121
Medical, precision and optical instruments, watches and clocks	BBBB	33	84	87	90
Motor vehicles, trailers and semi-trailers	BBBC	34	70	68	69
Other transport equipment	BBBD	35	80	83	74
Furniture and manufacturing not elsewhere classified	BBBE	36	60	63	65
Total	BAZY		60	58	58
Ratio 2 Imports/Home Demand plus Exports					
Other mining and quarrying	BBBH	14	53	54	57
Food products and beverages	BBBI	15	21	23	23
Tobacco products	BBBJ	16	11	11	11
Textiles	BAZN	17	52	53	55
Wearing apparel: Dressing and dyeing of fur	BAZO	18	76	78	80
Tanning and dressing of leather: Luggage, handbags, saddlery, harness and footwear	BBBK	19	77	84	85
Wood products of wood and cork (except furniture) articles of straw and plaiting materials	BBBL	20	35	36	35
Pulp, paper and paper products	BBBM	21	35	35	33
Publishing, printing and reproduction of recorded media	BBBN	22	5	5	5
Chemicals and chemical products	BAZP	24	42	44	45
Rubber and plastic products	BBBO	25	26	27	28
Other non metallic mineral products	BBBP	26	21	21	21
Basic metals	BBBQ	27	46	49	50
Fabricated metal products (except machinery and equipment)	BBBR	28	44	22	21
Machinery and equipment not elsewhere classified	BBBS	29	40	41	40
Office machinery and computers	BBBT	30	70	72	77
Electrical machinery not elsewhere classified	BBBU	31	43	44	45
Radio, television and communication equipment and apparatus	BBBV	32	60	67	68
Medical, precision and optical instruments, watches and clocks	BBBW	33	46	47	49
Motor vehicles, trailers and semi-trailers	BBBX	34	49	48	48
Other transport equipment	BBBY	35	46	43	39
Furniture and manufacturing not elsewhere classified	BBBZ	36	48	49	51
Total	BBBF		41	40	41

19.2

Import penetration and export sales ratios for products of manufacturing industry[1,2]

continued

United Kingdom: Standard Industrial Classification 1992

Ratios

			2002	2003	2004
Ratio 3 Exports/Sales		SIC Division			
Other mining and quarrying	BBCM	14	143	152	147
Food products and beverages	BBCN	15	15	15	15
Tobacco products	BBCO	16	52	49	40
Textiles	BAZR	17	53	60	63
Wearing apparel: Dressing and dyeing of fur	BAZS	18	77	90	100
Tanning and dressing of leather: Luggage, handbags, saddlery, harness and footwear	BBCP	19	88	124	135
Wood products of wood and cork (except furniture) articles of straw and plaiting materials	BBCQ	20	7	8	7
Pulp, paper and paper products	BBCR	21	21	21	19
Publishing, printing and reproduction of recorded media	BBCS	22	8	9	9
Chemicals and chemical products	BAZT	24	81	88	88
Rubber and plastic products	BBCT	25	25	26	26
Other non metallic mineral products	BBCU	26	18	18	18
Basic metals	BBCV	27	70	76	83
Fabricated metal products (except machinery and equipment)	BBCW	28	72	21	20
Machinery and equipment not elsewhere classified	BBCX	29	62	67	64
Office machinery and computers	BBCY	30	176	168	202
Electrical machinery not elsewhere classified	BBDK	31	68	71	69
Radio, television and communication equipment and apparatus	BBDL	32	192	171	138
Medical, precision and optical instruments, watches and clocks	BBDM	33	84	86	89
Motor vehicles, trailers and semi-trailers	BBDN	34	59	57	59
Other transport equipment	BBDO	35	79	85	77
Furniture and manufacturing not elsewhere classified	BBDP	36	39	42	43
Total	BBCK		54	51	50
Ratio 4 Exports/Sales plus Imports					
Other mining and quarrying	BBDS	14	68	70	64
Food products and beverages	BBDT	15	12	12	11
Tobacco products	BBDU	16	46	44	36
Textiles	BAZV	17	26	28	28
Wearing apparel: Dressing and dyeing of fur	BAZW	18	19	20	20
Tanning and dressing of leather: Luggage, handbags, saddlery, harness and footwear	BBDV	19	21	20	20
Wood products of wood and cork (except furniture) articles of straw and plaiting materials	BBDW	20	4	5	5
Pulp, paper and paper products	BBDX	21	14	14	13
Publishing, printing and reproduction of recorded media	BBDY	22	8	9	9
Chemicals and chemical products	BAZX	24	47	49	48
Rubber and plastic products	BBDZ	25	19	19	19
Other non-metallic mineral products	BBEA	26	14	14	14
Basic metals	BBEB	27	38	39	41
Fabricated metal products (except machinery and equipment)	BBEC	28	40	16	16
Machinery and equipment not elsewhere classified	BBED	29	37	39	38
Office machinery and computers	BBEE	30	53	47	45
Electrical machinery not elsewhere classified	BBEF	31	39	40	38
Radio, television and communication equipment and apparatus	BBEG	32	77	56	44
Medical, precision and optical instruments, watches and clocks	BBEH	33	45	46	46
Motor vehicles, trailers and semi-trailers	BBEI	34	30	30	30
Other transport equipment	BBEJ	35	43	49	47
Furniture and manufacturing not elsewhere classified	BBEK	36	20	21	21
Total	BBDQ		32	31	29

1 See chapter text.
2 Division 13 (Mining of metal ores) has not been published since 1995. Division 23 (Coke, refined petroleum products and nuclear fuel) and SIC 24610 (Manufacture of explosives) are excluded from the analysis. SIC 27100 (Basic iron and steel and ferro-alloys) is not incorporated in PRODCOM and therefore also does not form part of the analysis.

Source: Office for National Statistics: 01633 813065

19.3 United Kingdom exports: by commodity[1,2]
Seasonally adjusted

£ million

		1995	1996	1997	1998	1999	2000	2001	2002	2003	2004
0. Food and live animals	BOGG	7 079	6 997	6 581	6 286	5 925	5 827	5 499	5 693	6 481	6 462
of which:											
01. Meat and meat preparations	BOGS	1 466	1 081	925	746	657	642	428	516	606	667
02. Dairy products and eggs	BQMS	820	732	745	745	689	660	621	625	760	780
04 & 08. Cereals and animal feeding stuffs	BQMT	1 702	2 008	1 800	1 714	1 568	1 604	1 392	1 444	1 681	1 553
05. Vegetables and fruit	BQMU	456	470	455	408	437	403	405	433	475	508
1. Beverages and tobacco	BQMZ	4 113	4 331	4 522	3 930	4 022	4 081	4 151	4 299	4 405	4 116
11. Beverages	BQNB	2 986	3 138	3 305	2 875	3 004	3 065	3 225	3 320	3 481	3 354
12. Tobacco	BQOW	1 127	1 193	1 217	1 055	1 018	1 016	926	979	924	762
2. Crude materials	BQOX	2 725	2 583	2 489	2 267	2 087	2 447	2 429	2 645	3 071	3 566
of which:											
24. Wood, lumber and cork	BQOY	46	52	52	55	66	72	72	81	106	117
25. Pulp and waste paper	BQOZ	66	57	64	47	54	78	80	106	180	244
26. Textile fibres	BQPA	636	611	568	493	447	496	446	472	492	520
28. Metal ores	BQPB	771	657	642	560	518	759	819	928	1 194	1 605
3. Fuels	BOPN	9 942	11 578	11 016	7 513	9 929	17 057	16 381	15 997	16 558	17 941
33. Petroleum and petroleum products	ELBL	9 384	10 928	10 239	7 018	9 123	15 584	14 811	14 318	14 608	16 256
32, 34 & 35. Coal, gas and electricity	BOQI	558	650	777	495	806	1 473	1 570	1 679	1 950	1 685
4. Animal and vegetable oils and fats	BQPI	221	207	264	245	197	156	150	210	266	205
5. Chemicals	ENDG	20 999	22 166	21 901	22 102	23 071	24 992	27 607	28 385	31 403	32 008
of which:											
51. Organic chemicals	BQPJ	4 923	5 152	4 974	4 914	5 494	5 718	6 108	5 698	6 076	6 040
52. Inorganic chemicals	BQPK	1 236	1 190	1 183	1 153	1 137	1 491	1 643	1 367	1 461	1 543
53. Colouring materials	CSCE	1 618	1 641	1 578	1 542	1 534	1 555	1 528	1 583	1 629	1 630
54. Medicinal products	BQPL	4 926	5 333	5 416	5 850	6 279	7 217	9 100	10 103	11 908	12 326
55. Toilet preparations	CSCF	2 124	2 409	2 569	2 446	2 462	2 597	2 718	2 822	3 125	3 105
57 & 58. Plastics	BQQA	3 276	3 294	3 166	3 194	3 144	3 366	3 422	3 526	3 706	3 846
6. Manufactures classified chiefly by material	BQQB	22 459	23 142	22 675	21 243	20 302	22 673	22 837	21 836	23 136	24 458
of which:											
63. Wood and cork manufactures	BQQC	189	228	250	253	278	255	262	270	323	291
64. Paper and paperboard manufactures	BQQD	2 350	2 343	2 309	2 197	2 020	2 096	2 088	2 019	2 099	1 996
65. Textile manufactures	BQQE	3 282	3 471	3 421	3 259	3 020	3 051	3 026	2 847	2 958	2 846
67. Iron and steel	BQQF	4 345	4 059	3 637	3 321	2 576	2 848	2 885	2 916	3 322	4 245
68. Non-ferrous metals	BQQG	2 864	2 680	2 774	2 433	2 130	3 171	3 044	2 552	2 569	3 229
69. Metal manufactures	BQQH	3 086	3 346	3 368	3 591	3 553	3 595	3 864	3 660	3 770	3 856
7. Machinery and transport equipment[3]	BQQI	65 353	73 366	79 002	78 011	78 875	87 812	87 804	84 389	79 815	78 377
71 - 716, 72, 73 & 74. Mechanical machinery	BQQK	18 337	20 481	22 329	22 695	21 888	22 140	24 488	22 703	24 302	23 810
716, 75, 76 & 77. Electrical machinery	BQQL	30 652	32 939	34 252	34 464	36 012	42 681	42 230	38 703	30 706	28 623
78. Road vehicles	BQQM	11 644	14 278	14 811	14 550	15 077	15 604	13 929	16 314	17 513	18 489
79. Other transport equipment	BQQN	4 720	5 668	7 610	6 302	5 898	7 387	7 157	6 669	7 294	7 455
8. Miscellaneous manufactures[3]	BQQO	18 859	20 873	21 530	20 563	20 263	21 206	22 158	21 984	22 612	22 919
of which:											
84. Clothing	CSCN	3 056	3 356	3 259	2 976	2 804	2 722	2 592	2 507	2 713	2 729
85. Footwear	CSCP	519	595	605	535	532	514	494	452	427	419
87 & 88. Scientific and photographic	BQQQ	5 900	6 594	6 974	6 705	6 732	7 333	7 856	7 212	7 302	7 041
9. Other commodities and transactions	BOQL	1 827	1 953	1 943	1 896	1 495	1 685	1 039	1 073	868	881
Total United Kingdom exports	BOKG	153 577	167 196	171 923	164 056	166 166	187 936	190 055	186 511	188 615	190 933

1 See chapter text. The numbers on the left hand side of the table refer to the code numbers of the *Standard International Trade Classification,* Revision 3, which was introduced in January 1988.
2 Balance of payments consistent basis.
3 Sections 7 and 8 are shown by broad economic category in table G2 of the *Monthly Review of External Trade Statistics.*

Source: Office for National Statistics: 020 7533 6064

19.4 United Kingdom imports: by commodity[1,2]
Seasonally adjusted

£ million

		1995	1996	1997	1998	1999	2000	2001	2002	2003	2004
0. Food and live animals	BQQR	12 923	14 030	13 318	13 223	13 336	13 310	14 286	14 873	16 459	17 208
of which:											
01. Meat and meat preparations	BQQS	2 237	2 540	2 231	2 006	2 144	2 366	2 692	2 792	3 268	3 439
02. Dairy products and eggs	BQQT	1 077	1 194	1 101	1 112	1 167	1 165	1 243	1 291	1 501	1 609
04 & 08. Cereals and animal feeding stuffs	BQQU	1 781	1 915	1 991	1 806	1 719	1 762	1 964	1 985	2 219	2 308
05. Vegetables and fruit	BQQV	3 820	4 173	3 898	4 017	4 040	3 894	4 102	4 374	4 768	4 918
1. Beverages and tobacco	BQQW	2 638	3 392	3 593	4 027	4 451	4 350	4 220	4 499	4 736	4 939
11. Beverages	EGAT	2 065	2 479	2 610	2 881	3 064	2 910	2 858	3 027	3 238	3 474
12. Tobacco	EMAI	573	913	983	1 146	1 387	1 440	1 362	1 472	1 498	1 465
2. Crude materials	ENVB	5 893	5 859	5 670	5 076	4 861	5 816	5 934	5 421	5 530	5 718
of which:											
24. Wood, lumber and cork	ENVC	1 142	1 202	1 239	1 100	1 088	1 193	1 160	1 236	1 367	1 337
25. Pulp and waste paper	EQAH	979	656	572	477	510	763	612	488	490	480
26. Textile fibres	EQAP	636	639	590	452	413	412	398	361	338	340
28. Metal ores	EHAA	1 358	1 474	1 460	1 314	1 308	1 811	2 008	1 448	1 431	1 648
3. Fuels	BQAT	6 161	7 284	6 824	4 892	5 428	10 016	10 502	9 646	11 563	16 824
33. Petroleum and petroleum products	ENXO	5 061	6 118	5 679	3 976	4 675	9 048	9 232	8 579	10 484	14 584
32, 34 & 35. Coal, gas and electricity	BPBI	1 100	1 166	1 145	916	753	968	1 270	1 067	1 079	2 240
4. Animal and vegetable oils and fats	EHAB	561	686	603	555	568	491	520	538	614	622
5. Chemicals	ENGA	17 481	18 095	17 405	17 379	18 619	20 633	22 836	23 983	26 168	27 927
of which:											
51. Organic chemicals	EHAC	4 670	4 719	4 462	4 508	4 788	5 374	5 548	5 672	6 111	6 801
52. Inorganic chemicals	EHAE	1 086	1 233	1 107	1 015	1 056	1 046	1 179	1 069	1 096	1 366
53. Colouring materials	CSCR	930	1 000	975	1 003	956	1 002	982	952	1 004	1 060
54. Medicinal products	EHAF	2 785	3 061	3 100	3 305	4 124	4 714	6 182	7 287	8 198	8 372
55. Toilet preparations	CSCS	1 364	1 477	1 506	1 617	1 774	2 005	2 267	2 498	2 747	2 881
57 & 58. Plastics	EHAG	4 597	4 338	4 168	3 903	3 819	4 144	4 103	4 063	4 406	4 749
6. Manufactures classified chiefly by material	EHAH	27 760	28 700	28 007	27 695	26 930	29 232	30 225	28 737	29 921	32 299
of which:											
63. Wood and cork manufactures	EHAI	1 037	1 078	1 083	1 089	1 145	1 245	1 347	1 437	1 450	1 585
64. Paper and paperboard manufactures	EHAJ	5 200	4 961	4 550	4 504	4 321	4 407	4 867	4 582	4 748	4 841
65. Textile manufactures	EHAK	4 806	5 075	5 003	4 862	4 380	4 365	4 316	4 150	4 092	4 124
67. Iron and steel	EHAL	3 620	3 604	3 337	3 337	3 205	2 473	2 731	3 055	3 238	4 198
68. Non-ferrous metals	EHAM	3 753	3 720	3 625	3 709	2 942	3 711	3 792	3 222	3 324	3 617
69. Metal manufactures	EHAN	3 239	3 492	3 561	3 721	3 789	4 065	4 337	4 501	4 769	4 977
7. Machinery and transport equipment[3]	EHAO	68 044	76 120	80 518	83 300	90 183	102 420	105 680	107 558	101 645	104 183
71 - 716, 72, 73 & 74. Mechanical machinery	EHAQ	15 148	16 540	17 037	17 156	17 313	17 867	18 767	18 902	18 993	19 725
716, 75, 76 & 77. Electrical machinery	EHAR	31 487	35 299	35 792	36 900	42 423	53 631	51 195	49 918	43 747	45 797
78. Road vehicles	EHAS	17 831	20 238	21 704	22 472	24 000	23 117	26 365	28 449	29 959	30 732
79. Other transport equipment	EHAT	3 578	4 043	5 985	6 772	6 447	7 805	9 353	10 289	8 946	7 929
8. Miscellaneous manufactures[3]	EHAU	22 522	24 987	26 568	27 917	29 042	32 798	35 220	36 893	38 235	39 820
of which:											
84. Clothing	CSDR	5 178	6 059	6 630	7 023	7 483	8 495	9 160	9 805	10 341	10 639
85. Footwear	CSDS	1 514	1 770	1 912	1 859	2 041	2 001	2 244	2 366	2 378	2 448
87 & 88. Scientific and photographic	EHAW	5 382	6 001	6 067	6 102	6 170	7 273	7 691	7 044	7 067	7 256
9. Other commodities and transactions	BQAW	1 617	1 765	1 759	1 805	1 799	1 846	1 280	1 450	1 608	1 807
Total United Kingdom imports	BOKH	165 600	180 918	184 265	185 869	195 217	220 912	230 703	233 598	236 479	251 347

1 See chapter text. The numbers on the left hand side of the table refer to the code numbers of the *Standard International Trade Classification*, Revision 3, which was introduced in January 1988.
2 Balance of payments consistent basis.
3 Sections 7 and 8 are shown by broad economic category in table G2 of the *Monthly Review of External Trade Statistics*.

Source: Office for National Statistics: 020 7533 6064

19.5 United Kingdom exports: by area[1,2]
Seasonally adjusted

£ million

		1995	1996	1997	1998	1999	2000	2001	2002	2003	2004
European Union:[3]	LGCK	..	..	..	98 995	101 191	111 955	113 893	114 123	110 589	110 898
EMU members:	QAKW	83 271	89 124	89 504	89 241	91 771	101 464	103 493	103 215	99 893	99 872
Austria	CHMY	1 122	1 263	1 159	1 190	1 168	1 146	1 224	1 265	1 264	1 095
Belgium & Luxembourg	CHNQ	8 298	8 522	8 451	8 445	9 241	10 322	9 893	10 553	11 373	10 512
Finland	CHMZ	1 716	1 810	1 570	1 434	1 354	1 471	1 610	1 442	1 493	1 363
France	ENYL	15 265	17 093	16 601	16 449	16 907	18 577	19 242	18 756	18 885	18 567
Germany	ENYO	20 242	20 715	20 685	20 590	20 464	22 789	23 647	22 062	20 805	21 673
Greece	CHNT	1 038	1 147	1 047	1 045	1 153	1 229	1 113	1 197	1 253	1 410
Irish Republic	CHNS	7 794	8 661	9 357	9 604	10 783	12 372	13 829	15 419	12 224	14 137
Italy	CHNO	7 883	8 027	8 214	8 608	7 831	8 429	8 400	8 506	8 603	8 401
Netherlands	CHNP	12 346	13 484	13 923	12 983	13 632	15 167	14 596	14 009	13 597	12 032
Portugal	CHNU	1 469	1 677	1 752	1 722	1 712	1 660	1 578	1 517	1 453	1 580
Spain	CHNV	6 098	6 725	6 745	7 171	7 526	8 302	8 361	8 489	8 943	9 102
Non-EMU members:[3]	BQIA	..	..	..	9 754	9 420	10 491	10 400	10 908	10 696	11 026
of which:											
Czech Rep	FKML	571	719	709	713	733	927	1 075	1 031	1 003	975
Denmark	CHNR	2 108	2 214	2 093	2 057	2 054	2 315	2 267	2 728	2 180	2 042
Hungary	QALC	296	351	435	498	486	613	612	750	856	933
Poland	ERDR	953	1 358	1 354	1 213	1 169	1 299	1 297	1 318	1 462	1 414
Sweden	CHNA	4 157	4 420	4 451	4 392	4 035	4 211	3 950	3 872	3 823	4 355
Other Western Europe:	HCJD	6 417	7 279	7 851	7 392	6 244	7 223	6 957	6 334	6 658	7 027
of which:											
Iceland	EPLW	138	152	157	158	159	193	154	131	141	167
Norway	EPLX	2 002	2 039	2 609	2 658	1 999	2 018	1 862	1 696	1 894	1 937
Switzerland	EPLV	2 729	3 166	2 955	2 892	2 768	3 061	3 581	3 080	2 798	2 840
Turkey	EOBA	1 149	1 545	1 734	1 562	1 198	1 800	1 179	1 287	1 645	1 903
North America:	HBZQ	20 450	22 341	23 817	24 091	27 582	33 714	33 774	32 261	33 044	32 766
of which:											
Canada	EOBC	1 804	1 963	2 146	2 147	2 532	3 487	3 240	3 107	3 249	3 340
Mexico	EPJX	277	316	428	516	577	675	689	704	689	629
USA	EOBB	17 901	19 753	20 853	21 082	24 040	29 276	29 562	28 197	28 780	28 591
Other OECD countries:	HCII	9 467	11 116	10 900	6 321	6 728	8 028	7 686	7 469	7 854	8 230
of which:											
Australia	EPMA	2 140	2 492	2 454	2 188	2 155	2 699	2 344	2 114	2 298	2 457
Japan	EOBD	3 814	4 296	4 180	3 127	3 300	3 672	3 744	3 583	3 723	3 864
New Zealand	EPMB	440	474	409	336	324	305	314	311	349	418
South Korea	ERDM	1 162	1 314	1 222	666	949	1 350	1 284	1 461	1 475	1 482
Oil exporting countries:	HDII	6 296	7 906	9 426	7 289	5 524	6 031	6 472	6 229	7 652	7 997
of which:											
Brunei	QALF	251	548	536	247	124	96	58	61	129	67
Dubai	QALI	701	746	866	830	790	966	1 011	940	1 388	2 018
Indonesia	FKMR	518	809	674	369	385	404	313	324	455	398
Kuwait	QATB	548	565	481	325	293	338	358	308	376	354
Nigeria	QATE	430	426	410	454	447	524	686	711	741	773
Saudi Arabia	ERDI	1 621	2 425	3 656	2 605	1 481	1 557	1 523	1 388	1 828	1 611
Rest of the World	HCHW	21 413	22 796	23 881	19 968	18 897	20 985	21 273	20 095	22 818	24 015
of which:											
Brazil	FKMO	679	853	1 030	899	739	775	819	880	828	790
China	ERDN	832	741	922	860	1 211	1 468	1 735	1 493	1 931	2 372
Egypt	QALL	385	434	501	505	539	498	458	463	459	668
Hong Kong	ERDG	2 664	2 943	3 215	2 671	2 312	2 673	2 717	2 411	2 490	2 635
India	ERDJ	1 689	1 718	1 576	1 242	1 450	2 058	1 797	1 755	2 293	2 236
Israel	ERDL	1 113	1 277	1 178	1 079	1 295	1 516	1 376	1 428	1 364	1 392
Malaysia	ERDK	1 192	1 169	1 206	677	934	907	1 045	877	1 031	995
Pakistan	FKMU	342	347	271	228	221	207	234	240	294	344
Philippines	FKMX	436	398	601	301	239	273	397	352	378	315
Russia	ERDQ	871	1 018	1 233	929	532	668	903	981	1 426	1 468
Singapore	ERDH	2 072	2 158	2 047	1 598	1 597	1 625	1 613	1 445	1 587	1 711
South Africa	EPME	1 837	1 894	1 646	1 520	1 281	1 413	1 558	1 597	1 772	1 879
Taiwan	ERDP	965	945	1 036	867	865	1 015	890	848	898	951
Thailand	ERDO	838	981	863	386	463	582	601	529	573	638

1 See chapter text.
2 Balance of payments consistent basis.
3 Includes the ten countries which joined the EU on 1 May 2004: Cyprus, Czech Republic, Estonia, Hungary, Latvia, Lithuania, Malta, Poland, Slovakia, Slovenia.

Source: Office for National Statistics: 020 7533 6064

19.6 United Kingdom imports: by area[1,2]
Seasonally adjusted

£ million

		1995	1996	1997	1998	1999	2000	2001	2002	2003	2004
European Union:[3]	LGDC	..	..	..	104 737	109 286	117 217	126 077	136 140	136 417	141 722
EMU members	QAKX	87 323	93 503	93 507	95 466	99 258	105 678	113 842	122 992	122 452	126 375
Austria	CHNB	925	1 155	1 393	1 411	1 453	1 410	1 888	2 392	2 772	2 356
Belgium & Luxembourg	CHNY	8 130	8 895	9 390	9 831	10 156	10 927	12 159	13 204	13 169	13 860
Finland	CHNC	2 500	2 643	2 544	2 328	2 364	2 765	2 962	2 786	2 660	2 340
France	ENYP	16 457	18 090	18 020	17 956	18 415	18 642	20 116	20 776	20 360	20 155
Germany	ENYS	26 234	27 173	25 632	25 095	26 817	28 461	29 884	32 407	33 620	35 417
Greece	CHOB	429	395	396	363	399	443	476	538	625	634
Irish Republic	CHOA	7 045	7 236	7 391	7 802	8 708	10 261	12 136	13 164	9 908	10 145
Italy	CHNW	8 264	8 805	9 548	9 744	9 385	9 516	9 855	10 663	11 466	12 197
Netherlands	CHNX	11 516	12 407	12 328	13 408	13 772	15 379	15 387	16 123	16 672	18 214
Portugal	CHOC	1 467	1 661	1 763	1 790	1 822	1 734	1 624	1 759	1 964	1 929
Spain	CHOD	4 356	5 043	5 102	5 738	5 967	6 140	7 355	9 180	9 236	9 128
Non-EMU members:[3]	BQIB	..	..	..	9 271	10 028	11 539	12 235	13 148	13 965	15 347
of which:											
Czech Rep	FKMM	312	353	450	561	579	802	1 097	1 248	1 409	1 291
Denmark	CHNZ	2 199	2 356	2 316	2 156	2 342	2 631	2 921	3 590	3 394	3 360
Hungary	QALD	358	402	465	544	668	683	710	846	1 118	1 579
Poland	ERED	616	570	597	668	676	905	1 166	1 264	1 543	1 833
Sweden	CHND	4 537	4 769	4 693	4 361	4 649	4 950	4 666	4 324	4 565	5 125
Other Western Europe:	HBTS	10 341	11 315	10 755	9 701	10 554	13 040	12 404	12 509	13 362	15 707
of which:											
Iceland	EPMW	244	255	229	251	282	365	286	289	297	355
Norway	EPMX	4 175	4 751	4 666	3 440	3 546	5 563	5 596	5 251	6 441	8 470
Switzerland	EPMV	4 981	5 183	4 636	4 755	5 341	5 485	4 604	4 590	3 768	3 436
Turkey	EOBU	768	892	990	1 103	1 204	1 450	1 692	2 162	2 622	3 239
North America:	HCRB	22 293	25 130	27 277	27 815	28 035	33 460	34 904	29 615	27 348	26 873
of which:											
Canada	EOBW	2 300	2 409	2 480	2 519	3 026	4 009	3 693	3 537	3 645	4 154
Mexico	EPJY	288	326	371	366	395	613	686	502	490	410
USA	EOBV	19 615	22 287	24 329	24 785	24 360	28 416	29 589	24 986	22 746	21 892
Other OECD countries:	HDJQ	13 762	13 699	14 636	13 205	13 805	15 717	14 268	12 958	12 953	13 567
of which:											
Australia	EPNA	1 068	1 230	1 320	1 363	1 338	1 543	1 792	1 681	1 784	1 857
Japan	EOBX	9 276	8 545	9 031	9 124	9 118	10 214	9 151	8 040	8 062	8 066
New Zealand	EPNB	555	602	555	517	565	544	549	521	551	581
South Korea	ERDY	1 505	1 935	2 147	2 201	2 784	3 416	2 776	2 716	2 556	3 063
Oil exporting countries:	HCPC	2 930	3 266	3 351	3 201	3 228	4 258	3 971	3 768	3 921	4 849
of which:											
Brunei	QALG	111	251	282	161	66	95	34	33	52	63
Dubai	QALJ	169	208	286	337	433	401	398	497	719	576
Indonesia	FKMS	814	852	862	854	931	1 081	1 128	1 002	878	915
Kuwait	QATC	133	158	168	164	121	314	297	271	314	394
Nigeria	QATF	163	254	100	121	112	89	65	90	82	105
Saudi Arabia	ERDU	649	654	841	791	783	977	931	673	713	1 156
Rest of the World	HCIF	22 215	26 880	27 730	27 210	30 309	37 220	39 079	38 608	42 478	48 629
of which:											
Brazil	FKMP	936	942	911	883	910	1 114	1 287	1 358	1 472	1 540
China	ERDZ	1 843	2 110	2 379	2 816	3 384	4 826	5 775	6 693	8 321	10 360
Egypt	QALM	235	271	256	277	255	411	408	414	430	495
Hong Kong	ERDS	3 364	3 904	4 146	4 391	4 909	5 917	5 793	5 535	5 486	5 745
India	ERDV	1 363	1 542	1 546	1 382	1 426	1 651	1 825	1 794	2 088	2 280
Israel	ERDX	659	796	839	875	996	1 025	947	873	857	918
Malaysia	ERDW	1 414	2 280	1 931	1 892	1 961	2 288	1 951	1 723	1 862	2 013
Pakistan	FKMV	344	375	362	340	318	363	426	468	518	550
Philippines	FKMY	335	858	726	855	983	1 155	1 163	940	710	653
Russia	EREC	916	1 222	1 418	1 406	1 324	1 496	2 061	1 940	2 449	3 496
Singapore	ERDT	2 101	2 465	2 585	2 343	2 348	2 395	2 079	1 949	2 663	3 367
South Africa	EPNE	1 058	1 170	1 323	1 351	1 636	2 553	2 861	2 671	2 940	3 262
Taiwan	EREB	1 640	2 001	2 230	2 217	2 626	3 561	2 803	2 373	2 193	2 333
Thailand	EREA	987	1 140	1 166	1 264	1 291	1 602	1 617	1 544	1 643	1 755

1 See chapter text.
2 Balance of payments consistent basis.
3 Includes the ten countries which joined the EU on 1 May 2004: Cyprus, Czech Republic, Estonia, Hungary, Latvia, Lithuania, Malta, Poland, Slovakia, Slovenia.

Source: Office for National Statistics: 020 7533 6064

19.7 Services supplied (exports) and purchased (imports),[1],[2]: 2003

£ million

	Exports	Imports	Net
Business services			
Legal	1 935	454	1 482
Accounting	683	299	384
Management consulting	1 146	517	629
Advertising	1 789	752	1 037
Market research	366	195	170
Research and development	3 904	1 268	2 636
Insurance: premiums	13	186	-173
claims	20	4	16
Insurance broking	1 249	29	1 220
Financial Services	3 945	870	3 075
Property	84	46	38
Management charges	1 669	1 046	623
Procurement	56	60	-4
Publishing services	276	94	182
Recruitment and training	234	136	98
Other business services	1 398	571	827
Telecommunications services			
Communications	1 129	1 396	-266
Computer	3 740	1 318	2 422
Information	1 400	313	1 087
Technical services			
Architectural	106	50	56
Engineering (consulting, process etc.)	3 475	958	2 517
Surveying	58	25	34
Construction	205	99	106
Agriculture and mining	77	30	46
Other technical	1 753	392	1 362
Miscellaneous services			
Operational leasing	232	228	4
Cultural services			
TV and radio services	172	39	132
Music services (excluding royalties)	30	20	11
Other cultural	301	159	142
Royalties	5 912	3 651	2 262
Trade related services			
Own account earning	372	35	337
Commission	1 425	572	853
Commodity trading	394	181	213
Management services to affiliated companies	2 356	1 131	1 226
All other services	1 345	740	606
World Total	**43 252**	**17 862**	**25 390**

1 See chapter text.
2 Due to rounding, the sum of constituent items may not always equal the total shown. Data excludes the following industries: Financial, Film and TV, Travel and Transport, Public Sector (including Education) and Law Society members.

Source: Office for National Statistics: 01633 813109

19.8 International trade in services:[1,2] by country, 2003

£ million

	Exports	Imports	Net
European Union			
Austria	109	105	4
Belgium/Luxembourg	1 504	586	918
Denmark	476	162	313
Finland	457	77	380
France	1 758	1 691	67
Germany	2 770	1 658	1 112
Greece	151	56	95
Irish Republic	2 753	586	2 167
Italy	835	541	294
Netherlands	2 609	951	1 658
Spain	692	377	315
Sweden	676	596	80
Portugal and EU Institutions	173	79	94
EFTA			
Iceland	15	2	13
Liechtenstein	20	2	19
Norway	575	197	378
Switzerland	2 682	655	2 027
Other European countries			
Czech Republic	71	33	38
Poland	103	41	62
Russia	194	70	124
Channel Islands	393	85	308
Isle of Man	25	9	16
Turkey	73	32	41
Rest of Europe	400	157	243
Europe Unallocated	2 031	639	1 392
Africa			
South Africa	302	88	213
Rest of Africa	704	288	416
Africa Unallocated	138	24	113
America			
Brazil	61	30	30
Canada	368	174	194
Mexico	85	20	65
USA	10 835	4 760	6 076
Rest of America	1 332	295	1 038
America Unallocated	383	77	306
Asia			
China	293	65	228
Hong Kong	309	185	124
India	144	158	-14
Indonesia	44	109	-64
Israel	111	117	-6
Japan	1 933	626	1 307
Malaysia	156	17	138
Pakistan	23	35	-12
Phillippines	24	21	3
Singapore	1 243	109	1 134
South Korea	130	22	107
Taiwan	93	42	51
Thailand	46	23	23
Rest of Asia	2 107	794	1 313
Asia Unallocated	205	47	158
Australia and Oceania			
Australia	409	211	198
New Zealand	44	15	30
Rest of Australia and Oceania	61	14	47
Oceania Unallocated	7	4	3
Rest of World Unallocated and other orgainisations	115	103	12
World Total	**43 252**	**17 862**	**25 389**
Economic Zones			
OCED	31 457	14 188	17 269
NAFTA	10 701	4 953	5 748
Central and Eastern Europe	433	156	278
OPEC	2 086	814	1 272
ASEAN	1 538	283	1 255
CIS	469	169	300
NICs1	1 775	358	1 417
Offshore Financial centres	2 736	575	2 161
ACP	616	389	227

1 See chapter text.
2 Due to rounding, the sum of constituent items may not always equal the total shown. Data excludes the following industries: Financial, Film and TV, Travel and Transport, Public Sector (including Education) and Law Society members.

Source: Office for National Statistics: 01633 813109

19.9 Summary of balance of payments,[1] 2004
United Kingdom

£ million

	Credits	Debits
1. Current account		
A. Goods and services	293 949	332 927
1. Goods	190 933	251 347
2. Services	103 016	81 580
2.1. Transportation	16 343	18 851
2.2. Travel	15 414	30 873
2.3. Communications	2 703	2 042
2.4. Construction	278	142
2.5. Insurance	6 425	830
2.6. Financial	16 107	3 425
2.7. Computer and information	5 683	1 937
2.8. Royalties and licence fees	6 434	5 007
2.9. Other business	29 457	15 237
2.10. Personal, cultural and recreational	2 189	839
2.11. Government	1 983	2 397
B. Income	142 085	115 364
1. Compensation of employees	1 171	1 100
2. Investment income	140 914	114 264
2.1 Direct investment	64 218	27 700
2.2 Portfolio investment	36 708	36 250
2.3 Other investment (including earnings on reserve assets)	39 988	50 314
C. Current transfers	12 560	23 500
1. Central government	4 000	12 300
2. Other sectors	8 560	11 200
Total current account	**448 594**	**471 791**
2. Capital and financial accounts		
A. Capital account	3 602	1 716
1. Capital transfers	3 409	1 204
2. Acquisition/disposal of non-produced, non-financial assets	193	512
B. Financial account	542 583	527 201
1. Direct investment	42 395	52 564
Abroad		52 564
1.1. Equity capital		17 207
1.2. Reinvested earnings		32 425
1.3. Other capital[2]		2 932
In United Kingdom	42 395	
1.1. Equity capital	24 400	
1.2. Reinvested earnings	9 299	
1.3. Other capital[3]	8 696	
2. Portfolio investment	86 382	140 853
Assets		140 853
2.1. Equity securities		56 647
2.2. Debt securities		84 206
Liabilities	86 382	
2.1. Equity securities	−8 387	
2.2. Debt securities	94 769	
3. Financial derivatives (net)		7 875
4. Other investment	413 806	325 713
Assets		325 713
4.1 Trade credits		−336
4.2 Loans		112 264
4.3 Currency and deposits		213 735
4.4 Other assets		50
Liabilities	413 806	
4.1. Trade credits	−	
4.2. Loans	106 076	
4.3. Currency and deposits	307 734	
4.4. Other liabilities	−4	
5. Reserve assets		196
5.1. Monetary gold		−2
5.2. Special drawing rights		−35
5.3. Reserve position in the IMF		−558
5.4. Foreign exchange		809
Total capital and financial accounts	**546 185**	**528 917**
Total current, capital and financial accounts	**994 779**	**1 000 708**
Net errors and omissions	6 152	

1 See chapter text.
2 Other capital transaction on direct investment abroad represents claims on
  affiliated enterprises less liabilities to affiliated enterprises
3 Other capital transactions on direct investment in the United Kingdom
  represents liabilities to direct investors less claims on direct investors

Source: Office for National Statistics

External trade and investment

19.10 Summary of balance of payments: balances (credits less debits)[1]
United Kingdom

£ million

	Current account											
	Trade in goods	Trade in services	Total goods and services	Compensati-on of employees	Investment income	Total income	Current transfers	Current balance	Current balance as % of GDP[2]	Capital account	Financial account	Net errors & omissions
	LQCT	KTMS	KTMY	KTMP	HMBM	HMBP	KTNF	HBOG	AA6H	FKMJ	HBNT	HHDH
1951	−692	32	−660	−21	322	301	29	−330	−2.3	−15	426	−81
1952	−272	123	−149	−22	231	209	169	229	1.4	−15	−229	15
1953	−244	123	−121	−25	207	182	143	204	1.2	−13	−177	−14
1954	−210	115	−95	−27	227	200	55	160	0.9	−13	−174	27
1955	−315	42	−273	−27	149	122	43	−108	−0.6	−15	34	89
1956	50	26	76	−30	203	173	2	251	1.2	−13	−250	12
1957	−29	121	92	−32	223	191	−5	278	1.3	−13	−313	48
1958	34	119	153	−34	261	227	4	384	1.7	−10	−411	37
1959	−116	118	2	−37	233	196	−	198	0.8	−5	−68	−125
1960	−404	39	−365	−35	201	166	−6	−205	−0.8	−6	−7	218
1961	−144	51	−93	−35	223	188	−9	86	0.3	−12	23	−97
1962	−104	50	−54	−37	301	264	−14	196	0.7	−12	−195	11
1963	−123	4	−119	−38	364	326	−37	170	0.6	−16	−30	−124
1964	−551	−34	−585	−33	365	332	−74	−327	−1.0	−17	392	−48
1965	−263	−66	−329	−34	405	371	−75	−33	−0.1	−18	49	2
1966	−111	44	−67	−39	358	319	−91	161	0.4	−19	22	−164
1967	−601	157	−444	−39	354	315	−118	−247	−0.6	−25	179	93
1968	−708	341	−367	−48	303	255	−119	−231	−0.5	−26	688	−431
1969	−214	392	178	−47	468	421	−109	490	1.0	−23	−794	327
1970	−18	455	437	−56	527	471	−89	819	1.6	−22	−818	21
1971	205	590	795	−63	481	418	−90	1 123	2.0	−23	−1 330	230
1972	−736	665	−71	−52	407	355	−142	142	0.2	−35	477	−584
1973	−2 573	803	−1 770	−68	1 074	1 006	−336	−1 100	−1.5	−39	1 031	108
1974	−5 241	1 118	−4 123	−92	1 184	1 092	−302	−3 333	−4.0	−34	3 185	182
1975	−3 245	1 447	−1 798	−102	518	416	−313	−1 695	−1.6	−36	1 569	162
1976	−3 930	2 532	−1 398	−140	1 100	960	−534	−972	−0.8	−12	507	477
1977	−2 271	3 306	1 035	−152	−280	−432	−889	−286	−0.2	11	−3 286	3 561
1978	−1 534	3 777	2 243	−140	138	−2	−1 420	821	0.5	−79	−2 655	1 913
1979	−3 326	4 076	750	−130	155	25	−1 777	−1 002	−0.5	−103	864	241
1980	1 329	3 829	5 158	−82	−1 683	−1 765	−1 653	1 740	0.8	−4	−2 157	421
1981	3 238	3 951	7 189	−66	−1 058	−1 124	−1 219	4 846	1.9	−79	−5 312	545
1982	1 879	3 198	5 077	−95	−1 273	−1 368	−1 476	2 233	0.8	6	−1 233	−1 006
1983	−1 618	4 076	2 458	−89	280	191	−1 391	1 258	0.4	75	−3 287	1 954
1984	−5 409	4 491	−918	−94	1 284	1 190	−1 566	−1 294	−0.4	107	−7 130	8 317
1985	−3 416	6 767	3 351	−120	−877	−997	−2 924	−570	−0.2	185	−1 657	2 042
1986	−9 617	6 403	−3 214	−156	1 850	1 694	−2 094	−3 614	−0.9	135	−122	3 601
1987	−11 698	6 813	−4 885	−174	1 091	917	−3 570	−7 538	−1.8	333	10 764	−3 559
1988	−21 553	4 450	−17 103	−64	817	753	−3 500	−19 850	−4.2	235	17 201	2 414
1989	−24 724	3 643	−21 081	−138	−654	−792	−4 448	−26 321	−5.1	270	18 001	8 050
1990	−18 707	4 337	−14 370	−110	−2 869	−2 979	−4 932	−22 281	−4.0	497	15 083	6 701
1991	−10 223	4 102	−6 121	−63	−3 244	−3 307	−1 231	−10 659	−1.8	290	5 269	5 100
1992	−13 050	5 482	−7 568	−49	177	128	−5 534	−12 974	−2.1	421	5 089	7 464
1993	−13 066	6 581	−6 485	35	−226	−191	−5 243	−11 919	−1.9	309	11 330	280
1994	−11 126	6 379	−4 747	−170	3 518	3 348	−5 369	−6 768	−1.0	33	2 126	4 609
1995	−12 023	8 481	−3 542	−296	2 397	2 101	−7 574	−9 015	−1.3	533	5 005	3 477
1996	−13 722	10 372	−3 350	93	688	781	−4 755	−7 324	−1.0	1 260	4 036	2 028
1997	−12 342	13 198	856	83	3 193	3 276	−5 918	−1 786	−0.2	982	−9 769	10 573
1998	−21 813	13 869	−7 944	−10	12 314	12 304	−8 374	−4 014	−0.5	516	10 292	−6 794
1999	−29 051	13 634	−15 417	201	−1 661	−1 460	−7 383	−24 260	−2.7	773	22 113	1 374
2000	−32 976	13 726	−19 250	150	4 433	4 583	−9 752	−24 419	−2.6	1 527	13 706	9 186
2001	−40 648	13 703	−26 945	66	11 305	11 371	−6 611	−22 185	−2.2	1 206	19 310	1 669
2002	−47 087	15 536	−31 551	67	23 612	23 679	−8 615	−16 487	−1.6	868	8 027	7 592
2003	−47 864	16 882	−30 982	59	24 936	24 995	−9 961	−15 948	−1.4	1 296	28 894	−14 242
2004	−60 470	21 430	−39 040	71	26 342	26 413	−10 940	−23 567	−2.0	1 939	15 476	6 152
2005	−65 631	18 734	−46 897	80	27 328	27 408	−12 401	−31 890	−2.6	2 301	24 811	4 778

1 See chapter text.
2 Using series YBHA: GDP at current market prices.

Source: Office for National Statistics

19.11 Balance of payments:[1] current account
United Kingdom

£ million

		1995	1996	1997	1998	1999	2000	2001	2002	2003	2004	2005
Credits												
Exports of goods and services												
Exports of goods	LQAD	153 577	167 196	171 923	164 056	166 166	187 936	190 055	186 511	188 615	190 933	..
Exports of services	KTMQ	49 932	56 973	60 964	66 978	73 328	79 411	83 061	88 434	93 616	103 016	..
Total exports of goods and services	KTMW	203 509	224 169	232 887	231 034	239 494	267 347	273 116	274 945	282 231	293 949	..
Income												
Compensation of employees	KTMN	887	911	1 007	840	960	1 032	1 087	1 121	1 116	1 171	..
Investment income	HMBN	87 132	91 343	95 129	103 029	99 290	133 787	139 487	123 641	125 154	140 914	..
Total income	HMBQ	88 019	92 254	96 136	103 869	100 250	134 819	140 574	124 762	126 270	142 085	..
Current transfers												
Central government	FJUM	1 730	2 828	2 173	1 767	3 542	2 465	4 991	3 663	3 968	4 000	..
Other sectors	FJUN	10 821	17 201	10 898	10 597	9 828	8 336	9 601	9 038	8 400	8 560	..
Total current transfers	KTND	12 551	20 029	13 071	12 364	13 370	10 801	14 592	12 701	12 368	12 560	..
Total	HBOE	304 079	336 452	342 094	347 267	353 114	412 967	428 282	412 408	420 869	448 594	..
Debits												
Imports of goods and services												
Imports of goods	LQBL	165 600	180 918	184 265	185 869	195 217	220 912	230 703	233 598	236 479	251 347	..
Imports of services	KTMR	41 451	46 601	47 766	53 109	59 694	65 685	69 358	72 898	76 734	81 580	..
Total imports of goods and services	KTMX	207 051	227 519	232 031	238 978	254 911	286 597	300 061	306 496	313 213	332 927	..
Income												
Compensation of employees	KTMO	1 183	818	924	850	759	882	1 021	1 054	1 057	1 100	..
Investment income	HMBO	84 735	90 655	91 936	90 715	100 951	129 354	128 182	100 029	100 218	114 264	..
Total income	HMBR	85 918	91 473	92 860	91 565	101 710	130 236	129 203	101 083	101 275	115 364	..
Current transfers												
Central government	FJUO	5 022	5 297	5 260	6 787	7 482	8 015	7 584	9 296	10 939	12 300	..
Other sectors	FJUP	15 103	19 487	13 729	13 951	13 271	12 538	13 619	12 020	11 390	11 200	..
Total current transfers	KTNE	20 125	24 784	18 989	20 738	20 753	20 553	21 203	21 316	22 329	23 500	..
Total	HBOF	313 094	343 776	343 880	351 281	377 374	437 386	450 467	428 895	436 817	471 791	..
Balances												
Trade in goods and services												
Trade in goods	LQCT	−12 023	−13 722	−12 342	−21 813	−29 051	−32 976	−40 648	−47 087	−47 864	−60 470	−65 631
Trade in services	KTMS	8 481	10 372	13 198	13 869	13 634	13 726	13 703	15 536	16 882	21 430	18 734
Total trade in goods and services	KTMY	−3 542	−3 350	856	−7 944	−15 417	−19 250	−26 945	−31 551	−30 982	−39 040	−46 897
Income												
Compensation of employees	KTMP	−296	93	83	−10	201	150	66	67	59	71	80
Investment income	HMBM	2 397	688	3 193	12 314	−1 661	4 433	11 305	23 612	24 936	26 342	27 328
Total income	HMBP	2 101	781	3 276	12 304	−1 460	4 583	11 371	23 679	24 995	26 413	27 408
Current transfers												
Central government	FJUQ	−3 292	−2 469	−3 087	−5 020	−3 940	−5 550	−2 593	−5 633	−6 971	−8 300	..
Other sectors	FJUR	−4 282	−2 286	−2 831	−3 354	−3 443	−4 202	−4 018	−2 982	−2 990	−2 640	..
Total current transfers	KTNF	−7 574	−4 755	−5 918	−8 374	−7 383	−9 752	−6 611	−8 615	−9 961	−10 940	−12 401
Total (Current balance)	HBOG	−9 015	−7 324	−1 786	−4 014	−24 260	−24 419	−22 185	−16 487	−15 948	−23 567	−31 890

1 See chapter text.

Source: Office for National Statistics

19.12 Balance of payments:[1] summary of international investment position, financial account and investment income

United Kingdom

£ billion

		1994	1995	1996	1997	1998	1999	2000	2001	2002	2003	2004
Investment abroad												
International investment position												
Direct investment	HBWD	176.1	203.7	201.6	223.3	299.6	428.1	607.4	603.3	621.4	668.8	661.1
Portfolio investment	HHZZ	429.8	499.3	548.3	651.0	703.8	838.3	906.1	937.4	844.1	935.9	1 092.3
Other investment	HLXV	708.6	808.1	851.7	1 068.0	1 105.4	1 129.7	1 427.6	1 573.1	1 638.6	1 890.8	2 156.5
Reserve assets	LTEB	30.7	31.8	27.3	22.8	23.3	22.2	28.8	25.6	25.5	23.8	23.3
Total	HBQA	1 345.2	1 542.9	1 628.9	1 965.1	2 132.2	2 418.2	2 969.9	3 139.5	3 129.6	3 519.3	3 933.2
Financial account transactions												
Direct investment	-HJYP	22.7	28.7	22.3	38.2	73.3	125.0	155.0	41.3	34.5	37.3	52.6
Portfolio investment	-HHZC	-21.8	39.3	59.8	51.9	32.1	21.4	65.6	86.6	1.0	36.3	140.9
Financial derivatives (net)	-ZPNN	-2.4	-1.7	-1.0	-1.2	3.0	-2.7	-1.6	-8.4	-1.0	5.4	7.9
Other investment	-XBMM	27.8	47.5	136.7	169.5	15.0	59.4	275.6	173.8	96.9	259.2	325.7
Reserve assets	-LTCV	1.0	-0.2	-0.5	-2.4	-0.2	-0.6	3.9	-3.1	-0.5	-1.6	0.2
Total	-HBNR	27.3	113.6	217.2	256.1	123.2	202.4	498.5	290.1	131.0	336.6	527.2
Investment income												
Direct investment	HJYW	21.9	24.8	28.5	29.4	29.8	33.1	44.9	46.6	51.3	54.9	64.2
Portfolio investment	HLYX	16.4	19.7	20.2	23.8	29.3	25.7	33.0	34.9	32.5	32.6	36.7
Other investment	AIOP	33.8	41.0	41.0	40.5	42.8	39.4	54.9	57.0	39.0	36.9	39.3
Reserve assets	HHCB	1.6	1.7	1.6	1.4	1.1	1.2	1.0	1.0	0.8	0.8	0.7
Total	HMBN	73.7	87.1	91.3	95.1	103.0	99.3	133.8	139.5	123.6	125.2	140.9
Investment in the UK												
International investment position												
Direct investment	HBWI	129.9	146.2	152.6	173.7	213.6	250.3	310.4	363.6	339.8	355.1	383.9
Portfolio investment	HLXW	320.0	406.3	479.8	583.1	692.6	828.4	998.0	958.4	892.3	1 046.2	1 170.8
Other investment	HLYD	877.4	1 013.0	1 061.7	1 274.3	1 355.0	1 403.9	1 696.4	1 889.6	1 945.8	2 183.3	2 523.9
Total	HBQB	1 327.3	1 565.5	1 694.2	2 031.2	2 261.3	2 482.5	3 004.8	3 211.6	3 177.9	3 584.6	4 078.6
Financial account transactions												
Direct investment	HJYU	7.1	13.8	17.6	22.9	45.1	55.1	80.6	37.3	16.8	16.8	42.4
Portfolio investment	HHZF	30.7	37.3	43.0	26.8	20.8	114.0	164.6	48.1	51.0	95.9	86.4
Other investment	XBMN	-8.3	67.5	160.7	196.7	67.6	55.5	267.0	224.0	71.2	252.8	413.8
Total	HBNS	29.5	118.6	221.3	246.4	133.5	224.6	512.2	309.5	139.0	365.5	542.6
Investment income												
Direct investment	HJYX	10.6	13.8	16.6	14.9	8.6	17.0	27.4	21.4	16.0	21.8	27.7
Portfolio investment	HLZC	17.2	20.6	23.8	26.6	29.1	31.2	30.7	34.5	32.1	31.6	36.3
Other investment	HLZN	42.5	50.3	50.3	50.5	53.0	52.8	71.2	72.3	52.0	46.8	50.3
Total	HMBO	70.2	84.7	90.7	91.9	90.7	101.0	129.4	128.2	100.0	100.2	114.3
Net investment												
International investment position												
Direct investment	HBWQ	46.2	57.5	49.0	49.5	85.9	177.8	297.1	239.7	281.7	313.7	277.2
Portfolio investment	CGNH	109.8	93.0	68.5	67.8	11.2	9.9	-92.0	-21.0	-48.2	-110.3	-78.5
Other investment	CGNG	-168.8	-204.9	-210.1	-206.4	-249.6	-274.2	-268.8	-316.5	-307.2	-292.5	-367.4
Reserve assets	LTEB	30.7	31.8	27.3	22.8	23.3	22.2	28.8	25.6	25.5	23.8	23.3
Net investment position	HBQC	17.9	-22.6	-65.3	-66.1	-129.1	-64.3	-34.9	-72.1	-48.3	-65.4	-145.5
Financial account transactions												
Direct investment	HJYV	-15.6	-14.9	-4.7	-15.3	-28.3	-70.0	-74.4	-4.0	-17.7	-20.5	-10.2
Portfolio investment	HHZD	52.5	-2.0	-16.8	-25.2	-11.2	92.6	99.1	-38.4	50.0	59.6	-54.5
Financial derivatives	ZPNN	2.4	1.7	1.0	1.2	-3.0	2.7	1.6	8.4	1.0	-5.4	-7.9
Other investment	HHYR	-36.1	20.0	24.1	27.2	52.7	-3.9	-8.6	50.2	-25.7	-6.3	88.1
Reserve assets	LTCV	-1.0	0.2	0.5	2.4	0.2	0.6	-3.9	3.1	0.5	1.6	-0.2
Net transactions	HBNT	2.1	5.0	4.0	-9.8	10.3	22.1	13.7	19.3	8.0	28.9	15.5
Investment income												
Direct investment	HJYE	11.4	10.9	11.9	14.5	21.3	16.1	17.6	25.2	35.4	33.1	36.5
Portfolio investment	HLZX	-0.8	-0.9	-3.5	-2.7	0.2	-5.5	2.3	0.4	0.4	1.0	0.5
Other investment	CGNA	-8.7	-9.4	-9.2	-9.9	-10.2	-13.4	-16.4	-15.3	-13.0	-9.9	-11.1
Reserve assets	HHCB	1.6	1.7	1.6	1.4	1.1	1.2	1.0	1.0	0.8	0.8	0.7
Net earnings	HMBM	3.5	2.4	0.7	3.2	12.3	-1.7	4.4	11.3	23.6	24.9	26.3

1 See chapter text.

Source: Office for National Statistics

19.13 Net outward foreign direct investment by United Kingdom companies:[1,2] by area and main country

£ million

		2000	2001	2002	2003	2004
Europe	GQBX	127 448	13 743	27 300	16 600	10 440
EU25	DG7S	125 075	12 507	28 865	13 339	11 616
Austria	CBJD	240	1 628	797	165	1 308
Belgium	HIIL	1 643	103	1 046	−1 241	88
Cyprus	DG8D	42	−13	−79	−53	31
Czech Republic	DG8O	4	216	49	142	2
Denmark	CAUW	−67	−423	543	−53	431
Estonia	DG8E	..	6	5	4	21
Finland	CBJE	−196	61	1 124	99	−39
France	CAUX	6 398	2 794	4 112	6 627	617
Germany	CAUY	113 762	724	8 473	1 552	−361
Greece	CAUZ	624	156	−65	229	−252
Hungary	DG8F	544	746	163	527	316
Irish Republic	CAVA	4 679	2 698	1 674	985	3 387
Italy	CAVB	327	612	572	500	944
Latvia	DG8G	2	..	1	..	1
Lithuania	DG8H	..	..	..	..	1
Luxembourg	HIIM	−1 495	1 019	−2 046	1 313	−988
Malta	DG8I	4	32	..	58	..
Netherlands	CAVC	−4 335	4 324	13 152	728	5 000
Poland	DG8J	38	304	431	4	141
Portugal	CAVD	105	144	88	308	459
Slovakia	DG8K	..	−8	−22	−11	18
Slovenia	DG8L	..	..	..	37	..
Spain	CAVE	1 574	−1 564	288	626	1 090
Sweden	CBJG	1 309	−1 134	−35	794	451
EFTA	CAVG	408	−1 569	994	2 313	−6 578
of which						
Norway	CBJF	−75	508	−329	−274	365
Switzerland	CBJH	483	−2 077	1 329	2 591	−6 913
Other European Countries	DG8M	1 965	2 805	−2 559	948	5 404
of which						
Russia	GLAA	246	498	108	2 030	1 755
UK offshore islands	GLAC	1 952	1 346	−1 249	−1 031	3 478
America	GQBZ	29 558	23 987	−5 150	15 959	26 818
of which						
Bermuda	CBKZ	−270	801	−4 371	−2 613	6 278
Brazil	CBLA	596	352	17	786	247
Canada	CAVK	2 566	4 142	536	2 521	1 288
Chile	GQCA	295	292	1 021	290	673
Colombia	GQCB	58	57	−385	78	283
Mexico	GLAD	195	−139	939	261	1 392
Panama	GLAE	19	−19	..	58	12
USA	CAVJ	24 249	15 865	−984	19 300	12 917
Asia	GQCI	−3 568	524	5 538	3 601	7 306
Near and Middle East Countries	CBKF	43	822	376	82	315
of which						
Gulf Arabian countries[3]	GQCC	−13	738	369	−85	128
Other Asian Countries	GQCD	−3 611	−297	5 162	3 518	6 991
of which						
China	HIIN	410	662	757	309	517
Hong Kong	CAVN	−3 309	590	1 186	1 285	5 340
India	GLAF	287	135	276	193	269
Indonesia	GLAG	122	−31	70	481	−290
Japan	CAVM	1 390	−4 219	388	338	38
Malaysia	CBKN	−250	−321	334	277	424
Singapore	CBKQ	−3 387	1 681	1 619	−449	−356
South Korea	GLAH	−30	−	174	332	268
Thailand	GLAI	257	173	−55	155	167
Australasia and Oceania	GQCE	−595	1 478	3 677	−1 524	1 464
of which						
Australia	CBJO	−482	1 787	3 322	−492	1 163
New Zealand	CBJP	−53	−323	337	−1 017	254
Africa	GQCF	1 401	1 152	2 196	3 454	5 783
of which						
Kenya	GLAJ	137	42	32	58	58
Nigeria	CBJY	57	74	220	19	−23
South Africa	CAVO	629	325	2 265	2 222	3 828
Zimbabwe	CBKD	38	40	33	37	92
World Total	CDQD	154 242	40 884	33 561	38 088	51 812
OECD	GQCG	153 389	28 633	36 096	37 030	23 410
Central and Eastern Europe[4]	GQCH	263	1 543	654	156	−10

1 See chapter text. Net investment includes re-invested earnings.
2 Minus sign indicates net disinvestment abroad.
3 Includes Abu Dhabi, Bahrain, Dubai, Iraq, Kuwait, Oman, Other Gulf States, Qatar, Saudi Arabia and Yemen.

4 Includes Albania, Bulgaria, Croatia, Czech Republic, Estonia, Hungary, Latvia, Lithuania, Poland, Romania, Serbia and Montenegro, Slovakia, Bosnia and Herzegovina, Macedonia FYR and Slovenia.

Source: ONS FDI Inquiries: 01633 813314; Bank of England

19.14 United Kingdom outward foreign direct international investment position: book value of net assets: by area and main country[1]

At year end

£ million

		2000	2001	2002	2003	2004
Europe	GQCJ	384 204	368 465	390 359	408 881	381 066
EU25	DG8P	357 724	330 183	343 931	354 707	348 291
Austria	CDLZ	1 054	2 428	2 679	3 339	4 119
Belgium	HIIO	7 299	6 175	10 364	8 662	8 401
Cyprus	DG8Q	74	92	84	80	97
Czech Republic	DG8R	489	858	1 088	954	820
Denmark	CDLP	2 143	2 607	3 165	3 021	5 253
Estonia	DG8S	..	29	29	21	78
Finland	CDMA	597	640	580	588	695
France	CDLQ	21 845	24 683	31 928	31 460	30 918
Germany	CDLR	23 354	13 448	13 924	13 486	11 861
Greece	CDLS	1 001	1 155	498	460	455
Hungary	DG8T	410	1 185	1 403	1 722	1 537
Irish Republic	CDLT	33 305	23 033	29 944	29 989	33 875
Italy	CDLU	3 643	4 267	5 505	10 178	11 637
Latvia	DG8U	3	..	51	13	25
Lithuania	DG8V	..	..	24	16	22
Luxembourg	HIIP	52 499	64 042	62 556	79 208	80 524
Malta	DG8W	36	−9	−24	264	−1 321
Netherlands	CDLV	182 944	164 973	158 478	146 345	134 232
Poland	DG8X	1 037	1 749	2 809	2 900	2 348
Portugal	CDLW	1 069	918	629	973	1 659
Slovakia	DG8Y	−34	−18	261	332	102
Slovenia	DG8Z	..	89	92	128	88
Spain	CDLX	5 907	7 091	7 156	9 460	11 004
Sweden	CDMD	19 064	10 747	10 712	11 108	9 864
EFTA	CDLY	10 708	18 931	22 069	27 187	13 748
of which						
Norway	CDMC	4 236	4 340	4 904	4 900	4 933
Switzerland	CDME	6 466	14 584	17 164	21 913	8 387
Other European Countries	DG92	15 772	19 351	24 359	26 987	19 027
of which						
Russia	GQAA	283	1 062	744	777	1 579
UK offshore islands	GQAB	14 930	16 579	15 203	22 717	15 287
America	GQCU	173 409	176 685	167 345	178 599	188 599
of which						
Bermuda	CDOA	6 054	6 689	4 929	1 554	7 581
Brazil	CDOB	3 281	2 976	2 050	2 532	2 925
Canada	CDML	10 142	10 328	8 209	8 537	8 119
Chile	GQCT	1 506	1 895	2 036	1 919	2 129
Colombia	GQCS	1 691	1 272	1 752	2 434	1 933
Mexico	GQAC	1 018	887	1 450	1 431	2 460
Panama	GQAD	226	204	..	153	131
USA	CDMM	141 355	143 359	131 800	150 021	148 569
Asia	GQCL	24 616	30 044	28 914	43 118	47 014
Near and Middle East Countries	CDNH	1 760	2 344	1 619	1 559	2 816
of which						
Gulf Arabian countries[2]	GQCM	704	1 482	1 027	1 211	1 876
Other Asian Countries	GQCR	22 856	27 700	27 295	41 559	44 198
of which						
China	HIIQ	1 505	2 106	3 212	1 809	1 887
Hong Kong	CDNN	4 745	6 638	5 872	17 221	19 210
India	GQAE	1 204	1 488	1 409	1 555	1 674
Indonesia	GQAF	611	1 612	1 014	1 309	1 176
Japan	CDMP	4 613	1 754	1 896	2 361	5 819
Malaysia	CDNQ	2 423	2 390	1 214	1 476	1 586
Singapore	CDNT	3 286	5 947	6 797	9 510	6 180
South Korea	GQAG	443	547	927	1 339	1 120
Thailand	GQAH	682	831	1 513	1 357	932
Australasia and Oceania	GQCN	10 080	15 487	16 652	17 486	22 844
of which						
Australia	CDMO	8 101	13 700	13 936	16 283	21 139
New Zealand	CDMQ	1 701	1 560	2 524	1 060	1 461
Africa	GQCQ	9 383	8 948	13 516	17 039	17 272
of which						
Kenya	GQAI	373	294	278	285	235
Nigeria	CDNA	906	1 044	1 012	1 028	970
South Africa	CDMR	3 747	4 148	8 765	11 250	10 939
Zimbabwe	CDNF	130	166	62	48	103
World Total	CDOO	601 692	599 628	616 786	665 123	656 794
OECD	GQCO	536 232	522 287	527 681	563 769	553 089
Central & Eastern Europe[3]	GQCP	2 032	4 349	6 449	560	601

1 See chapter text.
2 Includes Abu Dhabi, Bahrain, Dubai, Iraq, Kuwait, Oman, Other Gulf States, Qatar, Saudi Arabia and Yemen.

3 Includes Albania, Bulgaria, Croatia, Czech Republic, Estonia, Hungary, Latvia, Lithuania, Poland, Romania, Serbia and Montenegro, Slovakia, Bosnia and Herzegovina, Macedonia FYR and Slovenia.

Sources: ONS Foreign Direct Investment Inquiries: 01633 813314; Bank of England

19.15 Net earnings from foreign direct investment overseas by United Kingdom companies:[1,2] by area and main country

£ million

		2000	2001	2002	2003	2004
Europe	GQCV	21 760	24 719	26 598	26 857	27 210
EU25	DG93	17 843	22 092	23 151	22 972	21 746
Austria	CBLQ	77	68	267	317	301
Belgium	HIIR	480	570	549	324	652
Cyprus	DG94	11	26	93	20	22
Czech Republic	DG95	57	132	115	165	183
Denmark	CAWI	248	227	54	197	272
Estonia	DG96	..	2	4	9	3
Finland	CBLR	95	73	95	103	112
France	CAWJ	1 693	1 610	1 904	1 714	2 000
Germany	CAWK	946	679	2 199	1 592	2 300
Greece	CAWL	72	95	120	120	100
Hungary	DG97	282	182	232	241	277
Irish Republic	CAWM	1 638	2 123	1 553	2 197	2 646
Italy	CAWN	539	585	517	639	718
Latvia	DG98	..	..	..	–	–
Lithuania	DG99	..	..	..	–	–
Luxembourg	HIIS	1 672	2 163	1 822	1 500	2 269
Malta	DG9A	28	24	36	41	480
Netherlands	CAWO	8 348	11 465	11 395	11 691	6 820
Poland	DG9B	27	194	210	290	329
Portugal	CAWP	174	182	115	175	205
Slovakia	DG9C	9	..	21	..	..
Slovenia	DG9D	26	..	..	..	..
Spain	CAWQ	749	627	672	576	697
Sweden	CBLT	668	970	1 115	959	1 251
EFTA	CAWS	2 393	1 010	1 643	1 761	2 379
of which						
Norway	CBLS	409	450	293	319	297
Switzerland	CBLU	1 983	559	1 349	1 441	2 080
Other European Countries	DG9E	1 524	1 617	1 804	2 124	3 085
of which						
Russia	GQAJ	62	297	334	345	983
UK offshore islands	GQAK	1 172	916	1 127	1 332	1 615
America	GQCX	14 886	13 529	14 716	17 586	21 403
of which						
Bermuda	CBNK	344	−90	203	1 254	1 645
Brazil	CBNL	256	344	378	291	552
Canada	CAWW	1 140	864	1 015	1 055	1 388
Chile	GQCY	236	156	199	273	819
Colombia	GQCZ	293	190	200	234	379
Mexico	GQAL	105	−48	295	207	486
Panama	GQAM	46	45	44	55	44
USA	CAWV	11 142	10 646	11 461	12 723	14 658
Asia	GQDA	4 434	4 356	4 755	5 108	8 040
Near and Middle East Countries	CBMS	908	596	398	461	689
of which						
Gulf Arabian countries[3]	GQDB	721	420	335	370	547
Other Asian Countries	GQDC	3 527	3 761	4 357	4 647	7 351
of which						
China	HIIT	74	340	255	278	447
Hong Kong	CAYB	708	341	610	1 083	2 539
India	GQAN	311	324	496	511	424
Indonesia	GQAO	81	150	132	184	155
Japan	CAWY	505	382	181	332	440
Malaysia	CBNA	400	277	448	477	524
Singapore	CBND	902	1 276	1 053	911	1 598
South Korea	GQAP	37	111	233	237	340
Thailand	GQAQ	90	166	162	160	158
Australasia and Oceania	GQDD	1 591	1 651	2 337	2 022	3 140
of which						
Australia	CBMB	1 393	1 337	1 818	1 518	2 828
New Zealand	CBMC	171	304	488	478	278
Africa	GQDE	1 567	1 849	2 973	2 959	3 964
of which						
Kenya	GQAR	71	70	64	81	64
Nigeria	CBML	88	95	282	122	153
South Africa	CAWZ	734	983	1 784	1 693	2 713
Zimbabwe	CBMQ	60	61	37	43	87
World Total	GLAB	44 237	46 103	51 379	54 531	63 757
OECD	GQDF	34 824	36 732	40 229	41 353	44 181
Central & Eastern Europe[4]	GQDG	465	791	802	195	216

1 See chapter text. A minus sign indicates net losses.
2 Net earnings equal profits of overseas branches plus UK companies' receipts of interest and their share of profits of overseas subsidiaries and associates. Earnings are after deducting provisions for depreciation and withholding tax on profits, dividends and interest.
3 Includes Abu Dhabi, Bahrain, Dubai, Iraq, Kuwait, Oman, Other Gulf States, Qatar, Saudi Arabia and Yemen.

4 Includes Albania, Bulgaria, Croatia, Czech Republic, Estonia, Hungary, Latvia, Lithuania, Poland, Romania, Serbia and Montenegro, Slovakia, Bosnia and Herzegovina, Macedonia FYR and Slovenia.

Source: ONS FDI Inquiries: 01633 813314; Bank of England

329

19.16 Net inward foreign direct investment in the United Kingdom:[1,2] by area and main country

£ million

		2000	2001	2002	2003	2004
Europe	GQDH	53 839	17 213	15 431	7 013	27 903
EU25	DG9F	52 404	17 509	15 721	5 498	24 797
Austria	CBOB	175	−149	..	8	−29
Belgium	HIIU	137	−23	−333	218	1 760
Cyprus	DG9G	2	1	−3	−	−
Czech Republic	DG9H	..	2	..	−	−
Denmark	CAYQ	481	195	114	321	−31
Estonia	DG9I	..	..	..	−	−
Finland	CBOC	87	26	5	26	−171
France	CAYR	31 722	8 779	1 460	414	1 870
Germany	CAYS	10 564	279	11 340	1 437	10 309
Greece	CAYT	..	4	7	33	13
Hungary	DG9J	1	1	..	−	..
Irish Republic	CAYU	384	755	210	206	905
Italy	CAYV	469	2 848	−208	−468	−632
Latvia	DG9K	..	..	..	..	−
Lithuania	DG9L	..	..	..	−	..
Luxembourg	HIIV	688	196	1	−105	−115
Malta	DG9M	..	1	..	−	−
Netherlands	CAYW	4 629	4 256	1 756	2 452	2 282
Poland	DG9N	4	4	1	−	..
Portugal	CAYX	−6	7	−12	..	..
Slovakia	DG9O	..	..	..	..	..
Slovenia	DG9P	..	..	..	..	..
Spain	CAYY	..	224	232	518	..
Sweden	CBOE	657	106	493	406	−40
EFTA of which	CAZB	740	−944	−298	1 408	2 616
Norway	CBOD	−392	−227	−137	−179	−806
Switzerland	CBOF	1 119	−775	−162	1 411	3 025
Other European Countries of which	DG9Q	695	648	9	107	490
Russia	GQAS	..	19	..	..	..
UK offshore islands	GQAT	646	622	−8	32	432
America of which	GQDJ	15 032	16 056	−2 051	3 396	−2 550
Canada	CAZF	1 882	−261	562	−325	871
USA	CAZE	12 741	15 025	−2 157	2 676	−3 678
Asia	GQDK	7 725	3 132	2 551	−449	3 964
Near and Middle East Countries	GQAU	88	287	−26	−34	317
Other Asian Countries of which	GQAV	7 637	2 845	2 579	−415	3 647
Hong Kong	GQAW	921	70	63	63	..
Japan	CAZH	5 765	2 572	2 352	−543	861
Singapore	GQAX	800	78	157	−76	14
South Korea	GQAY	−18	1	−26	−20	−117
Australasia and Oceania of which	GQDL	1 483	92	31	310	1 432
Australia	CBOJ	1 440	112	14	309	1 404
New Zealand	CBOK	40	−24	18	2	8
Africa of which	GQAZ	416	63	71	7	−43
South Africa	CAZJ	378	51	63	21	−35
World Total	CBDH	78 495	36 555	16 033	10 276	30 703
OECD	GQBA	74 995	33 980	16 194	8 984	26 708
Central & Eastern Europe[4]	GQBB	8	10	−	4	29

1 See chapter text. Net investment includes reinvested earnings.
2 A minus sign indicates net disinvestment in the UK.
3 Includes Albania, Bulgaria, Croatia, Czech Republic, Estonia, Hungary, Latvia, Lithuania, Poland, Romania, Serbia and Montenegro, Slovakia, Bosnia and Herzegovina, Macedonia FYR and Slovenia.

Sources: ONS Foreign Direct Investment Inquiries: 01633 813314;
Bank of England

19.17 United Kingdom inward foreign direct international investment position: book value of net liabilities: by area and main country[1]

At year end   £ million

		2000	2001	2002	2003	2004
Europe	GQDM	150 203	166 532	157 313	158 903	185 773
EU25	DG9R	136 893	151 245	142 514	142 240	166 592
Austria	CDPF	565	385	1 003	349	367
Belgium	HIIW	2 200	2 208	1 765	1 987	3 822
Cyprus	DG9S	122	177	68	67	39
Czech Republic	DG9T	..	14	3	9	6
Denmark	CDOV	2 758	3 955	2 358	2 086	2 201
Estonia	DG9U	..	..	..	−	−
Finland	CDPG	1 042	1 084	767	946	658
France	CDOW	48 947	35 213	37 195	36 565	41 432
Germany	CDOX	26 140	29 731	37 737	32 260	44 278
Greece	CDOY	..	92	89	86	100
Hungary	DG9V	9	13	8	9	12
Irish Republic	CDOZ	3 474	4 209	4 544	4 769	5 954
Italy	CDPA	2 415	6 522	5 788	4 580	4 825
Latvia	DG9W	..	..	..	..	−
Lithuania	DG9X	..	..	..	..	..
Luxembourg	HIIX	1 854	2 330	4 985	5 627	6 604
Malta	DG9Y	17	24	22	21	5
Netherlands	CDPB	41 565	60 920	39 512	46 876	48 064
Poland	DG9Z	47	19	13	10	7
Portugal	CDPC	180	129	97	115	108
Slovakia	DGA2	..	..	..	..	..
Slovenia	DGA3	..	..	..	..	..
Spain	CDPD	475	606	2 303	3 344	5 296
Sweden	CDPI	3 929	3 613	4 254	2 527	2 811
EFTA	CDPE	10 103	10 465	10 951	13 758	14 647
of which						
Norway	CDPH	854	832	1 019	831	234
Switzerland	CDPJ	9 091	9 341	9 717	12 439	13 573
Other European Countries	DGA4	3 207	4 822	3 849	2 906	4 534
of which						
Russia	GQBC	..	..	..	..	..
UK offshore islands	GQBD	2 774	4 366	3 393	2 361	3 915
America	GQDU	113 882	151 338	138 156	145 973	138 898
of which						
Canada	CDPM	9 307	8 693	8 718	11 176	12 611
USA	CDPN	101 245	136 967	124 597	130 512	121 408
Asia	GQDO	17 890	19 388	20 323	19 869	24 580
Near and Middle East Countries	GQBE	1 370	1 788	1 697	1 627	2 650
Other Asian Countries	GQBF	16 520	17 600	18 626	18 242	21 931
of which						
Hong Kong	GQBG	..	3 613	..	..	..
Japan	CDPQ	10 545	10 900	11 791	11 949	12 233
Singapore	GQBH	1 656	1 591	1 684	830	925
South Korea	GQBI	−245	108	448	635	634
Australasia and Oceania	GQDP	10 661	11 167	8 462	14 336	16 787
of which						
Australia	CDPP	9 875	10 997	8 309	14 160	16 615
New Zealand	CDPR	780	149	134	158	153
Africa	GQBJ	1 312	917	427	560	495
of which						
South Africa	CDPS	969	757	250	387	275
World Total	CDPZ	293 949	349 342	324 680	339 641	366 534
OECD	GQBK	278 358	329 296	307 395	324 491	344 836
Central & Eastern Europe[2]	GQBL	110	84	58	34	..

1 See chapter text.
2 Includes Albania, Bulgaria, Croatia, Czech Republic, Estonia, Hungary, Latvia, Lithuania, Poland, Romania, Serbia and Montenegro, Slovakia, Bosnia and Herzegovina, Macedonia FYR and Slovenia.

Sources: ONS Foreign Direct Investment Inquiries: 01633 813314;
Bank of England

19.18 Net earnings from foreign direct investment in the United Kingdom:[1],[2] by area and main country

£ million

		2000	2001	2002	2003	2004
Europe	GQDQ	15 304	11 250	5 475	10 158	12 740
EU25	DGA5	13 817	10 086	4 447	9 011	11 144
Austria	CBOR	79	93	176	111	61
Belgium	HIIY	−27	79	38	165	243
Cyprus	DGA6	9	16	16	24	20
Czech Republic	DGA7	..	1	..	−	−
Denmark	CBDL	373	259	253	305	311
Estonia	DGA8	..	..	..	−	−
Finland	CBOS	207	197	70	36	−50
France	CBDM	2 186	1 632	1 322	2 743	3 889
Germany	CBDN	2 233	−633	−1 109	1 754	2 732
Greece	CBDO	21	46	64	4	−4
Hungary	DGA9	..	..	..	−	−
Irish Republic	CBDP	422	426	561	578	503
Italy	CBDQ	155	375	−148	174	298
Latvia	DGB2	..	..	..	..	−
Lithuania	DGB3	..	..	..	−	..
Luxembourg	HIIZ	164	74	87	196	282
Malta	DGB4	..	1	..	−	−
Netherlands	CBDR	7 611	6 972	2 455	2 405	2 855
Poland	DGB5	..	2	1	−	−
Portugal	CBDS	9	6	13	49	47
Slovakia	DGB6	..	..	..	..	..
Slovenia	DGB7	..	..	..	..	..
Spain	CBDT	88	203	52	298	−71
Sweden	CBOU	280	337	599	167	21
EFTA	CBDW	1 451	816	735	822	1 038
of which						
Norway	CBOT	120	59	40	−	−20
Switzerland	CBOV	1 323	749	692	794	1 008
Other European Countries	DGB8	36	348	293	325	558
of which						
Russia	GQBM	..	..	..	..	..
UK offshore islands	GQBN	−34	313	267	287	527
America	GQDV	8 482	7 385	7 314	10 013	12 406
of which						
Canada	CBEA	774	147	659	639	1 182
USA	CBDZ	7 789	7 204	6 623	9 054	10 963
Asia	GQDS	1 227	1 099	1 214	−781	142
Near and Middle East Countries	GQBO	68	154	33	114	173
Other Asian Countries	GQBP	1 159	945	1 182	−895	−30
of which						
Hong Kong	GQBQ	36	11	−52	−456	−474
Japan	CBEC	925	684	1 022	−538	688
Singapore	GQBS	235	114	100	62	32
South Korea	GQBT	−85	3	16	−54	−289
Australasia and Oceania	GQDT	222	82	432	835	721
of which						
Australia	CBOZ	195	17	396	802	694
New Zealand	CBPA	21	15	3	4	5
Africa	GQBU	180	154	99	59	59
of which						
South Africa	CBED	167	122	97	50	26
World Total	CBEV	25 415	19 971	14 534	20 283	26 068
OECD	GQBV	24 907	18 988	13 904	19 715	25 391
Central & Eastern Europe[3]	GQBW	5	5	2	1	1

1 See chapter text. A minus sign indicates net losses.
2 Net earnings equal profits of UK branches plus overseas investors' receipts of interest and their share of the profits of UK subsidiaries and associates. Earnings are after deducting provisions for depreciation and withholding tax on profits and interest.
3 Includes Albania, Bulgaria, Croatia, Czech Republic, Estonia, Hungary, Latvia, Lithuania, Poland, Romania, Serbia and Montenegro, Slovakia, Bosnia and Herzegovina, Macedonia FYR and Slovenia.

Sources: ONS Foreign Direct Investment Inquiries: 01633 813314; Bank of England

Research and development

Chapter 20

Research and development

Research and experimental development (R&D) is defined for statistical purposes as 'creative work undertaken on a systematic basis in order to increase the stock of knowledge, including knowledge of man, culture and society, and the use of this stock of knowledge to devise new applications'.

R&D is financed and carried out mainly by businesses, the Government, and institutions of higher education. A small amount is performed by non-profit-making bodies. Gross Expenditure on R&D (GERD) is an indicator of the total amount of R&D performed within the UK: it has been approximately two per cent of GDP in recent years. Detailed figures are reported each year in a First Release published in March and the August edition of the Office for National Statistics (ONS) publication *Economic Trends*. Table 20.1 shows the main components of GERD. ONS conducts an annual survey of expenditure and employment on R&D performed by Government, and of Government funding of R&D. The survey collects data on outturn and planning years. Until 1993 the detailed results were reported in the *Annual Review of Government Funded R&D* produced by the Office of Science and Technology (OST). From 1997 the results have appeared in OST's *Science, Engineering and Technology Statistics* publication. Table 20.2 gives some broad totals for gross expenditure by Government (expenditure before deducting funds received by Government for R&D). Table 20.3 gives a breakdown of net expenditure (receipts are deducted).

ONS conducts an annual survey of R&D in business. Table 20.5 gives a summary of the main trends up to 2004. The latest set of results from the survey will be available in a First Release dated 24 November 2006 and a Business Monitor (MA14) published on 19 January 2007.

Statistics on expenditure and employment on R&D in Higher Education Institutions (HEIs) are based on information collected by Higher Education Funding Councils and HESA (Higher Education Statistics Agency). In 1994 a new methodology was introduced to estimate expenditure on R&D in HEIs. This is based on the allocation of various Funding Council Grants. Full details of the new methodology are contained in SET Statistics available on the Office of Science and Technology website at www.ost.gov.uk/setstats/.

The most comprehensive international comparisons of resources devoted to R&D appear in Main Science and Technology Indicators published by the organisation for Economic Co-operation and Development (OECD). The Statistical Office of the European Union and the United Nations also compile R&D statistics based on figures supplied by member states. To make international comparisons more reliable the OECD have published a series of manuals giving guidance on how to measure various components of R&D inputs and outputs. The most important of these is the Frascati Manual, which defines R&D and recommends how resources for R&D should be measured. The UK follows the Frascati Manual as far as possible. For information on available aggregated data on Research and Development please contact Julie Owens on 01633 812789 (e-mail Julie.owens@ons.gsi.gov.uk).

20.1 Cost of research and development: by sector[1]
United Kingdom

£ million and percentages

	1998		1999		2000		2001		2002		2003		2004	
	£m	%	£m	%	£m	%	£m	%	£m	%	£m	%	£m	%
Sector carrying out the work **Cash terms (£ million)**														
Government	1 471	10	1 464	9	1 593	9	1 160	6	1 053	5	1 243	6	1 234	6
Research councils	591	4	622	4	646	4	670	4	699	4	788	4	849	4
Business enterprise	10 133	66	11 302	67	11 510	65	12 336	66	13 110	66	13 687	66	13 504	64
Higher education	3 040	20	3 324	20	3 648	21	4 034	22	4 416	22	4 454	21	4 753	23
Private non-profit	226	1	257	2	322	2	423	2	539	3	669	3	666	3
Total	15 460	100	16 969	100	17 718	100	18 623	100	19 817	100	20 842	100	21 006	100
Sector providing the funds **Cash terms (£ million)**														
Government	2 564	16	2 712	16	2 763	16	2 440	13	2 178	11	2 925	14	3 026	14
Research councils	1 139	7	1 211	7	1 317	8	1 512	8	1 713	9	1 947	9	2 084	10
Higher education funding councils	1 085	7	1 157	7	1 276	7	1 474	8	1 626	8	1 665	8	1 084	9
Higher education	130	1	143	1	158	1	177	1	196	1	199	1	214	1
Business enterprise[2]	7 331	48	8 137	48	8 559	49	8 740	47	9 138	46	9 139	44	9 067	43
Private non-profit	621	4	701	4	815	5	888	5	963	5	931	4	960	5
Abroad	2 590	17	2 908	17	2 830	16	3 392	18	4 003	20	4 035	19	3 850	18
Total	15 460	100	16 969	100	17 547	100	18 623	100	19 817	100	20 842	100	21 006	100

1 See chapter text.
2 Including research associations and public corporations.

Source: Office for National Statistics: 01633 812789

20.2 Gross central government expenditure on research and development[1]
United Kingdom

£ million

	1998/99		1999/00		2000/01		2001/02		2002/03		2003/04	
	Intra-mural	Extra-mural[2]	Intra-mural	Extra-mural[2]	Intra-mural	Extra-mural[2]	Intra-mural	Extra-mural[2]	Intra-mural	Extra-mural[2]	Intra-mural	Extra-mural[2]
Defence[3]	801	..	798	..	932	..	419	1 685	288	2 502	380	2 364
Research councils	608	865	644	894	667	1 024	695	1 244	725	1 457	811	1 643
Higher education institutes	-	1 085	-	1 157	-	1 276	-	1 474	-	1 626	-	1 665
Other programmes	266	714	274	810	283	841	282	982	297	1 178	338	1 149
Total (excluding NHS)	1 692	..	1 703	..	1 778	..	1 396	5 385	1 310	6 763	1 529	6 820

1 See chapter text.
2 Extramural Includes work performed overseas and excludes monies spent with other government departments.
3 .. Denotes figures no longer available due to MOD revision between the years 1997 - 2000. The details are outlined in Defence Statistics Bulletin 6, which is available at the following web address: www.dasa.mod.uk

Source: Office for National Statistics: 01633 812789

20.3 Net central government expenditure on research and development:[1] by European Union objectives for research and development expenditure

United Kingdom

£ million

		1993/94	1994/95	1995/96	1996/97	1997/98	1998/99	1999/00	2000/01	2001/02	2002/03	2003/04
Exploration and exploitation of the earth	KDVP	98.8	106.8	105.2	95.4	81.3	78.5	79.5	85.5	106.0	138.3	176.8
Infrastructure and general planning of land-use	KDVQ	96.7	98.1	94.1	98.8	98.9	103.5	104.4	102.4	100.3	101.0	118.7
Control of environmental pollution	KDVR	108.7	117.2	131.8	128.7	136.2	142.8	147.0	151.1	129.1	126.5	150.1
Protection and promotion of human health (ex NHS)	KDVS	383.1	397.2	416.0	427.4	444.8	450.1	519.5	530.6	571.6	597.8	1 163.7
Production, distribution and rational utilisation of energy	KDVT	96.8	55.5	52.3	43.2	41.0	28.0	29.0	31.9	36.8	40.3	28.4
Agricultural production and technology	KDVU	284.6	263.4	281.9	257.0	268.9	255.5	260.6	266.6	265.2	267.8	275.9
Industrial production and technology	KDVV	458.7	184.4	165.8	144.6	116.9	61.6	56.5	109.2	237.0	423.4	426.5
Social structures and relationships	KDVW	149.1	141.9	137.1	120.7	113.8	154.7	217.6	270.2	268.8	293.4	226.7
Exploration and exploitation of space	KDVX	187.4	161.5	153.0	164.1	164.4	142.5	142.7	146.3	139.8	155.5	168.6
Research financed from general university funds	KDVY	968.4	1 017.9	1 018.6	1 027.5	1 033.3	1 085.1	1 157.1	1 276.1	1 473.5	1 626.4	1 664.6
Non-oriented research	KDVZ	267.3	612.5	653.5	680.5	671.0	677.0	700.5	789.3	918.2	1 071.6	1 290.9
Other civil research	KDWA	34.0	22.2	24.7	20.5	21.6	25.8	20.6	22.3	19.7	36.3	39.9
Defence	KDWB	2 278.5	2 033.6	2 071.7	2 237.0	2 317.2	2 144.2	2 275.9	2 245.1	2 063.0	2 739.7	2 682.2
Total (excluding NHS)	KDWC	5 412.1	5 212.2	5 305.7	5 445.4	5 509.3	5 349.3	5 710.9	6 026.6	6 329.0	7 618.0	8 413.5

1 See chapter text.

Source: Office for National Statistics: 01633 812789

20.4 Intramural expenditure on Business Enterprise research and development:[1] by industry

United Kingdom: At Current Prices and Constant 2004 Prices

£ million

		Total				Civil				Defence		
		2002	2003	2004		2002	2003	2004		2002	2003	2004
Current Prices												
Chemicals	KDWF	3 887	3 793	3 810	KDWP	3 885	3 793	..	KDWZ	2	–	..
Mechanical engineering	KDWG	826	1 032	1 111	KDWQ	524	466	505	KDXA	302	566	606
Electrical machinery	KJRT	1 565	1 449	1 283	KJTC	1 204	1 131	996	KJUL	361	318	287
Aerospace	KDWJ	1 347	1 652	2 000	KDWT	645	859	917	KDXD	702	792	1 082
Transport equipment	KDWK	1 244	1 346	994	KDWU	..	..	898	KDXE	..	..	96
Other manufacturing	KDWL	1 272	1 264	1 154	KDWV	..	..	..	KDXF	..	..	..
Manufacturing: Total	KDWE	10 140	10 535	10 352	KDWO	8 626	8 754	8 257	KDWY	1 514	1 781	2 094
Services	KDWM	2 645	2 876	2 855	KDWW	2 511	2 709	2 694	KDXG	135	167	161
Agriculture, hunting and forestry; fishing	HFRV	122	121	107	HFSA	122	121	107	MKFC	..	..	1
Extractive industries	HFRW	52	56	108	HFSB	52	56	108	MKFD	..	..	–
Electricity, gas and water supply	HFRX	116	69	43	HFSC	116	69	43	MKFE	..	..	–
Construction	HFRY	35	30	40	HFSE	35	30	39	MKFF	..	..	–
Other: Total	HFRU	324	276	298	HFRZ	324	276	297	MKFB	..	..	1
Total	KDWD	13 110	13 687	13 504	KDWN	11 461	11 739	11 248	KDWX	1 649	1 948	2 256
2004 Prices												
Chemicals	HFXA	4 077	3 876	3 810	HFXJ	4 074	3 876	..	HFYO	2	–	..
Mechanical engineering	HFXB	866	1 055	1 111	HFXK	550	476	505	HFYP	317	578	606
Electrical machinery	HFXC	1 641	1 481	1 283	HFYH	1 263	1 156	996	HFYQ	379	325	287
Aerospace	HFXD	1 413	1 688	2 000	HFYI	676	878	917	HFYR	736	809	1 082
Transport equipment	HFXE	1 305	1 376	994	HFYJ	..	..	898	HFYS	..	..	96
Other manufacturing	HFXF	1 334	1 292	1 154	HFYK	..	..	..	HFYT	..	..	..
Manufacturing: Total	HFWZ	10 635	10 766	10 352	HFXI	9 047	8 946	8 257	HFYN	1 588	1 820	2 094
Services	HFXG	2 774	2 939	2 855	HFYL	2 633	2 768	2 694	HFYU	142	171	161
Agriculture, hunting and forestry: fishing	HFSG	128	124	107	HFSL	128	124	107	MKFH	..	..	1
Extractive industries	HFSH	55	57	108	HFSM	55	57	108	MKFI	..	..	–
Electricity, gas and water supply	HFSI	122	71	43	HFSN	122	71	43	MKFJ	..	..	–
Construction	HFSJ	37	31	40	HFSO	37	31	39	MKFK	..	..	–
Other: Total	HFSF	340	282	298	HFSK	340	282	297	MKFG	..	..	1
Total	HFWY	13 749	13 987	13 504	HFXH	12 020	11 997	11 248	HFYM	1 729	1 991	2 256

1 See chapter text.

Source: Office for National Statistics: 01633 812789

20.5 Sources of funds for research and development within Business Enterprises[1]
United Kingdom

£ million and percentages

		Total				Civil				Defence		
		2002	2003	2004		2002	2003	2004		2002	2003	2004
Cash terms (£ million)												
Government funds	KDYM	884	1 487	1 602	KDYU	193	447	257	KDZC	691	1 040	1 346
Overseas funds	KDYN	3 567	3 554	3 336	KDYV	3 026	3 008	2 748	KDZD	541	546	588
Mainly own funds	KDYO	8 658	8 645	8 565	KDYW	8 242	8 283	8 243	KDZE	417	362	323
Total	KDYL	13 110	13 687	13 504	KDYT	11 461	11 739	11 248	KDZB	1 649	1 948	2 256
Percentages												
Government funds	KDYQ	7	11	12	KDYY	2	4	2	KDZG	42	53	60
Overseas funds	KDYR	27	26	25	KDYZ	26	26	24	KDZH	33	28	26
Mainly own funds	KDYS	66	63	63	KDZA	72	71	73	KDZI	25	19	14
Total	KDYP	100	100	100	KDYX	100	100	100	KDZF	100	100	100

1 See chapter text.

Source: Office for National Statistics: 01633 812789

Agriculture, fisheries and food

Chapter 21

Agriculture, fisheries and food

Output and input

(Tables 21.1 and 21.2)

For both tables, output is a net of VAT collected on the sale of non-edible products. Figures for total output include subsidies on products, but not other subsidies.

Unspecified crops include turf, other minor crops and arable area payments for fodder maize. Eggs include the value of duck eggs and exports of eggs for hatching. Landlords' expenses are included within farm maintenance, miscellaneous expenditure and depreciation of buildings and works. Also included within 'other farming costs' are livestock and crop costs, water costs, insurance premia, bank charges, professional fees, rates, and other farming costs.

Other subsidies

Agri-Environment schemes include Environmentally and Nitrate Sensitive Areas, Countryside Stewardship, Countryside Premium, Tir Cymen, Tir Gofal, Moorland, Habitat, Farm Woodland and Organic Farming Schemes. Included in 'other' subsidies are guidance premium for beef and sheep meat production, Pilot Beef and Sheep Extensification Scheme, non-agricultural horse grazing and farm accounts grant as well as historic data for fertiliser and lime grant and payments to small scale cereal producers.

Compensation of employees and interest charges

Total compensation of employees excludes the value of work done by farm labour on own account capital formation in buildings and work. 'Interest' relates to interest charges on loans for current farming purposes and buildings and less interest on money held on short-term deposit.

Rent

Rent paid (after deductions) is the rent paid on all tenanted land including 'conacre' land in Northern Ireland, *less* landlords' expenses and the benefit value of dwellings on that land. Rent received (after deductions) is the rent received by farming landowners from renting of land to other farmers, *less* landlords' expenses and the benefit value of dwellings on that land. Total net rent is the net rent flowing out of the agricultural sector paid to non-farming landowners, including that part of tenanted land in Northern Ireland. (Although there has been

some updating of the technical procedures for calculating this figure, it corresponds with the previous net rent variable.)

Agricultural censuses and surveys

(Tables 21.3, 21.5 and 21.13)

The coverage for holdings includes all main and minor holdings for each country. Northern Ireland data are now based on all active farm business.

Estimated quantity of crops and grass harvested

(Table 21.4)

The estimated yields of sugar beet and hops are obtained from production figures supplied by British Sugar plc, and the main hop producers in England and Wales. In Great Britain potato yields are estimated in consultation with the British Potato Council.

Forestry

(Table 21.6)

Statistics for state forestry are from their management information systems

For private forestry in Great Britain, statistics on new planting and restocking are based on records of the Woodland Grant Scheme, and timber removals are estimated from a survey of the largest timber harvesting companies. Woodland area figures are based on data obtained from censuses of woodlands and adjusted to reflect subsequent changes. Figures are based on results from the 1995–1999 National Inventory of Woodlands and Trees.

Average weekly earnings and hours of agricultural and horticultural workers

(Tables 21.11 and 21.12)

Prior to 1998, data were collected from a monthly postal survey, which mainly covered male full-time workers. Between 1998 and 2002 the survey collected information on an annual basis via a telephone survey. The survey was reviewed in 2002 and it was concluded that the frequency of the survey should be increased to four times per year to enable the production of more representative annual estimates. The annual sample size has been retained and has been split between four quarterly telephone surveys.

Results for other quarters can be found on the Department for Environment, Food and Rural Affairs DEFRA (website www,defra.gov.uk).

The survey covers seven main categories of workers and provides data which are used by the Agricultural Wages Board when considering wage claims and by in considering the cost of labour in agriculture and horticulture.

Data on earnings represents the total earnings of regular full-time male workers, aged 20 and over. Figures include all payments-in-kind, valued where applicable in accordance with the Agricultural Wages Order. The earnings and hours of hire farm managers are excluded. Part-time workers are defined as those working less than 39 basic hours per week. Casual workers are those employed on a temporary basis.

Fisheries

(Tables 21.14 and 21.15)

Data relating to the weight and value of landings of fish in the United Kingdom (Table 21.14) is generally obtained from sales notes completed at fish market auctions.

Fishing fleet information (Table 21.15) is obtained from vessel registers maintained by DEFRA in England and Wales and the Scottish Executive Agriculture and Fisheries Department.

Estimated average household food consumption – 'Family Food' Expenditure and Food Survey

(Table 21.16)

The Expenditure and Food Survey replaced both the National Food Survey and the Family Expenditure Survey in April 2001. The new survey is a voluntary sample survey of private households throughout the United Kingdom and the results are produced for the financial year ending 31 March each year. This represents a break in the continuity of the data as results from the National Food Survey were produced for Great Britain and for the calendar year ended 31 December.

The basic unit of the survey is the household which is defined as a group of persons living at the same address and sharing common catering arrangements. Each individual aged 16 or over in the household visited is asked to keep diary records, for a two-week period, of daily expenditure on and weight/volume of food and drink brought into the home and expenditure on food and drink eaten out. Children aged between 7 and 15 are asked to keep simplified diaries.

For the year 2001/02 the sample size includes nearly 7,500 households and over 18,000 persons.

21.1 Production and income account at current prices[1]
United Kingdom

£ million

		1995	1996	1997	1998	1999	2000	2001	2002	2003	2004[2]
Output[3]											
1. Total cereals:	C5X5	3 285.0	3 593.0	2 906.9	2 502.3	2 324.8	2 335.9	2 022.8	2 180.2	2 331.9	2 397.8
Wheat	KFKA	2 078.7	2 315.1	1 851.0	1 652.3	1 524.9	1 577.9	1 227.0	1 479.5	1 532.4	1 663.4
Rye	VQBG	5.1	5.6	5.4	5.0	3.5	3.1	2.8	2.2	2.3	2.8
Barley	KFKB	1 108.5	1 183.4	976.8	781.3	733.9	685.1	724.1	623.8	719.3	660.0
Oats and summer cereal mixtures	KFKC	89.0	85.6	70.6	60.5	58.2	65.0	64.9	70.0	72.6	65.4
Other cereals	VQBH	3.7	3.3	3.1	3.2	4.2	4.8	4.1	4.7	5.4	6.0
2.Total industrial crops	VQBI	1 150.8	1 107.1	1 007.7	1 011.7	1 011.8	776.4	810.2	899.4	1 067.3	1 040.3
Oilseeds	VQBJ	427.8	473.7	457.5	485.3	502.6	283.2	291.4	303.6	435.6	392.4
Oilseed rape	KFKG	387.3	434.3	406.0	417.4	370.5	248.9	275.5	297.9	417.2	376.3
Other oil seeds	KIBT	40.6	39.4	51.5	67.9	132.1	34.3	15.9	5.7	18.5	16.1
Sugar beet	KFKH	354.9	358.2	329.1	298.5	279.7	252.1	256.4	282.9	320.9	298.4
Other industrial crops	VQBK	368.0	275.2	221.1	227.9	229.6	241.1	262.4	312.9	310.8	349.5
Fibre plants	VQBL	14.2	17.0	15.2	12.8	11.4	8.4	3.5	1.9	3.0	2.1
Hops	KFKI	16.7	19.5	19.6	14.1	13.3	11.5	9.9	8.1	6.8	6.7
Others[4]	VQBM	337.1	238.6	186.3	201.0	204.9	221.3	249.0	302.9	301.0	340.6
3.Total forage plants	VQBO	171.5	170.8	159.4	141.1	145.4	138.7	169.6	156.4	175.7	163.0
4.Total vegetables and horticultural products	VQBP	1 692.2	1 753.4	1 628.1	1 634.6	1 673.6	1 565.9	1 710.3	1 701.5	1 768.7	1 731.9
5.Total potatoes (including seeds)	KFKO	1 095.1	636.3	390.0	629.4	749.2	452.7	655.3	479.7	518.2	680.0
6.Total fruit	KFKQ	257.6	292.0	198.5	258.8	256.9	232.2	238.8	243.3	307.0	315.6
7.Other crop products including seeds	VQBQ	41.5	43.3	47.6	43.7	46.2	40.4	39.9	26.9	34.0	33.2
8.Total crop output (Sum 1 to 7)	VQBR	7 693.7	7 595.8	6 338.3	6 221.6	6 207.9	5 542.2	5 647.0	5 687.4	6 202.8	6 361.8
9.Total livestock production	VQBS	7 236.3	7 441.9	7 020.6	6 040.0	5 560.8	5 516.4	5 177.0	5 718.0	5 965.5	6 026.5
Primarily for meat	KFLA	6 540.4	6 852.0	6 297.7	5 445.4	5 163.6	5 127.0	4 577.2	5 023.9	5 217.3	5 341.3
Cattle	KFKU	2 579.4	2 545.9	2 276.5	1 975.8	2 047.2	1 993.1	1 786.3	2 126.3	2 178.3	2 256.0
Pigs	KFKW	1 169.7	1 363.2	1 201.5	882.8	784.8	794.0	748.6	681.6	669.7	680.8
Sheep	VQBT	1 305.3	1 273.9	1 176.5	1 109.6	984.4	953.8	621.6	888.0	977.1	1 008.8
Poultry	KFXX	1 351.7	1 526.2	1 494.1	1 328.4	1 198.3	1 233.4	1 265.7	1 170.3	1 230.9	1 229.8
Other animals	KFKY	134.3	142.8	149.1	148.8	148.9	152.6	154.9	157.7	161.2	165.9
Gross fixed capital formation	KFLI	695.9	589.9	722.9	594.6	397.2	389.4	599.8	694.2	748.2	685.1
Cattle	KUJZ	408.4	289.3	377.9	296.9	206.9	188.5	344.7	381.0	459.8	374.1
Pigs	LUKB	15.4	19.1	15.2	5.6	6.8	5.6	5.3	7.4	6.9	8.5
Sheep	LUKA	151.1	152.4	198.6	155.3	56.7	63.8	122.4	177.4	153.8	172.2
Poultry	LUKC	121.0	129.2	131.1	136.8	126.8	131.4	127.4	128.4	127.7	130.4
10.Total livestock products	KFLF	3 948.5	4 006.6	3 625.5	3 132.4	3 042.5	2 791.5	3 201.7	2 876.2	3 101.2	3 208.1
Milk	KFLB	3 497.7	3 494.7	3 153.6	2 709.0	2 653.4	2 393.0	2 821.6	2 466.2	2 626.6	2 727.6
Eggs	KFLC	380.6	448.3	411.6	378.5	342.0	353.2	341.6	356.3	408.5	432.1
Raw wool	KFLD	45.9	39.9	35.1	23.9	21.4	22.7	17.3	19.1	20.8	20.6
Other animal products	KFLE	24.4	23.7	25.3	21.0	25.7	22.6	21.3	34.5	45.3	27.9
11.Total livestock output (9+10)	VQBV	11 184.8	11 448.6	10 646.1	9 172.4	8 603.3	8 307.8	8 378.8	8 594.2	9 066.7	9 234.6
12.Total other agricultural activities	LUOS	713.0	791.1	722.3	689.2	726.0	637.6	636.9	649.6	650.1	701.6
Agricultural services	LUKD	552.9	608.0	575.0	570.2	609.5	586.5	608.5	606.5	608.7	639.9
Leasing out quota	VQBW	160.1	183.1	147.2	119.1	116.5	51.2	28.3	43.1	41.4	61.7
13.Total inseparable non-agricultural activities	LUOT	326.6	362.1	371.6	421.1	430.4	465.8	604.1	542.0	576.1	609.4
14.Gross output at basic prices (8+11+12+13)	KFLT	19 918.0	20 197.7	18 078.3	16 504.3	15 967.6	14 953.4	15 266.7	15 473.2	16 495.6	16 907.4
15.Total subsidies (less taxes) on product	LUOU	2 106.9	2 782.1	2 587.8	2 436.1	2 373.2	2 187.0	1 923.3	2 132.4	2 179.6	2 345.2
16.Output at market prices (14-15)	LUOV	17 811.2	17 415.5	15 490.6	14 068.2	13 594.4	12 766.4	13 343.5	13 340.8	14 316.0	14 562.2
of which transactions within the agricultural industry											
Feed wheat	LUNQ	55.4	67.0	77.3	78.8	64.4	39.8	43.1	39.0	79.0	84.7
Feed barley	LUNR	198.9	205.6	192.8	163.6	147.9	136.9	151.9	142.9	159.3	119.5
Feed oats	LUNS	16.5	16.1	11.8	11.5	14.5	12.6	13.1	10.5	10.8	15.9
Seed potatoes	LUNT	41.1	33.7	9.2	12.7	28.8	8.3	17.3	15.5	5.1	6.7
Straw	LUNU	308.0	211.6	160.3	173.0	174.8	190.4	219.2	271.3	269.2	299.3
Contract work	LUNV	552.9	608.0	575.0	570.2	609.5	586.5	608.5	606.5	608.7	639.9
Leasing of quota	LUNW	160.1	183.1	147.2	119.1	116.5	51.2	28.3	43.1	41.4	61.7
Total capital formation in livestock	LUNX	695.9	589.9	722.9	594.6	397.2	389.4	599.8	694.2	748.2	685.1

21.1 Production and income account at current prices[1]
United Kingdom
continued

£ million

		1994	1995	1996	1997	1998	1999	2000	2001	2002	2003[2]	2004
Intermediate consumption												
17.Seeds	KFME	326.2	384.0	380.5	337.2	332.1	327.4	263.4	291.1	276.1	285.7	273.1
Cereals	KFMC	112.3	121.2	123.7	103.5	84.2	87.1	71.2	74.7	63.8	66.1	60.5
Other	KFMD	213.9	262.8	256.8	233.8	247.9	240.3	192.2	216.4	212.3	219.6	212.6
18.Energy	VQDO	586.5	590.9	647.4	629.9	598.3	621.9	695.0	685.7	647.3	604.6	716.8
Electricity	VQDQ	243.4	237.0	247.6	232.7	231.0	221.7	230.2	242.0	236.5	207.4	255.3
Fuels	VQDV	343.1	353.8	399.8	397.2	367.3	400.2	464.8	443.7	410.9	397.2	461.5
19.Fertilisers	KFMM	768.7	926.0	1 043.3	1 006.9	831.7	756.0	737.8	760.3	757.3	706.0	766.9
20.Pesticides	KFMN	557.3	590.0	646.9	674.6	653.7	621.0	579.4	530.9	533.6	509.2	532.8
21.Veterinary expenses	KCPC	274.3	289.2	297.7	307.8	288.0	270.0	255.8	242.7	250.4	254.9	261.8
22.Animal feed	KFMB	2 874.5	3 040.2	3 185.4	2 804.0	2 444.4	2 260.9	2 139.6	2 367.3	2 218.9	2 364.7	2 467.6
Compounds	LUNY	1 689.1	1 806.2	1 959.5	1 772.2	1 523.5	1 402.4	1 283.3	1 398.2	1 376.9	1 348.1	1 441.3
Straights	LUNZ	888.3	963.3	937.3	749.9	667.0	631.7	667.0	760.9	649.6	767.5	806.2
Feed purchased from other farms	LUOA	297.1	270.8	288.6	281.9	253.9	226.8	189.3	208.1	192.4	249.1	220.1
23.Total maintenance[5]	VQDW	977.3	1 089.4	1 110.3	1 091.2	1 024.5	1 016.4	941.5	982.2	957.7	1 044.2	1 082.2
Materials	KFMO	631.3	721.3	745.3	720.9	699.2	698.2	650.5	659.3	633.7	698.4	726.6
Buildings	KCPB	346.1	368.1	365.0	370.3	325.4	318.2	291.0	323.0	324.0	345.8	355.6
24.Agricultural services	LUOE	501.8	552.9	608.0	575.0	570.2	609.5	586.5	608.5	606.5	608.7	639.9
25.Other goods and services[5,6]	VQDX	2 060.5	2 186.7	2 277.4	2 314.7	2 251.3	2 267.9	2 085.7	2 053.3	2 082.1	2 166.2	2 261.3
26.Total intermediate consumption (Sum 17 to 25)	KCPM	8 927.1	9 649.3	10 197.0	9 741.3	8 994.2	8 750.9	8 284.8	8 522.0	8 330.0	8 544.1	9 002.4
27.Gross value added at basic prices (14-26)	LUOG	9 379.1	10 268.7	10 000.7	8 337.0	7 510.2	7 216.7	6 668.7	6 744.7	7 143.2	7 951.5	7 905.0
28.Total consumption of Fixed Capital	KCPS	2 549.5	2 592.1	2 622.8	2 675.0	2 594.7	2 432.1	2 481.4	2 560.2	2 558.9	2 614.5	2 548.6
Equipment	KCPR	1 175.8	1 226.2	1 291.1	1 318.6	1 323.0	1 309.7	1 256.0	1 249.8	1 248.0	1 197.6	1 190.0
Buildings[5,7]	LUOH	581.5	640.1	681.4	671.9	683.8	701.5	691.6	686.8	689.7	649.6	632.6
Livestock	VQEA	792.2	725.8	650.2	684.6	587.9	421.0	533.9	623.6	621.3	767.3	726.0
Cattle	LUOI	528.3	415.3	313.7	391.9	314.7	208.3	278.2	321.9	341.5	461.1	425.2
Pigs	LUOK	14.7	16.7	17.4	14.6	8.4	7.6	7.9	6.2	7.8	7.3	8.7
Sheep	LUOJ	143.3	175.8	191.6	157.1	119.0	69.6	120.1	169.1	142.6	173.0	168.0
Poultry	LUOL	105.9	118.0	127.6	120.9	145.8	135.4	127.7	126.5	129.4	125.9	124.1
29.Net value added at basic prices (27-28)	KCPT	6 829.6	7 676.5	7 377.9	5 662.0	4 915.5	4 784.6	4 187.2	4 184.5	4 584.3	5 337.0	5 356.4
30.Compensation of employees[8]	LUOR	1 827.5	1 836.3	1 880.9	1 929.8	1 975.3	2 029.0	1 893.3	1 942.6	1 957.7	1 915.6	2 004.3
31.Other taxes on production	VQEB	−68.1	−73.2	−81.5	−84.4	−88.9	−92.3	−92.1	−77.8	−80.9	−90.6	−92.8
32.Other subsidies on production	VQEC	261.3	266.4	243.1	188.9	209.5	318.3	296.7	536.5	555.9	622.1	579.6
Animal disease compensation	LUOM	6.8	6.9	5.5	15.3	14.3	19.8	29.4	23.2	54.1	60.6	54.8
Set-aside	LUON	206.3	198.4	159.5	90.2	87.7	170.0	127.3	180.1	142.5	176.7	130.6
Agri-environment schemes[9]	ZBXC	48.2	61.1	77.9	83.4	107.5	128.5	140.1	168.3	194.6	222.7	243.8
Other including Less Favoured Areas schemes[10]	VQED	–	–	0.2	0.1	–	–	–	164.9	164.6	162.2	150.4
33.Net value added at factor cost (29+31+32)	LUOQ	7 022.7	7 869.8	7 539.5	5 766.5	5 036.1	5 010.6	4 391.9	4 643.1	5 059.4	5 868.6	5 843.2
34.Rent	KCPV	181.6	175.5	228.7	255.8	250.1	239.7	223.7	251.4	239.7	295.5	299.5
Paid[11]	ZBXE	181.6	175.5	302.8	335.8	330.6	322.1	302.5	329.6	337.4	387.2	394.9
Received[12]	ZBXF	–	–	−74.1	−80.1	−80.5	−82.4	−78.9	−78.2	−97.7	−91.7	−95.4
35.Interest[13]	KCPU	536.2	587.3	553.3	621.2	688.6	594.2	628.2	557.2	482.8	470.9	525.6
Total income from farming (33-30-34-35)	KCQB	4 477.4	5 270.7	4 876.6	2 959.7	2 122.1	2 147.7	1 646.7	1 891.9	2 379.2	3 186.5	3 013.8

1 See chapter text.
2 Provisional.
3 Output is net of VAT collected on the sale of non-edible products. Figures for total output include subsidies on products, but not other subsidies.
4 Includes straw and minor crops.
5 Landlords' expenses are included within 'Total maintenance', 'Other goods and services' and 'Total consumption of Fixed Capital of buildings'.
6 Includes livestock and crop costs, water costs, insurance premiums, bank charges, professional fees, rates and other farming costs.
7 A more empirically based methodology for calculating landlords' consumption of fixed capital was introduced in 2000. The new series has been linked with the old one using a smoothing procedure for the transition year of 1996.
8 Excludes the value of work done by farm labour on own account capital formation in buildings and works.

9 Includes Environmentally and Nitrate Sensitive Areas, Countryside Stewardship and other management schemes, and Moorland, Habitat, Farm Woodland and Organic Farming Schemes.
10 Land area based schemes which replaced the Hill Livestock Compensatory Allowance Scheme in 2001. These are Tir Mynydd in Wales, Less Favoured Area Compensatory Scheme in Northern Ireland, Less Favoured Areas Support Scheme in Scotland and Hill Farm Allowance in England.
11 Rent paid on all tenanted land (including 'conacre' land in Northern Ireland) less landlords' expenses, landlords' consumption of fixed capital and the benefit value of dwellings on that land.
12 Rent received by farming landowners from renting of land to other farmers less landlords' expenses. This series starts in 1996 following a revision to the methodology of calculating net rent.
13 Interest charges on loans for current farming purposes and buildings and works less interest on money held on short term deposit.

Source: Department for Environment, Food and Rural Affairs: 01904 455080

21.2 Output and input volume indices[1]
United Kingdom

Indices (1995=100)

		1994	1995	1996	1997	1998	1999	2000	2001	2002	2003	2004
Outputs[2]												
1. Total cereals:	VQAN	89.1	100.0	87.9	85.2	98.5	146.0	176.2	121.5	141.5	135.5	136.4
Wheat	LUKH	93.2	100.0	112.2	104.1	107.5	103.4	116.2	81.2	111.4	99.7	108.1
Rye	VQAO	96.1	100.0	110.3	115.5	113.3	120.5	85.6	82.4	92.5	97.6	93.2
Barley	LUKI	103.1	100.0	116.6	131.2	139.9	161.6	81.9	83.7	100.7	126.3	116.5
Oats and summer cereal mixtures	LUKJ	101.8	100.0	117.5	131.0	135.0	134.7	93.0	96.3	119.6	145.7	134.7
Other cereals	VQAP	116.0	100.0	107.3	131.7	177.6	374.9	52.9	47.7	22.6	73.1	64.2
2. Total industrial crops:	VQAQ	103.4	100.0	123.6	131.5	118.6	125.5	107.7	98.9	113.4	108.7	105.0
Oil seeds	VQAR	81.4	100.0	89.7	80.4	74.3	66.7	67.3	63.5	65.0	61.6	60.7
Oilseed rape	VQAS	97.2	100.0	130.5	132.4	108.8	106.7	69.8	42.2	23.9	39.9	27.2
Other oil seeds	LUKN	108.3	100.0	126.2	119.6	81.9	69.8	62.1	58.6	58.7	44.1	44.1
Sugar beet	C5X4	103.4	100.0	123.6	131.5	118.6	125.5	107.7	98.9	113.4	108.7	105.0
Other industrial crops	VQAU	122.4	100.0	101.7	117.3	109.6	119.6	124.5	144.0	144.8	143.7	139.9
Fibre plants	VQAV	97.2	100.0	130.5	132.4	108.8	106.7	69.8	42.2	23.9	39.9	27.2
Hops	LUKP	103.6	100.0	101.4	99.9	97.4	99.4	96.9	93.6	93.3	89.9	91.7
Others[3]	VQAW	105.9	100.0	105.8	100.8	98.7	99.6	93.4	90.0	83.5	81.4	81.2
3. Total forage plants	VQAX	122.4	100.0	101.7	117.3	109.6	119.6	124.5	144.0	144.8	143.7	139.9
4. Total vegetables and horticultural Products:	VQAY	103.6	100.0	101.4	99.9	97.4	99.4	96.9	93.6	93.3	89.9	91.7
Fresh vegetables	LUKX	105.2	100.0	103.5	70.1	88.7	91.9	85.9	90.7	82.3	92.6	108.4
Plants and flowers	LUKZ	99.9	100.0	94.7	98.0	95.0	98.5	101.0	98.0	107.7	102.3	107.3
5. Total potatoes (including seeds)	LUKW	98.3	100.0	107.7	102.3	90.3	107.2	94.4	100.0	100.9	87.0	99.0
6. Total fruit	LUKY	109.3	100.0	90.8	99.6	92.0	102.4	98.6	98.0	68.2	81.0	83.1
7. Other crop products including seeds	VQAZ	106.4	100.0	101.0	110.8	112.3	103.1	86.9	79.7	76.1	67.2	68.5
8. Total crop output (Sum 1 to 7)	VQBA	97.0	100.0	107.9	104.6	101.8	104.5	100.0	91.5	98.8	96.1	..
9. Total livestock production	VQBB	96.3	100.0	103.6	106.1	105.2	100.5	101.4	105.1	102.3	104.2	109.9
Mainly for meat processing	LULH	100.1	100.0	101.8	102.3	102.3	101.7	101.7	101.4	101.6	101.0	101.0
Cattle	LULC	105.4	100.0	98.2	106.2	104.2	97.4	86.1	99.7	99.7	92.7	94.2
Pigs	LULE	100.6	100.0	99.8	98.4	96.0	96.6	84.4	97.9	93.1	94.2	91.2
Sheep	LULD	115.6	100.0	109.9	115.5	87.1	97.7	66.6	56.2	83.9	67.3	69.3
Poultry	LULF	125.4	100.0	90.8	117.9	122.7	92.4	62.6	97.4	108.4	77.9	89.0
Other animals	LULG	100.5	100.0	101.7	109.1	102.9	97.0	100.4	96.2	95.6	95.2	97.2
Gross fixed capital formation	LULR	105.4	100.0	98.2	106.2	104.2	97.4	86.1	99.7	99.7	92.7	94.2
Cattle	LULN	102.2	100.0	99.5	100.8	99.6	101.3	98.7	99.7	100.7	102.0	99.1
Pigs	LULP	102.4	100.0	99.6	100.5	99.0	101.4	98.6	99.8	100.9	102.0	99.1
Sheep	LULO	101.7	100.0	100.1	103.7	105.4	101.8	101.4	102.1	99.8	99.8	101.3
Poultry	LULQ	96.7	100.0	95.1	97.0	103.3	95.3	91.7	76.2	79.2	77.4	77.1
10. Total livestock products	LULM	102.2	100.0	99.5	100.8	99.6	101.3	98.7	99.7	100.7	102.0	99.1
Milk	LULI	102.4	100.0	99.6	100.5	99.0	101.4	98.6	99.8	100.9	102.0	99.1
Eggs	LULJ	101.7	100.0	100.1	103.7	105.4	101.8	101.4	102.1	99.8	99.8	101.3
Raw wool	LULK	95.0	100.0	108.7	104.1	103.7	109.0	93.7	93.5	95.3	95.2	92.7
Other animal products	LULL	98.8	100.0	107.8	109.4	115.2	123.2	116.2	120.6	120.2	120.6	120.7
11. Total livestock output (9+10)	VQBC	101.3	100.0	92.6	97.1	97.7	96.9	92.9	88.5	92.2	92.0	91.5
12. Total other agricultural activities	VQBD	95.0	100.0	108.7	104.1	103.7	109.0	93.7	93.5	95.3	95.2	92.7
Agricultural services	VQBE	99.5	100.0	99.0	100.4	100.0	100.8	96.4	91.5	95.9	94.7	95.3
Leasing out quota	VQBF	82.2	100.0	111.7	87.1	68.1	65.6	28.0	15.2	22.8	21.2	15.0
13. Total inseparable non-agricultural Activities	LULX	103.2	100.0	108.7	108.0	119.0	120.0	125.7	158.7	138.1	141.7	143.9

21.2 Output and input volume indices[1]
United Kingdom
continued

Indices (1995=100)

		1994	1995	1996	1997	1998	1999	2000	2001	2002	2003	2004
14.Gross output (at basic prices) (8+11+12+13)	LULY	99.5	100.0	99.0	100.4	100.0	100.8	96.4	91.5	95.9	94.7	95.3
15.Total subsidies (less taxes) on product	VQEE	145.7	100.0	121.5	176.0	209.9	175.0	120.1	115.1	123.9	196.1	209.5
16.Output at market prices (14-15)	VQEG	119.4	100.0	89.2	81.6	100.1	118.2	108.8	112.4	105.6	104.7	140.5
of which transactions within the agricultural industry												
Feed wheat	LULZ	98.8	100.0	107.8	109.4	115.2	123.2	116.2	120.6	120.2	120.6	120.7
Feed barley	LUMA	82.2	100.0	111.7	87.1	68.1	65.6	28.0	15.2	22.8	21.2	15.0
Feed oats	LUMB	105.4	100.0	98.2	106.2	104.2	97.4	86.1	99.8	99.7	92.8	94.2
Seed potatoes	LUMC	87.8	100.0	119.1	84.1	82.3	82.1	70.4	80.0	83.5	33.9	28.1
Straw	LUMD	77.6	100.0	84.5	73.3	69.5	61.1	63.8	60.4	62.4	58.8	57.9
Contract work	LUME	98.8	100.0	107.8	109.4	115.2	123.2	116.2	120.6	120.2	120.6	120.7
Leasing of quota	LUMF	98.1	100.0	102.4	99.2	95.2	95.1	90.5	94.5	90.1	89.2	87.1
Total capital formation in livestock	LUMG	95.0	100.0	104.5	95.1	83.1	86.3	73.0	75.1	66.2	65.1	61.5
Intermediate Consumption												
17.Seeds	LUMO	101.2	100.0	99.5	97.4	106.6	101.3	93.7	102.2	104.1	85.0	92.2
Cereals	LUMM	95.2	100.0	110.9	107.4	109.5	102.0	92.1	90.8	88.5	77.8	81.4
Other	LUMN	99.6	100.0	101.4	101.1	100.6	99.2	98.6	103.5	101.1	100.4	99.0
18.Energy	VQEH	97.6	100.0	106.3	103.3	108.3	101.6	92.5	94.3	93.4	80.0	84.8
Electricity	VQEI	93.0	100.0	103.1	106.7	111.2	108.1	106.7	101.0	102.6	98.0	100.6
Fuels	VQEJ	95.2	100.0	110.9	107.4	109.5	102.0	92.1	90.8	88.5	77.8	81.4
19.Fertilisers	VQEK	93.4	100.0	105.3	114.7	107.5	100.5	88.0	77.5	80.9	69.8	68.5
20.Pesticides	LUMQ	100.4	100.0	101.3	97.3	94.9	97.5	89.6	92.3	91.7	91.6	92.0
21.Veterinary expenses	LUMW	114.1	100.0	107.5	133.2	139.8	126.5	113.8	119.7	126.5	136.4	114.8
22.Animal feed	LUML	93.6	100.0	97.5	94.6	88.7	87.0	79.1	80.6	75.8	78.7	78.2
Compounds	LUMH	90.8	100.0	97.6	93.8	91.1	89.0	81.2	80.0	73.6	76.4	76.1
Straights	LUMI	99.0	100.0	97.1	96.3	84.0	83.1	74.9	82.0	80.6	83.8	82.9
Feed purchased from other farms	LUMJ	114.1	100.0	107.5	133.2	139.8	126.5	113.8	119.7	126.5	136.4	114.8
23.Total maintenance[4]	VQEL	93.6	100.0	97.5	94.6	88.7	87.0	79.1	80.6	75.8	78.7	78.2
Materials	LUMU	97.3	100.0	103.8	103.2	96.1	93.0	82.9	79.2	77.4	78.0	77.0
Buildings	LUMT	99.0	100.0	97.1	96.3	84.0	83.1	74.9	82.0	80.6	83.8	82.9
24.Agricultural services	VQEM	98.8	100.0	107.8	109.4	115.2	123.2	116.2	120.6	120.2	120.6	120.7
25.Other goods and services[4,5]	VQEO	97.3	100.0	103.8	103.2	96.1	93.0	82.9	79.2	77.4	78.0	77.0
26.Total intermediate consumption (Sum 17 to 25)	LUNE	99.2	100.0	101.3	101.2	96.6	93.8	92.7	92.7	92.6	93.1	92.9
27.Gross value added at basic prices (14-26)	LUNF	93.5	100.0	102.5	91.9	93.4	94.8	100.5	96.5	80.9	84.6	87.8
28.Total consumption of Fixed Capital	LUNN	110.4	100.0	92.7	101.0	108.2	97.5	82.7	56.9	82.3	65.2	66.0
Equipment	LUNI	102.6	100.0	96.7	80.6	82.7	92.5	97.2	117.1	76.9	75.4	75.1
Buildings[4,6]	LUNG	98.7	100.0	103.0	103.5	111.1	105.4	100.5	98.5	99.2	96.7	95.3
Livestock	VQES	93.5	100.0	102.5	91.9	93.4	94.8	100.5	96.5	80.9	84.6	87.8
Cattle	LUNJ	103.2	100.0	94.9	101.0	105.4	112.9	112.2	95.4	120.0	117.4	119.6
Pigs	LUNL	110.4	100.0	92.7	101.0	108.2	97.5	82.7	56.9	82.3	65.2	66.0
Sheep	LUNK	102.6	100.0	96.7	80.6	82.7	92.5	97.2	117.1	76.9	75.4	75.1
Poultry	LUNM	98.7	100.0	103.0	103.5	111.1	105.4	100.5	98.5	99.2	96.7	95.3
29.Net value added at basic prices (27-28)	LUNO	103.2	100.0	94.9	101.0	105.4	112.9	112.2	95.4	120.0	117.4	119.6

1 See chapter text.
2 Output is net of VAT collected on the sale of non-edible products. Figures for total output include subsidies on products, but not other subsidies.
3 Includes straw and minor crops.
4 Landlords' expenses are included within 'Total maintenance', 'Other goods and services' and 'Total consumption of Fixed Capital of buildings'.

5 Includes livestock and crop costs, water costs, insurance premiums, bank charges, professional fees, rates, and other farming costs.
6 A more empirically based methodology for calculating landlords' depreciation was introduced in 2000. The new series has been linked with the old one using a smoothing procedure for the transition year of 1996.

Source: Department for Environment, Food and Rural Affairs: 01904 455080

21.3 Agriculture land-use
United Kingdom
Area at the June census[1]

Thousand hectares

		1995	1996	1997	1998	1999	2000	2001	2002	2003	2004	2005
Total agricultural area	BFAH	18 746	18 750	18 653	18 604	18 579	18 311	18 555	18 388	18 438	18 437	18 509
Crops	BFAA	4 544	4 722	4 990	4 971	4 709	4 665	4 454	4 573	4 478	4 593	4 443
Bare fallow	BFAB	43	37	29	34	33	37	43	33	29	29	140
Total tillage	KIJR	4 586	4 759	5 020	5 005	4 742	4 702	4 497	4 605	4 507	4 623	4 583
All grass under 5 years old	KFEM	1 407	1 395	1 405	1 301	1 226	1 226	1 205	1 230	1 201	1 246	1 193
Total arable land	KFEN	5 993	6 154	6 425	6 306	5 968	5 928	5 702	5 835	5 708	5 869	5 777
All grasses 5 years old and over	KFEO	5 375	5 354	5 282	5 364	5 449	5 364	5 584	5 422	5 683	5 620	5 711
Total tillage and grass	KFEP	11 368	11 507	11 706	11 671	11 417	11 292	11 286	11 257	11 391	11 489	11 488
Sole right rough grazing	BFAD	4 785	4 760	4 657	4 621	4 575	4 445	4 435	4 484	4 329	4 326	4 354
Set aside	DMNF	633	509	306	313	572	567	800	611	689	560	559
All other land on agricultural holdings including woodland	BFAE	734	751	763	773	789	780	801	802	792	825	872
Total land on agricultural holdings	BFAF	17 520	17 527	17 432	17 377	17 352	17 083	17 323	17 154	17 202	17 200	17 273
Common rough grazing (estimated)	BFAG	1 226	1 223	1 221	1 227	1 227	1 228	1 232	1 234	1 236	1 237	1 236
Crops	BFAA	4 544	4 722	4 990	4 971	4 709	4 665	4 454	4 573	4 478	4 593	4 443
Cereals	BFAJ	3 182	3 359	3 514	3 418	3 141	3 348	3 014	3 245	3 059	3 133	2 925
Wheat	BFAK	1 859	1 976	2 036	2 045	1 847	2 086	1 635	1 996	1 837	1 990	1 868
Barley	BFAL	1 193	1 269	1 359	1 253	1 179	1 128	1 245	1 101	1 078	1 010	942
Oats	BFAM	112	96	100	98	92	109	112	126	122	108	91
Mixed corn	BFAN	3	3	2	2	2	2	3	4	4	..	..
Rye[2]	BFAO	8	8	9	10	8	7	5	5	4	6	..
Triticale	DMNH	7	7	8	11	13	16	14	14	15	..	..
Other arable crops (excluding potatoes)	DMNI	993	937	1 125	1 210	1 211	979	1 103	993	1 098	1 137	1 280
Oilseed rape	BFAP	354	356	445	507	417	332	404	357	460	498	519
Sugar beet not for stock feeding[2]	BFAQ	196	199	196	189	183	173	177	169	162	154	148
Hops[3]	DMNJ	3	3	3	3	3	2	1	2	2	2	..
Peas for harvesting dry and field beans	DMNK	195	178	197	213	202	208	276	249	235	242	239
Linseed	DMNL	54	49	73	100	209	71	31	12	32	30	..
Other crops	DMNM	195	204	210	200	197	192	214	204	207	211	306
Potatoes	BFAR	172	178	166	164	178	166	165	158	145	149	137
Horticultural	BFAV	187	189	184	180	179	172	173	176	176	175	170
Vegetables grown in the open	DMNN	130	132	126	125	126	119	120	124	125	125	121
Orchard fruit[4]	BFBG	28	28	30	30	28	28	28	26	25	24	..
Soft fruit	DMNO	12	12	11	10	9	10	9	9	9	9	..
Ornamentals	DMNP	15	14	14	14	13	14	14	15	14	15	14
Glasshouse crops	DMNQ	2	2	2	2	2	2	2	2	2	2	2

1 Includes estimates for minor holdings for all countries. See chapter text.
2 Figures are for England and Wales only.
3 Figures are for England only.
4 Includes non-commercial orchards.

Source: Agricultural Departments: 01904 455332

21.4 Estimated quantity of crops and grass harvested[1]
United Kingdom

Thousand tonnes

		1994	1995	1996	1997	1998	1999	2000	2001	2002	2003	2004
Agricultural crops												
Wheat	BADO	13 320	14 310	16 100	15 020	16 449	14 867	16 704	11 580	15 973	14 288	15 473
Barley (Winter and Spring) .	BADP	5 950	6 840	7 790	7 830	6 623	6 581	6 492	6 660	6 126	6 370	5 815
Oats	BADQ	600	615	590	575	586	541	640	621	753	749	630
Sugar beet[2]	BADR	8 720	8 431	10 420	11 084	10 002	10 584	9 079	8 335	9 557	9 168	8 850
Potatoes	BADS	6 542	6 404	7 228	7 128	6 422	7 131	6 636	6 649	6 966	5 918	6 316
		1994 /95	1995 /96	1996 /97	1997 /98	1998 /99	1999 /00	2000 /01	2001 /02	2002 /03	2003 /04	2004 /05
Horticultural crops												
Field vegetables												
Brussels sprouts	BADT	93.5	74.3	82.6	74.2	72.5	78.5	67.3	54.8	42.7	55.8	42.5
Cabbage (including savoys and spring greens)	BADU	381.4	401.8	377.5	304.9	308.9	295.2	273.2	295.4	255.2	245.6	290.9
Cauliflowers	BADV	267.6	247.3	217.1	191.0	191.7	172.4	156.1	107.4	115.8	126.3	165.3
Carrots	BADW	566.6	524.6	679.5	591.4	617.6	673.2	725.8	760.0	731.2	614.3	659.8
Turnips and swedes	BADX	137.1	124.2	135.6	106.9	117.5	123.3	132.1	141.8	104.7	96.5	103.8
Beetroot	BADY	88.9	72.1	72.1	72.4	69.5	63.4	67.1	68.6	56.3	58.8	53.9
Onions, dry bulb	BADZ	245.0	254.3	313.3	329.3	342.0	391.4	392.7	374.9	283.4	373.6	340.9
Peas, green for market (in pod weight)	BAEA	5.6	8.4	6.7	8.2	7.0	7.0	6.7	6.2	7.2	5.9	5.9
Peas, green for processing (shelled weight)	BAEB	181.0	198.0	215.5	167.9	152.0	143.1	184.5	161.0	169.3	167.6	130.3
Lettuce	BAEC	179.2	191.9	187.5	157.7	151.8	155.2	135.8	123.9	109.9	125.6	140.9
Protected crops												
Tomatoes	BAED	108.9	112.8	115.5	114.0	107.6	116.6	113.0	109.1	100.9	75.6	78.5
Cucumbers	BAEE	83.2	88.4	85.6	81.7	83.8	83.8	79.8	71.5	73.6	77.0	61.4
Lettuce	BAEF	33.1	29.7	26.5	24.1	20.6	19.9	18.7	20.9	16.0	16.6	10.8
Fruit												
Dessert apples	BFCD	167.7	118.5	116.3	71.1	97.8	133.9	101.3	104.4	84.0	69.0	96.3
Cooking apples	BFCE	144.8	129.6	108.7	82.4	85.9	112.4	107.5	107.4	95.3	74.9	78.2
Soft fruit	BFCF	76.6	75.6	82.2	59.4	60.1	65.9	65.4	64.6	66.7	79.6	85.9
Pears	BFBQ	25.6	35.3	40.1	24.4	26.3	22.7	26.6	38.5	34.2	29.6	22.7

1 See chapter text.
2 Figures are adjusted to constant 16% sugar content.

Source: Agricultural Departments: 01904 455332

21.5 Cattle, sheep, pigs and poultry on agricultural holdings[1]
United Kingdom
At June each year

Thousands

		1995	1996	1997	1998	1999	2000	2001	2002	2003	2004	2005
Total cattle and calves	BFCG	11 857	12 040	11 637	11 519	11 423	11 135	10 602	10 345	10 517	10 603	10 414
of which:												
dairy cows	BFCH	2 603	2 587	2 478	2 439	2 440	2 336	2 251	2 227	2 192	2 131	2 065
beef cows	BFCI	1 840	1 864	1 862	1 947	1 924	1 842	1 708	1 657	1 700	1 739	1 768
heifers in calf	BFCJ	775	818	848	787	763	718	701	728	680	691	639
Total sheep and lambs	BFCM	43 304	42 086	42 823	44 471	44 656	42 264	36 716	35 834	35 846	35 890	35 531
of which:												
ewes and shearlings	CKUQ	20 830	20 550	20 696	21 260	21 458	20 449	17 921	17 630	17 599	17 665	16 998
lambs under one year old	BFCP	21 350	20 443	21 032	22 138	22 092	20 857	17 769	17 310	17 335	17 275	17 537
Total pigs	BFCQ	7 627	7 590	8 072	8 146	7 284	6 482	5 845	5 588	5 047	5 161	4 864
of which:												
sows in pig and other sows for breeding	CKUU	654	649	683	675	603	537	527	483	443	449	403
gilts in pig	CKUR	101	107	116	103	85	73	71	74	73	66	67
Total fowls	KPSV	127 035	..	..	..	..	..	..	..	165 324	165 931	160 528
of which:												
table fowls including broilers	CKUT	77 177	..	..	98 244	101 625	105 689	112 531	105 137	116 774	119 912	111 487
laying fowls[2]	CKUV	31 837	..	34 286	29 483	29 258	28 687	29 895	28 778	29 274	29 662	29 550
growing pullets	CKUW	10 210	..	11 510	9 860	9 583	9 461	9 367	9 784	8 286	8 156	10 929

1 Includes estimates for minor holdings for all countries. See chapter text.
2 Excludes fowls laying eggs for hatching.

Sources: Department for Environment, Food and Rural Affairs;
Farming Statistics: 01904 455332

21.6 Forestry[1]
United Kingdom

		1980	1990	2000	2001	2002	2003	2004	2005
Woodland area[2] - (Thousand hectares)									
United Kingdom	C5OF	2 175	2 400	2 793	2 790	2 800	2 807	2 817	2 825
England[3]	C5OG	948	958	1 103	1 100	1 104	1 110	1 115	1 119
Wales[3]	C5OI	241	248	289	289	288	285	286	286
Scotland[3]	C5OH	920	1 120	1 318	1 317	1 324	1 327	1 330	1 334
Northern Ireland	C5OJ	67	74	83	83	84	85	86	85
Forestry Commission/Forest Service	C5OK		946	956	886	861[4]	855	848	842	838
Other[5]	C5OL		1 230	1 443	1 907	1 929	1 945	1 960	1 976	1 987
Conifer	C5OM		1 372	1 576	1 663	1 660	1 658	1 652	1 651	1 647
Broadleaved[6]	C5ON		804	824	1 131	1 130	1 143	1 155	1 166	1 178

		1994/95	1995/96	1996/97	1997/98	1998/99	1999/00	2000/01	2001/02	2002/03	2003/04	2004/05
New Planting[7] - (Thousand hectares)												
United Kingdom	C5OO	19.9	16.4	17.2	16.7	16.7	17.4	18.3	13.9	13.0	11.8	11.3
England	C5OP	5.1	4.4	4.4	4.1	4.9	5.5	5.5	4.9	5.3	4.1	4.7
Wales	C5OR	0.6	0.4	0.4	0.5	0.6	0.7	0.4	0.3	0.3	0.5	0.5
Scotland	C5OQ	13.4	10.6	11.7	11.4	10.5	10.4	11.7	8.0	6.7	6.8	5.7
Northern Ireland	C5OS	0.9	1.0	0.8	0.6	0.7	0.8	0.7	0.7	0.6	0.5	0.4
Forestry Commission/Forest Service	C5OT	1.2	0.6	0.6	0.2	0.2	0.3	0.3	0.8	0.9	0.3	0.1
Other[8]	C5OU	18.7	15.8	16.6	16.4	16.5	17.2	18.0	13.1	12.1	11.6	11.2
Conifer	C5OV	9.4	7.4	7.7	7.0	6.6	6.5	5.2	3.9	4.0	2.9	2.1
Broadleaved	C5OW	10.5	8.9	9.5	9.7	10.1	10.9	13.2	10.0	8.9	8.9	9.2
Restocking[7] - (Thousand hectares)												
United Kingdom	C5OX	14.6	13.9	15.0	14.1	14.0	15.1	15.2	13.7	14.3	14.8	14.5
England	C5OY	4.9	4.2	4.3	4.3	4.0	3.8	3.8	3.3	3.2	3.0	2.4
Wales	C5P2	2.6	2.3	3.0	2.7	3.0	2.6	2.2	1.9	1.9	1.8	1.6
Scotland	C5OZ	6.6	6.8	7.2	6.3	6.3	8.0	8.0	7.8	8.5	8.9	9.5
Northern Ireland	C5P3	0.6	0.6	0.6	0.7	0.6	0.6	1.1	0.8	0.7	1.0	1.0
Forestry Commission/Forest Service	C5P4	8.4	8.4	8.4	8.5	8.5	8.8	8.9	9.1	9.1	9.9	9.1
Other[8]	C5P5	6.2	6.6	6.6	5.6	5.6	6.3	6.2	4.6	5.2	4.9	5.4
Conifer	C5P6	11.0	10.9	11.4	11.2	11.3	11.9	12.2	11.4	12.0	12.1	11.8
Broadleaved	C5P7	3.6	3.0	3.4	2.9	2.8	3.2	2.9	2.3	2.3	2.6	2.7

		1996	1997	1998	1999	2000	2001	2002	2003	2004
Wood Production (volume - Thousand green tonnes[9])										
United Kingdom	C5P8	7 280	7 610	7 540	7 960	8 090	8 150	8 300	8 970	9 580
Softwood total	C5PA	6 480	6 790	6 830	7 280	7 430	7 500	7 680	8 410	9 070
Forestry Commission/Forest Service	C5PB	3 720	3 950	4 190	4 730	4 850	4 600	4 650	4 820	4 890
Non-Forestry Commission/Forest Service	C5PC	2 760	2 850	2 640	2 550	2 580	2 900	3 030	3 590	4 170
Hardwood[10]	C5PD	800	820	720	680	660	640	620	560	510

1 See chapter text.
2 Areas as at 31 March.
3 For England, Wales and Scotland, 1980 woodland area figures are the published results from the 1979-1982 Census of Woodlands and Trees and figures for 1990 are adjusted to reflect subsequent changes. From 1998 onwards they are based on results from the 1995-1999 National Inventory of Woodlands and Trees, adjusted to reflect subsequent changes.
4 The apparent fall in woodland cover in 2001 is due to the reclassification of Forestry Commission open land within the forest.
5 Includes private woodland and non-Forestry Commission / Forest Service public woodland.
6 Broadleaved includes coppice. For data based on 1979-82 Census, all scrub and other non-plantation woodland have been assumed to be broadleaved.
7 Figures shown are for the areas of new planting and restocking in the year to 31 March.
8 Includes grant aided planting on non-Forestry Commission/ Forest Service woodland. It excludes areas planted without the aid of grants.
9 Figures have been rounded to the nearest 10 thousand green tonnes.
10 Hardwood is timber from broadleaved species. Most hardwood production comes from non-FC/FS woodland; the figures are estimates based on reported deliveries to wood processing industries.

*Sources: Forest Service Agency;
Department of Agriculture and Rural Development (Northern Ireland);
Forestry Commission: 0131 334 0303*

21.7 Sales for food of agricultural produce and livestock
United Kingdom

			1994	1995	1996	1997	1998	1999	2000	2001	2002	2003	2004
Cereals:		Thousand											
Wheat[1]	KCQK	tonnes	4 300	4 673	4 842	4 737	4 676	4 826	4 707	4 885	4 768	4 825	4 839
Barley	KCQL	"	3 232	3 818	3 734	3 453	3 525	3 454	3 802	2 669	3 015	3 121	2 488
Oats[2]	KCQM	"	215	216	235	259	273	270	263	283	311	323	317
Potatoes[3]	KCQN	"	6 519	5 961	6 146	6 279	5 997	6 210	6 675	6 606	6 892	6 448	6 539
Milk[4]:		Million litres											
Utilised for liquid consumption	KCQO	Million litres	6 926	6 922	6 838	6 748	6 739	6 853	6 768	6 761	6 756	6 629	6 518
Utilised for manufacture	KCQP	"	7 134	6 918	6 934	7 059	6 821	6 988	6 550	6 741	6 965	7 281	6 922
Total available for domestic use[5]	KCQQ	"	14 420	14 255	14 194	14 258	13 973	14 233	13 738	13 940	14 099	14 289	13 762
Hen eggs in shell	KCQR	Million dozens	787	774	775	794	792	738	713	753	746	729	776
Animals slaughtered:													
Cattle and calves:													
Cattle	KCQS	Thousands	3 089	3 266	2 291	2 264	2 297	2 217	2 275	2 072	2 184	2 175	2 259
Calves	KCQT	"	22	26	24	20	32	75	152	92	98	87	102
Total	KCQU	"	3 111	3 292	2 315	2 284	2 329	2 292	2 427	2 164	2 282	2 262	2 361
Sheep and lambs	KCQV	"	18 962	19 311	18 049	16 660	18 688	19 116	18 442	12 964	14 993	14 924	15 195
Pigs:													
Clean pigs	MBGD	"	14 681	14 021	13 897	15 132	15 872	14 350	12 370	10 446	10 260	9 115	9 129
Sows and boars	KCQZ	"	389	355	324	363	415	379	321	180	314	240	239
Total	KCRA	"	15 069	14 376	14 221	15 496	16 286	14 728	12 692	10 626	10 575	9 355	9 368
Poultry[6]	KCRB	Millions	761	783	823	850	857	863	843	866	862	882	882

Note: The figures for cereals and for animals slaughtered relate to periods of 52 weeks

1 Flour millers' receipts of home-grown wheat.
2 Oatmeal millers' receipts of home-grown oats.
3 Total sales for human consumption in the UK. Figures for 2004 are provisional.
4 Data to 1994 sourced from the Milk Marketing Boards. Data from 1995 sourced from surveys run by the agricultural departments. 1994 includes two months of data sourced from the surveys run by the agricultural departments.

5 The totals of liquid consumption and milk used for manufacture may not add up to the total available for domestic use because of adjustments for dairy wastage, stock changes and other uses, such as farmhouse consumption, milk fed to stock and on farm waste.
6 Total fowls, ducks, geese and turkeys.

Source: Department for Environment, Food and Rural Affairs: 01904 455332

21.8 Stocks of food and feedingstuffs[1]
United Kingdom
At end December each year

Thousand tonnes

		1994	1995	1996	1997	1998	1999	2000	2001	2002	2003	2004
Wheat and flour (as wheat)	KCRC	1 237	1 074	1 031	992	1 000	869	826	719	833	852	766
Barley (GB only)	KCRD	1 406	1 574	1 534	1 472	1 327	1 404	1 372	1 315	1 300	1 340	1 162
Maize	KCRE	32	33	25	45	67	43	37	36	66	52	63
Oilcake and meal[2,7]	KCRF	108	103	89	79	69	72	..	..	..	..	..
Oilseeds and nuts (crude oil equivalent)[7]	KCRG	28	34	28	19	13	20	10	17	10	13	..
Vegetable oil (as crude oil)	KCRI	109	96	101	101	99	98	84	96	89	86	..
Marine oil (as crude oil)	KCRJ	18	17	10	4	..	..	..	..	..	..	—
Butter[3]	KCRK	19	11	14	7	11	22	17	18	19	17	9
Meat and offal[4]	KCRL	103	77	129	162	157	84	54	57	49	47	49
Raw coffee[5]	KCRM	13	11	8	7	8	7	8	13	9	9	11
Tea[6]	KCRN	43	38	39	37	38	38	28	31	29	25	19
Sugar	KCRO	1 016	766	807	1 003	928	..	..	..	..	..	..

1 Recorded stocks, including stocks in bond or held by the main processors.
2 Excluding castor meal, cocoa cake and meal.
3 In addition to stocks in public cold stores surveyed by DEFRA, closing stocks include all intervention stocks in private cold stores.
4 Stocks of imported and home-produced mean and offal held in public cold stores, excluding poultrymeat, bacon and ham.
5 Including manufacturers' stocks and additional public warehouses.

6 Covering stocks held by primary wholesalers and held in public/private warehouses.
7 For confidentiality reasons, these data are no longer available for publication.
Source: Department for Environment, Food and Rural Affairs: 01904 455332

21.9 Processed food and animal feedingstuffs: production
United Kingdom

Thousand tonnes

		1994	1995	1996	1997	1998	1999	2000	2001	2002	2003	2004
Flour milling:												
Wheat milling: total	KFTA	5 355	5 343	5 501	5 535	5 707	5 668	5 617	5 667	5 616	5 572	5 576
Home produced	KFTB	4 171	4 603	4 772	4 667	4 582	4 701	4 609	4 790	4 648	4 726	4 772
Imported	KFTC	1 184	740	729	868	1 125	966	1 008	877	968	846	804
Flour produced	KFTD	4 282	4 298	4 454	4 439	4 526	4 497	4 486	4 487	4 413	4 370	4 423
Offals produced	KFTE	1 094	1 081	1 111	1 111	1 221	1 181	1 148	1 169	1 179	1 170	1 124
Oat milling:												
Oats milled by oatmeal millers	KFTF	209	217	250	259	272	266	261	287	312	322	321
Products of oat milling	KFTG	102	110	123	129	154	157	155	171	186	191	190
Seed crushing:												
Oilseeds and nuts processed[1]	KFTH	2 035	2 122	2 466	2 587	2 683	2 398	2 380	2 252	2 332	2 210	..
Crude oil produced, including production of maize oil[1]	KFTI	739	779	862	909	915	832	820	786	805	769	..
Oilcake and meal produced, excluding castor meal, cocoa cake and meal[1]	KFTJ	1 242	1 305	1 541	1 614	1 687	1 484	1 475	1 396	1 451	1 361	..
Production of home-killed meat: total including meat subsequently canned	KFTK	2 380	2 383	2 084	2 157	2 273	2 136	2 058	1 757	1 871	1 828	1 898
Beef	KFTL	915	973	701	695	704	675	703	649	690	694	721
Veal	KFTM	1	1	1	1	1	2	4	2	3	2	3
Mutton and lamb	KFTN	352	364	345	321	356	361	361	259	300	300	312
Pork	KFTO	807	752	769	871	934	823	721	596	621	578	597
Offal[2]	KFTP	305	293	268	269	278	275	270	250	258	255	264
Production of poultry meat[3]	KFTQ	1 370	1 427	1 481	1 527	1 548	1 549	1 514	1 566	1 556	1 569	1 564
Production of bacon and ham, including meat subsequently canned	KFTR	233	247	243	242	240	243	224	216	215	214	211
Production of milk products:												
Butter[4]	KFTS	148	133	130	139	137	141	132	126	136	131	122
Cheese (including farmhouse)	KFTT	341	362	377	377	366	368	340	395	380	363	373
Condensed milk: includes skim concentrate and condensed milk used in manufacture of chocolate crumb	KFTU	196	181	206	214	192	177	162	161	174	158	161
Milk powder: excluding buttermilk and whey powder												
Full cream	KFTV	83	90	83	96	97	102	105	87	105	101	80
Skimmed	KFTW	142	117	108	109	107	102	83	71	87	115	87
Cream, fresh and sterilised; including farm cream[5]	KFTX	274	281	281	268	266	275	270	290	290	330	364
Sugar: production from home-grown sugar-beet (as refined sugar)	KFTY	1 263	1 469	1 324	1 524	1 439	1 548	1 325	1 222	1 430	1 368	1 350
Production of compound fats:												
Margarine and other table spreads	KFTZ	487	490	491	461	448	421	388	409	415	442	431
Solid cooking fats	KFUA	109	110	123	109	131	125	135	121	114	131	132
Production of other processed foods:												
Syrup and treacle[5]	KFUC	50	48	..	..	..	..	..	..	..	..	..
Chocolate confectionery	KSJS	573	592	608	569	567	553	544	559	584	600	602
Sugar confectionery	KSJT	322	322	351	345	337	317	307	322	338	333	324
Cocoa beans excluding re-exports	KFVX	163	160	189	174	172	168	..	..	..	..	..
Breakfast cereals, other than oatmeal and oatmeal flakes	KFUJ	325	335	343	359	349	354	334	344	343	323	346
Glucose	KFUM	593	607	642	637	644	630	657	701	727	735	737
Compound feedingstuffs: total[6]	KFUP	11 402	11 609	11 801	11 304	11 206	11 404	10 604	10 888	10 762	10 771	10 904
Cattle food	KFUQ	4 347	4 476	4 430	3 926	3 844	4 264	4 038	4 327	4 212	4 490	4 466
Calf food	KFUR	286	307	277	227	198	187	184	180	177	193	200
Pig food	KFUS	2 547	2 453	2 566	2 659	2 740	2 435	2 082	1 930	1 777	1 536	1 591
Poultry food	KFUT	3 179	3 243	3 280	3 324	3 213	3 139	3 064	3 246	3 458	3 340	3 375
Other compounds	KFUU	1 043	1 130	1 249	1 168	1 210	1 378	1 236	1 204	1 138	1 212	1 272

Note: The figures relate to periods of 52 weeks (53 weeks in 1998 and 2004) with the following exceptions which are on a calendar year basis: butter, cheese, cream, canned meat, soft drinks, condensed milk and milk powder, canned vegetables, canned and bottled fruit, jam and marmalade, and soups.
1 For confidentiality reasons these data are no longer available for publication.

2 Including poultry offal.
3 Total of fowl, ducks, geese and turkeys (carcase weight).
4 Includes cream from the residual elements of low fat milk production.
5 This survey ceased at the end of 1995.
6 Feed produced for retail sale only.

Source: Department for Environment, Food and Rural Affairs: 01904 455332

21.10 Food and animal feedingstuffs: disposals

Thousand tonnes

		1994	1995	1996	1997	1998	1999	2000	2001	2002	2003	2004
Flour	KFPU	4 250	4 297	4 457	4 434	4 529	4 487	4 489	4 481	4 408	4 359	4 426
Sugar (as refined sugar): total disposals	KFPV	2 196	2 177	2 200	2 040	2 143	..	..	..	..	..	..
For food in the United Kingdom[1]	KFPW	2 165	2 157	2 180	2 007	2 106	..	..	..	..	..	..
Syrup and treacle[2]	KFPX	50	48	..	..	..	..	..	..	..	..	..
Meat and fish:												
Fresh and frozen meat and offal, including usage for canning:												
Beef and veal	KFPY	1 228	1 206	804	865	872	942	921	907	996	1 001	1 039
Mutton and lamb	KFPZ	474	504	501	468	496	497	496	373	423	435	455
Pork	KFVA	922	917	954	1 035	1 092	1 056	990	851	929	991	1 014
Offal[3]	KFVB	351	354	312	320	316	324	328	306	318	326	339
Poultry-meat[4,5]	KFVC	1 473	1 511	1 587	1 567	1 651	1 721	1 709	1 717	1 718	1 710	1 786
Bacon and ham, including usage for canning	KFVD	457	476	505	481	472	471	492	497	509	514	511
Dairy products:												
Butter	KFVI	284	255	240	256	238	244	255	240	250	251	244
Cheese	KFVJ	559	577	617	614	632	645	595	664	668	684	703
Condensed milk[6]	KFVK	208	195	217	229	205	190	178	172	187	179	186
Milk powder, excluding buttermilk and whey powder:												
Full cream	KFVM	91	97	94	105	106	111	117	92	115	116	98
Skimmed	KFVN	149	138	95	103	91	131	162	86	89	125	169
Hen eggs in shell[7]	KFVO	837	818	833	838	795	779	781	847	858	871	914
Oils (as crude oil):												
Vegetable oil	KFVP	1 567	1 905	1 960	2 010	1 780	2 449	2 452	2 052	2 036	2 195	..
Marine oil for the manufacture of margarine and compound fat	KFVQ	105	100	52	31	8	8	2	2	2	2	2
Potatoes[8]	KFVR	7 835	7 055	7 661	7 938	7 626	7 584	8 297	7 793	8 382	7 684	7 838
Other foods:												
Chocolate confectionery	KFVT	696	674	698	668	681	681	669	672	668	679	695
Sugar confectionery, excluding medicated	KFVU	382	380	416	410	409	393	393	400	387	387	357
Tea excluding re-exports	KFVV	149	141	148	152	145	133	144	133	136	121	156
Raw coffee	KFVW	119	105	116	118	122	115	109	105	116	109	129
Barley:												
For brewing and distilling and for food	KFVY	3 134	3 616	3 621	3 481	3 544	3 366	3 694	2 623	2 878	3 074	2 534
Maize (including maize meal): total disposals	KFVZ	1 367	1 411	1 389	1 439	1 448	1 256	1 184	1 243	1 231	1 202	1 112
Animal feed	KCRT	158	156	174	184	197	216	232	260	271	297	221
Oilcake and meal	KCRQ	4 152	4 462	4 429	4 041	3 677	4 035	..	..	..	..	..
Wheat milling offals	KCRR	1 137	1 132	1 157	1 158	1 273	1 209	1 176	1 205	1 220	1 216	1 163
Fish and poultry meal for animal feed,[9] (figures relate to sales)	KCRS	385	378	257	233	216	194	192	180	162	145	136

Note: The figures relate to periods of 52 weeks with the following exceptions which are on a calendar year basis: fish and potatoes; condensed milk; milk powder; butter and sugar.

1 Including sugar used in the manufacture of other foods subsequently exported. Excluding sugar in imported manufactured foods.
2 This survey ceased at the end of 1995.
3 Including poultry offal.
4 Carcase weight.
5 Total of fowls, ducks, geese and turkeys.
6 Includes skim concentrate and condensed milk used in the manufacture of chocolate crumb.
7 Million dozen eggs
8 2004 data are provisional.
9 Before a ban on 29 March 1996 this included poultry meat as well as mammalian meat and bonemeal.

Source: Department for Environment, Food and Rural Affairs: 01904 455332

21.11 Average weekly and hourly earnings and hours of full-time male agricultural workers[1]

England and Wales: At September each year

		1999	2000	2001	2002	2003	2004
Average weekly earnings (£) 95% confidence interval	LQML	301.22 (+/-£11.88)	298.24 (+/-£13.84)	332.66 (+/-£15.08)	366.82 (+/-£18.88)	352.88 (+/-£30.30)	380.75 (+/-£28.79)
Average weekly hours worked 95% confidence interval	LQMM	50.9 (+/-1.4)	49.0 (+/-1.4)	51.9 (+/-1.7)	54.1 (+/-2.1)	51.1 (+/-3.0)	51.0 (+/-£2.8)
Average earnings/hours (£) 95% confidence interval	LQMN	5.92 (+/-£0.15)	6.09 (+/-£0.18)	6.42 (+/-£0.20)	6.78 (+/-£0.19)	6.91 (+/-£0.31)	7.46 (+/-£0.31)
Number of workers in the sample		292	234	251	204	72	94

1 See chapter text.

Source: Department for Environment, Food and Rural Affairs: 01904 455332

21.12 Average weekly and hourly earnings and hours of agricultural workers[1] : by type 2004

England and Wales: At September

	Full-time		Part-time		Casual		Managers
	Male	Female	Male	Female	Male	Female	
Average weekly earnings (£) 95% confidence interval	380.75 (+/-£30.30)	277.99 (+/-£23.84)	132.36 (+/-£20.43)	144.01 (+/-£15.27)	305.50 (+/-£37.00)	194.55 (+/-£39.78)	491.29 (+/-£45.36)
Average weekly hours worked 95% confidence interval	51.0 (+/-3.0)	42.2 (+/-1.4)	22.5 (+/-3.2)	24.4 (+/-2.5)	48.0 (+/-5.3)	34.9 (+/-7.2)	..
Average earnings/hour (£) 95% confidence interval	7.46 (+/-£0.31)	6.59 (+/-£0.51)	5.88 (+/-£0.41)	5.91 (+/-£0.38)	6.37 (+/-£0.32)	5.57 (+/-£0.41)	..
Number of workers in the sample	94	41	40	30	74	24	76

1 See chapter text.

Source: Department for Environment, Food and Rural Affairs: 01904 455332

21.13 Workers employed in agriculture [1,2]: by type

United Kingdom

At June each year

Thousands

	Regular					Seasonal or casual			All			Salaried managers[3]
	Total	Full - time		Part - time		Total	Male	Female	Total	Male	Female	
		Male	Female	Male	Female							
	BANC	BAMY	BAMZ	BANA	BANB	BANF	BAND	BANE	BANI	BANG	BANH	KAYG
1993	165.3	96.5	13.7	29.8	25.3	85.4	55.0	30.4	250.7	181.3	69.4	7.6
1994	161.0	93.6	13.2	30.0	24.2	82.2	53.9	28.4	243.2	177.5	65.7	7.8
1995	157.4	90.4	13.0	30.0	24.1	83.7	56.5	27.2	241.2	176.8	64.3	7.7
1996	156.4	89.2	12.6	31.2	23.4	81.5	55.6	25.8	237.9	176.0	61.9	7.8
1997	154.4	87.5	12.6	31.2	23.1	80.9	55.3	25.5	235.2	174.0	61.2	7.8
1998[4,5]	155.6	88.0	13.1	29.7	24.7	79.5	55.6	23.8	235.0	172.8	62.2	12.1
1999	144.7	82.7	11.9	27.5	22.6	73.0	51.8	21.2	217.7	162.0	55.6	13.8
2000	128.9	73.4	10.3	24.6	20.6	64.4	45.9	18.5	193.3	143.9	49.4	11.1
2001[6]	120.8	69.0	10.9	22.0	18.9	63.2	44.6	18.6	184.0	135.6	48.5	13.4
	123.5	70.3	11.2	22.5	19.4	64.1	45.4	18.8	187.6	138.2	49.4	14.1
2002	116.3	64.7	11.5	21.7	18.4	64.2	46.2	18.0	180.6	132.6	47.9	13.4
2003	108.4	60.4	10.0	21.0	17.0	62.6	44.8	17.8	170.9	126.2	44.8	12.7
2004 Jun	108.8	58.1	9.8	23.5	17.4	68.3	49.6	18.6	177.0	131.2	45.8	15.2
2005 Jun	109.2	57.2	10.3	24.5	17.2	65.1	46.4	18.7	174.3	128.1	46.2	15.7

1 See chapter text. Includes estimates for minor holdings for all countries.
2 Figures exclude school children, farmers, partners, directors and their spouses and most trainees.
3 Great Britain only.
4 Results from 1998 onwards are not comparable with previous years, due to changes in the labour questions on the June Agricultural and Horticultural Census in England, Wales and Scotland.

5 From 1998, all farmers managing holdings for limited companies or other institutions in England and Wales were asked to classify themselves as salaried managers.
6 Due to an English register improvement only the top figure for 2001 is directly comparable with 2000, while the bottom figure for 2001 is only comparable with data from 2002.

Sources: Department for Environment, Food and Rural Affairs; Farming Statistics: 01904 455332

21.14 Landings of fish by United Kingdom vessels: live weight and value[1]
into United Kingdom

		Quantity (thousand tonnes)							Value (£ thousand)					
		1999	2000	2001	2002	2003	2004		1999	2000	2001	2002	2003	2004
Total all species	KSJU	506.5	464.7	458.3	465.6	451.5	461.5	KSLN	464 131	422 063	423 687	414 689	396 902	405 636
Total wet fish	KSJV	389.8	337.6	322.2	334.9	315.8	335.4	KSLO	297 831	268 816	256 364	250 845	218 408	232 497
Brill	KSJX	0.3	0.4	0.4	0.4	0.4	0.3	KSLP	1 405	1 839	2 032	1 785	1 635	1 391
Catfish	KSJY	0.7	0.8	0.7	0.5	0.5	0.4	KSLQ	1 006	1 081	896	738	821	522
Cod	KSJZ	46.8	37.0	28.1	25.7	15.5	15.2	KSLR	62 587	50 635	37 368	35 009	22 320	22 727
Dogfish	KSKA	6.9	7.3	7.0	5.8	6.7	4.6	KSLS	5 295	5 862	6 280	5 433	6 504	4 467
Haddock	KSKB	71.3	50.3	42.3	51.9	40.7	45.4	KSLT	59 286	51 181	36 295	34 631	27 515	32 732
Hake	KSKC	3.9	3.5	2.2	2.1	1.9	2.2	KSLU	7 839	6 941	5 303	5 646	4 558	5 273
Lemon Soles	KSKD	4.5	4.0	3.6	2.3	2.2	2.1	KSLV	10 374	9 934	9 937	7 313	6 712	6 034
Ling	KSKE	8.8	7.6	6.9	7.2	4.5	4.3	KSLW	8 502	7 571	7 384	7 654	4 649	4 397
Megrims	KSKF	5.0	5.0	4.3	4.0	3.6	3.4	KSLX	9 326	8 914	7 035	7 991	7 648	7 708
Monks or Anglers	KSKG	15.5	14.7	15.1	13.1	10.2	10.8	KSLY	35 591	33 609	33 789	27 927	20 923	22 732
Plaice	KSKH	9.5	8.6	7.7	5.9	4.4	3.5	KSLZ	12 549	9 869	9 011	6 645	5 215	4 282
Pollack (Lythe)	KSKI	2.3	2.5	2.6	2.5	2.5	2.1	KSMA	2 734	3 197	3 300	3 026	3 616	2 703
Saithe	KSKJ	10.4	10.2	9.7	9.9	8.5	9.0	KSMB	4 878	4 089	4 258	4 130	3 490	3 751
Sand Eels	KSKK	6.8	9.7	1.3	1.2	0.2	0.6	KSMC	283	400	..	55	10	37
Skates and Rays	KSKL	5.6	5.5	5.5	5.3	5.8	4.3	KSMD	5 380	5 677	5 679	5 299	5 808	4 472
Soles	KSKM	2.0	1.9	2.1	2.1	2.3	2.0	KSME	13 829	11 295	13 223	12 751	14 337	12 858
Turbot	KSKN	0.5	0.5	0.5	0.6	0.5	0.4	KSMF	2 918	2 859	3 277	4 192	2 715	2 382
Whiting	KSKO	25.4	23.3	15.1	11.4	8.2	7.4	KSMG	14 010	14 317	9 913	6 603	5 071	5 002
Whiting, Blue	KSKP	38.4	17.7	20.0	8.6	9.7	25.0	KSMH	1 476	743	936	561	670	1 345
Witches	KSKQ	2.2	2.4	2.7	2.2	2.4	2.2	KSMI	2 202	2 352	2 678	2 478	3 271	3 664
Other Demersal[2]	KSKR	15.7	14.6	17.7	15.1	13.0	10.5	KSMJ	18 559	16 025	19 765	18 513	17 571	17 383
Total Demersal[3]	KSKS	282.6	227.3	195.5	178.1	143.6	155.8	KSMK	280 028	248 392	218 414	198 381	165 058	165 862
Herring[4]	KSKT	45.3	39.5	43.8	42.5	55.4	56.2	KSML	5 057	4 073	10 447	6 873	7 125	7 646
Horse Mackerel	KSKU	2.1	2.7	3.5	1.8	2.0	2.5	KSMM	304	440	587	367	295	441
Mackerel[4]	KSKV	41.3	54.6	63.9	96.6	106.4	115.3	KSMN	9 544	13 848	23 877	42 694	44 325	57 019
Pilchards	KSKW	3.5	2.9	6.8	5.8	2.7	1.3	KSMO	550	602	1 665	1 005	711	596
Sprats	KSKX	14.3	8.3	5.1	5.7	5.5	3.9	KSMP	2 053	1 040	607	677	804	734
Tuna	KSKY	0.1	..	..	–	–	–	KSMQ	111	20	..	–	1	–
Other Pelagic	KSKZ	0.6	2.3	3.6	4.4	0.1	0.4	KSMR	184	401	762	848	89	198
Total Pelagic	KSLA	107.2	110.3	126.7	156.8	172.2	179.6	KSMS	17 803	20 424	37 949	52 464	53 350	66 635
Cockles	KSLB	14.2	20.3	19.0	14.3	31.4	12.9	KSMT	2 526	2 953	3 832	4 170	19 113	10 067
Crabs	KSLC	23.0	25.7	25.0	23.3	25.4	21.7	KSMU	26 983	28 036	27 830	26 014	28 066	23 541
Lobsters	KSLD	1.8	1.2	1.1	1.2	1.4	1.4	KSMV	14 928	12 458	11 436	11 680	13 920	12 636
Mussels	KSLE	8.4	7.5	14.9	17.2	3.1	12.1	KSMW	2 107	1 442	4 835	4 515	1 659	2 017
Nephrops	KSLF	31.1	28.3	28.4	28.4	27.7	30.4	KSMX	74 327	60 778	68 433	68 754	64 788	70 296
Periwinkles	KSLG	1.2	1.1	0.8	0.2	0.2	0.1	KSMY	1 165	1 089	791	221	157	72
Queens	KSLH	5.9	5.3	8.7	10.8	7.3	5.1	KSMZ	2 563	2 292	3 667	4 156	2 855	1 879
Scallops	KSLI	19.1	19.7	19.5	18.8	19.3	21.1	KSNA	29 145	30 741	29 853	27 963	29 394	31 809
Shrimps/Prawns	KSLJ	2.0	1.6	2.6	1.5	0.7	0.5	KSNB	2 931	2 062	3 566	2 574	1 081	686
Squid	KSLK	2.1	1.4	1.4	2.1	3.0	2.9	KSNC	4 190	2 716	3 903	4 908	6 776	7 765
Other shellfish	KSLL	8.0	14.8	14.9	13.1	16.3	18.0	KSND	5 434	8 680	9 177	8 889	10 685	12 370
Total shellfish	KSLM	116.7	127.0	136.2	130.7	135.7	126.1	KSNE	166 299	153 247	167 323	163 844	178 494	173 139

1 See chapter text.
2 Includes roes and livers.
3 Includes fish roes.

4 Includes transshipments, i.e. caught by UK boats but not actually landing at UK ports. These quantities are transshipped to foreign vessels in coastal waters and are later recorded as exports.

Source: Department for Environment, Food and Rural Affairs: 01904 455332

21.15 Fishing fleet[1]
United Kingdom
At 31 December each year

Numbers

		1994	1995	1996	1997	1998	1999	2000	2001	2002	2003	2004
By size												
10m and under	KSNF	7 195	6 320	5 606	5 474	5 487	5 409	5 273	5 227	5 287	5 113	5 092
10.01 - 12.19m	KSNG	1 167	1 016	800	732	628	577	547	536	514	486	465
12.20 - 17.00m	KSNH	680	622	540	523	491	468	467	442	409	405	393
17.01 - 18.29m	KSNI	193	187	164	162	154	154	131	143	129	121	115
18.30 - 24.38m	KSNJ	610	574	509	471	443	414	406	405	322	271	257
24.39 - 30.48m	KSNK	211	212	223	227	226	224	219	218	185	156	147
30.49 - 36.58m	KSNL	126	127	114	104	89	80	77	75	65	63	60
over 36.58m	KSNM	116	117	117	119	121	122	122	123	122	120	112
Total over 10m	KSNN	3 103	2 855	2 467	2 338	2 152	2 039	1 969	1 942	1 746	1 622	1 549
Total UK fleet[2]	KSNO	10 297	9 174	8 073	7 812	7 639	7 448	7 242	7 169	7 033	6 735	6 641
By segment												
Pelagic gears	KSNP	68	67	58	49	50	46	44	47	45	42	31
Beam trawl	KSNQ	212	220	215	153	123	114	111	116	113	162	102
Demersal trawls and seines	KXET	..	..	1 040	..	..	..	..	..	..	..	..
Demersal trawls	KSIX	854	856	..	..	..	..	..	..	..	..	..
Nephrop trawls	KSIY	593	528	411	..	..	..	..	..	..	..	..
Seines	KSIZ	197	165	..	..	..	..	..	..	..	..	..
Demersal, Seines and Nephrops	JZCI	..	..	..	1 428	1 318	1 235	1 208	1 158	969	853	852
Lines and Nets	KSNR	300	267	224	214	187	172	165	146	136	118	123
Shellfish: mobile	KSNS	206	194	265	227	241	243	211	229	228	191	166
Shellfish: fixed	KSNT	305	283	339	352	311	301	297	301	304	307	253
Distant water	KSNU	13	12	15	13	14	12	13	11	10	8	10
Under 10m	KSNV	7 607	6 757	6 091	6 022	6 027	5 916	5 769	5 713	5 773	5 587	5 395
Non-active/non-TAC	KSNW	472	371	–	–	–	–	–	–	–	–	..
Other: Mussel Dredgers	JZCJ	..	..	..	3	2	2	2	7	15	15	13
Total UK fleet[3]	KSNX	10 827	9 720	8 658	8 461	8 273	8 041	7 820	7 728	7 593	7 283	6 945

1 See chapter text.
2 Excluding Channel Islands and Isle of Man.
3 Including Channel Islands and Isle of Man.

Source: Department for Environment, Food and Rural Affairs: 01904 455332

355

21.16 Estimated household food consumption[1]

		Great Britain										United Kingdom	
		1992	1993	1994	1995	1996	1997	1998	1999	2000		2001/02	2002/03
Liquid wholemilk[2] (ml)	KPQM	995	898	870	812	776	712	693	634	664	VQEW	599	555
Fully skimmed (ml)	KZBH	213	217	207	204	137	158	164	167	164	VQEX	160	166
Semi skimmed (ml)	KZBI	752	814	863	899	935	978	945	958	975	VQEZ	931	919
Other milk and cream (ml)	KZBJ	262	249	252	255	259	248	243	248	278	VQFA	333	350
Cheese	KPQO	114	109	106	108	111	109	104	104	110	VQFB	112	112
Butter	KPQP	41	40	39	36	39	38	39	37	39	VQFC	42	37
Margarine	KPQQ	79	70	43	41	36	26	26	20	21	VQFD	13	13
Low and reduced fat spreads	KZBK	51	52	74	72	79	77	69	71	68	VQFE	72	70
All other oils and fats (ml for oils)	KPQR	74	69	70	69	71	62	62	58	58	VQFF	70	70
Eggs (number)	KPQS	2	2	2	2	2	2	2	2	2	VQFG	2	2
Preserves and honey	KPQT	45	42	43	39	41	41	38	33	33	VQFH	35	34
Sugar	KPQU	156	151	144	136	144	128	119	107	105	VQFI	112	111
Beef and veal	KPQV	141	133	131	121	101	110	109	110	124	VQFJ	118	118
Mutton and lamb	KPQW	71	66	54	54	66	56	59	57	55	VQFK	51	51
Pork	KPQX	72	80	77	71	73	75	76	69	68	VQFL	61	61
Bacon and ham, uncooked	KPQY	77	77	77	76	77	72	76	68	71	VQFM	68	69
Bacon and ham, cooked (including canned)	KPQZ	33	35	38	39	33	41	40	39	41	VQFN	45	45
Poultry uncooked	JZCH	216	222	209	215	233	221	218	201	214	VQFO	206	199
Cooked poultry (not purchased in cans)	KYBP	15	16	20	22	23	33	33	35	39	VQFQ	43	44
Other cooked and canned meats	KPRB	68	60	63	63	62	52	49	48	51	VQFR	54	59
Offals	KPRC	12	11	9	9	7	7	5	5	5	VQFS	6	6
Sausages, uncooked	KPRD	61	60	61	63	63	63	60	58	60	VQFT	66	66
Other meat products	KPRE	183	194	203	211	207	209	216	221	239	VQFU	313	319
Fish, fresh and processed (including shellfish)	KPRF	67	71	71	68	72	70	70	70	67			
Canned fish	KPRG	32	30	30	29	31	31	29	31	32			
Fish and fish products, frozen	KPRH	43	44	44	46	50	46	46	42	44			
Fish, fresh chilled or frozen											VQAI	51	48
Other fish and fish products											VQAJ	105	106
Potatoes (excluding processed)	KPRI	901	875	812	803	805	745	715	673	707	VQFY	647	617
Fresh green vegetables	KPRJ	250	240	245	225	233	251	246	245	240	VQAK	229	231
Other fresh vegetables	KPRK	475	477	464	470	489	497	486	500	492	VQAL	502	505
Frozen potato products	KYBQ	92	98	103	99	113	106	111	113	120			
Other frozen vegetables	KPRL	106	105	107	101	94	94	88	87	80			
Potato products not frozen	JZCF	75	80	82	89	92	90	89	86	82			
Canned beans	KPRM	120	112	111	117	125	122	118	112	114			
Other canned vegetables (excl. potatoes)	KPRN	124	114	103	110	113	104	99	92	97			
Other processed vegetables (excl. potatoes)	LQZH	50	52	55	48	55	52	54	59	54			
All processed vegetables											VQAM	620	613
Apples	KPRO	187	179	180	183	175	179	181	169	180	VQGN	175	172
Bananas	KPRP	144	151	162	176	185	195	198	202	206	VQGO	203	208
Oranges	KPRQ	72	62	65	66	63	62	63	50	54	VQGP	55	62
All other fresh fruit	KPRR	216	224	238	247	263	276	274	290	304	VQGS	318	351
Canned fruit	KPRS	51	48	46	45	43	44	37	38	38	VQGT	40	39
Dried fruit, nuts and fruit and nut products	KPRT	38	39	36	34	36	35	34	30	35	VQGU	39	41
Fruit juices (ml)	KPRU	222	236	240	244	258	277	304	284	303	VQGX	327	333
Flour	KPRV	81	82	62	57	70	54	55	56	67	VQGY	55	61
Bread	KPRW	755	757	758	756	752	746	742	717	720	VQGZ	769	756
Buns, scones and teacakes	KPRX	40	39	38	36	47	43	41	40	43	VQHA	37	41
Cakes and pastries	KPRY	76	79	85	85	87	93	88	87	89	VQHB	139	122
Biscuits	KPRZ	148	142	138	135	150	138	137	132	141	VQHC	166	174
Breakfast cereals	KPSA	132	129	134	135	140	135	136	134	143	VQHE	133	132
Oatmeal and oat products	KPSB	15	14	11	11	13	16	11	13	15	VQHF	12	13
Other cereals and cereal products	JZCG	217	218	218	251	304	293	270	284	291	VQHG	345	366
Tea	KPSC	39	36	38	39	38	36	35	32	34	VQHK	34	34
Instant coffee	KPSD	14	13	13	12	13	11	12	11	11	VQHL	13	12
Canned soups	KPSE	70	66	68	64	72	70	71	67	71	VQHM	79	80
Pickles and sauces	KPSF	72	77	77	80	84	92	96	91	107	VQHN	121	123

1 See chapter text.
2 Including also school and welfare milk.

Sources: Expenditure and Food Survey;
Department for Environment Food and Rural Affairs: 01904 455077

Production

Chapter 22

Production

Annual Business Inquiry

(Table 22.1)

The Annual Business Inquiry (ABI) estimates cover all UK businesses registered for Value Added Tax (VAT) and/ or Pay As You Earn (PAYE), classified to the 1992 Standard Industrial Classification (SIC(92)) headings listed in the tables. The ABI obtains details on these businesses from the Office for National Statistics (ONS) Inter-Departmental Business Register (IDBR).

As with all its statistical inquiries, ONS is concerned to minimise the form-filling burden of individual contributors and as such the ABI is a sample inquiry. The sample was designed as a stratified random sample of about 69,600 businesses, the inquiry population is stratified by SIC(92) and employment using the information from the register.

The inquiry results are grossed up to the total population, so that they relate to all active UK businesses on the IDBR for the sectors covered.

The results meet a wide range of needs for government, economic analysts and the business community at large. In official statistics the inquiry is an important source for the national accounts and input-output tables, but also provides weights for the indices of production and producer prices. Inquiry results also enable the United Kingdom to meet statistical requirements of the European Union.

Data from 1995 and 1996 were calculated on a different basis from those for 1997 and later years. In order to provide a link between the two data series, the 1995 and 1996 data were subsequently reworked to provide estimates on a consistent basis.

Revised Annual Business Inquiry results down to SIC(92) 4 digit class level for 1995–2001, giving both analysis and tabular detail, are now available free of charge from the National Statistics website at *www.statistics.gov.uk/abi/*, with further extracts and bespoke analyses available on request. This service replaces existing publications.

Manufacturers' sales by industry

(Table 22.2)

This table shows the total manufacturers' sales for products classified to the 1992 Standard Industrial Classification and collected under the PRODCOM (Products of the European Community) Inquiry since its introduction in 1993. Some data are not available for confidentiality reasons or where data have not been published for a given period. Detailed product sales data together with exports and imports data are available in the Product Sales and Trade quarterly and annual reports (PRQ and PRA series).

Number of VAT based local units in manufacturing industries in 2005

(Table 22.3)

This table shows the number of local units (sites) in manufacturing by employment size bands. The classification breakdown is at division level (2 digit) as classified to the 2003 Standard Industrial Classification held on the Inter-Departmental Business Register (IDBR). This register became fully operational in 1995 and combines information on VAT traders and PAYE employers in a statistical register comprising 2.1 million enterprises (businesses), representing nearly 99 per cent of economic activity. UK Business: Activity, Size and Location (formerly Business Monitor – PA1003) 2005 provides further details and contains detailed information on enterprises in the UK including size, classification and location. Additionally, this information is available for whole economy local units.

For further information on the IDBR see the National Statistics website at www.statistics.gov.uk/idbr.

Production of primary fuels

(Table 22.4)

This table shows indigenous production of primary fuels. It includes the extraction or capture of primary commodities and the generation or manufacture of secondary commodities. Production is always gross; that is, it includes the quantities used during the extraction or manufacturing process. Primary fuels are coal, natural gas (including colliery methane), oil, primary electricity (i.e. electricity generated by hydro, nuclear wind and tide stations and also electricity imported from France through the interconnector) and renewables (includes solid renewables such as wood, straw and waste and gaseous renewables such as landfill gas and sewage gas). The figures are presented on a common basis, expressed in million tonnes of oil equivalent. Estimates of the gross calorific values used for converting the statistics for the various fuels to these are given in the *Digest of UK Energy Statistics* (published by The Stationery Office and available on the Department of Trade and Industry (DTI) website at www.dti.gov.uk/energy/inform/dukes/). Chapter 1 of the *Digest of UK Energy Statistics* gives more information on these figures.

Total inland energy consumption

(Table 22.5)

This table shows energy consumption by fuel and final energy consumption by fuel and class of consumer. Primary energy consumption covers consumption of all primary fuels (defined above) for energy purposes. This measure of energy consumption includes energy that is lost by converting primary fuels into secondary fuels, i.e. the energy lost burning coal to generate electricity or the energy used by refineries to separate crude oil into fractions, in addition to losses in distribution. The other common way of measuring energy consumption is to measure the energy content of the fuels supplied to consumers. This is called final energy consumption. It is net of fuel used by the energy industries, conversion, transmission and distribution losses. The figures are presented on a common basis, measured as energy supplied and expressed in million tonnes of oil equivalent. Estimates of the gross calorific values used for converting the statistics for the various fuels to these are given in the *Digest of UK Energy Statistics* (published by The Stationery Office and available on the DTI website at www.dti.gov.uk/energy/inform/dukes/). So far as practicable the user categories have been grouped on the basis of the SIC(2003) although the methods used by each of the supply industries to identify end users are slightly different. Chapter 1 of the *Digest of UK Energy Statistics* gives more information on these figures.

Coal

(Table 22.6)

Since 1995, aggregate data on coal production have been obtained from the Coal Authority. In addition, main coal producers provide data in response to an annual DTI inquiry which covers production (deepmined and opencast), trade, stocks and disposals. HM Revenue and Customs also provide trade data for solid fuels. The DTI collects information on the use of coal from UK Iron and Steel Statistics Bureau, and consumption of coal for electricity generation is covered by data provided by the electricity generators.

Gas

(Table 22.7)

Production figures, covering the production of gas from the UKCS offshore and onshore gas fields and gas obtained during the production of oil, are obtained from returns made under the DTI's Petroleum Production Reporting System. Additional information is used on imports and exports of gas and details from the operators of gas terminals in the UK to complete the picture.

It is no longer possible to present information on fuels input into the gas industry and gas output and sales in the same format as in previous editions of this table. As such, users are directed to Chapter 4 of the 2002 edition of the *Digest of UK Energy Statistics*, where more detailed information on gas production and consumption in the UK is available.

DTI carry out an annual survey of gas suppliers to obtain details of gas sales to the various categories of consumer. Estimates are included for the suppliers with the smallest market share since the DTI inquiry covers only the largest suppliers (i.e. those more than about 0.5 per cent share of the UK market up to 1997 and those known to supply more than 1,750 GWh per year from 1998 onwards).

Electricity

(Tables 22.8 to 22.10)

The electricity Tables 22.8 to 22.10 cover all generators and suppliers of electricity in the United Kingdom.

The relationship between generation, supply, availability and consumption is as follows:

Electricity generated

less	electricity used on works
equals	electricity supplied (gross)
less	electricity used in pumping at pumped storage stations
equals	electricity supplied (net)
plus	imports (net of exports) of electricity
equals	electricity available
less	losses and statistical differences
equals	electricity consumed.

In Table 22.8 'major power producers' are those generating companies corresponding to the old public sector supply system, i.e. AES Electric Ltd., Anglian Power Generation., Baglan Generation Ltd., BNFL Magnox, British Energy plc., Centrica plc., Coolkeeragh Power Ltd., Corby Power Ltd., Coryton Energy Company Ltd., Deeside Power, Derwent Cogeneration Ltd., Drax Power Ltd., EDF Energy Plc, Edison Mission Energy Ltd., Enfield Energy Centre Ltd., Fellside Heat and Power Ltd., Fibrogen Ltd., Fibropower Ltd., Fibrothetford Ltd., Great Yarmouth Power Ltd., Humber Power Ltd., Immingham CHP., International Power plc., National Grid Company (Kielder), NIGEN, Peterborough Power Ltd., Premier Power Ltd., Regional Power Generators Ltd., Rocksavage Power Company Ltd., RWE Innogy plc., Saltend Co-generation Company Ltd., Scottish Power plc., Scottish and Southern

Production

Energy plc., Seabank Power Ltd., SELCHP Ltd. (South East London Combined Heat & Power Ltd.), Thames Power Services Ltd, Western Power Generation Ltd.

In Table 22.10 all fuels are converted to the common unit of million tonnes of oil equivalent, which is equal to 10^3 kilocalaries.

More detailed statistics on energy are given in the *Digest of United Kingdom Energy Statistics* 2005. Readers may wish to note that the production and consumption of fuels are presented using commodity balances. A commodity balance shows the flows of an individual fuel through from production to final consumption, showing its use in transformation and energy industry own use.

Oil and oil products

(Tables 22.11 to 22.13)

The data on the production of crude oil, condensates and natural gases given in Table 22.11 are collected by the DTI direct from the operators of production facilities and terminals situated on UK territory, either onshore or offshore, i.e. on the UK Continental Shelf. Data are also collected from the companies on their trade in oil and oil products. These data are used in preference to the foreign trade as recorded by HM Revenue and Customs in the *Overseas Trade Statistics*.

Data on the internal UK oil industry (i.e. on the supply, refining and distribution of oil and oil products in the UK) are collected by the DTI from the UK Petroleum Industry Association members and other contributors. These data, reported by individual refining companies and wholesalers, and supplemented where necessary by data from other sources, provide the contents of Tables 22.12 and 22.13. The data are presented in terms of deliveries to the inland UK market. This is regarded as an acceptable proxy for actual consumption of products. The main shortcoming is that, whilst changes in stocks held by companies in central storage areas are taken into account, changes in the levels of stocks further down the retail ladder (such as stocks held on petrol station forecourts) are not. This is not thought to result in a significant degree of difference in the data.

Iron and steel

(Tables 22.14 to 22.16)

Iron and steel industry

The general definition of the UK iron and steel industry is based on groups 271 'ECSC iron and steel', 272 'Tubes', and 273 'Primary Transformation' of the UK Standard Industrial Classification (1992), except those parts of groups 272 and 273

which cover cast iron pipes, drawn wire, cold formed sections and Ferro alloys.

The definition excludes certain products which may be made by works within the industry, such as refined iron, finished steel castings, steel tyres, wheels, axles and rolled rings, open and closed die forgings, colliery arches and springs. Iron foundries and steel stockholders are also considered to be outside of the industry.

Statistics

The statistics for the UK iron and steel industry are compiled by the Iron and Steel Statistics Bureau (ISSB Ltd). from data collected from UK steel producing companies with the exception of trade data which is based on HM Customs data.

Crude steel is the total of usable ingots, usable continuously cast semi-finished products and liquid steel for castings.

Production of finished products is the total production at the mill of that product after deduction of any material which is immediately scrapped.

Deliveries are based on invoiced tonnages and will include deliveries made to steel stockholders and service centres by the UK steel industry.

For more detailed information on definitions etc please contact ISSB Ltd. on 020 7343 3900.

Fertilisers

(Table 22.18)

This data set provides an estimate of the quantities of major fertiliser nutrients and compound fertiliser product tonnage delivered to farm in the UK for the fertiliser seasons ending in June of each year. This table has previously included only fertiliser quantities delivered by Members of the Agricultural Industries Confederation (AIC) – Fertiliser sector (previously the Fertiliser Manufacturers Association (FMA). The table has now been fully revised to provide estimates of total UK fertiliser market in order to give more complete data and to eliminate fluctuations which could be caused by any change of membership within the AIC.

This table 22.18 is therefore completely revised from those published in previous editions.

Minerals

(Table 22.19)

Table 22.19 gives, separately for Great Britain and Northern Ireland, the production of minerals extracted from the ground. The figures for chemicals and metals are estimated from the quality of the ore which is extracted. The data come from an annual census of the quarrying industry which, for Great Britain, is conducted by ONS for the Department for Communities and Local Government and the DTI.

Building Materials

(Table 22.20)

Table 22.20 gives the production of a number of building materials which are closely associated with material extracted from the ground. The data come from surveys conducted by ONS on behalf of the DTI.

Construction

(Tables 22.21 to 22.22)

Table 22.21 shows the value of contractors' output in the construction industry in Great Britain. Output is defined as the amount chargeable to customers for building and civil engineering work done in the relevant period plus that done by public sector direct labour. The data come from surveys run by the DTI. As well as being an important input to the National Accounts, it is used by the government and the construction industry in their efforts to fully understand the industry, and also by Eurostat.

Table 22.22 shows the value of new orders in the construction industry; this is also collected by DTI. This information relates to contracts for new construction work awarded to main contractors by clients in both the public and private sectors; it also includes speculative work, undertaken on the initiative of the firm, where no contract is awarded. New orders are used as a good indicator of future output.

Motor vehicle production

(Table 22.25)

The figures represent the output of United Kingdom based manufacturers classified to Class 34.10 (motor vehicles) of the Standard Industrial Classification 2003. They are derived from the Motor Vehicle Production Inquiry (MVPI).

These figures include vehicles produced in the form of kits for assembly. The value of the kit must be 50 per cent or more of the value of a corresponding complete vehicle.

Drink and tobacco

(Tables 22.26 and 22.27)

Data for these tables are derived by HM Revenue and Customs from the systems for collecting excise duties. Alcoholic drinks and tobacco products become liable to duty when released for

consumption in the UK. Figures for releases include both home-produced products and commercial imports. Production figures are also available for potable spirits distilled and beer brewed in the UK.

Alcoholic drink

(Table 22.26)

The figures for Imported and other spirits released for home consumption include gin and other UK produced spirits, for which a breakdown is not available.

Since June 1993 beer duty has been charged when the beer leaves the brewery or other registered premises. Previously duty was chargeable at an earlier stage (the worts stage) in the brewing process, and an allowance was made for wastage. Figures prior to 1994 include adjustments to bring them into line with current data. The change in June 1993 also led to the availability of data on the strength; a series in hectolitres of pure alcohol is shown from 1994.

Made wine with alcoholic strength from 1.2 per cent to 5.5 per cent is termed 'coolers'. Included in coolers are alcoholic lemonade and similar products of appropriate strength. From 28 April 2002, duty on spirit-based 'coolers' (ready to drink products) is charged at the same rate as spirits per litre of alcohol. Made wine coolers include only wine based 'coolers' from this period.

Tobacco Products

(Table 22.27)

Releases of cigarettes and other tobacco products tend to be higher in the period before a Budget. Products may then be stocked, duty paid, before being sold.

22.1 Production and construction:[1] summary table
United Kingdom
Standard Industrial Classfication 1992: Estimates for all firms

£ million

	Total turnover	Gross value added	Stocks and work in progress		Capital expenditure *less* disposals	Total employment costs
			At end of year	Change during year		

Standard Industrial Classification: Revised 1992

Production and construction
Sections C-F

	ZIYQ	KSCD	KSCE	KSCF	KSCG	AWKC
1998	631 265	212 933	70 062	365	34 097	112 326
1999	644 749	220 338	66 400	1 539	30 007	114 584
2000	675 149	228 161	66 571	3 962	27 478	115 943
2001	674 274	229 773	65 831	713	28 823	117 560
2002	669 855	228 613	70 233	520	27 116	119 037

Production industries (Revised definitions)
Sections C-E

	ZIYR	KSCL	KSCM	KSCN	KSCO	AWKH
1998	528 819	178 459	55 354	−601	32 275	93 692
1999	533 384	181 189	54 867	204	28 139	93 774
2000	553 601	185 886	54 945	3 200	25 261	94 209
2001	544 210	182 243	52 732	−824	25 716	93 993
2002	529 380	178 828	50 261	−753	23 182	93 098

Mining and quarrying
Section C

	ZIYS	KSCT	KSCU	KSCV	KSCW	AWKI
1998	23 953	13 120	1 138	55	6 303	2 542
1999	26 270	15 245	1 138	−5	4 058	2 469
2000	36 513	22 289	957	−2	2 810	2 669
2001	37 057	22 560	958	64	4 272	2 698
2002	32 950	19 279	882	30	4 813	2 682

Mining and quarrying of energy producing materials
Subsection CA

	ZIYT	KSDB	KSDC	KSDD	KSDE	KSDF
1998	19 866	11 512	732	23	5 985	1 862
1999	21 975	13 615	850	−19	3 738	1 765
2000	31 704	20 489	657	−24	2 572	1 905
2001	32 237	20 765	658	33	4 008	1 945
2002	28 406	17 827	612	7	4 563	1 974

Mining and quarrying except energy producing materials
Subsection CB

	ZIYU	KSDJ	KSDK	KSDL	KSDM	KSDN
1998	4 087	1 609	406	32	318	680
1999	4 295	1 630	289	14	320	704
2000	4 809	1 800	300	21	237	765
2001	4 820	1 795	300	31	264	752
2002	4 544	1 452	271	23	249	708

Manufacturing (Revised definition)
Section D

	ZIYV	KSDR	KSDS	KSDT	KSDU	AWKL
1998	460 677	149 892	52 675	−643	20 386	87 079
1999	461 771	150 449	52 005	309	18 125	87 334
2000	469 146	148 793	52 167	3 150	17 004	87 456
2001	461 898	145 230	50 038	−816	16 278	87 574
2002	450 090	144 149	47 669	−667	13 237	86 691

22.1 continued

Production and construction:[1] summary table
United Kingdom
Standard Industrial Classfication 1992: Estimates for all firms

£ million

	Total turnover	Gross value added	Stocks and work in progress		Capital expenditure *less* disposals	Total employment costs
			At end of year	Change during year		

Standard Industrial Classification: Revised 1992

Manufacture of food; beverages and tobacco
Subsection DA

	ZIYW	KSDZ	KSEA	KSEB	KSEC	AWKM
1998	73 482	19 351	8 023	−221	2 763	9 333
1999	73 655	19 977	7 958	−62	2 725	9 885
2000	73 872	20 184	7 605	−88	2 271	9 929
2001	74 692	20 324	7 633	87	2 638	10 045
2002	76 764	20 721	7 557	53	2 161	10 416

Manufacture of textile and textile products
Subsection DB

	ZIYX	KSEH	KSEI	KSEJ	KSEK	AWKN
1998	17 365	6 699	2 906	−140	552	4 476
1999	16 137	5 930	2 610	−67	460	4 035
2000	14 358	5 506	2 285	−19	275	3 541
2001	13 229	5 051	2 046	41	258	3 096
2002	12 203	4 480	1 881	41	307	2 894

Manufacture of leather and leather products
Subsection DC

	ZIYY	KSEP	KSEQ	KSER	KSES	AWKO
1998	2 005	689	301	−11	42	461
1999	1 819	673	243	−2	38	360
2000	1 728	676	230	−18	9	330
2001	1 758	595	230	−28	23	320
2002	1 541	571	228	−3	18	275

Manufacture of wood and wood products
Subsection DD

	ZIYZ	KSEX	KSEY	KSEZ	KSFA	AWKP
1998	5 797	2 270	593	6	255	1 360
1999	5 838	2 101	508	−14	238	1 246
2000	6 186	2 303	610	30	227	1 292
2001	6 571	2 315	585	−17	219	1 374
2002	7 016	2 459	658	37	186	1 626

Manufacture of pulp, paper and paper products; publishing and printing
Subsection DE

	ZIZA	KSFF	KSFG	KSFH	KSFI	AWKQ
1998	42 734	18 309	2 660	−28	1 957	10 277
1999	43 387	19 280	2 608	71	1 719	10 260
2000	45 291	19 492	2 544	125	1 813	10 857
2001	44 922	19 425	2 606	25	1 657	10 856
2002	45 317	19 294	2 651	104	1 477	10 927

Manufacture of coke, refined petroleum products and nuclear fuel
Subsection DF

	ZIZB	KSFN	KSFO	KSFP	KSFQ	AWKR
1998	23 322	2 289	885	−196	730	923
1999	25 310	3 087	1 333	449	766	912
2000	27 855	2 302	1 199	114	623	920
2001	25 369	2 401	1 000	−190	705	898
2002	24 255	2 502	1 287	190	473	1 099

22.1
continued

Production and construction:[1] summary table
United Kingdom
Standard Industrial Classfication 1992: Estimates for all firms

£ million

	Total turnover	Gross value added	Stocks and work in progress		Capital expenditure *less* disposals	Total employment costs
			At end of year	Change during year		

Standard Industrial Classification: Revised 1992

Manufacture of chemicals, chemical products and man-made fibres
Subsection DG

	ZIZC	KSFV	KSFW	KSFX	KSFY	AWKS
1998	44 825	14 341	5 659	114	3 161	7 374
1999	46 282	14 939	5 911	75	2 830	7 710
2000	47 544	15 069	6 249	481	2 729	7 549
2001	48 915	15 821	6 205	−8	2 473	7 959
2002	48 759	15 847	6 208	−14	2 147	8 295

Manufacture of rubber and plastic products
Subsection DH

	ZIZD	KSGD	KSGE	KSGF	KSGG	AWKT
1998	20 420	8 062	2 021	54	1 102	4 855
1999	19 520	7 554	1 898	24	1 088	4 940
2000	19 743	7 644	1 824	59	961	4 767
2001	19 869	7 716	1 833	−1	742	4 769
2002	19 637	7 536	1 769	27	690	4 694

Manufacture of other non-metallic mineral products
Subsection DI

	ZIZE	KSGL	KSGM	KSGN	KSGO	AWKU
1998	11 346	4 904	1 420	29	656	2 771
1999	11 710	4 865	1 364	−106	747	2 759
2000	12 014	5 154	1 460	94	621	2 821
2001	11 656	4 895	1 332	−4	488	2 828
2002	12 139	5 011	1 354	21	602	2 755

Manufacture of basic iron and of ferro-alloys
Subsection DJ

	ZIZF	KSGT	KSGU	KSGV	KSGW	AWKV
1998	44 399	17 030	4 255	−203	2 024	10 713
1999	40 879	15 941	4 047	99	1 464	10 450
2000	41 028	15 912	4 063	192	1 334	10 340
2001	40 660	15 316	3 920	−43	1 122	10 098
2002	38 360	14 640	3 626	88	1 179	9 649

Manufacture of machinery and equipment not elsewhere specified
Subsection DK

	ZIZG	KSHB	KSHC	KSHD	KSHE	AWKW
1998	35 580	13 414	5 084	46	982	8 637
1999	33 306	12 254	5 044	−230	954	8 356
2000	33 821	12 286	4 826	−40	872	8 437
2001	32 825	11 770	4 460	−73	792	8 302
2002	32 247	11 841	4 118	−141	673	8 114

Manufacture of electrical and optical equipment
Subsection DL

	ZIZH	KSHJ	KSHK	KSHL	KSHM	AWKX
1998	61 037	19 202	6 832	−10	2 688	11 568
1999	64 891	19 587	7 014	119	1 861	11 881
2000	69 110	20 504	8 521	1 700	2 331	12 587
2001	63 227	15 813	7 280	−1 130	1 950	12 576
2002	53 048	15 960	6 107	−693	868	11 292

22.1

Production and construction:[1] summary table
United Kingdom
Standard Industrial Classfication 1992: Estimates for all firms

£ million

	Total turnover	Gross value added	Stocks and work in progress		Capital expenditure *less* disposals	Total employment costs
			At end of year	Change during year		

Standard Industrial Classification: Revised 1992

Manufacture of transport equipment
Subsection DM

	ZIZI	KSHR	KSHS	KSHT	KSHU	AWKY
1998	63 009	17 179	10 463	−193	2 948	10 840
1999	63 239	17 955	9 648	−128	2 749	10 866
2000	60 440	15 553	9 048	454	2 444	10 520
2001	61 366	17 322	9 206	444	2 740	10 740
2002	61 550	16 925	8 581	−473	2 028	10 808

Manufacture not elsewhere classified
Subsection DN

	ZIZJ	KSHZ	KSIA	KSIB	KSIC	AWKZ
1998	15 356	6 153	1 574	110	528	3 493
1999	15 798	6 306	1 820	82	485	3 674
2000	16 156	6 208	1 703	67	496	3 565
2001	16 839	6 468	1 701	81	471	3 714
2002	17 254	6 361	1 643	94	428	3 846

Electricity, gas and water supply
Section E

	ZIZK	KSIH	KSII	KSIJ	KSIK	AWLA
1998	44 189	15 446	1 542	−14	5 586	4 071
1999	45 342	15 496	1 723	−100	5 955	3 970
2000	47 942	14 804	1 821	52	5 448	4 084
2001	45 256	14 453	1 736	−72	5 165	3 721
2002	46 341	15 399	1 709	−116	5 132	3 725

Construction
Section F

	ZIZL	KSIP	KSIQ	KSIR	KSIS	AWLB
1998	102 446	34 474	14 708	966	1 822	18 634
1999	111 365	39 150	11 533	1 335	1 869	20 810
2000	121 549	42 275	11 626	762	2 216	21 734
2001	130 064	47 530	13 099	1 537	3 107	23 567
2002	140 475	49 785	19 973	1 272	3 934	25 939

1 See chapter text.

Source: Office for National Statistics: 01633 812435

22.2 Manufacturers' sales: by industry[1]
United Kingdom
Standard Industrial Classification 1992

£ million

Industry		SIC (92)	2001	2002	2003	2004
Other mining and quarrying						
Quarrying of stone for construction	KSPF	14110	..	..	..	..
Quarrying of limestone, gypsum and chalk	KSPG	14120	..	..	..	..
Quarrying of slate	KSPH	14130	..	..	..	..
Operation of gravel and sand pits	KSPJ	14210	1 978	..	2 192	2 098
Mining of clays and kaolin	KSPK	14220	..	..	..	..
Mining of chemical and fertilizer minerals	KSPL	14300	79	82	..	..
Production of salt	KSPM	14400	..	..	..	..
Other mining and quarrying not elsewhere classified	KSPN	14500	66	57	62	49
Manufacture of food products and beverages						
Production and preserving of meat	KSPO	15110	2 999	3 373	3 627	3 889
Production and preserving of poultry meat	KSPP	15120	..	..	1 930	..
Bacon and ham production	KSPQ	15131	1 110	1 152	1 264	1 288
Other meat and poultry meat processing	KSPR	15139	4 025	3 911	3 997	4 057
Processing and preserving of fish and fish products	KSPS	15200	1 710	1 640	1 715	1 761
Processing and preserving of potatoes	KSPT	15310	1 211	1 224	..	1 496
Fruit and vegetable juice	KSPU	15320	544	..	554	583
Processing and preserving of fruit and vegetables not elsewhere classified	KSPV	15330	2 456	2 488	2 387	2 521
Crude oils and fats	KSPW	15410	457	437	430	402
Refined oils and fats	KSPX	15420	462	514	611	906
Margarine and similar edible fats	KSPY	15430	..	545	476	..
Operation of dairies	KTEH	15510	5 291	5 210	5 606	5 630
Ice cream	KSPZ	15520	..	498	..	..
Grain mill products	KSQA	15610	2 485	2 755	2 693	2 788
Starches and starch products	KSQB	15620	401	399	389	390
Prepared feeds for farm animals	KSPI	15710	2 021	2 127	2 104	2 387
Prepared pet foods	KSQC	15720	1 034	921	929	976
Bread; fresh pastry goods and cakes	KSQD	15810	3 884	3 977	4 365	4 482
Rusks and biscuits; preserved pastry goods and cakes	KSQE	15820	2 772	2 887	..	..
Sugar	KSQF	15830	1 140	1 110	1 153	1 133
Cocoa; chocolate and sugar confectionery	KSQG	15840	3 319	3 474	3 528	..
Macaroni, noodles, couscous and similar farinaceous products	KSQH	15850	488	503	503	..
Processing of tea and coffee	KSQI	15860	1 380	1 393	1 428	1 394
Condiments and seasonings	KSQJ	15870	1 126	1 168	1 055	1 195
Homogenised food preparations and dietetic foods	KSQK	15880	131	67	67	58
Manufacture of other food products not elsewhere classified	KSQL	15890	2 109	1 974	2 033	2 058
Distilled potable alcoholic beverages	KSQM	15910	2 016	2 181	..	2 251
Production of ethyl alcohol from fermented materials	KSQN	15920	..	..	116	..
Wines	KSQO	15930	..	..	..	..
Cider and other fruit wines	KSQP	15940	412	444	529	419
Other non-distilled fermented beverages	KSQQ	15950	–	–	–	–
Beer	KSQR	15960	3 638	3 708	3 782	4 229
Malt	KSQS	15970	247	260	253	250
Mineral waters and soft drinks	KSQT	15980	..	..	..	..
Manufacture of tobacco products						
Tobacco products	KSQU	16000	1 796	1 825	1 829	1 838
Manufacture of textiles						
Preparation and spinning of textile fibres	KSQV	17100	672	556	448	486
Textile weaving	KSQW	17200	825	737	726	690
Finishing of textiles	KSQX	17300	518	530	483	472
Soft furnishings	KSQY	17401	544	529	592	576
Canvas goods, sacks etc	KSQZ	17402	137	120	113	101
Household textiles	KSRA	17403	897	783	731	654
Carpets and rugs	KSRB	17510	902	841	751	690
Cordage, rope, twine and netting	KSRC	17520	102	..	87	76

22.2

Manufacturers' sales: by industry[1]
United Kingdom
Standard Industrial Classification 1992

£ million

Industry	SIC (92)	2001	2002	2003	2004
Manufacture of textiles continued					
Nonwovens and articles made from nonwovens, except apparel	KSRD 17530	169	167	153	149
Lace	KSRE 17541	28	23	18	16
Narrow fabrics	KSRF 17542	193	187	160	145
Other textiles not elsewhere classified	KSRG 17549	491	438	452	435
Knitted and crocheted fabrics	KSRH 17600	..	244	203	197
Knitted and crocheted hosiery	KSRI 17710	282	..	..	..
Knitted and crocheted pullovers, cardigans and similar	KSRJ 17720	407	351	312	219
Manufacture of wearing apparel; dressing and dyeing of fur					
Leather clothes	KSRK 18100	13	..	9	7
Workwear	KSRL 18210	244	271	287	263
Men's outerwear	KSRM 18221	329	297	292	249
Other women's outerwear	KSRN 18222	789	873	845	792
Men's underwear	KSRO 18231	230	224	195	171
Women's underwear	KSRP 18232	612	553	461	392
Hats	KSRQ 18241	..	45	37	35
Other wearing apparel and accessories	KSRR 18249	458	426	362	315
Dressing/dyeing of fur; articles of fur	KSRS 18300	7	6	4	4
Tanning and dressing of leather; manufacture of luggage, handbags, saddlery, harness and footwear					
Tanning and dressing of leather	KSRT 19100	312	270	..	..
Luggage, handbags and the like, saddlery and harness	KSRU 19200	189	192	167	140
Footwear	KSRV 19300	627	563	292	248
Manufacture of wood and of products of wood and cork, except furniture; manufacture of articles of straw and plaiting materials					
Sawmilling and planing of wood, impregnation of wood	KSRW 20100	646	696	730	744
Veneer sheets	KSRX 20200	687	708	768	831
Builders' carpentry and joinery	KSRY 20300	2 867	3 106	2 984	3 285
Wooden containers	KSRZ 20400	408	401	350	412
Other products of wood	KSSA 20510	422	378	380	386
Articles of cork, straw and plaiting materials	KSSB 20520	5	5	6	6
Manufacture of pulp, paper and paper products					
Paper and paperboard	KSSC 21120	3 129	3 019	3 107	2 761
Corrugated paper and paperboard, sacks and bags	KSSD 21211	565	568	559	471
Cartons, boxes, cases and other containers	KSSE 21219	3 237	3 087	2 746	3 089
Household and sanitary goods and toilet requisites	KSSF 21220	1 510	..	1 792	1 994
Paper stationery	KSSG 21230	667	623	663	645
Wallpaper	KSSH 21240	..	..	188	184
Manufacture of printed labels	EQ2T 21251	445	429	454	467
Manufacture of unprinted labels	EQ2U 21252	46	33	40	..
Manufacture of other articles of paper and paperboard not elsewhere classified	EQ2V 21259	304	331	361	300
Publishing, printing and reproduction of recorded media					
Publishing of books	KSSJ 22110	3 250	3 191	2 995	3 204
Publishing of newspapers	KSSK 22120	3 882	4 122	4 200	4 429
Publishing of journals and periodicals	KSSL 22130	7 158	6 952	7 130	7 200
Publishing of sound recordings	KSSM 22140	..	207	220	..
Other publishing	KSSN 22150	546	500	514	539
Printing of newspapers	KSSO 22210	241	195	205	235
Printing not elsewhere classified	KSSP 22220	9 320	9 296	9 010	9 230
Bookbinding and finishing	KSSQ 22230	473	456	442	475
Composition and plate-making	KSSR 22240	516	412	396	346
Other activities related to printing	KSSS 22250	848	884	701	827
Reproduction of sound recording	KSST 22310	381	..	254	..
Reproduction of video recording	KSSU 22320	198	203	220	248
Reproduction of computer media	KSSV 22330	83	82	27	..
Manufacture of chemicals and chemical products					
Industrial gases	KSSW 24110	538	508	525	528
Dyes and pigments	KSSX 24120	1 073	1 022	971	936
Other inorganic basic chemicals	KSSY 24130	1 148	1 109	1 084	1 090
Other organic basic chemicals	KSSZ 24140	5 716	5 454	5 169	5 825
Fertilizers and nitrogen compounds	KSTA 24150	592	699	811	786

22.2
Manufacturers' sales: by industry[1]
United Kingdom
Standard Industrial Classification 1992

£ million

Industry	SIC (92)	2001	2002	2003	2004
Manufacture of chemicals and chemical products continued					
Plastics in primary forms	KSTB 24160	3 640	3 414	3 471	3 740
Synthetic rubber in primary forms	KSTC 24170	324	..	..	..
Pesticides and other agro-chemical products	KSTD 24200	1 137	483	474	470
Paints, varnishes and similar coatings, printing ink and mastic	KSTE 24300	2 530	2 726	2 795	2 776
Basic pharmaceutical products	KSTF 24410	679	864	741	734
Pharmaceutical preparations	KSTG 24420	8 004	8 290	9 240	8 761
Soap and detergents, cleaning and polishing preparations	KSTH 24510	1 963	1 891	1 718	1 805
Perfumes and toilet preparations	KSTI 24520	2 640	2 377	2 314	2 171
Explosives	KSTJ 24610	..	..	105	110
Glues and gelatines	KSTK 24620	376	358	371	400
Essential oils	KSTL 24630	582	548	..	..
Photographic chemical material	KSTM 24640	342	307	317	250
Prepared unrecorded media	KSTN 24650	..	124	127	75
Other chemical products not elsewhere classified	KSTO 24660	2 078	1 939	1 766	1 992
Man-made fibres	KSTP 24700	656	602	618	587
Manufacture of rubber and plastic products					
Rubber tyres and tubes	KSTQ 25110	808	867	778	704
Retreading and rebuilding of rubber tyres	KSTR 25120	105	..	..	106
Other rubber products	KSTS 25130	1 614	1 591	1 585	1 630
Plastic plates, sheets, tubes and profiles	KSTT 25210	3 230	3 449	3 525	3 628
Plastic packing goods	KSTU 25220	2 691	..	..	..
Builders' ware of plastic	KSTV 25230	4 070	4 313	4 676	4 501
Other plastic products	KSTW 25240	3 594	3 279	3 310	3 477
Manufacture of other non-metallic mineral products					
Flat glass	KSTX 26110	235	260	280	..
Shaping and processing of flat glass	KSTY 26120	844	907	969	1 056
Hollow glass	KSTZ 26130	..	630	626	639
Glass fibres	KSUA 26140	290	306	319	300
Manufacturing and processing of other glass including technical glassware	KSUB 26150	284	267	259	278
Ceramic household and ornamental articles	KSUC 26210	469	462	424	..
Ceramic sanitary fixtures	KSUD 26220	199	205	..	..
Ceramic insulators and insulating fittings	KSUE 26230	..	25	..	..
Other technical ceramic products	KSUF 26240	..	22	22	21
Other ceramic products	KSUG 26250	16	20	18	..
Refractory ceramic products	KSUH 26260	415	372	345	344
Ceramic tiles and flags	KSUI 26300	91	82	90	98
Bricks, tiles and construction products in baked clay	KSUJ 26400	632	..	..	632
Cement	KSUK 26510	819	758	778	765
Lime	KSUL 26520	..	..	60	..
Plaster	KSUM 26530	113	109	123	133
Concrete products for construction purposes	KSUN 26610	1 753	..	..	2 243
Plaster products for construction purposes	KSUO 26620	..	..	385	..
Ready mixed concrete	KSUP 26630	1 251	960	..	1 016
Mortars	KSUQ 26640	..	112	124	143
Fibre cement	KSUR 26650	76	76	89	97
Other articles of concrete, plaster and cement	KSUS 26660	..	111	105	111
Cutting, shaping and finishing of stone	KSUT 26700	341	..	441	..
Abrasive products	KSUU 26810	183	178	157	166
Other non-metallic mineral products not elsewhere classified	KSUV 26820	640	639	..	653
Manufacture of basic metals					
Cast iron tubes	KSUW 27210	..	..	..	161
Steel tubes	KSUX 27220	985	858	741	841
Cold drawing	KSUY 27310	123	111	113	142

22.2
continued

Manufacturers' sales: by industry[1]
United Kingdom
Standard Industrial Classification 1992

£ million

Industry	SIC (92)	2001	2002	2003	2004
Manufacture of basic metals continued					
Cold rolling of narrow strip	KSUZ 27320	87	76	71	113
Cold forming or folding	KSVA 27330	122	..	113	..
Wire drawing	KSVB 27340	256	237	244	..
Other first processing of iron and steel not elsewhere classified	KSVC 27350		..		..
Precious metals production	KSVD 27410	341	271	197	251
Aluminium production	KSVE 27420	2 208	1 977	1 793	1 640
Lead, zinc and tin production	KSVF 27430	371	362	258	271
Copper production	KSVG 27440	739	684	624	767
Other non-ferrous metal production	KSVH 27450	593	499	457	637
Casting of iron	KSVI 27510	517	491	439	434
Casting of steel	KSVJ 27520	163	126	103	105
Casting of light metals	KSVK 27530	299	303	288	280
Casting of other non-ferrous metals	KSVL 27540	415	387	374	305
Manufacture of fabricated metal products, except machinery and equipment					
Metal structures and parts of structures	KSVM 28110	5 118	5 033	4 792	5 093
Builders' carpentry and joinery of metal	KSVN 28120	941	1 025	933	968
Tanks, reservoirs and containers of metal	KSVO 28210	333	344	282	281
Central heating radiators and boilers	KSVP 28220	589	521	586	659
Steam generators, except central heating hot water boilers	KSVQ 28300	509	527		
Forging, pressing, stamping and roll forming of metal	KSVR 28400	1 954	1 850	1 787	1 790
Treatment and coating of metals	KSVS 28510	1 184	1 085	1 089	1 147
General mechanical engineering	KSVT 28520	2 783	2 817	2 598	3 011
Cutlery	KSVU 28610	..	..	..	25
Tools	KSVV 28620	997	875	835	812
Locks and hinges	KSVW 28630	583	552	573	594
Steel drums and similar containers	KSVX 28710	138	127	113	119
Light metal packaging	KSVY 28720	..	1 096	1 031	1 019
Wire products	KSVZ 28730	486	460	481	513
Fasteners, screw machine products, chain and spring	KSWA 28740	613	616	612	629
Other fabricated metal products not elsewhere classified	KSWB 28750	1 634	1 548	1 664	1 748
Manufacture of machinery and equipment not elsewhere classified					
Engines and turbines, except aircraft, vehicles and cycle engines	KSWC 29110	2 284	2 059	1 990	2 089
Pumps	KSWD 29121	990	1 026	1 133	1 157
Compressors	KSWE 29122	1 236	1 112	1 142	1 177
Taps and valves	KSWF 29130	1 162	1 149	1 103	1 164
Bearings, gears, gearing and driving elements	KSWG 29140	956	908	841	863
Furnaces and furnace burners	KSWH 29210	294	282	255	269
Lifting and handling equipment	KSWI 29220	2 940	2 718	2 776	3 002
Non-domestic cooling and ventilation equipment	KSWJ 29230	..	..	2 720	2 829
Other general purpose machinery not elsewhere classified	KSWK 29240	2 057	1 978	1 987	1 982
Agricultural tractors	KSWL 29310	811	871	773	752
Other agricultural and forestry machinery	KSWM 29320	426	441	454	481
Manufacture of portable hand held power tools	EQ2W 29410	338	309	229	134
Manufacture of other metal working machine tools	EQ2X 29420	755	591	539	526
Manufacture of other machine tools n.e.c.	EQ2Y 29430	498	405	364	384
Machinery for metallurgy	KSWO 29510	93	92	83	74
Machinery for mining	KSWP 29521	476	486	422	630
Earth-moving equipment	KSWQ 29522	976	938	1 017	1 174
Equipment for concrete crushing and screening and roadworks	KSWR 29523	..	525	558	592
Machinery for food, beverage and tobacco processing	KSWS 29530	582	581	609	662
Machinery for textile, apparel and leather production	KSWT 29540	154	135	129	108
Machinery for paper and paperboard production	KSWU 29550	202	213	220	212
Other special purpose machinery not elsewhere classified	KSWV 29560	2 029	1 765	1 617	1 706
Weapons and ammunition	KSWW 29600	1 384	1 468	1 621	2 081

22.2
continued

Manufacturers' sales: by industry[1]
United Kingdom
Standard Industrial Classification 1992

£ million

Industry	SIC (92)	2001	2002	2003	2004
Manufacture of machinery and equipment not elsewhere classified continued					
Electric domestic appliances	KSYR 29710	1 922	1 895	1 928	2 096
Non-electric domestic appliances	KSWX 29720	534	520	473	448
Manufacture of office machinery and computers					
Office machinery	KSWY 30010	..	781	..	358
Computers and other information processing equipment	KSWZ 30020	8 284	5 631	5 243	3 990
Manufacture of electrical machinery and apparatus not elsewhere classified					
Electric motors, generators and transformers	KSXA 31100	2 503	2 087	2 081	2 249
Electricity, distribution and control apparatus	KSXB 31200	2 607	2 314	2 376	2 417
Insulated wire and cable	KSXC 31300	1 436	917	868	983
Accumulators, primary cells and batteries	KSXD 31400	405	376	330	326
Lighting equipment and electric lamps	KSXE 31500	1 058	1 014	1 040	1 078
Electrical equipment for engines and vehicles not elsewhere classified	KSXF 31610	..	..	987	1 011
Other electrical equipment not elsewhere classified	KSXG 31620	1 993	1 870	1 785	1 782
Manufacture of radio, television and communication equipment and apparatus					
Electronic valves and tubes and other electronic components	KSXH 32100	3 762	3 299	2 951	3 004
Telegraph and telephone apparatus and equipment	KSXI 32201	4 550	1 963	943	973
Radio and electronic capital goods	KSXJ 32202	..	..	..	1 755
Television and radio receivers, sound or video recording etc	KSXK 32300	3 144	2 594	2 310	2 541
Manufacture of medical, precision and optical instruments, watches and clocks					
Medical and surgical equipment and orthopaedic appliances	KSXL 33100	1 948	2 159	2 086	2 183
Instruments and appliances for measuring, checking, testing etc	KSXM 33200	5 430	5 148	5 123	4 919
Industrial process control equipment	KSXN 33300	696	724	646	660
Optical instruments and photographic equipment	KSXO 33400	975	758	811	895
Watches and clocks	KSXP 33500	54	54	51	50
Manufacture of motor vehicles, trailers and semi-trailers					
Motor vehicles	KSXQ 34100	17 899	20 428	22 427	22 514
Bodies (coachwork) for motor vehicles (excluding caravans)	KSXR 34201	855	857	930	842
Trailers and semi-trailers	KSXS 34202	915	844	885	999
Caravans	KSXT 34203	402	451	..	594
Parts and accessories for motor vehicles and their engines	KSXU 34300	8 371	8 912	9 989	9 843
Manufacture of other transport equipment					
Building and repairing of ships	KSXV 35110	1 597	1 658	1 426	1 612
Building and repairing of pleasure and sporting boats	KSXW 35120	599	620	596	647
Railway and tramway locomotives and rolling stock	KSXX 35200	1 453	1 528	1 668	2 036
Aircraft and spacecraft	KSXY 35300	11 719	11 362	11 723	11 806
Motorcycles	KSXZ 35410	..	..	..	..
Bicycles	KSYA 35420	103	96	59	54
Invalid carriages	KSYB 35430	118	110	113	..
Other transport equipment not elsewhere classified.	KSYC 35500	86	86	..	..
Manufacture of furniture; manufacturing not elsewhere classified					
Chairs and seats	KSYD 36110	2 706	2 842	2 927	2 867
Other office and shop furniture	KSYE 36120	1 186	1 040	962	937
Other kitchen furniture	KSYF 36130	942	1 014	959	974
Other furniture	KSYG 36140	2 220	2 272	2 230	1 997
Mattresses	KSYH 36150	575	571	569	588
Striking of coins and medals	KSYI 36210	..	..	..	..
Jewellery and related articles not elsewhere classified	KSYJ 36220	479	360	430	358
Musical instruments	KSYK 36300	44	42	41	44
Sports goods	KSYL 36400	288	312	335	339
Games and toys	KSYM 36500	424	429	367	358
Imitation jewellery	KSYN 36610	34	25	..	27
Brooms and brushes	KSYO 36620	155	150	..	131
Miscellaneous stationers' goods	KSYP 36631	..	194	..	..
Other manufacturing not elsewhere classified	KSYQ 36639	461	432	447	377

1 See chapter text. PRODCOM data is published on the ONS website in the PRA and PRQ series of reports.

Source: Office for National Statistics: 01633 813065

22.3 Number of local units in manufacturing industries, March 2005[1]
United Kingdom
Standard Industrial Classification 2003 Division by Employment Sizeband

Numbers

		Employment size									Total
		0 - 4	5 - 9	10 - 19	20 - 49	50 - 99	100 - 249	250 - 499	500 - 999	1,000+	
Division											
15/16	Food products; beverages and tobacco	3 215	2 035	1 395	1 145	570	590	270	135	30	9 385
17	Textiles and textile products	2 400	845	575	505	275	165	30	10	0	4 800
18	Wearing apparel; dressing and dyeing of fur	2 265	780	465	340	95	40	10	0	0	3 995
19	Leather and leather products	345	160	90	70	25	20	0	0	0	710
20	Wood and wood products	4 750	1 680	895	590	165	75	15	5	0	8 175
21	Pulp, paper and paper products	905	330	280	370	190	190	40	5	0	2 310
22	Publishing, printing and reproduction of recorded media	18 285	4 470	2 495	1 600	590	360	115	40	15	27 970
23	Coke, refined petroleum products and nuclear fuel	90	40	25	30	25	5	10	5	5	235
24	Chemicals, chemical products and man-made fibres	1 505	620	525	565	360	270	120	60	15	4 035
25	Rubber and plastic products	2 665	1 465	1 180	1 195	545	370	90	20	5	7 530
26	Other non-metallic mineral products	3 280	1 090	695	605	295	195	50	10	0	6 215
27	Basic metals	770	305	225	285	185	110	40	10	5	1 940
28	Fabricated metal products, except machinery and equipment	14 560	5 410	3 600	2 640	845	335	60	10	5	27 455
29	Machinery and equipment not elsewhere classified	6 020	2 315	1 865	1 515	625	365	130	30	15	12 875
30	Office machinery and computers	540	140	75	100	45	40	10	10	5	965
31	Electrical machinery and apparatus not elsewhere classified	2 435	830	695	650	290	200	75	25	0	5 205
32	Radio, television and communication equipment and apparatus	1 395	345	245	265	115	95	30	25	5	2 515
33	Medical, precision and optical instruments, watches and clocks	2 065	845	615	610	255	155	40	20	5	4 615
34	Motor vehicles, trailers and semi-trailers	1 145	455	315	390	180	185	95	35	25	2 830
35	Other transport equipment	1 195	385	245	195	115	115	50	35	25	2 360
36/37	Manufacturing not elsewhere classified	11 960	3 300	1 675	1 020	360	205	60	20	0	18 600
Total manufacturing (15/37)		81 795	27 835	18 175	14 685	6 155	4 080	1 335	505	160	154 730

1 The data in this table is taken from the NS publication, UK Business: Activity, Size and Location - 2005. The count of units refers to local units, ie. individual sites, rather than whole businesses. All counts have been rounded to avoid disclosure.

Source: Office for National Statistics: 01633 812293

Production

22.4 Production of primary fuels[1]
United Kingdom

Million tonnes of oil equivalent

		1995	1996	1997	1998	1999	2000	2001	2002	2003	2004	2005[2]
Coal	HFZQ	32.8	31.1	30.3	25.8	23.2	19.6	20.0	18.8	17.6	15.7	12.9
Petroleum[3]	HGCY	142.7	142.1	140.4	145.3	150.2	138.3	127.8	127.0	116.2	104.5	92.8
Natural Gas[4]	HGDB	70.8	84.2	85.9	90.2	99.1	108.4	105.9	103.6	102.9	96.0	88.1
Primary electricity[5]	HGDN	21.7	22.4	23.5	24.0	22.9	20.2	21.2	20.6	20.4	18.8	19.1
Renewables and waste[6]	HGDO	1.7	1.8	1.9	2.1	2.2	2.3	2.6	2.8	3.1	3.3	3.4
Total Production	HGDP	269.7	281.6	282.1	287.2	297.7	288.7	277.5	272.8	260.3	238.3	216.2

1 See chapter text.
2 Provisional.
3 Crude oil plus all condensates and petroleum gases extracted at gas separation plants.
4 Includes colliery methane.

5 Includes nuclear, hydro and other non-thermal renewables (wind, tide etc).
6 Includes biofuels and waste, solar heating and photovoltaics, and geothermal aquifers.

Source: Department of Trade and Industry: 020 7215 2710

22.5 Total inland energy consumption
United Kingdom

Heat supplied basis

Million tonnes of oil equivalent

		1995	1996	1997	1998	1999	2000	2001	2002	2003	2004	2005
Inland energy consumption of primary fuels and equivalents[1]	KLWA	218.4	230.1	226.8	230.8	230.4	233.0	236.8	230.3	232.5	234.8	236.5
Coal[2]	KLWB	48.9	45.7	40.8	40.9	36.7	37.9	41.2	37.7	40.0	39.3	40.6
Petroleum[3]	KLWC	75.4	77.8	75.5	76.1	76.0	75.9	75.6	74.4	74.3	76.5	78.6
Primary electricity	KLWD	23.1	23.8	25.0	25.0	24.2	21.4	22.1	21.3	20.6	19.4	19.7
Natural gas	KLWE	69.2	81.0	83.5	86.9	91.4	95.6	95.4	94.2	94.5	96.1	93.9
Renewables and waste	GYUY	1.7	1.8	1.9	2.1	2.2	2.3	2.6	2.8	3.2	3.6	3.8
less Energy used by fuel producers and losses in conversion and distribution	KLWF	68.0	73.0	72.9	75.0	74.2	74.7	75.3	73.2	73.9	73.6	73.6
Total consumption by final users[1]	KLWG	150.4	157.0	153.9	155.8	156.2	158.3	161.5	157.1	158.6	161.1	163.2
Final energy consumption by type of fuel												
Coal (direct use)	KLWH	5.3	4.4	4.3	3.7	3.5	2.0	3.0	2.2	1.6	2.1	1.9
Coke and breeze	KLWI	3.9	1.0	0.8	0.9	0.9	0.8	0.8	0.7	0.7	0.6	0.5
Other solid fuel[4]	KLWJ	0.7	0.8	0.7	0.7	0.6	0.4	0.5	0.5	0.3	0.3	0.5
Coke oven gas	KLWK	0.6	0.4	0.5	0.4	0.2	0.2	0.2	0.1	0.1	0.1	0.3
Natural gas (direct use)	KLWL	50.1	56.5	54.2	55.9	55.1	57.1	57.8	55.2	56.7	56.0	55.9
Electricity	KLWM	25.3	26.5	26.8	27.1	27.8	28.3	28.6	28.7	29.0	29.2	29.6
Petroleum (direct use)[5]	KLWN	63.7	66.1	65.4	66.0	65.7	66.2	67.5	66.5	67.5	69.8	71.5
Renewables	GYVA	1.0	1.0	0.9	0.9	0.7	0.6	0.6	0.7	0.7	0.7	0.7
Final energy consumption by class of consumer												
Agriculture	KLWP	1.3	1.4	1.3	1.4	1.3	1.2	1.3	1.2	1.0	0.9	1.4
Iron and steel industry	KLWQ	6.9	4.2	4.2	4.0	3.8	2.2	2.5	2.0	1.9	1.8	1.9
Other industries	KLWR	29.4	30.3	30.4	30.5	30.9	32.3	33.4	31.7	32.3	32.3	31.7
Railways[6]	KLWS	1.3	1.3	1.2	1.3	1.2	1.2	1.2	1.1	1.1	0.9	1.1
Road transport	KLWT	39.3	40.8	41.3	41.0	41.4	41.1	41.1	41.9	41.8	42.2	42.3
Water transport	KLWU	1.2	1.3	1.3	1.2	1.1	1.0	0.8	0.7	1.2	1.2	1.4
Air transport	KLWV	8.5	8.9	9.3	10.2	11.0	12.0	11.8	11.7	11.9	13.2	14.1
Domestic	KLWW	42.7	48.1	44.8	46.1	46.1	46.9	48.5	47.9	48.3	48.7	49.1
Public administration	KLWX	8.5	8.8	8.4	8.1	8.4	8.1	8.1	7.1	6.9	7.3	7.3
Commercial and other services	KLWY	11.3	11.9	11.7	12.0	11.9	12.2	12.8	11.6	12.0	12.6	12.8

1 Includes heat sold from 1999.
2 Includes net trade and stock change in other solid fuels.
3 Refinery throughput of crude oil, *plus* net foreign trade and stock change in petroleum products. Petroleum products not used as fuels (chemical feedstock, industrial and white spirits, lubricants, bitumen and wax) are excluded.

4 Includes briquettes, ovoids, Phurnacite, Coalite, etc, and wood, waste etc, used for heat generation.
5 Includes manufactured liquid fuels.
6 Includes fuel used at transport premises.

Source: Department of Trade and Industry: 020 7215 2710

22.6 Coal: supply and demand[1]
United Kingdom

Million tonnes

			1994	1995	1996	1997	1998	1999	2000	2001	2002	2003	2004
Supply													
Production of deep-mined coal	KLXA		31.9	35.2	32.2	30.3	25.7	20.9	17.2	17.3	16.4	15.6	12.5
Production of opencast coal	KLXB		16.8	16.4	16.3	16.7	14.3	15.3	13.4	14.2	13.1	12.1	12.0
Total	KLXC		48.7	51.5	48.5	47.0	40.0	36.2	30.6	31.5	29.5	27.8	24.5
Recovered slurry, fines, etc	KLXD		0.1	1.5	1.7	1.5	1.1	0.9	0.6	0.4	0.5	0.5	0.6
Imports	KLXE		15.1	15.9	17.8	19.8	21.2	20.3	23.4	35.5	28.7	31.9	36.2
Total	KLXF		64.9	68.9	68.0	68.3	62.4	57.4	54.6	67.5	58.7	60.2	61.3
Change in colliery stocks	KLXG	KSOL	−4.2	−4.2	−3.0	0.7	−0.2	0.6	−3.5	−0.1	0.9	−0.9	−0.4
Change in stocks at opencast sites	KLXH		−0.5										
Total supply	KLXI		69.6	73.1	70.9	67.6	62.7	56.8	58.2	67.5	57.8	61.0	61.7
Home consumption													
Total home consumption	KLXW		81.7	76.9	71.4	63.1	63.2	55.7	58.9	64.2	58.7	62.3	60.7
Overseas shipments and bunkers	KLXX		1.2	0.9	1.0	1.1	1.0	0.8	0.7	0.5	0.5	0.5	0.6
Total consumption and shipments	KLXY		82.9	77.8	72.4	64.2	64.1	56.5	59.5	64.8	59.2	62.8	61.3
Change in distributed stocks[2]	KLXZ		−13.9	−4.4	−0.9	3.0	−1.2	0.6	−1.2	2.9	−1.2	−1.6	0.2
Balance[3]	KLYA		0.6	−0.3	−0.5	0.3	−0.3	−0.3	−0.2	−0.2	−0.2	−0.2	0.1
Stocks at end of year													
Distributed[2]	KLYB		16.0	11.6	10.8	13.8	12.6	13.2	12.0	15.0	13.7	12.1	12.3
At collieries	KLYC	KSOM	8.5	7.1	4.2	4.8	4.6	5.2	1.6	1.6	2.5	1.6	1.2
At opencast sites	KLYD		2.8										
Total stocks	KLYE		27.3	18.7	14.9	18.6	17.2	18.3	13.7	16.5	16.2	13.7	13.5

1 See chapter text. Figures relate to periods of 52 weeks. For 1998, figures relate to 52 weeks estimate for period ended 26 December 1998.
2 Excludes distributed stocks held in merchant yards etc, mainly for the domestic market, and stocks held by the industrial sector.

3 This is the balance between supply and consumption, shipments and changes in known distributed stocks.

Source: Department of Trade and Industry: 020 7215 2717

22.7 Fuel input and gas output: gas sales[1]
United Kingdom

Public supply

Giga-watt hours

		1994	1995	1996	1997	1998	1999	2000	2001	2002	2003	2004
Analysis of gas sales												
Fuel producers												
Power stations[2]	KIKK	114 575	145 790	201 929	251 787	267 703	315 400	324 563	312 939	329 847	324 579	338 748
Coal extraction and manufacture of solid fuels	KIKL	266	368	344	193	67	14	6	4	–	1	1
Coke ovens	KIKM	1	1	–	–	–	–	–	–	–	–	..
Petroleum refineries	KIKN	1 933	2 922	2 907	3 002	3 753	4 155	3 641	4 189	3 350	2 773	2 204
Nuclear fuel production	KIKO	550	467	874	923	989	1 021	472	1 210	402	369	201
Production and distribution of other energy	KIKP	114	352	437	487	549	629	619	451	709	726	721
Total final producers	KIKQ	117 439	149 900	206 491	256 392	273 061	321 219	329 301	318 793	334 308	328 448	341 875
Final users:												
Iron and steel industry	KIKR	20 327	19 988	20 940	20 577	20 105	21 622	8 953	8 502	8 791	10 327	8 837
Other industries	KIKS	143 979	150 697	142 820	151 013	155 979	155 193	174 488	171 341	156 375	155 890	136 394
Domestic	KIKT	329 710	326 010	375 841	345 532	355 895	358 066	369 909	379 426	376 372	386 486	396 411
Public administration	KIKU	41 119	46 308	51 411	52 315	51 976	43 253	44 552	46 232	42 998	44 362	45 825
Agriculture	KIKV	1 227	1 210	1 417	1 440	953	1 155	1 522	2 329	2 346	2 324	2 355
Miscellaneous	KIKW	58 790	61 502	65 080	59 022	64 695	62 079	78 978	75 923	66 269	69 652	71 947
Total final users	KIKX	595 152	605 715	657 509	629 899	649 603	641 368	678 402	683 753	653 151	669 041	661 769
Total sales	KIKY	712 592	755 615	864 000	886 291	922 664	962 587	1 007 703	1 002 546	987 459	997 489	1 003 644

1 See chapter text. The breakdown of consumption by industrial users is made according to the 2003 Standard Industrial Classification.
2 Includes auto-production of electricity.

Source: Department of Trade and Industry: 020 7215 2717

22.8 Electricity: generation, supply and consumption[1]
United Kingdom

Gigawatt-hours

		1994	1995	1996	1997	1998	1999	2000	2001	2002	2003	2004
Electricity generated												
Major power producers: total	KLUA	306 726	313 958	326 235	324 133	333 764	336 608	341 783	353 066	353 994	362 600	358 659
Conventional thermal and other[2]	AWLC	175 187	170 056	160 791	133 591	134 009	118 762	131 062	132 744	126 694	146 382	141 026
Combined cycle gas turbine stations	KJCS	36 971	48 720	65 880	86 974	93 832	114 620	117 935	123 846	132 016	121 076	129 261
Nuclear stations	KLUC	88 282	88 964	94 671	98 146	99 486	95 133	85 063	90 093	87 848	88 686	79 999
Hydro-electric stations:												
Natural flow	KLUE	4 317	4 096	2 801	3 337	4 237	4 431	4 331	3 215	3 927	2 568	4 253
Pumped storage	KLUF	1 463	1 552	1 556	1 486	1 624	2 902	2 694	2 422	2 652	2 734	2 649
Renewables other than hydro	KLUG	506	570	536	599	576	761	698	738	856	1 154	1 471
Other generators: total	KLUH	18 252	20 084	24 632	26 534	28 938	31 543	35 285	31 721	33 252	35 866	36 969
Conventional thermal and other[2]	AWLD	14 263	15 387	18 334	18 629	19 091	19 419	19 094	16 621	15 788	18 591	16 833
Combined cycle gas turbine stations	KJCT	1 505	2 126	3 535	4 412	5 428	7 141	10 859	8 979	10 577	11 068	11 113
Hydro-electric stations (natural flow)	KLUK	777	742	592	832	881	905	755	840	860	660	677
Renewables other than hydro	KILA	1 707	1 829	2 171	2 661	3 538	4 078	4 577	5 283	6 028	5 547	8 346
All generating companies: total	KLUL	324 978	334 042	350 867	350 667	362 702	368 151	377 068	384 787	387 246	398 467	395 628
Conventional thermal and other[2]	AWYH	189 451	185 443	179 125	152 220	153 100	138 181	150 156	149 365	142 482	164 973	157 859
Combined cycle gas turbine stations	KJCU	38 475	50 846	69 415	91 386	99 260	121 761	128 794	132 825	142 593	132 144	140 374
Nuclear stations	KLUN	88 282	88 964	94 671	98 146	99 486	95 133	85 063	90 093	87 848	88 686	79 999
Hydro-electric stations:												
Natural flow	KLUP	5 094	4 838	3 393	4 169	5 118	5 336	5 086	4 055	4 787	3 228	4 930
Pumped storage	KLUQ	1 463	1 552	1 556	1 486	1 624	2 902	2 694	2 422	2 652	2 734	2 649
Renewables other than hydro	KLUR	2 213	2 399	2 707	3 260	4 114	4 839	5 275	6 021	6 884	6 701	9 817
Electricity used on works: Total	KLUS	17 491	17 411	16 078	16 560	17 408	16 706	16 304	17 394	17 126	18 185	17 171
Major generating companies	KLUT	16 696	16 510	14 967	15 411	16 140	15 461	14 952	16 066	15 746	16 747	15 590
Other generators	KLUU	795	901	1 111	1 149	1 268	1 245	1 352	1 328	1 380	1 439	1 581
Electricity supplied (gross)												
Major power producers: total	KLUV	290 780	299 000	311 268	308 722	317 624	321 147	326 831	336 999	338 248	345 854	343 068
Conventional thermal and other[2]	AWYI	167 866	163 818	155 086	127 419	127 788	112 919	124 828	126 434	120 495	139 137	134 033
Combined cycle gas turbine stations	KJCV	36 815	48 525	65 604	86 682	93 005	112 768	116 110	121 344	129 384	118 546	127 189
Nuclear stations	KLUX	79 962	80 598	85 820	89 341	90 590	87 672	78 334	82 985	81 090	81 911	73 682
Hydro-electric stations:												
Natural flow	KLUZ	4 265	4 051	2 763	3 299	4 225	4 409	4 316	3 203	3 914	2 559	4 238
Pumped storage	KLVA	1 417	1 502	1 507	1 439	1 569	2 804	2 603	2 340	2 562	2 641	2 559
Renewables other than hydro	KLVB	455	506	488	542	447	574	640	692	802	1 059	1 367
Other generators: total	KLVC	18 207	20 909	23 521	25 385	27 670	30 298	33 933	30 393	31 873	34 427	35 388
Conventional thermal and other[2]	AWYJ	14 333	16 338	17 492	17 815	18 250	18 643	18 499	15 996	15 211	16 758	16 260
Combined cycle gas turbine stations	KJCW	1 466	2 100	3 358	4 192	5 157	6 785	10 318	8 531	10 049	10 516	10 559
Hydro-electric stations (natural flow)	KLVF	769	733	584	822	869	894	743	829	849	653	676
Renewables other than hydro	KIKZ	1 639	1 738	2 085	2 555	3 393	3 977	4 374	5 037	5 764	6 500	7 893
All generating companies: total	KLVG	308 987	319 909	334 789	334 107	345 294	351 445	360 764	367 392	370 121	380 281	378 456
Conventional thermal and other[2]	AWYK	182 199	180 156	172 578	145 234	146 038	131 562	143 327	142 430	135 706	155 895	150 293
Combined cycle gas turbine stations	KJCX	38 281	50 625	68 962	90 874	98 162	119 553	126 428	129 875	139 433	129 062	137 748
Nuclear stations	KLVI	79 962	80 598	85 820	89 341	90 590	87 672	78 334	82 985	81 090	81 911	73 682
Hydro-electric stations:												
Natural flow	KLVK	5 034	4 784	3 347	4 121	5 094	5 303	5 059	4 032	4 763	3 212	4 914
Pumped storage	KLVL	1 417	1 502	1 507	1 439	1 569	2 804	2 603	2 340	2 562	2 641	2 559
Renewables other than hydro	KLVM	2 094	2 244	2 573	3 097	3 840	4 551	5 014	5 729	6 566	7 559	9 260
Electricity used in pumping												
Major power producers	KLVN	2 051	2 282	2 430	2 477	2 594	3 774	3 499	3 210	3 463	3 546	3 497
Electricity supplied (net): Total	KLVO	306 936	317 627	332 359	331 630	342 700	347 671	357 266	364 182	366 657	376 735	374 959
Major power producers	KLVP	288 729	296 718	308 838	306 245	315 030	317 373	323 332	333 789	334 785	342 308	339 571
Other generators	KLVQ	18 207	20 909	23 521	25 385	27 670	30 298	33 933	30 393	31 873	34 427	35 388
Net imports	KGEZ	16 887	16 313	16 755	16 574	12 468	14 244	14 174	10 399	8 414	2 160	7 490
Electricity available	KGIZ	323 830	333 940	349 114	348 203	355 168	361 915	371 440	374 581	375 072	378 895	382 449
Losses in transmission etc	KGKW	31 000	30 020	29 335	27 138	29 818	29 862	31 146	32 077	30 963	30 934	32 035
Electricity consumption: Total	KGKX	292 830	303 920	319 779	321 065	325 350	332 053	340 294	342 504	344 109	347 961	350 414
Fuel industries	KGKY	7 518	8 070	9 211	8 624	8 406	8 037	9 703	8 625	10 060	9 893	9 733
Final users: total	KGKZ	285 310	295 849	310 567	312 441	316 944	324 016	330 593	333 879	334 049	338 067	340 667
Industrial sector	KGLZ	96 120	101 780	107 631	108 102	108 443	112 250	115 286	112 495	113 296	114 947	117 774
Domestic sector	KGMZ	101 407	102 210	107 513	104 455	109 410	110 308	111 842	115 337	114 534	115 761	115 526
Other sectors	KGNZ	87 790	91 860	95 423	99 884	99 091	101 457	103 465	106 047	106 219	107 359	107 367

1 See chapter text.
2 Includes electricity supplied by gas turbines and oil engines and plants producing electricity from renewable resources other than hydro.

Source: Department of Trade and Industry: 020 7215 5190

22.9 Electricity: plant capacity and demand
United Kingdom
At end of December[1]

Megawatts

		1996		1997	1998	1999	2000	2001	2002	2003	2004
Major power producers:[2]											
Total declared net capability	KGON	68 860	GUFY	68 140	68 312	70 245	72 193	73 382	70 369	71 500	73 308
Conventional steam stations	KGOO	38 230	GUFZ	37 395	35 081	35 647	34 835	34 835	30 687	30 327	31 182
Combined cycle gas turbine stations	KJCZ	12 052	GUGA	12 252	14 618	16 110	19 349	20 517	21 800	23 577	24 591
Nuclear stations[3]	KGOP	12 916	GUGB	12 946	12 956	12 956	12 486	12 486	12 240	11 852	11 852
Gas turbines and oil engines	KGOQ	1 491	GUGC	1 378	1 434	1 301	1 291	1 291	1 433	1 537	1 477
Hydro-electric stations:											
Natural flow	KGOR	1 313	GUGD	1 311	1 327	1 327	1 327	1 348	1 304	1 302	1 301
Pumped storage	KGOS	2 788	GUGE	2 788	2 788	2 788	2 788	2 788	2 788	2 788	2 788
Renewables other than hydro	KGOT	70	GUGF	70	108	117	117	117	117	117	117
Other generators:											
Total capacity of own generating plant[4]	KGOU	4 409	GUGG	4 625	4 990	5 388	6 258	6 296	6 336	6 829	7 062
Conventional steam stations[5]	KGOV	3 229	GUGH	3 240	3 248	3 315	3 544	3 464	3 325	3 451	3 450
Combined cycle gas turbine stations	KJDA	608	GUGI	757	1 005	1 243	1 709	1 777	1 854	1 856	1 980
Hydro-electric stations (natural flow)	KGOX	135	GUGJ	145	148	150	158	160	162	166	159
Renewables other than hydro	KILB	437	GUGK	483	589	680	847	895	995	1 256	1 473
All generating companies: Total capacity[4]	KGOY	73 269	GUGL	72 765	73 302	75 633	78 451	79 678	76 705	78 329	80 370
Conventional steam stations[5]	KGOZ	41 459	GUGM	40 635	38 329	38 962	38 379	38 299	34 012	33 778	34 632
Combined cycle gas turbine stations	KJDC	12 660	GUGN	13 009	15 623	17 353	21 058	22 294	23 654	25 533	26 571
Nuclear stations	KGPM	12 916	GUGO	12 946	12 956	12 956	12 486	12 486	12 240	11 852	11 852
Gas turbines and oil engines	KGPN	1 491	GUGP	1 378	1 434	1 301	1 291	1 291	1 433	1 537	1 477
Hydro-electric stations:											
Natural flow	KGPO	1 448	GUGQ	1 456	1 475	1 477	1 485	1 508	1 466	1 468	1 460
Pumped storage	KGPP	2 788	GUGR	2 788	2 788	2 788	2 788	2 788	2 788	2 788	2 788
Renewables other than hydro	KGPQ	507	GUGS	553	697	797	964	1 012	1 112	1 373	1 590
Major power producers:[2]											
Simultaneous maximum load met[6]	KGPR	56 815	GUGT	56 965	56 312	57 849	58 452	58 589	61 717	60 501	61 013
System load factor[7] (percentages)	KGQY	*67.0*	GUGU	*66.0*	*68.0*	*67.0*	*67.0*	*69.0*	*65.0*	*67.0*	*66.0*

1 1996 data are at end of March.
2 See chapter text.
3 Nuclear generators are now included under "major power producers" only.
4 Capacity figures for other generators are as at end-December of the previous year.

5 For other generators, conventional steam stations cover all types of stations not separately listed.
6 Maximum load in year to end of March.
7 The average hourly quantity of electricity available during the year ending March expressed as a percentage of the maximum demand.

Source: Department of Trade and Industry: 020 7215 5190

22.10 Electricity: fuel used in generation
United Kingdom

Million tonnes of oil equivalent

		1994	1995	1996	1997	1998	1999	2000	2001	2002	2003	2004
Major power producers:[1] total all fuels	KGPS	71.70	72.70	74.60	71.50	74.90	73.60	74.40	77.38	75.79	77.53	76.84
Coal	FTAJ	35.89	35.02	32.40	27.10	28.70	24.50	27.80	30.60	28.60	31.60	30.40
Oil[2]	FTAK	3.58	3.13	3.00	1.20	0.80	0.80	0.80	0.80	0.70	0.70	0.60
Gas	KGPT	9.1	11.4	15.2	19.3	20.3	24.2	24.4	23.8	25.0	24.5	26.2
Nuclear[3]	FTAL	21.20	21.25	22.20	22.00	23.40	22.20	19.60	20.80	20.10	20.00	18.20
Hydro (natural flow)	FTAM	0.37	0.34	0.20	0.30	0.40	0.40	0.40	0.30	0.30	0.20	0.40
Other fuels used by UK companies	KGPU	0.1	0.1	0.1	0.2	0.2	0.2	0.2	0.3	0.3	0.4	0.5
Net imports	KGPV	1.5	1.4	1.4	1.4	1.1	1.2	1.2	0.9	0.7	0.2	0.6
Other generators: total all fuels	KGPW	3.5	5.8	6.4	6.7	7.1	7.3	8.0	7.6	8.0	9.1	8.5
Transport undertakings												
Gas	KGPX	0.2	0.2	0.2	0.2	0.2	0.2	0.2	0.2	0.2	–	–
Undertakings in industrial sector												
Coal	KGPY	1.2	1.3	1.2	1.2	1.2	1.0	0.9	1.0	1.0	1.0	1.0
Oil	KGPZ	0.5	1.0	0.9	0.8	0.7	0.7	0.8	0.6	0.6	0.5	0.6
Gas	KGQM	0.6	1.6	1.9	2.2	2.5	2.7	3.3	2.9	3.2	3.4	2.9
Hydro (natural flow)	KGQO	0.1	0.1	0.1	0.1	0.1	0.1	0.1	0.1	0.1	0.1	0.1
Other fuels	KGQP	1.000	1.700	2.037	2.186	2.420	2.640	2.770	2.740	2.968	4.068	3.996
All generating companies: total fuels	KGQQ	75.20	78.60	81.03	78.20	82.00	80.90	82.40	84.90	83.80	86.60	85.40
Coal	KGQR	37.1	36.3	33.6	28.3	29.9	25.5	28.7	31.6	29.6	32.5	31.3
Oil	KGQS	4.1	4.1	4.0	2.0	1.5	1.5	1.5	1.4	1.3	1.2	1.1
Gas	KGQT	9.9	13.3	17.4	21.7	23.0	27.1	27.9	26.9	28.4	27.9	29.1
Nuclear[3]	KGQU	21.2	21.3	22.2	22.0	23.4	22.2	19.6	20.8	20.1	20.0	18.2
Hydro (natural flow)	KGQV	0.4	0.4	0.3	0.4	0.4	0.5	0.4	0.3	0.4	0.3	0.4
Other fuels used by UK companies[4]	KGQW	1.100	1.800	2.183	2.351	2.597	2.863	3.007	2.993	3.242	4.449	4.536
Net imports	KGQX	1.5	1.4	1.4	1.4	1.1	1.2	1.2	0.9	0.7	0.2	0.6

1 See chapter text.
2 Includes oil used in gas turbine and diesel plant for lighting up coal fired boilers and Orimulsion.

3 Nuclear generators are now included under "major power producers" only.
4 Main fuels included are coke oven gas, blast furnace gas, waste products from chemical processes and sludge gas.

Source: Department of Trade and Industry: 020 7215 5190

22.11 Indigenous petroleum production, refinery receipts, imports and exports of oil[1]

Thousand tonnes

		1994	1995	1996	1997	1998	1999	2000	2001	2002	2003	2004
Total indigenous petroleum production[2]	KMBA	126 812	129 894	129 742	128 234	132 363	137 099	126 245	116 678	115 944	106 073	95 374
Crude petroleum:[3]												
Refinery receipts total	KMBB	93 771	93 572	96 660	97 023	93 797	88 286	88 014	83 343	84 784	84 585	89 821
Foreign trade[4]												
Imports	KMBF	53 096	48 749	50 099	49 994	47 958	44 869	54 387	53 551	56 968	54 177	62 516
Exports	AXRB	83 205	84 578	81 563	79 400	84 610	91 797	92 918	86 930	87 144	74 898	64 504
Net imports	AXRC	−30 109	−35 829	−31 464	−29 406	−36 652	−46 928	−38 531	−33 378	−30 176	−20 720	−1 988
Petroleum products												
Foreign trade												
Imports[4]	BHMI	10 441	9 878	9 315	8 705	11 327	13 896	14 212	17 466	15 269	17 286	19 435
Exports[4]	AXRD	22 157	21 614	23 681	26 755	24 375	21 730	20 677	19 088	23 444	23 323	30 270
Net imports[4]	AXRE	−11 716	−11 736	−14 366	−18 049	−12 957	−7 834	−6 464	−1 622	−8 175	−6 037	−10 835
International marine bunkers	BHMK	2 313	2 465	2 664	2 961	3 080	2 329	2 079	2 274	1 913	1 764	2 085

1 See chapter text. The term 'indigenous' is used in this table to cover oil produced on the UK Continental Shelf. This includes small amounts produced onshore.
2 Crude oil *plus* condensates and petroleum gases derived at onshore treatment plants.

3 Includes process (partly refined) oils.
4 Foreign trade as recorded by the petroleum industry and may differ from figures published in *Overseas Trade Statistics*.

Source: Department of Trade and Industry: 020 7215 5184

22.12 Throughput of crude and process oils and output of refined products from refineries[1]

United Kingdom

Thousand tonnes

		1994	1995	1996	1997	1998	1999	2000	2001	2002	2003	2004
Throughput of crude and process oils	KMAU	93 162	92 743	96 661	97 024	93 797	88 285	88 014	83 343	84 784	84 585	89 821
less: Refinery fuel:	KMAA	6 256	6 481	6 623	6 572	6 468	5 969	5 252	5 059	5 677	5 528	5 453
Losses	KMAB	261	129	152	86	1 005	1 554	1 632	1 233	788	56	−7
Total output of refined products	KMAC	86 645	86 133	89 885	90 366	86 615	81 195	81 130	77 051	78 319	79 001	84 375
Gases:												
Butane and propane	KMAE	1 605	1 815	1 828	1 950	1 961	1 975	1 917	1 764	2 139	2 281	2 152
Other petroleum	KMAF	132	133	144	139	394	361	288	272	537	645	484
Naphtha and other feedstock	KMAG	2 794	2 711	2 824	2 854	2 316	2 430	3 082	3 428	3 153	3 503	3 168
Aviation spirit	KMAH	–	–	–	–	–	16	30	101	28	26	31
Motor spirit	KMAJ	27 562	27 254	28 046	28 260	27 166	25 230	23 445	21 455	22 944	22 627	24 589
Industrial and white spirit	KMAK	143	143	136	128	135	129	122	121	121	104	100
Kerosene:												
Aviation turbine fuel	KMAL	7 697	7 837	8 305	8 342	7 876	7 249	6 484	5 910	5 365	5 277	5 615
Burning oil	KMAM	2 967	2 924	3 510	3 336	3 442	3 553	3 078	3 088	3 506	3 521	3 613
Gas/diesel oil	KMAN	27 137	27 169	28 903	28 778	27 532	25 750	28 229	26 748	28 343	27 380	28 647
Fuel oil	KMAO	11 378	10 969	11 479	11 747	11 125	10 446	10 296	10 179	8 507	9 495	11 308
Lubricating oil	KMAP	1 296	1 261	1 111	1 231	1 125	907	702	656	509	576	1 136
Bitumen	KMAQ	2 569	2 459	2 189	2 258	2 172	1 644	1 438	1 707	1 918	1 925	2 196
Petroleum wax	KMAR	64	46	41	65	59	261	437	416	430	460	94
Petroleum coke	KMAS	679	759	714	598	678	648	657	513	441	612	633
Other products	KMAT	623	653	655	680	634	596	927	692	378	569	607

1 See chapter text. Crude and process oils comprise all feedstocks, other than distillation benzines, for treatment at refinery plants. Refinery production does not cover further treatment of finished products for special grades such as in distillation plant for the preparation of industrial spirits.

Source: Department of Trade and Industry: 020 7215 5184

22.13 Deliveries of petroleum products for inland consumption[1]
United Kingdom

Thousand tonnes

		1994	1995	1996	1997	1998	1999	2000	2001	2002	2003	2004
Total (including refinery fuel)	KMCA	81 213	80 175	82 013	79 073	78 437	77 985	77 197	76 646	76 603	77 966	80 226
Total (excluding refinery fuel)	KMCB	74 957	73 694	75 390	72 501	71 969	72 009	71 796	71 586	70 926	72 438	74 773
Butane and propane	ECAQ	2 486	2 481	2 439	2 426	2 368	2 249	2 030	2 097	2 553	3 017	3 114
Other Petroleum Gases (includes Ethane)	ECAR	1 459	1 489	1 482	1 561	1 534	1 829	1 886	2 077	2 181	2 043	1 883
Naphtha	ECAS	2 866	2 885	3 010	2 640	2 882	3 100	2 344	1 592	1 592	2 332	2 029
Aviation spirit	KMCI	29	29	32	37	36	45	52	59	50	46	49
Motor spirit:												
Retail deliveries:												
Leaded Premium / Lead Replacement Petrol	KMCK	9 503	7 993	7 043	6 138	4 595	2 629	1 462	838	401	183	74
Super Premium Unleaded	KMCL	1 323	925	698	506	409	473	403	420	706	861	810
Premium Unleaded	KMCM	11 536	12 603	14 228	15 188	16 432	18 307	19 008	19 100	19 167	18 291	17 795
Total Retail Deliveries	ECAT	22 362	21 521	21 969	21 832	21 436	21 409	20 873	20 358	20 274	19 335	18 679
Commercial consumers:												
Leaded Premium / Lead Replacement Petrol	KMCO	178	149	135	112	91	61	44	34	19	19	14
Super Premium Unleaded	KMCP	26	17	11	9	4	6	6	9	17	22	26
Premium Unleaded	KMCQ	277	285	294	298	318	311	480	538	499	542	765
Total Commercial Consumers	ECAU	481	451	440	419	413	378	530	581	535	583	805
Total Motor spirit	BHOD	22 843	21 972	22 409	22 251	21 849	21 787	21 403	20 939	20 809	19 918	19 484
Industrial and white spirits	KMCS	170	178	184	195	179	174	170	151	157	147	281
Kerosene:												
Aviation turbine fuel	BHOE	7 284	7 660	8 049	8 411	9 241	9 939	10 806	10 614	10 519	10 765	11 862
Burning oil	KMCT	2 655	2 774	3 336	3 343	3 575	3 633	3 839	4 236	3 578	3 569	3 950
Gas/diesel oil:												
Derv fuel:												
Retail Deliveries	ECAV	4 345	4 814	5 537	6 127	6 602	7 137	7 181	7 846	8 153	9 057	9 517
Commercial Consumers	ECAW	8 569	8 643	8 828	8 849	8 541	8 371	8 451	8 213	8 774	8 655	8 997
Total Derv fuel	BHOI	12 914	13 457	14 365	14 976	15 143	15 508	15 632	16 059	16 927	17 712	18 514
Other gas/diesel oil (includes Mdf)	ECAX	8 167	7 879	8 349	8 053	8 005	7 196	7 528	6 960	6 099	6 326	6 023
Fuel oil	BHOK	9 275	7 975	6 854	3 936	2 935	2 415	1 833	2 806	2 091	2 352	3 005
Lubricating oils	BHOL	795	895	864	872	813	790	801	846	829	868	914
Bitumen	BHOM	2 595	2 420	2 146	2 015	1 967	1 928	1 975	1 935	2 002	1 959	1 991
Petroleum wax	KMCU	47	44	44	44	18	37	32	33	51	57	50
Petroleum coke	KMCV	911	1 008	1 210	1 095	887	660	776	702	893	880	1 145
Miscellaneous products	KMCW	461	548	617	646	537	719	463	475	596	449	476

1 See chapter text.

Source: Department of Trade and Industry: 020 7215 5184

22.14 Iron and steel:[1] summary of steel supplies, deliveries and stocks
United Kingdom

		1994	1995	1996	1997	1998	1999	2000	2001	2002	2003	2004
Supply, disposal and consumption - (Finished product weight - Thousand tonnes)												
UK producers' home deliveries	KLTA	7 827	8 257	8 383	8 626	8 260	7 652	7 255	6 762	6 506	6 227	7 083
Imports excluding steelworks receipts	KLTB	5 012	5 384	5 147	5 894	6 466	6 014	6 387	6 978	6 793	6 893	7 272
Total deliveries to home market (a)	KLTC	12 839	13 641	13 530	14 520	14 726	13 666	13 642	13 740	13 299	13 120	14 355
Total exports (producers, consumers, merchants)	KLTD	8 120	8 228	8 917	9 060	8 008	7 623	7 446	6 512	6 320	7 007	7 455
Exports by UK producers	KLTE	7 873	7 828	8 305	8 534	7 876	7 416	7 163	6 182	5 594	6 202	6 275
Derived consumers' and merchants' exports (b)	KLTF	247	400	612	526	132	207	283	330	708	806	1 179
Net home disposals (a)-(b)	KLTG	12 592	13 241	12 918	13 994	14 594	13 460	13 359	13 410	12 591	12 314	13 176
Consumers' and merchants' stock change	KLTH	390	..	..	..	..	..	..	..	..	..	..
Estimated home consumption	KLTI	12 202	13 241	12 918	13 994	14 594	13 460	13 359	13 410	12 591	12 114	13 176
Stocks - (Finished product weight - Thousand tonnes)												
Producers - ingots & semis	KLTJ	946	1 068	767	946	717	747	727	705	690	706	765
- finished steel	KLTK	1 389	1 274	1 515	1 358	1 495	1 318	1 039	981	932	917	901
Consumers	KLTL	1 470	..	..	..	..	..	..	..	..	..	..
Merchants	KLTM	1 280	..	..	..	..	..	..	..	..	..	..
Estimated home consumption - (Crude steel equivalent - Million tonnes)												
Crude steel production[2]	KLTN	17.28	17.60	17.99	18.50	17.32	16.28	15.15	13.54	11.53	13.13	13.77
Producers' stock change	KLTO	−0.12	0.01	−0.07	0.03	−0.11	−0.19	−0.33	−0.14	−0.08	..	..
Re-usable material	KLTP	0.09	0.08	0.07	0.06	0.02	..	..	..	..	..	..
Total supply from home sources	KLTQ	17.49	17.67	18.13	18.53	17.45	16.47	15.48	13.68	11.61	13.13	13.77
Total imports[3]	KLTR	6.58	7.05	7.01	7.49	8.38	7.81	8.43	9.11	9.86	9.32	10.31
Total exports[3]	KLTS	9.55	9.63	10.26	10.43	9.25	8.70	8.61	7.53	7.39	8.65	9.15
Net home disposals	KLTT	14.52	15.09	14.88	15.59	16.58	15.58	15.30	15.26	14.08	13.80	14.86
Consumers' and merchants' stock change	KLTU	0.48	..	..	..	..	..	..	..	..	..	..
Estimated home consumption	KLTV	14.04	15.09	14.88	15.59	16.58	15.58	15.30	15.26	14.08	13.80	14.86

1 See chapter text. The figures relate to periods of 52 weeks.
2 Includes liquid steel for castings only up to 2003.

3 Based on HM Customs Statistics, reflecting total trade rather than producers' trade.

Source: Iron and Steel Statistics Bureau: 020 8686 9050 ext 126

22.15 Iron and steel:[1] iron ore, manganese ore, pig iron and iron and steel scrap
United Kingdom

Thousand tonnes

		1994	1995	1996	1997	1998	1999	2000	2001	2002	2003	2004
Iron ore[2]	KLOF	18 161	18 670	19 720	20 820	19 532	18 754	16 991	15 113	13 185	15 766	16 013
Manganese ore[2]	KLOG	64	32	48	37	22	14	36	4	4	–	6
Pig iron (and blast furnace ferro-alloys)												
Average number of furnaces in blast during period	KLOH	8	8	9	9	9	9	8	7	5	6	6
Production												
Steelmaking iron	KLOI	11 943	12 236	12 830	13 054	12 746	12 139	10 890	9 870	8 561	10 228	10 180
Speigeleisen and ferromanganese	KLOK	..	..	..	..	..	..	..	..	..	..	..
In blast furnaces: total	KLOL	11 943	12 236	12 830	13 054	12 746	12 139	10 890	9 870	8 561	10 228	10 180
In steel works	KLOM	11 889	12 121	12 753	13 044	12 746	12 139	10 890	9 870	8 561	10 228	10 180
Consumption of pig iron: total	KLOO	11 889	12 121	12 753	13 044	12 746	12 139	10 890	9 870	8 561	10 228	10 180
Iron and steel scrap												
Steelworks and steel foundries												
Circulating scrap	KLOQ	2 326	2 390	2 639	2 459	2 380	2 488	2 287	2 019	1 882	1 926	1 787
Purchased receipts	KLOR	4 533	4 688	4 130	5 418	4 045	3 433	3 327	3 001	2 271	2 617	3 371
Consumption	KLOS	6 874	7 012	6 828	7 207	6 408	5 884	5 675	5 006	4 216	4 469	5 123
Stocks (end of period)	KLOT	253	319	260	236	253	290	229	224	161	234	242

1 See chapter text. The figures relate to periods of 52 weeks.
2 Consumption.

Source: Iron and Steel Statistics Bureau: 020 8686 9050 ext 126

22.16 Iron and steel:[1] furnaces and production of steel
United Kingdom

Number and thousand tonnes

		1994	1995	1996	1997	1998	1999	2000	2001	2002	2003	2004
Steel furnaces (numbers[2])	KLPA	202	192	192	192	190	181	181	181	173	..	..
Oxygen converters	KLPC	11	11	11	11	11	11	11	11	8	..	..
Electric	KLPD	191	181	181	181	179	170	170	170	165	..	..
Production of crude steel	KLPF	17 286	17 604	17 992	18 499	17 315	16 284	15 155	13 543	11 667	13 268	13 766
by process												
Oxygen converters	KLPH	12 909	13 082	13 758	13 986	13 426	12 634	11 551	10 271	8 956	10 630	10 667
Electric	KLPI	4 377	4 522	4 234	4 513	3 889	3 650	3 604	3 272	2 711	2 639	3 099
by cast method												
Cast to ingot	KLPK	2 033	2 174	1 892	1 660	784	534	539	369	339	354	383
Continuously cast	KLPL	15 079	15 250	15 912	16 653	16 346	15 637	14 470	13 024	11 182	12 766	13 383
Steel for castings	KLPM	174	180	188	186	185	127	146	150	146	148	..
by quality												
Non alloy steel	KLPN	16 062	16 243	16 708	17 193	16 145	15 263	14 004	12 482	10 657	12 294	12 809
Stainless and other alloy steel	KLPO	1 224	1 361	1 284	1 306	1 170	1 035	1 151	1 061	1 010	974	957
Production of finished steel products (All quantities)[3]												
Rods and bars for reinforcement (in coil and lengths)	KLPP	1 269	1 154	1 182	1 118	1 133	893	812	755	487	294	769
Wire rods and other rods and bars in coil	KLPQ	1 524	1 642	1 536	1 565	1 492	1 407	1 408	1 389	1 394	1 316	1 392
Hot rolled bars in lengths	KLPR	1 275	1 311	1 499	1 716	1 791	1 542	1 545	1 449	1 267	1 107	1 179
Bright steel bars[4]	KLPS	363	424	357	385	336	311	337	296	271	273	277
Light sections other than rails	KLPT	306	286	298	302	318	264	183	201	188	116	136
Heavy sections	KGQZ	2 412	2 549	2 557	2 397	2 346	2 303	1 915	1 931	1 873	1 774	1 694
Hot rolled plates, sheets and strip in coil and lengths	KLPW	7 715	8 077	8 512	8 956	8 454	7 893	7 293	5 841	5 756	6 145	6 437
Cold rolled plates and sheets in coil and lengths	KLPX	3 835	4 100	4 221	4 437	4 288	3 914	3 612	2 944	2 951	2 958	3 001
Cold rolled strip[4]	KLPZ	243	267	246	255	259	233	218	201	179	186	156
Tinplate	KLQW	767	791	739	754	772	736	753	602	562	493	507
Other coated sheet	KLQX	2 021	2 306	2 366	2 534	2 610	2 475	2 471	1 773	1 786	1 811	1 713
Tubes and pipes[4]	KLQY	1 136	1 183	1 317	1 310	1 276	1 100	1 061	1 096	940	1 066	1 076
Forged bars[4]	KLQZ	2	3	3	3	3	2	1	1	1	..	..

1 See chapter text. The figures relate to periods of 52 weeks.
2 Includes steel furnaces at steel foundries, only up to 2003.

3 Includes material for conversion into other products listed in the table.
4 Based on producers' deliveries.

Source: Iron and Steel Statistics Bureau: 020 8686 9050 ext 126

22.17
Non-ferrous metals
United Kingdom

Thousand tonnes

		1994	1995	1996	1997	1998	1999	2000	2001	2002	2003	2004
Copper												
Production of refined copper:												
Primary	KLAA	11.1	12.0	13.0	9.1	6.4	1.7	–	–	–	–	–
Secondary	KLAB	35.6	43.0	43.6	51.3	47.4	48.6	–	–	–	–	–
Home consumption:												
Refined	KLAC	377.3	397.9	396.0	408.3	374.1	305.3	322.7	285.9	260.8	242.2	243.4
Scrap (metal content)	KLAD	88.0	81.0	81.0	69.0	64.6	112.5	132.4	127.0	120.0	120.0	120.0
Stocks (end of period)[1,2]	KLAE	8.1	7.5	6.6	12.8	7.5	7.3	10.4	7.3	..	..	..
Analysis of home consumption												
(refined and scrap):[3,4] total	KLAF	468.0	493.2	477.3	477.4	438.7	417.8	455.5	212.7	..	..	..
Wire[5]	KLAG	306.2	321.4	309.4	312.5	287.2	276.1	310.2	151.8	..	..	..
Rods, bars and sections	KLAH	54.9	59.0	58.3	58.3	53.6	46.9	43.6	21.6	..	..	..
Sheet, strip and plate	KLAI	33.0	37.1	34.0	36.5	30.5	27.7	32.3	16.9	..	..	..
Tubes	KLAJ	73.9	75.7	75.6	70.1	67.4	67.1	69.4	22.4	..	..	..
Zinc												
Slab zinc:												
Production	KLAL	101.3	106.0	96.9	107.7	99.6	132.8	99.6	99.6	99.6	16.6	–
Home consumption	KLAM	196.5	198.4	195.7	194.8	187.9	198.9	206.5	197.1	202.4	176.2	150.1
Stocks (end of period)	KLAN	10.5	9.8	10.5	10.1	10.6	10.9	10.9	9.5	9.2	8.9	8.9
Other zinc (metal content):												
Consumption	KLAO	45.0	46.8	41.3	41.5	37.3	41.6	46.3	48.2	51.8	52.5	55.4
Analysis of home consumption												
(slab and scrap): total	KLAP	241.5	245.2	237.1	236.3	226.2	236.7	242.5	231.2	234.6	233.7	238.9
Brass	KLAQ	42.6	45.2	39.1	41.6	36.6	33.6	34.4	32.2	30.0	30.0	31.2
Galvanized products	KLAR	107.4	110.7	110.3	108.4	103.8	116.6	120.9	111.8	117.3	115.5	118.5
Zinc sheet and strip	KLAS	4.6	3.0	3.0	3.3	3.3	3.3	3.3	3.3	3.4	3.3	3.3
Zinc alloy die castings	KLAT	46.5	46.5	46.5	46.5	46.5	46.5	46.5	46.5	46.5	46.5	46.5
Zinc oxide	KLAU	21.6	21.6	20.7	20.6	20.4	21.1	21.8	21.8	22.2	22.9	23.9
Other products	KLAV	18.8	18.2	17.5	16.1	11.0	11.0	–	–	–	–	–
Refined lead												
Production[6,7]	KLAW	352.5	320.7	351.4	384.1	349.7	351.0	328.0	366.3	366.3	364.6	245.9
Home consumption[7,8]												
Refined lead	KLAX	267.6	285.4	272.8	270.4	275.5	283.3	294.0	298.3	298.3	314.7	260.5
Scrap and remelted lead[7]	KLAY	38.5	41.6	43.4	39.1	38.4	32.2	40.9	40.7	40.7	40.7	41.5
Stocks (end of period)[9]												
Lead bullion	KLAZ	10.2	9.5	32.9	15.5	20.9	17.1	10.0	17.2	17.2	17.2	23.0
Refined soft lead at consumers	KLBA	23.5	24.9	28.8	29.1	27.4	25.7	25.8	26.1	26.1	25.3	25.9
In LME Warehouses (UK)	KLBB	6.1	0.4	3.0	2.4	0.1	0.1	0.1	0.1	0.1	0.1	0.1
Analysis of home consumption												
(refined and scrap): total	KLBC	306.1	327.0	316.2	309.5	313.9	315.5	333.5	338.9	347.3	354.8	302.0
Cables	KLBD	9.3	9.8	9.8	9.7	9.7	9.7	9.6	9.6	9.7	9.7	9.7
Batteries (excluding oxides)	KLBE	52.5	52.7	52.3	54.7	51.6	47.4	50.5	48.2	48.2	48.2	54.1
Oxides and compounds:												
Batteries	KLBF	55.2	56.2	54.9	56.1	54.4	53.1	55.9	54.7	54.7	55.9	59.0
Other uses	KLBG	53.9	53.8	56.1	54.5	56.4	57.0	56.8	53.8	53.8	49.8	56.4
Sheets and pipes	KLBH	84.6	101.2	94.1	91.1	96.1	94.9	102.3	102.3	102.3	109.8	111.4
Solder	KLBJ	7.4	7.4	7.4	7.4	7.4	7.4	7.4	7.4	7.4	7.3	7.4
Alloys	KLBK	15.3	15.9	12.1	9.4	9.4	11.9	15.2	24.3	24.3	24.3	33.3
Other uses	KLBL	27.9	30.0	29.5	26.6	28.9	34.1	35.8	38.6	38.6	38.6	39.9

Production

22.17
continued

Non-ferrous metals
United Kingdom

		1994	1995	1996	1997	1998	1999	2000	2001	2002	2003	2004
Tin												
Tin ore (metal content):												
Production	KLBM	1.9	2.0	2.1	2.3	0.4	0.4	..	..	1.9	1.9	–
Tin metal:[10]												
Production[11]	KLBO	–	–	–	–	..	..	..	..	1.9	1.9	–
Home consumption[11]	VQIX	10.6	10.5	10.5	10.4	10.6	9.6	10.0	10.3	6.9	7.1	5.3
Exports and re-exports[12]	KLBQ	1.2	2.7	0.6	0.3	3.4	0.1	0.1	0.4	1.9	1.9	0.6
Stocks (end of period):												
Consumers	KLBR	1.0	1.0	1.0	1.0	1.0	1.0	1.0	1.0	1.9	1.9	1.0
Analysis of home consumption												
(excluding scrap): total	KLBT	10.5	10.6	10.5	10.4	17.5	16.5	17.0	18.8	18.8	1.9	18.4
Tinplate	KLBU	3.6	3.6	3.6	2.8	2.6	3.0	3.0	3.0	1.9	1.9	3.0
Alloys	KLBV	3.3	3.4	3.5	3.4	12.1	11.2	11.6	2.6	1.9	1.9	2.6
Solder	KLBW	1.5	1.1	1.1	1.1	1.1	0.6	0.8	1.5	1.9	1.9	1.5
Other uses	KLBX	2.4	0.4	0.4	0.4	0.4	0.4	0.4	0.4	1.9	1.9	0.4
Aluminium												
Ingot production												
Primary	KLBY	231.2	237.9	240.0	247.7	258.4	269.7	305.1	340.8	344.3	342.7	359.6
Secondary[13]	KLCA	224.3	229.7	260.0	242.7	274.8	285.3	237.7	248.6	205.4	205.4	205.4
Wrought remelt production[14]	C6EW	519.7	546.5	527.8	561.2	583.5	596.2	567.0	585.3	565.1	580.0	599.1
Wrought and cast despatches												
Bar, section and tube[15]	C6EX	142.7	142.1	149.6	160.8	168.0	181.7	184.7	177.1	168.3	158.7	157.0
Plate, sheet, strip and circles	C6EY	346.4	359.2	327.9	350.4	352.5	349.7	419.1	384.8	312.2	274.3	267.3
Castings	KLCH	143.4	147.0	156.0	152.4	148.0	137.3	134.9	138.2	159.4	127.5	139.7
Exports												
Primary ingot	C6EZ	95.2	159.4	53.1	219.6	68.7	233.6	347.7	203.4	214.7	244.3	305.1
Secondary ingot	KLCC	124.8	145.8	152.2	153.3	156.6	143.1	84.2	59.9	35.7	26.9	30.8
Extruded products	C6F2	40.9	65.8	45.8	56.8	59.7	47.5	25.5	20.7	15.3	14.2	15.8
Rolled products	C6F3	177.7	185.6	155.5	157.7	160.1	166.6	222.9	198.3	208.8	193.9	192.2
Refined nickel												
Production (including ferro-nickel)	KLCM	28.4	35.1	38.6	36.1	39.1	39.5	38.0	33.8	33.8	26.8	38.6

1 Unwrought copper (electrolytic, fire refined and blister).
2 Reported stocks of refined copper held by consumers and those held in London Metal Exchange (LME) warehouses in the United Kingdom.
3 2001 figures only cover the period January to June.
4 Copper content.
5 Consumption for high-conductivity copper and cadmium copper wire represented by consumption of wire rods, production of which for export is also included.
6 Lead reclaimed from secondary and scrap material and lead refined from bullion and domestic ores.

7 Figures for production and consumption of refined lead include antimonial lead, and for scrap and remelted lead, exclude secondary antimonial lead.
8 Including toll transactions involving fabrication.
9 Excluding goverment stocks.
10 Including production from imported scrap and residues refined on toll.
11 Primary and secondary metal.
12 Including re-exports on toll transactions.
13 Predominantly from old scrap.
14 Predominantly using recycled scrap from fabrication.
15 Excluding forging bars

Sources: World Bureau of Metal Statistics: 01920 461274;
Aluminium Federation: 0121 456 1103

22.18 Fertilisers[1]
Years ending 30 June

Thousand tonnes

		1995	1996	1997	1998	1999	2000	2001	2002	2003	2004	2005
Nutrient Content												
Nitrogen (N):												
Straight	KGRM	855	858	957	912	819	819	714	751	664	662	685
Compounds	KGRN	493	475	483	463	465	449	448	446	467	463	371
Phosphate (P_2O_5)	KGRO	405	394	412	383	347	317	279	283	282	278	246
Potash (K_2O)	KGRP	476	471	501	487	451	409	369	391	375	375	341
Compounds - total product	KGRQ	3 201	3 115	3 238	3 037	3 013	2 851	2 471	2 511	2 558	2 550	2 161

1 See chapter text

Source: Agricultural Industries Confederation: 01733 385230

22.19 Minerals: production[1]
United Kingdom

Thousand tonnes

		1994	1995	1996	1997	1998	1999	2000	2001	2002	2003	2004
Great Britain												
Limestone	KLEA	102 844	90 933	82 442	84 252	85 382	82 714	80 810	83 492	88 013	84 445	86 846
Sandstone	KLEB	13 494	15 017	12 581	12 457	13 545	11 870	12 056	11 897	11 788	11 665	11 929
Igneous rock	KLEC	50 014	49 641	43 731	42 370	39 838	45 294	44 633	45 053	44 544	45 305	46 193
Clay/shale	KLED	12 464	13 930	11 804	11 322	12 230	11 355	10 838	10 426	10 306	10 680	11 164
Industrial sand	KLEE	4 038	4 344	4 861	4 704	4 662	4 092	4 095	3 848	3 833	4 073	5 011
Chalk	KLEF	10 236	9 949	9 239	9 550	9 934	9 667	9 213	8 205	8 587	8 066	7 997
Fireclay	KLEG	679	708	536	338	577	545	595	459	491	528	402
Barium sulphate	KLEH	34	74	93	57	64	59	54	70	56	..	..
Calcium fluoride	KLEI	50	46	..	58	52	46	21	46	22	..	..
Copper	KLEJ	–	–	–	–	–	–	–	–	–	–	..
Lead	KLEK	2	..	..	..	1	1	..	1	–	–	..
Tin	KLEL	1.9	2.0	2.1	2.0	–	–	–	–	–	–	..
Zinc	KLEM	..	..	..	–	–	–	–	–	–	–	..
Iron ore: crude	KLEN	2	2	1	2	2	1	1	1	1	–	..
Iron ore: iron content	KLEO	1	1	1	1	1	1	1	..	..	–	..
Calcspar	KLEP	..	..	..	13	15	..	..	12	..	–	..
China clay	KLEQ KILC	2 977	3 076	2 654	2 798	2 866	2 841	2 779	2 804	2 467	2 378	2 148
Ball clay	KIMS	913	..	..	..	..	..	..	..	..	..	..
Chert and flint	KLER	..	..	..	..	..	6	..	2	2	..	2
Fuller's earth	KLES	193	150	183	162	111	83	103	..	33	19	11
Lignite	KLET	2	–	–	–	–	–	–	–	–	–	..
Rock salt	KLEU	..	..	..	..	..	..	..	..	..	..	..
Salt from brine	KLEV	..	..	..	..	..	..	..	..	..	..	..
Salt in brine	KLEW	4 009	3 548	3 512	3 561	..	..	..	..	..	..	..
Anhydrite	KLEX	..	..	–	–	–	–	–	–	–	–	..
Dolomite	KLEY	17 616	17 966	16 555	17 282	15 632	13 698	13 069	14 314	12 946	..	..
Gypsum	KLEZ	..	..	..	..	..	..	..	..	..	..	1 686
Slate[2]	KLFA	402	275	408	347	425	361	479	551	742	832	901
Soapstone and talc	KLFB	5	4	5	5	5	6	5	5	6	6	4
Sand and gravel (land-won)	KLFC	86 341	78 031	70 489	74 362	73 016	74 785	74 877	74 599	69 889	68 090	73 061
Sand and gravel (marine dredged)	KLFD	11 331	11 625	11 508	12 004	12 952	13 424	14 356	13 611	12 832	12 131	12 996
Northern Ireland												
Sand and gravel	KLFG	5 109	5 262	7 684	5 138	5 300	5 517	5 073	6 194	5 512	4 894	5 084
Basalt and igneous rock (other than granite)	KLFH	6 480	7 564	6 974	6 286	6 107	7 861	9 480	6 448	6 681	6 051	6 844
Limestone	KLFI	..	3 703	4 122	3 500	3 892	4 219	3 538	4 746	4 514	4 887	5 634
Sandstone[3]	KLFJ	5 480	4 779	4 941	6 042	6 584	3 615	2 844	8 070	6 574	6 594	6 915
Granite	KLFL	..	..	–	–	–	–	–	–	–	–	..
Others[4]	KLFN	896	812	1 392	625	473	1 579	3 098	753	242	1 055	1 266

1 See chapter text.
2 Includes waste used for constructional fill, and powder and granules used in manufacturing.

3 Prior to 1993 the 'Sandstone' heading was called 'Grit and conglomerate'. The new heading is all encompassing and was confirmed as correct with the Geological Survey in Northern Ireland.
4 Rock salt, Chalk, Diatomite and Fireclay.

Source: Office for National Statistics: 01633 812082

22.20 Building materials and components: production[1]
Great Britain

			1995	1996	1997	1998	1999	2000	2001	2002	2003	2004	2005
Building bricks[2]	KLGA	Millions	3 256	3 046	2 997	3 000	2 939	2 864	2 754	2 750	2 772	2 868	2 752
Common bricks	GRTD	"	480	401	422	385	367	342	320	332	315	318	320
Facing bricks	GRTE	"	2 546	2 430	2 386	2 411	2 369	2 287	2 211	2 209	2 244	2 327	2 204
Engineering bricks	GRTF	"	230	216	190	204	204	235	223	210	213	224	227
Clay bricks (including sand-lime)	GRTG	"	3 065	2 880	2 828	2 830	2 759	2 694	2 595	2 600	2 606	2 707	2 604
Concrete bricks	GRTH	"	191	166	169	171	180	170	159	150	167	161	148
Cement (grey Portland)[3]	KLGB	Thousand tonnes	11 805	12 214	12 638	12 409	12 697	12 452	11 090	11 089	11 215	11 405	..
Sand and gravel	GRTI	"	89 656	81 997	86 366	85 968	88 209	89 234	88 210	82 721	80 221	86 057	81 058
Building sand[4]	KLGC	"	17 389	14 655	15 337	13 810	13 941	14 219	13 772	13 221	13 617	13 125	14 227
Concreting sand	KLGD	"	29 390	28 659	30 130	30 244	31 730	31 167	31 656	31 224	31 411	32 529	30 765
Gravel[5]	KLGE	"	42 877	38 683	40 899	41 914	42 538	43 847	42 782	38 276	35 193	40 404	36 066
Crushed rock	GRTJ	"	150 838	132 894	133 787	131 716	132 598	130 307	133 759	126 568	122 885	127 674	..
Coated roadstone	KLGF	"	28 972	26 270	23 906	23 131	22 260	21 785	23 340	23 281	23 139	18 721	..
Uncoated roadstone	KLGG	"	49 307	40 893	40 186	36 816	38 114	36 509	34 638	27 323	28 950	25 260	..
Fill and ballast	KLGH	"	56 140	50 982	51 396	51 623	52 144	53 417	47 225	49 622	42 208	62 460	..
Concrete aggregate	KLGI	"	16 419	14 748	18 300	20 146	20 080	18 595	28 556	26 342	28 588	21 231	..
Ready mixed concrete[6]	GRXA	Thousand cubic metres	21 676	20 892	22 327	22 983	23 550	23 043	23 008	22 597	22 289	22 856	22 432
Concrete building blocks	GRTK	Thousand square metres	78 287	75 866	82 537	84 662	87 767	90 219	87 922	91 474	95 645	96 256	89 997
Dense aggregate	KLGN	"	36 933	34 996	37 250	39 439	38 439	37 629	36 598	35 744	36 745	37 677	36 188
Lightweight aggregate	KLGO	"	18 147	16 316	17 783	19 110	20 830	22 991	22 684	23 478	24 991	25 462	25 561
Aerated concrete	KLGP	"	23 207	24 554	27 505	26 113	28 497	29 599	28 639	32 252	33 909	33 117	28 248
Concrete roofing tiles	KLGM	"	26 118	24 651	24 958	24 981	25 972	26 765	24 825	25 023	21 437	20 739	25 719
Roofing and architectural slates	GRXB	Tonnes	42 030	48 474	44 578	46 159	46 998	41 214	45 604	50 530	50 094	..	..
Fibre cement products	KLGK	Thousand tonnes	160.5	146.2	163.5	160.9	156.2	..	..	..	..	..	..

1 See chapter text.
2 Excluding refractory and glazed bricks.
3 United Kingdom up until 2000. Great Britain for 2001 onwards.
4 Includes sand and gravel used for coating.
5 Includes hoggin.
6 United Kingdom.

Source: Department of Trade & Industry: 020 7215 1555

22.21 Construction: value of output in Great Britain[1]
Standard Industrial Classification 1992

£ million

		1995	1996	1997	1998	1999	2000	2001	2002	2003	2004	2005
All work: total	FGAY	52 643	55 243	58 352	62 060	65 704	69 676	74 703	83 592	93 284	102 363	107 006
New work: total	BLAB	26 672	27 926	29 928	32 491	35 587	37 660	39 974	45 370	50 353	57 238	59 412
New housing: total	KLQA	7 135	7 013	7 983	8 430	8 418	9 985	10 234	12 089	15 362	19 447	21 063
For public sector	BLAC	1 660	1 421	1 232	1 069	1 012	1 319	1 437	1 716	2 032	2 628	2 680
For private sector	BLAD	5 475	5 592	6 751	7 361	7 406	8 666	8 797	10 373	13 330	16 818	18 383
Infrastructure: total	KIAM	5 660	6 338	6 311	6 182	6 200	6 453	7 147	8 077	7 363	6 491	6 499
Other new work: total (excluding infrastructure)	KLQB	13 877	14 575	15 635	17 879	20 969	21 222	22 594	25 204	27 628	31 301	31 850
For public sector	BLAE	4 661	4 441	3 756	4 151	4 919	4 854	5 330	6 865	8 875	10 516	10 191
For private sector	KLQC	9 217	10 134	11 879	13 728	16 049	16 369	17 263	18 339	18 753	20 785	21 659
Private Industrial	BLAF	3 008	3 119	3 491	3 810	3 973	3 716	3 702	3 374	3 644	3 978	4 291
Private Commercial	BLAG	6 209	7 015	8 388	9 917	12 076	12 653	13 562	14 965	15 109	16 807	17 369
Repair and maintenance: total	BLAH	25 971	27 317	28 423	29 569	30 117	32 016	34 729	38 222	42 931	45 125	47 594
Housing: total	KLQD	14 595	15 035	15 754	16 202	16 370	16 907	17 626	19 170	21 315	23 229	23 937
For public sector	BLBK	6 465	6 637	6 629	6 506	6 485	6 552	6 632	6 412	7 451	8 302	8 598
For private sector	BLBL	8 130	8 398	9 126	9 696	9 885	10 354	10 994	12 758	13 864	14 927	15 339
Public other work	BLAJ	5 398	5 252	5 079	5 220	5 371	5 685	6 111	6 712	7 930	8 015	8 939
Private other work	BLAK	5 978	7 030	7 590	8 147	8 376	9 424	10 992	12 340	13 686	13 881	14 718

1 See chapter text. Output by contractors, including unrecorded estimates by small firms and self-employed workers, and output by public sector direct labour departments - classified to construction in the *1992 Standard Industrial Classification*.

Source: Department of Trade and Industry: 020 7215 1953

22.22 Construction: value of new orders obtained by contractors[1]
Great Britain

Standard Industrial Classification 1992

£ million

		1995	1996	1997	1998	1999	2000	2001	2002	2003	2004	2005
New work: total	FHAA	22 065	22 834	24 806	27 477	26 079	28 120	29 643	33 411	33 951	39 089	43 932
Public housing	BLBC	1 182	1 073	995	933	969	910	1 084	1 129	1 340	1 697	1 951
Private housing[2]	BLBD	4 905	5 416	6 253	5 997	5 901	6 085	6 525	8 088	9 471	12 153	13 171
New housing: total	FGAU	6 087	6 487	7 248	6 930	6 869	6 995	7 610	9 217	10 812	13 850	15 122
Infrastructure:												
Water	KIBV	500	640	733	957	760	1 084	531	936	677	601	1 200
Sewerage	KIBW	394	481	656	737	789	380	540	524	423	393	429
Electricity	KIBX	218	294	382	359	254	244	279	294	255	356	561
Roads	KIBY	1 531	1 710	928	821	957	1 445	1 572	1 999	1 424	1 092	1 559
Gas, communications, air	KIBZ	904	745	693	745	713	1 085	584	485	699	480	694
Railways	KIDP	351	524	416	573	471	539	1 271	1 052	1 189	672	781
Harbours	KIDQ	273	270	182	287	250	215	377	264	228	178	319
Total	BAWT	4 170	4 664	3 991	4 479	4 195	4 992	5 154	5 555	4 894	3 772	5 532
of which												
- Public	KIDS	2 327	1 671	1 352	1 505	1 495	1 430	2 085	2 491	1 781	1 291	1 949
- Private	KIDT	1 843	2 993	2 639	2 974	2 700	3 562	3 068	3 064	3 113	2 480	3 584
Other public non-housing:												
Factories	KIDU	94	91	72	84	72	64	30	65	121	85	48
Warehouses	KIDV	29	14	27	20	24	12	10	11	27	25	26
Oil, steel, coal	KIDW	13	4	4	2	5	1	8	1	4	1	2
Schools and colleges	KIDX	710	707	749	770	791	986	1 498	1 397	1 988	2 586	2 735
Universities	KIDY	373	355	273	405	345	329	378	667	760	704	904
Health	KIDZ	717	681	491	769	635	685	813	1 065	1 114	1 378	1 049
Offices	KIFP	393	379	391	292	390	291	395	854	588	785	566
Entertainment	KIFQ	285	259	342	432	435	359	392	400	543	503	668
Garages	KIFR	51	28	34	19	36	44	30	53	34	56	54
Shops	KIFS	21	12	35	35	29	34	38	53	50	60	40
Agriculture	KIFT	12	8	33	17	9	12	46	16	10	4	6
Miscellaneous	KIFU	508	418	441	660	503	999	479	1 328	903	660	600
Total	BAWU	3 206	2 956	2 894	3 504	3 273	3 815	4 117	5 910	6 142	6 847	6 694
Private industrial:[2]												
Factories	KIFW	2 055	1 603	2 184	1 878	1 698	1 444	1 588	1 341	1 442	1 321	1 753
Warehouses	KIFX	594	663	901	1 014	821	1 110	911	866	867	1 158	1 569
Oil, steel, coal	KIFY	76	71	64	79	38	34	43	40	74	115	99
Total	BAWV	2 725	2 337	3 149	2 971	2 558	2 589	2 542	2 247	2 383	2 593	3 421
Private commercial:[2]												
Schools, universities	KIHP	105	156	189	351	393	577	702	850	873	744	1 479
Health	KIHQ	288	277	356	651	411	455	349	575	744	1 376	1 323
Offices	KIHR	2 123	2 169	2 506	3 472	3 566	4 384	4 748	3 947	3 253	3 555	4 306
Entertainment	KIHS	940	1 407	1 847	2 244	2 224	1 873	1 674	1 861	1 521	2 059	2 118
Garages	KIHT	301	265	344	315	266	169	190	199	194	272	263
Shops	KIHU	1 871	1 795	1 937	2 154	1 901	1 889	2 212	2 570	2 675	2 893	3 142
Agriculture	KIBN	124	123	148	146	100	77	105	107	158	149	154
Miscellaneous	KIBO	126	198	198	259	321	305	242	374	301	978	387
Total	BAWW	5 877	6 390	7 525	9 593	9 184	9 729	10 221	10 482	9 721	12 026	13 163

1 See chapter text. Classified to construction in the *1992 Standard Industrial Classification*.

2 Figures for private sector include work to be carried out by contractors on their own initiative for sale.

Source: Department of Trade and Industry: 020 7215 1953

22.23 Total engineering: total turnover of UK based manufacturers[1]
Standard Industrial Classification 2003

£ million

Activity heading Product group		1999	2000	2001	2002	2003	2004
Class 29: Manufacture of machinery and equipment not elsewhere classified							
2911 Manufacture of engines and turbines except aircraft, vehicle and cycle engines	MXVO	1 359.4	1 445.3	1 911.8	1 823.9	1 716.6	1 631.8
2912 Manufacture of pumps and compressors	MXXO	2 393.0	2 481.5	2 337.4	2 537.3	2 607.7	2 957.1
2913 Manufacture of taps and valves	MXZH	1 218.5	1 346.2	1 358.2	1 330.9	1 281.5	1 205.7
2914 Manufacture of bearings, gears, gearing and driving elements	MYCT	1 344.9	1 282.8	1 227.0	1 004.9	882.4	988.4
2922 Manufacture of lifting and handling equipment	MYLS	3 881.5	3 687.8	3 348.7	3 080.7	2 991.9	3 141.9
2923 Manufacture of non-domestic cooling and ventilation equipment	MYPT	3 082.0	3 160.0	3 411.9	3 298.7	3 194.3	3 339.7
2924 Manufacture of other general purpose machinery not elsewhere classified	MYRM	2 715.0	2 693.3	2 947.6	2 573.4	2 650.4	2 946.4
2941/3 Manufacture of other machine tools	MYYP	839.5	777.3	834.3	745.7	842.3	788.5
2942 Manufacture of metalworking machine tools	MYWY	866.9	937.0	912.6	738.6	689.9	603.4
2952 Manufacture of machinery for mining, quarrying and construction	MZCE	2 339.0	2 434.8	2 392.4	2 215.9	2 549.2	2 932.8
2953 Manufacture of machinery for food, beverage and tobacco processing	MZFS	576.0	593.8	629.1	710.8	802.9	949.9
2954 Manufacture of machinery for textile, apparel and leather production	MZJP	203.1	207.6	194.7	158.0	145.9	172.3
2956 Manufacture of other special purpose machinery not elsewhere classified	MZQF	2 360.8	2 153.9	2 148.8	2 187.1	2 239.7	2 218.3
2971 Manufacture of electric domestic appliances	MZTZ	2 008.9	2 046.7	2 230.9	2 196.4	2 177.2	2 450.4
Class 30: Manufacture of electrical and optical equipment							
3001 Manufacture of office machinery	MZXQ	1 409.3	1 528.6	1 481.1	1 129.8	919.0	815.2
3002 Manufacture of computers and other information processing equipment	VBCE	13 452.6	12 410.7	12 086.4	8 915.6	7 533.8	5 014.2
Class 31 : Manufacture of electrical machinery and apparatus not elsewhere classified							
3110 Manufacture of electric motors, generators and transformers	VBEB	3 150.0	3 302.5	3 287.6	2 732.3	2 620.5	2 330.8
3120 Manufacture of electricity distribution and control apparatus	VBFU	3 813.9	4 213.0	4 090.5	3 736.1	3 558.4	3 641.3
3130 Manufacture of insulated wire and cable	VBHW	1 739.2	1 753.7	1 414.7	1 271.6	1 140.0	1 122.9
3140 Manufacture of accumulators, primary cells and primary batteries	VBJW	587.5	606.2	493.7	444.6	451.9	460.9
3150 Manufacture of lighting equipment and electric lamps	VBLP	1 913.2	1 865.8	1 712.1	1 487.0	1 402.1	1 442.2
3161 Manufacture of other electrical equipment for engines and vehicles not otherwise classified	VBNI	1 068.5	1 030.6	1 034.2	1 042.5	1 037.3	1 006.2
3162 Manufacture of other electrical equipment not elsewhere classified	VBPK	3 438.5	2 756.5	2 728.1	2 480.9	2 384.4	2 639.0
Class 32: Manufacture of radio, television and communication equipment and apparatus							
3210 Manufacture of electronic valves and tubes and other electronic components	VBRI	4 652.9	6 695.8	4 460.0	4 063.0	4 132.7	4 214.9
3220 Manufacture of television and radio transmitters and apparatus for line telephony and line telegraphy	VBTF	11 881.6	15 349.1	10 527.5	7 112.6	4 088.3	4 170.1
3230 Manufacture of television and radio receivers, sound or video recording or reproducing apparatus and associated goods	VBVJ	3 826.5	4 044.2	4 038.0	3 192.4	3 262.3	3 781.1
Class 33: Manufacture of medical, precision and optical instruments, watches and clocks							
3310 Manufacture of medical and surgical equipment and orthopaedic appliances	VBXH	2 597.0	2 691.2	2 967.5	3 167.7	3 538.6	3 542.5
3320 Manufacture of instruments and appliances for measuring, checking, testing, navigating and other purposes, except industrial process control equipment	VBZF	6 261.8	6 541.0	7 104.8	6 378.5	6 748.6	7 046.2
3340 Manufacture of optical instruments and photographic equipment	VCCV	935.1	998.4	999.6	1 027.2	1 031.0	1 069.8

1 The figures shown represent the output of UK based manufacturers classified to Subsections DK and DL of the Standard Industrial Classification 2003. The figures shown are derived from the monthly production inquiry (MPI) and include estimates for non-responders and for establishments which are not sampled. Orders on hand figures are given for the end of the period to which they relate.

Source: Office for National Statistics: 01633 812786

22.24 Volume index numbers of turnover and orders for the engineering industries
United Kingdom
Standard Industrial Classification 1992

Indices (2000=100)

	Total			Home			Export		
	Orders on hand[1]	New orders[2]	Turnover	Orders on hand[1]	New orders[2]	Turnover	Orders on hand[1]	New orders[2]	Turnover

Total Engineering industries
SIC 1992 Division 29, 30, 31, 32 and 33

	JIQI	JIQH	JIQJ	JIQC	JIQB	JIQD	JIQF	JIQE	JIQG
1998	81.9	84.2	87.8	79.1	82.5	88.3	86.7	86.4	87.3
1999	92.0	91.8	91.9	92.8	94.2	93.5	90.8	88.6	89.9
2000	103.4	100.0	100.0	104.9	100.0	100.0	100.8	100.0	100.0
2001	94.4	89.5	95.3	104.6	94.5	98.4	77.2	82.9	91.2
2002	92.7	80.8	84.5	104.8	88.0	91.8	72.1	71.2	74.8
2003	92.7	78.9	81.6	108.7	87.9	90.2	65.5	66.8	70.3
2004	89.3	78.3	82.1	103.2	84.0	89.3	65.8	70.8	72.6

Manufacture of Machinery and Equipment
SIC 1992 Division 29

	JINX	JINW	JINY	JINR	JINQ	JINS	JINU	JINT	JINV
1998	92.6	97.9	106.0	91.0	97.7	106.8	96.1	98.3	104.6
1999	95.1	99.5	100.4	96.9	96.3	103.6	91.2	89.9	94.6
2000	99.9	100.0	100.0	99.1	100.0	100.0	101.7	100.0	100.0
2001	95.0	97.2	100.8	95.1	100.8	103.3	94.9	91.0	96.4
2002	99.9	95.6	95.4	99.9	98.8	97.1	99.8	90.1	92.4
2003	110.7	99.7	97.1	120.1	105.2	97.5	89.9	90.2	96.5
2004	106.6	99.3	102.5	112.3	96.5	100.1	93.9	104.1	106.7

Manufacture of Electrical and Optical Equipment
SIC 1992 Division 30, 31, 32 and 33

	JIPQ	JIPP	JIPR	JIPK	JIPJ	JIPL	JIPN	JIPM	JIPO
1998	75.1	78.0	79.5	70.3	74.7	78.2	82.1	82.2	81.1
1999	90.0	88.4	88.1	89.7	88.6	88.0	90.5	88.1	88.2
2000	105.7	100.0	100.0	109.3	100.0	100.0	100.4	100.0	100.0
2001	94.0	86.1	92.8	111.7	91.2	95.8	68.4	80.0	89.4
2002	88.1	74.2	79.5	108.5	82.4	89.0	58.5	64.4	68.5
2003	81.1	69.6	74.5	100.2	78.9	86.2	53.5	58.4	60.9
2004	78.2	69.0	72.7	96.4	77.6	83.3	51.9	58.8	60.5

1 At end of period, rather than the average value for that period, so the annual
value shown for 2000 may not equal 100.
2 Net of cancellations.

Source: Office for National Statistics: 01633 812786

387

22.25 Motor vehicle production[1]
United Kingdom

		1995	1996	1997	1998	1999	2000	2001	2002	2003	2004	2005
Motor vehicles												
SIC 1992, Class 34-10												
Passenger cars: total	JCYM	1 532 084	1 686 134	1 698 001	1 748 258	1 786 623	1 641 452	1 492 365	1 629 744	1 657 558	1 646 750	1 595 697
1 000 c.c. and under	GKAB	95 198	108 645	119 894	112 044	113 204	96 043	93 695	79 545	23 985	15 471	6 111
Over 1 000 c.c. but not over 1 600 c.c.	GKAD	814 873	845 084	829 079	814 595	776 111	676 438	632 747	711 553	750 840	796 174	854 687
Over 1 600 c.c. but not over 2 800 c.c.	GKAF	528 444	635 861	653 147	720 556	758 478	723 294	634 573	720 067	740 486	690 759	546 744
Over 2 800 c.c.	GKAH	93 569	96 544	95 881	101 063	138 830	145 677	131 350	118 579	142 247	144 346	188 155
Commercial vehicles: total	JCYG	233 001	238 314	237 706	227 379	185 905	172 442	192 873	191 267	188 871	209 293	206 753
Of which:												
Light commercial vehicles	GKDH	199 346	205 372	210 942	203 629	162 176	145 655	169 705	168 311	166 359	178 887	171 866
Trucks:												
Under 7.5 tonnes	GKDJ	9 523	8 913	6 254	5 006	4 107	5 160	5 000	4 600	4 151	4 977	5 533
Over 7.5 tonnes	GKDL	11 727	10 128	7 932	7 002	6 443	6 849	7 359	7 357	7 779	8 537	9 756
Motive units for articulated vehicles	GKCV	3 476	2 631	2 574	2 492	2 739	2 673	2 539	1 795	2 095	2 558	2 755
Buses, coaches and mini buses	GKDN	8 939	11 270	10 004	9 250	10 440	12 105	8 270	9 204	8 487	14 334	16 843

1 See chapter text. Figures for motor vehicles relate to periods of 52 weeks (53 weeks in 1993).

Source: Office for National Statistics: 01633 812394

22.26 Alcoholic drink[1]
United Kingdom

			1995	1996	1997	1998	1999	2000	2001	2002	2003	2004	2005
Spirits[2]		Thousand hectolitres of alcohol											
Production	KMEA	"	4 507	4 868	5 297	5 145	4 705	4 210	4 368	4 508	4 553	4 081	4 365
Released for home consumption													
Home produced whisky	KMEE	"	310	321	312	289	323	314	321	321	318	319	301
Spirit-based Ready-to-drink[3]	SNET	"	..	..	..	..	..	..	..	105	124	114	84
Imported and other	KMEG	"	481	495	533	505	596	615	647	689	744	792	822
Total	KMEH	"	791	815	845	794	919	929	968	1 115	1 187	1 226	1 207
Beer[4]		Thousand hectolitres											
Production	BFNK	"	56 800	58 072	59 139	56 652	57 854	55 279	56 802	56 672	58 014	57 459	56 021
Released for home consumption	BAYL	"	59 129	59 894	61 114	58 835	58 917	57 007	58 234	59 384	60 301	59 195	57 563
Production	JYXJ	Thousand hectolitres of pure alcohol	2 298	2 360	2 406	2 333	2 364	2 299	2 358	2 352	2 414	2 433	2 329
Released for home consumption	JYXK	alcohol	2 410	2 448	2 504	2 439	2 428	2 382	2 429	2 473	2 515	2 499	2 398
Wine of fresh grapes													
Released for home consumption		Thousand hectolitres											
Fortified	KMEM	"	330	331	323	370	316	289	287	325	296	298	306
Still table	KMEN	"	6 576	6 995	7 653	7 979	8 391	8 864	9 534	10 319	10 647	11 768	12 117
Sparkling	KMEO	"	315	358	382	416	576	543	515	578	640	676	721
Total	KMEP	"	7 221	7 684	8 358	8 765	9 284	9 696	10 336	11 222	11 584	12 742	13 143
Made-wine													
Released for home consumption													
Other than coolers	KMEQ	"	516	513	485	406	416	431	364	367	339	351	334
Coolers[3]	KJDD	"	903	1 781	1 153	1 244	1 802	2 800	3 712	1 606	423	508	597
Cider and perry													
Released for home consumption	KMER	"	5 575	5 656	5 513	5 548	6 022	6 006	5 911	5 939	5 876	6 139	6 377

1 See chapter text.
2 Potable spirits distilled.
3 Made wine with alcoholic strength 1.2% to 5.5%. Includes alcoholic lemonade of appropriate strength and similar products. From 28 April 2002, duty on spirit-based "coolers" is charged at the same rate as spirits per litre of alcohol. Coolers for calendar year 2002 includes only wine based "coolers".

4 A new system was introduced for beer duty in June 1993. The figures in this table include adjustments to data prior to this date to bring them into line with current data.

Source: HM Revenue & Customs: 020 7865 5323

22.27

Tobacco products: released for home consumption[1]
United Kingdom

			1995	1996	1997	1998	1999	2000	2001	2002	2003	2004	2005
Cigarettes:		Thousand million											
Home produced	KMFA	"	70.8	73.8	71.1	67.8	28.2	49.3	47.7	49.6	49.1	48.2	45.9
Imported	KMFB	"	9.5	9.5	9.9	7.5	6.0	7.3	6.8	6.5	4.9	4.5	4.3
Total[2]	KMFC	"	80.3	83.3	81.0	75.3	34.2	56.6	54.5	56.1	54.0	52.6	50.2
Cigars:		Million kg											
Home produced	KMFD	"	1.5	1.4	1.3	1.2	0.9	1.0	0.9	0.9	0.8	0.7	0.6
Imported	KMFE	"	0.1	0.1	0.1	0.1	0.1	0.1	0.1	0.1	0.1	0.1	0.1
Total[2]	KMFF	"	1.6	1.5	1.4	1.3	1.0	1.1	1.0	1.0	0.9	0.8	0.8
Hand-rolling tobacco:													
Home produced	KMFG	"	2.4	2.1	1.8	1.7	2.0	2.1	2.8	2.8	2.9	3.0	3.2
Imported	KMFH	"	0.1	0.1	0.1	0.1	–	–	–	–	–	..	..
Total[2]	KMFI	"	2.6	2.3	1.9	1.8	2.0	2.2	2.8	2.8	2.9	3.1	3.2
Other smoking and chewing tobacco:													
Home produced	KMFJ	"	1.3	1.2	1.1	1.0	0.6	0.7	0.7	0.6	0.5	0.5	0.4
Imported	KMFK	"	0.1	0.1	0.1	0.1	0.1	0.1	0.1	0.1	0.1	0.1	0.1
Total[2]	KMFL	"	1.4	1.3	1.2	1.1	0.7	0.8	0.8	0.7	0.6	0.6	0.5

1 See chapter text.
2 Any apparent discrepency between totals and the sum of the constituents is
  due to rounding.

Source: HM Revenue and Customs: 020 7147 0593

Banking, insurance etc

Chapter 23

Banking, insurance etc

Other banks' balance sheet

(Table 23.3)

The implementation of the review of banking statistics at end-September 1997 has resulted in several changes to this table:

(a)   The table now includes the business of all monthly and quarterly reporting banks in the UK; it formerly covered only the business of monthly reporting institutions.

(b)   The Channel Islands and Isle of Man are no longer treated as part of the UK for statistical purposes. Banking institutions in the Channel Islands and Isle of Man no longer have the option of being within the UK banking sector and their business, along with the business of offshore island branches of UK mainland banks, is now excluded from the figures within this table. Additionally, the business of the UK banking sector with offshore island residents and entities has been reclassified from UK residents to non-residents.

(c)   The table now contains more comprehensive detail of business with building societies. This business was previously included indistinguishably within the UK private sector elements of the table.

(d)   The aggregate balance sheet of the banking sector has been inflated because it is now reported on an accrual basis rather than a cash basis (accrued amounts payable/receivable are shown under liabilities and assets respectively). Additionally, acceptances have been brought onto the balance sheet and are shown under both liabilities and assets.

With effect from 1998, the balance sheet of the Banking Department of the Bank of England is excluded from this table, and other banks' business with the Issue Department is reclassified from 'UK public sector' to 'UK banks'.

Data for 1999 reflect the acquisition of Birmingham Midshires Building Society by Halifax during that year.

Data for end-2000 reflect the entry of Bradford and Bingley plc to the banking sector during the year. Data for end-2000 also reflect the new reporting during the year of agency business as a result of collateral management via repos and reverse repos.

Bank lending to, and bank deposits from, UK residents

(Tables 23.4 and 23.5)

These are series of statistics based on the Standard Industrial Classification 1992.

Table 23.4 comprises loans, advances (including under reverse repos), finance leasing, acceptances, facilities and holdings of sterling and euro commercial paper. It includes lending under the Department of Trade and Industry (DTI) special scheme for domestic shipbuilding. Holdings of investments and bills and adjustments for transit items are not included.

Table 23.5 includes borrowing under sale and repurchase agreements (repro). Adjustments for transit items are not included.

Figures for both tables are supplied by monthly reporting banks and grossed to cover quarterly reporters. They exclude lending to building societies and to residents of the Channel Islands and Isle of Man.

Building societies

(Table 23.13)

Building society figures are sourced from societies' annual returns and for each year relate to accounting years ending on dates between 1 February and 31 January of the following year. Figures are society-only as opposed to group consolidated.

Consumer credit

(Table 23.14)

Figures for net lending refer to changes in amounts outstanding adjusted to remove distortions caused by revaluations of debt outstanding, such as write-offs. Lending by retailers refers to self-financed credit advanced by food retailers, clothing retailers, household goods retailers, mixed business retailers (other than co-operative societies) and general mail order houses. Class 3 loans are advanced under the terms of the Building Societies' Act 1986. Loans on personal accounts exclude loans for house purchase and bridging finance.

Data relating to the narrower coverage cover finance houses and other specialist credit grantors, bank credit cards (operated under the VISA and Mastercard systems), and secured loans by building societies. A high proportion of credit advanced in certain types of agreement, notably on credit cards, is repaid within a month. This reflects use of such agreements as a method of payment rather than a way of obtaining credit.

23.1 Bank of England
At December

£ million

		1995	1996	1997	1998	1999	2000	2001	2002	2003	2004	2005
Issue Department[1]												
Liabilities:												
Notes in circulation	AEFA	21 262	22 407	23 715	24 573	27 232	29 412	32 226	33 639	35 524	37 212	39 329
Notes in Banking Department	AEFB	3	12	5	7	8	8	4	1	6	8	1
Assets:												
Government securities[2]	AEFC	15 510	16 524	16 416	15 826	17 264	13 498	13 996	13 841	13 573	14 870	13 370
Other securities[3]	AEFD	6 210	5 896	7 304	8 754	9 976	15 921	18 234	19 799	21 957	22 350	25 960
Banking Department[1]												
Liabilities:												
Public deposits[4]	AEFF	1 281	1 001	1 192	237	195	391	437	414	542	517	615
Bankers' deposits[5]	AEFH	2 131	2 021	2 800	1 388	1 357	1 520	2 354	1 722	2 320	2 162	3 117
Reserves and other accounts[6]	AEFI	3 150	3 193	3 214	5 163	50 506	8 471	9 834	12 215	15 190	17 767	21 095
Total[7]	AEFE	6 576	6 229	7 221	6 802	52 072	10 397	12 639	14 366	18 066	20 461	24 841
Assets:												
Government securities	AEFJ	1 191	1 232	1 373	1 352	1 444	1 504	1 795	1 510	1 672	1 810	2 126
Advances and other accounts	AEFK	5 388	2 339	5 388	3 302	46 895	6 533	6 413	6 938	9 173	12 093	14 977
Premises, equipment and other securities[6]	AEFL	1 039	2 646	455	2 141	3 724	2 352	4 428	5 917	7 214	6 550	7 737
Notes and coin	AEFM	3	12	5	7	8	8	4	1	6	8	1
Total	KCYT	6 576	6 229	7 221	6 802	52 071	10 397	12 640	14 366	18 065	20 454	24 841

1 Total assets may not equal total liabilities for the Issue Department or for the Banking Department, due to rounding.
2 Including the historic liability of the Treasury of £11 million until 1993 (repaid on 27 July 1994).
3 Including gilt and Treasury bill repurchase agreements from 1994 (previously in "Government securities").
4 Excluding local government and public corporations' deposits which are included under Reserves and other accounts.
5 These consist of operational deposits held mainly by the clearing banks and non-operational cash ratio deposits for which institutions authorised under the Financial Services and Markets Act, deposit - taking UK branches of "European Authorised Institutions" and (from 1998) building societies are liable.
6 Large increases from 1999 arise from the Bank of England's role in TARGET, as a result of which other European central banks may hold substantial credit balances or overdrafts with the Bank.
7 The only liability not shown separately is the Bank's capital (held by the Treasury) which has been constant at £14.6 million.

Source: Bank of England: 020 7601 3236

23.2 Value of inter-bank clearings
United Kingdom

£ billion

		1995	1996	1997	1998	1999	2000	2001	2002	2003	2004	2005
Bulk paper clearings[1]												
Cheque (formerly general)	KCYY	1 097	1 161	1 200	1 214	1 226	1 214	1 210	1 178	1 141	1 111	1 062
Credit	KCYZ	92	94	94	92	88	82	80	75	69	63	57
High-value clearings												
Town	KCZA	59	–	–	–	–	–	–	–	–	–	–
CHAPS Sterling only	KCZB	26 719	28 881	36 032	41 501	44 704	49 146	52 913	51 896	51 613	52 348	52 672
Electronic clearing (BACS)	KCZC	1 055	1 250	1 432	1 602	1 761	1 922	2 166	2 382	2 574	2 883	3 150

1 Excludes inter-branch clearings and clearings in Scotland and Northern Ireland.

Source: APACS - The UK payments association: 020 7711 6323

23.3 Other banks' balance sheet[1]

£ million

		1996	1997[2]	1998[3]	1999[4]	2000[5,6]	2001	2002	2003	2004	2005
Sterling liabilities											
Notes outstanding & cash loaded cards	TBFA	2 717	2 832	2 929	3 311	3 359	3 866	3 957	4 207	4 338	4 534
Sight deposits[7]											
UK banks	TBFB	20 138	44 573	37 839	33 463	40 054	59 573	101 905	99 208	109 866	148 202
UK building societies	TBFC	..	950	1 277	841	1 168	1 466	2 403	1 736	1 697	2 314
UK public sector[8]	TBFD	3 641	3 781	3 003	3 450	3 403	4 283	3 997	5 679	6 635	7 341
Other UK residents	TBFE	211 179	271 233	295 068	325 392	372 725	415 180	457 077	502 359	566 524	637 725
Non-residents	TBFF	17 707	37 730	43 528	44 581	55 489	55 837	57 218	65 157	72 452	83 608
Time deposits											
UK banks	TBFG	95 798	99 782	111 970	112 530	110 955	125 261	141 401	164 433	230 749	289 656
UK building societies	TBFH	–	5 682	4 361	4 253	4 688	4 856	4 487	3 643	4 045	4 098
UK public sector[8]	TBFI	6 087	9 059	9 748	8 064	8 241	8 306	8 936	8 934	10 872	11 378
Other UK residents	TBFJ	210 045	284 629	295 924	282 789	301 007	302 715	306 453	313 244	322 603	354 441
of which TESSAs	TBFK	9 389	20 394	21 568	22 868	24 265	9 752	5 235	1 832	–	
of which SAYE	TBFL	–	2 254	2 604	2 840	2 726	2 439	2 367	2 226	2 301	2 164
of which cash ISAs	TFDG	..	..	..	5 210	13 684	31 298	42 269	52 118	61 033	68 584
Non-residents	TBFM	63 995	91 040	97 953	116 967	134 844	150 964	151 304	166 449	177 381	203 777
Acceptances granted	TBFN	–	19 952	16 658	12 854	10 012	10 627	9 954	2 856	1 446	928
Liabilities under sale and repurchase agreements											
of which British govt. securities	TBFU	22 668	47 297	55 561	56 145	83 819	83 330	78 155	114 468	109 692	180 087
UK banks[8,9]	TBFP	13 718	29 089	43 314	48 213	56 408	60 551	52 079	95 922	86 876	133 938
UK building societies	TBFQ	..	20	32	200	36	–	107	170	62	345
UK public sector[8,9]	TBFR	2 279	6 044	–	–	14 351	5 127	1 402	1 521	113	155
Other UK residents	TBFS	7 703	18 114	20 918	17 165	22 974	25 732	19 759	19 906	35 038	55 378
Non-residents	TBFT	–	5 664	5 469	5 542	9 849	8 643	19 072	18 475	26 669	40 012
CDs and other short-term paper issued	TBFV	96 390	119 266	138 248	158 826	151 153	153 768	157 354	148 606	160 173	165 923
Total sterling deposits	TBFW	749 364	1 046 609	1 125 311	1 175 130	1 297 356	1 392 890	1 494 908	1 618 298	1 813 197	2 139 217
Sterling items in suspense and transmission	TBFX	12 120	16 054	15 714	17 307	15 261	16 702	13 318	18 371	17 923	27 479
Net derivatives	TBFY	..	8 186	8 342	8 324	10 992	4 029	2 491	–10 672	–15 457	9 894
Accrued amounts payable	TBFZ	..	20 713	24 632	22 122	23 726	22 836	21 541	22 624	26 262	27 108
Sterling capital and other internal funds	TBGA	90 464	103 462	103 868	100 575	133 436	148 294	173 320	204 295	265 344	245 812
Total sterling liabilities	TBGB	854 666	1 197 856	1 280 796	1 326 769	1 484 130	1 588 618	1 709 535	1 857 123	2 111 607	2 454 045
Foreign currency liabilities											
Sight and time deposits											
UK banks[10]	TBGC	91 314	90 858	77 128	77 684	99 447	106 368	111 536	139 018	151 946	153 024
UK building societies	TBGD	..	1 027	639	681	233	279	373	550	310	615
UK public sector[8]	TBGE	..	226	149	126	1 808	926	833	865	898	1 098
Other UK residents	TBGF	..	64 188	60 513	65 203	79 627	95 666	81 590	89 034	111 035	137 651
Non-residents	TBGG	605 439	716 573	766 934	736 792	914 888	1 001 321	997 398	1 055 183	1 185 037	1 427 857
Acceptances granted	TBGH	..	743	729	619	689	638	754	751	890	846
Sale and repurchase agreements											
UK banks	TBGJ	17 114	21 311	30 669	25 170	38 901	54 499	90 407	224 743	243 933	265 239
UK building societies	TBGK	..	–	–	–	–	1	–	–	–	–
UK public sector	TBGL	..	22	–	–	468	1	71	844	858	391
Other UK residents	TBGM	..	25 716	26 742	21 997	35 145	52 438	54 463	73 477	67 544	79 689
Non-residents	TBGN	61 307	100 936	118 909	115 357	139 656	154 976	211 276	289 674	379 695	433 712
CDs and other short-term paper issued	TBGO	101 005	131 620	124 151	151 009	199 510	224 225	234 731	255 590	278 440	341 866
Total foreign currency deposits	TBGP	975 619	1 153 220	1 206 562	1 194 637	1 510 373	1 691 336	1 783 432	2 129 730	2 420 587	2 841 988
Items in suspense and transmission	TBGQ	21 272	35 713	25 026	30 548	46 678	47 363	38 355	60 465	92 173	108 217
Net derivatives	TBGR	..	8 654	2 656	3 704	–4 472	–3 854	5 816	14 774	22 765	3 347
Accrued amounts payable	TBGS	..	21 996	25 184	18 080	18 568	17 756	16 312	15 708	18 214	23 015
Capital and other internal funds	TBGT	25 535	31 676	46 952	69 798	89 359	85 489	87 047	81 778	45 835	93 991
Total foreign currency liabilities	TBGU	1 022 426	1 251 258	1 306 380	1 316 767	1 660 506	1 838 090	1 930 961	2 302 455	2 599 575	3 070 557
Total liabilities	TBGV	1 877 092	2 449 114	2 587 177	2 643 536	3 144 636	3 426 708	3 640 497	4 159 579	4 711 182	5 524 602

23.3 Other banks' balance sheet[1]
continued

£ million

		1996	1997[2]	1998[3]	1999[4]	2000[5,6]	2001	2002	2003	2004	2005
Sterling assets											
Notes and coins	TBGW	4 812	5 225	6 699	9 047	8 007	6 566	6 621	7 464	10 559	9 500
With UK central bank											
Cash ratio deposits	TBGX	1 888	2 566	1 068	1 141	1 275	1 386	1 495	1 609	1 759	1 953
Other	TBGY	533	216	383	676	117	143	249	54	100	1 388
Market loans											
UK banks[7]	TBGZ	109 500	139 996	148 138	144 537	149 174	181 350	237 771	263 004	342 699	438 572
UK bank CDs	TBHB	36 922	62 584	65 510	75 071	65 156	68 868	68 728	55 053	59 505	58 780
UK bank commercial paper	TBHC	..	29	130	208	8	52	62	5	54	75
UK building societies CDs etc and deposits	TBHD	4 891	4 242	4 505	5 093	4 748	3 933	4 293	7 200	7 222	5 655
Non-residents	TBHE	50 585	79 368	84 162	74 403	94 381	102 404	89 848	109 665	102 286	128 343
Acceptances granted											
UK building societies	TBHF	..	–	–	–	–	–	–	–	–	–
UK public sector[8]	TBHG	..	–	–	–	–	–	–	–	–	–
Other UK residents	TBHH	..	18 573	15 394	11 933	9 496	9 992	9 111	2 777	1 348	817
Non-residents	TBHI	..	1 379	1 264	920	516	635	842	79	99	111
Bills											
Treasury bills	TBHJ	1 652	554	779	2 749	1 612	8 474	18 752	18 265	14 507	15 707
UK bank bills	TBHA	..	18 221	14 110	11 426	7 011	8 098	8 491	1 265	646	24
UK building societies	TBHK	..	–	–	–	–	–	–	–	–	–
Other UK	TBHL	..	1 116	1 221	818	1 202	1 601	485	1 013	955	779
Non-residents	TBHM	..	309	207	206	287	744	979	733	702	1 063
Claims under sale and repurchase agreements											
of which British govt. securities	TBHT	26 030	47 158	56 639	64 943	86 362	84 068	77 460	114 091	116 652	187 606
UK banks	TBHO	16 853	27 611	41 969	39 667	46 088	46 585	37 197	77 691	64 353	113 540
UK building societies	TBHP	..	345	134	91	116	327	86	114	263	1 048
UK public sector	TBHQ	..	–	–	–	9 067	4 692	5 159	5 231	10 801	11 695
Other UK residents	TBHR	..	21 283	23 803	30 338	35 058	36 222	31 363	35 885	50 371	61 311
Non-residents	TBHS	..	6 873	5 907	6 310	7 266	7 010	14 271	12 981	20 456	36 261
Advances											
UK public sector	TBHU	2 912	3 872	3 403	2 567	2 746	2 442	3 783	4 414	6 078	6 838
Other UK residents[11]	TBHV	460 107	636 162	672 812	732 649	823 787	891 790	986 835	1 062 650	1 159 833	1 253 553
Non-residents	TBHW	16 759	21 102	21 039	23 364	24 494	29 483	31 380	34 603	38 447	49 223
Banking dept. lending to central govt. (net)	TBNU	948	–2 741	–	–	–	–	–	–	–	–
Investments											
British government stocks	TBHX	19 910	23 078	14 714	9 243	2 867	499	–3 545	–8 525	–4 210	–6 203
Other public sector	TBHY	303	283	215	124	88	116	158	385	328	459
UK banks[12]	TBHZ	..	11 922	13 415	13 584	22 935	23 965	23 542	34 971	34 664	36 365
UK building societies	TBIA	4 898	2 875	2 223	2 506	2 251	2 099	1 835	1 700	1 889	2 068
Other UK residents[13]	TBIB	..	45 134	48 781	57 391	77 647	82 013	76 773	84 813	100 892	112 593
Non-residents	TBIC	..	9 343	11 834	13 775	20 572	23 462	22 821	22 505	26 029	30 487
Items in suspense and collection	TBID	19 830	23 526	23 888	23 441	21 982	24 024	19 577	22 434	22 066	31 417
Accrued amounts receivable	TBIE	..	15 003	17 352	15 173	15 919	13 528	15 486	17 204	19 987	19 510
Other assets	TBIF	10 267	12 218	12 593	13 036	12 654	12 876	12 685	11 955	12 875	15 522
Total sterling assets[14]	TBIG	852 075	1 192 264	1 257 652	1 321 486	1 468 527	1 595 380	1 727 136	1 889 200	2 107 562	2 438 452

23.3 Other banks' balance sheet[1]
continued

£ million

Foreign currency assets		1996	1997[2]	1998[3]	1999[4]	2000[5,6]	2001	2002	2003	2004	2005
Market loans and advances											
UK banks[10]	TBIH	83 920	90 367	72 263	74 250	93 269	104 107	114 809	137 417	149 119	146 316
UK banks' CDs etc	TBII	7 793	13 633	11 065	14 364	13 171	13 298	10 128	13 162	11 026	18 412
UK building societies CDs etc. and deposits	TBIJ	..	83	259	451	173	354	357	591	448	411
UK public sector[8]	TBIK	36	25	45	20	30	13	83	91	50	153
Other UK residents	TBIL	72 213	76 356	83 968	88 847	107 707	118 106	117 669	134 894	153 574	161 488
Non-residents	TBIM	505 953	598 541	616 832	599 146	743 781	783 057	783 168	779 983	839 535	1 013 764
Claims under sale and repurchase agreement											
UK banks	TBIO	21 189	24 184	31 900	28 008	41 801	61 188	91 488	225 027	250 209	272 361
UK building societies	TBIP	..	–	–	–	–	–	–	–	–	100
UK public sector[8]	TBIQ	..	22	–	–	737	23	486	1 420	1 590	1 125
Other UK residents	TBIR	..	55 945	39 764	33 027	57 876	73 237	86 866	100 817	106 973	135 018
Non-residents	TBIS	75 376	121 101	147 562	146 756	199 990	219 449	256 663	382 672	506 157	612 065
Acceptances granted	TBIT	..	743	729	619	689	638	754	751	890	846
Bills	TBIU	9 660	12 728	15 239	19 508	21 878	25 399	20 803	31 429	24 250	24 230
Investments											
British government stocks	TBIV	..	3 453	4 755	4 473	3 518	890	226	19	−20	−30
Other public sector	TBIW	..	–	–	–	–	4	18	7	–	–
UK banks	TBIX	..	2 850	4 310	8 607	11 706	10 633	10 298	11 688	13 187	13 176
UK building societies	TBIY	701	414	526	631	939	850	1 170	1 570	2 400	2 974
Other UK residents	TBIZ	..	4 055	4 584	5 679	12 298	18 129	20 130	21 846	32 882	45 283
Non-residents	TBJA	161 045	186 288	234 563	243 147	297 404	324 073	326 035	334 371	398 040	484 874
Items in suspense and collection	TBJB	21 664	40 175	30 229	29 706	44 885	55 026	44 037	60 804	81 937	112 089
Accrued amounts receivable	TBJC	..	23 673	27 821	20 163	21 279	18 969	19 434	18 129	19 561	22 397
Other assets	TBJD	1 809	2 215	3 111	4 648	2 978	3 880	8 735	13 683	11 802	19 089
Total foreign currency assets[15]	TBJE	1 025 017	1 256 850	1 329 525	1 322 050	1 676 109	1 831 322	1 913 355	2 270 372	2 603 610	3 086 141
Total assets	TBJF	1 877 092	2 449 114	2 587 177	2 643 536	3 144 636	3 426 702	3 640 491	4 159 572	4 711 173	5 524 593
Holdings of own sterling acceptances	TBJG	21 521	1 823	2 137	1 725	1 231	916	1 220	411	265	24
Holdings of own FC acceptances	TBJH	1 031	291	170	150	135	118	58	104	170	222
Eligible banks' total sterling acceptances	TBJI	21 220	21 366	18 722	14 523	10 597	11 320	10 805	3 035	1 217	152
Eligible liabilities	TBJJ	564 648	766 683	807 803	849 289	952 062	1 012 194	1 087 877	1 163 917	1 266 726	1 419 326

1 The implementation of the review of banking at end-September 1997 has resulted in several changes to this table. Details are given in the chapter text.

2 Data for 1997 reflect the entry of Northern Rock plc to the banking sector during the year.

3 With effect from 1998 the balance sheet of the Banking Department of the Bank of England is excluded from these data.

4 Data for 1999 reflect the acquisition of Birmingham Midshires Building Society by Halifax during that year.

5 Data for 2000 reflect the entry of Bradford & Bingley plc to the banking sector during the year.

6 Data for 2000 reflect the new reporting during the year of agency business as a result of collateral management via repos and reverse repos.

7 Sterling sight deposits from UK banks and sterling market loans to UK banks in 2003 were depressed by £19 bn following the consolidation of two banks balance sheets.

8 From 2000 the UK public sector series reflects assumption by the Debt Management Office (an executive agency of HM Treasury) of responsibility for government cash management.

9 There is a break in this series in 1998 as a result of the reclassification of the Issue Department of the Bank of England from UK public sector to UK banks.

10 Foreign currency sight and time deposits from UK banks and foreign currency market loans and advances to UK banks in 2001, 2003 and 2004 were each depressed by £14.5 bn, £0.5 bn and £4.7 bn respectively as a result of positions being consolidated out on the merger of two banks.

11 During 2000, 2001, 2002, 2003, 2004 and 2005 sterling advances to other UK residents were reduced by £10.3 bn, £12.9 bn, £16.2 bn, £29.1bn, £30.4bn and £33.6 bn respectively as a result of securitisations and other loan transfers to non-banks or non-residents.

12 Sterling investments in UK banks in 2000 were boosted by Barclay's £5.8 bn investment in Woolwich.

13 Sterling investments in other UK residents in 2000 were boosted by Lloyds TSB's £5.8 bn investment in Scottish Widows Group.

14 Changes in the reporting populations in 1998, 1999, 2000, 2001, 2003 and 2004 account for a net decrease of £7.3 bn, £11.3 bn £0.8 bn, £0.7bn, £0.2 bn and £4.5 bn respectively in sterling assets outstanding.

15 Changes in the reporting populations in 1998, 1999, 2000, 2001, 2003 and 2004 account for a net decrease of £4.6 bn, £6.6 bn, £0.2 bn, £0.2 bn £0.2 bn and £5.2 bn of foreign currency assets outstanding.

Source: Bank of England: 020 7601 3236

23.4 Industrial analysis of bank lending to UK residents[1]
Not seasonally adjusted

£ million

	UK residents					Manufacturing			
	Total	of which sterling	Agriculture, hunting and forestry	Fishing	Mining & quarrying	Total	Food, beverages & tobacco	Textiles & leather	Pulp, paper, publishing & printing
Amounts outstanding (sterling & other currencies)									
Loans & advances (including under repo & sterling commercial paper)									
	TBOA	TBOB	TBOC	TBOD	TBOE	TBOF	TBOG	TBOH	TBOI
2004	1 490 670	1 227 856	8 288	387	2 326	40 896	8 814	1 753	5 563
2005	1 633 521	1 334 349	9 363	371	3 262	48 485	11 817	1 641	6 931
Acceptances									
	TBQA	TBQB	TBQC	TBQD	TBQE	TBQF	TBQG	TBQH	TBQI
2004	1 588	1 346	–	–	77	418	126	35	8
2005	1 015	816	–	1	2	83	7	26	1
Total									
	TBSA		TBSC	TBSD	TBSE	TBSF	TBSG	TBSH	TBSI
2004	1 492 258		8 288	387	2 403	41 315	8 939	1 788	5 571
2005	1 634 536		9 363	371	3 264	48 568	11 824	1 668	6 932
of which in sterling									
	TBUA		TBUC	TBUD	TBUE	TBUF	TBUG	TBUH	TBUI
2004	1 229 202		8 179	380	1 249	29 102	7 280	1 235	4 376
2005	1 335 165		9 218	360	1 352	31 509	9 180	1 100	4 898
Facilities granted									
	TCAA		TCAC	TCAD	TCAE	TCAF	TCAG	TCAH	TCAI
2004	1 823 061		10 762	449	9 251	80 540	19 765	2 518	10 675
2005	1 988 039		11 700	463	11 483	87 320	23 519	2 488	11 885
of which in sterling									
	TCCA		TCCC	TCCD	TCCE	TCCF	TCCG	TCCH	TCCI
2004	1 491 778		..	441	2 547	51 962	12 556	1 881	7 183
2005	1 602 021		..	452	2 534	52 314	14 792	1 677	7 056

	Manufacturing					Electricity, gas and water supply		
	Chemicals, man-made fibres, rubber & plastics	Non-metallic mineral products & metals	Machinery, equipment & transport equipment	Electrical, medical & optical equipment	Other manufacturing	Electricity, gas & heated water	Cold water purification & supply	Construction
Amounts outstanding (sterling & other currencies)								
Loans & advances (including under repo & sterling commercial paper)								
	TBOJ	TBOK	TBOL	TBOM	TBON	TBOO	TBOP	TBOQ
2004	4 497	5 026	6 427	3 797	5 020	3 876	1 474	17 363
2005	6 253	5 242	7 085	4 267	5 250	4 992	1 163	19 154
Acceptances								
	TBQJ	TBQK	TBQL	TBQM	TBQN	TBQO	TBQP	TBQQ
2004	31	13	55	106	45	–	–	9
2005	5	9	8	7	19	–	2	2
Total								
	TBSJ	TBSK	TBSL	TBSM	TBSN	TBSO	TBSP	TBSQ
2004	..	5 039	6 482	..	5 065	3 876	1 474	17 372
2005	..	5 251	7 093	..	5 269	4 992	1 165	19 155
of which in sterling								
	TBUJ	TBUK	TBUL	TBUM	TBUN	TBUO	TBUP	TBUQ
2004	2 678	3 413	3 827	2 380	3 915	2 761	1 429	16 872
2005	2 933	2 951	3 875	2 468	4 105	4 149	1 130	18 545
Facilities granted								
	TCAJ	TCAK	TCAL	TCAM	TCAN	TCAO	TCAP	TCAQ
2004	..	8 979	12 882	6 950	7 959	13 223	5 382	28 591
2005	..	8 896	12 912	7 053	8 107	13 456	6 079	32 720
of which in sterling								
	TCCJ	TCCK	TCCL	TCCM	TCCN	TCCO	TCCP	TCCQ
2004	6 101	6 149	8 115	4 164	5 814	8 740	4 487	26 765
2005	5 680	5 445	7 749	4 008	5 908	8 576	4 944	29 988

23.4 continued
Industrial analysis of bank lending to UK residents[1]
Not seasonally adjusted

£ million

		Wholesale and retail trade					Real estate, renting, computer and other business activities		
	Total	Sale & repair of motor vehicles & fuel	Other wholesale trade	Other retail trade & repair	Hotels and restaurants	Transport, storage & communication	Total	Development, buying, selling, renting of real estate	Renting of machinery & equipment

Amounts outstanding (sterling & other currencies)

Loans & advances (including under repo & sterling commercial paper)

	TBOR	TBOS	TBOT	TBOU	TBOV	TBOW	TBOX	TBOY	TBPA
2004	35 473	9 634	11 508	14 331	23 600	20 545	149 028	116 051	5 836
2005	40 548	9 293	13 312	17 943	25 064	20 836	177 151	137 281	6 661

Acceptances

	TBQR	TBQS	TBQT	TBQU	TBQV	TBQW	TBQX	TBQY	TBRA
2004	370	25	260	85	1	–	449	430	1
2005	151	7	120	25	–	–	721	714	–

Total

	TBSR	TBSS	TBST	TBSU	TBSV	TBSW	TBSX	TBSY	TBTA
2004	35 843	9 659	11 768	14 416	..	20 545	149 477	116 481	5 837
2005	40 699	9 300	13 431	17 968	..	20 837	177 873	137 995	6 662

of which in sterling

	TBUR	TBUS	TBUT	TBUU	TBUV	TBUW	TBUX	TBUY	TBVA
2004	31 016	9 368	8 432	13 216	21 658	16 888	144 108	114 936	5 331
2005	34 325	8 787	9 644	15 894	23 568	16 531	169 826	135 928	6 028

Facilities granted

	TCAR	TCAS	TCAT	TCAU	TCAV	TCAW	TCAX	TCAY	TCBA
2004	58 212	12 329	18 835	27 048	30 842	41 661	196 919	148 825	7 024
2005	64 698	12 315	20 760	31 623	32 991	40 836	231 334	174 198	8 583

of which in sterling

	TCCR	TCCS	TCCT	TCCU	TCCV	TCCW	TCCX	TCCY	TCDA
2004	49 079	11 627	14 091	23 361	27 763	28 676	186 881	145 742	6 177
2005	52 234	11 344	14 861	26 029	29 915	26 062	216 641	169 994	7 529

Real estate, renting, computer and other business activities					Recreational, personal & community service activities		Financial intermediation (excl. insurance & pension funds)	
Computer & related activities	Legal, accountancy, consultancy & other business activities	Public administration & defence	Education	Health & social work	Recreational, cultural & sporting activities	Personal & community services activities	Total	Financial leasing corporations

Amounts outstanding (sterling & other currencies)

Loans & advances (including under repo & sterling commercial paper)

	TBPB	TBPC	TBPD	TBPE	TBPF	TBPH	TBPG	TBPI	TBPJ
2004	2 869	24 273	18 302	5 231	10 327	8 712	4 755	393 419	34 066
2005	3 752	29 458	19 590	6 317	12 729	10 025	5 304	423 088	36 770

Acceptances

	TBRB	TBRC	TBRD	TBRE	TBRF	TBRH	TBRG	TBRI	TBRJ
2004	2	16	–	–	–	40	4	218	75
2005	–	7	–	–	–	–	4	48	–

Total

	TBTB	TBTC	TBTD	TBTE	TBTF	TBTH	TBTG	TBTI	TBTJ
2004	2 871	..	18 302	5 231	10 327	8 752	4 759	393 637	34 141
2005	3 752	..	19 590	6 317	12 729	10 025	5 308	423 136	36 770

of which in sterling

	TBVB	TBVC	TBVD	TBVE	TBVF	TBVH	TBVG	TBVI	TBVJ
2004	2 234	21 607	16 669	5 163	10 263	8 006	4 395	194 870	31 547
2005	2 658	25 212	18 266	6 263	12 522	9 073	4 619	206 494	32 472

Facilities granted

	TCBB	TCBC	TCBD	TCBE	TCBF	TCBH	TCBG	TCBI	TCBJ
2004	4 527	36 543	20 196	6 791	12 621	13 928	6 370	438 728	39 208
2005	5 730	42 823	21 857	8 551	15 651	15 786	7 281	473 278	42 091

of which in sterling

	TCDB	TCDC	TCDD	TCDE	TCDF	TCDH	TCDG	TCDI	TCDJ
2004	3 460	31 501	18 388	6 722	12 439	11 853	5 888	225 207	36 125
2005	3 956	35 162	20 426	8 397	15 275	13 148	6 324	235 343	37 390

23.4 continued Industrial analysis of bank lending to UK residents[1]
Not seasonally adjusted

£ million

| | Financial intermediation (excl. insurance & pension funds) | | | | | | | | |
	Non-bank credit grantors, excl. credit unions	Credit unions	Factoring corporations	Mortgage & housing credit corporations	Investment & unit trusts excl. money market mutual funds	Money market mutual funds	Bank holding companies	Securities dealers (f)	Other financial intermediaries
Amounts outstanding (sterling & other currencies)									
Loans & advances (including under repo & sterling commercial paper)									
	TBPK	TBPL	TBPM	TBPN	TBPO	TBPP	TBPQ	TBPR	TBPS
2004	15 318	4	4 143	52 656	16 662	970	16 896	166 097	86 607
2005	17 833	28	4 633	62 869	20 394	1 377	19 707	165 562	93 916
Acceptances									
	TBRK	TBRL	TBRM	TBRN	TBRO	TBRP	TBRQ	TBRR	TBRS
2004	17	5	70	–	–	–	–	–	49
2005	15	5	–	–	–	–	–	–	27
Total									
	TBTK	TBTL	TBTM	TBTN	TBTO	TBTP	TBTQ	TBTR	TBTS
2004	15 335	9	4 213	52 656	16 662	970	16 896	166 097	86 657
2005	17 848	33	4 633	62 869	20 394	1 377	19 707	165 562	93 943
of which in sterling									
	TBVK	TBVL	TBVM	TBVN	TBVO	TBVP	TBVQ	TBVR	TBVS
2004	13 937	8	3 425	52 260	4 922	275	11 653	24 094	52 748
2005	16 512	33	3 914	58 500	5 743	265	13 084	22 948	53 024
Facilities granted									
	TCBK	TCBL	TCBM	TCBN	TCBO	TCBP	TCBQ	TCBR	TCBS
2004	18 082	35	4 588	55 419	27 302	1 016	17 131	169 311	106 635
2005	20 883	39	4 994	65 575	28 756	1 425	20 534	168 931	120 052
of which in sterling									
	TCDK	TCDL	TCDM	TCDN	TCDO	TCDP	TCDQ	TCDR	TCDS
2004	16 394	10	3 764	54 996	13 706	275	11 817	25 147	62 974
2005	18 998	39	4 235	61 111	12 176	266	13 329	23 822	63 977

| | Activities auxiliary to financial intermediation | | | Individuals & individual trusts | | |
	Insurance companies & pension funds	Fund management activities	Other	Total	Lending secured on dwellings inc. bridging finance	Other loans & advances
Amounts outstanding (sterling & other currencies)						
Loans & advances (including under repo & sterling commercial paper)						
	TBPT	TBPU	TBPV	TBPW	TBPX	TBPY
2004	20 059	14 038	44 955	667 615	529 661	137 954
2005	23 331	26 669	53 903	702 175	558 805	143 371
Acceptances						
	TBRT	TBRU	TBRV			
2004	–	–	–			
2005	1	–	–			
Total						
	TBTT	TBTU	TBTV	TBTW	TBTX	TBTY
2004	20 060	14 038	44 955	667 615	529 661	137 954
2005	23 331	26 669	53 903	702 175	558 805	143 371
of which in sterling						
	TBVT	TBVU	TBVV	TBVW	TBVX	TBVY
2004	18 895	10 453	20 031	666 816	..	137 270
2005	21 584	16 520	28 090	701 220	..	142 605
Facilities granted						
	TCBT	TCBU	TCBV	TCBW	TCBX	TCBY
2004	29 331	18 366	46 102	754 796	573 784	181 012
2005	32 931	30 745	55 894	792 985	605 078	187 907
of which in sterling						
	TCDT	TCDU	TCDV	TCDW	TCDX	TCDY
2004	25 339	13 301	20 878	753 817	573 654	180 162
2005	27 554	19 438	29 203	791 769	604 884	186 885

1 See chapter text.

Source: Bank of England: 020 7601 3236

Banking, insurance etc.

23.5 Industrial analysis of bank deposits from UK residents[1]

£ million

	Total from UK residents	Agriculture, hunting and forestry	Fishing	Mining & quarrying	Manufacturing			
					Total	Food, beverages & tobacco	Textiles & leather	Pulp, paper, publishing & printing
Amounts outstanding (sterling & other currencies)								
Deposit liabilities (including under repos)								
	TDAA	TDAB	TDAC	TDAD	TDAE	TDAF	TDAG	TDAH
2004	1 122 119	3 803	149	5 473	35 365	3 735	1 190	3 977
2005	1 285 133	3 608	192	7 399	38 471	3 272	1 165	4 262
of which in sterling								
	TDCA	TDCB	TDCC	TDCD	TDCE	TDCF	TDCG	TDCH
2004	941 784	3 760	139	2 272	25 444	2 913	1 008	3 319
2005	1 066 445	3 552	178	3 607	27 337	2 678	983	3 556

	Manufacturing					Electricity, gas and water supply		
	Chemicals, man-made fibres, rubber & plastics	Non-metallic mineral products & metals	Machinery, equipment & transport equipment	Electrical, medical & optical equipment	Other manufacturing	Electricity, gas & heated water	Cold water purification & supply	Construction
Amounts outstanding (sterling & other currencies)								
Deposit liabilities (including under repos)								
	TDAI	TDAJ	TDAK	TDAL	TDAM	TDAN	TDAO	TDAP
2004	4 705	3 878	7 801	6 447	3 631	3 915	1 940	13 390
2005	5 332	4 236	9 754	6 637	3 813	4 782	1 843	14 999
of which in sterling								
	TDCI	TDCJ	TDCK	TDCL	TDCM	TDCN	TDCO	TDCP
2004	2 997	3 145	5 420	3 614	3 029	3 581	1 912	13 182
2005	3 218	3 556	6 617	3 490	3 239	4 122	1 778	14 697

	Wholesale and retail trade				Hotels and restaurants	Transport, storage & communication	Real estate, renting, computer and other business activities		
	Total	Sale & repair of motor vehicles & fuel	Other wholesale trade	Other retail trade & repair			Total	Development, buying, selling, renting of real estate	Renting of machinery & equipment
Amounts outstanding (sterling & other currencies)									
Deposit liabilities (including under repos)									
	TDAQ	TDAR	TDAS	TDAT	TDAU	TDAV	TDAW	TDAX	TDAY
2004	28 892	3 322	12 816	12 754	4 275	18 865	82 820	24 383	1 311
2005	28 901	3 295	13 338	12 268	5 351	18 275	96 900	28 428	1 366
of which in sterling									
	TDCQ	TDCR	TDCS	TDCT	TDCU	TDCV	TDCW	TDCX	TDCY
2004	24 816	3 168	9 680	11 968	4 038	15 397	77 561	24 070	1 247
2005	24 407	3 080	9 952	11 375	5 111	15 038	90 444	27 884	1 294

23.5 Industrial analysis of bank deposits from UK residents[1]
continued

£ million

	Real estate, renting, computer and other business activities					Recreational, personal & community service activities			Financial intermediation (excl. insurance & pension funds)
	Computer & related activities	Legal, accountancy, consultancy & other business activities	Public administration & defence	Education	Health & social work	Recreational, cultural & sporting activities	Personal & community services activities	Total	Financial leasing corporations

Amounts outstanding (sterling & other currencies)

Deposit liabilities (including under repos)

	TDAZ	TDBA	TDBB	TDBC	TDBD	TDBF	TDBE	TDBG	TDBH
2004	6 968	50 157	16 753	6 367	9 546	10 776	13 149	191 077	4 002
2005	7 348	59 758	17 433	7 137	10 617	12 426	13 123	259 657	4 863

of which in sterling

	TDCZ	TDDA	TDDB	TDDC	TDDD	TDDF	TDDE	TDDG	TDDH
2004	5 710	46 535	14 956	6 156	9 278	10 047	12 690	92 704	2 901
2005	6 240	55 025	16 004	6 827	10 282	11 366	12 696	123 601	3 764

Financial intermediation (excl. insurance & pension funds)

	Non-bank credit grantors, excl. credit unions	Credit unions	Factoring corporations	Mortgage & housing credit corporations	Investment & unit trusts excl. money market mutual funds	Money market mutual funds	Bank holding companies	Securities dealers	Other financial intermediaries

Amounts outstanding (sterling & other currencies)

Deposit liabilities (including under repos)

	TDBI	TDBJ	TDBK	TDBL	TDBM	TDBN	TDBO	TDBP	TDBQ
2004	5 803	315	726	8 197	21 026	453	16 006	69 860	64 689
2005	8 120	384	622	9 325	28 754	187	19 853	95 940	91 609

of which in sterling

	TDDI	TDDJ	TDDK	TDDL	TDDM	TDDN	TDDO	TDDP	TDDQ
2004	4 989	315	405	7 913	12 231	149	5 978	18 200	39 623
2005	5 136	383	454	9 047	14 639	106	7 765	22 461	59 847

Insurance companies & pension funds	Activities auxiliary to financial intermediation		Individuals & individual trusts
	Placed by fund managers	Other	

Amounts outstanding (sterling & other currencies)

Deposit liabilities (including under repos)

	TDBR	TDBS	TDBT	TDBU
2004	55 561	47 586	53 948	518 469
2005	66 347	54 237	67 266	556 169

of which in sterling

	TDDR	TDDS	TDDT	TDDU
2004	48 645	30 019	29 219	515 967
2005	58 843	35 676	47 318	553 563

1 See chapter text.

Source: Bank of England: 020 7601 3236

23.6 Public sector net cash requirement and other counterparts to changes in money stock during the year

Not seasonally adjusted

£ million

		1995	1996	1997	1998	1999	2000	2001	2002	2003	2004	2005
Public sector net cash requirement (surplus)	ABEN	35 374	24 703	12 010	−6 622	−1 607	−37 389	−2 749	18 316	38 829	41 387	41 425
Sales of public sector debt to M4 private sector	KHGZ	−21 635	−18 972	−16 074	1 603	−1 538	13 536	7 748	−9 193	−32 510	..	..
M4 lending[1]	AVBS	57 744	59 129	68 208	63 954	78 088	111 224	82 446	107 655	127 712	156 087	155 934
External and foreign currency finance of the public sector	KHJP	−3 640	−10 884	−2 453	−4 717	6 198	3 616	3 875	2 486	−13 442	..	..
Other external and foreign currency flows[2]	AVBW	−3 456	18 020	24 565	14 033	−44 911	7 153	−21 607	−25 113	−27 161	4 463	27 388
Net non-deposit liabilities (increase)	AVBX	−8 565	−12 652	−5 812	−8 222	−2 936	−31 025	−10 815	−25 149	−20 341	−67 477	−34 362
Money stock (M4)	AUZI	55 885	59 336	80 362	60 125	33 386	67 220	58 868	68 936	73 163	100 115	148 151

1 Bank and building society lending, plus holdings of commercial bills by the Issue Department of the Bank of England.
2 Including sterling lending to non-residents sector.

Source: Bank of England: 020 7601 5468

23.7 Money stock and liquidity

£ million

		1995	1996	1997	1998	1999	2000	2001	2002	2003	2004	2005
Amounts outstanding at end-year												
Notes and coin in circulation with the M4 private sector[1]	VQKT	19 847	20 642	22 242	23 705	26 269	28 174	30 450	31 889	34 010	36 458	37 881
UK private sector sterling non-interest bearing sight deposits[2,3]	AUYA	35 450	38 447	38 937	37 262	43 011	46 604	50 205	46 144	51 160	50 421	56 622
Money stock (M2)[3,4]	VQXV	436 957	460 108	484 659	515 005	559 214	598 260	649 636	704 470	777 233	845 278	923 467
Money stock M4[3]	AUYM	623 385	682 786	721 977	783 240	816 545	884 839	942 433	1 008 678	1 081 121	1 179 117	1 325 278
Changes during the year[5]												
Notes and coin in circulation with the M4 private sector[1]	VQLU	1 178	798	1 609	1 501	2 582	1 957	2 284	1 493	2 189	2 509	1 481
UK private sector sterling non-interest bearing sight deposits[2,3]	AUZA	1 782	3 530	5 350	−624	5 758	3 364	3 831	−5 760	4 575	−512	6 352
Money stock (M2)[3,4]	AUZE	26 570	24 358	36 019	30 910	42 397	38 953	51 730	54 704	71 518	..	..
Money stock M4[3]	AUZI	55 885	59 336	80 362	60 125	33 386	67 220	58 868	68 936	73 163	100 115	148 151

1 The estimates of levels of coin in circulation include allowance for wastage, hoarding, etc.
2 Non-interest bearing deposits are confined to those with institutions included in the United Kingdom banks sector (See Table 23.3).
3 Revised rules on netting of customers' credit balances against their borrowing increased the UK private sector's outstanding balances of deposits and borrowing by £2.5bn at end-December 1993. Within retail deposit, £1.7bn of the increase was in NIB bank deposits. Re-netting during 1994 amounted to £1.7bn. Changes data have been adjusted to exclude these effects. Building societies' data from 1992 onwards are affected by the revised treatment of building society transit items within M4.

4 M2 comprises the UK non-monetary financial institutions and non-public sector, i.e. M4 private sector's holdings of notes and coin together with its sterling denominated retail deposits with UK monetary financial institutions.
5 As far as possible the changes exclude the effect of changes in the number of contributors to the series, and also of the introduction of new statistical returns. Changes are not seasonally adjusted.

Source: Bank of England: 020 7601 5468

23.8 Selected retail banks' base rate[1]
Operative between dates shown

Percentage rates

Date of change	New rate	Date of change	New rate	Date of change	New rate
1986 Jan 9	12.50	Aug 9	11.00		
Mar 19	11.50	Aug 25	11.00-12.00	1997 May 6	6.25
Apr 8	11.00-11.50	Aug 26	12.00	Jun 6	6.25-6.50
Apr 9	11.00	Nov 25	13.00	Jun 9	6.50
Apr 21	10.50			Jul 10	6.75
May 23	10.00-10.50	1989 May 24	14.00	Aug 7	7.00
May 27	10.00	Oct 5	15.00	Nov 6	7.25
Oct 14	10.00-11.00				
Oct 15	11.00	1990 Oct 8	14.00	1998 Jun 4	7.50
				Oct 8	7.25
1987 Mar 10	10.50	1991 Feb 13	13.50	Nov 5	6.75
Mar 18	10.00-10.50	Feb 27	13.00	Dec 10	6.25
Mar 19	10.00	Mar 22	12.50		
Apr 28	9.50-10.00	Apr 12	12.00	1999 Jan 7	6.00
Apr 29	9.50	May 24	11.50	Feb 4	5.50
May 11	9.00	Jul 12	11.00	Apr 8	5.25
Aug 6	9.00-10.00	Sep 4	10.50	Jun 10	5.00
Aug 7	10.00			Sep 8	5.00-5.25
Oct 23	9.50-10.00	1992 May 5	10.00	Sep 10	5.25
Oct 29	9.50	Sep 16[2]	12.00	Nov 4	5.50
Nov 4	9.00-9.50	Sep 17[2]	10.00-12.00		
Nov 5	9.00	Sep 18	10.00	2000 Jan 13	5.75
Dec 4	8.50	Sep 22	9.00	Feb 10	6.00
		Oct 16	8.00-9.00		
1988 Feb 2	9.00	Oct 19	8.00	2001 Feb 8	5.75
Mar 17	8.50-9.00	Nov 13	7.00	Apr 5	5.50
Mar 18	8.50			May 10	5.25
Apr 11	8.00	1993 Jan 26	6.00	Aug 2	5.00
May 17	7.50-8.00	Nov 23	5.50	Sep 18	4.75
May 18	7.50			Oct 4	4.50
Jun 2	7.50-8.00	1994 Feb 8	5.25	Nov 8	4.00
Jun 3	8.00	Sep 12	5.75		
Jun 6	8.00-8.50	Dec 7	6.25	2003 Feb 6	3.75
Jun 7	8.50			Jul 10	3.50
Jun 22	8.50-9.00	1995 Feb 2[2]	6.25-6.75	Nov 6	3.75
Jun 23	9.00	Feb 3	6.75		
Jun 28	9.00-9.50	Dec 13	6.50	2004 Feb 5	4.00
Jun 29	9.50			May 6	4.25
Jul 4	9.50-10.00	1996 Jan 18	6.25	Jun 10	4.50
Jul 5	10.00	Mar 8	6.00	Aug 5	4.75
Jul 18	10.00-10.50	Jun 6	5.75		
Jul 19	10.50	Oct 30	5.75-6.00	2005 Aug 4	4.50
Aug 8	10.50-11.00	Oct 31	6.00		

1 Data obtained from Barclays Bank, Lloyds/TSB Bank, HSBC Bank and National Westminster Bank whose rates are used to compile this series.
2 Where all the rates did not change on the same day a spread is shown.

Source: Bank of England: 020 7601 3644

23.9 Average three month sterling money market rates[1]

Percentage rates

	1995	1996	1997	1998	1999	2000	2001	2002	2003	2004	2005
Treasury bills:[2] KDMM											
January	5.93	6.08	6.01	6.80	5.28	5.72	5.49	3.83	3.80	3.90	4.66
February	6.16	5.94	5.81	6.88	5.04	5.83	5.46	3.87	3.50	3.98	4.69
March	6.09	5.79	5.92	6.95	4.92	5.86	5.23	3.97	3.47	4.10	4.77
April	6.30	5.80	6.09	7.00	4.90	5.92	5.12	3.97	3.45	4.19	4.70
May	6.20	5.82	6.15	7.01	4.93	5.95	4.98	3.95	3.44	4.34	4.66
June	6.37	5.58	6.37	7.29	4.76	5.85	4.99	3.98	3.47	4.58	4.62
July	6.62	5.49	6.63	7.22	4.76	5.83	5.01	3.84	3.31	4.64	4.46
August	6.58	5.54	6.83	7.19	4.85	5.81	4.72	3.77	3.40	4.72	4.41
September	6.51	5.54	6.88	6.94	5.12	5.78	4.43	3.79	3.52	4.69	4.40
October	6.57	5.61	6.94	6.54	5.23	5.75	4.16	3.75	3.65	4.68	4.40
November	6.40	6.05	7.09	6.31	5.20	5.68	3.78	3.80	3.81	4.66	4.42
December	6.20	6.05	7.07	5.72	5.46	5.62	3.83	3.84	3.83	4.68	4.43
Eligible bill: KDMY[3]											
January	6.41	6.18	6.15	7.28	5.63	5.90	5.64	3.91	3.87	3.94	4.75
February	6.54	6.00	5.99	7.24	5.28	6.01	5.56	3.92	3.65	4.06	4.78
March	6.40	5.87	6.01	7.25	5.11	5.98	5.37	3.99	3.54	4.19	4.88
April	6.44	5.83	6.26	7.24	5.02	6.05	5.21	4.04	3.52	4.28	4.84
May	6.54	5.85	6.31	7.20	5.08	6.09	5.06	4.01	3.52	4.42	4.80
June	6.44	5.66	6.50	7.42	4.94	6.03	5.08	4.04	3.45	4.68	4.76
July	6.66	5.57	6.80	7.49	4.89	5.97	5.07	3.94	3.39	4.75	4.57
August	6.64	5.60	6.95	7.40	4.94	5.97	4.82	3.86	3.42	4.85	4.51
September	6.55	5.63	7.02	7.20	5.16	5.95	4.57	3.86	3.59	4.83	..
October	6.58	5.76	7.10	6.91	5.42	5.92	4.26	3.82	3.69	4.79	..
November	6.49	6.10	7.27	6.52	5.43	5.88	3.85	3.84	3.88	4.78	..
December	6.29	6.18	7.31	6.05	5.59	5.78	3.88	3.71	3.90	4.77	..
Interbank rate: AMIJ											
January	6.56	6.36	6.32	7.48	5.80	6.06	5.76	3.98	3.91	3.99	4.80
February	6.75	6.16	6.19	7.46	5.43	6.15	5.69	3.98	3.69	4.10	4.82
March	6.66	6.05	6.20	7.48	5.30	6.15	5.47	4.06	3.58	4.23	4.92
April	6.67	6.00	6.38	7.44	5.23	6.21	5.33	4.11	3.58	4.33	4.88
May	6.72	6.02	6.45	7.41	5.25	6.23	5.17	4.08	3.57	4.46	4.83
June	6.64	5.85	6.66	7.63	5.12	6.14	5.19	4.11	3.57	4.73	4.78
July	6.80	5.73	6.96	7.71	5.07	6.11	5.19	3.99	3.42	4.79	4.59
August	6.79	5.75	7.15	7.66	5.18	6.14	4.93	3.92	3.45	4.89	4.53
September	6.72	5.77	7.21	7.38	5.32	6.12	4.65	3.93	3.63	4.87	4.54
October	6.73	5.94	7.26	7.14	5.94	6.08	4.36	3.90	3.73	4.83	4.53
November	6.64	6.30	7.54	6.89	5.78	6.00	3.93	3.91	3.91	4.82	4.56
December	6.49	6.35	7.62	6.38	5.97	5.89	3.99	3.95	3.95	4.81	4.59
Certificate of deposits: KOSA											
January	6.48	6.31	6.27	7.44	5.74	6.02	5.73	3.96	3.90	3.98	4.80
February	6.67	6.11	6.14	7.42	5.38	6.10	5.66	3.96	3.68	4.09	4.82
March	6.59	6.01	6.15	7.43	5.26	6.09	5.44	4.04	3.57	4.22	4.91
April	6.62	5.96	6.33	7.40	5.19	6.17	5.30	4.08	3.57	4.32	4.86
May	6.66	5.98	6.39	7.37	5.22	6.19	5.15	4.06	3.56	4.45	4.82
June	6.56	5.79	6.62	7.59	5.09	6.10	5.16	4.09	3.56	4.72	4.78
July	6.72	5.69	6.92	7.66	5.03	6.08	5.17	3.97	3.41	4.79	4.60
August	6.73	5.71	7.12	7.61	5.14	6.08	4.90	3.90	3.44	4.89	4.53
September	6.66	5.74	7.17	7.34	5.28	6.08	4.62	3.91	3.62	4.87	4.54
October	6.68	5.89	7.22	7.09	5.86	6.05	4.33	3.88	3.72	4.83	4.53
November	6.58	6.25	7.50	6.82	5.72	5.98	3.91	3.89	3.90	4.81	4.57
December	6.44	6.29	7.57	6.32	5.89	5.85	3.96	3.93	3.94	4.80	4.59
Local authority deposits: KDPX[4]											
January	6.52	6.31	6.27	7.43	5.76	6.03	5.73	3.85	3.87	3.91	..
February	6.69	6.13	6.15	7.40	5.38	6.09	5.62	3.88	3.61	4.08	..
March	6.59	6.02	6.14	7.40	5.27	6.08	5.39	4.01	3.55	4.12	..
April	6.60	5.98	6.33	7.38	5.17	6.12	5.26	4.05	3.54	4.31	..
May	6.68	6.00	6.38	7.34	5.19	6.14	5.13	4.06	3.54	4.45	..
June	6.58	5.80	6.57	7.56	5.07	6.09	5.10	4.05	3.57	4.75	..
July	6.76	5.69	6.90	7.64	5.01	6.04	5.12	3.95	3.39	4.82	..
August	6.74	5.71	7.11	7.55	5.11	6.06	4.86	3.87	3.43	4.92	..
September	6.65	5.72	7.19	7.35	5.19	6.05	4.58	3.88	3.61	4.90	..
October	6.68	5.86	7.21	7.08	5.83	6.03	4.29	3.86	3.71	4.85	..
November	6.60	6.24	7.49	6.85	5.64	5.96	3.82	3.87	3.90	4.84	..
December	6.43	6.30	7.56	6.35	5.88	5.80	3.87	3.93	3.92	4.82	..

1 A full definition of these series is given in Section 7 of the ONS Financial Statistics Explanatory Handbook.
2 Average rate of discount at weekly (Friday) tender.
3 This series discontinued at end of August 2005.
4 This series discontinued at end of December 2004.

Source: Bank of England: 020 7601 3644

23.10 Average foreign exchange rates[1]

	1995	1996	1997	1998	1999	2000	2001	2002	2003	2004	2005
Sterling exchange rate index (1990 = 100) AGBG											
January	88.5	83.2	95.9	104.7	99.6	108.5	104.4	106.9	104.0	102.4	102.1
February	87.4	83.8	97.4	104.7	100.8	108.4	104.1	107.4	102.4	104.8	103.3
March	85.6	83.5	97.4	106.8	102.8	108.4	105.0	106.5	100.6	105.0	103.2
April	84.5	83.8	99.5	107.1	103.4	110.1	105.8	107.1	99.8	105.2	104.4
May	84.3	84.6	99.0	103.4	104.2	108.5	106.6	105.3	97.9	104.6	103.6
June	84.1	86.0	100.4	105.4	104.7	104.6	106.8	103.6	99.6	105.8	104.9
July	83.6	85.7	104.5	105.3	103.5	105.6	107.2	105.3	99.4	105.9	102.1
August	84.4	84.7	102.5	104.6	103.3	107.4	105.1	105.4	99.0	105.2	102.8
September	84.8	86.1	100.4	103.3	104.7	106.2	106.1	106.5	99.2	103.3	103.9
October	84.3	88.4	101.1	100.7	105.4	109.2	105.8	106.7	99.8	102.2	103.1
November	83.3	92.0	103.8	100.6	105.7	107.3	106.1	105.9	100.4	101.7	103.2
December	82.9	93.8	104.4	100.4	106.7	106.4	106.5	105.5	100.3	103.2	103.3
Sterling/US Dollar AUSS											
January	1.5747	1.5306	1.6587	1.6353	1.6509	1.6402	1.4769	1.4323	1.6169	1.8234	1.8764
February	1.5720	1.5364	1.6246	1.6407	1.6276	1.5998	1.4529	1.4231	1.6046	1.8673	1.8871
March	1.6005	1.5271	1.6063	1.6620	1.6220	1.5802	1.4454	1.4225	1.5836	1.8267	1.9078
April	1.6074	1.5145	1.6295	1.6733	1.6105	1.5837	1.4350	1.4434	1.5747	1.8005	1.8960
May	1.5868	1.5152	1.6334	1.6366	1.6154	1.5075	1.4259	1.4593	1.6230	1.7876	1.8538
June	1.5949	1.5418	1.6446	1.6507	1.5950	1.5089	1.4014	1.4863	1.6606	1.8275	1.8179
July	1.5953	1.5539	1.6702	1.6437	1.5747	1.5088	1.4139	1.5546	1.6242	1.8429	1.7509
August	1.5681	1.5502	1.6034	1.6320	1.6073	1.4910	1.4365	1.5377	1.5950	1.8216	1.7943
September	1.5584	1.5597	1.6015	1.6822	1.6243	1.4355	1.4635	1.5561	1.6131	1.7922	1.8081
October	1.5779	1.5862	1.6329	1.6952	1.6572	1.4511	1.4517	1.5574	1.6787	1.8065	1.7640
November	1.5623	1.6626	1.6890	1.6620	1.6214	1.4256	1.4358	1.5723	1.6901	1.8603	1.7341
December	1.5398	1.6647	1.6597	1.6705	1.6132	1.4625	1.4409	1.5863	1.7507	1.9275	1.7462
Sterling/Euro THAP											
January	1.2525	1.1631	1.3559	1.5166	1.4236	1.6201	1.5753	1.6222	1.5222	1.4447	1.4331
February	1.2331	1.1707	1.3906	1.5196	1.4534	1.6266	1.5786	1.6348	1.4893	1.4774	1.4499
March	1.2038	1.1692	1.3944	1.5507	1.4902	1.6377	1.5901	1.6224	1.4649	1.4890	1.4440
April	1.1890	1.1763	1.4243	1.5490	1.5051	1.6730	1.6084	1.6282	1.4505	1.5022	1.4652
May	1.1893	1.1923	1.4217	1.4834	1.5185	1.6655	1.6304	1.5914	1.4030	1.4894	1.4611
June	1.1828	1.2094	1.4499	1.5110	1.5374	1.5882	1.6434	1.5515	1.4234	1.5050	1.4952
July	1.1693	1.2007	1.5247	1.5091	1.5204	1.6052	1.6433	1.5665	1.4277	1.5023	1.4547
August	1.1836	1.1845	1.5043	1.4912	1.5146	1.6478	1.5955	1.5723	1.4286	1.4933	1.4592
September	1.1903	1.2066	1.4591	1.4617	1.5458	1.6471	1.6060	1.5861	1.4338	1.4676	1.4761
October	1.1759	1.2407	1.4623	1.4200	1.5491	1.6994	1.6024	1.5868	1.4334	1.4455	1.4674
November	1.1612	1.2873	1.4914	1.4290	1.5706	1.6664	1.6166	1.5694	1.4426	1.4311	1.4719
December	1.1589	1.3192	1.5053	1.4254	1.5953	1.6302	1.6151	1.5566	1.4246	1.4401	1.4725

1 Working day average. A full definition of these series is given in Section 7 of the ONS Explanatory Handbook.

Source: Bank of England: 020 7601 3644

23.11 Average zero coupon yields[1]

Percentage rates

	1995	1996	1997	1998	1999	2000	2001	2002	2003	2004	2005
Nominal Five Year Yield ZBRG											
January	8.63	6.85	7.15	6.18	4.30	6.28	5.07	4.90	4.15	4.61	4.43
February	8.53	7.12	6.82	6.10	4.46	6.13	5.04	4.94	3.88	4.63	4.53
March	8.45	7.45	7.07	6.09	4.69	5.89	4.86	5.22	3.94	4.56	4.73
April	8.25	7.52	7.28	5.93	4.66	5.80	4.96	5.21	4.10	4.80	4.54
May	7.95	7.53	6.94	5.95	4.95	5.82	5.14	5.22	3.85	5.01	4.31
June	7.77	7.46	6.96	6.04	5.28	5.61	5.25	5.05	3.72	5.15	4.17
July	7.89	7.30	7.01	6.12	5.49	5.58	5.26	4.88	3.98	5.07	4.16
August	7.70	7.19	6.97	5.80	5.75	5.65	5.03	4.54	4.36	4.96	4.23
September	7.47	7.18	6.72	5.32	6.00	5.65	4.90	4.31	4.46	4.83	4.12
October	7.56	6.97	6.51	4.94	6.25	5.46	4.74	4.36	4.73	4.66	4.26
November	7.21	7.18	6.69	4.92	5.86	5.33	4.55	4.38	4.91	4.58	4.29
December	6.88	7.20	6.46	4.51	5.90	5.14	4.88	4.34	4.71	4.43	4.21
Nominal Ten Year Yield ZBRH											
January	8.57	7.46	7.52	5.96	4.24	5.62	4.75	4.85	4.39	4.76	4.50
February	8.50	7.80	7.15	5.91	4.39	5.44	4.90	4.90	4.25	4.78	4.54
March	8.45	8.08	7.41	5.85	4.60	5.18	4.64	5.18	4.35	4.67	4.74
April	8.31	8.06	7.58	5.69	4.53	5.14	4.90	5.19	4.49	4.92	4.57
May	8.07	8.10	7.08	5.73	4.83	5.23	5.05	5.22	4.24	5.06	4.38
June	8.04	8.09	7.04	5.60	5.07	5.05	5.11	5.05	4.13	5.13	4.25
July	8.20	7.96	6.92	5.65	5.24	5.09	5.10	4.95	4.43	5.04	4.27
August	8.07	7.86	6.97	5.41	5.25	5.18	4.88	4.68	4.59	4.95	4.29
September	7.93	7.86	6.70	5.03	5.51	5.25	4.91	4.47	4.68	4.86	4.17
October	8.09	7.56	6.37	4.93	5.68	5.09	4.77	4.60	4.88	4.72	4.31
November	7.78	7.56	6.46	4.83	5.11	4.98	4.58	4.62	5.03	4.65	4.26
December	7.52	7.52	6.22	4.44	5.19	4.80	4.83	4.55	4.87	4.49	4.17
Nominal Twenty Year Yield ZBRI											
January	8.23	7.89	7.74	5.94	4.36	4.45	4.33	4.69	4.46	4.70	4.43
February	8.16	8.19	7.39	5.88	4.44	4.38	4.42	4.72	4.40	4.73	4.44
March	8.15	8.37	7.59	5.78	4.60	4.25	4.45	4.99	4.56	4.63	4.66
April	8.09	8.30	7.73	5.61	4.53	4.35	4.76	5.02	4.69	4.81	4.53
May	7.92	8.38	7.16	5.67	4.75	4.40	4.87	5.08	4.49	4.91	4.37
June	7.98	8.41	7.08	5.42	4.77	4.37	4.98	4.93	4.44	4.89	4.27
July	8.24	8.34	6.80	5.45	4.67	4.38	4.90	4.82	4.71	4.82	4.31
August	8.14	8.26	6.86	5.30	4.53	4.49	4.69	4.57	4.69	4.70	4.31
September	8.05	8.27	6.64	4.91	4.62	4.63	4.88	4.40	4.74	4.65	4.19
October	8.30	7.98	6.36	4.87	4.56	4.61	4.92	4.54	4.82	4.59	4.28
November	7.98	7.81	6.37	4.73	4.07	4.39	4.53	4.60	4.88	4.50	4.18
December	7.80	7.67	6.17	4.47	4.20	4.30	4.65	4.59	4.77	4.40	4.06
Real Ten Year Yield ZBRJ											
January	3.87	3.42	3.45	3.10	2.00	2.10	2.22	2.52	2.00	1.94	1.75
February	3.86	3.54	3.27	3.06	1.91	2.17	2.27	2.50	1.74	1.96	1.77
March	3.87	3.67	3.43	3.00	1.85	2.05	2.33	2.53	1.79	1.81	1.87
April	3.79	3.63	3.56	2.91	1.70	2.08	2.56	2.43	1.96	1.93	1.76
May	3.57	3.72	3.57	2.92	1.91	2.14	2.58	2.43	1.81	2.05	1.70
June	3.56	3.77	3.66	2.85	1.89	2.12	2.54	2.33	1.67	2.10	1.65
July	3.58	3.70	3.62	2.77	1.90	2.14	2.56	2.42	1.83	2.07	1.65
August	3.48	3.58	3.60	2.65	2.19	2.25	2.42	2.33	1.95	2.04	1.61
September	3.45	3.57	3.52	2.59	2.31	2.28	2.51	2.20	2.04	1.97	1.51
October	3.63	3.41	3.23	2.67	2.26	2.33	2.53	2.36	2.15	1.89	1.57
November	3.52	3.43	3.25	2.40	2.05	2.34	2.39	2.33	2.21	1.88	1.54
December	3.43	3.42	3.11	2.11	1.98	2.23	2.58	2.24	2.03	1.76	1.47
Real Twenty Year Yield ZBRK											
January	3.89	..	3.67	3.06	2.07	2.01	1.88	2.26	2.07	1.96	1.59
February	3.89	3.79	3.49	3.05	1.99	1.95	1.88	2.30	1.96	1.90	1.59
March	3.88	3.81	3.59	2.98	1.93	1.78	1.99	2.32	2.05	1.77	1.72
April	3.80	3.75	3.68	2.85	1.81	1.84	2.25	2.25	2.13	1.85	1.64
May	3.64	3.82	3.66	2.83	1.99	1.91	2.32	2.25	2.04	1.88	1.57
June	3.69	3.86	3.69	2.63	1.97	1.87	2.27	2.17	1.99	1.88	1.53
July	3.71	3.81	3.57	2.58	2.00	1.90	2.24	2.24	2.16	1.87	1.54
August	3.62	3.75	3.57	2.53	2.14	1.96	2.16	2.15	2.14	1.82	1.49
September	3.61	3.76	3.48	2.49	2.26	1.96	2.31	2.06	2.18	1.80	1.40
October	3.73	3.61	3.22	2.59	2.22	1.99	2.32	2.22	2.22	1.77	1.40
November	3.61	3.62	3.18	2.36	1.92	1.94	2.12	2.25	2.21	1.71	1.29
December	3.56	3.62	3.06	2.14	1.87	1.87	2.24	2.21	2.08	1.60	1.20

1 Working day average. Calculated using the Variable Roughness Penalty (VRP) model.

Source: Bank of England: 020 7601 3644

23.12 Average rates on representative British Government Stocks[1]

Percentage rates

	1995	1996	1997	1998	1999	2000	2001	2002	2003	2004	2005
5 Year Conventional Rate KORP											
January	8.61	6.78	7.19	6.33	4.25	6.36	5.17	4.94	4.15	4.59	4.43
February	8.52	7.02	6.86	6.24	4.41	6.23	5.13	4.96	3.88	4.46	4.61
March	8.44	7.56	7.08	6.26	4.65	6.01	4.94	5.23	3.93	4.44	4.77
April	8.26	7.43	7.30	6.11	4.66	5.95	4.97	5.26	4.08	4.66	4.58
May	7.96	7.61	6.98	6.14	4.93	5.97	5.15	5.48	3.83	4.89	4.36
June	7.79	7.52	7.01	6.31	5.27	5.78	5.32	5.10	3.68	5.08	4.24
July	7.90	7.35	7.09	6.14	5.49	5.75	5.34	4.92	3.72	4.98	4.11
August	7.69	7.21	7.02	5.84	5.80	5.81	5.09	4.57	4.30	4.88	4.22
September	7.45	7.20	6.78	5.34	6.04	5.81	4.94	4.25	4.42	4.76	4.18
October	7.54	7.01	6.59	4.88	6.24	5.66	4.78	4.38	4.70	4.57	4.23
November	7.16	7.22	6.79	4.86	5.89	5.50	4.59	4.40	4.88	4.52	4.31
December	6.83	7.26	6.60	4.45	5.91	5.27	4.88	4.34	4.68	4.42	4.27
10 year Conventional Rate KORQ											
January	8.66	7.42	7.53	6.07	4.16	5.75	4.86	4.84	4.37	4.78	4.51
February	8.59	7.75	7.17	6.02	4.32	5.56	4.88	4.91	4.25	4.75	4.60
March	8.53	8.05	7.41	5.97	4.54	5.29	4.75	5.15	4.51	4.65	4.79
April	8.39	8.05	7.60	5.81	4.48	5.25	4.95	5.23	4.64	4.91	4.60
May	8.12	8.08	7.13	5.85	4.77	5.35	5.13	5.51	4.26	5.07	4.38
June	8.08	8.04	7.10	5.77	5.02	5.15	5.09	5.06	4.38	5.19	4.23
July	8.23	7.91	7.01	5.67	5.20	5.18	5.16	4.94	4.23	5.10	4.20
August	8.10	7.81	7.05	5.56	5.24	5.27	4.92	4.66	4.59	4.99	4.25
September	7.92	7.80	6.77	5.10	5.52	5.32	4.92	4.46	4.69	4.89	4.16
October	8.08	7.51	6.47	4.93	5.70	5.15	4.76	4.57	4.89	4.73	4.31
November	7.75	7.56	6.59	4.87	5.16	5.06	4.58	4.59	5.04	4.66	4.33
December	7.45	7.54	6.34	4.49	5.24	4.88	4.88	4.52	4.94	4.50	4.27
20 Year Conventional Rate KORR											
January	8.45	7.73	7.71	6.04	4.36	4.91	4.52	4.81	4.46	4.73	4.55
February	8.43	8.04	7.35	5.98	4.47	4.80	4.58	4.83	4.37	4.80	4.58
March	8.40	8.28	7.58	5.90	4.64	4.64	4.56	5.12	4.51	4.69	4.79
April	8.30	8.26	7.74	5.73	4.58	4.71	4.84	5.14	4.64	4.91	4.63
May	8.09	8.31	7.21	5.79	4.83	4.77	4.98	5.45	4.44	5.03	4.43
June	8.08	8.31	7.15	5.59	4.92	4.68	5.10	5.03	4.38	5.07	4.30
July	8.30	8.21	6.93	5.63	4.88	4.70	5.05	4.92	4.59	4.99	4.33
August	8.19	8.12	6.98	5.43	4.82	4.79	4.83	4.65	4.67	4.88	4.34
September	8.06	8.11	6.74	5.02	4.97	4.90	4.94	4.46	4.74	4.83	4.24
October	8.26	7.84	6.45	4.92	4.97	4.84	4.80	4.59	4.85	4.73	4.37
November	7.93	7.77	6.50	4.79	4.46	4.64	4.55	4.65	4.93	4.64	4.31
December	7.70	7.67	6.32	4.49	4.56	4.51	4.75	4.61	4.80	4.53	4.22
10 Year Index-Linked Rate KORS											
January	3.89	3.42	3.44	3.01	2.00	2.11	2.21	2.61	2.07	1.88	1.73
February	3.87	3.57	3.23	2.94	1.94	2.16	2.30	2.53	1.81	1.90	1.81
March	3.86	3.70	3.41	2.89	1.90	2.06	2.34	2.55	1.88	1.76	1.99
April	3.79	3.66	3.55	2.80	1.74	2.08	2.55	2.45	1.90	1.94	1.83
May	3.58	3.74	3.52	2.83	1.96	2.15	2.61	2.58	1.74	2.10	1.71
June	3.58	3.80	3.62	2.81	1.93	2.13	2.56	2.35	1.59	2.17	1.67
July	3.61	3.82	3.68	2.67	1.93	2.14	2.57	2.46	1.67	2.12	1.66
August	3.52	3.59	3.59	2.55	2.20	2.25	2.45	2.37	1.89	2.04	1.63
September	3.46	3.57	3.47	2.59	2.32	2.29	2.56	2.24	1.99	1.95	1.49
October	3.65	3.41	3.17	2.66	2.26	2.33	2.55	2.42	2.08	1.83	1.89
November	3.54	3.42	3.23	2.39	2.03	2.32	2.42	2.39	2.16	1.85	1.64
December	3.45	3.41	3.01	2.11	1.99	2.20	2.65	2.30	1.97	1.74	1.27
20 Year Index-Linked rate KORT											
January	3.91	3.58	3.62	3.01	2.06	2.01	1.96	2.35	2.10	1.95	1.68
February	3.89	3.70	3.43	3.01	1.97	1.98	1.99	2.36	1.99	1.94	1.72
March	3.89	3.82	3.55	2.92	1.93	1.83	2.09	2.39	2.07	1.80	1.89
April	3.81	3.77	3.65	2.80	1.81	1.90	2.35	2.32	2.10	1.91	1.77
May	3.64	3.84	3.61	2.79	1.99	1.97	2.41	2.43	2.00	1.99	1.67
June	3.67	3.88	3.65	2.61	1.97	1.94	2.38	2.23	1.93	2.01	1.63
July	3.71	3.72	3.68	2.56	1.97	1.96	2.36	2.30	2.05	1.99	1.63
August	3.62	3.75	3.54	2.51	2.12	2.03	2.25	2.21	2.09	1.93	1.58
September	3.60	3.74	3.43	2.51	2.23	2.04	2.39	2.12	2.13	1.89	1.48
October	3.74	3.60	3.17	2.58	2.18	2.08	2.38	2.29	2.17	1.84	1.51
November	3.62	3.59	3.16	2.35	1.91	2.02	2.19	2.31	2.16	1.80	1.45
December	3.55	3.58	3.02	2.12	1.88	1.94	2.33	2.26	2.04	1.69	1.38

1 Working day average.

Source: Bank of England: 020 7601 3644

23.13 Building societies[1,2]
United Kingdom

		1994	1995[3]	1996[3]	1997[3]	1998[3]	1999[3]	2000[4]	2001	2002	2003
Number and balance sheets											
Societies on register (numbers)	KRNA	96	94	88	82	78	72	68	65	65	63
Share investors (thousands)	KRNB	38 150	38 998	37 768	19 234	21 195	21 774	22 237	20 311	20 724	20 901
Depositors (thousands)	KRNC	5 369	6 143	6 718	882	820	642	660	501	440	452
Borrowers (thousands)	KRND	7 222	6 906	6 586	2 703	2 934	2 868	2 925	2 579	2 520	2 520
Assets and liabilities (£ million)											
Liabilities:											
Shares	KRNE	201 812.2	200 682.0	196 546.4	90 092.8	103 289.8	109 137.7	119 298.5	119 815.2	132 372.9	142 477.1
Deposits and loans	KRNF	69 925.2	67 513.8	73 919.1	31 033.7	33 311.2	34 746.6	44 262.4	37 358.9	37 933.0	49 552.6
Taxation and other	KRNG	2 939.2	3 306.2	3 727.4	1 338.8	1 586.4	1 665.4	1 664.0	1 244.9	1 088.4	1 179.0
General reserves	KRNH	16 312.3	17 218.3	17 940.3	7 331.2	7 926.4	8 301.5	8 987.1	8 511.2	9 043.4	9 489.8
Other Capital	KRNI	4 125.7	3 498.0	4 762.3	1 643.9	1 550.7	1 529.2	1 861.0	1 416.1	1 709.2	2 534.7
Assets:											
Mortgages	KRNK	240 297.2	236 841.0	241 472.9	107 531.5	118 288.4	123 183.4	137 072.3	130 229.6	140 839.7	159 938.2
Investments and cash	KHVZ	50 786.7	50 894.1	51 016.7	21 869.8	27 102.0	29 917.8	36 574.2	35 925.9	38 952.7	43 067.9
Other	KRNN	4 030.7	4 483.2	4 405.9	2 039.1	2 274.1	2 279.2	2 426.6	2 190.7	2 354.4	2 226.9
Total	KRNJ	295 114.6	292 218.3	296 895.5	131 440.4	147 664.5	155 380.4	176 073.0	168 346.2	182 146.8	205 233.1
Current transactions (£ million)											
Mortgage advances	KRNU	34 829.0	34 673.0	38 488.0	28 771.7	21 988.3	23 997.9	28 233.6	29 320.0	33 077.0	43 392.4
Management expenses	KRNX	3 136.7	3 352.6	3 555.3	2 270.5	1 501.7	1 573.8	1 640.7	1 528.0	1 623.6	1 746.4

1 See chapter text.

2 The figures for each year relate to accounting years ending on dates between 1 February of that year and 31 January of the following year.

3 The societies which have converted to the banking sector, namely Cheltenham & Gloucester (August 1995), National & Provincial (August 1996), Alliance & Leicester (April 1997), Halifax (June 1997), Woolwich (July 1997), Bristol & West (July 1997), Northern Rock (October 1997), and Birmingham Midshires (April 1999) have been included in flow figures (using flows up to the date of conversion), but have been excluded from the end of year balances.

4 Bradford & Bingley, which converted to the banking sector in December 2000, is included within flow figures and the end of year balances.

Source: Financial Services Authority: 020 7066 1000

23.14 Consumer credit[1]
United Kingdom

£ million

		1995	1996	1997	1998	1999	2000	2001	2002	2003	2004
Total amount outstanding	VZRD	68 202	77 478	88 081	102 222	116 155	128 041	141 718	157 844	167 049	182 856
Total net lending	VZQC	8 234	11 213	12 015	14 511	14 858	14 235	17 719	21 154	20 169	22 941
Retailers	AAPP	−133	75	208	7	103	−285	−27	59	−396	−206
Building societies' class 3 loans	ALPY	238	383	120	–	11	111	68	187	179	171
Banks	AIKN	5 606	7 682	9 027	11 709	10 999	13 195	16 181	17 352	15 377	19 366
of which											
Credit cards	VZQS	2 103	3 029	3 507	4 858	5 676	6 686	6 229	7 579	8 710	9 998
Loans on personal accounts	VTGA	..	..	..	..	..	..	..	..	..	..
Other	VZQT	6 132	8 184	8 509	9 656	9 182	7 550	11 492	13 577	11 459	12 944
Insurance companies	RSBK	39	−83	6	−16	224	−265	−19	4	−481	−40
Non-bank credit companies	-AGSJ	2 222	2 805	2 287	2 409	2 928	676	980	2 865	4 893	3 106
Other specialist lenders	VZQQ	2 485	3 156	2 654	2 810	3 521	1 478	1 516	3 553	5 490	3 650
Total gross lending	VZQG	89 114	103 215	116 079	133 710	147 015	158 711	175 056	193 938	204 570	218 504

1 See chapter text.

Source: Office for National Statistics: 01633 812776

23.15 End-year assets and liabilities of investment trust companies, unit trusts[1] and property unit trusts[2]

United Kingdom

£ million

		1994	1995	1996	1997	1998	1999	2000	2001	2002	2003	2004
Investment trust companies												
Short-term assets and liabilities (net):	CBPL	273	627	1 076	1 157	2 263	71	423	161	–	73	866
Cash and UK bank deposits	AHAG	1 006	1 660	1 424	1 577	2 647	1 227	2 202	2 513	1 821	1 346	1 756
Other short-term assets	CBPN	772	738	794	1 445	1 734	1 097	1 082	656	805	1 189	1 344
Short-term liabilities	-CBPS	–942	–1 120	–805	–1 865	–2 118	–2 253	–2 861	–3 008	–2 626	–2 462	–2 234
Medium and long-term liabilities and capital:	-CBPO	–40 180	–43 882	–50 911	–54 117	–49 985	–57 616	–60 412	–54 630	–38 054	–48 076	–48 627
Issued share and loan capital	-CBPQ	–10 978	–13 250	–8 330	–8 625	–8 837	–8 565	–8 934	–8 796	–8 711	–9 873	–8 210
Foreign currency borrowing	-CBPR	–354	–1 061	–638	–658	–607	–880	–994	–933	–780	–682	–607
Other borrowing	-CBQA	–1 354	–622	–823	–1 296	–1 723	–1 716	–2 503	–3 251	–2 246	–2 181	–1 728
Reserves and provisions, etc	-AHBC	–27 494	–28 949	–41 120	–43 538	–38 818	–46 455	–47 981	–41 650	–26 317	–35 340	–38 082
Investments:	CBPM	39 586	43 410	50 034	53 076	46 313	56 491	59 948	54 822	37 748	48 035	47 212
British government securities	AHBF	2 490	1 194	1 422	1 052	815	1 217	821	645	471	303	466
UK company securities:												
Loan capital and preference shares	CBGZ	1 000	846	832	1 320	1 351	1 425	1 654	1 516	946	1 079	1 270
Ordinary and deferred shares	CBGY	15 926	19 384	25 046	29 082	24 729	28 010	33 456	30 338	19 475	23 292	23 941
Overseas company securities:												
Loan capital and preference shares	CBHA	896	740	279	1 165	768	979	963	1 143	458	603	682
Ordinary and deferred shares	AHCC	17 873	19 485	21 047	17 747	17 741	23 330	21 355	19 476	14 453	20 294	18 967
Other investments	CBPT	1 401	1 761	1 408	2 868	1 051	1 530	1 699	1 704	1 945	2 464	1 886
Unit trusts												
Short-term assets and liabilities:	CBPU	3 266	3 116	3 822	5 048	6 883	5 894	8 340	7 979	8 041	10 256	10 229
Cash and UK bank deposits	AGYE	3 102	3 326	3 895	4 731	6 020	4 797	6 969	5 748	5 321	5 243	6 302
Other short-term assets	CBPW	1 364	986	1 201	869	1 343	1 545	2 319	2 763	3 072	5 990	4 390
Short-term liabilities	-CBPX	–1 200	–1 196	–1 274	–552	–480	–448	–948	–532	–352	–977	–463
Foreign currency borrowing	-AGYK	–21	–1	–	–	–	–	–	–	–	–	–
Investments:	CBPZ	83 495	104 069	125 841	144 038	162 929	213 553	222 844	204 899	210 002	245 516	269 064
British government securities	CBHT	1 414	1 774	2 716	3 087	3 771	3 627	4 693	4 690	7 077	9 125	9 768
UK company securities:												
Loan capital and preference shares	CBHU	2 970	3 298	5 029	6 494	9 290	13 322	14 654	16 318	21 152	23 972	22 467
Ordinary and deferred shares	RLIB	43 335	59 122	67 509	85 742	93 291	119 496	116 808	103 704	82 851	116 407	130 230
Overseas company securities:												
Loan capital and preference shares	CBHV	1 001	2 145	1 288	1 834	1 801	3 032	3 212	4 113	5 916	9 840	13 142
Ordinary and deferred shares	RLIC	33 473	36 062	47 346	42 898	51 119	70 256	79 601	71 329	63 152	75 074	81 034
Other assets	CBQE	1 302	1 668	1 953	2 518	3 657	3 820	3 876	4 800	9 997	11 098	12 801
Property unit trusts												
Short-term assets and liabilities (net)	AGVC	119	280	255	328	176	205	285	247	242	459	466
Property	CBQG	2 197	1 807	2 582	3 895	2 740	2 722	3 488	2 078	4 026	5 125	5 909
Other assets	AGVL	11	11	11	168	202	436	380	151	677	373	1 366
Long-term borrowing	-AGVM	–	–131	–45	–247	–106	–75	–391	–90	–75	–76	–63

Note: Assets are shown as positive: liabilities as negative.
1 Including open ended investment companies (OEICs).
2 Investments are at market value.

Source: Office for National Statistics: 01633 812789

23.16 Self-administered pension funds: market value of assets

United Kingdom

End year

£ million

		1992	1993	1994	1995	1996	1997	1998	1999	2000	2001	2002	2003	2004
Total pension funds[1]														
Total net assets	AHVA	381 997	480 547	443 467	508 581	543 879	656 874	699 191	812 228	765 199	711 572	610 441	692 694	761 066
Short-term assets	RYIQ	18 492	20 279	22 617	26 114	31 521	35 368	39 005	32 703	36 638	31 337	30 700	46 091	57 476
British government securities	AHVK	25 188	34 279	41 854	52 659	57 783	80 533	91 084	98 882	92 458	83 754	84 461	88 803	87 579
UK local authority long-term debt	AHVO	34	81	250	83	89	156	183	133	177	125	42	8	4
Overseas government securities	AHVT	10 529	11 044	11 092	11 721	11 800	13 079	15 493	16 684	19 206	20 383	16 031	16 340	15 075
UK company securities														
Ordinary shares	AHVP	202 311	251 099	219 189	256 625	276 001	339 687	334 648	357 230	299 318	260 696	186 437	186 426	180 561
Other	AHVQ	5 905	5 758	3 935	7 064	6 180	5 618	8 168	9 258	16 978	22 301	30 450	37 082	43 027
Overseas company securities														
Ordinary shares	AHVR	63 276	84 118	74 813	82 164	84 163	104 187	108 884	148 335	135 514	127 893	104 392	125 740	140 282
Other	AHVS	1 787	2 103	3 045	1 184	4 909	3 851	3 842	5 099	12 736	11 781	11 386	12 475	15 996
UK loans and mortgages	RLDQ	232	260	44	34	83	160	22	14	7	3	–	35	44
UK land, property and ground rent	AHWA	19 914	21 932	24 353	21 317	21 637	24 176	24 355	31 107	32 945	30 617	31 658	30 619	30 552
Authorised unit trust units	AHVU	8 569	13 188	13 345	15 212	17 267	21 979	30 596	33 731	34 587	38 083	36 530	62 029	67 482
Property unit trusts	AHVW	1 745	1 905	2 463	2 485	2 666	3 219	3 211	5 498	4 835	5 280	5 869	6 761	10 444
Other assets	RKPL	28 794	38 761	31 318	36 352	30 628	32 978	47 136	82 273	90 841	90 139	82 490	107 229	152 170
Total liabilities	GQFX	4 781	4 261	4 852	4 412	5 347	8 118	7 436	8 719	11 041	10 819	10 005	26 944	39 626

1 These figures cover funded schemes only and therefore exclude the main superannuation arrangements in the central government sector.

Source: Office for National Statistics: 01633 812726

23.17 Insurance companies: balance sheet market values
United Kingdom
End year

£ million

		1995	1996	1997	1998	1999	2000	2001	2002	2003	2004
Long-term insurance companies											
Assets											
Total current assets (gross)	RYEW	24 171	31 699	42 795	46 165	56 360	62 937	63 855	58 122	58 518	63 407
Agents' and reinsurance balances (net)	AHNY	−157	−232	155	1 383	508	384	..	6 373	4 720	..
Other debtors[1]	RKPN	7 565	12 982	15 708	18 210	18 613	21 045	..	34 391	35 414	..
British government securities	AHNJ	80 268	90 996	107 847	127 903	126 223	116 734	119 513	131 305	142 920	157 019
UK local authority securities etc	AHNN	1 322	1 088	914	1 722	1 456	1 170	1 407	1 427	1 547	2 044
UK company securities[2]	RKPO	272 554	304 587	386 734	438 666	539 834	557 293	..	443 535	468 910	..
Overseas company securities	RKPP	59 950	62 378	73 428	82 122	120 665	107 439	..	110 738	110 193	..
Overseas government securities	AHNS	8 793	7 554	8 471	17 515	18 494	18 004	21 285	19 762	20 561	20 161
Loans and mortgages	RKPQ	7 305	6 653	8 271	11 027	10 914	9 687	..	10 994	12 107	..
UK land, property and ground rent	AHNX	35 596	36 209	42 275	45 903	50 387	49 705	53 726	52 658	57 174	60 502
Overseas land, property and ground rent	RGCP	118	114	98	252	206	1 975	498	158	184	94
Other investments	RKPR	2 162	3 886	3 416	5 654	8 334	8 385	..	9 513	17 985	..
Total	RFXN	499 647	557 914	690 112	796 522	951 994	954 760	938 609	878 979	930 233	994 015
Net value of direct investment in:											
Non-insurance subsidiaries and associate companies in the United Kingdom	RYET	2 773	3 033	3 426	3 035	3 045	6 133	4 486	4 577	4 191	3 971
UK associate and subsidiary insurance companies and insurance holding companies	RYEU	701	575	−239	148	2 245	3 586	4 206	4 569	5 054	3 473
Overseas subsidiaries and associates	RYEV	987	986	1 104	1 087	3 638	4 002	5 581	5 463	6 330	2 181
Total assets	RKBI	504 108	562 508	694 403	800 792	960 922	968 481	952 882	893 588	945 808	1 003 640
Liabilities											
Borrowing:											
Borrowing from UK banks	RGDF	1 907	2 234	3 027	3 252	6 064	8 272	8 790	4 958	4 164	5 358
Other UK borrowing	RGDE	796	1 349	786	1 040	3 070	2 823	5 350	7 406	10 923	8 385
Borrowing from overseas	RGDD	79	90	104	148	159	38	81	800	530	793
Long-term business:											
Funds	RKDC	424 866	470 893	581 009	669 301	800 184	838 485	831 051	794 177	824 766	873 071
Claims admitted but not paid	RKBM	1 419	1 441	1 436	1 712	2 032	2 249	2 547	3 234	3 699	3 579
Provision for taxation net of amounts receivable:											
UK authorities	RYPI	502	2 568	4 207	5 443	6 344	5 381	3 951	2 803	4 055	4 881
Overseas authorities	RYPJ	−11	9	25	67	314	67	45	−20	2	−13
Provision for recommended dividends	RYPK	195	276	368	359	201	183	87	32	27	93
Other creditors and liabilities	RYPL	5 979	6 303	8 083	12 509	17 042	19 031	18 468	23 261	15 870	16 738
Excess of assets over above liabilities:											
Excess of value of assets over liabilities in respect of long-term funds	RKBR	63 255	71 817	89 790	96 456	116 951	79 173	63 337	36 517	62 546	65 641
Minority interests in UK subsidiary companies	RKTI	3	–	2	–	25	–	–	–	1	267
Shareholders' capital and reserves in respect of general business	RKBS	2 050	2 576	3 862	6 299	6 139	10 287	17 044	18 629	15 698	20 719
Other reserves including profit and loss account balances	RKBT	3 068	2 952	1 704	4 206	2 396	2 492	2 130	1 791	3 527	4 129
Total liabilities	RKBI	504 108	562 508	694 403	800 792	960 922	968 481	952 882	893 588	945 808	1 003 640

23.17 continued
Insurance companies: balance sheet market values
United Kingdom
End year

£ million

		1995	1996	1997	1998	1999	2000	2001	2002	2003	2004
Other than long-term insurance companies											
Assets											
Total current assets (gross)	RYME	8 318	11 559	12 628	8 524	10 468	8 772	12 264	17 671	20 036	29 258
Agents' and reinsurance balances (net)	AHMX	7 494	11 569	9 405	10 528	12 177	8 362	..	9 492	9 890	..
Other debtors[1]	RKPS	3 403	6 097	5 998	6 277	7 059	7 179	..	14 437	13 255	..
British government securities	AHMJ	14 363	16 893	15 666	16 409	15 938	14 561	15 064	18 390	19 645	19 662
UK local authority securities etc	AHMN	56	42	16	14	10	8	6	10	10	49
UK company securities[2]	RKPT	17 425	17 825	18 845	18 440	18 800	18 585	..	15 362	15 153	..
Overseas company securities	RKPU	4 422	5 072	6 594	8 676	6 284	8 190	..	7 394	7 124	..
Overseas government securities	AHMS	6 511	9 546	8 215	10 459	7 980	6 849	7 134	7 156	5 720	6 662
Loans and mortgages	RKPV	1 337	1 593	1 385	1 335	1 070	1 429	..	1 063	1 400	..
UK land, property and ground rent	AHMW	2 100	2 077	2 842	1 146	1 085	1 069	860	805	859	893
Overseas land, property and ground rent	RYNK	128	120	149	107	83	45	4	1	4	5
Other investments	RKPW	665	716	2 465	2 366	2 638	2 294	..	2 182	1 408	..
Total	RKAL	66 222	83 106	84 208	84 281	84 027	77 343	78 789	93 965	94 504	115 356
Net value of direct investment in:											
Non-insurance subsidiaries and associate companies in the United Kingdom	RYNR	2 449	3 195	6 950	5 553	7 074	7 038	10 456	11 706	13 408	19 028
UK associate and subsidiary insurance companies and insurance holding companies	RYNS	1 642	7 170	4 204	6 424	5 617	5 400	8 837	7 190	2 918	2 280
Overseas subsidiaries and associates	RYNT	15 485	14 859	16 402	14 239	17 775	15 993	14 260	9 014	5 718	5 507
Total assets	RKBY	85 798	108 330	111 764	110 497	114 493	105 774	112 342	121 875	116 548	142 171
Liabilities											
Borrowing:											
Borrowing from UK banks	RYMB	1 584	1 524	3 029	1 825	1 392	783	481	1 384	2 046	4 519
Other UK borrowing	RYMC	2 370	2 536	2 996	1 551	3 186	4 239	10 621	10 472	9 342	10 261
Borrowing from overseas	RYMD	1 876	1 976	1 202	1 600	3 045	1 867	1 964	2 916	2 918	2 476
General business technical reserves	RKCT	47 493	58 618	59 527	60 775	59 455	60 236	60 995	62 776	63 463	67 241
Long-term business:											
Funds	RKTF	–	–	–	–	–	–	–	–	–	–
Claims admitted but not paid	RKTK	–	–	–	–	–	–	–	–	–	–
Provision for taxation net of amounts receivable:											
UK authorities	RYPO	841	807	1 253	1 197	939	874	594	941	834	1 094
Overseas authorities	RYPP	16	22	7	11	11	11	7	5	84	24
Provision for recommended dividends	RYPQ	1 098	1 407	2 048	1 318	1 817	2 682	1 957	958	1 082	1 311
Other creditors and liabilities	RYPR	2 955	3 886	3 873	3 793	4 981	6 293	6 410	8 025	9 567	10 817
Excess of assets over above liabilities:											
Excess of value of assets over liabilities in respect of long-term funds	RKCG	–	–	–	–	–	–	–	–	–	–
Minority interests in UK subsidiary companies	RKCH	22	24	60	68	29	33	276	4	6	6
Shareholders' capital and reserves in respect of general business	RKCI	25 545	35 069	35 172	34 397	35 372	24 699	26 190	31 982	25 153	39 695
Other reserves including profit and loss account balances	RKCJ	1 998	2 461	2 597	4 215	4 265	4 056	2 847	2 411	2 053	4 727
Total liabilities	RKBY	85 798	108 330	111 764	110 497	114 493	105 774	112 342	121 875	116 548	142 171

1 Including outstanding interest, dividends and rents (net).
2 Including authorised unit trust units.

Source: Office for National Statistics: 01633 812726

23.18 Individual insolvencies
United Kingdom

		1994	1995	1996	1997	1998	1999	2000	2001	2002	2003	2004
England and Wales												
Bankruptcies[1]	AIHW	25 634	21 933	21 803	19 892	19 647	21 611	21 550	23 447	24 292	28 021	35 898
Individual voluntary arrangements[2,3]	AIHI	5 105	4 386	4 468	4 549	4 902	7 195	7 978	6 298	6 295	7 583	10 752
Total	AIHK	30 739	26 319	26 271	24 441	24 549	28 806	29 528	29 775	30 587	35 604	46 650
Scotland												
Sequestrations[4]	KRHA	2 182	2 188	2 503	2 502	3 016	3 195	2 965	3 048	3 215	3 328	3 297
Northern Ireland												
Bankruptcies[5]	KRHB	438	399	415	393	394	401	347	292	334	516	666
Individual voluntary arrangements[3,6]	KJRK	84	64	101	84	122	173	260	177	206	314	461
Total	KRHD	522	463	516	477	516	574	607	469	540	830	1 127

1 Comprises receiving and administration orders under the Bankruptcy Act 1914 and bankruptcy orders under the Insolvency Act 1986. Orders later consolidated or rescinded are included in these figures.
2 Introduced under the Insolvency Act 1986.
3 For statistical purposes deeds of arrangement are now included with individual voluntary arrangements.
4 Sequestrations awarded but not brought into operation are included in these figures.

5 Comprises bankruptcy adjudication orders, arrangement protection orders and orders for the administration of estates of deceased insolvents. Orders later set aside or dismissed are included in these figures.
6 Introduced under the Insolvency Northern Ireland order 1989.

Source: Department of Trade and Industry: 020 7215 3291/3305

23.19 Company insolvencies[1]
United Kingdom

		1995	1996	1997	1998	1999	2000	2001	2002	2003	2004	2005
England and Wales												
Compulsory liquidations	AIHR	5 519	5 080	4 735	5 216	5 209	4 925	4 675	6 231	5 234	4 584	5 233
Creditors' voluntary liquidations	AIHS	9 017	8 381	7 875	7 987	9 071	9 392	10 297	10 075	8 950	7 608	7 660
Total	AIHQ	14 536	13 461	12 610	13 203	14 280	14 317	14 972	16 306	14 184	12 192	12 893
Scotland												
Compulsory liquidations	KRGA	252	266	254	338	364	344	378	556	436	431	420
Creditors' voluntary liquidations	KRGB	189	175	223	228	208	239	224	232	195	190	149
Total	KRGC	441	441	477	566	572	583	602	788	631	621	569
Northern Ireland												
Compulsory liquidations	KRGD	72	68	60	53	58	83	60	49	95	73	49
Creditors' voluntary liquidations	KRGE	37	54	53	46	45	53	40	53	48	45	53
Total	KRGF	109	122	113	99	103	136	100	102	143	118	102

1 Prior to 2005Q4 the Department of Trade and Industry published these figures.

Source: Insolvency Service: 020 7637 6504/6443

23.20 Industry analysis: bankruptcies[1,2]
England and Wales

Numbers

		1995	1996	1997	1998	1999	2000	2001	2002	2003	2004	2005
Industry												
Self-employed												
Agriculture and horticulture	KRFY	218	168	155	157	183	173	183	132	151	204	195
Manufacturing:												
Food, drink and tobacco	KRFZ	30	31	18	21	17	18	10	19	14	7	15
Chemicals	KRLA	8	5	5	7	4	2	2	6	2	6	2
Metals and engineering	KRLB	396	411	413	378	385	306	339	257	242	376	228
Textiles and clothing	KRLC	114	91	76	81	87	81	75	33	46	27	28
Timber and furniture	KRLD	158	118	98	96	94	90	88	59	82	65	82
Paper, printing and publishing	KRLE	142	117	104	101	112	80	75	70	58	63	67
Other	KRLF	146	117	116	110	111	84	79	111	100	90	140
Total	KRLG	994	890	830	794	810	661	668	555	544	634	562
Construction and transport:												
Construction	KRLH	2 783	2 713	2 182	1 919	1 911	1 741	1 783	1 637	1 781	1 658	1 976
Transport and communication	KRLI	1 138	1 227	1 162	1 060	1 187	1 120	1 134	1 095	1 116	1 249	1 334
Total	KHGP	3 921	3 940	3 344	2 979	3 098	2 861	2 917	2 732	2 897	2 907	3 310
Wholesaling:												
Food, drink and tobacco	KRLJ	103	77	62	53	45	49	40	48	33	28	29
Motor vehicles	KRLK	33	36	28	20	22	29	20	14	15	13	12
Other	KRLL	122	101	78	92	83	83	61	44	47	40	40
Total	KHGQ	258	214	168	165	150	161	121	106	95	81	81
Retailing:												
Food, drink and tobacco	KRLM	782	662	546	514	438	424	347	311	251	280	256
Motor vehicles and filling stations	KRLN	316	327	276	238	241	237	199	138	128	136	121
Other	KRLO	1 566	1 268	1 048	971	1 032	801	792	680	609	621	772
Total	KHGR	2 664	2 257	1 870	1 723	1 711	1 462	1 338	1 129	988	1 037	1 149
Services:												
Financial institutions	KRLP	185	125	105	79	54	45	39	31	24	28	22
Business services	KRLQ	1 354	1 176	1 117	1 057	1 162	1 127	1 107	1 057	1 023	1 242	1 416
Hotels and catering	KRLR	1 956	1 736	1 603	1 309	1 376	1 263	1 187	1 041	1 038	951	1 125
Total	KHGS	3 495	3 037	2 825	2 445	2 592	2 435	2 333	2 129	2 085	2 221	2 563
Other	KHGT	1 732	2 161	2 077	2 157	2 179	2 199	2 279	2 071	2 379	2 480	2 979
Total	KRLT	13 282	12 667	11 269	10 420	10 723	9 952	9 839	8 854	9 139	9 564	10 839
Other individuals												
Employees	KRLU	1 981	2 471	2 625	3 141	4 357	4 601	5 525	5 900	7 101	9 528	13 626
No occupation and unemployed	KRLV	2 859	3 294	3 051	3 384	4 457	4 856	5 848	6 965	8 978	12 643	17 105
Directors and promoters of companies	KRLW	484	368	310	272	330	296	328	323	420	458	503
Occupation unknown	KRLX	3 327	3 003	2 637	2 430	1 744	1 845	1 937	2 250	2 383	3 705	5 218
Total	KRLY	8 651	9 136	8 623	9 227	10 888	11 598	13 638	15 438	18 882	26 334	36 452
Total bankruptcies	KRLZ	21 933	21 803	19 892	19 647	21 611	21 550	23 477	24 292	28 021	35 898	47 291

1 From January 1991 Industrial Analysis excludes Deeds of Arrangement.
2 Prior to 2005Q4 the Department of Trade and Industry published these figures.

Source: Insolvency Service: 020 7637 6504/6443

Service industry

23.21 Industry analysis: company insolvencies[1,2]
England and Wales

Numbers

Industry		1995	1996	1997	1998	1999	2000	2001	2002	2003	2004	2005
Agriculture and horticulture	KRMA	99	89	51	65	75	67	90	76	52	35	35
Manufacturing:												
Food, drink and tobacco	KRMB	130	163	93	89	67	104	71	61	69	38	43
Chemicals	KRMC	69	65	31	57	35	61	37	46	30	21	34
Metals and engineering	KRMD	681	658	591	594	698	683	704	739	828	630	591
Textiles and clothing	KRME	567	568	596	526	419	423	320	304	244	168	172
Timber and furniture	KRMF	267	249	181	149	190	187	199	179	92	69	85
Paper, printing and publishing	KRMG	452	438	364	426	387	386	484	545	376	291	253
Other	KRMH	681	599	613	652	780	678	717	768	430	379	441
Total	KRMI	2 847	2 740	2 469	2 493	2 576	2 522	2 532	2 642	2 069	1 596	1 619
Construction and transport:												
Construction	KRMJ	1 844	1 610	1 419	1 325	1 529	1 474	1 509	1 840	1 728	1 653	1 775
Transport and communication	KRMK	706	682	540	504	443	526	481	652	694	596	624
Total	KHGU	2 550	2 292	1 959	1 829	1 972	2 000	1 990	2 492	2 422	2 249	2 399
Wholesaling:												
Food, drink and tobacco	KRML	205	183	158	139	187	150	125	142	108	124	82
Motor vehicles	KRMM	83	95	41	60	38	29	24	64	208	210	198
Other	KRMN	678	429	340	364	394	391	363	512	788	486	487
Total	KHGV	966	707	539	563	619	570	512	718	1 104	820	767
Retailing:												
Food, drink and tobacco	KRMO	246	236	219	186	193	200	114	132	159	121	176
Motor vehicles and filling stations	KRMP	195	227	132	120	142	141	172	174	59	45	59
Other	KRMQ	1 127	956	891	847	919	853	833	902	578	548	626
Total	KHGW	1 568	1 419	1 242	1 153	1 254	1 194	1 119	1 208	796	714	861
Services:												
Financial institutions	KRMR	198	222	111	101	118	57	28	35	48	49	60
Business services	KRMS	1 525	1 500	1 528	1 617	1 831	1 605	1 618	3 215	3 886	3 392	3 462
Hotels and catering	KRMT	692	708	609	626	562	530	538	740	566	511	584
Total	KJRS	2 415	2 430	2 248	2 344	2 511	2 192	2 184	3 990	4 500	3 952	4 106
Other	KHGX	4 091	3 784	4 102	4 756	5 273	5 772	6 545	5 180	3 241	2 826	3 106
Total company insolvencies	KHGY	14 536	13 461	12 610	13 203	14 280	14 317	14 972	16 306	14 184	12 192	12 893

1 Including partnerships.
2 Prior to 2005Q4 the Department of Trade and Industry published these figures.

Source: Insolvency Service: 020 7637 6504/6443

414

Service industry

Chapter 24

Service industry

Annual Business Inquiry

(Tables 24.1, 24.3 and 24.4)

For details of the Annual Business Inquiry, see the text accompanying Table 22.1.

Retail trade: index numbers of value and volume

(Table 24.2)

The main purpose of the Retail Sales Inquiry (RSI) is to provide up to date information on short period movements in the level of retail sales. In principle, the RSI covers the retail activity of every business classified in the retail sector (Division 52 of the 2003 Standard Industrial Classification) in Great Britain. A business will be classified to the retail sector if its main activity is one of the individual 4 digit SIC categories within Division 52. The retail activity of a business is then defined by its retail turnover, i.e. the sale of all retail goods (note that petrol, for example, is not a retail good).

The RSI is compiled from the information returned to the statutory inquiries into the distribution and services sector. The inquiry is addressed to a stratified sample of 5,000 businesses classified to the retail sector, the stratification being by 'type of store' (the individual 4 digit SIC categories within Division 52) and by size. The sample structure is designed to ensure that the inquiry estimates are as accurate as possible. In terms of the selection, this means that:

> each of the individual 4 digit SIC categories are represented, their coverage depending upon the relative size of the category and the variability of the data;

> within each 4 digit SIC category, the larger retailers tend to be fully enumerated with decreasing proportions of medium and smaller retailers.

The structure of the inquiry is updated periodically, by reference to the more comprehensive results of the Annual Business Inquiry (ABI). The monthly inquiry also incorporates a rotation element for the smallest retailers. This helps to spread the burden more fairly, as well as improving the representativeness between successive benchmarks.

During 2003, the retail sales index was rebased using detailed information from the 2000 annual business inquiry. The reference year is now set at 2000=100.

The latest summary statistics are published each month by First Release. More disaggregated value indices (not seasonally adjusted) are published each month in Business Monitor SDM28, via the National Statistics website: www.statistics.gov.uk/rsi.

24.1
Retail businesses[1]
United Kingdom

£ million and percentages

		1999	2000	2001	2002
Number of businesses	ZABE	216 826	214 876	210 691	207 513
Total turnover[2]	ZABL	230 822	241 418	251 624	265 577
Value Added Tax in total turnover	ZABM	22 494	23 695	25 249	26 907
Retail turnover[2]	ZABN	209 962	218 013	227 298	238 456
Non-retail turnover[2]	ZABO	20 860	23 406	24 327	27 121
Other income					
Value of commercial insurance claims received	ZABP	85	88	89	105
Subsidies received from UK government sources and the EC	ZAEN	19	7	24	4
Employment costs[3]	ZABQ	25 072	26 475	28 036	29 779
Gross wages and salaries	ZABR	22 430	23 857	25 320	26 933
Redundancy and severance payments	ZABS	329	144	130	130
Employers' National Insurance contributions	ZABT	1 547	1 650	1 733	1 805
Contributions to pension funds	ZABU	767	824	853	911
Stocks					
Increase during year	ZABV	1 271	735	900	1 284
Value at end of year	ZABW	21 095	21 150	21 509	22 400
Total turnover[3] divided by end-year stocks (Quotient)	ZABX	9.9	10.3	10.5	10.7
Purchases of goods, materials and services[3]	ZABY	161 841	168 520	175 593	185 875
Goods bought for resale without processing	ZABZ	135 830	141 330	147 791	155 608
Energy and water products for own consumption	ZACA	1 826	1 921	2 028	1 918
Goods and materials	ZACB	3 484	3 413	3 544	3 845
Hiring, leasing or renting of plant, machinery and vehicles	ZACC	761	828	788	924
Commercial insurance premiums	ZACD	582	616	688	827
Road transport services	ZACE	1 627	1 784	1 945	2 137
Telecommunication services	ZACF	506	558	603	561
Computer and related services	ZACG	636	661	581	756
Advertising and marketing services	ZACH	2 771	2 772	2 881	3 047
Other services	ZACI	13 818	14 638	14 745	16 252
Taxes, duties and levies	ZACJ	3 987	4 132	4 432	4 576
National non-domestic (business) rates	ZACK	3 253	3 353	3 616	3 726
Other amounts paid for taxes, duties and levies	ZACL	734	779	816	850
Capital expenditure					
Cost of acquisitions	ZACM	8 215	8 312	8 469	9 355
Proceeds from disposals	ZACN	2 270	1 683	1 606	1 240
Net capital expenditure	ZACO	5 945	6 629	6 863	8 115
Amount included in acquisitions for assets under finance leasing arrangements	ZACP	498	531	474	587
Work of a capital nature carried out by own staff (included in acquisitions)	ZACQ	78	79	144	128
Gross margin					
Amount	ZACR	72 655	75 929	78 913	83 708
As a percentage of adjusted turnover[4]	ZACS	*34.9*	*34.9*	*34.9*	*34.9*
Approximate gross value added at basic prices	ZACT	47 287	49 415	51 201	53 545

24.1 Retail businesses[1]
United Kingdom

continued

£ million

		1999	2000	2001	2002
Total turnover	ZABL	230 822	241 418	251 624	265 577
Retail turnover	ZABN	209 962	218 013	227 298	238 456
1 Fruit (including fresh, chilled, dried, frozen, canned and processed)	DSSX	3 960	3 999	4 112	3 997
2 Vegetables (including fresh, chilled, dried, frozen, canned and processed)	DSSY	5 403	5 802	6 662	6 871
3 Meat (including fresh, chilled, smoked, frozen, canned and processed)	DSSZ	11 334	10 729	11 133	11 671
4 Fish, crustaceans and molluscs (including fresh, chilled, frozen, canned and processed)	DSTA	2 092	2 180	2 200	2 299
5 Bakery products and cereals (including rice and pasta products)	DSTC	8 510	9 067	9 424	9 661
6 Sugar, jam, honey, chocolate and confectionery (including ice-cream)	DSTD	6 009	6 040	6 289	6 469
7 Alcoholic drink	DSTE	9 947	10 579	10 625	11 301
8 Non-alcoholic beverages (including tea, coffee, fruit drinks and vegetable drinks)	DSTF	5 546	5 587	5 717	6 476
9 Tobacco (excluding smokers requisites, eg pipes, lighters, etc)	DSTG	8 845	8 293	8 616	9 016
10 Milk, cheese and eggs (including yoghurts and cream)	DSTH	6 866	6 933	7 032	7 233
11 Oils and fats (including butter and margarine)	DSTI	1 113	1 245	1 314	1 222
12 Food products not elsewhere classified (including sauces, herbs, spices and soups)	DSTJ	10 121	9 998	9 986	9 185
13 Pharmaceutical products	DSTK	1 930	2 432	2 744	2 911
14 National Health Receipts	DSTL	5 799	6 412	6 981	7 740
15 Other medical products and therapeutic appliances and equipment	DSTN	2 267	2 690	2 737	2 753
16 Other appliances, articles and products for personal care	DSTO	7 506	8 099	8 543	9 611
17 Other articles of clothing, accessories for making clothing	DSTP	1 356	1 520	1 253	1 293
18 Garments	DSTQ	26 092	25 542	26 777	28 331
19 Footwear (excluding sports shoes)	DSTR	4 213	4 380	4 629	5 270
20 Travel goods and other personal effects not elsewhere classified	DSTT	644	683	848	1 007
21 Household textiles (including furnishing fabrics, curtains, etc)	DSTV	3 478	3 369	3 568	3 656
22 Household and personal appliances whether electric or not	DSUA	5 088	5 477	6 499	6 580
23 Glassware, tableware and household utensils (including non-electric)	DSUB	2 815	2 651	2 748	2 823
24 Furniture and furnishings	DSUC	10 353	10 630	11 065	12 094
25 Audio and visual equipment (including radios, televisions and video recorders)	DSUE	3 770	4 064	4 500	4 781
26 Recording material for pictures and sound (including audio and video tapes, blank and pre-recorded records, etc)	DSUG	3 080	3 436	3 304	3 591
27 Information processing equipment (including printers, software, calculators and typewriters)	DSUL	2 953	3 205	3 175	3 056
28 Decorating and DIY supplies	DSUM	5 019	5 488	6 279	6 548
29 Tools and equipment for house and garden	DSUN	2 165	2 451	2 669	3 007
30 Books	DSUP	2 226	2 252	2 366	2 752
31 Newspapers and periodicals	DSUQ	3 503	3 541	3 652	3 709
32 Stationery and drawing materials and miscellaneous printed matter	DSUW	3 648	3 768	3 601	3 864
33 Carpets and other floor coverings (excluding bathroom mats, rush and door mats)	DSUX	2 944	3 123	3 182	3 411
34 Photographic and cinematographic equipment and optical instruments	DSUZ	968	1 062	1 059	1 402
35 Telephone and telefax equipment (including mobile phones)	DSVA	1 503	2 264	2 398	2 238
36 Jewellery, silverware and plate; watches and clocks	DSVB	2 806	3 448	3 774	4 387
37 Works of art and antiques (including furniture, floor coverings and jewellery)	DSVF	1 666	1 585	1 820	1 509
38 Equipment and accessories for sport, camping, recreation and musical instruments	DSVH	3 520	3 725	3 861	3 624
39 Spare part and accessories for all types of vehicle and sales of bicycles	DSVI	558	652	752	1 082
40 Games, toys, hobbies (including video game software, video game computers that plug into the tv, video-games cassettes and CD-ROMs)	DSVM	3 744	4 204	4 624	5 468
41 Other goods not elsewhere classified (including sale of new postage stamps and sales of liquid and solid fuels)	DSVN	5 029	5 420	3 745	3 359
42 Non-durable household goods (including household cleaning, maintenance products) and paper products and other non-durable household goods	DSVO	3 609	4 043	4 352	4 405
43 Natural or artificial plants and flowers	DSVQ	2 456	2 653	3 028	3 266
44 Pets and related products (including pet food)	DSVR	2 241	2 348	2 724	2 497
45 Repair of household and personal items	DSVS	1 266	944	927	1 031

1 See chapter text.
2 Inclusive of VAT.
3 Exclusive of VAT.
4 Turnover is adjusted to take out VAT.

Source: Office for National Statistics: 01633 812435

24.2

Retail trade: index numbers of value and volume of sales[1]
Great Britain
Not seasonally adjusted

Weekly average (2000=100)

		Sales in 2000 £ million	1995	1996	1997	1998	1999	2000	2001	2002	2003	2004	2005
Value													
All retailing	EAFY	207 149	80.2	84.6	89.9	93.4	96.5	100.0	105.9	110.6	113.7	118.7	119.8
Large	EAFZ	153 022	76	81	87	92	96	100	107	112	118	124	126
Small	EAGA	54 128	94	97	97	99	98	100	104	106	101	104	103
Predominantly food stores	EAFS	89 041	80.3	84.6	88.9	93.4	96.6	100.0	106.0	110.4	114.8	119.6	123.5
Predominantly non-food stores	EAFT	106 359	79.8	84.4	90.6	93.2	96.3	100.0	106.1	111.1	114.6	119.8	119.2
Non specialised predominantly non-food stores	EAGE	18 781	79.2	85.7	91.5	92.6	95.2	100.0	105.0	107.4	109.2	111.2	110.9
Textiles, clothing, footwear and leather	EAFU	27 880	83.5	87.0	93.4	93.8	96.0	100.0	105.8	112.4	118.3	124.5	126.3
Household goods stores	EAFV	27 699	73.4	79.2	86.8	91.6	95.7	100.0	107.6	113.1	113.4	117.2	112.9
Other specialised non-food stores	EAFW	31 999	81.2	84.5	89.3	93.1	96.8	100.0	105.8	110.5	115.6	123.0	123.1
Other retail sale (non-store) and repair	EAFX	11 749	85.3	87.6	91.8	97.1	98.8	100.0	103.2	106.7	97.6	102.5	98.5
Volume													
All retailing	EAHC	207 149	82.8	85.4	89.9	92.5	95.7	100.0	106.1	112.2	116.3	123.2	125.7
Predominantly food stores	EAGW	89 041	87.7	89.3	92.9	95.5	97.2	100.0	104.1	108.2	111.9	116.5	119.5
Predominantly non-food stores	EAGX	106 359	78.6	82.1	87.4	89.9	94.3	100.0	107.8	115.5	121.1	129.6	131.9
Non specialised predominantly non-food stores	EAHI	18 781	82.0	86.9	91.5	91.5	94.0	100.0	106.0	110.5	113.8	118.0	119.4
Textiles,clothing, footwear and leather	EAGY	27 880	79.3	82.7	88.1	88.8	92.9	100.0	109.4	121.0	128.9	139.1	143.8
Household goods stores	EAGZ	27 699	68.5	73.2	80.3	85.8	92.6	100.0	109.6	117.8	122.3	130.8	131.2
Other specialised non-food stores	EAHA	31 999	85.8	86.9	90.7	93.6	97.1	100.0	105.9	111.6	117.4	127.0	129.3
Other retail sale (non-store) and repair	EAHB	11 749	83.5	84.6	88.2	93.2	96.2	100.0	106.0	113.3	107.0	116.9	117.4

1 See chapter text.

Source: Office for National Statistics: 01633 812713

24.3 Motor trades[1]
United Kingdom

£ million and percentages

		Sale, maintenance and repair of motor vehicles and motorcycles; retail sale of automotive fuel (SIC 92 50.00)					Sale of motor vehicles (SIC 92 50.10)			
		1999	2000	2001	2002		1999	2000	2001	2002
Number of businesses	MKEQ	72 298	71 413	70 942	70 338	MKER	29 761	27 948	26 801	25 856
Total turnover	CMRH	128 956	129 675	136 398	141 867	EWRI	88 644	86 755	92 063	96 968
Motor trades turnover	CMRI	125 752	126 357	131 908	136 346	FDFZ	87 918	86 160	91 015	95 885
Retail sales of:										
New cars	CMRJ	25 992	24 377	28 891	28 433	FDGA	25 073	23 185	27 583	27 065
Other new motor vehicles and motorcycles	CMRK	3 598	3 543	4 011	4 404	FDGB	2 977	2 476	3 514	3 876
Sales to other dealers of:										
New cars	CMRL	16 780	16 241	16 720	20 867	FDGC	16 752	16 228	16 693	20 773
Other new motor vehicles and motorcycles	CMRM	2 936	3 101	3 282	3 703	FDGD	2 622	2 741	2 844	3 085
Gross sales of used motor vehicles and motorcycles	CMRN	28 233	30 126	29 434	27 939	FDGE	26 063	28 254	26 906	26 337
Turnover from sales of petrol, diesel, oil and other petroleum products	CMRO	15 448	17 090	16 750	16 978	FDGF	1 335	1 112	1 087	782
Other motor trades sales and receipts (including parts and accessories, workshop receipts)	CMRP	32 765	31 881	32 819	14 256	FDGG	13 095	12 164	12 387	4 916
Non-motor trades turnover	CMRQ	3 204	3 318	4 490	5 521	FDHJ	726	594	1 049	1 083
Purchases of goods, materials and services										
Total purchases	CMNR	111 324	112 157	116 458	120 819	FDGH	78 607	76 980	80 657	84 354
Energy, water and materials	CMRS	1 280	1 354	1 441	1 379	FDGI	632	629	630	542
Used motor vehicles and motorcycles	COBU	25 223	26 931	26 166	24 391	FDGJ	23 444	25 367	24 100	22 939
Parts used solely in repair and servicing activities	CMRT	6 249	5 181	5 787	6 397	FDGK	2 720	2 050	2 290	2 616
Other goods for resale	CMRU	71 895	71 589	75 855	80 726	FDGL	47 629	44 428	49 125	53 512
Hiring, leasing and renting of plant, machinery and vehicles	CMRV	247	282	270	326	FDGM	74	64	62	131
Commercial insurance premiums	CMRW	360	398	435	465	FDGN	177	163	190	198
Road transport services	CMRX	356	402	452	740	FDGO	196	240	268	373
Telecommunication services	CMRY	282	280	274	278	FDGP	151	137	127	129
Computer and related services	CMRZ	232	229	269	306	FDGQ	142	140	162	174
Advertising and marketing services	CMSA	1 713	1 630	1 644	1 847	FDGR	1 462	1 373	1 412	1 611
Other services	CMSB	3 488	3 881	3 866	3 964	FDGS	1 979	2 388	2 289	2 130
Taxes, duties and levies										
Total taxes and levies	CMSC	904	873	936	1 002	FDGT	543	482	529	519
National (non-domestic business) rates	CMSD	535	538	586	536	FDGU	246	225	261	245
Other amounts paid for taxes, duties and levies	CMSE	369	335	350	466	FDGV	297	257	268	275
Capital expenditure										
Cost of acquisitions	CMSF	1 964	1 938	2 093	2 216	FDGW	1 211	1 112	1 289	1 374
Cost of disposals	CMSG	685	658	798	846	FDGX	461	463	553	593
Net capital expenditure	CMSH	1 280	1 280	1 295	1 370	FDGY	749	649	736	781
Work of a capital nature carried out by own staff (included in acquisitions)	CMSI	21	9	14	12	FDGZ	13	6	9	6
Stocks										
Increase during year	CMSJ	1 042	616	828	886	FDHA	995	561	667	661
Value at end of year	CMSK	13 738	13 364	12 155	13 217	FDHB	10 797	10 405	9 005	9 913
Total turnover divided by end-year stocks (Quotient)	CMSL	9.4	9.7	11.2	10.7	FDHC	8.2	8.3	10.2	9.6
Employment costs										
Total employment costs	CMSM	8 179	8 261	9 069	9 400	FDHD	4 285	4 341	4 751	5 024
Gross wages and salaries paid	COBP	7 295	7 376	8 127	8 409	FDHE	3 815	3 859	4 232	4 470
National insurance and pension contributions	COBQ	884	885	942	991	FDHF	469	483	520	554
Gross margin										
Amount	COBR	26 398	26 279	29 335	31 064	FDHG	15 676	15 255	17 169	18 536
As a percentage of adjusted turnover	COBS	*21.5*	*20.3*	*21.5*	*22.0*	FDHH	*18.2*	*17.6*	*18.6*	*19.7*
Approximate gross value added at basic prices	COBT	18 726	18 214	20 710	21 777	FDHI	11 064	10 335	12 039	13 259

24.3 Motor trades[1]
United Kingdom
continued

		Maintenance and repair of motor vehicles (SIC 92 50.20)					Sale of motor vehicle parts and accessories (SIC 92 50.30)			
		1999	2000	2001	2002		1999	2000	2001	2002
Number of businesses	MKES	26 089	27 202	27 862	28 438	MKET	7 630	7 757	7 800	7 715
Total turnover	FDHK	11 118	11 218	11 890	11 964	FDIW	11 128	11 094	11 752	11 068
Motor trades turnover	FDHL	10 951	10 992	11 493	11 658	FDIX	11 085	11 014	11 557	10 567
Retail sales of:										
New cars	FDHM	724	977	1 099	1 206	FDIY	46	–	22	19
Other new motor vehicles and motorcycles	FDHN	61	567	..	162	FDIZ	34	83	..	161
Sales to other dealers of:										
New cars	FDHO	22	12	..	4	FDJA	1	–	..	89
Other new motor vehicles and motorcycles	FDHP	8	32	..	–	FDJB	–	–	..	–
Gross sales of used motor vehicles and motorcycles	FDHQ	1 416	1 169	1 574	1 079	FDJC	112	82	173	143
Turnover from sales of petrol, diesel, oil and other petroleum products	FDHR	656	387	371	334	FDJD	73	60	200	85
Other motor trades sales and receipts (including parts and accessories, workshop receipts)	FDHS	8 063	7 847	8 424	7 891	FDJE	10 819	10 789	11 096	1 029
Non-motor trades turnover	FDHT	167	226	397	306	FDJF	44	81	195	501
Purchases of goods, materials and services										
Total purchases	FDHU	7 236	7 375	7 817	7 806	FDJG	8 825	8 903	9 387	8 611
Energy, water and materials	FDHV	298	366	367	528	FDJH	257	260	299	171
Used motor vehicles and motorcycles	FDHW	1 150	965	1 347	892	FDJI	103	71	145	91
Parts used solely in repair and servicing activities	FDHX	3 080	2 606	2 734	3 053	FDJJ	290	293	574	544
Other goods for resale	FDHY	1 590	2 313	2 127	2 170	FDJK	7 359	7 424	7 405	6 657
Hiring, leasing and renting of plant, machinery and vehicles	FDHZ	115	138	146	75	FDJL	49	57	45	60
Commercial insurance premiums	FDIA	116	147	147	139	FDJM	36	52	64	85
Road transport services	FDIB	33	21	30	13	FDJN	76	92	86	228
Telecommunication services	FDIC	66	71	65	70	FDJO	46	49	60	57
Computer and related services	FDID	35	42	44	34	FDJP	39	31	50	78
Advertising and marketing services	FDIE	92	90	98	109	FDJQ	118	89	76	70
Other services	FDIF	661	615	713	724	FDJR	452	484	581	568
Taxes, duties and levies										
Total taxes and levies	FDIG	172	183	196	194	FDJS	97	104	104	90
National (non-domestic business) rates	FDIH	132	141	146	142	FDJT	85	87	80	74
Other amounts paid for taxes, duties and levies	FDII	39	42	49	52	FDJU	13	18	25	16
Capital expenditure										
Cost of acquisitions	FDIJ	389	358	396	376	FDJV	193	212	207	170
Cost of disposals	FDIK	86	75	89	84	FDJW	67	50	91	106
Net capital expenditure	FDIL	303	283	307	292	FDJX	126	162	115	64
Work of a capital nature carried out by own staff (included in acquisitions)	FDIM	7	2	3	2	FDJY	1	1	2	3
Stocks										
Increase during year	FDIN	–3	–43	79	51	FDJZ	31	35	43	66
Value at end of year	FDIO	747	670	809	805	FDKA	1 403	1 440	1 492	1 498
Total turnover divided by end-year stocks (Quotient)	FDIP	14.9	16.7	14.7	14.6	FDKB	7.9	7.7	7.9	7.8
Employment costs										
Total employment costs	FDIQ	1 930	1 919	2 176	2 298	FDKC	1 295	1 353	1 461	1 348
Gross wages and salaries paid	FDIR	1 725	1 715	1 961	2 075	FDKD	1 151	1 210	1 312	1 209
National insurance and pension contributions	FDIS	205	204	215	223	FDKE	144	144	149	139
Gross margin										
Amount	FDIT	5 283	5 236	5 741	5 878	FDKF	3 401	3 328	3 654	3 833
As a percentage of adjusted turnover	FDIU	*65.7*	*46.7*	*48.3*	*49.0*	FDKG	*31.4*	*30.0*	*31.1*	*30.6*
Approximate gross value added at basic prices	FDIV	3 898	3 883	4 134	4 187	FDKH	2 332	2 219	2 392	2 514

£ million and percentages

		Sale, maintenance and repair of motorcycles and related parts and accessories (SIC 92 50.40)					Retail sale of automotive fuel (SIC 92 50.50)			
		1999	2000	2001	2002		1999	2000	2001	2002
Number of businesses	MKEU	2 077	2 277	2 402	2 513	MKEV	6 741	6 229	6 077	5 816
Total turnover	FDKI	1 665	1 827	1 722	1 812	FDLV	16 401	18 781	18 971	20 056
Motor trades turnover	FDKJ	1 626	1 819	1 707	1 737	FDLW	14 173	16 372	16 136	16 500
Retail sales of:										
New cars	FDKK	17	22	–	–	FDLX	130	192	186	142
Other new motor vehicles and motorcycles	FDKL	526	416	433	194	FDLY	–	1	3	11
Sales to other dealers of:										
New cars	FDKM	–	–	–	–	FDLZ	5	–	–	–
Other new motor vehicles and motorcycles	FDKN	306	328	436	618	FDMA	1	–	1	–
Gross sales of used motor vehicles and motorcycles	FDKO	342	386	329	186	FDMB	300	234	452	193
Turnover from sales of petrol, diesel, oil and other petroleum products	FDKP	3	1	1	–	FDMC	13 382	15 530	15 091	15 776
Other motor trades sales and receipts (including parts and accessories, workshop receipts)	FDKQ	432	667	508	172	FDMD	356	414	404	248
Non-motor trades turnover	FDKR	40	8	15	75	FDME	2 228	2 409	2 835	3 556
Purchases of goods, materials and services										
Total purchases	FDKT	1 423	1 488	1 367	1 493	FDMF	15 232	17 411	17 230	18 554
Energy, water and materials	FDKU	10	26	33	39	FDMG	82	71	112	99
Used motor vehicles and motorcycles	FDKV	314	330	228	142	FDMH	213	197	345	328
Parts used solely in repair and servicing activities	FDKW	55	124	75	112	FDMI	105	109	114	72
Other goods for resale	FDKX	958	889	919	1 049	FDMJ	14 357	16 534	16 278	17 338
Hiring, leasing and renting of plant, machinery and vehicles	FDKY	1	1	4	4	FDMK	8	22	11	56
Commercial insurance premiums	FDKZ	7	9	11	9	FDML	24	27	24	34
Road transport services	FDLA	6	6	4	33	COBV	46	42	64	93
Telecommunication services	FDLB	4	6	6	5	COBW	15	17	16	17
Computer and related services	FDLC	3	3	3	3	COBX	13	12	10	17
Advertising and marketing services	FDLD	22	24	24	35	COBY	18	53	33	22
Other services	FDLE	44	68	60	63	COBZ	351	326	222	479
Taxes, duties and levies										
Total taxes and levies	FDLF	18	22	20	15	COCA	73	81	87	183
National (non-domestic business) rates	FDLG	7	12	15	..	COCB	65	74	84	..
Other amounts paid for taxes, duties and levies	FDLH	11	11	5	..	COCC	9	8	3	..
Capital expenditure										
Cost of acquisitions	FDLI	23	29	25	34	COCD	149	227	176	263
Cost of disposals	FDLJ	3	11	20	5	COCE	67	59	45	58
Net capital expenditure	FDLK	20	18	5	29	COCF	82	168	131	205
Work of a capital nature carried out by own staff (included in acquisitions)	FDLL	1	–	–	1	COCG	–	–	–	–
Stocks										
Increase during year	FDLM	–24	27	–11	35	COCH	43	36	50	72
Value at end of year	FDLN	291	361	378	302	COCI	502	488	471	698
Total turnover divided by end-year stocks (Quotient)	FDLO	5.7	5.1	4.6	6.2	COCJ	32.7	38.5	40.3	28.8
Employment costs										
Total employment costs	FDLP	128	90	132	144	COCK	541	557	548	587
Gross wages and salaries paid	FDLQ	115	81	120	127	COCL	488	512	503	528
National insurance and pension contributions	FDLR	13	9	13	17	COCM	53	46	45	59
Gross margin										
Amount	FDLS	313	501	488	542	COCN	1 725	1 960	2 283	2 275
As a percentage of adjusted turnover	FDLT	*19.5*	*27.4*	*28.3*	*31.0*	CMQN	*10.6*	*10.4*	*12.0*	*11.4*
Approximate gross value added at basic prices	FDLU	218	370	346	353	CMQO	1 215	1 407	1 799	1 464

1 See chapter text. Figures are exclusive of VAT.

Source: Office for National Statistics: 01633 812435

24.4 Catering and allied trades[1]
United Kingdom

£ million and percentages

		Total catering and allied trades (SIC 92 55.00)					Hotels and motels (SIC 92 55.11 and 55.12)			
		1999	2000	2001	2002		1999	2000	2001	2002
Number of businesses	MKEK	114 353	116 568	118 988	122 714	MKEL	11 381	11 188	10 890	10 800
Total turnover[2]	CMKX	51 315	55 058	57 738	60 603	CMLW	10 970	11 595	12 047	11 824
Taxes and levies[3]										
Total taxes and levies	CMLM	1 295	1 343	1 505	1 594	CMML	269	300	371	373
National (non-domestic business) rates	CMLJ	1 156	1 251	1 347	1 481	CMMI	260	292	350	359
Other amounts paid for taxes duties and levies	CMLL	139	92	158	113	CMMK	9	8	21	14
Capital expenditure[3]										
Capital acquisitions	CMLP	4 793	4 945	4 923	4 491	CMMO	1 333	1 402	1 201	1 127
Capital disposals	CMLQ	649	484	520	670	CMMP	203	106	81	225
Net capital expenditure	CMLK	4 144	4 461	4 404	3 820	CMMJ	1 130	1 296	1 120	902
Work of a capital nature carried out by your own staff (included in acquisitions)	CMLR	49	35	28	25	CMMQ	8	10	6	13
Stocks[3]										
Increase during year	CMLN	60	36	63	44	CMMM	−5	−3	–	−12
Value at end of year	CMLO	1 067	1 077	1 247	1 132	CMMN	208	181	207	231
Purchases of goods and services[3]										
Total purchases	CMLI	23 856	25 130	26 160	27 408	CMMH	3 817	3 947	4 135	4 327
Energy, water and materials	CMKZ	8 848	10 136	10 938	10 608	CMLY	1 667	1 793	1 766	1 729
Goods for resale	CMLA	8 028	7 757	7 556	8 173	CMLZ	450	383	469	468
Hiring, leasing of plant, machinery etc.	CMLB	306	344	277	350	CMMA	65	64	50	51
Commercial insurance premiums	CMLC	272	370	374	430	CMMB	67	71	82	106
Road transport services	CMLD	100	101	99	115	CMMC	25	28	19	19
Telecommunication services	CMLE	213	232	235	239	CMMD	60	56	63	61
Computer and related services	CMLF	105	115	130	141	CMME	36	29	31	45
Advertising and marketing services	CMLG	608	628	597	661	CMMF	167	182	177	178
Other services	CMLH	5 377	5 446	5 956	6 691	CMMG	1 280	1 340	1 475	1 670
Employment costs[3]										
Total employment costs	CMKY	11 012	11 668	12 965	13 504	CMLX	2 605	2 775	3 005	3 021
Gross wages and salaries paid	CMKV	10 169	10 777	11 971	12 475	CMLU	2 392	2 539	2 755	2 760
National insurance and pension contributions	CMKW	844	891	994	1 029	CMLV	213	236	250	260
Gross margin[4]										
Amount	CMQP	36 159	39 528	41 918	43 943	CMQS	8 922	9 542	9 825	9 610
As a percentage of turnover	CMQQ	*81.5*	*83.4*	*84.5*	*84.2*	CMQT	*95.0*	*95.9*	*95.2*	*95.5*
Value added at basic prices[4]	CMQR	20 568	22 326	23 466	24 786	CMQU	5 595	6 012	6 191	5 759
Accommodation										
Number of establishments	CMLS	23 667	25 589	23 584	23 559	CMMR	12 583	13 803	12 470	12 874
Letting bedplaces	CMLT	1 731 601	1 788 115	1 903 585	2 071 308	CMMS	757 491	780 158	819 116	1 022 079

£ million and percentages

		Camping sites and other provision of short-stay accommodation (SIC 92 55.21 to 55.23)					Restaurants or cafes, take-away food shops (SIC 92 55.30)			
		1999	2000	2001	2002		1999	2000	2001	2002
Number of businesses	MKEM	3 688	3 851	3 928	4 175	MKEN	49 955	51 395	52 633	54 340
Total turnover[2]	CMMV	1 932	2 152	2 220	2 631	CMNU	14 618	16 934	18 323	18 843
Taxes and levies[3]										
Total taxes and levies	CMNK	61	69	77	74	CMOJ	386	405	466	508
National (non-domestic business) rates	CMNH	53	63	74	73	CMOG	360	383	398	468
Other amounts paid for taxes duties and levies	CMNJ	8	6	3	1	CMOI	26	23	67	40
Capital expenditure[3]										
Capital acquisitions	CMNN	274	228	291	364	CMOM	1 048	1 305	1 351	1 222
Capital disposals	CMNO	38	46	22	38	CMON	137	128	128	112
Net capital expenditure	CMNI	236	182	269	326	CMOH	911	1 176	1 223	1 110
Work of a capital nature carried out by your own staff (included in acquisitions)	CMNP	7	5	7	–	CMOO	7	2	5	4
Stocks[3]										
Increase during year	CMNL	3	–4	48	4	CMOK	26	12	14	25
Value at end of year	CMNM	85	84	141	89	CMOL	291	274	298	295
Purchases of goods and services[3]										
Total purchases	CMNG	852	887	1 102	1 184	CMOF	7 079	7 962	8 544	8 637
Energy, water and materials	CMMX	184	201	233	249	CMNW	3 183	3 791	4 231	4 144
Goods for resale	CMMY	220	243	311	390	CMNX	1 934	2 120	2 154	2 067
Hiring, leasing of plant, machinery etc.	CMMZ	5	9	6	9	CMNY	53	45	42	62
Commercial insurance premiums	CMNA	28	35	32	29	CMNZ	70	92	94	119
Road transport services	CMNB	10	10	4	10	CMOA	29	36	33	38
Telecommunication services	CMNC	12	14	15	12	CMOB	61	64	62	67
Computer and related services	CMND	6	9	20	7	CMOC	19	29	35	28
Advertising and marketing services	CMNE	66	57	78	73	CMOD	200	232	203	248
Other services	CMNF	321	308	402	405	CMOE	1 530	1 555	1 689	1 865
Employment costs[3]										
Total employment costs	CMMW	355	405	428	488	CMNV	2 985	3 318	3 790	4 031
Gross wages and salaries paid	CMMT	325	370	392	450	CMNS	2 762	3 071	3 508	3 751
National insurance and pension contributions	CMMU	30	35	36	38	CMNT	223	247	282	280
Gross margin[4]										
Amount	CMQV	1 460	1 615	1 623	1 921	CMQY	10 665	12 375	13 533	14 085
As a percentage of turnover	CMQW	*85.3*	*85.4*	*83.8*	*83.2*	CMQZ	*84.5*	*85.2*	*86.0*	*87.6*
Value added at basic prices[4]	CMQX	865	1 003	888	1 128	CMRA	5 592	6 564	7 164	7 544
Accommodation										
Number of establishments	CMNQ	4 913	4 827	4 564	4 247	CMOP	1 033	1 053	1 106	1 809
Letting bedplaces	CMRR	844 311	860 261	940 003	895 191	CMOQ	45 449	60 329	55 590	55 406

24.4 Catering and allied trades[1]
United Kingdom

£ million and percentages

		Licensed clubs with entertainment, independent, tenanted, managed public houses or wine bars (SIC 92 55.40)[5]					Canteen operator, catering contractor (SIC 92 55.51 and 55.52)			
		1999	2000	2001	2002		1999	2000	2001	2002
Number of businesses	MKEO	44 647	45 139	46 320	47 914	MKEP	4 682	4 995	5 217	5 485
Total turnover[2]	CMOT	18 423	18 578	19 163	20 681	CMPS	5 372	5 799	5 985	6 624
Taxes and levies[3]										
Total taxes and levies	CMPI	551	538	559	611	CMQH	28	31	33	27
National (non-domestic business) rates	CMPF	460	484	497	557	CMQE	23	30	28	24
Other amounts paid for taxes duties and levies	CMPH	92	54	62	54	CMQG	5	1	4	3
Capital expenditure[3]										
Capital acquisitions	CMPL	2 032	1 861	1 895	1 634	CMQK	106	148	185	144
Capital disposals	CMPM	263	196	273	284	CMQL	8	7	15	12
Net capital expenditure	CMPG	1 769	1 665	1 622	1 350	CMQF	99	141	169	132
Work of a capital nature carried out by your own staff (included in acquisitions)	CMPN	25	18	11	8	CMQM	2	–	–	–
Stocks[3]										
Increase during year	CMPJ	24	32	−11	19	CMQI	12	−1	11	8
Value at end of year	CMPK	392	432	486	414	CMQJ	92	104	115	102
Purchases of goods and services[3]										
Total purchases	CMPE	9 386	9 486	9 423	10 222	CMQD	2 721	2 848	2 956	3 037
Energy, water and materials	CMOV	2 028	2 366	2 756	2 408	CMPU	1 785	1 986	1 951	2 078
Goods for resale	CMOW	4 924	4 525	4 166	4 836	CMPV	500	486	455	411
Hiring, leasing of plant, machinery etc.	CMOX	147	193	145	188	CMPW	35	32	34	42
Commercial insurance premiums	CMOY	91	152	141	148	CMPX	17	20	24	27
Road transport services	CMOZ	15	15	16	26	CMPY	21	13	27	23
Telecommunication services	CMPA	67	80	77	79	CMPZ	14	18	17	20
Computer and related services	CMPB	28	34	23	39	CMQA	15	14	20	22
Advertising and marketing services	CMPC	161	137	114	136	CMQB	14	20	25	26
Other services	CMPD	1 925	1 982	1 984	2 362	CMQC	321	261	405	389
Employment costs[3]										
Total employment costs	CMOU	3 206	3 170	3 647	3 745	CMPT	1 861	1 999	2 095	2 219
Gross wages and salaries paid	CMOR	2 975	2 954	3 390	3 484	CMPQ	1 715	1 842	1 926	2 029
National insurance and pension contributions	CMOS	231	216	257	260	CMPR	146	157	169	190
Gross margin[4]										
Amount	CMRB	10 762	11 343	12 126	12 819	CMRE	4 349	4 653	4 811	5 508
As a percentage of turnover	CMRC	*68.1*	*71.3*	*74.2*	*72.7*	CMRF	*89.9*	*90.3*	*91.3*	*90.9*
Value added at basic prices[4]	CMRD	6 383	6 432	6 902	7 469	CMRG	2 133	2 315	2 321	2 885
Accommodation										
Number of establishments	CMPO	5 137	5 906	5 445	3 970					
Letting bedplaces	CMPP	84 351	87 366	88 877	71 214					

1 See chapter text.
2 Inclusive of VAT.
3 Exclusive of VAT.

4 The total turnover figure used to calculate these data excludes VAT.
5 Includes figures for managed public houses owned by breweries.

Source: Office for National Statistics: 01633 812435

Sources

This index of sources gives the titles of official publications or other sources containing statistics allied to those in the tables of this *Annual Abstract.* These publications provide more detailed analyses than are shown in the *Annual Abstract.* This index includes publications to which reference should be made for short-term (monthly or quarterly) series. Further advice on published statistical sources is available from the National Statistics Customer Contact Centre on the numbers provided on page ii.

Table number and subject in Abstract	Government department or other organisation	Official publication or other source
1. Area		
1.1	Ordnance Survey	
	Ordnance Survey of Northern Ireland	
	Office for National Statistics	Regional Trends (annual, Palgrave Macmillan)
2. Parliamentary elections		
Elections		
2.1	University of Plymouth for the Electoral Commission	British Electoral Facts 1832–1999 (Ashgate) Dod's Parliamentary Companion (annual)
By–elections		
2.2	University of Plymouth for the Electoral Commission	Vachers Parliamentary Companion (quarterly) Social Trends (annual, Palgrave Macmillan)
3. International development		
3.1, 3.2	Department for International Development	Statistics on International Development 2000/01–2004/05, Tables 1,2 and 12
4. Defence		
4.1 – 4.11	Ministry of Defence/DASA	UK Defence Statistics 2003 (The Stationery Office (TSO))
5. Population and vital statistics		
Population		**Census**
5.1 – 5.3, 5.5	Office for National Statistics	*England and Wales*: Census reports 1911, 1921, 1931, 1951, 1961, 1971, 1981, 1991 and 2001 Census 1991, Key Population and Vital Statistics; Great Britain Digest of Welsh Statistics (annual, National Assembly for Wales)
	General Register Office (Scotland)	*Scotland:* Census reports 1951, 1961, 1971, 1981 1991 and 2001 Census 1991, Key statistics for urban areas: Scotland

Table number and subject in Abstract	Government department or other organisation	Official publication or other source
	Northern Ireland Statistics and Research Agency	*Northern Ireland:* Census of population 1951, 1961, 1966 and 1971, 1981 and 1991
5.1 – 5.3, 5.5	Office for National Statistics	**Resident population: mid–year estimates** *England and Wales:* Series FM (Family statistics), DH (Deaths), MB (Morbidity), PP (Population estimates and projections), MN (Migration) and VS (Key population and vital statistics) Series PP1, Population estimates: The Registrar General's estimates of the population of regions and local government areas of England and Wales Population Trends (quarterly, Palgrave Macmillan) Health Statistics Quarterly, (Palgrave Macmillan)
	General Register Office (Scotland)	*Scotland:* Annual report of the Registrar General for Scotland Annual estimate of the population of Scotland
	Northern Ireland Statistics and Research Agency	*Northern Ireland:* Annual report of the Registrar General
5.6	Office for National Statistics	
Projections 5.1 – 5.3	Government Actuary's Department	
	Office for National Statistics Government Actuary's Department	Series PP2, Population projections – national figures
Migration 5.7, 5.8, 5.9	Office for National Statistics	International Migration – first release of 2004 estimates Series MN (International migration) Population Trends (quarterly, Palgrave Macmillan)
5.10, 5.11	Home Office	Control of immigration statistics United Kingdom (annual) Asylum Statistics United Kingdom (annual)
Vital statistics 5.4, 5.12 – 5.22	Office for National Statistics	*England and Wales:* Series FM (Births, marriages and divorce statistics), DH (Deaths), MB (Morbidity), PP (Population estimates and projections), MN (International migration) and VS (Key population and vital statistics) Population Trends (quarterly, Palgrave Macmillan)
5.4, 5.12 – 5.21	General Register Office (Scotland)	*Scotland:* Annual report of the Registrar General for Scotland Quarterly return of births, deaths and marriages
	Northern Ireland Statistics and Research Agency	*Northern Ireland:* Annual report of the Registrar General Quarterly return of births, deaths and marriages

Sources

Table number and subject in Abstract	Government department or other organisation	Official publication or other source
5.14	Northern Ireland Court Service	Northern Ireland Judicial Statistics (annual)
5.18	Scottish Executive Department of Health	
5.22	Government Actuary's Department	*England and Wales*: Interim Life Table *Scotland*: Interim Life Table *Northern Ireland*: Annual Report of the Registrar General
5.23	Office for National Statistics General Register Office (Scotland) Northern Ireland Statistics and Research Agency	

6. Education

6.1 – 6.11	Department for Education and Skills	Education and Training Statistics for the United Kingdom (annual, TSO)
	National Assembly for Wales	Digest of Welsh Statistics (annual) Statistics of education and training in Wales (annual and ad–hoc, NAfW)
	Scottish Executive	Scottish educational statistics (annual and ad–hoc, SE) Scottish Social Statistics (annual)
	Northern Ireland Department of Education	Annual Abstract of Statistics, Northern Ireland (annual, DENI) Northern Ireland education statistics (annual and ad–hoc, DENI)
	Northern Ireland Department for Employment and Learning	Northern Ireland further and higher education statistics (annual and ad–hoc, DELNI)

7. Labour market

Labour Force Survey 7.1 – 7.3, 7.6, 7.6, 7.9, 7.10, 7.12, 7.15 – 7.17	Office for National Statistics	Labour Market Trends (monthly, Palgrave Macmillan)
7.4, 7.5	Office for National Statistics	
7.7	Cabinet Office	Civil Service Statistics (annual) Monthly Digest of Statistics (Palgrave Macmillan)
7.8	Office for National Statistics	Labour Market Trends (monthly, Palgrave Macmillan)

Table number and subject in Abstract	Government department or other organisation	Official publication or other source
Claimant count 7.11, 7.13 7.14, 7.25	Office for National Statistics	Labour Market Trends (monthly, Palgrave Macmillan)
7.18	Office for National Statistics	Labour Market Trends (monthly, Palgrave Macmillan) Monthly Digest of Statistics (Palgrave Macmillan)
Annual Survey of Hours and Earnings 7.19, 7.20, 7.23, 7.24	Office for National Statistics	Annual Survey of Hours and Earnings (annual, ONS)
Average Earnings Index 7.21, 7.22	Office for National Statistics	Labour Market Trends (monthly, Palgrave Macmillan) Monthly Digest of Statistics (Palgrave Macmillan)
7.25	Department of Trade and Industry	

8. Personal income, expenditure and wealth

8.1	Office for National Statistics	Economic Trends, May (monthly, Palgrave Macmillan)
8.2	Board of HM Revenue and Customs	HMRC National Statistics www.hmrc.gov.uk<http://www.hmrc.gov.uk> Economic Trends (monthly, Palgrave Macmillan)
8.3 – 8.5	Office for National Statistics	Expenditure and Food Survey, annual) (1990 onwards edition-Family Spending) (annual, Palgrave Macmillan)

9. Health

National Health Service 9.1	Department of Health service	Appropriation Accounts (annual) www.statswales.gov.uk Health and Personal Social Services Statistics for England (annual)
	National Assembly for Wales	Health Statistics Wales (annual)
9.2	Scottish Executive, NHS National Services Scotland	
9.3	Department of Health, Social Services and Public Safety (Northern Ireland)	Summary of Health and Personal Social Services (Northern Ireland) Accounts (annual) Hospital Statistics (annual)

Sources

Table number and subject in Abstract	Government department or other organisation	Official publication or other source
9.4, 9.5	Information Centre for Health and Social Care National Assembly for Wales Scottish Health Service, NHS National Services Scotland	Health and Personal Social Services Statistics for England (annual) Department of Health, Medical and Dental Workforce Census
Public health 9.6	Office for National Statistics General Register Office (Scotland) Northern Ireland Statistics and Research Agency	
9.7	HPA Centre for Infections	Communicable Disease Statistics Series MB2 (annual) Annual Review of Communicable Diseases
	NHS in Scotland NHS National Services Scotland	Scottish Health Statistics (annual)
	Communicable Disease Surveillance Centre (NI)	Annual report of the Registrar General Northern Ireland Quarterly return of births, deaths and marriages
9.8 – 9.10	Health and Safety Executive	Health and Safety Statistics (annual)

10. Social protection

Social security pensions, benefits and allowances 10.1	Department for Work and Pensions H M Revenue and Customs Department of Health, Social Services and Public Safety (Northern Ireland)	National Insurance Fund Account (annual)
10.2	Department for Work and Pensions	
10.3, 10.5	Department for Work and Pensions (Information and Analysis Directorate) Ministry of Defence/DASA (Pay and Pensions) H M Revenue and Customs	
10.4	H M Revenue and Customs	

Table number and subject in Abstract	Government department or other organisation	Official publication or other source
10.6 – 10.8, 10.12 – 10.19	Department for Work and Pensions (Information and Analysis Directorate)	
10.9, 10.11	H M Revenue and Customs	
10.15	Ministry of Defence/DASA (Pay and Pensions)	
Working Family Tax Credit 10.10	H M Revenue and Customs Department for Work and Pensions (Information and Analysis Directorate)	Quarterly Enquiry United Kingdom (quarterly)
Social services 10.20,10.21 – 10.24	Office for National Statistics Department for Education and Skills	Appropriation (annual) Northern Ireland Annual Abstract of Statistics
10.20	HM Treasury	HM Treasury Expenditure Statistical Analyses
Housing and community amenities 10.25	Office for National Statistics	

11. Crime and justice

11.1	Home Office	Police Service Strength England and Wales 2002/03 Home Office Statistical Bulletin 11/03
	Scottish Executive Justice Department	Scotland: Report of Her Majesty's Chief Inspector of Constabulary for Scotland (annual)
	The Police Service of Northern Ireland	The Chief Constable's Annual Report
11.2	Home Office	Crime in England and Wales 2003/04 Home Office Statistical Bulletin 10/04
11.3 – 11.9	Home Office	Criminal Statistics, England and Wales (annual) (TSO) Offender Management Caseload Statistics 2003 (annual) Digest of Welsh Statistics (annual, Welsh Office)
11.10 – 11.11	Home Office	Offender Management Caseload Statistics 2003
11.12	Home Office	HM Prison Service Annual Report and Accounts April 2003 – March 2004

Sources

Table number and subject in Abstract	Government department or other organisation	Official publication or other source
11.13	Scottish Executive Justice Department	Recorded Crime in Scotland, 2004/05
11.14 – 11.17	Scottish Executive Justice Department	Criminal Proceedings in Scottish Courts, 2002
11.18, 11.19	Scottish Executive Justice Department	Prison Statistics Scotland, 2003 Scottish Prison Service Annual Report and Accounts 2001–03
11.20	The Police Service of Northern Ireland	
11.21 – 11.23	Northern Ireland Office	A Commentary on Northern Ireland Crime Statistics 2003 A Commentary on Northern Ireland Crime Statistics 2004
12. Lifestyles		
12.1	Department for Culture, Media and Sport	Department for Culture, Media and Sport Annual Report 2002
12.2	Department for Culture, Media and Sport	Table B17 – Labour Market Trends (monthly, Palgrave Macmillan)
12.3	Cinema Advertising Association	
12.4	UK Film Council	
12.5	VisitBritain	Sightseeing in the UK 2002
12.6	VisitBritain Wales Tourist Board VisitScotland Northern Ireland Tourist Board	The UK Tourist: Statistics (annual) www.staruk.org.uk The national tourism statistics website
12.7 – 12.8	Office for National Statistics	Travel Trends (annual, Palgrave Macmillan) Overseas Travel and Tourism First Release Monthly Digest of Statistics (Palgrave Macmillan) International Passenger Survey MQ6 Overseas Travel and Tourism
12.9	Target Group Index, BMRB International	
12.10	Department for Culture, Media and Sport	Camelot – National Lottery Press Releases
	Gaming Board for Great Britain	The Gaming Board for Great Britain Annual Report www.gbgb.org.uk

Table number and subject in Abstract	Government department or other organisation	Official publication or other source
13. Environment		
13.1, 13.20	Office for National Statistics	Environmental Accounts (2006) Spring edition (biennial) www.statistics.gov.uk/statbase/ Product.asp?vlnk=3698
13.2 – 13.7, 13.9, 13.13, 13.14, 13.16 –13.18, 13.21	Department for Environment, Food and Rural Affairs	e–Digest of Environmental Statistics (annual) www.defra.gov.uk/environment/statistics/index.htm The Environment in your Pocket (annual)
13.8	Centre for Ecology and Hydrology, Wallingford	www.ceh–nerc.ac.uk/data/NWA.htm
	The Met Office	www.met–office.gov.uk
13.10	Scottish Environment Protection Agency	www.sepa.org.uk/pdf/data/classification/water
13.11	Centre for Ecology and Hydrology, Wallingford	www.ceh–nerc.ac.uk/data/NWA.htm
	Environment Agency	www.environment–agency.gov.uk
	Water plcs	
13.12	Office of Water Services (OFWAT)	Companies 2004 June Return to OFWAT (annual)
13.15	Environment Agency	
13.19	The Chartered Institute of Environmental Health	
14. Housing		
14.1	Department for Communities and Local Government National Assembly for Wales Scottish Executive Department for Social Development, Northern Ireland	
14.2	Office for National Statistics	General Household Survey
14.3	Department for Communities and Local Government	www.housing.odpm.gov.uk/statistics (Live Tables 241–247)
	National Assembly for Wales	Welsh Housing Statistics (annual, NAfW)

Sources

Table number and subject in Abstract	Government department or other organisation	Official publication or other source
	Scottish Executive	Statistical Bulletins on Housing (SE)
	Department for Social Development, Northern Ireland	Northern Ireland Housing Statistics (annual)
14.4	Department for Communities and Local Government	www.odpm.gov.uk
14.5	Department for Communities and Local Government National Assembly for Wales	
14.6	Council of Mortgage Lenders Department for Communities and Local Government	
14.7	The Court Service Northern Ireland Court Service	
14.8	Department for Communities and Local Government National Assembly for Wales Scottish Executive	
14.9	Department for Communities and Local Government	Homelessness Statistical Release (quarterly) www.odpm.gov.uk

15. Transport and communications

General
15.1, 15.2, 15.4	Department for Transport	
15.3	Office for National Statistics	

Road transport
15.5 – 15.12	Department for Transport	Transport Statistics Great Britain (annual, TSO) Vehicle Licensing Statistics (annual, TSO) Monthly Digest of Statistics (Palgrave Macmillan) Road accidents in Great Britain (annual, TSO) Road accidents Wales (annual, National Assembly for Wales)
15.11	Driving Standards Agency	
15.13, 15.14	Department of Regional Development, Northern Ireland	Transport Statistics NI

Table number and subject in Abstract	Government department or other organisation	Official publication or other source
Rail transport 15.20, 15.21	Department for Transport	Transport Statistics Great Britain (annual, TSO) Health and Safety Executive: Industry and Services (annual) Bulletin of Rail Statistics (quarterly)
15.22, 15.23	Department of Regional Development, Northern Ireland	Driver and Vehicle Licensing, Northern Ireland
Air transport 15.24 – 15.28	Civil Aviation Authority	Monthly Digest of Statistics (Palgrave Macmillan) Civil Aviation Authority; Annual Statements of Movements, Passengers and Cargo Civil Aviation Authority; Monthly Statements of Movements, Passengers and Cargo
Sea transport 15.29, 15.30	Department for Transport	Maritime Statistics (annual, TSO) Monthly Digest of Statistics (Palgrave Macmillan)
Passenger movement 15.31	Department for Transport Civil Aviation Authority	Monthly Digest of Statistics (Palgrave Macmillan) movement
Communications 15.32	Royal Mail Parcel Force Capita Business Services Ltd. Post Office Counters Ltd.	Monthly Digest of Statistics (Palgrave Macmillan) Post Office report and accounts (annual)
16. National accounts		
16.1 – 16.22	Office for National Statistics	United Kingdom National Accounts (annual, Palgrave Macmillan) Monthly Digest of Statistics (Palgrave Macmillan)
17. Prices		
Producer prices 17.1, 17.2	Office for National Statistics	Producer Price Index Press Notice (monthly) Business Monitor MM22, Producer Price Indices Monthly Digest of Statistics (Palgrave Macmillan)
Consumer prices 17.3 – 17.6	Office for National Statistics	Monthly Digest of Statistics (Palgrave Macmillan) Labour Market Trends (monthly, Palgrave Macmillan) Focus on Consumer Price Indices (monthly, ONS)
17.7, 17.8	Department for Environment, Food and Rural Affairs	Agriculture in the UK (annual) Agricultural Price Indices, Statistical notice (monthly)

Sources

Table number and subject in Abstract	Government department or other organisation	Official publication or other source
		Monthly Digest of Statistics (Palgrave Macmillan)
17.9	Department for Environment, Food and Rural Affairs	Economic Trends (monthly, Palgrave Macmillan) Agriculture in the UK (annual) UK Economic Accounts (quarterly, Palgrave Macmillan)

18. Government finance

Central government

18.1 – 18.3	Office for National Statistics	Financial Statistics (monthly, Palgrave Macmillan)
18.4	HM Treasury	Consolidated Fund and National Loans Fund Accounts
	Office for National Statistics	Financial Statistics (monthly, Palgrave Macmillan)
18.5	Office for National Statistics	United Kingdom National Accounts (annual, Palgrave Macmillan)
18.6 – 18.7	HM Treasury	Consolidated Fund and National Loans Fund Accounts
	Office for National Statistics	Financial Statistics (monthly, Palgrave Macmillan)
18.8	Bank of England	

Central government

18.9, 18.10	HM Revenue and Customs	IHMRC

Rateable values

18.11	HM Revenue and Customs	IHMRC

Local authorities

18.12, 18.13	Department for Communities and Local Government	Local government financial statistics (England) (annual)
	National Assembly for Wales	Welsh local government financial statistics (annual)
	Public Works Loan Board	Annual report of the Public Works Loan Board
	Scottish Executive, Economic Advice and Statistics	Local financial returns (Scotland) (annual)
	Department of Finance and Personnel for Northern Ireland	
	Department of the Environment for	

Table number and subject in Abstract	Government department or other organisation	Official publication or other source
	Northern Ireland	
	Chartered Institute of Public Finance and Accountancy	
18.14	Department for Communities and Local Government	Local government financial statistics (England) (annual)
	National Assembly for Wales	Welsh local government financial statistics (annual)
18.15, 18.16	Department for Communities and Local Government	Local government financial statistics (England) (annual)
18.17 – 18.19	Scottish Executive, Economic Advice and Statistics	Local financial returns (Scotland) (annual)
18.20	Department of the Environment for Northern Ireland	District Council – Summary of Statement of Accounts (annual)

19. External trade and investment

19.1 – 19.8	HM Revenue and Customs	OTS1 – Overseas Trade Statistics – Extra EC, (formerly MM20) (monthly)
		OTS2 – Overseas Trade Statistics – Intra EC and World, (formerly MM20A) (monthly)
		OTSQ – Overseas Trade Statistics – Intra EC, (formerly MQ20) (quarterly)
		OTSA – Overseas Trade Statistics – Extra and Intra EC, (formerly MA20) (annual)
	Office for National Statistics	Business Monitor MM24, Monthly Review of External Trade Statistics (monthly, ONS)
		Overseas Trade Analysed in Terms of Industries MQ10 (quarterly, ONS)
		Monthly Digest of Statistics (monthly, Palgrave Macmillan)
19.9 – 19.18	Office for National Statistics	United Kingdom Balance of Payments (annual, Palgrave Macmillan)
	Bank of England	(quarterly, Palgrave Macmillan) UK Economic Accounts Financial Statistics (monthly, Palgrave Macmillan) Foreign Direct Investment MA4 (annual, National Statistics website)

Sources

Table number and subject in Abstract	Government department or other organisation	Official publication or other source
20. Research and development		
20.1 – 20.5	Office for National Statistics	Business Monitor MA14, Research and Development in UK Business (annual, ONS), Economic Trends (monthly, Palgrave Macmillan), Gross Domestic Expenditure on Research and Development (annual, ONS)
21. Agriculture, fisheries and food		
Agriculture		
21.1, 21.2	Department for Environment, Food and Rural Affairs	Agriculture in the United Kingdom (annual)
21.3 – 21.5	Department for Environment, Food and Rural Affairs	Agricultural Statistics; United Kingdom (annual) Scottish Agricultural Economics (annual) Welsh Agricultural Statistics (annual, National Assembly for Wales)
21.6	Forestry Commission	Great Britain: Forestry Statistics (annual)
	Department of Agriculture and Rural Development (Northern Ireland)	Northern Ireland Annual Abstract of Statistics
21.7, 21.8	Department for Environment, Food and Rural Affairs	DEFRA Statistical Notice
Food		
21.9 – 21.12	Department for Environment, Food and Rural Affairs	Monthly Digest of Statistics (Palgrave Macmillan)
21.13	Department for Environment, Food and Rural Affairs	Agricultural Statistics, United Kingdom (annual)
Fisheries		
21.14, 21.15	Department of Environment, Food and Rural Affairs	England and Wales: Sea fisheries statistical tables (annual)
	Scottish Executive Agricultural Departments	Scotland: Fisheries of Scotland report (annual) Scottish Sea fisheries statistics (annual, TSO)
Family Food		
21.16	Department for Environment, Food and Rural Affairs	Expenditure and Food Survey

Table number and subject in Abstract	Government department or other organisation	Official publication or other source
22. Production		
Production and construction 22.1	Office for National Statistics	Annual Business Inquiry (www.statistics.gov.uk/abi/)
Manufacturers sales 22.2	Office for National Statistics	ProdCom: Product Sales and Trade Annual Reports – PRA series (annual, ONS) Product Sales and Trade Quarterly Reports – PRQ series (quarterly, ONS)
22.3	Office for National Statistics	UK Business: Activity, Size and Location (formerly Business Monitor PA1003) (annual, ONS)
Energy 22.4 – 22.13	Department of Trade and Industry (Energy Strategy Unit)	Digest of United Kingdom Energy Statistics (annual) Energy Trends (monthly and quarterly) Annual Business Inquiry (www.statistics.gov.uk/abi/)
Iron and steel 22.14 – 22.16	Iron and Steel Statistics Bureau Limited	Iron and steel industry: annual statistics: Iron and Steel Statistics Bureau Limited Regional Trends (annual, Palgrave Macmillan)
Industrial materials 22.17	World Bureau of Metal Statistics Aluminium Federation	World Metal Statistics (monthly) Annual Business Inquiry (www.statistics.gov.uk/abi/)
22.18	Fertiliser Manufacturers' Association	Monthly Digest of Statistics (Palgrave Macmillan) Annual Business Inquiry (www.statistics.gov.uk/abi/)
Minerals 22.19	Department for Communities and Local Government	Minerals (Business Monitor PA 1007) (annual, ONS) Natural Environment Research Council: United Kingdom
	Department of Trade and Industry	Minerals Yearbook
	Department of Economic Development (Northern Ireland)	Northern Ireland Annual Abstract of Statistics
Building Materials 22.20	Department of Trade and Industry	Monthly Statistics of Building Materials and Components (DTI) Monthly Digest of Statistics (Palgrave Macmillan)

Sources

Table number and subject in Abstract	Government department or other organisation	Official publication or other source
Construction (output) 22.21	Department of Trade and Industry	Construction Statistics Annual (DTI)
Construction (new orders) 22.22	Department of Trade and Industry	Construction Statistics Annual (DTI)
Engineering 22.23, 22.24	Office for National Statistics	Annual Business Inquiry (www.statistics.gov.uk/abi/) Business Monitor PA1003 – Size Analysis of United Kingdom Businesses 2002
Motor vehicle production 22.25	Office for National Statistics	Business Monitor PM 34.10, (monthly, ONS) Annual Business Inquiry (www.statistics.gov.uk/abi/)
Drink and tobacco 22.26, 22.27	HM Revenue and Customs	Annual report of the Commissioners of HMRC
	Office for National Statistics	Monthly Digest of Statistics (Palgrave Macmillan)

23. Banking, insurance, etc

Banking 23.1	Bank of England	Bank of England Annual Report and Accounts
23.2	APACS – The UK payments association	Yearbook of Payment Statistics 2005 or UK Payment Statistics for figures 1995–2005
23.3 – 22.5	Bank of England	Bank of England, Statistical Interactive Database
23.6	Bank of England	Bank of England, Statistical Interactive Database
23.7	Bank of England	Bank of England, Statistical Interactive Database
23.8	Bank of England	Bank of England Quarterly Bulletin
23.9 – 23.12	Bank of England	Monthly Digest of Statistics (Palgrave Macmillan) Financial Statistics (monthly, Palgrave Macmillan)

Table number and subject in Abstract	Government department or other organisation	Official publication or other source
Other financial institutions 23.13	Financial Services Authority	Building Societies: Statistical Tables www.fsa.gov.uk/pubs/annual/ar03_04/bs_statistics.html
23.14	Office for National Statistics	Business Monitor SDQ7, Assets and Liabilities of Finance Houses and Other Credit Companies (quarterly, ONS)
23.15	Office for National Statistics	Financial Statistics (monthly, Palgrave Macmillan) Monthly Digest of Statistics (Palgrave Macmillan) Business Monitor MQ5, Insurance Companies; Pension Funds and Trusts Investments (quarterly, ONS) First Release
23.16, 23.17	Office for National Statistics	Financial Statistics (monthly, Palgrave Macmillan) Business Monitor MQ5, Insurance Companies; Pension Funds and Insolvency Trusts Investments (quarterly, ONS)
23.18 – 23.21	Department of Trade and Industry	Insolvency Annual Report (DTI) and Industry Companies (DTI) Financial Statistics (monthly, Palgrave Macmillan)

24. Service industry

Retail trades 24.1	Office for National Statistics	Annual Business Inquiry (www.statistics.gov.uk/abi/)
24.2	Office for National Statistics	Business Monitor SDM 28 (www.statistics.gov.uk/rsi)
Motor trades 24.3	Office for National Statistics	Annual Business Inquiry (www.statistics.gov.uk/abi/)
Catering 24.4	Office for National Statistics	Annual Business Inquiry (www.statistics.gov.uk/abi/)

Index - figures indicate table numbers

A

Abortions, 5.18
Absolute discharge, 11.7, 11.23
Acceptances for settlement, 5.10
Accidents:
  airways, 15.27
  coal–mining, 9.10
  industrial, 9.10
  road, 15.17
  transport, 9.10
Acid rain, 13.1
Adoptions, 5.23
Aerodromes: activity, 15.28
Aerospace industry: cost of research, 20.4
Agriculture:
  crops and grass, 21.4
  index of prices, 17.7, 17.8
  land use, 21.3
  livestock, 21.5
  machinery, 22.2
  numbers employed, 21.13
  production and income, 21.1, 21.2
  sales for food, 21.7
  stocks, 21.8
Agriculture, fisheries and food, 21.1– 21.16
Agriculture, forestry and fishing:
  commodity price trends, 17.8
  earnings of agricultural workers, 7.19, 7.22, 21.11, 21.12
  employment, 7.5, 21.13
  gross value added, 16.4
  index of average earnings, 7.22
  index numbers of output, 16.5
  injuries to workers, 9.10
  production and disposals, 21.1, 21.2
  waste from, 13.17
  woodland area, 21.6
  wood production, 21.6
Aid, overseas, UK expenditure:
  by country, 3.2
  by organisation, 3.1
Aids: deaths from, 9.6
Air quality, 13.1
Air transport, 15.4, 15.24–15.28
Aircraft noise, 13.19
Airlines, UK:
  accidents on, 15.27
  operations and traffic, 15.26, 15.28
Alcoholic drink:
  beer, spirits and wine: production and consumption, 22.26

catering and allied trades, 24.4
household expenditure, 16.15
Retail Prices Index, 17.4
Alcohol abuse: deaths from, 9.6
Allowance:
  Attendance, 10.3, 10.5, 10.24
  Child's special, 10.1
  Disability living, 10.3, 10.5
  Guardian's 10.1, 10.3
  Jobseeker's, 10.1, 10.3, 10.5, 10.6, 10.24
  Invalidity, 10.3
  Mobility, 10.3
Aluminium:
  packaging: recycling, 13.18
  production and consumption, 22.17
Alzheimer's disease: deaths from, 9.6
Ambulances:
  licences, current, 15.13
  new registrations, 15.14
Animal feedingstuffs:
  agricultural input, 21.1, 21.2
  disposals, 21.10
  exports, 19.3
  imports, 19.4
  prices, 17.7
  production, 21.9
Animals: see also Livestock
  exports, 19.3
  imports, 19.4
  on agricultural holdings, 21.5
  price index, 17.8, 17.9
  sold for slaughter, 21.9
Area:
  by country, standard region, 1.1
  cities, 5.5
  conurbations, 5.5
  crops, 21.3
  forest, 21.6
  land:
    agricultural, 21.3
    total, 1.1
  rural districts, 5.5
  standard regions, 5.5
  urban, 5.5
Armed Forces, see Army, Royal Air Force, Royal Navy and Royal Marines
Army:
  cadet forces, 4.5
  civilian manpower, 4.6
  deaths, 4.9
  defence services and the civilian community, 4.11
  deployment of service personnel, 4.8

HM Forces employment, 7.4
formation, 4.3
medical staff, 4.10
outflow, 4.4
recruitment, 4.2
strength, 4.5
uniformed medical staff, 4.10
Asbestosis: occupational deaths from, 9.9
Assault offences, 11.3, 11.4, 11.13, 11.20–11.22
Assets, 23.3
Asthma: deaths from, 9.6
Atmospheric emissions, 13.1
Attendance allowance, 10.3, 10.24
Attendance at leisure and cultural activities, 12.9
Attendance centre orders, 11.7
Average earnings: see Earnings
Aviation: civil accidents, 15.27
Aviation spirit:
  deliveries, 22.13
  output, 22.12

B

Bacon and ham:
  disposals, 21.10
  production, 21.9
Balance of payments, 19.9–19.12
  current balance, 19.11
  investment and other capital flows, 19.9
  official financing:
  overseas investment, 19.13–19.18
  summary, 19.9
Bank advances, 23.4
Bank clearings, 23.2
Bank deposits, 23.5
Banking, finance, insurance, etc:
  employment, 7.5
Banking, insurance, etc, 23.1–23.21
Bank of England, 23.1
Bankruptcies, 23.20
Barley:
  area, 21.3
  disposals, 21.10
  harvested, 21.4
  output, 21.1, 21.2
  sales, 21.7
  stocks, 21.8
Base rates, 23.8
Bathing water, 13.14
Beef production, 21.9

Beer: production and consumption, 22.26

Bereavement benefits, 10.13

Betting and gaming:
    expenditure, 12.10
    offences, 11.3

Bicycles – *see* Cycles, pedal

Births:
    annual changes, 5.2
    by age of mother, 5.17
    inside and outside marriage, 5.16
    live births, 5.15
    occurrences, 5.16
    outside marriage, 5.16
    stillbirths, 5.15

Bitumen:
    deliveries, 22.13
    output, 22.12

Blood diseases: deaths from, 9.6

Books: retail trade, 24.1

Bricks: production, 22.20

Bronchitis: deaths from, 9.6

Building materials: production, 22.20

Building societies:
    balance sheet, 23.13
    current transactions, 23.13
    payment of interest on shares and deposits, 23.13

Bulk carriers: tonnage, 15.29

Burglary offences, 11.2–11.4

Buses, coaches, etc:
    fares, indices of, 15.16
    licences current, 15.8, 15.13
    new vehicle registrations, 15.9, 15.14
    passenger journeys, 15.4, 15.15
    production, 22.25

Butane and propane:
    deliveries, 22.13
    output, 22.12

Butter:
    disposals, 21.10
    production, 21.9
    stocks, 21.8

C

Calcspar: production, 22.19

Cameras: sales, 22.23

Camping sites, 24.4

Canals: biological and chemical quality, 13.9, 13.10

Cancer: deaths from, 9.6

Capital formation, 16.19–16.22

Caravans: sales, 22.2

Cars: *see also* Motor vehicles
    households with use of, 15.12
    licences current, 15.8, 15.13
    new registrations, 15.9, 15.14
    production, 22.25

Carbon dioxide: total emissions, 13.2

Carbon monoxide: emissions by source, 13.6

Cargo liners: tonnage, 15.29

Casualties in road accidents, 15.17

Catering trades:
    contractors, 24.4
    employment, 7.5
    hotels and motels, 24.4
    licensed clubs, 24.4
    restaurants and cafes, 24.4
    turnover, 24.4

Cattle:
    agricultural output, 21.1, 21.2
    on agricultural holdings, 21.5
    prices, 17.8, 17.9
    slaughtered, 21.7

Cement: production, 22.20

Central government expenditure:
    education, 10.21
    housing and community amenities, 10.25
    National Health Service, 10.22
    social security benefits, 10.24
    welfare services, 10.23
    social services and housing, 10.20

Census of:
    marital condition, 5.4
    population, 5.1–5.5
    production, 22.1

Cereals, *see also* Wheat, Barley, Oats
    area, 21.3
    disposals, 21.10
    exports, 19.3
    harvested, 21.4
    imports, 19.4
    prices, 17.7–17.9
    sales, 21.7
    stocks, 21.8

Cerebrovascular disease: deaths from, 9.6

Chalk: production, 22.19

Channel Tunnel, 15.30

Cheese:
    disposals, 21.10
    production, 21.9

Chemicals:
    exports, 19.3
    imports, 19.4
    sales ratio, 19.2

Chemical industry
    census of production, 22.1
    employment, 7.5
    expenditure on research and development, 20.4
    index of average earnings, 7.22
    materials and fuels used, 17.1
    producer price index, 17.1, 17.2
    size of establishments, 22.3

Chert and flint: production, 22.19

Child Benefit, 10.3, 10.9, 10.24

Child population, 5.3

Childbirth: deaths in, 9.6

Child's special allowance, 10.1

Child Tax Credit, 10.11

China clay: production, 22.19

Chocolate confectionery:
    disposals, 21.10
    production, 21.9

Cider and perry, 22.26

Cinema, 12.4

Cities: population, 5.5

Citizenship: country of last/next residence, 5.9

Civil aviation:
    accidents, 15.27
    activity at aerodromes, 15.28

Civil Service staff, 7.7

Civilian community and defence services, 4.11

Civilian migration, 5.7–5.9

Claimant count, 7.11, 7.13–7.14

Clay: production, 22.19

Clearing banks, 23.2

Clothing and footwear:
    Consumer Prices Index, 17.4
    employment, 7.5
    expenditure on, 16.14
    exports, 19.3
    imports, 19.4
    retail trades, 24.1, 24.2

Coaches, buses, etc, *see* Buses, coaches, etc

Coaches (railway): in use, 15.22

Coal
    census of production, 22.1
    consumption, 22.5
    opencast production, 22.6
    production, 22.4, 22.6
    stocks and supply, 22.6

Coal extraction and solid fuels:
    deaths and injuries, 9.10
    gross value added, 16.4

Cocoa beans: production, 21.9

Coffee:
    disposals, 21.10
    stocks, 21.8

Commercial vehicles, production, 22.25

Commodity price trends, 17.9

Commonwealth migration into and out of the United Kingdom, 5.9

Community punishment order, 11.7

Companies:
    insolvencies, 23.19, 23.21
    gross fixed capital formation, 16.19, 16.21

Compound feedstuffs: prices, 17.7

Index

Concrete:
    blocks, bricks, etc, production, 22.20
    ready mixed, production, 22.20
Conditional discharge, 11.7, 11.23
Confectionery:
    disposals, 21.10
    production, 21.9
Congenital anomalies: deaths from, 9.6
Consolidated Fund:
    assets and liabilities, 18.7
    revenue and expenditure, 18.4
Construction:
    average earnings, 7.19, 7.22
    production, 22.1
    employment, 7.5
    gross value added, 16.4
    industrial stoppages, 7.18
    injuries to workers, 9.10
    new work (value), 22.21
    noise from, 13.19
    output:
        index numbers, 16.5
        value, 22.22
    waste from, 13.17
Consumer credit, 23.14
Consumer Prices Index, 17.4
Contributory pensions, 10.14
Conurbations: population, 5.5
Copper:
    production, consumption and stocks,
        22.17
    recycling, 13.18
    tubing production, 22.17
Corn, mixed:
    acreage, 21.3
Corporate income: 16.6, 16.7
County Court mortgage possession
    orders, 14.7
Courts:
    offenders found guilty, 11.3, 11.5,
        11.21, 11.22
    people called to, 11.15
    sentences, 11.7, 11.8, 11.23
Cream: production, 21.9
Crime and justice, 11.1–11.24
Criminal damage,
    11.2–11.4, 11.20–11.22
Criminal offences:
    age analysis, 11.5, 11.6, 11.17
    sex analysis, 11.5–11.7, 11.17
    juvenile offenders, 11.5, 11.6, 11.17,
        11.22
    proceedings in court, 11.7, 11.14,
        11.21–11.23
    type of offence, 11.2–11.4, 11.13,
        11.14, 11.20–11.22
Crops:
    area 21.3
    harvested, 21.4

input/output volume, 21.2
producer price index, 17.8
production and income account
Crude oil:
    refinery throughput, 22.12
    supply and disposals, 22.13
Cultural activities, 12.9
Culture, media and sport: expenditure,
    12.1
Cycles, pedal:
    accidents, 15.17
    offences, 11.3
    road traffic, 15.4, 15.7

D

Dairy product:
    disposals, 21.10
    exports, 19.3
    imports, 19.4
    production, 21.9
Death rates, 5.21
Deaths:
    age and sex analysis, 5.19
    armed forces, 4.9
    average annual changes, 5.2
    by cause, 9.6
    infant and maternal, 5.20
    fatal accidents:
        air, 15.27
        due to occupationally related lung
            disease, 9.9
        industrial, 9.10
        motor vehicle, 15.17
Debt:
    local authorities, 18.12
    public sector, 18.3
Decrees absolute: granted, 5.13, 5.14
Defence:
    accommodation, 4.7
    armed forces, 4.5
    civilian manpower, 4.6
    deaths of service personnel, 4.9
    expenditure on, 4.1
    formation, 4.3
    location 4.8
    manpower strengths, 4.5
    outflow, 4.4
    recruitment, 4.2
    research, cost of, 20.3
    services and the civilian community,
        4.11
Degrees obtained: by subject and
    gender, 6.10
Demolition: waste from, 13.17
Dental services: government
    expenditure, 10.22

Dentists:
    numbers on list, 9.1–9.5
    payments, 9.1–9.3
Designated areas: by region, 13.21
Diesel oil, see Gas/diesel oil
Disablement benefits, 10.3, 10.5, 10.15,
    10.18
Diseases:
    deaths from, 9.6
    industrial, 9.8, 9.9
    notification, 9.7
Distribution, hotels and catering, repairs:
    employment, 7.5
    gross fixed capital formation, 16.21–
        16.22
Divorce:
    by age, 5.13
    proceedings, 5.14
Doctors:
    numbers on list, 9.1–9.5
    patients per doctor, 9.1–9.3
    payments to, 9.1–9.3
Domestic premises: noise from, 13.19
Domestic tourism, 12.6
Drink industry, see Food, drink and
    tobacco industry
Driving licences, 15.11
Driving test pass rates, 15.10
Drug offences:
    persons found guilty, 11.3, 11.4
    persons serving sentences, 11.11
    recorded, 11.2, 11.13, 11.20
Drunk driving, 11.13, 11.14
Drunkenness, 11.3, 11.4, 11.13, 11.14
Durable goods, 8.5, 16.14, 16.15
Dwellings:
    gains and losses, 14.4
    stock of, 14.1, 14.4
Dysentery: notifications, 9.7

E

Earnings:
    average, 7.19–7.24
    agricultural workers, 21.11, 21.12
Earth–moving machinery: sales, 22.2
Economic activity, 7.15
Economic inactivity, 7.16–7.17
Education, see also Schools, Students,
    Teachers, Higher Education,
    Universities, 6.1–6.11
    average earnings, 7.19, 7.22
    employment, 7.5
    government expenditure, 10.20,
        18.13, 18.15, 18.17
    grants to, 18.19
    gross value added by industry, 16.4–
        16.5

higher and further, 6.1, 6.6–6.10
labour disputes, 7.18
nursery, 6.1, 6.3, 6.11
primary and secondary, 6.1–6.5, 6.11
pupils' qualifications, 6.5
Eggs:
    disposals, 21.10
    output, 21.1, 21.2
    prices, 17.8, 17.9
    sales, 21.7
Elections, Parliamentary:
    by–elections, 2.2
    electorate, 2.1
    General elections, 2.1
Electrical appliances: turnover, 22.23
Electrical and electronic engineering:
    employment, 7.5
    expenditure on research and
    development, 20.4
    producer price index, 17.2
    production, 22.1
    size of units, 22.3
    turnover, 22.23, 22.24
Electrical machinery:
    exports, 19.3
    imports, 19.4
    sales, 22.2, 22.23
Electricity:
    capacity of generating plant, 22.9
    consumption, production and sales,
    22.8
Electronics equipment: turnover, 22.24
Emigration, 5.7, 5.8
Employers and self–employed, 7.4
Employment see also individual
    industries, 7.1–7.5
    agricultural, 21.13
    by age, 7.3
    by industry, 7.5
    by size of establishment, 22.3
    Civil Service, 7.7
    occupational analysis, 7.5
    self–employment, 7.2, 7.4
    status, 7.2
Energy, 22.4–22.13
    consumption, 22.5
    used in agriculture, price, 17.7
Energy and water supply industry:
    average earnings, 7.19, 7.22
    bank lending, 23.4
    employees, 7.5
    household expenditure, 16.15–16.17
    injuries to workers, 9.10
    producer price index, 17.1, 17.2
    water industry expenditure, 13.12
Energy consumption: total inland, 22.5
Entertainments: expenditure on, 16.17
Ethnic group, 5.6

Exchange rates, 23.10
Exchequer, see Consolidated Fund and
    National Loans Fund
Expectation of life, 5.22
Expenditure and Food Survey:
    food consumption, 21.16
    households and their expenditure, 8.4
    household durable goods, 8.5
    sources of household income, 8.3
Expenditure:
    by Department for Culture, Media
    and Sport, 12.1
    by households, 8.4
    by Government, 10.20 – 10.25
    on penal establishments, 11.12, 11.19
Exports:
    balance of payments, 19.9
    basic materials, 19.3
    basic metals 19.2
    by commodity, 19.3
    by destination, 19.5
    food, beverages and tobacco, 19.2,
    19.3
    manufactured goods, 19.3
    mineral fuels and lubricants, 19.2,
    19.3
    sales and import penetration, 19.2
    value, 19.1
External trade, 19.1–19.8

F

Family Credit, 10.3, 10.5, 10.10, 10.24
Family health services:
    England and Wales, 9.1
    Great Britain, 9.5
Feedingstuffs:
    agricultural input, 21.1, 21.2
    disposals, 21.10
    prices, 17.7
    production, 21.9
Ferry traffic, 15.30
Fertilisers:
    agricultural input, 21.1, 21.2
    prices, 17.7
    production and deliveries, 22.18
Fertility statistics, 5.15–5.17
Films, 12.4
Finance houses, 23.14
Fines:
    imprisoned due to default, 11.10,
    11.18, 11.24
    sentenced, 11.7, 11.16, 11.23
Fire clay: production, 22.19
Fire engines: licences current, 15.13
Fish:
    disposal, 21.10
    landings, 21.14

Fishery protection, 4.11
Fishing industry, 21.14, 21.15
    average earnings, 7.19
    employment, 7.5
    size of fleet, 21.15
Flour:
    disposals, 21.10
    production, 21.9
Flowers and plants:
    agricultural output, 21.1, 21.2
    prices, 17.8
Fodder crops:
    area, 21.3
    harvested, 21.4
Food:
    catering, allied trades, 24.4
    Consumer Prices Index, 17.4
    consumption, 21.16
    disposals, 21.10
    exports, 19.3
    household expenditure, 16.14–16.17
    imports, 19.4
    index of producer prices, 17.8
    production, 21.9
    Retail Prices Index, 17.5
    retail trade, 24.1, 24.2
    sales of agricultural produce, 21.7
    stocks, 21.8
Food, drink, and tobacco industry:
    census of production, 22.1
    employment, 7.5
    average earnings, 7.22
    size of establishments, 22.3
Food poisoning, notifications, 9.7
Food processing: machinery sales, 22.2
Footwear, see Clothing and footwear
Forces, see Army, Royal Air Force,
Royal Navy and Royal Marines
Foreign trade:
    imports and exports, 19.1–19.8
    seaborne trade, 15.29
Foreign visitors, see Migration
Forest area, 21.6
Forestry industry, 21.6
Fraud and forgery, 11.2–11.4, 11.11,
    11.20–11.22
Freight transport see also Goods
    transport, 15.3, 15.18, 15.19, 15.21
Fresh fruit: producer price, 17.8
Fruit:
    agricultural output, 21.1, 21.2
    area, 21.3
    commodity prices, 17.9
Fuel and power:
    Consumer Prices Index, 17.4
    household expenditure, 16.14
    retail price index, 17.5

Fuel consumption:
by class of consumer, 22.5
by type of fuel, 22.6, 22.7, 22.8
Fuel oil:
deliveries, 22.13
outputs, 22.12
Furniture industry, *see* Timber and
wooden furniture industries
Further education, 6.1, 6.6, 6.7

G

Gambling, 12.10
Gas
census of production, 22.1
gross value added 16.4, 16.5
production, sales, 22.7
Gas/diesel oil:
deliveries, 22.13
output, 22.7
General health services in N. Ireland, 9.3
Glass industry, 22.2
Glass recycling, 13.18
Glucose: production, 21.9
Goods transport:
railway, 15.3, 15.21
road, 15.3, 15.18, 15.19
water, 15.3
Goods vehicles:
licences current, 15.8, 15.13
registrations, 15.9, 15.14
Government:
consolidated fund assets and
liabilities, 18.7
exchequer financing, 18.4, 18.5
overseas trade, 19.8
securities, 23.1
Government expenditure:
education, 10.20
housing, 10.20, 10.24
National Health Service, 10.20, 10.22
research and development, 20.2–20.3
school meals, 10.21
social security benefits, 10.24
social services, 10.20, 10.23
welfare services, 10.20, 10.23
Grass:
acreage, 21.3
harvest, 21.4
Gravel and sand: production, 22.19
Greenhouse gases: emissions, 13.1,
13.2
Gross Domestic Product (GDP), 16.1–
16.3
Gross National Index (GNI), 16.1–16.3
Guardians' allowances, 10.1, 10.3,
Gypsum: production, 22.19

H

Hay: harvested, 21.4
Health, 9.1–9.10. *see also* National
Health Service, 9.1–9.10
average earnings, 7.19, 7.22
central government expenditure,
10.20, 10.22, 10.24
employment, 7.5
grants to local authorities, 18.15,
18.19
labour disputes, 7.18
local authority expenditure, 10.20,
18.13, 18.15, 18.17, 18.20
Heart disease: deaths from: 9.6
Heavy goods vehicles: registrations,
15.9
Higher education: 6.8–6.10
courses taken, 6.9
degrees and diplomas obtained, 6.10
expenditure on Research and
Development, 20.1, 20.2
government expenditure, 10.19
National Diplomas/Certificates, 6.10
students, 6.8–6.9
Hire purchase and loans, 23.14
HM Forces, *see* Army, Royal Air Force,
Royal Navy and Royal Marines
Holidays, 12.6–12.8
Home population, 5.1, 5.3, 5.5
Hops:
agricultural output, 21.1, 21.2
area, 21.3
harvested, 21.4
prices, 17.9
Horticultural crops: land use, 21.3
Hospitals: services, 9.1–9.5, 10.22
Hotels and motels, 24.4
employment, 7.5
Hours worked, 7.6, 7.19, 7.20, 7.24
Housebreaking offences, 11.13
Housebuilding completions, 14.5
Household goods:
Consumer Prices Index, 17.4
household expenditure, 16.15
Retail Prices Index, 17.5
retail trade, 24.1, 24.2
Households:
average incomes, 8.2
expenditure, 8.5, 16.14 – 16.17
food consumption, 21.16
in temporary accommodation, 14.9
source of income, 8.3
Housing:
Benefit, 10.5
central government expenditure,
10.20, 10.24
Consumer Prices Index, 17.4
dwellings completed, 14.3
grants to local authorities, 18.19,

homeless households, 14.9
household expenditure, 16.16
local authority expenditure, 10.20,
10.24, 18.13, 18.15, 18.17, 18.20
mortgages, 14.6
output by contractors, 22.24
Retail Prices Index, 17.4
stock of dwellings, 14.1
tenure, 14.2
Hypertensive disease: deaths from, 9.6

I

Igneous rock: production, 22.19
IMF, official financing, 19.9
Immigration, 5.8, 5.9
acceptances for settlement by
nationality, 5.10
Imports:
analysis by source, 19.6
balance of payments, 19.1, 19.9,
19.10
by commodity, 19.4
food, beverages and tobacco, 19.4
manufactured goods, 19.4
mineral fuels and lubricants, 19.4
penetration and export sales, 19.2
Imprisonment, 11.7, 11.8
Incapacity benefit, 10.1, 10.7, 10.8,
10.24
Income:
before and after tax, 8.1
GDP, income based, 16.2
local authorities, 18.13–18.16, 18.18,
18.19
national, 16.2
of households, 8.2, 8.3
personal, 16.2
Income support, 10.3, 10.5, 10.6, 10.16,
10.18, 10.24
Income tax:
allowances, 18.9
personal incomes before and after,
8.2
rates, 18.10
Index number of:
agricultural prices, 17.7, 17.8
average earnings, 7.21, 7.22
Consumer Prices Index, 17.4
Gross Domestic Product (GDP), 16.1
Gross National Index (GNI), 16.1
producer prices, 17.1–17.7
retail prices, 17.5
retail trade sales, 24.2
tax and price, 17.6
Indictable offences:
juveniles found guilty, 11.22
offenders cautioned, 11.4, 11.6

offenders found guilty, 11.3, 11.5, 11.21, 11.22
sentence or order, 11.7
Industrial:
deaths from accidents, 9.10
disablement pensions, 10.3, 10.5
diseases, 9.8–9.9
injuries benefit, 10.3, 10.24
premises, noise from, 13.19
production, index of 22.1
spirit:
deliveries, 22.13
output, 22.12
stoppages, 7.18
waste arisings, 13.17
Infant mortality, 5.20
Infectious diseases:
deaths from, 9.6
notifications, 9.7
Influenza: deaths from, 9.6
Insolvencies:
company, 23.19, 23.21
individual, 23.18
Instrument engineering:
sales, 22.24
size of establishments, 22.3
Insurance, see also National Insurance, 23.17
Insurance companies balance sheet, 23.17
International tourism, 12.7
Intoxication offences, 11.3, 11.13, 11.14
Invalidity benefits, 10.3, 10.7–10.8, 10.24
Investment overseas, 19.13–19.18
Investment trusts, 23.15
Iron and steel:
exports, 22.17
furnaces, 22.16
imports, 22.15
industry, fuel consumption, 22.5, 22.7
production, 22.14–22.16
scrap, 22.15
supplies, deliveries and stocks, 22.14

J

Jam and marmalade: production, 21.10
Jobseeker's Allowance, 10.1, 10.3, 10.5, 10.6, 10.24

K

Kerosene:
deliveries, 22.13
output, 22.12

L

Labour disputes, 7.18
Labour force, 7.1
Lamps, electric: sales, 22.23
Land:
area, 1.1
held by Ministry of Defence, 4.7
Law enforcement, 11.1–11.24
Lead:
production, consumption and stocks, 22.17
recycling, 13.18
Leather and leather goods:
census of production, 22.1
employment, 7.5
size of establishments, 22.3
Leisure activities, 12.9
Letter post, 15.32
Leukaemia: deaths from, 9.6
Liabilities:
foreign currency, 23.3
sterling, 23.3
Licences:
driving, 15.11
television, 15.32
vehicle, 15.8, 15.13
Life assurance:
industrial business, 23.17
market value of insurance companies, 23.17
Life tables, 5.22
Light rail: transport, 15.20
Limestone: production, 22.19
Liquidations, 23.19
Livestock:
agricultural input and output, 21.1, 21.2
on agricultural holdings, 21.5
prices, 17.8
purchase for slaughter, 21.7
Local authorities:
education, 10.21
expenditure on housing, 10.20, 10.25
expenditure on the National Health Service, 10.22
grants by central government, 18.20
income and expenditure, 18.13–18.20
loan debt, 18.12
sales and transfers of dwellings, 14.8
social services expenditure, 10.20, 10.23
welfare services expenditure, 10.23
Locomotives: railway, Northern Ireland, 15.22
London Regional Transport, 15.15, 15.16, 15.20

Lubricating oil:
deliveries, 22.13
output, 22.12
Lung disease: deaths, 9.9

M

Machinery:
sales, 22.23
exports, 19.3
imports, 19.2, 19.4
Magnesium and magnesium alloys:
production and consumption, 22.19
Maize:
disposals, 21.10
harvested, 21.4
stocks, 21.8
Malicious damage, 11.3
Manpower:
armed forces, 4.5
Civil Service, 7.7
National Health Service, 9.4, 9.5
number of employees in industry, 7.5
Manslaughter, offences, 11.3
Manufactured goods:
exports, 19.2, 19.3
imports, 19.2, 19.4
production, 22.23
Manufacturing industries:
capital formation, 16.19–16.22
census of production, 22.1
earnings, 7.19–7.22
employment, 7.5
expenditure on research and development, 20.4, 20.5
hours worked, 7.19, 7.20
index of average earnings, 7.21
index of materials and fuels purchased 17.1
injuries to workers, 9.10
labour disputes, 7.18
units by size, 22.3
Margarine: production, 21.9
Marital condition, 5.4
by age and sex, 5.12
status, 5.12
Marriages, 5.12
Material flows, 13.20
Maternal death rates, 5.20
Maternity benefits, 10.1, 10.3, 10.24
Measles: notifications of, 9.7
Meat:
disposals, 21.10
prices, 17.8, 17.9
production, 21.9
stocks, 21.8

Mechanical engineering industry:
    expenditure on research and
    development, 20.5
    index of average earnings, 7.22
    size of establishments, 22.3
Mechanical handling equipment: sales,
    22.23
Medical services, 9.1–9.5
Members of Parliament, elected, 2.1
Mental disorders: deaths from, 9.6
Metal goods engineering and vehicle
    industries:
    census of production, 22.1
    producer price index, 17.1, 17.2
    size of establishments, 22.3
    total sales, 22.23
Midwifery staff, 9.2–9.5
Migration, 5.2, 5.7–5.9
    acceptances for settlement by
    nationality, 5.10
    by sex, 5.8
    citizenship, 5.9
    country of last or next residence, 5.9
    usual occupation, 5.8
Milk:
    agricultural output, 21.1, 21.2
    prices, 17.8, 17.9
    sales, 21.7
Milk products:
    disposals, 21.10
    production, 21.9
Mineral oil and natural gas: extraction
    of, 22.1
Minerals: production, 22.19
Mining and quarrying:
    employment, 7.5
    injuries to workers, 9.10
    waste from, 13.17
Mining machinery, sales, 22.23
Mobility allowance, 10.3, 10.24
Money and bill rates, 23.9
Money stock, 23.6, 23.7
Mortality tables, 5.19
Mortgages, 14.6
Motor cycles:
    licences current, 15.8, 15.13
    new registrations, 15.9, 15.14
Motoring offences:
    called for trial, 11.14
    recorded by police (Scotland), 11.13
    offenders found guilty, 11.3
    offenders cautioned, 11.4
Motor spirit:
    deliveries, 22.13
    output, 22.12
Motor trades: commodity sales, 24.3
Motor vehicles:
    employment, 7.5
    household expenditure, 16.16

licenced, 15.8, 15.13
production, 22.25
registrations, 15.9, 15.14
repairs and servicing, 24.3
Motorways:
    length of, 15.6
    vehicle traffic, 15.5
Municipal waste, 13.17
Murder: persons found guilty, 11.3,
    11.20
Musculo–skeletal diseases: deaths from,
    9.6
Mutton and lamb: production, 21.9

N

National accounts, 16.1–16.22
National debt:
    borrowing and repayment, 18.6
    nominal amount outstanding, 18.3,
    18.7
National Health Service, 9.1–9.5, 10.22,
National insurance, 10.1, 10.2, 10.4,
    10.24
National Loans Fund:
    assets and liabilities, 18.7
    receipts and payments, 18.4
National Lottery, 12.10
National Rail see Rail transport and
    Railways
Natural gas, see Gas
Neoplasms: deaths from, 9.6
Nickel: production, 22.17
Nitrogen: production and deliveries,
    22.18
Nitrogen oxides: emissions by source,
    13.5
Nitrous oxide: total emissions, 13.2
Noise: complaints received, 13.19
Non–contributory benefits: expenditure,
    10.24
Nuclear energy, 22.8–22.10
Nursery schools, 6.1, 6.3, 6.11
Nursing staff in hospital, 9.2–9.4

O

Oats:
    agricultural output, 21.1, 21.2
    area, 21.3
    harvested, 21.4
    milled, production, 21.9
    prices, 17.7–17.9
    sales, 21.7
Occupation see Employment
Offal: production, 21.9
Offences, recorded, 11.2, 11.13, 11.20

Offenders:
    by age, 11.5, 11.17
    by previous convictions, 11.8
    cautioned, 11.4, 11.6
    found guilty, 11.3, 11.5, 11.16, 11.17,
    11.21, 11.22
    sentenced, 11.7, 11.8, 11.23
Office machinery and data processing
    equipment:
    producer price index, 17.1, 17.2
Official reserves, 19.9
Oilcake and meal:
    disposals, 21.10
    production, 21.9
    stocks, 21.8
Oil refining, 22.11, 22.12
Oils and fats:
    disposals, 21.10
    exports, 19.3
    imports, 19.4
    seed crushing production, 21.9
    stocks, 21.8
Oilseeds and nuts:
    agricultural output, 21.1, 21.2
    harvested, 21.4
    processed, 21.9
    stocks, 21.8
Opencast coal production, 22.6
Ophthalmic services, 9.1–9.5
Overseas
    aid, 3.1, 3.2
    trade in services, 19.8

P

Packaging products:
    manufacturers' sales, 22.2
    recycling, 13.18
Paper, printing and publishing:
    census of production, 22.1
    employment, 7.5
    exports, 19.2, 19.3
    imports, 19.4
    producer price index, 17.1, 17.2
    recycling, 13.18
    size of establishments, 22.3
Passenger movement, 15.4, 15.31
Peas for stockfeed:
    agricultural output, 21.1, 21.2
    harvested, 21.4
Pedal cycles, see Cycles, pedal
Pensioners:
    estimated number, 10.5, 10.14
    pensions, 10.1, 10.3, 10.5, 10.12,
    10.14, 10.15, 10.24
Pensions:
    credits, 10.17, 10.19
    disablement, 10.3, 10.5
    fund assets, 23.16

government expenditure, 10.24
    retirement, 10.1, 10.3, 10.5, 10.14,
      10.24
    war, 10.3, 10.5, 10.15, 10.24
    widow's, 10.1, 10.3, 10.5, 10.12,
      10.15
Personal income, expenditure and
    wealth, 8.1–8.5
Personal social services: work force,
    9.5
Pesticides, agricultural input, 21.1, 21.2
Petrol, *see* Motor spirit
Petroleum:
    consumption for fuel, 22.5
    exports, 19.3
    imports, 19.4
    production, 22.12
    retail sales, 24.3
Petroleum products:
    deliveries of, 22.13
    refined, 22.12
Petroleum coke, deliveries, 22.13
Pharmaceutical services, 9.1–9.3, 10.22
Phosphate: production and deliveries,
    22.18
Photographic: equipment sales, 22.23
Pig iron: production, 22.15
Pigs:
    agricultural output, 21.1, 21.2
    on agricultural holdings, 21.5
    prices, 17.7–17.9
    sales, 21.7
Pipelines, goods transport, 15.3
Plastics recycling, 13.18
PM10 emissions, 13.4
Pneumonia: deaths from, 9.6
Police:
    establishment and strength, 11.1
    expenditure of local authorities, 18.13
      18.15, 18.17
Population and vital statistics, 5.1–5.23
    age and sex distribution, 5.1, 5.3
    census based, 5.1, 5.4, 5.5
    cities, 5.5
    changes in, 5.2
    electorate, 2.1
    ethnic group, 5.6
    life tables, 5.22
    mid–year estimates, 5.1, 5.3, 5.5
    migration, 5.2, 5.7–5.9
    projections, 5.1, 5.3
    regional distribution, 5.5
    summary, 5.1
    working, 7.1–7.5
Pork: production, 21.9
Postal and postal order services, 15.32
Postgraduate awards, 6.10

Potash: deliveries, 22.18
Potatoes:
    agricultural output, 21.1, 21.2
    area, 21.3
    disposals, 21.10
    harvested, 21.4
    prices, 17.8, 17.9
    sales, 21.7
Poultry:
    agricultural output, 21.1, 21.2
    meat production, 21.9
    on agricultural holdings, 21.5
    prices, 17.7–17.9
    sales, 21.7
Pregnancy complications, deaths from,
    9.6
Prescriptions:
    cost, 9.1–9.3
    dispensed, 9.1–9.3
Prices, 17.1–17.9
Prices:
    agricultural, 17.7–17.9
    Consumer Prices Index, 17.4
    producer, 17.1, 17.2
    Retail Prices Index, 17.5
    tax and price index, 17.6
Primary care services, in Scotland, 9.2
Primary fuels, 22.4
Primary schools, 6.1, 6.4
Printing industry, *see* Paper, printing and
    publishing
Prisons:
    expenditure on, 11.12, 11.19
    persons sentenced to, 11.7, 11.16,
      11.23
    receptions and population, 11.9–
      11.11, 11.18, 11.24
Private sector liquidity, 23.7
Probation, 11.16
Producer price index, 17.1, 17.2
Production, 22.1–22.27
    average earnings, 7.21
Production: Census of, 22.1
Propane deliveries, 22.13
Property income: from abroad (net),
    16.1
Public administration:
    average earnings, 7.22
    labour disputes, 7.18
Public sector:
    debt, 18.3
    net cash requirement, 18.1, 18.2,
      23.6
Publishing industry, *see* Paper, printing
    and publishing
Pupils: in schools, 6.2–6.4
Purchasing power of the pound, 17.3

Q

Qualification obtained:
    by age, 6.5
    by higher education students, 6.10
Quarrying, *see* Clay, Stone and slate
    production

R

Radio and electronic goods: sales,
    22.23
Radioactive waste: stocks and
    arisings, 13.16
Rail transport, 15.4, 15.20–15.23
Railways:
    fatal injuries, 9.10
    fuel consumption, 22.5
    goods traffic, 15.3, 15.21
    London Regional Transport, 15.20
    offences, 11.3
    passenger transport 15.4, 15.20
    permanent way, 15.20, 15.22
    stations, 15.20
Rainfall, 13.8
Rateable values, 18.11
Rates (Scotland):
    local authorities' income from, 18.18
    rebate grant, 18.18
Recorded crime statistics:
    England and Wales, 11.2
    Northern Ireland, 11.20
    Scotland, 11.13
Recycling of selected materials, 13.18
Refinery fuel, 22.11, 22.12
Refinery receipts, 22.11
Refrigerating machinery: manufacture of,
    22.23
Regional statistics:
    area, 5.5
    population, 5.5
    unemployment, 7.12–7.14
Rent:
    corporate income of central
    government, 16.8
    imputed – of owner–occupied
    dwellings, 16.5
    local authorities, 18.15, 18.18
Research and development, 20.1–20.5
    analysis by sector, 20.1
    expenditure by industry, 20.4, 20.5
    government expenditure, 20.2, 20.3
Reservoir stocks: water, 13.11
Restaurants and cafes, 24.4
Retail Prices Index, 17.5
Retail trade:
    average earnings, 7.22
    turnover, 24.1

value of sales, 24.2
volume index numbers, 24.2
Retirement pensions, 10.1, 10.3, 10.5, 10.12, 10.24
Revenue:
central government, 18.4, 18.5
local authorities, 18.13–18.15, 18.18, 18.19
Rivers: biological and chemical quality, 13.9, 13.10
Road transport, 15.1–15.19
Roads:
casualties, 15.17
goods transported by 15.3, 15.18, 15.19
length of, 15.6
traffic on, 15.5, 15.7
traffic noise, 13.19
road works, noise from, 13.19
Robbery, 11.2–11.4, 11.11, 11.13, 11.14, 11.20–11.22
Rolling stock: railway (Northern Ireland), 15.22
Roofing tiles, production, 22.20
Royal Air Force, Royal Navy and Royal Marines:
cadet forces, 4.5
civilian manpower, 4.6
deaths, 4.9
deployment of, 4.8
HM Forces employment, 7.4
fishery protection, 4.11
formation, 4.3
medical staff, 4.10
outflow, 4.4
recruitment, 4.2
regular reserves, 4.5
search and rescue operations, 4.11
strength, 4.5
volunteer reserves and auxiliary forces,   4.5
Rural districts:
area, 5.5
population, 5.5
Rye (grain):
acreage, 21.3
harvested, 21.4

S

Sales: manufacturers by industry, 22.2
Salt: production, 22.19
Sand:
building and concreting, 22.20
industrial, 22.19
Sandstone: production, 22.19
Scarlet fever: notifications of, 9.7

Schools:
government expenditure on meals, 10.21
number of, by type, 6.1
pupils:
by age and sex, 6.2
by school type, 6.3
special educational needs, 6.4
pupil/teacher ratios, 6.3
special, 6.4
teachers in, 6.3, 6.11
Scientific research: cost and expenditure, 20.1, 20.5
Sea transport:
balance of payments, 19.9
goods transport, 15.3, 15.29
Seaport traffic, 15.29, 15.30
Search and rescue operations: by Services, 4.11
Securities: government and government guaranteed, 18.8
Seed crushing: production, 21.9
Seeds:
agricultural input and output, 21.1, 21.2
index of purchase price, 17.7
Self–employed, 7.2, 7.4
Services:
supplied and purchased, 19.7
overseas trade, 19.8
Sewage:
disposal, 13.12
sludge, 13.17
Sexual offences, 11.2–11.4, 11.11, 11.13, 11.14, 11.20–11.22
Sheep and lambs:
agricultural output, 21.1, 21.2
on agricultural holdings, 21.5
prices, 17.7, 17.8
sales, 21.7
Sickness benefit, 10.5, 10.7, 10.8, 10.24
Slate: production, 22.19, 22.20
Social conditions, 10.1–10.24
Social services:
expenditure on, 10.23
workforce, 9.5
Social security benefits: expenditure on, 10.20, 10.24
Solid fuels, see Coal, Coal extraction and solid fuels
Space research: central government expenditure on, 20.3
Spectacles: supplied, 9.1–9.3
Spirit, industrial and white:
deliveries, 22.13
refining, 22.12
Spirits, alcoholic: production and consumption, 22.26

Stateless persons, 5.11
Steel, see Iron and steel
Stillbirths, 5.20
Stock of dwellings, 14.1
Stone and slate:
production, 22.19, 22.20
Strikes, 7.18
Students:
further education, 6.6, 6.7
higher education, 6.8, 6.9
qualifications, 6.5, 6.10
Subsidies, 16.1,
Sugar and sugar confectionery:
disposals, 21.10
production, 21.9
stocks, 21.8
Sugar beet:
area, 21.3
agricultural output, 21.1, 21.2
harvested, 21.4
prices, 17.7, 17.8
Suicide: deaths by, 9.6
Sulphur dioxide: emissions by source, 13.3
Summary offences:
offenders cautioned, 11.4, 11.6
offenders found guilty, 11.3, 11.5, 11.21, 11.22
Suspended sentences, 11.7, 11.23
Syrup and treacle:
disposals, 21.10
production, 21.9

T

Take-away food shops, 24.4
Tax and price index, 17.6
Taxes:
on expenditure, 16.8, 16.9
on income, 16.9, 16.11
paid by UK residents, 18.5
total income before and after, 8.1
Taxis:
licences current, 15.13
new registrations, 15.9, 15.14
traffic on road, 15.5, 15.7
Tea:
disposals, 21.10
stocks, 21.8
Teachers:
full-time, 6.3, 6.11
part-time, 6.11
pupils per, 6.3
Television:
licences, 15.32
manufacture of, 22.23
Temporary accommodation: homeless households, 14.9

Tenure of accommodation, 14.2
Textile industry:
administrative, technical and clerical
employees:
employment, 7.5
exports, 19.2, 19.3
imports, 19.2, 19.4
index of average earnings, 7.22
producer price index numbers,
17.1, 17.2
size of establishments, 22.3
Textile machinery: manufacture of,
22.23
Theft, 11.2–11.4, 11.11, 11.13, 11.14,
11.20–11.22
Tiles: production, 22.20
Timber and wooden furniture industries:
producer price index, 17.1, 17.2
size of establishments, 22.3
wood production, 21.6
Tin:
exports, 22.17
production, consumption and stocks,
22.17
Tobacco:
clearances and stocks, 22.27
Consumer Prices Index, 17.4
household expenditure, 16.14–16.16
Retail Prices Index, 17.5
Tobacco industry, see Food, drink and
tobacco industry
Tourism:
domestic, 12.6
employment in, 12.2
international, 12.7
Tourist:
attractions. 12.5
expenditure in United Kingdom, 12.7
Tractors, agricultural:
licences current, 15.8, 15.13
registrations, 15.9, 15.14
sales, 22.2
Trade, external:
balance of payments, 19.9–19.12
value, 19.1–19.8
Trade unions, 7.25
Traffic accidents: deaths and injuries,
15.17
Traffic offences:
persons found guilty, 11.3, 11.21,
11.22
recorded by the police, 11.13
Trailers: sales of 22.25
Trams: passenger transport, 15.20
Transport and communications,
15.1–15.32
Transport:
air, 15.24–15.28
cost, 15.2

employment, 7.5
goods, 15.3
local authority expenditure and
receipts, 18.15, 18.17
passenger, 15.4
rail, 15.20–15.23
road, 15.6–15.19
sea, 15.29
shipping, 15.29, 15.30
Transport industry, see Motor vehicles
Travel:
balance of payments, 19.9, 19.10
household expenditure, 16.16, 16.17
passenger movement, 15.31
Trawler fleet, 21.15
Treasury bills:
assets, 23.3
increase in, 18.5
outstanding, 18.7
Trips, 15.1, 12.6
Tuberculosis:
deaths from, 9.6
notifications, 9.7
Turbines: manufacture of 22.23
Typhoid fever: notifications, 9.7

U

Unemployment: 7.1, 7.4, 7.8–7.14
Unemployment benefit (Jobseeker's
allowance), 10.1, 10.3, 10.5, 10.6,
10.24
Unit trusts: assets, 23.16
Universities:
government expenditure, 10.21
numbers, 6.1
Urban districts:
area, 5.5
population, 5.5

V

Vagrancy offences, 11.3
Vandalism, see also Criminal damage
11.13
Veal: production, 21.9
Vegetables:
agricultural output, 21.1, 21.2
area, 21.3
harvested, 21.4
prices, 17.8, 17.9
Vehicles, see Motor vehicles
Vehicles, machinery and equipment in
streets: noise from, 13.19
Veterinary services: prices, 17.7
Video rental, 12.4
Violence against the person:
offence recorded, 11.2, 11.13, 11.20
offenders cautioned, 11.4

offenders found guilty, 11.3, 11.21,
11.22
prison population serving sentences,
11.11
Visits to tourist attractions, 12.5
Vital statistics, see also Population
birth rates, 5.15
outside marriage births, 5.16
death rates:
infant, 5.20
maternal, 5.20
deaths:
by age and sex, 5.19
by cause, 9.6
divorce, 5.13, 5.14
life tables, 5.22
marital condition, 5.4
marriages, 5.12
still–births, 5.15
Volatile organic compounds: emissions
by source, 13.7

W

War pensions, 10.3, 10.5, 10.15, 10.24
Waste material:
annual arisings, 13.17
radioactive, 13.16
Watches: manufacture of 22.23
Water:
abstractions, 13.15
household expenditure, 16.16
industry expenditure, 13.12
inland area, 1.1
goods transport, 15.3
pollution incidents, 13.13
reservoir stocks, 13.11
Water supply industry, see Energy and
water supply industry
Welfare services: government
expenditure, 10.20, 10.23
Wheat:
agricultural output, 21.1, 21.2
area, 21.3
harvested, 21.4
milled:
prices, 17.7–17.9
production, 21.9
sales, 21.7
stocks, 21.8
Wheat milling offals:
disposals, 21.10
production, 21.9
White spirit:
deliveries, 22.13
output, 22.12
Whooping cough: notifications of 9.7
Widow's pension and benefits, 10.1,
10.3, 10.5, 10.14, 10.15, 10.24

Wine consumption, 22.26
Women's Forces:
   outflow, 4.4
   recruitment, 4.2
Woodland area, 21.6
Wood production, 21.6
Wool:
   agricultural output, 21.1, 21.2
   prices, 17.7–17.9
Work related diseases,
Workers *see* Employment
Working Family Tax Credit, 10.10
Working population, 7.4
Working Tax Credit awards, 10.11
Wounding offences, 11.3, 11.4

Y

Youth custody, 11.10, 11.16–11.18,
   11.23, 11.24

Z

Zero coupon yields, 23.11
Zinc:
   production, consumption and stocks,
      22.17
   recycling, 13.18

183001

183001